REQUIEM FOR THE TIMELESS

VOLUME 1

By the same author

Timeless Flight: The Definitive Biography Of The Byrds
Neil Young: Here We Are In The Years
Roxy Music: Style With Substance
Van Morrison: A Portrait Of The Artist
The Kinks: The Sound And The Fury
Wham! (Confidential) The Death Of A Supergroup
Starmakers & Svengalis: The History Of British Pop Management
The Football Managers
The Guinness Encyclopaedia Of Popular Music (co-ed.)
Morrissey & Marr: The Severed Alliance
The Smiths: The Visual Documentary
The Complete Guide To The Music Of The Smiths & Morrissey/Marr
The Complete Guide To The Music Of Neil Young
Crosby, Stills, Nash & Young: The Visual Documentary
The Complete Guide To The Music Of John Lennon
The Byrds: Timeless Flight Revisited – The Sequel
The Complete Guide To The Music Of The Kinks
Neil Young: Zero To Sixty: A Critical Biography
Van Morrison: No Surrender
Morrissey: The Albums
Lennon: The Albums

Anthology Contributions

The Bowie Companion
The Encyclopedia Of Popular Music
The Mojo Collection
Oxford Dictionary Of National Biography
Oxford Originals: An Anthology Of Writing From Lady Margaret Hall, 1879–2001

BYRDS
REQUIEM FOR THE TIMELESS

VOLUME 1

Johnny Rogan

© Johnny Rogan 2011, 2012

ISBN 978-0-095295-408-8

The right of Johnny Rogan to be identified as Author of this work has been asserted by him in accordance with the Copyright, Designs and Patents Act, 1988.

All rights reserved. No part of this book may be reproduced in any form or by electronic or mechanical means, including information storage or retrieval systems, without permission in writing from the publisher.

Personal orders/correspondence:
email: R.H.bksbyrds@hotmail.com

Exclusive distributors:
Music Sales Ltd
Newmarket Road
Bury St Edmunds
Ipswich
IP33 3YB

A catalogue record for this book is available from the British Library.

Photo credits: Front Cover: Courtesy of Jim Dickson. Centre Spread – Plate I: Jim Dickson collection at Henry Diltz; Plates II–III: Author's collection; Plate IV: Repro magazine *Cosmopolitan* (US)/William Claxton; Plate V: courtesy of Jim Dickson; Plates VI–VII: courtesy of CBS Records; Plate VIII: Author's collection; Plate IX: courtesy of CBS Records; Plates X–XI: Author's collection; Plates XII–XIII: Jim Dickson collection at Henry Diltz; Plate XIV: courtesy of CBS Records; Plate XV: Author's collection; Plate XVI: Jim Dickson collection at Henry Diltz; Plate XVII: courtesy of Sony Music Entertainment Inc/Don Hunstein photographer; Plates XVIII– XIX: Author's collection; Plates XX–XXI: Jim Dickson collection at Henry Diltz; Plate XXII–XXIV: Author's collection; Plate XXV: courtesy of Sony Music Entertainment Inc/Don Hunstein photographer; Plate XXVI–XXVII: Author's collection: Plate XXVIII: courtesy of Dorothy McGuinn; Plate XXIX: courtesy of Beat Publications; Plate XXX–XXXI: courtesy of Sony Music Entertainment Inc/Don Hunstein photographer; Plate XXXII: Author's collection, courtesy of John Delgatto; Plate XXXIII: courtesy of Sony Music Entertainment Inc/Don Hunstein photographer; Plates XXXIV–XXXV: courtesy of Jim Seiter; Plate XXXVI: courtesy of Raffaele Galli; Plate XXXVII: courtesy of CBS Records; Plate XXXVIII: courtesy of Lou Cohan; Plate XXXIX: courtesy of Jim Seiter; Plate XL: courtesy of Dorothy McGuinn; Plate XLI: courtesy of George Guttler; Plate XLII: courtesy of CBS Records; Plate XLIII: courtesy of Dorothy McGuinn; Plate XLIV: author's collection, original source Byrds International Fan Club; Plate XLV: Author's collection: Plates XLVI–XLVII: Author's collection, original photographer assumed Suzanne Litwornia; Plate XLVIII: courtesy of Asylum Records, photographer Henry Diltz; Plate XLIX: courtesy of Lou Cohan; Plate L: courtesy of Capitol Records; Plate LI (top left): Scorpion Publications/Dark Star book cover; Plate LII (top right): Square 1 Books cover; Plate LIII: Rogan House book cover.

Produced by R/H, Calidore & Sterne
Published by R/H [R. House]
Typeset by Galleon Typesetting, Ipswich

Even such is time which takes in trust
Our youth our joys and all we have,
And pays us but with age and dust:
Who in the dark and silent grave
When we have wandered all our ways
Shuts off the story of our days.
And from which earth and grave and dust
The Lord shall raise me up, I trust.

Sir Walter Ralegh

Critical reaction to Rogan's previous shorter books on the Byrds *Timeless Flight* and *Timeless Flight Revisited – The Sequel:*

"This is the closest to heaven it's possible to come." **MOJO**

"This is, at least, the best biography of a group ever written . . ." **Q**

"It's impossible not to admire Rogan, a man whose approach to popular music is academically exhaustive, and yet who still manages to write with an ease and generosity that puts younger gunslinger dudes to shame. Note the splendid introductory chapter where Rogan enthuses about the day when he first heard 'Mr Tambourine Man' in a flat near Dolphin Square still powered by gas. This is a book that is worth every penny and about a group that fully merits such a retrospective." **TIME OUT**

"As with all the best works in rock biography, this will send you back to the music with fresh ears. In a word: definitive." **UNCUT**

"Expansive enough to rival *War And Peace,* Rogan's definitive Byrds biography comes close to matching the emotional, if not geographical, range of Tolstoy's epic novel. One of the achievements of *Timeless Flight Revisited* is the way in which it matches its narrative flair with the incisiveness of its critical comment . . . But it's the narrative drive that makes the book so extraordinary. With its detailed research and fascinating interview material, it is a compelling portrait of collective turmoil, peopled by characters who win our sympathy at the same time as they earn our disbelief."
RECORD COLLECTOR

"A writer of real integrity." **SUNDAY TELEGRAPH**

"Rogan displays the rare ability to recall and report every minute detail of the band's career without relinquishing anything in the way of readability." **VOX**

"Johnny Rogan's epic biography sets a new standard . . . *Timeless Flight Revisited: The Sequel,* which has been lauded by the British music press, raises the bar in rock biographies and serves notice that rock 'n' roll can be worthy of the kind of critical analysis jazz has enjoyed." **MONTREAL GAZETTE**

"Rogan unsparingly assesses both the Byrds' music and their personal failings . . . His reporting on Crosby's near fatal cocaine addiction is at once poignant and horrifying . . . *Timeless Flight Revisited* is a scrupulously fair, cleanly written, and thoroughly researched take on one of the most important American groups of the Sixties." **BILLBOARD**

"A detailed, gripping account of the birth and death of a dream . . . *Timeless Flight* is one of the best rock biographies ever written."
RECORD COLLECTOR

"This is a remarkable book." **COUNTRY MUSIC WORLD**

"Johnny Rogan's expertise is beyond question." **Q**

"Dense and intriguing. If you ever loved the Byrds you'll find it rewarding and, even if you didn't, it's still a fascinating slice of rock history." **MELODY MAKER**

"Invaluable . . . One of the most detailed studies available of the rise and fall of a popular group." **SOUNDS**

"Rogan is obsessive and detail hungry." **NEW MUSICAL EXPRESS**

"The definitive history of one of the most volatile stories in pop history." **MANCHESTER EVENING NEWS**

"Johnny Rogan is pop's most eccentric biographer, a fanatical searcher after truth." **CITY LIFE**

"Rogan is a rock biographer's biographer. The guy is literally a method writer." **WHAT'S ON IN LONDON**

NOTES TO THE READER

Within the main text, albums are printed in italics, along with books, poems, radio and television programmes, plays, magazines and newspapers. Songs are in single inverted commas as are single word quotes, newspaper headlines, review titles, aphorisms and short phrases; interview quotes and citations from books are in double inverted commas. Numerical units are written up to ten and numbered thereafter, except in the use of birthdays, centuries, chart positions, measurements, money, musical time, percentages and specific usages such as '8-track recordings'. Acronyms have full points omitted, but names of people do not. Group/band names are preceded by a lower case 'the' and only painters are 'artists'. The abbreviation of microphone is still 'mike', as it always was until tape manufacturers started printing 'mic' on their products. Decades are capitalized in order to distinguish them from ages (thus 'the Sixties' versus 'in my sixties').

English usage, not American, applies throughout so it's 'any more' not 'anymore', 'archaeological' not 'archelogical', 'artefact' not 'artifact', 'baulk' not 'balk', 'behaviour' not 'behavior', 'cheque' not 'check', 'colour' not 'color' etc, with the exception of place names such as Pearl *Harbor* and different pronunciation from American interviewees (for example 'airplanes' instead of the English trisyllabic 'aeroplanes' and 'specialty' instead of 'speciality' – although English spelling is used for these words in the narrative). End spellings of verbs are 'ize' in accordance with *The Oxford English Dictionary* rather than computer spell checkers, with the obvious exceptions of words such as advertise, analyse, comprise, improvise, supervise, surprise, televise et al. Although some people erroneously believe that the 'ize' ending is an Americanism, this is not the case. It has been consistently used in English since the sixteenth century.

Song and album titles are generally displayed as they appear on the record, even if inaccurately spelt or lacking necessary commas/apostrophes. Nouns and noun compounds are usually not hyphenated except when attributive. In modern English there is a tendency to avoid such hyphenation, but exceptions apply. American English has a greater number of previously hyphenated compound words that now form a single word, whereas in British English we tend to split them into two words. Other rulings are mainly in accordance with *The New Oxford Dictionary For Writers And Editors*.

CONTENTS

Acknowledgements		xi
Preface: The Ghost Of Electricity Revisited		1
Chapter One	The Secret Origins Of The Byrds	21
Chapter Two	The Jet Set	37
Chapter Three	Preflyte	51
Chapter Four	Dylan's Charm Offensive	63
Chapter Five	Mr Tambourine Man	75
Chapter Six	The New Pop Way Of Living	87
Chapter Seven	Ciro's Magic	100
Chapter Eight	Positive Thinking	114
Chapter Nine	The First Album	125
Chapter Ten	Hollywood Parties	136
Chapter Eleven	The British Tour	148
Chapter Twelve	The Death Of Folk Rock	176
Chapter Thirteen	Non-Aristotelian Systems	195
Chapter Fourteen	Fracas And Fistfights	206
Chapter Fifteen	Turn! Turn! Turn!	222
Chapter Sixteen	Eight Miles High	242
Chapter Seventeen	Fear Of Flying	262
Chapter Eighteen	Space And Drugs	281
Chapter Nineteen	Courage	299
Chapter Twenty	Renaissance	310
Chapter Twenty-One	The Gathering Of The Tribes	331
Chapter Twenty-Two	Mutiny And Monterey	348
Chapter Twenty-Three	The Great Conflict	366
Chapter Twenty-Four	Crosby Fired! – Clark Hired!	380
Chapter Twenty-Five	The Notorious Byrd Brothers	397
Chapter Twenty-Six	Nashville	414
Chapter Twenty-Seven	Stonehenge	434
Chapter Twenty-Eight	South Africa	458
Chapter Twenty-Nine	Sweetheart Of The Rodeo	471
Chapter Thirty	Reconstruction	484
Chapter Thirty-One	Dr Byrds & Mr Hyde	497

REQUIEM FOR THE TIMELESS — VOLUME 1

Chapter Thirty-Two	Uncertain Riders	515
Chapter Thirty-Three	Just A Season	533
Chapter Thirty-Four	Expensive	552
Chapter Thirty-Five	Farther Along	575
Chapter Thirty-Six	Dissolution	590
Chapter Thirty-Seven	Full Circle	612
Chapter Thirty-Eight	Separation	630
Chapter Thirty-Nine	Interlude – Three Byrds Land In London	651
Chapter Forty	The Negotiation	662
Chapter Forty-One	The Cocaine Wars	676
Chapter Forty-Two	Burn Out	690
Chapter Forty-Three	The Dark Decade	710
Chapter Forty-Four	The Third Coming	738
Chapter Forty-Five	The Hall Of Fame	762
Chapter Forty-Six	Fatalities	774
Chapter Forty-Seven	End Of The Century	789
Chapter Forty-Eight	The Absence Of Charity	804
Chapter Forty-Nine	Survivors	816
Chapter Fifty	The Reaper's Blade	836
Epilogue		855
Notes		873
Sessionography		1016
Unreleased Material		1038
Byrds Discography		1043
Byrds Bootlegs		1087
Television Appearances/Videos/DVDs		1146
Index		1161

ACKNOWLEDGEMENTS

Requiem For The Timeless is a multi-volume book covering the complete history of the Byrds. The first volume is a group biography, detailing the life and work of the Byrds, including details of the interaction between the original members after the break-up of the band. In the second volume, the focus is on the lives of those former Byrds now dead and complements the story herein.

Research on this project began in earnest during the mid-Seventies when I was writing my first book, *Timeless Flight*. In the Nineties, I returned to the saga with the extensive *Timeless Flight Revisited* in which I promised a hopefully definitive work sometime in the next century. These are the results. As the dating in the endnotes confirm, this epic represents a veritable lifetime's work, comprising research, analyses and interviews conducted over a period of four decades.

This book may appear intimidatingly large, but its scope demands space. Combining the material into two volumes was the only solution to what might otherwise have been a production nightmare of broken spines, headache inducing miniscule type and see-though paper. Although the results are well in excess of 900,000 words and more than 2,000 pages, spread across the first two volumes, this account is by no means exhaustive.

It was not the mountains of interview tapes, transcripts and research notes that determined the page length, but the sheer scale of the tale. The Byrds' saga is not merely an account of the trials and tribulations of a legendary group, but a simultaneous treatise and mini-history of Sixties' California music. It is also the story of the evolution of pop into rock, the shift in cultural emphasis from the single to the album format, the rise and fall of folk rock, the emergence of country rock, the grand idea of the supergroup, the new age of the singer-songwriter, the drug culture and invention of the cocaine cowboy, the devolution of Sixties idealism into

Seventies hedonism, the cult of celebrity death, the rock reunion game and its psychological consequences, and the struggle to adapt to changing times when your life has been defined by a particular epoch.

Both volumes feature a cast list of crucially important players whose interaction defined their times. The Byrds continue to serve as a blueprint and metaphor for West Coast American music of the late twentieth century, a claim which might sound hyperbolic until you consider the range of talents and spectacular offshoots emanating from their central core.

The interviews conducted for this book span the decades. Looking back I am indebted to the many players, musical and otherwise, who agreed to lend their time and support in order to provide me with extensive first-hand material. Firstly, the original five Byrds: James Roger McGuinn, Gene Clark, David Crosby, Michael Clarke and Chris Hillman. Later Byrds: John York, Gene Parsons and Skip Battin. Original managers: Jim Dickson and Eddie Tickner. Producer Terry Melcher. Publicist Derek Taylor. Road managers Jim Seiter, Carlos Bernal and Al Hersh. In addition to this loquacious core group were a wealth of other speakers featuring, in alphabetical order: James Aderholt, Mark Adzick, Mark Andes, Matt Andes, Jesse Barish, Michael Barnes, Patricia Battin (née Cartabiano), Garth Beckington, Hillary Beckington (née Kontos), Linda Loo Bopp, Sharon Garrett Brooks, Jack Carchio, Jim Carlton, Rick Clark, Connie Cohen, Jon Corneal, Michael Curtis, Brian Cutean, Chris Darrow, Dale Davis, Muff Davis, Saul Davis, Jeff Dexter, Suzy Dick, Vicki Doney (née McClure), Lizzie Donohue, Ian Dunlop, Chris Ethridge, Jon Faurot, Kim Fowley, Carl Franzoni, Barry Friedman, Jimmy Weston Gavin, John 'Jack' Godden, Steve Green, Charlie Greene, Gib Guilbeau, Bobby Hamilton, Mike Hardwick, Trace Harrill, Sam Hutt, Bob Hyde, Bob Irwin, David Jackson, Pete Jamieson, Art Johnson, Patti Johnson, Rosemarie Johnson (née White), Andy Kandanes, Dennis J. Kelley, Joe Kelly, Michelle Kerr, Jesse Lee Kincaid, Gene Leedy, Kenny Lynch, John Manikoff, Gary Marker, Dewey Martin, Moon Martin, Lanny Mathyssen (aka Mathijssen), Elliot Mazer, Marc McClure, Patti McCormick, Chester 'Chet' McCracken, Camilla

ACKNOWLEDGEMENTS

McGuinn (née Spaul), Dorothy McGuinn, Henry McGuinn, Patrick McGuinn, Barry McGuire, Michael McRae, Terri Messina, Wayne Moore, David Muse, Scott Nienhaus, Philip O'Leno, Andrew Oldham, Peter Oliva, Carla Olson, Shannon O'Neill, Larry Page, Bruce Palmer, Van Dyke Parks, Michelle Phillips, Bill Plummer, Ron Rainey, Bob 'Ras' Rassmussen, Pat Robinson, Terry Rogers, Jason Ronard, Al Rosenberg (aka Al Ross), Bill Siddons, Tom Slocum, Kassy Stone, Joey Stec, Paul Surratt, Barry Tashian, Charlie Taylor, Peggy Taylor, Greg Thomas, Dolores Tickner (formerly McGuinn, née DeLeon), Cyriel Van den Hemel, Bo Wagner, Bob Warford, Joanne White, Michelle White, Roland White, William 'Bill' Wolff, Steve Young – and many more.

The extensive endnotes in both volumes of *Requiem For The Timeless* detail interview dates and information sources. Photos presented in the book over the years come courtesy of Capitol Records, CBS Records and Sony Records/Don Hunstein. Additional thanks to Barry Ballard, Lou Cohan, John Delgatto, Jim Dickson, Pete Frame, Raffaele Galli, Suzanne Litwornia, Pete Long, Dorothy McGuinn, Chrissie Oakes, Nick Ralph, Jim Seiter, Gary Strobl (at Henry Diltz Photography) and Jessica Sowin. (See imprint page for further details).

Thanking everyone over four decades is a daunting task for the memory banks. Pete Frame was around when I first started all this, and is still a supporter. In the mid-Seventies, he provided previously unpublished interview tapes with Clarence White, Roger McGuinn and Byron Berline. Frame wanted me to complete a serialization on the Byrds' career for *Zigzag* magazine. Alas, by the time these were done punk was about to engulf the nation and a change in editorship at the magazine meant there was more interest in Johnny Rotten than there was in Johnny Rogan's Byrds' writings. Nevertheless, *Zigzag* did commission and publish highlights from an interview I conducted with Roger McGuinn in 1977, which was a great boost. McGuinn kindly agreed to a far lengthier session soon after. By that stage I'd already interviewed Chris Hillman followed by Gene Clark and was contributing to another West Coast-inspired 'zine, *Dark Star*. That publication's founder Nick Ralph, along with contributor and polymath publisher Colin Larkin, were catalysts in the production of the first *Timeless Flight*, which was probably about a tenth of the size of the present tome. Larkin continued to pop up in my writing life, not least when he approached me to join him in the co-writing of that grand vision, *The Encyclopedia of Popular Music*.

In Byrds' lore, there are two indispensable figures whom I have now known for around 40 years. Chrissie Oakes founded the Byrds Appreciation Society as a teenager and we became regular correspondents during the Seventies and still exchange Christmas cards. She went on to edit the superb fanzine *Full Circle*, which was always a joy to read and is still missed. Among its chief contributors was Barry Ballard, another Byrds' fan who, like me, had been there since the beginning of the trip with 'Mr Tambourine Man'. Although we attended many of the same Byrds' concerts, including Gram Parsons' and Kevin Kelley's famous appearance at the Royal Albert Hall, I don't think we actually met until the mid-Seventies when he started writing for *Omaha Rainbow*. We've been swapping Byrds' information ever since and I have the utmost respect for his integrity, conscientiousness, generosity and continued interest.

Four other people who deserve special mention are my fellow CSN&Y/Neil Young aficionado Pete Long; George Guttler, my mainman Byrdswise in the States; Doug Hinman, fellow researcher from the days before the internet made people lazy; and Peter Doggett, whose musical tastes so often dovetailed with my own and who is now a full-time writer of considerable standing and a fine, judicious critic. Praise to them all.

Andy Neill provided some last-minute editorial assistance and I was greatly impressed by his attention to detail and willingness to debate the more arcane aspects of pop history with such pedantic passion. Designer Lisa Pettibone for patience in going back to the drawing board until I found the perfect cover photograph. Additional thanks to Ken Shiplee at Galleon for his courtesy, efficiency and punctual delivery of such lengthy proofs.

Thanks also to all at Random House and Music Sales for allowing me the time to complete this project.

Over the years many others have helped in numerous ways or simply written informative, enthusiastic letters. So, in alphabetical order, hello and thanks to Liz Beamish, David Belbin, Debbie

ACKNOWLEDGEMENTS

Bennett, Keith Bickerton, David Blackmore, Johanne Bodde, Adrian Booth, John Brindle, Dennis Brown, Neal Clark, Douglas Coates, Francis Constantine, Geraint Davies, John Delgatto, Dennis Dragon, Simon Drew, John Einarson, Scott Erickson, Elio Espana, John Etherington, John Fallon, Hector Feliciano, Ray Frieders, Raffaele Galli, Bill Gilroy, Bill Gore, John Graves, Sid Griffin, Jun Harada, Steve Harvey, Christopher Hjort, Peter Curt Holmstedt, Tom Isenhour, Ian Jones, Hans Kamermans, Harvey Kubernik, Roger Leighton, Huw Lewis, Mike Masterson, Max Merry, David N. Meyer, Chris Mills, Jon Monnickendam, Jean-Pierre Morisset, Akihide Nakamura, John Nork, John O'Brien, Peter O'Brien, Whin Oppice, Bob Parsons, Stephen Peeples, Tom Pickles, Tony Poole, David Prockter, Viv Pyne, Geoff Reynolds, Jo Saker, Jessica Sowin, John Tobler, Raoul Verolleman (founder of the internet site Byrds Flyte), John Ward and Dave Zimmer.

Going back far further, I always remember schoolfriends, primary and secondary, including Alan Culligan, Alan Roberts, Alan Russell, Eddie Lagan, Keith Rodger, Raj Mathur, plus Pimlico School's Anne Cesek, Deborah Novotny, George Kenyon, Wally Hammond, Sean Morris – and the rest of the ghostly crew.

From university and beyond, the wonderful Cathy Shea, Gill Chester, Anne MacInnes, Siobhan Dowd, Lory Laskey, Teresa Walsh (also for some passing musical observations) – and others.

On a personal level, family members, now all long, long dead. R.I.P. Plus nephews and cousins, some actually still living. Jackie Cuddihy in Tramore for all her love and support over recent years. Never to be underestimated.

In conclusion, it is the Byrds themselves that keep the passion burning and that is why the story is so important. The Byrds were there for me since the beginning of adolescence and I have little doubt that I will still be writing about them at the end of my life. Symbolically, maybe they *were* my life in a way that I have never quite articulated, even to myself – and so it goes on till the grave beckons, and time bids 'be gone'.

Johnny Rogan

PREFACE

The Ghost Of Electricity Revisited

CURIOUS readers have often asked me why I became so immersed in the saga of the Byrds. Americans have additionally wondered what it must have been like to experience California's answer to the Beatles at a time when all things British seemed unassailable. Usually, I respond with references to changing cultural trends in popular music, but that is an academic's answer. The truth is at once more simple and more complicated. Recalling the origins of the Byrds' phenomenon takes me back to a time just before I was a teenager. Treasured memories are sometimes tarnished, if not eroded, by passing decades until only the basic outlines remain. The intensity of the detail is lost as new experiences crowd the mind leaving only an overfamiliar, emasculated litany of events. But event can be transformed into myth and memory maintained through mental exercise. Even today, I still think about that time. Walking the streets at three or four in the morning, as is my wont, my mind commutes back to that period, as it has always done. At such moments, songs, feelings and experiences are regrounded firmly in the present. To this day, I can tell you every number 1 single of 1965 in chronological order, complete with label details and other minutiae, but this is no mnemonic party trick but something closer to an act of emotional catharsis, almost as if the recordings and events are happening in real time. It is a mysterious process and, somehow, the Byrds are at the centre of it. This is where it all began.

1965 was a fascinating year whose unfolding drama I can effortlessly conjure partly thanks to the exceptional number of superb singles that were released on an almost weekly basis. The Beatles and the Rolling Stones were in full blossom, carving up the charts with a series of number 1 hits, every one of them a classic: 'I Feel Fine', 'Ticket To Ride', 'The Last Time', 'Help!', '(I Can't Get No) Satisfaction', 'Get Off Of My Cloud', 'We Can Work It Out'/'Day Tripper'. In any other year, such a treasure trove of singles from the UK's top two groups would have been reason enough to inspire a young kid to devote his forthcoming teenage life to all things pop. The fact that there were equally great releases on offer from such acts as the Kinks, the Animals, the Who and the Yardbirds testified to a pop renaissance, whose profound influence is still felt decades on.

What was most gratifying about that time was the strong sense of democracy in pop. This was an era when pre-teens, teenagers and young adults could appreciate pop music that was not aggressively marketed for their benefit only. Easy-listening balladeers, thumping beat merchants, R&B shouters and aspiring protest singers could appear alongside each other on *Top Of The Pops* without the audience feeling any sense of incongruity. This lack of snobbishness was marvellous to behold and would soon be lost as pop music became deconstructed and classified into convenient categories and target groups for advertisers, marketing departments and counterculture chancers.

Post-punk feminist critics have often casually dismissed mid-Sixties pop as a barren ground for women, but such a sweeping assertion ignores the startling number of female artistes that congregated in the charts during that remarkable year of 1965. In the first few months alone, the list included Cilla Black, Dusty Springfield, Sandie Shaw, Petula Clark, Lulu, Twinkle, Francoise Hardy, Marianne Faithfull, Keely Smith and Jackie Trent. Indeed, it could be argued that female performers had never been better represented.

Back then, I still had the enviable ability to appreciate the momentous in the moment with a passion and sense of wonder that is always freshest in an impressionable young mind. Spoiled by the sheer number of brilliant singles, I assumed that the proliferation of pop groups and increasingly interesting records would carry on forever. Every week there was something new to discover as the tide of hits, ravenously demanded by record companies, seemed unstoppable. Great pop is best captured amid a feeling of temporal dislocation – an intense absorption in the moment, reinforced by the feeling that the instant is of such significance that it will later be recalled with similar and, possibly even greater, intensity. In late March, I heard a new single, so unusual in its vocal execution and literacy that it caused a shiver of excitement. The pop press had belatedly discovered Bob Dylan, the newly-dubbed 'king of folk', whose 'The Times They Are A-Changin'' was heading towards the Top 10. Soon after, it was joined by the contrasting 'Subterranean Homesick Blues', whose amphetamine-fuelled lyrics were sung at a blistering speed that made you marvel at the ingenuity of the performance.

The arrival of Bob Dylan in Britain that year transformed the pop landscape. His presence affected everybody on the scene and even reached a pre-teen like me. Suddenly, there was the realization that pop was not only entertaining and exciting, but erudite too. From March through to the summer, I was keenly aware of an intense feeling of anticipation that something important was about to happen. It was almost tangible. Subconsciously, perhaps, I was awaiting the emergence of a group that I could call my own, whose presence might capture my time as effectively as the Beatles had galvanized the lives of my close elders two years before. Back then, I had watched the Fab Four phenomenon with intense fascination and considerable excitement but always, it seemed, ever so slightly from the outside. They would always be my *second* favourite group. When Jim McGuinn later explained that there was a gap in the musical spectrum somewhere between the Beatles and Bob Dylan, that was precisely where my heart secretly lay.

While growing up in Pimlico, in the City of Westminster, the Swinging Sixties were swirling all around me, but that world existed largely in the minds of glossy magazine writers rather than in the daily lives of ordinary people. For all the superficial glitz, London in 1965 was still a city attuned to the austerity of the Fifties. What was left of my death ravaged family lived in rented rooms in a street opposite Dolphin Square, a world famous luxury block populated by actors, pop stars, politicians, doctors, minor royals and privileged professionals. Super vigilant nocturnalists might even have spotted Phil Spector there on his London visit the previous year, but you were more likely to see former pop idol turned variety star Craig Douglas, or the perfectly enunciated Eurovision presenter and Camay soap beauty, Katie Boyle. The opulence of Dolphin Square, with its beautiful gardens, fountain, swimming pool, squash court and enticingly labyrinthine basements, provided the perfect playground for illegal outsiders who knew its secret entrances and exits. Those sociologists who spoke of a new egalitarianism would have found Pimlico a classic case of the wealthy and the needy living almost next door to each other in a continual culture clash. Across the road from Dolphin Square, I dreamed not only of the Beatles and Bob Dylan, but of the wonders of electricity. Our rooms were entirely lit by gaslight, just like you see in Victorian melodramas. The communal hall, always atmospheric, had no light at all and getting around the place meant holding candles or learning to see in the dark. The city was not yet a smokeless zone, so heating came from coal fires and burnt wooden fruit crates taken from the greengrocers and chopped up with a hatchet. Removing ashes from the grate and emptying the urine-filled chamber pot were usually the first tasks of the day. There was no private toilet or bathroom.

Bizarrely, light entertainment was offered courtesy of cable radio, a system that required neither electricity nor batteries, but was pumped through from the local British Relay in Moreton Street. The set stood in the kitchen, with a switch offering only two channels: the Light Programme and the Home Service. Visualizing the room, I can see a second-hand Queen Ann chair, a marble table for baking and pencilling, a pre-War coal-black iron oven, a Butler sink with a single cold water tap underneath which is a bucket lined with one-inch of disinfectant mixed with water for lavatorial use. On a fading green linoleum floor, the smile of Wayne Fontana beams from the front page of issue 945 of the *New Musical Express*, while a coal fire burns, its flames competing with an adjacent gaslight, whose eroding mantle leaks a peek-a-boo blue-and-orange flame. There is a food cupboard, or 'press' as we call it, on top of which lies a never-to-be-opened packet of pretzels, itself part of a package of dangerously exotic American food that had been presented to the poor of Pimlico several years before following a glorious kids' party at the US Embassy in Grosvenor Square, during which a number of my fellow supposedly underprivileged tykes tore down the Stars And Stripes flag.

On reflection, this kitchen scene sounds like some post-modern urban fantasy, in which wildly contrasting cultural artefacts have collided to create an almost Orwellian setting. While Victorian gaslight bathed the room in its eerie glow, the strangely futuristic cable radio offered state sanctioned music played on shows whose very titles, *Housewives' Choice* and *Workers' Playtime*, betrayed the lingering, benign condescension of a broadcasting company that still prided itself on knowing what was best. The Home Service spoke reverentially of Winston Churchill, a far from popular figure in our household, whose funeral had recently taken place at nearby Westminster Abbey. It was one afternoon in this austere, storybook house that I first learned of the Byrds.

On Wednesday, 2 June 1965, I came home at lunchtime from school, ate two chocolate biscuits with a saucepan-heated milky coffee – my sole culinary skill as a 12-year-old – and opened the pages of that week's *New Musical Express*, which I had been religiously purchasing since the start of the year. Sandie Shaw was at number 1 with 'Long Live Love', but the Top 10 resembled a chart from another era, one that I still treasured as some kind of lost golden age. The two highest climbers were the Everly Brothers' 'The Price Of Love' and Elvis Presley's 'Crying In The Chapel' and it seemed to me at that time-bending moment that we might be about to witness some kind of Fifties' revival. That, in itself, was terribly exciting, akin to a science fiction fantasy. The *NME* even allowed you to project yourself, as if by magic, into another time zone by printing weekly charts from five and ten years ago. Spookily, the Everlys were top this same week in 1960 with 'Cathy's Clown', and I remembered that song with great fondness – even my brother and sister were alive and well back then. Maybe if I concentrated enough I could mentally travel back into that time of innocence and wonder.

However, it was the 1955 chart that proved most perplexing. Many of the song titles and performers prompted no immediate recognition whatsoever, but surely they had to be there buried deep in my subconscious. Perhaps if I concentrated enough I could bring them back. How could 'Give Me Your Word' by Tennessee Ernie (Ford) be number 1 for so long (seven weeks) without me being able even to hum the tune? Why weren't old pop hits ever played on the radio? I was amazed to see three versions of 'Unchained Melody' in the 1955 Top 10, including a rendition by someone called Les Baxter who, it would later transpire, was a bit player in the David Crosby story. Remarkably, a tune titled 'Cherry Pink' was both number 1 and 2 and there were also two versions of 'Stranger In Paradise' in the Top 10. All this conjured up visions of a deeply deprived pop culture wherein there were only a limited number of songs, most of which seemed to hang around the upper regions of the charts forever. Slim Whitman's 'Rose Marie' reigned at the top in 1955 for 11 consecutive weeks. I concluded that all this was a musical equivalent of post-war rationing. We now lived in different times, albeit without electricity, bath or toilet, and still grateful for the second-hand clothes bought from the stalls of Chapel Street market, off the Edgware Road. But Dylan was correct to proclaim that the times were changing.

The year 1965 was all about movement and rapid change, but it was salutary to consider that, a mere decade before, pop music had been rationed like bacon and eggs, and the world revolved at around 16 rpm. Ending this reverie about passing time which the *NME* had unintentionally inspired, my eyes lowered to scan the 'Round The World' charts, an entertaining interlude which offered the opportunity to marvel at the eccentricities of other nations: Denmark had the Beatles' 'Rock And Roll Music' at number 1; the theme from *Zorba The Greek* was top in the Lebanon, where former chart star Brenda Lee was challenging in second place; Bermuda's biggest hits this week featured such obscure names as Billy Stewart, Lou Johnson and Gene Chandler, all singing songs I would never hear. Alas, this procession of featured nations varied weekly, but I assumed Kathy Kirby's 'I Belong' (again unheard) was probably still top in Israel and the Ventures were no doubt dominant in Japan, having bagged the top two positions the week before. Of course, all this proved that the only thing that mattered chart wise was

THE GHOST OF ELECTRICITY REVISITED

NME and maybe *Billboard* – the rest of the world existed in a bizarre musical dimension beyond reason or imagination.

Seeking affirmation of this unholy notion, I scanned the listing of the 'Best Selling LPs in Britain' and took a kid's delight in the fact that my current hero, the newly lauded Bob Dylan, was holding off the irredeemably square *The Sound Of Music* soundtrack from the number 1 spot with his ultra hip *Bringing It All Back Home*. As always, I concluded my chart check by browsing through the 'Best Selling Pop Records In US', published 'courtesy of *Billboard*'. Bermuda, Japan and the Lebanon were all there for my xenophobic amusement, but America was always important and intriguing, as it sometimes provided accurate glimpses into the future. Admittedly, it overstated the chart potential of various Tamla Motown releases relative to the UK and made acts like Gary Lewis & The Playboys false gods, whom we disdainfully rejected. That said, the cultural divide in the wake of the Beatles had narrowed. I was always on the lookout for something unusual in their listing, a portal into an unknown future. On that memorable afternoon of 2 June, I spotted something worth further investigation. Suddenly, there it was, sandwiched between Herman's Hermits' 'Silhouettes' and Freddie And The Dreamers' 'Do The Freddie'. You couldn't miss it – it was the week's highest chart entry – 'Mr Tambourine Man' by the Byrds.

It was the song title and strange name that first struck me. At that stage I was completely unaware of Dylan's involvement, for he still existed primarily as a singles exponent in my limited world-view. While intrigued by *Bringing It All Back Home* and *Highway 61 Revisited*, they were album titles whose contents you never heard on the radio and certainly could not yet afford to buy without a massive investment. I coveted them, but waited. In 1965, I felt attuned to all things Dylan, but I discovered the Byrds by accident. The eye-catching title 'Mr Tambourine Man' was so exotic and unusual that you knew instantly this was a song you had to hear. As for the group name, that was even more perplexing. At first glance, and for some days afterwards, I innocently assumed it must be pronounced "Bye-Rids", which sounded positively weird.

I watched excitedly as the record headed for number 1 in *Billboard* and was then released here. I first heard it during that opening week of June, and it certainly was different. McGuinn's strange vocal inflexions, that distinctive Rickenbacker chime and the sumptuous harmonies all contributed to a record that sounded unlike anything I had ever heard before. It was almost as powerful as hearing 'Heartbreak Hotel' when I was about four years old – a treasured childhood memory. Several radio plays later, I was completely entranced and watched with vicarious pride as the song leapt to number 1.

The Byrds wasted no time in exploiting their new-found fame in England. While it has understandably gone down in the annals as a disaster, the group's tour of the UK won many lasting converts. I managed to see them playing *Top Of The Pops* and *Ready, Steady, Go!* and was amazed to discover that the image was as powerful and invigorating as the music. They looked infinitely hipper than the Beatles, the Rolling Stones, the Yardbirds, the Kinks, the Who, or anybody else. Their appearance seemed almost otherworldly. Crosby resembled a comic book hero come to life with his extraordinary cape; McGuinn's dark, rectangular, granny glasses, never before seen in this country, seemed specifically designed to provide him with an air of Dickensian disdain, broken only by a disconcertingly manic grin; Gene Clark, the well-toned extra vocalist with striking raven hair, played a tambourine, in keeping with the group's hit song; bassist Chris Hillman betrayed a look of childlike bemusement, like some lost character in *Peter Pan*; and the drummer, Michael Clarke, resembled a younger, taller and more glamorous Brian Jones.

Rushing home one lunchtime to catch *The Top Ten Game* on the Light Programme, I was thrilled to hear a studio audience unanimously vote the newly released 'All I Really Want To Do' number 1, thereby dislodging 'Mr Tambourine Man' in their fantasy chart. The very idea of the Byrds at numbers 1 *and* 2 was a thrill to be savoured. Despite all the bitchiness later evident in reviews of the Byrds' stage act, there was no doubting their greatness on record. Their first two singles enlivened the greatest summer that pop music has ever known, and saw them challenge the Beatles' 'Help!', Bob Dylan's 'Like A Rolling Stone' and the Rolling Stones' '(I Can't Get No) Satisfaction' for ultimate chart honours.

THE GHOST OF ELECTRICITY REVISITED

Back then, the acid test for any great group lay in the quality of their B-sides. In some ways, that told you all you needed to know about long-term potential, and the Byrds never disappointed. A single listen to 'I Knew I'd Want You' or 'Feel A Whole Lot Better' indicated hidden depths and tremendous reserves of strength that augured well for a wonderful future.

The Byrds left England on a sour note, replaced in the public's affection by the newly arrived Sonny & Cher. Folk rock continued to stay in vogue for several months, but that was not enough to rescue the third single, 'Turn! Turn! Turn!', which barely scraped into the charts, despite its enormous success in America. From that point on, following the group required a strong immunity to the vagaries of public taste. I remained optimistic that they might recover lost ground in Britain, wrongly predicting another number 1 in the near future, which surely would have been followed by a tour. Meanwhile, there was the challenge of keeping up with their recorded output. Saving up for records was a perverse luxury when you didn't have electricity. Singles were acceptable in limited doses but, at 32/6d, albums required months of careful saving and were impossible to justify if you didn't even own a record player. In a remarkable act of subterfuge, I squirreled away some Christmas paper round tips and ten bob Irish postal orders, then shamelessly went out and bought a couple of LP record tokens at nearby Recordsville in Wilton Road. Fearing rebuke for such a secret and wilfully extravagant purchase, I then mailed the tokens to my address at 16 Colchester Street, accompanied by a note of congratulations from an unnamed imaginary DJ for having supposedly won a competition on Radio Luxembourg. That was how I came to purchase the first albums I ever owned: *Mr Tambourine Man* and *Turn! Turn! Turn!*.

Deprivation brings its own frustrations and rewards and actually hearing these records was not always easy. I can remember some nights sitting alone in the kitchen, staring at those alluring Byrds sleeves and longing for the opportunity to hear such oddities as 'We'll Meet Again', 'Oh! Susannah' and the many new Dylan songs and group originals on offer. There was even an ode to JFK – mysteriously devoid of a writing credit on the record – which reminded me of the time I had seen the doomed president and his iconic first lady Jackie in Victoria Street, just months before his assassination. The Byrds were always good at conjuring up poignant memories, even ones you didn't know you treasured. The longing to hear those albums made the listening experience an event in itself. Occasionally, more affluent friends with record players or family radiograms came to the rescue, but all too often that seemed to be by special appointment only. Less well-off families, including my own, were reluctant to allow anybody inside their homes. Neighbouring kids usually remained outside on the doorstep. Funnily enough, it was exclusively on summer visits to Ireland that I could listen to all these records uninterrupted through long rain-tinged weeks. At the barracks at the top of Doneraile Walk, Tramore, we may not have had baths, fridges or inside toilets, but electricity was in plentiful supply and you could blast out the Byrds and Dylan from the back parlour, loud and proud.

Back in London, radio offered solace whenever staring at unplayable records proved tantalizing. Cheap transistors were all the rage and when Sid the Paper Man upped my paper round money to 10 shillings a week I wasted no time in purchasing a set for 19/6d at Piercy's electrical shop in Lupus Street. Both the pirates and Radio Luxembourg offered aural exotica beyond the imaginations of those responsible for the Light Programme's bland playlist. I clearly remember wandering around a bomb site in Cornwall Street, Pimlico, surveying the desolate rubble, as my transistor played an entrancing new release: 'Set You Free This Time'. The ravaged setting added an even greater poignancy to Gene Clark's word-packed tale of fractured love. The next day I rushed out of the school gates and bought the single at the Army & Navy Stores in Victoria Street, insisting that the sales assistant play it twice before handing over my money. At that moment, in that listening booth, I realized the Byrds had reached a new plateau and would survive with or without Dylan's patronage.

Not long after, I learned the sad news that Gene Clark had left the group. 'Eight Miles High' followed, a mind-blowing single that never dated and sounded better and better with each passing year. It elevated the Byrds in the eyes of discerning critics, even though many in the music press remained sceptical. Although played frequently on pirate radio, the track was only a minor hit in the UK. Its supposed drug connotations provoked no comment at all, although a radio ban was reported in the US, which seemed faintly ludicrous. The remainder of the year was a quiet period for the Byrds. I missed Clark's songwriting on their third album, with its relatively meagre 11 songs, and wondered whether they could survive and thrive without him.

1966 was the year of the Anglophiles. England, and more especially London, was deemed the music and fashion capital of the world. Riding around on my bicycle, buying records, bunking into Battersea Fun Fair to save the 6d entrance fee, sampling bottles of Guinness and cider or wandering around pinball arcades in Soho, I felt the empowering, if delusory, swagger of youth unbound. A general sense of optimism was palpable on the streets. Attitudes were changing and the media seemed to be kneeling in gratuitous homage before the inviolable altar of youth. Although I didn't know it at the time, the Small Faces had recently moved in down the road, consuming drugs and women in spendthrift abandon at their rave pad in Westmoreland Terrace, across the road from the Stanley Arms. Every evening I passed by their house on my bike delivering papers for Sid the Paper Man, unaware of the pop saturnalia in my midst.

This focus on all things English was hardly good news for the Byrds. They no longer featured in the *NME*, appeared on *Top Of The Pops* or graced the Top 20, so it became increasingly difficult to justify their existence to sceptical schoolfriends. At that time, certainly for kids of my age and background, there was no concept of cult status or indie credibility. If you wanted to champion the obscure, you were old and elitist and probably listened to jazz or folk, not pop. For young kids, it was all about hits and misses, and the fact that so many great singles charted proved the wisdom of that brutal commercial logic.

The Byrds re-emerged in early 1967 with 'So You Want To Be A Rock 'n' Roll Star' and tantalized a nation by appearing on *Top Of The Pops*, yet neglecting to undertake a major tour. The release of the single coincided with the enforced demolition of our house, which saddened me greatly, but it was amusing to graduate to a council flat which boasted a toilet, bathroom and even a private bedroom. A first bath felt like sinking into the sea, only warmer, but the experience was eclipsed by the miracle of electricity. There were sockets all over the flat, positively inviting consumer durables, although absurd, undreamed of luxuries like fridges, washing machines and vacuum cleaners were clearly out of the question. To this day, I question their relevance, like an acoustic folkie still baffled by electricity. Nevertheless, a rented black and white television with three channels ushered in a new era. I celebrated this technological good fortune by trading in my sadly departed sister's old manual typewriter for a record player. For the remainder of the decade the Byrds' story unfolded against a virtually non-stop soundtrack of their every song played over and over on my faithful phonogram. At night, when the record player was off, I'd often stay up till 2 am listening to the transistor, and awaiting that thrill of excitement whenever the pirates played a Byrds' song alongside the familiar hits of the time. I was late for school every day of the week, including lunch times, when I insisted on listening to an entire LP of theirs uninterrupted. It was a daily ritual.

The Byrds' successive chart failures brought moments of suffering, but every time they released a new record it was a wondrous event. *Younger Than Yesterday* provided the final conviction, and one was needed then, that they were arguably the greatest group of the era. This was a period when they had acquired that almost indescribable touch of greatness, spread over an entire album's worth of songs. Suddenly, David Crosby was a songwriter *par excellence*, right up there with Clark and McGuinn. Even Hillman, the once shy bass player, was composing instant classics. Was there no end to this group's talent? I thought the Byrds had outdone the Beatles on *Younger Than Yesterday* and reckoned them to be at the forefront of a new revolution in popular music. These were heady considerations at such a young age. There was no UK underground press back then to offer interviews or commentaries on the group or their music, and filtering news meant scouring other music papers like *Disc* and *Record Mirror*, or catching nuggets of news in columns like *America Calling*.

THE GHOST OF ELECTRICITY REVISITED

The disintegration of the Byrds in late 1967 came via conflicting, desultory and belated bulletins. Crosby was out, Clark was back, then Clark had left again. Little or no explanation was given for this cataclysmic series of changes. 'Byrds Make Trio Debut', headlined the *NME* when reviewing their single 'Goin' Back' in Christmas week, but by then Michael Clarke had gone too. I was so deflated by the news that I delayed purchasing *The Notorious Byrd Brothers* for nearly two months, assuming that it must be a severely watered-down work. I was astounded to hear how strong the album sounded given the obvious conflict surrounding its creation. Even at their apparent weakest, the Byrds could still challenge and match the Beatles to my mind.

The recruitment of Gram Parsons and the abrupt move towards country music no doubt bewildered some fans, but by this time I was ready to expect anything from this group. They seldom ceased to astound. In 1968, they played their grandest show yet in the UK, appearing with new boy Parsons at the Royal Albert Hall. Wow! It was an eventful Sunday evening when I took the 52 bus from Victoria to the RAH, completely unaware of what might happen. Assuming there was probably some formal dress code at this magnificent institution, I wore a Burton's suit, recently purchased by my mother. That detail is also revealing. Fridges, phones, washing machines and vacuum cleaners may have been beyond the family budget or imagination but, as Mr Dick had suggested in *David Copperfield*, it was very important to have a suit for Sunday best. Fortunately, I was not alone. Both McGuinn and Parsons also wore fine suits that evening. Gram's had a reddish hue and was the most striking garment I'd seen since David Crosby's impossibly fab green suede cape.

It is difficult to convey the sense of expectation, even consternation, surrounding this crucial concert. Since their controversial 1965 UK tour, the one constant in reports of the Byrds had been their disappointing live performances. At the height of Crosby's dominance, transatlantic bulletins reviewing their LA shows were full of acerbic put-downs of their onstage cool and interminable tuning sessions between songs. Even Derek Taylor, their own publicist, had heretically described their appearances at the Whisky as "terrible". Now they were descending on the Royal Albert Hall in the full glare of the British music press, not to mention an audience that included rock's hip elite, among whom was an assortment of Beatles and Rolling Stones. Equally worrying was the concert's line-up of up-and-coming stars (Joe Cocker, Grapefruit, the Alan Bown, the Easybeats and the Bonzo Dog Doo-Dah Band) any one of whom might distract attention from the Byrds. Most disconcerting of all, however, was the presence of the Move who, unlike their American rivals, were chart regulars and boasted one of the most exciting stage acts of the period. They even featured a cover of 'So You Want To Be A Rock 'n' Roll Star' in their set, although it would not be played on this all-important evening. As if inviting disaster, the Byrds had agreed to close the first half of the concert, leaving the Move the honour of ending the night and, most likely, stealing the show. Fortunately, it was the Byrds who won the accolades with a thrilling set that secured them their first major headline in *NME* since the glory days of 'Mr Tambourine Man' and 'All I Really Want To Do'. One of my abiding memories is the thrill of hearing the shout "bring back the Byrds" during the second half of the concert, as if confirming that the old prejudices about their live shows had finally been put to rest.

Some latter-day music historians insist that *Sweetheart Of The Rodeo* was greeted with bewilderment and contempt. "Country fans despised it and Byrds fans thought it was a counter revolutionary joke," was one recent revisionist assessment. While this may have been true among the counterculture elite in America, it was clearly not the case throughout England, where 'You Ain't Going Nowhere' had reached the lower regions of the chart and was frequently played on both the Light Programme and the pirate radio stations. Whatever anyone thought of the Byrds' new musical direction, it was no longer a massive shock by the time *Sweetheart Of The Rodeo* appeared at the end of September 1968. The album was a challenging but beautiful piece which confirmed my growing belief that the Byrds could conquer almost any musical genre.

Of course, they had to spoil it, as usual, with more damaging line-up changes. At the end of 1968, even I thought they must be finished and mourned their passing that Christmas. Two months later, they re-emerged with a great new single and the adventure began all over again. That same year, my history teacher allowed me to submit 'the history of pop music' as a CSE project for examination. Needless to say, the Byrds featured heavily.

In 1970, I was transferred to the newly built Pimlico School which, rather poignantly, stood on the very spot where our gaslit house had once been. The new decade saw a confident counter-culture largely unaffected by events such as the Altamont tragedy or the break-up of the Beatles. It would be some time yet before the Sixties' party was officially deemed over. Three years after Haight-Ashbury, LSD reached Pimlico's working classes and it was intriguing to witness recently skinheaded hooligans growing their hair, abandoning allegiances to Chelsea Football Club and proclaiming the wonders of the heaven and hell drug. Nobody came out with any negative or condescending comments about the Byrds any more. They were back in vogue thanks to the best-selling *(Untitled)* and 'Chestnut Mare', their first UK Top 20 hit in four years. Their final two albums for CBS were not the strongest by their standards, but still received far more press attention than their brilliant mid-period work.

By this point, the Byrds had decided that the UK was a cool outpost for touring purposes. The McGuinn/White/Parsons/Battin line-up played here regularly and their live shows were invariably excellent. Like many fans of that time, I have fond memories of performances at the Royal Albert Hall and the Rainbow and I was lucky enough to attend a *Top Of The Pops'* recording where they played their new single, 'I Trust'. In August 1971, they appeared at the Lincoln Folk Festival, billed as 'the acoustic Byrds'. I slept in a graveyard after the festival, then made my way home.

At the end of the following year, they split. I was still a teenager, at 19, but it seemed that they had already taken me through an entire lifetime. Their reunion album was released in the year after I finally left school. I returned shaven-headed from a monastery on a mountain in Ireland in time to savour this unlikely turn of events. I had never expected a groundbreaking work in the tradition of *Younger Than Yesterday* or *Notorious* so I loved the record at the time, which easily eclipsed *Byrdmaniax* and *Farther Along*. Not long after, Clarence White and Gram Parsons both died in tragic circumstances. I still had fond recollections of Gram and Kevin Kelley and more recently had been thrilled to see the New Kentucky Colonels whom Clarence had brought to Europe.

I had hoped that the original members of the Byrds would persevere with a follow-up album and tour, but that proved a false dream. In the end, it didn't matter that much. There were already enough offshoot ventures, from the Flying Burrito Brothers through Dillard & Clark and Crosby, Stills, Nash & Young to keep you in listening pleasure for years. Looking back, the Byrds single-handedly spawned an entire subgenre of LA rock, which is a lasting testament to the immense talent contained within their ranks.

For the next seven years after their demise, I was at university, first studying English Language & Literature in Newcastle upon Tyne, then as a postgraduate in Nova Scotia, and finally at Lady Margaret Hall, Oxford. During those years I wrote about the Byrds in specialist music magazines like *Zigzag* and *Dark Star* and made the bold decision to write a book on them. Collating research material was no easy task in those days and arranging interviews as a student without a phone sometimes proved problematical. But I was nothing if not determined. After winning a fellowship and scholarship for work in Anglo Saxon, I completed a Masters degree in double quick time and used the remaining money to finance a spell in Hollywood, where many of the original interviews for the book were done back in the Seventies. Since then there have been countless more interviews with scores of their associates, and I don't suppose this book will be the last word from me on the subject.

From a writer's viewpoint, the Byrds were always great interviewees, even when they weren't being too co-operative. Their story was a highly emotive drama and I was always impressed by the forthright tone and unflinching honesty with which they recalled their darker moments. During the late Seventies there was a lot of cocaine around, which no doubt added an impressive air of candid acidity to their world-view. Then again, the Byrds always did tread a fine line between idealism and cynicism: listen to 'Renaissance Fair' and 'So You Want To Be A Rock 'n' Roll Star', respectively, for two contrasting views of the rock world.

THE GHOST OF ELECTRICITY REVISITED

Apart from Crosby's famous recommendation of LSD, onstage at the Monterey Pop Festival, the Byrds were reasonably discreet about their drug use. Still, they could always surprise you. When three of the originals arrived here on a package tour in 1977, RSO Records threw a lavish party for them across from the Mayfair Hotel. I can fondly remember bumping into McGuinn in a toilet there and he immediately produced some cocaine, which he offered as though it were a packet of cigarettes. When a friend added, "I never tried that", McGuinn replied: "I don't want to corrupt you." I excused myself and returned upstairs where Gene Clark and Tommy Kaye were proving that alcoholism was alive and well. Clark stood up and toasted me that evening in front of the entire assembly. He was both cordial and enigmatic on that tour, and we got on well. Hillman was sharp, funny, engaging, likeable and extremely professional, but in the end he was the one who left the tour and returned home.

By the time I caught up with them again, back in the States, they were experiencing new-found fame as McGuinn, Clark & Hillman. But you didn't have to be a psychologist to detect an iciness in their interaction. Los Angeles in the late Seventies was characterized by a wilfully blind and peculiarly insular hedonism in which the attendant Caesars continued to drink from the demulcent dregs of a once golden cup, already tarnished by cocaine excess. At its most delusory, it resembled a never ending party – even several of the old Ciro's set were still around happy to be interviewed into the early hours – but once you left the City of Angels, it was clear that an era was coming to an end. The Eighties were upon us and the Byrds were scattered once more.

All the original members seemed adept at pushing themselves towards the edge, but not all were capable of avoiding the abyss. Crosby's cocaine addiction seemed certain to end his career and probably his life. One year on, back in London, I remember asking him how much time he felt he had left as he inhaled hungrily from his pipe. "About five years or so," he mused. It was difficult to decide whether he was referring to his career or his life. On reflection, it was probably both.

Crosby was staying at a small guest house in Denbigh Street, adjacent to Pimlico School on whose site, 15 years before, I had first learned of the Byrds' existence. I tried to take him to the Lord High Admiral or across to Recordsville to see a different world, but he wouldn't be distracted from his stash. His descent into freebase hell later in the decade could not disguise a resilient spirit, whose corrosive ego provided both the reason for his doom and the means of his salvation. He was a burning mass of passion, pride, hubris and regret, but blessed with a clear-eyed, almost painful honesty, that was genuinely moving. Always the most articulate of the Byrds, he gave me the best interview of my life. It was an extremely moving experience, never to be forgotten.

Back then, I was an intensely interrogative interviewer, still immersed in academe, who saw the role of the detached commentator and critic as crucially important. "Don't get *too* close" was a dictum to be followed, no matter how much you were enjoying an opportunity to socialize. When Crosby proudly showed a picture of his boat, the *Mayan*, and suggested a visit to San Francisco and even dangled a tentative, if unlikely, book project, it was difficult not to be swept along by the sheer force of his passion. He seemed to care about the Byrds and its legacy far more than McGuinn did at the time, and was more trusting than Hillman and a better communicator than Clark. Of course, there was always the danger of factions and competing loves with the Byrds. It was important to obtain an uncompromising interview and for that you had to be impartial at all costs. Schmoozing was enjoyable, ego-gratifying and tempting, but so is the devil. For a writer, the performer as surrogate friend is invariably a dangerous trade-off. Familiarity often leads to favouritism, complacency and even contempt. There are further complications. If you get too close, you're in danger of losing the magic that got you interested in the first place. Over the years, I had plenty of opportunities to hang out, and often did, but I always remembered that writing a group biography meant knowing when to leave the party with your impartiality and integrity intact. It probably helped that I loved them all equally for different reasons at different times. That still holds to this day.

When I first started writing about the Byrds all of the above seemed terribly important. We were only a decade away from the

THE GHOST OF ELECTRICITY REVISITED

glory days of 'Mr Tambourine Man' and there was a lot at stake. I still vainly hoped they might reunite and fulfil McGuinn's dream of creating something as significant as 'Eight Miles High' or *The Notorious Byrd Brothers*. Rather than revelling in their past greatness and flattering their achievements, my approach as an interviewer was to encourage them to try even harder. With albums like Crosby's *If I Could Only Remember My Name* and Clark's *No Other*, there was evidence of great innovation but, unreasonably at times, I believed they needed to sustain this standard and eclipse all comers. I was always greedy for greatness on their behalf.

Of course, by the Eighties you were pathetically happy just to hear them still record *anything*. By then they were part of rock's history rather than its future. Nevertheless, their influence was everywhere and the phrase 'Byrds-like' had virtually become a cliché. By the end of the decade, their past was being reassembled in the manner of an archaeological dig, courtesy of the many unearthed tapes recorded during their golden era. Soon after, Sony Records generously offered me a sizeable fee to provide song notes, memorabilia and feedback for the extensive reissue series. Songs doomed to extinction 40 years ago suddenly found a new life on CD; innumerable backing tracks, alternate takes and long forgotten snippets of in-studio argument were tagged on at the end of their reissued albums. There was a strange poetic justice at work here as the ghostly voices of their former selves laid claim to a destiny that was denied them all those years ago. In the end, the Byrds' myth conquered even time itself, or so it seemed.

The deaths of Gene Clark and Michael Clarke ended the dream of any full-scale reunion, just as Lennon's assassination had done with the Beatles' myth. Anything else would be merely partial and inadequate, although nostalgists, promoters and the surviving Byrds would all have benefited on some level.

After all I had written about the group, I was amazed to discover that there was still more to be discovered and learned – and it was all great stuff. I never stopped writing or listening. I kept going back. The research, conversations and interviews with an extended cast have continued up until this very day. I'm still searching, reflecting and trying to improve my own understanding and appreciation of the story. It has taken an entire lifetime. Gloriously, their music continues to resonate with new meaning as well as reaffirming the beauty of a treasured past. One thing I never wanted to do was choose between them, nor make any one of them a hero or villain. They were all fallible, like the best of Shakespearean characters, and almost as fascinating. As this first volume shows, the Byrds' saga is a remarkable adventure and a parable of the age in which they lived.

CHAPTER ONE

The Secret Origins Of The Byrds

A HARRIED scriptwriter could not have conceived a more unlikely story than the formation of the Byrds. Rock mythology tells us that Jim McGuinn, Gene Clark and David Crosby first combined their talents to form a Beatles-influenced trio, the Jet Set, which later expanded with the addition of drummer Michael Clarke and bassist Chris Hillman. Unlike many band histories though, this was not the familiar saga of teenage friends finding fame together or garage group aspirants in search of glory. The players came from different parts of America, and boasted varying musical backgrounds that ranged from folk, R&B and rock 'n' roll to country & western and bluegrass. Some of them had fortuitously crossed paths before, without ever realizing that they might be drawn together in this unique enterprise. The British beat boom clearly played a crucial part in their creation, but that was only part of the tale. More important was the rebellious zest and wide-eyed enthusiasm of five young people, the majority still in their teens, pooling together their limited playing experience to fashion a new American music, the impact of which still seems as potent today as it was nearly half a century ago. Every member of the original Byrds deserves a full-scale biography of their own, but it is their star-crossed story in the mother group that remains the stuff of rock legend.

James Joseph McGuinn III, born in Chicago on 13 July 1942, had the most colourful pre-Byrd history of all. His parents, James and Dorothy, were involved in journalism and public relations and during his childhood penned a best-seller humorously titled *Parents*

Can't Win. They toured extensively across the States and James Jnr attended a variety of schools. He first became interested in popular music after hearing Elvis Presley's 'Heartbreak Hotel', which hogged the top of the US charts for eight weeks in the spring of 1956. There was something indefinably arresting about the disc, which sounded unlike anything McGuinn had ever heard before. That voice, so youthful and yet so mournful, sang in almost elegiac recognition of a loneliness beyond redemption. For a lapsed Catholic like McGuinn, it was the closest verbal articulation of his religion's greatest taboo, despair. The stark piano accompaniment, in curious contrast to a throbbing bass line, merely added to the drama. All this might have proven academic were it not for the physical presence of Presley himself, whose aura of brooding sexuality and unspecified rebellion threatened the very fabric of apple pie American morality. For even liberal parents, Elvis seemed the latest and most provocative example of unfettered youth, swaggering triumphantly in obscene arrogance on prime time television. Those with long memories called this new music another fad which wouldn't last the year. For teenagers bereft of the prejudice of historical perspective, it was something more: an engagement with the present that glorified in its own wilful instant gratification.

The Presley phenomenon so captured McGuinn's imagination that he asked his parents to buy him a Harmony six-string acoustic guitar for his 14th birthday. In his spare time he began playing the rock 'n' roll hits of the period and soon boasted a jukebox-like repertoire featuring the works of Gene Vincent, Carl Perkins, the Everly Brothers and, of course, Elvis Presley. Many youths lost their appetite for rock 'n' roll during the late Fifties when Presley was inducted into the US forces and the music became pasteurized. McGuinn was spared any pangs of disillusionment, for he had already moved on.

McGuinn's fascination for rock 'n' roll was replaced by a new musical passion, which unexpectedly emerged in the school classroom. His music teacher, Louise Ganton, was acquainted with the folk musician Bob Gibson and invited him to play some songs for the kids one afternoon in the autumn of 1957. This made a great impression on McGuinn who embraced folk with the zeal of a convert. Subsequently, Miss Ganton suggested that he enrol at Chicago's Old Town School Of Folk Music where, for $10.00 a lesson, he could master the five-string banjo and hone his guitar skills. One of his tutors was Frank Hamilton (later of the Weavers) who introduced him to the work of Pete Seeger, Big Bill Broonzy and Leadbelly. McGuinn also studied the 12-string guitar, an instrument once popular but under-used in contemporary music. Even at this stage, the teenager was blessed with a folklorist's appetite and loved discovering new styles of music to add to his collection. He occasionally taped himself on a reel to reel and some songs survive from this period, including 'In The Evenin'' and the traditional 'To Morrow', an American-Irish tune detailing a trip to the town of Morrow in Ohio.

By now, McGuinn felt confident enough to appear at local coffee houses on Chicago's Rush Street. Although still a minor, he frequented Albert Grossman's Gate Of Horn where he remembers seeing Odetta and Josh White and hearing the entire Ewan MacColl songbook of sea shanties. Years later, he would remember those impressionable moments in the tribute song 'Gate Of Horn', which appeared on his second solo album, *Peace On You,* and he would return to the period again in compiling his 'Folk Den' recordings.

One evening, Alex Hassilev of the Limeliters invited McGuinn to play banjo at an after hours jam. It went so well that he was asked to attend an audition the following day. McGuinn stayed up all night learning their songs and impressed the elder musicians with his commitment and enthusiasm. "I was a little shaky, but I got through it," he recalls. A job offer followed, but he reluctantly declined, explaining that he was obliged to complete his final year at high school and could not tour.

Fortunately, the Limeliters still needed an accompanist some months later. A few days after leaving school, McGuinn received a telegram requesting his presence on the West Coast. His parents signed a letter of permission and, on 3 July 1960, still ten days short of his eighteenth birthday, he boarded a plane for Los Angeles. Over the next month, he played at the celebrated folk mecca, the Ash Grove, appeared at the Hollywood Bowl on a bill including Eartha Kitt, and guested on the Limeliters' live recording *Tonight In*

Person. Any hopes of further glory were postponed when his cost-cutting employers dispensed with his services after only six weeks. Undeterred, he started hanging out at clubs like the Troubadour in Hollywood, which is where he first met his later co-writer R.J. ('Bob') Hippard, who was then working as a road manager for Hoyt Axton and the folk duo, Art And Paul. Fully embracing the West Coast experience, McGuinn moved to San Francisco, performing regularly at the Hungry i, where he befriended several members of the Gateway Singers and the Kingston Trio, as well as discovering the delights of strong marijuana. He also began experimenting with LSD for the first time and placed great faith in the mind-expanding properties of the drug, which was then still legal.

The teenage troubadour found himself in demand again when the Chad Mitchell Trio telephoned through an irresistible offer from New York. Mitchell and his cohorts were part of the more commercial area of folk music and could afford to pay good wages. McGuinn stayed with them for two-and-a-half years, toured across America and played on their albums *Mighty Day On Campus* and *Live At The Bitter End*. Along the way, he enjoyed some notable adventures, not least a trip to South America, sponsored by the State Department. According to McGuinn, the visit came about following their recording of Michael Brown's political satire 'The John Birch Society', a lighter stab at the right-wing institution pilloried on Dylan's hilariously acerbic, 'Talkin' John Birch Paranoid Blues'. "Somebody in John F. Kennedy's State Department thought it would be funny to send us down to South America as musical ambassadors," he recalls.

After hearing the sound of gunfire on the streets, McGuinn sought tranquillity alone with his guitar. One day, he walked to the top of a cliff in Santa Domingo overlooking the ocean. A Bach-like lilt filled his head which he played on his guitar, then filed away for future reference. The melody would unexpectedly reappear years later as the central section of 'Chestnut Mare'.

Life as the unheralded fourth member of the Chad Mitchell Trio brought its own frustrations. Since they were all singers, McGuinn's role could never rise above that of an invisible accompanist at the side of the stage. The experience was invaluable, but he eventually became disenchanted. "They wouldn't let me sing and I had to do all the playing," he told me. "They treated me like James the Butler, so it was a little frustrating, but I did enjoy working with them. It wasn't entirely a negative experience. They were quite good at what they did but they didn't know that much about real folk music and I didn't feel they had the integrity of the people I'd followed. I wanted to get better. It seemed time was slipping by. So I started practising more, using a metronome. They found it difficult to sing along with a steady beat as they weren't used to strict tempo."

As part of his act, McGuinn liked to clown around in the shadows, making faces onstage. One evening at the Crescendo, the Trio were opening for comedian Lenny Bruce, unaware that singer Bobby Darin was in the audience. Darin was one of the most astute pop singers of his era and immediately saw McGuinn's potential. Having moved from the bubblegum pop of 'Splish Splash' and 'Queen Of The Hop' to the supper club circuit sophistication of 'Mack The Knife', Darin needed a guitarist to add a musical punch to his folk routine. At the end of the gig, he asked McGuinn how much he was being paid by Chad Mitchell. "I'll double it," he added, almost before the startled guitarist could answer the question.

Darin's offer, allegedly occurring on McGuinn's twentieth birthday, came just in time to prevent the accompanist from accepting an invitation to team up with the New Christy Minstrels. Instead, Jim spent the latter part of 1962 playing upmarket cabaret. Midway through his set, Darin featured a folk music segment, backed by his new guitarist. "The big band would take a break and it would be down to a stand-up bass and me on the 12-string," McGuinn remembers. "I don't think we even had drums, just bass and guitar. We would play 15 minutes of folk songs, real folk music in the middle of his show. Then I'd go away and he'd do his Frank Sinatra kind of stuff."

The showbiz discipline demanded by Darin was quite a revelation to the ex-folkie, who suddenly found himself purchasing expensive mohair suits and ultra smart shoes. "He was a great influence on me," McGuinn maintains. "He was old school showbusiness – the work ethic. He was able to give me some really helpful hints on how to pursue a career in the music business." Darin was full of instant aphorisms such as "Get in front of an audience," and "Always be on time, always be in tune". Under the singer's tutelage, McGuinn learned that presentation and image were a crucial part of performing and should not be ignored.

Darin's precarious health temporarily stopped him from performing but he offered McGuinn a job at his New York publishing company for $35.00 per week. During early 1963, he was hard at work in the cubicles of the Brill Building, which also housed such protégés as Neil Sedaka, Gerry Goffin and Carole King. While there, McGuinn and co-writer Frank Gari came up with 'Beach Ball', a Beach Boys pastiche released on Capitol under the banner of the City Surfers. It was a typical studio creation which failed to sell, in spite of the presence of Terry Melcher (piano) and Bobby Darin (drums). At this point, McGuinn was a skilled arranger rather than a natural songwriter, but he took heart when informed that 'Beach Ball' had become a minor hit in Australia for television presenter Jimmy Hannan.

Working with Darin brought McGuinn good money and during this period he married for the first time, but it was not to last. "I wouldn't say that was a responsible part of my life," McGuinn reflects. "It wasn't like buying a little house, settling down and having a day job kind of marriage. It was more a staying up till five in the morning and sleeping till one marriage. It only lasted six months before it was annulled. I wouldn't say it was a real marriage, just kids playing." It was Darin's priapic urges that brought the marriage to an abrupt end but, despite witnessing that betrayal, McGuinn has never had a bad word to say about his mentor.

During visits to the West Coast, McGuinn also teamed up with California-based composer, Jane Schorr (wife of the songwriter Walter Schorr). The pair copyrighted two songs, 'Love Beyond Compare' and 'You Are The One', but neither made any impact commercially. "I don't even remember writing them," McGuinn confesses. "I couldn't even hum them now. They're just lost in my memory. Jane was a songwriter of sorts and we used to hang out together."

Despite his brief time in the Brill Building, McGuinn was never a prolific writer and preferred practising his guitar scales while dreaming of a performing career. From his conversations with Darin, he realized that his best option was to play solo. Before leaving his employer, he sought his advice on how to become famous. Darin's reply was perceptive: "The way to start off is to be a rock 'n' roll singer." It would be some time yet before McGuinn actually followed this good advice. In the meantime, he played to his strengths. He was already a strong musician and gained valuable experience in session work, arranging for and accompanying Hoyt Axton, the Irish Ramblers, Judy Collins and Tom and Jerry (who later emerged as Simon & Garfunkel). Additionally, McGuinn appeared on several instrumental albums, playing banjo and 12-string guitar. While guesting at Greenwich Village hootenannies he had also seen the competition that included the soon-to-be-famous Bob Dylan. At that point, McGuinn regarded the un-crowned king of folk as "just another imitator", while Dylan merely smiled inscrutably at his uncool mohair suit.

Shortly after his 21st birthday, McGuinn had an important appointment with the United States Armed Forces. The prospect of serving in Vietnam was anathema to the peaceniks of the folk movement but at this stage avoiding the draft was not especially difficult. "I was exempt," McGuinn recalls. "I had taken the physical and they didn't want me. They seemed to think that I would be more trouble than I was worth. That was the attitude. I went in there and I was not as co-operative as they would have wanted. I didn't just want to waltz off to war. So it was as easy as that. I got out of it. I got a 4-F. It could have been devastating. Look what happened to Elvis."

By the end of 1963, McGuinn had become fixated with the Beatles, who were about to conquer the American charts. While playing New York coffee houses, he started adding a back beat to traditional folk songs like 'Wild Mountain Thyme'. One club owner placed a sign advertising for "Beatles imitators" and McGuinn took the gig, playing Fab Four covers, even though he still had short hair and wore glasses. Once, while walking down Bleecker Street in Greenwich Village, two would-be managers in search of a Beatles' copy band, eyed him enviously and declared: "What we need is four of *him*." The endorsement amused McGuinn and boosted his confidence at a time when other folkies were quick to deride his Fab Four affectations.

At this point, McGuinn still saw himself as a Beatles imitator, and it took a figure from an earlier era in pop to show him the future. "I had been mixing the Beatle beat with folk music when Dion DiMucci came by the hotel where I was staying. I guess he'd heard about me because of Darin and was looking for a sideman, a guitar player. I showed him what I was doing and he said, 'You're on to something, you should go ahead and pursue that.' He gave me that encouragement."

At first, McGuinn was perplexed and said, "I'm just doing the Beatles!"

Dion shook his head and insisted: "No, what *you're* doing is different, it's not the Beatles." Always a good listener, McGuinn was impressed by the enthusiasm of the former doo-wop king, who had already shown an astute grasp of changes in pop by re-launching himself as a solo and acting out the loneliness, insecurity and macho narcissism of adolescent life in such teenage mini-operas as 'Runaround Sue' and 'The Wanderer'.

Soon after the exchange with Dion, McGuinn received a phone call from his friend Bob Hippard in Hollywood informing him that the Troubadour's owner Doug Weston needed someone to open for Roger Miller and Hoyt Axton. McGuinn relocated to LA but initially found great difficulty in persuading the denizens of the Troubadour that he was a credible performer. The traditionalists in the audience felt his Beatles copies were laughable, and he sneered back at them. One evening, Roger Miller took him aside and told him to grit his teeth, smile hypocritically, and ignore the hecklers. As the weeks passed, McGuinn improved and, before long, his repertoire came to the attention of another Beatles' fan in search of a sympathetic writing partner.

Harold Eugene Clark had yet to assimilate McGuinn's vast experience of the different spectrums of the music business, but his road to the Troubadour was far from uneventful. Born in Tipton, Missouri on 17 November 1944, Clark was reared on country, bluegrass and rockabilly and, like McGuinn, became a folk music aficionado in his teens. At high school in Kansas City, he joined his first group, Joe Meyers and the Sharks, then began that prolific songwriting spree which was to characterize his later stint in the Byrds. In 1958, the Sharks recorded one of his compositions, 'Blue Ribbons', which was purportedly issued on a local label and played on national television. For 14-year-old Gene, this was quite an ego boost. School groups seldom last, however, and Clark went through several, including the Rum Runners and the Surf Riders. The latter looked particularly promising and during late 1962 they could be seen playing Kingston Trio-influenced material at the Castaways club in Kansas City. The following summer, the New Christy Minstrels came to town and a couple of their members caught the Surf Riders' set and were pleasantly surprised. Christy supremo Randy Sparks arrived next to gauge their potential and wasted no time in commandeering the entire group. Clark's erstwhile partners, Jimmy Glover and Michael Crumm (aka Crowley), were subsequently despatched to the Back Porch Majority while he was offered a spot in the Minstrels.

The timing could not have been better. The Christies had just recorded the album *Ramblin'* and their latest single 'Green Green', featuring the gravel-voiced Barry McGuire, was about to become a smash hit. The Minstrels toured extensively and slotted in recording schedules whenever time permitted. On one hot summer's day, Gene found himself in the studio putting down tracks for a festive album, *Merry Christmas*. When a second Top 30 hit occurred with 'Saturday Night' in November 1963, Clark became strangely uneasy. Their hectic schedule, especially the long, tension-filled aeroplane flights, started playing on his nerves.

During the first ravages of American Beatlemania, Clark was entertaining President Lyndon B. Johnson at the White House. However, the prestige of Minstreldom could not entirely compensate for his subordinate role in the ensemble. He contributed towards one more album, *Land Of Giants*, before half-reluctantly returning to California to stake out the local clubs. One evening, he visited the Troubadour and saw McGuinn playing Beatle-songs on a 12-string guitar and introducing rock arrangements of famous folk songs. Suitably impressed, Gene suggested that they form a duo in imitation of the British group, Peter And Gordon. The pairing was to prove short-lived, but memorable.

"Gene and I actually started it," McGuinn says. "We met at the Troubadour and we were both guitar-playing, singing, writing people and we wanted to get a thing going. We were playing around in coffee houses and running around trying to find places to play all night long, and there weren't many out here. So we'd wind up at somebody's house and that was the pattern– no pressure at all, no responsibility, just get up and feed yourself, find a place to play all night."

At the same point in time, another young, impressionable folk singer was regularly frequenting the Troubadour. Born in Los Angeles on 14 August 1941, David Van Cortlandt Crosby hailed from a high society family. His mother Aliph was a former débutante and his father Floyd was a respected director of photography. As well as winning Academy Awards for his work on *High Noon* and *Tabu*, Floyd was also responsible for the photography on a whole series of Roger Corman films, including such classics as *The Raven*, *The Pit And The Pendulum* and *The Fall Of The House Of Usher*. Music was very much a part of David's early life and even before he learned guitar he enjoyed scat-singing along with his elder brother, Chip.

By the time he reached late adolescence Crosby had a long history as a troublemaker. An incorrigible pupil, he was expelled from some of the best private schools in Hollywood and was generally regarded as a precocious, car-crazed, girl-chasing, rich kid. In spite of his affluent background, he was always restless and rebellious and briefly took up housebreaking with a couple of local accomplices. Predictably, it all ended in tears.

"I used to make a joke that was the way I worked my way through school," he told me, "but the truth was that we did it more for the rush than anything else. We did it a number of times. I worked out a system which worked pretty well. I did it until once I had to confront a woman whose house we had ransacked. She wanted her wallet back. It had the only existing picture of her old man who had died in the war. She was in tears, you know. And it changed it completely. It was not just taking stuff. All of a sudden it was somebody's precious things. It made quite an impression on me and I would never take anything now. It's just not right." Crosby's punishment was a term of probation and a visit to a therapist. His mother was suitably mortified.

After graduating from Santa Barbara College, Crosby enrolled at the Pasadena Playhouse acting school, but soon dropped out to become a folk singer. He appeared in coffee houses with a repertoire that included 'Motherless Children', 'Anathea', 'God Bless The Child' and a startling jazz-influenced version of Gershwin's 'Summertime', complete with scat singing. There was also more brooding material like 'It's Been Raining', which prefigured his work as a singer-songwriter later in the decade.

"When I started playing music, there was no money to be made," he recalls. "Peter, Paul & Mary hadn't made their first record, and neither had Dylan. I was a folkie and I played because I loved it and I wanted to get the attention of girls. I passed a basket around after my set. Five bucks was a big night."

The music did attract female attention, but this was not always to his benefit. After impregnating a budding acting student, Celia (Cindy) Crawford, David ignobly fled from responsibility and took off across America. The child was given up for adoption and reared as James Raymond, unaware that his father was a world famous musician. It would be over 30 years before Crosby met his lost son. Nor would this be the last occasion on which one of his mystery offspring would dramatically reappear.

While living out a Woody Guthrie fantasy, Crosby met a number of influential musicians including Travis Edmonson and Fred Neil, both of whom greatly influenced his guitar playing. Edmonson also recorded Crosby's first composition, 'Cross The Plains' and introduced him to the thrill of marijuana. After a year on the road, David relocated to San Francisco, where he shared a houseboat with Dino Valenti. Eventually, he moved into a semi-communal household in Venice which boasted some interesting names, including Paul Kantner and David Freiberg. Most of their time was spent sitting around playing guitars and smoking dope. Always the experimentalist, Crosby even smoked aspirin, which no doubt provided a less than satisfactory high.

The proto-hippie lifestyle was eventually replaced by an urgent need for cash so Crosby joined the Les Baxter Balladeers, another of those commercialized folk aggregations. Dressed in cute, red jackets, Crosby and his friends (including brother Chip, Bobby Ingram and Michael Clough) toured the States and were even captured on vinyl on the rare *Jack Linkletter Presents A Folk Festival*. Life as a Les Baxter 'Little Dear' eventually took its embarrassing toll and Crosby returned to playing solo in Hollywood, hanging out at clubs like the Unicorn. The patrons were largely unimpressed with his jazz-tinged repertoire, but there was one man who listened closely and spotted something special.

James Thomas Buchanan Dickson (b. 17 January 1931, Los Angeles, California) was ten years older than Crosby and had already lived a full life by 1963. From military service in Japan at the age of 15 to motorcycle gangs and sales work, he suddenly found himself in the music business after discovering and recording the legendary comedian/satirist Lord Buckley in 1951. Always a pioneer and risk taker, Jim formed an independent label VAYA Records ("Vaya means go as in 'Go, man, go!'") which released Buckley recordings and other Dickson-produced albums by the Page Cavanaugh Trio, Herb Jeffries and Jimmy Gavin. During the mid-Fifties, Dickson married the glamorous Academy Award nominated actress Diane Varsi and worked in films, both as a sound engineer and assistant cameraman. One of these was 1960's *The Little Shop Of Horrors*, directed by Roger Corman, on which Dickson toiled alongside Floyd Crosby, David's father. Inspired by his good friend, Barry Feinstein, Dickson later took up photography as a possible career, but this always overlapped with music. Elektra Records' founder Jac Holzman, an astute talent spotter, hired his services as an A&R director and producer. Dickson was wonderfully eclectic in his tastes, equally at home with jazz, folk and bluegrass. He recorded various musicians at the Club Renaissance, where he also screened avant-garde films made at UCLA for the hipper patrons. Dickson produced a number of albums by artistes including Dian & The Greenbriar Boys, the Dillards, Eric Weissberg & Marshall Brickman, Fred Engelberg, the Modern Folk Quartet, Odetta and Hamilton Camp, among many others.

Dickson sought to increase his own standing in the industry by branching out into the potentially lucrative field of music publishing. He found the perfect complementary partnership working with Eddie Tickner, an ex-Army auditor turned business manager. Born 18 October 1927, Tickner had moved from Philadelphia to LA after the dissolution of his first marriage and had been sleeping on Barry Feinstein's couch when he first encountered Dickson. Later they both stayed in apartments at the Park Sunset and met regularly at the hotel's coffee shop where they shared stories about the music business. One of Dickson's gripes was the difficulty of finding publishers willing to take on certain songs. Tickner provided an easy solution.

"I knew Jim Dickson from the Club Renaissance days. I was doing business management, working with Odetta, a black folk-singer-songwriter. Jim was producing records and since I was experienced in accounts he asked me if I'd like to go into publishing. He was working mainly in jazz and he was in a position to get the publishing and needed somebody to take care of the publishing work. So, during the latter part of 1963 we each put up $100.00 and formed Tickson Music."

The first song that Tickson Music published was Dino Valenti's 'Get Together', although they were later pressurized into selling the copyright to Frank Werber of SFO Music, publishers of the Kingston Trio. With Dino Valenti languishing in Folsom Prison, the only means of securing his release was bail money offered by Werber and his partner Rene Cardenas in return for the outright sale of the copyright. Its loss would cost Tickson Music millions, as it later became a much covered folk-rock standard. It also taught Valenti a salutary lesson about the importance of publishing, although he remained stoical about the lost copyright, arguing that he could always write another song, but could never have won back the years he might have wasted in jail.

The fact that Dickson had recorded Valenti impressed David Crosby as he came offstage at the Unicorn. More importantly, Dickson had recently produced a best-selling guitar instrumental album for World-Pacific Records and, as a reward, label owner Dick Bock allowed him free access to their studio after midnight.

This meant he was in a position to offer aspiring performers a shot at recording some demos. Soon after their meeting, Crosby cut several songs under Dickson's supervision, two of which popped up in the late Sixties on the archival album *Early LA*. The tracks provide a revealing insight into Crosby's pre-Byrd repertoire. Ray Charles' 'Come Back Baby' displays his youthful voice, strikingly higher in range than some of his later work. 'Willie Gene' [later correctly titled 'Willie Jean'], written by Hoyt Axton, is even better, an absolute showcase for that crystal-clear enunciation with some sparse backing, unobtrusive percussion and a surprisingly effective blues guitar. Three other demos, the aforementioned 'Get Together', Crosby's 'Brotherhood Of The Blues' and a version of the Civil War song 'Jack O' Diamonds' completed the session. Dickson was hopeful that a major label would be interested. He approached Joe Smith of Warner Brothers, but met with a cool response, much to Crosby's disappointment.

Although Crosby's voice was distinctive, it was not considered strong enough to secure a major deal in the competitive folk market of the time. "When he wrote songs with verses and choruses in them they were OK," Dickson says. "They weren't great though. Certainly, they weren't enough to found a career on. They tended to be songs that showed him off as a singer." Never a prolific songwriter, most of Crosby's unreleased recordings from 1963–64 were adaptations of public domain songs such as 'Motherless Children' and 'I Know You Rider'. One notable exception was the extraordinary 'Everybody's Been Burned', which remained dormant for several years before finally appearing on *Younger Than Yesterday*. Although the song is regarded, particularly by this author, as one of Crosby's greatest, Dickson was less than overwhelmed.

"I used to have tapes of David doing it on his own and they're not that good. I suspect that when he was complaining about being burned somebody said to him – 'Everybody's been burned, David', and he wrote the song . . . It reflected the period of his life before he had approval of any kind from anybody, when he tried to deal with his unhappiness by himself. We published it before the Byrds. In fact, it was one of the first songs we published. If I had been able to get that deal from Warner Brothers for David Crosby as a solo singer with a back-up band then it would have been one of the best songs on the album. No question. That's assuming we were going to use stuff from him. I was also impressed by David singing 'Motherless Children', which is in a similar vein. Hundreds of people have sung 'Motherless Children' but I think it's a better song. 'Everybody's Been Burned' is a nightclub ballad that would fit into the late Fifties or early Sixties. It would have been sung well by a Ruth Price or Chris Connor. The people that sprang from singers like Peggy Lee and Ella Fitzgerald, the later imitators of that kind of person. A girl torch singer would be the one to sing the hell out of 'Everybody's Been Burned' – somebody with a lot of feeling . . . David, in fact, sang that kind of ballad similar to a girl singer . . . It's gentle, it's reaching for a shared experience, it doesn't have the aggression of Sinatra."

Although some of Crosby's solo demos survive, including 'Get Together' which Dickson remixed at the Historical Society in Nashville during the Nineties and later sanctioned for inclusion on *The Preflyte Sessions*, many others were either lost, taped over or destroyed. Crosby had yet to reach his full potential, but the early recordings demonstrate a unique talent, all the more fascinating in light of his subsequent success.

Without a record contract, Crosby had little choice but to continue playing the local circuit as a struggling folk singer. Dickson had instilled the need to find other players to work alongside in a possible group and Crosby was eagle-eyed. Among those he reputedly approached was the talented Van Dyke Parks, who proved a reluctant recruit. "I could have been a Byrd," Parks fantasizes. "I tell myself that when I'm alone . . . the blinding lights, the screaming girls, the page boy haircuts. But I really wanted to be off-camera. The fox lies low." Crosby's invitation sounded more like a casual conversation and he did not even bother to report the incident back to Dickson.

During the same period, Crosby found more receptive candidates while visiting the Troubadour. Gene Clark remembers that he and McGuinn were strumming together in the front room of the Troubadour bar which was called 'The Folk Den'. "We started to write a few songs and then one night we went along to a hootenanny and there was this guy David Crosby who came onstage and played a few songs. I told McGuinn that I thought he was good. He said that he had worked with him before, that they were friends and had hung out in the Village together. We went into the lobby and started picking on the stairway where the echo was good and David came walking up and just started singing away with us doing the harmony part . . . We hadn't even approached him."

Clark's merry account fails to mention McGuinn's initial scepticism. Several years before, he had indeed socialized with Crosby, whom he met while playing with the Limeliters at the Ash Grove. Crosby was still acting at the time, but was clearly keen to succeed as a singer. He ferried McGuinn around in his convertible, taught him to drive, and took him home to Santa Barbara where his mother Aliph prepared them lamb and avocado sandwiches. Crosby proved a fine host but McGuinn was put off by his brash behaviour and sharp manner. Faced with Crosby's irrepressible enthusiasm at the Folk Den, McGuinn was still unsure but the promise of instant access to a recording studio rendered any reservations irrelevant.

Crosby immediately introduced the duo to Jim Dickson, who was quick to see their potential. Years before Dickson had seen a one-off performance featuring Bob Gibson, Bob Camp and Jimmy Gavin that made a huge impression on his thinking. "In folk music that was the first time I thought three guys singing together could be magical. They were the best thing I'd ever heard and none of them had a big audience by themselves. That was in the back of my head. You could take three guys who couldn't do it on their own, put them together and get a powerful sound." Impressed by Crosby's discoveries, Dickson took on the responsibilities of management, even providing rent-free accommodation and a daily cheeseburger allowance. It was a loose arrangement and much depended upon what the trio could produce in the studio over the next few months.

CHAPTER TWO

The Jet Set

DICKSON's continuing friendship with World-Pacific's Dick Bock meant that he had a luxury that many fledgling producers and inchoate groups would have envied: unlimited studio time. McGuinn, Clark and Crosby soon became nocturnal creatures, playing on into the early hours of the morning. Their vigilant manager/producer kept the tapes rolling, encouraging them to record take after take until the harmonies gelled. Already, Dickson was convinced that they could bridge the gap between the soft folk sound of Peter, Paul & Mary and the sparky pop of the new British groups. A less open mind might have chosen one direction to the detriment of the other, but Dickson saw the possibility of a fusion that might just work commercially.

"It was his idea," Crosby enthuses. "He thought it up. Jim's a good man. He helped us a lot. He helped me to shape my whole attitude toward the world. He instilled in me a lot of healthy cynicism, and at the same time he had a lot of humour. He was one of the smartest men I'd ever met, up until that time. He had a vantage point that none of us had . . . he'd been around showbusiness for years. He already knew what the scams were. He knew that the record companies were totally dishonest and unscrupulous and couldn't give a rat's ass about music, which is still true, even to this day."

During the first months of painful rehearsal, the boys sought a catchy name and McGuinn came up with the Jet Set. Although Dickson felt it was highly inappropriate, the monicker was accepted, at least for the present. One of the first recordings made by the Jet

Set was 'The Only Girl', later included on *Early LA*, which came out as a cross between the Beatles and the Everly Brothers. Certainly, the trio was unique: three solo folk singers, each with a 12-string acoustic guitar, attempting to play rock 'n' roll. For Crosby, it seemed a natural transition. "I really wasn't suited to folk music. They used to say, 'Hey, you sing like a rock 'n' roll singer', and I used to play with a flat pick on a very loud acoustic 12-string. I couldn't pick; I don't know how to pick. I played rhythm guitar all along. I made a terrible folk singer . . . McGuinn too. We were ill-suited to the folk field because we were already half grown into rock 'n' roll."

The beat influence was hardly surprising given recent events. Since the beginning of 1964, the Beatles had dominated American pop music in devastating fashion. Their first appearance on *The Ed Sullivan Show* was seen by a record-breaking 73 million viewers. By April *Billboard* showed the group holding the first five places in the singles charts with records on four different labels: 'Can't Buy Me Love' (Capitol); 'Twist And Shout' (Tollie); 'She Loves You' (Swan); 'I Want To Hold Your Hand' (Capitol) and 'Please Please Me' (Vee Jay). In Canada, the phenomenon was even more pronounced with nine Beatles singles hogging the Top 10. McGuinn, Clark and Crosby were exhilarated by the group's dramatic rise and incorporated strong Merseybeat elements into their songs. The leading light in the group at this stage was undoubtedly Gene Clark, who excelled in the studio and contributed the bulk of the Fab Four pastiches. By the time the Beatles returned for their second tour of the States during the summer, they were playing the celebrated Hollywood Bowl, pre-empting a new era of stadium rock. The Liverpudlians had also completed their first film, *A Hard Day's Night*, which was premiered in the US during August. The Jet Set religiously attended a screening and came out as Beatles' converts. Crosby remembers being so energized by the movie that he was swinging around poles in the street outside. Conjuring an image of Crosby as a gymnast is a formidable test for the imagination, but testifies to the phenomenal potency of the Beatles during 1964. The more laid-back McGuinn reacted more pragmatically. The following day, he traded in his banjo for a 12-string electric guitar, a decision that would shortly transform the group's sound.

Dickson, with his interest in photography, was keen for the Jet Set to develop a strong visual image. They were already starting to grow their hair in imitation of the Beatles, but still had a long way to go before they looked the part. Meanwhile, they needed a drummer whose presence would make them appear more like a pop group than a long-haired folk trio. The perfect candidate appeared like a ghostly vision on Santa Monica Boulevard, almost as though he had been scripted for the part.

Michael James Dick was born on 3 June 1946 at the Sacred Heart Hospital in Spokane, Washington, the eldest of three children. "My childhood was like anyone else's," he told me wistfully. "I was a child! Then two sisters arrived, Judi and Debbie. My parents got me a full set of little drums when I was only five and I opened them on Christmas morning and was banging on them loudly. They had to get up and re-wrap everything. Possibly that doesn't hit home with everyone, but if you want something – go for it."

James and Suzy Dick were solicitous parents who encouraged their son's creative inclinations. Suzy sang, and James painted, so it was not too surprising that Michael inherited both their talents. His maternal grandmother had played piano in the silent movie houses and Suzy had appeared in jazz bands since the age of 14, a career interrupted by her marriage. Michael was quick to discover percussive musical interests. "He could play on anything since he was a tiny boy," his mother remembers. "He was beating on everything under the sun. We'd got him a little child's drum when he was five, but it wasn't a set as he says. We didn't get him a set of drums until he was at high school and even then it was only part of a set that my husband got at a hock shop. He didn't have a foot pedal or a cymbal. The truth is stranger than fiction."

"It didn't have a goddamn bass drum," Michael told me. "I stole a cymbal from somewhere. I did it. I loaded the cymbal out of a window, down under the floor, and picked it up as I walked out. It wasn't very nice of me, but I had to have it. I needed it and didn't have the money to buy it."

Michael's high school record was appalling and before long he was missing classes regularly and arguing with his father, whose Texas upbringing and Air Force background engendered a respect for authority that had the unintended effect of exacerbating his son's rebellious streak. Jimmy Dick had flown 64 missions over Europe as a tail gunner, but his impressive war record was not enough to tame his wayward son.

"You couldn't punish Michael," his mother concedes. "His father learned that from a very early age. Michael and I always had a good relationship and were really close because of our interests, but he and his dad rubbed each other the wrong way. Jimmy had been a Southerner and wanted everybody to say 'ma'am' and 'sir' all the time and Michael wasn't going to be that type of child. They loved each other dearly, but they were at each other's throats a lot of the time. His dad was a disciplinarian and expected too much from Michael who was independent and couldn't handle that."

In an attempt to improve Michael's grades, his parents enrolled him in summer school, but all too often he would abscond, causing further conflicts with his teachers. "I'd take him to school and he'd walk through the building and out the other side," says his mother. "Teachers were frustrated because he had a brain and was smart but he never did finish any of it. He just didn't want to be there." At home, he could often be found in the basement, banging away on a drumkit and extolling the brilliance of Joe Morello. "My husband wasn't a musician so he didn't always appreciate the noise," Suzy recalls. "Michael would turn his record player up full blast and drum along to Dave Brubeck and George Shearing as loud as he could. He had a little group of musicians he worked with and they practised at the house. I played with them a couple of times. They opened up a store that belonged to the father of one of the kids, playing in the front window. They wanted me to play with them because the kid who played piano couldn't go, but they had an organ, and I'm not an organist, so I didn't do it. They would get together for fun and they weren't too bad. When I played with them we did 'Misty', but it was basically R&B."

Always popular with the local girls, Michael strutted around Spokane with a confidence well beyond his years. He was restive of spirit and longed for the excitement of big city life. "Michael seemed to be driven by something inside," Suzy remembers. "He had talent, he could paint and do everything. He could sing really well, but he never wanted to. He'd say, 'I'm not going to be one of those drummers that sings, I want to be a different type.' He went far without any real lessons of any kind and I thought he did real well from what he had to start with."

After flunking school, Michael saw no reason to be constrained by the limited opportunities available to a coltish youth in Spokane. A free spirit, he saw himself as a young beatnik and wasted no time in emulating Jack Kerouac by taking off on his travels. Before leaving home for the first time at 16, he informed his mother, "I'm going to be in the big time."

Over the next two years, he travelled to and fro from San Francisco, enjoying a freedom and new-found hedonism that remained part of his character for the remainder of his life. His parents grew accustomed to receiving late night collect calls during which he would relate censored versions of his exciting exploits. One of his most effusive calls occurred after he met his hero Joe Morello and persuaded the great drummer to provide a lesson. "It was his great claim to fame," Suzy remembers, but even bigger things were to follow.

Like most aspiring teenage beatniks, Michael was often in need of accommodation and sustenance. His parents occasionally sent him money and his grandmother posted "care boxes" full of candy and cookies but, most of the time, he had to fend for himself. Back in Spokane, his mother was under no illusion about his ability to survive in the city. "I often wondered," she reflects. "But if you knew how Michael could snow the women, they'd practically stand on their heads to do things for him. They would feed him and take care of him and do whatever was needed! He really had a knack with the females. I don't think he ever had to worry if he could find a woman. That's a terrible thing to say, but I don't think he saw it that way. There was never a woman he couldn't conquer, I tell you."

In order to gain access to bars, Michael used a fake ID under the name Tom Raymouth. Like Bob Dylan, he enjoyed using different aliases and by late 1963 he decided to jettison his real surname, settling on a nomenclature borrowed from one of pop's most famous broadcasters: Dick Clark. An 'e' was fortuitously added which later helped distinguish him from Gene Clark, his namesake and best friend in the Jet Set. Going one step further, Clarke also reinvented his birthplace, claiming that he was a born and bred New Yorker and came from Stockbridge, just like Peter Yarrow, from Peter, Paul & Mary.

Such revisionism was amusing, but unnecessary. With his bright blue eyes, Brian Jones' styled sheepdog hair and sensual Jaggeresque lips, the 6 foot 2 inch youth was classic pop star material. Enjoying his beatnik credibility, Clarke spent time painting rocks on the beach and playing congas in coffee houses. He had first met Jim McGuinn at the Coffee and Confusion in San Francisco when the guitarist was still with the Chad Mitchell Trio. Michael claims he played along on a conga while McGuinn sang some Chuck Berry songs. Later, Clarke appeared alongside Crosby's friend Dino Valenti, a connection that no doubt impressed David. It was at the Redwood Lodge in Big Sur that Clarke first came face to face with Crosby, who was smoking dope in a room and causing unintended havoc among the local beatniks who suspected he was an undercover cop. After sorting out the matter, Crosby explained that he was working with a couple of folk musicians and a producer in Hollywood. They were keen to use a drummer who looked right and David was convinced that Michael was the man. "Meet me at the Troubadour," was his parting message.

In June 1964, Clarke returned home to celebrate his eighteenth birthday and was glowing with good news. "He said he was going down to California and was going to get into this group," Suzy recalls. "Michael was a vagabond, he would have gone anywhere at any time." After a few days in Spokane, he took off on his grand adventure, hitchhiking part of the way. He arrived on the Sunset Strip in search of the Troubadour, slightly dishevelled, but undeniably cool in appearance and attitude.

From the first moment they saw Clarke, the Jet Set knew that they had someone special. "I remember Michael was walking down Santa Monica Boulevard on his way to the Troubadour," McGuinn recalls. "He had this Brian Jones haircut which looked really neat.

We said, 'Hey, how would you like to be our drummer?' and he said, 'Sure.' David already knew him from Big Sur and I'd seen him play congas when I was in this folk club in San Francisco. I reckoned he could learn to play drums pretty quickly, though he really couldn't play when we hired him."

"We only used the trio for about a month or six weeks before we got Michael," Dickson estimates. "David brought him to World-Pacific, which is where I met Gene and McGuinn too. I could easily tell he wasn't a drummer, but I wasn't too concerned about it. It was better than not having him. David could have brought anyone in and I wouldn't have checked their credentials. All David said was, 'I found us a drummer, man! He's played congas with Dino Valenti.' Michael was great, like a tall Brian Jones. He already had the long hair that they were still beginning to grow and was everybody's dream to be in one of those groups. Michael being attractive was not lost on Crosby. He certainly didn't get him because he thought he was a great drummer. None of these guys had worked much with drummers, so they weren't great critics. They didn't hear Michael's deficiencies or show any concern about them. I don't know that they were adamant about making a record, but they needed him to play live. Michael didn't have any drums so we set him up with a cardboard box which we found in a locker at World-Pacific. They were full of empty tape boxes. He put a tambourine on top and made himself a couple of tom toms and a snare."

Michael Clarke spent a long time banging away on his cardboard boxes and although some of the tapes of those sessions survive, most were destroyed. The group struggled as a quartet, with Crosby uneasily attempting to master the bass and sing harmony at the same time. Watching on, Dickson decided that the time was right for a new experiment. Having saved some money, he decided to finance a professional recording and produce the group, with the assistance of Paul Rothchild. Ray Pohlman, musical director of *Shindig!* and an important ally during the group's early days, appeared on bass, while the drums were handled by the renowned session player Earl Palmer. With Gene Clark on acoustic guitar, McGuinn on electric 12-string and Crosby adding harmony vocals, the results were primitive yet endearing. Two tracks were completed for a projected single: 'Please Let Me Love You'/'Don't Be Long' (the B-side being an earlier version of 'It Won't Be Wrong'). Both songs were co-written by Harvey Gerst, a friend of McGuinn's from the Troubadour, who later went on to join the 13-piece folk aggregation, the Men. "Jim and I wrote 'Don't Be Long' in about five minutes while sitting in the bar at the front of the Troubadour one night," Gerst recalls. "We wrote most of 'Please Let Me Love You' next, but it took Gene's added bridge to make it great."

During the late summer, Dickson approached Jac Holzman of Elektra Records, who offered a one-off deal that erred on the side of caution. "It was my first attempt at recording them with studio musicians," Dickson says. "I didn't know where we were going to take it. I didn't know what we had in mind when we were recording it other than to see what we could do. Having spent the money and wanting to get it back, us all being broke, it was submitted to Jac Holzman. It was submitted, *not* to get a hit record, but as a means to get signed. We didn't have an entrée to CBS, and we'd only checked out a couple of other small labels. I still needed money ($5,000) to get them instruments. Michael was still playing cardboard boxes then and I don't think the Rickenbacker is on those cuts, is it? I think it's a 12-string with a pick-up. We were trying to see what a finished record would sound like, trying to get it going. I made a deal with Jac Holzman to release the record but he couldn't associate it with them. He couldn't use their names or the group name. It would have prejudiced our chances of signing to another label. We didn't want to use it up . . . The deal was OK. We got our money back – $750.00 – and that's all we cared about."

The main aim of the Elektra recording was to provide the group with some valuable experience in preparation for what lay ahead. It also served as a strong morale booster, particularly for David Crosby. "It was a funny thing," he told me, twinkle-eyed. "We just thought it was great to be able to make a record. I guess we didn't know what to think really. We were kids. We didn't have any idea."

Immediately after the Elektra recording, there was a significant addition to the Jet Set line-up. Crosby's attempts at playing bass were not proving fruitful and both Dickson and the group realized that something had to be done. "David had got a six-string bass and tried but couldn't do it," Dickson explains. "Playing the bass was very hard for David. He finds it hard to play the brunt of anything. He plays accent rhythm; he wants to be the one to make it swing, not the one to put the mark down where you swing from. But he struggled along with it for some time. Finally, we knew we couldn't make it work with David." Intriguingly, Crosby's replacement as bassist would be a musician who was even less experienced on the instrument.

Christopher Hillman, the third of four children, was born in Los Angeles on 4 December 1944. In 1948, the family moved to San Diego, where Chris was raised on a small ranch. Much of his leisure time was spent riding his pet horse Ranger and watching Western adventures on the television. All the family loved music and his parents' interest in Forties' big bands meant that the house swung to the sounds of Duke Ellington, Count Basie, Benny Goodman et al. One of Hillman's earliest musical memories was discovering a 78 rpm album of Josh White in his father's collection, after which he was always receptive to blues and folk music. The rock 'n' roll explosion of the mid-Fifties captured his young imagination but, like Crosby and McGuinn, he became disillusioned with the state of pop music towards the end of the decade and turned towards more traditional forms. At the time, Hillman's elder sister was studying at the University of Colorado and returned home one summer clutching an armful of albums featuring such names as Woody Guthrie, the Weavers and Cisco Houston. The folk revival proved inspirational for Hillman and he decided to study guitar, initially purchasing a $10 instrument in Tijuana. Although he appreciated the commercial folk offered by the Kingston Trio, he was more intrigued by the ethnic stylings of earlier singers. He also enjoyed country music and tuned in regularly to the local television shows *Cal's Corral* and *Town Hall Party*, which featured many of the leading bluegrass players of the time. A local guitar tutor, who had played in country bands, worked at Hillman's high school and took on a mentor role, introducing the boy to songs by everyone from Hank Williams to Buck Owens. Along with a fellow student, Hillman started playing guitar at parties in San Diego, which is where he first connected with Kenny Wertz and Gary Carr. The youngsters shared a love of folk, bluegrass and country and frequently made pilgrimages to the Ash Grove in Los Angeles, where proprietor Ed Pearl booked the most respected players in the field.

Hillman was also attracted to the revivalist old string bands such as the New Lost City Ramblers who copied hillbilly recordings from decades before. Among their ranks was multi-instrumentalist and folklorist Mike Seeger, the younger half-brother of Pete Seeger. Hillman was impressed by Mike's prowess as a mandolinist and fell in love with the instrument. After saving all summer, he purchased a Gibson model and began practising up to eight hours a day under the tutelage of Scott Hambley and, later, Roland White.

Back in San Diego, Hillman's family was undergoing various changes and upheavals. His brother was joining the Air Force and his elder sister was also leaving home to get married. But it was his father's fate that proved the most disturbing. Chris was barely 16 when he suffered the traumatic news that the head of the family had committed suicide. It was a scar that the teenager found difficult to bear and no doubt caused him to become a more withdrawn figure over the next few years. The powerful remembrance of the suicide and its effects on his life were poignantly revealed in the song 'Running'. Significantly, it took nearly 30 years before Hillman was able to express his troubled feelings about the tragedy in song.

Along with his mother and younger sister, Hillman moved to an apartment in LA. He was soon drawn back to San Diego following a call from his old friend Kenny Wertz, who was about to join the Scottsville Squirrel Barkers, a bluegrass group which included Larry Murray, who subsequently wrote 'Bugler'. Completing the line-up was guitarist Gary Carr and the senatorial Ed Douglas, a recent retiree from the San Diego Police Department. Douglas and Murray co-owned the Blue Guitar, a store that sold instruments and was also used at the weekend for low-key performances. The Barkers played there regularly and also ventured to LA to appear at bluegrass events. While there, they sought a record deal and Douglas contacted Jim Dickson at World-Pacific. Dickson was not in a position to offer a contract, but was impressed by the band, particularly the young mandolin player. Dickson suggested that they approach the nearby Crown Records, a low budget outfit that manufactured albums, which were distributed for sale in supermarkets. It seemed an inauspicious debut, but the results were surprisingly pleasing.

Blue Grass Favorites featured ten tracks, all exuberantly executed, with mandolinist Hillman in shining form, most notably on their concert favourite, 'Three Finger Breakdown' and the vocal showcase 'Reuben's Train'. "It was completed in a day," Hillman marvels. "Just a few hours. Then it came out. You could buy the record for something like 79 cents then. We thought it would help us get more gigs. The deal was simple and there were no publishing royalties to worry about as it was public domain stuff. They gave us a box of records." Looking back with charitable hindsight, Hillman now sees the supermarket album as perfectly capturing a moment in time. "It might be one of the best records I ever made because we played with a wild abandon and no fear."

One of Hillman's favourite bluegrass ensembles at this time was the Golden State Boys who performed on *Cal's Corral*, the local television show hosted by car dealer Cal Worthington. Chris was thrilled to meet their banjo player Don Parmley at a bluegrass evening at the Ice House in Pasadena. That contact became useful by early 1963 when Hillman found himself without work. The Barkers had drifted apart and he took off to San Francisco, fruitlessly searching for a new direction. One day, he received a telegram from his former colleague Ed Douglas with the exciting news that Parmley was looking for a replacement for guitarist Hal Poindexter in the Golden State Boys. Hillman was surprised to pass the audition and took on mandolin duties in the new line-up alongside Parmley and brothers Vern and Rex Gosdin. "This was my window on authenticity," he reflects. "These guys were ten years older than I was. Don was from Kentucky and the Gosdins were from Alabama and they sang like the Louvin Brothers."

Soon, Hillman was playing in casinos, country bars and appearing regularly on *Cal's Corral*. Like Michael Clarke, he used a fake ID to make himself appear older, glorifying in the name Chris Hardin. As a result of the change in their line-up, the Golden State Boys decided to find a new title, initially settling on the Blue

Diamond Boys. Meanwhile, Hillman had phoned Jim Dickson, who agreed to help them find a record deal. Along with his associate Eddie Tickner, he came up with a catchier appellation for the quartet. "We changed their name to the Hillmen after the 17-year-old genius mandolin player," Tickner wryly recalls. "I thought it would focus attention on Chris because he didn't sing much," Dickson adds.

The newly christened Hillmen became regular visitors to World-Pacific Studios and Dickson persevered with them in the same way that he later nurtured the Jet Set. Unfortunately, the big break remained frustratingly elusive. "I'd been taping Chris for over a year at World-Pacific long before there was any Byrds. He was there overlapping the stuff I did with Crosby independently. I'd recorded 16–18 sides with him and the Gosdin Brothers and we'd done the same thing, taping over and over until we'd built an entire album with choices. It was aimed at Elektra Records, but they turned it down."

It would be a further five years before Chris' work was revealed to the world on the archive album *The Hillmen*. The opening track was the traditional 'Fair And Tender Ladies', later attempted by the Byrds in 1972 for their reunion album and subsequently recorded by Gene Clark. There was also a rare co-songwriting credit for Hillman on the vibrant instrumental, 'Blue Grass Chopper'. Interestingly, the work also included two Bob Dylan songs, most notably a somewhat muted 'When The Ship Comes In', on which Hillman was billed as 'lead vocalist'. Who would have thought Hillman would be the first of the original Byrds to sing a Dylan composition on a studio recording?

"I knew something about Chris Hillman that nobody else knew," Dickson says. "When he first came in with the Scottsville Squirrel Barkers and they auditioned for me at World-Pacific, Chris sang a country ballad and he was able to do that because I was totally anonymous to him. He didn't know me yet. That was the first time I saw him. I was very impressed by his vocal ability. And I never saw it again. I got him to sing that Dylan song ['When The Ship Comes In'] on the Hillmen album and he could hardly sing. He wouldn't put anything into it. It had to be carried by the harmony."

THE JET SET

After the break-up of the Hillmen, Chris went through a directionless period and found employment in the Green Grass Group, a mainstream bluegrass outfit formed by the ubiquitous Randy Sparks, creator of the New Christy Minstrels. They played a regular weekend residency at Spark's club Ledbetter's in Westwood, California. Like McGuinn and Clark in their earlier commercial folk ventures, Hillman rapidly became disillusioned. When Dickson approached him about a possible opening in a Beatle-influenced beat group, he was taken aback, but intrigued. Although he did not want to lose the $100.00 a week that he could earn playing watered-down bluegrass, the chance to try something new was both tempting and appealing.

Dickson appreciated Hillman's dilemma. "He was very flighty. He'd already gone through a long period with me of recording as the Hillmen and nothing had come of it. On the other hand, this new group looked like the future. He didn't play with the Randy Sparks group because he had respect for them. It was just like working at Woolworth's to him. I tried to figure out how to get Chris into the group and not interfere with the Green Grass Group. Randy Sparks didn't want him to do both. We didn't care if he did both because we never played on a Friday or Saturday night . . . Chris didn't come into the Jet Set until a *long time* after Michael, and long after David had given up trying to play the bass and decided not to play anything. Chris was a little surprised I let him come in . . . David had a passing knowledge of him, but I don't think any of them really knew Chris Hillman. But he was immediately better off on the bass than Crosby. Right off. David just couldn't handle it. He never became a lead player either. Single note playing isn't where Crosby's at and when he came to sing, the minute he'd come in, he'd blow it. You could see it was going to be hopeless and he was certainly more valuable as a harmony singer than as a bass player."

As a compromise, Hillman initially intended to join the Jet Set on a temporary basis. However, once he visited World-Pacific and checked out their repertoire, his appreciation grew. At this early stage, a lack of funds meant that he was forced to practise on a cheap little red Japanese bass, which was probably as effectual as

Clarke's cardboard boxes. It hardly mattered. The fact that they were so young and still seemed to be finding their way with this new music was a bonus. "Michael had enough time to learn to play the drums for music as simple as this," Dickson concludes. "He could keep time and play a fill now and then. I had no fear of that, just as I knew that Chris would play the bass adequately, especially if he knew what to play. He put a lot of melody into his bass playing, which was what I wanted. I wanted to create counter melody and you could see indications of it at the time, like the kind of energy in Roy Orbison's 'Oh Pretty Woman'. It was only a riff there but it gave the song a level of energy which, if you took it out, would be underwhelming."

For Hillman, the prospect of playing a new instrument was a challenge that seemed surmountable in such an untested group. "I was a mandolin player and didn't know how to play bass, but they didn't know how to play their instruments either, so I didn't feel too bad about it. None of us were rock 'n' rollers; we were all folk musicians and, although it was tremendously exciting, it was such an alien thing to be getting into..."

That sense of the unknown was part of the thrill. But it could also prove intimidating. The Jet Set felt that they were channelling the zeitgeist, but who could be sure? Apart from Dickson, who else genuinely believed in their potential? Was Los Angeles ready for this odd combination of folk musicians playing like a British beat group? Could they even perform live without making fools of themselves? Was it possible to find a sympathetic audience or establish a following? After the recent failed experiment with Elektra would any other record company be remotely interested in offering a deal? As autumn 1964 darkened, the questions continued to multiply.

CHAPTER THREE

Preflyte

ALTHOUGH the Jet Set line-up seemed settled, the unit remained dangerously volatile. At this point, McGuinn and Clark were the dominant forces at World-Pacific, but Crosby had firm views of his own which were not always appreciated. Dickson had already been through some arguments with David during their time recording together, but the others were still coming to terms with his mood swings. Crosby realized that he was third in line in the group, with far less professional experience than McGuinn or Clark, but he had travelled widely and knew more about harmony singing and jazz than either of them. Clearly, he was the most articulate member but, for all his verbal skills, he lacked the ability to convert ideas into songs. At times, McGuinn and Clark found his criticisms exasperating and tough to swallow, particularly considering his own lack of material. Although Crosby could be the world's greatest enthusiast when things went right, he was equally merciless when the music offended his sensibilities.

The first serious flare-up with David occurred at World-Pacific, long before the group had even released a record. It was a key incident that provided a prophetic glimpse into the fundamental fragility of the group. Without an explanation, beyond general disgruntlement, McGuinn and company abruptly decided that they could work better without Crosby's overbearing presence. Having brought the Jet Set to Dickson and World-Pacific, Crosby was stunned when his comrades turned on him. During a rehearsal break, he was ignominiously turfed out of the group and left the building with tears in his eyes.

"He went out the back door at World-Pacific," Dickson recalls, "and they came into the booth and told me: 'We just fired David. He's gone.' I said, 'If he's gone, I'm gone.' Then, they looked at each other, and McGuinn and Clark went out that door and brought him back with their arms around him. David was all shook up. They were saying, 'We love you like a brother, and you *can't* go.' I thought: 'Boy, these guys are good at hypocrisy!' I was surprised at their ability to be so sincere. It was actually heartening that they could be such actors. It took some acting on their part too. I was sensitive to that and I was also ambivalent about it. I was glad that they brought him back because I felt they needed him in the sound. It wasn't rich enough without him."

Always a barometer of feeling, Crosby was again in tears as they embraced him and his emotion spilled forth on the next few songs they taped. It seemed that such cathartic moments invariably brought out his best as a performer. When his ego was bruised and pride was at stake, anything could happen. He could bring the group crashing down into petty conflict or transform them into one of the most exciting musical forces of their generation. The price they would have to pay for harnessing that unique talent would be calculated in countless minor skirmishes over the next three years.

After further practice sessions, the young musicians were suddenly eager to be seen and decided to turn up unannounced at the Troubadour and perform some songs in front of the folk crowd. Crosby was still without an instrument at this stage but convinced himself that he could impress the audience by wiggling his thighs and backside like a sexy, rock 'n' roll singer. It looked passable when he gyrated in front of his bedroom mirror, but less convincing onstage at the Troubadour. Dickson laughed at the spectacle. "David without a guitar in his hand was a comedy act. Trying to wiggle and act like a rock 'n' roller was pretty funny to see from the audience. He knew it and they knew it. Everybody said it. Nobody felt any necessity to be kind to David in those days. He was of no stature in a folk club like the Troubadour. This was a hoot night where they lined up to play three songs. The Troubadour was about four blocks from World-Pacific so we just packed everything up and moved it all out there. They weren't even booked to play."

The public humiliation dented Crosby's ego and may have had some bearing on the next minor clash in the Jet Set. Coincidentally or not, it was after the hoot that David first voiced concern about Gene Clark's abilities as a rhythm guitarist. Dickson was perplexed by this sudden objection and still believes that the mocking laugher at the Troubadour convinced Crosby that he needed an instrument to hide behind. "When Gene came in with McGuinn, David said, 'These guys *both* play guitar better than me, I'm just going to sing harmony.' That's what he first said to me. After the experience at the Troubadour, David started telling Gene his timing wasn't good and shaking his confidence. There wasn't anything wrong with Gene's timing. It wasn't imaginative, but it was straight. He played straight time. He was pretty much on the money, as good as the rest of them. We tried them all with a metronome and he certainly wasn't the worst. But I'd seen it happen in jazz where you could shake someone's confidence. I saw one bass player shake the confidence of another by just circulating the rumour that his timing was bad. By the time it got around, it had become bad. David did that to Gene. It was a self-fulfilling prophecy, to use your phrase. I don't remember a whole lot of resistance on Gene's part and I had to agree that David was better with a guitar in his hands than without one . . . but I believe David needed that guitar to hide behind and improve his presence onstage. When you have a bunch of your friends laugh at you – that's painful."

Viewing from a distance, Eddie Tickner recalled, "there was a hustle – and Crosby took the guitar out of Gene Clark's hands." Crosby himself was unaware of any deep psychology regarding the switch of instrumentation, which he felt was perfectly justified.

"I don't think I *literally* took the guitar out of Gene's hands," he stresses. "But that was certainly the effect of what I did. I am aggressive. Gene played very poorly and his time sense was atrocious. He would play really monotonously and very behind the beat. He would start behind the beat and slow down from there. He dragged heavily, and with a drummer like Michael Clarke (who at that time wasn't a drummer) it was a disaster. And I was a good rhythm-guitar player already."

Characteristically, Clark accepted the decision without rancour, narrowly avoiding another possible split in the ranks. In fairness, Crosby soon proved that he was a superior rhythm player, full of verve and invention. He still spent time looking in the mirror, but now it was to see how well a guitar looked strapped across his chest. "It was like role playing then," he says. "We had all been to see *A Hard Day's Night* and that was the model."

While the Jet Set were finding a suitable identity, their act still required polish. There were several visitors to World-Pacific during those late-night sessions, including a dance instructor whom Dickson had enlisted to assist with their stage presence. He attempted to teach them some rudimentary steps but gave up within a week when confronted by their barely disguised disdain. Dickson also remembers "a guy named Jimmy" who hired the Jet Set to back him on some surf tunes. Later, he took Dickson aside and told him he was wasting his time with Beatle-influenced pop and should fully embrace the surf boom. The mysterious 'Jimmy' may well have been the aforementioned Jimmy Hannan, who had already scored a surprise hit in Australia in February 1964 with a cover of McGuinn's Brill Building surf spoof, 'Beach Ball'.

During the first week of October, Jac Holzman confirmed that the Merseybeat-styled 'Please Let Me Love You' was to be the thirteenth single released by Elektra and copies were immediately despatched. Unfortunately, erratic distribution meant that the record would not reach many stores until as late as December. Faced with the problem of finding a pseudonym for the Jet Set, Holzman had decided to exploit the group's long-haired image and cash in on the British Invasion. He needed a quintessential English-sounding name and suddenly realized that the answer was staring him in the face. On a gin bottle nearby was a brand name that conjured up visions of the Tower of London: 'Beefeaters'.

"Jac wanted to dress them up in Beefeaters' uniforms," Dickson reveals. "They never even considered that. When McGuinn heard it was going to be called Beefeaters, he was disgusted . . . 'Beefeaters?' It was ugly, not like the Jet Set. Who wanted to be known for eating beef? It was a name that they *never* used themselves. The odds that Jac could successfully promote a single at that time were very thin. I was confident that it was going to go down the drain. We only did it to get some money back. Jac had hoped to talk them into more involvement once the record had been made. If we'd had any money we'd have left it in the can."

'Please Let Me Love You' emerged as a self-conscious beat ballad, with strong Beatles' overtones. "When you'd listen to the playback it would make you giggle," Dickson says. "It sounded and felt legitimate while they were doing it, but I don't think any of them, when they heard it back enough times, wanted to continue sounding British." Dickson was neither surprised nor upset by the subsequent failure of the single. He knew that a small independent label like Elektra, with no experience of the singles market, had only a slim chance of breaking a record nationally. Indeed, it probably came as a relief that the song did not draw attention to the group, especially as they were already searching for a deal with a bigger company. In many ways, the Beefeaters' saga precipitated the inevitable move away from Beatle-imitation. Although they all adored the Fab Four, McGuinn, Clark and Crosby were never mere copyists. In fact, it was impossible for the Jet Set/Beefeaters to capture the Liverpool sound effectively because their backgrounds were so far removed from the British beat tradition. Without even realizing it, the trio were on the brink of discovering a new style which would transform their lives and alter the direction of pop music over the next few years.

The genesis of the group's experimentation remains in a small cache of three-track tapes surviving from the World-Pacific period. Dozens of takes spanning over 100 minutes provide an intriguing insight into the Jet Set's primal sound. Sadly, from the many months of rehearsals, only 15 different actual songs (excluding the Beefeaters' tracks) are now in existence and one of these, Gene Clark's 'Maybe You Think', is still unreleased. The remainder show the group at various stages of development, from their most primitive to the moments when they were close to major label stature. Crosby has always credited his former manager for having had the foresight to play back the rehearsal tapes endlessly until the rough-hewed musicians righted their flaws. "It might have taken us a couple of years to learn how to play and sing together," he points out, "but because of that we were ready in eight months. But it was brutal. You can hear it on *Preflyte*. It wasn't good enough at that point. I would never have put those songs on a record and released it."

Preflyte (later issued with additional tracks and alternate takes as *In The Beginning* and *The Preflyte Sessions*) was a retrospective collection from the World-Pacific period that offers a revealing secret glimpse into the Jet Set's experimentation. "It was an exciting process, a struggling process," Dickson acknowledges. "But it had its rewarding moments in the studio. I wouldn't say the best things they ever did in the studio were saved or ended up on *Preflyte* and *In The Beginning*. They were just the best of what was left in the boxes when we moved on. Some of the *Preflyte* cuts had Michael on cardboard boxes, but we saved more of the tapes with real drums. But he played a lot longer with the cardboard boxes than with the drums. Once we got the drums, we didn't save much of the rest. They did those songs thousands of times on tape."

Contrary to Crosby's comments, the songs that survive are a veritable treasure trove of Byrds juvenilia. Only five of these tracks appeared on their first official album and the prototype versions are, not surprisingly, weaker, both vocally and instrumentally. Strangely, it is the minimalist nature of the recordings that makes them so appealing. There is an intangible feeling of lost innocence and yearning eroticism permeating almost every song. These sessions are not only a pleasant revelation but a highly important artistic statement in themselves, a point that needs to be widely acknowledged. What the Jet Set achieve in their understated way is nothing less than a musical blueprint for a new, young generation of performers.

'You Showed Me', one of the earliest compositions from McGuinn and Clark, had been written when they sang in the Troubadour's Folk Den during their Peter And Gordon days. Unlike some of the other songs featured from the sessions, this was a fairly late recording undertaken after the group had received new instruments. The strong influence of the Fab Four and the overtly sentimental lyrics meant that it did not survive the transition from World-Pacific to CBS (Columbia). However, it gained its writers some belated royalties when the Turtles transformed the song into a

Top 10 US hit five years later. Subsequent hit covers by Salt 'n' Pepa, the Lightning Seeds, and a sampling by U2, testify to the surprising durability of the composition.

A second McGuinn/Clark collaboration, 'It's No Use', looked to the future, with its more pronounced guitar work. Although less sophisticated lyrically than Clark's solo offerings, the vocals are reasonably strong. "Gene and McGuinn would both be singing melody, like a double lead, and Crosby would sing the only harmony," Dickson notes. "I tried to get Gene and McGuinn to drop down and sing a third part in the chorus sometimes. They had difficulty trying to do three-part harmony. But the three-part harmony gave David more freedom. The only problem with those early attempts at freedom is that the chord structures didn't support some of the lyrics. Crosby would rehearse the songs vocally with them and they'd sound great. But when you put them on top of the music they were playing, they sounded a little sour. Crosby later found the chords that would fit the harmonies."

One of the great surprises of *Preflyte* was hearing Crosby sing crystal-clear lead on 'The Airport Song', a beautiful composition, which featured Clark on harmonica and McGuinn offering some striking flourishes of guitar glory towards the close. "I collaborated with Crosby on 'The Airport Song' but it was basically my idea to do it," McGuinn told me. "It was written about LA Airport where we used to spend a lot of time just hanging about getting drunk and watching the planes coming in . . . Looking back I guess the song was OK. It's a pity it didn't make the first album but these things happen."

With its slight jazz inflections and sophisticated air, 'The Airport Song' sounded unlike anything else in the Jet Set's repertoire or indeed anything else in contemporaneous pop. It is akin to entering a parallel world in which Crosby becomes the creative force in the Byrds. A lovely missing link, the song was never considered part of the group's future, having been recorded during their final days in the studio especially for use on a subsequently aborted film soundtrack. "It got included on *Preflyte* because I felt there should be some example of how Crosby sang at the time," Dickson explains. "The problem was finding the right song for that voice and getting people to accept him for who he was and not who he thought he was. I suppose we could have put 'The Airport Song' on the first album but since it wasn't intended for that, it never occurred to us. At the time it sounded too much like an ordinary pop song. It was pleasant, enjoyable and had a nice mood but it didn't sound like the new wave of music that we were interested in and trying to promote. It was better than much of the stuff on *Preflyte* but that was because most of those songs were never intended for release. They were originally for copyright purposes or with the idea to use the songs to try and get auditions, gigs or television shows." One can only wonder what might have happened if Crosby had been encouraged to write or record more material in this vein. Already, he was the Byrds' secret weapon – a powerful presence whose songwriting talent would not be fully unveiled until several years later.

Two of the more nondescript tracks from the period were the pleasant but derivative 'You Movin'' and the dated 'Boston', a pastiche of Chuck Berry's 'Memphis Tennessee', complete with plodding bass and simple, copycat lyrics. "That was stuff to play at dances," Dickson stresses. "Both were *never* intended to go any further. They were derivative and they couldn't play them well and they weren't that good. We did every song over and over . . . there were probably a hundred versions of 'You Movin''." Clark was clearly inspired by the success of Johnny Rivers, whose streamlined rock 'n' roll covers were popular at clubs like Gazzari's and the Whisky A Go-Go, resulting in a best-selling 'live' album and a number 2 hit with 'Memphis' that same summer. The Jet Set were happy to rehearse their own imitation rock 'n' roll songs to death, knowing that they would be rewarded with an enthusiastic response from the freakier dancers among their following.

The remaining songs from the pen of Gene Clark were uniformly excellent. 'Here Without You', although still in primitive form, sounds even more haunting and vulnerable in its stark state. 'I Knew I'd Want You' and 'You Won't Have To Cry' proved the key survivors at this transitional phase, boasting engagingly tentative harmonies, marked by careful enunciation and delightfully precarious instrumentation. The catchy 'She Has A Way', although not the best song on offer here, would make the short list for the first album sessions, only to be rejected at the eleventh hour. "Looking back, 'She Has A Way' was really partly my fault for playing on the Everly Brothers," says Dickson. "I was trying to get them to see how tight harmony sounded. That was sort of Gene's Everly Brothers' song in his mind. David loved it when Gene first wrote it because he liked doing the harmony, but then he got tired of it very early on."

Three more songs from Clark would never get beyond the World-Pacific nights, despite their obvious qualities. 'The Reason Why', a brooding ballad which takes teenage angst to the precipice of neuroticism, combined the best of the Beatles/Everly Brothers influence, with Clarke providing some intuitive drumming and McGuinn offering a decisive solo. Clark's pained admission of emotional vulnerability still sounds immensely moving, even several decades on.

'For Me Again' was even better. Against an impressively sensual and sensitive backing, Clark sang words which mixed moments of melancholy with flashes of self-revelation. He expresses the transformative powers of love though simple nature imagery invoking the shifting seasons, the moon and sun and wind and rain. The song was akin to a Gene Clark primer and it says much about the changes that the group were to undergo over the next few months that they could afford to abandon a composition of this quality.

The last track to be issued from the World-Pacific sessions was Clark's 'Tomorrow Is A Long Ways Away', a title no doubt inspired by Dylan's 'Tomorrow Is A Long Time'. Clark's voice is at its deepest on the acoustic version, premiered on *In The Beginning*, and it was precisely for this reason that the song failed to stay in their set. "Gene's vocal bothered everybody," Dickson admits. "We tried to get the vibrato out of his voice and find some way to deal with it, but we couldn't."

Although the Jet Set were regularly covering Beatles' songs throughout their tenure at World-Pacific, none remain on tape. Interestingly, the only extraneous composition extant was the most important of their entire career: 'Mr Tambourine Man'. The *Preflyte* version still sounds remarkable. McGuinn's lead guitar work is already good and will soon be better; Crosby shows signs of uncertainty and nervousness in his harmony, but, as always, the diction is crystal clear. The most perplexing feature of this early version however is Clarke's drumming. For some reason he has adapted the song to a military school beat which sounds completely inappropriate, yet extremely interesting. The attention of the listener is distracted from Bob Dylan's poetic lyrics as a result of the unusual arrangement, which partly transforms the number into an old-fashioned marching song.

The story of how 'Mr Tambourine Man' reached the Jet Set is almost worthy of a chapter in itself. McGuinn assumed that it was an unsolicited gift from Bob Dylan who "laid this dub" on Dickson. "It hadn't been released on the previous album because of a contract release problem with Jack Elliott," McGuinn said. "It was sloppy, kind of 'Hey Hey Mr Tambourine Man' – the words weren't all clear– it was groovy though . . . had its charm."

Eddie Tickner provided a more plausible explanation, pointing out that "Dickson had heard Dylan do 'Mr Tambourine Man' in concert, but it hadn't been recorded. He requested a demo of the song from the publisher and when it arrived it had Jack Elliott on it too."

The concert mentioned by Tickner was the 1964 Monterey Folk Festival (30–31 May) which Dickson attended, accompanied by the Hillmen, who'd won a competition to appear on the main showstand. To be precise, it was not the actual concert grounds at which Dickson saw Dylan, but afterwards in a hotel room where the master unveiled a stunning new repertoire. Two weeks before, he had appeared at London's Royal Albert Hall performing a set that included two songs which would have a particular resonance for Dickson: 'Mr Tambourine Man' and 'Chimes Of Freedom'.

"Dylan, to me, was a very unassuming guy and easy to rap with. He was amusing, charming and I had not been a big Dylan fan from the very first moment I heard him, which was when Victor [Maymudes] played me an acetate of his first album. But I ran into him again at Monterey, sat in a hotel room and listened to a dozen or so new songs and came away a believer . . . From that moment on, I started to record Dylan songs on folk labels. He became a source of new material when all the other stuff was tired. So I paid very careful attention to everything new of Dylan's at that time. It was a serious business for me and I'd recorded a lot of his songs by then . . . I'd heard about a song that Jack Elliott, who'd been a friend of mine for many years, had been invited to sing with Dylan. I thought that was really wonderful of Dylan. It made me feel good about him that he would give Jack a piece of the light because he'd almost made him obsolete. I was sad to hear Jack had got drunk on the session and it was too sloppy to use, but I wanted to hear the song. When I finally got the acetate for 'Mr Tambourine Man', it was the most magical song I had ever heard in that genre."

Dickson credits a genial West Coast promotions person named Jack Mass for promptly securing him the acetate that would shortly transform his group into international stars. The demo had been recorded on 9 June, with Ramblin' Jack Elliott attempting harmony on the chorus. Despite McGuinn's comments, Dylan's diction was fine throughout and there should have been no trouble interpreting the lyrics. Apart from Elliott's difficulty in the chorus, there were a couple of tentative moments on the vocal, and at one point Dylan sang the wrong lyrics midway through a verse. Other than that, the song was superb and it is hardly surprising that Dickson was overwhelmed by its potential. That he could see the composition as part of the Jet Set's repertoire required a prescient leap of the imagination that was even more remarkable.

Even when presented with the song that would change their entire lives, Dickson's protégés were frustratingly obdurate. It was only under great pressure that they were persuaded to attempt the song. Clark was the sole lead vocalist then, but he was lukewarm about the track, much to Dickson's frustration. "They started off hating 'Mr Tambourine Man'. They went ahead and rehearsed it a little bit, tried to do it . . . I doubt we ever rolled tape at World-Pacific with Gene singing 'Tambourine Man'. I think we just listened and tried to work it up." Eventually, everyone agreed that it was not working and it was temporarily dropped. McGuinn then intervened and volunteered to sing lead, bringing a fresh dimension to the track. "McGuinn began to like it because he was singing it. When it became *his* number, he stopped being resistant to it. Now, with McGuinn on your side, you could bring it back."

Dickson's euphoria did not last. Before long, Crosby, who objected to the song most vociferously of all, persuaded the others that it was not worth working on. He argued that it was too long, too obscure and not commercial enough for radio play. Although Dickson had already encouraged them to cut down the verses and add a rock beat, they were still unconvinced. "David politicked within the group to stop it. McGuinn was ambivalent because he wanted to be able to do as well as Dylan, and not lean on Dylan. He said he'd felt a little competitive with Dylan at an earlier stage and Dylan shocked everybody with how much he grew during that period. Gene didn't see it as part of the music they were doing anyway, he was easy to persuade out of it . . . Gene's songs had nothing in common with 'Mr Tambourine Man'."

With greatness at their fingertips, the group was on the brink of throwing everything away. They rejected the song outright, refused to play it at rehearsals and left Dickson in a very bad temper. "Doing the song at that point was more important to me than the group. Without 'Mr Tambourine Man', we didn't have a chance. I'd have done what I could but a lot of the time you start on projects and they just fade out or disappear." In such circumstances desperate measures were called for, so Dickson decided to seek the patronage of the highest authority available.

CHAPTER FOUR

Dylan's Charm Offensive

BOB Dylan was a little mystified by the invitation to see the Jet Set. All he knew was that a bunch of Beatles-freaks were rehearsing their repertoire at Hollywood's World-Pacific Studios and had requested one of his still unreleased demos: 'Mr Tambourine Man'. He knew their mentor Dickson as an A&R scout who had always allowed him to get in free at the Ash Grove. They'd hung out together at the Troubadour and other haunts and got along well, so it seemed churlish not to pay a visit. Dylan also had reasons of his own that made him curious. After hearing 'I Want To Hold Your Hand', he became intrigued by the Beatles' sound and since touring England in the spring, he had emerged as a secret convert. "They were doing things nobody else was doing," Dylan enthused. "Their chords were outrageous, just outrageous, and their harmonies made it all valid. You could only do that with other musicians. Even if you're playing your own chords you had to have other people playing with you. That was obvious. And it started me thinking about other people. But I just kept it to myself that I really dug them. Everybody else thought they were for teenyboppers, that they were going to pass right away. But it was obvious to me that they had staying power. I knew they were pointing the direction of where music had to go. I was not about to put up with other musicians, but in my head the Beatles were *it* . . . There was a lot of hypocrisy all around, people saying it had to be either folk or rock. But I knew it didn't have to be like that. I dug what the Beatles were doing and I always kept them in mind . . ."

The notion of a West Coast equivalent of the Beatles playing a song like 'Mr Tambourine Man' was novel and amusing, but perhaps not as crazy as it seemed. Even while Dylan was heading towards World-Pacific, the Animals had just released 'House Of The Rising Sun' in the US and were heading for number 1. Dylan was fascinated by the arrangement which threatened to bridge the gap between the contrasting worlds of folk and pop. If Dickson's protégés were already on the same track, they were definitely worth a listen.

The news that Dylan would be attending their rehearsals was enough to persuade the Jet Set to practise the dreaded 'Mr Tambourine Man' once more, although it was still in primitive form. "When I told them Dylan was coming down they rehearsed it a couple of times," Dickson recalls. "They didn't want to embarrass themselves in front of somebody *they'd* been putting down."

Dylan arrived in exuberant mood, accompanied by his roadie and acolytes Bobby Neuwirth and Victor Maymudes. Rather than playing the cool songwriter, he went out of his way to greet each of the musicians in turn. They were a little nervous about playing their still shaky version of 'Mr Tambourine Man', but after hearing the song, Dylan remarked, "Wow, man! You can dance to that!" It was a charitable comment, but sounded sincere enough to bring a collective glow to the group, who were pleased to find such an enthusiastic and supportive voice. They were even more taken aback when he suggested sitting in on some songs. "He didn't have a guitar with him," Dickson recalls, "but there was a piano at World-Pacific, so he played a little piano with them. When they'd played him 'Mr Tambourine Man', he just did a lot of smiling. He thought it was cute. Gene and Michael were very personable to Dylan. McGuinn was just standing there, looking stunned. David had been against doing the song, and Chris didn't do anything. He never does – he just stood there and played his part."

Whatever reservations they had about Dylan's visit were rapidly forgotten. He genuinely enjoyed their quirky Beatles imitations and the notion of hearing his own work performed in such a fashion seemed invigorating. Looking on, Dickson realized that the young songwriter was astute enough to understand the cultural and financial potential of having his songs cross over to a younger audience.

"Dylan was a very adept song-plugger. I saw that side of him. His biggest successes and money had come from Peter, Paul & Mary, not from his own records. So he came down and he charmed them. He not only approved of what they were doing, but found Michael Clarke playing the tambourine on a cardboard box delightful. The funny beat gave it a half-jug band sound. The next thing Dylan did outside of enjoying the music and putting them at ease was having a good time with them. He got them to like him, and once the song came back, it never dropped out of the set again. At the end of the session, I knew I'd won. All the hostility and jealousy over Dylan was gone. Crosby dropped the subject! He'd lost. Crosby was prepared to lose in those days. Later, he wouldn't lose; he'd continue to fight until he'd won or destroyed it. But he wasn't ready to give up what was going on just to keep 'Mr Tambourine Man' out."

The excitement over Dylan's visit, the recording for Elektra and the arrival of Hillman all buoyed the Jet Set's spirits at crucial moments. There was further good news along the way. Although Jac Holzman had declined to risk money purchasing the group proper equipment, another interested party emerged courtesy of Dickson's management partner Eddie Tickner. "One of my clients at the time was Naomi Hirshhorn," Tickner recalls. "I solicited her to invest $5,000 for a five per cent interest in the Byrds. She was an artist and an art collector and an off-Broadway producer of shows and small theatre."

Naomi, the daughter of multimillionaire Caryl Hirshhorn, was a keen patron of the arts whose own musical talents were never fully realized. In 1963, she sang lead and composed the music for *Spoon River*, produced by the Theatre Group at UCLA. It later switched to Broadway for 111 performances with Joseph Cates as producer. "She did a lot of other things in entertainment as an angel," recalls Jim Dickson. "Eddie was managing her personal money and brought her in. I recorded her playing the piano and singing songs she had written and gave her the tapes. It was a courtesy to Eddie's client."

Spoon River, an intriguing mixture of folk songs, adaptations and originals, gave some indication of why Hirshhorn took a chance on the Jet Set's odd hybrid of Dylan-inspired folk and Merseybeat. Her investment was also the first example of the group finding favour with a culturally sophisticated outsider who normally would have had no involvement in the realm of pop music. "I saw one of her musical shows and it wasn't bad, it was certainly interesting," Dickson recalls. "I also went to an exhibit of her art. Every painting was a picture of a heart with a piece out of it. She had everything, but she was on the other side, and seemed a little pitiful too. Like a poor little Jewish girl with a broken heart. She tried very hard and she was very nice to everybody and backed all these different shows that she was in. They weren't hits, but they were respectable and she was happy with them." Her father disapproved of such largesse and, according to Tickner, cut her off from the family fortune. But her gamble with the Jet Set would eventually prove a big winner. "She must have made well over $100,000 on that $5,000 investment," Dickson estimates. "She got 5 per cent out of our percentage, not the Byrds' percentage. When it first started, there were the three 'Byrds' and me. We each had 25 per cent. Then I got Eddie, and split with him. Then we got Naomi: me and Eddie gave her 2.5 per cent each out of our percentage to make her 5 per cent."

The injection of funds transformed the group, both visually and instrumentally. They returned to the cinema to watch *A Hard Day's Night* once more, this time carefully noting the instruments that the Beatles played before placing an order with Naomi's money. Soon after, Michael received his long-overdue Ludwig drum kit; Chris was given a Fender; a Gretsch Tennessean rhythm guitar was purchased for Clark, then passed on to Crosby, and McGuinn replaced his previous guitar with a gleaming new George Harrison-style 12-string Rickenbacker 360. Harrison had done wonders for the sale of the guitar since acquiring the model from Rickenbacker president Francis C. Hall at the start of the Beatles' first US tour back in February. With expensive instruments to practise on, the Jet Set's morale improved, and so did their work at World-Pacific. "At first the songs were dull and we didn't know how to sharpen them up," McGuinn remembers. "The Rickenbacker added a lot of tone. Once we got the instruments, it gave us a lot of focus. The only one we avoided was Paul McCartney's Hofner bass, which would have been too obvious a Beatles' copy. Even we couldn't have got away with that."

DYLAN'S CHARM OFFENSIVE

One member who was initially intimidated by the instrumental upgrade was their still inexperienced drummer. "Michael thought he was going to be fired so he decided to beat us to the punch and quit," says Dickson. "He set up his drums, hit the snare a couple of times, then whacked the tom tom and the sticks flew out of his hands. He thought, 'It's all over. I'm not going to fool anyone any more.' But, in the first place, I wasn't fooled, and I don't think they were. They were too self-involved to look closely at what the other guy was doing. You're trying to do your thing and if Michael throws you off, that's one thing, but if he doesn't you're not going to look for the finer points of whether he's done something wonderful. And he soon proved with 'The Bells Of Rhymney' that he was capable of doing something wonderful!"

Adjusting to the new instruments still took some time. Even the experienced McGuinn caused some unintended amusement when Dickson walked in to find him practising with a capo on the neck of his Rickenbacker. "I just laughed," Dickson fondly remembers. "I'd never seen a capo on an electric guitar before. I'd seen millions of folk singers use them. They played in the key that was comfortable. He did the same thing with the Rickenbacker. I didn't mean to laugh. It just struck me as funny instantly to see it. So I went to talk to him about it and he looked embarrassed and he didn't say too much because he's not too wordy. Then, a couple of weeks later, he came back without the capo on the Rickenbacker and played the scales in every key right in my face. That also made me laugh. He was being kind of defiant at what he thought was an insult. But I doubt he'd known that I'd been so proud of his achievement. I don't think he understood how I thought then."

While Dickson was a creative force at this point, Eddie Tickner remained a silent partner whose input was yet to be measured. It was only Naomi Hirshhorn's investment that concentrated his attention. He felt responsible for encouraging her to take a gamble on the group and secretly feared that they might split before any remuneration was received. Tickner could do little for them at this stage so left all the creative management decisions to Dickson. "When I first started with Eddie I saw him as somebody to keep the books, to be a partner and to keep track of it. To me, a partner was an equal partner. I didn't think of him as an equal contributor, but if you make somebody a partner you play straight with them. I can't imagine a 60:40 partnership. It's beyond my imagination to do that. Eddie never came to World-Pacific that I can remember and he didn't interfere in the music. He didn't have anything to say about the music then. It was only when he took over the responsibility of dealing with all the live performances [in 1965] that he began to enjoy the Byrds."

The Jet Set were eager to enhance their 'Beatles image' with a suitably modern look in keeping with the British groups of the period. Somewhat reluctantly, Dickson agreed to use their Naomi Hirshhorn funds to finance the sartorial makeover. "It was certainly their idea to buy those little black suits. It was the closest thing they could find to what the Beatles were wearing. They wanted them, they got them, they put them on and, later down the line, a picture was taken. But once we got them, they began not to like the suits. Having bought them with borrowed money and insisted upon having them, along with the instruments, the novelty wore off. I didn't care to have the suits. That kind of look wasn't important, or even positive to me, although it looked really good in the picture that was used by Columbia the following year."

One afternoon, the group visited the home of local impresario Benny Shapiro to play him some demos on their portable tape recorder. Nothing amazing was expected of the meeting but since Shapiro could get them gigs his support would be an asset. The Jet Set unpacked their equipment in the promoter's cathedral-like living room and McGuinn, Clark and Crosby sang along to the tape, creating an impressive double-tracked three-part harmony. Suddenly, Shapiro's daughter Michelle ran into the room, overwhelmed by a sound which conjured up visions of the Beatles. For one magic moment, she believed that the Fab Four might actually be singing live in her house. Her father related this funny episode to Miles Davis shortly afterwards and the great horn player repeated the tale to his record company. In a seemingly casual but pertinent aside, he advised CBS executive Irving Townsend to consider signing the group. According to McGuinn, Davis had never even met the Byrds or heard any of the World-Pacific tapes. He had crossed paths with Dickson in his years playing the jazz circuit, but they were hardly close friends. His recommendation was pure serendipity, but it was seized upon by Dickson who was now able to open communication links with CBS. The future of the Jet Set now lay in the hands of CBS' West Coast A&R representative, Allen Stanton.

Dickson's rhetoric, supported by Miles Davis' cursory advocacy, probably swayed Stanton, but he had another good reason for expressing interest in the group. The phenomenal success of the Beatles had provided a wake-up call for every A&R rep in search of the next big thing. CBS' Columbia imprint was still regarded as a rather 'square' label by many in the industry. The visionary John Hammond had signed Pete Seeger and Bob Dylan, which brought credibility, but there was a lingering distaste for anything resembling rock 'n' roll. Even on the folk front, the company looked as though it was more comfortable with the overtly commercial work of the New Christy Minstrels. The influence of Mitch Miller, who became head of A&R at CBS in 1950, was still profound among the company elite. As a producer, arranger and policy maker he had helped establish the company as a market leader in the Fifties, with acts such as Doris Day, Frankie Laine, Rosemary Clooney, Patti Page, Guy Mitchell and Tony Bennett. His own recordings, most notably the million-selling 'The Yellow Rose Of Texas', reinforced his position and accentuated his musical prejudices. Famously, he baulked at Colonel Tom Parker's valuation of Elvis Presley, turned down Buddy Holly, and regarded rock 'n' roll as nothing more than a superficial fad. "Rock 'n' roll is musical baby food," Miller proclaimed in 1958. "It is the worship of mediocrity brought about by a passion for conformity."

Inevitably, CBS fared less well in the pop market than its rivals, but that was not seen as a major problem during the early Sixties. They had a strong roster of easy listening artistes – including Johnny Mathis, Percy Faith, Andy Williams and Barbra Streisand – who were well established in the albums market and guaranteed regular income with minimal promotional effort. The company's other great money-spinner came via soundtracks with massive sales from the original cast recordings of *My Fair Lady* and *South Pacific*. They could afford to be complacent, but not forever.

Musically, Allen Stanton probably had more in common with Andy Williams and Percy Faith than he had with the Jet Set, but he knew the company needed a Beatles-style act for the gaping pop market. The Mitch Miller era had now passed into history and the great man would retire from CBS within a year. Stanton was no radical, but he was practical enough to appreciate market forces. He also understood the importance of competition within the company. Politically, there was considerable rivalry between the East and West coast branches of CBS, so signing an LA-based act was akin to sending a message of one-upmanship to his counterparts in New York.

It was this combination of timing, circumstance and policy change that won the Jet Set their much coveted recording contract. The document, dated 10 November 1964, contained only three signatures: James J. McGuinn, David Crosby and Harold E. Clark. Although Hillman and Clarke were regarded as fully fledged Jet Setters by this time, and not merely a live adjunct to the group, CBS insisted on signing vocalists only. It would be another four months before Chris' and Michael's names were added to the contract.

What seemed a major breakthrough was cautiously viewed by Dickson. He knew that the deal far from guaranteed long-term commitment, let alone imminent success. The 12-page contract reveals that Columbia's obligations did not extend far beyond recording, as opposed to releasing, four titles. Nor were those titles to be chosen and controlled by the group. "The musical compositions to be recorded shall be designated by us" the agreement stated unambiguously, adding that "each master recording shall be subject to our approval". The Byrds were obliged to record exclusively at CBS' studios and no recordings were allowed to be made "by unauthorized dubbing". Certain aspects of the contract appeared almost archaic, with little acknowledgement of the revolutionary changes that had taken place in the music industry over the past ten years. The Byrds' commitments were to produce "a minimum of four 78 rpm sides, or their equivalent" and, in recognition of CBS' strong association with Broadway shows, they were even obliged to contribute to soundtrack albums, if requested.

Clause 2 (b) stated: "Accordingly, you agree that when we record such albums, we may require you to cooperate with us by performing for recordings of individual compositions from such shows." In other words, if CBS decided to release any musical soundtrack from *Porgy & Bess* to *Mary Poppins* or *My Fair Lady*, they could quite legitimately demand that the Byrds sing along.

If the group or their management were hoping for some immediate financial reward from signing to one of the biggest music corporations in America, they were to be disappointed. There was no advance at all. Not a penny. All CBS were willing to offer was payment for studio work at union scale to be remitted 14 days after the completion of their first recording which, of course, would be deducted from any future royalties, always assuming the record would be released in the first place. They did promise an aggregate royalty of "10 per cent of the applicable wholesale price (less any taxes) in respect of 90 per cent of all phonograph records . . . manufactured and sold by us." The agreement was valid for only six months with regular renewal options extending to five years at the discretion of CBS. If the recordings were successful, the company would no doubt take up their five-year option, but failure would probably leave the group label-less again.

Within days of the signing, everyone agreed that a new name was required in place of the Jet Set. CBS pointed out that an English group of the same appellation existed, so it was imperative to find an alternate title. That same month, the UK version of the Jet Set, a soul-influenced beat group featuring Lisa Strike, released 'You Got Me Hooked' on Parlophone, home of the Beatles. Bizarrely, another far more arcane outfit named the Jet Set had previously issued the single 'VC 10' b/w 'Cruising 600' as a private pressing on Delta Records. They were hardly high profile and their Shadows' style instrumentals were a world away from what McGuinn and company were recording at the time. In all likelihood, CBS could have allowed their group to retain the name Jet Set without worrying about these obscure English competitors. What probably forced their hand was the news that Capitol Records were preparing to release 'You Got Me Hooked' early in 1965. A name change was now a necessity.

McGuinn had already suffered some ribbing over the title Jet Set from those who laughed at the idea of these struggling folkies seemingly regarding themselves as sophisticates. "I didn't like Jet Set," Dickson says. "I didn't think that's what they were. That was something McGuinn aspired to but, to me, Jet Set was Peter Lawford, Jill St John, people that jetted around the world and went to all these exotic places. It certainly wasn't somebody who just flew to New York and back to Chicago with an acoustic guitar."

Although the 10 November contract referred to the group as the 'Jet Set', that name was crossed out early the following year and replaced with a more evocative title. "McGuinn was enchanted with jets," says Dickson. "They were fairly new and he wanted to be the Jet Set. So I needed to get something that would appease him. One of the names I came up with was the Eagles, but he said, 'No, that's a bird of prey.' It seemed every bird that you'd want to use was a bird of prey. We were hardly going to call them the Sparrows. So we got down to 'Birds'."

Unknown to Dickson, there was also a British group signed to Decca named the Birds, although CBS' head of A&R Allen Stanton failed to mention them. Stanton was more concerned with an American country outfit named the Birds who were about to release a single. Their existence caused further prevarication, not least because 6 (b) of the group's contract included a warranty that they owned all rights to their designated name and would indemnify CBS for any infringement. Meanwhile, Dickson and McGuinn were still riffing on an alternative to Birds. "McGuinn went through the vowels and when he got to 'Burds' he said, 'That sounds like turds.' Finally we went with 'Byrds' because it sounded and looked English." Stanton accepted the suggestion but advised them to ratify the decision immediately.

On 26 November, the entire group convened for a Thanksgiving celebration at Eddie Tickner's home where the issue of the name was finally resolved. Gene Clark has an interesting spin on the story. "We were still trying to think of another name and I remembered a song that Dino Valenti had written called 'Birdses', so I suggested that we call ourselves the Birdses because I really liked the song. They were serving turkey dinner – that's how I flashed on it." The other members were less than thrilled by Clark's brainwave. 'Birdses', the bizarrely voiced flip-side of Valenti's 'Don't Let It Down' (Elektra EKSN 45 012), was the record that immediately preceded the Beefeaters' release on the label, so there was a subtle significance in its name and association. Crosby was a good friend of Dino Valenti but he wasn't sure whether the Birdses was an appropriate pop group name. Dickson, who produced 'Birdses', was not only dismissive, but denies that it was ever even mentioned.

As the discussion continued, McGuinn reiterated his fondness for a title that conjured images of soaring flight, similar to the Jet Set. Tickner mused over the Birds, unaware that Allen Stanton had already questioned its use. As it transpired, the others objected too, pointing out that it was English slang for girls and might therefore cause confusion about their sex. "They'll think we're faggots!" they laughed. Still imitating their beloved Beatles, they then agreed to alter the vowel in Birds, and McGuinn patiently pointed out that 'Berds' and 'Burds' were inappropriate. The classically English 'Byrds' sounded Elizabethan and everyone agreed that it was the best suggestion thus far. While McGuinn was still stressing the importance of flight, aviator Admiral Byrd's name entered the conversation, reinforcing the relevance of Byrds as the perfect moniker. After weeks of considering possible names, the Byrds were at last christened and ready to start their career as Columbia recording artistes. Tickner credits McGuinn and Dickson for selecting the name Byrds. "They thought it was a great idea because it had the magic 'B' as in Beatles and Beach Boys."

The Thanksgiving saga is such a wonderful tale that it seems almost churlish to challenge its mythological significance. Over the years, it has been assumed that the debate over the name Byrds began and ended on that eventful night but, as Dickson confirms, the title had already been discussed and thrashed out with McGuinn in advance of the dinner. "We did go to Thanksgiving. That's true. Eddie's wife Rita was a marvellous cook and she cooked Thanksgiving dinner for all of us. We were all there to finalize the name because CBS had said, 'You've got to make a decision.' But

I'd already had that conversation with Allen Stanton and he'd said, 'OK' to the Byrds. Everyone agreed with it at that Thanksgiving meeting. But Eddie wasn't involved in any of those discussions I'd already had with McGuinn. Eddie never once came to World-Pacific when I was working with them. And, contrary to what Gene Clark says, the name had nothing to do with the turkey! Gene wasn't in on the previous conversations. It was McGuinn who wanted the Jet Set originally and it was him alone I had to persuade. No one else ever took any interest in it or said anything about it. I never got the feeling that they cared what they were named. So, although it was *finalized* at Thanksgiving, it had been discussed between Jim McGuinn and me and Allen Stanton about a month before."

CHAPTER FIVE

Mr Tambourine Man

THE Byrds barely had time to congratulate themselves on their new recording star status when their line-up was again put at risk. Having already attempted to fire David Crosby and risked losing Gene Clark in the instrument switch, they next faced a walk-out from Chris Hillman. The drama occurred one afternoon when they were called together by Dickson for a photo shoot. Each member was taken to a hairdresser and Hillman had his curls straightened to achieve the much desired Beatle look. The beautifully coiffeured quintet then gathered over lunch, accompanied by an effervescent girl, whose presence would soon prove a major distraction.

Catherine James was a young teenager then living at a Jewish institution that looked after kids with family problems. Dickson had recorded her mother, Dian James, at World-Pacific and felt a fatherly affection for the girl. He had first met her when she turned up at the studio with a broken arm and since then had acted as her unofficial guardian. Under Dickson's supervision, she could roam reasonably freely, although he was still responsible for signing her out for the day and ensuring she returned safely. Jim often played the role of protector to troubled youngsters and had recently married a 17-year-old, Harley Stevens, who urgently needed to escape from a dysfunctional family and alcoholic father. "It was only intended for the marriage to last until after she was 18. We drove to Arizona in Dino Valenti's car to get married. I said to my lawyer, 'Won't I get into trouble taking a 17-year-old girl across the border?' He said, 'You can get arrested for taking a minor across a border for immoral purposes. Getting married is *not* an immoral purpose.' So we did that, but it wasn't a profound relationship, like my first marriage had been."

Both Harley and Catherine James had much in common with the current generation of Hollywood kids, many of whom were coming to terms with family upheavals in the Sixties. Catherine was affable, bright, sparky and loved music. Hanging out with musicians and eating cheeseburgers was part of the fun. She had been one of the first people to spot McGuinn playing Beatles songs at the Troubadour and also knew Hillman. Indeed, she remembers one occasion when she got up onstage and performed with the Hillmen at the Troubadour during a break in their World-Pacific recordings. That was quite a thrill for the youngster. Everyone said that Chris was the quietest of the Byrds, but for many girls that was part of his attraction.

Unfortunately, this was a bad day for young romance. While the four Byrds and Dickson waited downstairs, Hillman had left the building with Catherine, recklessly exposing his carefully groomed hair to the winter elements. Meanwhile, back inside, tensions mounted. As time passed, the group grew restless and began to complain about the delay. Dickson recalls McGuinn "looking as if he was going to come out of his skin as he began to realize that Chris and Catherine weren't coming down from the restaurant".

Eventually, it occurred to Dickson that the pair might be at Chris' home, which was only a few blocks away. "I went over to Hillman's house just fuming that he would do this. It wasn't that I suspected a whole lot about him and the girl – although it turned out that I should have. I was as much, if not more, pissed off that he had blown what we were there for . . . It was hard to get them all together, to get all their hair done at the same time and get a good picture."

By the time Dickson arrived at Hillman's door, he was in no mood for excuses or explanations: "I went over, kicked down Chris Hillman's door and punched the shit out of him. She ran into the closet with her pants. I prevented anything that might have happened by arriving in timely fashion. Nothing did happen between them . . . I caught him right in the face and he was bloody. I cut his face and his mouth, I suppose, maybe gave him a bloody nose. I didn't stick around. I told Catherine to put her pants on and took her back to where she belonged and went home. When I got back, the rest of the band had left – so I dismissed the photographer."

The drama didn't end there. For a time it seemed that the Byrds might be without a bassist. "Hillman left and ran away," Dickson confirms. "I think he went to a friend's place in Northern California. Then I got a letter from him, written in a childish scrawl. I still have it somewhere. It said, 'I don't deserve a friend like you. Please don't let the Byrds fall apart on account of me', and he added that he was sorry. At that moment, he accepted that the whole incident was his fault. I felt it was too. I never regretted punching him out over that. He wrote the letter, he calmed down and came back. I hadn't thrown him out. He had run away and he came home. I didn't find it a great big thing to forgive him. The milk was spilt, the picture didn't get taken, we'd wasted our last $50.00. He knew I had an attachment to the girl. I never had a relationship with her, other than as a bit of a protector. I thought she was a cute little girl and enjoyed her company."

Soon after the Hillman incident, there was more romantic drama when McGuinn became involved with a young waitress whom he would later marry. Dolores DeLeon had moved to Hollywood from Tucson after winning a place at Los Angeles City College, where she majored in journalism. She hoped to work as an artist, but took a job at the Ash Grove, the spiritual home of folk, where many musicians, young and old, enjoyed hanging out. Dolores started dating guitarist Nick Gerlach, the nephew of folk tutor Fred Gerlach. "We actually lived together for a time and were going to get married," she reveals. "His father said, 'How can you marry someone without a pot to piss in?' It's so true." Halted by parental disapproval, the relationship cooled. Gerlach was moving back and forth to Boston working with the then unknown Taj Mahal. Soon, Gerlach would change his name to Jesse Lee Kincaid and form the Rising Sons, whose ranks included Mahal, the wunderkind slide guitarist Ry Cooder and, later down the line, Hillman's cousin, Kevin Kelley.

Dolores first noticed McGuinn when he started turning up at the Ash Grove, sometimes accompanied by several other fledgling

Byrds, all of whom were still rehearsing at World-Pacific. "Later, Chris came in on his own," she says, "and I asked him who was the guy I'd seen him with. He said, 'That's Jimmy McGuinn!' I don't know how, but somehow we got together."

Not long after, Gerlach turned up to confront his former fiancée. "He said, 'I hear you're seeing this McGuinn guy. Well, what are you going to do? Are you going to see him or me?' I said, 'Well, I guess I'm going to see *him*!' He had this Martin D-28 which he picked up and crashed on the floor in the office of the Ash Grove." When McGuinn learned about this outburst he was nonplussed, but no doubt flattered.

Like Dickson and his cheeseburgers, Dolores became a valued source for the provision of fast food. "I would save my tips and that's what we'd eat on. I was the only one making money at that point. I had a little Renault that I bought from Ed Pearl [owner of the Ash Grove] for $50 and all of us used to pile in that, even though the engine would die and we'd all have to get out and push it." Hillman, now fully recovered from his assault by Dickson, also became involved with an Hispanic waitress named Vickie, who worked at the Old Manhole. "The four of us used to hang out a lot together," says Dolores. "Chris and [McGuinn] were the only two that were dating. The others were just looking for girls." Hillman would remain with Vickie until the Byrds secured their first residency at Ciro's, at which point he moved on to the more exotic world of "sexy babes and go-go dancers". McGuinn, by contrast, seemed immune to such temptations and his relationship with Dolores deepened, eventually leading to marriage and children.

After a dramatic conclusion to 1964, the Byrds opened the New Year still intact and slightly nervous about their forthcoming recording date at Columbia. Crosby suggested that an addendum be attached to their management contract requiring Dickson and Tickner "to provide the valium" for the session. McGuinn, meanwhile, sought relief in spiritual contemplation. Jim Dickson's young wife Harley recommended that he attend a meeting of the international spiritual movement, Subud.

Founded in Java, Indonesia, back in the Thirties by Bapak

Muhammad Subuh Sumohadiwidjojo, the organization adopted the acronym Subud in 1947. Its full title *Susila Budhi Dharma* suggested the 'good character of man' and the force of the inner self with an emphasis on 'patience, submission and sincerity'.

McGuinn had first encountered Subud shortly before leaving New York. While wandering around Greenwich Village with his folk musician friend Bob Kerry, McGuinn was openly smoking a joint in the street. The pair met up with mime artiste Richmond Shepard (formerly Lionel Shepard), whom McGuinn handed a reefer, only to be rebuffed by the words, "No thanks, I've got something better." Intrigued and eager to sample Shepard's supposedly superior stash, McGuinn demanded more information. "I'd envisaged something you put in your coffee," he recalls. It transpired that Shepard wasn't talking about drugs at all, but a relatively new free-form 'quasi-religion' that offered spiritual highs through meditation. Although sceptical of organized religions and a lapsed Catholic to boot, McGuinn attended a Subud meeting and found the experience rewarding. He was informed that Subud was not a religion or didactic system but a spiritual exercise whose aim was to free the individual 'from the influence of the passions'. It seemed ideally suited to McGuinn's pacific personality. As Harley Dickson confirmed, the organization was even more popular on the West Coast and had already attracted a number of minor Hollywood celebrities and musicians who were attracted by its informal style and emphasis on the self.

On 10 January 1965, McGuinn was initiated into Subud, following an experience that was to have a profound effect on his thinking hereafter. He practised the *latihan*, a meditation in which he opened himself to receiving spiritual guidance. The exercise of 'opening' his heart to the whole universe or the essential life force would later be partly translated into song via some key lines in the quasi-mystical/relativity anthem '5 D (Fifth Dimension)'. God's message reached him in a flash of light, which sounded like a cross between Saul on the road to Damascus and a scene from Mary Shelley's *Frankenstein*.

"You do what they call an exercise," McGuinn recounted. "The third or fourth one I did was as if I'd been electrocuted . . . as if they'd put electrodes in my head and turned on 5,000 volts. Pow! I'm serious, man. I saw blue lights and it just went through me and lasted for about 15 or so minutes. It was an electro-spiritual-tactile-visual hallucination without any drugs. It has never been so heavy for me since, because that first experience got rid of a lot of things I'd been through – all the forces which were not necessarily good or which I'd been subjected to for the past 22 years, which is how old I was then."

While McGuinn was finding spiritual enlightenment, the Byrds were placed in the hands of an ambitious young producer. Terry Melcher (b. Terry Jorden, 8 February 1942, New York) was the only son of CBS' recording artiste and actress Doris Day. In 1962, he had been signed to the company as Terry Day, under which name he had recorded the failed 45s, 'That's All I Want' and 'Be A Soldier'. A greater interest in A&R encouraged him to enrol in the company's trainee producer programme. Over the next two years, he produced singles by Emil O'Connor, Eddie Hodges, the Rip Chords and Frankie Laine, among others. He attempted to revitalize Laine's career by utilizing the services of young writers, such as Barry Mann & Cynthia Weil and Randy Newman. Melcher's cachet at CBS increased when the Rip Chords secured a US Top 5 hit with 'Hey Little Cobra' in January 1964. Later that year, while the Byrds were rehearsing at World-Pacific, Doris Day's seductive 'Move Over Darling' reached the Top 10 in England. Melcher had produced and co-written the song, proof enough of his all-round abilities. He seemed the perfect candidate to oversee the Byrds at their first recording session. His age meant that he could relate to them more easily than one of the senior producers and it probably helped that he had briefly worked with McGuinn in the Bobby Darin days when he played piano on 'Beach Ball'.

"I was a staff producer at Columbia and at the time they didn't have any rock 'n' roll groups," Melcher told me. "The next youngest producer was about 20 years older, so the Byrds were allocated to me. CBS had originally signed me as an artiste, then I met Bruce Johnston and formed a duo, Bruce & Terry. I'd produced about four or five hit records and was well known as part of the Jan and Dean, Beach Boys, LA rock 'n' roll set."

Initially, Melcher and Dickson proved a superb combination and were in total agreement that the Byrds' first single should be 'Mr Tambourine Man', backed with the Gene Clark song 'I Knew I'd Want You'. Melcher liked the group's striking image but upon first being presented with a promotional photograph pointed at Crosby and said, "Do we really need this guy?" By uncanny coincidence, Melcher had fingered the single person in the group who would ultimately cause him the greatest grief. Dickson patiently explained that Crosby was the harmony singer, adding that his contribution was indispensable. Melcher nodded, instantly forgetting the point as they went on to discuss more serious matters.

Since the recording deal with CBS only featured the three singing Byrds, Dickson was obliged to find some additional session players to flesh out the track. He boasted that he could recruit some of the best around, including pianist/arranger Leon Russell, guitarist Jerry Cole, bassist Larry Knechtel and drummer Hal Blaine. "That was the most interesting thing for Terry," Dickson notes. "Not that I wanted to get them – he was sceptical that I *could* get them. But these guys were more than willing to help. They were working on stuff outside the studio, listening to what we were up to so that they would be prepared and efficient when they got to the studio. When Terry checked with these people and found that this was all true and that these guys were involved, he was enthused. He looked up to these people, as well he might. I did too . . . The people I'd chosen to back them were heroes of his and had played on Beach Boys records. Hal Blaine, not Dennis Wilson, played on those Beach Boys hits. Nobody in California would ever have questioned our use of those session musicians. They were the guys that everybody used in some sort of combination."

That last point is crucially important. Ridiculous emphasis has since been placed on the fact that McGuinn was the sole Byrds' instrumental player invited to appear at this session. Latter-day critics and lazy rock historians often confuse matters by suggesting that McGuinn was the only Byrd to appear on the single, forgetting the all-important vocal contributions of Clark and Crosby and failing to understand that Hillman and Clarke were contractually not yet official members of the group at the time of the session.

Compared to many groups of the period, it is actually extremely impressive that all three original Byrds were involved in the creative process.

On 20 January 1965, Melcher recorded 'Mr Tambourine Man', with McGuinn contributing that distinctive Rickenbacker chime. Coincidentally, Dylan had finally recorded his own version in New York, only five days before. According to the union contract for the American Federation Of Musicians, the session leader at the Byrds' recording was Melcher's friend Roger Webster, brother of photographer Guy Webster, and son of Paul Francis Webster, who co-wrote the standard, 'The Twelfth Of Never'. "When I saw the AFM contract for the first time I asked Terry why [Roger] Webster got twice as much as the other session guys who actually played on the song," McGuinn recalls. "He told me the leader always gets double scale. From that point on, I was the 'leader' of the Byrds."

Dickson was mildly amused by McGuinn's machinations. "The responsibilities of the leader was to get twice as much money to do the same work. McGuinn never accepted any responsibilities as leader in the studio or on the road. But he was [later listed as] 'musical leader'. David didn't argue because he was the third one in, so he certainly wasn't going to be leader: it was either Gene or McGuinn. Gene didn't argue; Gene didn't care. At World-Pacific he went ahead and did all the work that a leader would do as far as being the coach. He'd say, 'Come on, guys, let's go, let's get it done. Stop goofing off. We could do better.' They were mostly his songs and he was the energy force then. Just as David was the energy force when they went onstage. When the money for leader came to be paid when they did an album, neither Eddie nor I was prepared to have McGuinn paid twice as much, so we rotated it. Everybody got the same money and, if they didn't, we'd try to make it up some place else."

Famed Wrecking Crew guitarist Bill Pittman was also listed as present at the 'Mr Tambourine Man' session. Dickson had originally wanted to use Glen Campbell, but took a gamble that the Byrds' lead guitarist was now experienced enough to make the grade. "McGuinn playing on that date could have been marginal. There was nobody else to replace him quickly. I'd already tried to see what Glen Campbell could do with the Rickenbacker and it wasn't appropriate. But McGuinn began to get wonderful with it, and he was beginning to stretch out. He grew faster than the rest of them, especially after he got the Rickenbacker. There weren't many of them around, even over here. Everyone was using session musicians. When McGuinn walked in to play, I was very sceptical that it was going to be good enough. He had to play with those guys and he did it. Boy, he could surprise you. It's not the strongest 12-string he ever played, but there was a lot of strength there. He was nervous because he was playing on that track, but he was OK. He would never cease to amaze me when he'd come up with an arrangement on 12-string."

The evolution of 'Mr Tambourine Man' was a story in itself with Melcher employing a rhythm feel inspired by the Beach Boys' 'Don't Worry Baby' and suggesting that classic opening bass line, to which McGuinn added a Bach-inspired lilt. "The bass part was Terry's main contribution," Dickson agrees. "There's no dispute about it. The naked 12-string was a little shaky, but the minute we heard the bass nobody said no. Once Terry had put in that bass line, we didn't try to restructure or rearrange anything. We sat there and listened, trying to find what Jerry Cole should play on his rhythm guitar. We were getting that kind of samba beat because we'd overdubbed the military drums. They were overdubbed over the straight rock 'n' roll drums. Most people never heard that but it's there and if you take it out it's an entirely different record. It was that same little military beat that Michael had provided on *Preflyte* – Hal Blaine overdubbed that on his basic drum pattern and got that movement. McGuinn picked up on it and accented it, which he'd never done before. Then Jerry Cole tried to be funky playing 'chink chink'. 'Do you want something like this?' He was probably expecting to get balled out for wasting time, but Terry and I just looked at each other. It sounded perfect. 'Yes! Don't change it!' He almost forgot what he was doing because it wasn't worked up but Cole's little combination at that moment really made the record have the right feel."

Twenty-two takes were required before Melcher was fully satisfied. Listening to the recording tapes, he sounds fully in control of the session, instructing McGuinn on the tempo and urging Blaine to play heavier on the snare drum. During the eighth take, he advises McGuinn: "Jim, try not to make any string noise when you come in there . . ." Melcher's familiarity with the musicians is evident from the juvenile humour between takes as they engage in sexual banter, joking about pubic hair and fags. "It's a bit draggy," Melcher remarks, before asking Pittman, "Are you in drag, Bill?" The mild teasing puts the musicians at ease, but there can be no denying Melcher's serious intent. By take 11, he's telling McGuinn: "Jim, do some kind of fill in 21, like bar 21 and 22 go into 'Take me for a trip . . .'" McGuinn accepts these instructions without reply, except for the occasional apology. But Melcher is relentless. "Let's take another one" is his constant refrain. "Everybody attack, really attack bar 5," he interrupts. "Jerry and Bill and Leon – everybody! When everybody comes in, there just isn't enough there. And a little more attack on the first note too, Jim." Melcher's carrot and stick approach saves the session, just as the musicians are flagging during take 21. "Do you want to go on, or do you want to rest for a minute?" he enquires. "You want to rest?! Well, let's try one more while it feels good. One more while you're resting! You've been resting through the whole thing anyway, for Christ's sake." It is only after this last take that Melcher seems satisfied with the backing track, but his enthusiasm is irrepressible.

When it came time to overdub the vocal, McGuinn proved equally inspired. Ten days after his initiation into Subud, he was now appreciating 'Mr Tambourine Man', not as a drug song or an exercise in symbolist poetry, but as a submission to the power of God. According to Dickson, McGuinn told him that he was thinking "take me away from the Bomb" when he sang the lyrics, but the singer later suggested a more spiritual motivation.

In the late Sixties, he described the song as "a sort of Islamic concept", adding that during the recording he was surrendering his spirit to Allah. Thirty years on, he related the same story, albeit with less emphasis on Eastern religion. "Underneath the lyrics to 'Mr Tambourine Man', regardless of what Dylan meant when he wrote it, I was turning it into a prayer. I was singing to God and I was saying that God was the Tambourine Man and I was saying to

Him, 'Hey, God, take me for a trip and I'll follow you anywhere.' It was a prayer of submission."

After focusing his mind on the spiritual aspects of 'Mr Tambourine Man', McGuinn was ready to attempt one of his most moving and expressive vocal performances. In order to bolster his confidence, he approached the song like an actor. Dickson had already encouraged him to appreciate the work of Konstantin Stanislavski and consider method acting. "My problem with all of them was that there was no feeling in the singing," Dickson says. "Sometimes there was when David was in a good mood, but McGuinn had no expression. I said, 'You need to have an image in your head to decide who you are when you perform the song.'" McGuinn was intrigued both by the notion of vocal role-playing and Stanislavki's concept of the importance of emotional memory and what he termed "the conscious road to the gates of unconsciousness." McGuinn's response to all this was an ingenious reprogramming of his voice so that it sounded like a cross between John Lennon and Bob Dylan.

"In the spectrum of music at the time, that was the niche I saw vacant. I saw this gap, with them leaning towards each other in concept. That's what we aimed at and hit it. We caught it from there and worked it up in a more contemporary style at the time, the beat and the wispy kind of freaked-out vocal treatment. The unison sounds came from the 12-string guitar doing plagal cadences – like the Joan Baez thing. It sounded different with electric."

The difference in quality between the World-Pacific 'Mr Tambourine Man' and the Columbia version was staggering in itself, but it was salutary to consider how close the Byrds had come to abandoning the song. At a very early stage, the lead vocal had switched from Gene Clark to McGuinn, but there was little trace of the former's contribution in the final recording. "Terry mixed out Gene Clark's vocal," Dickson points out. "You've got to be magic to hear that. It's only bleed from the other mikes four feet away. He also mixed out Leon Russell. It wasn't out of disrespect though. The electric piano just wasn't working. By the time they added the drums, they had enough. It had come together."

At the last minute Dickson suggested that they should hire his old friend Douglas Dillard to add a banjo to the recording. Terry Melcher looked around quizzically and decreed: "Man, you'd be gilding the lily. You've already got a *great* record."

Melcher was correct and the whole ensemble agreed that the end product had a marvellous sound. The recording seemed to unite the three singing Byrds, who acted more friendly towards each other now that they were achieving a common goal. In one of his more effusive moments, Crosby could even be heard crowing, "Man, we've got the best lead guitar player in the world." Clark and Crosby sang their parts with pride and the projected B-side 'I Knew I'd Want You' also turned out extremely well. Whether Crosby received the valium that he'd humorously demanded prior to the session is not known, but there was little sign of his customary awkwardness at any time during the recording. He seemed more than relieved to have survived his first test and conjured a beautiful harmony part without criticism. "It was a scary business going into that big Columbia studio with them trying to be professional musicians," Dickson stresses. "They were in a state of awe, but that didn't last very long at all. David was rising above it and putting it behind him. Within six months he would be ready to dump Columbia as being inadequate to his needs. It would go from overwhelming to inadequate before we had even finished the first album."

CHAPTER SIX

The New Pop Way Of Living

HAVING successfully completed 'Mr Tambourine Man' the Byrds were left in limbo when CBS delayed the release of the song for several months. This was particularly worrying as everyone knew that CBS was not obligated to do more than four songs under the terms of the present contract. Nobody could be certain that the label would release a single, and rumours from New York suggested that it might be shelved. The conservative elements at the company were still stuck in the era of Fifties balladeers and easy listening. When John Hammond had signed Bob Dylan in 1962, his detractors called the singer "Hammond's Folly". Although Dylan was now a best-selling albums artiste and the Beatles were international stars for rivals Capitol Records, some of the old prejudices remained. Who knew the long-term potential of pop groups?

The idea of releasing a composition like the poetic 'Mr Tambourine Man' into the pop marketplace seemed too risky a venture to warrant serious consideration. "They wanted 'I Knew I'd Want You' to be the A-side," claims Dickson. "It was only Terry Melcher's intervention that saved that. If we'd had some other house producer who didn't have the pull then Gene's song might have been the A-side, and it would have failed. The Byrds wouldn't have been any better than the Beau Brummels. But Terry, believing that there was no future for them in rock 'n' roll, wanted 'Mr Tambourine Man'." Dickson encouraged Melcher, feeding him every possible line to reinforce his commitment to the song, and the producer needed no persuading. Having heard demos like 'Boston', he couldn't see the

Byrds as a convincing beat group, but liked the idea of capturing a young audience of disenfranchised folkies, newly attuned to the pop market.

Even after Melcher had won over the company sceptics in New York, there was another hurdle to surmount: Albert Grossman. Although Dickson had previously recorded Dylan songs for folk acts, he was none too confident about the singer's imperious manager agreeing to sanction an A-side release by a pop group. "I was concerned that Grossman would say, 'No'," Dickson told me. "That's why I went to Dylan. I had to win Dylan. It was important to me that Dylan said 'Yes'. If Dylan had said, 'No', it was the end of our career. We weren't going to get a second chance at CBS. They'd only done us a favour because Miles Davis had made that call. In the end our involvement with CBS was very tenuous. Nobody at CBS was excited about the Byrds. The engineers felt insulted that these scruffy kids came into their studios and treated them contemptuously. They only did such a good job because Terry Melcher was somebody in their eyes. He was Doris Day's son, so he had the respect of the engineers. I don't know whether it was a respect for what he could accomplish or a respect for who he was. You don't mess with Doris Day's son! Doris Day was one of the biggest things that ever happened in music . . . and she was on Columbia. She was the biggest thing CBS had. They'd even given her shares during World War II as a way of paying her for what she'd done. The older guys at the company treated her like royalty and spoke about her in hushed tones. You'd think they were talking about the Queen."

On 4 February, the Byrds followed up their impromptu appearance at the Troubadour with their first paid gig: an afternoon show advertised as the 'Howdy Hop' at East Los Angeles City College. The date came courtesy of Dickson's friendly networking. During the World-Pacific period, he had invited the controversial comedian/satirist Lenny Bruce to see the Jet Set rehearse. Bruce, whom Dickson had previously recorded, was impressed enough to recommend the group to his mother, Sally Marr, a former burlesque teacher and occasional agent. "She liked to see young people get a job," says Dickson. "I'd first met her at the very beginning of my record career when working with Lord Buckley and she became a good friend. She was married to a guy younger than Lenny who cut my hair. Sally was on the scene all the time. When I was working at Barry Feinstein's [photography] studio, we'd help her get pictures, so she helped us get work."

Reputedly, the 'Howdy Hop' was the first time that Crosby had played his Gretsch before a live audience since taking the instrument from Clark after the humiliation at the Troubadour. It certainly improved his confidence. Playing at noon was also a novel experience. The group set up their equipment ("nothing more than an extension cord and their little amplifiers") in the middle of the college playground and received a good reception from the young students, eager to hear anything vaguely resembling the Beatles. Running through their brief repertoire, the Byrds performed some self-penned material, mixed with such Beatles' songs as 'Things We Said Today' and the Fab Four's version of Chuck Berry's 'Roll Over Beethoven'. The $50.00 fee was greatly welcomed too.

In a prophetic piece of advertising, the college newspaper referred to the group as 'The Byrds, US answer to the Beatles', a phrase that would later be used in slightly different form when, much to their chagrin, they were promoted as 'America's Answer To The Beatles' during their summer tour of England. The visionaries at the college newspaper were less reliable in predicting that the Byrds' debut single would be issued in "about three weeks". A series of delays, combined with record company indecision meant that there was a worrying three-month gap between the recording and release of 'Mr Tambourine Man'.

The Byrds did receive an acetate of their recording, which they played incessantly, as if to prove that they were genuine contenders. Gene Clark was still the cheerleader, eagerly informing anyone in his vicinity that the Byrds had a potential number 1 on their hands. He even sought psychic validation for his outrageous prophecy. "I might not have convinced them, but I had this strange feeling," he told me. "We used to play spin the bottle – not the kissing game – but looking for a sign. We were stuck in this hotel, playing our demo pressing of 'Mr Tambourine Man' to death while McGuinn spun a Coke bottle on a table over and over again. Every time it stopped, it pointed towards the window, out into space. I told him, 'That must be a sign, man.' He thought about my prediction and said, 'Well, I don't know, maybe you're right!'"

Despite Gene's predictions, there was still considerable uncertainly about the future. David Crosby had even returned to playing some solo dates at the New Balladeer during February, while Hillman must have been questioning the wisdom of abandoning the regular income provided by Randy Sparks. Eddie Tickner attempted to keep the momentum going by securing some low-key gigs. Fearful that there was a danger of Naomi Hirshhorn losing her $5,000 investment, he was not particularly discriminating in accepting bookings, one of which took place in the humiliating setting of a bowling alley. "I stayed away," Dickson recalls. "We were in debt to Naomi, but playing there was meaningless to me. What good could come from playing in a bowling alley in Torrance, or wherever? You should play in places where you'll be seen and heard that is relevant to the music business. I knew they wouldn't enjoy it and they did have a terrible time."

McGuinn was appalled and outspoken on the subject. "It was awful. I think there were about 20 people scattered around the room that held 100, with cocktails in their hands, totally apathetic, all looking at the floor. We'd had two sets of suits to wear which were both stolen, so we started wearing blue jeans which stayed. Anyway, we played to these mannequins with their martinis, and the bowling pins were going smash as we sang."

After the gig, the Byrds threatened to break up, but eventually calmed down. Nevertheless, McGuinn was growing restless. In a capricious moment, he fell under the spell of Dino Valenti, who voiced the view that the Byrds were a joke. He had seen them at World-Pacific in more primitive mode and could not imagine their progress or the greatness they had already touched with 'Mr Tambourine Man'. Preying on McGuinn's doubts, Valenti almost persuaded him to form what sounded like a novelty act. "He had this great idea for a group," McGuinn remembers. "He had designed costumes with radio transmitters built into the jackets, a place in your belt buckle to plug in your guitar, and it was a workable idea . . . The delay between the recording and release of 'Mr

Tambourine Man' seemed like forever. Columbia Records weren't too excited about us, Dino was anxious to do something, and it sounded like fun. He said he was getting spacesuits and wireless microphones. He hit me on the technological area which I was really keen on."

When Dickson learned of these casual machinations, he was understandably furious. "I was very angry that Dino would even try to do that, and I was angry that McGuinn would consider it. Dino gave McGuinn an expensive leather jacket that he wore on the cover of the first album and on the front of your first book. The idea that I'd gone to all that trouble and the guy was going to leave because someone gave him a leather jacket! It was difficult for me to deal with . . . Dino was aware that McGuinn was a good lead guitar player and Dino was a remarkable rhythm guitar player who developed the amphetamine strum, second only to Bob Gibson, and maybe better. But there was no way he could ever have been in the Byrds, even if he'd wanted to be. He was way too volatile. Dino Valenti made David Crosby look like a pussycat. He had far too much energy for you to want to deal with. At that time, he was the best singer I'd heard in that genre. He had everything the folkies had, but he also had everything Neil Diamond later had. Dino needed somebody who had a lot more resources than me – like a big band and an arranger. He thought we were laughable then. Dino's attitude was 'Tell McGuinn to get out of it because it's a waste of time.' I think he believed it too. He was aware that the entire folk community in New York were laughing at us, saying: 'Dickson's out there with McGuinn and all those losers trying to put together a group.' There was a grapevine that had been established through the folk community and that's what you'd hear from New York."

Dickson was mightily relieved when the deadlock over the release of 'Mr Tambourine Man' was finally broken. First came the good news via Albert Grossman's office that there was no objection to the song's release. "We'd sent Dylan the acetate and he and Bobby Neuwirth listened to it until they wore it out. Dylan was not entirely sure but Bobby Neuwirth was a big persuader. He told Dylan: 'Hey man, are you crazy – that's great.' Dylan began to like it, warmed to it and *told* Albert Grossman we could do it. It was in the can by then and we were on our way."

Dylan's endorsement assuaged many of the misgivings at CBS New York, but they were even more impressed after learning that the Byrds had been featured in a photo shoot for the forthcoming March issue of fashion magazine *Cosmopolitan*. "CBS thought I'd pulled some sort of magic trick," Dickson recalls. "Their art director couldn't figure out how I'd got the Byrds in *Cosmopolitan* on my own, and I didn't really tell them anything. I just said, 'Well, you know, things happen.' I wanted to keep the mystery. The photo was taken before the Byrds had even signed to CBS."

As was often the case in the early history of the group, this unexpected break was down to serendipity. While they were still rehearsing at World-Pacific around October 1964, studio owner Dick Bock received a call from fashion designer Rudy Gernreich asking to photograph a hip jazz or pop group in rehearsal. The fledgling Byrds, still the Jet Set at the time, were the lucky choice. Celebrity photographer William Claxton took the shot, which featured four 'Byrds', dressed casually, clutching electric instruments. Crosby, who was not playing rhythm guitar at that point, was conspicuous by his absence, either because he was superfluous to requirements, disobedient or busy elsewhere. The black and white photo is endearingly innocent. Model Peggy Moffitt stands high on an equipment case, centre stage, while three Byrds sit around her like children, with Gene standing nearby, singing, eyes closed, and playing the gleaming Gretsch which Crosby will soon covet. In a beautiful piece of flirtatious condescension, Moffitt places her hand on McGuinn's recently grown mop-top in what the magazine describes as her "off-the-top-of-my-head action dance".

The Byrds were slightly bemused by the fashion shoot, but thought little about its significance in late 1964. "It was all very foreign to them," Dickson says. They had almost forgotten about the photo when it belatedly appeared in *Cosmo* four months later as part of an eight-page spread under the modish title, 'The Gernreich Girls: New Pop Way Of Living'. Without even trying, the Byrds were suddenly bracketed as players among a new 'pop elite', whose membership included several stars whom they would later befriend or work alongside. The strangely prophetic photo shoot included actor Steve McQueen, sipping champagne with Peggy Moffit in his Ferrari, already looking like a role model for Gene Clark; Terry Southern, author of the novel *Candy* and later a scriptwriter for *Easy Rider*, poses with girls beside a TWA Super Jet, just like McGuinn might do; and there is a location shot taken at the 'Pop Art home' of Dickson's old friend and nemesis, Dennis Hopper, future co-star of *Easy Rider*.

Since signing to CBS, the Byrds had not been allowed to practise at World-Pacific, but found a new rehearsal room in the basement of a counterculture sculptor named Vito, a local legend, whose free thinking lifestyle and artistic passion inspired beatniks, aspiring existentialists and Valley girls in need of rebellion. "I can't remember who made the initial contact with Vito," says Dickson. "None of the Byrds seem to recall it either. But we knew that he was a sculptor and had students, lots of them. At the end of a class he'd take his people on to the street and go from club to club dancing – he'd done that for years. They were a sight. They were all in costume and looked 'out there', particularly Carl Franzoni. There was another guy who used to jump up and down in one place who did weird paintings of angular blocks. It was exciting to go out with Vito. He was like a travelling show. Vito reminded me of a miniature Lord Buckley in that he was absolutely positive about everything he ever said, and he was happy to give us a room to rehearse."

Vitautus Alfonso Paulekas (b. 20 May 1913, Massachusetts) was the son of a Lithuanian sausage maker with artistic aspirations and a talent for wood carving that he inherited from his grandfather. An ageless bohemian, his life was characterized by a reckless *carpe diem* that proved infectious to his young, impressionable following. In 1932, he had entered a marathon dance competition in the style of *They Shoot Horses Don't They* and somehow came away with prize money totalling $1,000. He genuinely believed that he would never have to work again. Six years later, he was broke and turned to crime. With a stocking over his head, he attempted to rob a movie theatre of its takings, but was caught and sentenced to 25 years' imprisonment. He was saved by the advent of World War II. Having served four years in jail, the government agreed to his release in 1942 on condition that he joined the merchant marines and help the war effort. When hostilities ended, he relocated to Los Angeles and attempted to make a living as an artist and sculptor. In July 1961, he married 18-year-old Sue Anne Shaffer, a former cheerleader nearly 30 years his junior, who designed clothes and adopted the more exotic monicker, Szou. "The day she was 18, her father came to Vito's house," a friend recalls. "He said, 'Have you seen my daughter?' She was in the other room. He asked her if she was coming home to dinner and she told him, 'I got married today!'" Szou's brightly plumaged fashions soon attracted a host of teenage girls to Vito's art studio, Clay Vito, which doubled as a clothes boutique. Even before the term came into common parlance, his studio was a "happening place".

During 1963, Vito came to the attention of an ebullient priapic figure who would later become his first lieutenant of dance. Carl Orestes Franzoni (b. 1932, Cincinnati, Ohio) first saw Vito on television when the artist was a guest on the *Steve Allen Show*. At the time, Franzoni was making money in the mail order business selling breast inflating pumps and penis enlargers. Despite his later reputation, there was nothing particularly bohemian about Franzoni then. He had short hair, wore a suit and looked at girls and women with a lustful leer, more befitting an oversexed teenage jock in a frathouse. At least his libido fitted his trade. Franzoni regularly ate at Ben Franks on the Sunset Strip, which was where he encountered Mary Mancini, a young art student, who painted at Vito's studio "on the corner of Laurel Avenue and Beverly". She invited Franzoni over and, flush with money from his mail order business, he purchased one of her paintings and subsequently employed her as his secretary. But the intoxication of Vito's proved irresistible. "His studio was downstairs," Franzoni recalls. "It was illuminated with florescent light and looked like some Mayan tomb. He did a lot of sculptures expressing how people felt and whatever was happening currently. They were all over the wall and on shelves. Vito was an entity I became curious about even though I was in straight business then."

THE NEW POP WAY OF LIVING

Every evening after sculpting lessons, Vito would accompany his artistic troupe to one of the nearby eateries and then visit a local club to dance the night hours away. Franzoni was initially intimidated by the confidence of the free-form dancers and declined to join in. Within a few months, however, he was not only regularly hitting the dance floor but leading the cast. Among countless adventures, Franzoni recalls Vito entering the black neighbourhood of Watts and challenging the police, a year or more before the riots began. They even met Muhammad Ali in the street, when he was still Cassius Clay, just before his first victory over Sonny Liston. The boxer was as animated as his public persona, but friendlier in person. Franzoni, a decade older than the other young dancers, grew his hair into wild curls, dressed outrageously and took free-form dancing to new levels of weirdness. His favourite band was an obscure 11-piece revue, the Gauchos, who dressed in sombrero hats and sounded like a cross between James Brown's Famous Flames and a Mexicana ensemble. 'La Bamba' was their showstopper. It was all a long way from the Byrds but, by early 1965, Vito's studio was attracting an even younger, vibrant set, dominated by a gang of girls, many from Santa Monica, aged between 16 and 18. Armed with fake IDs, a sense of adventure and a love of late-night dancing, they would soon become a crucial addendum to the Byrds' live show.

Clay Vito's motley collection of exotically dressed teens and twenties were eager to bring their art on to the streets of LA. Although there were a handful of men on the scene, including the inveterate socialite Kim Fowley and Franzoni's young friend Bob Roberts (Beatle Bob), it was the girls who attracted most of the attention. Among the retinue was the teenager Michelle Kerr who joined the troupe shortly after the Byrds arrived for rehearsals. "Vito had a studio, a store and his living quarters in the same building," she remembers. "People used to go over there for sculpting lessons and exercise classes. He was a weird artist, the original beatnik – he looked about 61 then! Carl Franzoni lived upstairs. Kim Fowley had seen me and Karen Yum Yum at Ciro's and asked us to come over to Vito's. The Byrds were rehearsing in Vito's basement and got to know Carl, and gradually it all came together."

The basement sessions were conducted in a fashionably stoned atmosphere, with the Byrds working up new material while smoking endless joints and experimenting with LSD. "We used to all smoke pot with them," Chris Hillman confesses, "and Beatle Bob would come over and play congas with us. When we later worked out 'The Bells Of Rhymney' at Vito's art studio, we were all on acid . . . Beatle Bob wasn't even a musician, he was just one of the crowd with Beatle long hair."

Even the unflappable McGuinn felt a little overwhelmed by the bohemian saturnalia in his midst. "These people were amazing, just bizarre. They were really there too, it wasn't just an act. They were very artistic people. It was almost lunacy. 'Fellini film' says it perfectly. We'd rehearse every day in that basement on LSD and we smoked a lot of pot. That was a staple. We used to have it for breakfast back then. Like drinking caffeine."

While the Byrds rehearsed, Eddie Tickner elected to take on full responsibilities for organizing the group's live performances. Despite the infamous "bowling alley" gig, he was determined to keep the boys working and displayed a similar parental concern to Dickson over whether they were eating properly or had enough money. It was Tickner who secured the group their now legendary first season at Ciro's, a once glitzy supperclub from the golden era of Hollywood, previously frequented by movie legends such as Errol Flynn, Humphrey Bogart, Cary Grant, Judy Garland, Lana Turner and Marilyn Monroe. It had also been a regular haunt for Frank Sinatra and the Rat Pack and famously launched the careers of Jerry Lewis and Dean Martin as a comedy duo. The Sunset Boulevard club closed in 1959, a victim of changing times. The lure of Las Vegas and its sumptuous casinos spelt the end for many LA nightclubs and Ciro's seemed consigned to the history books until its recent relaunch by new owner Frank Sennes. The Byrds were scheduled to play Ciro's for an entire week at the end of March, appearing five times every night. At this same point, they also learned that their management had appointed an English publicist whose love for the Byrds would shortly be translated into reams of fulsome praise.

The urbane Derek Taylor (b. 7 May 1932, Liverpool, England) had recently landed in Hollywood following a very successful tenure as the Beatles' press officer. A year younger than Jim Dickson, he had served in the army, then worked as a journalist before the onset of Beatlemania changed his life. He was employed as a ghostwriter for George Harrison in the *Daily Express* and penned Brian Epstein's autobiography *A Cellarful Of Noise*. His effortless, cheery prose also enlivened the liner notes for *Beatles For Sale* and his diplomatic skills dealing with hardened journalists were already much admired. The lure of new challenges brought him to America, but even Hollywood seemed a little tame after the Beatles. Taylor was working for Bob Eubanks of *The Dating Game* and gradually pooling a motley crew of clients, who provided money but offered little in the way of excitement or passion. Dickson had heard about the Englishman from a photographer friend, Curt Gunther, who had also worked with the Beatles. Taylor was doing some promotion for KRLA when Dickson accosted him with an acetate of 'Mr Tambourine Man'. "The Byrds came in off the street through Eddie and Jim," Taylor told me. "It was those two and the acetate that convinced me. After hearing 'Mr Tambourine Man' I had to get involved. I felt that enormous possessive sense that you did as a youth – somehow I *must* get involved in this thing. For the specific job for which God had sent me to LA, I wanted it. That's why I took this tenuous offer of two-and-a-half per cent of bugger all."

Dickson knew that he could not afford to pay Taylor a retainer, so came up with the intriguing idea of offering the Liverpudlian a commission of the group's earnings. It was a loose arrangement which proved highly successful and the terms were never revoked or challenged, even after the Byrds' rise to fame. "It wasn't even on paper," Dickson notes. "We never talked about it. It never came up. I guess when Derek left we never paid him any more. It wasn't ownership in the way Naomi Hirshhorn, who actually put up cash, continued to get paid." Taylor's percentage came out of the management's cut, as did another two-and-a-half percent which Dickson gave to his lawyers McDaniel & McDaniel, who had completed the original negotiations with CBS and would continue to represent the Byrds until 1967. Taylor's remit was loose, but Dickson hoped that he might use his former newspaper contacts to help the group secure some publicity and pirate radio play back in England.

While the Byrds were rehearsing for their Ciro's debut, Vito invited them to play at an anti-Vietnam War concert. There was some confusion about attending an audition and indignation when the Byrds seemingly went missing. Franzoni remembers someone sending one of Vito's actor friends to a cold water apartment in West Hollywood where several of the group were hanging out. The actor had appeared in some B-movie horror flicks and had a fearsome enough visage to shock them into instant contrition. Evidently, they were not entirely at fault. The group had recently returned from a visit to San Francisco where they had played before a couple of hundred school kids, a pleasant experience marred only by a break-in during which they'd lost some vital equipment and, presumably, whatever was left of their stage wear.

Vito's 'Stop The War In Vietnam' protest attracted a sizeable teenage following, keen to see the Byrds. It was an unpublicized gig, situated in a large rented room on Melrose Avenue which the artist had decorated with newspaper collages and painted signs denouncing the war. "There were pews there, like a church," Franzoni says. "He charged $1.50, I believe, and the place was packed. Vito knew about Vietnam before any of us. Who else was doing anything like that in early 1965? At the end, McGuinn told everyone, 'We're playing at Ciro's tomorrow night. Come along!'"

The first Ciro's residency (21–27 March) was attended by the Byrds' management, their publicist and some of Vito's crowd. It only took a few days before the numbers increased. "When we first turned up, there was hardly anyone there, literally about 16 of us," Derek Taylor remembers. "From then on, though, it was always packed. The sound was new and exciting. McGuinn was terrific. He had a certain abstraction about him which was fascinating; and then there were those incredible dancers. I can vividly recall this young girl dancing on her own, wearing McGuinn's glasses. I was captivated."

Michelle Kerr, the girl who was sporting those strange, rectangular granny glasses, was only one of a number of exotic creatures congregating on the dance floor. Vito's entourage provided the perfect backdrop for a living art movie starring the Byrds. The dancers were an incredible sight with their outlandish costumes and weird names like Beatle Bob, Karen Yum Yum, Linda Bopp, Emerald and Butchie. After seeing the Byrds' opening nights at Ciro's some spectators, including the impressionable Derek Taylor, felt that both the group and their followers were permanently stoned. Several certainly indulged heavily, but Michelle was a notable abstainer. "I was never on drugs," she says. "Ciro's was such a high. I'd be just in another world. None of the Byrds were *really* gone on drugs either. They weren't into it to any great degree."

The group were quietly thrilled to receive their first press notice in the showbiz bible *Variety* at the end of March. The paper had been alerted to their Ciro's debut and agreed to run a short piece. Written in a distinctly beatnik idiom, the review identified that odd combination of folk and Merseybeat as a possible winner. "At last a rock 'n' roll group that's considerate of the listener as well as the gyrating, beat-happy terper who couldn't care less about a lyric! True, it's another long-locked turtle-necked fivesome physically resembling sundry deportees from Liverpool – but that's where the similarity stops. Recently inked by Columbia Records, the five all-American-type lads, four converts from the folk-tunery circuit, where material is all-important."

Eleven days before opening at Ciro's, the Byrds' contract with CBS was amended. Both Chris Hillman and Michael Clarke had voiced dissatisfaction with the group's musical policy and told Dickson that they wanted to become "a blues band". He laughed at their audacity, but understood their frustration concerning their lesser role in the group. They were the only two members that did not appear at the sessions for the first single and their names were also absent from the record company contract. As far as CBS was concerned, the group contractually consisted of McGuinn, Clark and Crosby. The other two were merely hired hands for live performances. That anomaly was rectified by a letter dated 12 March, which confirmed Hillman and Clarke's new status as fully-fledged Byrds. By the time 'Mr Tambourine Man' was set for release, the group was *officially* a quintet.

CHAPTER SEVEN

Ciro's Magic

CIRO's represented David Crosby's epiphany as a live performer. After facing years of indifference on the folk club circuit, he was suddenly being treated like a star. Only a few months before, he had suffered some ridicule at the Troubadour when trying to wiggle like a pop star, but now people were listening, applauding and cheering his every note and utterance. "Coming off the street, they had no confidence at one time," Dickson recalls. "But David's belief and energy made it happen. I remember him coming out of Ciro's when people started liking him, and his eyes were wide. He said, 'They think we're real! We got away with it!' That gives you a good insight into his frame of mind then. He didn't think of himself as real. He felt like a fraud. Now he'll talk like he invented the world. It just amazes me."

The excitement that the Byrds generated at Ciro's was enough to encourage Bob Dylan to check out what was happening. He had already seen the group rehearse at World-Pacific and was delighted by their reworking of 'Mr Tambourine Man', the acetate of which he had almost worn out. News that they were currently working in the studio on more of his songs piqued Dylan's interest. The same week that the Byrds made their debut at Ciro's, CBS had released the great *Bringing It All Back Home*, which featured the master's 'Mr Tambourine Man' in all its acoustic glory. On the evocative album sleeve, Dylan had placed a copy of the Dickson-produced *The Best Of Lord Buckley* on the mantelpiece, as if sending out one of his gnomic messages. The album opened with the amphetamine-tinged 'Subterranean Homesick Blues', which was simultaneously issued as a single and testified to its composer's determination to use electric instrumentation in the future. Although the single reached the Top 5 in the UK, it would peak at a lowly number 39 in the US, a sure sign that Dylan had some way to go before breaking the charts as a rock performer. What the Byrds offered Dylan was an inspiring example of how to fuse acoustic folk with electric rock and create something fresh and exciting. In an impromptu gesture of solidarity, Dylan joined the Byrds on stage for their arresting version of his own composition, 'All I Really Want To Do' and added some harmonica to their cover of Jimmy Reed's 'Baby, What You Want Me To Do'. Once more, Dylan was intrigued by their ability to translate his material so radically into a pop context. According to McGuinn: "We played some of his other songs at Ciro's that night and he didn't even recognize them."

Dylan's motives in patronizing the Byrds were partly altruistic, but he was astute enough to realize what they might come to represent at a later date. As Derek Taylor pointed out: "Dylan was then [the] super-hero but his impact had yet to be measured in record sales. It looked as if he was bestowing his presence upon them, but the Byrds were doing him a favour as much as he was doing them. I always thought they had a good deal going together."

Dickson had similar feelings and was keen to capture their on-stage get-together for posterity. "I asked Dylan if it was all right to take some pictures. I wanted to make sure I had permission. He said, 'Sure, go ahead.' I don't think the Byrds consulted him about what songs to play, he just went on with his harmonica. I gave that picture to CBS and they put it on the back of the first album. That's how it worked out. Everyone was casual friends then. It wasn't a big deal to be a friend of Bob Dylan. All you had to be was friendly to him, I thought. The Byrds had let Mary Travers get up onstage before that. Barry, Mary Travers' husband at the time, has a wonderful picture of David Crosby and Mary Travers singing together on one mike at a private party. It's a great picture. They look as if they've been singing together all their lives. The whole band was there, but the picture was a close-up. Mary sang with a lot of heart."

Dylan was so enthusiastic about the Byrds' performance at Ciro's that he invited them to a prestigious party that Columbia was organizing in his honour. He seemed indignant upon learning that the group had not already received an official invitation. For Dickson, it was a great opportunity to show CBS how important an asset the Byrds were to the company. "Dylan had finally achieved some credential at CBS. He had become important. They were slow realizing that . . . but they were making up for lost time in treating Dylan good. They threw that party for Dylan, and the Byrds weren't even invited. Dylan said: 'If they don't come, then I don't come.' That had tremendous repercussions against the kind of people that were working for CBS then, who were stuffy, holier than thou and looked down on everybody in the world because they were part of CBS. But Dylan had big power. I remember that party at that Japanese place and Dylan standing up for us. I felt so grateful when they tried to take pictures of Dylan and he said: 'I want my friends in this picture.' He made sure they got lots of pictures with him and the Byrds."

At one point, Dylan invited photographers outside and sat on some steps, with the Byrds huddled around him as though they were his best friends. "In the photo Dylan had his index finger pointing at his head," McGuinn reminds us. "It seemed to me that he was being very cool, as if he were saying, 'I'm not sure I should be here, but I'm here.'"

From a PR point of view it was another heaven-sent photo opportunity, as Derek Taylor was only too aware. "Dylan didn't go out of his way to do anything that wasn't meaningful to him. He knew what his presence meant and it would only be given to people he utterly respected. And everyone was very impressed. Dylan was a strange, elusive creature of the night, like the Shadow or the Invisible Man. He was Superman, really."

Underground journalist Paul Jay Robbins secured an enlightening interview with 'Superman' immediately after his guest appearance at Ciro's. Incredibly, Dylan not only mentioned the still unknown Byrds, but spoke of them with near reverence. "They're doing something really new now. It's like a danceable Bach sound. Like '[The] Bells Of Rhymney'. They're cutting across all kinds of barriers, which most people who sing aren't even hip to. They know it all. If they don't close their minds, they'll come up with something pretty fantastic." For a group that had not yet issued a record or even played anywhere of note beyond Sunset Strip, this was praise beyond measure. It was almost too much too soon, but by some strange quirk of mid-Sixties journalistic scheduling, the piece would not appear until over five months later.

Thrilled by Dylan's appreciation of the Byrds, Dickson introduced him to his multimillionaire friend, Lance Reventlow. Even the discerning Dylan was impressed by the good-looking 29-year-old, whose playboy exploits could not disguise an admirably adventurous spirit. London-born Reventlow was the unique offspring of Danish monarchy and Hollywood royalty: his father was Count Kurt von Haugwitz-Hardenberg-Reventlow and his mother was Woolworth's heiress, Barbara Hutton. A ward of court at the age of two, Reventlow was the subject of custody battles throughout his childhood, but settled with his mother in Hollywood after she married her next husband, actor Cary Grant. By the mid-Fifties, Lance had spent a small fortune developing the Scarab – America's fastest racing car – and became a celebrated driver on the track. He befriended Dylan's former idol James Dean and was among the last people to see him before he drove to his death in 1955. Living the Hollywood dream, Reventlow married starlet Jill St John in 1960. His love of fast cars almost cost him his life three years later when he careered off Mulholland Drive. After retiring from racing, he spent more time sailing, skiing and flying, and while the fledging Byrds were starting at World-Pacific in the summer of 1964, he wed for the second time to Walt Disney Mouseketeer Cheryl Holdridge. Although seemingly far removed from the nascent counterculture, the connection with Dickson allowed Reventlow a glimpse into this new community, which already boasted Jack Nicholson, Dennis Hopper and Peter Fonda among its hip following.

Dylan was sufficiently caught up in the magic of Ciro's to accept an invitation to join Dickson and McGuinn for a trip on Reventlow's lavish yacht. Also in the party was McGuinn's partner Dolores, Dylan's road manager Victor Maymudes (aka Maimudes) and the irrepressible 'Butchie' Cho (formerly Jean Carole Webber), a wealthy folk music aficionado and Byrds fan who had travelled from the East Coast to Hawaii before settling in Hollywood. "It was Dylan's relationship with me that got him on Lance's boat," Dickson recalls. "Lance didn't know Dylan and his wife was very nonplussed by him."

The sailing trip proved eventful. "It was very funny," Dolores says. "I can remember Butchie telling me, 'I'm not happy unless I can spend $50 a day.' She seemed very domineering to me, but they were all characters on that boat. I recall Dylan sitting on the cabin deck, which was elevated a little higher than the other part of the boat. He was sitting there and she was sitting below him sucking his big toe. It was awful. I thought, 'Oh my God, in broad daylight, on a boat with everyone around.' I'll never forget that. I was disgusted. I kept thinking, 'Oh my God, people will stoop to anything to get this guy!' But I'm sure he's had worse things done to him. I'm sure he's had more come-ons than anyone in the world . . ."

Butchie's playfulness provoked no comment from the perennially phlegmatic Jim McGuinn, but amused Dickson who always appreciated her humour. "That wasn't out of her range," he laughs. "She wasn't easily grossed out. All the girls at Ciro's were jealous of her because they were younger and prettier, but she could get near to their heroes . . . Butchie always had aristocratic and eclectic tastes." The teasing flirtation, if that's what it was, ended when Dylan's customary cool was defeated by a sudden bout of seasickness. "He wasn't feeling too well and went down into the hatch. Lance had to unblock a toilet." Any chance of reminiscing about James Dean ended there.

On 26 March, coinciding with Dylan's visit to Ciro's, the Byrds could be seen for the first time on local television, appearing on KCOP Channel 13. The occasion was a talent showcase for pop, folk and rock 'n' rollers, hosted by KRLA DJ Charlie O'Donnell. Titled *Bash!*, the programme was most notable for the appearance of Jackie De Shannon, who was already championing the Byrds and experimenting with folk rock herself. At Ciro's, one of the Byrds' most popular covers was her composition, 'When You Walk In The Room', which had been an international hit for the Searchers several months before. The commotion at Ciro's, along with the *Bash!* special and the *Cosmopolitan* shoot, encouraged another

KCOP presenter, Lloyd Thaxton, to book the Byrds for his own show the following month.

A fortnight after the Ciro's summit between Dylan and the Byrds, the long-delayed 'Mr Tambourine Man' was released on 12 April. With Columbia publicist Billy James extolling the virtues of the group and hip young disc jockeys hearing something that sounded amazingly fresh, the single became a word-of-mouth cult sensation on the West Coast. Gene Clark carefully monitored the progress of the disc during its first few weeks of release. "It was picked up by Tom Donahue at KYA in San Francisco because David Crosby was a friend of Tom's and David flew up there with an acetate which Tom listened to and right away he decided to put it on the radio. He put it on air, Top 40 air, and from San Francisco it was picked up in Sacramento, Fresno and into LA and the thing broke within three weeks. It was getting pretty crazy."

The Byrds played a second season at Ciro's during the first week of April and by this point their local reputation was such that long queues formed along the Strip. When the single received airplay in San Francisco a contingent of proto-hippies trekked to Hollywood convinced that the Byrds were preaching the LSD gospel. Suddenly, Ciro's became both a counterculture mecca and one of the most hip and fashionable places to be seen. On the dance floor Vito's wife Szou undulated dreamily, with a baby suckling at her breast, while the other members of his wildly plumaged flock performed their free-form routines, watched by a battalion of amazed spectators, who soon joined them in festive revelry. Scattered amongst the fans, freaks and dancers was a combination of established stars and the soon-to-be-famous: Jack Nicholson, Barry McGuire, Major Lance, Little Richard, Judy Henske, Mary Travers, Buffy Saint-Marie and Sonny & Cher. Dickson spread the word like a prophet, calling in favours from old acquaintances and ensuring that Ciro's was filled to the rafters with his friends, associates and rivals.

"We had all the up-and-coming elite who wanted to know what was going on. All the young Hollywood people came there. If you were in Hollywood and on the way up, or even trying to be, it was too big an event to miss. Even people who had nothing to do with it came. Sal Mineo arrived in a tuxedo because the last time he'd been at Ciro's that's what you wore. He had that tuxedo and a black tie and ordered champagne in a bucket. He was the only one in the room with that kind of set-up. None of us were impressed with Sal Mineo as an actor, performer or hero. But to have him show up and to be able to say: 'Hey, that's Sal Mineo over there!' was neat. Jack Nicholson was a more familiar part of our community. All these actors came in, lots of people I'd known. We'd call them up on the phone every day, everybody. They'd have a good time then come back with somebody else. Everybody had a great time at Ciro's. That's why they're still talking and writing about it over 30 years later. It was just mind-boggling – and for Eddie Tickner too! For me, to see Eddie at a Byrds show *every night* was surprising then."

Other people who attended the shows were no less extravagant in their praise and speak in epochal terms about the Byrds' performances. Dancer Michelle Kerr maintains that the happening at Ciro's was the harbinger of a cultural revolution. "We started the hippie movement. We were the first groupies who were known. Jim Dickson started calling us groupies, but at that time it wasn't a put-down. After that, when everybody else started following the groups around, it became a lower-class thing."

David Crosby concurs. "Dickson engineered a lot of that. He phoned every movie star he could find and encouraged people to come down and help turn it into a scene. As soon as people found out there were rich people and movie stars hanging around this scruffy band, it got to be the hip thing to do. Unquestionably, it put us on the map. There'd be prototypes of hippies there, lots of actors and actresses, Hollywood people, racing drivers. It was an eclectic mix. I think the whole countercultural movement started on the Strip."

Watching the instant happenings at Ciro's, Derek Taylor convinced himself that he had entered an *Alice In Wonderland* setting, in which the Byrds and their retinue took on mythical qualities. "The dance floor was a madhouse. A hard-core of Byrd followers – wayward painters, disinherited sons and heirs, bearded sculptors, misty-eyed nymphs and assorted oddballs – suddenly taught Hollywood to dance again."

Among the dancers was the extrovert Kim Fowley, a scenester

supreme and a Hollywood hustler and womanizer, not known for starry-eyed sentimentality. Yet even he found a moment in heaven at Ciro's and spoke about the experience with uncharacteristic effusion and reverence. "It was Sherwood Forest in a nightclub. The Byrds were more than just a band. Every time they played at Ciro's, it was wonderful. This was ascension music. It was illuminating. It was Disney and Christmas time combined. It was probably the best acid trip anybody was ever on. They were the group for that time and they reinvented a lot of things. We didn't have a religion, but this was a religious experience. That's what the Byrds really were. It wasn't a hype. It was astounding. This was the true magic that showed how a favourite band can make lives better and work through all our pain and suffering. It doesn't happen too often in music where you can go somewhere and have your life changed in a 25-minute set."

The Byrds' five-set sessions at Ciro's were always unpredictable and daringly erratic. During the first couple of sets they seemed nervous, off-key and out of place. McGuinn appeared tentative, Crosby "looked at the guitar as if it was a foreign object" while Clarke appeared to be asking "What do I do with these drumsticks?" Once Crosby's mood lightened, however, the entire group would surge. Just as Clark had galvanized the Byrds' spirits during sessions at World-Pacific, so Crosby was responsible for their abrupt shifts to brilliance during live performance. Dickson pinpoints David's backing vocal on the Beatles' 'Things We Said Today' as the pivotal moment. As soon as he uttered the words, "Me, I'm just the lucky kind", he seemed to realize the full implications of the words and, smiling that cute crooked smile, would take the Byrds towards musical nirvana.

"When David was positive he made the whole band shine," says Dickson. "I used to watch it every night and wait for that moment in the middle of the third set when they sang 'Things We Said Today'. When the Byrds did a reunion album years later that was one of the songs I wanted them to do because they always sang it great. When David's part came in, it would light him up onstage and from there on the set would be great."

For Dickson, the other hero of Ciro's was Michael Clarke, whose drumming on his home territory, orchestrated by a legion of dancers, was so magnificent that it defied belief. "Michael's ability to keep good time and happen depended upon everybody else's ability to do it. And with a roomful of dancers, maybe 300 to 400 people dedicated to time, then it *would* happen. It's like trying to march out of step with a military band. When somebody's playing one of those John Philip Sousa marches it's more difficult to walk out of step than to walk in step. When the sense of rhythm in a room is so solid from everybody contributing to it, including the audience jumping up and down in time, then Michael would get grand. Michael would play on 'The Bells Of Rhymney' so marvellously that it would blow your mind every single night."

Clarke's new-found musical confidence surprised everybody. Only a few months before he had been playing on cardboard boxes. He was even ready to leave the group after the comical humiliation of seeing the drumsticks fly from his hands when trying out his first proper kit. Now people were actually congratulating him for his rudimentary playing ability. At the end of April, Major Lance followed the Byrds at Ciro's and enlisted Clarke as a substitute drummer. "Michael sat in for him," Hillman recalls. "Oblivious to who he was, Major Lance, at the end of the night, turned to him and said, 'Hey, drummer! Here you go, buddy' and threw him five bucks. Michael goes, 'Five bucks? Thanks, Mr Rockefeller!'"

The Byrds' inspired but strangely erratic performances were to remain a constant for the next few years. During those early days of 1965 they had the capacity to move from poor to brilliant in the space of an evening and the following night the process would be repeated. It was this aberrant quality which won them a fanatical following in Hollywood. What was most surprising was their ability to transform cerebral folk into a form of dance music. In achieving this alchemy, they no longer required derivative crowd pleasers like 'You Movin'' or 'Boston' but instead chose to forge ahead with their unique brand of Dylan-inspired rock and ever stronger and stranger songs of fractured romance, characterized by inspired arrangements and an unrelenting folk beat. Even the sober-blooded Dickson, who had worked with many great jazz and folk musicians, was completely overwhelmed and mystified by the Byrds' ability to reach inexplicable musical heights as if by sorcery. Ciro's weaved its own magic on those entering its portals and, amid the sensory delights, time itself appeared to stand still.

"Each night was a week," Dickson insists. "They seemed to have played there for months. Every night was so exciting that it was a high moment in your life. You'd go back there the next night and it would be a higher moment in your life. It would be more exciting than all sorts of alternatives in life. It was more fun than anything that any of us or any of the audience had ever experienced. It made people fanatically crazy for the Byrds. It made the Byrds seem bigger than life. By the third set, they were playing great. By the end of the night, it was like Temple Music. It was perfect. It was majestic. It compelled you to dance. I hadn't danced in 15 years since I was a young kid. I found myself out there dancing with Odetta, with Mary Travers. It's hard for me to get an image of myself and Odetta boogying to the Byrds. I can't even imagine that any more. I remember her saying: 'Gee, Jim, I didn't know you could dance.' Even she was amazed. When the Byrds left Ciro's after a night of exhausting sets, they went in five different directions and did entirely different things. They had a tremendous amount of local attention. Having spent all that time living on cheeseburgers, they hadn't had much interaction with the glamorous world around them. Suddenly, people were willing to take them to their homes and invite them to dinner. The audiences were more than prepared to shower them with all the goodies of Hollywood. Teenyboppers and stars who'd thought you were nobody were now taking you seriously, sharing insights and experiences. They'd all go off and have a grand time. Time stood still in those Ciro's times in a way I can't explain. It did for everybody."

Local reporters were not only amazed but puzzled by the phenomenon. Reviewing the second season at Ciro's, a journalist from the *Los Angeles Times* spent an entire paragraph attempting to deconstruct the meaning of Carl Franzoni's bizarre writhings. "A man whose chin was thrust behind a large beard stood up and jigged toward the dance floor. Now, we have all become used to seeing young moderns twitch without touching their partners, but, aside from the Middle East, we have never seen a man writhe on the floor, wholly unaccompanied. For one full set, the bewhiskered man performed his solo, occasionally stretching both arms toward the ceiling as if offering personal sacrifice and plucking notice from some pagan deity."

The circle of musicians, actors and writers that surrounded the Byrds were eager to provide assistance when called upon. Chief amongst them was Paul Jay Robbins, an astute writer for the hip *Los Angeles Free Press*. Robbins had already interviewed Dylan at length, and his intellectual prose, almost unheard of at that time in connection with chart pop, made the Byrds sound like the most important group in the world. Observing their performance at Ciro's, he courageously attempted to define the nature of their appeal, extravagantly proclaiming: "What the Byrds signify . . . is a concept deeply applied to unification and empathy and a rich joy of life – together with a positive recognition of the bulbous clusters of sickness around us. It represents a passing through negative apathy and an approach into involvement . . . Their singular method is so unique, in a dynamic and irresistible adventure, the technique and honesty of folk music, the joy and immediacy of r&r, and the virtuosity of jazz . . . In their brief span of professional life, the Byrds have gone through the Beatles and into a totally novel and fascinating place. They successfully united an audience of average teenagers, Bach, Bartok, and Cage, aesthetics, folkniks, sophisticated middle-agers, r&r devotees, and serious hippies into one joyous movement . . . The sound is so damned right that you can't deny it. The modes of dancing which the Byrds incite, is a thing of open loveliness to behold and a state of ecstasy to involve yourself in. Dancing with the Byrds becomes a mystic loss of ego and tangibility, you become pure energy some place between sound and motion, and the involvement is total . . . However, hearing a Byrds record is like listening to a record of *The Rite Of Spring*. The dynamic empathy is rich, but it just doesn't compare to the direct gestalt of music, dancing, aura and communication."

Such flattering, intellectual prose about a young American pop group was virtually unprecedented, but McGuinn accepted the plaudits with honour. "We were seen as a symbol of something good, something new away from the stagnation that had occurred in music. Also, we were the first group to incorporate any intellectual value to speak of. Up until then it had all been 'baby, I love you, see you at the drive-in tonight'. And Dylan's lyrical intellect was an innovation."

All of those in attendance at Ciro's appear to have understood that something revolutionary was taking place. Some were eager to take advantage of the phenomenon. Sonny Bono who, along with arranger Jack Nitszche and Jackie De Shannon, had written the Searchers' UK chart-topping 'Needles And Pins', was quick to spot a new trend and keen to profit from the Byrds' pioneering work. Ostensibly a young buck with a strikingly attractive teenage companion, he was actually 30 years old, only four years younger than the Byrds' manager Jim Dickson. Bono had previously worked at Art Rupe's Specialty Records, home of Little Richard, Larry Williams and Sam Cooke. Ever astute, he persuaded the great Phil Spector to hire him as West Coast promotion person for the Philles label. While there, Bono played on various sessions, joining the backing singers, and simultaneously involving his girl Cher, who even released her own single under the name Bonnie Jo Mason. Previously the inveterate apprentice, Bono was determined to advance his cause as a producer, songwriter and singer. He had already recorded with Cher under the name Caesar & Cleo and was ripe for reinvention. A secret master of pop realpolitik, Bono always gravitated towards the most cunning power players in his orbit. He next hired former New York publicists Charlie Greene and Brian Stone as his managers and publishers. They effortlessly assumed their role as a more ruthless version of Dickson and Tickner. In a supreme example of brinksmanship, they resold Caesar & Cleo as Sonny & Cher, and later acquired solo deals for each artiste on different labels, as if they were shares on the stock market. Meanwhile, Bono watched the Byrds with hawkish vigilance, eager to learn whether this new phenomenon could possibly break out of LA into the wider market.

Another figure studiously observing events at Ciro's was producer Lou Adler, who had recently formed his own label, Dunhill Records. Terry Melcher had just given him a copy of Dylan's new album, *Bringing It All Back Home*, the most important and talked about record of the year so far. Adler passed on his copy to a teenage client Phil (P.F.) Sloan, supposedly along with a pair of Chelsea boots and a folk singer's cap, and suggested he write a bunch of songs along similar lines. It was akin to asking a Brill Building writer to mimic Dylan but, amazingly, Sloan was up to the task. Both Adler and Sloan had visited Ciro's and saw the future, not merely onstage, but on the dance floor. "The Byrds were playing," Adler remembers. "It was the beginning of the freak period – there was this subculture that no one in LA knew about, not even me, and it was growing. The Byrds were the leaders of the cult, and the place was jam-packed, spilling out into the streets. In the middle of it was this guy in furs, with long hair, and dancing. I thought he looked like the leader of a movement." The dancer was not Carl Franzoni nor one of Vito's crew, but another disenfranchised folkie, suddenly adrift in LA.

Dancing at Ciro's, Barry McGuire found himself in the right place at the perfect time. He had been somewhat bemused to discover that his former bandmate Gene Clark, to all intents a reject from the New Christy Minstrels, was now in the most talked about group in town. That their ranks also included Jim McGuinn, David Crosby and Chris Hillman, musicians who had previously appeared in lesser rival aggregations to the Christies, was all the more baffling and frustrating. "When I left the Christy Minstrels and tried to get a job, nobody had the time of day for me," McGuire recalls. "I couldn't believe it. I'd been three years on the road, playing 300 gigs a year, appeared on Andy Williams shows and had a hit record ['Green Green'] on which I was the lead vocalist and co-writer. It was the only big hit the Christies ever had. And nobody wanted me. One day, McGuinn gave me a ride across town and told me he'd got this group together and they'd just recorded a Dylan tune. He sang it to me a cappella as we were driving down La Cienega Boulevard. It was 'Mr Tambourine Man'. I thought, 'Wow, that's incredible!', even with him just singing it. Then he invited me to their opening night at Ciro's, and they were all there playing 'The Bells Of Rhymney' and all these great songs."

McGuire's primary interest was finding a suitable girl for the evening and dancing all night. His life changed when he was accosted by Adler, who suggested he record some of Sloan's compositions, which were pitched to RCA Records later that year. Among the batch were the word-packed, harmonica-tinged 'Child Of Our Times', the evocative 'Upon A Painted Ocean' whose opening lyrics "come gather round . . ." were taken verbatim from 'The Times They Are A-Changin'', and a portentous, doom-laden reflection on the state of the world, ominously titled 'Eve Of Destruction'. Whether these songs had any commercial potential rested largely on what the Byrds would achieve over the next few months. A new age was underway.

CHAPTER EIGHT

Positive Thinking

TERRY Melcher was eager for the Byrds to re-enter the studio in search of a quick follow-up to 'Mr Tambourine Man', which he suspected might peak as a regional hit. Although its impact on the West Coast assured the Byrds further studio time, their long-term prospects could only be guaranteed by an across the board national hit. At first, the group seemed rusty and Melcher quickly rejected some Gene Clark material, including 'She Has A Way' and the recently composed live favourite 'You And Me'. However, after completing their second residency at Ciro's in mid-April, the Byrds sounded much fresher and hit a rich vein of form, concluding an album's worth of songs in two long sessions.

The sessionography suggests that the album was a breeze to complete, but the bare details patch over countless hours of patience, pain, exhilaration and frustration. The first hurdle to overcome was deciding who would play on the record. "Columbia wanted us to do the first album with session men," Crosby recalls, "and we threatened to quit. We didn't like that at all."

Dickson was disappointed by their insistence on the subject of session musicians. All the other groups he knew used top players to bring out their best qualities in a studio setting, so why did the Byrds have to be different? Faced with their stony determination to complete the album without outside assistance, Dickson backed down, but suggested a compromise: "I wanted to use Leon Russell for the whole of the first album, no matter who else the other guys were, because I wanted them to learn from him. What an opportunity. What a great teacher. Here was a guy who'd directed symphony orchestras at 19 and had produced many pop smash hits. He was totally versatile and had a full box of paints of musical colours. He could do anything you wanted. He could speak Italian notation, work without music – play him a record and he'd play it back to you with a whole new arrangement out of his head. Play him a song and he'd make up another one on the spot."

Despite Dickson's protestations, the Byrds stood firm and Leon Russell's contributions were not required. It was a considerable slight to Russell and the session men, but proof of the group's new-found confidence and sense of cool. Already the gods of Hollywood, the Byrds typified the 'me' generation at its youthful zenith. Like Dylan at his most aloof, the Byrds refused to play the pop game according to the age-old rules of the industry. Having won the support of the greatest session musicians of the era, they were willing to dispense with their services with scarcely a second thought. It was an attitude that Dickson could understand, but one for which he felt little sympathy. "These people were very hurt when David Crosby went around calling them 'meccano musicians', and they were *never* invited back. They came in the studio and made a number 1 record and the guys never got called back. That was very uncommon in Hollywood in those days. I felt bad about it and they felt terrible about it. 'What a bunch of ungrateful people!' And they had so much to offer. Hal Blaine had helped Michael to learn to play drums on the side of all this. Helping Michael to set up his drums took time. These were nice people, they weren't like the Byrds! They were good, nice, honest, very straightforward people that were happy to help if you were trying to get somewhere. If they saw you struggling with a package, they'd help you. The generation the Byrds were in wouldn't help you. They were incredibly more self-centred. I grew up in the early Forties, so I had different values. I had more radical values in some ways, and more traditional values in other ways."

Melcher was initially sceptical about the Byrds' ability to work on their own tracks, but he was won over by the quality of the material they were presenting. Their decision to cover some Dylan songs resulted in an effervescent version of 'All I Really Want To Do', which sounded like a definite hit. Equally impressive was a surprise composition from Gene Clark titled 'Feel A Whole Lot Better', which reminded Melcher of the Searchers' 'Needles And Pins'. Having previously jettisoned a couple of Clark songs, Melcher began to see the Missouri singer-songwriter in a more positive light. Dickson was also impressed with their progress and marvelled at McGuinn's virtuosity on the Rickenbacker, which was already providing the Byrds with a sound unique in pop. Against the odds, they had risen to the challenge of working under intense pressure and were creating some of the finest music of the era. Completing the album took its toll, however, especially on Dickson, whose love of perfection was almost proving his undoing.

Lizzie Donohue, another of Vito's dancing troupe, attended a recording session, which suddenly turned very ugly. "It was clear that David Crosby wasn't getting along with Jim Dickson," she recalls. "Jim had David on the floor and he was choking him. David seemed to have a problem with everybody. He was always at odds with someone, but we all got on really well."

The incident that Donohue describes actually occurred on the very last day of the recording sessions for the first album. For Dickson it was a cathartic moment, which left him emotionally drained. Recalling his fracas with Crosby, he felt justified that the circumstances demanded firm action: "Lizzie said I was choking him! It probably looked that way from the booth. I wasn't choking him though. I had him by the shoulders. David Crosby had cut the last track for the album, 'Chimes Of Freedom'. He then announced that he wasn't going to sing on it, he was leaving. Trying to get him through the first album, I sat on his chest and said: 'The only way you're going to get through that door is over my dead body. I will physically stop you with every bit of energy I have. You're going to stay in this room until you do the vocal.' And David broke into tears. There were a lot of people there apart from Lizzie. People were there from CBS who'd come to see them for the first time. It was not the moment that one would choose to have that kind of conflict, but it was either finished or to hell with it all."

Within a month of completing the album sessions, the Byrds set out on a seven-day West Coast tour supporting the Rolling Stones, who were soon to break big in America with the chart-topping

'(I Can't Get No) Satisfaction', which they had first recorded at Chess Studios in Chicago and completed in California. Crosby had picked up some of the Stones' sexism of the time and, when confronted by McGuinn's girlfriend, Dolores, acted like the narrator of 'Under My Thumb'. "David said, 'No chicks in the limousine,'" she laughs. "[McGuinn] told him, 'Dolores is coming', so I got into the limo with them. David was just beside himself. He was so angry because I was always there. There were no other girls at Long Beach and I was like the little mascot. I used to always have this nightmare that I would go out of the fencing area and try to come back in and no one would let me in and I wouldn't have a ride home. But I was pretty independent. I didn't hang out. I would always walk around. I wasn't afraid because I just felt like I *could* come back. Surely, there was always someone that would let me back in." At Long Beach, Dolores almost realized her worst nightmare. This was the Byrds' first experience of playing large venues and provided a frightening insight into the dangers of fan mania.

"Long Beach was a disaster," Dickson recollects. "The police beat up the fans – it cost one girl her fingers. They got on top of the Stones' car when they were leaving. I remember Mick Jagger saying how the roof of their station wagon was collapsing. The girls had their hands on the luggage rack on the top of the car and the cops were hitting their hands and blood was running down the windows."

Fortunately, the tour was not all blood and gore. At San Diego, the Byrds were forced to extend their set when the Stones failed to reach the venue on time. After exhausting their repertoire of Dylan covers and originals, McGuinn and Clark attempted some Stones' numbers, cleverly mixing the Bo Diddley beat of 'Don't Doubt Yourself Babe' with 'Not Fade Away' and others. Michael Clarke was in his element playing in the R&B style that he so enjoyed, while Crosby improvised on rhythm guitar. Everyone was enormously grateful to the Byrds that evening for pacifying a potentially hostile crowd. "When you open for the Rolling Stones and the Rolling Stones aren't there, people are likely to get crazy," Dickson says. "There was a sense of danger. The Rolling Stones were desperately trying to get there before there was a riot. The story they tell is that when they arrived the Byrds were playing all their songs. The Byrds had run out of their own songs, but I don't recall them doing *many* Rolling Stones' songs. But that's what the Stones said and who's going to argue? They were complimenting the Byrds."

The Byrds returned the compliment not long after when they played 'Not Fade Away' on *Shindig!*, a clear indication of their positive feelings about the group. Mick Jagger continued to compliment them in print, while Brian Jones emerged as an early supporter. "We spent seven nights with the Byrds, so I had plenty of time to get to know them," he recalled, "especially Mike Clarke and guitarist Dave Crosby. They are very nice fellows. Mike is very much like me, only much taller. We were always being mistaken for each other and we seemed to be meeting the same girls. I went to dinner with Dave a few times and we talked about the music scene in Britain. The Byrds seemed very anxious to make it in England – even more so than in America . . . Like me, the Byrds are night people. They like to stay out late. Dylan thinks a lot of the Byrds. I met Dylan at his hotel while he was in London, and he was playing 'Mr Tambourine Man' all the time. He just loves the sound of them."

If the Rolling Stones' tour brought the Byrds immense gratification, then an even greater buzz was forthcoming during late May when 'Mr Tambourine Man' exploded across the country. After three weeks in the *Billboard* Hot 100, it suddenly jumped from number 55 to number 17, then rose inexorably to the top spot. The chart surge was pre-empted by a moment of revelation that stunned everyone in the group. "We were driving along in a black station wagon that we'd bought from Odetta," Crosby recalls. "All of us were in the car – and on radio station KRLA comes 'Mr Tambourine Man' *three times in a row*. The biggest radio station in LA and they played it three times in a row. We just sat there and drooled. We went crazy. It was so good. We knew we'd won."

As the momentum gathered, CBS publicist Billy James worked overtime by promoting the group at every opportunity, recruiting new fans and encouraging them to spread the word. Television promotion was a crucial part of their ascent and, just before the Stones' shows, they had been flown to New York for a prestigious plug on

POSITIVE THINKING

NBC's high-rating *Hullabaloo*. While there, they visited CBS' offices in Manhattan, but some of the executives were nonplussed, much to Dickson's amusement. "They were very disenchanted when they saw the Byrds live in their office. They weren't wearing their little black suits. They were in jeans and looked scruffy, having been out all night in the Village. Columbia thought they were going to meet these nice, tidy, polite, young gentlemen."

Tensions were mounting as the group prepared for the *Hullabaloo* broadcast. Although they had performed several times on screen back in Los Angeles, this was different. Even the perennially cool McGuinn was nervous. "We'd never experienced the pressure of a live television show before, and this was a national broadcast. They had these big colour television cameras coming in on us and it was pretty unnerving. The guy at the mixing board couldn't get our voices right and I didn't like my vocal on 'Mr Tambourine Man', which came out very shaky, probably because we were so nervous."

The Byrds performed two numbers on *Hullabaloo*, a slightly slower than expected 'Feel A Whole Lot Better' and a nervous, but ultimately rewarding, 'Mr Tambourine Man'. The playing was competent, with Clarke abandoning his unusual military style of drumming, as demonstrated on *Preflyte*, and effectively duplicating Hal Blaine's work on their hit. The Byrds were a little ragged but sounded strangely appealing and their casual clothes made them look suitably nonconformist.

Unfortunately, not everyone was pleased by their hip attire. Against Dickson's advice, Crosby had insisted upon wearing a pea coat on the show, which made him seem bloated from certain camera angles. When he saw the broadcast, he was furious and screamed at Dickson: "Why didn't you tear the coat off me?" It was not long after this incident that Crosby bought an extraordinary green suede cape, a garment that sanctified his appeal as a *bona fide* sex symbol pop star. With McGuinn's rectangular granny glasses, Clarke's sheepdog bangs, Clark's muscular presence and Hillman's non-expressive visage, the Byrds looked the coolest group in the world. The image was immensely powerful, but Crosby still insists that the Byrds' otherworldly ambience and groomed prettiness were not premeditated fashion statements.

"We didn't look at it that way. I naturally smile all the time. I didn't do it as an act. I have no act. And you know it because you've seen me. The green cape and the glasses we did use to look far-out to jazz people. I admit that. But we dispensed with them pretty quickly and rested it almost solely on the music. We were trying to be avant-garde, new, fresh, noticeable and positive. McGuinn was a good force there. His 'I trust it will turn out all right', and things like that, were a very positive force. The guy really meant it and really played his role in the group that way. It was a very good thing in that sense. He was a very positive force and I liked him for it. I thought it was good and I respected him. But none of us bought the star bullshit. Star is the *übermensch* mistake – it means somebody bigger than life. And nobody is. There's no such damn thing. They try and tell you that you're solid chrome, 11 foot tall, you've got wings and, sweetie baby, everything you say is deathless prose. But it's pure, unadulterated, misleading bullshit. It's one of the peripheral things that pulls you away from the music. That fame and glory shot, and the chicks and money and 'Oh my God, I must be smart, look at how many people are listening to me.' All those things are mistakes. They all pull you away from the music. And we tried very hard, consciously, to avoid them and to stay concerned with the music and with what we were saying. We thought we were wordsmiths too by the time we got into it, and we at least liked the things that we were saying. But I don't think that any of us bought that star bullshit. Not any of us. I'd give every guy in the band credit for not going for it. I can remember McGuinn, before we even really started, saying, 'Man, we'll be like princes.' But even he didn't buy it in terms of thinking of himself as any different. Maybe he did, but I don't think he did. I'd give him credit for being smarter than that."

The positive philosophy that Crosby remembers emanating from McGuinn came about partly thanks to Jim's mother Dorothy, who had mailed him a copy of the best-selling book *The Power Of Positive Thinking* by Norman Vincent Peale. McGuinn immediately adopted the author's words "I trust everything will turn out all right" as his catchphrase and determined to transform the Byrds into a vehicle for positive thinking, an ambition that would not prove easy to achieve. "I'd been through Catholicism, went through an agnostic period, then got into Subud," McGuinn recalls. "So I was looking for God. I figured, 'OK, there's a God somewhere, let's find Him.' I read the Peale book and even though he was coming from a Christian base, I didn't really buy into that part of it. I just took it for the psychological value of positive thinking. And positive thinking works. If you really focus on the positive side of every issue and don't let yourself get bogged down in negativity then you will have more success in life. It's a simple fact and it worked for me."

The combination of positivity and coolness made the Byrds seem unfathomable. Like Dylan, they gave the impression that they had discovered some great secret, which they were unwilling to impart to the uninitiated. Unlike many groups of their era, the Byrds were not forced to fashion an image to please their managers or record company, for they were already a marketing man's dream. Onstage, they created their own image of unpredictability and eccentric genius, both in their unconventional dress and their moody, erratic performances. "The Byrds' management let them control their own image," Derek Taylor told me. "The group did it all themselves. The Tickner/Dickson thing was just right for the Byrds, just relaxed enough for them. Had they had an Elliot Roberts or Irv Azoff type, it might have frightened them. They were so scruffy, and their attitude towards the audience was so blasé. They were often quite bad onstage, but they had this relaxed management who said: 'That's cool!' Dickson really knew what being laid-back meant. He was so laid-back himself; no middle-aged, middle-class hang-ups. Everything went with Dickson. His attitude was, 'If David Crosby wants to do this, let him do it.' Eddie curbed Jim's wilder instincts. It was a good partnership."

In one sense, Taylor was right about Dickson's easy-going attitude, but the manager could also be volatile and even violent if roused. His determination to save the Byrds from themselves and play the father figure ignited strong passions that were not always easy to control. "Eddie Tickner is more laid-back than me," Dickson points out. "He's more organized. I don't know if I'm as laid-back as Derek says. To him, I was. To East Coasters I guess I was. But I didn't think I was any more laid-back than the average

Californian goof-off. I came from a community that felt that if you had to get a job to make a living then you were a failure. If you couldn't make it by your wits, you weren't worth it . . . The times that I got upset with the Byrds were all reactions. They weren't instigated by me. I never said, 'You're going to do what I say.' I wasn't domineering that way. I tried to persuade them one at a time. I suppose that looks duplicitous because you're telling five people a different story to get the same end. But I had to take into consideration who they were. You've got to say something different to McGuinn to get him to understand the same thing as Michael. You'd have to take time to explain something to Michael, and different values are involved. If something had five positives you might mention two of them to one person if you knew they cared and some other point to somebody else to get them on your side. It was merely politicking."

The management duo needed new offices now that the Byrds were breaking big. It was Tickner who decided that they should move into 9000 Sunset Boulevard, a skyscraper that symbolized the corporate avarice of Hollywood and, equally importantly, stood across the road from his favourite delicatessen, the Gaiety. The building was still under construction when they moved in and finances were so tight that Dickson had to borrow $3,000 from Lance Reventlow while awaiting the first royalty cheque from CBS. With publicist Derek Taylor joining them in an adjacent office, the Byrds' management set-up now looked considerably more organized and efficient. Tickner's wife Rita Rendall, who had formerly worked as a controller for Albert Grossman, was also involved in looking after the accounts and reluctantly tolerating the craziness.

"Rita didn't want any messing," Derek Taylor remarks. "And with this thing we were in, it was all messing. She couldn't believe she was involved in such confusion. Bad boys! Eddie getting involved with these teenagers and this piss-arsed Englishman who was so charming and unreliable and always late with his rent. Never mind!"

Taylor may have been a little wayward in Rita Rendall's eyes, but his laconic charm and eloquent prose often saved the Byrds during moments of minor crisis. Dickson remembers one spot of trouble when the Byrds found themselves booked into a small club across the road from Ciro's, just as 'Mr Tambourine Man' was starting to break. They pointedly refused to play the date despite Tickner's concern that the club would sue for breach of contract. Having reached an impasse, Tickner sent Taylor on a mission of diplomacy with instructions to placate the owners. Several days later, a strange package arrived at the Byrds' office, which was passed over to Dickson. Inside, he found a home-made cake, iced with the words 'Get Well Soon Byrds'. Beside it was a contract, torn in half. "What Derek did blew my mind," Dickson enthuses. "He told them some story about the Byrds being sick and created so much sympathy that they not only dropped the contract, but actually baked a cake. They'd let us off the hook. That was Derek at his finest."

At the beginning of June, the Byrds returned to Ciro's for a two-week engagement. With packed houses now a guarantee, the establishment owner's son took exception to the Vito's gang receiving preferential treatment. "We'd let them in free because we knew they had no money," Dickson explains. "Frank Sennes Jr was very upset about that, especially when there were 300 people in line and we'd open the rope and let 30 of Vito's people in. It's times like that when you need David Crosby on your side, and you let him go. He told Frank, 'If you don't let them in, we won't play a single note!' Eddie and me were there cringing. But Frank backed down. David gets away with so much in his life. When he's on your side you chuckle, but when he's against you . . . whoa!"

At Ciro's, McGuinn continued to sport the rectangular granny glasses which Michelle Kerr and others were also wearing as a fashion statement. Although credited with their discovery, McGuinn admits that he first saw them the previous year in New York's Greenwich Village. The Lovin' Spoonful's John Sebastian, more famous for his round spectacles, was wearing a pair and told McGuinn he could achieve a miniature psychedelic high by staring at street lights while shaking his head from side to side. It was hardly a substitute for LSD, but McGuinn appreciated the advice. He may have been tripping at the time, which would have helped. After forming the Byrds, McGuinn found a pair for sale at De Voss' boutique on Sunset Strip. He instructed his optician to replace the dark lenses with a cobalt blue effect.

The marketing potential of the glasses was fully realized when the Byrds appeared on ABC's *Shindig!* on 23 June. The show's producer was Jack Good, a bombastic, outrageous and passionate believer in the potency of pop music, who had already proven himself as an inspired broadcaster while working on BBC's groundbreaking *6.5 Special* in England during the late Fifties. He later produced a rival show, *Oh Boy*, which helped break Cliff Richard and Billy Fury in the UK. Good's visual flair was perfectly demonstrated in the strange transformation of Gene Vincent. When he arrived in England, the partially crippled, alcoholic wildcat Virginian was conservatively dressed and disarmingly unassuming. It took the perverse logic of Good to encourage his metamorphosis into a cross between Hamlet and Richard III, complete with a black leather makeover and an accentuated limp which emphasized his deformity. Backstage at *Shindig!*, Good noticed McGuinn sheepishly adjusting his granny glasses, apparently uncertain if they were suitable for a television show. Good exploded into animation, not only insisting that he must use them on screen but bluntly telling him that he had to wear them all the time – day and night, if necessary. McGuinn, once a big fan of Gene Vincent, quietly concurred. "We had a big hit, we did *Shindig!*, and my glasses became a bit of a style item." The positive thinking was working wonders.

CHAPTER NINE

The First Album

BY the time the Byrds reached number 1 on 26 June, CBS had rush released the group's first album and their next single in the USA. It seemed a crazy situation. There was 'Mr Tambourine Man' a week away from topping the *Billboard* chart and the record company was recklessly pushing 'All I Really Want To Do' into the marketplace. What forced CBS' hand was the ominous news that Cher was issuing a rival version on Imperial. The Byrds' management were horrified to learn that Sonny & Cher had taped a Byrds' performance at Ciro's without permission and, after listening back, were aiming to use their cover material to their own advantage. As well as 'All I Really Want To Do', Cher was recording 'The Bells Of Rhymney' for her debut album, and throwing in some Dylan folk rock covers. The duo's astute managers Charlie Greene and Brian Stone were shrewd New York hustlers who enjoyed the cut and thrust of staying ahead of the game and had no ethical quibbles about copping another act's intended song. When Dickson confronted Charlie Greene about the copycat tactics, he simply laughed in his face. "Sonny was a good thief," he says, still laughing. "He felt that was very clever espionage."

Of course, the CBS corporation was not about to allow Imperial Records to secure a Top 40 hit from the live set of one of their own acts without a fight, even if that meant interfering with the Byrds' release schedule. The chart race began in earnest, probably to the detriment of both artistes. Fearing the worst, the Byrds' management considered a tactical withdrawal, but they were overtaken by the speed of events. "We resented Columbia issuing 'All I Really

Want To Do'," Eddie Tickner told me. "Columbia decided that they were going to bury Imperial. Dickson got upset about that and wanted them to give it up. We were willing to let Sonny & Cher get away with it. We were against releasing it. We weren't interested in a fight. It became a political thing between the two companies."

Reigning at number 1 meant that the Byrds were likely to win the chart battle and there was no disputing that they had adapted Dylan's song to great effect. Their single of 'All I Really Want To Do' was a different take from the album version, with a more abrasive sound, enticing diction and forceful vocal. Terry Melcher was surprised to be reminded that the Byrds had taken the time to re-cut the song: "I remember remixing it for the single. I used to always speed tracks up for singles but I can't remember the details of any re-recording. But if you say the words are different then we must have re-recorded it. It was put on the album first but I thought it was a bad move for a single because Cher's version had just entered the US charts."

In fact, both Cher and the Byrds entered the Hot 100 during the same week. For three weeks, the Byrds stayed ahead, at which point the split sales seemed likely to kill both records. Dickson then got his way and the B-side 'Feel A Whole Lot Better' was promoted in its own right as an alternate A-side. By the end of July, Cher's 'All I Really Want To Do' stood at number 42, with the Byrds' version only three places lower, while 'Feel A Whole Lot Better' charted in its own right at number 103. The following week Cher broke away, buoyed by the concomitant chart success of 'I Got You Babe', which was on its way to number 1 for her and husband Sonny. The Byrds' 'All I Really Want To Do' eventually peaked at number 40, while Cher reached number 15. As their publicist and tireless proselytizer, Derek Taylor was severely disappointed by this self-defeating chart battle: "I was not only disappointed, I was disgusted. Sonny & Cher went to Ciro's and ripped off the Byrds and, being obsessive, I could not get this out of my mind that Sonny & Cher had done this terrible thing. I didn't know that much about the record business, and in my experience with the Beatles, cover versions didn't make any difference. But by covering the Byrds, it seemed that you could knock them off the perch. And Sonny &

THE FIRST ALBUM

Cher, in my opinion, stole that song at Ciro's and interfered with the Byrds' career and very nearly blew them out of the game."

Taylor's wrath was not entirely shared by the group or their management, who felt it was uncool to make a big fuss. McGuinn was rightly concerned that the mercurial Dylan might get mad at him for losing out to Cher, but otherwise took a detached and forcefully positive view of the new opposition. "I didn't really mind Sonny & Cher as competitive artistes," he reflects. "It was fair game that they went down there and taped it. It was OK that they liked our stuff enough to want to emulate it, but the fact that they beat us out with a Dylan song and he would come back at us bothered me. But it was nothing new to borrow things that weren't your own . . . It was a bit of industrial espionage and seemed a little underhand, now that you mention it. But, basically, what's the difference if you tape somebody or go in and listen to it and get the idea? It's just a matter of mechanics."

With Cher diluting the impact of their second single, the Byrds needed a boost. Fortunately, their debut album, *Mr Tambourine Man* restored them to chart glory, peaking at number 6 in *Billboard*. It was a highly impressive record, most noticeable for its homogeneity of sound – a fascinating fusion of chiming Rickenbacker solos, folk melodies and compressed, interlocking harmonies. It was also evident how much the group had moved away from their earlier Beatles fixation and found their own unique style, which the press was already labelling folk rock.

The album's title track was the perfect opener, establishing once and forever the Byrds' supremacy during the summer of 1965. For McGuinn, the song represented a baptism of fire. It was his first time playing at CBS, among musicians of far greater experience, but he was not over-awed and rose to the challenge in a fashion that typified his youthful ambition and persistence. For McGuinn, 'Mr Tambourine Man' was more than a number 1 chart record, for it represented a personal dialogue with God – a spiritual testimonial. "I got this overwhelming feeling of electricity with it," he adds. "Like 'my hands can't feel to grip.' It was such an experience that I couldn't do anything except submit."

'Feel A Whole Lot Better', the B-side that was momentarily an

A-side, was one of the most satisfying and durable tracks on the album. It contained the essence of the Byrds' sound, the pounding tambourine, the exceptional jingle-jangle Rickenbacker breaks and some great criss-crossing vocals between Clark and McGuinn. Terry Melcher was overwhelmed by the quality of the composition, which helped transform his view of Gene Clark and the Byrds.

Dickson was equally impressed and, years later, would record Gene singing the same song as a solo artiste. From his viewpoint, the track represented the perfect bridge between Clark's early sentimental love songs and the more ambitious Dylan-inspired material that Gene would compose later in the year. "There was always something to unravel in those songs – the non-explanation of the complex feeling. For instance, if you remember 'Feel A Whole Lot Better', it doesn't say: 'I'll feel a whole lot better when you're gone', but 'I'll *probably* feel a whole lot better'. For me, that makes the song. There's a statement followed by hesitation: 'Hey, I'm a little unsure!' I've heard Gene sing the song without the 'probably'. He got tired of singing it for a while in later years . . . I remember him laying behind the beat and not having that right-on feeling that he had in the beginning. He started economizing on words because of gum disease. I said to him: 'But, Gene, you can't leave out the *probably* – I can't live with that, Gene!' He said: 'What do you mean?' The part that was most remarkable to me was probably just some way that he filled up the chorus at the time. I think we all tend to find things in songs that songwriters don't necessarily intend. But that's OK. A good song always allows the listener to make up his own mind."

According to Clark, 'Feel A Whole Lot Better' was originally conceived during their residency at Ciro's when he became involved with a girl whose emotional demands proved overwhelming. "I remember her," says Dickson. "She was a little, blonde girl, a specific person and he thought he'd feel a whole lot better if she was gone because she was making him nervous and driving him crazy. The Byrds had been used to these folk chicks who were laid-back, then all of a sudden they were faced with high pressure girls who weren't prepared to just sit and adore you like a simple girl from home. They had complex desires and wishes, and places where they wanted to go and be seen with you. Gene had to ease himself into it.

He came to love it all and wallow in it and hurt himself with it, but at that moment he was resistant."

'Spanish Harlem Incident' was one of three Dylan songs on the album to be taken from *Another Side Of Bob Dylan*, which had been released while the group were recording at World-Pacific. Neither Dylan nor the Byrds performed the song much in concert, although it was played during the Ciro's residency. Its dramatic, headline grabbing title was an invitation into an impressionistic songscape of rich imagery in which the heat of a Harlem night is captured in all its passionate incandescence and embodied in the sensual, mysterious, wildcat Gypsy gal. McGuinn's unusually sassy vocal and the short-playing time ensured that it was not one of their best Dylan covers. There's a brilliant moment of *audio-vérité* when Hillman's E string appears to snap as McGuinn sings: "I've been wondering all about me." "Not a lot of people have found that," Dickson notes. "Chris made a mistake, and it just goes flat. The strings flap against the stringboard and make a bad sound. Terry let it go and it came out on the record." If nothing else, it proved that the Byrds played on their own records, mistakes and all. Dylan never raised any objections to the original Byrds' treatment of his material. "After Jim Dickson picked 'Mr Tambourine Man' we got into Dylan," McGuinn says. "It was a mutual decision. I'd come up with the guitar part and Chris would come up with the bass part. Dylan was aware of what we were doing and liked the idea."

'You Won't Have To Cry', co-written by Clark and McGuinn, was arguably the most moving and accomplished of Gene's early love ballads. A welcome survivor from the World-Pacific sessions, the song was beautifully arranged with some excellent Rickenbacker picking and sumptuous harmony work. Unlike 'She Has A Way' and 'Feel A Whole Lot Better', this song presented the woman as the wronged victim rather than the scheming predator. It was noticeable that Clark's compositions fell into two broad categories, either celebrating love and apotheosizing womankind or presenting a darker vision of loneliness and unrequited desire. Here he offers an emotional paradise free from pain and betrayal. It was an enticing invitation.

'Here Without You', written solely by Clark, was definitely in the category of lost love. Its lyrical theme was similar to Hal David's contemporaneous '(There's) Always Something There To Remind Me', a composition that detailed a neurotically nostalgic trip through city streets in which every physical object serves as a painful reminder of all that had been lost in a relationship. Like Hal David, whose lyric ended with a vestige of hope, Clark knew the importance of providing a bittersweet feel to the composition and concluded his doomy narrative with the uplifting "I know it won't last, I'll see you someday", indicating that the separation might be merely temporary. The emotional power was amplified by the quality of the harmony, on which Crosby was the master. "The trouble with a lot of harmony singers is that they don't sing with any expression," Dickson contends. "David, when he was willing to, had the ability to sing with the others' expression and feeling. He could do that with Gene, even though he might have preferred to sing with different phrasing or a different attitude. Gene couldn't come to him, but he'd go to Gene. He could get on Gene's trip, as he put it. He didn't want to, but he could do it. All of a sudden you'd hear some magic in the song. The nervous tension in Gene's voice would be smoothed out by David's harmony and it would work every time. Gene would build up some tension, then the harmony would hit and relieve that tension. It was dramatically perfect, automatically. You couldn't ask for more."

'The Bells Of Rhymney' was a late addition to the Byrds' repertoire, coming together magically during their residency at Ciro's. Originally a lyric poem by Welshman Idris Davies and published in his 1938 work *Gwalia Deserta*, it was inspired by the 1926 General Strike and the failure of the miners to achieve social justice. Davies had lost a finger while working at the coalface in Rhymney, marched in the strike, and later became a teacher and lifelong socialist. His poetry was subsequently championed by T.S. Eliot, who brought him to the publishers Faber & Faber. Davies' poetry was aimed at everyman, and for 'The Bells Of Rhymney' he employed the nursery rhyme 'Oranges And Lemons' (which details a conversation between the bells of famous London ecclesiastical landmarks) as an ironic metrical backdrop to his bitter litany. The use of place names to tell the tale – Rhymney, Merthyr, Rhondda,

THE FIRST ALBUM

Blaina, Newport, Caerphilly, Neath, Swansea, Cardiff and Wye – add a political dimension to the work. Although the bells condemn the exploitation and heartlessness of the mine owners, there is also a suggestion of betrayal within. The prevarication of Cardiff ("all will be well if if if . . ."), the condescension of Wye ("why so worried sisters why?") and some reactionary voices in Newport ("throw the vandals in court") indicate the class divisions, ambivalence and lack of empathy felt by some non-mining communities during the heart of the struggle.

The great egalitarian Pete Seeger first discovered Idris' work in a poetry book by Dylan Thomas and adapted 'The Bells Of Rhymney' to music, using a familiar pattern that reminded him of 'Twinkle Twinkle Little Star'. He introduced the song to the folk community during a recorded performance at New York's Carnegie Hall in 1957, after which it appeared on an album and EP. McGuinn was listening attentively and subsequently arranged the song for *Judy Collins 3*. Having successfully adapted Dylan to Rickenbacker rock, it was a welcome challenge to translate Seeger's work in similar fashion. The favourable response of the Byrds' audience at Ciro's, where they first played the song live, ensured that it was an automatic choice for the album. McGuinn was reasonably faithful to the original lyric, although he excised one stanza, in favour of a reprise of the first verse. The missing part was the most graphic, with Neath portraying the mine bosses as feral creatures with "fangs and teeth", while Swansea describes divine disapprobation ("even God is uneasy"). Intentionally or not, McGuinn also changed one word in the song, substituting "who *killed* the miner?" for the less dramatic verb "robbed". No doubt it was this subtle alteration that wrongly convinced publicist Billy James that the lyric was about a "Welsh mine disaster". That canard was included in the liner notes to the Byrds' first album and carried forward in many later commentaries on the song. In tackling the composition, McGuinn added some passing chords to enliven the tempo and create a more upbeat reading. There was a decisive move away from the group's pseudo-Merseybeat beginnings at World-Pacific to a more familiar folk-rock sound, the distinctive 'aaahhs' replacing the Beatles' 'oh yeah' phrasing. Special care was taken with the pronunciation of tricky Welsh place names although 'Rhymney' was actually mispronounced. "I didn't know any better," Seeger sheepishly admits, having only seen the town's name in a book. It would be over 30 years later before McGuinn learned of this and he has since sung 'Rumney' at every concert, usually prefacing the song with the story of how someone in Wales wrote a letter correcting him on his phrasing. Although he still omits the 'Swansea' verse live, he did sing that stanza on the 1998 Seeger tribute album, *Where Have All The Flowers Gone*.

Prior to the first take of 'The Bells Of Rhymney', Crosby was sufficiently concerned by the quality of the diction to remind everybody "It's miners and mine-owners". Despite the sombre theme, the composition became one of the Byrds' most popular tunes, prompting everybody to congregate on the dance floor at Ciro's. Dickson credits Michael Clarke's chiming cymbals as the most inspiring moment on the record and although they still sound great on headphones, the Byrds' manager feels they should have been even more prominent. "The only mix of Terry's that I was disappointed with was 'The Bells Of Rhymney' because he automatically shut Michael's cymbals down. It was the only time Michael ever had something important on the cymbals that was part of the music. It was just overlooked in the process. Ordinarily, it would have been a good idea to turn them down and just concentrate on the snare and bass drum and forget about Michael's tom-tom and cymbals. He wasn't that good at them, but on *that* song, he had it. The fact that we never got 'The Bells Of Rhymney' on tape anything like the way it was at Ciro's was just a terrible thing. Later on, I wanted CBS to release 'Chimes Of Freedom' with 'The Bells Of Rhymney' on the back as a single so that we'd have a chance to remix it as a single. Terry would always remix for singles and do a much better job."

The album version of 'All I Really Want To Do' used the grammatically unsound opening "I ain't looking to compete with you" rather than the single's "I don't want to compete with you". In almost every respect the single was a better take, but the album version would be used on most compilations hereafter. Alas, no one thought to record Dylan's appearance on this song at Ciro's, despite the fact that a photo of that evening was proudly displayed on the back cover of the Byrds' album.

'I Knew I'd Want You', originally the B-side of their first single, was early proof that the Byrds were more than capable of composing their own material. If New York executives had prevailed this might have been the group's first A-side, but it is difficult to imagine the song as a smash Top 40 hit. Clark's vocal is moving, if a little mannered in execution, while Larry Knechtel provides the rumbling bass line. Clark's romantic lyrics even include some uncharacteristic hip parlance: "You've had me on your trip . . ." There was also a strong hint of the Beatles with the suffix "oh yeah" added to the chorus. As Crosby notes: "Gene did try to emulate the Beatles, and he would try to play folk changes rather than standard rock 'n' roll changes. His songs had good chord structures. You'll notice that they never had just three chords; there were several chords involved, and they were strong chord structures with good melody. Gene had a pretty good way of stringing the melody across chords."

'It's No Use', the second Clark/McGuinn collaboration on the album, was a harder-edged song than most of the material they recorded during this period. A sister song to the later 'Feel A Whole Lot Better' lyrically, it lacked the subtlety of emotion that characterized Clark's best work relying on a macho aggression unleavened by doubt or self-examination. McGuinn provided a defiantly driving Rickenbacker break that contained more than a hint of early acid rock. Although the song dated back to the World-Pacific period, it also anticipated the work they would be undertaking one year later. In that sense, it was the classic transitional track, bordering two different ages of rock.

'Don't Doubt Yourself Babe', written by Jackie De Shannon, was another of the new songs that they had introduced to their set at Ciro's. With its maracas and tambourine, the number came out sounding not unlike the Rolling Stones' 'Not Fade Away'. There was even a clever guitar effect at the end, which was a nice touch. The Byrds had already betrayed a strong inclination for De Shannon's material and even appeared as backing musicians on her demo of 'Splendor In The Grass'. Dickson was determined that they should record at least one of her songs as a thank-you note for her unstinting support and insisted that this was a matter of honour: "Jackie De Shannon was the first professional person in rock 'n' roll to risk her credibility by saying that the Byrds were great and helping them to get work. She had put herself on the line. Jackie had a reputation good enough to have sung [as support act] with the Beatles when they first came over. She was a little piece of the American new dream and already had a career and success. She'd written hit songs and made hit records. With no hesitation at all, Jackie looked everybody in the eye and said: 'The Byrds are the greatest!' She said wonderful things about them. I wanted to do one of her songs to repay her and 'Don't Doubt Yourself Babe' became that one. McGuinn decided that this was the time to do the Rolling Stones' rhythm part with the Bo Diddley feel. They'd lapse into it, come out of it, go into straight time and then play it again. Michael always wanted to play something like that anyway. He'd try to figure out how to do it. They played it and they didn't think much of it. In truth, it never amounted to that much. But I had a feeling, and it came from an older part of Hollywood, that you paid back debts and didn't overlook favours."

The final Dylan composition on the album was the majestic 'Chimes Of Freedom', which became one of the Byrds' most enduring and loved cover songs. McGuinn's vocal has seldom been bettered, while his Rickenbacker playing still sounds exemplary. Recorded on the final day of the first album sessions, this was the song that prompted Dickson to sit on Crosby's chest and physically restrain him from leaving the studio until he completed his vocal. "It was one of those cathartic moments. David had been saying, 'Ah, it's a dumb cowboy song, it's no good!' Then he played this line. It was the first time he'd played a line instead of straight rhythm and it was beautiful and worked really well. Terry liked it, I liked it, *everybody* liked it. Then David said, 'I can't play it and sing it onstage.' I suppose he was thinking of his past experience with the bass. I told him, 'Play something different live. It doesn't matter. This is good. This is what we need for the record.' David wanted to make a point out of it. I really believe he held out hopes of getting 'Hey Joe' on there which he knew I was bitterly opposed to. So then he had a little cry. He got it out of his system and sang like an angel. He never sang better. It was a beautiful sound. He was entranced with how well this turned out." After listening to the playback, Crosby had tears in his eyes and, turning to his manager, said: "When am I going to realize that it's only my own bullshit that hangs me up?" Dickson considered this one of the finest and funniest rhetorical questions he'd ever heard. He could only reply, "I don't know", while later acknowledging, "I doubted then that he ever would learn."

The closing track on the album, 'We'll Meet Again', was the biggest surprise of all. Best known as a wartime anthem by British singer Vera Lynn, the song came into the group's set after it was used at the close of the movie *Dr Strangelove*. At Ciro's the Byrds dedicated the number to Stanley Kubrick, Peter Sellers and Slim Pickens (the director and stars of the film, respectively). Although their polite reading of the song was heavily laced with irony, it sounded faithful enough to convince many of their following that it was a fairly straight signing-off song. At a time when albums largely consisted of boring filler for undiscriminating teenagers, a sardonic yet sensitively played song like this was an audacious and delightfully humorous move.

CHAPTER TEN

Hollywood Parties

THE Byrds could afford to be sanguine about performing 'We'll Meet Again', a British wartime song of hope, even though the threat of induction to the Armed Forces was an ever present fear among American youth. The spectre of Vietnam loomed large and each Byrd had a brush with the draft board, somewhere along the line. Elder members McGuinn and Crosby had been exempted prior to the formation of the group, but the younger triumvirate of Clark, Clarke and Hillman each received the call. Hillman came under the closest scrutiny and ended up briefly marrying Dickson's friend Jeannie Cho (Butchie), who had known the group since the World-Pacific days and later hung out at Ciro's and travelled with Carl Franzoni's dance troupe. Considerably older than Hillman and the mother of two children from her previous marriage, she was the perfect choice. Having achieved his deferrable 'husband' status, Hillman swiftly returned to happy bachelorhood, later marrying Anya Butler, daughter of Richard Cadbury Butler, and secretary to the Who's manager, Kit Lambert.

Gene and Michael were also concerned about the draft and, like Hillman, went to considerable lengths to resist induction. Gene had previously escaped due to a knee injury incurred when he played football in his teens. But the diagnosis of Osgood-Schlatters disease was remedied by rest and physiotherapy, so it was not long before he was re-examined. This time, he feigned madness, employing whatever drugs were at his disposal to enhance the desired effects. "Gene was living with me at the time," Clarke told me. "We did a programme and it was hard getting Gene out of the draft.

They weren't buying that bullshit about his leg. I kept him up for a week. Thanks to massive amounts of dexedrine he screwed up all the tests. They looked up his ass. It was seriously demeaning. But we were the best of brothers and I helped get him out."

As the last Byrd to attract the attention of the draft board, Michael Clarke was equally determined not to be enlisted. His father, Jimmy Dick, had been in the Air Force during World War II and at one time Michael had tinkered with the idea of joining the US Navy. "At least I'd be in the water, diving and stuff," he told me. Once that whim passed, the prospect of joining the Forces was seen as the ultimate nightmare and the certain end to the bohemian life in which the Byrds revelled. The folk fraternity were expert draft dodgers and champions of 4-F status, with a book of tricks that included simulated psychosis through drugs, marriages of convenience, feigned homosexuality and, in the most extreme cases, amputation of a big toe. Knowing that the other Byrds had escaped induction made Michael more resolute than ever about remaining a civilian. He stayed up for several nights with the assistance of more dexedrine, dressed himself in shabby clothes and, psyched up by Gene Clark, he set off for his induction interview eager to provide an Oscar-winning performance. His vivid and uncensored recollection of that day was imparted with a raconteur's glee.

"When I went in, it was major shit. I wore these stupid pants and sandals. I sat there cross-legged and suggested I had a problem. They were waiting for somebody to try and get out and their attitude was 'You're front line, dude.' I got through the tests. There was a form with the question, 'Are you a homosexual?' I wrote 'No!', then changed it to 'Yes', then 'No' again, then crossed it out a few times. I knew all the answers and freaked out. I followed the yellow line and I had to take a piss. They give you this thing to carry and I threw it down on the floor and went over in the corner and took a piss. The guy said, 'This is very serious . . . You can't do that!' I turned around and accidentally ended up pissing on him. Then somebody tried to take my stuff, so I jumped in and said, 'Take your hands off my stuff or I'll kill you. I'm serious.' I'd got my hands round this guy's neck. Right away, they sent me to the psychiatrist's office. They were looking at me thinking, 'Is he for real or is he bullshitting us?' There was one guy there with long hair who went to Vietnam, but I didn't. You had to be good. The psychiatrist asked me, 'Have you ever done it with a woman?' I said, 'No!' He said, 'Have you ever wanted to?' I said, 'No!' He said, 'Have you ever done it with a man?' I said, 'No!' He was just looking at me – that's all he was doing. Finally, he said, 'Get the hell out of here.' They ran me down the red line and booted my ass out of there – 'Get out of here, you faggot bastard, schizoid homosexual, not fit for military service at any time – 4-F.' I ran out the door, jumped in my Porsche, beat it back to the beach and was laughing all the way. If you think I wanted to go to Vietnam, you were out of your mind. I was making too much goddamn money."

With hit records in the charts and a best-selling album, the Byrds were now in even greater demand among the Hollywood elite. They had already entered the exclusive environs of the private Tinseltown party, courtesy of Lance Reventlow, who was eager to show them off to his rich friends. The result was a housewarming with a difference. "It was a new house up above Beverly Hills with a swimming pool that came into the front room, and all that stuff," Dickson recalls. "They hadn't moved in or put the carpet down yet, but they threw a party. I thought it was a way to get some of Lance's friends interested in the Byrds. Back then, I was trying to expand their world and get anybody and everybody interested. Parties have a life of their own. They played and must have been there for four or five hours until everybody was worn out. Carl and the girls came, all the freaks. Lance had an English butler, Dudley, whom his mother had given him. When he saw them coming he expected the place would be wrecked. But he was very impressed and amazed. None of the family silver went missing and they even used coasters for their drinks. Everybody treated the place like they were perfect gentlemen."

On 4 July, the Byrds appeared at an even more prestigious gathering. The occasion was Jane Fonda's Independence Day Party in Malibu, on the edge of the Pacific Ocean. The star-studded guest list included Louis Jordan, Steve McQueen, Diahann Carroll, Roddy McDowell, Mia Farrow, Warren Beatty, Peter Finch, James

HOLLYWOOD PARTIES

Fox, Dennis Hopper, David McCallum, Sidney Poitier, John Leyton, Leslie Caron, Ronald Fraser, Jill Ireland and Jane's fiancé, Roger Vadim. Peter Fonda studiously organized the affair, playing the perfect host. His father, Henry, hovered in the background, roasting a pig on a spit while conversing with the stars from his generation, including Gene Kelly and Lauren Bacall. Publicist Derek Taylor watched in fascination as the evening's entertainment unfolded. "I was thinking 'This is really something,' and hoping that the Byrds would behave. I still had this rather suburban view of life that when people came to a party they should be wearing suits. Brian Epstein had always made sure that if the 'boys' had been going to a party where Henry Fonda was going to be with his friends, then they would be suitably dressed and well-behaved. Even into 1965, when the Beatles were going to special evenings they would look nice. But when the Byrds turned up, they were just the Byrds. And when Carl Franzoni and Vito came, I got into a terrible panic."

Taylor had not expected to see Vito's entourage who had no trouble gaining access to the private party. "Our roadie Bryan MacLean knew all those people," says Franzoni. "His father was a famous architect, so he'd hung out with the Fondas when he was a kid on the beach. He was able to take us right into the house. Vito's wife Szou goosed Jane Fonda while we were dancing in the sand and that perked her up. She was thinking, 'What is this woman doing to me?'"

Taylor looked on at Vito's motley entourage, fearing the worst. Turning to Jim Dickson, he whispered: "Jim, this is terrible. These people look a mess."

Nonplussed, Dickson retorted, "Well, they always look a mess! You don't understand. This is Hollywood. They're used to this kind of thing. It's been going on for 30–40 years!"

At one point, Henry Fonda questioned why the Byrds had to play so loudly, but otherwise he seemed unfazed by his children's new friends. "Socially, it was a very successful evening," Taylor concludes. "There was no bad behaviour. I saw Fonda and his wife pinned against a wall by the writhings of Carl Franzoni and company. They seemed to be saying, 'We are the new Americans and we're out of our heads.' They were not going to go there and just have a glass of sherry. But it was a good night. Jane Fonda was a lovely girl and Roger Vadim was suitably interested in these new people."

During the early hours, Taylor took McGuinn aside to tell him he had arranged a major interview with a British music paper. Its prominence depended upon the success of 'Mr Tambourine Man' which had just entered the *NME* charts. There was already premature talk of a UK tour, possibly with several of the Vito's dancers in tow, if the budget could be stretched. Primed with these vague details, McGuinn provided the *NME* with an effusive three in the morning phone interview during which he sounded like a stereotypical American Anglophile. "We wanna buy some mod clothes in Carnaby Street," he gushed, "then we'll be able to look even more English. And I wanna meet John Lennon, he sounds like a man after my own heart. Who knows, maybe we'll come home with English accents. Crazy!"

There was no rest for the Byrds in America for the remainder of July. They could be seen on *Where The Action Is* singing 'All I Really Want To Do' and Dickson's favourite 'The Bells Of Rhymney', and for those who missed their television spots there was a fair chance of catching them live. A gruelling tour of the Midwest was organized by the Willard Alexander Agency, bookers for Frank Sinatra and Count Basie. The concept was masterminded by Eddie Tickner, who had the inspired idea of adding five members of Vito's female entourage for visual effect. "We went out on a dance tour and played five sets a night in ballrooms," he recalls. "We brought our own go-go dancers, but we put them on the floor and not in costume and created a scene. I felt that was the next step in the evolution of rock. I thought my vision was correct but they weren't ready for it. It wasted them."

Amazingly, the tour began the evening after Jane Fonda's Hollywood party, in faraway Denver, Colorado. In order to make the journey more pleasant, Crosby kept a substantial stash of marijuana on board which was liberally distributed among the group and their following. On a couple of occasions, the group were stopped by the police, and it was only a combination of luck, swift action and barefaced effrontery that saved them from arrest.

"I was 17 when we went on tour," recalls Lizzie Donohue, a member of their hand-picked travelling dance troupe. "We took a Trailways bus – the Byrds, Bryan MacLean [equipment roadie], Carl, Karen Yum Yum, Jeanine and me. Linda [Loo] Bopp and Butchie followed in a car. I remember we all got high in a bathroom on the bus, especially David Crosby. In Duluth, Minnesota, the police searched the bus and I remember David having to throw his stash out of the window."

A second police confrontation was more alarming. As a precaution, Dickson had appointed his best friend John Barrick to act as road manager on the tour, accompanied by photographer Barry Feinstein, but neither could control Crosby, who defied authority with a brass neck wilfulness that astonished everybody. "Somewhere along the trip, another sheriff stopped them and asked to search the bus. David had a pound of grass and he went to the top of the bus, stood in the door and said, 'You're not getting on this bus!' There wasn't anybody there that had that much nerve. Jim McGuinn told me that he was petrified. He thought it was all over. They all knew there was a pound on the bus and the cops couldn't miss it. But David stood there and defied the police and convinced them that they had no right to get on *his* bus. 'We're travelling interstate and . . .' He'd make it up as he was going along, like he does. John Barrick, who had become totally disillusioned with David by then, just couldn't believe his eyes, couldn't accept what he was hearing. David stood nose to nose with this nasty cop and he backed the cop down. Everybody felt sure the cop would lose patience and arrest David for what he was saying. But, instead they drove away without a search."

When the Byrds arrived in town, they often faced hostility from audiences still coming to terms with the new youth movement. Seeing a group like the Byrds was adventurous enough, but with Vito's crew along for the ride, the ensemble resembled a hippie circus. In the smaller towns they visited, pandemonium was always a distinct possibility. On one occasion, the irrepressible Carl Franzoni took to the dance floor in his black and yellow tights and was bodily removed by two strapping youths, who took great pleasure in beating him up. Franzoni was too cool to be intimidated for long and returned more irreverent than ever, strutting in imitation of a demented chicken and sticking out his tongue like a cross between a kid in a playground and some sex-crazed pervert.

Two weeks into the tour, the Byrds had a very important date at the Columbia Records Convention in Miami. As part of the weekend event, they were invited to perform in front of a thousand teenagers who had won complimentary tickets from local radio stations. Columbia personnel, including the A&R and sales teams, watched their golden asset with corporate pride. In order to impress the executives, who were eager for the Byrds to unearth more Dylan material, the group had entered the studio in late June and ran through two very rough versions of 'The Times They Are A-Changin'' and 'It's All Over Now, Baby Blue', which were taped as works in progress. These were played for the CBS hierarchy without any accompanying sales pitch. Predictably, the Byrds seemed more interested in cavorting with various beauty queens on the beach, although this at least provided a unique photo opportunity of the barechested group in swimming trunks. At the convention, other acts were primed to suck up to officialdom, but the Byrds were inevitably too cool to care, despite the presence of such influential figures as Goddard Lieberson and Clive Davis.

"The big cheese was Clive Davis," Derek Taylor notes. "He was more accessible than Lieberson. But he wasn't as interested in the Byrds as he was in Paul Revere. They were the ones who were thought to be the item. And, indeed, Chad & Jeremy were thought to be more important because they were easier to handle, and there were only two of them. The Byrds were very tough for a record executive to get a handle on. They were the kind of people who'd wander around a room. They weren't disciplined. They weren't trained like soldiers. There'd be three of them on a sofa, one would be somewhere else, and Crosby would be doing something weird, just to be a nuisance. Record companies weren't used to this nonsense. And Dickson was right – Columbia did not know what they had, although certain people at Columbia like Billy James most certainly did. And so did Terry Melcher. He had clout and skill and was a jolly good asset."

Neither the female dancers nor Franzoni were invited to the

Miami convention, but stayed back at a hotel in Chicago. When the Byrds returned a couple of days later, there was a detectable change in their demeanour. "I thought Miami screwed the Byrds up," says Franzoni. "Up until then they were regular guys, but after that they knew they were in another world. When they came back they were different people. It was like they'd seen money and been bought by the music business."

Franzoni detected a new confidence in the Byrds and increasingly felt that they were acting like stars rather than artistic collaborators. Nevertheless, he still testified to their greatness as a live act during the Midwest tour. Predictably, it was 'The Bells Of Rhymney', featuring Clarke's tour de force cymbal playing and McGuinn's Rickenbacker chime, that was still the most memorable number for the dancers. "I always think of dancing to 'The Bells Of Rhymney'," Franzoni says. "They could have started their own church with that kind of music . . . that 12-string worked really good." More surprising was the positive reaction to Crosby's fast, punky version of 'Hey Joe'. "We would just yell and scream when David was doing that. He would raise the temperature on the dance floor with that one." Although the Byrds' performing abilities would later be examined severely, Franzoni and his followers were always adamant about their brilliance. "The Byrds were the best dance band without horns. For a small group playing Dylan music and so forth, they were on fire. They were always fighting with each other but when they got on to that stage, it was like they had turned on the whole world. That was the best dance tour I was ever on. Vito later called them the best dance band of the Sixties."

The dynamic between the individual Byrds was always fascinating to observe. Franzoni was aware that McGuinn and Crosby were slightly older than the others, but also noted their greater sophistication, especially compared with Clark and Clarke who evidently came from humbler backgrounds and spent money with reckless disregard for the future. Interestingly, it was the quieter Chris Hillman whom Franzoni felt most comfortable around. "Chris was my favourite Byrd. When you're on the dance floor, you look up and you make contact with whoever it is. I always made contact with the bass player. I could talk to Chris about what was happening. David was a cantankerous son of a bitch who would always start everything, but you knew that there was a fine player there." There was speculation among the dancers, completely wrongly as it turned out, that their blond, baby-faced equipment roadie might eventually join the Byrds in some capacity. "Bryan MacLean was like the sixth guy," says Franzoni. "He was like the rookie they were bringing around. He only played rhythm guitar but we always thought he might get in the band later on. At that time, I was helping him pick up their equipment."

The standoffish McGuinn remained an enigma to Franzoni, who found it difficult to gauge his feelings. "McGuinn was the distant guy. He didn't want us on the tour. I think he was afraid we were going to upstage him. That was another thing about the Byrds. Throughout that whole tour they never once told the audience we were part of their situation. We were almost taboo. We would just hang out with them, and live with them on the bus. But it was really McGuinn that did that. He was the announcer and he should have told the audience who we were."

Franzoni may have misread McGuinn's motives and actions. The coolest aspect of the troupe was that they seemed to have appeared from nowhere, like ghostly visions conjured from a different universe. Most onlookers assumed the dancers were following the Byrds across the country out of some perverse love for this strange, new phenomenon. Their outrageous garb also suggested that they were not mere fashion accessories, but something weirder. When they gyrated on the dance floor, their sense of abandonment was almost frightening, as well as provocative. They not only challenged the standard rules of formal dance but lost themselves in the music. For some Midwestern audiences this must have been a supreme culture shock, akin to witnessing cult worshippers celebrating a new religion to which the Byrds were providing the musical soundtrack. Maintaining that distance between the stage and the floor was crucial to the magic trick. By making no reference to the dancers, McGuinn was removing them from the orbit of the Byrds and thereby making them more real. "I see what you're saying," Franzoni acknowledges. "We were seen as people that just happened to show up – and there we were, dancing!"

Such nuances were lost on Franzoni back in 1965. At the next Byrds date in Youngstown, Ohio, he was punched in the stomach during one of his spirited gambols. "It was amazing," Lizzie Donohue reflects. "I don't think the Midwest was ready for Carl Franzoni and the whole troupe of us. We'd go into restaurants and they wouldn't wait on us. They thought we were something from outer space. In Paris, Illinois, they actually threw us off the dance floor. I think they cancelled the gig that night."

Franzoni also blamed the reactionary response on an uptight middle America, whose only defence against the new counterculture was ridicule and aggression. "We were all long-haired and we dressed the same all the time. I never came out of tights and boots, even at previews. Once, we stopped at this forlorn coffee shop and people went through this whole thing of crying and laughing at us and jeering, 'Where do you people come from? Mars?'"

It was not only the dancers that provoked a negative reaction. In the elevator of a hotel, Crosby turned to a middle-aged woman and politely said: "I think I'm on the wrong floor." Observing his green suede cape and long hair, she retorted: "Boy, you're on the wrong world!" Crosby was steely enough to laugh off such jibes but Ohio robbed him of more than dignity. There was still a sizeable slab of marijuana left over to keep everyone blissful, but a lapse of concentration saw the stash finally disappear. "Crosby had got that pound of grass in Chicago," recalls Franzoni. "It was for all of us, but he'd bought it. He was supposed to be taking care of it but when we were in Ohio, he left the goddamn thing in his hotel room. The grass was left on the cocktail cabinet in his room." Fortunately, it was either confiscated by a cleaner or, more likely, thrown away. No police were contacted. This would not be the last time that Crosby's carefree, irresponsible absentmindedness would endanger the group.

During the final days of the Midwest tour, the Byrds' electrification of Dylan's material received further vindication from the master himself, who released the epic single, 'Like A Rolling Stone'. A week later, he took the stage at the Newport Folk Festival on 25 July backed by the Paul Butterfield Blues Band. His decision to play an electric set at deafeningly loud volume became a *cause célèbre* and a defining moment in his career. Coaxed back onstage for an acoustic encore, he offered 'It's All Over Now, Baby Blue' as a coded farewell to the folk crowd, then ended the evening with 'Mr Tambourine Man' which, thanks to the Byrds, was now even more famous as an electric single. Its success prompted him to push further into electrified rock. "He had a sound in his mind," says guitarist Mike Bloomfield. "He had heard records by the Byrds that knocked him out. He wanted me to play like McGuinn. That's what he was shooting for. It was even discussed. He said, 'I don't want any of that B.B. King shit, man.' Dylan would play me Cher's versions of his songs, and different English versions, Animals' versions, but the Byrds' sound was what he wanted to get in his sessions."

Back on the Byrds tour, the lascivious Carl Franzoni was tortured by sexual frustration, made worse by the presence of the female dancers, all of whom were resistant to his ever flicking tongue and lofty protestations about the virtues of free love. The 17-year-old Lizzie Donohoe evidently drove him crazy. "Lizzie! God. Oh, boy! I was always trying to get in her pants, but she'd never let me in there." Franzoni's failed amours were amplified by the female hysteria surrounding the Byrds. Gene Clark and Michael Clarke confided their conquests while pointing out that the real conquerors were the insatiable young girls. "They told me the story," Franzoni says. "It was like this. What would you do if at 12 o'clock at night, after you'd done a gig, you opened your motel room door and two or three girls are standing there naked? You can't tell their age. So you either scoop them up or shut the door in their faces. I don't think they did much door slamming."

Finally, the frustrated Franzoni found a teenager who was keen to explore her sexual horizons and equally eager to move to Hollywood. "I had my own personal groupie," he says. Unfortunately, the Byrds refused to allow the ingénue on the bus. They muttered something about insurance, but Franzoni wasn't listening. Their objections may have been sounder than he assumed. After all, the young Linda Bopp had been chaperoned by the elder 'Butchie' Cho and they travelled separately by car. Following a heated exchange, Franzoni offered the ultimatum on behalf of his teenage conquest:

either she goes, or I don't. The bus left without him. At the next date, Derek Taylor arrived with a cameraman, hoping to film the dancers. Franzoni's absence was not appreciated. Upon returning to LA, he was given a cheque for outstanding monies and told he was fired. He would never work with the Byrds again.

The same fate befell roadie Bryan MacLean who was now considered out of his depth. "I didn't do well on the tour," he admitted. "I began to break down physically. We did 30 one-nighters. I was so exhausted I started to hallucinate." The female dancers remained staunch friends, but they too were sacrificed as further touring opportunities were deemed uneconomical. For the original troupe, it seemed like the end of an era.

CHAPTER ELEVEN

The British Tour

TOWARDS the end of their Midwest tour, the Byrds received some exciting news. 'Mr Tambourine Man' had topped the UK charts, dislodging the Hollies 'I'm Alive'. As in America, the Byrds' single was initially slow to receive airplay but once the pirate radio stations picked up on the disc, it catapulted to number 1. Eddie Tickner was pleasantly surprised to receive an offer to tour England from promoters Mervyn Conn and Joe Collins (father of Joan and Jackie Collins). Conn had seen the Byrds in San Francisco and excitedly noted, "With their Dylan image I think they will be a shot in the arm for the group scene here, which has been in the doldrums."

Derek Taylor was equally excited by the idea of taking the Byrds to England, realizing that they might yet become a worldwide phenomenon. His only reservation lay in the tone of Mervyn Conn's correspondence and some of the venues mentioned. "What I brought to the Byrds was an expertise from British newspapers," Taylor told me. "I'd come from Fleet Street newspapers to the Beatles knowing nothing about the world of rock 'n' roll. I didn't know anything about gigs or bookings, all that was done for me. I was an innocent so I wasn't able to give the best advice to Eddie about the halls they would be playing. All I did know was that the correspondence from Mervyn Conn didn't assure me. It didn't seem like the world I'd left – the Epstein world. I kept expressing doubts about the content of the letters. There was something about the grammar. You know, 'I'll give you a deal' and 'we'll get you some good gigs'. The whole thing was very much showbusiness, almost pantomime showbusiness."

THE BRITISH TOUR

Despite niggling concerns, Taylor could not resist the prospect of introducing the Byrds to an England then at its zenith as the world centre of fashion and music. "I was much more of a follower and wouldn't really interfere with management. Eddie wanted them to go and he came to me and I said, 'Yes'. If Tickner wanted them to go then I would give him all the reasons why. I wanted them to meet the Beatles and England was where you had to be in those days. Everybody wanted to go to England and get to the clubs and sit in the Ad Lib with the Beatles and be recognized and meet people in Carnaby Street and the King's Road." Although the Byrds had no time to recuperate from their recent US tour, the chance to meet the Beatles and sample new adulation in Swinging London was irresistible.

Dickson was sceptical about the tour from the outset but, faced with the combined wills of Tickner, Taylor and the Byrds, kept his counsel to himself. "Eddie believed whatever Derek told him. I didn't want them to go to England after completing a 30-day tour. They didn't have to go, and they could still have vetoed it. They got big at doing that. Going out and playing lost a lot of appeal after that beat up road trip. I disagreed with Eddie, but how far are you going to take it? Every single person wanted them to go: Eddie, Derek, the Byrds themselves. You've just come off a tour and someone says, 'How'd you like to go to England, have fun and meet the Beatles?' 'Sure!' They had no idea what they were going to face. They didn't know they'd be double booked, and exhausted from playing and fulfilling social responsibilities. They should have booked a few important dates which they could have been rested and prepared for. If that had happened I'm sure they might have come away with some good press. But to do a torture tour of England with jet lag, illness and exhaustion . . ."

Despite Dickson's reservations, the UK tour was important and necessary. The Byrds needed to establish themselves in the world market and the chart-topping success of 'Mr Tambourine Man' suggested that this was the perfect moment. Any delay could have proven fatal in the fast changing pop world of 1965. The Byrdmania currently sweeping the States was already gaining a foothold in England. Derek Taylor had been prescient enough to send promotional photos and extravagant press releases to selected UK editors and journalists, resulting in effusive articles, backed by some promotional overkill. Unknown to the Byrds, Mervyn Conn had been busy proclaiming the group 'America's Answer To The Beatles'. All over London, placards began to appear bearing the enigmatic message: 'The Byrds Is Coming'. Exactly two years before, Alfred Hitchcock's film *The Birds* had received a similar pre-release poster campaign, so the public would have appreciated the in-joke. As excitement about the Byrds' arrival intensified, a handful of articles appeared in the music weeklies. Although most English journalists had only heard 'Mr Tambourine Man', they were more than willing to echo the words of Mervyn Conn's posters, with such headlines as 'Byrds Biggest Craze Since Beatles' and 'Byrds – America's Biggest Ever Group?' The *NME*'s Chris Hutchins was convinced that the Byrds' visit would be the greatest pop event of the year, and we were warned to take heed: "Unless I am very much mistaken August is going to see Britain gripped by a new phenomenon – BYRDMANIA. Stand by for the biggest explosion of hysteria since the Beatles first sent love From Me To You, when the Byrds fly from Hollywood to cash in on the success of this week's haunting chart topper. Mothers should take heed of the warning and lock up their daughters, for I have it on good authority that the group has Pied Piper habits, and at this very moment birds are following Byrds by the coach-load across the breadth of America."

Hutchins' allusion to the coach-load of birds was a reminder of the fate of Carl Franzoni and the female dancers, who missed the opportunity to transform the English pop landscape that summer. "It was my fault that we didn't go," says Franzoni. "I screwed that whole thing up when I tried to take that teenager on the bus. I never realized how different the culture was in Europe." Whether the Byrds could have stretched the finances to accommodate a section of the Vito's crowd is debatable, but their presence would certainly have caused a sensation and perhaps distracted some of the negative attention later focused on the Byrds.

Even as Chris Hutchins was stirring up the hype, Mervyn Conn faced a heart-stopping moment. For one terrible week, it seemed that the imperious Musicians Union might put paid to the visit, but they relented on condition that the Dave Clark Five could enjoy a reciprocal trip to the States. A series of dates were hastily finalized and on 30 July, the Byrds were plastered across the front page of the *NME*, their five faces framed by a tambourine, alongside which was that familiar litany 'The Byrds Is Coming!!' Suddenly, it was impossible to pick up any teenage magazine that did not include a long list of the Byrds' vital statistics and various likes and dislikes. Their 'Life Lines', printed in the *NME*, and sanctioned by the Byrds' office, included some vital misinformation about birth dates and certain family details, which would be carried forward for decades afterwards.

Opinions were sought from leading pop stars about the significance of the visit, as if the Byrds were on a mission of state. In *Disc*, Mick Jagger praised them highly and seemed remarkably knowledgeable about their history. "Their manager is a very close friend of Dylan and so he often hears his numbers before Bob has recorded them. That was the case with 'Mr Tambourine Man'." Amazingly, Jagger even knew about the original, then unknown and unpublicized, World-Pacific demo of the song. "They did it in march time and didn't like the results. So they kept it on one side and didn't release the results. Then they re-recorded the number and the result is this hit."

Fellow pop intellectual and Dylan enthusiast Paul Jones was also questioned about the quality and meaning of the new single, which he admitted had made a deep impression. "I wouldn't want to be drawn into a discussion as to whether Dylan's 'Mr Tambourine Man' is better than the Byrds' version. Or vice versa. I prefer Dylan's recording – but not because it is more 'genuine', and less of a pop record. I wouldn't even say 'Mr Tambourine Man' is folk. What is folk anyway? Maybe you and me walking down the street and singing is folk! If I had to generalize about folk, I would say it is more in keeping for one man to sing folk songs than groups . . . like Dylan or Donovan. But even if people consider that 'Mr Tambourine Man' is a folk song – just because it is composed by Dylan – and that it should be sung by Dylan or a so-called folk singer, I wouldn't agree. Not only is it a very commercial record, it's very good too. And I still think this despite the opinion of the Ivy League's Ken Lewis that the record is technically terrible. I wouldn't argue with Ken on technical grounds. But he has some strange ideas."

Finally, the Byrds' new pal Brian Jones was approached on the subject and added, "It seems that the Byrds have brought the folk music technique to the electric guitar group sound – sort of given folk a rock 'n' roll sound." Alone among his peers, he warned that British audiences might find the Byrds' live act alien and understated. "They don't go in for any showmanship onstage – but I wouldn't like them if they did. They are very static, in fact." Those prophetic words were tagged on at the end of his interview, almost as an afterthought. Nobody registered their significance. With all the pre-flyte publicity, anticipation of the tour remained feverishly high.

The Byrds arrived at London Airport from Chicago at 8 am on Monday 2 August looking jet-lagged and prematurely stoned. They were greeted by a coach-load of fans who had waited patiently just to get a glimpse of their new heroes. A less amiable greeting came from British mod group, the Birds, who presented their American counterparts with seven writs claiming infringement of their group's registered name and damages for loss of earnings following the release of 'Mr Tambourine Man'. Mervyn Conn was appalled by this affront and sniffed, "It's just a nasty publicity stunt."

In what was indicative of things to come, the Byrds were offered no afternoon nap but found themselves speeding towards the plush Savoy Hotel for a reception at which they were introduced to the ladies and gentlemen of the press. Among those in attendance was the Rolling Stones' manager Andrew Oldham, who turned to Derek Taylor and said: "You should be very pleased to come back with a hit act. This proves you can do it."

The Byrds made quite an impression on the assembly, prompting more lavish headlines. Indeed, there was almost too passive and too positive an acceptance of their pop godhead. Before hearing a note of live music, the *NME*'s Norrie Drummond rushed to his typewriter and casually observed: "Although the group has had only one hit record, the Byrds will very probably become the biggest ever group to come from America. Already in the US they are hailed as the leaders of a new cult in pop music, and it shouldn't be long before the same happens in Britain. They are untidy, long-haired, intelligent and extremely modern. They are all devoted to music and regard Bob Dylan as the master of tune-making."

Following the reception, the Byrds retired to the Europa Hotel in Grosvenor Square. One of their visitors was Dickson's friend, the folk singer Jimmy Gavin, who had recently moved to England. An advocate of Subud, and now renamed Weston Gavin, he had crossed paths with both McGuinn and Crosby many times during their pre-Byrds days. As he entered their suite, he was amazed to hear McGuinn enquiring, "Where's the hairdryer?" It was confirmation of their complete transformation from folkies to pop stars.

The Byrds smoked several joints and stayed in their rooms until dark fell. They were then whisked across to the Scotch of St James, the favourite watering home of the UK's pop aristocracy. Although no strangers to celebrity, the Byrds were thrilled to meet several leading members of the British beat boom. Paul McCartney acted as unofficial host, first introducing them to his charming and sophisticated girlfriend, actress Jane Asher. Gene Clark was fascinated to encounter the sister of Peter Asher, whose duo Peter And Gordon had first inspired him and McGuinn to combine forces at the Troubadour, a decision that led to the creation of the Byrds. Mick Jagger and model Chrissie Shrimpton, English pop's second most famous couple, were also present, along with Stones' drummer Charlie Watts and his wife, Shirley. As drinks flowed, a constellation of stars passed their table, including the Kinks' Dave Davies, American expatriate P.J. Proby and several delegates from the Animals, Hollies, Dave Clark Five and Georgie Fame's Blue Flames. The Byrds eagerly sampled the beat groups' preferred tipple, Scotch and coke, but expressed a greater fondness for their own hidden stash of illicit substances.

The whiff of marijuana was seldom absent from hotel suites and dressing rooms frequented by the Byrds, and they invariably brought a touch of psychedelic bliss to their dull surroundings. "They had crystals and coloured cubes," Derek Taylor told me. "Chamber maids were saying, 'I don't know what they're doing in that room. They've got all these things piled up like children's bricks on the table. And what are they doing with the towels?'" Taylor knew that the towels placed on the bottom of doors were to prevent marijuana smoke escaping from the room while they got happily stoned watching their collection of coloured objects.

The bizarre behaviour proved all too much for their cockney roadie Bobby Hamilton, who quit after a few days. Looking back, he pictures the group as almost otherworldly: "They floated out of the hotel, floated into the car, floated onstage, floated offstage, floated back to the hotel, shut the bedroom door and that was it. It was reefers from day one. You could never socialize with them. They were away. Smoke was everywhere."

"The dope smoking was chronic," Derek Taylor confirms. "And we were taking purple hearts, which I bought from some bloke who came up from W.10. He said, 'What do you want, buddy?' I said, 'I don't know. What have you got?' He said, 'These are 15 quid a hundred.' So I said, 'Give us them.' I distributed the purple hearts and generally behaved irresponsibly, I would say."

As it turned out, the Byrds could hardly have survived the week without some kind of artificial stimulation. Within a day of their arrival, they opened the ill-fated tour on 3 August at the Imperial Ballroom in Nelson, Lancashire. Even before they reached the stage, there was a casualty in the ranks. The normally robust Chris Hillman collapsed in the dressing room, suffering from "acute asthma and bronchitis" and a doctor was rushed to the scene to administer emergency penicillin injections. He also prescribed a cough mixture for Michael Clarke, accompanied by dire warnings about the dangers of ingesting too much of the potion. After a 30-minute delay, Hillman recovered sufficiently to appear onstage. As a result of the drama, not much attention was paid to the show. Instead, journalists gathered around and took photos of McGuinn offering medication to the beleaguered bassist, who was huddled up in a corner like a war refugee.

The following day the Byrds headed south, appearing on the regional television programme *Scene At 6.30* and playing a seaside date at the Pier Pavilion, Morecambe. On 6 August, they faced their sternest test to date with three shows in an evening, beginning at Croydon's Fairfield Hall and concluding at the new nightclub Blaises, situated at Queen's Gate in London's fashionable Knightsbridge. Several of the capital's critics made the trip to Croydon, but seemed a little bemused by proceedings. *Disc*'s Nigel Hunter delivered a tentative but sympathetic report of the evening's entertainment and seemed unfazed by the group's evident aloofness: "The Byrds walked on to a hearty wall of welcoming screams. Actually, they didn't walk on. They wandered on with that unique air of detached vagueness. Each move by each Byrd was calculated. They drifted across the stage in a seemingly aimless fashion but each went to his allotted place and plugged in or set up. Nothing was hurried. Everything was casual and slow-paced but everyone knew what they were doing and did it on time . . . The boys were singing into their mikes and vocal sounds were coming through, but there was no definition. The tune and chord progression was there, but the words were nowhere."

Despite their excessive tuning-up and niggling sound problems, the Byrds ran through a lively seven-song set comprising: 'The Times They Are A-Changin'', 'Don't Doubt Yourself Babe', 'All I Really Want To Do', 'Chimes Of Freedom', 'The Bells Of Rhymney', 'We'll Meet Again' and 'Mr Tambourine Man'. It was a classic folk rock repertoire, dominated by Dylan songs and although the set list may now appear parsimonious, its length was fairly typical of the period. Having performed their early evening set, the group returned at 9 pm for a second show at the venue.

In keeping with the British sense of fair play, *Disc* decided to send along a second reviewer in the person of Manfred Mann's lead singer, Paul Jones. His refreshing comments on their stage performance and musicianship were the most positive and perceptive heard during the tour. Summing up that remarkable evening, he concluded: "I liked them very much. They're a very good group. I don't think I heard them at their best at Fairfield Halls because they had a bit of trouble with the mikes. I couldn't hear all the words, which was a bit of a shame considering they do so much Dylan in their act. Dylan's words are worth hearing . . . The stage act is good. I wondered about them when they first came on. They seemed a little too casual in their manner. But it's all well drilled and nice and cool and relaxed and the way they drift on to the stage is obviously well worked out. I'm not sure about their amplification . . . I thought the Byrds overdid theirs a bit. The lead guitar wasn't bad, but the rhythm guitar was near distortion. I especially liked their version of 'We'll Meet Again'. That's what I call Pop Art. The re-presentation of something familiar in a way that makes you sit up and notice . . . I think they're going to be a lot better in the future."

Returning from Croydon that evening, the Byrds still had a long night ahead as they drove towards Knightsbridge for their third gig in seven hours. The astute Jim Carter-Fea, owner of the hip hangout Blaises, was happy enough to have secured the group for a bargain £175. Packed inside his club was a select gathering which included John Lennon, George Harrison, Brian Jones, Bill Wyman, Pete Townshend, Denny Laine, Perry Ford, various Pretty Things, Dana Gillespie and singer/actress Adrienne Posta. Derek Taylor remembered that late night with mixed feelings: "Blaises was a place where people wouldn't mind being seen, but it wasn't an ideal gig. The stage was the size of a sofa and the Byrds played extraordinarily loud and appeared both awkward and temperamental. Still, I loved them, and George Harrison and John Lennon were also impressed."

The Byrds were embarrassed as they came offstage at Blaises. Hillman had broken a bass string during the show and Crosby and McGuinn had been forced to use the same amp, which severely distorted the sound. None of this seemed to bother the celebrity guests, who applauded the Byrds for their efforts. After the show, the Americans fraternized with Lennon and Harrison and found common ground. The myopic Lennon was intrigued by McGuinn's rectangular glasses, particularly when he discovered they were prescription spectacles. He admitted that he was barely able to see the other Beatles onstage, let alone the audience. Lennon's acerbic wit was also in evidence, which was enough to intimidate that lord of silence, Chris Hillman, who preferred to avoid eye contact with the Beatle. Eventually, Lennon enquired sarcastically, "Does the bass player speak?" prompting everyone to gaze on Hillman, who visibly reddened, without finding a reply.

Over several bottles of wine, the musicians bonded, and Derek Taylor proved the perfect diplomat, uniting the two parties. The entire troupe then returned to Brian Jones' flat, where they stayed up until the early hours of the morning, drinking, and smoking dope. On their way back to the Europa they at least managed to purchase some well-deserved hamburgers from an all-night eaterie.

With little time for sleep after their riotous night of pop star entertainment, the Byrds consumed more pills and prepared for an action-packed weekend. On Friday, they could be seen on television's *Ready, Steady, Go!* having received the honour of a whole show seemingly built around them. Later that evening, they were due to play at an all-nighter (midnight to 5 am) at that bastion of bluebeat and R&B, the Flamingo, a club whose regular acts included Georgie Fame and the Blue Flames, John Mayall's Bluesbreakers, Zoot Money and Chris Farlowe. It was an incongruous booking for a supposedly folk-rock act and tested the nerves of everybody present. "The Flamingo Club was awful," Taylor lamented. "Paul McCartney came to that and there were people with blood-stained shirts when we arrived. It was quite the wrong place."

After Geno Washington and the Ram Jam Band warmed up the audience, the Byrds took the stage at 2 am. On hand to document proceedings was *Melody Maker*'s late-night clubber Chris Welch. Crushed in the middle of an overheated audience, he observed unsympathetically: "Enough people packed in for it to take on the appearance of the Black Hole of Calcutta. Apart from being utterly airless, the heat was intense enough to bake bread or fry eggs on the floor, if anybody felt so inclined . . . A roar of applause greeted the Byrds when they finally arrived and fought their way to the stand. Paul McCartney was among the Byrd diggers which helped to raise the temperatures of several young ladies present even more. Eventually, the Byrds began their act, lasting only half an hour, during which they performed about six numbers, mostly in the familiar Dylan-cum-Tambourine Man-cum-Searchers mould. Their reception grew markedly tepid and the biggest applause came when club proprietor Rik Gunnell announced that gramophone records would be played and the return of Geno Washington and the Ram Jam Band was imminent."

In the early hours of Saturday morning, Gunnell was busily counting the door money, but found time to offer his own negative review. "The Animals are still the top for attendance figures," he declared, "then Georgie Fame, and the Byrds, in that order. I think there are a lot better pop groups in this country than the Byrds. They are definitely a miss!" At least Paul McCartney proved the perfect host, graciously driving the Byrds back to their hotel after the gig in his Aston Martin. Despite the hostile response earlier that night, the group were happy enough to have received the continued patronage of a Beatle.

Unbelievably, the Byrds faced three more gigs the next evening, including another all-nighter. Saturday 7 August was not a particularly pleasant day for the group as they set out for their two shows at the Adelphi, Slough, the first scheduled for 6 pm and the second 9 pm. They reached the town early that evening, by which time Taylor was in urgent need of promotional copies of their album, which had just been issued. Scouring the town centre, he was relieved to find a record store with the album prominently displayed in the window. Unfortunately, the closed sign had just been placed on the shop door. Taylor succeeded in winning the proprietor's attention, but it was to no avail. "I had the five Byrds outside and there was a nasty shopkeeper inside," he told me. "He said: 'Can't you see the fucking notice?' I said, 'Can't you see the fucking Byrds' and pointed at them and the albums, and he pointed back at the closed sign. I told him, 'You don't realize what you've got, you're typical English, you've never known what you've got. You've got no class or style. These people will come in and sign the record. Give us a copy.'" Unimpressed by Taylor's uncharacteristic lapse in diplomacy, the Slough shopkeeper concluded matters with the unhelpful rejoinder, "Come back on Monday!"

Although the Adelphi, Slough was a fine pop venue, familiar to Taylor from his Beatles' days, the Byrds had another torrid evening. Their main problem was coming to terms with the new WEMs equipment that had been loaned to them during the tour. Despite the presence of an engineer, the group was still unhappy about playing with unfamiliar amps and spent too much time tuning up. They also tended to overcompensate by playing too loudly. "They were always too loud, except at Ciro's," Taylor says. "They lost some swing voters, especially when they got hold of those big

WEMs amps. I always thought Crosby was turning up. I used to watch him overdoing it. That's how rock stars are. The besetting sin of rock stars in those days was turning up too loud. Also, audiences were used to the Beatles and Gerry and Freddie running straight on doing 12 songs in 25 minutes and then off. With the Beatles, it was 'nice to see you; this is the B-side of our latest record . . .' That was the paradigm. The Byrds didn't know that. They didn't talk to the audience and there was no 'nice to see you'. Chris was virtually behind a curtain."

After their second performance of the evening, the Byrds relaxed by climbing on to a nearby rooftop and smoking some dope with Donovan, who informed them that he had just written a new song, 'Breezes Of Patchouli', which he insisted was based on their vocal arrangement of 'Chimes Of Freedom'. The Byrds liked the 19-year-old Donovan, whose evocative songwriting, soft-spoken nature and wide-eyed enthusiasm proved irresistibly charming. Since entering the UK charts with 'Catch The Wind' and 'Colours' he had survived damaging comparisons with Dylan and established himself as Swinging London's premier beat poet turned pop star. Like the Byrds and Dylan, he saw no contradiction between ethnic folk credibility and mass popularity. The Byrds were more than happy to have him open several of their shows during the tour.

Hanging out with a fellow folk enthusiast was a joy compared to the prospect of playing another gig that night, but the Byrds still had a booking to fulfil at the Pontiac Club in Putney. This was another R&B stronghold at which the Byrds sounded completely out of place. Once again, they took the stage in the early hours of the morning and played their standard 30-minute set of Dylan covers, with a twist of Pete Seeger and Vera Lynn, while weary spectators looked on in bemusement. The Byrds' ice-cool persona remained unruffled throughout and the Putney audience watched as one song melted into the next, without introduction or explanation. Eventually, one girl became so exasperated that she cried out: "Aren't you going to say anything?" Crosby looked up for a second and said, "Goodbye!", upon which the Byrds departed the stage and left the club.

Melody Maker now had a headline that seemed to sum up the

tour: 'Fans Go Cool Over The Too-Cool Byrds'. Once again, it was Chris Welch sharpening his pencil to decree: "Flopsville was London's verdict on the much-publicized Byrds following their weekend club appearances. They left a trail of hot, tired, bored and disappointed fans, who waited hours to see them give a performance described as 'very, very dull'." Strangely enough, the person providing the "dull" accusation was no fellow critic or club owner, but Denise Hall, a 19-year-old whom Welch had arbitrarily plucked from the packed audience in order to obtain an instant review. She proved suitably forthcoming. "I think they are a drag. Absolutely no stage presentation and they ignore the audience. All their numbers sound like 'Mr Tambourine Man'. They are completely competent but they don't go out of their way to do anything. They are not bad, just very, very dull." With the cynical voice of youth on his side, the *Melody Maker* reporter was free to conclude on a note of jingoistic condescension: "It seems a shame to be so hard on our American guests especially after the receptions British groups have got in the States, but it proves they can't beat the Beatles yet."

For all their problems playing live, the Byrds still commanded respect as recording artistes, even among their sterner UK critics. Dickson had hoped that 'Chimes Of Freedom' and 'The Bells Of Rhymney' might be issued in the UK, but CBS wisely went with the more commercial 'All I Really Want To Do'. *NME*'s Derek Johnson headlined his review with the qualified prediction: "Another Byrds No. 1?" Although slightly cagey, he seemed pretty confident that the new single would emulate the chart-topping success of 'Mr Tambourine Man'.

"The Beatles and the Stones may prevent the Byrds' new one reaching the top, but in all other respects 'All I Really Want To Do' (CBS) has that No. 1 look about it. The pattern is very much the same as before, with those familiar high-register harmonies – clearly influenced by the West Coast surf sound – coupled with strident twangs throughout, rattling tambourine and crashing cymbals. Another Bob Dylan composition, it has a haunting melody – particularly in the oft-repeated title phrase, which you find yourself singing over and over once you've heard the disc. It can't miss!

Fractionally faster is 'Feel A Whole Lot Better'. Leader dual tracks with chanting support and a storming, driving shake beat. An excellent flip."

When the single smashed into the Top 20 the following week, the Byrds were invited to appear on *Top Of The Pops*. They had already featured on the show the previous month, courtesy of a filmed performance of 'Mr Tambourine Man', but this was arguably even more important. They certainly looked startling that evening. McGuinn was positively otherworldly, the consummate method actor, staring deep into the camera lens over those weird rectangular glasses; Crosby smiled seductively, both innocent and mischievous in the same shot; Clark grinned, while slapping the tambourine, occasionally; Hillman barely moved, a statuesque paragon of cool furtiveness, partly hidden beneath his pulled up jacket collar; Clarke, dressed in an English tweed jacket and polo neck, just like McGuinn, affected an abstract disdain, cupping a drumstick in one hand while playing peek-a-boo beneath that long, blond hair. The performance was brilliantly captured by the *Top Of The Pops* crew, who studiously honed in on each individual Byrd as if they were undertaking an ornithological study of a new species.

The Byrds' appearance was one of the great television moments that summer, but it was typical of their laid-back approach that this crucially important plug was almost forfeited. "We missed the plane to Manchester because I bought them a slap-up meal at the restaurant in Heathrow," Taylor admits. "There were misjudgements everywhere. I was not a punctual man then. I had no Neil Aspinall or Brian Epstein! So I will blame myself for some of the unpunctuality and general chaos. I had a terrific desire to make them enjoy England, so if there was a chance of a meal or some social discourse, I would encourage that, which was to the detriment of their general health and punctuality . . . I certainly overemphasized the social context because my primary aim then was the old Liverpool theme of a laugh and a shout, which I would normally put above almost everything. And they were up for that. I always believed that the show must go on, but before the show went on, I was always up for a laugh and a shout, and certainly after the gig too."

The combination of late nights, double bookings, pep pills and testing schedules soon caught up with McGuinn, who followed Hillman into the realms of the afflicted. "I got sick. I had something like 103 temperature fever. We were at the BBC studio doing some show and the doctor came in and said: 'This guy shouldn't work, send him home to bed.' And they said: 'He's got to work.' So I'm laying on a couch or something there and everybody's going crazy, nobody has any organization any more."

As a result of McGuinn's illness, gigs in Newbury and Basingstoke were cancelled and the future of the tour was placed in doubt. More problems followed. Even while a doctor attended to McGuinn, Beatlemaniac Michael Clarke became the third victim of the Byrds' plague. He had received a cough mixture from a doctor earlier in the tour, but was now taking incautious doses and found that it made him drowsy. "That wasn't conducive to working," he admits. "When they tell you to take a teaspoonful, they mean it! Otherwise you're dead beat." Nobody seemed too interested in his self-inflicted plight, so he went off on his own to get some fresh air while the group prepared for an appearance on BBC's *Gadzooks*. As showtime grew closer, everybody was in a panic, believing that he might not reappear. The usually unflappable Derek Taylor was caught up in the chaos and had to employ his finest diplomatic skills: "Mike Clarke was also ill during that BBC session and I seem to remember that the others weren't particularly sympathetic, so he imitated Ringo's stunt in *A Hard Day's Night* and vanished. He returned literally one second before the live show was due to begin."

The Byrds were not amused by this stunt, and soon began arguing among themselves whether Clarke ought to be fired or not. It was all hot air, of course, for they knew that Michael's irresponsibility was ultimately part of his maddening charm. After receiving some harsh words, he shrugged his shoulders and breezed through this mini-crisis with characteristic nonchalance. "You couldn't make Michael suffer," Dickson says. "He'd just go away. He'd take off and hang out with somebody that was fun. He wouldn't put up with it. Then he'd show up for that show unrehearsed and not ready for it. But Michael was always the only one that never hesitated to apologize. For David Crosby, it's the most difficult thing in his life to have to admit he was wrong. For Michael, it came really easy. 'Hey, man, I'm sorry, I'm an asshole, I'll try and do better. What do you say?' He'd beat you to the punch. He'd punish himself before you got a chance."

Not surprisingly, by the end of the evening the discussion had switched from Michael Clarke's transgression to a more general weariness of life on the road. At one point, they all decided to call it a day and return home, but the whim soon passed and the tour resumed. They were still in a weakened state during the latter half of the itinerary and the speed they had ingested was now repaying them with bouts of exhaustion. Derek Taylor diagnosed their problems most perceptively: "Their resistance was low. Mike was ill, Hillman was ill, McGuinn was ill. As soon as you took them out of Hollywood and put them into a proper climate it seemed to affect them. They were not leading healthy lives or eating good food, and they were overworked by Mervyn Conn, God bless him."

"The illnesses were wonderful," Clarke concludes. "It was just that we sometimes had to do three shows a night in different places, and it was difficult to get there. As a result we got sick with flu. I have a basic tolerance, but it crept up on me. I got it from them. We were doing television and I was seriously sick of doing press. They'd badgered us to the point of no return. Mervyn Conn at night and Derek Taylor in the morning – think of that!"

The redoubtable Mervyn Conn was obviously used to dealing with artistes of greater stamina and clearly felt that every opportunity to promote 'America's Answer To The Beatles' should be grasped while they still held the public's attention. He was not to know that the group had already wasted themselves on a 30-date tour of the USA and were now living on artificial energy in order to take advantage of London's night life. Within six days of arriving in England, they had conducted a full-scale press conference, appeared on several television shows and played 13 gigs, including three consecutive all-nighters. Post-midnight supplemental bookings were clearly asking for trouble, for the Byrds weren't the kind of act to return to their hotel and settle into bed with a cup of cocoa. The temptation to socialize with the Beatles and Stones from daybreak onwards was irresistible, no matter what schedule was placed before them.

Conn seemed unperturbed by the cancellations and promised that the Byrds would stay on an extra few days to compensate for the missed shows. Amazingly, he even spoke of the distinct possibility of a follow-on European tour, with appearances in France and Germany. He further revealed that he was planning to bring the Byrds back for a Christmas show at the Hammersmith Odeon on a bill that would also feature Bob Dylan and Joan Baez. The music press could barely keep up with Conn's hyperbole. When questioned about the disappointing cancellations, he turned the conversation to the Byrds' advantage by focusing on their brilliant new single. "My prediction that they will knock the Beatles off the top will come true," he insisted.

As it turned out, Conn's prediction was not far wrong. 'All I Really Want To Do' soon joined 'Mr Tambourine Man' in the upper regions of the chart, prompting pundits to predict a certain number 1. For once, the timing seemed perfect. After all, it was August, and as everyone in the music world knows, the summer months are invariably the dreariest for quality singles. Unfortunately for the Byrds, a series of staggeringly good new releases transformed their summer of chart glory into one of ultimate disappointment. Firstly, Cher's rival version of 'All I Really Want To Do' also became a Top 10 hit and although the Byrds outsold and outcharted her in Britain, they were seriously affected by the split sales. The sleepy summer months might normally have left the Byrds relatively unaffected by a cover version, but this was no ordinary August. Incredibly, three of the year's finest singles were released almost simultaneously, and the Byrds found themselves sandwiched between the Rolling Stones' '(I Can't Get No) Satisfaction' and Bob Dylan's 'Like A Rolling Stone', while competing against the Beatles' 'Help!'. As Derek Johnson had forecast, they needed to sell a vast amount of records to overcome a combined Beatles/Stones threat, with or without Cher's spoiling tactics.

Despite mounting criticism in the music press, the Byrds still looked likely to triumph in the UK on the strength of their studio work. Their debut album received a full-page review in *Disc*, with extensive track-by-track analysis, a privilege that even the Beatles would have envied. *Melody Maker*, so far the greatest critics of their stage act, was also effusive: "If you dig the Byrds' style on 'Mr Tambourine Man' then this album is for you. Nine of the 12 tracks start with Jim McGuinn's characteristic 12-string guitar . . . Considered the best group to ever perform Dylan numbers, 'Chimes Of Freedom', the longest track on the album, is an excellent example of the Byrds-Dylan combination. All the tracks are tremendous singly, but the overall sound is too samey despite different tempos and composers. They are a very good group and we're going to hear a lot more of the Byrds."

In circulation terms, the key review was from the *New Musical Express*, the one paper yet to show its hand concerning the Byrds' stage act. Like *Disc* and *Melody Maker*, they were positive, headlining their review with the words, 'Versatile Album From Byrds'. Reviewer Allen Evans enthused: "They look like a rock group, but they are really a fine folk unit. They play their stringed instruments with great skill and invention against the rock-steady drumming. Their voices merge well. Before joining up, they had a fine grounding in folk with various units – Chad Mitchell Trio, Christy Minstrels, etc. Result is good music, easy to listen to and yet in the modern idiom. As the first group to bridge the gap between beat and folk, they deserve to be winners."

As *Mr Tambourine Man* entered the album charts, soon climbing into the Top 5, the Byrds resumed their tour, with appearances in East Grinstead, Bristol, Hove, Worthing and Ipswich. It seemed that they might yet rescue their reputation in the UK, but they were dealt a fatal blow by the presence of their deadliest rivals. "Sonny & Cher became a haunting," Taylor told me, and his words were well-chosen. From the very moment that the Byrds arrived in Britain, the selling of Sonny & Cher was well underway. Their UK representative Larry Page placed an advertisement in the *NME* officially welcoming the duo and he also ensured that they appeared on *Ready, Steady, Go!* alongside their rivals. Although the Byrds were winning the war over 'All I Really Want To Do', they could do little about the infectious 'I Got You Babe', a wonderful amalgam of Dylan-inspired folk rock and Phil Spector-styled production, whose lyrics updated the early Sixties ideals of teenage romance with a smidgen of hippie rebellion. The song served as the perfect anthem for the pair. On television, Sonny & Cher pointedly stared into each other's eyes, cooed unctuously, smiled blissfully and presented themselves as star-crossed lovers, doomed to be misunderstood simply because they were young and in love. Despite Sonny's evident seniority, he somehow managed to pass himself off as a man barely out of his teens. It was a performance guaranteed to melt the hearts of frosty parents who would never have allowed their own children to dress or behave in such an ostentatious manner. Unlike the cool Byrds, Sonny & Cher proved more loveable darlings of the anti-establishment and gained a great deal of publicity and public sympathy by being refused admittance to London's more elite hotels because of their eccentric clothing. The Byrds, by contrast, were safely ensconced at the Europa and had even been given a reception at the Savoy. Although they were clearly more genuine spokespersons for non-conformist youth, it was Sonny & Cher that caught the imagination late that summer. There was even a report, apparently true, that a sheikh had offered a million dollars to purchase Cher for his harem. Suddenly, the fickle teenzines, which had devoted so much time to Crosby's green suede cape and McGuinn's groovy rectangular mini-shades, were now obsessed with Sonny's furs and Cher's hair and striped, bell-bottomed trousers.

Unlike the Byrds, the Californian duo did not have to prove themselves on a stamina-sapping live circuit. They came to London simply to relax, talk to journalists and undertake some easy-going promotion and key television appearances. When the Byrds played their final London gig at the Astoria, Finsbury Park, Sonny & Cher turned up along with the *NME*'s star journalist Keith Altham and received a round of applause from the audience. It was an ominous start to another disappointing evening. In a typically arbitrary mid-Sixties pop package, the Byrds shared the bill with a line-up comprising Boz, Elkie Brooks, Johnnie B. Great, Charles Dickens, Kenny Lynch, Them and Donovan. While the Byrds' super-cool stage persona had worked wonders back at Ciro's, the response at the Finsbury Park Astoria was much more muted.

"I loved the band," says Kenny Lynch, "but it was just too long waiting for them to play each song. They'd come on and they'd go down great for the first couple of songs. The crowd was ready to go potty. But then they'd start tuning up. They'd tune up for five minutes, sometimes between each song. They never said anything to anybody and would tune for what seemed hours. That's all I remember about that tour. The promoter wanted to cut down everybody else's set because they were taking so long." Lynch gamely volunteered to shorten his already slight repertoire. "They thought I was being a good chap, but I didn't want to be onstage and was happy to finish early and go around the pub, being a lazy bastard. The promoter was very pissed off with the Byrds. At one point I thought they might be thrown off the bill, but 'Mr Tambourine Man' was number 1 when we started the tour so he had to keep them on. He thought they were a nightmare, and they were. Christ, you don't tune up after every song. I was left thinking what it must have been like for them in America, playing bigger places." In fairness, the Byrds were severely hindered by the unfamiliar equipment, although that meant little to hardened showbiz troupers like Lynch. "Whatever mike they put in front of me, I just used to sing. I didn't care what the gear was."

Viewing proceedings with a jaundiced eye, Keith Altham seemed convinced that 'America's Answer To The Beatles' were nothing more than pretenders to the throne and spared few adjectives in exposing them. With Sonny & Cher and Larry Page by his side, Altham was not among the Byrds' greatest supporters and shared their criticisms of the group. Observing their second set, he complained about the bad playing and atrocious sound quality noting: "After tuning up for a full five minutes behind the curtain, they were treated to a traditional slow handclap by the impatient audience. Then their first two numbers were completely drowned by over-amplification. I have it on good authority from Cher that the first number was 'Feel A Whole Lot Better', but the vocals of that and the next number were inaudible. The 'chiming whining' effect which runs through their numbers may be good for a few, but not for all seven tunes in their repertoire. Stage presentation is non-existent and so is any communication with the audience, although at one stage Jim McGuinn did say 'Hello'."

With Sonny & Cher in tow, Altham managed to get backstage

after the show and gamely attempted to interview the Byrds. "I thought we were good tonight," Crosby told him, without apparent irony, adding "We don't talk much to the audience because we like our music to speak for us. I wonder if people realized how tired we are? We had a month's tour of America before coming here and we're knocked out." Having provided a reasonable defence of the Byrds' shortcomings, Crosby immediately lost interest in the reporter and turned away to continue a conversation with Donovan. Altham, who was used to receiving greater respect from pop musicians, was not impressed. Moving on to McGuinn, he found the Byrds' leader "more likeable", despite a niggling tendency to converse in a whisper. As for the others, they were clearly caught up in their own insular world: "Gene Clark walks around in a Mountie's hat, saying 'Hi, all!' Chris Hillman seldom says anything and Mike, the drummer, reads papers through a fringe combed over his nose. He says: 'Cool it' and 'When do we eat?' occasionally."

Like a newly-appointed headmaster, faced with a bunch of recalcitrant young pupils, Altham concluded sternly: "The Byrds biggest fault is this 'cool, couldn't-care-less' attitude onstage and off. The audience didn't like it. Neither did I." Years later, Crosby admitted that the super-cool persona was partly inspired by imitation. "We were really studying the example of the Beatles and Dylan and the way they handled things. It suited us perfectly. We were a little aloof, but it was more that we weren't in awe of the press. It was like that bit in *A Hard Day's Night* where someone asks, 'How do you find America? . . . Turn left at Greenland'. That was the attitude we wanted. A little bit funny and sarcastic. Certainly not respectful of the press. And we got good at it." Unfortunately, the effect was largely lost on British journalists like Altham, and understandably so. Unlike Lennon or Dylan, who combined acid wit with a dash of humour, sprinkled with engaging one-liners and sardonic smiles, the Byrds all too often came across as aloof, distant or downright surly. Any leavening irony was buried beneath a deceptively over-confident and defensive exterior.

The adverse comments of Altham and some of his colleagues may have been justified, but there also seemed to be strong overtones of partisanship in a number of the reviews. As a former reporter, Derek Taylor felt that the criticisms were unduly harsh in both their content and attitude. "The press was, as usual, the press," he wearily observed. "Unfortunately, the British press tends to get together on such occasions and there was a lot of aggression over the Byrds. One of the Byrds' characteristics was that they could be objectionable by not performing very well and not being consistently good. I loved them as if they were my own children, but unfortunately they weren't as well-behaved as my own children! I found the concerts very unnerving. I had tears in my eyes every night, I thought it was so wonderful. But the audiences had gone expecting heaven. They'd been told that this was a very important group."

McGuinn was charged by Derek Taylor with the task of rescuing the Byrds' reputation via some well-placed diplomatic words. He rose to the occasion, employing a combination of detached humility, politeness and partial culpability. "Yes, the press comment has been harsh," he concurred. "But I was brought up by my parents – who are both in the public relations business – to believe that any publicity is good. And we've had so much, in your national press as well as the music papers. It has been fair. We've been quoted correctly on the whole. We have no complaints. In fact, we're grateful because we've learned a lot about communication with people from reading the reactions to us . . . With a few exceptions, we've found British audiences very similar to those in the States. In some cases our reception has been a little ahead of what we've been used to. I think that's because the lyrics of our numbers are poetry and appeal to those who have a cultural heritage a little in advance of some of the isolated agricultural communities we've been playing to back in America." Complimenting the English on their cultural heritage, while showing that the group were not merely arrogant Americans too cool to care, might have helped the Byrds in different circumstances. Unfortunately, the bad press was steamrolling them into disrepute by now and McGuinn's ambassadorial apologia was not published in *NME* or *Melody Maker*, but the less regarded and lower circulation *Record Mirror*.

After the Astoria show, the Byrds completed their itinerary with appearances in Bournemouth and Bath. Before the Bournemouth performance on 15 August, McGuinn instructed Taylor to capture the screams of the fans on to a cassette tape recorder which he had recently purchased in London. The device was so new that most people had never even seen such a machine. Two years later, Jim would exhume the recording for inclusion on the suitably ironic 'So You Want To Be A Rock 'n' Roll Star'.

The final date of the tour at the Guildhall, Portsmouth, was cancelled, reportedly due to "indifferent support at the box office". At least, this gave the Byrds some extra time to spend shopping. For all their bad impressions of England, they had few complaints as tourists. Op Art was in the ascendant, miniskirted girls and mohair-suited young men filled fashionable clubs like the Ad-Lib and Scotch of St James, and Carnaby Street offered untold delights for those in search of garish garb. Having squandered money frivolously on room service at the Europa, the Byrds spent even more purchasing polo neck sweaters, tweed jackets, leathers and brogues. Despite the problems with the press, they still allowed *Melody Maker* into their rooms and dutifully reviewed some records for the paper's Blind Date column. McGuinn and Clarke were full of praise for the Stones and Dylan, leaving Hillman to play the hard man on some of the other releases. After listening to Peter Jay & The Jaywalkers' 'Before The Beginning', McGuinn charitably observed, "For an instrumental, it's interesting." Reclining forward, Hillman retorted, "It's plain dull!" As for Ray Charles' 'Love's Gonna Live Here', Chris revealed his country leanings, adding, "Buck Owens did this and I liked it better."

In a final attempt to boost 'All I Really Want To Do' to number 1, the Byrds pre-recorded an appearance on television's *Thank Your Lucky Stars*. Although the record was the fastest-selling UK single in the history of CBS, it was immediately overhauled by Sonny & Cher's 'I Got You Babe'. As the Byrds packed to leave, their great rivals were on their way to achieving the impossible. The final chart of August said everything there was to say about the Byrds' mission that summer. It read: 1. 'I Got You Babe' – Sonny & Cher; 2. 'Help!' – the Beatles; 3. '(I Can't Get No) Satisfaction' – the Rolling Stones; 4. 'All I Really Want To Do' – the Byrds.

The letters column of the *New Musical Express* left one last bitter taste with a mocking caption: 'The Byrds Get The Bird'. Underneath were a handful of anti-Byrds missives, including one which read: "My friend and I went to Slough to see the Byrds and thought they were terrible. The sound was awful, they didn't bother to introduce any of the songs, they tuned up onstage, and altogether they had no talent or personality."

On 19 August, the Byrds checked out of the Europa Hotel and headed for London Airport. They were in a downbeat mood, having suffered a severely damaged reputation and personal losses including both a stolen Rickenbacker and the commemorative disc awarded to them for sales of 'Mr Tambourine Man'. One passing reporter, no doubt recalling Mervyn Conn's extravagant suggestions of a possible Dylan/Byrds tour in December, had the nerve to ask whether they would be returning soon. "There is absolutely no question of a Christmas show," Taylor answered with strained patience. "The group will return when the bill is right and at the right time and the right place. They have immensely enjoyed the tour; they've learned a tremendous amount . . . It's been hard but invaluable experience."

Taylor's words were not entirely PR blarney. Although the Byrds had fallen ill, suffered exhaustion and been pilloried in certain sections of the music press, their memories of England were not all bad. "They did an awful lot of things they wanted to do," Taylor points out. "They met the Beatles and were worshipped by them, and hung out with a couple of Stones and saw Swinging London. It wasn't as bad as they painted, but it wasn't as good as they would have liked."

Characteristically, it was the irreverent David Crosby who seemed least perturbed by all that had gone wrong during the tour. Turning to Taylor on the plane back to America, he produced his stash of marijuana and, with a twinkle in his eye, announced: "If we did nothing else, even if our music is shit, we got you high."

After returning to the States, Taylor placed a full-page advertisement in *Disc*, inset with press cuttings and framed with words borrowed from their recent single, "In Britain we did all we really wanted to do . . . and now we feel a whole lot better."

"There was enough good press to extract some warm quotes,"

Taylor recalls, "but, by and large, what we left behind was a feeling of disappointment. I think the Byrds felt they'd blown it. The next thing to decide was how we were going to cheer them up."

The Byrds might have been cheered if they'd continued reading the British music press in the wake of their departure. After all the criticisms of the previous month, there was an unexpected backlash in favour of the group. Both *NME* and *Melody Maker* printed effusive letters, either defending or celebrating the Byrds. A. Barnes of Wilts, wrote: "After reading the knocking letters, I was dubious about going to see the Byrds, but now I'm certainly glad I did go. They are wonderful, and they're still my favourite group."

Reader J. Meenan added: "Bravo Byrds! Just because they didn't get up onstage and make fools of themselves by dancing around they are criticized."

More pointedly, Ana Joyce of Crouch End, London tackled *Melody Maker*'s editorial policy, demanding: "How could you allow Chris Welch's article to be printed? I would remind him that the Byrds were cramming into a short time as many performances as our groups do in twice the time."

Both the positive and anti-Byrds letters were largely the indignant reactions of spurned pop fans, but they did point to the possibility of a nationalistic bias in the reporting. America had been relatively slow to react to the Beatles' explosion with a group of similar scope and imagination, and by the time the Byrds arrived in Britain attitudes were so entrenched in favour of UK pop groups that a US invasion seemed ludicrous. With a better structured PR campaign and a tour that concentrated on unstressful promotion, rather than energy-sapping engagements, the Byrds might have left the country in triumph. Instead, the heavy-handed advertising proclaiming them 'America's Answer To The Beatles', combined with a studied cool easily misinterpreted as arrogance, lost them vital support at a crucial moment.

The snapshot views of aggrieved critics and blindly faithful followers were played out in the pages of the music press, but there was little opportunity to analyse what went wrong. Interestingly, the only journalist to attempt an overview was Brighton-based columnist Anne Nightingale, who felt that England had seriously misjudged the Byrds. She detected a worrying partisanship in the press and, no doubt with Chris Welch and Keith Altham in mind, concluded that a cultural clash had exacerbated the Byrds' bad reputation.

"The Byrds did try to make friends," Nightingale argued. "But a kind of national prejudice was working against them. They just looked too English, with their long hair and hip clothes. And it seemed to strike their critics that the Byrds, being essentially a pop group, were trying to crash a scene which till then had been totally British... People who met the Byrds in the flurry of a press conference or the backstage confusion of a one-nighter, put them down as detached and arrogant when spoken to, and remote onstage. The detachment, I suspect, was a simple misinterpretation. The Byrds look like any British group, but their language is different. They talk Dylan talk, sprinkled with expressions like 'where it's at', 'up tight' and 'hung up'. Some of their conversations needed a translator to unravel the hip West Coast slang. All the Byrds have an indirect manner of speaking and, James Dean-like, they tend to mumble. But in Britain, the Byrds weren't arrogant, just bewildered by the harsh reception from the country they'd set their hearts on visiting."

Seizing on this heartening appraisal, Derek Taylor realized some reflective or appeasing comments from the Byrds might further shift the focus in their favour. Needless to say, they weren't remotely interested in addressing their present status in Britain, having already written off the trip as a mistake. Apart from some trendy clothes and an introduction to the Beatles' coveted circle, the visit only brought back painful memories of their own inadequacies. With neither of the senior Byrds available for interview, Taylor turned to the unlikely figure of Chris Hillman, whose shy, silent persona had already provoked condescending comments in the music press. According to *Melody Maker*, he agreed to a transatlantic phone interview, but no journalist's name was appended to the resulting article, which was probably ghosted by Taylor and planted for PR purposes. Hillman's defence of the Byrds was cleverly worded, mixing indignation, arrogance, flashes of humility and a hint of a conspiracy. The following read suspiciously like a script straight from Taylor's school of journalism, but succeeded in presenting Hillman as a much more articulate character than previously imagined.

> We feel there was a slightly negative reaction towards us as Americans, and as a rock 'n' roll group offering what was interpreted as a challenge to the British. This seemed to be based particularly on the way we dressed, on the length of our hair and on our music. The British seemed to take the view that it all started in England, or more particularly Liverpool . . . The negative feeling wasn't around all the time, it was just a certain atmosphere we sensed now and again. We certainly didn't receive it from the Beatles. They were marvellous from the outset and we certainly hadn't expected them to make a special visit to a club to see us.
>
> What we wanted to do in England, we did. We wanted to play to British audiences and absorb some of the vitality which has been around the London scene since the Beatles first became famous. We were heard by many thousands of people and, so far as we could hear from the screaming, most of them seemed to enjoy themselves. The criticism that we were too cool onstage may be justified. We are not 'Jimmy and the Jets'. We don't have any choreography or unified stage movements. We don't laugh and joke with the audience and maybe we were a little cool. But it wasn't intended to be an affront to the audience. Nor did it mean that we didn't want to communicate. It was simply that we expected our music to do the communicating for us. One of the results of the criticism was that we did examine our stage lighting and we did learn to make announcements onstage. Maybe we didn't speak for very long but at least we did say 'Hello' and 'Goodbye'. So we learned something in that respect.
>
> The people handling our equipment tried manfully to provide us with our sound but somehow we never quite achieved the sound we got in America. We are grateful, especially, for the sharp scrutiny of the musical and national press, though naturally the criticisms stung. We will certainly be back, but in

the right places at the right time and we are going to have a few nights off to relax with some of the many friends we met.
  Thank you for having us. We will see you all again in 1966.

The 'Hillman' apologia was not taken up by any of the other music papers and proved insufficient to reverse the negative memories associated with the tour. In subsequent interviews, the Byrds would reinforce the view that the 1965 UK visit was a complete disaster and it would be several years before they undertook another tour on British soil.

CHAPTER TWELVE

The Death Of Folk Rock

ON the evening of 25 August 1965, there was a meeting of frazzled minds in Benedict Canyon, Beverly Hills. The Beatles were holding court and had invited the Byrds to a supergroup summit. Details of the Fab Four's address had already filtered through to the street and Sunset Boulevard was chock-a-block with cars, all heading towards their Spanish villa in the mountains. Some of the wealthier Hollywood kids had even hired helicopters in the hope of photographing the Beatles in their swimming pool. With the police force providing a safe escort, the Byrds were allowed through to the house, where they were soon joined by actor friend Peter Fonda. An acid-drenched evening stretched into the night and continued the following morning. During the revels, Fonda recalled a near-death-experience while on the operating table and kept repeating the words: "I know what it's like to be dead." Chilled by the mournful tone, John Lennon told him to shut up, but the words stuck in his head and would later form the chorus of the Beatles' 'She Said She Said'.

Fonda was not the only influence on the Beatles' songwriting that evening. An informal jamming session took place which would prove significant. "We were sitting around on acid playing 12-strings in the shower," McGuinn told me. "We were in this large bathtub which used to belong to the Gabors. John, George, David and I were just sitting there playing. We were showing them what we knew about Ravi Shankar and they'd never heard of him."

The Byrds, of course, had an edge on the Beatles thanks to Jim Dickson, who had taken Crosby to a Shankar session during the

World-Pacific days. The influence of Eastern music on both acts would be forthcoming before the end of the year. McGuinn, already a dedicated student of Subud, steered the conversation towards Eastern religion, but was met with cool indifference from George Harrison, who drawled, "We don't believe." McGuinn was taken aback, not by Harrison's agnosticism, but the absolute conviction with which he spoke for all four of the Beatles. Despite their differing personalities, they seemed to exist as a collective consciousness, complete with their own Beatles' philosophy. It would never have struck McGuinn or Crosby to speak in such terms. "We were competitive in the Byrds," says McGuinn, "and wouldn't have thought of protecting each other in the way the Beatles did. They had real unity. Of course, they'd been together for years and grew up in the same place."

When the stoned musicians emerged from the bathtub, somebody pointed out that it had been an age since any of them had eaten. Unfortunately, a sterling attempt to prepare some food in the kitchen caused further problems as the LSD exaggerated their spatial perspective. Some found they had too much food, others not enough. Meanwhile, John Lennon lost the ability to operate a knife and fork and went through a torment worthy of Tantalus as his food moved around the plate, frustratingly out of mouth's reach. Eventually, he poured the contents onto the floor, unsure how to proceed thereafter.

Presumably, the Byrds had come down from their trip by late the following evening, when they played a 'welcome home' gig at the Palladium in Hollywood. Titled the 'Byrds Ball' and promoted by Dickson's pal John Barrick, the performance proved something of an anticlimax with a noticeably low turn-out. "The 'right' people were there, such as Peter Fonda and company," Derek Taylor recalls, "but the punters were not there in large numbers." The group felt close enough to their hip followers to wander into the audience and chat between sets. Unfortunately for Crosby, the support act were the Leaves, who would soon hijack his version of 'Hey Joe', much to his chagrin. Reviewers, normally used to the Byrds' legendary coolness, responded positively to their unaccustomed cordiality.

Three days later, there was an unexpected PR opportunity when the Beatles attended a crowded press conference to coincide with their appearance at the Hollywood Bowl. Taylor and Dickson ensured that their mutual friend Curt Gunther was planted among the journalists and primed to ask the Fabs to name their favourite US group. Happy to oblige their former press officer, the Beatles announced: "The Byrds". Capitol Records, whose other major signing was the Beach Boys, were furious when they learned of this clever manoeuvring.

In late August, the Byrds returned to the studio in an attempt to complete their third single. They had recently cut a promising B-side, Gene Clark's 'She Don't Care About Time', and had just selected 'The Times They Are A-Changin'' as their next Dylan A-side. Dickson remembers his excitement after learning that they had incorporated the song into their set while touring the UK. "It was on the same tape [from Bournemouth] that has the screams which they later put on 'So You Want To Be A Rock 'n' Roll Star'. It was a very important song and I thought they should record it right away." The session proved one of the most eventful of their career thanks to the surprise arrival of George Harrison and Paul McCartney, still buzzing from the recent drug extravaganza back in Beverly Hills. Dozens of fans waited outside Columbia Records studios on Sunset, only to miss Harrison, who arrived in Derek Taylor's unostentatious Simca car. Heading straight for the recording booth, Harrison was introduced to Terry Melcher, then waved to Crosby through the glass partition separating the musicians from the control room. The Byrds were over-eager to impress, but their attempt at 'The Times They Are A-Changin'' was not proving fruitful. Since recording the song for Columbia at the end of June, they had performed the number in England, but still felt uncomfortable with the arrangement. McGuinn had adopted a more irreverent, ironic vocal which only served to drain the song of its polemical thrust. Melcher hastily faded the track and attempted to boost everyone's confidence by playing George 'She Don't Care About Time', which the Byrds had successfully completed the previous week. Turning to Taylor, Harrison remarked, "Don't they phrase beautifully? Listen to the clever work in the chorus . . ."

THE DEATH OF FOLK ROCK

During a break in the session, Paul McCartney arrived outside in a black limousine, pursued by dozens of cars. After dodging the outstretched arms of fans, he was ushered into the building and joined his fellow Beatle in the recording studio. He seemed particularly interested in the technical aspects of Melcher's production, carefully noting the recording levels. Further work commenced on the Byrds' Dylan cover, but the presence of the two Beatles proved distracting. "It was sloppier than anything on the first album in terms of playing," Melcher complained. Towards the end of the session, the Byrds spent time trying to perfect a harmonica part, even inviting George and Paul to have a go at the instrument. "It's a pity John's not here," McCartney noted. "He would have been glad to help." After Jim and Gene laid down a harmonica break, Michael Clarke stepped up with one of his own, which turned out best. Looking on, Dickson was surprised to see the drummer outpointing Clark and McGuinn in front of the Beatles. As they finished up, Harrison listened back to the rudimentary recording of 'The Times They Are A-Changin'' and was impressed enough to ask for a dub version. "If I know anything about record companies, it won't be released until Christmas at least," he joked, not realizing that the single would never actually appear.

While the Beatles and the Byrds were happily socializing, a drama was underway of which they were completely oblivious. Derek Taylor's wife Joan had just phoned to tell him that the police were at their house, asking a number of awkward questions about drugs. Worse, they were on their way to the studio. By the time the message was relayed, an FBI agent was already closing in and it was too late to extricate the Beatles from an embarrassing situation, which looked likely to end in a drugs bust. "They came down and sealed off CBS," Dickson recalls.

Trapped inside the studio, there was no escape, so they sent Taylor to greet the FBI man. It rapidly transpired that Derek Taylor was his major suspect. The police had been alerted by the airlines that some marijuana had been found in a cigarette packet on the plane on which the Byrds had flown back from England. "David Crosby had put some drugs in an empty cigarette packet, not wishing to risk going through customs," Dickson points out.

When the police checked their files and discovered that a certain Derek Taylor was on the flight, they were convinced that they had their man. A marijuana grower of the same name lived not far from Taylor, a coincidence that often plagued him at airports. The FBI agent seemed puzzled upon being introduced to Taylor and agreed to accompany him across the road for a drink to discuss the matter.

Although it was evident that they had the wrong Derek Taylor, there was still a possibility that the studio might be searched and police might even be heading for the Byrds' homes. Dickson was amazed when an agitated Taylor suddenly re-entered the studio. "He'd told the FBI guy that he had to go to the men's room in the bar, then he climbed out of the window and came over to tell us what was going on. Terry was kept in the dark. He didn't know anything about the Byrds smoking grass on the plane and nobody wanted to tell him about it, or include him."

Instructions were immediately passed on to clear the Byrds' houses of any drugs. Taylor then slipped back across the road and continued drinking with his new friend. "I didn't smoke hash at that time," Taylor reminded me, "although Crosby had given me a joint. He takes great pride in that. I was not a doper, which was why I was able to deal with that FBI fellow. I told him, 'I don't know anything about that stuff. You and I are drinking men.' And I got him very pissed. I could drink any of those fuckers under the table."

By the end of the evening, the 'FBI fellow' was so enamoured of his new drinking pal that he declined to follow up the investigation. In any case the Byrds had flown, accompanied by Paul and George. As one news report noted: "George slipped out of a side door with David Crosby and the two of them went to Benedict Canyon Drive. Paul, after side-stepping attempts to get him on the air, also escaped. The session ended and the remaining four Byrds followed in their cars on the familiar journey to Benedict Canyon."

Although nobody was there to report what happened when the two groups arrived back at the Canyon, their previous visit strongly suggests that they got royally stoned. With the Byrds' houses cleared of drugs, they still had the perfect opportunity to end the evening on a high note, irrespective of police cordons and prying FBI investigators.

THE DEATH OF FOLK ROCK

Taylor's astute rescue job ensured that he was firmly back in favour with the Byrds' management, who had been a little concerned after hearing about the disaster in England. The Byrds had overspent on the tour, running up silly bills for sandwiches and snacks at the Europa Hotel and liberally dipping into their limited slush fund. "When Derek took them to England, he spent a lot of their money and he was ready for it to be at an end," Dickson claims. "He'd been irresponsible enough to get himself fired. I think he expected to get fired and wanted to because there's a lot of pain in the ass connected with dealing with the Byrds. It's not all rewards. There were a lot of rewards too, high, wonderful, exciting moments. But Derek was at the brunt. He had to cover up all these misadventures and make a business out of it. So he was ready to bail out or be fired . . . and Eddie Tickner boxed him in. He wasn't mad. He didn't bawl out Derek for being imprudent. He said, 'It's going to work out, we'll straighten it out, don't worry about it.' There was no way for Derek to quit honourably."

Dickson had overestimated Taylor's sensitivity. Despite the swashbuckling adventures in England, the overspending, and the hard diplomacy that the Byrds sometimes brought to bear on his PR shoulders, Taylor could never lose his sentimental affection for them. "I never wanted to be fired," he stresses. "And certainly didn't expect to be fired. It was the last thing I expected and it never came up. Eddie may have said *something*." It was typical of Tickner's laid-back approach that, even in the act of reprimanding Taylor, he was so subtle that the Liverpudlian remained blissfully unaware that he was being taken to task or persuaded to stay on. "The thing about Jim and Eddie, which must be stressed, is that they never complained about anything I did, or they did!"

The fact that Taylor had saved the Byrds' reputation within a couple of weeks of returning from England ensured that any further criticisms of his largesse were forgotten. "It took a crisis to get the best out of Derek," Dickson notes, "and what he did at that Columbia session with the FBI astounded me."

Despite surviving police scrutiny and enjoying the patronage of the Beatles, the Byrds were not immune to self-doubt. The ghost of Sonny & Cher had continued to haunt them upon their return to the States and there was a growing feeling among their critics that they had been outmanoeuvred. Even the faithful Bob Dylan could not resist a dig and taunted and embarrassed McGuinn for losing the US chart race over 'All I Really Want To Do'. As the Byrds' leader confessed: "What really got to me most was Dylan coming up to me and saying, 'They beat you man,' and he lost faith in me. He was shattered. His material had been bastardized. There we were, the defenders and protectors of his music, and we'd let Sonny & Cher get away with it."

To rub salt in the wounds, Dylan attended a Sonny & Cher recording session that September, as if hinting that he might yet switch loyalties. The *New Musical Express* even printed a rumour that he was planning to compose a new single for Sonny & Cher. Of course, it was part of Dylan's nature to play mind games and nobody could be absolutely sure how he felt about any given subject. McGuinn realized as much, while acknowledging the gap between them. When Dylan stayed at a hotel, he would socialize, but never let play get in the way of work. "He had a typewriter on the balcony," McGuinn recalls. "He'd sit there and write a song a day. We were really impressed by that. We never did it, though. It was too hard. He was miles above us. He'd kind of humour us a little bit. He was Dylan, and we were this band who did one of his songs and happened to have a hit with it. That was his attitude. We weren't *really* close."

Like the Beatles only a week before, Dylan played a sold-out show at the Hollywood Bowl on 3 September, after which he was invited to a celebrity party at Benny Shapiro's house. The effusive agent and club owner brought together a spectacular gathering, including actors Burgess Meredith, Dennis Hopper, John Barrymore Jr and James Coburn. But what really impressed Dylan was the presence of Marlon Brando, whom he had idolized since his youth. Several of the Byrds also attended the party, but McGuinn was distracted for much of the evening. He later admitted feeling uncomfortable when Brando started hitting on his wife-to-be, Dolores. "There were tons of people there because Dylan was in town," she remembers. "Marlon Brando was drunk and stumbling around. He told me, 'You are the girl of my dreams!' He was sitting on this little settee and everyone was sitting around in awe of what he was saying." McGuinn looked on, unsure how to react but trusting everything would turn out all right. According to Dolores, he finally registered his disapproval with the cutting line: "If that's your partner, you can go with him, or you can go with me." Looking back, she jokes, "And I was stupid enough to go with him! But I always thought he valued his relationship with me a little more because Brando had paid attention to me. I always credited Brando with that. It may have cemented the relationship, although we were already living together."

While McGuinn was busily pondering his romantic life, David Crosby was pursuing a charm offensive on Dylan. He ingratiated himself to such an extent that he was allowed to tag along to a Dylan press conference the next morning at the Beverly Hills Hotel. McGuinn could be forgiven for thinking that this was another gnomic slight from Dylan, who knew that Crosby was his chief rival in the group. Realizing that Crosby had always been the Byrd most resistant to Dylan's influence somehow made it worse. While Dylan may have taken mischievous delight in befriending Crosby at the expense of McGuinn, it is equally likely that he simply enjoyed his company. "Crosby was a colourful and unpredictable character," Dylan later acknowledged, "wore a Mandrake the Magician cape, didn't get along with too many people and had a beautiful voice – an architect of harmony. He was tottering on the brink of death even then and could freak out a whole city block all by himself, but I liked him a lot. He was out of place in the Byrds. He could be an obstreperous companion."

That same month, Dylan could be seen hanging out with Michael Clarke at the coffee shop Fred C. Dobbs. "Bob wanted a bottle of wine, a bottle of red," Clarke told me, "and he called it Lee J. Cobbs. When he said it, it was hilarious. It was the funniest thing I ever heard. Bob and I were sitting there hating everybody. He hated everybody too! He was tired of having to talk to the press – you get that way sometimes."

Dolores also remembers Dylan frequenting Fred C. Dobbs with Clarke and affecting an air of mystery. He spent much of the evening scribbling enigmatic phrases on the inside flaps of the free paper matchbooks on display. Like a myopic scientist peering through a microscope, he would hold these close up to his eye, pen in hand, while people looked on intrigued and amazed. "Everyone was so scared of Dylan," Dolores recalls. "He wouldn't tolerate anyone and always had the best of everything. The best pot around. When he was in town, everything was happening. It had been the same when he walked into Ciro's earlier. Everyone would hush up and you could feel the excitement in the air. It was just like the Beatles. Those were great days. He was so mysterious. We all went to Ollie Hammond's Steak House on Wiltshire/N. La Cienega Boulevard. It was 24-hour service. Everyone was bowing down to Dylan, but when he'd gone to the Ash Grove earlier with his little entourage, Ed Pearl made him pay. He was used to saying, 'I'm Bob Dylan.' I reminded him of that and we had a little argument. Everyone was so fearful of him, and I hated that. It seemed like you had to be on tiptoes around him. When I spoke up [McGuinn] said I was a suffragette!"

Dylan might have been aloof and tired of the press, but he wasn't tired of the Byrds, irrespective of his previously catty comments to McGuinn. Soon after, he would be full of praise for their interpretation of 'Lay Down Your Weary Tune' and continued championing them in the press. It helped enormously that his endorsement to Paul Jay Robbins back in March had belatedly appeared in the September edition of the *Los Angeles Free Press*, just when it was most needed. Readers, unaware that the interview emanated from the Ciro's days, must have assumed that Dylan was now their greatest fan when he said: "They know it all. If they do not close their minds, they'll come up with something pretty fantastic."

At the beginning of October, the Byrds opened at Elmer Valentine's new venue the Trip, which had replaced the old jazz club, the Crescendo. It proved a strange time for Dolores, who suddenly found herself the centre of attention. "We were walking down Sunset Boulevard and David Crosby was the first to meet us outside the Trip. He said, 'Dolores, we love you. We think you're the best!'" Crosby's unexpected words of support instantly rang alarm bells. Only a few months before, he had tried to prevent her getting on the group's bus, now he was charm personified. "I was thinking,

THE DEATH OF FOLK ROCK

'What's going on here?' Everyone was being over-friendly to me. Something was weird. Then we went into the dressing room and there was this big painted graffiti which said, 'Dolores Is A Mexican Bitch'. It was kind of sad because suddenly I realized that not everyone liked me." McGuinn was stunned by the racial slur, but somehow kept his cool and remained silent. The perpetrator was never discovered, but Dolores could easily identify the most likely culprits. "I'm sure it would have been one of the groupie girls. That's who I always charged it off to. The next day they painted it over and it was gone."

It was not only McGuinn's girlfriend who was the butt of bad vibes at the Trip. McGuinn himself was lampooned by visiting celebrity Peter Noone, whose Manchester group Herman's Hermits were then kings of America, with a flurry of 1965 hits, including two anachronistic chart-topping million sellers borrowed from the British music hall era: 'Mrs Brown You've Got A Lovely Daughter' and 'I'm Henry VIII, I Am'. The ever protective Derek Taylor was sufficiently peeved to reprimand Noone in his column for the UK music paper *Disc*. "Little Mr Noone was in the Trip, Hollywood's new, hip club, twice this week, gazing in wonderment at the electricity generated by the Byrds. On the second visit he and one of his guitarists – the one who wears glasses – leaned against the bar, sniggered between themselves, attempted a brief impersonation of Byrd-leader Jim McGuinn with the glasses on the end of his nose, and then walked out with the approximation of a swagger . . . I suppose McGuinn can take it."

David Crosby was also in mischievous mood during the two-week Trip residency. Like Herman, he displayed a touch of condescension directed towards one of the support acts: the Skip Battyn Trio. Among their ranks was the talented composer Van Dyke Parks, who had once turned down Crosby's advances at a time when he was searching for musicians to form a group, just prior to finding the Byrds. "I was playing keyboards for Skip, who was the opening act," he recalls. "As we were exiting the stage, ever affable David Crosby mounted with the rest of the Byrds. He came up to me in his cape and page boy [haircut]. With a victorious taunt, he said, 'I told you so!' David didn't understand that performing in front of screaming fans would never really satisfy my aims. I don't regret my reticence as a team player. Further, I love that I had a cameo in public with the Byrds."

Another visitor reminded of vanished opportunities was the outrageous Carl Franzoni. He still regretted missing out on the Byrds' infamous UK tour and secretly felt that McGuinn had been wary of the wild dancers upstaging him on foreign soil. "He apologized to me at the Trip," Franzoni says. "He just said he was sorry. I didn't let him expound on it. I just said, 'OK, Jim, everything's cool' – and I walked away."

Completing the weird vibe at the Trip was an excitable Gene Clark, who sounded as if he had just discovered the secrets of the universe. He'd always considered himself blessed with some psychic ability and some of his oft-kilter statements were portentous enough to impress his fellow members. He'd rightly predicted that 'Mr Tambourine Man' would top the charts, although precisely when he said those words nobody could quite remember. In later years, he insisted that he had foreseen the Byrds' signing to Columbia and recalled doodling the CBS logo, as if that were an example of automatic writing. Of course, it hardly needed pointing out that he had already recorded for the label with the New Christy Minstrels, so the company logo was hardly alien to his subconscious. Coincidentally or not, he had that familiarly strange feeling at the Trip and was keen to try out his latest prediction on the most unlikely recipient. Kim Fowley, the cynic's cynic, was probably the most grounded freak attached to the Vito's crowd. He never took drugs and his greatest joy was sashaying across Sunset Boulevard in search of young girls and quick fire business opportunities. A gangly giant of a man, he spoke with the speed and mental dexterity of a seasoned hustler and, despite his youth, had already been involved in the music business for nearly a decade during which he had worked as a producer, PR man, record label opportunist, and much else. Clark knew that he also had family links with old Hollywood and was the perfect person to try out his latest pet theory which, as it transpired, was more sociological than psychical.

"Gene was like a singing Robert Mitchum," Fowley remembers. "At the Trip he was predicting the future. It was quite astounding to hear him saying what the rest of the century was going to be like. He came up to me and said, 'You're smart and I want to see if you agree with me on this.' I was curious and listened. He told me, 'The 1960s are the 1920s and that's how people are going to judge it in the twenty-first century. Do you agree?' I said, 'Wow, yes.' He talked about bathtub gin and bootlegging and all the illegal prohibition stuff and said it was the same with drugs. 'It was alcohol that fuelled literature and music in the 1920s and ours is a drug fuelled music and literature. Don't you see the parallels?' I then started calling it the Silver Sixties. He laughed at that and then we drank some beer. I don't know where he got that from but he just had to share it. He thought we were now in the Roaring Twenties and that's what was happening to us. Hair had changed, music had changed and everything was changing because of it. He was pretty deep."

Clark walked off feeling mighty pleased with himself. Usually it was McGuinn who took the intellectual plaudits by comparing the modern Jet Age with the sound of the 1940s, but Clark's theory somehow sounded sharper. It's a pity he never had the confidence to push his homespun philosophies into the public arena, but he was acutely aware that he lacked the easy articulacy of David Crosby or the languid, detached wit of McGuinn.

The complex group dynamics within the Byrds were reaching intense levels and their position as America's top new group was seriously under threat, but there was still optimism in the camp. Public support from both the Beatles and Dylan was a welcome ego boost but everyone knew they still needed another hit to re-establish themselves commercially and outwit the marauding Sonny & Cher. Derek Taylor remained endearingly obsessive about the duo's ripping off the Byrds but was calmed down by some sagacious words from Dickson: "You're over-exaggerating Sonny & Cher's impact, the Byrds will outlast them."

In the late autumn of 1965, however, it seemed as though Taylor's worst fears were about to be realized. While the Byrds plotted their next move and fretted over the release of 'The Times They Are A-Changin'', Sonny & Cher, as a duo and as soloists, notched up no fewer than six Top 30 entries in two months: 'I Got You Babe', 'All I Really Want To Do', 'Laugh At Me', 'Baby Don't

Go', 'Just You' and 'But You're Mine'. The Byrds were also facing competition on the folk-rock front from the Turtles, whose catchy interpretation of Dylan's 'It Ain't Me Babe' was a sizeable hit. We Five also stormed the US charts with 'You Were On My Mind', but the biggest sensation turned out to be a former New Christy Minstrel and Ciro's habitué, Barry McGuire, whose gritty reading of P.F. Sloan's controversial 'Eve Of Destruction' survived a radio ban and rocketed to number 1.

P.F. Sloan, a belated Dylan disciple, was thrilled when his mentor invited him to a personal audience at his suite in the Beverly Hills Hotel. The occasion was a private listening to the newly pressed *Highway 61 Revisited*. Midway through, David Crosby unexpectedly entered the suite, then disappeared with Dylan into an adjoining room. After a brief interval, two topless women emerged from the room and pointedly sat opposite the bemused Sloan. They did not speak a single word. Suddenly, a character dressed as Zorro, complete with black mask, hat and cape, burst through an open window. Without explanation, he joined the women on the couch and proceeded to stare into Sloan's eyes, never uttering a word. A quarter of an hour later, the silent interlopers got up and left the room. Finally, Dylan and Crosby emerged from another room, like actors taking the stage. As Sloan recalls: "David . . . shakes hands with me and Bob continues to play me the rest of the album . . . I can only imagine that Bob had set this up, but I don't know."

The elaborate charade was a depressing comment on the condescending, sanctimonious attitudes displayed towards Sloan by his elder folk-rock contemporaries, most of whom dismissed 'Eve Of Destruction' as a cash-in, novelty protest. Among the musicians involved in the contentious single were Hal Blaine and Larry Knechtel, who had previously contributed to 'Mr Tambourine Man'. That irony was not lost on the Byrds who had, unintentionally, created the circumstances resulting in the recording. It was at Ciro's that McGuire had been introduced to songwriter P.F. Sloan and subsequently recorded several of his compositions. Originally, 'Eve Of Destruction' had been considered as a B-side, but the topicality of Byrds-inspired folk rock persuaded producer Lou

Adler to risk a radio ban and push the composition as a single. At an earlier point, he had offered Terry Melcher a shot at the song and, recognizing its hit potential, the producer urged the Byrds to consider releasing this catch-all protest as a follow-up to 'All I Really Want To Do'.

Dickson was appalled by the suggestion. "It was the first song that Terry tried to push on them. I was 100 per cent against it. To me, 'Eve Of Destruction' was the kind of song that ends your career. I agreed with Terry that it could be a number 1 hit if it was done well. He came in with it, wanted to do it, and was all excited. P.F. Sloan was a writer who could write all different kinds of songs. He could probably have written a song for his mother. We knew the song was powerful and would win, but I didn't think a song about the end of the world was a good statement for the Byrds to make. In the first place, it's patently ridiculous, it's certainly an attention getter and what do you sing after that, 'Rainbows And Lollipops'? I sincerely believe that with a new artiste, you are what you sing. That's the real way that people think they know you – through the songs. They may pore through fan magazines and try to figure it all out, but your real identity is right there in the play itself."

Dickson's scepticism about 'Eve Of Destruction' proved well-founded. The iconoclast Barry McGuire failed to register a follow-up hit, despite recording further material from the busy pen of P.F. Sloan. More importantly, the success of this ultimate protest song provoked sharp reactions from the folk and rock communities which were to have far-reaching implications. Mick Jagger took particular exception to 'Eve Of Destruction', slamming its sentiments as "phoney" and "awful rubbish". The sensationalist aspect of the song elicited similar rebukes from Mary Travers of Peter, Paul & Mary, who was disenchanted by its apparent negativity: "I think 'Eve Of Destruction' is a terribly depressing song and it doesn't point the way. Maybe it just stirs thing up, but it doesn't offer a solution."

That bastion of the folk community, *Sing Out!*, ran articles condemning the commercialization of protest, with such headings as 'Folk + Rock = Profits'. Leading with a provocative piece titled 'Folk Rot', Tom Paxton mercilessly laid into the new prophets of doom and trendy harbingers of social change, by focusing on their naivety. "Nothing could be more ridiculous than to suppose that while swimming and frugging the kids are going to be contemplating Red China," he sneered. "They are going to dance and dance only and any apologist or pundit who would have you believe otherwise is putting you on. These protesters are protesting because it pays. It isn't folk, it isn't very good rock, it is fraudulent protest – but it does pay well. When it stops paying it will disappear."

Manfred Mann's Paul Jones joined in the critical mauling, insisting, " 'Eve Of Destruction' protests about nothing. It is simply a 'Thy Doom Is At Hand' song with no point. Sweeping generalizations like 'Look at all the hate there is in Red China' don't strike me as the observations of someone out to promote peace. That kind of comment deserves to get the record banned." Having also alluded to McGuire in his 'Red China' reference, Paxton blamed Dylan ("the Chief Oracle and Originator") for the proliferation of beat group protest as personified by the Byrds: "Hanging desperately to his coat-tails are a swarm of beat groups, their hair grown hopefully long and their expressions surly from long hours of practice. Unwilling to admit to the altogether normal desire to be rich and famous musicians, they instead piously declare that they want to 'get the message through'. They want to be 'where it's at'. 'Where it's at' is a euphemism for 'rich'. Many of them, especially the ones who left folk music, explain that they want to reach 'a larger audience'. One group [the Byrds] claims that if just one line of 'Mr Tambourine Man' gets through to the teenies it will have been worth it. They are doomed to disappointment, which I trust they'll survive . . . The fact that there has been a response by the young to these 'protest' songs is no cause for rejoicing . . . Anyone who asks of these idols that they probe a bit deeper will be disappointed because these songs never intended to tell them anything more than Mom and Dad don't understand them."

The Byrds declined to involve themselves in *Sing Out*'s debate on the commercial evils of folk rock. Although McGuinn still read the magazine, he deliberately averted his eyes from the offending article, not wishing to taint the positive outlook that he still currently enjoyed. "I only read the title 'Folk Rot', then decided I didn't need it," he stresses. "But I could understand where he was coming from. He was basically being put out of business. The folk music boom was falling flat and we were partly responsible. But it had already gone flat because the Beatles came in and changed the folk music boom to a British Invasion boom."

Paxton's righteous indignation was understandable but, in many ways, he missed the crucial point. Whatever its origins or true motivation, the music *did* make a difference. Not only was it far more intelligent than the usual mindless, singalong Tin Pan Alley pop, but it provided a sense of empowerment for teenagers and promoted idealism, albeit tinged with cynicism. 'Eve Of Destruction' was a great pop song couched in the rhetoric of folk protest. For purists, it was a sell-out, but for pop fans it articulated, however clumsily, an adolescent frustration and sense of unease about the cumulative ills of the world.

Barry McGuire was understandably deflated by the harsher criticisms which he also felt were misconceived. "It was a phenomenon and I never thought it would be," he says of the song. "People said I did it for commercial reasons. Are you kidding, man? It was supposed to be a B-side, even Lou Adler thought that, but it had a life of its own. It just did what it did and I was as amazed as everyone else. It was labelled a protest song, but it wasn't saying anything was right or wrong. It was a mirror. But people didn't want to look into that mirror, so they called it a protest song. Dylan's music was mirror music too, it was mirroring society. I realized that's what all prophets do: they mirror society."

While folk aficionados were concerned with the question of authenticity, the pop marketplace consumed so-called protest music without a care for any distinctions between the genuine and the artificial. This was the crucial difference between the folk and pop consumers. Folk was about movements and communities, pop was about individual expression. Donovan's contemporary reading of Buffy Saint-Marie's 'Universal Soldier' was generally regarded as legitimate protest, but it was effectively aimed at the same market as 'Eve Of Destruction'. Everyone was jumping on the protest bandwagon and differentiating between the committed and the cynical was no easy task. Even McGuinn's old mentor Bobby Darin had reinvented himself as a protest singer with a single whose title echoed the words that every troubled or whinging adolescent had once said to their chastizing parents: 'We Didn't Ask To Be Brought Here'.

Over in England, the charts showed an even greater preponderance of Dylan-inspired protest hits including Manfred Mann's 'If You Gotta Go, Go Now', Joan Baez's 'It's All Over Now, Baby Blue' and Johnny Cash's 'It Ain't Me Babe'. Still at the cover version stage, the Animals nevertheless voiced a sense of social and personal unrest with the hits 'We Gotta Get Out Of This Place' and 'It's My Life'. A new strain of self-penned beat group protest completely transformed pop radio during the latter half of 1965. The Rolling Stones' '(I Can't Get No) Satisfaction' and 'Get Off Of My Cloud' sounded disgruntled enough with the world to be classified under the 'protest' banner, even if the targets were suitably vague. The Who had even commandeered the moral vacuity at the centre of mod culture to proclaim the triumph of selfish youth in 'My Generation'. And then there were the clever pretenders. Jonathan King, a Cambridge undergraduate and therefore an instant pop intellectual in class-conscious Britain, charted with 'Everyone's Gone To The Moon', a quaint but meaningless song of unconnected images that nevertheless fulfilled the criterion of sounding like a pseudo-profound commentary on the human condition. Later that year, King managed Hedgehopper's Anonymous, whose hit 'It's Good News Week' opened with the sardonic observation "Someone's dropped a bomb somewhere". It was a wonderful comment on the times that this anti-establishment litany should be written by musicians still in the secure employ of the Royal Air Force.

The assimilation of protest and folk music by Tin Pan Alley writers ultimately confirmed its demise as a soundtrack for youth, just as Tom Paxton had predicted. By the end of 1965, protest records were still charting, but the angry voice of youth had lost its resonance, grown shrill with hectoring. In Paxton's world-view, all this was evidence enough that the pop protest boom had been merely an ephemeral fashion. But that was not the whole story. Ultimately, the ensuing creative fall-out proved Paxton completely wrong. A legion of young, self-conscious would-be poets found their voice, and many turned their anger and angst inwards, transforming public sloganeering into a personal confessional style that reached its apogee at the end of the decade with the rise of the sensitive singer-songwriter. It was ironic that an age which held a mirror up to society to proclaim the dangers of the bomb would end the decade locked in introspective romantic isolation. As Dylan had rightly predicted in 'My Back Pages', the radicalism of youth was a rage that would finally give way to an understanding of personal inadequacy and a realization that black and white issues become greyer with age.

The Byrds were the beat group most closely associated with Dylanesque protest but, like their mentor, they never swallowed the ideology whole. Although they sincerely believed in the sentiments of their songs, they refused to be shackled by the dictates of the folk community. McGuinn had already experienced the sanctimonious scorn of the dogmatic folk elite during his time in New York when he chose to perform with Bobby Darin. During the World-Pacific and early Columbia period, those on the East Coast who knew of the Byrds' folk-rock experiments derided these young men. "We were an easy target for ridicule from folkies," Dickson says. "Especially playing electric music. Look at Dylan. They crucified him when he first played electric. They would have crucified McGuinn if he had been worthy in their minds, but it was just something to laugh at . . . McGuinn wanted to embrace the new technology and not be folkie any more. People in the Village, who'd never been to the country in their lives, were the biggest critics of people who weren't 'genuine'. And McGuinn had been exposed to that . . ."

McGuinn was not the only member of the Byrds to rise above the politics of folk. As Dickson notes: "Coming out of folk music, everybody tried to keep up some kind of front as to who they were. You couldn't take anyone seriously who said they were interested in the money. Nobody said that, no matter how true or part true it might be. David Crosby broke all those rules because he had no respect for the ethnic side of folk music anyway. He didn't care what *Village Voice* said, and neither did I. That was one of many things that David and I agreed on that neither of us mentioned much."

Although the Byrds were inextricably linked with the 'folk rock' phenomenon they never felt bound by its traditions or precepts. In their discussions with the Beatles they eagerly spoke of new musical ideas and themes that transcended the public's limited conception of their role as Dylan disciples. They would soon realize, in the wake of Sonny & Cher and Barry McGuire, that it was time to move on from the sound they had pioneered, but in the meantime more product was required. Although they had recently released an album, CBS demanded they complete another during the autumn, in anticipation of the Christmas market. With their ongoing touring commitments, there had been little time to rehearse new material and suddenly they were under even greater pressure.

CHAPTER THIRTEEN

Non-Aristotelian Systems

DECIDING upon a follow-up single to 'All I Really Want To Do' was causing untold problems for the Byrds. Their lack-lustre attempt at 'The Times They Are A-Changin'' remained undeveloped and was temporarily consigned to the tape vault. The general consensus was that they should continue covering Dylan material so 'It's All Over Now, Baby Blue' was selected from *Bringing It All Back Home*. Arranger Jack Nitzsche was commissioned by Melcher to produce a demo of the song designed to bridge the gap between the Spector-influenced sound of Sonny & Cher and the more fluid folk rock of the Byrds. Nitzsche hired a local group and came back with two Dylan songs, 'I Don't Believe You' and 'It's All Over Now, Baby Blue'. The unnamed, rented session group boasted a female vocalist with a fairly strong, bluesy delivery and arrangements that McGuinn could easily duplicate. This made sense to Melcher who had worked with Nitzsche as arranger and conductor on many recordings, including his own debut single as Terry Day back in 1962. Melcher was eager to experiment with the new material, but met resistance from Dickson who felt that the musical direction was wrong. "I didn't want to do them. I already didn't like Jack Nitzsche and I didn't like the tracks. Terry wanted it to sound more like Sonny & Cher. He felt the Byrds weren't getting that big sound and so, when he bought those tracks, he thought, 'That sounds like those Sonny & Cher records.' I didn't want to sound like Sonny & Cher. I was absolutely satisfied with the way we sounded . . . There were improvements we could make, but I didn't want to change things."

What was additionally alarming was Melcher's decision to employ McGuinn on the track without recourse to Crosby or Clark. This was the first indication of Melcher's growing alliance with McGuinn in what was to become a political battle of wills. As it turned out, the recording proved unsuccessful. According to Dickson, "McGuinn came into the booth and he was about to overdub the 12-string on 'It's All Over Now, Baby Blue' and he played until he found a wrong chord in the track. Then he stopped and said, 'The next track is wrong, we'll cut it ourselves.' Terry didn't want to do that."

Realizing that the Byrds were unlikely to produce a track highlighting the full-blown sound he had envisaged, Melcher curtailed the session and departed for a weekend in Palm Springs. In the interim, Dickson persevered with the song, bringing in the other Byrds in the hope of achieving a reasonable take. Although he was adamantly against following any Sonny & Cher pattern, the opportunity to record a strong Dylan composition was always irresistible.

A rough version of 'It's All Over Now, Baby Blue' was completed, with Dickson producing, assisted by engineer Tom May. McGuinn provided another fine acting performance, replacing Dylan's studied venom with a cocky, self-assured air and a faster arrangement with a chunky rhythm. A short but distinctive Rickenbacker break added a touch of drama to the song. One of the people attending the session was the programme director of KRLA, who was impressed enough with the track to play it on air. When Melcher learned of this turn of events, he was appalled. He felt the track was even more sloppy than their recent attempt at 'The Times The Are A-Changin''.

Melcher was particularly annoyed that the KRLA director, a close friend, had been encouraged to plug the song without his permission. Not for the first time, he suspected that Dickson was attempting to usurp his authority. The Byrds' manager pleaded his innocence, but to no avail. "I didn't do it behind his back," Dickson still insists. "I did it to cut the track, not to trick Melcher. He wasn't standing waiting for the Byrds. He had a life outside of the group. If Melcher or the Byrds didn't want to do it, he'd walk away. He'd go to Palm Springs. 'You don't want to do it? See you next time.' I thought we should do the song. I liked 'It's All Over Now, Baby Blue'. What I expected to do was to go in and cut it with Tom May on Saturday, bring it back, have Terry polish it, transfer it to 8-track and finish it up. I didn't expect him to be upset by it. I wasn't trying to defy him. He just wasn't there and we had a chance to go in and do it. I felt they did a pretty fair performance although we didn't have Ray Gerhardt (the engineer) to help. You're not allowed to touch the knobs at CBS. Whether I could have done it better at the time, I'm not sure, but I think I could have with the right help. We didn't have our A-team. I thought when Terry finally came back and listened to it he'd say: 'Let's take it back down into the studio, clean it up and make it better.' We thought he'd make a good mix and be delighted. But when Terry heard that it got played on the radio he became very angry and uptight. What could you say? 'I'm sorry you didn't like it.'"

The hostility over the recording of 'It's All Over Now, Baby Blue' was the second occasion on which Melcher had cause to cross swords with Dickson. Earlier, there had been some horse trading over publishing rights, with Melcher maintaining that he was in a better position to exploit the group's song catalogue in the marketplace. Dickson was coldly unimpressed. "The first time I wanted to get rid of Terry Melcher was when he gave us the ultimatum that if we didn't turn over the publishing then he wasn't going to produce them any more. I said, 'OK, don't produce them any more!' His stepfather put him up to that. 'Don't produce records and make them hits without the publishing.' It's well enough for a father to say, but it seemed a little inappropriate to me since I'd worked a year with them and Terry had worked a couple of months. But his stepfather was much more powerful than Terry. Marty Melcher was a very powerful man and I expect that if I'd been Terry, I'd have done what my father said too! I didn't fault him for it, but I said that I wasn't going to do it. I certainly wasn't going to turn over the publishing."

What Melcher did not know was that Dickson was already planning to transfer half the publishing to all five Byrds on condition that they completed a second or third album. He was already aware of the growing resentment shown towards Clark and, to a lesser extent, McGuinn, over the question of publishing income. "Michael, Chris and David were very short-suited in the publishing, yet they were very helpful in making the songs hits. It seemed unfair to me to continue to be a 50:50 publisher."

Once the discussion over publishing was resolved, Melcher settled into his role as producer with great aplomb and determination. In many respects, the Byrds could hardly have found a better producer at CBS. Melcher was young, enthusiastic, empathetic and, in his own way, as musically accomplished as any of them. The extant session tapes from the first two albums underline the extent of his contribution, carefully guiding the group through endless takes, singing along on the trickier choruses and ironing out their deficiencies with a confidence and humour that should have won considerable respect.

"When Terry got excited and energized and liked what he was doing, he'd contribute a lot," says Dickson. "When he would get rejected, and sometimes he'd have to be rejected, he'd withdraw. He wanted to sing with them, not just be a producer. As Bruce & Terry he'd sung on records and he wanted to get in the studio and be part of it. To be a producer at Columbia, one of the things you had to be able to do was read and understand music. Terry could play the piano and had musical training. None of the Byrds had that."

Unfortunately, Melcher's standing with the Byrds was always under subtle threat, his obvious credentials notwithstanding. Apparently, it was not enough that he had just produced a number 1 single and a best-selling album. Crosby, for reasons that he could not quite articulate, took a dislike to the son of Doris Day, whose Hollywood upbringing was not so far removed in privilege from his own. It is one of the great ironies of this early phase of Byrds history that Melcher's ultimate fall from grace probably stemmed from a commendable desire to get closer to the group. After 'Mr Tambourine Man' broke and Melcher realized that the Byrds could play pretty well and write good material, he was in a celebratory mood and full of confidence about the future. "Terry brought in a bottle of vodka and orange juice for us," Dickson remembers. "He was trying to become friends with these guys who were remote. He had all the good feelings that this was going to work out and it was more interesting than Paul Revere & The Raiders. He wanted to loosen up the session. He was going to go out on the hook for more studio time and to hell with Allen Stanton, Columbia and their tight schedules. Terry was ready to push it as part of his production budget and get in there and work with the guys. And none of them would take a drink with him. Not even Gene. Drinking was unhip, especially in the folk world . . . I had one drink with Terry, just to be sociable. But Terry had so much to drink that he went to sleep on the couch. We cut several tracks without him, just went right on ahead. He was out of it. But when he woke up, he did all the mixes and sorted through it all . . . But that instilled in David Crosby the idea that we could do it without him. He said, 'We don't need Terry Melcher because, look, he's passed out drunk!' I didn't like it that he was drunk and I eventually used it against him, and I don't feel proud that I did."

Melcher's misdemeanour hardly seemed major and wouldn't have happened at all if the Byrds had accepted his hospitality. Although McGuinn and Clarke became friendly with the producer, with Michael even staying at his house for a brief spell, Crosby remained unimpressed. It might have helped if Terry had been an ardent supporter of Crosby's compositions but he tended to agree with Dickson about their questionable quality.

"There was resistance to me getting stuff on the records," Crosby contends, "probably from Dickson, whom I love and he's a good cat. But he felt it was in the group's interest to do Dylan songs, which was absolutely true, and he loved Gene Clark songs. So it was hard for me to get songs in there . . . I just kept growing and I don't think that sat well with McGuinn. I think he wanted me to stay subservient to him, and Dickson reinforced his position very strongly and wanted it to stay that way too and, I think, wrongly."

Crosby's argument had merit but, at this point, his fascination with the nascent counterculture was uneasily translated into song. Some hints of what was to come could be gleaned from 'Flower Bomb Song' and 'Stranger In A Strange Land', both of which adopted the hippie ethic a full two years before the Summer of Love. Unfortunately, Crosby could get little support for these songs from anybody connected with the group and his attempt to break the Clark/McGuinn songwriting duopoly failed miserably. Regrettably, his groundbreaking experiments, which would have added a new dimension to the Byrds' story, were lost to posterity. In common with Dino Valenti's 'Get Together', the intriguing 'Stranger In A Strange Land' was passed on to Frank Werber's SFO Music. The song was later recorded by San Franciscan duo Blackburn & Snow, with Crosby's writing credit mysteriously altered to a pseudonym, 'Samuel F. Omar'. Even two years on, with the hippie counter-culture at its zenith, the song undeservedly languished in obscurity. "'Stranger In A Strange Land' was a very unsophisticated, childish rendering of that ethic," Crosby confessed to me with undue modesty. "I don't think it was a very good song, but I was greatly influenced by Robert [A.] Heinlein and always loved science fiction."

It spoke volumes about Dickson's reaction to Crosby's early songwriting that he would sell the copyright of one of his songs. "That was the only Byrds' copyright we ever sold. Somebody that David was talking to was supposedly making a movie. We were pretty confident that the song was worthless and that the movie would never be made. David had read the book, and we'd all read it long ago. He set great store in it. It represented a search for his idea of a new lifestyle. Years later, he'd use the 'water brothers' line in his song 'Triad', which also came from *Stranger In A Strange Land*. David's ability to write songs then was only just beginning."

The infamous 'Flower Bomb Song', which boasted an equally memorable melody that promised much, embarrassed the group with its exotic lyrics which spoke of "the love gun that will blow your mind". Although Dickson enjoyed smoking dope with Crosby, he was not about to nail the Byrds to the wall as counter-culture gurus and lambasted the song unmercifully. "Everybody, myself included, felt that 'Flower Bomb' had no business being a song, let alone being part of the Byrds. It was not a song with a verse or a chorus. He was trying to embrace the hippie thing and wasn't too successful. The phrase 'flower child' was popular in LA then, even in the summer of 1965."

Having failed to persuade his comrades to include either of his songs on the new album, Crosby's defeat was completed when his championing of Dino Valenti's 'I Don't Ever Want To Spoil Your Party' was also omitted. Dickson remained staunchly unconvinced of Crosby's merits as a lead vocalist within the Byrds, maintaining that he would be better employed as a harmony singer, a view with which Melcher concurred. Although these decisions were accepted by Crosby initially, his frustrations about playing second fiddle to McGuinn and Clark were never far away. "Suddenly there were insecurities and cracks in the relationship," Derek Taylor reflects. "David was getting awkward and they were getting on each other's nerves. They were too busy arguing and, as a result, they were not singing well."

Frustration was evident in the group's attempt to fashion a new single under pressure from CBS. Since abandoning 'It's All Over Now, Baby Blue', they had again settled on Dylan's 'The Times They Are A-Changin'' as a suitable substitute. When the Beatles had attended their recording session they rushed through an unfinished version, then seemed to lose confidence in themselves and the song. "They could have done it so much better had they recorded it once more, but they gave up on it," Taylor remembers. "They just said, 'We can't!' Dickson was crazy with anger about it because he was a perfectionist in his own way. I'd seen them perform a beautiful version of the song onstage, but in the studio they couldn't get it right."

Columbia pressed thousands of sleeves for 'The Times They Are A-Changin'', only to be told by Dickson that the Byrds were dissatisfied with the recording. Although they agreed to perform the song on *Hullabaloo*, this television opportunity was wasted, as another single was already in the works. The replacement was a song McGuinn had previously arranged for the third Judy Collins album. 'Turn! Turn! Turn! (To Everything There Is A Season)', with lyrics adapted by Pete Seeger from the *Book of Ecclesiastes*, fitted perfectly into the folk-rock idiom when played on a Rickenbacker 12-string guitar. The idea of reviving the song had originally come up on the group's first US tour. Sitting at the back of their bus, McGuinn's girlfriend, and later wife, Dolores, requested the tune, which Jim dutifully played. His expressive reading sounded fresh and distinctive, an inevitable result of his current immersion in folk rock. "It was a standard folk song by that time," McGuinn admits, "but I played it, and it came out rock 'n' roll because that's what I was programmed to do like a computer. I couldn't do it as it was done traditionally. It came out with that samba beat, and we thought it would make a good single. It had everything: a good message, a good melody and the beat was there. It fit right into the commercial formula of the time."

McGuinn had a secondary motive in pushing Seeger's song forward as a single. Years before, on the Judy Collins album, he had been prevented from playing guitar on 'Hey Nelly Nelly' and 'The Bells Of Rhymney' by Jac Holzman, who had elected to employ the more experienced session guitarist, Walter Raim. "The fact that he was replaced for what Jac Holzman thought were two important songs made him very unhappy," Dickson points out. "He talked about it a number of times, and those two songs were 'The Bells Of Rhymney' and 'Turn! Turn! Turn!' [*sic*]. They were important songs because they were Pete Seeger's, so Jac hired somebody more expensive and special. That's why McGuinn did those songs with the Byrds. Part of it was to show Jac Holzman that he could play them. I doubt whether Jac would have even remembered that those were the songs he replaced McGuinn on."

Back at their rehearsal room at 9000 Sunset Boulevard, McGuinn worked on the arrangement with Crosby, who came up with the distinctive off-beat opening and helped construct the chorus. Hillman was quietly impressed, but said little. He had been a fan of Pete Seeger for years but, strangely enough, had never heard the song until McGuinn played it on the tour bus. Clark was happy to go along with the majority rule and Clarke enjoyed the challenge of playing in tune and perfecting that clever 'off-time' beat.

McGuinn's enthusiasm and belief in 'Turn! Turn! Turn!' ensured that it became a recording priority, but there was still uncertainty about its merits as a Byrds' single. In the eyes of some record company executives, and a large proportion of the general public, the group's name was still synonymous with Dylan compositions. They had already invested some effort tinkering with 'The Times They Are A-Changin'' and 'It's All Over Now, Baby Blue' and now they were abandoning Dylan and working on a song that threatened to exceed the three-minute barrier. McGuinn might have expected some support from Jim Dickson, who had already championed their version of Pete Seeger's 'The Bells Of Rhymney' as one of his favourite songs. Instead, he reacted coldly, arguing that 'Turn! Turn! Turn!' was totally inappropriate for the Byrds. Fortunately, McGuinn found the perfect ally in Terry Melcher, who recognized the anthemic power of the tune when translated into folk rock and picketed for its release. "McGuinn and I were the only people who thought it was a good idea," Melcher told me. "Dickson and I disagreed over it. He felt it didn't have hit potential because it was a lyric from the Bible."

Dickson's reservations seemed perplexing. At this point in their career, it would have been inappropriate for the young rebels to record a song like 'The Christian Life', but 'Turn! Turn! Turn!' was hardly a religious song in the psalmodic sense. There was no mention of God in the lyrics and its stoical tone sounded more classical than Christian. The sentiments of the song were essentially philosophic and even included mild political overtones in keeping with the times. Such considerations failed to convince Dickson, who remained dogmatically opposed to the lyrics, even arguing that they were a betrayal of what the Byrds represented: "I thought 'Turn! Turn! Turn!' was an either/or song that didn't fit with the kind of poetry we could get from Dylan, which was light years ahead philosophically. The philosophy that you've got only two alternatives went against everything that I thought we were about. It conflicted with that. It wasn't that it was biblical or that I was uninterested in purveying religion. That hadn't stopped me from doing all kinds of bluegrass songs and other gospel songs, if they were appropriate for the time. McGuinn and Melcher chose to think that I didn't like it because it was from the Bible, but the real reason was that it was philosophically simplistic."

It is difficult to resist the impression that Dickson was so distracted by what he considered the distasteful dualism in the song that he chose to overlook its universal appeal, not merely to the young pop audience but to the more discerning listeners who applauded the Byrds for their sophistication. Within the context of pop music, 'Turn! Turn! Turn!' was far from an intellectual sell-out, but rather another step forward. In an era when the Vietnam War played on the conscience of the American nation, the song's final line, "A time for peace, I swear it's not too late", had a deep resonance. More importantly, the song was the perfect panacea to Barry McGuire's doom-laden 'Eve Of Destruction' and revealed the Byrds pedalling a more positive view of contemporary life by falling back on the age-old cycle of life/death and destruction/renewal. "That's the essence of the song," McGuinn agrees. "There's a time for everything. A time for war and a time for peace. And this is a time of peace, and I believe that's what people picked up on at that point because there was a longing in the world for peace."

While the song's upbeat sentiments, reinforced by McGuinn's joyful Rickenbacker breaks, suggested an optimistic world-view, Dickson could only see the dark side. "It's a laundry list!" he protests. "I don't see it as optimistic at all. Except for the last line, the rest is very pessimistic to me. Especially when it says there's only two answers to everything. It features that concept that it's either a time to reap or sow. It might be a time to go fishing, to care or not care, or to care a little. It says you have to do everything in its time – it's inflexible. The whole problem's Aristotelian. There's an insanity to it in my mind. Read Alfred Korzybski's *Science And Sanity: An Introduction To Non-Aristotelian Systems And General Semantics* [first published, 1933]. One chapter deals with the confusion of orders of abstraction. I don't expect to convince you, and I don't expect to be swayed . . . I went though Korzybski and you can't come away from that and want 'Turn! Turn! Turn!' to be how you identify something. It's like going to the dark ages philosophically. There's a bail out line at the end, 'A time for peace – I swear it's not too late'. That's fine, but that's Pete Seeger's contribution to it, not the biblical part. The intellectual revolution that would turn you against that song happened in the Fifties. I think Dylan, especially at that time, would have understood clearly why I wouldn't want to do it. Everything he wrote avoided that. One of the things that appealed to me was that he never violated that. He created multiple choices that never existed! 'I don't want to fake you out . . . etc' [from 'All I Really Want To Do'] is a simple example of that. Listen to 'Chimes Of Freedom'. What lines it had. That was the ultimate Byrds song to my mind – along with 'Mr Tambourine Man'. 'Chimes Of Freedom' and not 'Turn! Turn! Turn!' is what the Byrds ought to sing . . . I still contend, and I haven't changed my mind, that when you come along with a song which is a bigger success than what you'd done before or may do later, that is who you are to many people. And that's not who I wanted them to be. I'm not likely to be shaken from my point of view, even though I know McGuinn doesn't know what I'm talking about."

Whatever his reservations about the lyrics, even Dickson could not deny the commercial power or musical craftsmanship evident on the track. Fired by a self-belief in the song, Melcher persevered, forcing the group to play take after take until he was satisfied. He later complained to me that he had to spend five days in a studio in order to get the Byrds playing in time to his satisfaction. At least there was no problem choosing a suitable flip-side. George Harrison had already praised Gene Clark's 'She Don't Care About Time', which included a beautiful guitar arrangement of Bach's *Jesu Joy Of Man's Desiring*, which McGuinn had previously played on a banjo album. Clark's composition featured densely packed lines, anticipating his later work, complete with references to hallways, staircases, a white-walled room and a loved one located "on the end of time". Even by his standards this was a fascinating apotheosis in which naturalistic detail and abstraction coalesced. Who else but Clark would write a song combining love and metaphysics? And who else but McGuinn would condense Bach into a Rickenbacker solo?

CHAPTER FOURTEEN

Fracas And Fistfights

EVEN after recording 'Turn! Turn! Turn!' the Byrds found it difficult to complete their second album on time. As the sessions dragged on towards the end of October, CBS feared that the work would not be ready in time for the lucrative Christmas market. Immense pressure bore down on the group, which inevitably produced more tensions in the studio. Dickson was still unconvinced by 'Turn! Turn! Turn!', while Crosby seemed irked that his work had been rejected in favour of Gene Clark's ballads and some older McGuinn adaptations. Tempers frayed, loyalties divided, and the continual arguments created warring factions.

Terry Melcher found himself caught up in the maelstrom. "There was friction between McGuinn and Dickson and it became a sort of McGuinn and Melcher versus Dickson and Crosby situation. I think that McGuinn figured that with me on his side he'd have a greater say in the albums. Gene, Chris and Michael were pretty much neutral at this point. Crosby had probably the biggest ego and he was causing a lot of problems in the studio. In the middle of one session, Crosby became extremely objectionable because Gene had been playing a rhythm guitar. Anyway, Mike was always a fairly passive guy but, shortly after this incident, I remember he left his drums, walked over to Crosby, and smashed him in the mouth. He literally knocked him off his stool and just said: 'I've wanted to do that for a long time.'"

When Crosby recovered his poise, he turned on the drummer and told him in true Hollywood fashion: "You'll never work in this business again!" Clarke escaped further censure thanks to his usual boyish charm and when I questioned him about the incident, he merely said, "I slapped him because he was being an asshole. He wasn't producing. It was necessary." Surprisingly, the violent outburst even received a passing mention in the American teenzine, *16*, albeit several months after the event. "David was punched by drummer Mike Clarke at the session for the album *Turn! Turn! Turn!*" they reported. "Mike said Dave was off the beat." The irony of Clarke supposedly complaining about Crosby's bad timing was priceless, as was the reportedly happy conclusion ("the boys shook hands and made-up").

Fractious outbursts became more frequent as the album neared completion. Although Dickson had been a powerful influence during the recording of *Mr Tambourine Man*, his authority weakened as the Byrds grew more confident in their own abilities. Different factions had clearly emerged, but they lacked any consistent game plan. Sometimes Crosby sided with Dickson, but at other times they would be at loggerheads. McGuinn's cool persona ensured that his allegiance to any one party could not easily be gauged, while Clark was both hero and villain, respected when he wrote a great song and the subject of envy when royalties were distributed. Dickson often needed to assert his will to keep the Byrds focused yet, in doing so, he risked rebellion and retribution. "They all ganged up on Dickson," Melcher recalls. "They felt he'd been bullying them. They were doing some filming on the beach, and suddenly they jumped him."

The 'beach incident' was a pivotal moment in Dickson's relationship with the Byrds and emphasized the extent of their volatility at a time when they should have been concentrating on restoring their status as America's new number 1 group. Money had been received from the BBC to shoot a promotional film for Gene Clark's 'Set You Free This Time'. It was an enormous compliment to the songwriter that his composition had been specifically selected, but the decision did not please everybody. Crosby felt the wrong song had been chosen and betrayed scant enthusiasm for the entire idea. "He was a complete drag about it, no help at all," Dickson says. "He didn't want to be there. I saw it as an opportunity to make a film that far surpassed what they had asked for and also have it for our own use. I wanted to start at the beach and write 'Set You Free This Time' in the sand, getting the title in and letting a wave run over it. Then we were going to pan up and feature Gene all by himself, walking down the beach, this lonely guy. When the harmony came in, the entire band would appear from nowhere and go through the frame. That was the first scene on location."

From the very moment they arrived at the beach, the Byrds were in an unruly mood. Filming commenced, with photographer Barry Feinstein setting up the camera to shoot footage of Clark walking across the sand. In order to align all five members within the correct angle of the lens, the taller Michael Clarke was ordered to move further back. Crosby, realizing that he could have some fun at Clarke's expense, began goading the drummer by telling him that he was being ignored and denigrated. Take after take was wasted as Clarke crept closer to the camera, ensuring that the head shots were out of line. Eventually, a fuming Dickson lost patience and slapped the drummer across the face for wasting time. Michael reacted with the shocked surprise of a boy who had been ritually humiliated into silence. "David was the one who fucked it up, not me," Clarke told me. "He kept saying to me: 'Don't let him do that to you. Get right in front of the camera. We need you.' It's the truth!"

McGuinn watched the proceedings with the fascinated disinterest of a pacifist, whose temperament always ensured that he avoided the violent emotions which overpowered his fellow Byrds. Years later, McGuinn remembered the ensuing fracas with a mixture of incredulity and amusement: "Someone wasn't looking right or something, some dumb thing like that. Then, Michael started to get really uptight, you know, he said: 'This is stupid.' And Dickson said: 'You'd better stay in' and got everyone back in line. So then Crosby just hauled off, let off, and punched Dickson in the mouth. And Dickson said: 'Wow, you loosened my tooth' or some number like that, and he had him down in a stranglehold. Dickson was twice as big as Crosby. This is on the beach, and Gene Clark went and grabbed him off of Crosby . . . and we straightened everything out."

Crosby confirms that he was rescued from a salutary beating after audaciously striking his mentor in the face. "I slugged Jim once," he admits. "Hard! I was mad at him. Fortunately, for me, Barry Feinstein threw me up on the ice plant and helped to restrain him. Dickson could have beaten me to a pulp. Jim's a big man: 250 lb, 6 foot 2 inches."

On reflection, it's fortunate that the filming did not degenerate into a full-scale brawl. Apart from McGuinn and Hillman, everybody there seemed involved in some physical altercation and, if the camera had still been rolling, there might have been footage worthy of a rock 'n' roll Keystone Cops. Dickson's vivid recollections of that fateful afternoon underline the extent of his ambition and the fragility of his relationship with the boys at a still crucial time in their career: "I felt we could make the equivalent of a modern-day video. I'd had strong ideas and training and had gone to school and worked with Barry Feinstein for years to figure out how to cut film to music, and make it work. I figured that sooner or later people would make films good enough to have a show, like a hit parade of them or something. But, for David Crosby, it was the wrong song. It wasn't a matter of choice. The BBC picked the song to do – not us . . . David said, 'This is a bunch of bullshit', then he'd tell Michael, 'You're the best looking one. How long are you going to take being put in the background?' So Michael would come down and walk through at the wrong place. I had to explain it to Michael. He'd say, 'Sure, sure.' Then David would get him down there and say, 'Bullshit, man. Don't listen to him. He's trying to fuck you over.' And he'd do it again. I finally got so exasperated with Michael that I slapped him across the face. It didn't hurt Michael or really upset him a whole lot. But David started to run away up the hill and leave. 'That's it!' He was looking for an excuse to leave. We had a lot more shooting to do that day. That was just the first part of the first verse! We wanted to go to other locations. So I ran after him, and Gene Clark ran after me. He caught me around the neck before I caught David and pulled me backwards. Gene was incredibly strong. He had me by the neck and I couldn't move. David turned around, came back and hit me in the face. Gene, seeing that was unfair, let me go. Then David said: 'Grab him again, Gene, I want to hit him again.'"

Clark faced a moral dilemma in deciding whether to release

Dickson or hold him in thrall. If he failed to loosen his grip, then Crosby would land another blow and cause even more problems by hitting Dickson while he was unable to defend himself. On the other hand, Dickson was so enraged that he was likely to pummel Crosby for ruining the film. Either way, Clark would be blamed by somebody whichever course of action he decided upon. In the end, his conscience was salvaged by a sudden intervention, as Dickson explains: "Barry Feinstein arrived, went up to Gene Clark and wouldn't let him grab me again. Barry was unfamiliar and had enough authority that Gene obeyed him. To Barry, from a distance, it must have looked like one guy was going to hold me while the other beat me up. He wasn't going to allow that to happen. Barry had been a football player and was the guy that stood at the goal posts with his arms out when his team played Notre Dame. He got creamed by 11 Notre Dame players who broke his face for making fun of Jesus. Barry Feinstein was fearless and a lot more gifted at handling himself than any of us. I found it really funny reading your first book that on that day Crosby said I was 6 foot 2 inches and 250 lb. I've never been more than 5 foot 10 inches, an inch or so taller than David. I may weigh 250 lb now but then I wasn't more than 180 lb. David likes to blow things out of proportion. But that wasn't who I was! In order for him to hit me while I was being held by Gene Clark I'd better be a pretty *big* guy. David was 24 years old, he wasn't a child but a full-grown man. I was 34. I was almost too old for that kind of shit. I didn't feel that I had any intrinsic advantage over David Crosby other than that he would be frightened."

What is interesting, however, is that the normally reliable McGuinn also pictured Dickson as "twice as big as Crosby". Listening to the Byrds recall the debacle, it is not merely the all-action sequences that prove revealing, but the almost child-like way they still perceive Dickson's size and power. The incidents as described by McGuinn and Crosby are accurate enough, yet strangely reminiscent of the way adults remember key childhood experiences. Physical objects and charismatic characters somehow become bigger and brighter than they actually were as everyday event is magically transformed into myth.

FRACAS AND FISTFIGHTS

In many ways, the beach saga enshrined the Byrds' myth in microcosm: Crosby's passion and petulance; Clark's moral indecision and uncertainty about his role; Dickson's creative vision, blurred by frustration and anger; McGuinn, coldly observing events and disguising his feelings; Hillman absenting himself from the action; Clarke stumbling into conflicts that he barely understood. With so many disparate personalities and conflicting points of view, it was a miracle that the Byrds ever recorded their second album.

A strange combination of passion and cool fuelled the dynamic at the centre of the Byrds. Crosby's passion collided head-on with McGuinn's reserve to create an inner tension that would never be adequately resolved. The reasoning side of Dickson's mind veered towards McGuinn, but emotionally he was closer to Crosby. "People have stronger feelings about David Crosby. I love David more than the rest and I hate him more than the rest. I love McGuinn the least, and I hate him the least, because he doesn't give you emotional feedback. You don't get a chance. The hate is in equal proportion to how much you love them, how much you hope for them, how much you care for them as people and want them to make it happen and do the right thing."

Passionate ambivalence was the hallmark of Dickson's relationship with Crosby. The fistfights, the bitter comments, the strained affection and the sense of betrayal were all characteristics of a love/hate relationship that embraced dope-smoking camaraderie, musical kinship and the terrible beauty of unleashed rage. For Jim McGuinn, such public displays of emotion were uncomfortable to witness and his only response was to remain aloof and offer the tired adage, "I trust everything will turn out all right". His calculated cool was only partly convincing.

"McGuinn was horrified by the undercurrent of violence in me and Crosby, and later, Hillman," Dickson observes. "He can't deal with that. He's more like Eddie Tickner. With Eddie, when somebody starts to get a little violent, he just freezes. He panics. He can't talk, can't deal with it. He isn't aggressive, nobody is ever aggressive to him. He has no habit of it."

McGuinn disguised his negative feelings about the Byrds at this point but, as Dickson noted, he was shaken by the violent undercurrents. "It was upsetting to me that people were hitting each other in the studio and other places," he admits. "Dickson was a violent man. Crosby and Michael Clarke could be provoked to violence, and even Hillman was violent. Dickson had hit Hillman because of some girl and then Crosby and Michael got into it, and Dickson and Crosby. It was like a jungle in there. I was trying to be positive about it and just keep out of trouble."

McGuinn's passivity was not always appreciated. Dickson often found it difficult to get through to him, especially when attempting to act as go-between. Even Michael Clarke sometimes exploded with sarcastic exasperation and taunted McGuinn with the words, "You're supposed to be the leader. *Lead!*"

Melcher was equally concerned and confused about the fiery politics inside and outside of the recording studio. He had assumed that Dickson and Crosby had formed a pact against him in some way, but he also knew that they were at each other's throats. They posed little threat in a political sense because they were never unified for any length of time. Increasingly, Melcher realized that Dickson's passion for the Byrds would prove his undoing. Unlike Brian Epstein, who dared not attempt to influence the Beatles' music, the Byrds' manager wanted to be part of the creative process and relentlessly pushed his protégés in a specific direction. When they rebelled, in true character, the conflict could be bloody.

"Dickson was becoming too emotional," Melcher observed. "He seemed to see the Byrds as his revenge on the music business. There was so much fighting and arguing, especially between McGuinn and Crosby. Dickson should have been the father figure but he wasn't ready to step up and pacify everyone. He should have kept everybody happy but he did nothing to quell the unrest and, if anything, contributed to it. If Tickner had taken a more active role at this point things might have been different."

For David Crosby, the suggestion that his manager was incapable of playing a role *in loco parentis* was anathema, especially when coming from the mouth of Melcher. "That's pure, unadulterated bullshit," he insists with conviction. "He *was* the father figure to us. He did quell the unrest between us. He did everything he could to keep that band together and to keep us working together. When I

FRACAS AND FISTFIGHTS

would get mad at McGuinn, he would say, 'Listen, now look at it from his point of view . . . understand that he's always going to react to that particular thing, so cool it. Do it this way and it will work. You'll get exactly what you want anyway.' He was a practical man and he was a lot older than any of us and he knew how to make it work. He did exactly that, and it worked very well for all of us."

From Crosby's position, it was Melcher who was stifling their creativity in the studio. Ever since the vodka incident, Crosby had maintained, against considerable evidence to the contrary, that the Byrds could produce themselves. What he really desired was a return to those late nights at World-Pacific when Dickson weaned them through months of tortured rehearsals and helped hone their sound. Reacting to Melcher's criticisms of Dickson, Crosby's view hardened to such an extent that he lashed out against the entire set-up at Columbia. Ignoring most of Melcher's positive points, he could see only his shortcomings as the man who had stepped into the position that Dickson once held. Whatever vision Crosby had of the Byrds was not one to be shared with the young producer. "Melcher's an idiot," Crosby barks impatiently. "He had almost nothing to do with it. He was an obstruction to it. Terry's a nice guy, but he's a dummy. He's not real bright. He didn't know anything about it. He didn't understand what we were trying to do and I don't think he does yet. He was just in the way. He was a hindrance, as was Columbia. What Terry said about us taking sides was somewhat true, but McGuinn wasn't really on Terry Melcher's side. McGuinn thought Terry Melcher was a dummy too. And Terry Melcher was a dummy."

Such an outrageously antagonistic view of Melcher was not shared by McGuinn, nor even Dickson, whom Crosby felt he was defending. Contrary to Crosby's put-down, Melcher was affable, astute, articulate and a guiding force in the studio. The power of Melcher at Columbia had played an important part in bringing the Byrds to fame and Dickson was well aware of his considerable contribution, especially during the recording of 'Mr Tambourine Man'. Crosby's lack of respect for Melcher was no doubt clouded by memories of growing up in Hollywood with other rich young men, whose wealth outstripped their talent and ambition. A sense of rivalry, of knowing a higher purpose and moving in hipper circles, convinced Crosby that he was far removed from the Tinseltown values of Doris Day's son. Crosby liked Peter Fonda and selected members of the young Hollywood elite, but looked down on Melcher, whose background, tastes and world-view were still far closer to his own than those of any member of the Byrds. In different circumstances, they might even have been friends, but it was not to be.

As Dickson says: "Although Terry liked what he could do with David's voice, he didn't like putting up with his bullshit. Nobody was comfortable with that . . . David Crosby's vibe to Terry Melcher was 'You're on another side of the wall of life from me.' He was part of the enemy. I couldn't see Terry that way. He just had a different upbringing. Terry Melcher was the kind of kid that David's mother would have liked David to be: polite, well-mannered, not rude . . . Although certain things about Terry were disappointing, there were others that were very pleasant. I never felt that he had to be exactly like us."

McGuinn agrees that a rift was developing in the group as a result of his close involvement with Melcher, although he saw nothing wrong in fostering that friendship. "I was hanging out with Terry and I could see his point of view more clearly than I saw Crosby's. Basically, Crosby and I were competitors trying to get songs on the album, even though Gene Clark had that sewn up for the first album. Once we got past that, we got our songs on. I wouldn't say I was hanging out with Terry for that reason. I really enjoyed Terry. I thought he was a good producer and a good friend. I liked him a lot. It was a matter of allegiance. Dickson and Crosby had been working together before the Byrds came along and I didn't ever develop a strong relationship with Dickson. He was a sort of father figure, but a stern, disciplinarian father. I liked Crosby, but we weren't great buddies. There was always that competitive edge between us, but Melcher and I hit it off."

In adopting the role of father figure within the Byrds, Dickson also had to show an even-handed concern for the needs of the younger members. Often, it was all too easy to be distracted by the demands of Crosby and McGuinn which, in turn, caused concern to their comrades. Gene Clark was still in the ascendant creatively and needed no prompting to produce a catalogue of songs, including such outtakes and compositions as 'The Day Walk', 'The Emptiness' and 'That's What You Want'. Positive reports from Dylan ("Gene Clark intrigues me more and more") ensured that his confidence was not dented, while a string of girlfriends distracted him romantically. Despite this, it was disconcerting to witness the conflicts within the Byrds and, as the months passed, Clark became more distant from the central action. Michael Clarke, despite occasional flare-ups, also kept out of the politics and concentrated on enjoying himself. The member most likely to be ignored was Chris Hillman, whose shyness could mistakenly be read as easygoing acquiescence.

Since the Catherine James incident, Hillman had successfully avoided any conflict with Dickson, but appearances proved deceptive. There was clearly a lot more to Hillman than the humble bassist whom the pop press called "the quiet one" and the shy guy who seemed to hide away from audiences. "That's what we all saw," Dickson recalls. "I believed it. But I understand that he was suppressing a tremendous amount of stress and anger. Chris Hillman's father committed suicide when he was younger, which I didn't know yet. And there were times when I realized that I was being punished for his father committing suicide. There was a transference happening. Chris didn't start to get surly until after the hit record. He was very quiet, but he wasn't at peace. At Ciro's, he stayed in the background and would say, 'You guys won't let me sing.' They said: 'Come right up and sing.' Nobody ever said, 'We don't want you to sing, don't try it.' Nobody ever stopped him, but he blamed everybody for him not singing. And he'd continue to do it and they'd continue to say, 'Come and do it, double my part, do what you want, write a song.' Nobody ever stopped Chris Hillman but his sense that they would."

Hillman later admitted that he was scared to death during the early days of the Byrds. The only time he recalled singing at Ciro's was a one-off performance of Dylan's 'Maggie's Farm'. His father's suicide, followed by a level of fame undreamed of when he was playing bluegrass music, left him uncertain and noticeably reserved. Dickson, the surrogate father, attempted to boost his confidence, but it was no easy task. "They always encouraged him," Dickson says of the other Byrds. "Nobody picked on Chris Hillman. He imagined it all. Nobody ever tried to make him less. He made himself less. I used to try and build him up and tell him how important the bass was, how I saw it as the foundation, how the sound of the bass and the 12-string made the Byrds' sound unique. The sound that's identifiable doesn't exist. You can change every other part, except the bass and the 12-string. If you've got that sweeping, sustaining bass with the 12-string, people are going to say it's the Byrds. And when somebody else does it, it's Byrds' derivative. That's the signature. It started with the bass and 12-string opening of 'Mr Tambourine Man', and it never left that marriage of sound. I'd say all that, knowing it was a simplification and that there's a hell of a lot more to it, and that the vocals were just as, if not more, important, and the songs were more important. But I tried to boost him, and I didn't do it alone. I cannot think of any occasion in my early period with the Byrds where anybody did anything to try and intimidate, restrict or slow down Chris Hillman."

The Byrds were becoming a classic study of conflicting group dynamics, a powerhouse of petty jealousies, growing resentments and lingering suspicions that would eventually tear them apart. Yet, there was also a calm at the eye of the hurricane, a preternatural cool that they donned to mask their inner feelings. They were at once deeply concerned about the group yet remarkably jaundiced about their fate. Their simultaneous strength and weakness stemmed from their youth and lack of awareness about all that they could achieve. There was nothing self-conscious about the Byrds beyond the affectations of the age. Had they realized the unique quality of their teaming, they might have tried harder to maintain a saner equilibrium, but that would have made them less dangerous and less interesting. Their lack of respect for each other was reminiscent of a family in which caprices are tolerated, harsh words are spoken and relationships continue because that is the accepted order of the world. Outside the Byrds, most of the members led very separate lives. McGuinn and Crosby were the antithesis of Lennon and

McCartney or Jagger and Richards, who fed off each other for mutual benefit and forged deep and lasting relationships. Clark was also a loner creatively, his collaborations with McGuinn and girl-hunting expeditions with Michael Clarke notwithstanding. Despite all these differences, the Byrds were capable of great love and a sense of unity when great music was at stake. As Dickson concludes: "When everyone was contributing equally and they played with one mind and feeling, the Byrds were unbeatable."

As the group completed the sessions for their new album, some felt more than ever that a gap was beginning to emerge between McGuinn and the rest due to his close involvement with Melcher. "The opinion was that Melcher was playing favourites in the group," Tickner observes. "He became fast friends with McGuinn, and was isolating the other members of the group." There was some evidence for this theory, not least Melcher's love of introducing the McGuinns to the social and gastronomic delights of Hollywood. He regularly took them to the Villa Carpi, a favourite haunt of movies stars, situated on 6735 Yucca, a block north of Hollywood Boulevard. The restaurant effectively served as a clubhouse for Frank Sinatra and various members of the Rat Pack. Melcher's standing as Doris Day's son ensured that he was always welcomed.

Melcher had already singled out McGuinn as the most stable member of the Byrds and the one most likely to achieve long-term success. "He liked his music," says Dolores. "He felt more comfortable around him, than he did with the others. [McGuinn] had a way of charming people, as did David Crosby. They seemed more intellectual. [McGuinn's] parents were in public relations and they knew a lot of people and read books. But David didn't respect Terry's judgement. He was a conceited mug know-it-all and had to put his two cents into everything. He just thought, 'Oh, he's Doris Day's son, he doesn't know what he's talking about, and I'm David Crosby, and I know.' I think that's where the conflicts started. Terry really had a wonderful ear. I felt he did a lot for the Byrds, as much as he could have done in his position. But he didn't think David's opinion mattered as much as [McGuinn's]. Of course, David was always a thorn in everyone's side."

Melcher's use of McGuinn as a soloist on the rejected 'It's All

Over Now, Baby Blue' underlined this partisanship. The producer felt that he could circumvent many of the problems if he could win McGuinn's consent and muffle the voices of Dickson and Crosby. It wasn't that big a deal but proved sufficiently sensitive to disturb the delicate balance that kept the Byrds in uneasy equipoise. "I think McGuinn and Terry tried to use each other for mutual benefit," Dickson argues. "And I had no real objection to it. Terry focused on McGuinn, and McGuinn, knowing that [connection] was there, saw that he had an opportunity to go directly to Terry and get his way and leave Jim Dickson and David Crosby and the rest out of the picture. The reason that the other people aren't mentioned is that Gene Clark didn't fight for any point of view. Mike Clarke and Chris Hillman didn't have any opinion about these things. So if I disagreed with something McGuinn and Terry wanted to do, I had only Crosby to enlist. If Crosby disagreed, he had only me to come to. If I disagreed with Crosby and sided with McGuinn, Crosby lost. If Crosby agreed with me against Melcher and McGuinn, there's a good chance they'd win. David and I certainly weren't strong enough to stop a determined McGuinn and Terry."

The funny thing about Crosby was that it wasn't these convoluted arguments over musical direction that caused his next minor flare-up, but an objection based on something far more trivial and pettily materialistic. In spite of their folk origins, the Byrds had no aversion to material wealth. Already, Crosby was telling journalists of his ambition to own a yacht. At this stage, money from the hit singles and first album was only beginning to meander through to them and they were still living fairly modestly, although that would soon change. The American obsession with cars would presently dominate their thoughts, causing amusing exchanges and crazy demands. Initially, Crosby preferred to roar down Sunset Boulevard on a motorbike loaned to him by actor friend Peter Fonda. With his green suede cape blowing in the wind and a bulbous crash helmet on his head, Crosby resembled a Californian hippie Arab and briefly acquired the nickname Lawrence of Laurel Canyon. For Fonda, Crosby was the best mannered and most generous of the Byrds, but he was also the most acquisitive and demanding.

McGuinn was living more modestly than his partner, with no

great material advantage to cause envy. The major problem in that area was Gene Clark, whose publishing money would soon transform his life. Jim McGuinn was still adapting to LA and, for a time, was without transport. He had hired a car, but it broke down on the freeway and was repossessed, leaving him financially embarrassed. On a couple of occasions, he had even suffered the indignity of travelling to rehearsals on the city bus, an ordeal made worse by the catcalls he received for sporting Beatle-styled hair. Terry Melcher was amused by McGuinn's car troubles and made another of those magnanimous gestures that backfired. Having failed to win over the Byrds with vodka, he now attempted to impress McGuinn with a convertible.

"Terry was trying to bridge the gap," Dickson recalls, "certainly more than they were trying to bridge the gap with him. He was destined to fail, but since McGuinn is quiet like he is, you don't know you're failing. Terry would loan him a Cadillac, and that made the group very jealous and very uptight. It was the same when Gene bought the Ferrari, everybody got uptight with Gene. 'He's got it, and I don't!' . . . McGuinn got tight with Terry Melcher and was out there driving around in a Cadillac and David Crosby is still a pedestrian!"

Although Melcher was probably just trying to be friendly, there was some suspicion that he might attempt to woo McGuinn away from the group and employ his musicianship exclusively to save time. This had less impact on the Byrds than the more visible evidence of a Cadillac for his exclusive use. As the group prepared for their second nationwide bus tour, Crosby offered his management an ultimatum. Dickson recalls his protégé waltzing into the office and saying, "If I don't have a Bentley when I come back from this tour you're through and all this is over." The comment was typical of Crosby at this time and was never acted upon or mentioned again. "He's fond of making threats like that," Dickson adds. "He later got most of his drug money that way."

With the new album completed, Columbia commissioned photographer Guy Webster to take a moody portrait shot of the group against a blue backdrop. Publicist Derek Taylor had the inspired idea of composing some liner notes with a difference, in keeping with Webster's illustration. Instead of the usual fawning prose, he produced a demythologizing fly on the wall analysis of the album sessions, complete with some painfully revealing insights into the Byrds at their most unattractive. The results were remarkable and completely unprecedented in 1965. Jim Dickson approved the copy, as did Terry Melcher, but the executives at Columbia, notably Allen Stanton, were so shocked that they demanded a complete rewrite. Taylor received a terse message complaining that the notes were "unsuitable and appear to be anti-Byrd." Given the content, he could hardly have been surprised. As he said at the time: "Really, Columbia was quite right. The notes were fairly eccentric and might – to young minds – appear to be anti-Byrd. In fact, I like the Byrds very much and they respond magnificently to rudeness. I respect Columbia's opinion and the rewriting was a pleasant exercise. What I was attempting to do was to skirt the clichés and nonsense of showbusiness and, at the same time, entertain anyone with an odd turn of mind."

It speaks volumes for the coolness of the individual Byrds that they made no attempt to censor Taylor's sleevenotes or even comment on the contents. Perhaps they never saw them. As a commentary on the group at the peak of their success the notes are priceless and testify to the complex group dynamics that were already threatening their stability. Inevitably, Taylor's first target was the ever controversial David Crosby. "He wears a green and brown suede cloak – who doesn't? – and if there is a more impossible human being than this man then I'd be interested to meet him. He was struck across the face during a recording session the other day. 'I'll get you for that,' he told his attacker, the drummer Mike Clarke. He didn't get him at all. What he did do was sulk for a week and ruin every recording session. When Jim Dickson asked him to behave himself, he said, '*You* didn't get two *Help!* albums sent to you personally by George Harrison of the Beatles,' which was true enough, if irrelevant."

Taylor was even more forthcoming about Gene Clark and threatened to make public the hounding of the tambourine man. "Jim McGuinn is the leader and boy, has *he* an ego! Gene Clark, who meanders across the stage banging a tambourine, well he used to play guitar but McGuinn and Crosby soon fixed that. They nipped at his confidence so that now with a guitar he looks like a spastic carrying an anvil. His answer was to write more songs than Crosby and McGuinn and they met this bleak challenge by letting time run out on the sessions so that only three Gene Clark songs made the album. Gene should worry. He's making more bread than all the rest of the Byrds heaped together."

Even Taylor at his satirical darkest was hard pushed to find too much to complain about Hillman and Clarke, but he still managed to throw in a few unexpected barbs. "Hillman is a bluegrass man and he's fed up with the whole rock scene, except that he enjoys being told that he's become the best mandolin player to play bass, which he probably is. The competition's negligible anyway so there's nothing for Hillman to get so big-time about. Or Mike Clarke for that matter. He's got a nice smile. So had Hitler." It says much for Taylor that when he was ordered back to the drawing board by Columbia, he emerged with a new set of sleevenotes that were positive and uplifting, yet still managed to sneak in a reference to "a dozen fistfights and great mouthfuls of awful abuse". Nor were the dramas anywhere near over.

CHAPTER FIFTEEN

Turn! Turn! Turn!

DURING November 1965, the Byrds were shuttled off on an arduous bus tour – Dick Clark's Caravan Of Stars – accompanied by We Five, Paul Revere & The Raiders, Bo Diddley and his cat-suited guitarist, the Duchess. The Byrds had little in common with the other acts, Diddley excepted, and seemed to live in their own stoned world aboard a rented mobile home. To soundtrack the tour, McGuinn taped a couple of Crosby's favourite John Coltrane albums, *Impressions* and *Africa/Brass*, plus a selection of material from Ravi Shankar. For the next few weeks, the group force-fed themselves Coltrane and Shankar with no escape. "I had a physical response to that Coltrane album the first time I heard it," says McGuinn. "It felt like a white hot poker searing through my chest. It cut deep into me and it was a little painful. But I loved it. It opened up some areas in my heart and head that I hadn't known about. What I loved about *Africa/Brass* was the improvisation, of course, but his attitude came through: a forceful, rebellious attitude, like rock 'n' roll. It really knocked me out." At one point, their bus stopped at a railroad crossing and a train whizzed by carrying coal. "It's a coal train!", punned Crosby, as the jazz saxophonist blared in the background. The combined influences of Coltrane and Shankar would soon transform the sound of the Byrds in as radical a fashion as anyone could imagine.

While the Byrds were touring America, their third single, 'Turn! Turn! Turn!' was rapidly climbing the charts. Once again, a white label copy of the single received radio airplay and this time the reaction was favourable, in spite of some departmental rivalry unwittingly caused by Taylor. "I slipped the single to KRLA and got into trouble with CBS," he told me. "Their promotions man said, 'I'll bury that bloody record', but he couldn't and it made number 1."

When the single replaced the Supremes' 'I Hear A Symphony' at the top on 30 November 1965, the Byrds could once again lay claim to the title of America's top group. Suddenly, Sonny & Cher and Barry McGuire seemed a long way in the past. Within the space of six months, the group had registered two number 1 hits and were perfectly placed for a long-term career that should have made them all millionaires and established their supremacy at the cutting edge of American rock for the remainder of the decade. Despite selling a million copies in the US, 'Turn! Turn! Turn!' faced stiffer competition in the traditionally competitive UK seasonal singles market and peaked at a disappointing number 28 in the *NME*, a fact that caused George Harrison to comment, "I felt sorry for the people who didn't buy it."

During the same week that 'Turn! Turn! Turn!' reached number 1 in America, the Beatles released their new album *Rubber Soul*. The Byrds received an advance copy, accompanied by a letter from Harrison to Derek Taylor, which read: "Tell Jim [McGuinn] and David [Crosby] that 'If I Needed Someone' is the riff from 'The Bells Of Rhymney' and the drumming from 'She Don't Care About Time', or my impression of it." It was immensely flattering to the Byrds that Harrison had paid so much attention to their work. Memories of those stoned discussions between the groups back in Benedict Canyon during the summer could also be heard on the raga-influenced 'Norwegian Wood'. Like the Byrds, the Beatles borrowed freely from different musical traditions and after Crosby had introduced Harrison to Shankar, the Liverpudlian wasted no time in incorporating the sitar into the group's repertoire. The folk-rock boom had signalled the possibility of a new literary awareness in pop and both groups were at pivotal moments in their careers, uneasily attempting the transition from uncomplicated teen idols to rock gurus.

One week after *Rubber Soul* was issued, Columbia rush released *Turn! Turn! Turn!* in the USA, just in time to capture the Christmas market. The cover of the album showed the group sitting for their portrait photograph with serious, blank expressions, the epitome of 1965 cool. Structurally, the album was similar to its predecessor and served as a perfect companion piece. McGuinn later noted, with some precision, that the second side could have been a bit stronger, but few noticed that in the mid-Sixties when the general standard of pop albums was low. The high quality of the majority of the tracks made the work seem like a significant step forward for the group, prompting Derek Taylor's effusive and memorable opening liner notes: "Didn't our grannies wag their wise and withered heads and tell us that good things are worth waiting for. This album was as long in the making as a President. But, as Jim McGuinn trusted it would, everything's worked out all right. Personally, I think it's a beautiful piece of work, and maybe the Byrds were right to linger over it. After all, a great record album is to the 1960s what a piece of sculpture is to the Middle Ages. Isn't it?"

The opening 'Turn! Turn! Turn!' was a highly sculpted recording. According to legend, it took between 50 and 78 takes to complete. Crosby believed it was a significant progression from their earlier work. "We thought that it was better, it sounded more real. It had gone from being the commercial meat-grinder process to a wholly organic thing that we were doing ourselves. McGuinn did the arrangement and I thought up that opening lick." Unlike Dickson, Crosby had no problems with the song's lyrics or its implicit message. "It's so unassuming and so unpretentious and so clear. It's really a wonderful piece of poetry and it just translated into our thing. It hit our chemistry perfectly. It made a great record for our kind of music. And when we did it live everybody loved it. It was a natural for us. I think it's mostly because of the poetry. The music was excellent too, but as a piece of poetry, it was just perfect."

Although 'Turn! Turn! Turn!' was not quite as big a hit internationally as 'Mr Tambourine Man', it still made quite an impact around the world. "I heard that in Catholic schools the nuns were using it in classes," McGuinn says. "In South Africa, they banned it because it came from the Bible. They're so reactionary and strait-laced, and yet hypocritical, that they couldn't justify a religious song being done by a rock 'n' roll group, which is connected with dope and sin and sex . . . they thought it was blasphemous for us to do it."

Following the excellence of 'Turn! Turn! Turn!' was a revival of the Beefeaters' 'Don't Be Long', retitled 'It Won't Be Wrong'. It came as a surprise when McGuinn suggested the song, as most of the compositions from the pre-Columbia days were now regarded as ancient history. A further complication was that Jac Holzman owned half the publishing on the Beefeaters' tracks and might even block its release unless the terms were right. Dickson decided to gamble on the publishing money by approaching Holzman with a tantalizing offer: "You take everything on one side of the Beefeaters' single, and I'll take everything on the other side." Holzman, still unaware of McGuinn's intention to re-record 'Don't Be Long', agreed. "Jac chose and I had my fingers crossed behind my back," Dickson remembers. "He chose the one I thought he would, 'Please Let Me Love You', which we would never have recorded again. It was too ersatz Beatles. We'd given up on that British accent thing. That had disappeared along the way."

The difference in quality between 'Don't Be Long' and 'It Won't Be Wrong' was startling. Gone was the lacklustre Beefeaters' effort, replaced by the driving beat of a Byrds rock classic, complete with strident guitars and improved harmonies that transformed the song's sentiments from an ineffectual statement to a passionate plea. "We were all satisfied with 'It Won't Be Wrong'," says Terry Melcher, echoing the favourable impressions of the Byrds to the revamped version. "The production was really tight."

The most astonishing song on the album was surely Gene Clark's 'Set You Free This Time', which was undoubtedly the Byrds' finest lyric to date. Having already established himself as the master of the torch ballad, Clark found fresh inspiration with this densely worded lyric, clearly influenced by Bob Dylan. There was a strangely stoical, almost contemplative air about the composition in which Clark somehow manages to convey a sense of bitterness and veiled vengeance, couched in courtly love magnanimity. It opens with a stark acknowledgement of his newly beloved's intellectual and emotional superiority, reinforced by a conviction that she is sure to make a fool of him in time. His own inadequacies are alluded to via her conviction that he has nothing that can challenge or "go beyond" her own intellect. These convoluted thoughts arguably reveal more about the narrator's state of mind and self-image than the girl's supposed coldness. Although she is ultimately reduced to a pathetic figure, pleading "please be kind", the emphasis remains on his own existential hurt, with flashbacks of previous relationships and memories that tear away at his mind. It is a lovingly created composition of self-deception and self-realization. At times it evokes the emotional selfishness of adolescence, cleverly disguised and exonerated by an analytical tone and wordiness designed to suggest a clinical impartiality. The vocal is tender and humble, yet the subtext is quiet vengeance. Even the song's title presents rejection as if it were an act of kindness. The composition was originally written during the British tour, following a late-night drinking session with Paul McCartney and various members of the Animals at London's Scotch of St James. Gene remembered what happened next: "When I reached my room, I got out my acoustic guitar and started picking out a tune. In a couple of hours I was finished, literally! I slept for a full 12 hours after that."

While 'Set You Free This Time' should have established Clark as a singer-songwriter of distinction, it was largely ignored, particularly by the other Byrds. Recalling the session, which admittedly involved many takes, Melcher claims: "The Byrds left the studio before Gene had even completed the vocals. Gene was always very tolerant, but I remember him being a little upset about their attitude. There seemed to be an element of resentment on the part of the other Byrds because he was making the most money as the main songwriter in the group."

'Lay Down Your Weary Tune' was the first of two Dylan songs on the album. While other groups tackled Dylan's sparkier, pop-orientated material, the Byrds were never afraid to interpret his more abstract work, this time settling on an inspired outtake from his 1963 album, *The Times They Are A-Changin'*. The song had a hymnal quality and striking lyrics that aligned allusions to the forces of nature with the sound of particular musical instruments. As Dylan scholar Michael Gray perceptively wrote: "Never before or since has Dylan created a pantheistic vision – a vision of the world, that is, in which nature appears not as a manifestation of God but as containing God within its every aspect. Underlying an exhilaration so intense as to be saddening, there is a profound composure in the face of a world in which all elements of beauty are infused with the light of God."

McGuinn retained three of the five verses for the Byrds' version, while Gene Clark later borrowed some key lines in the chorus to compose his own cosmological anthem, 'Strength Of Strings'. Within the Byrds' circle the ambitious attempt to capture the incantatory quality of 'Lay Down Your Weary Tune' produced conflicting responses. Melcher admitted that "the production was lousy" and felt the final recording was "sloppy from start to finish". Dickson, who claims to have recommended the song, was equally disappointed. "They didn't do it as well as they could have done. They should have left it off and tried again later. I loved the song. I just didn't like the way they did it. It was monotonous and didn't bring its message across. The lyrics didn't come across in the music."

Part of the problem was that there was no time in the three-and-a-half minute format to include a distinctive Rickenbacker solo, which would surely have enlivened the track. McGuinn enunciated the words clearly but mechanically, and there was a lack of animation in the arrangement which a guitar break would surely have mended. Nevertheless, the decision to tackle an obscure Dylan composition with some conviction won the approval of the master. Given Dylan's well-documented appreciation of 'Mr Tambourine Man', his latest broadcast to McGuinn sounded strangely contradictory. "It was 'Lay Down Your Weary Tune' that finally convinced Dylan that we were really something. I was at this apartment in New York and he came up to me and said: 'Up until I heard this I thought you were just another imitator and didn't like what you were doing. But this has got real feeling to it.' That was the first time he'd realized that I could do something different with his material."

'He Was A Friend Of Mine' had been performed by many folk singers, including Bob Dylan, who recorded his version in 1962. Jim McGuinn provided a contemporary slant to the tune one year later when the world was shocked by the slaying of JFK. Like all good tribute songs, this one succeeded precisely because it was so delicately understated. The sparse backing complements perfectly McGuinn's personal statement: "I wrote that song the night John F. Kennedy was assassinated (22 November 1963). I suppose you could say it's one of the earliest Byrds songs. The arrangement used for *Turn! Turn! Turn!* was as I'd always sung it. I just thought it was a good idea to include it on the album."

David Crosby was less than pleased with one aspect of the production: "Remember that organ note that goes all the way through it that seems very out of place? Terry put it on after we finished the song without even asking us, and mixed it that way. And the tambourine... I could have popped him in the lip for that."

'The World Turns All Around Her', which opens the second half of the album, was a textbook example of how a plaintive love song could be combined with a rock beat in such a fashion that the lyrical impact is not negated but reinforced. This composition was a return to Gene Clark's tortured songs of teen romance, complete with the moral of understanding through loss. There is an acknowledgement of the mystery of love and the tortured realization that abandoning a partner in a moment of doubt may rebound upon the perpetrator ("Now, whenever I see her with you, I realize how much I didn't know"). Romantic envy is couched in noble rhetoric towards the end, while the final line (". . . if you should set her free") sounds like a link to 'Set You Free This Time'. In many ways this was the consummate Clark composition of apotheosis and longing, loss and envy, culminating in an almost neurotic romanticism. The harmonies are among the best on the album and although the instrumental work could have been tighter in places, Clark was clearly satisfied with the finished take. "I liked the song very much," he told me. "I thought the fast, electric treatment worked out OK."

'Satisfied Mind', a country standard made famous by Porter Wagoner, was recorded by the Byrds at the suggestion of Chris Hillman. Although he was familiar with Wagoner's 1955 version, it was Hamilton Camp's revival on the 1964 Dickson-produced *Paths Of Victory* that inspired this surprise cover. Composed by Jack Rhodes and Red Hayes, the song's anti-materialist sentiments made it popular as a contemporary hymn, just like 'Turn! Turn! Turn!'. "The song came from my mother," Red Hayes remembers. "Everything in the song are things I heard from her over the years. I put a lot of thought into it before I came up with the title. One day, my father-in-law asked me who I thought the richest man in the world was, and I mentioned some names. He said, 'You're wrong, it is the man with a satisfied mind.' [The song] has been done a lot in churches. I came out of the [Grand Ole] Opry one night and a church service was going on nearby. The first thing I heard was the congregation singing 'Satisfied Mind'. I got down on my knees."

Dickson was enthusiastic about reviving Camp's version of 'Satisfied Mind' in the Byrds' style, but less convinced by the results. "It's a great song, which I've always loved, but they did a bad job. Once they did it and heard it they should have left it off . . ." As the earliest example of the Byrds' excursion into country music, the song was interesting, but hardly riveting. It might have proven an excellent opportunity for Hillman to advance his cause as a vocalist, but with competition from Clark, Crosby and McGuinn, that prospect was probably too intimidating. "All he did was grumble about his small role in it," says Dickson. "But he never offered an alternative. What did he expect us to do? He said: 'You won't let me sing.' Every single person said, 'Sing!' The answer was 'Nah, man.' He wouldn't do it. He'd bitch about it and then he wouldn't do it."

'If You're Gone' was another of Clark's lyrical admissions of emotional insecurity, albeit without the melodic uplift of his finest work. Like a singer-songwriter reincarnation of Rudyard Kipling, he frames the entire composition around the theme of 'If'. It was already evident to the other Byrds that Clark's complicated love life played a key part in inspiring his muse. "David Crosby was very aware of that," says Dickson. "He would kind of promote it and say, 'Well, as soon as he breaks up with her we'll get another song' and stuff like that." Probably the most interesting aspect of 'If You're Gone' was the unusual harmonic blend, which Melcher credits to McGuinn. "He had this good idea for using a fifth harmony to create a droning effect, like that of a bagpipe or drum. On the album it really does sound like another instrument."

Indeed, the drone effect adds depth to the composition, accentuating the mournful tone. Instead of the expected uplift of a 'la la' backing, McGuinn offers the funereal keening of a tragic folk song to tease out the bleaker aspects of Clark's grim meditation.

'The Times They Are A-Changin'', once considered a single, ended up sounding so contrived that it was almost sardonic. McGuinn tries desperately to sound full of spunky venom, while Clarke's deliberately ostentatious drum rolls and clashing cymbals create a curious dichotomy. An earlier version of the song, which they also played in concert and on television, was much more convincing. "We were going to do a great version of that," Dickson remembers. "It seemed to me that it was such a significant Dylan song that they shouldn't bypass it. It was an anthem for the time, even though it was an older Dylan song." The track would probably have been a mistake as a single, mainly because Dylan's own version had been issued in that format earlier in 1965 and was already familiar to the pop audience internationally. While it was sensible to cover Dylan's album tracks, adapting his singles was far riskier. CBS England subsequently compromised by issuing 'The Times They Are A-Changin'' as the lead track of an EP, which enjoyed modest success.

'Wait And See' was the first Byrds song credited to McGuinn/Crosby, although they had previously combined forces for the then unreleased 'The Airport Song'. It is difficult to decide to what extent this new Crosby/McGuinn collaboration was included for aesthetic reasons, rather than simply to break Clark's songwriting monopoly. Eddie Tickner recalls that "Crosby and McGuinn wanted to move away from the simple boy/girl songs." Ironically, 'Wait And See' was far more a "simple boy/girl song" than any of Clark's new material. It was almost as if McGuinn and Crosby had consciously constructed a composition based on World-Pacific period Gene Clark. They managed to capture the romantic innocence but none of the emotional complexity that characterized Clark's tortured love songs. 'Wait And See', catchy and instantly acceptable to the Byrds' young teen audience, was nevertheless a step backwards to the pre-'Mr Tambourine Man' period. It was largely salvaged by an exuberant backing track that deserved better lyrics. Considering the times and the marketplace, its inclusion made sense, but also testified to a lack of adventure or, more likely, an obstinate adherence to what constituted a 'Byrds song'. Crosby later wiped the composition from his memory banks and, when interviewed, could not even remember the title, let alone his role as a collaborator. The song was a calculated compromise on an album that had already deemed Crosby's 'Stranger In A Strange Land' pretentiously hip and Clark's 'The Day Walk' lyrically abstruse and over imitative of Dylan. That the latter would have made far better choices is easy wisdom after the event and fails to appreciate the artistic confines forced upon performers producing album tracks in the golden age of the pop single.

The rocked-up 'Oh! Susannah' closes the album on a humorous and inventive note. McGuinn hijacked Stephen Foster's nineteenth-century minstrel tune and attempted to transform it into pure Byrds by the simple expedient of replacing a banjo with an electric Rickenbacker, speeding up the tempo and singing in a distinctive world-weary drawl. Clarke was given leave to resurrect his bizarre military-style drumming which suited this traditional standard. It was never a song that was likely to be featured on a Byrds anthology, but worked well in its day when albums were applauded as much for variety as artistic merit. Dickson still reckons McGuinn unwittingly cajoled Melcher into accepting the song: "Terry was too intimidated and felt that it was something hip that he didn't understand. There was maybe some hip humour in there. I didn't think it was appropriate for the Byrds. It wasn't my idea of humour . . . I'd once wanted to do Count Basie and Ray Charles performing the Stephen Foster songbook. In fact, the first person I wanted to do it with was Miles Davis. I thought that would have been an extraordinarily funny irony, almost like a Lenny Bruce comment on racism. A great idea. You try and puzzle people to figure it out and ask: 'What does he mean by that?' You'd get a lot of press out of it. It's only speculation, but I think McGuinn heard my comment about the Stephen Foster songbook and accepted there was some humour there, not realizing that it wasn't appropriate for him. You had to have a black musician of stature. McGuinn was pushing for 'Oh! Susannah' but nobody knew how to stop it. Terry was trying to be positive because we'd already punished him for not being positive. I guess Terry hoped I'd put up a fight. Maybe it was all right, he wasn't sure. I don't think anybody felt confident about it, Michael least of all. I remember him sitting there playing on it and saying, 'Are you sure we want to do this?'" Once assured, Clarke came up with that endearingly playful percussive accompaniment, employing the regimental style previously used on 'Mr Tambourine Man' during the World-Pacific period.

Although McGuinn had pushed for 'Oh! Susannah' he was also retrospectively critical: "I'm not too happy with the last four cuts of that album. I'm sorry about 'Oh! Susannah'. That was a joke, but it didn't come off, it was poorly told. It was a private joke between Dylan and I, actually. I was riffing with this song – we were trying to rock anything and Stephen Foster was a funny thing to rock with. Dylan said, 'Yeah, you've got to do that on your next album, right?' . . . He didn't think I had the guts to do it . . . We could have done it much better. If we had, it would have been funny." McGuinn never fully explained the joke and has since forgotten the punchline, but the idea of transposing a Foster minstrel song like 'Oh! Susannah', 'Campdown Racetrack' or 'My Old Kentucky Home' into the sardonic, cutting edge world of folk rock was a novel conceit that appealed to Dylan's sense of humour. He later embraced the minstrel era as an inspirational source for part of his great 2001 album, *Love & Theft*. Whatever its shortcomings, 'Oh! Susannah' served its purpose by continuing the tradition of ending Byrds albums on a wry and unexpected note.

Within a month of the release of *Turn! Turn! Turn!* Terry Melcher returned from a trip to England, only to be informed that he was no longer the Byrds' producer. It seemed a remarkable decision in view of the album's success and the fact that the single had topped the charts for three weeks. At a point when the Byrds needed the clout of CBS to exploit their latest good fortune, they were risking a great deal by crossing Melcher. The circumstances of his dismissal were far from clear-cut, but there was a degree of Machiavellian expediency, not least in dragging up the innocuous 'vodka incident' from months before as an excuse. Dickson performed the execution with uncharacteristic ruthlessness.

"When the Byrds wrote me a letter from the road saying, 'Get rid of Terry Melcher', I had to go to New York to get him fired. He had a good record in the eyes of CBS. They said, 'You guys are doing well together.' I showed them the letter, told them what had happened and I mentioned that he'd gotten drunk and fallen asleep, and I may not have mentioned his good intentions. It was my job to get him fired. There was no replacement in mind."

It seems remarkable that Melcher should be dismissed for something that happened during the sessions for the first album, and even more strange that all five Byrds concurred with the decision. McGuinn, who signed Melcher's death warrant along with the rest, maintains that the sacking was a political manoeuvre: "Jim Dickson believed that if he got rid of Melcher then he would be the one to produce us. He didn't realize that CBS would stick another of their producers on us. It was Jim Dickson's political ambitions. Melcher was doing a fine job though. Dickson convinced everybody that Melcher was a fuck-up, getting drunk on the set and all that stuff. He made us all believe that he could do a better job . . . But if you listen to the things he did with us, they weren't as good as what Melcher did. Melcher had a really good ear for what we did best. Maybe I'm subjective about that because what Melcher would focus on were my guitar and vocals and that was what Crosby wanted to get away from. He wanted more air space for his work."

When faced with the accusations of inebriation, Melcher was understandably dismissive of their credence, and pointed to other factors: "Getting drunk on the set? That's funny, especially when you consider that they were all high. No, the real problem on the set was that 'Turn! Turn! Turn!' was number 1. My theory has always been that Dickson was embarrassed because he made such a great point about 'Turn! Turn! Turn!' being such a blatant error on my part."

Dickson's lingering antipathy to 'Turn! Turn! Turn!' may have been a factor, but co-manager Eddie Tickner felt that Melcher probably misconstrued his partner's reasoning: "It wasn't so much that Dickson didn't want to put it out. He wasn't opposed to the 'Turn! Turn! Turn!' release as much as the timing. He felt that something was needed before it. Dickson felt that 'Turn! Turn!

Turn!' was too good to put out then. He said that if it was released at that point then they would never get another number 1 – and they never did."

Indeed, Dickson had already taken McGuinn to one side and given him that stark prediction. "I told him that he'd never have another number 1 because he was going to lose the intelligentsia that had given us gratuitous praise. It wouldn't hurt us in *Tiger Beat* or with the teenyboppers, but I felt we were going to lose that Carl Sandburg world that had made such a difference to how the Byrds were looked at."

There is no doubt that Dickson lost ground in influencing the musical direction of the Byrds during the sessions for the second album when he was effectively banned from the studio. David Crosby clearly felt that his mentor would be in a stronger position without Melcher's involvement, and Dickson probably assumed the same. In this sense, Melcher was a victim of his own success. Politics loomed large in this scenario and, as Tickner quite rightly reminds us, Dickson's original ambitions for his protégés extended far beyond a chart-topping single: "Dickson's vision of the Byrds was beyond Terry Melcher's imagination. There are people who have such a strong vision, such an intense vision and sense of direction that nobody else's voice can be heard. Dickson found it difficult to compromise when something interfered with that vision."

With hindsight, Dickson concurs with this personality reading, admitting that his autocratic concept of the Byrds could never easily be translated to a third party. "Good or bad I was probably guilty of that. I knew what I wanted the Byrds to be and I was as inflexible as I could get away with being. I compromised when I felt I had to, and I did it reluctantly. I felt sincerely that I was a better judge of material than anybody else available for those purposes. I wasn't prepared to say: 'David Crosby is a better judge of material for what he wants to do.' If those directions weren't left to me they'd break down the team and send a message of who the Byrds were that wasn't what I thought would be pertinent to the future."

Although Dickson was not always in agreement with Melcher over material or direction, he was never at loggerheads with the producer and understood the depth of his contribution, from 'Mr Tambourine Man' onwards. While Crosby hoped that Melcher's departure might pave the way for Dickson to take over the producer's chair, union rules made the dream impossible. "It must have been the biggest frustration of his whole life," Crosby stresses. "He could mix that stuff ten times as well as they could. He could hear the music really well. He knew what we were trying to do. He knew how to structure it, and he knew how to get it out of us."

Dickson plays down those political ambitions, maintaining that he never deluded himself about replacing Terry Melcher, irrespective of the claims of McGuinn and Crosby. "I couldn't produce at CBS. The fact was you had to be a musician or a Columbia employee. They only used in-house producers, so when I signed them to Columbia I never felt that I would be able to produce. Allen Stanton, when he got Terry, suggested that he take his lead from me. I could work on all the sessions, but I couldn't produce. Once Terry cut 'Mr Tambourine Man' and did such a great job I didn't feel any real need to be the producer."

The removal of Melcher meant that McGuinn had lost an important ally and threatened to tilt the balance of power in Crosby's favour. It says much for McGuinn's self-confidence, but less about his personal courage, that he agreed to Melcher's sacking, seemingly without resistance. With the Byrds' hit sound so closely connected with his voice and guitar, McGuinn knew that he had established a powerful position for himself and would not easily be dislodged. Others in the Byrds' camp had come to the same conclusion. "McGuinn was a most unlikely case to look at," Derek Taylor reflects, "and that voice was not an ordinary rock 'n' roll voice. He had a kind of sexuality because people followed him, but it was not an obvious one. Crosby was very much more upfront with the cape and everything and in his determination to amount to something, rooted, I'm sure, in his childhood, where he'd been much belittled. Through all of that, I felt McGuinn would be the one to carry it, if he so chose and it got that nasty."

Taylor was indiscreet and drunk enough to voice those feelings during an evening at Phil Spector's house following the Byrds' appearance on the *The Big TNT Show*. Sitting around a long table, with Spector, Dickson and Joan Baez, Taylor, drink in hand, turned to McGuinn and told him his future. "I was being outrageously tactless," Taylor recalls. "I began quoting from the prayer book [*Book Of Common Prayer*], as is my wont, and said, 'All things end in corruption and decay and moths and dust and tears, and when it all has gone, as I fear it will, that voice, that chord, that 12-string, that personality and that iron will shall result in you taking on the Byrds as your own.' I thought it was obvious."

Somebody laughed and cried "It's sedition!", but Taylor's words had a haunting ring. Not long afterwards, Dickson also came to realize the strength of McGuinn's steely resolve and marvelled at his power in assuming leadership of the Byrds through a passive force of will, so different from the passion exhibited by himself and Crosby. "As remarkable as McGuinn would be, I didn't find myself having deep feelings about him . . . I don't remember ever being really angry with McGuinn and if he was angry with me, then I was never able to see it. We had some differences of opinion and the way he explained it at the time was that 'You had the ball, I got in a position to take the ball, I took it, isn't that the name of the game?' I didn't have an answer to that. It was his rite of passage."

With all the emphasis on powerplays featuring Melcher and Dickson or McGuinn and Crosby, it was easy to forget the dilemmas facing the group's other creative presence, Gene Clark. More than any other member, his life had been transformed by a combination of sudden fame and songwriting income. Having written the B-sides to two million sellers within the space of a year, he found himself in a different financial league from his fellow Byrds. Crosby and McGuinn may have been older and more sophisticated, but they hadn't fully grasped how much money could be generated from songwriting. Clark's compositions on the first album had also netted him substantial sums and although McGuinn had consciously capped his prolific pen on the recent follow-up, he was still their leading songsmith. His confidence may have been bruised by Crosby's criticisms, but he still seemed capable of meeting the challenges presented by the Byrds. Ever since touring with the New Christy Minstrels, he had disliked travelling, particularly flying, but that had not stopped him visiting England. The recent Caravan of

Stars tour had been wearying for everybody but Clark had voiced no complaints or presented any problems. Upon his return to Hollywood, he still seemed upbeat and positive about the future.

Months before, Clark had appeared shy in the company of California girls, most of whom seemed impossibly worldly in comparison to those he had known back in Kansas. Pop star success rapidly changed his outlook. Suddenly, girls were throwing themselves at his feet, clubs were eagerly encouraging his patronage and even movie stars would stop by his table. Lithe, glamorous dancers held a particular attraction for the tambourine man, but he was seemingly too intense to sustain a long-term relationship and too eager to play the field. He responded badly to rejection, slipping into sudden melancholy which would usually manifest and resolve itself in song. Clark's best ballads came from the heart. Suitably cleansed, he would follow Michael Clarke on some girl-hunting expedition and the process would be repeated. "Dancers were not rare in Hollywood," Dickson wryly notes.

Despite their new-found stardom, even the Byrds were impressed when Jackie Levy, the sultry, dark-haired main dancer from television's *Hollywood A Go-Go*, entered their circle. They had recently promoted 'Turn! Turn! Turn!' on the show and she clearly liked them. "Jackie showed up in a Thunderbird to begin with," Dickson recalls. "She was from a Beverly Hills family and was very comfortable. Other girls danced at the Whisky, but she didn't. She was financially independent and was already on television." Levy was confident, effervescent and had a good sense of humour. "She told me she used to imagine the camera lens as a big penis that she was making it with, and that was the secret of how she came across so well on screen," adds Dickson. Evidently ready to date a Byrd, she was initially attracted to the group's most outgoing, flamboyant and gregarious member. "She went after David first, and he said to her, 'You're steak and I'm used to hamburger!' He didn't mean to be insulting, but in her mind he was comparing her with a piece of meat. That turned her off, so she went to Gene and they hung out for a while." Eleven months older than Gene, Jackie was years in advance of the Missourian in terms of sophistication. "They played at being Sonny & Cher with fur coats. It was really funny . . . David used to say, quite rightly, that whenever Gene got a new girlfriend you could count on one song for the beginning and another one for the ending."

Swanning around with Jackie Levy was a lot more fun than traipsing across America in a Winnebago. Knowing that she'd chosen him instead of Crosby must have been an even greater ego boost. And to top it all, the Byrds had just been invited to appear on *The Ed Sullivan Show*, the ultimate confirmation of national, mainstream acceptance. Even Clark's friends and family in Kansas would all be watching that epoch. Sullivan had been an American institution for years and among the acts who most benefited from exposure on his show were Elvis Presley and the Beatles. Fittingly, the Byrds performed their two number 1 hits: 'Mr Tambourine Man' and 'Turn! Turn! Turn!'. Visually, they were stunning: Gene Clark stood stage centre, tambourine in hand in a blue jacket and wine red polo neck; McGuinn's rectangular blue-tinted glasses looked groovier than ever in full colour; Clarke seemed confident beyond his years and was even miming along with the vocalists; Hillman came across as distant and statuesque; Crosby, resplendent in cape, grinned mischievously, as if he was privy to some secret that had brought him immense satisfaction.

Crosby's demeanour was an accurate barometer of the tempestuous events that had preceded the live broadcast. During rehearsal, Crosby, had become embroiled in a furious argument with the show's producer Bob Precht. Insisting that the engineers and sound recorders were not up to his standards, Crosby embarrassed everybody. Precht was no mere floor manager, but the son-in-law of Ed Sullivan, whose power was formidable. When Precht berated Crosby, several personnel in the adjoining booth supposedly burst into spontaneous applause. The Byrds were told that they would never appear on Sullivan's show again. Precht's prediction proved correct, although it probably owed more to their commercial decline than Crosby's insurrection. He could at least claim to have joined a merry band of rebels who had dared defy Sullivan's dictates. That list included Buddy Holly, whose objections pre-empted Crosby's comments about the programme's inability to capture a convincing rock 'n' roll sound. Bo Diddley, the Byrds' recent companion on the 'Caravan Of Stars' tour, had also been 'banned' following a performance in 1955 during which he had played a different song from the one Sullivan demanded. More recently, in May 1963, Bob Dylan had declined to appear when the network's censor had refused to allow him to sing the controversial 'Talkin' John Birch Paranoid Blues'. Crosby could rightly point out that the Byrds were in good company, but his tendency to sabotage opportunities, consciously or otherwise, was becoming wearying for his fellow members.

The group's gigging schedule was reduced after the 'Caravan Of Stars' and they were happy to learn that they could close 1965 with a visit to Hawaii. Gene Clark seemed at his apogee as the New Year approached. For once, he was looking forward to travelling and eagerly anticipating a new recording jointly written by himself, McGuinn and Crosby. Barry McGuire remembers the moment when Clark was atop the wheel of fortune. "The best quality time I had with him was when he lived right across the street from me. He was going to Hawaii and I was leaving for New York. He came over and we sat out on the lawn and smoked a joint. He just looked absolutely beautiful, sitting there in the Hollywood Hills, passing a joint back and forth, and talking about music. It was incredible. I'll always remember his dark, sable brown hair; it was cut so perfectly. He said, 'I'm going west and you're going east, and here we are now in the California sunshine.' Finally, we shook hands and said, 'Have a good trip, see you later.' That was one of the last meaningful conversations and moments I ever had with Gene. It taught me – when you shake somebody's hand, you never know if it's going to be the last time you see them."

Anticipation was high for the Hawaii trip, which included a stay in Honolulu. Recently, the group had bought some new amplifiers and sounded better than ever. "It was the first really good live sound they got," Dickson explains. "You could hear them from the parking lot. Gene Clark was magnificent in Hawaii. I'd never seen him sing better, mostly to a group of grammar school children. It startled me how good he was onstage. He came through that curtain before it opened with 'Feel A Whole Lot Better' and just nailed everybody to the wall, including me. I couldn't believe it. A great set."

Celebrating the closing days of 1965, the group decided to explore the island, and split into two groups. McGuinn and Crosby had differing social commitments, so Dickson led a party including the other Byrds and road managers John Barrick and Roger Di Fiore. "We'd done the two shows and had a day off to go play," says Dickson, "so we went to the other side of the island, and dropped some acid." The LSD they consumed provided some strange trips. Chris Hillman suffered a nightmarish mind invasion after hearing the screams of a pig that was being slaughtered across the river. On acid, the squeals sounded so intense that Hillman simply ran off in terror.

Gene Clark, whose use of the heaven and hell drug was usually ill-advised given his nervy disposition and overactive imagination, was preternaturally calm throughout the expedition. Improbably, he found himself invested with the super strength of a comic book hero and dazzled his manager with a display of muscular might that defied logic. "Gene picked up a coconut with the green husk still on it. It was very fibrous on top and hard to get through. You'd have to open it with a machete. He stuck his thumb into it, lightly pulled and said, 'Gee, it's just like a zipper.' Next, he pulled a section off the surface of the inner nut, put his hands in and just ripped the green shell off that coconut. It was a feat of strength that astounded me. There was about an inch-and-a-half wide wedge pointed at each end that I tried to remove with a tyre iron off this [car] bumper and I couldn't. But he'd pulled off the whole part with his bare hands. That was an impossible feat of strength. I could hardly believe my eyes."

After rippling his muscles, Clark descended into a Zen-like calm and allowed the acid to take him on a trip through the ages. "We were in this little river," Dickson recalls, "and Gene got in a rowing boat, picked up an oar and sensed all the people that had worked or handled that oar through time and said, 'I don't know. I think I'll stay here. I don't want to leave.' I didn't even know where we were. We were in somebody else's jungle!"

When they finally emerged, there were further problems. Already "nervous about Gene's driving" they had parked the car in advance of the expedition, and now realized it had been stolen. Like an absent-minded professor, Clark had left the keys in the ignition and some local hoods, seizing an opportunity, secured an unexpected haul. Dickson was devastated. "We lost the car, the $5,000 overrun money, my camera and film. We had to be rescued by the police and go on the plane barefoot. When the police arrived we were kind of hoping they wouldn't find the car in case we got into even more trouble. That was the end of the Hawaii trip. McGuinn and Crosby were certainly not pleased with that performance because they had stayed out of it."

It was a novel experience to be berated by David Crosby for the crime of irresponsibility. As they flew back to Los Angeles, the Byrds could nevertheless reflect on an incredible year that had literally transformed their lives. For all the recent tensions, they still seemed a formidable unit with a great future. Their twin assault on the top of the charts ensured that they were arguably the biggest group in America, surging ahead of the Beach Boys in terms of popularity and innovation. Sustaining that momentum would prove the next big challenge, but nobody could have predicted how quickly they would be eaten away by external pressures and another crisis from within their own camp.

CHAPTER SIXTEEN

Eight Miles High

THE pop universe that the Byrds inhabited looked comfortable as 1966 beckoned. 'Turn! Turn! Turn!' was still number 1 back in LA, but the outside world was unaware how far they had moved on even from that epoch. After the 'Caravan Of Stars' tour, they had presented Dickson with a new song, so astonishing in its daring and ambition that it threatened to transform the career of the group and the development of rock music. The Coltrane-inspired 'Eight Miles High' was the culmination of those stoned exchanges between the Byrds and the Beatles back in Benedict Canyon. A combination of LSD, Dylan-influenced folk, Indian ragas and progressive jazz had inflamed the imaginations of both groups. Lennon would go on to compose 'Tomorrow Never Knows' and other acid-inspired work, but that was still many months away. What was most incredible about 'Eight Miles High' was the timing. It was still 1965, the era of 'Turn! Turn! Turn!' and 'Day Tripper'/'We Can Work It Out', when the Byrds entered the studios of RCA Victor, three days before Christmas, to lay down the original 'Eight Miles High'.

Dickson was too excited to wait for CBS and with Melcher no longer on board, he produced this extraordinary work, assisted by engineer Dave Hassinger. Unfortunately, when they attempted to proceed with plans to release the track, they were thwarted by their own record company. "Columbia wouldn't let us release it because it had been cut at another studio," Chris Hillman explains. "We cut this really hot version and we were trying to sneak it on to a single and an album but they caught us and we had to re-cut it."

McGuinn felt that the RCA cut had a more spontaneous guitar break, but soon realized that the Byrds would have to re-record the track because of the union rules at CBS. Crosby was appalled by the decision and always maintained that Dickson's original was superior. "It was a stunner, it was better," he told me. "It was stronger. It had more flow to it. It was the way we wanted it to be. When we did the other one, we had to force it. I promise you, it's better. It has a better solo on it."

It was another 22 years before the original was finally revealed to the world and, as promised, it was a more spontaneous reading, though never likely to replace the power of the later hit version in the listener's consciousness. Judging the original as a finished work would be wrong however since it was never intended to be released in such crude form without adding considerable work. "It was just demonstration vocals on the RCA version," says Dickson. "The problem with it when we finally put it out on *Never Before* was that it came from a quick mixdown on the four track. The whole band is on one track, McGuinn's on another and two tracks are vocals. That's only four track and you can't open up the mix and get it all back. The way we had intended to do it was to take the four band tracks that had the drums and guitar separated, transfer them to 8-track at CBS, then do the vocals and a new guitar. We had the choice of saving the guitar because it was on a separate track. We could have used part of it, all of it or we could have given McGuinn several passes at bettering himself."

The RCA session also saw the debut of 'Why', the Crosby song that was based on the work of Ravi Shankar and would shortly inspire the term 'raga rock'. David's enthusiasm for ragas originally stemmed from his passing friendship with guitarist Eric Hord, who could play in that distinctive drone-like style. An abiding love of Indian music had been consummated when Crosby accepted Jim Dickson's invitation to attend a Ravi Shankar recording at World-Pacific. "David was energetic," Dickson recalls. "He was always trying to stay on top of what was going on. He got all that raga stuff from Eric Hord, who was into raga on the guitar and open tunings with no success before the Byrds even got moving. That was no secret to people who knew about Shankar. I took

David to a Shankar session and that's where he first heard him. It blew his mind. Ravi Shankar is a little hard to follow for some people if you're just playing the record. But if you're there while it's going on with all that mystery and magic, it's different. They were sitting on an Oriental carpet in the studio playing instruments that looked as though they were made by a master craftsman and everyone was concentrating because you had to be quiet in the booth. Getting David's attention was the hardest part. Stopping him from thinking about what he's doing or wants and getting him to consider what you're saying . . . And when he saw Ravi Shankar, it blew him away. He was all excited. He gets hyper from things like that. It was fun to turn him on to stuff. It's always fun to turn on somebody who appreciates. Somebody who is cool like McGuinn, who will say, 'Yeah, I could do that' and gives you no feedback for having brought him along or shown him something is disappointing. It was always more fun to show stuff to Crosby."

Crosby's infectious enthusiasm for Shankar spilled over into such effusion that he later enchanted George Harrison with tales of Indian magic and sitar solos. "Shankar's sound always intrigued me," David says. "I played some of his records for George Harrison and it turned him on. He bought [a sitar], which the Beatles used on 'Norwegian Wood'." During the Dick Clark bus tour, Crosby performed the same sorcery on McGuinn. "I played him Coltrane and Shankar until it was coming out of his ears."

McGuinn, of course, needed little persuasion. "David didn't *make* us listen to it," he stresses. "Once I heard Coltrane and Shankar, I loved them both." When McGuinn imitated the sound of these greats on his Rickenbacker it created a sound that nobody had ever heard before. Crosby's chunky rhythm playing, Hillman's loping bass line and the electrifying raga drone combined to produce an outstanding performance made perfect by that sitar-like solo at the end of the song. When they came to re-record the composition at CBS, the 'sitar' on 'Why' sounded even more prominent, thanks to some ingenious tinkering. "It was not a sitar on 'Why'," McGuinn admits, "but a 12-string Rickenbacker. We used this special gadget I had made. It was an amplifier from a Philips portable record player and a two-and-a-half inch loudspeaker from a walkie-talkie placed in a wooden cigar box which ran on batteries, and it had such a tremendous sustain that it sounded very much like a sitar. When I plugged my guitar into it, it had a very thin and sustaining sound."

Crosby had good cause to be pleased with 'Why', but it stuck in his throat when McGuinn's name appeared on the disc as co-writer. "Did I give somebody credit for that?" he remarks incredulously. "It was all me! Every word, every note, totally, solely mine. Nobody else had anything to do with it. I finished it before I played it for anybody. You see what I had to do . . . It was not changed one bit. McGuinn added *nothing*."

Although Crosby certainly had completed the song before it was presented to the Byrds, his memory banks have erased a crucial piece of information. It was Dave Hassinger who first voiced reservations about 'Why'. He was impressed by the power of the backing track and expected some aggressive lyrics from Crosby. Instead, the opening line offered the childish plea: "You keep saying no to *me* since I was a baby". Everyone at the session felt embarrassed that Crosby had seemingly written a song complaining about his mother's dominance during his adolescence. Dickson was mortified.

"When I heard the track 'Why', I thought it was magnificent," he says. "When I heard the lyric, I thought it was atrocious. McGuinn came up with a brilliant idea to save it, and that was to change the words 'You keep saying no to *me*' to 'You keep saying no to *her*'. Take that out and it wasn't a song whimpering to mama. It then became a song about a mother who had restricted her girl, which made it more suitable in my mind for the Byrds. It was the kind of message we wanted to say like Jackie De Shannon's 'Don't Doubt Yourself Babe', which encouraged the girl to look after herself. One word changed the whole thing and McGuinn thought it up. It was an inspired thought in a crisis. We saw eye to eye in instant agreement. I never felt more in tune with McGuinn than in that short moment. And David saw it too . . . He never said another word about having done it. I don't know whether he was embarrassed or just saw the wisdom in it . . . I don't know what he thought, but he did it, and it stayed changed."

Completing the RCA sessions was yet another attempt at 'The

Times They Are A-Changin'', which Dickson still believed could make a strong single. Crosby rebelled, refusing to sing on the track, which was left as an unused instrumental. David's disenchantment was understandable. With 'Eight Miles High' the Byrds had proven that they were beyond covering Dylan material and it made no sense to record another version of 'The Times They Are A-Changin'' three weeks after the song had been released on their second album. That moment had long passed, despite Dickson's continued push for Dylan material. "Well, I still wanted to get something out that had quality," Dickson demurs. "When they came back off the road and had 'Eight Miles High' nobody was more enthusiastic about it than I was, but I didn't feel it had to be the next single. We could have done 'The Times They Are A-Changin'' which CBS had printed sleeves for and, win or lose, we'd still have 'Eight Miles High' ready to go. I think David was afraid that 'Why' would be left off [the B-side] which wasn't the case. There was a big row with Crosby because he didn't want me cutting 'The Times They Are A-Changin'' so he walked out without doing the vocal. They'd already done a very poor job on it at CBS where the vocal just plodded along. Crosby would sabotage tracks when he didn't like the songs. He'd gone through this anti-Dylan thing. He was buddies with Dylan, then he was anti-Dylan again. Now he acts like he was always his best friend! But he used to say hateful things about Dylan [before the Byrds]. He said Dylan sang out of tune, but he'd never listened to him. I sat him down to listen to *Another Side Of Bob Dylan*, and when he heard all the words, he saw the humour in it. He was loaded, so he enjoyed it. He lightened up for a while, but he was still politicking against 'Mr Tambourine Man' in 1964–65. He followed Allen Stanton into the toilet to tell him, 'Jim Dickson doesn't know what he's doing and 'Mr Tambourine Man' is a big loser.' He tried to stop it, even then."

At the end of January 1966, the Byrds re-recorded the RCA versions of 'Eight Miles High' and 'Why' for CBS and, that same month, played their second season at the Trip, supported by the Paul Butterfield Blues Band. Audiences were surprised to discover that the group had already replaced many of their folk-rock tunes with heavier, jazz-orientated arrangements and were playing surprisingly well. "The Trip was good," Linda Loo Bopp drawls seductively, remembering the Byrds' transition from Ciro's heroes to counterculture gods. They still looked the same, although McGuinn would soon lose his trademark granny glasses, which subsequently flew off while he was riding on a motorcycle. Crosby retained his green suede cape and his young girlfriend Christine Hinton had bought him an additional brown leather version for extra, dazzling effect. "Crosby's cloak is the delight of both sexes," Derek Taylor told the world, "and *Newsweek* has noted its influence."

Although Linda Bopp stuck around for a while, most of Vito's crew had drifted off into alternative adventures after the Byrds were consumed by the masses. Rationalizing their shift to pop fame and beyond, Taylor painted a poignant picture of stars in the firmament of fame: "It's clear that the Byrds are no longer the private property of the little hippies on the Strip, for now they belong to too many others. The hippies long for the old days, when the Byrds *walked* up the Strip to play for $30 per man at Ciro's, the days when they had no homes to call their own, the days when the Byrds were the *new* thing, and about to make it. But, like the Beatles and the Stones, the Byrds found success brings an inevitable uprooting from old ways and former places; and when the Byrds left the Trip after their nightly stint last week, it was in Porsches equipped with stereo tape players, and it was to the fashionable hills they drove – away from the noise and lights of Sunset Boulevard, past the 15 cent coffee stands of yesterday."

Record buyers still had few clues about the group's new musical direction, although there was much to marvel at the newly released 'Set You Free This Time'. After three consecutive flip sides, Clark had finally been elevated to A-side status with his finest composition to date. Suddenly, he seemed more prominent than ever and could be seen singing the song on several US television shows including *Shivaree* and *Where The Action Is*. In the UK, the single appeared amid a bumper bundle of early '66 Byrds releases, including *The Times They Are A-Changin'* EP and their delayed second album. Initially, 'Set You Free This Time' looked like it might become a minor hit, but the much-touted promotional film that had recently caused a fistfight on the beach remained unseen. Worse followed, when the *NME* headlined their review: 'Byrds' Flip Is Best'. One week later, CBS announced that they were reversing the sides and promoting 'It Won't Be Wrong' instead.

The decision was echoed in the States where both tracks were pushed, causing confusion in the marketplace and curtailing radio play. In truth, both songs were superb. McGuinn/Gerst's 'It Won't Be Wrong' was probably the more commercial offering, containing the essence of the Byrds' sound, including a sprightly Rickenbacker with a discernible raga-like drone, delicately anticipating the more ambitious work ahead. However, it was 'Set You Free This Time' that attracted greater attention from those listeners who saw a connection between the Byrds and Dylan. Here was Gene Clark attempting a love song whose opening sentence was 24 words long and full of complex recriminations and romantic neuroses, far beyond anything he had ever attempted. It was doubly regrettable that Clark lost his A-side status, leaving 'It Won't Be Wrong' to enjoy a peak US chart position of number 63, while 'Set You Free This Time' foundered at number 79.

These were strange times for Gene Clark. Since his acid experience in Hawaii, he had become more remote from the Byrds. His desire to stay on the island and never leave was a dream not easily forgotten. Back in Hollywood, he was still enmeshed in an intense relationship with Jackie Levy, which was soon to end. Although Clark was well capable of moving on relatively quickly, his romantic fantasies always seemed accompanied by a purgatorial spell of dark melancholy. The recent reversal of fortune with 'Set You Free This Time', and the negative, apathetic attitude expressed towards the record by Crosby, McGuinn and Hillman, hardly lifted his spirits. But what bothered him most of all were the travelling and promotional expectations associated with being a Byrd. The group was already gearing up for the release of their innovative new work, 'Eight Miles High' b/w 'Why', produced by Columbia's West Coast Vice President, Allen Stanton. That meant media commitments and another arduous coast-to-coast tour.

On 22 February the group was scheduled to appear in New York for an important appearance on a television special hosted by the garrulous disc jockey Murray The K. As flight time approached, Clark became more nervous and neurotic. On the eve of departure, he visited the home of the Byrds' perennial mother hen Butchie Cho and poured out his fears and misgivings. He was not only anxious about the trip but concerned about his future with the group. He smoked a lot of dope, which rarely had the calming effect expected. Instead, it made him even more unpredictable. Nevertheless, he seemed reassured and prepared to endure the trip from LA to New York. But by the time he reached the airport the following day, he was in a dreadful state. Evidently, he had taken something to alleviate his tension, possibly a downer or, worse still, LSD. As he boarded the plane, his nerves were shredded. McGuinn, who disliked the rigmarole of checking in at airports, had a habit of arriving just as the flight was about to depart. Looking around, Clark became increasingly agitated by his partner's absence, as if it signified imminent doom.

"I got there late," McGuinn remembers, "just as the thing was closing up. I always do. Gene was already freaked out and they were holding his arms and he was saying: 'I got to get off, I got to get off, I can't stand this thing!' And he was vibrating with fear, it was like nine foot in diameter fear vibrations, very heavy panic. And I got into it and cold sweat came over me, you know. 'Wow! Maybe he's right. Maybe he's psychic and knows something I don't know.' But we stayed on and he got off. I said: 'Hey, man, if you get off it's going to blow it for you.' And he said: 'If I stay I'm going to blow it too.' So he got off and that was it, more or less."

When the group arrived in New York, an anxious Murray The K enquired about Clark only to be told by the deadpan McGuinn: "He broke a wing." One week later, the Byrds set out on their nationwide tour, reduced to a foursome. On 3 March, they appeared at the Whitefish Bay High School in Milwaukee in front of 1,250 fans and attempted to compensate for Clark's absence by turning up the volume. "Clark's contributions weren't missed," a local reviewer noted. "The sound level approximated what you'd get playing your stereo wide open in a closet. No one who was there may ever hear quite as well again." When confronted for an explanation about Clark's non-appearance, McGuinn was characteristically non-committal, simply saying that the tambourine man was back in LA suffering from a "nervous condition".

The tour continued without attracting too much scrutiny. At some shows, spectators shouted "Where's Gene?", but the group ignored the question and continued playing. They fared reasonably well in the circumstances, apart from a Sunday evening show in Chicago during which Hillman was injured in a fracas and a score of screaming fans besieged the stage. Back in Los Angeles, the Byrds' management urgently sought to resolve the Clark problem. "Eddie started working on him immediately," says Dickson. "He tried to get Gene across the country by train, but that wasn't fast enough. We tried everything. When I got back we both talked to him about it, but he said, 'No, man! No, man! I can't do it!' The other Byrds were pretty down on him by then."

In the circumstances, the most sensible solution was to allow Clark time to recover from what was described as "nervous exhaustion". *KRLA Beat* claimed that he was expected "to return to the group within the next five to six weeks". Ambiguous bulletins in the British music press also revealed that he had been forced to "temporarily" leave the Byrds and advised "not to undertake any personal appearances for the time being". Yet there was also a quote from Chris Hillman which hinted at a more permanent split: "I'll be doing more singing now that Gene has gone. It was his own decision and we're all sorry to see him go. There were no ill feelings within the group."

That unfortunate slip was steadied by a somewhat obfuscating explanation from Eddie Tickner indicating that Clark was evolving into a studio bound Byrd. "He's clearly not well enough to cope with the pressures and strains of one-night stands and cross-country travel. Gene, of course, remains a member of the group and will continue to write songs and work with them on their Columbia recordings." This hardly sounded reassuring, but there was still some hope that Clark might be ready to resume promotional and live appearances following a well-deserved rest.

When the Byrds returned to Hollywood at the beginning of April for another residency at the Trip, Clark was tentatively invited to join them onstage, but the atmosphere was frosty. It hardly helped when a reviewer from *Record Beat* dismissed the four piece Byrds as inadequate. "Their first set was disappointing: it was very short and it seemed that there were four individuals performing instead of a well-integrated group. The second set was different. Gene Clark came onstage first and the roar from the crowd was deafening. He introduced the group and started to step down, but the crowd wouldn't have it. They actually pushed him back onto the stage, and he did the set. It was Gene's show and, after every song, the crowd gave him a thundering ovation. At this writing, I don't know what will happen, but general opinion was that without Gene Clark, the Byrds didn't make it."

While Clark scuttled back into the shadows, the American pop media was distracted from his disappearance by Derek Taylor who focused on the musical innovations offered on their new single, 'Eight Miles High' b/w 'Why'. A special press conference was held and a sitar was hired to provide the assembled journalists with an insight into the wonders of 'raga rock'. The influence of Indian music on pop was now a major talking point among the rock elite, stretching from the Kinks' 'See My Friend' to the Yardbirds' 'Still I'm Sad', the Beatles' 'Norwegian Wood', the Rolling Stones' 'Paint It, Black' and the Byrds' new single. While McGuinn was photographed plucking at the sitar with studious intent, few realized that he could not actually play the instrument. Like the Kinks, the Byrds employed a raga drone without the need to hire a genuine sitar player. "I don't think there's a sitar on anything the Byrds ever did," McGuinn later told me. "We brought the concept of it into rock music. We were doing the same thing with John Coltrane. We weren't playing saxophone, we were playing 12-string Rickenbacker to sound like a saxophone, and the same goes for the sitar. It was our interpretation of those instruments and musical styles. We were translating it into a rock form. We later used backward tapes and gadgetry. We were just synthesizing those instruments with other electronics."

Fortunately, none of the assembled press people questioned the group about either Gene's absence or their sitar-playing abilities, so Crosby was free to wax lyrical on his jazz influences. Like a hip college professor, he explained the origins of the latest musical novelty to the raga-hungry journalists: "Every kid practically in the United States now knows what a sitar is because George Harrison played it on *Rubber Soul*. Most of them are becoming aware of where the sitar comes from – India. Some are even aware of Ravi Shankar, John Coltrane and a lot of other people too. I'm not trying to justify what we're doing with Indian music. We didn't plan it that way. We went into a room, sat down and played. And what came out was what we put down later on the record. It'll be our next single. We didn't write it or arrange it. The five of us just played music to each other until it gelled. And that's what it comes out as. I don't want to justify it either. We don't plan anything we do, we don't try to scheme trends. We just play music."

Do you think the public is ready to accept raga?
"We'll find out. Somebody's got to turn them on to it. It might bomb completely, you might never hear of the Byrds again. When we did 'Mr Tambourine Man' everybody said it was too far out. I think it's been to number 1 in all the English-speaking countries. We're not wanting to brag, it's just that the blue-chip thinkers were wrong."

Summing up the Byrds' forward thinking philosophy, Crosby concluded: "Most groups accomplish one thing. They achieve a static form and maintain it for security. In so doing they promptly go straight backwards. Every record we make will differ from every other record, I guarantee . . . Rock is going to keep growing. It has in it now African, South American, jazz, folk, church, Bach, Indian, Greek, country bluegrass."

By the end of the conference, the Byrds' explanations had caused so much confusion that the press forgot about the Coltrane-inspired jazz rock of 'Eight Miles High' and labelled both sides of the single 'raga rock', a term which Crosby patently disliked. His fears that the single "might bomb completely" were not unwarranted as the work was dangerously ambitious for pop radio. McGuinn took a demo to WNEW-FM in Manhattan, where he met Alison Steele ('The Nightbird'), a bright, young disc jockey who would later emerge as one of the great champions of progressive rock. After listening to the 'Eight Miles High' demo, she turned to

McGuinn with a quizzical expression and asked, "But where's the new single?" It was not an uncommon reaction. While its chart potential remained uncertain, the track was obviously one of the most sophisticated, daring and intelligent rock singles ever released. McGuinn's Coltrane-influenced guitar lines were so fresh and exciting that they transformed the airwaves. The single's unique qualities became even more apparent when compared to the other hit records of the period.

The Byrds were convinced they had recorded a winner and Derek Taylor dictated his latest effusive press release to his ever vigilant secretary Jackie Ingles. By now, 'Eight Miles High' had entered the US charts and required just one more push to send it spiralling into the Top 20. Characteristically, Taylor provided a critique of music business trends worthy of *Billboard*, even while addressing humble disc jockeys, pop scribes and CBS staff back in London.

Exaggerating certain chart statistics, he wrote: "The Byrds are waiting with the cool remote aplomb for which they are either admired or deplored for their third number 1 single in the United States. 'Eight Miles High', the fifth US single release, is at number 24 on the *Cash Box* chart, and no Byrd record has been played so hard coast to coast. The vital element in quick US chart busters is simultaneous nationwide airplay . . . ideally, New York should be playing a record at the same time as Chicago and Los Angeles. All three cities picked up on 'Eight Miles High' on the day of release; so, the Byrds are blandly optimistic. If they make it, their form will run 'Mr Tambourine Man' number 1, 'All I Really Want To Do' number 9, 'Turn! Turn! Turn!' number 1, 'It Won't Be Wrong, number 39, 'Eight Miles High', number 1. 'Eight Miles High' is the decider – this is the one which puts them way, way ahead of the field which is now seething with some tough new sprinters; Mamas & Papas, Spoonful, Revere and the Raiders, Turtles, and the distance runners like the Beach Boys. So here they are in their homes in the Hollywood Hills, smoking cigarettes under the Californian sun, patiently waiting for the charts to rain new glories."

Instead of new glories, the Byrds found themselves the victims of a record ban that threatened to destroy Taylor's chart dreams. On 29 April, *Bill Gavin's Record Report*, a weekly subscription sheet circulated to over a thousand US radio stations, took a moral stand on the subject of drugs in rock and fingered the current releases of Dylan and the Byrds as subversive. Dylan's new single 'Rainy Day Women # 12 & 35' included the chorus "everybody must get stoned", which the innocent general public took as an invitation to get drunk, while hipper listeners laughed at its celebration of drug-induced euphoria. Gavin had discovered that "a rainy day woman" was supposedly hippie slang for a "marijuana cigarette", while getting "eight miles high" was apparently "LSD talk".

Armed with these revelations, he announced: "We have dropped 'Rainy Day Women' and 'Eight Miles High' from our 'Recommended Playlist'. In our opinion, these records imply encouragement and/or approval of the use of marijuana or LSD. We cannot conscientiously recommend such records for airplay, despite their acknowledged sales. We reserve the right to distinguish between records that simply mention such drugs and those that imply approval of their use."

Gavin's condemnation had potentially dire consequences and arrested the progress of the single, which was banned in Washington, Baltimore and Houston within a week of the report. Derek Taylor wasted no time in despatching an indignant press release, clearly pointing out that 'Eight Miles High' had nothing to do with drugs. "The irony of it is that the Byrds and Dylan are, in their lyrical innocence, again linked in a drugs controversy. The first time this happened was in the middle of last year when pundits hazarded guesses that 'Mr Tambourine Man' referred to a drug peddler. As in the case of 'Eight Miles High' and 'Rainy Day Women', the implications failed to prevent 'Mr Tambourine Man' from reaching the top of the charts."

Taylor went on to explain Clark's role in writing the song ("with help from fellow Byrd-members Jim McGuinn and David Crosby") and provided a fascinating lyrical analysis, complete with sarcastic asides from the group's leader. "We could have called the song 'Forty-Two Thousand Two Hundred and Forty Feet', but somehow this didn't seem to be a very commercial song title and it certainly wouldn't have scanned," McGuinn observed.

In a later interview, he explained the genesis of the song: "We started it out as six miles high – Gene Clark and I wrote the lyrics – because that's the approximate altitude that commercial airlines fly. 42 or 43,000 feet, or about eight miles high, is the altitude reserved for military aircraft only; commercial aircraft have to fly below that – and that was one discrepancy which led people to believe it was about drugs and not about airplanes. But Gene said eight miles sounds better than six, and it did sound more poetic, and it was also around the time of 'Eight Days A Week' by the Beatles, so that was another hook or catch, if you like."

The Byrds patiently pointed out that the song's opening line was a reference to their plane touching down at London Airport upon their arrival in the city in August 1965. Their inability to come to terms with the apparently arbitrary placing of street signs on railings and walls inspired the lines "signs in the street that say where you're going are somewhere just being their own". As McGuinn elaborated: "You come over here and try to find the names of the streets and you find them tacked up on the sides of buildings if they haven't been torn down or fallen off. So that line refers to how difficult it is to find which street you're on. It's one of the things that strikes a visiting American."

The hostility of the UK pop press and the meanness of the British band, the Birds, who had served a writ on the Byrds as they stepped off the plane, were also documented in the lines: "Nowhere is there warmth to be found among those afraid of losing their ground". Taylor's missive explains that the line about "squares, huddled in storms", was a direct reference to a photo session that took place in rain-swept Trafalgar Square in one of the wettest London summers in recent memory. David Crosby had also taken up this allusion with his contribution to the song: "I wrote that verse beginning 'Rain grey town' and I think I contributed most of the last verse and some of the changes."

Summing up the unexpected ban, McGuinn said: "It seems extraordinary that a very pretty lyric about an intriguing city should be condemned because the phrases are couched in some sort of poetry. I daresay if we had sung, 'We dig London and its big, big beat but we don't dig the rain, and our feet get sore waiting for the limousine', we'd have been OK."

While Taylor's forceful publicity campaign attempted to undo any damage caused by the Gavin Report, Tickner and Dickson took more direct action, instructing their solicitors to seek a retraction.

On 20 May, Marshall L. McDaniel of McDaniel & McDaniel despatched a letter to *Bill Gavin's Record Report* in San Francisco headed 'Demand For Correction'. It read:

> Please be advised that the song 'Eight Miles High' relates to the airplane trip taken by its writers and 'The Byrds' from the United States for a performing engagement in England. The reference to 'eight miles high' as contained in the title and as also indicated in the words of the song relates to the height at which the aircraft flew over the earth. Neither the title of the song nor its words and lyrics indicate in any manner or to any extent that it relates to encouragement of or implies the use of marijuana or LSD, or any other substance.
>
> As a direct result of the incorrect information transmitted by *Bill Gavin's Record Report*, radio stations throughout the United States have discontinued playing Columbia Record No. 4378 entitled 'Eight Miles High'. This discontinuance of playing of the record has caused a decline in sales, and the decline in sales has resulted in damages to the author of 'Eight Miles High', to 'The Byrds', and to the group's managers and agents, and to Columbia Records.
>
> Demand is hereby made for a correction of the defamatory statements published and distributed by *Bill Gavin's Record Report* so as to reduce the continued general and special damages which the author of 'Eight Miles High', 'The Byrds', and others, have been and are now experiencing. Each of the parties who have been damaged by the defamatory statements made and published by *Bill Gavin's Record Report* reserve the right to seek recovery for general and special damages suffered by them, as well as exemplary damages.

One week after receiving this demand, Gavin reprinted the relevant portion of the letter explaining the meaning of the song, although he failed to offer any apology. By then, it was too late. 'Eight Miles

High' had peaked at number 14 on *Billboard* the previous week and was now on the way down. Whether it would have fared any better anyway is debatable, but the psychological effects of the controversy were real enough and the legal correspondence underlines how seriously the matter was taken by everyone in the Byrds' camp. McGuinn later pinpointed this setback as the moment when the Byrds lost their chance to re-establish themselves as America's premier group ahead of all competition.

One enduring mystery surrounding 'Eight Miles High' was the origin of authorship. In later years, Clark revealed that he had started writing the song in the unlikely company of Brian Jones. That claim was subsequently embellished to such an extent that Gene even claimed that part of the song was written in St Louis, Missouri during the US tour with the Rolling Stones in 1965. "Brian never wanted credit," he noted. "He never really got credit for it. But then me and Brian picked it up later down the line, the idea, and we groomed it for months, presented it back to Crosby and McGuinn, and they liked it so much that they went real deep into it, so it ended up all three of us writing it."

The key word in Clark's comment was 'idea' for whatever exchanges he had with Jones were likely to have been musical rather than lyrical. Jones always had problems with lyrics and it is clear from the words of 'Eight Miles High' that its theme was not developed until after the Byrds arrived in London. In another interview, Gene had Brian Jones merely looking on and making some positive comments while he scribbled down some words on a sheet of paper after a discussion about William Burroughs. After perusing Clark's poetry, Jones supposedly commented vaguely: "That's pretty good, you ought to work on that." Judging from the lyrics of the song, it seems unlikely that a single line could be apportioned to a time before the British visit. Clark and Jones did meet again during the Byrds' UK tour when Gene also wrote 'Set You Free This Time', so it is possible that some chords were strummed. The song remained undeveloped and was not ready in time for the *Turn! Turn! Turn!* sessions. As everyone confirms, it was during the Dick Clark Caravan Of Stars bus tour that the song finally took shape, with Clark completing the lyrics about the group's experiences of

London, Crosby adding the "rain grey town" and McGuinn incorporating the Coltrane elements.

"It was mostly Gene's tune," McGuinn admits. "He had the chord changes and the melody. It was my idea to write about the airplane ride, naturally. Then we worked out the lyrics, and Crosby's input was the 'rain grey town' and describing the fans, 'in places small faces unbound'."

Clark never seriously disputed this, although, like Crosby later down the line, he felt the writing collaboration was as much a political act as a creative move. "I wrote all the words except for one line that David wrote 'Rain, grey town . . .' and then McGuinn arranged it, so I had to part something with those guys . . . I decided that I wasn't going to get a single out of this deal because I'd already written so many songs that they were going to grab the singles for their own stuff, so I split it with them to get the single. That, and they did really help me to write it too. But one of the problems we had by the release of the second album was the animosity growing amongst the group. Especially about me, because I was making a lot more money than anybody else from the royalties."

While threats of a radio ban in America scuppered any dreams of the disc reaching the US Top 10, let alone number 1, there was no moral clampdown across the Atlantic. The BBC was relatively unfazed by obscure drug connotations in pop songs, which generally slipped through the censor's net undetected. Anodyne disc jockeys thought stoned meant 'squiffy' and saw the uproarious 'Rainy Day Women # 12 and 35' as no more dangerous or offensive than Dean Martin's 'Little Ole Wine Drinker, Me'. As for 'Eight Miles High', its Stateside 'banning' was seen as typical of the kind of American paranoia that wanted to burn communists at the stake during the Fifties. The only serious objection came from a 25-year-old Birmingham councillor who obviously read the music press and unsuccessfully called upon Home Secretary Roy Jenkins to ban both Dylan and the Byrds from the airwaves.

The major problem that 'Eight Miles High' faced in Britain was not its lyrical content, but the conservatism of the BBC Light Programme and the lack of an underground or alternative press to champion the record. *New Musical Express*, which boasted more sales than any music paper in the world and almost exceeded the combined circulations of its UK competitors, greeted the recording cautiously with the finger-wagging headline, 'This Won't Help Byrds'. Reviewer Derek Johnson carefully catalogued the song's constituent parts, but remained unmoved by its magic, and ultimately damned the disc with faint praise: "A compulsive fast-moving rhythm underlines the Byrds' vocal, complete with all the familiar characteristics – strident guitar, crashing cymbals, and a double-time shuffle. A lengthy instrumental intro precedes the vocal. But although the basic idea of the lyric is original and the title's intriguing, there's virtually no melody. And I thought the backing was far too complex. I rate it the group's most disappointing to date."

Although Johnson's comments may now seem sacrilegious, they echoed the aforementioned response of American DJ Alison Steele. Other reviewers also seemed puzzled or alienated by the song's remarkable ambition. *Melody Maker* reckoned it was "a very interesting, appealing record but maybe a little trying on the ears of the masses". *Record Mirror* thought it an "odd mixture of musical styles," adding "song isn't a knockout but the originality of style and the actual performance should see it into the charts – anyway, it's big in the States". But the weirdest and most dismissive comments came from the usually supportive *Disc*, whose reviewer lamented: "Before today, I used to look forward to every Byrds release knowing that the arrangement and production would be a dream. When I played this record I nearly ran out of the room. It is muzzy, badly-made, a terrible song, a bad copy of some of the worst British groups, nothing like the Byrds at all."

The pirate stations came to the rescue and played the record frequently during the evening, but in the end 'Eight Miles High' fared no better than 'Turn! Turn! Turn!' in the UK, charting for one week at number 28 on 1 June while the old enemy Cher was back flying high with 'Bang Bang'. Although the Byrds could rightly claim to have been ill-treated over the drugs controversy, the final irony was that 'Eight Miles High' was not an entirely innocent statement. "Of course it was a drug song," Crosby later told me. "We were stoned when we wrote it. We can also justifiably say that it wasn't a drug song because it was written about the trip to London. It was a drug song and it wasn't a drug song at the same time."

The moral ambiguity of 'Eight Miles High' was reflected in the paradoxical image of the Byrds. Despite their bohemian tendencies, they remained a pop group in the best tradition of the Beatles, hiding their private vices from the public but experimenting liberally with LSD, and taking daring musical steps with each new record. Although they were hip enough to deride the musical demands of the pop press, they were still acutely aware of their image. As Derek Taylor recalled with mild amusement, "Chris always used to wear a straightener in his hair and he hated it! I remember Gene returning from San Francisco and telling me, 'Long hair is all right but they look like girls out there. I mean you don't even know if it's clean, man.' The thing about [the] Byrds' long hair was that they were always washing and setting it."

Michael Clarke was equally fastidious and had recently established himself as the clothes horse in the group, obsessively changing his shirts and sweaters half-a-dozen times before venturing out from Dickson's basement in search of girls. Like the other Byrds he used and enjoyed recreational drugs, but showed little interest in booze, the legal drug that would eventually take his life.

Jim McGuinn had first taken LSD as early as 1962 and was still getting high on acid in a bathtub with the Beatles three years later. Upon waking every morning, he usually began the day with a joint and moved on to speed late in the evening. For all that, his lifestyle was the complete antithesis of the stereotypical degenerate doper, as Taylor testifies: "McGuinn got smashed with restraint. He was austere. His belongings were always in order and his electronics were always working. He had a very formal relationship with Dolores. I found him both exact and demanding. I was always surprised how easy he was to be with because he did have that fussy school-ma'am attitude."

Even Crosby, the most celebrated drugs proselytizer in the Byrds, was still a long way from experiencing his first rush of heroin, preferring the standard rock star diet of marijuana and acid. As their lifestyles indicated, the Byrds were perfectly poised to negotiate that delicate balance between pop star fame and progressive musicianship. Still accepted by teen audiences, in spite of the expanding competition, they were also the darlings of the non-conformist set and had shown with 'Eight Miles High' a degree of sophistication unrivalled by their contemporaries. For a while, it seemed that they might retain a pop and rock audience with the same confident equilibrium shown by the Beatles and the Rolling Stones, but that required regular hits as well as cult credibility. McGuinn was deflated by the 'banning' of 'Eight Miles High' and, in spite of its hit status, he later confessed to Derek Taylor: "It blew us out of the game." Typically, McGuinn had ignored a far more important setback that rendered the drugs controversy irrelevant and inconsequential by comparison. Amid the trauma of bans and disconcerting chart placings, news belatedly leaked out that sounded like a funeral notice – the recently absent Gene Clark had now officially left the Byrds.

CHAPTER SEVENTEEN

Fear Of Flying

AT first it seemed unbelievable. The Byrds were preparing to reach new heights with the self-sufficiency of their own songwriting talent and suddenly they were without their main composer. In 1966, personnel changes in a popular group were regarded as the cardinal sin, and Gene's departure threatened to signal the death-knell for their future. Although McGuinn was nominal leader, Clark was regarded by many as the central figure in the Byrds. He was the singer who stood stage centre, the tambourine man and, apparently, the only member capable of writing an album's worth of songs. What could possibly have persuaded him to abandon such a successful group?

The answers were, to say the least, complex. Initially, it seemed that his withdrawal might only be temporary, but it was not long before the press revealed to their readers the startling story of Clark's fear of flying. During his youth in Kansas, he had witnessed a plane crash. He had never forgotten the incident, which played on his nerves when air travel became more frequent during the period of the Byrds' greatest success. Playing the amateur psychologist, McGuinn provided a retrospective analysis of the neurosis that sounded surprisingly persuasive: "He reached the point of crisis, the mounting pressure of the whole gig, and, at that point, it was pretty intense. We had two number 1s, there was pressure from the press and we had to be good. We were shuffled around like cattle and you get that boxed-in feeling. And this is what ganged up on Gene. He's a country boy from Missouri, a farm boy who got into this high intensity thing, and the airplanes got to him."

Pinpointing where and why Clark had unravelled emotionally probably required the expertise of a therapist. His fairy-tale ascension from Midwest obscurity to preflyte fame in the New Christy Minstrels clearly came at a price. "Gene didn't like to fly even while he was with the Christies," says former member Barry McGuire. "I don't think he ever got over that fear." The Minstrels were run with the precision and fighting spirit of a baseball team. The leading members had big booming voices, well-rehearsed stage patter, comedic skills and dance moves. Plus they were very competitive with each other. Clark's social shyness, sensitivity and greater interest in musical expression than pure entertainment singled him out as an underachiever in the line-up. He was never likely to challenge the major voices in the group and in truth made little impression on them.

By the time he joined the fledgling Byrds, Clark settled into his role as lead singer, but his spot was always under threat. Outwardly confident, energetic and gregarious, he had a darker, vulnerable side, which was always likely to overwhelm him in moments of stress. "Gene was a little squirrelly to begin with," says Jim Dickson, "and I didn't know why. He stayed at my house when they first got going and he'd tell me about these weird dreams he'd have and how he'd roll downstairs wrapped in a carpet filled with tacks and glass. He had that strange side to him. Otherwise, he seemed like an ex-Christy Minstrel, an all-American boy. I saw him as the John Wayne of the group, and I wanted McGuinn to appear as the intellectual, which was a bit of a fraud. The tragedy was that David wanted to be things he couldn't pull off . . . trying to be too hip."

During the World-Pacific recordings, Clark was the creative giant, the true songwriter and the constant cheerleader. Unfortunately, his power was forever being chipped away. He lost the rhythm guitar to David Crosby and was supplanted by McGuinn as lead vocalist on the major hits 'Mr Tambourine Man', 'All I Really Want To Do' and 'Turn! Turn! Turn!'. Even Clark's songwriting monopoly, once welcomed and respected, was re-evaluated in a negative light by late 1965. Both Crosby and McGuinn became less enthusiastic about his contributions as the Byrds progressed, arguing that there was a need for more challenging material. "That was true," Crosby says. "I didn't think the lyrics were that good. I don't want to put him down. But all our songs were juvenile at that stage. Listen to the words. We were all kids. As we became more aware of Dylan and other sophisticated writers, we obviously pulled for the best we could. This upset Gene a little, but not much. Gene's smarter than he can articulate, and a lot smarter than most people gave him credit for being. We spent many years together and he was a good man and a good friend too, and a pretty loyal one."

The irony was that it was not Clark who was stuck in a one dimensional world of Beatle imitations. Crosby may have been attempting hipper songs like 'Stranger In A Strange Land' and 'Flower Bomb Song', but he was also locked into the old traditions, as evidenced by the appealing but lyrically banal McGuinn collaboration, 'Wait And See'. By contrast, Clark was experimenting daringly with a more ornate, poetic form in the mode of mid-period Dylan. One of the early examples, 'The Day Walk', with its portentous images of the righteous picking pieces of their minds up off the floor, was fascinating, but easily overlooked by the other Byrds. Dickson was intrigued by some lyrics but baffled by others, while McGuinn considered them mere Dylan imitations. "Gene was not Bob Dylan," he concludes.

Since the formation of the Byrds, a cache of Clark songs was regularly arriving on Dickson's desk. Some were fair, others very good to excellent, but the Byrds could never have included them all on albums. Perhaps the ease with which Clark churned them out convinced his fellow Byrds that the songs could not have been that great. Selecting material considered appropriate was always a challenge, as Dickson well knew. "Gene could write 15–20 songs a week and you had to find a good one whenever it came along because there were lots of them that you couldn't make head or tail of. They didn't mean anything. We all knew that. Gene would write a good one at a rate of just about one per girlfriend. Crosby was aware of that. He would even promote it and say, 'We've got to get Gene a new girlfriend and get a new song, a good one.' Crosby would say nasty things about Gene Clark songs and he would say good things about them. It depended upon who he was talking to and why he was talking to them."

At a time when there was growing resistance towards Clark's material, he remained in the ascendant. Although he had fewer songs on their second album, he was allowed a precious A-side single with 'Set You Free This Time', probably his most accomplished composition to date. Even that received a muted response from his fellow members. "I liked the sound and feel of it," says Dickson. "It was nice, but it wasn't an astounding 'tear your head off the wall' thing. Gene could write a song like 'Set You Free This Time' and it's hard to verbalize why that one's better than some of the others. You loved the song, Derek Taylor loved the song. He said, 'This is the Gene Clark song we've been waiting for!' He was more enthusiastic about it than anybody, and I wasn't quite sure why. And I was never quite sure why you picked up on it either. I seem vaguely to remember Dylan liking it too. Gene came in and told us: 'I played it for Dylan and he thought it was great.' CBS liked it enough to make it a single. The BBC wanted it. David obviously didn't want it to be a single and sabotaged that promotional film about it. When it became a single, it was hard for Gene to understand why the rest of the Byrds continued not to like it."

In a breathtaking example of reverse psychology, complete with a telling Freudian slip, McGuinn later posited a theory to explain one reason for Clark's departure. "Maybe the guilt factor was there because he was in Ferraris and things and we were still starving. He was making thousands and we weren't making anything yet."

But why should Clark feel 'guilty' about his songwriting success? It was hardly something which warranted shame. He was never a dictator when it came to including his songs on albums and had even allowed the B-side 'She Don't Care About Time' to be excluded from *Turn! Turn! Turn!* in the face of inferior material without a word of complaint. McGuinn himself admits that the Clark songwriting monopoly was as much to do with the lackadaisical attitude of his fellow members. "Gene was so prolific that there didn't seem to be any point in trying to compete with him." The 'guilt' factor, then, was hardly applicable, but McGuinn's other comment, "we were still starving" reveals undertones of mild resentment, even jealousy, on the part of the other Byrds.

Clark himself confirmed this conclusion. He was disappointed by the group's lack of support and, like Crosby in later times, felt resentful about sharing songwriting credits on compositions which he had largely instigated. One of the reasons he had presented the Byrds with 'Eight Miles High' and encouraged their participation as co-composers was to ensure that it would be released as an A-side. "I was making a lot more money than anybody else from the royalties," he stressed. "They didn't realize what had happened and they started knocking my material."

Derek Taylor also detected a lack of respect for Clark, which he found surprising and disconcerting. "I got the impression that Gene was not regarded as a first-class Byrd. I don't think it was the flying. He was not taken seriously enough."

The tendency of the Byrds to underestimate Clark's contribution was reinforced later in the Sixties when they enjoyed songwriting success of their own. In flippant moments, they would look back at the history of the group with an almost amnesiacal disregard of his importance. Hillman's description of Clark's original role in the group was a classic example of understatement and faint praise: "The five of us started out from scratch, you know, like playing on nothing. Michael Clarke was hitting cardboard boxes, I was playing a $20 Japanese bass, and McGuinn had an acoustic 12-string. That was the real Byrds. Gene didn't really add that much . . ."

Crosby sometimes sounded equally dismissive claming that "McGuinn, Christopher and I were the essential parts" adding that Gene, although a decent songwriter, was no great loss "as a singer or performer". McGuinn could also be resoundingly cynical when caught in world-weary mode. Rounding up the original Byrds for some carefree castigation, he was particularly critical of Clark's contribution, and not noticeably enthusiastic about anybody else: "Hillman was a good bass player. Crosby wasn't a hot guitarist, Michael wasn't a hot drummer. Gene Clark didn't really know how to keep time at all, at all. He was playing tambourine: 'Cah, Cah, Taw!' He was just spastic on the tambourine. I'm glad he left, actually. I'm glad everybody left."

Such words were not untypical of the Byrds at their most

unsympathetic. Crosby once described Hillman to me as "a mediocre bass player who only once in a while would ever come up with something" and McGuinn as "an off-the-wall guitarist". Like McGuinn, Crosby could be brutally harsh, yet also charitable and positive, especially when reminded of a particular song. Within the dynamic of the Byrds, McGuinn's attitude was generally blasé, Clarke's pally but powerless, Hillman's distant and Crosby's overly aggressive.

Eddie Tickner portrayed Crosby as Gene Clark's greatest tormentor and probably the key person in prompting his decision to quit. "I don't believe there was a conspiracy against Clark, at least not an overt conspiracy. I think the feeling was that it was Crosby who was tantalizing Gene. He was making Gene Clark feel insecure and criticizing him. He had already taken the guitar out of his hands."

Derek Taylor voiced similar feelings. "I felt an absolute sense of justice towards Gene, just as I would have felt to Michael or Chris or David who, in a way, was a less sympathetic character because he was more difficult, awkward and selfish. He too had to be treated with fairness. So that's why I thought they should have stuck up for Gene Clark. But they were definitely down on Gene, removing his instrument and not being too generous towards his songs . . . I'm really an all for one and one for all type. I don't like parties to break up, I don't like families to break up, I don't like marriages to break up. I don't like anything to break up. Musically, I felt they were losing something important and, anyway, I liked Gene as a chap."

When I confronted Crosby with Tickner's accusation about taking Clark's guitar from his hands, he was understandably defensive, but engagingly forthright. "I don't think it ever happened," he retorted. "Now the result of it was that, but I don't think I actually ever took the guitar out of Gene's hands. That would have been a little too rude. I don't think I did that. I intimidated Gene, I'm sure, but not consciously . . . I've got an enormous affection for Gene Clark. I really loved the cat, man. I thought he was a real good guy. What happened was over and over again he would be behind the beat, slow and awkward. He had no sense of time onstage. It would be really awkward. He'd come in a quarter of a beat late with the tambourine, playing it real loud behind the beat, which was wrong. It would drive me nuts because rhythm is one of my favourite things. Listen to a tape of us live and you'll understand the whole story. It wasn't good."

Crosby's affection for Gene Clark increased when he stood back and realized that he was not a threat, but an important asset to the Byrds whose contribution might be missed. By then, it was too late. Always a passionate man, Crosby had good reason for regretting his past insensitivity when he had made fun of Clark. The fact that he was number three in the group bruised Crosby's ego and all too often he would compensate for that deficit by playing up in front of audiences or photographers. His awkwardness and outspokenness were even bothering the normally unflappable Tickner. Derek Taylor remembers that during early 1966, there were discussions about the possibility of Crosby leaving the group. Nobody expected Clark to jump ship and perhaps if more attention had been paid to his problems, his exit might have been averted. Crosby was no doubt aware of this, but there was little that he could do to erase the past.

"There was guilt," Dickson concludes. "David understood when Gene left that 95 per cent of why Gene left could be brought back to him. Not so much directly, but including the politicking and snide remarks. David used to put rabbit ear signs with his fingers behind Gene's head when he'd be singing lead. Even at Ciro's he'd do stuff like that. He'd make nasty faces at him when Gene couldn't see him when he was in the middle of a lead and distract the audience from him. Those are just spiteful, mean little spoilt-kid tricks. Who thinks people are going to do that? I can't imagine David would defend that he did that any more. Maybe he'd deny it, but he did it in front of hundreds of people, everybody knows it. I watched Gene deteriorate and there was nothing I could do about it. David just wouldn't let up. Onstage, he'd ridicule him behind his back all the time. One of the things that cracked Gene was that he couldn't understand why this was happening. It just didn't make sense. He couldn't understand why David would focus so heavily on bringing him down. David said to me, 'Well, I want to be the co-pilot!' I said, 'That's just nonsense, David.'"

FEAR OF FLYING

Despite Dickson's criticisms there was some sign of belated remorse on Crosby's part. Eddie Tickner remembers that David was the Byrd most taken aback by the announcement that Clark was quitting: "Although David did tantalize Gene, when he finally quit Crosby was the first to demand that he not leave. He would not hear of it. He couldn't see the Byrds without Gene. As far as he was concerned, Gene Clark was Mr Tambourine Man."

Blaming Clark's departure on any particular Byrd misses the crucial point that he was a victim of his own demons and desires. Considering his neurotic personality, it seems likely that he would have suffered the same fate in any young group as internationally famous as the Byrds. One of the reasons that the group could distance themselves from Clark's migration was the knowledge that he had largely self-destructed. Since their first flush of success, the internal and external pressures had reached intolerable proportions for the tambourine man. The fear of flying, the apathetic attitude of the other Byrds towards his own material, the constant teasing by Crosby and the niggling pressures of deciding whether to remain in the group or pursue a solo career, had each taken their toll. Many of these problems might have been surmountable, but they were exacerbated by his worryingly intemperate lifestyle. "I always thought that David got smashed with a little abandon," Taylor told me, "but, as for Gene, he would do *anything*. He'd have a glass in one hand and a pill in another. He was an excessive."

It had not always been that way. Barry McGuire recalls him briefly smoking dope in the New Christy Minstrel days, but by the time Clark connected with McGuinn and Crosby, he was drug free. While staying at Dickson's house, he consumed food with the appetite of an athlete and maintained his focus during those long hours at World-Pacific. His fitness, energy levels and commitment impressed everybody. "When the Byrds first came together he was the only one I remember that *didn't* smoke grass," says Dickson. "And none of them drank then. David tried to make him hip and turn him on. David had great faith in grass. He was the one who said, 'Everyone should take drugs and the whole world will be OK.' But Gene got so instantly paranoid. Once it started, we all said he shouldn't smoke grass. He was too uptight. He already had enough trouble dealing with his psyche. He arrived with problems, but they just got incredibly expanded. If you've got a bit of depression and you find yourself in an enormously powerful situation, you'll get yourself a bigger depression. It all gets amplified. When you have that kind of success, your problems are bigger, your wins are bigger and the ups and downs become bigger."

It seemed that the greater the pressures became, the greater became Gene's fear of flying. And the stronger his fears, the more he drank. And when drink was not enough he would resort to drugs in order to deaden the dread. Taylor vividly recalls Clark sitting on a plane while under the influence of LSD and mistaking a ray of sunlight on the wing for a raging fire. His reaction was predictably traumatic. Patti McCormick, a friend from the Ciro's days, also felt that his use of LSD was ill-advised. "Gene warned me against taking LSD because when he'd taken it he stared out of a window for two hours. But the thing was, I could take LSD and Gene couldn't."

Chris Hillman also pinpointed the combination of Clark's excesses and neuroses as the primary reasons for his departure. "I don't know if there was any turmoil between him and any of the members. I think it was the whole experience that was driving him nuts . . . It was all too much. It was a lot for all of us . . . You really are susceptible to all the demons there are and it's very hard. If you're thrust into this spotlight of adulation, you're open for some good neuroses. We all got a little whacked out, it just got to Gene more."

The stoical McGuinn was sometimes bamboozled by the bright lights, but never affected as badly as his neurotic colleague. "Gene had the toughest time dealing with fame of anybody I ever met," he says. "I had a tough time dealing with it myself, so I understood it. I went through very dark times with it at first. Euphoric highs, then crashing lows and depression and anxiety attacks and all kinds of stuff that you get as a result of this emotional upheaval. I was more spiritually oriented, so that I had that release. I had that place to go to in my being, so I think that's what helped me."

Hillman's and McGuinn's diagnosis was supported by Clark himself, who admitted that the suddenness and intensity of pop star fame was proving overwhelming. "We'd been together eight months and we're already right in there with the Beatles and the Rolling Stones. They'd already been together like five years and had some time on it. We were just thrown in right into the winners' circle. It spun me out, madly, to deal with that kind of impact, coming into the thing real green. Here are these other guys who really had paid their dues, taken their knocks, then come all the way up the ladder – and we're just up there almost instantaneously. I think we weren't ready for it – our management or anybody."

Clark was a creature of extremes. Although he had been inculcated with a strong work ethic since childhood, he was always prone to manic excess. The sober, hard-working character that Dickson first observed was but one aspect of his personality. Insecurities were never far away. "One of the things I noticed about him was his indecisiveness," says Dickson. "He always wanted to be somebody, but who he wanted to be seemed to change from week to week. He had the energy to go places, but he wasn't sure where he was going. He'd been a Christy Minstrel, then he was singing with an English accent and trying to be the Beatles with McGuinn, then it was Dylan . . ."

Finally, he became 'The Byrd Who Could Not Fly', a neat headline and a handy epithet, but as an explanation for his departure, it was woefully inadequate. Nevertheless, there was an unintended underlying truth in McGuinn's related quip: "To be a Byrd, you have to fly". Punning aside, planes and flight had always been connected with the Byrds, even going back to their original name, the Jet Set. McGuinn and Crosby, the leading aviator fans in the band, had even written a tribute to the time they spent plane spotting at LAX: the beautiful love ballad, 'The Airport Song'. In interview comments, reproduced on the sleeve of their first album, McGuinn spoke about music representing the jet age and how the sound of Sinatra could be compared to a Forties' aircraft, whereas the Byrds were equated with "jet sound". Crosby used similar comparisons when discussing the group's musical themes. "There's a lot of motion. Sometimes it's trains, sometimes it's horseback, mostly it's jets because that's mostly what we ride, that's where our heads are."

That last point was no exaggeration. Both McGuinn and Crosby had befriended the aviator and adventurer John Lear (the son of jet-plane manufacturer William P. Lear), who was encouraging the Byrds, quite literally, to fly high. At the time, Lear was breaking speed records for round the world flights. In his most paranoid moments, Clark wondered whether his fellow members were attempting to oust him by teasingly playing on his flight phobia. These irrational fears reached their climax on the aircraft bound for New York when, according to McGuinn, Clark became deranged to such an extent that he believed Jim had planted a bomb on the plane. It was clearly part of the panic attack, for Clark and McGuinn had no history of conflict in the group. But alighting the aircraft symbolized Clark's abandonment of the Byrds. As McGuinn concluded: "We worked a couple of more gigs with him but we couldn't hold together. He went on his own."

For Dickson, watching Clark get off the plane was like witnessing the penultimate act of a torturous melodrama. "Several things had happened. In the Christy Minstrels, he didn't like to travel and didn't like the bus. He was getting kind of cuckoo. They said he seemed a little crazy. I didn't think he was dangerously crazy, maybe to himself a little bit, but not a lot. He had no particular vices, he was just a nervous kid. But when David got the guitar off of him – that was the beginning of the intimidation of Gene Clark. Before that he was more confident in himself. Even though he may have had some underlying problems, he did better with girls than David, and fronted himself very well. Really, it was the plane flight when he wouldn't go to New York. That was the sowing of the seeds of his finally leaving the group."

While fans were shocked by Clark's decision, his fellow Byrds were imperiously cool about the entire affair. Perversely, some of them may even have privately welcomed his decision. At best, they were unfazed. "I suspect Crosby probably saw it as an opportunity and McGuinn felt it would bring the focus towards him," Dickson contends. "I don't think they saw the gravity of it. I don't remember any one of them coming and saying: 'Man, why can't you do something about Gene?' Crosby may have gone to Eddie with a story after the event, but that still sounds apocryphal to me. I don't think it was a blow to any of the Byrds, except maybe Michael, and then only a little. McGuinn never understood it. To all of them, it was as casual as a guy getting up and leaving a coffee shop. McGuinn's response at the time was, 'Oh, we don't need Gene.' They needed him *terribly* as far as I was concerned. Gene Clark's voice was essential. Whatever balls the vocals had came from him. He was the deeper, stronger voice. The only other vocal element we had at the time, besides McGuinn, was Crosby and Clark together. Crosby didn't sing a lot of songs alone, only 'Hey Joe'. With Gene gone, I thought we'd lost so much ground that we might never recover."

Thirty years on, McGuinn confirmed that neither he nor the other Byrds made any serious attempt to dissuade Clark from leaving. "I guess we were real jealous that he'd had so many songs on the albums that we all wanted his air time," he frankly admits. "It's probably true. Too bad." With an absent-minded air, he trotted out some of the other reasons, as though they'd been learned by rote over the years. "Well. Whatever. Gene left. He didn't want to be in the Byrds at that point. He was really stressed out. You could feel the fear around him. If you got close to him, it was like a sense of panic. It was contagious . . . He was more important as a writer than as a singer. Although his baritone underneath mine when we used to do a unison blend made a third voice that was really interesting and gave a depth and a texture . . . He'd done some acid and he'd had a bad experience on it. I think that was more responsible for it. And he'd had a bad relationship with a dancer who hurt his feelings. Alcohol may have been a contributing factor, but I wouldn't put it down to that. He was basically a nervous guy anyway, even without drugs. If he smoked a joint he'd be a wreck."

Had the Byrds been wiser or more sympathetic, they might have retained Clark in a Brian Wilson role, leaving him to compose in isolation, while they toured. Over the years, he learned to live with a backlog of unrecorded songs and would probably have remained in the Byrds had he been able to win their full attention and respect as a singer-songwriter. Unfortunately, the competition and jealousy over songwriting and publishing ensured that this was never likely to happen. Clark would no doubt have enjoyed playing the genius in Hollywood exile, but that would have been anathema to the Byrds. Far from being intimidated by his departure, they would soon find a greater confidence in their own abilities. McGuinn always clung to a casual comment made some months later by George Harrison as a final vindication of Clark's exit. "In a way being four got us together," he reflects. "It became a much tighter organization. I remember a communication between Crosby and George Harrison at the time, and Harrison said, 'Isn't it lighter and nicer with just four?' And it was."

Derek Taylor appreciated Harrison's comments, but did not subscribe to the less is more theory. "It was a meaner, leaner unit if you like, as it was now a foursome like the Beatles. But I thought it was a great loss. It was like the Stones. I always thought the Stones had a great completeness with Brian Jones. That was a marvellous fivesome and again all had their place in this thing."

The timing of Clark's leaving proved particularly frustrating for manager Jim Dickson, who had gone to New York on that fateful plane trip in order to complete negotiations on a major new project. CBS had recently appointed a new art director who had previously worked for one of the major fashion magazines in Manhattan. He had also been involved in the production of a photo book of John F. Kennedy which had been window displayed across an entire city block in the Big Apple. With such a keen eye for photography, he immediately latched on to the untapped potential of the Byrds' image and contacted their management.

Dickson had been photographing the Byrds constantly for well over a year, until his camera had been stolen during the recent trip to Hawaii. Throughout that time, he had collected hundreds of photos, most of which had never been published. They included many personal, studio and location shots. There was even a complete 36 reel taken the night Dylan appeared with them at Ciro's. In addition to these, Tickner/Dickson had specifically commissioned both Curt Gunther and Barry Feinstein to tour with the Byrds, so their shots were also owned by the management. It was a stupendous portfolio. "I'd saved the best pictures all the way through so that we'd have a historical account of the Byrds' evolution," Dickson recalls. "CBS were so impressed that they decided to subsidize 200,000 copies of a programme book which they said would knock the socks off the Beatles. The art director was going out on a limb to get Avedon & Penn to compete with some of the best photographers in the world to shoot the Byrds. This was a major involvement from CBS."

Dickson desperately hoped to keep the project alive, but without Clark it was doomed. "CBS immediately cancelled the whole idea. Every picture we had with Gene was suddenly obsolete. A lot of fine photography. Gene Clark not getting on that plane and quitting the group not only destroyed those plans but made CBS realize that the Byrds was a pretty fragile thing to start getting behind. They thought, 'These guys are not professional or safe enough in what they're doing. They can self-destruct without any outside influence.' So there it was – all cancelled. This was supposed to be our big boost to catch up that I'd been working so hard to engineer. There had already been several trips to New York showing pictures and talking it through. To do all that groundwork and have it blown away by somebody who just got off a plane . . . It wasn't expected. He'd never got off a plane before. And when I heard McGuinn say in later years, 'If our management had been a bit smarter about it . . .' I think back about a lot of incidents like that where major chances to improve our situation were stopped by one or all of them."

McGuinn added one final twist to the tale, albeit decades on. In several interviews he put forward the conspiracy theory that the Byrds' management, specifically Dickson, had urged Clark to leave in order to create their version of Elvis Presley. In 1997, he told me: "Dickson was in hospital about 12 years ago and [my wife] Camilla and I went to see him. I don't think he was at death's door, but he was kind of confessional. He was telling me that around the time Gene left he and Tickner were romancing him to be a solo and be the next Elvis Presley." Considering the many problems Clark's departure caused, this still seems a remarkable allegation.

"It's not true," Dickson insists. "It's like the 'Beefeaters'. I've heard McGuinn say in interviews, '. . . and then we were the Beefeaters.' And that was just a name Jac Holzman used. It was a stupid name and when Jac wanted them to be called that we all said, 'No!' McGuinn doesn't really know what happened. I was never even a fan of Elvis Presley. Eddie maybe saw Gene as Elvis and talked about it one time. But that was much later. I certainly didn't ever think Gene would replace them or become bigger. That wasn't ever in the cards. I felt obliged to try and help him. He was still under contract. I was always trying to find a way to get him back. Later, I got Chris and Michael to play on his album. I was into the symbolism, trying to make it look like he was still in the family, so to speak. But he didn't want to go on the road any more."

Clark was frustratingly unpredictable and ambivalent about precisely what he wanted. At first, he merely demanded a break, then settled into the notion of writing and recording with the Byrds, but not touring. Only when that suggestion was vetoed did he stand firm about leaving. Resisting the entreaties of both Dickson and Tickner – whose respective artistic passion and business logic was a powerfully persuasive combination – underlined the extent of Clark's desperation. He knew he was quitting the Byrds when they were scaling new peaks creatively, but he left anyway. It was the first serious example of a self-destructive tendency that characterized his career hereafter. There was no apparent logic to his decision, beyond self-preservation. It was as if he was acting from instinct alone, like an animal sensing danger from afar. Clark always believed in intuition, convinced that he was blessed with the power of prophecy. Perhaps the incident on the plane was a manifestation of a deeper fear that he could never articulate.

There is a sense of doom that sometimes accompanies achievement, a realization that the moment may be fleeting and its essence must be grasped in all its evanescent glory. Clark had been experiencing such highs since the summer of 1965, but his psyche resembled an explosive thermometer. Hollywood had allowed him to reinvent himself, but at what cost? He was a feted pop star, who sometimes felt invincible, but at night his dreams were still plagued by intimidating visions of pain and torture, the recurring images of 'tacks and glass' that were attached to his body like thorns on the head of a martyr. Clark's *carpe diem* attitude to life failed to appreciate that living constantly in the present can be as dangerous as obsessive immersion in the past. There is always that furtive fear of the future, a dread so overwhelming that it almost makes perverse sense to destroy your gift or good fortune before it is stolen away by time or fate. Clark himself hinted at this while stumbling to articulate what was happening in his head during the early months of 1966.

"After 'Eight Miles High' I felt we had a direction to go that might have been absolutely incredible. We could have taken it from there, but I felt because of the confusion of egos, we were headed in a direction that wouldn't have that importance or impact. There was [a] slight falling out amongst members of the group . . . it was between everybody at that time and nobody knew who was right and who was wrong. So when I walked off that plane that day, it wasn't so much that I was afraid of flying as I was tired of flying. I felt as though I was just going to be travelling on in an aimless direction after really having achieved a high . . . I actually did not intend to leave the group when that happened. I only basically made an appeal to take a break. I thought we needed it. We'd been travelling too hard, we'd been touring intensely heavy schedules, trying to record in the meantime. Just nuts. By that time, I thought, 'Wait a minute . . . we're starting to lose our perspective.' Then, of course, that . . . was kind of a blow to the other guys. They felt as though I was slighting them, I felt as though they were slighting me, so all those facts involved overshadowed the flying thing."

There were no immediate prospects for Clark after leaving the Byrds, simply more trouble. Always prone to tricky romantic entanglements, he soon found himself enmeshed in a liaison with the embodiment of Californian perfection, Michelle Phillips. The lissome, blonde goddess from the Mamas & The Papas was temporarily estranged from her husband John Phillips and in search of new excitement. When the affair was later discovered, she was briefly fired from her group, a punishment which no doubt troubled and embarrassed Clark. "It was a fine romance if one was into danger, but Gene wasn't, not really," she recalls. "Gene was a farmer's boy, a lovely boy about my own age, but he was also a neurotic little Scorpio from Missouri . . . It was all a bit tense because he felt very guilty and didn't like the idea of having an affair with a married, albeit separated, woman. We couldn't go out together, couldn't be seen together; that would be blatant. He would sometimes wake up in the middle of the night and wake me up and tell me to go home. But we were together a lot."

Remarkably, the press failed to unearth or reveal the secret behind Michelle Phillips' dramatic dismissal from the Mamas & The Papas later that summer, so Clark was spared some unwanted attention. For much of that time, he preferred to lay low. "I didn't want to talk to anybody. I cut my telephone lines. I just stayed in my house for two months. I couldn't deal with it any more . . . It was just the intensity of 'What do we do now? How do we deal with this?' You're going well and none of it makes any sense. . . . We were starting to change producers, change this, change that. We already had a winning formula. I felt as though it was going to fall apart, and also there was the pressure. You had tremendous egos in that group, myself included . . . a tremendous amount of ego all the time." Still reeling from his nervous breakdown, he sought solace back home in Kansas before agreeing to a brief interview with the teen magazine *Flip*. Even then, he was noticeably shaken, and as reporter Michelle Straubing observed: "It was a new Gene Clark that walked through the door. Still recovering from his state of physical exhaustion he seemed quite pale and walked at a much slower pace. It was now even more apparent that he had been quite ill."

Speaking about his decision to leave the Byrds, he indicated that it was not taken hastily. "I had been thinking about it for some time. I finally made the decision that I wanted to leave and go solo. We sat down as a group and talked it over. We all agreed that it could be worked out and that the Byrds would continue as a group of four."

The rest was silence – at least as far as the other Byrds were concerned. Then, as now, the most appropriate way for a group to deal with the departure of a key member was to say as little as possible. Where appropriate, photos were cropped at CBS to remove Clark from the line-up and the publicity department was ordered to adopt a Stalinist revisionism. An International CBS memo to all its affiliates announced: "In order to preserve the continuity of the Byrds' popularity, this should not be treated as a special announcement. Instead, you should just begin to use four-man photographs in your publicity and advertisements. Inquiries as to why Gene Clark left the group should run something like this. 'Gene Clark for his own personal reasons felt he no longer wanted to perform with the group. He still retains a close friendship with the remaining members.'"

This was not the approach of Derek Taylor. Although he understood the machinations of PR, he was sufficiently moved by the loss of Gene Clark to pen a lengthy tribute that cut through the banality and cold expediency of record company politics. Taylor's message to the world bore scant resemblance to a public relations exercise and was closer in tone to an elegy. As if returning from a funeral and counselling an old friend, Taylor offered the following report in his finest bedside manner.

> They have recently survived a dramatic upheaval – the separation of Gene Clark, tambourine man, most prolific songwriter in the group, physically the strongest (the only one with obvious muscles), vocally the deepest, emotionally the warmest, and a founder member.
>
> He left not because of a row, and not because he was fired. He left because he was tired of the multitude of obligations facing successful rock 'n' roll groups. Tired of the travel, the hotels and the food. Tired of the pursuit of the most relentless autograph hunters, weary of the constant screaming. Bothered by the photographs and interviews, and exhausted by the whole punishing scene.
>
> Gene was a good friend and a valuable Byrd – and while fans were mourning his absence, the Byrds too were feeling an emptiness which they sublimated by tackling the problems of consolidating their unit into four . . . four, whom they knew would be expected to equate the impact of five.
>
> And such is the fickleness of fans and of all people, and such is the healing power of time, the foursome made it without Gene. Bass player Chris Hillman stepped forward from the shadows to take over David Crosby's mike, and to sing the vocal bottom. Crosby stepped to centre mike, where Gene had stood in the old days. McGuinn, King Byrd, stayed where he

was and adjusted his glasses, and trusted everything would work out all right . . . and started to talk to audiences. Yes – to talk. With wit and a firmness few had detected who did not know him well. And at the back of the stage, visible at last, Michael Clarke assumed tambourine responsibilities. Thus did the Byrds become four, and thus, since time began, have the ranks closed totally to conceal the absence of those who have gone.

Gene will always be a Byrd. For he wrote Byrd songs and, indeed, 'Eight Miles High' was his hymn to London – to the very strange and mystical impact the city had on the Byrds when they arrived last year to justify the intriguing reputation they had earned so swiftly with 'Mr Tambourine Man'."

Even the Byrds at their most eloquent and sympathetic could never have composed such a frank and poignant statement about their lost tambourine man. It would never have occurred to them to do so. As a quartet, they retained enough self-belief to convince themselves that his contribution would not be missed. Although Clark's exit was accepted by the public, there were many who felt that the original spirit of the group had been irrevocably lost as a result of his departure. The group's visionary founder Jim Dickson was not unsympathetic to such a view: "To each person the Byrds began when they arrived and ended when they left. David's no different. Chris is no different. McGuinn is the only one that didn't leave so there's no Byrds without him. To hear Gene Clark tell it, there's no Byrds without him. I'm the same. There's no right or wrong."

CHAPTER EIGHTEEN

Space And Drugs

WHILE the Byrds had dominated 1965 and could rightly claim to be America's most popular group, their standing in the wake of Gene Clark's departure was less secure. Competition on the folk-rock front had intensified to such a degree that the charts were dominated by groups reaping the rewards of the Byrds' groundbreaking work. In the month of Clark's leaving, the US Top 10 included hits from the Mamas & The Papas ('California Dreamin''), Simon & Garfunkel ('Homeward Bound') and the Lovin' Spoonful ('Daydream'). All three had oblique connections to the Byrds.

Simon & Garfunkel had headed the US charts during the last week of 1965 with the evocative 'The Sounds Of Silence', a composition that perfectly bookended the protest boom of that year. Producer Tom Wilson had manufactured this exercise in electric folk by overdubbing rock instrumentation on to an acoustic version of the song previously available on the duo's debut album, *Wednesday Morning 3AM*. That this had occurred while the Byrds were struggling to complete *Turn! Turn! Turn!* and vacillating over their choice of follow-up to Dylan's 'All I Really Want To Do' was no coincidence. As Jim Dickson confirms: "CBS were screaming for records and the Byrds couldn't come up with new songs. They couldn't put out enough product. CBS were upset. There mightn't have been a Simon & Garfunkel if the Byrds were able to deliver. 'The Sounds Of Silence' was made in reaction to the Byrds at CBS in New York. They took an old acoustic master and overdubbed it without their knowledge. Paul Simon later thanked us at Monterey.

He sought me out. I'd never met him before. He said: 'You guys are responsible for our success and I want to thank you for it.' I thought, 'How rare. How wonderful to find somebody that thoughtful in rock 'n' roll.'"

If the Byrds deserved a nod of thanks from Simon & Garfunkel, then similar gratitude was due from the Lovin' Spoonful. As early as August 1965, Crosby was telling British reporters that they would be the next big group, even though they had yet to release their first single. After 'Do You Believe In Magic?' charted the following October, the Byrds paid tribute by performing their own a cappella version on *Hullabaloo*. The easy-going relationship between the two groups was echoed in their mutual association with the Mamas & The Papas. The Spoonful's John Sebastian and Zal Yanovsky had previously played alongside Cass Elliot in the Big Three, and both Crosby and McGuinn knew this clique of musicians from their folk days. Although Gene Clark's adulterous affair with Michelle Phillips might have strained relations between the Mamas & The Papas and the Byrds, both camps remained close during this fertile period. As Michelle says: "There was never any sense of competition because we were all friends. I'd known David Crosby long before the Byrds, and McGuinn too. It was the same with John Sebastian and the Spoonful. We'd all come from the same place really. I think the fact that we were politically of the same mind helped to unify us."

There were many other Byrds' connections that spring of 1966. The Jefferson Airplane, which included Crosby's friend Paul Kantner, were preparing their debut album *Jefferson Airplane Takes Off* and had already been given carte blanche to use the Byrds' rehearsal room at the 9000 building. The first album from Love was also issued at this time and, amid their ranks, could be found former Byrds' roadie Bryan MacLean, who borrowed freely from the musical style of his ex-employees and hijacked their freakier following. Frank Zappa's newly formed Mothers Of Invention also had a ready-made audience consisting of Carl Franzoni and the Vito's crowd.

Another recently established group whose future would be linked with the Byrds was the Buffalo Springfield. While the Byrds were often slow to show magnanimity to each other, they proved surprisingly supportive of putative rivals. Stephen Stills remembers Chris Hillman in the surprising role as patron of the arts to his emerging group. "It was Chris who really got us off the ground to begin with. He was in the Byrds, who were really successful at the time, and he happened to come and see us rehearsing on what little equipment we had. He really dug us and literally got us off the street, borrowed equipment and really got us going."

Hillman not only advised the Springfield but approached Elmer Valentine and secured them their all-important debut gig at the Whisky. David Crosby tagged along and seemed initially cool but soon appreciated the dramatic guitar interplay between Stills and Young. Like the Byrds at Ciro's, Buffalo Springfield looked and sounded special and it was not long before interested parties arrived to check out their potential. Quite uncharacteristically, the normally reserved Hillman felt confident enough to consider the possibility of managing the group, with assistance from McGuinn. The idea of fellow performers attempting to manage any group, let alone one as volatile as the Springfield, seemed totally presumptuous and unworkable. McGuinn was sufficiently curious to attend one of their Whisky gigs but left unimpressed, prompting Hillman to abandon the management idea. Instead, the group were offered a support slot on some Southern California dates with the Byrds, which boosted their confidence and indicated that they might yet emerge as strong competition if they could only control their egos.

Buffalo Springfield would have been better advised to woo Jim Dickson, although he already had enough problems managing the Byrds. Tickner and Dickson had loaned the Springfield equipment belonging to the Dillards, but showed no great desire to oversee their career, perhaps feeling that it might result in a conflict of interest. Instead, Steve Stills and company signed to the old enemy Greene and Stone, who were still riding high with Sonny & Cher and had just launched Bob Lind, whose 'Elusive Butterfly' sounded like an instant standard. Terry Melcher, another ghost from the Byrds' recent past, had channelled his indignation into production work with the less talented Paul Revere & The Raiders, whose anti-drugs warning 'Kicks' outcharted 'Eight Miles High', much to

Crosby's fury. The chart statistics clearly showed that the Byrds could not afford to rest easily, while the emergence of rival underground groups threatened to steal away some of their hipper following.

Not that David Crosby could ever be accused of being anything but hip, certainly not in the spring of 1966 when he seemed attuned to every significant ruction in the musical and counter-culture climate of Los Angeles. One day he received a leaflet accompanied by a brochure with an enticing invitation: 'Jog your deep and merie way to the fourth annual Renaissance Pleasure Faire and May Market'. Originally founded by schoolteacher, Phyliss Patterson, the Faire was sponsored by KPFK Radio and drew 8,000 or more people to the Paramount Ranch in Agoura where the clock was turned back to the Elizabethan age, with a parachronistic dash of King Arthur's mythological court, complete with pageantry, knights in armour, comely maidens, costumed musicians and entertainers. There was even a celebration of Robin Hood's birthday. On arrival, the first spectators were greeted by heraldic banners and the sound of trumpets. At the heart of the event was the fair itself, carefully constructed by the Living Art Theater to recreate the vivacity of a springtime marketplace.

The other Byrds joined Crosby on the Pleasure Faire excursion, which they treated like a schoolday visit to a theme park. Some said the group looked Elizabethan, with their pageboy haircuts and Crosby's tunic style green-suede cape. Their music, particularly back in 1964, also had an Elizabethan quality, especially on songs like 'Tomorrow Is A Long Ways Away', the lilt of which was reminiscent of a sixteenth-century madrigal. Even their followers had been described as resembling stragglers from Sherwood Forest, a fitting image for the historically wayward Robin Hood anniversary promoted at the Faire. Crosby or McGuinn could probably have won an audition to play Alan-a-Dale in a theatrical reenactment.

Arriving at the entrance of the Paramount Ranch, the Byrds made their way down Green Meadow Lane to the Hawker's Market on Ha'Penny Hill, where the fair was in full swing. On sale were Florentine candlesticks, stained glass, spices, Robin Hood hats, frocks, flowers, rings, mystic charts, amulets, velvet money bags, bright beads, jewellery, pottery, stoneware and fool's caps. The grounds then spread outwards, leaving the group free to wander individually and experience different events and sideshows. Weavers and craftsmen demonstrated their skills; aspirant alchemists, sorcerers, soothsayers, clairvoyants and wizards promised magic; dancers gambolled around a May pole; games of skill included archery and darts tournaments, plus the scary 'slay the dragon'; medieval nuptials enticed young lovers, while dunking stools provided a reminder of the fate of witches. Food was available at quaintly titled stands such as 'Ye Feasting Stalls', 'Ye London Bakerie' and 'Ye Mead & Ale Stall'. High school dramatic societies performed Marlowe's *Dr Faustus* and Gay's *The Beggar's Opera* and, as Crosby recalls, there was music *everywhere*. Strolling players strummed lutes, the Neo-Romanesque Ensemble played a concert and there was a chance to attend the Musica Antiqua Consort of Rare Instruments. More earthy fare was on offer at Ye Angel & Strumpet Coffe Hous courtesy of bawdy balladeer Beverly Miller or the Fertility Song Lady, Donna Curry. It is not known whether Crosby was stoned during the Renaissance Faire, but you can only imagine how exhilarating, exciting or disorientating his surroundings would have felt in such circumstances. Either way, the event stimulated his imagination so much that he wrote an evocative musical memoir to be featured a year later on the Byrds' fourth album, *Younger Than Yesterday*.

Immediately after the Renaissance Pleasure Faire, Derek Taylor decided to enhance the group's profile by providing some free quotes to *Melody Maker* which they presented as a Crosby/McGuinn interview. The most striking part of the feature came towards the end where McGuinn spoke of his ambition "to make an experimental film using electronic colours", adding "but that's my personal project". More revealing was the surprise news of a Byrds film in the offing. "We're all hoping to act in a picture which we may even start work on this summer. We've got the script we like already. We're ready to go the straight acting route, with no stand-up guitar playing and singing scenes at all. That would all be in the background track. Now it all hinges on a certain director, who shall remain nameless . . . it's still being talked over and negotiated."

There was a bittersweet irony in McGuinn's words for the film project had already been causing headaches prior to his published interview. Earlier in the year, Dickson had offered $1,000 to Carole Eastman to write a film script inspired by the Byrds. It was a clever and audacious move as Eastman was a relative neophyte. Originally trained as a ballet dancer, her career was forestalled by a broken foot, after which she switched to modelling, then acting and screenwriting. While the Byrds were at Ciro's in April 1965, filming had begun on the quirky, existential Western *The Shooting*, starring Warren Oates and Jack Nicholson, for which Eastman had written the screenplay. It would be another two years before the movie was released. One of Eastman's closest friends was Dickson's former wife Diane Varsi, which meant she maintained a distant relationship with the Byrds' manager. "It was almost competitive," he says. "She was Diane's mentor in a way. When I married my second wife [Harley], Carole came along to tell me that I was making a big mistake. I don't really know what her motive was but she was very insistent that I shouldn't marry her. Maybe she thought I'd eventually get back with Diane or something."

Employing Eastman meant that Dickson had someone who not only appreciated the Byrds' myth but had seen it grow from nothing. "Carole was there before Derek Taylor, even before Eddie Tickner. She was in the studio at World-Pacific when I was rehearsing them. She had studied them very carefully and knew what they were about and what their limitations were." Eastman submitted a draft treatment to Tickner which included details of the early scenes. Dickson caught a glimpse and was immediately impressed. "When I read the first page, I knew she was on the right track. It began with Michael Clarke sitting in front of a big orange background. The opening was perfect. She knew what would be cinematic and Michael always looked great on film. I expect it would have been a very interesting and semi-abstract film. Way more abstract than pop films like *Help!*. It wouldn't have been like that at all. If you watch *Five Easy Pieces*, which she wrote, you'll get some idea."

Unfortunately, Eastman's original concept was scuppered the moment Gene Clark left the group. This was another example of the unforeseen repercussions of his abrupt departure. Forced to rewrite some scenes, she agreed to amend the script but must have wondered whether the Byrds would still be around by the time the film, if sold, was completed. Meanwhile, the group was adjusting to a future without their main songwriter.

McGuinn and Dolores were living in a modest abode on Woodrow Wilson Drive when Bob Dylan surprised them with a visit. The recent departure of Gene Clark and the radio censorship inflicted on 'Eight Miles High' and 'Rainy Day Women # 12 and 35' may have rekindled his interest in the Byrds. He was curious about McGuinn's state of mind and seemed both critical and appreciative in the same breath. "It was funny," says Dolores, "because Dylan was saying, 'You taught me how to sing my music.' Dylan had come into town with Allen Ginsberg and we were living in this tiny ranch-house. Dylan said, 'Oh, man, I thought you'd be living in a bigger home.' I guess he expected us to be living in some grand Hollywood mansion. He wanted or wished that [McGuinn] had made more money. He was going on like that."

McGuinn had his own unique perspective on Dylan's surprise visit. "He said to me, 'Look, I'm a millionaire, and I want you to get to the same place, and you're not going to do it singing with the Byrds.' He told me that I'd do it by writing songs. Writing 12 songs and throwing 11 away, every day. He was right, but I haven't found time to do that. I don't want to be a millionaire anyway."

Dylan seemed fixated with money during the conversation and kept returning to that theme before finally relaxing. McGuinn wondered what had prompted this outpouring. "I got the feeling that he was guilty about making all that bread. He said, 'I don't know, man, how are you ever going to make a million dollars? I'd like to help you somehow.' I figured he wanted someone to play with, to hang out with. He was into a talking thing. He'd vary at times, putting himself and everybody and me on, and then just talking straight. We got into some beautiful philosophical things about the nature of the universe, deep stuff, then we'd go back to trivia, riffing on words, playing word games, like the 17 extensions from a word. I sort of miss him."

The discussion with Dylan about "the nature of the universe" sounded suspiciously like the lyrics to a song McGuinn had recently completed. Minus Gene Clark, he had faced the daunting task of composing the Byrds' all-important new single and came up with '5 D (Fifth Dimension)', an abstract lyric set against a waltz-time arrangement. The composition had emerged in a flash of post-sleep inspiration. "When I wrote '5 D', I got up one morning, sat down on my couch . . . I don't usually pick up the guitar that early, but for some reason I did that morning and just strummed it out and wrote it in about ten minutes." Both Crosby and Hillman applauded his effort and producer Allen Stanton was also enthusiastic. The song was an exceedingly ambitious piece of work from the group, lacking even the hit potential of 'Eight Miles High'. McGuinn was upbeat about its chances though and seemed eager to explain the origins of the composition.

"'5 D' is a poem in *3/4* about a book I read *1-2-3-4, More, More, More, More* written by Don Landis and published by Dylart. If you can get your hands on a copy, you'll understand what I did in the song. If you don't it's sort of vague and philosophical. It's sort of weird but . . . what I'm talking about is the whole universe, the Fifth Dimension which is height, width, depth, time and something else. But there definitely are more dimensions than five. It's infinite. The Fifth Dimension is the threshold of scientific knowledge. See, there are people walking around practising fifth dimensional ways of life and the scientists are still on two or three dimensional levels. There's a conflict there. A lot of our world is very materialistic and scientific. It overlooks the beauty of the universe. That's what the song is about. Maybe it'll tell a few people what's going on in life. The organ player on it is Van Dyke Parks from Los Angeles. When he came into the studio I told him to think Bach. He was already thinking Bach before that anyway. I wrote that song but the arrangement just came out the way it did. We just sat down and did it."

Released in June 1966, '5 D' predictably failed to storm the US charts, peaking at number 44. Elsewhere, it would fare even worse. McGuinn defended the song with great eloquence, and in later interviews expressed despondency that the true message he was attempting to convey had been misinterpreted: "I was talking about something philosophical and very light and airy with that song, and everyone took it down . . . they took it down to drugs. They said it was a dope song and that I was on LSD, and it wasn't any of that, in fact. I was dealing with Einstein's theory of relativity, the fourth dimension being time and the fifth dimension not being specified . . . so it's open, channel five, the next step. I saw it to be a timelessness, a sort of void in space where time has no meaning. All I did was perceive something that was there. The catalyst to the whole idea was a booklet someone sent me called *1-2-3-4, More, More, More, More* which was about dimensions but explained in a cartoon way. It gave me the premise for the song, but I think that the booklet should've been issued with the song so people would have been able to understand. I gave the copy I had to Allen Stanton who read it and gave it to his kid because he thought it was a comic."

In many ways, '5 D' was not merely a science fiction song about other dimensions, but the culmination of McGuinn's experiences with the spiritual sect Subud. Fundamentally, it looked back to that moment in January 1965 when he had surrendered to Allah in a burning flash of spiritual enlightenment. Of all his lyrics, '5 D' came closest to fusing his twin interests in science and spirituality. As he elaborated: "It was an ethereal trip into metaphysics, into an almost Muslim submission to Allah, an almighty spirit, free-floating, the fifth dimension being that 'mesh' Einstein theorized about. He proved theoretically – and I choose to believe it – that there's an ethereal mesh in the universe, and probably the reason for the speed of light being what it is is because of the friction going through that mesh . . . We were talking about a way of life, sort of a submission to God or whatever you want to call that mesh, that life force. I believe the universe is alive. And I'm into science fiction to the point that I'm long past doubting that there's a way of exceeding the speed of light. I believe this race will eventually get into teleportation . . . I believe in the immortality of a spiritual essence of everyone."

The clash between materialism and spirituality was a familiar dialogue among the Byrds' contemporaries during 1966. Mind expanding drugs, money and a belief in artistic independence were constant subjects of discourse. Faced with the implicit contradictions between their lifestyles, status and inner beliefs, most decided to have their cake and eat it. In his previous conversation with McGuinn, Dylan had recognized the conflict between God and Mammon, but seemed remarkably adept at accepting both. He could switch from discussing house prices to pondering the meaning of life in consecutive sentences without any sense of incongruity. Others felt more conflicted. Barry McGuire had embraced the hedonism of the time with the same proselytizing zeal as David Crosby. "David was just like me," he says. "A womanizer. That was our whole thing. Get loaded, get laid, and sing songs. That was our life." But in the aftermath of 'Eve Of Destruction', McGuire found himself becoming more in tune with McGuinn's style of spirituality. "I got on this spiritual search in 1966 and was looking for the answer. That's when it really kicked in. Acid was like a sacrament that unlocked a door. I went to New Mexico and had an out of body LSD experience, and when I came back and re-entered reality my whole concept of death and the purpose of life had changed. I left the business, moved to Topanga Canyon, didn't hang out with Hollywood people or go to parties. I just stayed there in my swimming pool and smoked marijuana. Friends came out and visited me during the week."

It was at this pivotal point that McGuire briefly reconnected with McGuinn in a meeting that was to have a significant effect on his future spiritual direction. "He came to Topanga and we talked. 'McGuire,' he said, 'you have to know that there's something out there, some intellect beyond space itself, the infinite being that knows your name, and you can trust. Just trust this loving force and everything will turn out all right.' So I did." In effect, McGuinn was combining the Norman Vincent Peale motto "I trust . . ." with the lyrical sentiments of '5 D', plus a dash of Subud awareness, to promote a positive philosophy that McGuire found both appealing and profound.

McGuinn's contention that the philosophic '5 D' was perceived as a 'dope song', and may have suffered commercially as a result, was not far-fetched. Within a month of its release, the showbiz bible *Variety* ran the headline: 'Pop Music's Moral Crisis: Dope Tunes Fan DJ's Ire'. Highlighting what they saw as the greatest moral outrage since Elvis Presley's sexually explicit pelvic thrusts, the magazine announced: "A recent wave of pop songs contains references to getting high on dope or liquor, suicide, prostitution, and sundry other way out, offbeat and taboo subjects. The freedom of today's young songwriters and performers to tackle any subject is resulting in a rising tide of DJ protest." Inevitably, 'Eight Miles High' was back in the dock, but so too were the seemingly innocuous Lovin' Spoonful, whose name was supposedly junkie jargon for the instrument used for liquefying heroin powder. The group patiently pointed out that their name was taken from Mississippi John Hurt's 'Coffee Blues', whose lyrics featured the line "I love my baby by the lovin' spoonful". Producer Eric Jacobsen quipped: "For years, mothers all over the world have given their children a spoonful of sugar to help the medicine down. Even Mary Poppins did it."

In the same month that the drugs issue was under debate, the Byrds issued their third album, *Fifth Dimension*, its very title suggesting the kind of otherworldly experience liable to alert the media drug police. Although the work was seen to grow in stature over the years, it met a tepid critical reception during the summer of 1966. On the credit side, it showed that the Byrds had moved away from the familiar jingle-jangle sound of their previous recordings and were thinking more in terms of an 'album concept' rather than a collection of songs. The record was not without its flaws, however. Several songs lacked the familiar harmonic blend that characterized the Byrds' collaboration with Gene Clark. Some of the material had an unusually raw, metallic guitar sound which, although adventurous, seemed unfamiliar to pop audiences of the period. The Byrds were experimenting with new ideas but the results were hit and miss. Both the lyric writing and the melodies were sometimes intriguing, sometimes unmemorable.

The entire album appeared to have been put together hurriedly, under great pressure, a view reinforced by a scan of the session listings which show only one outtake, the traditional 'I Know My Rider' ('I Know You Rider'). As with *Turn! Turn! Turn!*, the Byrds were required to complete the album to a tight deadline and without Clark's usual backlog of songs, new material was at a premium. To make things even more difficult for themselves, the group had elected to break with tradition by not featuring a single Dylan song in the set, as if expunging the memories of former folk-rock triumphs. "Perhaps we were consciously trying to get away from it," McGuinn ponders. "I guess we were trying to show Dylan we didn't need him. But that was a mistake because his songs were good for us."

For younger purchasers, the fact that the album included 11 tracks instead of the usual 12, several of which had previously appeared on singles, meant that it was hardly a bargain in strictly economic terms. Such factors may seem trivial today, but back in 1966 they were important and disconcerting, especially considering that contemporary British Beatles albums contained up to 14 songs. At a time when the Byrds needed to look solid, confident and bountiful in the aftermath of Clark's loss, they placed themselves in a position where their work could be considered thin and meagre. It is easy to assume that mid-Sixties rock critics would have applauded a work as radically new as *Fifth Dimension*, but this was not the case. Even the highly respected underground rock writer Jon Landau felt uncertain about the new direction and expressed a preference for the more commercially acceptable folk-rock sound of the earlier albums. Sitting in judgement, he concluded: "This album, then, cannot be considered up to the standards set by the Byrds' first two and basically demonstrates that they should be thinking in terms of replacing Gene Clark, instead of just carrying on without him."

A few years later, McGuinn admitted that *Fifth Dimension* had not achieved everything he had hoped. "I think it was a disappointment to the public. They weren't ready for our material and, to be honest, I don't think it was up to the level we set out for ourselves. It was a step down in quality because we were new at it and to do something like that well takes a lot of practice."

In effect, *Fifth Dimension* was a transitional album, which showed that the Byrds were still capable of forging ahead into new musical territories, with or without Gene Clark. If they had been allowed an additional few months to adjust to Clark's creative loss, offered the opportunity to compose new material and structure the album more carefully, they might have produced a far more important work that would have enshrined their godhead at a crucial moment in rock history. As it was, they were hard pushed to compete against the Beatles' *Revolver*, the Rolling Stones' *Aftermath* or Dylan's *Blonde On Blonde* and faced competition from the Beach Boys' groundbreaking *Pet Sounds*, and the well-publicized debut albums of the Mothers Of Invention and Jefferson Airplane. All things considered, *Fifth Dimension* did well to reach number 24 in *Billboard*.

As expected, the work commenced with the recent single, '5 D (Fifth Dimension)'. This was the first occasion on which a Byrds album had not kicked off with a number 1 single. "I liked '5 D'," Jim Dickson says, a view supported by Crosby and Hillman. "I thought it was one of the better songs McGuinn did. The mistake was the Van Dyke Parks' tag at the end. If they'd made that the intro and set a mood before the singing started then that song could have been a hit."

Having previously pioneered Dylan folk rock, the Byrds returned to traditional material on the second track, 'Wild Mountain Thyme'. The song was a coffee house favourite from the pre-Byrds era, having been successfully adapted by the McPeake Family and the Clancy Brothers With Tommy Makem. "I played it in my folk days and took it from Pete Seeger," McGuinn remembers. All four Byrds received a publishing credit for their arrangement, which had a less pronounced ethnic feel, largely due to the orchestration. The strings had been suggested by producer Allen Stanton and sounded tasteful and unobtrusive enough not to over-sentimentalize the theme. "I went with it because I liked the idea of orchestration on those folky things," McGuinn concludes.

The Byrds' second excursion into the realms of science fiction (following '5 D') could be heard on 'Mr Spaceman', the song that provided the group with the tag 'space rock'. It was lighter in mood than the remaining material on the album and showed a closer affinity to their earlier work, with Clarke playing Gene's tambourine and McGuinn and Crosby weaving a fine harmonic blend set against a slightly countrified backing. McGuinn had originally intended to compose a serious dramatic song about a trip into outer space but, as the theme developed, it became more whimsical.

Dickson felt the humour was misplaced. "'Mr Spaceman' was too trivial," he says. "I didn't like the 'flies in my beard, toothpaste was smeared' line. It was a trashy lyric. The lines about 'please take me along, I won't do anything wrong' – that's where McGuinn's at. But the 'flies' was a very forced image and I don't like ugly images in songs for no reason. That song did better in foreign countries where they don't understand English. To this day, it earns more money abroad."

McGuinn felt serious enough about 'Mr Spaceman' to stress its more cerebral content: "I'm interested in astronomy and the possibility of connecting with extraterrestrial life and I thought that it might work the other way round, if we tried to contact them. I thought that the song being played on the air might be a way of getting through to them. But even if there had been anybody up there listening, they wouldn't have heard because I found out later that AM airwaves diffuse in space too rapidly."

In complete contrast, 'I See You', with its intricate, jagged, raga-inspired guitar work, veered towards psychedelia. Musically and lyrically, it lacked the power and intelligence of 'Eight Miles High' but provided a clear signpost for what would be happening in rock music in 1967. The lyrics, co-written by McGuinn and Crosby, were deliberately obscure and sung so fast that they were almost impossible to decipher. In many respects, this song was a turning point, revealing the Byrds moving away from their familiar lyrical tradition and concentrating less on dark romance than the dramatizing of psychological states. McGuinn suspects that they may have written the song well in advance of the album, although he cannot be sure. Given its sonic resemblance to Coltrane's *Impressions*, it seems likely that it was conceived on their Dick Clark package tour. Crosby was modest to the point of dismissive when reminded of this early effort: "It didn't turn me on that much, in retrospect."

He felt far happier with his first solo contribution to the Byrds, 'What's Happening?!?!', a stark and unusual composition expressing his pervasive sense of emotional confusion. "It's a very strange song," he admits. "It asks questions of what's going on here and who does it all belong to and why is it all going on. I just ask the questions because I don't really know the answers . . . Actually, each time I ask the questions, McGuinn answers them on the 12-string. He says that same thing with the instrument musically. You can tell it, you can feel it."

Striking and ambitious, 'What's Happening?!?!' continued the raga rock experiment begun on 'Why' with the addition of a droning guitar and lyrics that intentionally avoided the creation of a dramatic vehicle for the theme. At a time when McGuinn was still deeply involved in Subud, the song's agnostic perspective ably summarized Crosby's position. As he concludes: "It was one of the very first of my, 'Well, gee, who am I? What's going on here? Where's the instruction booklet? How come nobody knows what's going on?' songs. I've written a great many of those. I'm still writing them too."

The first half of the album closed with 'I Come And Stand At Every Door', which must qualify as the most macabre song that the Byrds ever recorded. Its lyrics were translated by Pete Seeger from a poem by Nâzim Hikmet Ran (originally titled *Kiz Çocugu* aka 'The Little Girl') and the melody was adapted from the traditional ballad 'Great Selchie Of Shule Skerry', which had appeared on the second Judy Collins album, *The Golden Apples Of The Sun*. In Hikmet Ran's poem, the narrator relates the story of a dead seven-year-old child, the victim of radiation fall-out following the bombing of Hiroshima, whose spirit walks the Earth in search of peace. The depiction of the aftermath of nuclear radiation is uncompromising, with graphic images of scorched hair, blindness and human bones transmuted into dust and scattered by the wind. Surprisingly, that great critic of negative lyrics, Jim Dickson, applauded the song: "'I Come And Stand At Every Door' was fine for McGuinn to do. It was depressing, but it was classy. It had more scope. I couldn't argue with it. McGuinn certainly should have been allowed to do it." Seeger had already recorded the song, providing a suitably stately yet sombre reading and McGuinn followed suit. His voice alone graced the opening four verses, while Michael Clarke was faced with the task of supplying a mournful beat that sounded like a death march. The stark arrangement climaxed in a moving final verse during which Crosby's harmony swept in relieving the tension and heightening the positive message about fighting for peace, a coda that echoed the last two lines of 'Turn! Turn! Turn!'. This was the third consecutive occasion on which the Byrds had included a Seeger song on an album.

'Eight Miles High' opened the second side of the long player, providing listeners with their first opportunity to hear the track in stereo. The curious will note that the four beat drum roll at the end of the mono version disappears here. It was largely the presence of this Byrds' classic that ensured the album would always be granted a positive critical reception in later years. Although it was probably asking too much at the time, the group urgently needed to produce a jazz-influenced classic of similar ambition to transform the album into a masterwork and eclipse their rivals. Had they succeeded, they would have been hailed as innovators.

Crosby's second solo offering on the album was a fast arrangement of 'Hey Joe'. The publishing history of this much covered song was a story in itself. Composer Billy Roberts sold the copyright to Dino Valenti, who later published the song under his pseudonym Chester Powers. Rival West Coast group Love had already recorded the song, but Crosby could not resist a reply. His recording was not exactly a favourite of the other Byrds, as McGuinn remembers: "The reason Crosby did lead on 'Hey Joe' was because it was *his* song. He didn't write it but he was responsible for finding it. He'd wanted to do it for years but we would never let him. Then both Love and the Leaves had a minor hit with it and David got so angry that we had to let him do it. His version wasn't that hot because he wasn't a strong lead vocalist."

Manager Jim Dickson was equally unenthusiastic: "Some of the songs that David would bring in from the outside were perfectly valid songs for other people, but did not seem to be compatible with the Byrds' myth. And he may not have liked the Byrds' myth. He fought for 'Hey Joe' and he did it. As long as I could say 'No!', I did, and when I couldn't any more they did it. You had to give him something somewhere. I just wish it was something else . . . 'Hey Joe' I was bitterly opposed to. A song about a guy who murders his girlfriend in a jealous rage and is on the way to Mexico with a gun in his hand. It was not what I saw as a Byrds' song."

Even Crosby later came to realize that the song did not deserve a place on the album and admitted that the recording was an error on his part. "It was a mistake," he atones. "I shouldn't have done it. Everybody makes mistakes."

'Captain Soul', originally the flip side of '5 D', was the first instrumental to be recorded by the Byrds. It proved a disappointment to some reviewers who saw the track as filler. Back in the Ciro's days, just before Clarke and Hillman were annexed to the Byrds' CBS contract, they had suggested, somewhat naïvely, that the group should play blues. This was the belated outcome of that conversation. It was recorded during a short break between sessions when the Byrds began improvising the riff of Lee Dorsey's 'Get Out Of My Life Woman'. Originally, the number was to be titled 'Thirty Minute Break' until Chris Hillman came up with 'Captain Soul'. Looking back, McGuinn feels that the instrumental was not without merit: "It wasn't really funky but it was interesting. Essentially, it was Mike Clarke's trip. He wanted us to do something soul-oriented so we did that for him."

The drummer also provided the distinctive, breathy harmonica break, which added atmosphere to the track. The instrumental ended up with a four-way writing credit, much to the annoyance of Clarke, who felt that he deserved a larger slice of the publishing and later flippantly damned his co-writers as "absolute cruel bastards". "It was basically my song," he claims. "I got one fourth credit for it, but I'll tell you what, I thought it was mainly mine and felt they fucked me on it. How's that?"

'John Riley' was a familiar traditional song, derived from Homer's *Odyssey* and mutated through the ballad tradition of seventeenth-century England. In the story, the wanderer returns from a quest to test his beloved's fidelity and finally rejoices in her faithfulness. The song was popularized in folk circles by Joan Baez, whom McGuinn first heard performing in 1960 at the Club 47 in Cambridge, Massachusetts. He was entranced by her expressive rendition and the delicate finger-picking guitar technique which she used. In reviving the ballad, McGuinn sang the lyrics with understated grace, while the string accompaniment added a suitable touch of drama. As was often the case with Byrds' adaptations, a verse was omitted: "I will die when the moon doth wane/If he's drowned in the deep salt sea/I'll be true to his memory". Along with 'Wild Mountain Thyme', the updating of 'John Riley' provided a pleasant complement to the electric folk-rock experiments on their previous two albums. When I asked McGuinn whether he was attempting to perpetuate the group's folk-rock image by unearthing such material, he responded angrily to my cynical enquiry. "I wasn't trying to perpetuate *anything*, except my love of folk music."

The final track on the album, '2-4-2 Fox Trot (The Lear Jet Song)' seemed another example of Byrds humour in the grand tradition of 'We'll Meet Again' and 'Oh! Susannah'. The bracketed title was a tribute to their aviator friend John Lear, whose personal jet had the registration number N242FT. For years this aural oddity prompted Byrds fans to speculate, with some amusement, whether or not the sound of the Learjet was caused by a vacuum cleaner. McGuinn failed to appreciate that joke: "It was not a vacuum cleaner, it was a Learjet. We went out to the airport with an Ampex tape recorder and recorded the jet starting up. I really resent the fact that some people think it's a vacuum cleaner. But, then again, I guess they sound pretty much the same on record."

Far from regarding the track as a joke ending to an album, McGuinn and Crosby considered their '2-4-2 Fox Trot' close to the cutting edge of avant-garde. Crosby was buoyant about the song at the time, feeling that the use of mechanical effects on records, in place of instruments, was extremely innovative. "It's another expansion for us," he crowed. "It's another direction that we've gone into. We've mixed the sound of the jet and the sound of the people talking on the radio and the sound of the instruments, and the entire sounds – all the sounds that you would go through if you were taking off in a Learjet. We mixed them with music, with songs, with words, and everything." Crosby was confident that such experimentation would soon be embraced by other artistes. When the Beatles released 'Yellow Submarine' during the summer, Crosby was delighted to discover that his prediction had been partly fulfilled. Once again, the Byrds were mentally back in tune with the Fab Four.

CHAPTER NINETEEN

Courage

THE Beatles were still reigning at number 1 in the US charts with 'Paperback Writer' as *Fifth Dimension* was about to be released. The cascading vocals perfected so masterfully by the Beatles inspired the Byrds to return to the studio post haste and attempt a fresh version of 'I Know My Rider' ('I Know You Rider'). News even filtered through to the British music press that this traditional tune would be their next single but, sadly, it failed to appear. According to Dickson: "They recorded 'I Know You Rider' on three separate occasions and worked hard on it. In every case, it was rejected. I think McGuinn was hoping for a single. There's a great danger in telling people your plans. They were never satisfied that the song was good enough. My input wasn't asked for but it would certainly have been not to do the song."

The disenchantment with 'I Know My Rider' is difficult to fathom. Its energetic tempo, staggered three-part harmony and searing guitar break made it excellent single material but, instead, it was consigned to the vaults for over 23 years. The same fate befell its probable B-side, 'Psychodrama City', a bluesy studio jam, with Crosby reflecting on various aspects of LA life, including a verse cruelly highlighting Gene Clark's fear of flying and departure from the group.

Shortly after these tracks were cut, the Byrds parted company with senatorial producer Allen Stanton, who left Columbia to join A&M. He was not mourned by the Byrds, who had preferred the younger and more vibrant Terry Melcher. "Allen Stanton was always difficult to work with," McGuinn insists. "He used to keep me after class as though we were at school and ask me, 'Why is David so hard to understand? Why can't this go this way? Why can't we do that?' It was ridiculous!"

Crosby was equally critical of his working relationship with Stanton, dismissing him with the same impatience that he reserved for all Columbia producers. "Allen Stanton knew nothing about music. He'd push a buzzer in the middle of a song and let the engineers take a union break. He'd say, 'Well, OK guys, we've got to take a break now.' And that would happen in the middle of a take!"

Dickson, observing from a distance, felt that Crosby and McGuinn were too censorious. "I think he did a reasonable job. I don't think he tried to put a lot of input into it. But he worked with Ray Gerhardt, the same engineer that had been recording them. I didn't find any flaws in what he did. He was a professional. I know he was distant from it, but he tried to understand. McGuinn said he used to call him in and talk to him and try to find out what was happening because he didn't have me there to call in any more. I liked Allen Stanton, he was never mean or unfriendly."

Stanton's replacement later that year would be the more innovative Gary Usher, fresh from working on Gene Clark's first solo album. Usher had been employed as a bank teller in Beverly Hills when he first entered the music business, rapidly rising to prominence after meeting Brian Wilson. With half-a-dozen co-writes on the first Beach Boys' LP, *Surfin' Safari*, and a couple more on successive albums, Usher could justifiably claim to have helped kick-start Wilson's writing career. Among the songs they completed were the hot rod anthem '409', the wistful 'Lonely Sea' and deeply introspective 'In My Room'. Although Usher would not be called upon to write with the Byrds, his production skills and love of experimentation would prove beneficial as they entered their most creative period.

The Byrds continued performing sporadically over the remaining months of 1966, but their live performances often left much to be desired. Since those days at Ciro's when they played 'Temple Music' and acquired a fanatical following, the group had been engagingly erratic. Written off as live performers on countless occasions, they were still capable of playing quite brilliantly, if you were lucky enough to attend the right gig. When they rehearsed and focused on their live shows, as they had done at the Trip and on other occasions, the magic would reveal itself. "The Byrds could play very good or very bad," Dickson remembers. "There was no upper limit to how great they could sound and no lower limit to how bad they could sound. There were times when the Byrds were more magical than any group you ever heard. More magical than the Beatles even. But not often."

At a time when some progressive groups were beginning to extend their sets, the Byrds seemed to be moving in the opposite direction. During the early summer, they played a two-month tour of the East Coast. Many of the venues were small clubs and ballrooms, not far removed from the shows they were playing in the Midwest a year before. Along the way, they made their debut in Canada, joining the 'Beach Boys Summer Spectacular' which took them to selected stadiums, but overall it was a gruelling and unrewarding experience. Almost every review made some disparaging remark about their excessive volume spoiling the performance, irrespective of the size of the venue. It was difficult to escape the conclusion that their crown was slipping.

The East Coast tour was a perplexing baptism for their new road manager, Jimmi Seiter. "The first time I worked with them, I didn't meet them," he says. "They arrived, did the show, and left. They never even said, 'Hello'. Eddie Tickner drove them there in a Cadillac. We were all fed up waiting for them. They came in, went into the dressing room, did the show, left and never said a single word. They were gone, across to the airport, and back to LA. I didn't take it personally. From the minute I joined them, I was handed the keys to the van and told, 'Go and deal with it!' I remember driving down Sunset and thinking 'I'm in charge of this band but I've no idea what that means.' And there wasn't anybody to help me. I was frightened about it but then I thought, 'It can't be that bad.' But after I saw them working in the recording studio I realized, 'God this *is* bad. These guys hate each other.' Then I started having fun and trying to get them to smile." Evidently, this was no easy task.

The group returned to Hollywood prematurely and several tour dates were cancelled, much to Tickner's frustration. The increasingly detached Dickson, who was uninvolved in the bookings, made no comment. Part of the frustration for the Byrds was that, beyond favourite places like the Trip, they were still treated like teenybop idols. This was a familiar dilemma in 1966 among those caught between the two disparate audiences of pop and rock. The Byrds were valiantly pushing forward musically, even though the majority of their following were still young teenagers who bought singles rather than albums and probably had only a limited knowledge of folk and jazz, let alone Indian music. This was a year when courage was required to risk all on releasing singles that were artistic, inventive and dared to confront the listener. The Byrds had risen to that challenge with 'Eight Miles High' and '5 D', but the chart rewards had been minimal. At this point, it was uncertain whether a former singles act could survive on album sales alone and although the industry was changing, chart action was still considered critical. Negotiating that divide would test the morale of the Byrds for the remainder of the year. Nor were they alone. Even the great untouchables – the Beatles and the Rolling Stones – faced similar questions. In the UK, the Stones' brave but sonically chaotic 'Have You Seen Your Mother, Baby, Standing In The Shadow?' enveloped listeners with the thrill of the new, but only reached number 5 in the charts, their most disappointing showing since their second single 'I Wanna Be Your Man' back in 1963. In June, the Beatles' 'Paperback Writer' had failed to enter the UK listings at number 1 during its first week of release, a state of affairs that prompted some music press doomsayers to question their continued popularity. Over the next year, there would be constant speculation that the gods of pop were maturing so quickly that they were in danger of losing sizeable sections of their audience.

As the Beatles could testify, the frustration was felt most keenly in live performance where artistic ambition was rendered meaningless by poor acoustics and a deafening wall of sound from screaming teenyboppers that made it impossible to hear your own voice. John Lennon later responded to the exigencies of touring with a characteristically jaundiced rejoinder. "We might as well have sent our four waxwork dummies for all the people cared about the sound."

In another interview, he complained that Beatles concerts had nothing to do with music. "They're just bloody tribal rites."

The Byrds may not have felt the same cynicism, but they understood what Lennon meant. For the Beatles the tribal rites were still a necessity at this point, so they agreed to schedule an American tour in August. This was welcome news for McGuinn and Crosby who were always pleased to see the Fab Four and could invariably rely on Derek Taylor to set up a meeting. The last summit between the groups had been the previous summer when they'd taken acid together, discussed Ravi Shankar and enjoyed the privilege of having Harrison and McCartney attend a recording session. Much had happened in the interim, not least the departure of Gene Clark, so there was a lot to catch up on.

The Beatles could be forgiven for thinking their 1966 tours were cursed by the god of hubris. After a nostalgic trip to Hamburg they encountered their first major obstacle in Tokyo. Upon arrival, they were told that a powerful group of militant students had objected to their proposed performance at Budokan as an offence against Japanese culture. Death threats had supposedly been received and, wary of the dangers of instigating an international incident, a massive security operation was set in place. It left the Beatles feeling more frightened than safe. But that was nothing compared to what awaited them in the Philippines. Prior to their performance in Manila, they had been invited to a palace party by the imposing first lady Imelda Marcos, wife of President Ferdinand Marcos. The group's manager Brian Epstein politely declined but his reply was either ignored or arrived too late to forestall the preparations. Next morning, a newspaper headline 'Beatles Snub President' fomented national wrath and placed the Beatles in fresh danger. The thriller in Manila ended in a near riot during which the group were verbally assaulted, jostled and kicked.

At least the Beatles could look forward to a more civilized reception in America. Even that dream ended weeks later when Epstein learned that Beatles records were being ceremoniously burned in several Southern states. In Mississippi, an imperial wizard of the Ku Klux Klan insisted that the group had been brainwashed by the Communist Party and declared a Holy War against their apostasy.

The cause of the bizarre furore could be located in an interview that Lennon had conducted with the London *Evening Standard* several months before. During a discussion about religion, he had casually remarked: "Christianity will go. It will go. It will vanish and shrink. I needn't argue about that. I'm right and I will be proved right. We are more popular than Jesus now. I don't know which will go first – rock 'n' roll or Christianity." In Britain, Lennon's words went largely unnoticed but when they were reprinted and given cover prominence in *Datebook*, an American teenzine, all hell broke loose. Overnight, the most celebrated group of the twentieth century became the object of a witch hunt almost unparalleled in pop history. When the Byrds heard the news, they were first stunned, then amazed. Derek Taylor told the press in suitably hushed tones: "I'm seriously worried about someone with a rifle. After all, there's no Kennedy any more, but you can always shoot John Lennon."

The US tour went ahead, but merely confirmed all the prejudices that the Beatles already felt about the futility of playing live. Prior to leaving England, they did not bother to rehearse anything new and declined to feature a single song from the recently released *Revolver*, preferring to rely on less adventurous material. It hardly seemed to matter. Audiences responded, as of old, with piercing screams and stage invasions, while the Beatles played for the obligatory 33 minutes. The tour ended in California, where McGuinn and Crosby awaited. During their stay, the Beatles were ensconced at a mansion in Beverly Hills, and David Crosby was pleased to play the gregarious Hollywood host, chauffeuring George Harrison around town in his Porsche on a whirlwind visit to the homes of the hip hierarchy. Harrison was curious about the fate of Gene Clark, who was currently in the studio recording. All Crosby could tell him was that the four Byrds were now a tighter unit in his absence.

A surprise interloper who squeezed into Crosby's car was Barry Tashian of the Boston-based Remains, who had secured a support spot on the Beatles' tour. Tashian was thrilled to receive an opportunity of a lifetime, courtesy of David Crosby. "It was a big night for me when we went out with George Harrison. First, we went to McGuinn's house and he showed us a film he had put together. It had abstract images, almost like an animation, and the soundtrack was the Beatles' 'Tomorrow Never Knows' from *Revolver*. There were a lot of stops that night. How many people get to go out in a Porsche with George Harrison and David Crosby visiting Mary Travers, Barry Feinstein, Mama Cass, Denny Doherty and Peter Tork? We ended up at Derek Taylor's house. John Lennon and Paul McCartney were sitting there with Carl and Brian Wilson and their wives. It was pretty heady company."

Crosby must have been practically purring. Here was the ultimate group summit: the Beatles, the Byrds and the Beach Boys – the magic Bs – together in the same room. Alas, there were no musical instruments but plenty of mutual respect. What was most extraordinary about the gathering was its timing. After the recent releases of *Pet Sounds*, *Fifth Dimension* and *Revolver*, all three acts were on the brink of who knew what? The possibilities were limitless.

On 28 August, Crosby accompanied the Beatles to LA's Dodger Stadium for the penultimate performance of their controversial America tour. They performed before 45,000 frenzied fans, who acted like it was still 1964. The next evening they played at San Francisco's Candlestick Park, returned to Beverly Hills, then headed home. On the plane back they made an unspeakable pact: they would never tour again.

Witnessing the spectacle of the Beatles at their apathetic apogee in Dodger Stadium left Crosby feeling ambivalent about stadium performances. The Fab Four's message seemed clear: studio recordings were the true aesthetic and could not be translated into a concert setting under current conditions. Dickson maintains, rightly or wrongly, that many Byrds' show became shorter and less focused during 1966 largely as a result of Crosby imitating the Beatles' aloofness and disillusionment with the live process. "David decided that the Byrds were going to do 25-minute sets, because that's what the Beatles did. The Beatles had done it because that's as long as they could play before the crowd got out of control and they had to leave. It wasn't because they didn't want to play more music. According to Derek, the event that Crosby saw [at the Dodger Stadium] was when the Beatles got off the stage because they were frightened. The audience was getting out of hand. They didn't think the police were going to be able to hold them back any longer. But that wasn't the case with the Byrds. The Byrds weren't working people up to a dangerous frenzy, but David thought that blank thing was hip. If you're going to do 25 minutes of music, you're going to play maybe six songs or so. You go all the way to a concert featuring the Byrds and that's what you get? I don't know if David would defend that now. He does long concerts and loves being out there. There's no better place for him to be. But back then he was absolute." The group's policy of performing desultory sets was greeted with disdain by certain promoters. "All of a sudden the bookings dried up," Dickson recalls.

On 1 September, the Byrds returned to their former stomping ground the Whisky A Go-Go. First night nerves spoiled an otherwise interesting set which included such eclectic fare as 'Don't Doubt Yourself Babe' and 'I See You'. The *Los Angeles Times* complained that the group were "extremely sloppy", adding, "they hit the wrong notes, played slightly off-time and occasionally sang bad or thin harmony". It rapidly became apparent that the real problem was Crosby's voice, which was rapidly failing during the opening set. Since Clark's departure, he had taken on more lead work and the strain was showing. With insufficient rehearsal time to rearrange the set, the group decided to re-enlist Gene for the remainder of the 12-day engagement. The announcement caused a frisson of excitement on Sunset Boulevard, then stretched across the Atlantic to the British music press, where hope was rekindled that Clark might rejoin on a permanent basis. As the *NME* enthused: "Hollywood kids were practically dancing in the streets with delight. The password around town was, 'Gene's back – isn't it wonderful!' Well, sometimes it was and sometimes it wasn't; it's been a long time since they worked and rehearsed together. Gene did fill in the weak points in harmony with the strength of his beautiful voice when David's fine voice was hushed to a whisper. The quality of performance was influenced also by sometimes malfunctioning equipment and the individual moods the boys were in. But when they were good, they were very good."

Unfortunately, the dream of an extended Byrds' reunion proved short-lived. In many respects, it was amazing that it had happened at all. According to roadie Jim Seiter, they were frequently wary of

Clark forcing himself back into the ranks. "At first, they showed me a picture of him, an old PR shot, and said, 'If this guy comes to a gig when we're in LA, don't let him near the stage because he'll want to play with us and it'll be terrible. Keep him away.' I said, 'Fine', but that's how I first met Gene, by keeping him away from them. For some reason he respected me because of the way I handled him. I treated him with respect and said, 'Look Gene, I understand your history with these guys, but please . . . they really don't want you to sit in with them.'"

Despite all the excitement, the group clearly preferred to continue as a four-piece. In any case, Clark had already signed with CBS for a solo album, which was due to be completed some weeks later. Meanwhile, the Byrds flew to New York during October for a historic appearance at Art D'Lugoff's Village Gate. It was fitting that this bastion of jazz and folk should choose the Byrds as its entrée into the rock world, for they had done more than any other group to translate those two musical forms into a pop context, from 'Mr Tambourine Man' to 'Eight Miles High'. As ever, the Byrds attracted a hip and star-studded clientele, ranging from Peter, Paul & Mary to the Hollies, the Lovin' Spoonful, the Fugs, the Velvet Underground and Timothy Leary. Linda Eastman, later to become Mrs McCartney, was also on hand to take some backstage pictures. As at Ciro's, the Byrds' audience once more attracted the interest of startled journalists, eager to spot the latest phenomenon. One spoke earnestly of "a scintillating, polka-dotted red, green, blue, brown, wriggling mass of human kaleidoscope. Young navels without jewels. Fresh soapy aromas. Earnest talk between sets, peering at each other through rimless spectacles. They had faces, but none were ugly and none were pretty. All were unique. And when the Byrds played all those incredible faces, all these bodies moving with the energy of now, stopped to hear some of the grooviest people of our time. You could look at the audience and know that the Village Gate was crowded with people who dug each other because they were all digging the Byrds."

The fashionable audience distracted attention from any musical shortcomings but, not for the first time, the Byrds rose to the occasion, finding a greater sense of purpose playing for onlookers hip to the jazz world. As usual, they played far too loud, but this was seen as evidence of empowerment or, as one critic called it, "loud music dancing on electric cable, music written in voltage." While New York critics praised the group for "their ingenious method of infusing the sitar-sound into today's popular repertoire", Columbia Records was rather more concerned with their chart profile.

That same month, 'Mr Spaceman' was issued as a single, complete with a spoof claim that the Byrds had been insured against abduction by space aliens. A poker-faced Eddie Tickner was quoted in the publicity memos as saying: "We live in weird times, and it would be foolish not to take seriously the possibility that there may be a response from outer space". Not surprisingly, the joke did not extend as far as actually forking out any money to protect the Byrds from this unlikely occurrence.

With a catchy and commercial single, whose title cleverly echoed that of their first number 1, the Byrds registered a minor hit, climbing to a modest number 36 on *Billboard*. The single's progress was also helped by some personal plugging from Michael Clarke, who was despatched across the country to make guest appearances at various radio stations. Characteristically, his PR work ended with an impromptu vacation. As Eddie Tickner told me with a wry smile: "Michael went out on the road. He got as far as Dallas. He was put on a plane for New Orleans but never arrived. He went to Canada instead."

Although the Byrds were still playing live and had survived Gene Clark's exit, they remained a fragile unit whose long-term future seemed uncertain. Observing the evident instability, Tickner decided that it was time to take some strong measures in order to ensure that a Byrds dissolution was not a financial disaster. "There was a separation at the time," he recalled. "Dickson had left, creatively, and Gene Clark had gone. The guys weren't very close. I said to them: 'Let's put our shoulders to the wheel, make another record, push it and I'll re-negotiate your contract and get $1,000,000. We'll all take $200,000 and call it a day.' The idea was 'Let's rob a bank', but in order to rob a bank you have to plan it. So the idea was spend a month writing, collecting material, spend a month rehearsing it, go into a studio, record and release a single. Then we'll all go to Europe, promote the single and then re-negotiate our contract. I wasn't too sure that there would be another album."

For the remainder of the year, Tickner's master-plan was adhered to very closely. Anxious to progress in their studio work and aware of the growing competition from other underground groups, the Byrds spent more time than ever rehearsing material in their room at 9000 Sunset Boulevard. At the end of November they entered Columbia Studios in Hollywood and during an amazingly productive 50 hours, spread over an 11-day period, recorded their fourth and finest album to date. The sessions proved trouble-free, except for one fiery moment when Crosby berated a Columbia promotions man for inviting 'Miss Teen Princess of Oklahoma' and her proud mother to see the Byrds at work. Derek Taylor remembers Crosby "moving across the studio floor like a crazed boar" and by the time he reached the control room, the interlopers were "already alarmed" by his intensity. Television's ABC network was also on hand to document part of the session, which featured the Byrds working on Miles Davis' 'Milestones', which McGuinn dubbed "garage jazz". Unfortunately, the group declined to issue this jazz/rock jam and the disappearance of the master tape from the vaults ensured that it would not appear on their remastered CD reissues 19 years later. Looking back, producer Gary Usher regretted its non-appearance. "I thought it was great. I always loved it. It was a five to six-minute cut and it was a song that David Crosby was behind. We worked on that song for a couple of days straight and the guys played great. To the guys though, it never came out 100 per cent and in a way they are right. There were timing problems but, overall, I wanted them to go ahead and finish up the record and take it to the next level. I thought it was a good departure for them, it showed another side of their talent."

Jim Dickson was ambivalent about the track. "When I heard they'd done it, I had two reactions. One, I was worried that they might do it so badly that they'd insult Miles Davis. But Miles Davis was instrumental in getting them signed to Columbia, so it would have been a nice way of paying him back if they'd put it on the album. I didn't know their motives, but it's shame we didn't put it out to thank Miles."

CHAPTER TWENTY

Renaissance

WHILE the Byrds were recording their new album, the Sunset Strip continued its metamorphosis into a teenage paradise. Legions of bright young things arrived daily, marshalling the hippie movement, which would reach its glorious apotheosis the following summer. Signs of a burgeoning counterculture were ever present. Expensive stores for spendthrift teens increasingly gave way to incense-filled boutiques offering garish T-shirts, expansive bell bottoms and chic posters. There was a boom in music venues and an endless supply of all-night eateries and health food stores for the sleepless hordes and late risers. This rapid influx of kids irked the city's bankers, restaurateurs and real estate elite who were intent on preserving the Strip as a high-rise financial district. Political pressure persuaded the authorities to clamp down on young offenders and soon the dream town turned into a nightmare zone. The LA Sheriff's office enforced draconian laws forcing kids under 18 off the street after 10 pm. Police harassment increased, with late-night restaurants providing easy targets for mass arrests. Hundreds of teenagers were picked up in armoured buses outside Ben Frank's, Stripcomer's, Gee Gee's and the delicatessen Canter's. Scores of summonses were issued for minor offences such as jay-walking, loitering and unlawful assembly. Meanwhile, Fred Rosenberg, chairman of the Sunset Strip Restaurant Association, complained that traffic congestion and juvenile problems were causing incalculable harm to local businesses and petitioned for a tow-away zone to be instituted along the entire Strip. Late night music clubs were also under threat and attempts were made to rescind their dance permits.

The Byrds, whose politics seldom extended beyond echoing Dylan's decreasingly unfocused protest, found themselves part of a new cause. Both Crosby and Dickson were concerned about the plight of the kids, many of whom were friends from the Ciro's days onwards. Leaflets were distributed and a mass protest was organized outside Pandora's Box on 12 November. Most of the teenagers, whose numbers swelled to over a thousand, protested in an orderly fashion. Some sang, some stood around, and a few carried banners saying 'Police Brutality', 'Cops Uncouth To Youth' and 'Give Us Back Our Streets'. Then the scene became very ugly. According to *The New York Times*: "Baton swinging armed officers marched shoulder to shoulder down Sunset Blvd, the main artery, shoving the protesters into side-streets or clubbing them to the pavement".

In *The Los Angeles Times*, the headline read: '1000 Youths Riot On Strip', although the kids insisted that there never had been a riot, just some thrown bottles and slight damage to a couple of city buses. Inevitably, the violence prompted some commentators to write excitedly about a generational conflict that would have far-reaching implications. Columnist Al Aronowitz spoke of "long-haired, bellbottomed teenagers who have become the shock troops of Hollywood's psychedelic revolution". Even as he wrote, public disturbances continued throughout December.

For many caught up in the conflict, the rhetoric of revolution seemed inappropriate and sensationalist. Byrds manager Jim Dickson was concerned about the dissemination of information through the mainstream press and the flippant way in which the word 'riot' was universally applied. Already there was talk of an exploitative movie, which would later emerge as *Riot On Sunset Strip*. Meanwhile, kids still suffered harassment and the power of the real estate magnates showed little sign of waning. Dickson decided to form a committee which would organize marches, issue a newspaper and provide funds for those fined or imprisoned.

CAFF (Community Action For Facts And Freedom) established its headquarters at the 9000 building and brought together several prominent and rich benefactors. Hollywood actors were particularly well represented with Dennis Hopper, Sal Mineo and Jill St John all responding to Dickson's call. The Byrds' old friend Peter

Fonda and actor pal Brandon deWilde had been handcuffed and arrested during the disturbances, and spoke out about police brutality. Woolworth's heir Lance Reventlow also offered his support as did Elmer Valentine (owner of the Whisky and the Trip) and the Buffalo Springfield's managers Charlie Greene and Brian Stone. The first meeting of the committee provided a sobering reminder that the counterculture did not necessarily occupy the moral high ground in all matters. Derek Taylor was disillusioned to discover that his prized Lucien Picard gold watch had been stolen while all those around him denounced the greed of rapacious restaurateurs and real estate speculators.

Dickson's increasing involvement in CAFF distracted him from the everyday problems of the Byrds, who seemed determined to pursue their own musical policies without his input or direction. Crosby had recently met a young manager, Larry Spector, who was representing several of his actor friends. One of his clients was the South African jazz trumpeter and bandleader Hugh Masekela, who had emigrated to the USA at the beginning of the Sixties and married 'Mama Africa' Miriam Makeba. Masekela had subsequently formed a production company and record label, Chisa, and was currently working with another South African singer, Letta Mbulu. When Spector invited Crosby to attend the sessions, he passed on the news to Hillman, who was happy to tag along. The day's recording proved a revelation for Hillman who experienced the equivalent of an evolutionary jump in time. "I went in there with my bass, playing with all these wonderful jazz guys. David was a good rhythm player and I played bass and it was the most exciting time I'd ever experienced up to that point in my life. It was totally outside of my arena of music." Hillman was quietly thrilled when, at the end of the session, Mbulu listened attentively to the playback, pushed the intercom button and said: "Chris, you're cooking on that bass, man!"

Hillman was still buzzing when he returned home, his head full of alluring melodies that demanded to be committed to tape. "For the next few days I stared writing songs. They were just coming out of me. It was like the cobwebs had come off of me."

Emerging from the shadows in the Byrds, Hillman was suddenly flowering as a bass player, vocalist and instant songwriter, penning such compositions as 'Time Between', 'Have You Seen Her Face', 'I Hear Singing', 'Time For Love', 'Remember Love', 'When Love Goes Bad' and 'Relax Your Mind'. This sudden outpouring instantly elevated his status in the group, ensuring that he would receive equal songwriting status on subsequent albums. "Chris had a lot of potential as a writer," says producer Gary Usher, "and it was his bluegrass background that added a nice mixture and influence to the group. Chris was a stabilizing force with his country music roots in the Byrds' sound mixture. I also think Chris saw from earlier albums how much money could be made from writing songs. Chris was a good songwriter, and he and McGuinn also wrote a lot of good songs together."

The most celebrated McGuinn/Hillman collaboration also emerged in the aftermath of the Letta Mbulu session. An insistent riff was swirling around inside Chris' head which would soon emerge as the opening part of 'So You Want To Be A Rock 'n' Roll Star'. Determined to complete the song, he phoned McGuinn who immediately popped over to provide assistance. With all the talk of South Africa, McGuinn recalled something he had once worked on with Miriam Makeba during his pre-Byrds days. Adapting the melody line, he came up with the perfect bridge, including the lines about making the charts and being torn apart by teenage fans, an experience he had encountered a couple of years before, which still haunted him on occasions. Trading lines and ideas in rapid fire fashion, the duo completed a composition that sounded clever, novel and surprisingly commercial. "We finished the song in about 30–40 minutes," Hillman still marvels.

The startling 'So You Want To Be A Rock 'n' Roll Star' was issued as a single in America on 9 January 1967. Its caustic lyrics were partly inspired by the recent publicity hype surrounding the Monkees, whose television series had launched them to international fame, accompanied by ludicrous suggestions that they might even topple the Beatles. Purists scoffed upon learning that they did not play on their records and ridiculed the concept of a 'manufactured' group, half of whose membership consisted of ex-actors. Hillman and McGuinn were not angry, but looked on with increasing jaundice at the current state of the pop world and fashioned a statement that served as their own instruction manual for instant pop stardom. To add greater momentum to the song, Crosby invited Masekela to play trumpet, while McGuinn added those taped screams that Derek Taylor had carefully recorded at the Byrds' show in Bournemouth, England during the notorious 1965 tour. The tone of 'So You Want To Be A Rock 'n' Roll Star' was heavily sarcastic, but there was enough deadpan humour to rescue the lyric from accusations of complete cynicism. As McGuinn observed: "Some people have accused us of being bitter for writing that song, but it's no more bitter than 'Positively 4th Street'. In fact, it isn't as bitter as that. We were thumbing through a teen magazine and looking at all the unfamiliar faces and we couldn't help thinking: 'Wow, what's happening . . . all of a sudden here is everyone and his brother and his sister-in-law and his mother and even his pet bullfrog singing rock 'n' roll.' So we wrote 'So You Want To Be A Rock 'n' Roll Star' to the audience of potential rock stars, those who were going to be, or who wanted to be, and those who actually did go on and realize their goals."

Hillman's daring in challenging the pop elite brought unexpected retribution. Within days of the release of 'So You Want To Be A Rock 'n' Roll Star', his rustic, mountain-top house was burned to the ground. Chris had returned home on his Triumph Bonneville TT motorcycle and accidentally kicked the vehicle over, fracturing the fuel tank and starting a fire which raced towards his veranda and razed his home. As he rolled on the ground to avoid the flames that had already singed his eyebrows, he was shocked by the devastation. All his instruments were lost in the blaze, including a prized Martin D-28 guitar, along with his telescope, camera, paintings, furniture and a favourite poster of Tijuana. The only clothes he had left to wear were those on his back. The fire alerted onlookers from all around, including McGuinn, who captured the conflagration on his new movie camera and turned bad fortune to his own advantage by selling the footage to the ABC TV network. They used it as a lead item on the evening news. McGuinn received $75.00 for the video footage and was advised by Taylor to pass it on to Hillman, "so it would look good in the papers". Whether

McGuinn took the advice is not known. Years later, Hillman added a mischievous footnote to the story. "Here's the twist on it," he jokes. "Crosby was in my house an hour before the blaze. I can't connect it yet – where the Satan factor came into play with David – but I'm working on it!"

February 1967 proved one of the most important months in the pop calendar. History tells us that this was the period when rock finally came of age, with the Beatles and the Stones reaching fresh peaks, Jimi Hendrix causing a sensation in London clubland, Cream enjoying albums success and a new generation of underground anti-heroes dethroning Tin Pan Alley's staid status quo. The reality was rather more sobering.

In England, reactionary forces were at work. Police descended in droves on Keith Richards' cottage in West Wittering, interrupting an acid soirée and busting the Stones' guitarist, his cohort Mick Jagger and art dealer Robert Fraser on highly tenuous drugs charges. The case subsequently dominated headlines and was rightly seen as symbolic of the battle between the old establishment and the new bohemian elite. That same clash was played out in the pop charts, the contents of which proved far more depressing than McGuinn or Hillman could ever have envisaged when they wrote 'So You Want To Be A Rock 'n' Roll Star'. The Monkees may have been the new pop pretenders, but compared to the other acts in their orbit, they seemed positively radical.

In Britain, the Rolling Stones released their formidable double A-side 'Let's Spend The Night Together'/'Ruby Tuesday', only to be blocked from number 1 by a combination of the Monkees and MOR vocalist Petula Clark, whose reading of Charlie Chaplin's 'This Is My Song' sold a million. A couple of weeks later, the Beatles entered the fray with their most adventurous single to date: 'Penny Lane'/'Strawberry Fields Forever'. Amazingly, it too failed to reach the top, losing out to Engelbert Humperdinck's lachrymose 'Release Me'. A glimpse at the best-selling records made salutary reading, with such artistes as Engelbert, Pet Clark, Vince Hill, Harry Secombe, Val Doonican and Frank and Nancy Sinatra dominating the listings. The albums chart was even more conservative with the immemorial *The Sound Of Music* celebrating its 100th week in the Top 10 and about to climb back to number 1, where it would successively outlast passing threats from the pop aristocracy. Beneath could be found two albums by Herb Alpert & the Tijuana Brass, and best-sellers from the Seekers, Jim Reeves, Tom Jones and Mantovani. If rock revolution was in the air, then the British public was lagging behind the zeitgeist and seeking contentment in easy listening music. It was difficult to resist the feeling that a strange war was underway between two generations of pop listeners in early 1967, and the early victors were those middle-aged consumers supposedly vanquished by the beat boom four years before.

In America, the Rolling Stones also faced the wrath of the moral majority and were humiliated into altering the words of 'Let's Spend The Night Together' before it could be performed on *The Ed Sullivan Show*. The enduring image of a grimacing Mick Jagger mouthing the words "let's spend some time together" spoke volumes about the establishment's desire to neuter great pop. Significantly, it was 'Ruby Tuesday' and 'Penny Lane' that climbed to the top in *Billboard*, while their more daring flip sides fared less well. Although the US charts were not quite as anachronistic as their UK counterparts, the continued presence of Herman's Hermits, Sonny & Cher, Johnny Rivers and the Bob Crewe Generation cast some doubts on the tastes of a "generation with the new explanation".

Since the banning of LSD in the US in October 1966, San Francisco had become a focal point for those in search of counter-culture revolution. For many pop kids, even those in nearby LA, Haight-Ashbury was still a place shrouded in some mystery, an alternate world about to be discovered and analysed by a sceptical, straight media. In February 1967, *KRLA Beat* responded to the phenomenon by belatedly alerting its readers to a new breed of pop fan: "They're called 'hippies' or 'happeners', seek intense sensual and emotional experiences as a way of widening their awareness of themselves, believe in 'consciousness expansion' by way of LSD and marijuana – though not all hippies use drugs. Other methods include yoga breathing, special diets, electronic music, light shows and sauna baths . . . But San Francisco's older generation finds the hippie anything but welcome. The Haight Street Merchants Association refuses to admit the hippie businessmen into their organization. So, the hippies who own approximately 25 shops have formed their own . . . Alcoholics Anonymous and the Salvation Army have nothing on the Haight-Ashbury hippies. There are phone numbers to call in case of police brutality or a bad 'trip'. The Artists Liberation Front proclaim free public entertainment and the Diggers offer free food and clothing with no questions asked . . . The Diggers gather rejected vegetables in the market and stale bread from the bakeries . . . Hippies fear that the National Guard is being readied against them and that the Federal Government is dispatching throngs of drug agents into the district to cut the flow of psychedelic drugs. But the agents have a hard time identifying LSD since it is odourless, colourless, tasteless and large quantities can be painted on the back of a postage stamp."

While the LSD detectors continued their surreptitious searches, the pop world enjoyed a memorable February. At the end of a ten-day period during which the Stones had been raided and the Beatles had issued their most eloquent single to date, the Byrds re-emerged with the awesome *Younger Than Yesterday*. The new album would achieve only moderate chart success, which was a terrible injustice, for it was not only a major progression for the Byrds, but also a giant step forward for rock music, predating *Sgt Pepper's Lonely Hearts Club Band* by several months.

As always, the new Byrds album commenced with their latest single. 'So You Want To Be A Rock 'n' Roll Star' was the pop equivalent of Shakespeare's Seven Ages Of Man, clinically delineating the thrills and perils of rock stardom. Its lasting significance lay in its timing. Although rightly regarded as a sardonic and precociously perceptive commentary on the pop process, it could also be viewed as a personal reflection on the Byrds' own career. The ironic tone was all the more powerful considering where the group stood commercially in early 1967. Like the imaginary pupils under tutelage in the song, they had already sold plastic ware, topped the charts and experienced the ambivalent delights of being chased and torn apart by screaming fans. Now they were actually living the final verse of the song – coming to terms with the 'strange game' of post-fame and its attendant anomie. The sense of unreality, of being "a little insane", summed up the group experience during their classic mid-period. And as the lyrics concluded, with chilling precision, they were now caught somewhere between a new age spirit of rebellious disenchantment and an old world-view that demanded they fulfil their appointed role in the pop circus: "don't forget what you are, you're a rock 'n' roll star". Consciously or not, the song was both an outward, detached reflection on the state of contemporary pop and an introspective examination of the Byrds' current place in the scheme of things. The bitter cynicism of 'So You Want To Be A Rock 'n' Roll Star' was brilliantly offset by Taylor's "good British screams", a gimmick that, intentionally or otherwise, appealed to certain disc jockeys. Unfortunately, the single could only reach number 29 in *Billboard* and failed to register in the UK charts, although it would later be accorded classic status.

Chris Hillman's first solo contribution to the Byrds, 'Have You Seen Her Face' was surprisingly inventive and commercial enough to be issued as a single in the USA. His emergence as a singer-songwriter of great charm and wit was a crucial development in the Byrds' story. Even more amazing was the realization that he had written more songs on the album than either of his more famous partners. The distinct, understated vocal style and McCartney-influenced melodic bass playing served as an effective contrast to the more ambitious work of McGuinn and Crosby, perfectly complementing their contributions. Always in search of new inventive touches, McGuinn borrowed Crosby's Gretsch to play that wonderfully twangy solo on the track. "It all came from that Hugh Masekela session," Hillman says. "I suddenly heard these new rhythms and they came out on the album. It was a fresh experience for me." Hillman's contributions were welcomed by his partners. He remembers with fondness McGuinn saying, "Chris was a late bloomer. But when he bloomed, he blossomed." Evidently, McGuinn was even more enthusiastic at the time of the recording and told Crosby, "You better hear what Chris just wrote. It's unbelievable." Hillman was humbled by the compliment. "That tells you they were never holding me back. I was holding myself back by being a little unsure. I was confident in my playing. I just needed a little more time to develop my singing confidence. David was such a good harmony singer. He made 'Time Between' sound great. He made 'Have You Seen Her Face' sound really good. His part was so well crafted. He came in and just found that part. It was so beautiful the way he weaves in and out of the lead vocal."

'CTA 102', like its 'space rock' predecessor 'Mr Spaceman', contained elements of whimsy, complete with gimmicky effects and simulated alien voices. Interviewed at the time of its release, McGuinn sounded like he might be putting on his inquisitor and having fun with his audience. "We have reason to believe that any intelligent life form on CTA 102 would probably be smaller than us," he said. "We have tried to speak to them by speeding up our voices to a higher pitch. This is more likely to stimulate the sounds that the CTA people would make." Considerable work went into achieving the desired sound effects in an age when synthesizers had yet to reach the rock elite. "We used earphones fed into microphones and talked into them, and then we speeded it up. It was just nonsense but we deliberately tried to make it sound like a backward tape so people would try and reverse it . . . we were playing a joke really because it was a big fad at the time to play things backwards. We used an oscillator with a telegraph key, and that booming bang that you hear is the sustain pedal of a piano being held down and banged with our fists . . . a sort of Stockhausen idea."

In common with the writing of 'Mr Spaceman', the original idea for 'CTA 102' was quite serious, with McGuinn and co-composer Bob Hippard speculating on the existence of a quasar that might be a source of intelligent life. "At the time we wrote it, I thought it might be possible to make contact with quasars, but later I found out that they were stars which are imploding at a tremendous velocity. They're condensing and spinning at the same time, and the nucleus is sending out tremendous amounts of radiation, some of which is audible as an electronic impulse on a computerized radio telescope. It comes out in a rhythmic pattern, but the frequency of the signal depends on the size, and originally, the radio astronomers who received these impulses thought they were from a life-form in space." McGuinn's wide-eyed love of science fiction later brought him unexpected fame when Dr Eugene Epstein, a radio astronomer at Jet Propulsion Laboratories, included a sly reference to 'CTA 102' in an article printed in *The Astrophysical Journal*.

The Byrds' versatility on *Younger Than Yesterday* was ably demonstrated by their effortless switch from the futuristic 'CTA 102' to the medieval ambience of 'Renaissance Fair'. Credited to McGuinn/Crosby, the composition was a vivid phantasmagoria inspired by David's memories of the previous spring's Renaissance Pleasure Faire. In common with 'What's Happening?!?!', the song concentrates not merely on a physical description of the event but the feelings of dislocation it produces in the narrator. Images pass in dream-like sequence, with Crosby focusing on the individual senses of hearing, smell and sight to convey his sense of wonder. Tellingly, there is no characterization. The arrangement proved equally noteworthy, with each layer of instrumentation being carefully added as the song developed. Crosby played a smooth *B5* arpeggio while McGuinn contributed some changes in dropped *D* tuning. Hillman's melodic, loping bass work was particularly strong, indicating the extent to which he had matured as a player. The soprano sax of Jay Migliori, evidently mixed out of existence, was originally intended to enhance the jazzy feel. Jim Dickson was impressed by the song and regretted being unable to offer Crosby some overdue moral support. "I wish that I had been there to give him the appreciation that he deserved but, by then, he and I were alienated. He'd found a niche and a song to write that expanded the Byrds without contradicting the Byrds. It worked with the rest and yet gave him a new flavour. It was different from McGuinn, Clark or Dylan, yet compatible for the Byrds. I've told him since, and I'm not sure he believes me, that 'Renaissance Fair' was the first good Byrds' song he ever wrote. It's still one of the best."

'Time Between' featured the Byrds' debut of Clarence White, whom Chris Hillman recruited to add a country tinge to the lead guitar break. Old friend Vern Gosdin added acoustic guitar. "He also sang a harmony part," says Hillman, "but then Crosby came in and got all his feathers ruffled and replaced it – though actually Vern's was better." At the time, the country influence was subtle enough to go unnoticed, especially with the added distraction of maracas. Hillman's lyrical playfulness, love of elongated rhymes and grasp of easy melody were all present on this track, which would have made a pleasant single. "'Time Between' was the first song I ever wrote," Chris told me. "So God knows what I was trying to do." Like the best of Hillman's songs, 'Time Between' was born of real emotion, albeit subtly expressed. It documented the early frustrations of his long distance romance with Anya Butler, secretary of the Who's manager Kit Lambert. Hillman would soon marry Butler, but the sense of anticipation in the song was irrepressible. She had recently returned to England and the geographical distance brought a new tension to the romance. The song begins with a petulant protest ("Don't say you love me, don't say you care") before resolving its inner conflict with an upbeat faith in the power of love and trust. Like 'Have You Seen Her Face', it advocates patience as emotional panacea. It was a resolution worthy of McGuinn at his most positive. The enduring quality of the composition was emphasized by its reappearance on an album 20 years later by Hillman's Desert Rose Band.

The final track on side one, 'Everybody's Been Burned', already familiar as a recent B-side, quietly threatened to dwarf everything else on the album. A magnificent vocal by Crosby was complemented by one of the most beautifully moving guitar solos of all time from McGuinn. Hillman's jazz-influenced bass work also reached unforeseen heights here. "Christopher did a real good job on that," Crosby enthuses. "I was real pleased with it." The composition was written by Crosby during his solo days and its quality emphasizes his greatness as a songwriter, even before he joined the Byrds. The expressive lyrics attempt a subtle balance between disillusionment, with the image of the door closing on the dream, and the determination to continue with a relationship: "But you die inside, if you choose to hide/So I guess, instead, I'll love you". Though less ambitious than either 'Renaissance Fair' or 'What's Happening?!?!' it was clearly superior, and stands alongside the greatest material recorded by the Byrds.

Crosby was fortunate that his manager Jim Dickson no longer had any creative or quality control for, in such circumstances, this most startling of compositions would have remained in the vaults.

"I would never have done 'Everybody's Been Burned' in the Byrds, no matter how well David sang it," Dickson admits, with brutal heresy. "To me, it's not a Byrds song. I would have been resistant to it because of the lyric. The expression 'burned' had come and gone. It was already part of the past before he did it. He sang that song long before the Byrds and we had the publishing on it. If I didn't want to do one of our songs, there must be a compelling reason. My reason was that it's negative. You've got images of 'dying inside' and 'being burned', which pop out before the sense of the song comes through. If it gave them a new level of sophistication, as you say, then it predated the Byrds. It wasn't a song that David wanted to do on the first album. He didn't perform it live and it didn't come up. He never said it was a Byrds song. I'd rather have done it than 'Hey Joe', it wasn't as negative as that! But David wanted 'Hey Joe' as a vehicle for his performance. 'Everybody's Been Burned' was café society sophistication. That's not what I wanted for the Byrds. You'll be singing Cole Porter songs next. David would probably be quite good at that sort of song now. He could have had a different career singing those kind of songs when no one else could. 'Everybody's Been Burned' was relatively inane compared to the music it was meant to imitate in the time before the Byrds. It's another style of music. It wasn't an advance for me, but a retreat to the past and a contradiction of the new music."

Arguably Hillman's finest solo composition, 'Thoughts And Words' fused two disparate musical genres, sounding at once like a romantic pop ballad and an LSD-influenced reflection on human relationships. The melody, possibly influenced by the Beatles' 'If I Needed Someone', was enhanced by the sitar-like sounds of guitars taped backwards. Both the title 'Thoughts And Words' and the reference to "mind" in the opening line imbued the song with a metaphysical air, making an apparently simple statement seem unusually profound. In common with his other two compositions on the album, time is an underlying theme, on this occasion expressed in a neurotic meditation on the passing minutes that occur between the lovers. Unusually for Hillman, there is a controlled passion in his near paranoid utterance, "I knew what you wanted to do", after which his words are drowned by the reverberating sound effects. "The backwards guitar insert was McGuinn and Gary Usher's idea," Hillman points out. "I didn't consciously borrow the melody from the Beatles. Any similarities are purely coincidental."

The ambitious 'Mind Gardens' revealed Crosby reaching his furthest extremes as a songwriter. He had to fight hard to include this atonal, experimental work on the album. Both the song's title and lyrics invited interpretation, even prompting some to refer loosely to the composition as "an allegory". However, it seems clear the content and theme are symbolic rather than allegorical. The garden, overprotected and free from harm, will be suffocated by its own security, unless it is allowed to feel pain as well as pleasure. We may see the garden as representative of woman, knowledge, truth or anything else that may suffer from being locked away or overprotected. Whether the composition is impressive or excessive remains a matter of burning controversy among the group's critics and aficionados. Many, not least McGuinn and Hillman, complained of its self-indulgence and tunelessness. The employment of those droning, sitar-like reversed taped 12-strings was made even more bombastic by Crosby's stentorian vocal and insistence on showing us that he had read some Shakespeare, citing the 'To Be Or Not To Be' soliloquy in the line: "The slings and arrows of outrageous fortune" (*Hamlet* III, i, 58). Despite such criticisms, the song still sounds fascinating and remains a unique and welcome example of Crosby's venture into psychedelia.

Alas, there were no welcoming voices during or after the session. "We fought Crosby on that," says Hillman, "but he managed to get it on the album anyway, and it's lousy. What's more Crosby later admitted that, looking back, he didn't think it was very good either."

For Jim Dickson, 'Mind Gardens' was a composition as far removed from his vision of the Byrds as imagination would allow. The kid who had once acted like Dickson's protégé would no longer be constrained by old notions about the group's jingle-jangle sound. He had been held back creatively two years before with the demotion of 'Stranger In A Strange Land' and 'Flower Bomb Song', but now there was nobody in the way and Crosby was eager to push the Byrds' music into uncharted areas. With 'Mind Gardens', artistic experimentation dwarfed any other consideration. "If I had a vote without hearing the song and I saw that title I'd have said 'No!'," Dickson admits. "You can rationalize that it has some kind of meaning, but I've heard you speak of it more profoundly than David ever could, even then. David collected a lot of thoughts and phrases to make him appear smart, but he was glib. He had the reasoning and logic ability of a 14–15 year old who has just reached the age of reason and is so astounded by himself and the fact that he can figure out something that he thinks he's somehow turned into a god."

Dickson's overly harsh view underplays the extent to which Crosby was developing as a brilliant player and writer during this period. There is nothing else in his catalogue that even approaches this composition in terms of atonal audacity. If 'Mind Gardens' had a fault it was less to do with its obtuse musical structure and lyrical pretensions than the fact that it rapidly dated as a period piece, typical of the San Franciscan school of psychedelic weirdness. Crosby later conceded that the track was a one-off and it was never attempted by him in live performance. Sadly, even the sitar-like guitar sound, which had previously been used to such exciting effect, was never employed on any subsequent Byrds number. The raga rock dream ended here.

In argument, Crosby accepted most of the above points, while retaining a strong distaste for classifications such as raga rock. Taking the offensive, he proclaimed: "There was never anything called raga rock. It didn't exist. It was something that some idiot at Columbia thought up. 'Mind Gardens' had nothing to do with ragas or rock. It had to do with the words. And they're good. It wasn't excessive. They're just good words. However, it was unusual and not everybody could understand it because they'd never heard anything like it before. At that time everything was supposed to have rhyme and have rhythm. And it neither rhymed nor had rhythm so it was outside of their experience, and they weren't able to get into it. The words are good. I used an acoustic 12-string taped backwards. It wasn't a success because of the rhythm and the rhyme. It was just a little story and what it said was true. It said that if you build walls around your mind to keep out the abuse and harshness of life and the pain, then you also shut out the joy and the love. That's all it said. There's nothing wrong with that."

Crosby's defence is persuasive, but even he realizes that a song cannot survive on its lyrics alone, and requires a complementary tune. Whether the "guitar taped backwards" compensates for the lack of melody in 'Mind Gardens' remains the debatable point. His objection to the term raga rock is another understandable overreaction. As a blanket term to cover all rock songs in which Indian instruments are played or imitated, it seems an effective genre classification. Certainly, raga rock has a far more comprehensible meaning than other vague labels such as folk rock. Although Crosby denies that the playing on 'Mind Gardens' had anything to do with ragas, he neglects the main point that the use of a guitar taped backwards is part of the raga-rock tradition since it was one of the ways in which musicians effectively imitated the sound of a sitar.

The placing of 'My Back Pages' directly after 'Mind Gardens' seemed, intentionally or otherwise, to signal the division between Crosby and his partners at this point. McGuinn, ready to record a Dylan number once more and anxious to use the theme for the title of the album, felt that 'My Back Pages' was an excellent choice. Crosby, on the other hand, complained that it was a regressive step to the days before *Fifth Dimension*. In one of his more invective and unexpected outbursts, he complained: "It was a cop-out, it was a total backward shot. It was 'Oh, let's make 'Tambourine Man' again.' It was a formula record, anybody could hear it. It was a piece of shit, had all the commitment and life of a four-day-old mackerel . . ."

While Crosby worried about selling out, critics rightly praised McGuinn for another memorable performance and a classic Rickenbacker solo. Since McGuinn and Hillman had tolerated the inclusion of 'Mind Gardens' on the record, Crosby's resistance to 'My Back Pages' sounded unreasonable, at best. He later qualified his harsh remarks. "There wasn't really a dispute over it," he told me. "I did think if there was a Dylan song that we really wanted to do, then we should do it. But I thought that putting a Dylan song in as a formula was dumb. 'My Back Pages' wasn't the best Dylan song, but it was OK. It didn't hurt."

Clarence White's second uncredited appearance on the album can be heard on the penultimate track, 'The Girl With No Name'. The anonymous girl in the title of the song was actually a name borrowed from a real person. Julia Dreyer was nicknamed 'Girl' as she was the only daughter in a family full of sons. During the pre-Byrds days, the teenager had hung out with Crosby and subsequently married David Freiberg of Quicksilver Messenger Service. Her unexpected appearance in a Byrds' song amused Dickson, who was equally surprised to see Hillman finally emerge as an accomplished songwriter. "I thought his stuff on *Younger Than Yesterday* was OK and I was glad to see him do it. It was better that there were more contributors from within the group. There were a lot of plusses with Chris writing. His songs weren't astounding, but they were good. They weren't as bad as their bad stuff or as good as their best stuff. I would have been happy to have had a couple of Hillman's songs at any time. I particularly liked them because of the country flavour. McGuinn, in spite of the later *Sweetheart Of The Rodeo*, has no sensitivity towards country music."

The final track on *Younger Than Yesterday*, 'Why', broke the tradition of joke endings to Byrds albums, or did it? The song was already a year old, and the raga version that appeared on the B-side of 'Eight Miles High' was infinitely superior to this watered-down copy. Why the Byrds bothered to issue an inferior version at so late a date remains a mystery. Jim Seiter, the Byrds' road manager at the time, maintains that it was Crosby's idea: "They weren't satisfied with what they had and David wanted equal time. 'Why' was a song that Crosby had written, so 'Why' was done as a stroke for David."

Dickson concurs with Seiter's theory: "When something's on a B-side to us, it was as if it never existed. B-sides of singles not getting on albums was CBS policy, so it took extra effort to get them on there. By the time *Younger Than Yesterday* emerged, you'll notice there's more Crosby and Hillman songs. That reflects how David's power in the group had increased. The attitude may have been: 'We'll do a better version.' Who says it's better? Gary Usher! David

Crosby! If they say it's better, it's better. Who cares, but David? McGuinn's always prepared to believe that he can do a better solo."

In retrospect, Crosby insists: "The version of 'Why' we did at RCA with Jim Dickson was the best one of all." Certainly, those stunning sitar-like breaks on the RCA and original CBS B-side versions seem far superior to the standard breaks on the *Younger Than Yesterday* track, though Dickson remains far from convinced. "I wouldn't say the solo wasn't as good," he counters. "I was later able to make what I thought was a stunning solo, one that made me question whether I should put out the RCA version on *Never Before*. I left it up to McGuinn. It was *his* solo. McGuinn agonized over it and said: 'I guess we should use the RCA version, though it's a lot rougher in some ways.' So it was not an easy decision to choose the best version, even recently."

While *Younger Than Yesterday* failed to sell a million, it helped to establish the Byrds as an albums band. The mainstream pop press paid scant attention to the record, but the difficult-to-find underground American rock magazine *Crawdaddy* included a lengthy review from Sandy Pearlman, whose stoned intellectualism found its perfect subject matter in the Byrds. The mid-section of his commentary, at times veering from insight to incoherence, was a brave and entertaining attempt to articulate the mystery at the heart of the Byrds' music:

> The Byrds have real formal constancy. From time immemorial they have grounded their music in what are – or what seem to be – obviously regular rhythmic patterns. It is out of this ground that all developments and variations seem to rise – as it were – to the surface. This sound is dense, but not obviously and impressively complicated . . . The Byrds' music is not at all progressive. In comparison to say the Jefferson Airplane, the Doors or the Yardbirds, it's awfully calm. It doesn't go anywhere. The resolutions are not dramatic. They don't obviously end anything. Instead they are cyclical. But the cycles aren't closed . . .
>
> When the Byrds started, somebody (in *Hit Parader*, I think)

said that their first album was very nice, but it all sounded the same. Now we are up to taking that. It's become a virtue. What started out as a folk-rock style on the first album has been turned, via repetition, into a form ... The latest works of the Byrds are on this album, ironically titled *Younger Than Yesterday*, on which the Byrds give us magic, science, religion, psychedelic sounds, lots of electronic stuff and technological tongues, love songs, Dylan, rock 'n' roll, science fiction, some Southern California local lore, an African trumpet guy, a country & western guitar guy, a little bit of raga and so forth. They refer to all sorts of people including their older selves and yet after a while it winds up sounding pretty close. Even the abundant amazing sounds are far too amazing to remain that way for long. They make themselves very familiar. That's how strong the form is. Unique to rock, the Byrds are so formalistic that even when they do something new it's hard to tell. But the Byrds are conscious not only of their peculiar form but also of their place in the rock firmament.

The extent of the Byrds' 'self-consciousness' was debatable, but it was a trait picked up by other commentators. In an overview of the season's album releases, the august *New York Times* failed to appreciate the group's innovative qualities, complaining: "On the whole, it seems to be an uninspired, self-conscious attempt to do something new. They throw in some avant-garde sound effects on several songs – electronic bleeps and tapes played backwards – but these devices are not put to good use." David Crosby's maturation as a writer was similarly dismissed in words that echoed uncannily some of Dickson's familiar prejudices: "There's also a good deal of intellectual pretentiousness in the lyrics. The sentiments in a song called 'Everybody's Been Burned' are certainly very contemporary, but the words are really nothing more than a string of fashionable pre-packaged notions about alienation, trust and love. It sounds like a cocktail party snow-job. Then there's 'Mind Gardens', which is sung free-form with a background of bleeps. And which represents the same notions in the form of a disastrously simple-minded allegory. On the credit side, there is a good original song, 'Renaissance

Fair', and a strong version of Bob Dylan's 'My Back Pages'. *Younger Than Yesterday* is a disappointment. The Byrds' *Turn! Turn! Turn!* ... was a classic of folk-rock style, but they haven't matched it since."

It must have been dispiriting to read such a negative appraisal, the more so considering the remarkable artistic advances that the Byrds had made over the past year. Then again, the group always had a cocksure cool, ably assisted by Crosby's egomaniacal confidence and McGuinn's sometimes perverse optimism. Crosby was ever capable of dismissing negative criticism as blind ignorance while McGuinn, employing his 'I trust' mantra, simply turned the page at the first sign of offence. Their reactions were understandable. Rock criticism was still in its infancy during early 1967 and it was revealing that even a broadsheet newspaper would cling to *Turn! Turn! Turn!* like a security blanket while resisting the many advances evident since 'Eight Miles High'. Fortunately, the Byrds still had friends among the rock aristocracy and the quality of their work was expanding the imagination of an impressionable, coming of age audience in search of rock innovation. The length and depth of the aforementioned *Crawdaddy* review emphasized how seriously they were now seen in the still emerging underground press.

Moreover, they retained a sizeable young teenage audience whose long-term allegiance was impossible to measure. Despite declining sales since their peak period, CBS Records remained hopeful of a commercial renaissance and the publicity department must have been pleased when *Time* magazine agreed to review the album. Tellingly, *Time* concentrated on the most newsworthy aspects of the record, namely the lingering Dylan influence and the presence of hidden drug references. "The Byrds first took wing as interpreters of Bob Dylan and on their fourth album soar highest with one of Dylan's old songs, 'My Back Pages'. Where Dylan himself sang the disillusioned sermon like a harsh and nasal backwoods evangelist, the Byrds weave it into a more mellifluous and harmonic song. They also chirp sweetly about what seem to be LSDelightful reveries ('Mind Gardens', 'Renaissance Fair')."

Although tensions within the group were increasing, they were now working at white heat and using their multiple talents to create music of immense power and promise. Their greatest challenge was maintaining unity and simply sticking together. They now boasted three singer-songwriters, each growing more powerful with every succeeding song. Once again, it seemed that the Byrds were in a position to challenge the Beatles artistically. With Hillman having assimilated and developed McCartney's melodic bass style, and threatening to emerge as an engaging tunesmith, everything seemed possible. McGuinn and Crosby were also peaking as songwriters and now had enough material to compensate for the loss of Gene Clark. From this point onwards, the Byrds should have dominated the remainder of the Sixties but, instead, they were threatening to implode in spectacular fashion.

CHAPTER TWENTY-ONE

The Gathering Of The Tribes

WITHIN days of the US release of *Younger Than Yesterday*, the Byrds appeared at a benefit concert for CAFF at the Valley Music Theatre, Woodland Hills. The event was staged to coincide with the birthday of George Washington (22 February) and featured an impressive line-up, comprising the Byrds, the Doors, Peter, Paul & Mary, Hugh Masekela and the Buffalo Springfield. Reviewer Tracy Thomas, reporting for *NME*, noted: "The Byrds closed the first half playing mostly songs from their new album. Unfortunately, the quartet will do anything for music but rehearse. One felt like introducing them to each other."

Stephen Stills' protest song 'For What It's Worth' provided the organizers with a ready anthem for the CAFF campaign and due to its chart success Buffalo Springfield were allowed to close the second half of the show. The erudite Derek Taylor acted as master of ceremonies, but it was Lance Reventlow who articulated the committee's aims most eloquently. Writing in the CAFF newspaper, he proclaimed: "Since Los Angeles is the first city in the US to have experienced a confrontation between youth and authority, it is to us that the rest of the nation will look for a precedent. Unless our community can provide a meaningful accommodation to the ideas and wishes of youth, we will find ourselves raising a generation of cop-haters and misfits, and will thus rob our society of its most valuable resource, its young citizens. Although great strides have been made recently in the field of Civil Rights, little thought has been given to the rights of young people. CAFF hopes to be able to present the problems of youth to the community in a responsible fashion. We beseech the support of all who believe, as we do, that our youth should not be swept under the rug."

The concert ultimately proved a watershed in the propaganda battle and helped cause a rethink at City Hall. As Dickson proudly concludes: "In the end the police backed off, the city officials backed off, the Strip did not become a high rise and the proposed Beverly Hills freeway was not built."

Immediately after the CAFF concert, the Byrds left for a lightning tour of Europe, appearing in England for the first time since the disastrous 1965 tour. 'So You Want To Be A Rock 'n' Roll Star' had just been released and was receiving generally positive reviews, accompanied by limited airplay. "Lovely title," exclaimed Penny Valentine in *Disc*, still the most supportive music paper for Byrds' product. "Since they and Terry Melcher split, a certain something has been missing from the Byrds records. This goes some way to getting it back. The sound is still too fuzzy, thank you, but this song has a fascination, especially the jokey part where fans scream terrifyingly near. In an odd way I think this may be why the record is good, because the bad balance and the screaming make it sound as though it was recorded live, and therefore adds excitement." *NME*'s senatorial Derek Johnson was more cautious in his response, arguing, "No one can deny that this disc has a sensational dance beat and a stimulating effect, even though it's a bit dated in conception. The Byrds generate a great sound and blend effectively in the vocal – which, by the way, will have considerable appeal for teenagers. But I didn't like the dubbed-in screams, and there's very little melody."

Tellingly, none of the reviews centred on the satirical aspects of the composition, nor its sardonic overtones. That same week, the Beatles had entered the charts at number 2 with arguably the greatest double A-side ever released, 'Penny Lane'/'Strawberry Fields Forever'. Paul McCartney was invited by *Melody Maker* to review some recent singles releases in their 'Blind Date' feature, and the Byrds' new record was included in the batch. The most diplomatic Beatle was more forthcoming than expected and gave the impression that the Byrds were not progressing quickly enough for their own good, at least on the evidence of their current single.

THE GATHERING OF THE TRIBES

"I don't know," he hesitated. "I think by now they should be getting off that style of 12-string guitar and that particular brand of harmony. They really should be splitting from that scene because they'll end up finding themselves caught up in it. Dave Crosby knows where they should be going. And so does Jim McGuinn. They know what's happening . . . They've done some good stuff on their albums. A funny group, you know? If they go on like this – that's just the same sound speeded up. Dave and Jim know they've got to put more of themselves into their music. I can't think why it's not happening. They've got to put more of themselves into it." Of course, *Younger Than Yesterday* was still two months away from release in the UK and McCartney did not say whether he'd listened to an import copy as yet. Certainly, the album addressed many of the points he was making but McCartney's standards were exceptionally high at the time as the Byrds were about to discover.

On the Byrds' first evening back in London, on 24 February, Crosby visited EMI Studios in Abbey Road, where the Beatles were busily completing the groundbreaking *Sgt Pepper's Lonely Hearts Club Band*. McCartney's critique had appeared in *Melody Maker* that very day, but no mention was made of it at the meeting. Not that it would have mattered. Crosby felt privileged to see the Beatles in the studio and was fascinated to hear what they were currently working on. His timing could hardly have been better. In a break between sessions, the Fab Four couldn't resist impressing their host by playing back their most ambitious and innovative composition to date. "They pushed two huge coffin-sized speakers up to either side of me on the stool in this enormous room. Then, giggling to themselves, scampered up the stairs into the control room and shut the door. Then they played 'A Day In The Life', which they had just finished. By the time it got to the end of that last piano chord ring-out, I was a dishrag. I was stunned."

Such was the close rapport between the Byrds and the Beatles that Crosby was given a pre-release tape of 'A Day In The Life', which he clutched proudly to his chest and later plugged relentlessly to fellow members of the rock elite. As a publicist Crosby was peerless and his social circle was expansive. While three of the Byrds stayed at the White House Hotel in Regent's Park, Crosby immediately checked out and relocated to the London flat of Graham and Rose Nash. The Hollies' high harmony singer was in awe of Crosby and they soon became firm friends, laying the foundations for a long-term musical partnership that would spark into life as the decade reached its close.

The following afternoon, the Byrds attended a 250-strong fan club gathering at the Roundhouse, Chalk Farm. This was a special thank you to the fans who had collected 1,700 signatures urging them to return to England. For the best part of two hours, the group autographed albums and chatted to fans while their records were played as background music. One fan had the foresight to ask Crosby if the Byrds were likely to split up. "Not a chance," he retorted, convincingly. McGuinn, meanwhile, captured part of the event on his new movie camera, just as he had done when filming Hillman's home burning to the ground the previous month. He also had footage of the plane landing in London and a blurry series of images taken during the taxi ride to their hotel.

During their stay in England, the Byrds undertook some promotion, including a splendid appearance on *Top Of The Pops* where they played a searing 'So You Want To Be A Rock 'n' Roll Star'. They also travelled to Denmark, Sweden and Italy – an excellent audio recording of their radio appearance in Stockholm would later be widely bootlegged.

On 10 March, they returned to London and, four days later, on the eve of their departure, played a surprise gig at the Speakeasy. It was another fascinating set with Crosby well represented on a song list that included 'Why', 'Renaissance Fair', 'What's Happening?!?!', 'So You Want To Be A Rock 'n' Roll Star', 'Hey Joe', 'The Bells Of Rhymney' and 'My Back Pages'. At this point few, if any, of the spectators would have been familiar with the *Younger Than Yesterday* material as there was a two-month gap between US and UK release dates, a schedule which even the Byrds' visit failed to reverse. As the show reached its climax, there were audible cries for 'Mr Tambourine Man', but Crosby would not be swayed. "Sorry," he interjected, "but that's going too far back." The audience, which included Scott Walker, Marianne Faithfull, Long John Baldry, and various members of the Who, Pretty Things and Moody Blues, responded enthusiastically to the show, but not everyone was impressed by Crosby's cool. *Disc*'s reviewer, Hugh Nolan, concluded, with a tinge of regret: "They didn't happen. Onstage they seemed bored, tired, brought down and completely out of touch with the packed audience . . . Dave Crosby, moustached and wearing a black sombrero, announced the numbers in a vague take-it-or-leave-it sort of way which couldn't have endeared non-Byrd followers . . . Maybe they should realize what the Beatles are up to and just record, forgetting all about personal appearances. But the sad thing is that the Byrds – one of the world's top groups as far as original ideas and making first-class records goes – left Britain for the second time without glory."

The Byrds' return to LA coincided with the release of an edited version of 'My Back Pages' with a verse omitted. Crosby still felt a little uneasy about issuing a Dylan cover and later denounced the single. "We were kind of uptight. We had done an album that was good – and we *needed* a single. So we sat in a studio and tried to figure out how many different ways we could sell out, essentially. I don't think anybody thought we were doing that, but the point is we came down to making a formula record, and that's a mistake." Few, if any, critics shared Crosby's disdain for the single, which is still regarded as a Byrds' classic. Although it provided the group with another US Top 30 hit, this was little consolation to Crosby who valued his reputation as an innovator and forward-thinking singer-songwriter. He would no doubt have been appalled by the attitude of CBS Vice President Clive Davis, who wrote to Eddie Tickner on the day of the single's release expressing his delight at their success in covering Dylan material. Davis' letter neatly summed up the company's policy of allowing some degree of experimentation as a trade-off for commercial product:

> Listening to the album of *Younger Than Yesterday*, it's evident that 'My Back Pages' is really in the Byrds' bag and stands out. Although the group will obviously continue to experiment, as they should, it is also abundantly clear that their major appeal is with the folk flavoured rock, melodic composition. It is with this that their special sound comes through and it's not

surprising that it's with these songs that they have had their brightest successes. Obviously, no one wants to interfere with their originality and creativity, but the group will have a long, long future if they continue to work with simple folk tunes, adding to it their unique artistry and sound. I would appreciate it if you would convey my thoughts to the group. Also convey my really high regard for their work. I know they have yet to achieve the tremendous potential they are capable of. I look forward to seeing you and them soon.

Many of Clive Davis' reservations about the Byrds were shared by Jim Dickson. He had not envisaged Crosby emerging as a lead singer on so many tracks and could see no future in either the overt experimentation of 'Mind Gardens' or the whisky sophistication of 'Everybody's Been Burned'. In Dickson's mind, the old sound still had value, and the idea of connecting with the perfect Dylan song was his vision of the Byrds at their best. It comes as little surprise to learn that Dickson was the instigator behind the recording of 'My Back Pages' but, not for the first time, his reasons for encouraging McGuinn were far from straightforward.

"'My Back Pages' was my suggestion to McGuinn from out of the window of my car. I think the rest of the band undersold him, but he sang it with great force. It was their last chart single. Many times, McGuinn thanked me for that. I just happened to pull up alongside him in traffic, a couple of blocks from CBS. I was out of the picture as far as the recordings were concerned. I was still manager, but we weren't speaking. I saw him there and I felt for him. I believed that I'd done something wrong, that McGuinn's reputation was built on songs that were over his head that I'd insisted on. That's how I felt at the time. All that Dylan stuff was just a little outside his grasp. Yet, he did them well and I was satisfied with how he did them. But I felt I'd left him with nowhere to go. 'My Back Pages' was Dylan getting off the pulpit and trying to free himself to do something else, and I hoped I could do the same for McGuinn. I don't know if McGuinn even knows that that was how I felt. But I wanted him to be free and to go on to do whatever he wanted. I had a lot of respect for his ability to grow apart and adjust. McGuinn astounded me so many times with what he could do."

Although Dickson was estranged from the Byrds creatively, he continued to involve himself in countercultural pursuits and CAFF-related activities. One of these was the organization of a festival titled 'The Gathering Of The Tribes'. The first gathering, punningly subtitled 'The Human Be-In', had taken place in San Francisco's Golden Gate Park in January, with a line-up including the Jefferson Airplane, the Grateful Dead and Quicksilver Messenger Service. The LA rock fraternity decided that a similar display of hippie solidarity could be achieved by planning a 'Love-In' at one of their own parks. John Carpenter of the *Los Angeles Oracle* met with Dickson, Troubadour owner Doug Weston, and Peter Bergman of Radio Free Oz to co-ordinate proceedings. Eventually Elysian Park was chosen as the venue and a date was set for 26 March (Easter Sunday). The focal point of the Love-In could be located, somewhat inappropriately, behind the Dodger Stadium parking area.

Dickson was confident that at least one member of the Byrds would definitely attend: David Crosby. The musician who had once boasted a green suede cape and spoke reverentially of John Coltrane was now a counterculture Zelig, who was known to appear at Beatles sessions and fraternize with many of San Francisco's leading players. His broad-brimmed Borsalino hat, slim moustache and flamboyant dress were sartorial pointers for many up-and-coming musicians who envied his style, social circle and familiarity with the best musicians in town. Crosby already felt he had outgrown Dickson's patronage, but retained a respect and admiration for his mentor, whose idealistic aims so often coincided with his own. Crosby was characteristically enthused when he received an invitation to attend a Dickson-involved Gathering Of The Tribes. Enclosed was a paper sheet offering a vague breakdown of the day, beginning with a 6 am Sunrise Service featuring 'Spontaneous Sound with Christopher Tree', at which "several religious leaders would participate". A number of acts were booked for the day, including the Turtles, the Daily Flash, the New Generation, the Dawn and the Peanut Butter Conspiracy. But what impressed Crosby most of all was the sense of spectacle and solidarity offered by the event. The Love-In invitation explained that, "Many of the 'tribes' will attend in procession form. All those attending are asked to please bring flowers, food, drums, bells, cymbals, incense, tambourines, love, colors, and their friends." Crosby was enchanted by the event and, following the festival, he immediately wrote a jazz-influenced tribute, 'Tribal Gathering', which he looked forward to recording on the next Byrds album. For the moment, all seemed deceptively well.

Younger Than Yesterday eventually peaked at number 24 in *Billboard*, a reasonable showing, but evidence enough that the Byrds still needed to make up ground if they were to re-establish themselves as America's most popular group. With Brian Wilson already in self-destructive freefall and unable to complete the legendary *Smile*, the Beach Boys' recent creative surge had effectively ground to a halt. Never again would they challenge the Beatles or find that Holy Grail link between the singles and albums markets. Even as they were losing their pop audience, their counterculture credentials were under scrutiny and would later be ridiculed in the new hip bible, *Rolling Stone*. The Byrds might have benefited from this power shift among rock's elite, but there were still other contenders, whose careers were then blossoming. The Mamas & The Papas were enjoying a resurgence of popularity with their cover of the Shirelles' 'Dedicated To The One I Love' and an excellent album *Deliver*, both of which climbed to number 2 in their respective US charts. Crosby's old friends the Jefferson Airplane were crossing similar boundaries with a Top 3 album, *Surrealistic Pillow*, which spawned two Top 10 singles, 'Somebody To Love' and 'White Rabbit'. And lurking in the wings were the Doors whose debut album would soon be released, accompanied by a US number 1 single, 'Light My Fire'.

On reflection, the spring of 1967 was a time when the Byrds needed to be at their best in order to exploit the dramatic changes in the pop/rock landscape. One year on from the departure of Gene Clark, they were back in the game in a big way, but had lost many friends and supporters during the interim. Without a massive single to their name, no sign of a coast-to-coast tour and an abject refusal to perform either of their number 1 hits in concert, they were increasingly reliant upon their underground following. The Byrds had grown accustomed to uncritical support from writers like Paul Jay Robbins but, two years on from the wonder days of Ciro's, they could no longer be certain of their standing amid a scene in which LA values were under siege from the hipper-than-thou avatars of San Francisco. Crosby remained the crucial link between the two communities, with the Byrds delicately poised in the middle. David's charisma frequently worked wonders for the Byrds' reputation, but he could also damage their precarious position in pop circles, where his fiery temperament was not always appreciated. When the Byrds squabbled or acted icy cool, rumours would inevitably circulate about their inherent instability. Dickson heard them all and, watching from the sidelines, he frequently feared the worst: "The future of the Byrds was up for new interpretation daily. KRLA, the station that broke them, said that the Byrds were finished and they didn't expect them to last the year. The Byrds had died and died, and they were still there! People weren't on their side the way they were before. When the Byrds first broke on to the scene in Hollywood, just about everybody was on their side. They were the only game in town. By 1967, they couldn't draw flies. A lot of that had to do with the bad performances that disappointed people and a lot had to do with who they turned out to be. Look at who David Crosby turned out to be. Loads of people in Hollywood have egos that they mostly try to control and be civilized about. There's a guy in the Byrds who's got a bigger ego than any movie star, than any musician, than *anybody*. People got soured. It's not important enough for them to put up with. I put up with a lot and the group put up with a lot from David Crosby, but people outside got tired of putting up with David Crosby. He's great when he's up, but when he's down he can ruin your day, your week, your month! The glitz was off, there were other bands. They weren't the only game in town any more. There were people that came along who were prepared to be a whole lot more fun to be around."

When they played live, the Byrds were increasingly dominated by Crosby, who not only took over centre stage and announced the songs, but heavily influenced the choice of material. McGuinn and Hillman reluctantly succumbed to Crosby's demand for a larger profile without necessarily believing that he deserved such attention. For students of group dynamics, the onstage antics provided revealing insights into a personality clash that was gradually degenerating into a long, cold war. "It was Crosby versus the rest onstage," recalls roadie Jim Seiter. "It was a joke. At times the audiences loved it. But back in LA it was dreadful."

Eddie Tickner noted the conflicts with increasing concern. "There was a point when if Crosby didn't get his own way he would be very brought down and his guitar playing would be affected. If he wasn't pleased, he would not play well onstage."

McGuinn was even more derogatory about Crosby's vocal displays and complained bitterly, "He'd be off, off out of tune. But when it came to one of *his* songs, he'd shine, man."

Crosby was appalled by McGuinn's put-down, telling me, "I don't think it's right or fair to say I sang out of tune. You can't play if it's out of tune." What no one disputes is the animosity that became increasingly noticeable whenever they took the stage. Although Crosby had insisted that the Byrds perform 40–45 minute sets, he still expected a degree of enthusiasm that his ultra cool partners were loath to display. One time, Crosby caught McGuinn staring at his watch in mid-set, as if impatient to return to the dressing room. For David, that was enough to destroy the mood of the entire evening. The formerly stage-shy Chris Hillman had also developed a cold arrogance and was not beyond missing a few notes in order to take a drag from his cigarette, a gesture which Crosby regarded as contemptuous. Such actions caused Crosby to freeze onstage and soon he allowed himself to become completely disillusioned by his fellow players' boredom and lack of commitment. They, in turn, felt alienated by his tendency to pontificate like a guru and would have much preferred to return to the days when there was no comment at all between songs. The bad feeling ensured that rehearsals were kept to a minimum, which made matters even worse.

On one infamous occasion, the ever experimental Crosby decided to confront the audience at San Francisco's Fillmore while in the midst of an LSD trip. "[It was] one of the few times that I ever tried to play behind acid and the strings became the size of ropes. Song? What song? Oh! It was too loose." The reaction of McGuinn and Hillman hardly needs stating. The next night in San Jose, it was McGuinn's turn to sabotage the show, albeit unintentionally. As the set reached its climax, the PA system spluttered to a halt. "The electronic complexities of lead guitarist Jim McGuinn's playing apparently proved too much for the sound equipment," a reviewer wryly noted.

Collecting criticisms of Crosby's behaviour during this period is easier than grasping frozen flakes in a snowstorm. Everyone attests to his extraordinary ego as if that was the whole story. What they all too frequently fail to acknowledge is the enormous leaps he was making as a singer-songwriter and musician. Moreover, he had become the perfect barometer of the age, a questing innovator forever looking ahead who saw himself as a standard-bearer for the young, hippie generation. He was the burning heart at the centre of the group. Crosby's self-belief should have been harnessed by the Byrds for their own advantage and benefit, but old and new rivalries made that dream impossible. That was the great tragedy of the Byrds story. Crosby was capable of great love, enthusiasm, support and generosity of spirit – far more than any of his fellow Byrds – but those positive traits could be suddenly erased by a thoughtless remark or action. He had so much to offer, but a sense of being held back compounded his frustrations. Crosby was instinctive rather than calculating and his acerbity was partially born of a deep sensitivity and vulnerability that few appreciated. He believed passionately in the concept of a new, free musical community and it was not always easy to reconcile that vision with the everyday reality of life in the Byrds. In different circumstances, McGuinn and Hillman might have healed the growing rift with Crosby by focusing on common ground and encouraging his creativity, but instead they remained aloof and allowed resentments to fester. Communication lines were frequently closed and for someone as verbally and musically empathetic as Crosby that was akin to slow torture. It was like the perfect marriage gone terribly wrong.

From 16–21 May, the Byrds were booked at the Whisky, supported by the up-and-coming Doors, whose aggressive lead singer Jim Morrison deeply offended Crosby. When challenged by a support act, Crosby's customary reaction was to assert control, but it was not easy to transform the Byrds into a tight unit between desultory sets. Instead, they would be reduced to musical stasis, while their disgruntled rhythm guitarist sought the perfection that only weeks in a rehearsal room could have produced. "David did some of the most unprofessional things ever onstage," Jim Seiter alleges. "He'd start a song, play a couple of bars, and then insist upon a five-minute tuning interlude. It was on a night like this that Hillman went up to the microphone and announced, 'Ladies and gentlemen – the David Crosby Show'. And Hillman never said much, but he'd sneak around and get his digs in."

"I remember that, it was at the Whisky," Crosby grimaces, still seemingly aggrieved. His reaction came as no surprise to Seiter, who saw it as a defining moment. "That was devastating – especially at the Whisky with all their crony friends. When Hillman said that, everyone in the audience laughed. That's what pissed David off so much. I would bet you anything that he still holds that against Chris."

When the group looked out into the audience or to the side of the stage, most of the reassuring faces from bygone days were long gone. "I never went to gigs any more because I couldn't stand being ashamed of the way they played," Dickson laments. "They played sloppy music sometimes, especially at the Whisky. And I felt unwelcome." Even the normally effusive Derek Taylor complained about their playing. In his traditionally partisan column in *Disc*, he strained his prose to breaking point while desperately seeking to convey an unconvincing ambivalence. "The Byrds, one of the best groups in the world, were again terrible at the Whisky . . . I cannot work it out. They seem to have a death-wish, which is only thwarted by their indomitable heartbeat. They will probably outlive us all. I love them and deplore them."

One week after their Whisky residency, the group played a few dates in the Washington area, which allowed Michael Clarke's parents a rare opportunity to see their only son play live. "It was their first concert at our coliseum here in Spokane," recalls Michael's mother, Suzy Dick. "Jefferson Airplane opened for them. That was when I met David Crosby, and I never liked him, although he's mellowed now, I'm sure. He was just a snot. He would hardly lower himself to talk to you, let alone cooperate with anything. He held up the show for I don't know how long because of the sound system, which wasn't to his liking. We all sat backstage while he held up everything. But that was the only time I ever did meet David, and I never talked to him on the phone. McGuinn I knew well, and Gene, and always Chris. He was a sweetie, and I loved him like a son."

Crosby was no doubt oblivious to the feelings of Mrs Dick. He was probably too busy ignoring the other Byrds and hanging out with his Jefferson Airplane friends. McGuinn and Hillman seemed increasingly distant, even mildly hostile to his ideas and wishes, while Clarke was funny but irritating. "David always underestimated me, and I always overestimated him," was one of Michael's favourite quips. In truth, their relationship had been fragile ever since that unfortunate incident back at the *Turn! Turn! Turn!* sessions where Clarke had shown the temerity to punch his colleague in the face. For his part, Crosby often complained about Clarke's drumming, just as he had criticized Gene Clark's sense of time. But Clarke's child-like enthusiasm ensured that it was impossible to stay mad at him for any length of time. Unlike McGuinn and Hillman, Clarke was too transparently fiery to indulge in the complex cold war tactics that characterized their interaction with Crosby. He always had the ability to laugh things off, play the fool, or simply find fun elsewhere. Retribution was not in his nature but, soon after, he found the ideal opportunity to wreak some mischief. Prior to a hip gathering at the Valley Music Theatre, featuring the Byrds, Kaleidoscope, Clear Light and the Fraternity Of Man, he imitated Crosby's recent display at the Fillmore by devouring some hallucinogens and playing the entire gig stoned. The performance was shambolic, but when they rounded on Clarke afterwards, he had the perfect riposte, blaming Crosby for setting a bad example at the Fillmore.

Conflict can produce strange responses that often seem weirdly out of character. For all his onstage exuberance, outspokenness and aggression, the ultra passionate Crosby was also deeply sensitive and capable of retreating into a dark shell of melancholic inertia. In those moments he was more remote than McGuinn at his frostiest. The Byrds continued to play out old roles, like hapless participants in a bad marriage. During this strangest of times in the Byrds' history, their personalities started to mirror each other's in bizarre ways. The perennially shy Hillman magically transformed into a pushier personality with a penchant for razor-sharp sarcasm. McGuinn, the king of icy cool, was also restive and acting oddly. While appearing on a CBS News documentary, *Inside Pop: The Rock Revolution*, he started sounding off like some San Franciscan radical, storming the gates of the establishment. Rather than the ever familiar apolitical McGuinn, viewers were confronted with a tough-talking activist full of iconoclastic zeal. It was as if he had suddenly turned into David Crosby. "We're out to break down those barriers that we see to be arbitrary," McGuinn announced. "The big fences that have been built, you know? The walls that will crumble if hit hard enough. And we're out there hitting them. We're cutting them subtly. We're cutting them with laser beams and not dynamite. We're doing other things here. We're cutting them with emotions, which are stronger than fists, and we're getting mass emotions involved. I feel there's some sort of guerrilla warfare going on. I feel like a guerrilla. I feel good." McGuinn would never speak like this in public again nor display the fiery political passion which Crosby would carry forward over the decades. The momentary mental transfer between the pair all but ended here.

The sense of an already insecure unit slipping away was confirmed by a shift in business personnel. Derek Taylor, whose effusive press releases and urbane manner had mollified many an angry journalist or fractured ego, had decided to move on. Meanwhile, Crosby had brought in an independent adviser who would have a profound impact on the future of the Byrds. "Larry Spector was a business manager for a lot of the young guys around Peter Fonda and Dennis Hopper, who were all friends with David Crosby," Tickner explains. "So David came in one day and said: 'I've found a business manager who will do really well.'"

Larry Spector's unexpected rise to power was a lasting testimony to Crosby's caprice during this period. Dickson was amazed by the suddenness with which the interloper usurped the Byrds' management, not least because Spector was largely unknown in the business. It was all the more intriguing that his entrée to the group came via Dennis Hopper, with whom Dickson had a tempestuous friendship, going back years. During the mid-Fifties, Hopper had become entangled in a torrid affair with Dickson's actress wife, Diane Varsi. The pair had been working on a film together when Dickson learnt of their fling. Inevitably, there were fireworks. "My first meeting with Dennis was when I took a swing at him," says Dickson. "He jumped behind the bed and said, 'Don't mess with me, I was Golden Gloves champion' – which, of course, wasn't true! I swung a chair at him and he ducked and ran. Diane was 19 years old and had received an academy nomination. All of a sudden, every ambitious actor in Hollywood was pursuing her with great aggression. I thought, 'Well, if all these pretty starlets came after me, I'd probably crack too.'" Hopper's motives were romantic rather than mercenary, and the blow-up with Dickson was soon forgotten. The following day, Hopper realized that he'd left behind a memento of the affair in Diane's room. "It was his hat, which he needed for a shoot. When he came back I was in bed with her. He gave us one of the best dramatic scenes I've ever seen Dennis Hopper do, and only Diane and I got to see it. He turned around to her with tears running down his face, his hat in his hand, and said, 'But I love you, asshole!' She just smiled. The scene was so intense that I can still picture it in my mind. If I'd got that on film, he would have received an academy award."

Over the years, Hopper and Dickson remained in contact, both sharing many friends in the film industry. The actor was also frequently on the scene during the Ciro's days and later at the CAFF benefits. His involvement with the still unknown Spector was pure kismet. "I was puzzled how it happened and Dennis told me the whole story," Dickson explains. "Dennis had an interview for a part in a movie. He had no manager because he was 'unmanageable'. He had a history of problems and he needed somebody quickly." At the time, Larry's mother was working as Hopper's accountant and bookkeeper and Dennis casually suggested he act as a silent intermediary at the meeting. "Dennis put him in a suit and told him,

'Don't say anything, I'll introduce you as my manager. Just sit there in your good suit and exchange pleasantries.' To talk to Larry Spector, the fact that he was well-educated was apparent. He wasn't some slob off the street. He was a relative in some way to the Max Factor fortune. At one time, I believe, the Spectors were the superior family and the Max Factors were almost like the poor cousins. Larry wanted to come out of college and be an executive rather than working his way up."

Spector already had several entrepreneurial schemes afoot involving real estate deals and a specialist laundry service that discreetly provided clean clothes for Hollywood stars. Thanks to Hopper's patronage, he was able to move into personal and business management in the film and music business. Before long, his client list featured several people closely connected with the Byrds' inner circle, including actor/singer Brandon deWilde, Ciro's habitué Peter Fonda, Hugh Masekela the trumpeter on 'So You Want To Be A Rock 'n' Roll Star', and Bob Denver, star of the television comedy series *Gilligan's Island* who was then married to Chris Hillman's ex-wife Butchie. It was unsurprising that Spector's networking would lead him to a Byrd, but it was to his lasting advantage that the first one he met was the gregarious David Crosby.

Crosby was initially impressed by Spector whose social background and movie star clientele seemed superficially impressive. That he was still a neophyte in the music business was evidently not considered important. "It was Larry's mother they should have been after," says Dickson. "David, easily taken in, hired Larry independently for his personal business." When he first arrived, Spector was not regarded as any threat by Dickson or Tickner, who merely saw him as David's latest find. "It didn't diminish what David had to pay off, it just meant he wasn't using Eddie's wife, Rita. The Byrds were paying her 5 per cent to be a mama and do stuff Eddie wouldn't do for them any more. He did everything in the beginning to help them, but when they became more helpless as it went along, he said, 'That's your personal business, not Byrds' business. Get somebody else to do it.'"

Rita Rendall was regarded as a godsend for the Byrds. She had been in the music business considerably longer than Tickner, having previously worked as a bookkeeper for Bob Dylan's manager Albert Grossman. Her stern, no-nonsense attitude was a welcome panacea to the countercultural vagueness favoured by many others in the business. "I really liked her a lot," says McGuinn's former wife, Dolores. "She was responsible for us owning a house. She would help us set aside the money to buy it."

What nobody had bargained on was Crosby the passionate proselytizer, who soon persuaded everybody that Spector could be the great saviour of the Byrds. Meanwhile, in his role as Crosby's new business manager, Spector caused a scene by shouting at Rendall and reducing her to tears. "I heard him railing at her from two offices away," says Dickson. "He was saying, 'I hire *you* and you do what I say!' She got up, cleared out all her stuff and never set foot in the office again. Left the music business too." This ritual humiliation did nothing to quell support for Spector, who unexpectedly won McGuinn over to his side.

Eddie Tickner had already seen enough to realize that the partnership was breaking up, with Crosby acting as executioner and kingmaker. "Some undercover things then went on," he told me. "A conspiracy to leave Tickner/Dickson and go with Larry as personal and business manager. Actually, I'd called it a day after Europe. Dickson came down from the hills and took over for the remaining period. We negotiated a settlement and we officially left on 30 June 1967. I still get a royalty cheque!"

Surrendering a bookkeeper as organized and efficient as Rita Rendall was bad enough, but switching management at such a decisive time in the group's history and employing a relative newcomer with limited experience of the rock business was obviously courting danger. "It was another example of going along with David's bad ideas," McGuinn laments. "Probably, it was the grass is greener because Larry had Peter Fonda and Hugh Masekela, who were our friends. We thought, 'This guy must be really great' and I guess we weren't doing as well with Dickson. He was on the sidelines because nobody got along with him. It was a mistake. I didn't realize how big a mistake it was."

CHAPTER TWENTY-TWO

Monterey And Mutiny

PRIOR to his departure from the Byrds, Terry Melcher had predicted that Dickson's intense emotional involvement with the group would eventually prove his undoing. "Dickson could be a svengali either on a positive or negative level," Hillman concurs. "Unfortunately, it got to him being mother hen and us being little chicks. He became so threatened by certain things, he turned on us and later on, in 1966–67, it became so uncomfortable we couldn't work with Jim. But initially he had this wonderful vision, one which we fought him on. He was an older guy, but he was really our Brian Epstein. Unfortunately, he got so emotionally involved with it beyond the business aspects it destroyed our relationship with him. If he had not become so emotionally involved, he probably would've kept this band together as the Byrds until 1970 as a major creative force."

Of course, if Dickson had not been "emotionally involved", it is doubtful whether he would have persevered with the Byrds during their painful, embryonic period at World-Pacific. "The problem is that if you close off that emotional sensitivity to protect your own feelings, you also close off your emotional sensitivity to the music and to the fire," Dickson says. "I could have disciplined myself to shut it all out, but then I wouldn't have been of any use. It's your responsibility to say, 'I think you'd better do it again.'"

Once Dickson had been cast in the mould of a father figure, he never found it easy to relinquish that role. It was another coincidence of Byrds/Beatles history that they should both lose their guardians at the same time. Epstein was already rumoured to be facing a future without the Fab Four. Within two months he would be found dead at his London home. During the same period, the Rolling Stones parted with their wunderkind svengali Andrew Oldham, who withdrew when the drug squad and the Grim Reaper threatened to destroy all that he had helped to build. Dickson, the great survivor, was another victim of the times. Pop stars, now enjoying more power and wealth than ever, felt uneasy with autocratic or charismatic managers, and many naively believed that they could control their own destinies. Even the great Dylan was about to abandon his immemorial mentor Albert Grossman. Against the odds, both the Beatles and the Rolling Stones survived the loss of their managers, but the Byrds were less stable and responded with scarcely credible displays of dolorous self-destructive behaviour, almost tearing the group asunder in their confusion. Dickson was also damaged by the experience, losing clout in the industry and temporarily retiring in order to take stock. Like Epstein and Oldham, his close relationship to the personalities in the group left him vulnerable to emotional expediency.

"I might have stayed more remote from it and kept in reserve more clout, not used it up so fast," Dickson reflects, with the wisdom of old age. "I really used it up by the end of the *first* album. These guys were so shaky . . . I spent too much personal currency, not money but self, in that period of time. I used myself up too much, did too much, went to too many places, hustled too hard, put too much on the line. Everything. Every friend I had, after ten years of accumulating friends and never asking anything, I asked *everybody everything* to help the Byrds. I used them up and then, having given the group tremendous credential by claiming how marvellous they were, when they turned on me, I was the discard."

The last month of Jim Dickson's tenure as manager could hardly have been more eventful, for the Byrds were booked to play at the International Monterey Pop Festival. Originally conceived by LA impresario Alan Pariser, who had helped produce the CAFF concert, it was the ultimate flowering of youth culture at a time when the musical divisions between pop and rock were still blurred. The organization for the festival passed from Pariser and his partner Benny Shapiro to Papa John Phillips and Dunhill Records' supremo Lou Adler. At first, the Byrds were not even invited, but Phillips finally confirmed a booking with Dickson, telling him that it would not feel right without the group. A more pressing problem facing Phillips and Adler was winning over the San Franciscan fraternity, who openly scorned the commerciality of Hollywood and derided LA scene makers as plastic hippies and bread heads. Several delegates were sent to Haight-Ashbury bearing promises that the festival would be a charitable event for the people. After much consideration, the Golden Gate gurus accepted the proposals. Perhaps the most remarkable aspect of Monterey was the amazingly eclectic line-up of musicians, with representatives from contrasting areas of the rock scene. The chart stars of LA rock were there in the form of the Mamas & The Papas, the Byrds, the Association, Buffalo Springfield, Scott McKenzie and Johnny Rivers; San Francisco offered the Grateful Dead, the Jefferson Airplane, Quicksilver Messenger Service, Steve Miller, Big Brother & The Holding Company and Country Joe & The Fish; New York was represented by Simon & Garfunkel and Laura Nyro; England sent over the Who and Eric Burdon & The Animals, and flew an Anglo-American flag with the Jimi Hendrix Experience; Stax and soul meant Booker T & The MGs and Otis Redding; a touch of cabaret was provided by Lou Rawls; and the 'international' tag was justified by the presence of South African émigré Hugh Masekela and India's most celebrated exponent of ragas, Ravi Shankar.

Faced with playing what was probably the most important gig of their career, even the Byrds were roused from their customary lethargy and spent weeks in the rehearsal room of the 9000 building in a determined attempt to prove their critics wrong. This should have been a unifying experience but, already, there was a lingering suspicion that Crosby might be disillusioned enough to seek employment elsewhere. The Buffalo Springfield's singer/guitarist Stephen Stills had long admired David's harmony powers and rhythm playing and made no secret of his desire to jam with the most sociable Byrd. "I knew Stephen was romancing David away," McGuinn insists. "I'd gone over to Stephen's house with David, and Stephen had a guitar out and was playing some blues licks. Then he turned to me and said, 'Can you do that?' It was something out of my arena, so I said, 'No'. Then, he turned to David and said, *'See!'* Stephen wanted to work with David, who was very unhappy about being in the Byrds."

Stills' attempt to humiliate McGuinn sowed the seeds of doubt in David's mind about the quality of the Byrds' musicianship. In such moods, Crosby was always likely to make an unintentionally cruel remark, but this time he excelled himself. As the Byrds were completing rehearsals, he casually informed McGuinn and Hillman, "You guys aren't good enough musicians to be playing with *me*". As McGuinn recalls, "We went, 'Gee, sorry David!' We knew it was just a matter of time."

Even when Crosby was contrite, his words grated with McGuinn, who felt he was being condescending at best. "He said, 'Look, I won't go out of loyalty to you guys.' And I said, 'Oh, come on – if you really want to do it, you should. You're not going to be of any use to us if you really want to be somewhere else.' But nevertheless he stuck it out and he eventually managed to get himself fired because of his attitude. He became a tyrant – even started to say, 'I won't do this.' I was the group leader. I had to decide whether to get rid of him."

On Sunday 11 June, a week before Monterey, the Byrds enjoyed a dry run, playing alongside the Doors, Jefferson Airplane, the Seeds and the Steve Miller Band for the Fantasy Faire and Magic Mountain Music Festival at Crosby's favourite spot, Mt Tamalpais. They were driven to the festival on the back of Hell's Angels' motorcycles, a firm indicator of Crosby's affiliations. More than 15,000 people turned up for this musical love-in, which featured an eclectic array ranging from singer-songwriters Tim Hardin, Tim Buckley and P.F. Sloan to hip newcomers the Merry-Go-Round, Blackburn & Snow, the Mojo Men and the Blues Magoos, plus Dionne Warwick and Motown legends, Smokey Robinson & the Miracles. The event boosted the Byrds' morale in preparation for the bigger event that followed. For McGuinn, the festival fitted in perfectly with his optimistic outlook. "We really believed all the peace and love stuff, and we thought we could change the world. And some things did change for the better. You can't say we didn't do anything. The feeling was a euphoric one. Aside from the substances, we were feeling really good about everything. It was a good time."

At this point, Crosby was momentarily distracted by a cry for help. His new friend Stephen Stills had recently suffered a major career setback when Neil Young abruptly left the Buffalo Springfield on the eve of a prestigious appearance on Johnny Carson's *The Tonight Show*. The group had attempted to fulfil some East Coast dates as a quartet but after a couple of poor performances in Boston, promoters told them bluntly, "Don't come back!" As fellow member Bruce Palmer succinctly noted: "They weren't the real deal without me and Neil." On the same day that the Byrds played at Mt Tamalpais, Buffalo Springfield recruited a replacement for Young in Doug Hastings, late of San Franciscan band, the Daily Flash. It was a welcome move but, with only days left before Monterey, the Springfield urgently needed extra ammunition. Magnanimous to a fault, Crosby instinctively offered his assistance, much to Stills' relief and joy. "I rehearsed with them for a few days," David recalls, "and I said I'd sit in with them. I was just trying to help. I had no intention of becoming a member of Buffalo Springfield."

For Crosby, the gesture of friendship to Stills was in keeping with the spirit of the festival, but he declined to tell McGuinn of his plans in advance. David was well aware that his partner was far more cautious about fraternizing so openly with potential competitors and did not wish to start another argument. Although Hillman was also friendly with Stills, even he questioned Crosby's loyalties, especially in view of his recent comments on the Byrds' musicianship. At a time when the world was about to celebrate the first great pop festival, Crosby felt their critical comments and petty jealousies were pathetic and unnecessary. "They were worried about my hanging around with Stills because they knew he was better than they were," he told me. Not only was Crosby willing to play with the Buffalo Springfield but he even helped Stills complete a Byrds-style melody about their mutual friend, Grace Slick: 'Rock & Roll Woman'. Crosby provided part of the melody and that wonderful opening choral sequence in the full knowledge that he could not receive a writing credit. The contractual conundrums and restrictions placed upon musicians were anathema to his hippie sensibility and generous personality. If record companies or publishers attempted to curtail his contributions, then he would give away his ideas and melodies to friends for nothing. David's rebellious streak and refusal to be held back by small-mindedness ensured that any adverse comments about his beneficent behaviour were merely likely to exacerbate matters. McGuinn's response, as ever, was to play it cool and trust that everything would turn out all right.

The three-day Monterey International Pop Festival (16–18 June) was to prove a landmark in rock history. Everyone agreed that its timing was in perfect synchronicity with some of the biggest pop events of the era. Two weeks before, the Beatles had issued the groundbreaking *Sgt Pepper's Lonely Hearts Club Band* and, on the first day of the festival, Paul McCartney was on the front page of *Life* testifying to the magic of LSD. Back in England, Mick Jagger and Keith Richards were in the middle of a nightmarish court case, while Brian Jones had also just been busted for possession of marijuana. That setback did not prevent Jones from attending Monterey and representing the Rolling Stones 'in spirit'. Amid glorious summer weather, the festival remained miraculously free from violence with only one arrest logged by the police. The event even had its own specially-tailored anthem from the pen of John Phillips. 'San Francisco', sung by Phillips' former folk buddy Scott McKenzie, became an instant flower power anthem that pullulated into a worldwide hit over the summer, even reaching number 1 in England. The Beatles, no longer performing live, responded to the vibes across the Atlantic by composing 'All You Need Is Love', which was broadcast across the world by satellite, within a week of the festival. Crosby endorsed their message of love: "God bless the Beatles! I picture them a lot of times as a big Coastguard icebreaker with a solid steel bow that's going to crash through idiocy and ignorance."

Crosby was in good spirits on the eve of Monterey, but his sense of mischief remained dangerously intact. The authorities frowned upon some hard-core pornographic pictures that were liberally displayed in his tent, while he lectured them about censorship and freedom of expression. He was still in proselytizing mood when the

Byrds took the stage. Musically, the group offered an extraordinary performance, oscillating from ramshackle to brilliant within the space of a song. McGuinn's jagged guitar lines brought a harsh metallic edge to reflective pieces like 'Renaissance Fair' and every number was taken at a frantic pace, folk rock mutating into garage punk as if in an amphetamine rush. Crosby dominated proceedings, cranking out a breathless 'Hey Joe' and even drowning Hillman's vocal on a slapdash, punky rendition of 'Have You Seen Her Face'. Frantic versions of 'Lady Friend' and 'I Know My Rider' added to the drama, with Crosby more animated than ever before. At one point, while they were tuning, a Boeing 707 came soaring over the festival site. The Byrds continued playing above the noise of the jet, adjusting the tempo to simulate the sound of the aircraft as it landed at a nearby aerodrome. The incident was a whimsical justification of McGuinn's concept of the Byrds as the first group of the jet age.

The Byrds' sense of adventure was conveyed to the audience by an adamant refusal to play old songs like 'Mr Tambourine Man', 'Turn! Turn! Turn!' or even 'Eight Miles High'. Responding to some disappointed groans, Crosby chided, "Hey, the only answer I can give you was written by somebody else – the times they *are* a-changin'," an allusion that brought him a round of applause. Despite Crosby's ineluctable insistence on modernity, the Byrds did not entirely block off their past. Jim Dickson was still keen to play the Dylan card and, just as he had done with 'My Back Pages' on *Younger Than Yesterday*, persuaded McGuinn to return to the master for inspiration.

"I was chasing around Monterey trying to find McGuinn the lyrics to 'Chimes Of Freedom'," Dickson recalls. "I had convinced him that this was a place where he ought to sing it." Even Crosby could not argue about the relevance or sentiments of the song, which rounded off the new set with some aplomb, despite McGuinn's failure to learn the words correctly. There was one final surprise when Crosby invited trumpeter Hugh Masekela and his drummer Big Black to join the Byrds onstage for a rousing finale of 'So You Want To Be A Rock 'n' Roll Star'. Taken at a faster tempo, with Masekela's horn blaring loudly in the background and McGuinn's Rickenbacker tearing through the song, it was the highlight of the set and a lasting aural document of the Byrds at their mid-period finest.

While the Monterey performance was fascinating on a musical level, it was overshadowed by Crosby's memorable broadsides on drugs and politics. He had already graced the stage in the early afternoon to introduce the Electric Flag and was still extolling the greatness of his idol Mike Bloomfield midway through the Byrds' set. With the audience transfixed by his rhetorical flourishes, he decided to use Monterey as an ideological platform for the hippie nation. "I'd like to tell you all something," he announced in a tone of urgency. "I don't know whether any of you have seen, probably a lot of you have, *Life* magazine this week. In it, there is a statement that affects our times and is gonna cause a lot of trouble. I'd like to quote it to you roughly. 'I believe that if we gave LSD to all the statesmen and the politicians in the world we might have a chance at stopping war.' That's a quote from Paul McCartney – *crowd applause* – I concur, heartily!"

While advocating LSD, Crosby wore an STP sticker on his guitar, mischievously subverting the logo of Scientifically Treated Petroleum into an advertisement for the drug dimethoxymethyl amphetamine (popularly nicknamed Serenity, Tranquillity and Peace). If the acid reference was controversial, then the political rant was more portentous still. As the Byrds prepared to play 'He Was A Friend Of Mine', Crosby informed the audience: "You know they're shooting this for television. I'm sure they'll edit this out the way they'll edit out Country Joe & The Fish's good things . . . but I want to say it anyway, even though they *will* edit it out. When President Kennedy was killed, he was not killed by one man, he was shot from a number of different directions by different guns. The story has been suppressed, witnesses have been killed, and this is your country, ladies and gentlemen."

Crosby's counterculture news reports irritated McGuinn and Hillman, who retained the icy aloofness of 1965 and had little in common with the political hard core of San Francisco hippiedom. "I respected Pete Seeger more for what he said than Crosby," McGuinn reflects. "I think he believed what he said, but many of the comments were outrageous, and not necessarily valid. He was speculating about the Warren Report onstage, but he didn't really have anything to say beyond what we all knew. He said that Paul McCartney had said, 'Everyone should take acid', which was unnecessary. I think he was just trying to be hip and I felt he should have been more discreet."

The cold response of McGuinn and Hillman nettled Crosby, who could see no reason for their complaint. They all took LSD, so surely it was a matter of honour and solidarity to assist McCartney and the Beatles in their hour of controversy. In pointing out the Kennedy conspiracy theories, Crosby also felt he was attacking a corrupt political system in the only manner available to him at that time. McGuinn felt ambivalent when his understated song of private grief for JFK was transformed into a political diatribe. Yet, he failed to raise any objection prior to the festival and allowed Crosby to voice the same sentiments at other concerts. Moreover, as victims of a drug ban for 'Eight Miles High', maybe the Byrds deserved to fight back politically and reveal the acid flashes that had partly inspired some of their recent work. "I probably did encourage people to drop acid because I thought it was a good idea," Crosby admits. "It did sort of blow us loose from the Fifties. And at the time, it seemed a great idea. I did say something about the Warren Report as an introduction to 'He Was A Friend Of Mine'. That's why I said it. It was pretty relevant, I thought."

Debates on drug use and political corruption were part of the cultural zeitgeist and Crosby's comments at Monterey were the same. His views should not be taken lightly and deserve serious consideration. For many, he was making an important and supportive gesture at a crucial moment. Why shouldn't he have done? Crosby lived those times and felt himself part of a capacious community. Only a fierce cynic would doubt his sincerity and commitment.

Some contemporaneous reviewers used the word 'sophomore' when discussing Crosby's political rants, but he still had his supporters. The ever amenable Derek Taylor rose above the controversy in his usual laid-back way. Although he always regarded Crosby as the most difficult Byrd, he was never offended by his public statements. "David's behaviour at Monterey didn't bother me at all. That STP stuff? No. I'd always been generous to the avant-garde and all this to me was avant-garde behaviour. Even if I didn't understand it, I welcomed it. I couldn't bear conventionality. That's what I liked about the Byrds. They were rebellious and defied society. I really had a delayed adolescence which had been going on for about 15 years. And they suited me very well. They wanted to set people free and break the curfews. They wanted young people to have a say, they wanted marijuana to be legalized and they wanted the war to end, and I loved all that stuff. Things got tense between the Byrds. But you know how people are."

Unfortunately, Crosby's contentious commentaries ensured that the Byrds were omitted from the proposed television coverage and the spin-off film, *Monterey Pop*. McGuinn and Hillman had good reason to be annoyed by this loss of exposure, but it was the events of the following day that irked them even more. His decision to appear onstage with the Buffalo Springfield was interpreted as an open act of defiance rather than a brotherly gesture to a fellow musician in trouble. The Springfield's set was less exciting than that of the Byrds, but Crosby was happy to sing 'Rock & Roll Woman', which showed just how well he and Stills could work together. It provided a brutal reminder to the Byrds that Crosby was not their exclusive property. "At Monterey he showed to the world that he'd rather play with the Buffalo Springfield," roadie Jim Seiter attests. "When he appeared with them he was God's gift to the harmony voice but he was terrible with us. David hated being a Byrd. He didn't consider it hip for some reason. He wanted to be a Buffalo Springfield, a Jefferson Airplane or a Door. David's a groupie, always was and always will be."

Crosby retorted that Seiter's view was "pure and unadulterated bullshit" and insisted that he had no intention of joining the Buffalo Springfield, despite all the rumours to the contrary. Moreover, he never liked the Doors, whom he felt "couldn't swing" and reserved particular contempt for Jim Morrison, whose drunken antics were invariably associated with the phrase 'bad vibe'. Watching the fragmenting Byrds from the sidelines, Dickson felt that Crosby's ego had reached a dangerously destructive level which McGuinn was finding difficult to accommodate or tolerate. "McGuinn would say things like, 'I don't know how much longer we can take David Crosby.'

They were very upset when David played with the Buffalo Springfield. I just felt looking at him onstage that he was continuing to make an ass of himself. I'd long ago given up personally trying to stop him making an ass out of himself. It was a hopeless job. There was a big dilemma. David seemed as if he was intent on destroying the group. I'm sure he didn't see it that way. He was just acting out of compulsive behaviour."

Seiter was the first to hear about Crosby's plans to appear with the Buffalo Springfield and watched the scenes unfold with a mixture of trepidation and voyeuristic satisfaction. "I remember vividly what happened," he says, "because I was onstage helping [lighting engineer] Chip Monck set up. David showed up with a guitar case. I asked him, 'What are you doing?' and he said, 'I'm sitting in with the Buffalo Springfield.' I thought, 'Holy shit! Where are the other Byrds? Are they here?' Yep, they were in the restaurant backstage. When we'd finished what we were doing onstage, I went back to the restaurant and was just sitting there with them, hanging out. There was a speaker in the restaurant, so they could hear what was going on. They were listening, and someone said, 'Oh, the Springfield, let's go and watch!' I thought to myself, 'This is going to be great!' They walked out, looked up and said, 'What's *he* doing with them?' I said, 'He's going to play!' They said, 'No way!' Now, Hillman was the one who'd found them, nurtured them and helped turn them on to record companies which got them a deal. He was the one that was into their music and even he was amazed that David would even *consider* doing that. Trust me, it did piss them off. I don't know where they went, but they left. Michael was still there because he was drinking and the liquor was free. I asked him, 'Where'd Hillman go?' He said, 'I don't know, man. They were pissed off with David.'"

Although the performance with the Springfield was seen by many as the catalyst to Crosby's departure, McGuinn maintains that it was the earlier incident at Stills' house and during rehearsals that caused the real friction. "I don't think playing with them was a big deal. What problem would there be if I wanted to sit in with another musician? I wouldn't see that as a betrayal of any kind. The betrayal was the fact that he didn't want to be in the Byrds, not that he wanted to sit in with the Springfield. He'd become discontent with the Byrds and insufferable."

The lack of encouragement that Crosby received from those in the Byrds' camp convinced him that they were petty, uptight, jealous and maybe even crypto-straights. His ego was powerful enough to withstand their silent censure, while the applause he received from the crowd indicated that they were firmly on his side. After the festival, Crosby was happy to find that he was also applauded by the underground press. Whatever the Byrds' faults, they were at least seen as an important part of the culture and for every critic who regarded Crosby as an ass, there was another who proclaimed him a crusader. Even Ralph Gleason, the doyen of the San Franciscan music scene, singled out Crosby for special and unexpected praise as Monterey's hip philosopher. Reviewing the show, Gleason concluded with a poignant flourish: "Early on Monday morning, a solitary guitarist was playing and singing on the grounds as the clean-up crew was working. He sang of peace and brotherhood and I thought of David Crosby's words after the show's conclusion. 'I hope the artists know what they have here; the power of it to do good. It's an international force.'"

Alas, Crosby's vision of brotherhood did not extend as far as embracing Jim McGuinn and Chris Hillman. In the aftermath of Monterey, they became more distant than ever. David could hardly be blamed for seeking companionship elsewhere. He thrived on musical camaraderie and felt deeply hurt when his contributions were undervalued. What he needed was love or support, not disdain or rejection. Although Crosby insisted that he was uninterested in teaming up with Stills in the Buffalo Springfield, he again came to their rescue when Richie Furay suffered a throat infection. Eyewitnesses recall two nights at the Hullabaloo in Hollywood during which Crosby sang Furay's parts. That same evening, an estranged Neil Young turned up and joined his old group for an unrehearsed version of 'Mr Soul'. At the second show, the convalescing Furay joined Crosby on harmony and David and Stephen completed their dream of marrying off every musician in the community by inviting Michael Clarke and Buddy Miles onstage for what the *Los Angeles Times* dubbed "the Electric-Buffalo-Springfield-Byrd jam".

Crosby was thrilled by these musical get-togethers, which spilled over into private jamming sessions over the next few days. Back at Stills' Malibu beach house, David played alongside Jimi Hendrix, Buddy Miles and Hugh Masekela, sometimes for stretches of 12 hours at a time, as copious intakes of LSD spurred them on into wilder and more adventurous improvisation. Crosby revelled in this exciting new circle of friends, some of whom he regarded with the same reverence previously reserved for such gods as John Coltrane and Ravi Shankar.

These empathetic jamming sessions convinced Crosby that something was rotting at the heart of the Byrds. He was insightful enough to understand that their personal conflicts were affecting live performances and weakening group morale, but resolving these issues was no easy task. "Rock 'n' roll groups have to use telepathic messages or else they can't play really good music," he explained. "You get up to about 70 per cent level with just sheer technique, but to really play the magic stuff you have to be in rapport with the other cats. You've got to know exactly what is happening on levels that are non-verbal. You've got to be linked with other people. The Byrds is a perfect example because if you watch us two nights in a row, you'll see us one night when we're not linked and we're shitty. Come back the next night and we love each other and we cook our brains off, take you right out for the full set! Oh, we've done it. It's dependent on a lot of variables; you can fuck us up with a bad sound system, a bad audience, or by putting us through bad scenes before we get there. Or it can happen by one of us, or two of us, or three of us, or all four of us getting our egos involved and forgetting we love each other, that we're all the same person and that it's cool . . . we do love each other. When we really remember *that*, we play. When we don't, we make noise." Whether the four Byrds could rekindle their love for each other was a conundrum that even the great Crosby found impossible to answer.

While his fellow Byrds became more aloof and uptight, Crosby abjectly refused to be bound by band loyalties which he increasingly regarded as an anachronistic leftover from the beat group era. He preferred to dream of a musical community in which performers could share ideas and play alongside each other freely.

McGuinn remained refrigerator cool when faced with Crosby's promiscuous group hopping and, for the moment, consciously retreated from open conflict. Not for the last time, he sought salvation in spirituality. Since his initiation into Subud in January 1965, he had retained a slightly distant air and quizzical demeanour, which would prove useful in the stormy months ahead. While the Byrds were discovering a new musical identity, he suddenly announced that he was changing his name from Jim to Roger. The decision came about when he and Dolores were seeking a name for their new-born child.

"When we had our son I named him James IV," McGuinn recalls. "Then we decided to send to Indonesia to find out what his name was, and it came back Patrick McGuinn. I thought, 'Wow, what a groovy name. That's a better name than I would have thought of.' So I was curious to see what mine was, and my wife and I both sent for our names. We got them, and she was Ianthe and I was Roger . . . you get a letter back that suggests the first letter of your name and suggests that you make up ten names that you might like to have. So I made up weird names like Retro and Rex and others. I put down nine ridiculous ones and Roger, sort of picking my own. I liked it because it was airplane talk, you know, 'Roger'. It had a very right, positive sound."

McGuinn's positivism was symbolized by the so-called Summer of Love, which some saw as a media creation, although the earnestness of many of its participants indicated that it was genuine enough. The Beatles' idealistic, if simplistic, anthem 'All You Need Is Love', ushered in that strange season, expounding the hippie doctrine, crystallized at Monterey. McGuinn spoke in revered tones about seeing cops at the festival with flowers in the antennae of their helmets, as if they had been converted to the countercultural customs of their youthful charges. 'Flower Power' was the current buzzword and became a much derided term that infantilized rather than empowered its exponents. Before autumn ended, flower power had already wilted, its bloom blighted by the canker of commercial exploitation. In addition to Scott McKenzie, the other beneficiaries of the universal love message were the perennially popular Mamas & The Papas, who had closed the show at

Monterey and released a quaintly autobiographical single, 'Creeque Alley', whose playful and witty lyrics documented their journey from relative folk obscurity in New York to mainstream pop success in the promised land of Los Angeles. In the song, they saluted their fellow travellers, namechecking John Sebastian, Zal Yanovsky, Barry McGuire, and Jim McGuinn.

McGuire was blissed out that summer, a not unusual occurrence, but his detachment meant that he missed partaking in the zeitgeist. Incredibly, he claims that he was totally unaware of Monterey, even though the festival had been organized by his former mentor Lou Adler and featured many of his musician friends. "I didn't even know it was happening till afterwards," he maintains. "I never understood why they didn't invite me to be part of that. I'd introduced Lou to the Mamas & The Papas, and they had to drive past my house in Topanga to get to Monterey."

Shortly after the festival, McGuire was driving east on Sunset Boulevard when he spotted McGuinn, heading in the opposite direction. The Byrd did a swift U-turn and McGuire applied the brakes at the same time. Soon they were exchanging pleasantries at a kerbside, while McGuire inspected his friend's new Cadillac. "Roger's Cadillac was specially wired. I'm sure he had one of the first car stereos in the United States. He always had the first of everything." McGuinn reminisced about Monterey, the Mamas & The Papas and positive thinking, while his car radio blared in the background. "We were sitting there on the front fender just talking about life," says McGuire, "when 'Creeque Alley' came on the radio. They were singing, 'McGuinn and McGuire just a-getting higher in LA, you know where that's at'. It was surreal, like I was living in a movie and thinking 'Who wrote this script?' When the song was over, Roger leaned over and said, 'Well, where *is* it at, man?' I told him, 'I don't know!' He said, 'Well, don't tell anybody because now they all think we know where it's at!' I thought, 'OK' and for the next three years I went around pretending I knew where it was at, but I didn't have a clue. Never did. Still don't. I didn't have the answer." Nevertheless, they continued to promote the 'I trust everything will turn out all right' stoicism as the most appropriate response to their changing circumstances.

Crosby was unimpressed by McGuinn's more serious spiritual dabblings and openly derided Subud as "the Oriental conspiracy to overcome the rock 'n' roll world". While McGuinn was settling down to his new life as a father, and at least thinking in terms of minimizing his drug consumption, Crosby was still hell-bent on pursuing hedonistic excesses. Back at his home in Beverly Glen, he was surrounded by beautiful, naked girls, a constant supply of dope and a steady stream of like-minded musical friends. Drugs and sex were akin to sacraments in the ultimate search for spiritual enlightenment, with Crosby cast in the role of high priest. "I smoke pot which helps," he said, "and once every two or three months I take an acid trip, which also helps. It clears the deck and shakes everything up and loosens up the whole thing and keeps it from getting too static. It seems to have a salutary effect; I can't really define what it does, because we don't have words yet for most of what goes on in a trip . . . I get high a lot of different ways mostly on myself; a lot on music, a lot on making love, when I'm lucky by sailing, playing my guitar; talking to people, drugs, groovy foods, making love, making love, making love as often as possible, which isn't *all* the time. That's not easy to say that I'm some weird kind of freak who fucks ten times a day or something. When it happens it's a groove. I get high on everything I can, man, and I'm trying to get high on everything."

At his egotistical, infelicitous best, Crosby sounded as though he had created his own universe at the centre of which he lorded over all creation. "Buddha and Christ and Shiva and Krishna and Mohammed and everybody all seem to say that you should get high on the flowers and on yourself and on making love and you *are* love, and thou art God, and God grok, and the grass is God and the grass grok, and everything is IT, and if you get into it the whole universe is yours; playground, playpen, universe! . . . The whole universe is your home, if you can get big enough to live in it. It's there. It doesn't care. You can come and go and live there. You just have to get big enough."

In full flow, Crosby talked excitedly about the secrets of the inner self, sometimes employing 'spaceship' similes straight out of the McGuinn school of extraterrestrial phenomenon. "The inside of your head is like a darkened control room for a gigantic spaceship and we are blinded babies walking around pulling switches, trying to find out how to turn on the light. The switch is there, the capability is there. You could be a full telepathic. You could surpass this entire plane and flick to a whole other thing instantly, if you knew how to do it! Anybody could do it if they found the controls, and the controls are in your head. So . . . get high and look."

McGuinn might well have approved of some of this, but he was less enamoured of Crosby's political musings and ex cathedra pronouncements, which were lapped up by the underground press. It says much about Crosby's stoned ramblings that he could switch instantly from speculations about God, inner space, LSD and love-making to the state of the nation, which he was all too willing to address with the seasoned aplomb of a political pundit. "I see President Johnson and these other cats with huge monster egos walking around like grunting gladiators in a ring, man! They don't realize that the world is the size of a golf ball; there isn't room to do that any more. It is like six cats in a closet; each has a hand grenade and they hate each other, anybody pulls the pin, they all get it! It's not a war, it's just a bad scene. We've got to find some way to cool out all the egos. Not just President Johnson's, but mine and everybody else's, a lot more than we're doing. Maybe my children will know how to do it if I don't teach them all that repressive stuff."

Crosby's expansive discourse enlivened many an evening and his dope remained the best in town. The relaxed atmosphere at Beverly Glen also inspired a series of stunning new songs, spearheaded by the brass-tinged 'Lady Friend', a work of great maturity that provided his first and only A-side in the Byrds. "That was just an idea of mine that I wanted to try," he says modestly. "I envisaged a little French horn fugue in the middle of it." In order to complete the track, a call was made to the local Musicians' Union and a brass section was quickly assembled. After arriving at the studio, their first words to a puzzled Crosby were "Where are the charts?" Unsurprisingly, none had been prepared. Instead, Crosby sang them the opening 'da da da' melody in his inimitable style. "They went, 'Huh? You don't have any charts?' An interesting moment as back then nobody could get away with that. Nobody had ever sung a part to these guys. It was that formal and stylized." Amazingly, Crosby was not even at his best when recording the vocal for this remarkable recording. As the tapes rolled, he spluttered contemptuously, "I can't even talk – how can I sing?", then proceeded to provide a flawless performance. The playing was surprisingly hard resulting in the loudest, fastest and rockiest Byrds' single to date, while the brass parts, which he wrote, provided even greater momentum. However, there was belated controversy over the vocal contributions, which left Crosby dissatisfied.

"He kicked us out of the studio because we weren't good enough to be on it," claims McGuinn. Hillman confirms the story. "David went back into the studio and put all the voices on and took ours off, and he made it this mishmash crazy sounding thing that had no personality. He ripped it of personality and loaded it up with tracks of vocals of his own and it was awful. But it was initially a great song. It's one of his better songs . . . The original was simple; it was great; we all sang it."

Contrary to Hillman's critical vitriol, the resulting 'Lady Friend' still sounds thrilling although, for some, the song was partly let down by Usher's unusual mix. Crosby was among the dissenters, even at the time of the record's release, when he complained: "The final mix of 'Lady Friend' sounds like mush. I can't hear anything distinguished out clearly and maybe that's my fault. I don't know. I felt it was a pretty record and it didn't make it."

While Crosby was scaling new heights creatively, McGuinn and Hillman were temporarily reduced to composing the banal, 90-second 'Don't Make Waves', an alternate take of which was used in the MGM beach movie of the same name. The song sounded like pure pastiche, a throwback to the Brill Building era when McGuinn co-wrote the equally risible 'Beach Ball'. 'Don't Make Waves' surely represented the nadir of McGuinn and Hillman's songwriting collaboration in the Byrds. At the end of the recording, Crosby took merciless and mischievous delight in sarcastically exclaiming, "Great, let's double it! Masterpiece!" Fortunately, better songs lay ahead.

CHAPTER TWENTY-THREE

The Great Conflict

THE Byrds' involvement with MGM refocused attention on their plans to make a movie of their own. Carole Eastman was still working on the screenplay she had begun the previous year, but nothing came of it. "We were still anxious to do it," Dickson recalls. "But when Gene left the group that was a setback, and then it fell apart. It started development but was cancelled when the Byrds left us to go with Larry Spector. So nothing was ever shot." The closest McGuinn and Hillman reached to celluloid fame was working with actor David Hemmings on the Dickson-produced album, *Happens*, where they contributed the music to several songs, including 'Talkin' L.A.' and 'War's Mystery'. In an affectionate farewell to the Byrds, Dickson also encouraged Hemmings to open the album with an unreleased Gene Clark composition, the opaque 'Back Street Mirror'.

While the Byrds' film ideas foundered, Crosby remained hopeful that 'Lady Friend' would restore their hit status and publicly establish his greatness as a songwriter. The group performed the song on Johnny Carson's *The Tonight Show*, along with 'Renaissance Fair' and Hillman's 'Have You Seen Her Face'. Three of the Byrds sported suits and ties for the occasion, while David preferred an ornate, Eastern-style top and his by now familiar Cossack hat. Comedian and guest host Bob Newhart introduced the group while pointing out that they were still tuning up. Ever indignant Crosby sneered back, "We tune because we care." The incident was eerily reminiscent of the time Crosby had insulted Ed Sullivan's son-in-law back in 1965, but he still seemed unconcerned about the consequences of his sarcasm. Despite the high-rating Carson appearance,

'Lady Friend' sold poorly in both the US and world markets. This disappointment punctured Crosby's more self-aggrandizing asides and convinced McGuinn and Hillman that he was fallible and far from indispensable. Their unwillingness to acknowledge the importance of 'Lady Friend' made Crosby even more irritable. He felt severely undervalued, but the more he criticized McGuinn and Hillman, the less they thought of his material. "The thing that made people underestimate him was his insistence on telling you how intelligent he was," McGuinn reasons. "He was so insecure that he had to lay it all out for you verbally, and when somebody does that you don't believe him. If you really are, you don't have to say it. But it so happens that he really *is* talented, but he said it anyway because he didn't believe it or something. He believes it now and doesn't say it that much."

The chart failure of 'Lady Friend' was in stark contrast to a new work, which seemed to underline Clive Davis' dictum that the Byrds' old sound was still their most viable commercial weapon. Responding to the group's recent minor chart success with 'So You Want To Be A Rock 'n' Roll Star' and 'My Back Pages', CBS sanctioned the summer release of *The Byrds' Greatest Hits*. The company had already issued *Bob Dylan Greatest Hits* earlier in the year and enjoyed high-profile Top 10 success. The Byrds did even better, peaking at number 6, their best showing on *Billboard* since their first album. Within a year, the record would be certified gold by the RIAA, outselling all previous Byrds LPs. Strangely enough, the underground press, traditionally wary of such blatantly commercial undertakings, greeted the compilation with warm compliments. Although the Byrds had not been actively involved in compiling the work, *Crawdaddy*'s Paul Williams took a delightfully eccentric standpoint, reviewing the product as if it had been conceived as a major artistic statement by the group:

> Any greatest hits album is insignificant. By definition it contains nothing unfamiliar; and yet this very fact offers great potential beauty, for a well-made greatest hits LP might then unleash the emotion of familiarity in an artistic context. The Byrds have achieved that goal; always masters of the form, they

have now taken the concept of a great hits anthology and created from it an essay into rediscovery. The opening is masterful. The listener, knowing this is a big hits album, knows he can only expect crass repetition of earlier recorded material; and yet, staring at the cover whose beauty has only just begun to work its magic on him, cannot help but feel that somehow something miraculous is going to take place. Never has there been a Byrds album without a stunning cover, and never has the record itself proved to be anything less than infinitely greater than its jacket. So you can't quite believe this will be an exception, and then you hear those beautiful notes that begin the [Mr] *Tambourine Man* album and the Byrds' careers, and you know that this album too is wonderful, for there is that same joy, that same perfection, but opening a *different* LP . . . and no matter how many times you've played the *Tambourine Man* LP over again, this is the first time since the first time that you have heard that opening as new, as a surprise. Only by somehow recording a new album that again started with '[Mr] Tambourine Man' could the Byrds restore the listener's virginity, make it possible for you to hear the same thing without ever having heard it before. This is the rediscovery of the world that so many are experiencing through drugs, and never before has music captured it so well.

For David Crosby, the success of a cash-in hits album was soured by the realization that the superior 'Lady Friend' had failed commercially. On 31 July, one week before the release of the hits package, the Byrds were back in the studio, working purposefully on their next album. They made a promising start, producing preliminary backing tracks for a new McGuinn/Hillman composition, tentatively titled 'Universal Mind Decoder', which Clarke found particularly appealing and provided a funky rhythm part in his inimitable style. Crosby was also enthusiastic. In a valiant attempt to display his full musical dexterity and break with convention, he offered to play bass guitar on the track. In doing so, he was re-writing the Byrds' musical history. This was the first time he'd picked up the instrument in earnest since usurping Gene Clark on

THE GREAT CONFLICT

rhythm guitar back in 1964, after which Hillman had been added as full-time bassist. Crosby also offered them a new composition, 'Draft Morning', a moving anti-war protest for which they provided a backing track and promised to complete at a later date. Before attempting any vocal parts, they were required to complete some dates in Hawaii, supported by the Young Rascals. This was a welcome break, during which they were allowed a few days' rest to enjoy the sunshine.

Hawaii always had a strange effect on the Byrds. When they'd previously appeared there at the end of 1965, Hillman had freaked out on an acid trip and Gene Clark had a spiritual communion with nature during which he expressed a wish to stay on the island forever. Coincidentally or not, he was never the same after he returned to LA. On this return trip, Michael Clarke had a similar epiphany. Away from the studio and surrounded by scantily-clad girls, sunshine, surf and stress free living, he acquired what McGuinn termed "Hawaii fever". Crosby also enjoyed this vacation and his enthusiasm lifted everybody's spirits. They even surprised themselves by making further headway on a couple of his new songs, both of which were impressive and augured well for the new record. "We first got 'Draft Morning' and 'Dolphin's Smile' together in Hawaii," Hillman remembers. "We were working there at this house on the other side of the island of Oahu – we worked those songs up there, ready to record when we got back."

Sadly, the sojourn in Hawaii proved a false dawn. Upon their return to Hollywood, all the recent resentments returned with a vengeance. A greater understanding of these conflicts can now be gleaned by eavesdropping on the recording sessions that took place that summer. Crosby, still in the creative ascendant, was rightly proud of his new material and eager for the Byrds to play at their best. Unfortunately, he caught Michael Clarke on a grumpy day, still suffering from Hawaii homesickness and irritated about being locked in a studio after such a brief holiday. Before long, the pair were re-enacting the conflict that had previously caused the drummer to punch Crosby in the face during the *Turn! Turn! Turn!* sessions. Initially, the problem seemed simple enough. David was attempting to complete the mellow, lilting 'Dolphin's Smile', which Clarke found unexciting. As usual, the drummer had been given little prior opportunity to rehearse the song and would have preferred something beefier to play. Crosby at first reacted sympathetically, adopting a cheerleader role and urging Clarke to improve. When that failed, the session turned hilariously vindictive. The extant tapes capture the highlights in brutal *audio-vérité*.

"If you really wanted to, you could do it", Crosby insists, but his encouragement is soon replaced by extreme condescension. Adopting a more haughty tone, he implores, "It's not beyond you, Michael, you're just doing a scene."

While Clarke becomes increasingly restive and impatient, the other Byrds start discussing him as though he was not there. "He always does the same thing," sighs an exasperated Crosby, referring to the disgraced drummer in a tone normally reserved for a disobedient child.

"So do you man," McGuinn spits back, having convinced himself that Crosby is deliberately irritating the drummer and intentionally feeding the dissension. "It's really a drag . . . you attacked me when I started playing the bass, man."

"The part of you that thinks it's being attacked, man, is your ego. E-G-O," Crosby retorts.

Exasperated by Crosby's nerve and audacity in actually complaining about somebody else's ego, McGuinn can only reply dismissively, "So do you, man."

With the Crosby/McGuinn conflict brimming nicely, Michael Clarke is left to explode in isolated frustration, at which point Crosby makes matters worse by shouting, "Try playing right!"

"What do you mean, 'Try playing right!'?", Clarke barks back, barely able to contain his anger. "What do you know what the fuck's right and what's wrong? What do you know, man? . . . You're not a musician."

The attack on Crosby's musical ability inevitably worsens matters, but Clarke is no longer content to accept such humiliation and announces loftily, "Send me away, man."

The hurt voice of Clarke is so full of comic pathos that it provokes sarcastic cries of "We love you!" and Crosby's pricelessly mocking, "Ah, the poor baby. Give him a pacifier!"

Instinctively, Clarke knows how to annoy Crosby in return and offers the dismissive, "I don't even like the song!"

A discussion next ensues as to why Michael is still in the group. "For the money," he tells them, unashamedly.

"You're not helping us to make any right now, man," Hillman reminds him. "You're helping us to lose it."

Unconcerned about his financial status, Michael shrugs, "It's all right. I get by."

Such humour serves to break the ice between Crosby and McGuinn who now join with Hillman in making fun of Michael with acid comments like, "We'll try Hal Blaine, man."

The threat of a session drummer, made in jest, is taken seriously by Clarke who calls their bluff with the riposte, "Do it. I don't mind. I really don't," followed by the damning admission that he doesn't like any of the songs anyway.

Over the next few days, more new Crosby songs were attempted, underlining his increasing involvement in the new album. Despite this flurry of creativity, he was far from happy by their responses. While Clarke's head was still in the Hawaii clouds, Crosby was dreaming of even more exotic environs. Wearied by the lack of appreciation shown towards his latest compositions, he found himself fantasizing about life beyond the Byrds. At his most extravagant, he spoke of escaping society completely, a fantasy already alluded to on 'Dolphin's Smile' and later captured in all its science fiction glory on the epic 'Wooden Ships'. "I'm going to buy a boat," he said. "I hope a lot of other people do too. Get a bunch of boats together travelling around together, a sea tribe of people that live mostly off what they get from the seas and a little of what they traded in various places, and some of their royalties from the songs they used to write. That's an interesting way to drop out. Nobody can tell you what to do, at all; paint yourself purple, have three wives, blow your house up every Thursday. No longer a concern to anybody else, except the dolphins who will watch you pretty closely, and their big brothers, the whales. Been saving and figuring, and learning, and hoping . . . dreaming and thinking about getting a boat for eight years or so. I'm taking a month off to go look for it in Scandinavia. I got the money in the bank . . . A boat is as graceful as a bird, and a piece of art, and your home. It's a good trip. Very meaningful."

Tensions continued to mount within the Byrds, made worse by Crosby's belief that they were not taking his work seriously. Nobody had commended him for 'Lady Friend' and its spectacular chart failure in the US was deemed reason enough to question whether it even deserved to be included on the new album. McGuinn and Hillman had allowed Crosby the chance to dictate their choice of single and he had not provided a hit. Maybe they could do better. Crosby was appalled by their apathetic and cynical response to what he considered one of his best songs. The knowledge that 'Lady Friend' was not automatically scheduled for the new album stirred deep feelings of betrayal. Recalling that moment in our most intense interview, he voiced an irrepressible anger.

"I thought up the brass parts and they all played on it, but the song never got put on a fucking record. Now, do you think I'm kidding you about not being able to get my stuff on a record? Was 'Lady Friend' good? Did you like it? I couldn't get it on the record. They wouldn't put it on the record because it was mine, and not theirs. It never got a chance, man, they wouldn't put it on a record. That's one of the reasons why there was a lot of bitterness on my part. It wasn't a joke, it was a very real problem I was up against. Do you understand that?"

Crosby's hurt was palpable and, intentionally or not, McGuinn was adept at turning the knife in insouciant fashion. When 'Lady Friend' was mentioned, he grimaced, "it went phut . . ." imitating the sound of a balloon bursting or a plane crashing to the ground. It was almost as if he was pleased it had failed. "Our latest things are very much in the jazz bag," he said at the time, before damning 'Lady Friend' as "an imitation of some commercial group like the Four Seasons . . . to make number 1 now, you've got to be a new group and have something fresh, or at least another viewpoint, to catch attention." In other words, 'Lady Friend' was supposedly old-fashioned, wilfully commercial and stale – the antithesis of everything Crosby stood for and railed against. This was as perverse an interpretation as Crosby's pungent remarks about the 'sell-out' 'My Back Pages'. Hillman also took pyrrhic satisfaction over

THE GREAT CONFLICT

Crosby's doomed single, indignantly noting how he had overdubbed their vocals with his own, but still couldn't get anywhere near the US charts.

Alas, the same fate befell the single in the UK, where it was issued at the beginning of September. *NME*'s Derek Johnson offered some kind words ("An incredible full sound . . . the arrangement is positively startling") but the review was the size of a postage stamp, relegating the Byrds to the status of also-rans in the British music press. The song received little or no airplay on the BBC's recently launched Radio 1, thereby sealing its fate. One supportive voice came from Graham Nash, who loved the single. That same month, the Hollies released Nash's 'King Midas In Reverse', their most adventurous recording to date. Like 'Lady Friend' it included brass augmentation, an array of flutes and what sounded like a full-scale orchestra wrapped in an epic production. For all its greatness, the single barely scraped into the UK Top 20, a commercial failure by Hollies' chart standards and a bitter blow to Nash's ambitions. His power base in the group was irrevocably damaged after this so he had good reason to empathize with Crosby.

While still fighting to feature his material on record, Crosby seemingly held sway in concert, where his charisma encouraged some onlookers to assume he had taken complete control of the group. Commenting on their latest appearance at the Whisky, one reviewer innocently noted: "David Crosby is evidently the lead singer, as Jim McGuinn had only one song in two sets. David has a lovely tenor folk voice which comes across very well on record, but in person he tries too hard to sound bluesy and loses the 'sweet' quality of his voice." Their Whisky set list provided another fascinating glimpse into the power structure and group dynamic. Alongside old favourites such as 'He Was A Friend Of Mine', 'The Bells Of Rhymney', 'Chimes Of Freedom', 'Turn! Turn! Turn!', 'I Know My Rider' and 'So You Want To Be A Rock 'n' Roll Star' were several Crosby cameos including 'Hey Joe', 'Renaissance Fair', 'Everybody's Been Burned' and 'Triad'. Another reviewer singled out "'The Universal Decoder' [the prototype of 'Change Is Now'] in which Crosby switched to bass guitar to set a compelling tempo." Reading the reviews, Hillman must have been sorely tempted to reprise his acerbic quip, "Ladies and gentlemen – the David Crosby Show".

Between residencies at the Whisky, a sore-throated Crosby appeared on B. Mitchell Reed's radio show on 30 August and spoke of his plans. He promised a new Byrds album in November and suggested that they all needed a vacation to recuperate from their recent studio tribulations. Still high from Monterey, he continued to promote his belief in a musical egalitarianism. "I see groups that three years ago were competing with each other. Now they go to each other's sessions and watch and laugh and say, 'Hey, man, can I help?' And people play for each other, man, and help each other and write tunes together and break rules. There's a lot of rule-breaking going on . . . and I really approve. That's the only way we're gonna improve the whole scene, man, is if all of us get by with a little help from our friends. If we don't help each other, who the hell is gonna?"

Outside the radio studio, Crosby continued his rap, more extravagantly than ever. "If we get together and help each other we can accomplish things. We can do it by buying land for people to live on, throwing free concerts to make people happy; we can do it by trying to help, any way we can, man! There's an international community of people who are creatively trying to live better and do something new."

While Crosby was projecting a musical utopia of communal trust, appreciation, land purchases, free concerts and unpaid session work, the Byrds were disintegrating amid petty recriminations, jealousy and a noticeable lack of fellowship. The recent studio outburst heralded the beginning of the end for the rebellious Michael Clarke, who carelessly accepted the group's decision to enlist the experienced Jim Gordon to complete virtually the remainder of the album. Crosby continued to appear at the sessions, encouraging the Byrds to do justice to his new songs. In order to placate any ill feelings over publishing, he offered McGuinn and Hillman a co-writing credit for their contributions to 'Dolphin's Smile' and agreed that Chris' work on 'Tribal Gathering' also deserved a part share of the royalties. Such open-handed gestures were not enough to convince McGuinn and Hillman to sanction the release of the third tune from those memorable mid-August sessions: 'Triad'.

THE GREAT CONFLICT

Crosby's mildly controversial *ménage à trois* ballad was fully in keeping with his hippie philosophies of the period. The content of the lyrics were not that far removed from the home life he enjoyed at Beverly Glen, where nudity and sexual freedom were accepted and even encouraged. The lyrics referred to "sister lovers" and "water brothers", allusions that Crosby borrowed from Robert A. Heinlein's *Stranger In A Strange Land*. Two years before, he had been blocked from releasing a song inspired by the book and now it was happening again. Crosby was crestfallen. He genuinely believed that 'Triad' was one of his best compositions of the period, a view reinforced by the Jefferson Airplane who applauded his beautiful vocal work. They eagerly accepted the song for their fourth album *Crown Of Creation*, which easily outsold the Byrds' current product in America.

The survival of 'Triad' as an Airplane track confirmed Crosby's suspicions that McGuinn and Hillman were vetoing his songs due to a warped sense of envy at his impending greatness. Later, he came to believe that 'Triad' had been censored because of McGuinn's squeamishness about the subject matter, which he'd supposedly derided as a "freak-out orgy tune". David liked the idea that his final days in the Byrds were spent fighting a moral crusade on behalf of outlawed material. For Hillman, though, the argument over 'Triad' was not based on repression, but a simple matter of personal taste. "We didn't like the song at the time," he bluntly admits. "I don't think it was a moral decision. The song just didn't work that well. David was drifting and bored and wanted to do something else, and that song just added fuel to the fire."

McGuinn agrees, adding that the composition played only a small part in turning himself and Hillman against Crosby. "'Triad' wasn't the crux of it, that was nothing really," he insists. "It was just a song that I didn't think was in particularly good taste."

The rejection of 'Triad' was made all the more bitter when McGuinn, Hillman and producer Gary Usher elected to cover Goffin/King's 'Goin' Back'. Crosby regarded the song as sentimental pap and unworthy of his attention. The idea that his flowering brilliance as a songwriter was about to be forestalled by a composition redolent of the Brill Building era seemed the ultimate insult. There he was presenting them with the songs of tomorrow and they preferred to seek material from the past. The only answer to such an affront was to absent himself from the recording. "David sat on a couch for three days with his hat over his eyes and didn't do a thing," Seiter recalls. "'Goin' Back' was in direct competition to 'Triad' for a place on the album and David had really wanted to do 'Triad'. He eventually went off to a Jefferson Airplane session and made them stop to listen to 'Dolphin's Smile'."

Seiter, who accompanied Crosby on this latest mission, was amazed by his audacity. "I was driving him home when he said, 'Come on, we're going to RCA to see Jefferson Airplane.' He had the tape of 'Dolphin's Smile' under his arm and he made them listen to it. On the way home I said: 'Jesus, David. McGuinn's going to go nuts if he finds out you played that for them.' He said, 'Well, don't tell him!' I knew he'd find out though. I told Crosby, 'He'll find out, they'll all find out, and they'll be pissed.' Sure as hell, three days later, it happened. The engineers at CBS knew that we'd taken the tape out and gone to RCA. Engineers talk to each other, and they told Roger. David said to me, 'You asshole, you told him, didn't you!' I had to tell him it was the engineers and he should go and tell them they were assholes!"

McGuinn was more infuriated by Crosby's mutinous apathy over 'Goin' Back' and pointedly completed the session with Hillman and drummer Jim Gordon, later assisted by some classical session players recruited by Gary Usher. When he heard the results, Crosby was predictably unimpressed. "I don't think David thought we would do it," says Usher. "The song started coming out great and one day David walked in the studio and listened to it and made some kind of comment like 'that really sucks', and refused to sing on it or be involved in any way. He thought the song was very wimpy. I just think this had been coming for a long time and McGuinn got to the point where he couldn't take any more, so finally he said, 'Crosby, I've had enough of your bullshit, if you don't want to be part of this song and the group just get your ass out of here. We don't want you, or even need you.' Well, that did it. Crosby turned red and you could sense him burning. He just picked up his guitar and walked out of the studio . . . If I remember correctly, after he walked out I looked at Roy Halee [the engineer] and he looked at me, and a pin could have dropped in the studio."

After the 'Goin' Back' furore, it was evident that the end was not far away. Crosby's disenchantment over 'Lady Friend' and 'Triad' festered during the autumn of 1967 as he pondered upon which of his new songs would appear on the forthcoming album. Meanwhile, the Byrds continued to play occasional gigs, but showed no interest in undertaking a strenuous coast-to-coast tour, let alone returning to Europe to improve their sales abroad. Crosby spent more and more time socializing with musician friends like Paul Kantner and Stephen Stills, whose support during this depressive period was greatly appreciated. McGuinn and Hillman still felt their partner was naïve and over-generous in his relationship with rival players. Both the Buffalo Springfield and the Jefferson Airplane had benefited from Crosby's creative input, but no obvious advantage had come to the Byrds as a result of David's largesse. McGuinn concluded that Crosby was using the Byrds to expand his social circle and needlessly giving away ideas, as he had always liked to do since turning on George Harrison to Ravi Shankar back in 1965.

Crosby was contemptuous of such creative covetousness and continued to flaunt his friendships without remorse. "They were worried by my hanging out with Stills," he told me, "and they were worried that I wasn't continually satisfied with that band. The reason was, quite simply, that it couldn't play. The Byrds couldn't play live. They never could. There was a clash onstage but it came from me feeling that the band was not good enough. Every time the Byrds went on, it was an embarrassing thing. It never was any good. I cannot remember us ever being good. That bummed me because I wanted to be in a good band . . . We'd get it on occasionally, but that used to frustrate me even more because I couldn't understand why we couldn't do it all the time."

What the Byrds needed to do was concentrate on their potential strengths live, rehearse more and expand their set. Instead, they continued to play the old 45-minute shows favoured by Crosby and approached performances like a chore. As they had shown at Monterey, the Byrds could be brilliant and terrible within the space of a few minutes. When they played badly, there was always somebody who pointed out that the Beatles could not play 'Strawberry Fields Forever' or *Sgt Pepper's* live, so why should the Byrds waste time perfecting their studio experiments for an inappropriate live setting. A creative manager might have persuaded them to focus their energies on improving performances and breaking into the potentially lucrative and rewarding concert market. Alas, they were already beyond such counsel.

Despite his protestations, Crosby had grown weary of competing with McGuinn and Hillman onstage and had also fallen out with manager Larry Spector, the false messiah he had brought in to replace Dickson and Tickner. Suddenly, the entire Byrds' organization was a terrible drag for Crosby, a realization made more bitter by the knowledge that they could still produce great music. Their work in the studio was as good, if not better, than ever. If they would only follow Crosby's logic, feature more of his songs, dump Spector and loosen up their uptight attitude towards his friends, then all might be well.

Sorting out the Byrds' complex group dynamics at this point was no easy task as Crosby became more despondent and disillusioned. "I remember the arguments quite well," notes Usher. "More than likely the arguments took place between McGuinn/Hillman and Crosby. Mike Clarke never really had that much musical input to be involved in these arguments. On most instances I sided with McGuinn/Hillman . . . David had a great ego and he could be very hard to work with if he didn't have his way. He knew what he wanted and could be very distasteful to be around."

Crosby had little respect for Usher, the more so when he failed to champion some of the fine work he was currently composing. As far as Crosby was concerned, Usher was merely another impediment to his artistic flowering and by aligning himself so closely with McGuinn and Hillman had shown a lack of radical thought and intent. He was the man who wanted 'Goin' Back' at a time when Crosby was concerned with pushing forward at all costs. It is easy to understand his frustration, particularly in late 1967 when rock musicians suddenly seemed capable of changing the world with groundbreaking albums. The souring politics within the group were wearing Crosby down, even though he was quite capable of fighting his corner. It made him uneasy, short-tempered and suspicious.

"David was always a very acidic character," McGuinn noted at the time. "He was always eating into somebody. He was starting to lose interest in the group. It was sort of an underground group by this time, and his buddies in Buffalo Springfield and Jefferson Airplane were saying, 'Come on, David, you can do better than this.' And he was saying, 'Yeah, man, but I've got to be loyal to McGuinn and Hillman, I can't let them down.' Being noble and everything. And all this time we were wishing he'd split because he was heavy, hard to handle, being a little outspoken and hip for the wrong reasons. And he started getting very like a tyrant on the material."

Road manager Jim Seiter was the next to fall victim to his wrath. "David got real uptight with me during his last days with the group. One night I received a call from a girl who lived in a house below his, and she asked me to come up there and keep him awake because he'd taken an overdose of something weird. He was passing out and she wanted to keep him together. So I went up to his house to keep him alive. He was in a sad shape. The next day I talked to Larry Spector and told him David was depressed. We went to San Francisco. The group stayed in one place and David stayed in another hotel, with me next door to him. That night Bill Graham asked us to play a slightly longer show. The first night they played 55 minutes instead of the usual 45 minutes. When they came offstage David was furious. He threw his guitar on the floor and yelled at me, saying that I'd better not ever let him play 55 minutes again. The next night I had a great big stopwatch onstage and I pushed it as soon as they started. They were off the stage to the second at 45 minutes, which annoyed Bill Graham. While I was putting some equipment away, David burst into my room, threw his guitar down, *again*, runs over and starts punching me in the head. As far as he was concerned, I'd left them onstage too long again. He wasn't in good shape, mentally. That night he called me up a hundred times, crying and apologizing over and over again."

CHAPTER TWENTY-FOUR

Crosby Fired! – Clark Hired!

CROSBY's last performance as a Byrd took place on Saturday 9 September 1967, the culmination of a three-night stint at the Fillmore. This was the evening after his clash with Seiter and, ironically, it was all smiles and good vibes. The trauma had temporarily passed but by then McGuinn and Hillman had already made a momentous decision. Their disenchantment was magnified by a wearisomely long list of Crosby's transgressions involving themselves, various producers, record company personnel and unspecified others. "People like Clive Davis had heard for years that David was a pain in the ass," Jim Seiter says. "And he didn't like that level of confrontation. Nobody does. David used to push these guys' buttons and they hated him for it. He wasn't really serious most of the time. He'd say it to their faces, but as soon as he walked away he'd be laughing and smiling about it. He was just kidding them in his own way. But Roger and Chris had to deal with that shit. Several things led up to their decision: stopping and tuning his guitar on *The Tonight Show,* playing badly onstage or out of tune, saying rude things to the audience. Monterey! This didn't just happen overnight. There were five or six things that happened leading up to their decision. David's a great harmony singer provided he's with people he can relate to personally. If he can't relate to you, he closes down that doorway and loses the love for doing it. There were years of bullshit between him and Roger. That's why he was fucking with us onstage. I watched it happen. He wouldn't sing his part sometimes and he'd try and blame me for not turning his mike up. I knew better and would tell him to his face. I'd say, 'Man, you're embarrassing us; you're embarrassing me, and I don't have to stand up onstage with you.'"

CROSBY FIRED! — CLARK HIRED!

Some of the criticisms may have been one-sided, self-justifying, unfair and unreasonable, but suddenly McGuinn and Hillman were resolute. On one fateful September day, they confronted Crosby with the news that he was no longer a member of the Byrds. The meeting is still indelibly etched on Crosby's mind, in images tinged with righteous indignation, bitterness and regret.

"They came over and said that they wanted to throw me out," he told me. "They came zooming up in their Porsches and said that I was impossible to work with and I wasn't very good anyway and they'd do better without me. And frankly, I've been laughing ever since. Fuck 'em. But it hurt like hell. Did I try to reason with them? No! I didn't try to reason with them. I just said, 'It's a shameful waste . . . *goodbye*.'"

This was not the entire story. As a parting gesture, Crosby told them, "You know, we could make great music together", only to be crushed by their riposte, "Yeah, and we could make great music *without* you." His ego was momentarily shattered by their absolute conviction that they could not only survive but *thrive* without his contribution. "That's what they said," he reiterates, as if the very notion was beyond human understanding. Crosby knew that he was emerging as a strong singer-songwriter intuitively attuned to the age, but McGuinn and Hillman seldom, if ever, complimented him on his artistic growth or recognized his budding brilliance. They reacted coolly at best to his latest batch of songs, seemingly convinced that they could provide compositions of equal or greater value. It was a reassuring delusion. Years later, particularly during the peak period of Crosby, Stills, Nash & Young, David would quietly gloat over how wrong they were about his worth. When pushed on the circumstances of his dismissal, he could rationalize their response, but found it difficult to contain his anger and sense of betrayal at the injustice of it all. It was a pain that burned deeply.

In an extremely moving combination of humility, wrath, love, pride and hubris, he confessed to me: "I'm a very opinionated person and I know that doesn't make it easy. But Spector had those guys pretty well fooled. It was a big mistake on my part getting him, but I'd already figured him out. He knew this, so he did his level best to set McGuinn and Hillman against me all the time. But, mainly, it was just ego on their part. They felt me getting stronger. I think they either resented it or were worried by it. The resistance to my material was like the resistance of the Hollies to Nash's material. It was just dumb. They were territorial; they were afraid. And I kept writing better and better songs. When they threw me out I had just written [or was writing] 'Guinnevere', 'Wooden Ships' and 'Laughing'. Now, who the hell do you think is the best writer there? They can't fight it, man. There isn't one of them can write as good as me, and you fucking know it. And that's the truth. I'm better than they are. I'm better than them put together. That's the truth. I'm a better writer. And they can't touch it. None of them has ever written anything as good as that . . . Do you understand what happened? Excuse me for being angry, but it was unjust what did happen. They didn't mean to do it. They didn't consciously set out to fuck me over, and they're OK guys. I don't hate them. But it hurt, and it was so frustrating that you couldn't believe it. I was writing good stuff and I wasn't getting credit for it. I was doing good work and I wasn't allowed to grow. And I was growing. Look what happened next. What did they do next, man? Compare them. What's the lasting worth of what they did next in comparison to what I did next?"

The firing of Crosby was one of the most shocking and self-destructive decisions in the history of Sixties' rock music. For a person as calculating as McGuinn, the final moments were akin to a rush of blood to the head. They had often moaned about Crosby's attitude and lost patience with his mood swings, but to sack him midway through an album, without even a replacement waiting in the wings, smacked of hot-headed lunacy. "Maybe it was a rash decision," McGuinn reflects. "I thought that afterwards at times. But he was impossible to work with and I just felt that firing him was the only solution. We had to get rid of him."

Reflecting on Crosby's three years in the Byrds, McGuinn recognized the artistic growth of a performer whose ego finally defeated his talent. In the end, the Byrds blinded themselves to Crosby's immense contribution amid the distractions of endless mind games and petty recriminations. Attempting a practical viewpoint, devoid of emotion, McGuinn summed up his reasons for forcing the departure of his fiery colleague.

"David Crosby at the time wasn't right for the job. He only regrets that I didn't quit myself – he thinks I should have buried it then so that he'd have a clean slate. But he and I are friendly now. Even though I didn't agree with David on certain issues – and he said things onstage which made me say them by proxy since we were a group – we always had this policy where you could wear what you liked, do anything you wanted to, onstage or off, and the fact that he was outspoken onstage wasn't the reason he was fired or asked to leave. It was really that he was becoming a dictator and was trying to dominate the present and the future of the Byrds . . . He was trying to dictate what our policies should be, which songs we shouldn't do. One of our big disagreements was over 'Goin' Back'. He didn't like that at all. So I thought his heart wasn't in it. At this point he was hanging out with the Buffalo Springfield a lot, playing around town with other groups, sort of shopping for a new position. I figured that he wanted to get out of it, and we did him a service."

Given Crosby's hurt, it was extremely disingenuous of McGuinn to suggest that he had done him a service. There was every possibility that Crosby's reputation as a viable recording artiste might have been irrevocably destroyed by his dismissal from the Byrds. At least some of the sting was taken out of the firing by a reasonable cash settlement, with which Crosby bought a boat, *The Mayan*. After his humiliation, he made a swift exit, sailing the ocean and stopping off in Florida, where he discovered Joni Mitchell and began the next stage of his career. McGuinn was left to carry a new reputation in the rock media as the man who had dared vanquish David Crosby. Few people knew about the role of manager Larry Spector within this dynamic, and even less consideration was given to Chris Hillman, whose unassuming nature disguised a strong and wilful temperament. "Chris was always the catalyst to these departures," McGuinn later noted in self-mitigation. "Everyone blames me because I was the figurehead, but Chris was always there in the background saying, 'Get rid of him.'"

If Hillman was becoming more powerful and opinionated, this was largely due to the increasing divisions in the group. In the past, Dickson had been cast in the role of hard man, father confessor and the one person capable of persuading each Byrd to compromise in support of some common cause. Ever the astute observer, Hillman had witnessed such techniques on numerous occasions and suddenly found himself taking on a similar role, playing the diplomat or the quiet persuader, while attempting to balance his own interests against considerably larger egos. "Chris would call everybody one at a time," claims Jim Seiter. "He knew exactly how to get Michael on his side. He would get Roger on his side. And he would get David on his side if he needed David to be against Roger . . . you know what I mean? Hillman was good at that stuff. Not that it wasn't necessary. There were times when it was very necessary. Nobody wanted to confront David and if it got down to an issue that was going to end up in an argument, you'd think, 'Nah' and walk away. When I needed a decision and couldn't get it, I would always call Chris."

Jim Dickson remained totally oblivious to Crosby's fate for some time. Like David, he had disappeared to sea soon after leaving the Byrds and it was only upon his return that he learned the scarcely believable news that his protégé had suffered the same fate as himself. The irony appealed to Dickson's humour, not least because he suspected that McGuinn and Hillman's powerplay was based on an authority that they had never really possessed.

"When I heard about it at first it didn't register as real because it never occurred to me that they could fire David. Later, I told him, 'David you bitched for years that they fired you. What made you think that they had any right to fire you?' He looked a little stunned and said, 'What, you mean they didn't?' There was no partnership agreement. I suspect that, if anything, he could fire Hillman but couldn't fire McGuinn. It would seem that he had more of a claim on being a Byrd than Chris Hillman. I asked him why he accepted it, and he had no answer. He just thought they could fire him. Two against one wasn't much of a majority. Michael wasn't a party to it. He wouldn't do anything like that. He stayed out of that shit . . . Crosby could have turned up at the next date. They would have had to settle it somehow, probably through an arbitration in the court. But who would take that on and who would defend it, and how would it work? Twenty years later they were still trying to figure out how to do it by stopping Michael playing as the Byrds. There was no provision in the contract for firing David Crosby. He would say, 'The guys are ganging up on me and want me out.' But it's like kids saying, 'You can't play with us!' Eddie Tickner once said that one of the most important things in putting anything together is to figure out how you would dissolve it. But who thinks of things like that when you're trying to move forward?"

The shock departure of Crosby was a bitter pill for fans to swallow, alleviated only partly by the unexpected news that Gene Clark was set to return as his replacement. Clark's much vaunted solo career had failed to bring any critical or public acclaim, in spite of the release of the excellent *Gene Clark With The Gosdin Brothers* and the stupendous 'Echoes', an elegiacal reflection on LA life in which he had damned the Byrds' machinations with the cryptic line "They team up to tear down each other's feelings." Dickson had recruited Leon Russell in the hope of launching Clark as the first of a new generation of LA singer-songwriters, but the commercial failure of the brilliant 'Echoes' proved a serious setback and the timing of the album, in direct competition with *Younger Than Yesterday*, proved fatal in the marketplace. With only one recording in 19 months, limited touring options and a low publicity profile, Clark's solo prospects were poor. Like his fellow Byrds, Gene had eventually decided to leave Tickner/Dickson Management and belatedly throw in his lot with Larry Spector. In what seemed an ingenious move, the much maligned Spector persuaded Clark to rejoin the Byrds and take up the rhythm guitarist's role that he had once held before Crosby. For fans, at least, this announcement momentarily distracted attention from the appalling news of Crosby's shock departure.

These latest series of melodramas urgently required the rhapsodic prose of Derek Taylor who stepped in to make sense of recent events for the readership of *Hit Parader*. His extended essay looked back over the past two years as if he was chronicling the rise and fall of an epoch.

> It is 1967 now and Sunset Strip isn't what it was, but then, in the spring of 1965, when the Byrds, young and ragged and starving thin, opened in Ciro's and the amps wouldn't work and the mikes were wrong and 18 of us were there for the first

set, jittering our way through the ice-bound two-drink minimum, wondering how either the Byrds or ourselves would sustain sufficient nervous energy to make it to the end of the set – even then in 1965, they were saying the Strip wasn't what it was and Ciro's wasn't like the old days and where was the bygone aura when Bogey kicked Barrymore in the stomach and Gable mourned the loss of Carole Lombard and all of that? Answer came there none. Well, the reality was that, of course, Ciro's had changed, for hadn't the whole world changed and maybe for the better?

The Byrds are, by the very nature of their art and its ancillaries, like truth and cool and deepening beauty, a symbol of the quietening of the Strip scene, and their transformation has been notable both for the dramatic changes in the physical characteristics of the group and for their ability to come through the torment of rock 'n' roll fame without a mystique-loss. Good, bad, rotten, lazy, fierce, nasty, lovely, crude or gentle as the Byrds can be, you cannot not want to live their changes with them. When the Byrds opened in Ciro's, as nervous adventurous translators of folk-into-rock, few of us knew the extent to which their innovations would influence popular music . . . The Byrds won their status because they deserved to and retained it because despite appalling internal grief and strife, they were too strong even for the forces of self-destruction, and the Byrds are still here because within us and without us they are invincible.

There are only a few groups with value, who relate to values beyond the sound of music. There are only a handful of those with the power to reach to the edge of the world and touch, just touch a human spirit and leave the touch to work and activate what it may. The Byrds are one of these groups and one cannot say why because if it isn't *felt*, then it isn't to be explained in words.

Summing up the current state of the Byrds, Taylor offered a snapshot of the latest line-up, not realizing that they were on the brink of further changes.

The Byrds have reached up and down the charted Top 40, and they have grown moustaches and beards and hats, and they have been through capes into velvet and denim into satin, through sunglasses into the fearless naked eye, through rumours of bust and break-up, through the fires of competition and the confusing misery of alternating criticism and adulation . . . It was Jim McGuinn once, and it was Gene Clark . . . Then it was Jim McGuinn, David Crosby, Chris Hillman and Mike Clarke.

Today it is 1967 and it is now Roger McGuinn, neat and egghead precise, lofty and loving, married and a father. Jim McGuinn, the bony, woolly one with the Byrd-glasses, and no domestic ties or ambition as far as the fan mags saw him, is dead by his own Roger-hand. With the name change and a rejection of euphoric short cuts, has come a better musician than ever and a man who knows who he is.

David Crosby is not in the group any more and it is probably right and healthy that this should be so, else why would it be so? But he is still 'a Byrd'. A part of him stayed behind with the group and something of what the group was, left when he left. He will be OK. He will.

Christopher Hillman has moved to the mountains beyond the brown smog-filth-haze and he knows what's what. He always did and he is still having fun behind the face that tells you nothing.

Gene Clark is back in the group, reinforcing the Byrds with his strength, rhythm and honesty.

I am tired and it is late – which is why Mike Clarke is spared the pain of description in words. He is a lovely man and he was a lovely child when the Byrds began.

Taylor's spirited appraisal might have had an impact had it been published promptly, but it was mysteriously delayed until the New Year by which time much of its contents would be old news, made history by the rapid speed of events. For manager Larry Spector, the task of keeping the Byrds' name alive and convincing Columbia that they were still a viable unit required the steely nerve of a seasoned salesman. Perhaps his greatest gamble was bringing back Gene Clark and attempting to convince everyone that all would be well. "Larry was an opportunist," Jim Seiter wryly notes. "He was a great business manager. His supposed forte was dealing with funds. He couldn't get a deal for Gene Clark, so he decided to get him back in the Byrds. Gene had no money in the bank but he owned two $35,000 Ferraris. That was Gene. We'd already done most of the album when he arrived. We were just about to set out on tour."

Seiter was intrigued by Clark, having only heard about his reputation second-hand from the other Byrds. He had seen him perform with the group onstage at the Whisky, but was aware that there was always an uneasiness between the parties. Previously, they had told him to beware of Clark turning up at gigs and possibly causing a scene, so it was a pleasant surprise to meet him in more positive times. On his first visit to pick up Clark at his home, he was taken aback and thought, "Jesus, he has a Ferrari parked outside this dog ass apartment? What is that all about?" That wasn't all. "He had a chick with him too. It seemed that there was always one hanging around."

More than anything else, Clark resembled the consummate singer-songwriter consumed by his gift. "Gene was like some wandering folk troubadour. He would always have his guitar with him, ready to sit down and play on his own. I never saw any of the other original Byrds doing that. Michael couldn't; Hillman probably did so in private; McGuinn might have played with some synthesizer or whatever weird instrument he had at home. But Gene was more like Bob Dylan. He'd pick up a guitar and play and if one string was out of tune, he thought, 'OK, I'll live with that.' Gene didn't care whether he was in tune or not. It didn't matter to him – and that's the way Dylan was. They both liked to sit down and play whenever they felt like it."

The intense pressures that had forced Clark to leave the group in 1966 seemed less threatening now that the Byrds had fallen from commercial grace and no longer boasted legions of teenage fans. Determined to re-establish his rightful place in the rock world, Gene expressed confidence in his ability to overcome his fear of flying, believing that the absence of screaming female fans, relentless autograph hunters and scoop-seeking reporters would enable him to function adequately in the new line-up. "Gene would have liked to have recorded with the Byrds but not appear with them, not go anywhere, not leave town," Dickson stresses. "He'd have stayed in the Byrds if all he had to do was record. But he never wanted to leave Hollywood. Hollywood's magnetic. When Hollywood likes you, boy, it's a marvellous experience. You get to see and do things you didn't believe existed. You go to parties that blow your mind. Gene had plenty of attention and was sought after by people, and he loved that. He'd go nightclubbing where none of the others did. He'd visit music business places where the hacks hung out. He'd dress up special and have his hair done real neat, and people would open doors for his girlfriends. You would never have caught McGuinn, Hillman or Crosby doing that, being a patron, hanging out with the elite and all that bullshit. It was already in my past, I'd rejected it too. But Gene was having too much fun to leave. Travelling was very upsetting for him. Everybody said so, even the guys from the New Christy Minstrels."

McGuinn and Hillman were aware of Clark's instability but convinced themselves that all might be well. They suddenly felt confident that they could surmount the loss of Crosby by working with a more amicable player, whose prolific writing abilities would ensure a steady flow of material should they run dry. More importantly, Clark was now severely subservient to both McGuinn and Hillman in the power structure and seemingly happy simply to be back in the group again. Dickson also suspects that Larry Spector initially felt that Clark's presence might prove an asset in renegotiating the group's contract with CBS, which was due for renewal a few months later. All things considered, it seemed a perfect solution from the point of view of both Clark and the Byrds, but nobody could have foreseen the calamitous weeks ahead.

At first, Clark was in deceptively good form. He dutifully appeared at some recording sessions, mainly as an observer rather than a participant. His major contribution was bizarrely uncredited. Outside the studio, he helped McGuinn complete the appealing 'Get To You', whose lyrics detailed a trip to London, just like the last great song on which they had collaborated: 'Eight Miles High'. Although McGuinn had recently formed a strong writing partnership with Hillman, he had never forgotten the early days when he and Clark co-wrote some beautiful love songs. Could they possibly do so again?

Clark's first major task as a re-enlisted Byrd wasn't too intimidating. The group had been booked for several television slots, including *The Smothers Brothers Comedy Hour*, on which they were not required to play or sing but merely mime 'Goin' Back' and 'Mr Spaceman'. It was typical of the Byrds' eccentricity that they kept plugging 'Mr Spaceman', ignoring the obvious fact that it was over a year old and therefore inappropriate for late 1967. They were filmed playing it aboard a mock spaceship suspended in space and on another occasion undertook a comic sketch in which Clark tempted fate by allowing himself to be chased by several frenzied girls as the group sang about friendly extraterrestrial visitations. Throughout these sequences Clark looked in good shape: clean-cut, slim and more photogenic than ever.

What the television cameras did not capture was the inner turmoil that was already threatening Clark's attempt to re-establish himself in the Byrds. Lip-synching on television was one thing but the prospect of playing live with the Byrds and travelling across the country was quite another. At their first rehearsal, Clark was tentative, clumsy and visibly agitated. "It was like eggshells," Seiter recalls. "You could tell this guy was ready to explode. Singing and playing the guitar, he was horrible. He couldn't hit a note if his life depended on it. I'd heard him sing great before. When he wasn't around those guys, he was fine. But as soon as he was with them, there was some weird chemistry. I don't know what it was, and I didn't care to know, but he was god-awful. And he *knew* he was awful." After the rehearsal, Seiter turned to Hillman and said, "Man, that was embarrassing", but the bass player maintained a stoical optimism worthy of McGuinn. "Don't worry, it will be all right," Chris insisted. "He'll be fine!"

The following day, Seiter confided his fears to Larry Spector, and met with a similar response. "I said, 'Larry, come on, this guy's not prepared to go onstage.' That's how Spector was bad. He didn't get it at all. He had Gene signed and probably felt sorry for him and wanted to get him back in the group." As an apologetic afterthought, Spector explained that Clark had decided to take a train to the first gig, but was otherwise more than willing to fly. "Please give me a break!" Seiter snorted. "Never mind that the rehearsals were terrible, that was another problem, right there and then."

By the time Clark rejoined the Byrds, every last vestige of his self-confidence had evaporated and all the old neuroses returned with a frightening vengeance. "We'd only rehearsed once or twice," Seiter recalls. "It was kind of strange. He was on the edge. We were booked for three days in Minneapolis and then New York. The first night was weird. It was like playing with a maniac. He was so scared. He was out there at the end of his mental capacity. He was totally frightened, looking around, shaking. For hours after he came offstage he kept asking everybody, 'Did I play good? Was I OK?' He was so insecure. I turned his rhythm guitar off. We weren't using it. He was singing flat. I turned his mike down. His own songs weren't so bad except that he'd get paranoid halfway through them. The guys couldn't believe what they'd let themselves in for. They were going to New York where they had a real big following, and they were really dreading it because Gene had been so bad."

On 10 November, the Byrds appeared at Minneapolis' Marigold Ballroom in front of 1,500 teenagers. "The show was a financial success for the promoter," a polite local reviewer observed, "but left much to be desired in the way of good, exciting entertainment. Instead, the show was something of a drag, as the Byrds appeared bored with the whole affair." The Byrds were not merely bored but stoned to the gills. Backstage, the tensions in the camp were alleviated by some pharmaceutical distractions, which only made matters worse. Working on a shoestring budget, Seiter was forced to recruit a couple of kids to help with the equipment and stage security. One of the helpers, Jim Dochniak, was a Byrds' fan who was soon divested of any starstruck illusions. "Sadly," he recalls, "this turned out to be the night that rock 'n' roll – at least the worship of rock 'n' roll stars – died for me. Before the concert, all but one of the band had dropped acid, and Gene Clark came drunk on Jack Daniels. They got through the first set OK. We got to their dressing room to say, 'Hi'. But then the acid was coming on, they were fighting and miserable. By the second set, they were so gone they couldn't play the same song. At one point, they were so confused about what to play I leaned over to McGuinn and whispered 'Eight Miles High' – they suffered through it, just barely."

There was another show in the Minneapolis area that was evidently no better as Clark continued to unravel. "I swear to God I've never seen anyone so nervous onstage in my life," says Seiter. "To this very day! When he walked on that stage, he was in panic mode. He was sweating and his hands were shaking. He was a fucking maniac. What caused it? I think his life had been so wrapped up in the Byrds' success and then he'd left and later felt rejected. Gene had a weird negative vibe which was very hard to explain. Once again, he came offstage and was saying 'Was it cool?' I just said, 'Jesus Christ, Gene, you were fine!' That night, I asked Hillman: 'You want to put some money on whether he'll get on the plane tomorrow? I'll bet you anything he won't.' Hillman wouldn't bet me. All he said was 'I'm not gonna bet!'" Before they retired for the night, Seiter quipped: "You won't have to worry about him in New York, man. He won't go."

Clark had faithfully promised them that he would fly at any cost, even if that meant deadening his fears with a cocktail of alcohol and tranquillizers. After the final Minneapolis gig, however, he stayed up all night in a cold sweat and early the next morning announced that he could not fly. While McGuinn suggested that they knock him out with pills, one person in the Byrds camp had the insensitivity to goad Gene with the rejoinder: "It's mother!" McGuinn described the ensuing argument as a melodramatic soap opera as Gene screamed back at his tormentor "You're damned right it's mother" then stormed off.

While it's difficult to avoid the impression that the other Byrds were taunting Clark in bullying schoolboy fashion, Seiter disagrees. "I don't think they were taunting him at all. I think that was an old joke. They were teasing him about something that he remembered from a long time before. That's the way Hillman was. Hillman was quiet and everybody said, 'Oh, Chris!' He used to stand back and not say much. But, man, when that fucker said something he could nail you to the wall with it. And he would only say one sentence. He was brutal, man. He had a way of getting to everybody. When he gets out of it and stuff, he can be very obnoxious."

Singling out Hillman was hardly fair. McGuinn's comments about knocking Gene out with pills was practical but insensitive and betrayed a similarly dark, offbeat humour. Seiter himself was constantly fomenting the banter with merciless one-liners and Michael Clarke was also drawn into the argument. "We were flying and Gene wanted to take the goddamn train," Clarke told me. "We said, 'Fuck it! You take the fucking train. Go for it!' I wish I'd gone with him. But you can't get a train from there to New York, so it never happened. That was his demise."

Chris Hillman, who had initially supported Clark's re-enlistment, only to realize that it was now a mismatch, was so bemused by the speed of events that he could barely recall the unfortunate saga. "It's almost like he came in through the door and went back out again. So quickly! . . . I can't even remember. It was so brief. It was like a wind hitting you."

The reactions of the Byrds to Clark's neuroses may seem harsh, even brutal, but they felt let down too. Always competitive, they did not see themselves as counsellors to the psychologically afflicted. As Clarke admits: "None of us were easy to work with. *Ever.* We were all bastards. Seriously. Just ask Jim Dickson!" Evidently, they regarded Clark as a decent person but a dangerous liability who could not be relied upon to fulfil his professional obligations. Looking back, they might have been more sympathetic, but probably felt they'd already offered the hand of friendship by allowing Clark back in the group for a second time. From their hardened viewpoint, he had blown it yet again and there was nothing more to add.

Clark concluded his second coming by taking a train back to Los Angeles. Even after returning to Hollywood, he was to discover that the nightmare of the past few weeks had not quite ended. Seiter provided the following sad footnote to the saga.

"We did a gig as a trio and it was even easier. The next day Larry asked me to go to the station and meet Gene as he'd only just arrived by train. When I got there and met him at the train, he just walked past me at a fast pace, and didn't say a word, got in a yellow cab and split to the office. Now, Gene was always afraid of small closed spaces. He never took elevators. We had this old-fashioned elevator in the office building and Gene never took it. But for some reason he did that day. When I arrived at the office the police are there and the Fire Department – someone is stuck in the lift. Gene is stuck in the lift for two-and-a-half hours. When they finally opened it he ran out, soaking with sweat, and split. I didn't see him for six or eight months after that. The inside of the elevator was totally scratched up where he'd tried to get out. You should have heard him screaming. Unbelievable. He was going crazy in that elevator. He screamed at the top of his lungs for almost an hour. Bad time for Gene."

With no suitable candidate available as a replacement for Clark, the Byrds determined to continue as a trio. A proposed major tour soon devolved into a sporadic series of concerts, largely concentrated in California. On an out-of-town jaunt to Las Vegas, McGuinn was amazed to discover that the support act was called the Jet Set. It felt eerily like going back in time. Having started as a vocal trio under that name, the Byrds were once again a threesome, albeit with Clarke and Hillman rather than Clark and Crosby. In order to compensate for those losses, the rhythm section became more pronounced with Hillman extending his bass runs and Clarke pushing for a more bluesy sound.

The late 1967 mini line-up was so short-lived that only one known concert review was ever published. The venue was the Hullabaloo on Sunset Boulevard, where the Byrds received a very charitable response from the underground magazine, *The Happening*. "The curtains open, and the three Byrds play. In the audience, there is silence. They succeed. Only Chris Hillman, Michael Clarke and newly moustachioed Roger McGuinn are onstage, but they've somewhat captured the spirit of their old music. The vocals need a little work, as Chris' harmonies sometimes overpower McGuinn's melodies, but the magic is still there. Once people get over the shock of seeing a trio in place of the familiar quartet or quintet, they'll come to realize this. It just takes a little time. Once you've been a big group like this, people demand more; it takes more to satisfy them and their beliefs. The Byrds are aware of this and are outdoing themselves in order to retain their status in the pop music world."

While such words were encouraging, the absolute lack of comment elsewhere testified to a general sense of apathy among reviewers and public alike. Writer and fan Bill Wasserzieher, who attended another of the trio's dates at the Golden Bear, Huntington Beach (16–19 November), recalls the enveloping feeling of disillusionment that was already threatening to overwhelm the group. "I remember the performance distinctly. Roger McGuinn was dejected enough to ask for requests from the stage and then apologize for not being able to duplicate the LP sound, and Chris Hillman played so loudly, perhaps to compensate, that my chest and stomach hurt from the pounding by the end of the evening. I remember it as a truly sad, desolate show, rain dripping in and the tables half empty, and roadie Jim Seiter standing forlornly in the back looking like it was all over. I figured it was."

Minus two of its original members, both of them talented singer-songwriters, it was difficult to imagine how the Byrds might compensate, let alone rescale past heights. Back in the studio, there had been some occasion for good cheer when Michael Clarke, responding to recent crises, elected to take up sticks again. He even co-wrote an impressive new song, 'Artificial Energy', which regrettably was the final track recorded by this particular line-up. Soon after finishing the album, the frequently absent Clarke was informed that he too was an ex-Byrd. He accepted the decision without rancour and sought no compensation, even though the group were poised to sign a lucrative new deal with CBS in the New Year which would have netted him a substantial sum. Later, he claimed that he was unaware of this impending windfall and might otherwise have stayed in the band a few months longer. But at heart he was a free spirit and ready to go. Weary of the recent group traumas, bored with LA, and unconcerned about the Byrds' finances or future, he took off for Hawaii and temporarily left the music business, securing a mundane job at a bay restaurant in Maui.

"I think he was on the point of quitting when we suggested that he should leave," McGuinn recalls. "He seemed to be depressed at the time and didn't want the responsibility of being a Byrd, although he didn't really have to do that much. Another factor was our audience which was changing. We weren't really pulling in any teenage girls and Michael missed that. He liked the idea of being a sex symbol."

David Crosby provided an assessment of Michael Clarke's contribution to the group: "Michael would turn the time round two or three times in a song back to front. But he improved steadily and he tried very hard to get better. He surprised me because he got better and better after he left the Byrds. He could play a groove quite well. Michael was a good guy. He meant well and I liked him a lot."

Jim Seiter regretted the drummer's departure. "Michael and I were really good friends, more so than I was with any of the other guys then. He was a child at heart and always had a good time. I knew all of his down points and failings, but I still loved the guy. He wasn't a real good musician but he had a feel for it and a soul for it, and he was just trying to make a living. I thought they fucked him every way they could at times . . . If any of them had called my ass into it [for a cynical comment on all their feuding] they'd have been in deeper shit with each another. There was some stupid stuff going around then and Larry Spector was in the middle of [the drama] too."

Clarke was ultimately a victim of his own carefree approach, both to the music and the business side of the Byrds. He was remarkably blasé about his departure, fully cognizant that it had largely been self-inflicted. No one remembers him being unhappy about leaving. Symbolically, his exit left the Byrds in a seemingly impossible position going into the New Year. The comings and goings at the end of 1967 had threatened the completion of their current album but McGuinn and Hillman were always determined to finish the project and succeeded with the help of some notable session players including Jim Gordon, Red Rhodes and Clarence White. Across the Atlantic, a new single, 'Goin' Back'/'Change Is Now', already a failure in the States, was released in Christmas week as a festive treat for British Byrd followers. It was treated as a more significant release than 'Lady Friend' and attracted a modicum of airplay, but not enough to provide a surprise hit. Ironically, publicity was given to the fact that the Byrds were now reduced to a trio. *NME* even provided a lead review, accompanied by a doctored photograph from 1965, featuring McGuinn, Hillman and Clarke. Few knew that the recent line-up changes had worsened rather than stabilized, and the situation was now critical.

CHAPTER TWENTY-FIVE

Wanted: The Notorious Byrd Brothers

AT the close of 1967, critics were sarcastically asking whether McGuinn and Hillman were poised to become a West Coast Simon & Garfunkel-type act. By the first week of January 1968, however, reports filtered through that the Byrds had found a new drummer. The first non-original Byrd had another distinctive quality; he was cousin to Chris Hillman.

Kevin Daniel Kelley (born Los Angeles, California, 25 March 1943) was the son of a prominent entertainment lawyer and grew up among the privileged of Beverly Hills. Always interested in music, he studied piano and guitar, sang in choirs and played in orchestras. He even appeared at the Hollywood Bowl, conducting the Beverly Hills School Band. Along the way, he took up drums, but had little interest in rock 'n' roll and always seemed more likely to pursue a career in classical music. He specialized in composing at both Santa Monica College and Los Angeles City College, but his path abruptly changed thereafter. Often regarded as a loner, he entered what he referred to as a state of confusion and enlisted in the Marine Corps for three years, including a year spent in Japan, where he "became interested in Far East religions". No Byrd had ever served in the forces, but Kelley had done so willingly, without the pressure of a draft notice. Some said he was trying to impress his father, a disciplinarian who had military honours. While in the services, Kelley gave up music completely but, after returning to civilian life, he followed his cousin into the LA music scene. In 1965, he joined Taj Mahal and Ry Cooder in the Rising Sons, replacing Ed Cassidy as drummer. Bassist Gary Marker remembers Kelley as officious and organized. Given his recent spell in the Marine Corps, that was hardly surprising.

The Rising Sons were a hugely talented ensemble, whose prospects were stifled during a troubled spell with CBS Records, where they worked with both Allen Stanton and Terry Melcher, but only released one single. After they split, Kelley teamed up with Marker in the jazz rock experimental band Fusion, but their progress was erratic and money was tight. By the time Chris Hillman reached his cousin, Kelley was working part-time in a men's clothing shop. Like Michael Clarke, his entry to the Byrds was sudden, unexpected and welcomed.

The prospects of the Byrds as a trio seemed slight, but they showed no signs of surrendering the name or abandoning the security that beckoned via a new contract. "I suppose McGuinn must have hoped that they'd continue for years to come," Dickson reflects. "He continued to do it. Was there any hope? I'm sure there were lots of people that had hope and there were a lot of people who thought it wasn't worth bothering with any more. I'm sure there were people who never thought it was worth bothering with in the first place."

Even the remaining original members of the Byrds were low on optimism as they set out on a tour of colleges and small clubs with Kelley as a trio. "There wasn't a lot of hope for the future," McGuinn admits. "I probably had more hope than Chris did because I've always had this internal optimism. But it was pretty bleak."

Those who had kept the faith were duly rewarded with the New Year release of *The Notorious Byrd Brothers*. Its appearance amazed many observers, as it was assumed that the work was still at the planning stage. However, the intense pressure of three departures in as many months spurred them into completing the album, with McGuinn and Hillman still working in the weeks up to Christmas in order to meet their deadline. "I think the stress we felt was a catalyst," McGuinn agrees. "We were going to show David – and it was competition again – and it worked." The album was a critical triumph, greeted with lengthy and effusive reviews in both *Rolling*

Stone and *Crawdaddy*. Among the underground rock writing hierarchy of the period, the Byrds were still regarded as one of the most inventive groups in America. Their new work proved a steady seller and performed particularly well in the British market, charting higher than any LP since *Turn! Turn! Turn!*.

Lyrically, musically and technically, the Byrds were pushing forward to new musical horizons, even as their ranks were diminishing to an alarming degree. Their achievement on *The Notorious Byrd Brothers* lay in creating a seamless mood piece from a variety of different musical sources, the whole bound together through studio ingenuity. The work retains its standing among their greatest triumphs and deserves special consideration.

The intriguing opening track, 'Artificial Energy', sounds unlike anything they'd recorded before. McGuinn's vocal is enmeshed in a weirdly pulsating brass accompaniment while Clarke's unrelenting drumming barrages through, as if he is oblivious to all the extraordinary effects. With 'Eight Miles High' and '5 D', the Byrds were unjustly accused of peddling 'drug songs'. Ironically, when they finally issued a composition dealing specifically with the subject, nobody blinked an eye. It was Chris Hillman who first suggested "Let's write a song about speed," after which drummer Michael Clarke came up with the title 'Artificial Energy' and provided enough lyrical input to secure a rare songwriting credit. Producer Gary Usher helped with the special effects, creating a bizarre mix of phased brass, undulating vocals and a ghostly piano accompaniment that percolates in and out of audibility. The entrance of the piano after they ask "do you think it's really the truth that you see" is positively spooky. 'Artificial Energy' is full of playful subtleties, including a wry nod to the Beatles' 'Ticket To Ride' (sung "ticket to ri-hi-hide"), another example of McGuinn using the media as a private communications device. Lyrically, the song proves equally fascinating, from its Dr Jekyll references to the effects of amphetamine ("powerful things are brewing inside") to that final horrific image of the drug taker imprisoned for murdering a homosexual ("I'm in jail 'cos I killed a queen"). Although unconfirmed, that last line sounds very much like one of Michael Clarke's darkly humorous gibes. The composition remains a brilliant testament to the group's love of experimentation during this period.

In his eccentrically opaque and impressionistic review of the album for *Crawdaddy*, Sandy Pearlman paid most attention to 'Artificial Energy', and with good reason. Its sonic appeal left him breathless with adjectives. "Rhythms against counter rhythms: John Philip Sousa's mechanical bass drum repetition (oom-pah, oom-pah etc) against Hillman's bass playing (so great and flexible) with its liquid (a beautiful tone) wavelike variable cycle bass patterns. Energy type against counter-energy. Linear brass (directionally moving at diagonals) against the flowing wave motion of the Byrds' chorale which is a specialization in ad hoc phrasing . . . The mix is with great delicacy, and the piano's appearance (at a barely audible level) as the vehicle for an instrumental resolution after the voices stop singing . . . is quite outasight. Another nice one is the electronic noise maker's fade into audibility at the fadeout."

Although McGuinn no doubt appreciated such unexpected praise, he was still a little critical. "It's a good strong track but we messed up the vocal. We did it electronically. We were trying for a hard sound which we'd never had. We sang it and then we took some kind of gadget that some guy brought in that we rented for 50 bucks. You plug into it and it distorts, but the voice came out more like Donald Duck than we wanted. The brass section was just studio cats and then we phased their stuff so it came out a little more soulful." Contrary to what McGuinn claims, the 'Donald Duck' effect transforms the song into something greater than the sum of its parts. The bizarre brass part is, in many ways, the key to the song's greatness. Crosby had previously persuaded the Byrds to use Hugh Masekela's trumpet on 'So You Want To Be A Rock 'n' Roll Star' and employ brass on 'Lady Friend', but Gary Usher and McGuinn take the idea one step further on 'Artificial Energy'. "I remember we had a really 'square' brass section," McGuinn says. "So I took this electronic device and made them boogie. They were doing Harry James-type swing music and I electronically modified an entire brass section by myself, with my right hand, and made it come out as it did."

The unearthly sounds that end 'Artificial Energy' abruptly

metamorphose into the opening strains of 'Goin' Back', a poignant song of nostalgia and lost innocence, in complete contrast to the grim realism of the first cut. Written by Gerry Goffin and Carole King, the song was already well known in Britain, having been a hit for Dusty Springfield in the summer of 1966. "Gary Usher got the tune and brought it to us in the studio and played it for us as a demo," McGuinn recalls. "I didn't know of Carole King, even though I had worked in the Brill Building earlier on. And I had never heard of the Goffin/King songwriting team, but I loved the tune and thought it was really good. Gary explained that they were Tin Pan Alley writers who had just kind of taken a sabbatical and come back and revamped their style to be more contemporary, like we were doing. So it really fit well, I thought. We learned it and put a kind of dreamy quality into it."

By altering the tempo, arrangement and lyrics, the Byrds make the song sound fresh and completely new. The alterations to the lyrics are subtle, but significant. Dusty Springfield had sung of "No More Colouring Books/No Christmas bells to chime" which the Byrds masculinized as "No more electric trains/No more trees to climb". Similarly, the Byrds' "Now I think I've got a lot more than just my toys to lend" had originally been the girly ". . . a lot more than a skipping rope to lend". Other changes were more gratuitous, but with pleasing results. They miss out the wonderful couplet, "I can play hide and seek with my fears/And live my days instead of counting my years", substituting "But thinking young and growing older is no sin/And I can play the game of life to win." The Byrds conclude their reading with the words "A little bit of courage is all we lack . . ." arguably an improvement on the original's more vague "A little . . . freedom is all we lack."

Having petitioned the group to record the composition, Usher worked particularly hard to ensure the production was top notch. At first, they overdubbed a glockenspiel, then attempted a take on which a veritable battalion of musicians was recruited to sweeten the track. Among the additional instruments employed are a celeste, harp, cello, violin, piano, pedal steel guitar and Moog synthesizer. Remarkably, the final production sounds both subtle and uncluttered, while the mixing is exemplary. It was almost as if

Usher was determined to show Crosby that he had made a mistake by not contributing to the recording. The streamlined Byrds' vocal performance is also exceptional with those distinctive 'ahhs' recalling earlier feats of harmony, an amazing achievement considering that they were bereft of Crosby's guiding genius. Michael Clarke is also absent from the session, but Jim Gordon steps in to provide a magnificent flourish, fondly remembered for that great drum roll towards the end of the song. It is also impressive how some of the aforementioned lyrical alterations tallied with the Byrds' recent changes. The theme of thinking young and growing older recalls the title of their last album, *Younger Than Yesterday*, which had touched on similar notions of wisdom in innocence. Even the song's reference to a "magic carpet ride" could not help but evoke visual memories of the striking front sleeve of *Fifth Dimension* with its own magic carpet. No wonder the song became such a Byrds' favourite, Crosby's antipathy notwithstanding.

Chris Hillman follows up his three songwriting credits on *Younger Than Yesterday* with the engaging, otherworldly ambience of 'Natural Harmony', a song which enacts the freedom longed for in 'Goin' Back'. Having asked us in 'Goin' Back' to return to the days when we were young enough to know the truth, the narrator of 'Natural Harmony' actually attempts to describe a feeling similar to a day of birth, "our first awakening to this Earth". It is easy to dismiss the Blakean 'merging with a grain of sand' lyrics as the expression of a drug-related experience, but such a view would be as reductive as the establishment's misguided commentaries on 'Eight Miles High' and '5 D'. The important point is that 'Natural Harmony', like 'Goin' Back', conveys a sense of irresistible longing for a golden age of childhood purity. Someone once asked why Hillman used the word 'graciously' and not, for example, 'gratefully'. The answer, of course, is that 'graciously' is far more evocative and closer in association to the orderly concept of natural harmony. It also describes more vividly the druggy, dream-like atmosphere, so reminiscent of the medieval-tinged 'Renaissance Fair' on the last album. Hillman's expression of idyllic bliss (with the image of the couple dancing through the streets, arms wide open) finds its musical equivalent in the eerie combination of Paul Beaver's Moog synthesizer and Clarence White's guitar.

Having already dealt with the subject of drugs, innocence and freedom, the Byrds next turn their attention to war with 'Draft Morning'. At the time Crosby wrote the song, Muhammad Ali had just been stripped of his world heavyweight championship title and sentenced to five years' imprisonment for refusing to be inducted into the United States Armed Forces. Soon after, President Lyndon B. Johnson announced that another 50,000 troops would be sent to Vietnam in 1968. The Byrds had kept quiet about their views on the war, even though Chris Hillman, Michael Clarke and Gene Clark each had untold stories about their scary encounters with the draft board. It was Crosby who finally articulated their feelings in print and his tone was sympathetic rather than shrill. "It's not a them-versus-us situation," he insisted. "They *are* us, man . . . The guy who shoots people in Vietnam lives in me because I have gotten mad and have hit people in my life and we're all the same person. He came from the same energy source that I did, and he'll go back into the same energy source that I will, and he is probably trying to get off the wheel too. I can't straighten him out without straightening myself out first. Somebody's got to straighten all of us out now, it's getting out of hand, man. People dying. It puts me uptight. It lives in my house and it lives in my head."

Crosby wrote 'Draft Morning' in that same ameliorating frame of mind. Despite his reputation for hectoring, his handling of the theme is both sensitive and understated. 'Draft Morning' builds subtly but powerfully, tracing the journey of a soldier from the morning of his induction to an imagined future on the battlefield. The first verse introduces the narrator, awakening to feel the warmth of the sun on his face and hearing a figure, presumably a loved one, moving below stairs. The quiet, homely atmosphere alters abruptly in the second stanza. Suddenly, we learn that this is the morning of the draft and the time approaches when the soldier must unwillingly be taught how to kill. A clarion of brass, reinforced by the steadily increasing volume of gunfire, creates a startling effect, resulting in a spatial and temporal shift. For when we next return to the narrator in the final few lines, he is no longer uneasily contemplating his approaching induction into the army but is already an active soldier. Note the move from the present to the past tense in the phrase "today *was* the day for action" (as opposed to "today *is* the day for action") implying that military service has already taken place and hinting, perhaps, that the gunfire we have heard was his own.

'Draft Morning' stands high as one of the finer songs in the Byrds' canon. Chris Hillman's melodic bass lines, set against the delicate cymbal opening, are positively spinetingling, while the inspired inclusion of gunfire courtesy of the Firesign Theatre (whom Gary Usher also produced) adds a suitably dramatic crescendo before the quiet fade. Despite such strengths, the composition became a subject of controversy and deep bitterness. Crosby had first played the song to the Byrds in Hawaii and an impressive backing track was duly completed. Unfortunately, he was fired before the vocal was laid down, which left McGuinn and Hillman facing a dilemma. They were unwilling to lose the track, so elected to add fresh lyrics of their own. As Hillman recalls: "Crosby had written the basic song but we had to rewrite some of the words because he had left right after introducing the song to us and we could hardly remember the lyrics."

Crosby was appalled by their seemingly cavalier decision to revamp the track and complained bitterly that this was an unethical act unworthy of them. "It was one of the sleaziest things they ever did," he told me. "I had an entire song finished. They just casually re-wrote it and decided to take half the credit. How's that? Without even asking me! That's bullshit. I had a finished song, entirely mine. I left. They did the song anyway. They re-wrote it and put it in their names. And mine was better. They just took it because they didn't have enough songs."

Nevertheless, the new interpretation sounds superb. In one of his greatest acting performances, McGuinn modulates his voice to sound uncannily like Crosby. Listening to the verse just prior to the gunfire, you can hear David's familiar phrasing channelled through McGuinn like a ghostly medium. Considering the antipathy between the parties, it is a tribute to the power of Crosby's composition that the other Byrds were so reluctant to abandon the track. They could easily have slotted Mike Brewer's 'Bound To Fall' in its place if a shortage of songs was their only problem.

Such polite reasoning leaves Crosby cold. He would never again return to his original recording or play the song live. Try telling him that McGuinn and Hillman were complimenting, or at least acknowledging, the importance of his songwriting contribution here, and he would explode with anger: "Man – they used it after they changed it, and took it for themselves without even asking me. That's theft! Do you understand? How would *you* feel? Suppose we were co-writing a book together, man, and you had just finished doing something with it and we split up. I said you were a piece of shit, and I walked. Then I rewrote all of your stuff in it and claimed that I had written the book. How would you feel? You'd be pissed off, wouldn't you? Well, I was pissed off. I'm *still* pissed off."

After the sombre approach of 'Draft Morning', the succeeding 'Wasn't Born To Follow' lightens the mood. Goffin and King's second contribution to the album saw them momentarily replace Bob Dylan as the Byrds' favourite outside composers. "Gary Usher knew Carole King and he was responsible for getting those songs for us," McGuinn remembers. "We felt they were suitable choices." The now divorced songwriting duo were attempting to adjust to changing times by writing more impressionistic material with a distinctly hippie ambience. Rather than producing a carbon copy of Carole King's slow, piano-led original demo, the Byrds completely restructured the melody and added some startling musical effects, juxtaposing Clarence White's country-style picking and a cascade of exotic phasing. "It was before electronic shifting, so we used two [8-track] tape machines out of phase with each other," McGuinn explains, "one going at a slightly different speed to the other. We had a speed variator on the other machine, so we went back and forth." As well as speeding up the tempo, the Byrds removed some lyrics. While retaining the first two verses, they cut and pasted the remainder. After the references to the rivers of our vision flowing into one another, King sang "And I'll stay awhile and wonder at the mist that they've created and lose myself within it, and cleanse my mind and body/And I know at that moment as I stand in that cathedral, I will want to die beneath the white cascading water . . ."

Similarly, in the closing stanza, beginning "She may beg, she may plead . . ." Goffin adds the ponderous qualification, ". . . though I doubt that she will ever come to understand my meaning, and in the end she will surely know, I was not born to follow." The Byrds' revisions are surprisingly effective, retaining the vivid imagery while removing the more meditative musings. The song's evocation of pastoral freedom and the implicit desire to escape from the restrictions of conventional society perfectly complement the Byrds' own compositions on the album. Significantly, the song was later chosen as the most suitable piece of music to express 'the search for America' in the motion picture *Easy Rider*.

'Wasn't Born To Follow' ends with what sounds like the slamming of a door. The Mamas & The Papas first used this trick on 'John's Music Box' to announce the conclusion of side one of *Deliver*, but here there is still one track remaining – the beautiful, lilting melody 'Get To You'. While the composing credits are given as Hillman-McGuinn, Chris concedes that the lyrics were almost entirely the work of his colleague and could not even remember his own contribution. His lapse of memory is unsurprising since, according to McGuinn, the composition should actually have been co-credited to Gene Clark. "I remember Gene coming to my house while I was working on the chords, and we took it from there. Part of our motivation was an 'I'll show David . . .' attitude, as he'd gone by then." McGuinn could not recall who was responsible for registering the album's writing credits, which seem arbitrarily ordered on various songs for no apparent reason. Sometimes Hillman is named first, other times McGuinn, without rhyme or reason. Evidently, Clark never asked for his name to be appended to 'Get To You' and the original LP credits are unaltered to this day.

Lyrically, 'Get To You' seems straightforward enough, documenting a plane trip to London just prior to the advent of autumn. But the listener is left with a riddle: who is the 'you' in the title? If we assume the speaker to be McGuinn, then it seems logical that the 'you' is London itself, which he did indeed wait 20 odd years to see before arriving with the Byrds in August 1965. Viewed from this perspective, the phrase "see *you* run my way" becomes a play on words, suggesting 'runway' and indicating the arrival of the plane at London Airport. Like 'Eight Miles High', which also used the plane trip to London as its central theme, 'Get To You' relishes its playful ambiguities. In the second line of the song, McGuinn complicates matters by including the phrase "back there *again*", which clearly suggests that the speaker has been to London two decades before ("it took me *20* years to get to *you*"). Perhaps it is safer to concede that the lyrics are only partly autobiographical with the 'you' representing both London and some idealized, perpetually faithful woman in the mould of John Riley's "fair young maid" or Homer's Penelope. The deceptively simple 'Get To You' remains a textbook lesson in the hidden complexities of Byrds' music, from the allusive lyrics to the delightfully unexpected shifts from *5/4* to *3/4* time between verses and choruses. Completing the mystery is the difficult-to-decipher refrain, conspicuously omitted from published songbooks and a source of widespread misinterpretation among Byrds' aficionados. "Actually, it's 'oh that's a little better'," McGuinn confirms. "I never realized how difficult that line was to decipher."

The opening track on side two, 'Change Is Now', was the first tune recorded for the album. Originally titled 'Universal Mind Decoder', it was championed by Michael Clarke and developed by Hillman and McGuinn, who are credited for the music and lyrics. Clarke's rhythmic drumming both propels and grounds the track, gliding through all its surprise sonic touches without distraction. Where we might have expected to hear a Rickenbacker break from McGuinn, there is an eerie yet scintillating 6-string Fender guitar solo, possibly fed through a Moog, that thrills to the quick. Equally notable is the understated chunky rhythm work that neatly complements McGuinn's extended solo and Clarence White's delicate picking. The other significant feature of the track is Hillman's absence on bass. "I played the bass," Crosby confirms. "What I did was a very simple thing . . . it was a picking pattern, an octave. It's the only time that I ever played bass on anything. I wasn't any good at bass and the only time I could get away with it was on that particular tune, because it was suited to it. Also, Chris really wanted to play guitar. He was turning into a damn good guitar-player by that time and that's the main reason why I was allowed to do it."

When I first confronted Crosby about his bass work, he simply referred to playing "on Hillman's tune", as if Chris had written only one song on the album. This led to the assumption that he meant 'Old John Robertson' but, such was Crosby's bitterness about the album, that he could barely remember the song titles, thus perpetuating this factoid. The giveaway reference to the 'octave' part confirms that 'Change Is Now' was the song in question, a view reinforced by contemporary concert reports which reference his surprise appearance on bass. 'Change Is Now' remains a wonderful fusion of different styles, mixing pastoral flourishes with flashes of psychedelia and experimental rock. This unusual combination works superbly with words that delicately balance country-style homilies alongside quasi-philosophical speculations in a fashion reminiscent of McGuinn's work on '5 D'. Lyrically, 'Change Is Now' celebrates a *carpe diem* philosophy, advising us to live life to the full. The underlying metaphysical speculations, including a stab at epiphenomenalism ("that which is not real does not exist") are subtle enough to pass almost unnoticed but serve as an excellent example of the Byrds' concern to avoid overstatement. Much of the composition reflects the mood of the album's first side, with subtle echoes from 'Natural Harmony'. We are told to keep in 'harmony' with love's sweet plan, while the "dancing through the streets side by side" of 'Natural Harmony' now becomes an admonition to "dance to the day when fear is gone". It is no wonder that the album has so often been applauded for its remarkable thematic and musical continuity. 'Change Is Now' is an important part of the overall puzzle or, as McGuinn flippantly remarks: "It's another of those guru-spiritual-mystic songs that no one understood."

'Old John Robertson' maintains the constantly shifting mood of the album with its evocative references to age, youth, childhood, death, laughter and tears. The song has a mythical, fairy-tale quality, although it is faithfully based on Hillman's memory of a larger than life local character. "I grew up in a small town of about 1,000 people, Rancho Santa Fe, San Diego County. There was an old man named John Robertson who retired there. He had been a movie director in the Twenties. He wore a Stetson hat and had this long, white handlebar moustache; quite an old cowboy character, but he was really nice to us kids." Hillman's characterization is full of pathos as he relates the children's cruel laughter at this colourful figure, whose presence prompts a strange combination of derision, fear and awe. Like 'Wasn't Born To Follow', 'Old John Robertson' contains a dramatic break midway through, this time via the intervention of orchestration. Although the song was originally conceived as a straight country tune, all that changed thanks to a wonderful stroke of serendipity. As McGuinn recalls: "We were just playing a country song and, all of a sudden, this harpsichord and baroque section walked in and sat down and played the break. Then they packed up their gear and split . . . We decided to leave it in."

The importance of *The Notorious Byrd Brothers* as a document of the Sixties was reflected in its songs of innocence, freedom, exploration and rejection of war. Crosby captured the moment in another evocative tribute, 'Tribal Gathering'. Swirling sound effects are evident throughout, but beneath the modern technology lurks a vocal arrangement that unmistakably harks back to David's youth when he listened to singers such as the Four Freshmen. Like 'Renaissance Fair', the song evokes the atmosphere of a public event as though it were a dream-like experience. According to McGuinn, "'Tribal Gathering' was about the feeling that what we were witnessing was a strange gathering of tribes – the Hell's Angels, the hippies, the straight people and the police, all getting together for a musical event that made everybody feel wonderful." McGuinn mistakenly assumed that Crosby was celebrating Monterey, while others have wrongly believed that the song was inspired by 'The Human Be-In' which took place in San Francisco's Golden Gate Park. Crosby confirms that the actual event was the first Love-In he attended at Elysian Park, an LA version of 'The Gathering Of The Tribes' staged on Easter Sunday, 1967.

'Dolphin's Smile', Crosby's song of the sea, concludes the many references to childhood, innocence and freedom that make up the main body of the album. Crosby had first used nautical imagery on 'It Happens Each Day', an outtake from *Younger Than Yesterday* that escaped his musical memory bank and remained unissued during the Byrds' lifetime. Dolphins symbolized the freedom that he was seeking at the time, as well as contributing to his personal philosophy of life. "I have found not one absolute in my whole life," he decreed, "only balancing and variables. Mostly by watching dolphins, porpoises. Have you ever been in the water with one? There's a consciousness expanding experience. They're heavy, man. Old souls. Many times around the wheel, feels like. And they feel groovy and they feel cool, they feel joyous and simple and clean and happy." In common with his reaction to 'Draft Morning', Crosby was upset that the Byrds chose to include 'Dolphin's Smile' on the album, although it was a completed take, credited to all three members. Crosby claims he agreed to share the publishing in return for their minor contributions, a decision that he later regretted. "It was my idea, my music and my lyrics," he maintains. "I gave McGuinn half the credit to get it on a fucking record. It was a political situation and very often I had to do that to get material recorded."

Publishing politics aside, it is clear that McGuinn contributed some fascinating musical suggestions which were taken up by Crosby during the recording process. The ingenious opening seconds of the track may sound like a school of dolphins in full song, but are actually McGuinn simulating those effects. "It was my idea to do the 'be-de-lum' introduction," he says. "That was my fingernails on the neck of the Rickenbacker with a lot of echo. I was heavily involved in all the effects."

The concluding track 'Space Odyssey' was effectively a sea shanty transposed to outer space, with the synthesizer accompanying McGuinn's folky vocal. Although the track was released prior to the film *2001: A Space Odyssey*, both Stanley Kubrick and McGuinn adapted the theme from the same source – Arthur C. Clarke's short story, *The Sentinel*. Despite its funereal tempo, the song became a long-time favourite of McGuinn's. He always enjoyed fusing the traditional with the futuristic, and was fascinated by speculation on the role of extraterrestrial life in the evolution of man. The song's placing on the album seemed a deliberate echo of 'We'll Meet Again' at the close of *Mr Tambourine Man*, which was also dedicated to Stanley Kubrick.

While the selection and sequencing of the tracks were applauded by many critics as one of the album's major strengths, McGuinn reveals that, in common with other great works, the final structuring was a seemingly spontaneous act. "It was purely accidental. We didn't plan it that way. It was natural. I think the only continuity occurred in the editing, the placement and the lead-in from one song to another. We did it arbitrarily in about 35 seconds. Gary Usher said: 'Let's work on that order.' He took a piece of paper and he said, 'Let's start off with 'Artificial Energy' and then end up with, um, 'Space Odyssey', OK?' And then he said, 'Let's see – side one – what do you want to do? OK, the last cut on side one, 'Get To You'.' Then he said, 'Goin' Back', then he had it all like that. And I looked at it and said, 'Man!' And I'm sure that he had no idea when he did it that it would come out the way it did. So it was a happy accident."

Usher, while not contradicting McGuinn, suggests that this was an oversimplification. "It was more a question of how the album would flow, what we were trying to say conceptually, how one song would fit together sequencing into another song, the key they were in and the overall performance. A lot of thought went into the final picking of the tracks. It was not just at random."

According to McGuinn, the album's remarkable front sleeve was another stroke of fate. The three Byrds had been photographed riding horses, then returned to the stable where they lined up, peering out of the stone building. Michael Clarke's horse wandered across to the light and poked its head through the windowless frame, while the drummer clasped its reins to ensure that the steed was part of the picture. Photographer Guy Webster snapped a beautiful portrait shot, which provided one of the best ever Byrds' covers. When the record was released, many critics believed that the inclusion of a horse where Crosby would have been was a malicious joke on McGuinn's part. The story became part of Byrds folklore despite Roger's insistence that the sleeve had no symbolic intent. "If we *had* intended to do that, we would have turned the horse around," he quips. It was quite simply one of life's accidents. Perhaps not surprisingly, Crosby was unconvinced by this plausible explanation and greeted McGuinn's account with open-mouthed incredulity: "An accident? An *accident*! He said that? Do you believe that? It's bullshit. You *know* it is. *You* know why he did it."

If the front sleeve of the album offended Crosby, then he was equally mortified by the rear on which personnel details were conspicuously absent. McGuinn and Hillman could rightly claim that there was nothing unusual or sinister about that. Neither *Fifth Dimension* nor *Younger Than Yesterday* had listed the musicians present, let alone provided a breakdown of who played on which track. Nevertheless, Crosby believed there was a conspiracy of silence, a view reinforced by critical reaction to the album, which heaped extravagant praise on McGuinn, Hillman and Usher for completing such an outstanding work, apparently without the assistance of the missing fourth member.

Understandably, Hillman and McGuinn neglected to emphasize Crosby's role during promotional interviews. Even in later years, Hillman casually observed, "It came down to McGuinn and me doing most of it." Some latter-day reviewers still make the mistake of acclaiming *The Notorious Byrd Brothers* without considering Crosby's contribution.

"That's dumb," he points out, referring to the vital lack of information on the original sleeve. "I'm all over that album, they just didn't give me credit. I played, I sang, I wrote, I even played bass on one track, and they tried to make out that I wasn't even on it, that they could be that good without me. And that was bullshit because I was there. You can tell from the bitterness in my voice that it was a strongly emotional problem. It hurt me a lot. McGuinn used to do that stuff regularly. He wanted to stay on top. He wanted to be the boss of that band. And I don't really allow anyone to be my boss. I won't have any bosses. I have partners, but nobody is my boss. *Ever.*"

At the time of the record's release, McGuinn revealed that he was disappointed with the finished product, and it was only in later years that he came to recognize the importance of the work. Hillman did not bother to keep a copy at his home and Crosby could never stomach listening to the album, even ignoring the remastered edition in 1997. For all of them, in different ways, it symbolized a period of pain and uncertainty. Along with *Younger Than Yesterday*, the album displayed the Byrds at the height of their creative powers, unravelling the complexity of their group dynamics as they spiralled towards greatness and self-immolation in the same breath. One cannot help wondering what might have been achieved had Crosby remained or had Gene Clark not been forced to leave after only a few weeks. Perhaps the quality of the group's studio work was a reflection of the tensions and pressures that forced them to extend their creative abilities to unforeseen heights. On the other hand, it is not inconceivable that an album of even greater stature than *The Notorious Byrd Brothers* might have been achieved if the final breakdown towards the end of 1967 had been averted.

For all the problems they faced in this unbelievably eventful year, the group achieved a mastery that few in rock music have ever held. Any fears about the Byrds' standing in the history of modern popular music were made redundant by the twin thrust of *Younger Than Yesterday* and *The Notorious Byrd Brothers*, a fact that even McGuinn would not dispute. "I feel that was the best stage we ever reached," he concludes.

Crosby, while not denying that his final year in the Byrds was their finest, is a little more critical: "I thought *Younger Than Yesterday* was real good. I thought *The Notorious Byrd Brothers* was considerably less good, and from there it went steadily downhill. I don't think it ever touched the stuff I did with them again."

Crosby's acidity cannot disguise, and should not distract from, an understanding of the enormity of all that had been lost. From 1965–67, the Byrds had undertaken an extraordinary odyssey and for a time acquired that almost mystical touch of greatness by which virtually everything they recorded was invested with distinction and grace. In falling victim to the ego battles that undermine so many successful groups, they revealed themselves as terribly wasteful and self-destructive, but also engagingly human. For a time, they had it all, and at their very best created some of the finest music written by anyone from their generation. Now, without Crosby, they were forced to re-establish their standing in the most difficult circumstances imaginable.

CHAPTER TWENTY-SIX

Nashville

FOLLOWING the release of *The Notorious Byrd Brothers*, the Byrds began touring as a trio with the recently recruited Kevin Kelley. It was a challenging period during which they secured regular bookings on the college circuit for the first time. Previously, Crosby had objected to performing for students on the grounds that rock music should not be intellectualized. The Byrds would henceforth ignore such taboos, eagerly playing before any audience or venue that would offer them a reasonable booking. Although gigs were forthcoming, it was clear that the Byrds found great difficulty performing their studio material live and required a fourth player before embarking on a major tour. "We were playing these little gigs and it was terrible," McGuinn recalls. "It was really not a good time with the three of us. We definitely needed someone."

In choosing the right candidate, hard decisions needed to be made concerning the group's musical direction following the stupendous *The Notorious Byrd Brothers*. The ambitious McGuinn felt that they should continue to experiment freely. Paul Beaver had played synthesizer on the last album and McGuinn also rented his own model, which had been employed on 'Moog Raga', a slightly whimsical fusion of electronic and Eastern music that had been dropped from *Notorious* at the eleventh hour. In addition to electronica, McGuinn was eager to continue the jazz-inspired rock previously perfected on 'Eight Miles High'. Hillman, always receptive to new ideas and a jazz buff himself, had no cause to disagree with McGuinn's latest ambitions. With the Byrds' continued good standing in the underground press it made perfect sense to capitalize on the excellent reviews of *The Notorious Byrd Brothers* and establish themselves in the newly thriving albums market. Accordingly, McGuinn decided to hire a keyboard player.

While the Byrds were pondering their musical future, business manager Larry Spector was eager to promote a new talent. Gram Parsons was an exotic country singer, whose background resembled the scarred pages of a Tennessee Williams play. Born Cecil Ingram Connor in Winter Haven, Florida, on 5 November 1946, he was the grandson of citrus fruit baron, John Snively. Despite all the material advantages of old Southern money, Ingram was surrounded by a dysfunctional family in which alcoholism was rife. His father, the preposterously named Coon Dog Connor, suffered terrible mood swings and abruptly took his own life on 23 December 1958. His wife, Avis, subsequently married Robert Parsons, whose surname was adopted by the boy. Henceforth, he would be known as Gram Parsons. For a time, the family found a stability of sorts until Avis rapidly descended into alcoholism, culminating in her death from cirrhosis of the liver.

As his family disintegrated around him, Gram developed strong musical interests. While barely in his teens, he played in cover groups such as the Pacers, the Legends and the Rumors. By the age of 16, he had graduated to folk music with the Village Vanguards and, in 1963, teamed up with his first professional outfit, the Shilos. Heavily influenced by the Kingston Trio and the Journeymen, the Shilos regularly played hootenannies, hospitals and high schools, punctuated by occasional big bookings such as a Cypress Gardens show in Chicago in honour of the visiting King Hussein of Jordan and a fund-raiser for an incoming Florida governor. Forays to Greenwich Village included appearances at the Bitter End and Gerde's Folk City. In March 1965, the group were booked to play the Bob Jones University, the degree mill from which the Reverend Ian Paisley received his postal doctorate. While there, they recorded some material at the college's radio station WMUU, which was finally released years later on the archive album, *The Early Years*. The work included a couple of Parsons' compositions and a reading of 'The Bells Of Rhymney' which, by uncanny coincidence, the Byrds were playing at Ciro's in Hollywood that same month. Not long after, Parsons fully realized the importance of Bob Dylan and was keen to pursue a folk-rock direction. He wrote to Shilos' bandmate Paul Surratt expressing such desires, but the group folded soon after.

Parsons quickly moved on, securing a place at Harvard, which accepted the rich kid in spite of his poor school record. His stay at the university was brief and inauspicious. He formed a new group, wrote songs, strummed guitar, dropped acid and dropped out. After falling in with child actor Brandon deWilde, he relocated to New York in late 1965 and formed the International Submarine Band, a vehicle for Parsons' pioneering fusion of soul and country, a form he later self-consciously dubbed 'Cosmic American Music'.

The tortuous career path of the International Submarine Band is dealt with extensively in the second volume of this book. Suffice to say, they recorded a couple of unsuccessful singles, 'The Russians Are Coming! The Russians Are Coming!' and 'Sum Up Broke', then moved to LA, where Parsons ingratiated himself with the hip elite of Hollywood. Peter Fonda invited the band to appear in the psychedelic movie *The Trip*, where they played a scene, miming to music actually recorded by the Electric Flag. Impressed by Parsons' promising songwriting and carefree style, Fonda even recorded one of his compositions, 'November Nights'. Crucially, Fonda also introduced Parsons to his business manager, Larry Spector.

After a few months, the ISB devolved into a bunch of jamming musicians, performing in bars around Southern California under a loose title coined by bassist Ian Dunlop: the Flying Burrito Brothers. With a line-up that included Barry Tashian and Billy Briggs of Boston's the Remains, this embryonic Burritos line-up played rockabilly and Western swing simply for enjoyment. Meanwhile, Gram fulfilled his Hank Williams' fantasies by appearing in various honky tonks and country bars, while celebrating the Bakersfield music scene of Buck Owens and Merle Haggard.

A contract with Lee Hazlewood's LHI Records saw Parsons working with guitarist John Nuese in a revamped International Submarine Band. In July 1967, they began an album which would not be released until the following spring. The delay distracted

Parsons, who always had the financial security to survive the worst of times in bacchanalian comfort. His wealthy Southern family had set up a trust fund in his name from which he was able to withdraw up to $100,000 a year. Appropriately enough, it was in a Beverly Hills bank during that same Summer of Love that he first met Chris Hillman.

A month before, Hillman had appeared at Monterey and was about to start work on *The Notorious Byrd Brothers*, an album that coincided with the most tempestuous changes in the group's fractious career. Hillman and Parsons did not form an instant friendship, but their social orbits collided infrequently over the succeeding months, usually at parties or other musicians' houses. They not only shared the same manager but also had a mutual love of country music which would prove crucial. In later years, Parsons claimed to have attended a session for the then untitled *The Notorious Byrd Brothers* during which the group playfully suggested calling their album *The Flying Burrito Brothers*. None of the other Byrds can now recall that evening, which may only have existed in Parsons' imagination, but considering all the turmoil they were experiencing, a memory lapse about such a trivial anecdote is hardly surprising. Several guests attended the *Notorious* recordings and it is probable that Parsons would have gained access to the sessions via Larry Spector. Significantly, Parsons told this story to reporters on at least two different occasions and the details were always unerringly consistent. "I was with Ian [Dunlop] while they were recording *The Notorious Byrd Brothers*, before they had a title for the album," Parsons insisted. "I just happened to go to a Byrds session . . . they were still doing their real Byrd tunes. Crosby was wearing his velvet hat. They said, 'Who are you playing with now?' and I said, 'Flying Burrito Brothers' over the microphone, because that's what we were calling the International Submarine Band, or some such nonsense. They all freaked out and wanted to use the name for the album and, if they had, we wouldn't have had a name. I told them they couldn't do it." Ian Dunlop, believes that Gram did attend a *Notorious* session and suspects that "moves were afoot [to join the Byrds] earlier than people are saying."

The canny Larry Spector had already sanctioned the reinstatement of Gene Clark after McGuinn and Hillman had fired David Crosby. When that failed to work out, it made sense to promote another of his clients who was more than eager to apply for a vacancy in the Byrds. "They needed another musician," Parsons recalled. "They were working as a trio at the time and they figured they needed a keyboard man." Parsons soon discovered that McGuinn was intent on projecting the group into the experimental area of future electronics and jazz.

"When I hired Gram Parsons, it was as a jazz pianist," McGuinn told me. "I had no idea that he was a Hank Williams character. He pretended to be a jazz player too . . . I was thinking more McCoy Tyner, who played with John Coltrane. That would have meant we could go further in *The Notorious Byrd Brothers* or 'Eight Miles High' direction." At a session break, Parsons thrilled Chris Hillman by singing Buck Owens' 'Under Your Spell Again', which was far removed from McGuinn's job requirements, but the Byrds' leader remained unfazed. While ignoring Parsons' other qualities, he accepted him solely on the strength of his keyboard abilities.

During February, Parsons augmented the trio for their East Coast/Midwest series of 'college dates'. At first, he was a low-key presence, largely unnoticed by reviewers, but when the Byrds played in Michigan, a sharp-eyed university reporter detailed key changes in the sound: "The organ adds needed depth to the concert performance but seriously detracts from the well-known Byrds style. The Byrds have always depended on crystal clear guitar work, threading the rhythm with the lead, to bring off their songs. But the organ muffles McGuinn's guitar to a great extent and the audience can only hear snatches of his beautiful riffs. The group definitely needs a good rhythm man again."

This was a rare occasion when the ghost of David Crosby returned to haunt the group, even though he was not mentioned by name. Generally, the college dates were well-received and McGuinn was particularly proud to receive a standing ovation in Michigan. Parsons was confident enough to feature a recently completed composition, 'Hickory Wind'. Hillman also revived 'Satisfied Mind', a song common to both the Byrds and the International Submarine

Band. Although they were still playing some material from *The Notorious Byrd Brothers*, the latest additions to the set suggested that the group was leaning more towards country rather than jazz or electronics.

While attempting to re-establish the group on the live circuit, McGuinn and Hillman were carefully ensuring that they took control of the Byrds' name. Manager Larry Spector negotiated a new contract with CBS on which there were only two signatories: Christopher Hillman and James Roger McGuinn. All subsequent Byrds would be hired hands, irrespective of their creative contributions.

On 29 February 1968, CBS despatched a new contract to Hillman and McGuinn, care of Larry Spector's office on Brighton Way, Beverly Hills. The document bound the duo to CBS for the next seven years, commencing on 1 March 1968. After four years with the company and a fairly good track record, the Byrds were obviously keen to improve upon the agreement they had signed back in November 1964. The major difference between the two contracts naturally lay in the advances and royalties. Before the era of 'Mr Tambourine Man', CBS had cautiously offered an 'advance' which merely consisted of a non-returnable payment at the rate of union scale following each recording session. The renewal offered an advance of $150,000, with $125,000 paid on signature, followed by annual payments of $5,000 on each succeeding year from 1969–73, inclusive. The original royalty of 10 per cent of the applicable wholesale price of a record was amended to 12 per cent, on condition that a Columbia staff producer was employed, with 2 per cent deducted if they chose an independent producer. After four years had elapsed, the group was promised a 14 per cent royalty on recordings after 1971, again with the proviso of a 2 per cent reduction should they employ an outside producer.

The remainder of the contract did not differ markedly from its 1964/65 counterpart and included some onerous stipulations, especially in the area of recordings required by CBS. For the next seven years, the Byrds were contracted to produce an annual minimum of "*four* long playing 33⅓ rpm record sides" which the company would record. The company also reserved the right to demand a further two record sides per year. This meant that CBS could effectively demand the equivalent of three albums a year from the Byrds and certainly expected a minimum of two albums annually. In addition, they reserved the right to record a fourth album in any single one-year period, although that was at least subject to the group's consent. The company's obligations did not extend beyond releasing one long playing album per year and "two single recordings" (one single). If the terms of the contract were adhered to then the Byrds could well be locked in the studio for months. The subsidiary clauses were more familiar, but no less revealing. CBS retained the right to appoint an A&R producer subject to the group's approval; the company would pay all "accompaniment costs" for hired musicians, plus studio and engineering charges, all of which would be treated as advances to be deducted from any future royalties. Finally, there were a long list of clauses allowing the company to reduce the aforementioned royalty rates by half. These included sales outside the USA; all sales of pre-recorded tape; "club operations" such as the Columbia Record Club; and records "sold to clients for promotional sales incentive or educational purposes". Overall, it was a tough contract, the chief advantage of which was the immediate injection of funds that did not have to be shared with David Crosby, Michael Clarke or Gene Clark. In this sense, the break-up of the Byrds in late 1967 had worked to McGuinn and Hillman's fiscal, if not artistic, benefit. Or so it seemed.

Relations between McGuinn, Hillman and Spector remained cordial, but ambivalent. Spector lacked the passion or belief of Jim Dickson, but that was not necessarily seen as a disadvantage at a time of rebuilding. The financial injection from CBS provided a boost for McGuinn and Hillman, but there is no evidence that they studied the new contract with a careful eye. Their publishing affairs had also altered significantly over the past year. In common with many managers acquiring an established act, Spector was keen to break with the past, wherever possible. Prior to *Younger Than Yesterday*, Dickson and Tickner had verbally agreed to split the publishing of Tickson Music with the group "in order to benefit Michael and Chris who weren't writing at the time". According to Dickson, he and Tickner were already paying out money on that basis, but all that changed after Crosby brought in Spector. As part of the negotiated settlement, it was agreed that the Byrds would surrender part of this improved share-out in order to break free and establish a new publishing company. "I assume Larry Spector's idea was that they would have all this great new stuff, and that little bits of the past wouldn't matter," says Dickson. "So they signed that back to us. As it turned out the future would be much bleaker than that. They'd traded away part of the past for the future."

Crosby had already issued bitter broadsides about Spector, but as he had also fallen out with Dickson, his opinions were seen as nothing more than sour grapes. Roadie Jim Seiter, although inexperienced in the world of finance, caught some of the negative feelings on visits to Spector's office and often wondered about his motives. He warned McGuinn to take a keener interest in the Byrds' business affairs, but his words fell on deaf ears. "McGuinn at the time was very aloof to it," he says. "He wouldn't go in the office much because Gene Clark was around there a lot. None of them really wanted to be near Gene, so they stayed away."

For a time, the Byrds spoke well of Spector and seemed impressed by his sophistication, breeding and manners. They'd heard about his connection with the Max Factor family, but weren't too sure what that actually entailed. There was a social gulf between Spector and the Byrds, and a sexual and emotional one too. But he certainly dressed and sounded like a gentleman and was regarded as a fine host. "He had this black maid who served dinner when he had people over," recalls McGuinn's then wife, Dolores. "The four of us were invited to Larry's – Roger and I, Chris and his wife, Anya. Larry had this guy who was sort of a gofer. We went up there and we were knocking on the door . . . and thinking, 'What's going on?' The kid opened the door and his hair was all mussed up. I didn't think anything of it until we left. When we were in the car, Chris and Roger were roaring and laughing about it. It didn't occur to me what was going on. I was always dumb about those things. That evening Roger wore this green mohair suit that had lapels on it. Later when Chris and Gram wrote that song ['Sin City'] I was always intrigued about that reference to 'green mohair suits'."

Although McGuinn and Hillman had secured complete control

of the Byrds' name, the recruitment of Gram Parsons was instantly threatening to take their music in an unexpected direction. "We had given him the opportunity of a lifetime," says Hillman. "We had just hired this kid off the street to join the Byrds. We were splintered. There were just two of us out of the original five and we were saying, 'What are we doing here?' We'd already [had] our minor success and tasted that. We were a bit like jaded guys by then, even though we were in our early twenties." Singing along with Gram on tunes he had himself played during his period with the Hillmen, Chris became convinced that the Byrds should reconsider their musical policy and add stronger country elements. He cited 'Time Between', with its distinctive Clarence White guitar picking, as evidence of the group's familiarity with the genre. More recent compositions such as 'Change Is Now' and 'Old John Robertson' had indicated that beneath the psychedelic sound effects there lurked a keen country influence which, in the wake of Crosby's departure, might be brought to the fore. Drummer Kevin Kelley enjoyed playing both country and jazz, which meant there was now a powerful lobby within the Byrds' camp eager to try something new. "I knew this music," says Hillman. "I was playing in hardcore country bars south of LA, with a fake ID, when I was 19. But Gram understood the music too, and he knew how to sing it . . . Gram was ambitious, full of vinegar and ready to go."

The problem lay in persuading McGuinn to take the country route which would, presumably, mean sacrificing his twin dream of an electronic-jazz Byrds. While McGuinn, with his folk background, would be capable of contributing significantly to such a work, there seemed little likelihood that he would agree to such a fundamental change of direction. Unbelievably, the head Byrd not only accepted the idea but offered his enthusiastic support. Like Hillman, he was impressed by Parsons' passion and agreed that the Byrds needed to expand their audience. The eloquent Parsons had conjured a wonderful piece of sophistry convincing them that country music produced in Nashville sold worldwide to millions of record buyers. His favourite aphorism was "Once the country audience accepts you, they stay with you forever". Evidently, nobody questioned his statistics or argued with his logic.

"We thought country was a fun place to dabble in," McGuinn says, "but Gram wanted to go there the whole hog. It was a burning desire on his part." McGuinn accepted that if they were to record some country tracks they should travel to Nashville. This was a daring proposition as no established rock group had ever attempted to bridge such disparate musical cultures.

Parsons was fearless in pursuing his ambitions, prompting McGuinn to quip, "it was like one of the Rolling Stones had just joined my band". At this point, however, McGuinn had no reason to assume his leadership was under challenge. Even though he had never played country music or shown any strong affinity for the genre, Roger had a musicologist's appetite for assimilating songs. He appreciated country within the context of the American folk tradition and anticipated the Nashville excursion as a brilliant opportunity to enhance his musical education. Like an academic investigating the South, McGuinn sounded as though he had just been perusing John Lomax's *Cowboy Songs And Other Frontier Ballads* or Cecil Sharp's *Folk Songs From The Southern Appalachians*, before concluding that country was now defiantly hip. "I loved it," he says. "I'd already been exposed to it through folk music. In fact country music is very closely related with folk music – the same sort of Anglo Saxon melodies that came out of the Appalachians. Same instruments. Bluegrass music was considered part of folk. It was like our country cousins and we were just going down there for a holiday."

Ever the method actor, even when playing the rustic visionary, McGuinn immersed himself in his new role. Much to the amazement of their Hollywood friends, Hillman and McGuinn cut inches off their hair, and Parsons and Kelley followed suit. It did not end there. They all bought cowboy boots and other paraphernalia and started acting like saloon outlaws in a Western movie: drinking whiskey and playing poker long into the night. It seemed the correct course of action. McGuinn went even further, visiting country bars and honky tonks like an explorer acclimatizing himself to an alien culture. At home, he switched his radio dial away from rock stations and listened only to country. He even bought a new Cadillac. With a minimum of exertion, Parsons and Hillman had effectively transformed McGuinn into a singing cowboy, ready to take on the Nashville establishment.

This was not the entire truth. Far from surrendering his grander ambitions, McGuinn had simply substituted one dream for another. Country, folk, jazz, electronic music – they were all contained within McGuinn's gargantuan scheme of things. It now occurred to him that even jazz and electronics were no longer adequate. What he desired was an even greater challenge and an opportunity to show the world that the Byrds could once again compete with the Beatles and push back the boundaries of popular music.

McGuinn's marvellous concept was a veritable history of twentieth-century music, beginning with traditional country, taking in R&B and rock, and ending with the most advanced form of electronic wizardry. "It was going to be a chronological thing," McGuinn recalls with a glint in his eye. "Like old-time bluegrass, modern country music, rock 'n' roll, then space music. It was meant to be a five-stage chronology." Gram Parsons was merely the key to stage one. Although it is difficult to imagine Parsons ever accepting the notion of 'space music', McGuinn spoke about his plans, confident that he had the full consent of the other members. They planned to cut 25 or 30 tracks, culminating in a double album which he promised would be released by early summer.

Before setting off for Nashville, Parsons had cause to consider his future with the International Submarine Band. He had not completely deserted them and was aware of his commitments to the LHI label, which was preparing for the spring release of the now overdue *Safe At Home*. "He's sort of up in the air between the International Submarine Band and us," McGuinn said at the time. "It depends on how their record goes." With each passing day, Parsons was drawn further away from his previous project which he now saw as a burden rather than an opportunity. It seemed increasingly likely that the Submarine Band would founder commercially, even with the extra publicity that Parsons' stint in the Byrds provided. Nevertheless, Parsons continued to string his former colleagues along, neither confirming nor denying his commitment to them.

The ISB's drummer Jon Corneal already suspected the worst.

NASHVILLE

Parsons had shown no interest in playing live with the band. Indeed, they had not performed a single gig since their reconstruction the previous summer. A conflict of interest emerged when the ISB were offered a touring opportunity, just as the Byrds were about to depart for Nashville. "We were supposed to open for the Turtles," Corneal recalls. "It was ten days for pretty good money and there were endorsements. We had Summ PA Systems and Ovation Guitars endorsing us and Ampeg were giving us a bass and an amp. Things were going our way." At the time, John Nuese's guitar lay in a repair shop. Corneal maintains Parsons used this as a pathetic excuse to defer a firm commitment to the tour. "John said it wasn't playing right, so all of a sudden he didn't have a guitar. It seemed a very small matter to me. You just get another guitar. Or we could have got another guitar player if Gram had wanted one. That was no problem – one phone call and I could've got someone. The bottom line was that Gram was using Nuese as an excuse to drop the whole deal and go with the Byrds. I thought that Larry Spector was a manipulator. I didn't ever see him socially. Gram had his meetings with him. I wasn't comfortable around the guy. I felt he was my enemy in that he pulled Gram away from the International Submarine Band before we really had a chance to do something. It was just very convenient for Gram to have an excuse to pull out of the whole deal."

The Byrds pencilled in a week-long session in Nashville, even though McGuinn and Hillman had no original material to record. Still reeling from the recent turmoil in the group, the frantic conclusion to *The Notorious Byrd Brothers* and weeks spent rehearsing with Kelley and Parsons for the 'college tour', Hillman had no time to put pen to paper. He still had some unused love songs lying around like 'Time For Love', 'Remember Love' and 'When Love Goes Bad', plus 'Relax Your Mind', but these were now deemed either stale or inappropriate for the new project. Parsons, never a prolific songwriter, only had two new compositions prepared, plus an oldie from the early ISB days. McGuinn had made no attempt at all, pointing out that he had zero experience of writing in a country vein. It hardly seemed to matter. There was a wealth of public domain songs at their disposal and no shortage of covers to choose from. More importantly, for the first time since 'My Back Pages', they were ready to re-enter the songbook of their former master.

At the beginning of 1968, Bob Dylan had just released *John Wesley Harding*, a stark but brilliant work, infused with biblical imagery, outlaw allegory and a landscape variously populated by the socially disadvantaged – the hobo, the drifter and the immigrant. After the electric maelstrom of 1966's *Blonde On Blonde*, its austere, acoustic setting was both challenging and prescriptive. But that was only part of the story. Critics and fans were equally intrigued by the recent missing link in Dylan's recording history that became known as the 'Basement Tapes'. In the aftermath of his 1966 motorcycle accident, Dylan – along with several members of what became the Band – lay low in Woodstock, filling up reels of tape in the basement of the house known as 'Big Pink'. The material anticipated the aural quietude of *John Wesley Harding*, but was more surreal lyrically and far more diverse in its musical palette. Steeped in the traditions of the great American songbook, the tapes revealed the extent of Dylan's range: at times playful, satirical and comedic; elsewhere grave, ascetic and apocalyptic. Amazingly, none of these songs was revived for inclusion on the recent *John Wesley Harding*. Instead, they lay untouched like a treasure trove of undiscovered gems.

Dylan had been absurdly prolific, even by his standards, and left behind a breathtaking number of compositions, enough to fill several archival albums. His astute manager Albert Grossman was keen to tap this unused material and soon a publisher's acetate of at least 14 songs was being channelled to various parties for consideration as covers. In the past, Dylan's music publishers would have contacted Jim Dickson directly about such material, but he was long gone. Surprisingly, it was Hillman who received either a reel tape or acetate in the mail, which he dutifully passed over to McGuinn for inspection. Everyone spoke about the 'Basement Tapes' in hushed whispers back then as we were still a year away from the 'release' of the first rock era bootleg album, *The Great White Wonder*, which featured several of its songs. What McGuinn heard was a mouth-watering collection of tunes, several of which seemed uncannily appropriate for their 'Nashville project'. "It was interesting to hear him simultaneously going in the same musical direction we were," he says. Impressed by the tone of the compositions, he imagined Dylan's frame of mind. "I can hear the despair, the way he was probably holed up after this motorcycle accident. He's immobilized, it's grey and cloudy, he's suffering from colour deprivation." Not that it was all bleak. Equally encouraging was the mounting evidence that some of this arcane work had undoubted commercial potential. Back in the UK, Manfred Mann – who had already enjoyed chart success with covers of 'If You Gotta Go, Go Now' and 'Just Like A Woman' – hit the jackpot with an exuberant reading of 'Mighty Quinn' which soared to number 1 in February. Even while McGuinn was deciding which 'Basement Tapes' selections to record, Julie Driscoll & The Brian Auger Trinity had cut a thrilling, jazz-tinged reworking of 'This Wheel's On Fire', which was soon heading towards the UK Top 5. If nothing else, it augured well for the Byrds.

On 9 March, the group arrived, uncharacteristically promptly, at Nashville Columbia's Studio A. They were greeted by steel guitarist Lloyd Green, a highly experienced session player who had worked with countless country legends from Porter Wagoner to Lynn Anderson. Fittingly, the first song they worked on that Saturday morning was Dylan's 'You Ain't Going Nowhere'. Sitting at the steel guitar, Green asked, "Where do you want me to play?" Almost in unison, they responded, "Everywhere!" Green was stunned. Nobody, during his entire working life in Nashville, had ever spoken to him with such imprecise instructions nor offered such unrestrained freedom. It was almost intimidating – and required considerable thought. They appeared to consider the arrangement as much his creation as their own. "I was used to doing an intro to a song, laying out for eight bars, then filling in at different spots. It was pretty formulaic . . . I came from a Nashville perspective, where everything is pristine and [there are] no flaws. Their music had a roughness, but it was part of the magic. This was the first time I'd cut anything with a group outside the country or gospel mainstream . . ."

That first day in Nashville ended on a high as Parsons introduced his latest composition, 'Hickory Wind', which had all the hallmarks of a Nashville standard. It was a brilliant start to the sessions and the Byrds wasted no time in celebrating their arrival at Music Row. Lloyd Green was fascinated to see that they had already armed themselves with a clay jar, brimming with Portuguese rosé wine. "I didn't smoke pot or anything, but I did drink a little of that wine," he remembers. "Every day they'd bring in a 12-bottle case, and by the end of the day all of it was gone. It tasted good in the moment, but I got the world's worst headaches. They were smoking a lot. That was the first time I saw the studio lit up with marijuana smoke. I was getting a little heady."

During their free Sunday, Parsons reconnected with the International Submarine Band's drummer Jon Corneal, who was currently completing a move from Nashville to Los Angeles. Corneal was concerned about his own future. He had agreed to relocate to LA solely to work with the ISB and here was Parsons in Nashville, seemingly committed to the Byrds. Increasingly sceptical about Gram's intentions, he sought clarification, but received only vague responses. Perhaps as a sop to Corneal, Parsons invited him to the studio the next day to play on 'Lazy Days', a year old composition of questionable quality. Parsons appeared to have a blind spot about the song. It had already been recorded by the original line-up of the International Submarine Band for possible inclusion in Roger Corman's drug-inspired movie *The Trip* but was roundly rejected as completely inappropriate. Heavily indebted to Chuck Berry, it seemed equally out of place here and was never seriously considered as a contender for the album. While Parsons may simply have been attempting to placate Corneal, there is good reason for assuming that he genuinely believed in the song's potential. A couple of years later it would be revived by the Flying Burrito Brothers and included on their second album, *Burrito Deluxe*.

Over the next four days, the Byrds completed 'Pretty Boy Floyd', 'I Am A Pilgrim', 'Nothing Was Delivered', plus two cuts that they ultimately rejected. Parsons' laborious reading of Tim Hardin's 'Reputation' sounded like a leftover from his coffee house days and had nothing in common with the country material they were recording. By contrast, McGuinn's 'Pretty Polly' was a traditional murder ballad that fitted well within the conceptual parameters of the album. A familiar staple in the repertoires of both country and folk performers, it had previously featured on the Dillards' 1964 album, *Live!!! Almost!!!,* produced by Jim Dickson. "I'd known the song since my days at the Old Town School of Folk Music," McGuinn recalls, "and had always loved the modal tuning on the banjo and guitar in spite of the morbid lyrics." In Nashville, he had a rare opportunity to play his 12-string Rickenbacker on the track. Although he felt it was a strong candidate for release, McGuinn soon met resistance from within the band. "Chris Hillman discouraged me. He knew 'Pretty Polly' from the bluegrass days and was probably sick of playing it." Already, it was evident that McGuinn was under pressure to defer to Hillman and Parsons in the choice of material. But a far bigger concession would soon follow.

Parsons took full advantage of his time in Music City, frequenting country bars, braving open mike nights and immersing himself in his George Jones persona. Sometimes the other Byrds tagged along. Gregarious road manager Jim Seiter also had fun impressing the locals with technological wonders and was treated like a cross between Alexander Graham Bell and the Wizard of Oz. Even the studio engineers raised their eyebrows when he rigged together two 8-track recorders and synchronized them to create a 16-track effect. "We had musicians from all over town coming down just to watch this," he says. "It was like a circus."

Lloyd Green, the venerable steel player who had suffered wine-induced headaches throughout the week, was mightily impressed by the Byrds' industry, audacity and courage. "Nobody of that calibre had even come to Nashville to perform before. And none of the other rock groups would have entertained the notion of making such an album. But the Byrds did it."

Not everything went according to plan. Midway through the week, the group were booked to appear on country DJ Ralph Emery's radio show on WSM to promote 'You Ain't Going Nowhere' (evidently earmarked as their next single). A culture clash ensued. The normally urbane host was unfamiliar with Hollywood based groups and suspicious of Bob Dylan, who was still seen as an icon of the counterculture and therefore an enemy of Nashville. "I don't think he liked what Dylan stood for," says McGuinn, "and he didn't like us either." Wary of broadcasting anything controversial, Emery turned to McGuinn and asked: "What's the song about?" Roger was amused by the question, which he knew was impossible to answer. "Well, it's a Bob Dylan song," he said, as if that was enough to explain everything.

Emery was unamused by the droll response, which he misinterpreted as disrespectful. The recording was reluctantly played without reference to its opaque lyrics, but there was a cold rapport between the DJ and his hosts. Off air, he even challenged Lloyd Green about his current choice of employment. "Ralph was outrageously confrontational," says Green. "Sarcastic and condescending. And he was a friend of mine! I recorded with this guy. He looked at me and said, 'Lloyd, what are you doing lending your talents to this kind of stuff?' It was almost like he was accusing me of committing a crime." Parsons was particularly soured by the experience and on a subsequent visit to London got together with McGuinn to compose a satiric reply, 'Drug Store Truck Drivin' Man'. Alas, it was never recorded while Parsons was in the group.

On 15 March, the Byrds made music book history as the first pop/rock group to perform at that bastion of country ideology, the *Grand Ole Opry*. Originally titled the *WSM Barn Dance* when it was first broadcast in 1925, it was renamed two years later, partly as an in-joke based on the fact that it was preceded on air by NBC's *Music Appreciation Hour*, which featured selections from grand opera. Over the years, the venue for the show was moved but since 1948 it had been housed in the majestic Ryman Auditorium. The *Opry* featured country music's elite performing before a partisan audience. At its peak it had been broadcast nationally and at the time of the Byrds' appearance reached approximately 30 US states. During its long history, the show had weathered a handful of minor controversies, largely of its own making. A strict ban on using drums had been flouted by Western swing king, Bob Wills; Hank Williams had been banned for missing some shows and stripped of his membership; Elvis Presley had appeared only once and was chastened by the experience, vowing never to return. The Byrds had no intention of offending their hosts and seemed keen to make a good impression. They dressed casually, but reasonably smartly by their standards, and Kelley agreed to appear onstage standing up with just a snare drum and brushes in acknowledgement of the strict rules.

There is no doubt that Parsons felt honoured to be allowed to perform. He was so thrilled by the prospect that he invited several members of his extended family to attend. Hillman was equally enthusiastic. "From my point of view, it was a great experience because I'd grown up worshipping the *Grand Ole Opry*. It was beyond my wildest dreams to have the chance to play there . . . If it hadn't been for CBS Records, who had considerable power and clout down there, we would never have got on. They just didn't want us down there at all. Don't get me wrong. Not everybody disliked us. People like John Hartford, Lloyd Green, Junior Huskey . . . helped us a lot. But there is a sort of Nashville establishment who are very critical of infiltrators coming along to nibble at their end of the music business, and they were staunch in the opposition to us."

"Nobody who was part of that scene wanted us to be on there," adds McGuinn, "and you could feel the resentment. They didn't think we were real and they were pretty protective of their little society."

It must have been intimidating as the Byrds entered the Auditorium. Parsons assumed the central microphone position, flanked by Kelley who looked strangely vulnerable standing head down, with only a single snare drum to his name. McGuinn and Hillman were located stage right, huddled together in front of a single microphone. They were dwarfed by a large sign placed by the *Opry*'s original sponsors, the National & Accident Insurance Company. "Life Insurance For Every Member Of The Family," it proclaimed, a firm reminder of Nashville's filial values. Before they played a single note, the Byrds were subjected to a smattering of mocking barbs from the more conservative members of the audience. Some chanted "tweet tweet" and "get your hair cut" – which was funny considering that the Byrds had all recently visited the barbers. Steel guitarist Lloyd Green had offered support by joining them and he seemed more shocked than anybody by the reception. "I was so embarrassed I wanted to crawl off the stage. I didn't believe they would get such rude redneck treatment. I'm from Mobile, Alabama, and I didn't have those biases. I felt sadness that people would do that to musicians just because of their hair."

The ridicule was by no means universal and in fact dissipated once the Byrds began playing 'You Ain't Going Nowhere'. It was immediately evident that the group could play country and the crowd responded positively. "Initially, they were making fun of us," Hillman says, "but once they heard us play, and they heard a very brave man, Lloyd Green, who had the guts to get up there and play with us – really going against the peer pressure of Nashville – they *liked* us."

Along with Skeeter Davis, the Byrds had been alloted to appear during the 30-minute slot hosted by Tompall Glaser & The Glaser Brothers. Prior to the show, Glaser had been informed of the song selection and, as a newspaper report revealed just after the show, it was "suggested that, for the sake of public relations, they use the current [country] number 1 song, 'Sing Me Back Home', for their encore number." It was at this point that Parsons broke with protocol and wrote himself into the annals of *Opry* history. As Hillman recounts: "On the air, Tompall said: 'You're going to do Merle Haggard's 'Sing Me Back Home', aren't you?' And Gram said, 'No, we're going to do 'Hickory Wind' for my grandmother.'" McGuinn and Hillman were taken aback but managed to cope. As they came offstage, however, they faced the combined wrath of *Opry* officialdom. Country star Roy Acuff was appalled. Tompall Glaser was so incensed that he could be heard yelling at Gram: "How dare you. You made me look like a fool on the radio! You'll never work at the *Opry* again." The Byrds' sole ally backstage was fellow guest Skeeter Davis who showered them with hugs and kisses as if they had just returned from a war. "She was always sort of wacko down in Nashville," Hillman reflects. It cannot have escaped the Byrds' well-tuned sense of irony that Skeeter was the former wife of their nemesis, Ralph Emery.

Parsons' rebellious act ensured that the group would never be invited to play the *Opry* again. Not that they were remotely concerned by this setback. They took great pleasure in milking Skeeter Davis' support and dined out on the story for years afterwards. In numerous interviews, Parsons' bold gesture was paraded as a classic example of rock rebellion and a courageous attack upon staid Nashville tradition. Hillman told the story that way for years, claiming Gram was "right on the money" while cheerleading his revolt against pompous officialdom. Recently he has had a change of heart and now regrets the "humiliation" of Tompall Glaser while dismissing Parsons' trick as egocentric and thoughtless. "You know what, he shouldn't have done that. He was a guest on the *Opry*. You should *not* do that. That is disrespectful." In terms of defiance, Gram's action was not that far removed from the insurrectionist tactics of David Crosby. The Byrds had lost one giant ego and apparently inherited an even larger one.

Immediately after leaving the *Opry*, the group were rushed over to Vanderbilt University, to be interviewed on Radio WRVU by Earl Scruggs' son, Gary. Still buzzing from the conflict with Glaser, they relaxed in Scruggs' company and conducted an informal phone-in, fielding questions from local listeners and old fans. There was one funny moment when a crazed caller accused the Byrds of being "dirty commies", but they soon twigged it was the mischievous Hillman, who had snuck downstairs to make the spoof call. At least the Byrds had ended their stay in Nashville on a humorous note.

CHAPTER TWENTY-SEVEN

Stonehenge

AFTER completing the Nashville sessions for their country album, the Byrds set out on a short tour, accompanied by a mystery steel guitarist, cryptically referred to as 'J.D'. This was, in fact, Jay Dee Maness, one of the session musicians who had assisted in the recording of the International Submarine Band's *Safe At Home*. One of the first gigs featuring the quintet took place at Derek Taylor's farewell party, on 28 March 1968. Rather fittingly, Taylor had chosen Ciro's, the venue at which the Byrds first received critical acclaim, as the site for his final night in Hollywood. It was a unique gathering of friends, old and new, and among the guests were several of the dance troupe who had religiously followed the original line-up back in 1965. When their time came to take the stage, the Byrds delighted the audience by combining their country & western style numbers with a series of familiars from their illustrious past, including 'Chimes Of Freedom', 'Mr Tambourine Man', 'Eight Miles High' and 'He Was A Friend Of Mine'. During the festivities, they were joined onstage by Gene Clark but it was not exactly a glorious reunion. As Derek Taylor remembered: "Gene was drunk. He sung a few songs with them but stayed up there too long. There was mild irritation. The Byrds never really got on. They were always marvellously dangerous."

Roadie Jim Seiter had been warned about Clark's likely intentions, but could do nothing to prevent him from securing the spotlight. "I couldn't have stopped him if I'd been 400 lb. They told me specifically that Gene was going to be there and that I had to keep him offstage as much as possible. 'He's going to be drunk, obnoxious, out of tune and he'll want to get onstage and, if he does, it will suck.' All I knew was that he was really drunk, and staggering. I'd never seen him quite like that before. Of course, I couldn't stop him. He virtually ran up on the stage from all the way across the floor, grabbed the mike and started singing. He sang 'Mr Tambourine Man' which sucked, then he pulled a harmonica out of his pocket, which I guess he hadn't played for a while."

Numerous attempts were made to coax Clark off the stage, but he was obviously enjoying himself too much to pay any attention to whispers from the wings. Observing from behind the amps, Seiter witnessed a preposterously melodramatic exit. "He fell flat on his back at my feet. McGuinn's old lady was tugging on him, trying to get him offstage. Then she lost hold of him. He slipped, fell backwards, fell over an amplifier and his head hit hard on the stage at my feet. And I looked down at him and the look in his eyes was incredible. He jumped up, almost superhumanly, and he ran off the stage, straight through the people and gone. We didn't see him for months after that. It was terrible. He did that many times. Gene's whole life got shattered when he left the group. All of a sudden he was walking around Hollywood and he wasn't a Byrd any more. That hit him hard, man. He came to many gigs, drunk as a skunk. He was just a slob and a mess and I had to deal with him and keep him away from the band when they were onstage, because he'd try and get up there." Seiter was astonished by Clark's drunken dexterity, but equally amazed by the deadpan reaction of the Byrds after his departure. "They just kept on playing and never said anything. Not a word. They didn't even acknowledge to the audience that anything had happened. I looked at Hillman and shrugged my shoulders. He shook his head and just looked down. Nothing more. I muttered, 'What can you do, man?' But Gene never appeared after that."

At the beginning of April, Columbia rushed out 'You Ain't Going Nowhere' in the US. Despite the country elements, most noticeably Lloyd Green's sterling steel guitar work, the single came as no great shock to critics or fans. It was very much in the classic Byrds tradition – an unreleased Dylan song, featuring McGuinn on lead vocal. Parsons' presence was undetectable vocally and radio listeners were reassured by Roger's familiar Dylanesque drawl from the very opening line of the song. In different circumstances, it might have been a hit. Unfortunately, promotional work on the single was limited and its timing regrettable. Only two days after its release, the group was scheduled to re-enter the studio to complete work on the new album.

McGuinn was still upbeat about the Byrds' future at this point. Prior to the recent Ciro's show, he had told journalist Jerry Hopkins that the current line-up was less problematical than its predecessors. "There are fewer hang-ups now. Before, we had some stars to contend with. It's much tighter now. The new group is better than the old one. There are fewer errors. There's no grandstanding." He was looking forward to recording the electronic segment of the album and had already ordered a synthesizer in anticipation. The 'chronology of twentieth-century music' concept was still uppermost in his mind. "We don't have a title for the album yet," he added. "That'll come in time. And it probably will have something to say about time – backward, forward, something – because the music we're doing will cover a lot of time."

Later that month, American television viewers could be forgiven for thinking that they were witnessing some unexplained time shift worthy of *The Twilight Zone*. While the group were promoting 'You Ain't Going Nowhere' on ABC's *American Bandstand*, rivals NBC broadcast a bizarre cameo on the *Where The Boys Are* special dating back to the *Notorious* period. A mimed performance of 'Mr Spaceman' featured McGuinn and Gene Clark backed by Jim Seiter (deputizing for Chris Hillman) and the Association's Ted Bluechel guesting on drums. In another part of the filmed sequence, Michael Clarke was suddenly the featured drummer. As an ironic visual commentary on the convoluted comings and goings during late 1967, this television oddity took some beating.

McGuinn must have thought that the old conflicts were now in the past, but further trouble was brewing. While he continued to dream and formulate vague plans for executing his grand design, a subtly different powerplay was underway. When the Byrds convened at CBS' Hollywood studio on 4 April, Parsons suddenly appeared to be calling the shots. Over the next few weeks, they would record 'Life In Prison', 'You're Still On My Mind' and 'The Christian Life' – all with Parsons as lead vocalist. Hillman proffered another pastoral chestnut 'Blue Canadian Rockies' and even Kevin Kelley was granted a lead vocal on the excellent outtake 'All I Have Are Memories'. In addition to Jay Dee Maness, Parsons roped in pianist Earl Ball, another session player previously employed by the International Submarine Band. Clarence White later brought along his trusty white Telecaster to countrify some of these songs. By now, McGuinn had been overtaken by events. Somewhere along the way, his plan to record the electronic part of the album was jettisoned in favour of a fully fledged country & western project. "We split into two different camps at that stage and the country thing won," McGuinn admits. "Chris, Gram and Gary Usher just didn't want to go along with the electronic music idea, so I was outvoted."

One year later, McGuinn looked back at these events as if he had experienced an *Alice Through The Looking Glass* moment. "We hired a piano player and it turned out to be Parsons. A monster in sheep's clothing. And he exploded out of this sheep's clothing – 'God! It's George Jones! In a big sequin suit!' And he's got his guitar and sidemen accompanying him. He took it right into the eye of the hurricane and raaaaaaooow: came out the other side. It was Japanese."

McGuinn was not the only person feeling slightly disorientated. Some of the session players found the experience of working with the Byrds more than challenging. Lloyd Green was later flown in from Nashville just to help with Parsons' final recording: 'One Hundred Years From Now'. It seemed an extravagant expense. Prior to that, pianist Earl Ball had the taxing task of working with Buck Owens during the day and the Byrds in the evening. The transition felt odd. Owens had a strong work ethic, which meant songs were usually completed in a single session, a far cry from the Byrds' studied nonchalance. Sometimes, Ball barely had time to change out of the suit he wore for the king of Bakersfield before rushing over to his younger employers. As well as the sartorial and time differences, there was a psychological adjustment to consider. "With Buck Owens we had to get at least three songs done in our three-hour period. Then I'd go over and record with the Byrds where, if you got one song all night, you were doing good . . . the first thing they'd do was get high and try to tune their guitars. That was a challenge. I'd show up when I was supposed to, and sometimes me and the engineer would be the only people there. But I adapt to my surroundings pretty well. I would have smoked some pot with them, but I thought, 'I'll be lost, too!' So I stayed straight . . . there were enough people over the edge without me getting there with them."

With more live dates to fulfil, Parsons tried to persuade McGuinn to employ Jay Dee Maness on a full-time basis. McGuinn held out, however, and refused to acknowledge Maness as anything other than a 'temporary Byrd', at least for the present. Although he agreed that the steel guitarist could accompany the group for selected dates, McGuinn was reluctant to expand the line-up just to improve Parsons' solo spot. Maness now claims that he was reluctant anyway, particularly after the recent Ciro's debacle with Gene Clark. "I was miserable," he admits. "The band was so loud, and the music was so different from the record."

Parsons next approached Lloyd Green, who was more keen. He even agreed to grow his hair like a Beatle, but could not commit to an overseas tour due to his session commitments in Nashville. Having failed to recruit Maness or Green, Parsons next pushed for Sneaky Pete Kleinow. With Hillman in agreement, McGuinn suddenly found himself under tremendous pressure from all sides. His dream of the 'electronic' album had been postponed, if not cancelled, and steel guitarists were being offered gigs with the group by Parsons, sometimes before McGuinn had even been approached or consulted. Even Crosby had seldom challenged his leadership so effectively, and though McGuinn still believed he could control the Byrds' musical direction, his power and influence were waning. "Gram and Chris took over at that stage of the game," he concedes. "They really brought it into the country thing. That wasn't my idea but I went along with it because it sounded fun. It was totally their trip. They actually wanted to fire me and get Sneaky Pete in my place. In essence, they later did this by getting the Flying Burrito Brothers together."

In late April the Byrds returned to the Troubadour for a four-night residency. Michael Clarke, still living in Maui, was visiting Hollywood at the time and sat in with them on their opening night. There was the expected mixture of country songs and old Byrds' hits, but some critics were reluctant to accept the latest changes. "Roger, formerly Jim, McGuinn played his unique 12-string guitar only on 'Bells Of Rhymney'," complained one reviewer. "New singer Gram Parsons' C&W contributions will never make the *Grand Ole Opry*," he added, clearly unaware that Gram had already secured that unexpected accolade.

On 7 May, the Byrds undertook a surprise mini-European jaunt, commencing with an appearance at the grandly named 'First European International Pop Festival'. Evidently, Rome's belated answer to the Monterey International Pop Festival, this was intended to show off the city's credential as a rock emporium. The organizers had even succeeded in winning the endorsement of Mick Jagger as their 'working sponsor', and an impressive list of performers were promised. Unfortunately, poor sales and bad planning blighted the enterprise. Several of the acts had already pulled out before showtime and those that remained faced an embarrassingly poor turnout. The Byrds were supposed to appear at the indoor arena Palazzo Dello Sport in front of an estimated 30,000 spectators. By the time they arrived, the festival was in such dire straits that their section of the show was relocated to the nearby Piper Club, with an 800 audience capacity. Despite all the problems, the Byrds received a rousing welcome and their set was broadcast on both Italian and Dutch radio, ensuring good quality bootleg tapes would eventually seep out over the years.

Despite Parsons' failure to enlist a steel player, McGuinn had allowed banjoist Doug Dillard to accompany the group, thereby ensuring that the country tunes had an additional authentic bite. Although suffering some tuning problems, particularly on Parsons' contributions, the Byrds played a memorable set, highlighted by Dillard's incongruous but fascinating banjo-picking alongside McGuinn's familiar Rickenbacker ring on 'Feel A Whole Lot Better' and 'Chimes Of Freedom'. Long-term road manager, Jim Seiter, who accompanied the Byrds on their essay into Europe, recalls a pleasant time but was struck by some unspoken divisions in the group. "The Byrds basically stayed to themselves. McGuinn was McGuinn, and Hillman was Hillman. We took Doug Dillard with us to Europe and he was the wild one. It would be Dillard, myself and Gram. Kevin was sitting over in a corner reading a book. That band was very unusual and I wasn't surprised at all by what happened later."

Four days after Rome, the Byrds were back in Britain. CBS had just rushed out their new single, 'You Ain't Going Nowhere', while the recently released *The Notorious Byrd Brothers* was defying all expectations by climbing to number 12 in the album charts, their best showing since the glory days of 1965–66. In the US, *Notorious* had peaked at number 47 so its success in the UK, without the benefit of a single live appearance, television promotion or attendant hit single, was all the more impressive. By this point, of course, album sales were starting to eclipse those of singles in the UK and there had been a growing market for 'progressive' American albums, particularly fashionable imports from the Doors, Jefferson Airplane and the Grateful Dead, among others. *Notorious* was also the first Byrds album more readily available in stereo than mono, a feature which proved particularly attractive to hi-fi lovers. This was reflected in several reviews. "In stereo, this is even better," *Record Mirror* enthused. "Just listen to the guitar break in 'Change Is Now' in stereo!" The other three music weeklies, *New Musical Express*, *Melody Maker* and *Disc*, all lavished praise on the album, even though their readership still consisted largely of pop fans. The smaller circulation *Beat Instrumental* went further, insisting: "It's true to say that the Byrds are one of the two best groups in the world. Nobody can say any different with the proof of this album." Although these were still primarily capsule reviews, in keeping with the UK pop press of the time, the universal admiration was significant. When the Byrds learned of their autumnal appeal in the UK – a territory that they assumed still held prejudices going back to the 'America's Answer To The Beatles' tour of 1965 – they were genuinely pleased. "We were kind of astonished when *The Notorious Byrd Brothers* was a hit in Britain," McGuinn informed *Melody Maker*. "We had sort of given Britain up after 'Turn! Turn! Turn!'."

STONEHENGE

On 11 May, the Byrds were set to play a two-set show at the Middle Earth club in London's Covent Garden. This bastion of hippiedom ensured that they would be greeted by a partisan audience at a time when they were suddenly in vogue among the underground fraternity. Jeff Dexter, the resident DJ at Middle Earth, visited the Byrds at their hotel prior to their Saturday night show. A former mod turned hippie, he was supportive of their new fusion of rock and country. "They knew I had a passion for country music, so we got on very well. Doug Dillard was with them and I already liked the Dillards. What struck me as funny was going into the restaurant at the Mayfair Hotel and Doug was smoking a pipe, which I did too. He'd sit there at breakfast and lunch smoking this pipe full of dope. The people in this posh hotel thought it was strange American tobacco, because that's what he'd tell them. We talked about leys and the other hippie, trippy shit of the time."

Dexter was aware that McGuinn was into science fiction and flying saucers, as was the new boy Gram Parsons, whom Dexter instantly warmed to as a kindred spirit. He presented them with a copy of John Michell's esoteric book, *The Flying Saucer Vision: The Holy Grail Restored*, a pre-New Age treatise, linking Arthurian legend with UFOs. Wisely, Dexter ensured roadie Jim Seiter looked after the 'sacred' tome, knowing that it would otherwise be mislaid before they even reached their hotel suite. "Jimmi looked after everything," he recalls. "He was a driving force then. He didn't just look after the gear, he looked after the *other* gear too. Anything that was going, he was doing it, fixing it and running it. We got on well, especially when he discovered I had loads of acid."

Dexter told them that he was planning to visit Glastonbury Tor and the Stonehenge monument after the Middle Earth gig, presumably in the hope of seeing a flying saucer. A friend had nominated himself as driver and, more importantly, had a sizeable stash of dope. Parsons was particularly keen to tag along and sample some of Dexter's acid. A promising night beckoned.

Even though the Byrds had received relatively sparse coverage in the UK pop press since the epoch of 'Mr Tambourine Man', they had always enjoyed the patronage of their peers, most notably the Beatles and the Rolling Stones who had both championed them since 1965. At the time of the Middle Earth gig, Brian Jones, their greatest supporter in the Stones, was only days away from an appearance at Great Marlborough Street Magistrates' Court on a charge of possessing marijuana. His colleagues, Jagger and Richards, were in more sociable mood and seemed very keen to hang out with the Byrds during their stay. *Rock Family Trees* chronicler, Pete Frame, still a year away from establishing the underground music magazine *Zigzag*, attended the Byrds' late show, unaware of the recent radical musical changes they had experienced. It turned out to be a memorable affair. "Mick Jagger and Marianne Faithfull came in to witness the gig and were assisted to the front by a minder," Frame remembers. "Gram was wearing a translucent, silky black shirt and he sat at an electric piano for most of the gig. He played acoustic guitar now and then. He sang lead on several songs, but sang harmony on most, and he left all the talking to McGuinn and Hillman . . . They played past favourites plus a whole tranche of country numbers, which neither I nor the audience were expecting . . . *The Notorious Byrd Brothers*, which I consider one of the greatest albums ever released, had only just come out and they appeared to have changed their style completely since then."

That last point was only partially true, but summed up the element of surprise felt by many in attendance. It was a strange experience witnessing the country-tinged Byrds, augmented by Doug Dillard, seemingly attempting to promote an album that represented their most progressive and pronounced foray into psychedelia. This inner conflict produced arguably the most eclectic and exhilarating repertoire that the group would ever perform. It was akin to watching two groups: the old Byrds and the new Byrds, functioning as one. McGuinn may not yet have achieved his aim of recording a history of twentieth-century music, but in concert he was providing a microcosm of that vision, ingeniously using the group to illuminate its own strange odyssey. At Middle Earth, and the following night's show at Blaises, the selection of songs was stupendous. There was 'Mr Tambourine Man', 'The Bells Of Rhymney', 'Feel A Whole Lot Better', 'Chimes Of Freedom', even 'We'll Meet Again' – all representing the all-important first album; more favourites followed, including 'Turn! Turn! Turn!', 'Eight Miles High',

STONEHENGE

'5 D', 'My Back Pages' segueing into 'Baby, What You Want Me To Do', 'So You Want To Be A Rock 'n' Roll Star' and onwards to 'Goin' Back', 'Tribal Gathering' and 'Space Odyssey'. Like a set within a set, Gram Parsons came forward to offer selections from their next album, including 'You Don't Miss Your Water' and 'The Christian Life', plus covers that would never be heard on any Byrds studio record such as Merle Haggard's 'Sing Me Back Home', Buck Owens' 'Under Your Spell Again' and the Owens/Harlan Howard collaboration, 'Excuse Me, I Think I've Got A Heartache'. McGuinn returned to his folk roots for 'Pretty Boy Floyd' and even Doug Dillard was allowed a cameo virtuoso banjo performance on Flatt & Scruggs' 'Foggy Mountain Breakdown'.

The critics in attendance were impressed. One report noted that the Byrds "were called back countless times by a mainly hippie audience, and DJ Jeff Dexter nearly ran out of nauseous hippie jargon with which to praise them." Decades on, Dexter reprises some of that old effusion. "It was fantastic. Listen, I was on a trip and enjoying every moment of it. A wonderful night. We were eight miles high. It was a wonder I could actually speak. What do you expect from a dodgy old hippie? It was beautiful the way Doug played banjo that night. I was going completely crazy because I loved that banjo. It was fabulous, especially on acid. And he smoked his pipe during the set as well!"

Politically, these gigs were a masterstroke. By featuring songs from every one of the Byrds' albums, McGuinn was asserting their historical importance, while placing Parsons in the subsidiary role as their 'new find'. McGuinn was simultaneously accommodating Parsons by allowing him full rein, while also proving emphatically that the Byrds was his own property. Inevitably, both Italian and British audiences warmed to the familiar Byrds' songs, while politely acknowledging the country numbers. This was a powerplay disguised as a welcome compromise. It is notable that in this battle of wills and egos, Hillman was squeezed out of the middle in live performance. His only vocal cameo was on 'Old John Robertson'. The opportunity to feature even one of his key contributions from *Younger Than Yesterday* ('Time Between', 'Have You Seen Her Face', 'Thoughts And Words', 'The Girl With No Name') in this onstage history lesson was never taken. Similarly, while Parsons introduced the country material from the new album, Hillman did not come to the microphone to attempt 'Blue Canadian Rockies' or 'I Am A Pilgrim'. He stood back while McGuinn and Parsons played out their creative battle for leadership and, like so many artistic conflicts in the Byrds, the true victors were ultimately the lucky listeners who heard more great music than they could ever have imagined.

There was more good news for McGuinn when the new single, 'You Ain't Going Nowhere', began to receive extensive airplay. This was the new country Byrds but it was also unmistakably McGuinn. Both critics and fans instantly picked up on the Dylan connection, re-establishing a link that went back to 'Mr Tambourine Man'. "Seems that everyone has discovered Bob Dylan all over again and is rushing to record his songs!" Derek Johnson exclaimed in *NME*. "Still we can hardly blame the Byrds for doing so, as they've been there from the beginning." Unsurprisingly, Parsons' name was not mentioned once. The other music papers also rallied around the Byrds, praising the new single, which sounded like a palpable hit. "This Dylan song must shoot the high-flying Byrds in the charts again," *Record Mirror* insisted. The paper wasn't too far wrong. Over the next month, the single hovered just below the charts, eventually peaking at number 45, the first time the Byrds had hit the UK Top 50 since 'Eight Miles High'.

Meanwhile, interviewers of the period flocked to McGuinn and Hillman for comments on the 'new' Byrds, and showed only passing interest in Parsons, who quickly realized that his domination of the group in Nashville meant little to the world's media. A telling photo shoot in the *Daily Mirror* newspaper pictured McGuinn and Hillman standing confidently in front of the camera, pointing at Parsons and Kelley in the background, as if they were salaried hands. It was an image that reflected an economic reality and also ingrained the notion that the Byrds were a two-tier group – the old and the new. McGuinn spoke unusually frankly to the press, providing shock revelations, most notably the previously unheard story of how he was the only Byrd to have played on the million-selling 'Mr Tambourine Man'. In this way, he asserted his importance as the man who had formulated the group's sound, and nobody could doubt that he was still King Byrd. Any hopes Parsons may have harboured of enforcing some kind of coup ended at this moment.

Having graced the Byrds with their presence at Middle Earth, Jagger and Richards decided to take them on a hip tourist trip to Stonehenge, the prehistoric archaeological wonder beloved of Druids and neo-pagans. Several small limousines were employed for the excursion which, in addition to the Byrds, included Mick and Keith's respective partners, Marianne Faithfull and Anita Pallenberg, McGuinn and Hillman's wives, Dolores DeLeon and Anya Butler, and photographer and friend of the Stones, Michael Cooper. Jeff Dexter, who had previously invited Parsons to join him on the trip, was swiftly jettisoned. "Gram came over and said, 'I'm not going with you, I'm going with *them*.' They'd hijacked him! I felt a bit miffed but I suppose if you're a rock 'n' roll star you want to go with other rock 'n' roll stars, not some dodgy DJ. I didn't think it was right to go to Stonehenge in a limo. We still got there before them, even though they had a limo, and I agreed to catch up with them the next day."

Stonehenge was a few hours' drive away and the intention was to see the stones at sunrise. This was a modern day 'pilgrimage' in which hunger and sore feet were replaced by pop star provisions and chauffeur-driven luxury. Unfortunately, when they reached the Wiltshire wilds, it was disconcertingly rainy and cold. It was also long after sunrise. Chilled to the bone in their flimsy rock finery, they fortified themselves with regular swigs from a bottle of Johnnie Walker Red whisky. Dolores remembers the limos could only get within about half a mile of the monuments, so they were forced to traipse through muddy fields in the misty rain, ruining several pairs of shoes. The ever courteous Jagger later sent out his driver to supply them all with a change of socks. "Mick and Keith were complete gentlemen, and they were very keen to take us on that trip in the middle of the night," says Hillman. "It was quite a nice early morning adventure . . . What I recall, most vividly, is walking through Stonehenge, and Roger and I chuckling, because Gram was running after Mick and Keith, like a little boy running after his mentors."

The women present were also amused by Gram's puppy dog enthusiasm but found this endearing rather than crass or embarrassing. "Anya felt Gram was attractive," says Dolores. "Everyone loved Gram. All the women did, anyway. He was just as smooth as silk. The Southern gentleman. He could have been one of those guys from the 1800s with the top hat. In fact, he actually did have a top hat at one point."

It was during the Stonehenge visit that Jagger and Richards learned of the Byrds' plans to tour South Africa later that summer. At first, they were too cool to challenge McGuinn and Hillman on the matter, but Parsons was quick to spot their unease. Later, back at Jagger's house in Chester Square, Belgravia, he broached the subject and Mick explained that it was a bad idea. Socially aware British musicians did not visit South Africa on principle. McGuinn was undaunted, however, and had already convinced the other Byrds that it would be an interesting experience. "It was to be an experiment," he told me. "I'd known Miriam Makeba, who'd grown up there and was aware of the situation. I wanted to see it for myself. Jagger was saying not to go, but Miriam had told me it was important to see the situation first hand. It wasn't an easy decision."

Keith Richards was also vocal about South Africa, albeit in private. He had warmed to Parsons and felt like an elder brother offering advice. "Gram was a lovely, warm, down-to-earth guy," Richards recalls. "He didn't know about the situation in South Africa, so Anita and I explained it to him in [art dealer] Robert Fraser's apartment. It was quite an intense way to meet a guy." When Parsons pushed him on the subject, the Stones' guitarist reputedly responded with the withering one-liner: "Well, put it this way, *we* wouldn't go." Those words would resonate in Gram's mind over the next couple of months.

After returning from Stonehenge, Jagger and Richards had a busy evening. The Stones made a surprise appearance at the *NME* Poll Winners' concert, promoting their new single, 'Jumpin' Jack Flash'. It was to prove Brian Jones' final public performance with the group he had formed. Later that night, the Byrds played at Blaises and Jagger and Richards again turned up to offer support and enjoy the show. Parsons' brief encounter with Richards had encouraged a certain outlaw recklessness that was demonstrated on the day of the Byrds' return to the States. As they headed for the airport, Parsons surreptitiously deposited a small chunk of hashish into Jim Seiter's briefcase. When they reached New York, there were gasps of trepidation from those Byrds aware of Parsons' mischief when customs officers searched the road manager's luggage. Miraculously, the stash was not discovered.

The Byrds, still accompanied by Doug Dillard, remained in New York for a weekend of performances at Manhattan's Fillmore East, where they were supported by songwriter Tim Buckley and the British soul/pop band, the Foundations. Later, backstage, McGuinn was approached by an attractive blonde, who introduced herself as the girlfriend of Jacques Levy, a former clinical psychologist who had abandoned his practice to become a writer and stage director. She explained that he was currently composing a musical destined for Broadway and was eager for McGuinn to provide the score. It was a flattering offer, and well-timed. With an album nearly completed, he was available to discuss this new project.

Back in California, McGuinn had good reason to feel satisfied. The Byrds' European jaunt, despite the fiasco in Rome, had proven memorable. He had effectively asserted his leadership abroad, curbing Parsons' overweening ambition, and established the 'new' Byrds as a formidable live act. While the forthcoming album would prove a major departure for the group, McGuinn contented himself with the knowledge that country music was a healthy reaction against the spate of psychedelic groups that had mushroomed in the wake of Monterey. The Byrds had pioneered jazz rock, raga rock and the birth of psychedelia, so it would be fitting that they should be the first to react to the overkill. With the country album completed, McGuinn hoped that the quartet would be ready and willing to move into another field, possibly even indulging his vision of electronic music.

Parsons also had cause to reflect on recent triumphs. He had seen swinging London, befriended Keith Richards, toured successfully with the Byrds, and was looking forward to the release of their country album, on which he was the dominant party. At one point, he had intended to keep the International Submarine Band going as a side project, but that no longer seemed relevant. Their album, *Safe At Home*, had been released to little fanfare, as expected. Parsons' presence in the Byrds had been enough to secure a couple of favourable reviews in *Hit Parader* and the *Los Angeles Times*, but advance sales were negligible. LHI Records had no clout in the marketplace and limited distribution. Tellingly, no one else on the label enjoyed chart success. Parsons probably felt that the publicity he had secured while in the Byrds had been of some small service to his now former band.

Label founder Lee Hazlewood did not share Parsons' sanguine viewpoint. Angered by his charge's defection to the Byrds, he exerted pressure on CBS Records, pointing out that Parsons still had commitments to LHI and was not a free agent. Rather than risk a lawsuit, CBS instructed McGuinn and Hillman to remove Parsons' lead vocals from the forthcoming album. It was an earth-shattering decision with bitter consequences. According to Terry Melcher, Gram became paranoid when McGuinn confirmed that his lead vocal contributions were to be erased. "Parsons got really mad because Roger told him CBS insisted on that," Melcher remembers, "but he didn't believe it. He thought it was Roger's own idea. But Parsons had a lot of things in life distorted. He and McGuinn were not friends for a while because of this."

Parsons claimed that Columbia took complete control, and the overdubs began in earnest. McGuinn even imitated Parsons' voice on certain songs in an attempt to maintain the country ambience. By the time Gram's contractual release had been confirmed, only 'Hickory Wind' supposedly remained in its original state.

"Things really came out well until this thing about the suit," Parsons recalled. "They had to pull a few things out of the can that we weren't going to use and they're on there anyway. Things like 'Life In Prison' and 'You're Still On My Mind'. Those are great songs, but we just did them as warm-up numbers or something. We could have done them a lot better. They were just about to scratch 'Hickory Wind' when somebody ran in with a piece of paper. It was the last one they saved."

With extensive tour commitments looming, and pressure from

Columbia to complete the record, there was apparently no time left to re-record the album. However, according to producer Gary Usher, the final running order, featuring a mixture of McGuinn and Parsons vocals, was a conscious choice that eventually resulted in a more appropriate and democratic album. "It is true that some of Parsons' leads were overdubbed because of legal problems," Usher points out, "but those problems were resolved. Once we were down in Nashville, the attorneys back in Los Angeles were able to work that out. Whoever sang lead on the songs was there not because of what we could do legally but because that's how we wanted to spice the album up. McGuinn was a little bit edgy that Parsons was getting a little bit too much out of this whole thing. I think McGuinn wanted to keep the Byrds in the Byrds' pocket which, at that point of time, was he and Chris. He didn't want the album to turn into a Gram Parsons album. We wanted to keep Gram's voice in there, but we also wanted the recognition to come to Hillman and McGuinn, obviously. You just don't take a hit group and interject a new singer for no reason. It was also a question as to how long Gram Parsons would be in the group . . . He had stars in his eyes. I really couldn't see him being a Byrd for too long. I knew he would be there for the album, but he just didn't seem to be the one who could fit within that framework with Hillman and McGuinn for any great length of time."

Usher's reasoning was sound, if not regrettable, inasmuch as the original performances from Parsons were generally superior to McGuinn's studied imitations. Parsons was upset by this turn of events but, with Usher in his corner, McGuinn was hardly likely to push for the deletion of his own lead vocal work. Moreover, it made sense to ensure that Parsons did not completely dominate proceedings. "There was a genuine concern that we would be sued if we kept Gram's vocals on it," McGuinn notes. "So we put mine on and then the contract dispute went away, so we got Gram back and kept *some* of his. Basically, it was a misunderstanding. I wouldn't have had any involvement at all if it had been up to Gram. I would have been a harmony singer. He was taking over the band, so we couldn't really let that happen. That's why I sang a couple of songs anyway. That was the balance."

It was evident that Parsons' forceful nature needed to be contained. In addition to his other demands, he was continuing to insist that Sneaky Pete be appointed on a permanent basis so that his material would sound more authentic in concert. As the summer approached, Parsons grew more restless. At one point, he pushed for a higher salary and even suggested that he deserved individual billing. Such demands were probably coloured by the relegation of his studio material, but McGuinn was unimpressed. Even Chris Hillman, who had supported Parsons from the outset, felt that his ego needed to be held in check. From a position of great power in the Byrds, Parsons was ultimately losing the creative struggle for leadership. For a brief period, he had all but ousted McGuinn in terms of plotting the group's musical direction but, at the last, his supremacy was severely qualified.

With the new album more closely resembling a group effort than a vehicle for Parsons' own ambitions, McGuinn plotted his next move. He invited Jacques Levy over to his house to learn more about the Broadway musical and was quickly won over by his enthusiasm. Six years older than McGuinn, Levy had already directed a production of Sam Shepard's *Red Cross*, followed by the off-Broadway anti-war drama *America Hurrah* and the comedy *Scuba Duba*; he would later direct the New York production of *Oh! Calcutta!*, another hit. McGuinn was impressed by his CV and quickly saw that he was a highly talented and imaginative lyricist with a storyteller's art. His fabulous idea was a rock musical, loosely based on Henrik Ibsen's verse play *Peer Gynt*. He outlined Ibsen's drama for McGuinn, explaining that it combined an array of scenes and geographical locations from Norway, through Morocco, Cairo and the Sahara Desert. Its titular hero, Peer Gynt takes on a variety of roles, "a fortune hunter, a bridegroom, a prophet, a Bedouin chief, an historian, and an old man." Along the way, he battles a shapeless monster, the Great Boyg, and has countless other adventures. McGuinn was intrigued enough by this, but Levy's ingenious adaptation proved even more alluring. He had decided to set the action in the south-west of America, sometime between 1840–80. It would resemble an early Western, and the leading character's name was to be Gene Tryp (an anagram of Peer Gynt).

STONEHENGE

Levy promised enough thrills and spills to keep contemporary audiences satisfied. His plotline included a bewildering series of set pieces, seemingly guaranteed to intoxicate McGuinn's imagination. There was to be a wedding scene in which Gene Tryp enters and steals the bride away, *á la* Dustin Hoffman in *The Graduate*. After escorting her to the High Country, Levy explained, Gene is abruptly smitten by a nubile young Indian with whom he becomes romantically involved. Incurring the wrath of the local tribe, Gene is forced to abandon her, and finally falls in love with a third girl, Kathleen. Together, they settle down and build a house on the prairie but, one evening, as Gene returns from chopping firewood, he discovers that his house has been surrounded by an impenetrable force-field. Suddenly, the Western becomes both fantasy and science fiction. Unable to return to the house, Tryp is forced to travel all the way around the world, which takes the remainder of his life. This odyssey would allow the writers to include many more scenes featuring Gene as an evangelist, a smuggler, a gun runner, a riverboat gambler, a presidential candidate and anything else that might later be adapted to the score. The musical was to end on a dramatic note with Gene finally returning to the Penelope-like Kathleen, only to die in her arms. How could it fail?

McGuinn was so blown away by all this that he suggested they start work immediately. With Levy providing the majority of the lyrics, the pressure was off, leaving McGuinn free to concentrate on the music. All being well, he envisaged another great career step as one of the first rock musicians to conquer Broadway. It was almost as ambitious an idea as his recent concept of creating an album documenting the history of twentieth-century music from old time country to futuristic electronics.

In early June, Levy was welcomed into McGuinn's den, where it was intended they would compose the work. For Levy, it was an extraordinary sight. Eddie Tickner had once said, only half-jokingly, "McGuinn's from Outer Space." Judging from his work room, the theory had some merit. Like the stranded alien played by David Bowie in the later film *The Man Who Fell To Earth*, McGuinn enjoyed watching six television sets simultaneously. "He wanted to watch all the networks, and there weren't that many then," says his former wife, Dolores. The sets were mounted on a mantle for McGuinn's instant edification. Whenever something caught his interest on a particular channel, he would amplify its sound via a remote control device which apparently worked on every set. He told Levy that the constant visual and aural stimulation would inspire their songwriting. Evidently, he was correct.

At the time of Levy's visit, McGuinn was caught up in the politics of the day. It was rare for any of the Byrds, bar Crosby, to reveal their political allegiances, but these were heady times. McGuinn, who had once written a tribute to the late John F. Kennedy, now saw the dead president's younger brother as a new symbol of hope.

On 16 March, Robert F. Kennedy had announced his intention to run for president on an anti-war ticket. The timing was significant as press reports were currently indicating that the Johnson Administration was planning to send another 200,000 soldiers to Vietnam. President Johnson's political career had effectively ended four days before in New Hampshire when he narrowly defeated Democratic Senator Eugene McCarthy in the first primary. Two weeks later, Johnson confirmed that he would not be seeking re-election. The following month, Dr Martin Luther King was assassinated. Amid the turmoil, Vice President Hubert Humphrey put himself forward as a presidential candidate, leaving Kennedy and McCarthy to fight it out in the primaries. During the campaign, Kennedy worked tirelessly and gave some electrifying speeches. He liked to paraphrase George Bernard Shaw, telling supporters: "Some people see things as they are and say 'Why?' I dream things that never were and say, 'Why not?'"

Although he had little or no appreciation of pop or rock culture, Kennedy was attuned to the youth vote and had a following that included actors, showbiz personalities and musicians. Chief amongst them was John Stewart, formerly of the Kingston Trio, who travelled with Kennedy throughout the campaign, during which he wrote one of his most enduring songs, 'Omaha Rainbow'. Andy Williams and McGuinn's former mentor Bobby Darin also offered support, and so did the Byrds. On 24 May, they appeared at a fund raiser (billed 'SRO for RFK') at LA's Memorial Sports Arena. It was a wonderfully incongruous billing that also featured Andy

Williams, Mahalia Jackson, Henry Mancini – and the old enemy, Sonny & Cher. "That was the only political benefit we ever played," says McGuinn. "I really believed in Bobby Kennedy."

On 4 June, Kennedy won the California primary, amid scenes of jubilation. Shortly after midnight, he addressed his campaign team at the Embassy Room of LA's Ambassador Hotel. McGuinn and Levy were in the den that evening, brainstorming song ideas, discussing *Gene Tryp*, dreaming of Broadway and reflecting on Kennedy's victory. "We were watching the California primary with the sound off and working on some songs," McGuinn remembers. "Then Jacques said, 'Hey, something's happening up there on the TV.'" What followed was the chilling and barely believable announcement that Kennedy had been gunned down in the kitchen of the Ambassador. McGuinn was shattered by the news. "I couldn't sit down for two hours. We'd just done a benefit for Bobby Kennedy two weeks before, and then he was dead. It really tore me up."

Dolores remembers being awoken by the words, "Bobby Kennedy has been shot . . . assassinated". In fact, there was lingering hope over the next 24 hours that he might miraculously survive. He had been taken to the nearby Central Receiving Hospital, then transferred to the Hospital of the Good Samaritan for an emergency operation. "Roger and Jacques were sitting there, glued to the TV," Dolores recalls. "They'd been writing the music to *Tryp* and then this happened." Crestfallen, Levy feared the worst. Turning to his partner, he said, "Oh, Roger, this country is in terrible trouble."

At 1:44 am on 6 June, 26 hours after the shooting, Robert Kennedy was declared dead.

McGuinn and Levy seemed momentarily shocked into silence. It was difficult to concentrate on composing a rock musical in such mournful circumstances, so they decided to pick up the project later in the year. Meanwhile, tributes poured in for Robert Kennedy, acknowledging his commitment to civil rights over the years, which had included a groundbreaking trip to South Africa in 1966. Kennedy had been welcomed by the black population and went out of his way to champion the enemies of apartheid. "Apartheid, the Afrikaans word for 'apartness', rigidly separates the races of South Africa . . ." he wrote. "Our aim was not simply to criticize but to engage in a dialogue to see if, together, we could elevate reason above prejudice and myth . . . In Durban, I was told the church to which most of the white population belongs teaches apartheid as a moral necessity. A questioner declared that few churches allow black Africans to pray with the white because the Bible says that is the way it should be, because God created Negroes to serve. 'But suppose God is black,' I replied. 'What if we go to Heaven and we, all our lives, have treated the Negro as an inferior, and God is there, and we look up and He is not white? What then is our response?' There was no answer. Only silence."

McGuinn was no Bobby Kennedy, but he seemed comfortable with the prospect of touring South Africa and Rhodesia in the summer. He knew that the South African Broadcasting Corporation had banned the Byrds' 'Turn! Turn! Turn!' for its heretical use of Biblical quotations, but was prepared to challenge such preconceptions. Like Kennedy, he seemed willing to "engage in dialogue" and sought to "elevate reason above prejudice and myth". Even the senator's assassination had not been enough to extinguish his enduringly positive 'I trust' philosophy. "I believe in getting through with our music," he told journalists, prior to his departure. "If we work there and they like us, they'll be a lot more ready to think about what we say . . . I've got great faith in humanity, and besides, good always wins in the end, just like the movies say."

A month before their overseas tour, the Byrds' on the road provider cum amanuensis Jim Seiter was nearly killed in a road accident on Mulholland Drive. He suffered pelvic injuries, severe bruising, and worse. While he convalesced over the next couple of months, a replacement roadie had to be found at short notice. Seiter recommended his pal, 22-year-old Carlos Bernal, who was about to embark on the adventure of a lifetime.

The group still had a couple of US dates to fulfil, during which Bernal became acquainted with the dynamics of the band. He spotted nothing untoward. "It was a tremendous gig for Gram," he stresses. "He got to be exposed to a lot of different audiences and was playing with some great musicians. They were singing harmonies on those Gram Parsons' songs. I know Roger was having one of the times of his life. He wanted to play that music and do those harmonies and there he was with one of the best, and the newest, Gram Parsons. We treated Gram real nice, I felt. Everybody was thrilled to have him there. The Byrds' corporation bent over backwards after his arrival. We wanted him to be comfortable and I know because I was at the service end. If he wanted a Fender Rhodes or an amp, or whatever, we'd get it and do whatever we needed to do. I thought the shows were tremendous."

On the eve of their departure from the US, Bernal was contacted by Seiter and offered some last minute advice: "Take your guitar with you." It seemed an odd request, but Seiter was known to cover all contingencies. Without Seiter or Larry Spector, the inexperienced Bernal would face considerable challenges over the next few weeks. Amazingly, this was his first overseas tour.

After arriving in England, the group played a warm-up gig at the Roundhouse, perfect preparation for their all-important appearance at the 'Sounds '68' charity spectacular at the Royal Albert Hall on Sunday 7 July. The organizers were thrilled when the Byrds agreed to play for no fee, along with seven other artistes. It was a great spectacle watched by a star-studded audience that included three Rolling Stones and two Beatles. The Byrds closed the first half of the show, while joint bill-toppers the Move ended the evening. Throughout the second half, there were cries of "bring back the Byrds", a firm indication that the Americans were the real stars of the night. The *NME* subsequently headlined with 'Byrds Long-Fly Worth It' and correctly noted that "there was a tremendous reception for the Byrds . . . A good section of the 4,000 audience was there to see them alone, and let them know it." Commencing with a stunning 'So You Want To Be A Rock 'n' Roll Star', the Byrds moved confidently through a series of hits and country songs and astounded the audience with a riveting version of 'Eight Miles High'. Parsons also enjoyed a cameo spot during which he sang 'Hickory Wind' and a moving rendition of Merle Haggard's 'Sing Me Back Home' which many of us present expected to appear on the next album. A memorable evening ended with the old Byrds' favourite 'Chimes Of Freedom'.

After the show, several of the Byrds' retinue went for a walk in nearby Hyde Park, then returned to the Grosvenor House Hotel in Park Lane. "Someone ordered room service and there was lots of great dope and good friends," recalls Jeff Dexter. "I was on LSD, of course. In those days, the trips lasted a while. I removed my shoes and got very comfortable and everyone was sitting around singing songs. McGuinn was being a bit weird and acting strange and Gram seemed in a bit of a state. He had some of my sunshine and was wondering where he was at . . . The atmosphere between Gram and Roger was deadly. Two of the Byrds wandered in and out, coming back and then going out. There was a kerfuffle in one of the lavatories but I didn't know exactly what was going on. There were definitely some strange vibes, man."

In the background was the simmering debate about South Africa, which was reaching boiling point. "There was a bit of ill feeling and mixed emotions," Dexter recalls. "Someone was saying, 'Well, if you had any real conscience none of you would go to South Africa . . .' and some business type person said, 'Yes, but you've got a contract to do it.'" Parsons seemed increasingly swayed by the weight of opinion, reinforced by memories of some withering comments from his new pals, Jagger and Richards. "He picked up the vibe from the people in London," says Dexter. "He'd been given the guilt trip by everybody." The tension was broken when somebody suggested a return visit to Hyde Park to cool down. Dexter warned them it was not a good idea, but went along anyway. "We walked around the outside of the park towards Speakers' Corner, then back to the hotel. Gram didn't turn up for another 45 minutes and when he came back into the room he made the announcement that he was not going to South Africa. He just said, 'I'm not going to go, so I guess I'll have to leave the group.' There was a tense moment in the room and, of course, everyone just really wanted to have a great party, so there was a lot of mixed feelings, especially from me, a little bloke sat in the middle listening to people he adored . . . There were some tears and sadness, but then Gram picked up the guitar, started singing and resolved his sadness, and everyone joined in. The last thing on Gram's mind was publicity. The condition he was in that night, it was outside his thoughts."

Just before 4 am, the hotel manager, accompanied by three

security officers, began hammering on Parsons' door following a series of complaints about the noise. All the guests were ejected, including Dexter, who walked home shoeless, still high, wondering about the fate of the Byrds.

A few hours later, the group were checking out of the hotel, evidently still uncertain of Parsons' intentions. As their bags were being removed, McGuinn and Hillman realized that Gram's threats were no stoned bluff. He would not be accompanying them to South Africa. "That was it," says a flabbergasted Chris Hillman. "No warning, he just pulled out. I really wanted to murder him at the time." After less than five months, the Parsons domination of the Byrds had ended with the most dramatic and unexpected of exits.

CHAPTER TWENTY-EIGHT

South Africa

ALTHOUGH the suddenness of Gram Parsons' departure was a shock, McGuinn appeared unconcerned, disguising any ill feeling with his customary cool. By contrast, the volatile Chris Hillman had already flown into a rage and subsequently vented his feelings to the press, denouncing Parsons as a sensation-seeking egotist. "He thought he was more important than the Byrds. He was a drag personally, but a good musician. He knew we were going to South Africa long before England, why the sudden announcement?"

Parsons' reasons for leaving the Byrds certainly seemed suspect. In a contemporaneous interview with *Melody Maker*, he explained: "I first heard about the South African tour two months ago. I knew right away when I heard about it that I didn't want to go. I stood firmly on my conviction. The Byrds are a very professional group and they thought it very unprofessional of me not to do it. I thought it was short-sighted saying it was confirmed without finding out about the South Africa situation first. It was just two conflicting opinions. I knew very little about South Africa before the tour was mentioned. I knew there was an intense problem but I didn't know what it was based on. I began to talk to people who had been born there and I found out."

As so often with Parsons' press interviews, contradictions were apparent. The contention that he stood firmly on his convictions was a nonsense given the timing of his leaving. It was clear to everyone that he had agreed to the tour months before and voiced no ultimatum until the morning the Byrds were scheduled to depart. Nevertheless, he was more than ready to play the race card.

Rationalizing his decision, he explained: "Something a lot of people don't know about me, I was brought up with a Negro for a brother – I was brought up with a spade brother. Like all Southern families, we had maids as servants, a whole family that took care of us called the Dixon family. Sammy Dixon was just a little older than me, and he just lived with me. He wasn't paid for doing it; he just grew up with me. I learned at a real close level that segregation was just not it."

Even with the benefit of several decades' hindsight, Hillman remains convinced that Parsons' comments on segregation were a red herring. "People to this day go on the premise that Gram did not want to go to South Africa because of racial reasons. That's not true. Gram wanted to stay in England and hang out with Mick and Keith and he did not want to fly . . . he didn't like to fly. He was a very sensitive guy and very socially aware of the situation he grew up with in the South, but the closest he came to black people was the servants he had in his home. So, the situation where he says, 'I'm not going to South Africa because of the apartheid' is garbage. He just didn't want to get on the plane, and he let us down."

The cynical view of Parsons suggests that his abrupt announcement was designed to give him a maximum of publicity. At the very least, it enabled him to win the sympathy of Jagger and Richards, whom he was keen to befriend. Apart from his racial conscience and reluctance to fly, it seems safe to assume that Parsons' differences with the Byrds played an equally important part in formulating his final decision. "Gram wasn't going on the tour because he couldn't have things just exactly as he wanted," insists Byrds' roadie Carlos Bernal. "The things he wanted, he could have had after a while, but he wanted them immediately. He wanted a steel guitar to do a lot of his tunes and things that the band wasn't prepared to jump into overnight."

Parsons played down any disagreements and rightly noted that McGuinn had been keen to push him into the spotlight. "I was originally hired as a keyboard player, but I had experience of being a front man and that came out immediately," he boasted. "Roger being a perceptive fellow saw that it would help the act and he started sticking me out front." Allowing Parsons prominence merely exacerbated his hunger for recognition which he realized could never be sated in an established group such as the Byrds. Short of replacing McGuinn, he would always be regarded as a subsidiary member. "Being with the Byrds confused me a little," he admitted. "I couldn't find my place. I didn't have enough say so."

Even if Parsons had relented later down the line and attempted to re-establish his standing in the Byrds, there was evidently no way back. "By refusing to go he had sealed his fate with the Byrds," says Hillman. "He was hired as a sideman, as an accompanist, as an extra singer. He turned out to be a really good songwriter, and we featured him and let him do as much as we could. But by not going to South Africa, and fulfilling his commitments as a member or sideman of the Byrds, he was gone."

The suspicion that Parsons was using the South Africa tour as an excuse to leave the Byrds was reinforced by the speed with which he formulated plans for his next project. While staying at Keith Richards' cottage, Redlands, he contacted Chris Ethridge and set about forming the Flying Burrito Brothers. In early July, he told the press, somewhat prematurely: "The group's already formed, although I can't say too much about it", adding that it was "basically a Southern soul group playing country and gospel-oriented music with a steel guitar."

What Parsons did not tell the music press was the extent of Mick Jagger's and Keith Richards' influence on his decision not to tour South Africa. His fascination for the group, which would remain for the rest of his life, eclipsed any lingering loyalty to the Byrds. The Stones' suggestion that it was uncool, and probably unethical, to undertake the tour proved enough to make up his mind. One aspect of his leaving that bothered him unduly was McGuinn's characteristically cool response upon hearing the news. "He just sort of pocketed it and included it in his definition of rock music being a joke," he complained. "And I walked away very disillusioned."

Having fired the great David Crosby, McGuinn was never likely to be overwhelmed by the loss of any fellow musician, even one as talented as Parsons. While Parsons could cite some of the objections to apartheid voiced by his friends in the Rolling Stones, McGuinn felt he held the higher moral ground, having received the

SOUTH AFRICA

blessing of the exiled black South African singer, civil rights campaigner and leading political activist, Miriam Makeba. Such reasoning was logical but naïve in view of the political climate in 1968. Writing over 20 years later, author and political/music columnist Robin Denselow observed: "It is ironic, putting it mildly, that Jagger and Richards – who don't rank as radical heroes these days – advised Gram Parsons to act in a way that would be applauded today by the UN and by the Anti-Apartheid Movement. It follows that Roger McGuinn should never have listened to Miriam Makeba, the early heroine of South Africa." What Denselow did not consider, and McGuinn seldom clarified, was the date of Makeba's advice. There is no evidence that he consulted her in the months prior to his departure but was instead relying upon guidance given many years before when he was a member of the Chad Mitchell Trio. Since then, the UN had hardened its stance and had McGuinn investigated the situation more thoroughly, he might well have reconsidered his position.

Although they were ill-equipped to compensate for the loss of Parsons, the Byrds decided to continue with the tour and boarded the plane to South Africa. It was a disastrous decision. McGuinn persuaded Byrds' roadie Carlos Bernal to play rhythm guitar, and the depleted unit was reduced to such absurdities as rehearsing its repertoire for the first time during the flight to Johannesburg. "Actually, there was no rehearsal," Carlos corrects. "I sat next to Roger on the plane and said, 'Shall I get my guitar?' He said, 'No', then held up his right arm and with his left hand he made a fingering configuration of a *G* chord and a *D* and a *C*. He said, 'One song goes like this and another like that, and that's about it. Anything you don't know, leave out.' That was the extent of the rehearsals for South Africa. I was pretty competent on the guitar, but I was no Roger McGuinn or Clarence White."

With Bernal masquerading as Parsons, the Byrds struggled through a gruelling series of concerts and during those ten days gave what were possibly the most unprofessional performances of their entire career. "It was pretty awkward," Bernal recalls. "We hired a guy to drive the truck and run the sound and I helped where I could. I was just following orders from Roger and Chris. They said,

'Be Gram', so I was. Then it was 'Be less Gram, be Carlos-Gram'. In the newspapers it was escalating or de-escalating as to whether I was Gram or Carlos. Carlos Parsons!'

The tour began with a three-night stint at Johannesburg's City Hall, where the Byrds played two short shows each evening in front of an all white audience. It was an inauspicious start. The press criticized every aspect of the group's performance, complaining about the sound, the presentation and the lackadaisical attitude. "The Byrds were unbelievably bad for a group which has just come from London's Albert Hall," wrote one reviewer. "Roger McGuinn, the leader, mumbled something into the mike every now and then to announce a new number. On occasions, he laughed to himself – but he was the only one laughing. The Byrds were dressed in clothes which one wears while working in the garden. It is hard to believe this is the group which has sold over 10 million records. What at one stage of the evening appeared to be the start of a number suddenly turned out to be a tuning session. The music was disjointed, sometimes out of tune, and shockingly loud. Hit records of yesterday were barely recognizable."

The group fared rather better during the afternoon when they were taken to the retail store OK Bazaars for a personal appearance during which they mimed to 'You Ain't Going Nowhere'. "There were some really nice people there and also backstage after the concerts," Bernal says. "Besides the people that were ugly about us being there, we met fans and it was terrific to hang out with them and see the city." McGuinn was also impressed by the reception from supporters, but shocked by the depth of racial prejudice. "I was walking down the street with a black girl and she was holding my hand, and she said, 'I want to thank you for what you're saying for my people. It's helping the morale.' And then I tried to get her in the concert, and they wouldn't let me in with her. It was terrible. I hated that whole audience. I wanted to get out of there."

There was still some optimism in the camp when they flew into Cape Town where they were greeted by over 300 well-wishers brandishing banners proclaiming 'Welcome The Byrds', 'The Byrds Are Great' and 'We Love You'.

Unfortunately, the fans' love was not reciprocated by the media,

SOUTH AFRICA

and McGuinn's stage patter only inflamed the negative reporting. His opening words at their first Cape Town performance were laced with sarcastic invective: "If there are any newspaper critics in the audience, would they please go home and blow their brains out?"

Instead, it was McGuinn who was hoist with his own petard. After the first show, he collapsed in his dressing room, the victim of a viral infection. He was rushed back to his hotel. Meanwhile, ticket holders at the Metro Theatre were informed that the second set had been cancelled. The plucky impresario attempted to assuage disappointed fans by offering them a free screening of *Zebra In The Kitchen*. How many accepted such a peculiar recompense is not recorded.

The next morning McGuinn convalesced, while perusing reviews of the previous night's disaster. There were the usual poisonous barbs, although even McGuinn must have formed a grim smile when reading a priceless description of the 'fake' Gram Parsons, Carlos Bernal: "If nothing else, the Byrds are original, looks-wise. One of them, who spent most of the time hammering a guitar, sulking with his back to the audience, had a head of luxurious black Shirley Temple curls which contrasted oddly with his droopy moustache."

Surprisingly, it was not all bad news. Amid the brickbats, was a sympathetic overview in the *Cape Argus* which challenged conventional opinion, even suggesting that the group's contemptuous attitude in concert was partly due to South Africa's misunderstanding of LA cool. "With all the unnerving experiences the Byrds have suffered in South Africa – of which McGuinn's collapse before the second performance last night and the terrifying bashing they received from Johannesburg critics were only two – it would be a pity to forget what this group can do when the circumstances are on their side. In London, where their appearances are still legend in pop circles, they produced professional results, well-balanced and original. Their unorthodox behaviour onstage passed almost unnoticed: not so here, with an audience of young people conditioned to rigid conventions of pop music in community halls, clubs, or onstage, rather than to the fluid, casual meanderings of the television camera. Here, in spite of loud protests of the contrary, the teenyboppers of this generation are surprisingly convention-bound."

In conclusion, reviewer Garner Thomson dared question his country's academic understanding of popular music. "Supporting the Byrds in a serious review is not without its hazards," he wrote. "One could, on one hand, be accused of banality – on the other, of intellectual bandwagoning. This must be one of the hazards of an age and a country where pop music is still not considered a music form in its own right. It seems a pity that the Byrds will almost inevitably leave South Africa on a down note – disappointing, perhaps at the collapse of what promised to be a golden tour. Certainly, they will leave in their wake a large number of young fans who will share their disappointment. They, like me, will be dogged by the vision of what might have been."

The Byrds could hardly have expected a rougher passage in South Africa and, in retrospect, it seems remarkable that the tour was even undertaken. Demoralized, buffeted by culture shock and still bitter about playing solely for white audiences, they were now regretting ever setting foot on the continent. Adversity can often bring people closer together, but the dynamic in the Byrds was too complex to allow such an easy solution. Old wounds were suddenly reopened. It was almost as if the anger over Parsons' departure had now turned inwards, eating away at every vestige of group solidarity. "The band wasn't really getting along with one another," Bernal admits. "Chris wasn't talking to anybody. Roger was ill and he was mad with Chris and going back about problems with the band. It was Chris against Roger, and Roger against Chris. I was just doing my job as road manager. I talked to McGuinn regarding business. We were friends, but we weren't very friendly on that tour."

While avoiding the cold war, Bernal found an unexpected ally in Kevin Kelley. "We were roommates on occasion. He was a pretty nice, easy-going guy. So we became pals on that tour. We went to museums and different places." Away from the tourist trail, the fearless duo decided to experience the inequities of apartheid first hand by visiting a township. After securing the assistance of the bell boys at their hotel, they were taken on the ultimate sightseeing adventure. "We hid under a blanket in the backseat of a car while they drove us to the township," Bernal recalls. "It was outside the perimeter of the city. We wanted to see what it was like for people living in the system of apartheid. I can remember this housing development complex. There were 18-storey brick high-rises, but they had no windows and the elevator didn't work, so people had to walk up. You could see fires flickering because they had no electricity there. It was pretty weird. We met some people who had books which they told us were banned. They said it was an offence for black people to have books or to be taught to read. Of course there was no television. I'm glad we went to that township, but I can see now it was pretty foolish. Chris and Roger didn't go, and we were lucky not to be caught. We could have ended up in prison like Mandela!"

Despite still feeling poorly, McGuinn somehow retained his humour, throwing out sarcastic one-liners to journalists, photographers and fans. In concert, he introduced 'Turn! Turn! Turn!', telling audiences that in America nuns taught schoolchildren the words, while in South Africa the broadcasting authority refused to sanction its biblically inspired lyrics. Like a stand-up comedian, he satirized the South African situation with withering comments, sometimes in an affected accent. "So ziz is Port Elizabeth," he announced at their opening show at the Showgrounds Hall. "Well, it's weird, man." Predictably, more criticisms followed. Even the great South African cricketer Graeme Pollock joined the debate, taking on an unlikely role as guest rock critic. "It was ridiculous," was his assessment of their performance. "I don't know how they got away with it. There was absolutely no contact between the band and the audience, and the music was far too loud."

By the time the Byrds reached Durban, they were no longer bothered about couching their criticisms in diplomatic understatement. "People at one of our shows were belching and making noises," McGuinn complained. "Your audiences must be the worst in the world. We were told not to come here but we wanted to see the country for ourselves . . . we will tell everyone at home not to come here."

While McGuinn concentrated on the audience response, Hillman offered a political assessment, guaranteed to provoke an incendiary response. "Apartheid is all wrong and the sooner they take away the 'Whites Only' signs the better. Your country is boring and about five years behind the times. I miss television and your apartheid laws are sick."

Years later, Hillman was still bitter about South Africa and regaled me with the story of how McGuinn succumbed to the mounting pressures during a performance at Durban's City Hall. "We got to the third song and Roger said, 'I got to get out of here!' and literally runs off the stage. It was a full house, and there's me having to take leads on the bass. He left me hanging in South Africa with a bunch of angry Afrikaners. Jesus Christ! That was a dumb tour to begin with. We should never have gone."

McGuinn was understandably prickly about the criticisms heaped upon him in the aftermath of the tour, and did not take Hillman's anecdotal account too kindly. Providing a more accurate appraisal of his apparent breakdown, he admits: "I did have a nervous reaction, it's true. For the whole tour I had a 102° temperature. We were under a lot of pressure because of the political statements we'd been making about apartheid. The people were against us and there was blatant hatred emanating from the audience. I'm very sensitive, but I didn't desert under fire. I was very polite about the whole thing. I walked up to the microphone and said: 'Ladies and Gentlemen, I've a touch of influenza and if you'd excuse me for ten minutes we'll be back.' We retired to the dressing room. I'd been trying to kick cigarettes at the time, so I had a cigarette, then recovered, went back onstage and finished the set. I didn't just run off leaving them onstage. That was an untrue accusation by Chris Hillman and I'll tell him when I see him. I've had similar feelings to that since then and I haven't left the stage, but just gone right through. I've learned to cope with that feeling of nervousness. It happens now and again for no apparent reason. It's like stage fright. It gets so intense you think you're going to die. You can't feel your hands, but you have to keep going and I've learned to function as though my body were a spaceship and I was the pilot. I think I've learned my lesson and can deal with that phenomenon."

Newspaper accounts confirm that McGuinn's account of his 'breakdown' was the more reliable one. The *Durban Mercury*

SOUTH AFRICA

reported: "During their second song in last night's final performance, Roger was unable to continue and apologized to the audience saying he was still suffering from the influenza which caused the group to cancel one of their Cape Town shows and asked to be excused for a few minutes. The packed audience waited patiently while a doctor was called. Five minutes later, the group reappeared amid cheers from the capacity audience and Roger McGuinn carried on. Several times during the show he apologized to the audience saying he felt dizzy, but they were in full sympathy and cheered him on. The group cut the show by about five songs, despite calls for more."

It is interesting to note that this particular audience was a lot more sympathetic than McGuinn remembered. Far from "emanating hatred", they appear to have shown a commendable degree of support and enthusiasm, which the Byrds did not fully deserve. One fan, who saw the Durban show, provided an amusing and perceptive account of the evening's entertainment: "The local press was pretty sympathetic, as was the national radio . . . Fair enough, they did speak their minds when they were down there and the situation does stink, but on a musical and personal level they had no cause to complain, because they were greeted with love that they did nothing to deserve. Imagine yourself at a Byrds concert; the curtain opens, there they are, wreathed in smiles, they step up to the mikes together and launch into a hideously unbalanced version of 'Feel A Whole Lot Better', with McGuinn singing lead and harmony! The thing got worse from there, with Bernal playing 'Turn! Turn! Turn!' in a different key from the others. Really, they were the worst professional group I had ever heard and they shouldn't have offered that crap to any audience, even one as starved of name bands as the South African freaks. Still . . . it would take more than that to put off a Byrd fanatic!"

Whatever sympathy McGuinn had won in Durban was immediately lost when their aforementioned interview comments were translated into a provocative headline that paraphrased their views on South Africa in three derogatory adjectives: 'Sick, Backward, Rude'. The rumpus inflamed nationalist opinion, prompting several abusive phone calls, culminating in an assassination threat directed at Chris Hillman. Responding to the intimidation, McGuinn explained, "They were obviously from cranks, but all the same it was all very upsetting."

Meanwhile, the group ran into more trouble. Crazy rumours were spread that they were certified drug addicts, a fabrication that McGuinn claims was corroborated by untrue statements from bell boys who had been bribed. As a result, some of their tour money was frozen and they were informed that they would not receive full payment unless they returned to the country to disprove the allegations. Even the terms of their contract had allegedly been altered, forcing them to play before segregated audiences until their arrival in Rhodesia at the end of the tour.

"Rhodesia was a great time," says Carlos Bernal, evidently happy to have escaped the press controversies. For their final show on the continent, they were booked to play the open-air Glamis Stadium in Salisbury before an estimated audience of six thousand. It turned out to be an anticlimactic finale for everyone, bar the drummer, who was praised to the hilt by an otherwise unimpressed reviewer. "The Byrds, still in travel clothes, provided an intelligent, well-trained sound, ranging from psychedelic to country & western. Drummer Kevin Kelley must be among the world's best. But I saw few genuinely excited reactions among the crowd. I left Glamis disappointed and with ears ringing . . . but the venue and sound amplification were a lot to blame."

The drama was almost over, but the Byrds faced one final hurdle. "Leaving Rhodesia and going back to South Africa and on to London to come home was a very tricky manoeuvre," Bernal remembers. "If it hadn't been for the nightclub owner in Rhodesia, a guy named Fisher, we might have been incarcerated in South Africa. The secret police were waiting there to arrest the Byrds for fraternizing and having drugs with people of a different colour in Johannesburg. Fisher found out about it and arranged for some people to meet us, change our flight tickets and put us on a different plane on the runway. We didn't have to go through the terminal, so we escaped the country. A true story."

Defeated, exhausted and morose, the Byrds returned to California knowing that they urgently required new blood. Chris

Hillman's preference was a musician whom he had known since his early bluegrass days. Unlike Gram Parsons, who was a talented singer-songwriter but a rudimentary guitarist, the new candidate had barely written a lyric in his life yet established a formidable reputation as an inspired player on both acoustic and electric guitar. Equally importantly, he had already appeared as a session player on *Younger Than Yesterday*, *The Notorious Byrd Brothers* and the country album they had recently completed in Nashville.

Clarence Joseph White (b. 7 June 1944, Lewiston, Maine) was a chapter unto himself in the annals of bluegrass music. His extensive pre-Byrds adventures will be documented at length in Volume 2 of this book. Suffice to say, he was a prodigy, who began strumming guitar at the age of six, after which he teamed up with his brothers Roland and Eric, occasionally accompanied by sister Joanne, in the family bluegrass group, the Country Boys. They evolved into the Kentucky Colonels, arguably one of the finest bluegrass bands of their era. The group recorded a couple of albums for World-Pacific, and White also worked with Jim Dickson, while guesting on the Elektra album, *New Dimensions In Banjo And Bluegrass*. At one point, Dickson suggested that the brothers should record an instrumental version of 'Mr Tambourine Man' but, Clarence apart, they staunchly resisted the notion of electric folk rock. White's breathtaking flat-picking had already singled him out as a player of great talent and originality, but the market for acoustic bluegrass was contracting by the mid-Sixties. Clarence subsequently moved into session work, following the lead of his idol James Burton. Switching from his acoustic Martin D–28 to a Fender Telecaster, he became a much sought after electric player. Complementing his session work, he appeared regularly in bar bands, whose names included the Reasons, the Roustabouts and Nashville West. All this was a perfect apprenticeship for membership of the Byrds. After years of struggling on the bluegrass circuit, White could not resist the opportunity to join a group with such an established reputation. The Byrds' recent move towards country music was another plus and ensured that he would be a valuable asset. He not only knew some of their material but was proficient enough to enhance their musicianship, both live and in the studio. Equally importantly, although ambitious, he was engagingly modest and a less conspicuously dominant personality than Gram Parsons. McGuinn was more than happy to add him to the ranks, albeit as a salaried member, in common with every other non-original Byrd.

With little time to rehearse, the new look Byrds made their performing debut on 3 August at the Berkeley Community Theatre. Mike Nesmith, still a Monkee but soon to become one of the great pioneers of a distinctive brand of country rock, joined them onstage. The next day, the Byrds flew in by helicopter to the Newport Pop Festival at the Orange County Grounds, Costa Mesa. The Californian festival featured the cream of San Francisco's rock community, including the Jefferson Airplane, the Grateful Dead and Quicksilver Messenger Service. Also lurking incongruously on the bill were the by now terminally unhip Sonny & Cher. Three years on from Ciro's, the duo had not lost the knack of haunting McGuinn in his darker hours. Nor had David Crosby, who was backstage joking with the Jefferson Airplane, who played his 'controversial' 'Triad' that evening. The Byrds were woefully ill-prepared for Newport, but gamely struggled through their set, hiding any concerns behind dark glasses and a cool exterior. A review in the *Los Angeles Times* dismissed their performance as 'mediocre', adding that they had "made little impression on the audience." Clearly, they had a lot of ground to recover after all their recent setbacks.

CHAPTER TWENTY-NINE

Sweetheart Of The Rodeo

AT the end of August, *Sweetheart Of The Rodeo* received its American release and met with a reasonable reception from the critics. It was such a drastic change from their previous album, however, that some of the group's stauncher hippie following were taken aback by the content. Once again, the Byrds were leading rather than following and even doubling back on themselves to cleanse rock music of its recent indulgences by seeking refuge in a lost golden age of dustbowl America in which images of pastoral bliss commingled uneasily with tales of hardship, alcoholism and prison life. The album was refreshing, challenging and, viewed in the context of its two predecessors, revealed the Byrds as the most eclectic and uncompromisingly risk-taking major act of their era. Both historically important and a beautiful work in its own right, *Sweetheart Of The Rodeo* was nevertheless haunted by the ghostly whispers of Gram Parsons, whose disenchantment over the vocal switches on certain tracks eventually turned him against the album. "A few songs they overdubbed completely," he complained, "things that shouldn't have been overdubbed. And my voice was used way in the background as a guide to go by. It gave it too much of that old Byrds' sound, which we were fighting against at that time, not because it wasn't any good but because there was all this other stuff to work with and we didn't need to look back, as Bob Dylan once sort of said."

'You Ain't Going Nowhere' characterizes the "old Byrds' sound" most noticeably but few, beyond Parsons, were complaining. Despite the radical change of musical style, the new Byrds had found a link with their heritage by opening the album with a Dylan composition, just as they had done with 'Mr Tambourine Man'. Steel guitarist Lloyd Green, who had been told to play "everywhere" on the track, duly obliges. Freed from the regimented conventions usually associated with Nashville, he improvises a beautiful soaring lilt, filling every available space until the chiming steel rings with the same clarity as Roger's Rickenbacker solos of yore. Kelley's precise drumming is solid but never intrusive while a subtle organ accompaniment, presumably the work of Parsons, provides added depth to the sound. Hillman seems equally at home, connecting well with his cousin to conjure a perfect rhythm, while offering a delicate but distinctive background harmony. McGuinn, meanwhile, falls into his Dylan role with relish. His vocal enunciations sound both mimetic and inventive, suggesting a playfulness that is echoed in the lyrics. Amid this freedom, McGuinn casually inverts a key line, altering the words from "pick up your money and pack up your tent" to "pack up your money and pick up your tent". Evidently irked by McGuinn's presumptuous poetic licence Dylan exclaimed in a re-recorded version (included on 1971's *More Bob Dylan Greatest Hits*): "Pack up your money, pull up your tent, McGuinn, *you* ain't going nowhere". Ever sensitive to the master's gnomic pronouncements, McGuinn was never quite sure whether Dylan was genuinely annoyed or merely having some fun at his expense.

'I Am A Pilgrim', arranged by Hillman and McGuinn, and featuring the former on lead vocal, was the group's first straight country & western outing and the second single to be taken from the album. It also proved the group's most serious foray into country music to date. Rock instrumentation is conspicuous by its absence, replaced by the fiddle of John Hartford and the string bass of Roy Huskey. Even McGuinn abandons his Rickenbacker guitar in favour of a banjo. At the time, it seemed strange to hear the Byrds singing a religious song, even though they had used biblical imagery previously on 'Turn! Turn! Turn!'. For Hillman, the song was an excellent opportunity to re-live his past. "It was my idea to do 'I Am A Pilgrim'," he told me. "I used to play that song with Clarence White during the bluegrass days." Hillman remains faithful to the memory of the original, although he subtly updates the archaic diction in places, removing awkward inversions for the benefit of younger listeners. The biblical power of "If I could touch but the hem of his garment" is replaced with the modern translation "If I could just touch . . .", a typical example of the folk process in motion.

'The Christian Life' continues to stress the religious theme, and to hear the Byrds celebrating the virtues of godliness seemed, to many listeners, almost ironic. Originally a starring vehicle for new boy Gram Parsons, this Louvin Brothers' standard first appeared on the duo's powerful 1959 gospel album, *Satan Is Real*, whose cover artwork featured a burning effigy of the Devil. The Louvins' fundamentalism was expressed in fire and brimstone preaching that offered a dizzying sense of an almost visible cosmology. "It's sweet to know that God is real," they sang, "but, sinner friend, Satan is real too, and Hell is a *real* place." Other songs like 'Are You Afraid To Die' and 'There's A Higher Power' offered the possibility of redemption in the face of sin. 'The Christian Life' was both a defiant affirmation of their religious conviction and a warning against the vanities of worldly wishes. Parsons' love of the Louvins was a testament to his own Southern upbringing. Even though he had not been raised in a traditionally devout Christian household, he was always fascinated by non-secular music and had a keen interest in theology and spiritual matters.

"Religion was deeply woven into the cultural fabric of the South," says Parsons' pre-Byrds colleague Barry Tashian. "Much more so than in the North where I was from. There was a large repertoire of bluegrass and gospel songs that Gram knew that are still sung and performed today." Parsons had a particular affection for strong, filial harmonies as demonstrated by his long-standing love of the Everly Brothers, the Osborne Brothers and the Louvin Brothers. While the Byrds' harmonic blend made it possible to do justice to such songs, it was no easy task. The group undertook several tuneless rehearsal takes of 'The Christian Life', with Parsons clearly struggling to achieve the desired connection between emotion and precision. By the eighth take, and on all subsequent recordings, one of the most powerful lines in the song ("I live without them, *it tortures my soul*") was amended to "I live without them, and walk in the light". Without fully realizing the impact of this casual alteration, Parsons had neutered the composition's theological complexity. The intensity of the Louvin Brothers' biblical allegiance was not merely that it involved sacrifice, but a complete abandonment of so much they held dear. Friends and loved ones, not blessed with the Word, were doomed to be lost in eternity. There is no spiritual smugness in the Louvins' cosmological coda, but rather a terrifying sense of loss expressed in imagery more appropriate to the pains of Hell. "It tortures my soul" applies to both the earthly and heavenly kingdoms, enforcing the notion that even salvation and sainthood can be accompanied by a profound sorrow for those wretches who have failed to heed "God's call". Parsons' platitudinous "walk in the light" is a pretty poor substitute for the Louvins' divinely inspired lyric. Worsening matters, McGuinn makes a belated appearance as Parsons' replacement on lead vocals. Despite his religious history, McGuinn had little empathy with fundamentalist Christianity at this point in his life. He had long since abandoned Roman Catholicism and was currently immersed in the free-form spiritual community, Subud. Hellfire warnings were regarded as archaic and treated with mild derision while a straight celebration of conservative Christianity seemed theologically and politically uncomfortable. Instead of singing 'The Christian Life' in his own style, McGuinn sought solace in method acting, even imitating Parsons' Southern accent. What was once intended as a complex celebration of the Christian faith ending up sounding strangely parodic.

 McGuinn fared much better on the cover of William Bell's 1961 Stax recording 'You Don't Miss Your Water'. The composition had already become a Southern soul classic, largely thanks to Otis Redding's rendition on the best-selling *Otis Blue*. The Byrds were not alone in reviving the number in 1968. Taj Mahal, Kevin Kelley's former bandmate in the Rising Sons, also included a version on his album, *The Natch'l Blues*. McGuinn reverts to his familiar vocal style, accompanied by Jay Dee Maness' pedal steel guitar and Earl Ball's honky tonk piano. The well-executed harmonies and the slowed-down ending give the song an authentic, bar-room feel, complete with a countrified coda. Comparing McGuinn's vocal overdub with Parsons' original is a vexatious task made more complicated by the realization that the released version, aurally familiar for decades, is difficult to dislodge from the memory. That said, both renditions have their appeal: Parsons has a richer resonance during some lines, but McGuinn has a greater vocal precision throughout. The song's fusion of soul and country anticipates the stylistic experimentation later favoured by Parsons in his pursuit of so-called 'Cosmic American Music'.

'You're Still On My Mind' was one of the tracks that Columbia supposedly retrieved from a rehearsal session and, according to Parsons, it was not originally intended for inclusion on *Sweetheart Of The Rodeo*. Both those assertions are now discredited and it is plain from the sheer number of outtakes that considerable work was invested in this track. Gram's Southern drawl, set beside a honky tonk piano backing, was well-suited to the sentiments of this song, which presented the classic country & western stereotype of the lovelorn alcoholic, unsuccessfully attempting to find salvation at the bottom of a bottle. Written by Luke Daniel, who recorded the song under his stage name Jeff Daniels, it had originally appeared as the B-side of his 1959 single 'Switch Blade Sam'. Parsons was probably more familiar with the 1962 version released by George Jones, which was a minor hit on the country charts.

With 'Pretty Boy Floyd', McGuinn returns to his folk days to resurrect Woody Guthrie's portrayal of the 'people's outlaw', Charles Arthur Floyd. A bank robber, convict and alleged killer, Floyd gained his cute nickname when a teller or payroll master referred to him in a police description as "a mere boy . . . a pretty boy with apple cheeks". Guthrie presents a highly sanitized version of Floyd's life, transforming him into a latter-day Robin Hood, and comparing his gun-toting exploits favourably with those larcenists who would "rob you with a fountain pen". This fairy-tale aspect is evident from the opening lines: "gather round me children, a story I will tell . . ." Floyd may have been a flawed character, but here the details of his life are airbrushed and mythologized for propagandist purpose. He becomes a defender of his wife's virtue, offended by "vulgar language", a victim of false crime statistics in Oklahoma, and a humanitarian providing dinner for families living on welfare.

Whether all this really happened is ultimately irrelevant since Guthrie is not striving for historical accuracy but creating a modern folk song. As listeners, we are invited to suspend our disbelief in the same way we do when we appreciate outlaw tales of Jesse James, Billy The Kid or Ned Kelly. Agitprop creates its own black and white universe populated not by authentic flesh and blood figures, but idealized constructs who happen to share the names of real people. While operating in this part-fictional panorama, both Guthrie and McGuinn tell us more about their understanding of the folk tradition than their accuracy as chroniclers. McGuinn sings the saga with great exuberance and conviction, fully engrossed in his role as storyteller. He changes a handful of Guthrie's lyrics ("trees and timber" become "tree and bushes"; a "note" is now a "letter") and there is no reference to the outlaw paying off mortgages and saving "little homes", or leaving a thousand dollar bill under a napkin. Other than that it is faithful to the original. What truly powers the song is the Byrds' spirited arrangement with fiddle, banjo, mandolin and stand-up bass each contributing splendidly to the overall effect.

'Hickory Wind' underlines how stupendous this album could have been with even one more original composition of this magnitude. Co-written by Gram with former International Submarine Band member Bob Buchanan, the song was completed during January 1968 on their train ride from Florida to Los Angeles. The alluring hickory wind serves as a powerful image for Parsons' bittersweet nostalgia, as he imagines an Edenic childhood of simple pleasures like climbing an oak tree. During successive verses, he reflects on the pursuit of fame, the curse of wealth without spiritual satisfaction and the perils of city life. Buchanan composed the second and most accomplished verse, beginning "I started out younger . . ." As he says: "Of all the people in my high school class, how many go out and do what I did? I was on the road and having adventures when I was 19 years old. I had a fancy sports car and motorcycle back in my house in Hollywood. I had all that and was still bankrupt. What else can life bring? Big deal with all the riches and pleasures – that wasn't the answer." The yearning lyrics are invested with an unbearable poignancy thanks to Parsons' achingly moving vocal, which combines with a superb steel guitar backing for maximum emotional effect. The result is nothing less than arguably Parsons' greatest moment on record.

"It's his signature song," insists Hillman, with considerable conviction. "If Gram had never written another song, 'Hickory Wind' would have put him on the map. The song says it all – it's very descriptive, with vivid imagery. It's actually quite literary, but Gram, as we know, was a very bright kid."

'One Hundred Years From Now' with its noticeable percussion, seems closer to country rock than the more traditional numbers on the album. The harmonies, which were substituted for Parsons' solo lead vocal, work very well and the song remains an interesting example of Gram's pre-Burrito style. Interestingly, the composition begins as a tale of an unsuitable suitor with wanderlust tendencies, but soon develops into a more portentous speculation on human vanities, with Parsons reflecting on attitudes one hundred years hence. Coincidentally, a song of the same title, composed and performed by the Gosdin Brothers, was produced by Chris Hillman. Many years later, an archival release included an additional version of the Byrds' track with the backing vocals of McGuinn and Hillman studiously removed in order to display Parsons' rich phrasing. Again, both renditions have their merits, although the artificial deletion of the original Byrds' harmonies meant it ended up sounding like a Parsons' solo version, thereby rendering the experiment inconclusive.

'Blue Canadian Rockies', featuring a vocal cameo from Hillman, harks back to the pre-rock 'n' roll era. Texan composer Cindy Walker was a seasoned songwriter whose sumptuous catalogue included numerous hits through the Forties courtesy of Western swing king Bob Wills & The Texas Playboys. Her paean to the Canadian Rockies became a country hit for Gene Autry & The Cass County Boys and featured in the George Archainbound directed 1952 sepia tone Western, *Blue Canadian Rockies*, starring Autry and his perennial companion, Champion the Wonder Horse. Remarkably, Walker's yearning, picturesque ballads still resonated in the Sixties, most notably with Roy Orbison's classic treatment of 'Dream Baby', Ray Charles' 'You Don't Know Me' and Jim

Reeves' 1966 posthumous chart topper 'Distant Drums' – one of the best-selling singles of the year in the UK. Hillman's decision to revive 'Blue Canadian Rockies' may have been a subliminal response to hearing Parsons' 'Hickory Wind'. If not, then it was a wonderful piece of serendipity. Both songs are imbued with a strong sense of place and a panoramic landscape in which strong visual details dominate. While Parsons focuses on the pine trees and oak of South Carolina, Walker vividly describes "golden poppies" blooming around the banks of Alberta's glacial Lake Louise. Her song is structurally more accomplished, with a secondary scene that combines the memory of an idyllic setting with the longing for a far-away love. Indeed, it may be the 'sweetheart' solely mentioned in this song that partly inspired the title of the album. The arrangement is both precise and confident, while Hillman's understated vocal works perfectly, never once lapsing into overt sentimentality or melodrama. Producer Gary Usher avoids any temptation to embellish the work and even the harmonies are restrained – a far cry from Autry's recording in which a histrionic choir of angelic voices intervene to sweeten Walker's delicate, yearning ballad.

'Life In Prison', in spite of its intriguing introduction, was definitely a warm-up number and Parsons felt bitterly disappointed that the group did not record a more competent version. Parsons clearly revered Merle Haggard as a musical influence and regularly featured his prison song 'Sing Me Back Home' in the Byrds' live shows during 1968. The maudlin 'Life In Prison' offers a veritable cornucopia of familiar country themes, detailing alcohol abuse, murder, fears of insanity and morbid preoccupation with death. Hillman considered the song inappropriate and damned it with the same faint praise he always reserved for *Sweetheart Of The Rodeo*. "Doing 'Life In Prison' was Gram's idea, and that's a silly song for a 22-year-old kid with a trust fund to sing. It didn't mean anything for him to be doing a song like that . . . *Sweetheart* was a great idea but it was real sophomore in its attempt at country music . . . It wasn't something we were very well-versed in." Hillman has a point. Parsons was no Merle Haggard, an ex-convict, whose first-hand experience of his subject matter brought a chilling authenticity to his work. But to portray Parsons merely as a rich dilettante is to deny his own family history. Alcoholism, insanity and death were themes familiar to the privileged Georgian during his adolescence. His awareness of tragic loss, including the suicide of his father and the alcohol ravaged demise of his mother, meant that he was well qualified to bring meaning to Haggard's lamentation. All that is missing is a sense of gravitas and maturity in the voice that only age could bring. Indeed, the slight increase in tempo makes the Byrds' version sound almost jaunty in comparison with Haggard's slower, more tortured reading. Parsons' carping about the recording remains puzzling. Its presence on the album merely reinforces the mystery surrounding the partial re-recording of *Sweetheart Of The Rodeo*. If the legal situation concerning Parsons' vocals was resolved, it seems strange that they could not find time to record songs that weren't simply guide versions, as Gram insisted this was. What seems doubly odd is that if the material included was not quite what they had originally intended, why did they not choose to feature one of the other songs recorded at the sessions, such as 'Reputation', 'Lazy Days', 'Pretty Polly' or Kevin Kelley's surprisingly effective 'All I Have Are Memories'? Perhaps, as Gary Usher insisted, the final running order was by far the best compromise available in view of the material on offer.

The closing cut on the album, 'Nothing Was Delivered', proved a surprise highlight with a brilliant vocal from McGuinn in his best Dylan-imitation voice. Kevin Kelley finally receives the chance to play in a rock style as the drums collide with the steel guitar in a startling crescendo. It was appropriate that the Byrds should commence and conclude their exploration of traditional country music by returning to the present day. As Hillman notes: "Roger and I had access to Dylan's tapes through Columbia and we chose 'Nothing Was Delivered' and 'You Ain't Going Nowhere' as the most appropriate songs for the album."

Despite its urbane tone, 'Nothing Was Delivered' is a strangely menacing song, although you would never guess that from either Dylan's or the Byrds' rendition. The narrator's matter of fact, conversational style distracts attention from a scary scene in which an unnamed individual is held hostage, accused of larceny, blatant lies, and failing to deliver promised goods, after which he is forced to confront his 'fate' which, although not spelt out, has ominous undertones. Retribution is offered in an acquiescent, apologetic voice ("I hope you won't object to this"), even though the demand is for complete and immediate restitution of *everything* that is owed. The chorus and pay-off line about taking care and getting plenty of rest seems like a pleasant homily but, within the context of the narrative, sounds bitterly ironic. Like a smiling Shakespearian villain or a pathological gangster schooled in sinister, sarcastic understatement, the narrator's 'concern' for his host suggests that he would do well to look after his precarious health. Although it is reductive to interpret the composition as the tale of a recalcitrant drug dealer failing to make a delivery and facing the inevitable consequences, that dramatic interpretation certainly fits.

Of course, like several Dylan compositions, the song could also be analysed on a more sophisticated level as a dialogue of self and soul: the artiste and songwriter confronting his own obligations and failures either towards his audience or his art. It is worth noting that, at the time of writing the song, Dylan had recently retreated from various business and artistic demands that were threatening to become overwhelming. Such tensions are as implicit in the Byrds' version as they were in Dylan's blithely executed original. McGuinn, perhaps unaware of the song's menacing undercurrent, sounds wonderfully detached, responding to the narrative with resigned fatalism. He even risks incurring the master's wrath once again by another subtle but significant lyric change, this time modernizing the words from the original manuscript's "*take heed of this*", then adapting the line "take care of yourself . . ." to "take care of your health . . .". His phrasing here implies a certain empathy, but there is no great compassion. Like his favourite mantra, "I trust everything will work out all right", it is a testament to inaction rather than involvement, and all the better for it.

The most intriguing aspect of *Sweetheart Of The Rodeo* was not that it was one of the first 'country rock' albums, as critics have often erroneously suggested, but rather that it stood alone as a work almost completely divorced from the prevailing rock culture. Its themes, mood and instrumentation looked back to another era at a time when the rest of America was still recovering from the recent assassinations of Martin Luther King and Robert Kennedy. The usually apolitical Byrds had played a fund-raising event for Kennedy not long before his death, although this went largely unnoticed in the wake of their South African excursion. Several years before, McGuinn had written a requiem to John F. Kennedy with 'He Was A Friend Of Mine' but, with Bobby's death, it was David Crosby who translated his feelings into song with the passionate plea 'Long Time Gone'. The second Kennedy assassination symbolized the trauma of a nation already at war with itself. With the attendant escalation of the conflict in Vietnam, peaceful demonstrations had given way to street rioting and hippies were usurped in the media by yippies and political pranksters, whose watchword was organized chaos. Across the Atlantic, the Beatles were ambiguously name-checking Chairman Mao in 'Revolution', while the Stones adopted a similarly hard edge when documenting the dilemma of a 'Street Fighting Man'.

Besides the Byrds, only Dylan's reflective *John Wesley Harding* and the Band's *Music From Big Pink* sounded a similar note of old wisdom amid the political hectoring of 1968. In many respects, the Byrds' recording was the most surprising of the three, for it displayed country & western roots without any fear of being branded reactionary or out of time. While the rock audience had finally caught up with the Byrds on *The Notorious Byrd Brothers*, this new work threatened to undo that progress. For those who clung to McGuinn's notions of extending the electronic dream begun on *Notorious* into even grander synthesizer works, *Sweetheart Of The Rodeo* must have seemed the ultimate volte-face. But for discerning listeners, whose minds were open to the philosophy encapsulated in 'Change Is Now', the album was nothing less than a delight.

Sweetheart Of The Rodeo was as impressive in its own way as *Younger Than Yesterday* and *The Notorious Byrd Brothers* and marred only by the underlying feeling that its greatest moments were not quite sustained over the entirety of the album. Its strengths easily outweighed such reservations, for here was a work that strove for those essential qualities of honesty and perspective that had been lost amid the musical saturnalias of the Summer of Love and the yippie yelps of the politically disillusioned. In a time of shifting moral values and self-questioning, *Sweetheart Of The Rodeo* provided a sense of place and a love of tradition. The landscape was far removed from the familiar environs of rock culture, offering sepia snapshots of South Carolina ('Hickory Wind'), Oklahoma City ('Pretty Boy Floyd'), and Dylan's personal Utopia ('You Ain't Going Nowhere'). More than anything, it was refreshing to see the Byrds refusing to rest on their musical laurels. *Sweetheart Of The Rodeo*, a full year ahead of Dylan's celebrated *Nashville Skyline*, was not only a healthy reaction against the excesses of psychedelia, but a landmark album that spearheaded an interest in country music, which would shortly become pervasive. It was probably the bravest move that the Byrds made in their entire career, risking everything in order to pursue a new musical goal. For the umpteenth time, it demonstrated the Byrds' uncanny ability to stay ahead of their nearest rivals. Even when looking back, they remained, as their press advertisements truly noted, "always beyond today".

Regrettably, the Byrds' innovation was not rewarded with profit and, despite initially promising returns, *Sweetheart Of The Rodeo* sold fewer copies than any of their previous albums. This was particularly alarming as, according to their recently renegotiated contract with CBS, they were now responsible for studio engineering costs and session fees, all of which would be deducted from future royalties. Suddenly, that impressive roll call of Nashville musicians listed on the back of their album read like a financial liability. This setback came at a bad time for everybody. Physically and mentally exhausted after the South African debacle, McGuinn briefly went through a period of apathy regarding the Byrds' future. He was defensive when questioned about the group's integrity by the liberal press but nevertheless took the opportunity to explain his reasoning in undertaking the tour.

Warming to his interrogator from *Jazz And Pop*, he offered an American rock performer's view of South Africa: "Let me tell you a little bit about the place. Television is illegal in South Africa, you know. They do not allow television, because it would drastically change the status quo if all these oppressed people saw what they were missing in the world. Even the tight control they would have had on it would leak something through. I proposed to some of the groovy people down there, of which there is a very small group, that they should start an underground television station. But you're not allowed to mention the Beatles on the air because of what they said about Jesus . . . We told the press various things, like they should take away the segregation signs, and they really blasted us. They hated us. I heard that we're banned in England because we went down there in the first place; the English Musicians' Union is banning all British groups who go down there, and I think that's ridiculous, man, because we did a painful, sacrificial missionary trip down there. We didn't make bread, we just sort of broke even. We went down there for more or less political reasons, to help straighten out the scene or agitate or try to change the status quo as much as we could. I thought I was going to get assassinated because of what we said in the papers. We were getting threats, and telephone calls saying, 'Get out of the country, man, or else' . . . It was like Nazi Germany before the war. There was a tremendous nationalistic feeling there, sort of a self-conscious, defensive attitude that we're right, even if we're wrong. They knew they were wrong, and they knew that we knew they were wrong, and they hated us for it."

When South African newspaper reports of the Byrds' controversial and derogatory remarks about apartheid reached England, the MU lifted the ban. The circumstances of the trip indicated to many that the Byrds had not toured South Africa for commercial gain, but with altruistic motives in mind. McGuinn no doubt made a mistake following Miriam Makeba's advice, yet he never used her to defend his actions when the press turned ugly. His suggestion that the tour was a "sacrificial missionary trip" sounded like a public relations exaggeration, understandable in view of the controversy. It was much more likely that McGuinn's original motivation was simply curiosity and a desire to see and experience the events in South Africa first hand. Without wishing to drag Makeba into the debate, he naturally outlined the horrors experienced by the Byrds as the final justification for his decision and proof positive that, unlike other entertainers, his motives were clearly not for financial gain. The Byrds had suffered by touring South Africa and the negative reaction they received threatened to destroy what little morale they retained upon their return to America.

CHAPTER THIRTY

Reconstruction

WHILE the induction of Clarence White promised stability, there was still uncertainty about the future of the Byrds. Chris Hillman had been out of sorts ever since Gram Parsons' departure and the South African experience had done nothing to improve his mood. Often adversity brings people together, but Hillman and McGuinn were no longer working as a team. Faced with a crisis, McGuinn's familiar defence was icy detachment, supported by the reassuring mantra, "I trust everything will turn out all right." Some found this frustrating, while others misinterpreted his self-protective aloofness as lazy apathy. Hillman, more ruled by his emotions when angered, preferred confrontation and direct action. Increasingly, he focused his discontent on the shortcomings of his manager who had been away from the action in America during both the Parsons and South Africa crises. "Chris never liked Larry Spector," says Carlos Bernal. "Not everybody did. Spector was the manager when we went to South Africa, so he was the guy responsible for us going there. I hadn't really given that any thought, but I do remember Larry had a history of being [wary of] Chris Hillman . . . Larry was a cute, tubby little cherub, a jovial doughboy. You'd hug him, you know. He wasn't hiding it. He wore his cashmere sweaters and his silk shirts and his Belgium riding pants. He was dapper. You could tell that he was a straight ahead Rodeo Drive kind of dude . . . I don't want to be harsh on Larry. I never saw Larry do anything untoward with anybody."

Like Crosby in 1967, Hillman had lost faith in Spector, but McGuinn remained loyal, or merely indifferent. Complicating matters was Hillman's waning commitment to the Byrds. In a remarkable display of charm, Gram Parsons had somehow ingratiated himself back into Hillman's company, armed with apologies and secret plans. Informally, they mentioned the possibility of forming a new group, an idea that evidently predated Parsons' departure from the Byrds. Unknown to McGuinn, there had been a low-key recording session, financed by Eddie Tickner, which anticipated future changes. Three tunes were cut by a line-up comprising Chris Hillman, Gram Parsons, Clarence White and drummer Gene Parsons. Guitarist/violinist Gib Guilbeau also maintains he was involved. "The group was a prototype Burritos," Gene claims. "Chris had asked Clarence to join the Byrds temporarily and later become a Burrito, but Clarence decided to stay with the Byrds because he felt it would be a safer bet." While White committed himself to the Byrds, Hillman continued to vacillate, seemingly still brooding on the implications of a momentous decision.

More unrest rapidly followed, this time fomented by the group's disarmingly quiet new member. White started questioning the drumming abilities of Kevin Kelley. The timing was odd, inasmuch as Kelley had been the only Byrd whose musicianship was praised during the recent South African tour. Moreover, as a renowned session player, White could have easily adapted to any style, and Kelley's competence had never previously been questioned. Behind the musical quibbles lay political intrigue. White's real intent was to recruit his friend, Gene Parsons, whom he had worked with at Bakersfield International and played alongside in the bar bands, the Reasons and Nashville West. After joining the Byrds, White promised that he would try and get Parsons involved should the opportunity arise. Unknown to Kelley, Gene was auditioned and the drummers compared. Suddenly, Kelley found himself in the firing line. McGuinn evidently had no firm opinion but was ready to sanction the executioner's axe, if necessary. Hillman, who might have been expected to rush to his cousin's defence, seemed frozen with conflicting feelings. In the end, he was given the unenviable task of informing Kelley that he was no longer a Byrd. "I'd got Clarence into the group, but it wasn't really happening the way it should have been. Kevin was a good drummer, but sometimes you need to cool out and have a rest. It got a little too much for Kevin for one reason and another, and so we got Gene in because he'd been playing with Clarence for a year or two, and Clarence reckoned that he was the right man for the job."

Gene Victor Parsons (b. 4 September 1944, Los Angeles, CA) was raised in the desert area of Morongo Valley and after learning guitar and banjo hung out at various folk clubs and coffee houses in Hollywood. While working in a music shop, he was discovered by an aspiring folk-rock group, the Castaways, whom he joined as bassist. The group split in 1963, but their singer Gib Guilbeau continued working with Parsons as Cajun Gib & Gene. Between dates, the duo found regular employment at Bakersfield International, working on countless sessions, often with Clarence White. After playing around the bars of California, Gib and Gene teamed up with the guitarist in the Reasons/Nashville West. It says much for their friendship that White brought Parsons into the Byrds barely a month after his own recruitment.

"Clarence convinced them that they needed me," says Parsons. "Kevin was Chris' cousin and he was not happy with him. I think they were looking for a heavier drummer. They auditioned me and had me play the same tunes as Kevin so that they could compare us. Strangely enough, I thought Kevin was a really good drummer. His work on *Sweetheart Of The Rodeo* was excellent."

The circumstances surrounding Kelley's sacking have always been understated in Byrds' histories. Hillman was consistently circumspect about the details and his cousin never spoke about the matter, even with musicians whom he worked with in later years. Gene Parsons, perhaps in defence of Clarence White, now suggests it was Hillman's dissatisfaction rather than White's machinations that proved crucial. Road manager Jim Seiter, who would later perform onstage with the Byrds as an additional percussionist, also believes Kelley's family ties with Hillman contributed to his departure. "You make a mistake when you play with relatives. Kevin was always treated as an outsider because he was Chris' cousin. Instead of dealing with Kevin directly, the other members of the band would complain to Chris. So Chris resented having that responsibility. They used an excuse that Kevin had got busted for something, but I think it was his playing that was the problem. He wasn't a rock drummer, he was more into jazz and country. Onstage, he'd never start a song the same way twice. Every time they started 'So You Want To Be A Rock 'n' Roll Star', Chris would look at me, as if to say, 'What's he going to do this time?' The tempo and rhythm pattern would be totally different."

Under further cross-examination Seiter elaborated on these comments (see Volume 2 for a fuller debate). His criticisms should not detract from Kelley's considerable contribution to the recording of *Sweetheart Of The Rodeo* nor undermine his undoubted skills as a country/jazz drummer, which were well appreciated elsewhere. "I enjoyed his drumming," says Marc McClure, one of his post-Byrds collaborators. "I can always recognize his drumming. He had an interesting approach with his tom toms and that was always his signature. He was an offbeat kind of R&B drummer. He played country but it certainly wasn't a country style when he played with us."

"Kevin was a *great* drummer," claims Nashville singer-songwriter Charlie Taylor, who also worked with Kelley during the Seventies. "He loved Art Tatum, Max Roach, Charles Mingus and Dizzy Gillespie – all the jazz guys. It's true that Kevin had more of a jazz spirit than he did a rock 'n' roll feel. I'd call him a world class R&B drummer. He played behind the beat and could syncopate as well as anybody. I think that's why some people from the rock 'n' roll world might not have liked him because rock drumming is pretty much on the money whereas Kevin would lay back. I tended to write R&B stuff so that's why we fell in together. There weren't many people that could play like that, especially in rock bands. Really, it was natural for him. He was into gospel music too. He listened to a variety of stuff and had a huge appetite for good music."

In different circumstances, Kelley's eclecticism might have saved his place in the Byrds, but these were strange times. "All of a sudden Kevin was gone," says Bernal, as if he had just witnessed a magic trick. "I met him at the place where we kept our equipment, and he picked up his drums. That was it. That's how you got thrown out of the Byrds. I'd meet you in the middle of the night some place and you'd take your stuff out, never to be seen again." Remarkably, Kelley never played with any member of the Byrds – past, present or future – for the remainder of his life. There were no guest appearances on any of his cousin's albums or sessions, and Kelley was the only surviving subsidiary member who declined to cash in on the tribute fiascos during the Eighties and Nineties. Pride and integrity were the major reasons for his aloofness. While other drummers played over-familiar covers in pick-up bar bands or lived off former glories, Kelley constantly challenged himself. His musical experimentation continued in a variety of promising ensembles such as Gas, Food & Lodging, whose membership consisted of accomplished jazz musicians and talented players. A busy schedule of session work over the next decade further underlined Kelley's importance as a studio player. Without retribution or rancour, he wiped the Byrds from his memory, seldom mentioning them again.

The new line-up of McGuinn, Hillman, White and Gene Parsons was introduced to the media via a brief interview with *Disc* columnist Judy Sims. McGuinn was remarkably upbeat about their future and provided a PR spin worthy of a seasoned politician. "We anticipated a negative reaction to country, but we're overwhelmed," he gushed. "The album is selling like hotcakes. The country market is open-minded enough to accept us . . . There are too many musicians playing 15-minute guitar solos in the key of *E*." McGuinn may even have believed his own rhetoric but, if so, he was neither studying chart positions nor record sales sheets. He had also underestimated further simmering tensions in the band. Within a month, there was more drama. Chris' already negative feelings about the Byrds were exacerbated by morale sapping financial wrangles. After re-signing with CBS, McGuinn and Hillman had retained joint ownership of the Byrds and elected to pay the subsidiary members a weekly salary. At one point, they each had over $50,000 in their bank accounts, but additional monies were unlikely in view of recent record sales and future royalty deductions for the studio work done in Nashville for *Sweetheart Of The Rodeo*. Since they had named Larry Spector as their legal representative, he had power of attorney over their affairs and was able to withdraw money at will. While he detailed bills and expenses, no doubt worsened by the

RECONSTRUCTION

South African tour and successive line-up changes, Hillman became increasingly impatient and disenchanted. It should be stressed that Spector's transactions on behalf of the Byrds were legal and valid, but Hillman was convinced that the steady drop in income was an alarming prelude to financial ruin.

On 15 September, the bassist's pent-up frustration and simmering anger could no longer be contained. After a performance at the Rose Bowl's 'American Music Show Festival' in Pasadena, he erupted in a violent outrage and pinned Spector against the dressing room wall. Realizing the futility of threatening behaviour, he released Spector from his grasp, then raised his prized Fender above his head and hurled it to the ground in disgust. As a symbol of his anger, the bruised Fender was a fitting comment on four years of hard service in the Byrds. McGuinn looked on, slightly bemused, but unemotional about the tempestuous scene. "It was irresponsible the way he left though," he later complained. "He threw his bass down on the floor and said, 'I don't know why I got stuck with this fucking thing in the first place.' He just threw it down, a good, beautiful bass, and went storming out for no apparent reason. There's nothing that triggered it off that I could see. It was just building up inside . . . he went through a whole transition. Maybe growing pains, you could call it."

Growing pains was an apt description for Hillman's life in the second half of 1968. He never recovered his belief in the Byrds after the South Africa disaster, he was furious with Spector, bitter about the money and, to top it all, his marriage to Anya Butler had hit troubled waters. Worse followed when he discovered that she was involved in an adulterous liaison with, of all people, the Byrds' young roadie, Carlos Bernal. As part of his chores, Bernal had been helpfully driving her around on errands and was tempted into a clandestine relationship which soon became public.

"She and I had a torrid affair," he admits. "It made things real bad for me and Chris Hillman. That was an awfully embarrassing thing . . . she was about two years older than me and knew what she was after. I don't know whether she wanted to cause a ruckus with Chris or whether she wanted to get out of her marriage and go back to England, but she picked me to flirt with. I fell for it hook, line and sinker because I was young and naïve. She was a cute, hot English babe in a miniskirt. Other guys were all fooling around, so I didn't know the deal. She was really encouraging me and pushing it, so I got trapped. The naïve young guy chasing the pussy. Unfortunately it was my boss's wife, Chris Hillman. We were good friends and I feel real bad about it to this day even."

According to Bernal, the Anya affair was exposed about a month before Hillman's departure from the group. "He was still in the Byrds. I remember we had some concerts up in San Francisco [in August]. Chris and I already had this falling out and it was public with the band. Jim Seiter said: 'You're not going to fight. You'll stay on one side of the stage and Chris will stay on the other.' Chris and I were fighting... I thought he'd beat me up every time he saw me. I remember Seiter saying, 'No fighting, Chris! I mean it.' We had to have a truce. Anya went after me and had her way with me, and Chris and I took years to heal it."

Others suggest that Hillman never forgave Bernal. The humiliation of being cuckolded by a mere roadie must have been a devastating blow to Hillman's ego. It surely soured his already negative attitude towards the Byrds and may well have been a contributory mood enhancer to the rage he unleashed on Spector and the others after the Rose Bowl concert. For Gene Parsons, it was an unpleasant introduction to the Byrds. "The first time I played was the night Chris quit. Shortly afterwards, we had a gig booked for Salt Lake City and were really hard pushed to find a bass player."

McGuinn remained characteristically cool in the crisis and predicted that Chris' tantrum would be resolved in a matter of days. It was a severe underestimation of the seriousness of Hillman's angry disappointment and his overwhelming desire to start afresh. He also had to deal with further fury upon learning that Anya had now run off with Carlos Bernal. "We ran away to hide and Chris Hillman chased us to New Mexico," the roadie recalls. "We were mainly concerned with our torrid love affair and not getting caught by Chris who was chasing us on his motorcycle. He chased us to El Vito, New Mexico, just north of Taos. We hid at the home of Victor Maymudes, Bob Dylan's first tour manager. He had built an Adobe mansion on this enormous expanse of land. It was a rambling ranch place. He was there with Maggie, as in 'I ain't gonna work on Maggie's Farm no more'. She was as nice as she could be but after being there for a few weeks she would fine you if you slammed the door. We stayed one winter there, hiding. Then I said, 'I ain't gonna work on Maggie's Farm either!'"

The tempestuous romance never went any further. "At the end of this ruckus, Anya left Hollywood and went back to London to work for Kit Lambert and the Who," Bernal concludes. "I went to visit her twice there, but each time it was diminishing returns. The affair was over."

McGuinn remembers Hillman buying some land in New Mexico with his Byrds' settlement, an interesting coincidence in the circumstances. Despite the attendant melodrama, Chris wasted no time re-orienting his personal and professional life. Within weeks, he was forging ahead on a new project: the Flying Burrito Brothers. This, in itself, was a remarkable turnaround. Only a couple of months before, Hillman had felt like murdering Gram Parsons, but now they were back together, the best of friends. As Hillman explains: "Gram came to me, hat in hand, and said, 'I'm sorry that I did that.' We made up and we embarked on a brand new journey, which was quite fruitful and exciting from the get-go." The pair ended up in a house on De Soto Avenue, Reseda, in the San Fernando Valley. Away from the temptations of Hollywood, they disciplined themselves sufficiently to compose close to an album's worth of material in a matter of weeks. Several of the songs were inspired by the recent personal and business problems they had suffered. Hillman was so bitter about the final days of the Byrds that he poured those feelings into that apocalyptic vision of Los Angeles, 'Sin City'. The acerbic line "On the 31st floor a gold plated door won't keep out the Lord's burning rain" was inspired by the address of Larry Spector's high-rise home. It was a singularly forthright attack from Hillman and Parsons, who enjoyed calling upon divine retribution.

McGuinn soldiered on with Spector and the new Byrds, but later claimed his manager had been wrong to negotiate a big advance to the detriment of other long-term clauses in the group's contract. Within a year, Spector would quit the management business and move to Big Sur, much to McGuinn's scornful disillusionment. Hillman continued to berate Spector in interviews down the years, far more so than any other ex-member of the Byrds. This was decidedly ironic since Hillman had come out of the deal far better than anyone else and had reason to be grateful for his good fortune. With his share of the advance money, he had been able to buy some land and in disentangling himself from CBS was free to seek new employment without a huge debt hanging over his head. McGuinn was not so fortunate and in continuing with the Byrds, he had numerous financial responsibilities, which were daunting in the wake of the poor sales of *Sweetheart Of The Rodeo*. Without Hillman to share the future financial burden, his problems were exacerbated. "McGuinn had to reimburse everybody," Dickson says. "Gene, David, Eddie, me, Naomi Hirshhorn, everybody that didn't get paid royalties. After that, CBS started accounting to everybody individually, including me."

While Spector's business management of the Byrds has been severely criticized by almost everybody connected with the group, Eddie Tickner reminds us that this was a period when desperate measures were required. "The game was pretty much over," he stresses. "It had all fallen apart. In order for it to work with anybody, it had to be put together piece by piece. That means taking the Porsches and the houses on the hill away from everybody, and going back to Rice Krispies and hamburgers."

With performing commitments to fulfill, McGuinn wasted no time in appointing Hillman's replacement. John York (b. John York Foley, 3 August 1946, White Plains, New York) had originally intended to pursue a career as an actor and dreamed of joining the Royal Academy of Dramatic Arts in London. Instead, he travelled to Hollywood in the hope of getting into the movies, before finding work as a musician. His first serious group was the Bees, who later became the W.C. Fields Electric String Band. With so many new groups congregating in LA after the Byrds' success, York's unit got lost in the shuffle. From 1966 onwards, he kept busy, touring with the Sir Douglas Quintet, the Mamas & The Papas and Gene Clark, and working on sessions with Johnny Rivers. The Gene Clark Group boasted a touring line-up that included York, drummer

RECONSTRUCTION

Eddie Hoh and Clarence White, with Larry Spector acting as business manager. In late 1967, Spector had needed to fill the vacancy created by David Crosby's dismissal and initially approached the good-looking York, who declined. "At the time, I wasn't interested," he admits. "But when the offer came around again when Chris Hillman left, I accepted. I'd hitchhiked to New York and had to be flown back to join the Byrds. There was no audition as I'd already played together with Clarence in Gene Clark's group."

Almost immediately after joining the Byrds, York unexpectedly feasted on the fruits of fame. The group were booked to appear on Hugh Hefner's *Playboy After Dark* and kitted themselves out in matching suits with white, ruffled shirts. They performed two *Basement Tape* songs, 'You Ain't Going Nowhere' and 'This Wheel's On Fire', and York later joined fellow guest Marvin Gaye on a comic singalong of 'Mary Had A Little Lamb'. But the actual performances were the least eventful part of the evening for the new bass player. Amorous roadie Carlos Bernal had decided to play Cupid and his sharpened arrows found an easy target. "I introduced John to one of the penthouse playmates," he says. "He ended up staying with this blonde for about five years, or so."

While York found love with a busty playmate, the Byrds were still struggling. The *Playboy After Dark* appearance would not be broadcast for several months and news about the group was terribly sparse. York's arrival received little or no publicity and most people in the music press appeared to believe that the Byrds had folded following Hillman's departure. In fact, the group were busy in the studio preparing an album, scheduled for release in the New Year. There were also a handful of break-out gigs, including short residencies at the Whisky and San Francisco's Avalon Ballroom. Caught between the past, the present and the future, the group were still playing Hillman's 'Time Between' and Parsons' 'Hickory Wind', alongside familiar Byrds hits and oddities, including the Carl Perkins/Elvis Presley rock 'n' roll evergreen 'Blue Suede Shoes', and the strangely disappointing McGuinn/Hippard composition, 'Stanley's Song'. Tellingly, these shows were largely ignored by concert reviewers of the period.

By the end of November, a confusing report reached Britain

suggesting that Roger McGuinn was the only surviving member, while adding, somewhat cryptically, that the Byrds was now the Byrd. Amid the confusion, some deflated fans, myself included, went through a second consecutive Christmas believing that the Byrds were dead.

The early months of 1969 saw the remnants of the Byrds coming to terms with their past. David Crosby had been left marinating in the juices of his own peculiar genius at the end of 1967, but was now back in the creative ascendant working on the first Crosby, Stills & Nash album; Hillman and Parsons were completing the celebrated *The Gilded Palace Of Sin*; Gene Clark was forging ahead with the memorable *The Fantastic Expedition Of Dillard And Clark* and Michael Clarke was preparing to tour with the Expedition, after which he would reunite with Chris as a Flying Burrito Brother. Meanwhile, McGuinn was desperately attempting to keep the Byrds together and effectively starting from scratch. He soon discovered how far the group had fallen from public favour. The lack of a best-selling album ensured that the once undisputed bill toppers were now playing the bread and butter circuit of high schools and community colleges while attempting to reforge their group identity.

When McGuinn returned to his home city, Chicago, for shows at the Kinetic Playground during the first weekend of the New Year, he received no charity from the local paper. The Byrds were described by the *Chicago Tribune* as "not very good, vocally or instrumentally". The following month they appeared at the Fillmore West for a show which was fortuitously test recorded and belatedly issued as an archive release in 2000. It was far from their best live work of the period, but revealed the group attempting to come to terms with changing times with a set that included old songs, selections from their soon-to-be released studio album, some blues-influenced rock and a liberal sprinkling of country material, including 'Buckaroo', 'Close Up The Honky Tonks' and 'Sing Me Back Home'.

Financially, McGuinn was still struggling to keep the Byrds solvent. With money owing to the airlines, he was forced to accept bookings that he would not normally have considered. On one occasion, they found themselves in Mexico City, appearing on the bill of a rock concert at the Sports City Stadium, Magdalena Mixhuca before 42,000 people. Following some crowd disturbance, the event degenerated into a full-scale riot. Bravely, the Byrds completed their scheduled ten-song set amid a barrage of flying bottles and broken chairs. While frantically fighting their way back to the dressing room, they fell victim to the avaricious mania of souvenir-seeking looters. "It was bedlam," McGuinn recalls. "We were surrounded by rioting people breaking up wooden chairs and slamming me over the head with them, and trying to strangle me with my guitar. They did manage to rip off our briefcase with our passports and all the money we'd made. Wonderful!"

While the Byrds were encountering problems restoring their reputation on the road, their new album was readied for release. Following Hillman's departure, McGuinn had hoped to pursue the electronic dream, but he soon realized that the desire was his alone. "It was just a concept of mine," he admits. "I did manage to record it after *Sweetheart Of The Rodeo*. I cut a number of hours of electronic stuff, but I didn't feel that the quality was sufficient to release it. I couldn't really pursue the electronic thing on our next album because I hadn't mastered the keyboard. I didn't get my synthesizer until late 1968. I'd never been a keyboard player and they hadn't come up with a realistic neck that worked for the synthesizer. Ultimately, I think the project would have been a Roger McGuinn album rather than a group work. It would have come out like Paul Beaver or Walter Carlos, one of those things."

With the early results of his electronic music experiments confined to his private tape vault, McGuinn contented himself with the knowledge that the new Byrds could provide a mixture of country and guitar-based rock. His dream was realized as early as January 1969, when the Byrds unexpectedly re-emerged with a brilliant new single, whose contrasting sides summed up their revitalized potential. 'Bad Night At The Whiskey', co-written by Joey Richards, a 250 lb teenager whom Roger had known through his association with Subud, remains one of the great neglected Byrds songs and the first indication to fans that the group was still a productive, ongoing venture. The intricate, ghostly guitar work and heavy rock flavouring suggested that the group might be entering an exciting new phase, but they never quite pursued the direction promised by this track. Even the song's title bore no relationship to the allusive lyrics, echoing Dylan's wilful obscurity on such classics as 'Positively 4th Street' and 'Rainy Day Women # 12 and 35'. According to McGuinn, he was driving Joey Richards home after a Subud meeting and was asked to consider adding music to some lyrics. The finished composition had no chorus but they found an unexpected song title after reflecting on a disappointing show that the Byrds had played during October at the Whisky A Go-Go. Part of the song's appeal lay in McGuinn's sour, world-weary Dylanesque protest and perhaps it was these negative sentiments that prevented its long-term inclusion in the Byrds' live set.

The contrasting flip-side, 'Drug Store Truck Drivin' Man', was equally intriguing, outshining many of the lesser tracks on *Sweetheart Of The Rodeo*. Co-written with Gram Parsons in London, just prior to the South African disaster, the song was a satiric riposte to the Nashville audience that had rejected the Byrds. The lyrics were directed more pointedly against Ralph ("This one's for you") Emery, the country music disc jockey who had denounced the Byrds on Radio WSM. Between record plays, Emery would announce commercials for various items such as truck components, and it was from this that McGuinn developed the image of the drug store truck driving man who was so reactionary that he might as well be the head of the Ku Klux Klan. The lyrics were undoubtedly the wittiest that the Byrds had ever produced and the only clue we have of what McGuinn and Parsons might have produced as a songwriting team. Musically, the composition was equally strong, with some striking steel guitar work from Lloyd Green backed by excellent harmonies. Very much in the Byrds tradition of 'You Ain't Going Nowhere', this song confirmed that the group were among the great precursors of country rock.

CHAPTER THIRTY-ONE

Dr Byrds & Mr Hyde

THE new album, *Dr Byrds & Mr Hyde*, issued in the US during March 1969, lacked the consistent excellence of 'Bad Night At The Whiskey'/'Drug Store Truck Drivin' Man' but showed great promise for the future. Its cover design, featuring portrayals of spacemen as cowboys, was McGuinn's idea and partly commented on the music, which veered between country and rock. "The concept was never realized on the cover," John York points out. "It came out totally wrong and missed the point. The idea was that we were going through another transition. The original concept was that the cover would be divided into four equal sections and each section would have a black and white photo of each musician. Coming out of the third eye in the middle of each forehead would be a small colour photo of that musician with a cowboy hat on. The idea was to have a photo like that of the early Beatles, but with a colour photo coming out of the third eye so that we'd have that mystical, raising-of-consciousness overtone connected with the more roots-like traditional Western figure. But they got it completely wrong. The way they reproduced the photos on the back was sort of what we wanted, but nowhere near as artistic as we'd hoped." Indeed, McGuinn had planned to rent a flying saucer for the shoot, but was told by Columbia that it was far too expensive, so they settled for horses instead. Despite the compromises, the cover was very striking.

Having lost their previous producer Gary Usher, who was fired from Columbia after spending too much money on Chad and Jeremy's artistically ambitious but poor-selling albums *Of Cabbages*

And Kings and *The Ark*, the Byrds chose Bob Johnston as a replacement. Johnston had impressive credentials, and his recent work with Bob Dylan and Johnny Cash had been highly commended. Initially, McGuinn praised his production on *Dr Byrds & Mr Hyde*, but later reversed that opinion. It seems safe to say that the remaining Byrds were disappointed from the outset. White, Parsons and York criticized the mixing of the album and accused Johnston of playing a passive role as producer. "Bob was a joy to work with," York stresses. "He was very patient and kept us amused. But sometimes it went too far in that direction in the sense that there was not always the feeling that work was being done. He didn't really understand what we were doing."

The main contention was that the mixing left little vestige of the familiar Byrds sound. Several critics complained that the jingle-jangle Rickenbacker chime was inaudible, but the same could not be said of McGuinn's expressive vocal, which linked the work with its great predecessors and provided that distinctive Byrds' texture. More than anything, the album underlined Roger's healthy determination to take control of proceedings at a crucial time. *Dr Byrds & Mr Hyde* remains the only Byrds album on which McGuinn takes the lead on every vocal cut.

Characteristically, the Byrds opened their new LP with an unreleased Dylan song, 'This Wheel's On Fire', their third borrowing from *The Basement Tapes*. On this occasion, they faced stern competition from rival versions courtesy of the Band and Julie Driscoll & the Brian Auger Trinity. McGuinn provided an acidulous vocal and encouraged Clarence White to take lead on fuzz guitar before adding some explosive synthesizer work at the end of the track. Producer Bob Johnston was also in experimental mode and instructed Parsons to tune his snare drum so loosely that it was almost impossible to play. Parsons later admitted that he felt as though he were hitting a paper towel. The manipulation of the instruments and mixing emphasized McGuinn's vocals, but provoked fierce criticisms from the subsidiary Byrds. It was certainly a departure for White, who claimed it was the worst track that he had ever recorded. He much preferred an alternate take recorded the same day and would have been happier if Johnston had brought in another lead guitarist to play his part. "I felt I was faking it." White admitted. "In bluegrass music there is a lot of gospel and blues influences and flavouring. So the blues part was in me, but there were so many people playing blues that I didn't ever feel that I could catch up with them. I just wanted to play honest music in an honest style that I believed in and felt at ease with. 'This Wheel's On Fire' was the most embarrassing thing I've ever done."

'Old Blue' was deliberately placed in stark contrast to the electronic fade-out of 'This Wheel's On Fire' to provide sweet relief and emphasize the Byrds' dual role as innovators and traditionalists. McGuinn was happy to return to his folk roots on a traditional tune that his former manager Jim Dickson had previously produced with the Dillards in one of their most exuberant live performances. "I'd heard it performed [earlier] live by Gibson & Camp at the Gate Of Horn in 1961 and had always loved it," McGuinn adds. The song had been popularized by both Pete Seeger and Joan Baez, whose renditions were sombre and moving, complete with poignant details of the dog's demise. In their hands, it was more a requiem than a wake. Interestingly, the Byrds' version followed the more upbeat country arrangements rather than the folkier ballad renditions. The song was also one of the first Byrds' tracks to feature the famous Parsons/White Pull String, a device that enabled Clarence to duplicate the sound of a steel guitar. "I designed the String Bender for his guitar in anticipation of him doing live performances with the Byrds," Parsons notes.

'Your Gentle Way Of Loving Me' was introduced to the Byrds by Gene Parsons, having been written by his former acolytes, Gib Guilbeau and Gary Paxton. This pleasant country number, with subtle echoes of 'Gentle On My Mind', would normally have been sung by the drummer, but McGuinn felt the public might be confused by new singers emerging from the reconstituted Byrds, so he wisely took the lead vocal. The homely harmonica contrasts strongly with the surprise reverberating conclusion, suggesting that the 'Dr Byrds versus Mr Hyde' concept was in McGuinn's mind during the recording. Originally, the song was mislabelled 'Your Gentle *Ways* Of Lovin' Me' on a pressing released by Cajun Gib & Gene and McGuinn actually sang the title using the plural.

"It's 'way', we didn't sing it as 'ways'," confirms Gib Guilbeau. "But I guess it doesn't matter, it's still the same thing, although I think 'your gentle *way* . . .' makes it a little more personal. We used to close our set with that song. Sometimes we wouldn't sing the whole thing, just do a part of it at the end. I liked the way McGuinn sang it. It had a good folk-rock feel to it. McGuinn is McGuinn. Give him a Dylan song or any song and it'll come out McGuinn."

'Child Of The Universe', written by McGuinn and Dave Grusin, was mixed twice, once for the film *Candy*, and once for this album. Whereas the soundtrack version features added brass and orchestration, the *Dr Byrds* mix is sparser. As a lyrical apotheosis of the movie's eponymous heroine, the song fitted vaguely into the Byrds' catalogue of science-fiction songs, complete with references to the cosmos and the universe. McGuinn had attended an early screening of the movie in the hope of finding some inspiration for the lyrics. In the film, Candy speaks of love and her desire "to give to whoever needs it", which was partly paraphrased to provide the song's opening lines. McGuinn never bothered to incorporate the composition into his live repertoire. "It was just an attempt to write a song for a movie," he says. "I thought the song was appropriate for the movie the way it turned out."

The square dance music of 'Nashville West' closes the first side of the album on a suitably exuberant note, culminating in a drunken free-for-all in the studio in which everyone contributed to the inaudible mumblings, including McGuinn's new friend, Jacques Levy. White and Parsons, whose theme song this once was, were critical of the new arrangement, preferring the version they had performed during the Bakersfield International days, when they played at the club Nashville West in El Monte, California.

'King Apathy III' was another of McGuinn's hidden gems in the Byrds' catalogue. The Chicago-born singer always retained a healthy cynicism towards politics which spilled over into this Dylanesque observation of universal apathy. "I guess I was imitating Dylan's style," he admits. "I was very disturbed by the fact that there was so much apathy in the world and that was just my comment on it." Combining blues and country elements, the song champions the rural idyll then in vogue among the rock elite, with McGuinn contributing some sinewy lead guitar work alongside Clarence White. The song fulfils the schizoid premise of the album's title, separating and combining country and rock in an attempt to continue the template established on the magisterial 'Change Is Now'. McGuinn clearly wanted the best of both worlds, utilizing the Dylansque cool and suppressed anger of 'Bad Night At The Whiskey' and 'King Apathy III', while allowing the new members to retain the country appeal, watered-down since *Sweetheart Of The Rodeo*. McGuinn did not want the Byrds to become a Flying Burrito Brothers or Poco, as that would minimize his contribution and take them too close to the precarious environs of country and compromise their appeal as a rock band.

John York receives his first co-writing credit on 'Candy', a charming period piece on which McGuinn once more assumes lead vocal. The guitar work is again notable, the singing high, and the lyrics far more appropriate to the subject matter of the movie. "We'd met the director and done some incidental music for the film," York recalls. "He wanted a theme song, so Roger and I wrote 'Candy' while we were in Nashville. My understanding is that the song was rejected because I was completely unknown and they wanted Roger to work with Dave Grusin, who was a well-established songwriter. The rest of us didn't think much of his song."

The concluding medley was as unusual and unexpected in its own way as those other album closers 'We'll Meet Again' and 'Oh! Susannah'. A tantalizing snatch of 'My Back Pages', minus the familiar jingle-jangle sound, is followed by a blues excursion, ending with a grammatically improved version of Jimmy Reed's 1959 classic 'Baby What You Want Me To Do', a number they had once performed onstage with Bob Dylan. The Byrds' signature tune of the period, 'Hold It!', already familiar to their new audience, completes the medley with McGuinn signing off and pointedly promising to return soon. According to John York, the medley was a theatrical touch, born of spontaneity. "Roger was willing to try anything at that point. We decided to leave the ending in to remind people of the live band. Most bands, when you see them perform, have a 'break song' that they play between sets. Being the Byrds, we only got to do one show, so we never had that. For fun, we started to play 'Hold It!', which a lot of groups in the Sixties used as a break song. We wanted to show the Byrds shifting once more into a new genre. It was supposed to have the feeling of us saying, 'We'll be right back . . . the Byrds are still here and are coming back stronger than ever.'"

Overall, the album demonstrated McGuinn's determination to keep the Byrds alive. The recruitment of Clarence White and Gene Parsons enabled him to retain a country element placed firmly within a rock framework. Essentially, the album was more 'Dr Byrds' than 'Mr Hyde'. The schizophrenic concept was ironically reflected in the disparity between the encouraging reviews and an appalling US chart performance. No Byrds album had ever failed to reach the *Billboard* Top 100 but this one stalled at a lowly number 153, 76 places below the uncommercial *Sweetheart Of The Rodeo*. By bizarre contrast, it climbed to number 15 in the UK, a far better showing than such sterling predecessors as *Fifth Dimension*, *Younger Than Yesterday* or *Sweetheart Of The Rodeo*. This statistic was all the more impressive considering that the Byrds had done nothing to promote the album outside of America. The major UK music weeklies all paid tribute with the *NME* headlining their review: 'Byrds Push Forward Into Country Music'. This was proof enough of the group's still untapped potential in Europe as a touring act.

It is worth stressing that *Dr Byrds & Mr Hyde* was critically applauded in its time, even in America. Historically, it was undermined by some negative comments from the subsidiary Byrds, who felt constrained by Bob Johnston's production and McGuinn's dominance as vocalist. Revisionist critics were also less than kind, indicating a vast chasm of contradiction between contemporaneous thought and modern appreciation. Or perhaps they were simply too influenced by the sour soundbites of Gene Parsons and Clarence White, which were widely reported. For those of us who championed the work vigorously and still regard it highly, its merits seem self-explanatory. The presence of York added a different flavour, complementing and reinforcing McGuinn's vocal. "I had the same voice as David," York notes, "the high voice that had been missing for a long time. I think Roger felt he finally had the band he wanted for the road. I thought of it as a period of reconstruction after a great battle."

Not everyone was pleased by McGuinn's dogged persistence in continuing with the Byrds' name. Although the press seemed reasonably supportive, a shower of brickbats was forthcoming from his former colleagues, Chris Hillman and Gram Parsons. With the term country rock still a neologism, the Flying Burrito Brothers had just completed the highly accomplished *The Gilded Palace Of Sin*. Dressed in garish, floral suits, courtesy of the country stars' tailor Nudie, they pioneered a confrontational musical style fusing urban blues with traditional country, behind a distinctly rock beat in which steel guitars and mandolins collided with advanced studio wizardry. This paradox was exhilarating as familiar country phrasing vied with synthesized brass and distorted guitars to proclaim the birth of a new musical genre. The songs featured righteous assaults on LA life ('Sin City'), drug abuse ('Juanita'), groupies ('Christine's Tune') and draft evasion ('My Uncle'). Like *Dr Byrds & Mr Hyde*, the Burritos' debut sold poorly and seemed equally lost on rednecks and mainstream rock fans, despite flattering reviews.

While promoting *The Gilded Palace Of Sin*, Hillman and Parsons could not resist attacking McGuinn, whom they seemed to regard as a pariah simply for carrying on with the Byrds. Parsons, knowing that McGuinn had no real authenticity as a country singer, questioned his credentials in performing such material and continued to bracket him and the Byrds as Dylan disciples. While Parsons saw himself as a self-destructive latter-day Hank Williams, he regarded McGuinn as a more reserved and distant figure, whose passions were firmly held in check. "He's always found a way to either buy the information or gather the information that he needs to keep up with what's going on," Parsons sneered. "He doesn't live that life, and he brings you down. Clarence White has always been right – but he's an original friend of Chris Hillman. McGuinn wouldn't know Clarence White from Mighty Sam if it wasn't for Chris. As a matter of fact, he probably never heard of Mighty Sam! . . . And everybody still writes all these comprehensive articles on him like *Crawdaddy* and all that analytical bullshit. Singing like Dylan, thinking like Dylan, selling like Dylan."

Although Hillman should have known better, he joined in the ritual mauling. Still smarting from the conflict with Larry Spector and completely disillusioned with the Byrds, he even took the unprecedented measure of momentarily siding with David Crosby when discussing the group's politics. "He [David] was up till half of the album *The Notorious Byrd Brothers*. Then he left. It got to be ridiculous. It's very difficult to work with McGuinn, you know, on anything. He's the type of guy that . . . it's just a job. He goes up onstage and becomes a musician. Offstage he's not. He doesn't buy records, he doesn't listen to the radio, he doesn't keep up with what's happening in music. The last album that they did, it was McGuinn and the rest was his hired group . . . They should have buried it – let it die, that was it, over. All McGuinn's doing now is riding it out till it ends, just for the money. It's not a creative, productive thing any more. He pays everybody's salary every week, and he's the head Byrd."

Hillman's gibe about "riding it out for the money" was terribly disingenuous given that he had just pocketed his remaining advance money and escaped from Spector and CBS, while the less canny McGuinn was still locked into that relationship and its attendant financial burdens. The reference to "hired musicians" was true, inasmuch as the rest of the group were paid on a weekly basis by McGuinn, but similar conditions of employment had been enforced when Chris had joint ownership of the Byrds, so little had changed. Given that neither the Byrds nor the Burritos were selling vast quantities of records or filling stadiums, the feuding talk sounded a little ludicrous. They might have been better advised to pool their resources for mutual benefit and, in fact, did precisely this both before and after the publication of Chris' and Gram's barbed comments.

It says much for McGuinn's level-headedness that he paid little, if any, attention to criticisms made by fellow Byrds in the press. All the members continued to be engagingly frank about each other over the years, but their comments did not always tally with their actions. On several occasions during 1969, the Byrds and Burritos appeared onstage together, celebrating their mutual heritage as country rock pioneers. The first of these get-togethers took place at the hip club, the Boston Tea Party. Their respective repertoires extended to include old and new songs; three strong Dylan renditions: 'You Ain't Going Nowhere', 'My Back Pages' and 'It's All Over Now, Baby Blue'; a stunning Gram Parsons solo set, including the haunting 'Hickory Wind', and Hillman reaching back to *Younger Than Yesterday* for 'Time Between'. Even McGuinn acknowledged the sense of occasion and included 'Pretty Boy Floyd' and 'The Christian Life' from the one album that the three had recorded together. The highlight of the evening, however, was a fine rendition of 'You Don't Miss Your Water' with Parsons singing lead, backed by McGuinn and Hillman. The performance provided a revealing insight for those who had wondered how *Sweetheart Of The Rodeo* might have sounded with Parsons singing lead throughout. Completing the set were three songs that would never appear on Byrds' albums: Gene Parsons' version of 'Take A City Bride' (later featured on his solo album *Kindling*), John York's reading of Danny Dill and Marijohn Wilkin's country standard 'Long Black Veil' and a McGuinn/York duet on 'Get Out Of My Life Woman' (the old Lee Dorsey hit that the Byrds, inspired and encouraged by Michael Clarke, had rearranged into 'Captain Soul').

When the two groups repeated the reunion at Carnegie Hall later in the year, Byrds' connoisseur George Guttler was on hand to provide an effusive commentary: "After the Byrds' typically outstanding set, instead of an encore, the Burritos came back out and the whole conglomeration went into 'You Ain't Going Nowhere' with Roger, Gram and Chris taking verses. What followed was Gram playing Roger's 12-string on 'Hickory Wind' and Gram, with Roger and Chris, on Merle Haggard's 'Sing Me Back Home', a tribute to the infamous night at the *Grand Ole Opry*. Chris took a turn on 'I Am A Pilgrim', freed up to play mandolin by John York on bass. Since the Byrds adapted the instrumental arrangement of 'Pilgrim' note-for-note from the Kentucky Colonels' *Appalachian Swing*, it was no surprise that Clarence played his acoustic guitar perfectly. Another nice bonus was Bernie Leadon on banjo during 'Pretty Boy Floyd'. They closed the show with 'Roll Over Beethoven' with Chris taking a very confident lead vocal and Roger, Sneaky Pete, Clarence and Bernie trading guitar leads. Needless to say, to a Byrds' fan this dual Byrds/Burritos show was a dream come true."

The success of these surprise get-togethers prompted music industry rumours that a joint album was in the offing. At a time when both groups needed a boost, this seemed an excellent idea, but the moment passed without anyone pursuing the venture. Alas, the hopes of further onstage reunions receded as both units fulfilled their respective recording commitments. For John York, the Byrds/Burrito package was a missed opportunity. "Those gigs were really magic," he enthuses. "Something more could have come from it. Someone should have booked a tour because, organically, it was already alive."

The new Byrds seemed in reasonable spirits as they began the long haul towards renewed commercial success. Nevertheless, there was an underlying realization that the group was still primarily a vehicle for McGuinn's music, with the subsidiary members cast in the role of hired hands. Like a schoolmaster unwilling to become too close to his students, McGuinn retained a slight distance from his new colleagues. "We were very different people," Gene Parsons stresses. "There were times when I really tried to make friends with Roger and there were times when I felt I was successful, but he would stay just a little aloof. He and I had difficulties with one another and personality conflicts, even early on."

For the more impressionable John York, McGuinn remained a frustrating enigma who showed flickers of warmth, punctuated by longer periods of emotional detachment. When York first joined the Byrds, McGuinn kindly offered to allow him to live at his house until he found a permanent home in Los Angeles. York politely declined, but appreciated the gesture. It was not long before the more glacial aspect of McGuinn's character manifested itself. "I didn't do the research," York regrets. "I should have said to myself, 'What has this guy been through?' I knew about Crosby and I knew that I was not going to have that kind of a relationship with him. I knew what it was like to be onstage with Gram and I knew the other guys, but I never stopped to think, 'What damage was done to Roger through all this?' And he presented himself as this immovable guy, this impervious, thick-skinned individual. Now I know why he was like that because he had gone through all these other ego maniacs."

Having survived the rock wars with Crosby and Parsons, McGuinn was unlikely to let his guard down in the future, especially in the company of relative neophytes. Throughout the Byrds' history, he had retained control by allowing his adversaries to overreach themselves in the struggle for power and he retained that tactic in his interaction with the second generation line-up. York recalls being taken aside by manager Larry Spector and told: "Roger's tactic is to do nothing. You'll have this feeling that everything's out of control, but it's just a tactic he's learned to deal with people. Don't let it throw you. That's just what he does. He won't do anything until he's backed so far up against a wall that he'll make a decision and it may appear heartless, but that's how he's learned to survive." York listened, but failed to grasp the sagacity and significance of Spector's comments. More than once, he would look at McGuinn and ask himself: "God, what is this guy? He's like a robot or something."

McGuinn's emotional disconnection provoked some humorous comments. On one occasion, he turned up with a new pair of dark tinted contact lenses which, when worn out of direct sunlight, had the disconcerting effect of blackening his pupils. Those addressing him would be greeted by a seemingly otherworldly automaton with expressionless eyes staring at them like black coals. Behind his back, the other Byrds used to joke, "He should wear those all the time because he really looks as though he has no heart." McGuinn affected a cool, unflappable persona and continued to avoid confrontation, unless it was absolutely necessary.

In spite of the Byrds' dissatisfaction with the mixing of *Dr Byrds & Mr Hyde*, producer Bob Johnston was retained for the new Byrds single, 'Lay Lady Lay'. The song fared badly in the States and was later heavily criticized by the group, who were incensed at Johnston's unilateral decision to back them with a wailing choir. They would never work with him again. "We loved 'Lay Lady Lay'," York says. "After *Nashville Skyline* Bob [Johnston] played us that cut at Roger's house and we decided to do it. But then, unknown to us, he overdubbed the girls' voices and it became an embarrassment. We felt it sounded like a parody. We even stopped doing it in concert."

Despite the Byrds' corrosive comments, not everyone was

dissatisfied with the track. Many felt the choral overdub added a dramatic touch which heightened the song's emotional appeal. In Britain, the *NME*'s singles reviewer Derek Johnson clearly supported his near namesake Bob Johnston all the way, and proclaimed: "A great version of one of the strongest numbers on Bob Dylan's LP. The harmonic support behind the solo vocal is really outstanding, largely because the Byrds have been augmented by a girl chorus. This, plus the familiar acoustic guitars, the attractive melody and the obstructive beat, makes it one of the group's best discs in ages."

The single even received a fair amount of airplay and became yet another in a long series of Byrds near misses. Its lack of commercial success hardened their conviction against the recording, but one wonders how they would have reacted if Johnston's choir had restored them to Top 10 glory. Their sense of an opportunity squandered was compounded soon afterwards when Dylan's original version was released and became a sizeable hit.

Still smarting from their involvement with Bob Johnston, the Byrds sought a more sympathetic producer. In an attempt to turn the clock back to the Byrds' golden era, McGuinn suggested Terry Melcher, whom he had always liked, despite having agreed to fire him after the recording of *Turn! Turn! Turn!*. Without the political distractions of the Crosby/Dickson axis to worry about, McGuinn felt confident that Melcher could work successfully with the group and assist their climb back towards the big time. Melcher was understandably cautious in his dealings with McGuinn, but came up with a perfect compromise. "Roger and Clarence came down to my house on the beach," he remembers, "and I agreed to become producer and personal manager, not wishing for a repetition of the Dickson affair."

With Melcher at the controls, the Byrds commenced work on their eighth studio album. Meanwhile, the group received a smidgen of additional publicity when Together Records issued the archival album *Preflyte* on 29 July. This welcome and wholly unexpected artefact allowed a secret glimpse into the group's pre-Columbia days. Although David Crosby was sensitive about sanctioning the album's release, he was finally won over by his new partner Graham Nash, whose enthusiasm for the recordings convinced him to sign the letter of permission required by former manager/producer Jim Dickson. "Graham Nash said that the songs were charming baby pictures," Dickson recalls. "You have to get a little older before you can tolerate seeing your baby pictures out there. We were all babies once! Graham just charmed David's socks off."

While *Preflyte* revealed the Byrds' secret origins, McGuinn still had eyes firmly focused on the future. In a break between sessions, he performed under his own name on the soundtrack album *Easy Rider*. The film had premiered the same month that *Preflyte* was issued and caused a sensation which was to have a profound and lasting effect on the movie industry. It was among a handful of films that spearheaded the emergence of the 'New Hollywood' in which young directors wrested creative control of film-making from their more conservative forebears and were proclaimed instant auteurs. The principals behind the movie both had bad boy reputations as anti-establishment Hollywood outlaws. Dennis Hopper had starred alongside James Dean in both *Rebel Without A Cause* and *Giant* in the mid-Fifties, but his confrontational personality and penchant for alcohol had torpedoed his career for most of the succeeding decade. In 1967, he had attended the Human Be-In in San Francisco, during which he swallowed copious amounts of LSD and emerged as a hippie convert, albeit one whose mantra was closer to chaos and violence than love and peace. The more pacific Peter Fonda was part of a Tinseltown dynasty, whose career thus far had been eclipsed by that of his more famous sister Jane and celebrated father, Henry. Peter's film career had begun innocently enough in 1963 with *Tammy And The Doctor*, but thereafter he sought out nonconformist roles, starring in the Roger Corman directed biker movie *The Wild Angels* and the LSD-inspired *The Trip*.

Easy Rider was originally conceived by Fonda as a modern Western in which cowboys were supplanted by biker hippies on a cross-country trek across the American hinterland. In a prescient moment, Hopper suggested that the characters carry cocaine which, a few years later, would become the drug of choice among rock stars. Fonda, in his role as producer, was effectively combining the themes of his recent film appearances – the result was a biker saga which included a memorable scene in which the participants experienced a psychedelic high. It sounded like *The Wild Angels* meets *The Trip*. In selecting music for his road movie, Fonda defied convention by bypassing familiar film composers in favour of his rock star friends and personal record collection.

It seemed inevitable that the Byrds would figure somewhere in his thinking as there were already any number of oblique links between them and the movie. Former manager Jim Dickson had known director Dennis Hopper since the Fifties and they'd even had a fistfight over actress Diane Varsi. Unintentionally, Hopper later helped deliver Crosby and other Byrds into the hands of Dickson and Tickner's successor, Larry Spector. Fonda, of course, had been a Byrds' fan since the Ciro's days and was a personal friend of both Crosby and McGuinn. The Byrds even played at his sister Jane's Independence Day party in Malibu, described in Chapter Ten. Peter had also accompanied the Byrds during their Hollywood acid soirée with the Beatles in August 1965 when he famously uttered the words "I know what it's like to be dead" (recalling a chilling memory of how he had shot himself in the stomach, aged 11, and a consequent operation), which John Lennon later used on 'She Said She Said'. Another associate was *Easy Rider*'s third leading man Jack Nicholson, whose film debut, *The Little Shop Of Horrors*, included camera work by Dickson and who was namechecked during the Byrds' Ciro's shows and on the back sleeve of *Mr Tambourine Man*. Also in the cast was Toni Basil, the dancer who had dated Michael Clarke back in 1965. *Easy Rider*'s screenwriter Terry Southern had previously worked on *Dr Strangelove*, which had inspired the Byrds to record 'We'll Meet Again' and he had also written the book *Candy*, the film of which included the group's music. Finally, among the cameramen was Barry Feinstein, who had photographed the Byrds on their bus tour and provided the iconic fish lens shot used for the cover of their first album. He had played the peacemaker during the Byrds' infamous fistfight on the beach amid the chaotic filming of 'Set You Free This Time'. While working on *Easy Rider*, he ended up in a brawl with Dennis Hopper.

Peter Fonda had intended to feature Bob Dylan's 'It's All Right Ma (I'm Only Bleeding)' in the film but after failing to license the track, he asked McGuinn to record his own interpretation. McGuinn also agreed to write the title song to the movie, which was played over the credits. Both songs were substantially different from the material that the Byrds were currently recording. McGuinn adopted his Dylan-imitation voice sounding like an ex-Greenwich Village folkie revisiting old memories. Gene Parsons added to the stark feel by playing bluesy harmonica. In addition to the solo material, Fonda wanted to include two tracks from *The Notorious Byrd Brothers*: 'Wasn't Born To Follow' and 'Draft Morning'. In the end, only the Goffin/King tune was featured. CBS later took advantage of this turn of fortune by issuing 'Wasn't Born To Follow' as a single in the vain hope that it might provide the Byrds with a fluke hit.

It is difficult to estimate the effect that the film *Easy Rider* had on the popularity of the Byrds, but it certainly put them back into the limelight. The characters played by Peter Fonda and Dennis Hopper bore a striking physical and psychological resemblance to McGuinn and Crosby, respectively, which was clearly no coincidence. "I loved the movie," McGuinn says. "I told Peter, 'Boy, I sure would have liked to have been in the movie.' And he said: 'You were!' Peter and Dennis Hopper were modelling their characters after David Crosby and me. Dennis got David down . . . and Peter was like, 'I trust it'll work out all right, it'll be cool, man.' That's what he meant [when he said] that I was in it. He was using me. It was a nice honour. I was really proud to have my music in it."

Crosby was also impressed by the accuracy of his own depiction. "Peter was just Peter, but Dennis was me, right down to the fringed jacket and the pocket-knife. He just saw that as a good image – kind of loose and crazy, laughing, fierce at times." Unintentionally, the Crosby/McGuinn rivalry was even played out in the choice of music. At one point, it was intended that CSN&Y's 'Find The Cost Of Freedom' would accompany the film's closing scene, but the ideas was jettisoned. "I sabotaged that," claims Hopper. "They picked me up in a limo at Columbia, and drove me over, played the music. I told Steve Stills, 'Look, you guys are really good musicians, but very honestly, anybody who rides in a limo can't comprehend my movie, so I'm going to say no to this, and if you guys try and get in the studio again, I may have to cause you bodily harm.'" Crosby claims that there was an invitation to provide further music, which was regrettably declined due to recording commitments for the first CS&N album. "We could have done one or the other. Very tough, because we wanted to do it. That was an amazing movie."

Instead, McGuinn took full advantage of the opportunity. Originally, he had assumed that *Easy Rider* was some independent motorcycle B-movie, but soon realized that it was likely to become a mainstream success. One person who seldom, if ever, receives any acknowledgement for behind the scenes work is Larry Spector. By the time the movie was released he had moved on, but he was a crucial player in putting it all together, not least because he managed Hopper, Fonda and the Byrds during its early production. Sensing a swing in the Byrds' favour, McGuinn announced that the group's next album would be titled 'Captain America' after the central character in *Easy Rider*. Anticipation was high for the new record but if the public were looking to McGuinn for counter-cultural anthems about freedom, motorbikes and revolution, then they were soon to be disappointed.

Melcher continued working on the 'Captain America' sessions through June–July, completing two final tracks, 'Fido' and 'Armstrong, Aldrin And Collins' in late August. By that point, it was a wonder that he could still concentrate on any work at all for, on 9 August, he had received the most horrifying and spinechilling news of his life. The house he had recently vacated on 10050 Cielo Drive had become the killing ground for one of the most gruesome mass murders in modern American history. The victims included the pregnant movie star Sharon Tate (carrying Roman Polanski's child), hairdresser-to-the-stars Jay Sebring, coffee heiress Abigail Folger and her friend Voytek Frykowsky. These brutal and senseless murders outraged the cosseted Hollywood elite and would shortly cast a dark shadow over the Summer of Love generation. Within 24 hours, a second series of slayings took place at 3301 Waverly Drive, near Griffith Park, when a middle-aged couple, Leno and Rosemary LaBianca, were hacked to death.

The macabre nature of the killings provoked crazy rumours of Satanic rites and ritual sacrifices inspired by nightmarish LSD visions. It was as if Roman Polanski's chilling movie *Rosemary's Baby* had come to life to haunt Hollywood. Fear spread like a contagion through Beverly Hills and Bel Air, prompting peaceniks to arm themselves against crazed demons, whose identities and motives remained unknown. It was alarming enough to learn that they had murdered Sharon Tate, the young blonde star of *Don't Make Waves*, whose film theme the Byrds had provided two years before. More worrying was the growing suspicion that the intended victim might be Terry Melcher, whose social circle included some of the richest and most talented members of the Californian rock aristocracy. John Phillips drowned such fears in nightly bottles of Tequila and acquired a variety of pistols and hunting knives for nocturnal company. David Crosby was equally alarmist and told me, "All those people were killed by mistake. That's how crazy those damn kids were. It was around then that I started carrying a gun." Melcher also armed himself, while still hoping that the Cielo Drive slaying was some bizarre coincidence that had no link with his past.

For those outside the mansions of Hollywood, life continued as mundanely as before. With *Preflyte* and the soon-to-be-released *Easy Rider* soundtrack, the Byrds had reminded the rock world that they were a group with a long and important history. Unfortunately, that history also contained a disproportionate amount of unrest and conflict, which was about to be revisited upon them. As they completed a successful summer tour, sandwiched between sessions for their current album, it became increasingly clear that all was not well with John York.

"I was very unhappy," he recalls. "I began to realize that what they wanted from me was pretty small in terms of what I could give them. I sing, play the piano, bass and write. Roger wanted to encourage those things in me, but he didn't want another Gram Parsons on his hands. I'd always known how to perform but I never really knew the business. Once we played somewhere and were two-and-a-half hours late. But the people were so patient; no stamping or anything. We went out and did a 35-minute set. I wanted to play all night. I felt we owed them more. I wanted to give them something they'd never forget. But I was embarrassing everyone by getting so upset. The other guys were saying, 'Cool it, man.' Had I been more professional, I would have said, 'We'll get them next time around', or realized that Roger knew what he was doing."

What York saw as integrity was interpreted by the other Byrds as an example of naivety and unprofessionalism. As the weeks passed, he became more alienated from his fellow members, who felt he was overreacting to irrelevancies. During the recording of their new album, he appeared restive and subdued. By the end of the sessions he considered handing in his notice, but then had a change of heart. Feeling that there was a possibility of contributing more material in the future, he decided to stay on.

CHAPTER THIRTY-TWO

Uncertain Riders

THE summer of 1969 was a great period for rock festivals and a golden opportunity to reach a mass audience with a minimum of effort. McGuinn was still attempting to re-establish the Byrds critically and commercially so he eagerly accepted bookings at three of the more prestigious musical events of the season. On 20 June, the Byrds appeared at Newport '69 on a bill that included Jimi Hendrix, Joe Cocker, Creedence Clearwater Revival, Jethro Tull and Steppenwolf; on 25 July, they played the Seattle Pop Festival alongside Led Zeppelin, the Doors, Chuck Berry, Bo Diddley, Vanilla Fudge and Chicago, and on 1 August they attended the Atlantic City Pop Festival with the Jefferson Airplane, Santana, Creedence, B.B. King and Iron Butterfly. For those three dates alone, the Byrds were heard by over a quarter of a million people. At any other time, this would have been an occasion for back-slapping congratulations but the rock zeitgeist was not to be found at Newport, Seattle or Atlanta. In the lottery of music festivals that summer, the Byrds had missed out on the one event that promised and provided instant worldwide recognition. "We were flying to a gig and Roger came up to us and said that a guy was putting on a festival in upstate New York," John York remembers. "But at that point they weren't paying all of the bands. He asked us if we wanted to do it and we said, 'No'. We had no idea what it was going to be. We were burned out and tired of the festival scene. You'd be there for hours and hours because they were so massive you couldn't just drive in and out. They were never running according to schedule, so you had to wait until it was your turn to play. It was more draining than a normal gig and usually there was no soundcheck. You ran up real quick and hoped for the best. So all of us said, 'No, we want a rest' and missed the best festival of all."

The Woodstock Music And Arts Fair: An Aquarian Exposition at Max Yasgur's farm in Bethal, New York, was the ultimate gathering of the tribes and a final communal flowering of Sixties' youth culture. It seemed a world away from the disturbing news of the Tate/LaBianca murders that had occurred the previous week. On the East Coast, it was a time to celebrate the generation that still believed in its powers to change the old order. At this point, the perpetrators of those crazy murders in Tinseltown were still undiscovered. Nobody knew their ages, backgrounds or motivation. Hollywood murder suggested movie excess or organized crime, scenarios far removed from the hippie culture, whose preoccupations were neatly summarized in the Woodstock subtext, 'peace, love and music'.

Between 15–17 August, an audience of close to half a million descended on the hamlet, while the numbers forced to turn back was greater than any single recorded concert or festival attendance. A stupendous line-up turned up to play, including Joan Baez, the Band, Blood Sweat & Tears, the Butterfield Blues Band, Canned Heat, Joe Cocker, Country Joe & The Fish, Creedence Clearwater Revival, the Grateful Dead, Arlo Guthrie, Tim Hardin, the Keef Hartley Band, Richie Havens, the Incredible String Band, Jimi Hendrix, Jefferson Airplane, Janis Joplin, Melanie, Quill, Santana, John Sebastian, Sha Na Na, Ravi Shankar, Sly & The Family Stone, Bert Sommer, Sweetwater, Ten Years After and the Who. But the musician whose presence was most closely associated with the festival was the man whom McGuinn had fired 23 months before.

The recently formed Crosby, Stills, Nash & Young, playing only their second gig in public, became the living embodiment of what was loosely termed the Woodstock Nation. They were among the first of the 'supergroups', a vainglorious concept that crystallized the vanities of artistic ambition amid the flowering of hippie idealism. Most of the species from Blind Faith to Humble Pie seemed ill-matched, often cancelling out each other's individual talents without necessarily adding to the whole. CSN&Y were different. There was nothing remote, distant or artificial about their music. This was not a combination of convenience but a natural evolution that promised a musical nirvana in which the beauty of the Byrds, the Hollies and Buffalo Springfield could be rechanneled into a completely new dynamic. David Crosby, already blossoming as a songwriter during the latter-days of the Byrds, had hit a rich vein of form in the succeeding months, completing a formidable catalogue of songs, including 'Guinnevere', 'Laughing', 'Long Time Gone', 'Games', 'Song With No Words', 'Is It Really Monday?', 'You Sit There', 'Wooden Ships' and 'The Wall Song'. The concomitant release of *Crosby, Stills & Nash* was a striking example of David's vocal and songwriting power, boasting exquisite harmonies, outstanding arrangements, advanced but subtle production and some highly accomplished playing, each contributing to a sound that proved remarkably fresh and hugely influential. From the jazzy time signatures of 'Guinnevere' to the politically incendiary 'Long Time Gone' and the co-written escapist fantasy 'Wooden Ships', the album cemented Crosby's reputation as the uncrowned king of the counterculture and gave notice to McGuinn that he had transcended his time in the Byrds and was now among rock's new elite.

If Woodstock, the festival of the people, precipitated the unstoppable rise of corporate rock in the Seventies, then David Crosby was part of that paradox. CSN&Y soon joined the biggest grossing acts of the era, spiralling heavenwards in a creative and fiscal explosion that would culminate in the release of the chart-topping *Déjà Vu* early the following year. Crosby's rise to superstardom came as a shock to McGuinn who had never anticipated such an outcome. It was the perfect vindication for David, public proof in his mind that he had been right all along in protesting that McGuinn had held back his genius in the Byrds. There was no urgent need to gloat or even mention the matter, as it was self-evident. Crosby's familiar visage could be seen in music papers and record stores all over the world. McGuinn was unsure how to react, so said little or nothing. But he was affected by Crosby's level of fame. "I was jealous, I must admit, when they were at their peak. I mean, I hired David Crosby and I fired the guy. I remember Dylan once said to me, 'Did you ever think David Crosby would make it as big as he did?', and I said, 'No', and he said, 'I didn't either'. Of course, Dylan will deny that if you ask him."

While Crosby was being lauded by the music press, McGuinn was still scratching for credibility and income with a Byrds' line-up whose pedigree remained uncertain. The summer that had brought unprecedented triumph for Crosby ended in further instability for the Byrds, whose cursed line-up changes showed no signs of decelerating. Before the end of September 1969, John York was officially asked to leave, apparently the victim of his own insecurity. "I was very depressed," he acknowledges. "I told Clarence and Gene that I planned to stay for three months more. I figured that would give them time to find a new bassist and get me some money to survive. Little did I know that they'd been monitoring me and had someone who was willing to join immediately."

York still recalls the fateful day Gene Parsons phoned with the stern warning, "John, sit down, boy!", followed by the crushing words, "You're not in the band any more." The bassist took the news stoically, although he was somewhat bemused by the method of execution. "Roger never fired me," he points out. "I thought it was ironic because Gene was not my employer, Roger was, but it didn't seem to matter at the time. I was glad they'd found somebody, and there were no bad feelings."

Oddly, McGuinn has subsequently put an improbable twist on the story. "There's a rumour going around that I fired him. I never did that. He left. It was his blonde girlfriend. She didn't want him going on the road. That was it. It was for a girl. I think he regrets it now." York was nonplussed by McGuinn's peculiar revisionism. "I guess he forgot I was fired. Maybe it makes him feel better to think that."

Although Parsons and White were responsible for finding a replacement, their decision to oust York was obviously supported by McGuinn, even if he delegated the sacking and distanced himself from the executioner's axe. "I loved John, he was a great guy and we were the best of friends," Gene Parsons adds. "But when you're young, you're filled with an idealism which isn't always founded on good logic. John didn't want to play old Byrds tunes. He kept saying, 'I want to do something else.' Obviously, we were into what we were doing. The rest of the band felt that if John was going to keep complaining and wasn't coming to work with the spirit we wanted, then he needed to move on, whether he needed the money or not. Since I was closest to him, I was designated to be the bearer of the news. I wasn't the one that actually caused him to be fired. It was the consensus. We decided that it was best, not only for us but for him because he was miserable. Maybe it was just who he was at that time in his life, but we needed somebody to be there 100 per cent."

Unusually eager to play the armchair psychologist, McGuinn concluded that the impressionable York was the victim of a doomed infatuation with the Byrds dating back to 1965. The pressure of living up to the image of being a Byrd was supposedly intolerable and McGuinn maintains that for York, "it was like being a Beatle". York, while not agreeing with McGuinn's personality profile, admitted that there were problems: "I was not a Byrds freak. I did really love 'Mr Tambourine Man' and the early songs, but after the second album I completely lost touch with their music. However, there is an element of truth in Roger's statement. I was beginning to feel like a computer part. Onstage, people would go bananas before we even played a note. I felt almost like a liar. What I had to give could never come across because it didn't seem to matter who the Byrds were. The people in the audience had this idea in mind and it didn't seem to matter who was there, as long as it was McGuinn and some other guys. I felt I was not giving. It was like living a lie. Leaving was a matter of integrity."

The dismissal of York was seen by some critics as further proof of McGuinn's dominance over the Byrds and refusal to compromise. Continued changes in the line-up earned McGuinn a reputation as a hirer/firer, a view reinforced by Hillman's revelations about the group being salaried hands. As so often in these scenarios, McGuinn's actions merely reflected the feelings of the majority of the group rather than some caprice of his own. Even after his firing, York refused to paint McGuinn as a heartless autocrat, but saw the Byrds' leader as a sympathetic character with a genuine interest in his future musical development. "People always say Roger is cold,"

York reflects, "but I would tell him exactly how I felt. I remember I went through a period when I was very unhappy and used to tell Roger what I thought was wrong with the group. He would say, 'This will be a good stepping stone for you when you leave.' But I would say, 'How can you talk about leaving?' I wanted to put energy into it. Roger advised me to leave if I didn't like the band, but I didn't want to split. I wanted to be part of it. But the part was so small. I used to think Roger was pushing me forward with one hand and holding me back with the other, but essentially I was doing it to myself. Roger was right, but at the time it seemed utter nonsense to me."

The new Byrd, Skip Battin (b. Clyde Raybould Battin, 18 February 1934, Gallipolis, Ohio) was, at 35, the oldest member, and also the one with the longest musical history. His pre-Byrd exploits, more properly documented in Volume 2 of this study, read like a bizarre journey through the backroads of US pop and rock. While at university, majoring in Physical Education, he played in country bars with a covers band, Earl Mock & The Mockingbirds, then teamed up with the eccentric pop polymath Gary Paxton. They recorded under a variety of aliases, including the Pledges and Clyde & Gary, before hitting big as Skip & Flip with the US Top 20 hits, 'It Was I' and 'Cherry Pie'. By 1961, Battin had moved to Los Angeles where he collaborated with the larger than life pop entrepreneur Kim Fowley on countless recording projects. Battin co-wrote songs, worked in A&R and even performed as a part-time actor, appearing in several films. He had an epiphany of sorts after seeing the Byrds at Ciro's in 1965 and attempted to transform himself into a folk rocker, working with Van Dyke Parks, Steve Young and Stephen Stills in the short-lived project, the Gas Company. After reverting to studio work, Battin re-emerged with a new band, the Evergreen Blueshoes. They lasted almost two years, during which they played the Hollywood club circuit, worked regularly at the Corral in Topanga Canyon, and released one album on Amos Records, *The Ballad Of Evergreen Blueshoes*. The record was an odd curio of diverse musical styles, clearly aimed at the progressive rock fan, but it died in the marketplace, much to Battin's disillusionment. Following the break-up of the group, he continued with his studio work and jammed for a few months with jazz guitarist Art Johnson.

After a decade in the music business Battin had vast experience, but never looked like repeating the commercial success of Skip & Flip. Ever conscious of passing time, he experimented with youth serums, took up Buddhism and networked like crazy. He had already crossed paths with Gene Parsons and Clarence White while doing studio sessions and was in the perfect position when John York was dismissed from the Byrds. Parsons secured him an audition and Battin seized the opportunity. "I practised and learned every Byrds song I could before I went along," he told me. "I didn't want to leave anything to chance. Roger was impressed – and I was in."

Towards the end of 1969, the Byrds found themselves back in the news. Apart from Battin's arrival, and all the publicity surrounding the *Easy Rider* soundtrack, news leaked out of the musical McGuinn had started co-writing with Jacques Levy the previous year. Still titled *Gene Tryp*, it was apparently destined for Broadway, with McGuinn boasting of an opening night as early as the autumn. McGuinn's flurry of activity was supposedly only a prelude to even loftier ambitions involving Gram Parsons and Michelle Phillips (as two intergalactic flower children!) in a science fiction movie, provisionally titled *Ecology 70*. There was also talk of Roger playing a junkie folk-singer in a movie directed by his old mentor, Bobby Darin. As the interviews multiplied, McGuinn even found himself denying rumours that he was abandoning rock 'n' roll to become a Broadway star. The great contemporary interest in rock as theatre attracted the press back to McGuinn at a crucial time and helped to defuse criticism about the instability of the current Byrds' line-up.

On 10 November 1969, the Byrds' new album *Ballad Of Easy Rider* was issued in America. Its title was a clever ploy to cash in on the success of the movie *Easy Rider*, but neither the music nor the artwork had much to do with the film or its theme. The album sleeve, later condemned by McGuinn as the Byrds' worst, resembled a parody of the biker movie. Instead of the drug-taking, freedom-loving, easy-riding hippies that were portrayed in the film, purchasers were confronted with an out of focus shot of Gene Parsons' father Lemuel, clutching a rifle and smiling inanely, while sitting, rather uncomfortably, on a 1928 Harley Davidson. The advertising department at CBS obviously did not agree with this interpretation and insisted upon equating the album with "a generation's search for freedom and expression". The implications of that phrase were that the album contained songs in the vein of 'The Pusher' or 'Born To Be Wild', which were included on the soundtrack album. Unfortunately, *Ballad Of Easy Rider* was a truer reflection of its strange cover than CBS assumed. Instead of powerful, hard-hitting biker songs, the Byrds were generally in reflective mood, with one eye looking back at the old world of *Sweetheart Of The Rodeo*, where bluegrass-influenced tunes and Woody Guthrie compositions held sway.

Ballad Of Easy Rider attracted considerable public interest and no doubt enticed many old Byrds fans back in search of such songs as 'Eight Miles High', '5 D' or 'So You Want To Be A Rock 'n' Roll Star'. What awaited them was not the shock of the new or the reassurance of the old, but a calmative, transitional album, seemingly designed to dampen expectations. Not only was the theme of *Easy Rider* conspicuously absent, but the presence of McGuinn seemed merely a mirage. On the previous album, he had co-written the majority of the material, but here he received only one songwriting and one arranging credit. The advance publicity with its lavish claim, "The movie gave you the facts, the *Ballad* interprets them", punctuated by promises of "a new feeling in American music" could hardly have been more inappropriate. On this occasion, the Byrds were not ready for any revolutionary changes, but seemed to be pacing themselves in preparation for a greater work.

'Ballad Of Easy Rider' opens the album on a deceptively strong note and remains one of McGuinn's most enduring melodies. On the *Easy Rider* soundtrack, he had performed a solo version, accompanied by acoustic guitar and Gene Parsons' harmonica, but this later arrangement reveals much more depth. Taken at a quicker pace, the song was lengthened by grafting the first verse on to the end of the second. The most significant alteration though was the striking and tasteful use of orchestration. "It was my idea to add the strings," Terry Melcher told me. "I was trying to make the song into a 'Gentle On My Mind' or 'Everybody's Talking'." McGuinn remembers sitting in the studio during the playback when Melcher's stunning actress girlfriend Candice Bergen entered. After listening attentively, she turned to McGuinn, tears in her eyes, and told him the song was absolutely beautiful. Unused to such an emotional reaction, he was temporarily lost for words. "Now she *really* liked the strings!" he says.

Although the writing credit for 'Ballad Of Easy Rider' reads 'Roger McGuinn', it is generally accepted that Bob Dylan was at least partially involved in its composition. In August 1971, McGuinn revealed: "When I wrote that track for the film, Dylan had something to do with it and so his name came up in the credits. He called me and said, 'Take that off, I told you not to give me any credit. I do things like that for people every day. I just gave you a line that's all.' Which actually was true, we hadn't really got deeply involved together over the song."

Gene Parsons later complicated matters by incorrectly suggesting that Dylan had written the lyrics, while McGuinn was only responsible for the melody. In later interviews, McGuinn confirmed that Dylan merely composed the opening two lines, which he had scribbled on a cocktail napkin and placed in the hands of Peter Fonda, accompanied by the words: "Give that to McGuinn. He'll know what to do with it."

Soon afterwards, Dylan disowned his contribution. As McGuinn told me: "The screen credit said, 'Ballad Of Easy Rider' by 'Roger McGuinn and Bob Dylan'. He said, 'Take it off!' because he didn't like the movie that much. He didn't like the ending. He wanted to see the truck blow up in order to get poetic justice. He didn't seem to understand Peter Fonda's anti-hero concept."

The second track on the album, 'Fido', succeeded 'Old Blue' as the latest in a series of Byrds' songs about dogs. It was also John York's first and last solo for the group, although unissued versions of 'Tulsa County Blue' and 'Way Behind The Sun' would later appear as bonus tracks in 1997. The story behind the writing of 'Fido' was surprisingly complicated for such a simple song. As York recalls: "We were in Kansas and I couldn't sleep. Everybody was out doing something and I was up in my room on the second storey of a motel. It was a hot night, my door was open and this dog came in and stayed in the room with me all night. I had nothing to give him, nothing to feed him with. I thought, 'Isn't this interesting? This dog is not at home; he's lonesome, curled up in the corner. Here I am, several thousand miles from home and I'm lonesome.' I saw the parallel between the lonely travelling artiste and the stray dog. So that was what the song was about. It was written in one night."

Terry Melcher, who at one time was interested in acquiring the publishing rights on 'Fido', suggests that the other Byrds were unenthusiastic. "'Fido' was a problem with Roger. The guys didn't like it too much. But York was a pro and a nice guy. He never showed up loaded and he worked hard." York, himself, was not entirely satisfied with the production. "I didn't like Melcher double-tracking my voice. The original idea was that Gene should have a drum solo, and at least he did get that opportunity. I wanted him to stretch out a bit because I really love the way he played, and the Byrds never had a drum solo. I was trying to bring a little bit more R&B and blues into it."

'Oil In My Lamp' was brought to the group by Gene Parsons, who fondly recalls the song from his childhood. "We used to sing it in the back of the school bus when I was going to school in 29 Palms, near Joshua Tree. I had about a 30-mile ride there and back, and that was one of the songs we'd sing." White remembered the tune and suggested they add some harmonies. Encouraged by Parsons, he sang lead for the first time since the Kentucky Colonels days. His enervating, nasal vocal adds a dirge-like feel to what was traditionally an uplifting children's hymn, often sung at weddings. The diction in the chorus is unclear (note the peculiar pronunciation of the word 'hosanna' in "Sing hosanna to the King"). Slowing the song's tempo to a *funereal* pace was unintentionally ironic as church authorities specifically warned against using the hymn at cremations due to the lyric "keep me *burning*". The Byrds' mournful rendition was far removed from what Gene Parsons had heard in the back of his school bus and adds a dark edge to the celebratory hymn.

For 'Tulsa County Blue', White introduced the Byrds to world champion fiddle player Byron Berline, who had recently begun working as a session player. The song is impressive with White's thrilling string bending to the fore. Once more the song came from outside the group. "'Tulsa County Blue' was a copyright I'd owned for a long time," Terry Melcher recalls. "It was a country hit for June Carter, written by Pam Polland who had a group called Gentle Soul who I cut an album with for Epic with Ry Cooder, Van Dyke Parks and Larry Knechtel. It was John York's idea to cover the song and I was obviously very pleased because it was my copyright." At several shows during this period, York took lead vocal on the composition, having been taught the arrangement by Gentle Soul's bassist, but the studio version features McGuinn.

'Jack Tarr The Sailor', another traditional tune, closes the first side of the album. During his youth, McGuinn enrolled at Chicago's Old Town School of Folk Music and honed his folk repertoire at the Gate Of Horn. This English sea shanty was an old favourite and features a verse that also appeared on the traditional 'New York Girls', which McGuinn later included in his Folk Den archive. Gene Parsons vividly recalls Roger getting drunk one night and convincing himself that he was a sailor, after which 'Jack Tarr The Sailor' was immediately recorded. McGuinn delivers the song in best British folk-cellar nasal style, adding an arrangement which recalls his work on 'I Come And Stand At Every Door' and 'Space Odyssey'. Always a lover of sea shanties, he would return to such material during his solo years on such songs as 'Heave Away' and 'Jolly Roger'.

With 'Jesus Is Just Alright', the Byrds turn their attention to gospel music. Parsons introduced the group to the song, having attended the original recording by the Art Reynolds Singers, who were produced by his former partner, Gib Guilbeau. As John York recalls: "Gene had this idea of an intro that started off with the voice, then added another and another, all building up to the actual song. We all really liked the idea and started performing it in concert and people really enjoyed it, so we decided to record it. When we came into the studio, Terry Melcher had a totally different idea of how to arrange it so that it would be more of a pop record. Now, when I hear it, I understand why he did it that way."

Melcher added to the effects by remembering an old trick borrowed from the days of *Turn! Turn! Turn!*: "I had a whole string section on 'Jesus Is Just Alright' that you probably never heard. I had them drone two notes through the entire record and I ran it through a tape phaser. The idea was an adaptation of McGuinn's drone concept on 'If You're Gone'."

Although 'Jesus Is Just Alright' failed to provide the Byrds with a hit single it was a live favourite, highlighted by some solid drumming, bass playing and the return of the tambourine. "Some of my drumming style I got from Jim Troxel," Parsons remembers, citing the former member of Duane Eddy's Rebel Rousers. "He was the hired drummer that Gary Paxton used quite often. I learned a lot from these guys who played with the Art Reynolds Singers. They had two ladies in the band that played tambourine and they would do tambourine solos that you couldn't believe." Ironically, in the wake of the Byrds' failure to find a hit, the Doobie Brothers covered the song with a similar arrangement and enjoyed considerable success. "If you listen to the two records, the Byrds' version is much more creative," York insists. "There's a certain celestial quality to it."

The Byrds first attempted 'It's All Over Now, Baby Blue' in 1965 when it was scheduled as a single. Back then, they approached the song with a sparky irreverence, but when McGuinn returned to the composition for this album, he and Melcher radically altered the tempo and arrangement to produce a more serious, elegiac reading. McGuinn was still dissatisfied with the number, which tended to drag alongside the other slower tracks on the album. Roger deliberately drags the syllables out of each word in order to provide the obligatory Dylanesque flavour, as if intent on emphasizing a world-weariness conspicuously absent from the Byrds' original version. Melcher put White's guitar through a Leslie speaker to create further delay.

The title of the song provided a prophetic warning to John York, who was about to be fired. "That was a time of turmoil," he remembers. "I walked out of that session. I played the bass on it, but I got the feeling that Terry Melcher wanted to be a rock 'n' roll singer so badly and there was only room for four voices at the time. I began to feel I was in the wrong place. I went into another room and played the piano while they did the vocals."

The decision to cover 'There Must Be Someone' was primarily instigated by Gene Parsons and Clarence White, who had already appeared on the song when it was issued as the B-side to the Gosdin Brothers' single 'Hanging On' in 1966. The circumstances surrounding its composition are particularly poignant. As John York remembers: "The story we got was that it was written when Vern Gosdin lived near to Clarence White. One night, Vern came home after playing a gig to find his house completely empty. His wife and kids were gone, the furniture was gone and there was a goodbye note from his wife. So he sat down and wrote 'There Must Be Someone'. Then the sun came up and he waited until he knew Clarence was awake, went over to his house and played him the song." Both Clarence and Gene picketed for the composition's inclusion on the album, even though it did not easily fit into the Byrds' canon. "There was some kind of conflict," York remembers. "Roger stayed in the control room and it's just Clarence, Gene and myself on that cut. We just said, 'We want to do this song, leave us alone.' And he said, 'OK, go in,' and we did it." Parsons believes that McGuinn was unsure about the song's suitability: "I think Roger might have questioned whether it was sufficiently Byrds-sounding, but he was very open to new musical ideas at the time, so he allowed it to be included."

'Gunga Din', arguably the best song ever written by Gene Parsons and a minor Byrds' classic, is a fascinating composition, with another intriguing storyline inspired by a real life incident. "The song was based on a series of events that happened on our visit to New York," Parsons recalls. "Part of it was written about John York and his mother. We always used to stay at the Gramercy Park Hotel and we spent hundreds of dollars there. On one occasion, John wanted to take his mother to dinner but they wouldn't let him in the restaurant because he had a leather jacket on. It was very upsetting and insulting. The song also documents a gig we played at Central Park, where Chuck Berry, 'Mr Rock 'n' Roll', failed to appear, and the crowd were really angry. Part of the song was written on the plane when we really were chasing the sun back to

LA. I threw in the 'Gunga Din' part to make up the rhyme." Musically, the song is most notable for its lilting melody and an attractive, intricate picking pattern created by its composer. "It took me a little time to get that pattern down," Parsons says. "Clarence could hear what I was going for and he just knew that it would take me a little time. The people in the control room were not as patient as maybe Clarence was. I had a particular sound I wanted and I knew I could get it if I just had a couple of more minutes... I was going for something with an open *D* tuning and I was having trouble getting it. The engineer said, 'Let's go back to another tuning or try something else.' Clarence was in the control room and said, '*No!* He's going for something, let him do it, let him go. You've got nothing but time, give him another 10 or 15 minutes.' So, because Clarence persevered, I was able to get that particular little thing which is sort of the signature on that track."

'Deportee (Plane Wreck At Los Gatos)' was the second Woody Guthrie song recorded by the Byrds, following their excellent rendition of 'Pretty Boy Floyd' on *Sweetheart Of The Rodeo*. McGuinn was very familiar with 'Deportee', having played on the version recorded on Judy Collins' third album in 1963. Guthrie had put the music to a poem about the California tradition of employing cheap labour to pick fruit. The poignant account of migrant exploitation and the callous disregard shown towards the immigrants' deaths ("the radio said they were just deportees") enhances the reflective mood of the album. As an isolated track, the Byrds' interpretation was impressive, but on an album already glutted with non-original material its inclusion seemed questionable. Nevertheless, it was rewarding to hear McGuinn take the lead vocal while simultaneously finding common musical ground with White and Parsons.

The Byrds had pioneered space rock with songs such as 'Mr Spaceman', 'CTA 102' and 'Space Odyssey', so it was appropriate that they should celebrate the year of the moon landing with a tribute to the three astronauts in 'Armstrong, Aldrin And Collins'. Rather than connecting with his usual 'space' co-writer Bob Hippard, McGuinn incorporated a song from outside the Byrds' camp. Zeke Manners' homily ends the album on an unusual note, although this was long part of the Byrds' tradition. "The Zeke Manners song was our joke, our 'We'll Meet Again'," Terry Melcher told me. "We were trying to get back to the feel of the first album. The song was originally very long when Zeke gave it to us, so we cut it down." The contrast between the folky delivery and the electronic wizardry was presumably designed to illustrate the importance of commonplace truths in the search for universal wisdom (i.e. they were launched into space by technology, but they had God's helping hand). If McGuinn's arrangement elucidated the moral, it did not drastically improve the song. His fusion of folk and electronics would not be perfected until as late as 'Time Cube' on his first solo album.

Overall, *Ballad Of Easy Rider* was an uneasy, transitional record that failed to match the quality of their greatest work. Gene Parsons admits that there was conflict with John York throughout the recording and expressed surprise that it turned out so well. Although the sound was impressive that had more to do with Melcher's crystal clear production than the quality of the songs. The album's major weakness was the absolute dearth of original material. Amazingly, only three songs came from within the Byrds' camp, with York offering the passable, if inconsequential, 'Fido' and Parsons contributing the excellent 'Gunga Din'. Elsewhere, the group seem content to cobble together extraneous material, borrowing freely from Art Reynolds, the Gosdin Brothers, Bob Dylan, Zeke Manners and the traditional folk song catalogue. Much of the material seemed ill-chosen, as if McGuinn was completely unfocused on the project. His role throughout was most perplexing. According to Parsons and York, he did not even appear on at least two of the tracks: 'There Must Be Someone' and 'Gunga Din'. He insisted on recording the jinxed 'It's All Over Now, Baby Blue' and agreed to its release, despite his dissatisfaction with the end product. As the session listings indicate, he had nothing in reserve beyond a rather bland reading of Jackson Browne's 'Mae Jean Goes To Hollywood' and a whimsical folk/moog experiment, 'Fiddler A Dram'. At a time when the Byrds needed to exploit the interest in their work resulting from the movie *Easy Rider*, McGuinn's cupboard was bare. What we were left with was a Byrds album bereft of a single *new* McGuinn composition — even the sumptuous title track had previously appeared in starker form on the *Easy Rider* soundtrack.

In many respects, *Ballad Of Easy Rider* was the victim of the Byrds' CBS contract, which demanded product voraciously. Ideally, McGuinn should have delayed the album until he had completed enough new songs to warrant a release, but in 1969 he did not have that luxury. Apart from his commitments to Columbia, he was distracted from writing for the Byrds by a more important project. Throughout the year, his creative energies had been channelled into the much-touted *Gene Tryp* musical, which McGuinn believed would transform his career. The results of those extracurricular activities were to be revealed in a series of new songs, which would be completed and released in the New Year. In the meantime, McGuinn could content himself with the knowledge that his latest album had at least reversed the Byrds' recent US chart decline.

One week after the release of *Ballad Of Easy Rider*, Terry Melcher's worst nightmares became terrifyingly real. The police had finally arrested the mass murderers responsible for the Tate/LaBianca slayings and the identity of the cult's psychotic manic-eyed figurehead was a person Melcher knew only too well.

Charles Manson had spent much of the early Sixties behind bars, but re-entered society just in time for the Summer of Love. He soon became the Mordred of hippie Camelot, subverting its permissive values for his own ends. After moving to the desert, he acquired a seraglio of supplicant hippie girls, high on drugs and free love. They became known as the Family, a motley assembly of impressionable miniature Trilbys, with Manson playing the deranged Svengali. With youth and sex at his fingertips, Manson insidiously infiltrated the movie and rock communities of Hollywood and rustic Laurel Canyon. He encountered several minor celebrities, including Neil Young, who was impressed enough by his psychotic presence and wayward, ill-defined music to recommend him to Warner Brothers. Manson was still too far out for most record company executives, but his supply of ever accommodating girls attracted the attention of Dennis Wilson, the hunky rebel of the Beach Boys, whose priapic urges and pharmaceutical desires all too often overwhelmed his better senses. Wilson was entranced by Manson, whose New

UNCERTAIN RIDERS

Age sophistry, occult dabbling, apocalyptic assertions and orgiastic promiscuity sated his impressionable followers, softening their will until morality became a meaningless abstraction.

After infiltrating his way into the Beach Boys' camp, Manson presented them with one of his compositions, 'Cease To Exist', which was partly rewritten as 'Never Learn Not To Love' and appeared on *20/20* and the B-side of 'Bluebirds Over The Mountain'. Manson uncharacteristically sacrificed his writing credit, but continued to pressurize Wilson into helping his cause. By the spring of 1969, Manson found a new focus of attention in Terry Melcher, whose wealthy background and connections in the movie and rock world proved an irresistible combination. Melcher listened to some Manson songs, while admiring the nubile, naked female flesh that served as a visual backdrop. After a second visit to the ramshackle ranch at which the Family were holed up, Melcher witnessed an outbreak of psychotic violence that convinced him Manson was unstable. Terry took his leave and, 11 days later, began work on the Byrds' *Ballad Of Easy Rider*. He did not expect to cross paths with Manson again.

Although Melcher always maintained that he had made no promises to Manson about his fantasy recording career, the Family's head felt angry at a non-committal which, to his twisted, psychotic logic, was perceived as some sort of betrayal. Whether the Tate murders were completely random acts of madness, a coded threat to Melcher, or a crazed attack against the weirdoes who later frequented Cielo Drive, remains unclear. However, Family member Susan Atkins subsequently testified that "the reason Charlie picked that house was to instill fear into Terry Melcher, because Terry had given us his word on a few things and never came through with them." Her words were enough to indicate that Manson bore some paranoid grudge against Melcher, who testified in court that he was terrified of the man. Even with Manson in custody there were rumours that members of the Family were roaming free, programmed like robots to fulfil their master's psychotic wishes. It was a chilling consideration. An intimidating letter was even sent to the peace-loving Derek Taylor for no apparent reason. The trial was a devastating experience for Melcher who admitted he was undergoing psychiatric treatment for his frazzled nerves, employing a bodyguard, and carrying a gun for protection.

While the Manson trial was taking place, American rock music suffered another fall from Eden with the tragic news of bloody carnage at the free festival at Altamont in Livermore, California. What was intended to serve as another mini-Woodstock ended as a dark mirror for all the optimism of the age. The fateful decision to employ Hell's Angels to police the event created a cauldron of smouldering intimidation and violence which eventually cost the life of Meredith Hunter, who was brutally slain while the Rolling Stones impotently looked on. The Altamont debacle was a convenient metaphor for the death of the Sixties and was witnessed by four of McGuinn's former colleagues in offshoot bands, the Flying Burrito Brothers and Crosby, Stills, Nash & Young. This was one festival that the Byrds were more than pleased to have avoided.

CHAPTER THIRTY-THREE

Just A Season

THE Byrds ended the Sixties on an upbeat note. Reviewers observed that even the normally undemonstrative McGuinn was more animated – talking, joking and actually dancing onstage. Interviewed after a December concert at East Orange, New Jersey, he provided an address to the Byrds' nation that testified to a new dawn. "Did you see the reaction we got tonight? Three standing ovations, and three encores. Have you ever seen the Byrds perform like that before? I consider it going uphill, slowly but surely; the whole thing is happening . . . We have a better, tighter, more responsible, more professional, more musical, more dynamic, more interesting, more delightful group than ever before. Forget who the Byrds were before, erase it! . . . My sights are set beyond the Fillmore East; my sights are set on Mars and Pluto and Venus and indeed other galaxies."

McGuinn's intergalactic ambitions confirmed that the old hunger was back, accompanied by a steely determination to re-establish the Byrds as a major creative force. Musically and financially, considerable work would be required to achieve his aim. Since the great splits of 1967–68, the group had been in a parlous financial state and lost ground on most of their rivals at a time when heavy rock and supergroups were in the ascendant. Although the Byrds' connection with *Easy Rider* had resulted in a small resurgence of critical and public interest at home, many still regarded the group as creatively bankrupt. *Ballad Of Easy Rider* was issued in the UK in January 1970, only to be greeted by general apathy. Whereas *Dr Byrds & Mr Hyde* had climbed as high as number 15, its successor not only failed to reach the Top 40, but did not even receive a single review in the weekly music press. It was almost as if CBS London had failed to receive any promotional stock to distribute. Although the album fared much better in the States, peaking at number 36, there was still a widespread belief that the group were treading water, with a lingering reputation for poor live performances. An overview in the underground rock magazine *Fusion* pinpointed the recent malaise:

> Dissension had always been an integral part of Byrds history, an ever present footnote to their musical changes. But for the past couple of years, things had been going just a little bit out of hand. Group members came and went like Volkswagen parts, leaving old Roger McGuinn the sole surviving member of the original band. Faceless names like Kevin Kelley and John York went through the motions of being the Byrds, but it just wasn't the same. A mirror reflection of the dissension within the band, their live shows were little more than a skeleton exercise in nostalgia . . . Only the presence of McGuinn gave any clues as to the identity of the band. This situation came to a head with *Ballad Of Easy Rider*. Clearly, it was the only blatantly mediocre album the Byrds have ever released, one which I called 'transitional' largely out of respect for their past. It was at times like these that the Byrds found out who their real friends were, for only the staunchest of fans could have weathered those lean times. And there were times when even the staunchest must have been tempted to give them up for dead.

Although neither *Ballad Of Easy Rider* nor the live shows were as bad or disappointing as suggested here, the sense of lost ground in terms of innovation was undeniable. Perhaps, in desperation, McGuinn saw the need to re-think his future, and concluded that a revival in the group's fortunes could only be effected through a more intensive work schedule.

Throughout 1970, the Byrds concentrated on perfecting their live shows as they prepared to haul themselves back into the premier league of US rock acts. What they required was a younger audience to complement their die-hard followers from the mid-Sixties. The only way to recruit new fans was literally to go out and play to them, in clubs, bars and universities. Over the next year, the Byrds would visit countless colleges across the face of America. The exhausting work schedule passed in a blur. As McGuinn remembers: "We were doing a lot of gigs, commuting from LA to New York every week, doing four days out and three days back. It was quite expensive but we had a lot of gigs booked on the East Coast."

With months of performing experience behind them, the Byrds felt confident enough to take a unique step in their career by recording their first live album. At the same time, it was felt that each member had sufficiently impressive material to donate to a new studio work. The dilemma was solved when they decided to record a double album incorporating both ideas. Producer Terry Melcher takes credit for the concept insisting, "It was my idea to do a double album, half live and half studio, and sell it for the price of a single album. One record was to enable us to toss in a load of hits, with live excitement, in order to get us back into the [albums] charts."

While the touring continued, the Byrds found themselves in the news pages again courtesy of their old mentor, Bob Dylan. In April, McGuinn revealed that the Byrds and Dylan were planning to record an album together. "We may be doing an album with Dylan soon, either here or in Nashville," he explained. "Yes, it is great. We don't have any concept in mind. He just said to bring some of our stuff and he'd bring some of his. He said he hasn't been writing much lately and he needs his new songs for his own album, so he may even want to do some Byrds songs. Who knows what will happen?"

Needless to say, nothing did happen. According to CBS' Clive Davis, McGuinn failed to attend the session, and by the time he was contacted it was discovered that the other Byrds had returned to Los Angeles. McGuinn tells a different story, blaming the failure of the project on the organizers, rather than the artistes. The Byrds had flown to New York for the weekend in order to perform two gigs at the Felt Forum and Queen's College. These were the all-important concerts from which the live part of their album would be selected. They expected to finalize the deal with Dylan but, claims McGuinn, the promised telephone call came too late. "It wasn't our fault," he adds defensively. "Clive Davis was supposed to meet us after the gig at Queen's College, the previous night, but he didn't show. I was expecting a call from Bob Johnston, whose job was to notify us of the time of the session, but he didn't call us either. Dylan was really mad about it."

McGuinn recalls that Parsons and Battin were on the plane when Dylan's call finally came through. "Some of the musicians had left already. I said, 'I'll be glad to come over Bob, but . . .' He said, 'I came all the way in from the country!' And I said, 'Well, I'm really sorry, man. I'll come over.' Then he got angry with me. He said, 'Musicians! Musicians! I can get musicians at the drop of a hat, man. I don't *need* you.' Which was a nasty thing to say, but he just lost his temper. I forgive him. Everyone gets grumpy once in a while."

The mix-up resulted in another of those temporary rifts between McGuinn and Dylan, following on from the mild irritation over the composing credits on 'Ballad Of Easy Rider'. As always with Dylan, the extent of his anger was difficult to ascertain. All McGuinn knew was that they didn't see each other for quite some time. The matter was never mentioned again. Looking back, McGuinn regretted the misunderstanding, but had no regrets about the failure of the project. "What he wanted was us to back him," he told me. "It wasn't our material and, from my point of view, it wasn't a very attractive project. It was like the Byrds being subservient to Dylan. It was just Clive Davis' idea to sell some records."

By the summer, the Byrds added a short tour of Europe to their apparently inexhaustible itinerary, and continental fans were overjoyed to see the group play in Frankfurt, Amsterdam and Rotterdam. The tour culminated in a memorable appearance at the Bath Festival. Rock giants Led Zeppelin had closed the evening's entertainment on 28 June, leaving the other acts to follow them during the early hours of Monday morning. The Byrds appeared towards dawn, but thunder, lightning and a torrential downpour prevented them from playing an electric set. Undaunted, they emerged with acoustic guitars, while Battin played bass standing safely on a rubber mat towards the back of the stage. Despite these setbacks, the group performed all their old classics, even 'Eight Miles High'.

The response was joyful, and McGuinn treasures the memory to this day.

A fan of the time summed up the general feeling of the crowd: "When the Airplane walked off the stage cursing the weather I was all set to turn my back on rock 'n' roll and all that it represented. But I stayed. I found the crowd fascinating. Half of them had already gone home, but those who remained were drenched through, miserable and defeated. It was pathetic. Like a refugee camp after the war. Then this solitary figure appeared onstage with an acoustic guitar and sang 'So You Want To Be A Rock 'n' Roll Star'. McGuinn summed it all up, just like that. The emotion of the moment was so great that I was not the only one of the crowd who cried for joy, I was so moved. The Byrds performed their entire repertoire and more, and saw us through that sad night. They gave us 'Mr Tambourine Man' just as the first ribbons of light appeared in the sky. They were magnificent." Capturing the moment, the Byrds finally exorcized bad memories of their British appearance five years earlier. This time, they left England triumphantly.

While McGuinn was attempting to revive the Byrds' flagging career, his former colleagues were adjusting to differing levels of fame. Chris Hillman had reunited with former manager Jim Dickson for the Flying Burrito Brothers' second album, *Burrito Deluxe*. Despite a handful of decent tracks, including the first release of Jagger/Richards' enticing 'Wild Horses', it was a pale imitation of its great predecessor *The Gilded Palace Of Sin* and revealed a Gram Parsons seemingly bored and in creative decline. Before long, he would be fired as frustration mounted at the band's inability to find commercial success. Gene Clark, meanwhile, had reached the end of the road with Dillard & Clark, whose patchy but pleasing country album *Through The Morning, Through The Night* also failed to emulate the sparkle of its excellent predecessor. With the singer-songwriter boom still a year away, Clark was in creative limbo and, like Hillman, turned to Dickson, who produced a couple of interim tracks ('She's The Kind Of Girl' and 'One In A Hundred'), recruiting various original Byrds for the musical backing.

Alone among the ex-Byrds, David Crosby was now a superstar. The celebrated *Déjà Vu* proved one of the biggest-selling albums of

1970 and momentarily transformed Crosby, Stills, Nash & Young into the highest earners working in the rock field. Since Woodstock, their reputation had grown to gargantuan proportions and Crosby could now afford to look back on the Byrds as a troubled apprenticeship from which he had emerged stronger and more talented than any of his fellows. Previously known for his harmonic quietude, he added a grittier edge to CSN&Y with the hectoring 'Almost Cut My Hair', one of his most passionate, compelling and heartfelt performances. Its power was complemented by the title track 'Déjà Vu', an eerie, complex composition of unusual time signatures that required close to a hundred hours of studio experimentation before completion. If the word 'supergroup' meant anything then CSN&Y were worthy recipients of the epithet.

McGuinn had not forgotten the competitive bond that existed between himself and the musician he had recklessly fired three years before. The success of CSN&Y made McGuinn more determined than ever to re-establish the Byrds with a hit album. Like Hillman and Clark, he looked to past business associates for inspiration, pooling together figures from the Byrds' golden era (Terry Melcher, Jim Dickson, Eddie Tickner and Derek Taylor) to add their particular magic to the new group of musicians currently in his employ. Although the prospect of Melcher and Dickson working together as producers seemed decidedly precarious, the pairing proved effective, partly thanks to a shift in the power structure. With Melcher now tied to McGuinn as personal manager, there was no possibility of the rivalry that existed when Crosby and Dickson formed an uneasy alliance back in 1965. "Getting Dickson was a magnanimous gesture on my part, almost revenge," Melcher gloated. "I didn't co-produce the album with Dickson. What I did was allow him to edit the live tapes while I was cutting the studio part of the album. On the live side, we came back with five hours of live music and I gave Dickson all the tapes. We got on well because he didn't have any power. One thing about Dickson though, he's got taste."

Melcher's comments notwithstanding, there is clear evidence that Dickson was involved in the studio recordings. He vetoed McGuinn singing 'Take A Whiff (On Me)' in favour of Clarence White and was present at all the playbacks. "Terry got me in for

(Untitled) because he was getting buried by the album and he wanted some help. At first, I took the band and rehearsed them at Gene Parsons' house, He had a place where he could play drums and they could all practise. It was a nice reunion with Clarence. I was a little surprised when he joined the Byrds. I spent more time with him and he was very supportive, probably more supportive than McGuinn, really. We went up there and we worked hard and then I brought them back. Terry was pleased and then we recorded and got the thing together. I was never as hostile to Terry as people like to believe. Remember, it was the original Byrds – all five – that signed a note saying 'Fire Terry Melcher' back in 1965."

One powerplay that Dickson did execute was putting the subsidiary Byrds in their place. "Gene Parsons and Skip Battin were concentrating on *their* songs and I told them: 'Your songs wouldn't see the light of day if wasn't for McGuinn.' I felt they were treating McGuinn shabbily. He had these songs that he thought were going to be in a Broadway play but they weren't impressed. I said, 'You need to give him support.' I was trying to protect McGuinn, and Clarence was right there with me. He treated it like, 'There's no question that you have to listen to Jim Dickson.' Clarence's manner was very deferential but he was strong. He didn't say a lot but, when he did, Parsons and Battin would pay attention."

The new album, *(Untitled)*, was released in the autumn to critical acclaim and surprise chart success in both the US and UK. For most fans, this was the long-awaited return to greatness that had been eagerly anticipated since the bitter personnel shift following the release of *The Notorious Byrd Brothers*. The work confirmed that McGuinn had at last found the stable line-up for which he had been searching since 1967. This was not only demonstrated through the music, but also suggested in the sleeve notes, with their discussion of discarded titles, such as 'Phoenix' and the frankly heretical 'The First Byrds Album'. McGuinn managed to forge musical links with the lost original Byrds, both in the choice of material on the live album and through his Rickenbacker playing, which combined beautifully with White's string-bending guitar runs.

The iconic cover artwork featured the Byrds at LA's Griffith

Observatory, a landmark previously made famous in the James Dean-starring movie, *Rebel Without A Cause*. The picture was colour tinted by artist/writer Eve Babitz, who was also responsible for the memorable collage on *Buffalo Springfield Again*. Inside, there was an equally striking shot of McGuinn in his den, sitting beneath a photo of Albert Einstein, while looking deep in thought and enigmatic, like some absent-minded professor. His wife Dolores found the visual image a little disturbing. "Our son Henry is crawling on the floor and Roger's looking off into the distance. He was facing to the right where the televisions were, directly across from the synthesizer. The chair he was sitting on was on castors and Henry is crawling near the chair. Every time I see it I cringe and think, 'Oh my gosh, he could have rolled over his fingers.' The baby seemed so vulnerable."

What also attracted attention to the album was its playful non-title which, according to McGuinn, was an accident: "Somebody from Columbia called up our manager and asked him what it was. He told them it was 'as yet untitled' and so they went ahead and printed that. Before that we were considering 'McGuinn, White, Parsons and Battin', but that would probably have been misinterpreted."

Melcher has a slightly different story. "I'll tell you what *really* happened," he confides. "It went from my office that way. On the label copy information, on which you list artiste, producer, song titles, writers, publishers and times, I put down 'Untitled'. 'Phoenix' had been considered but at that time they were still unsure. Before I knew it, they'd pressed it up as *(Untitled)*."

Interestingly, McGuinn not only lost control of the album's titling but was overruled on the matter of track sequencing. Understandably, he wanted to feature the studio recording on the first disc in order to highlight his songwriting collaborations with Jacques Levy, but Melcher had other ideas. "Terry was in total control," he admits. "I remember trying to change his mind about the order of things on *(Untitled)*. He said, 'No, I'm going to do it the other way.' I actually got angry for a minute and said, 'I demand that you do it.' And he said, 'Oh, you're *demanding* now? Well, I'm *still* doing it the other way.' I didn't have any control at all!"

The novel idea of issuing a live and studio album in one package appealed to record buyers and the results were stimulating. 'Lover Of The Bayou' opens the live segment, as it would do at most subsequent Byrds' shows, with White's interweaving guitar work providing the highlights. Dickson placed some tape delay to the drum track in order to brighten the performance. Originally, this McGuinn/Levy composition had been intended for inclusion in the *Gene Tryp* musical, but was later deleted from the score for financial reasons. "The bayou scene was cut because the play was already running too long," McGuinn explains. "The scene was set during the Civil War, and Gene Tryp was smuggling guns to the confederates. At the same time, he was selling drink and stuff to the bayou people." McGuinn's portrayal of the bayou witch doctor Big Cat, who attempts to frighten Gene Tryp by describing his own supernatural powers, is most convincing, with a suitably sour vocal abetted by a menacing musical backing. Lyrically, the song captures the ominous atmosphere, complete with references to Baron Samedi, the voodoo god of death. "That was a spoof on Dr John," McGuinn adds. "If you listen to the lyrics, they don't make any sense ("Learned to float in the water clock/Learned to capture the lightning shock"). We used a lot of terms, threw them around and made up some phrases that sounded like something, but weren't. Dr John probably did the same thing but everybody believed him."

On 'Positively 4th Street', McGuinn regresses five years to borrow one of Dylan's most bitter put-down songs. Given the falling-out between the two after the Byrds' failure to attend a session, it is tempting to interpret the song's inclusion as a coded dig at Dylan, but McGuinn denies this inference. Nevertheless, this would prove the last Dylan song to appear on a Byrds album, up until their semi-reunion at Nashville for 'Paths Of Victory' in 1990. Like 'Lover Of The Bayou', 'Positively 4th Street' has a slightly gruff vocal quality, which McGuinn claims was artificially created. "My voice got real hoarse. You can hear that on the live part of *(Untitled)*. That's a cocaine voice."

The remainder of the live album's first side consists of familiar Byrds' material. A pleasant, sprightly 'Nashville West', which Gene Parsons regarded as weaker than the version on *Dr Byrds & Mr*

Hyde, precedes three Byrds' classics from the David Crosby era. 'So You Want To Be A Rock 'n' Roll Star' is taken at a faster pace than the original and emerges as a surprise highlight; 'Mr Tambourine Man', that most famous of Byrds songs, had been excluded from live performances in 1967 but was now played at every show; and the slightly countrified 'Mr Spaceman', though less spectacular than the other songs on offer, proves a predictable crowd pleaser.

   The song selections indicate that McGuinn was cleverly placing his current group in an historical perspective. After all the niggling criticisms about the Byrds' live shows, he was determined to prove that they could perform the old songs as well as the new. The message clearly read that this was not merely McGuinn with three hired musicians, but four individuals who collectively saw themselves as the inheritors of a legacy founded by the original Byrds. "There was a time when there was a real brotherhood in the band," Gene Parsons remembers. "We'd sing together before we went onstage. We'd have a singing circle. It was a ritual for about a year. We were doing our best. We would get together in a circle for about half-an-hour and do our harmonies before we went out onstage. Roger had a band that was really behind him for a while there."

   The restructuring of 'Eight Miles High' represents nothing less than the ultimate fusion of the old Byrds and the new. While the other Byrds songs on side one of *(Untitled)* are faithful to their prototypes, the extended 'Eight Miles High' takes the group into a new dimension. The live version was initially part of a medley with 'Turn! Turn! Turn!' and 'Mr Tambourine Man', but during rehearsals the Byrds began jamming and an extended piece evolved. "There was a real charge of energy there that none of us expected," Skip Battin told me. The interplay between Parsons' intricate drumming and Battin's bass solo is at times breathtaking. Dramatic emphasis is added by the deliberate fading of McGuinn's guitar following the opening. He returns to the riff towards the end of the song, which culminates in a long-awaited vocal. Here, McGuinn is careful not to overdo the nostalgia and tantalizingly curtails the lyrics after a single verse to prevent the emotional climax from becoming overtly sentimental. The performance is a concrete realization of the balance McGuinn sought between his desire to sustain the spirit of the old Byrds, while simultaneously attempting something new. Although side long instrumentals were one of the more self-indulgent exercises of late Sixties/early Seventies rock, this survives the test of time better than most. While it is still dwarfed by the classic three-minute original, the live 'Eight Miles High' is a pleasing reminder of the Byrds in concert during their most well-travelled period.

The live segment ends with the Byrds' signature tune, 'Hold It!', which was first heard at the conclusion of the medley on *Dr Byrds & Mr Hyde*. According to Gene Parsons, the signature tune began as a joke but sounded so neat that the group retained it as the closing moment to every show, followed by McGuinn's grateful thanks to the audience for their patience and participation. The Byrds' pride in their live performance was emphasized in the words of McGuinn: "I preferred the live segment of *(Untitled)*. I thought the Clarence White Byrds were a better live band while the original Byrds were a better studio band."

While few could reasonably disagree with McGuinn's comments on the original Byrds, most would contest his view about the superiority of the live LP. It was the studio recording that proved the real surprise of the package. The opening 'Chestnut Mare', for example, was probably the most exciting track that the group had produced since their creative peak in 1967. Its lyrical content alone eclipses anything that had been written since Crosby's departure, with the possible exception of Parsons' 'Hickory Wind'. The distinctive melody, complete with a Bach-inspired centrepiece from the pre-Byrds era, is full of invention. A crudely edited version proved commercial enough to secure McGuinn his first UK Top 20 hit since 'All I Really Want To Do' in 1965. Musically, 'Chestnut Mare' recalls the sound of the old Byrds, with McGuinn's piercing 12-string jingle-jangle guitar work ably complemented by the subtlety of White's careful picking. The story of an individual's struggle to capture and tame a wild horse echoes the common Byrds' themes of nature, freedom and optimism. McGuinn's yearning vocal is powerfully accented even though, by his own admission, he fails to sustain the high note at the close of the song. "'Chestnut Mare' is the most impressive piece on *(Untitled)*. I only wish it would have been more perfect. Say the last note at the end where I run out of breath. It would take Ezio Pinza [the late Italian basso opera singer] to sing that song. There's no stop to it. It's really up there." Although the composition transcends its origins as a *Gene Tryp* composition, it was always intended as an important part of the musical. "We modified the story a little there," McGuinn adds. "Peer Gynt was trying to catch a reindeer or some animal like that, but we changed it to a horse to bring it back to America."

'Truck Stop Girl', known equally well as a Little Feat song, was introduced to the group by Clarence White. "I used to run into Lowell George a lot in the studio and he gave me some material on tape, and that was one of the songs." White's whining vocal works exceptionally well on this story of a tragic, violent death. The theme was made all the more poignant in view of the circumstances surrounding the singer's own death three years later.

'All The Things', the third *Gene Tryp* song on the album, sounds vaguely pantheistic, with its stress on the disillusionment resulting from a conscious decision to isolate oneself from the natural cycles of life. Although the song was written for the musical, McGuinn and Levy were able to stretch the *Peer Gynt* story to accommodate new lyrical ideas. Derek Taylor's liner notes reveal that Gram Parsons guested as harmony vocalist, an admission verified by Terry Melcher. "I'd have loved to see Gram back in the Byrds," the producer acknowledged. "I think I was drunk that night and he came in and asked to do the harmony."

Although Parsons' presence came as a surprise to some fans, he had already charmed his way back into McGuinn's good graces. "At that time, we were friends, partying, riding bikes and playing pool together at my house, so it was cool."

'Yesterday's Train', penned by Gene Parsons and Battin, features the former on vocals, acoustic guitar, harmonica and drums, with Sneaky Pete Kleinow on additional steel guitar. "We wrote it in a hotel," Battin told me. "Gene and I were sharing a room at the time and he actually began it. I was involved in Buddhism, so I latched on to the idea of reincarnation and the feeling you get when you feel you know somebody from a former life."

The final track on side one, 'Hungry Planet', was the first song written for the Byrds by the songwriting team of Skip Battin and Kim Fowley. It had already appeared, in different form, as 'The Hungry Planet' on Earth Island's ecologically enlightened album *We Must Survive*, and was also considered by the Turtles at one point. McGuinn's inclusion in the writing credits resulted from a restructuring of the tune. "The original melody was completely different," Battin told me. "On the *(Untitled)* version we tried to experiment. Roger wanted to do some work on the synthesizer, which he felt would be a good idea at the time. But none of us liked the way it turned out. It just fizzled."

'Just A Season', the final *Gene Tryp* song on the album, is a fascinating composition and one of the best Byrds tunes from the period. The jingle-jangle guitar work again recalls the early days of the group, evoking a sound much loved and only fleetingly heard since the time of their first two albums. Even the title, with its references to seasons, echoes the subtitle of 'Turn! Turn! Turn!' – 'To Everything There Is A Season'. The reflective lyrics sound intensely personal but were actually designed specifically for the musical. The references to "hills" and "circles without reason" correspond to the episode in which the hero Gene Tryp is forced to circumnavigate the globe in order to rediscover his loved one.

Leadbelly's 'Take A Whiff (On Me)', re-arranged by White and McGuinn, was originally slated for *Ballad Of Easy Rider*. Clarence first suggested the song but there was a general lack of enthusiasm from the other Byrds. Coincidentally, during *(Untitled)*, McGuinn resurrected the idea. "Roger said he'd like to do 'Take A Whiff', and he didn't remember me talking about it earlier," White recalled. "But later, he said, 'Yeah, seems I do remember you getting the lyrics to it.' Well, we started cutting it and I guess it was more of my type of song, though Roger performs those old folk songs really well. I arranged it because his version was too like Leadbelly's. We laid down the track and he started putting the voice on, with me singing harmony. But Jim Dickson said, 'Hold it, Roger, could I hear Clarence sing it by himself?' I used the words Roger had written down and not the ones I knew." McGuinn enjoyed the song but later joked that it probably had "too many whiffs in it".

Battin/Fowley's 'You All Look Alike' allowed champion fiddle player Byron Berline another guest appearance on a Byrds album. Although some suspected that the song might have been based on a real life drama, this was not the case. "It was not a true story but a fantasy," Battin told me. "At the time there was a newspaper report of a drummer who had been killed by his girlfriend. I was aware of that incident, but the song was not directly written about it." Fowley, who was responsible for the lyrics, offers a sardonic comment on people's supposed inability to distinguish individual physical traits when confronted by foreigners or different ethnic groups. "All white people look the same to black people; all black people look the same to white people; all Frenchmen look the same to Belgiums; all Koreans look the same to Japanese. It was one of those things, but it wasn't about a specific person."

The closing cut 'Well Come Back Home' proved one of the most intriguing songs on the album. Unlike the majority of Battin/Fowley collaborations, this was not a novelty, but an arresting lyric with strong political overtones. "I was personally touched by the Vietnam situation," Battin told me, "and my feelings about it came out in the song. I had a high school friend who died out there and I guess my thoughts were on him at the time. Roger heard me composing the song and he liked it. He suggested we record it. We were veering between the two titles 'Well Come Back Home' and 'Welcome Back Home'. I used to be a practising Buddhist and that's how the chant got in there. 'Nam Myoho Renge Kyo' is meant to be the highest sound in the universe. It was a one-take song and it really got loose at the end. It was probably the most serious song that I was ever involved in."

Battin's Buddhist interests prompted some to wonder about McGuinn's own spiritual state in 1970. Having ended his involvement in Subud, he seemed more worldly, but still pondered on the divine. Although intrigued by Battin's performance on 'Well Come Back Home', he was not about to follow his theological flight. "I'm not a Buddhist," he confirmed. "Nor am I any other form of organized religion, really. I'm sort of a free spirit . . . It embarrasses me how much he [Battin] chants every day. He chants for hours at a time. The thing about his thing that I don't understand is that he does it asking the spiritual forces for toys – whatever you want, you know? Goodies, cars, colour TV – and he gets it." Despite such passing cynicism, McGuinn felt Battin's personal and political anthem deserved a place on *(Untitled)*. Its length ensured that it was the obvious candidate to close the record. Intentionally or not, it also fitted the tradition of ending Byrds' albums in an oft-kilter fashion.

Critical reaction to *(Untitled)* was almost universally positive. In America, the mainstream rock press were supportive, but the most piercing review came from underground magazine *Fusion*: "The Byrds are alive and doing just fine . . . After the disappointment of *Ballad Of Easy Rider*, it is a pure joy to see that the Byrds are flying as high as ever. *(Untitled)* is a joyous reaffirmation of life; it is the story of a band reborn. It is especially gratifying to those of us who maintained, in the face of adversity, that the Byrds were everything we had initially taken them for. The welcoming home of old friends is always cause for celebration."

In the UK, where the album climbed as high as number 11, their best showing since the salad days of *Turn! Turn! Turn!,* there were similar accolades. *Melody Maker*'s erudite editor Richard Williams noted: "There are few bands whose music has the power to evoke nostalgia for an era rather than for an isolated moment of time. There are even fewer who can do it at the same time as making music which is completely representative of the present, too. The Byrds have this, and *(Untitled)*, apart from being simply their most satisfying work to date is full of these complex memory-folds . . . Simply a great album, and 'Chestnut Mare' . . . whew!"

(Untitled) received some additional publicity from a very unexpected quarter. On the same day that it was released in America, Vice President Spiro Agnew was in Las Vegas addressing a group of Republicans at a campaign dinner in advance of the forthcoming mid-terms. In his speech, Agnew complained about "radical liberals" corrupting American youth who were supposedly being "brainwashed into a drug culture" by rock music. His diatribe was more than a simplistic attack on youth and addressed the abuse of alcohol and barbiturates by his own generation, but it was the pervasive influence of rock culture that bothered him most. Agnew argued that many rock songs presented drug use in "such an

attractive light, that for the impressionable, turning on becomes the natural and even the approved thing to do." Unfortunately, when it came to demonstrating his viewpoint, the examples he chose were ill-advised. Attacking the Beatles, he centred on 'With A Little Help From My Friends' as a typical example, helpfully pointing out that the friends in question were transparently 'drugs', which probably came as a surprise even to those radio programmers that had banned 'A Day In The Life'. He also mentioned the Jefferson Airplane's 'White Rabbit' and condemned the Byrds' 'Eight Miles High'. The reaction from the Byrds' camp was mild indignation mixed with a grimace of satisfaction upon realizing that they were back in the news. It was the 1966 controversy all over again, reinvented for Republicans. And it was happening the same day that they had issued the live, elongated 'Eight Miles High' on their new double album. Uncanny.

As before, the Byrds released a press statement, this time via the laconic Eddie Tickner, whose weary response was syndicated in local newspapers all over the country. "A lot of hullabaloo was raised over the song," he said, "but if you listen to the lyrics, you'll see the song is about the group's first trip to England as rock 'n' roll stars. There isn't even any subtlety in that song advocating the use of drugs. Eight miles high refers to how high the airplane flies. Does 'Smoke Gets In Your Eyes' advocate the use of tobacco? That's how silly it could get." The Byrds were not slow to take advantage of the publicity as part of their stage act. During subsequent live performances, they altered the lyrics of Leadbelly's 'Take A Whiff' to throw in the sarcastic gibe: "Come on Spiro, take a whiff on me". Hipper audiences enjoyed the joke, and others innocently clapped along regardless.

The international success of *(Untitled)* was a just reward for the commitment and energy that everyone had invested in re-establishing the band's standing. McGuinn remembers 1970 as a time when the Byrds achieved both satisfaction and security: "We made a lot of money. That was a million dollar year for us, and it got us out of the red."

As 1970 closed, the Byrds were seemingly in the ascendant with a major selling album and a strong reputation as a live act. One idea that failed to reach fruition, however, was the launching of *Gene Tryp* on Broadway. Although Jacques Levy remained confident that the musical would be staged, there was some doubt about the funding and business management. Already, there was confusion as to precisely who would star in the show. Ideally, McGuinn wanted Dylan to play Gene Tryp but he also thought of auditioning himself. Other names were suggested, including Tim Buckley and Jon Voight, but nothing came of it. In spite of these setbacks, McGuinn remained extremely enthusiastic about the musical, and talked about the production at great length in several interviews of the period.

As the script shows, *Gene Tryp* was feasible enough and the many different scenes encouraged the use of a variety of musical forms from country and bayou to hard rock. Regrettably, the special effects were far too elaborate for a budget that had already been cut from $750,000 to $300,000. McGuinn spoke of rivers running onstage, a 23-piece pit band, tapes and liquid projections. Even the maximum $150,000 that Columbia had bid for the score was not enough to finance all this. Disturbed by the financial risks, the businessmen began to question the profitability of the venture. Millionaire David Merrick felt it would not last a year on Broadway, and bubblegum genius, Don Kirshner, after showing some initial interest, also withdrew his support.

While interest in the project waned, McGuinn was still convinced that *Gene Tryp* was a viable proposition. In 1971, he announced that Michael Butler, who had been involved in the staging of *Hair*, was showing some interest in the book, and the Byrds were awaiting his comments on the score. Assuming that Butler would support the project, McGuinn predicted that the musical would be staged in 1972, three years after it had first been announced.

As time passed, however, everyone agreed that *Gene Tryp* was just a giant white elephant which no reputable producer could afford to risk handling. If the work had been staged, many believe that it might have vicariously projected the Byrds into superstardom, but it soon became apparent that there would be no easy substitute for extensive touring.

In spite of the continual setbacks, McGuinn's optimism about the *Gene Tryp* venture seemed unquenchable and, as late as 1974, he was still toying with the idea, albeit in a somewhat modified form. "I have considered reconstructing the play as an audio-musical, just doing a soundtrack album," he announced. "I could have done it as a radio show where it would be narrated and say, 'Now such and such is happening.' You can get away with lots of flights of fantasy when you don't have actual sets to deal with. It would be a lot easier and a lot cheaper to do. It's a good idea for an album. I think Jacques Levy and I should adapt it for a radio show type of album. That's coming back into popularity, it would be a good country rock opera. Well, we have the book, we're sitting on it. We wrote it way back in 1968, it's been a long while."

Unfortunately, neither the album nor the soundtrack ever appeared and when I spoke to McGuinn in 1977, he was ready to admit that the project had failed. "It's passé," he lamented. "It wouldn't work today. It was good for 1968, but it wouldn't be good for 1978. I've had talks with Jacques Levy and he completely puts it down on the grounds that the novelty of country rock is over and the attitude of it is extremely male-chauvinistic, which just wouldn't go these days. Jacques is very cynical about the whole thing. He doesn't want to even think about it. I'd like to read the book again and check it out, but he's not interested, so it's just history. Too bad."

Although the musical never reached Broadway, it would be a mistake to write off *Gene Tryp* as a complete failure. Even during the Eighties, McGuinn continued to weave the songs from the musical into a rambling narrative, suitable for his solo concerts. In 1992, there was still enough interest in the project to inspire a student musical and the narrative format was subsequently adapted for the autobiographical in-concert album, *Live From Mar*s.

Without *Gene Tryp* we would never have heard such memorable Byrds songs as 'Lover Of The Bayou', 'Chestnut Mare', 'All The Things' and 'Just A Season'. It should be stressed that, minus those tracks, *(Untitled)* would hardly have been such a commercial success. More importantly, had it not been for *Gene Tryp*, McGuinn might never have established his successful songwriting partnership with

Jacques Levy. The former psychologist's influence on McGuinn should never be underestimated. At a time when McGuinn appeared to have run dry creatively, Levy inspired him to co-write approximately two dozen songs in under a month. The cream of those McGuinn/Levy collaborations transformed the group's atrophying song catalogue at the dawn of the Seventies and prompted a resurgence of public and critical interest in the Byrds.

CHAPTER THIRTY-FOUR

Expensive

THE Byrds' intense touring schedule throughout 1970 placed immense pressures on all of the members' personal lives. The road had become a virtual reality, a time free zone in which monogamy and fidelity were subjugated by imaginations contaminated with an excess of everything. Aberrant behaviour was not merely normalized but encouraged and pandered by thrill-seeking roadies, profit-loving drug dealers and starstruck supporters, all of whom expected their groups to act like self-indulgent Caesars. It was a subculture that flourished in the Seventies, powered by cocaine and new money. Even the most prudish acts found restraint an outmoded virtue – and the Byrds had never been known for spurning the zeitgeist.

Compared to David Crosby, then in the ascendant with CSN&Y, the Byrds were regarded as aspiring artisans, who worked hard on the road, but avoided the superstar excesses of the time. But the group were far from saints. The drug culture had permeated their work and leisure time, and the same was true of their road crew, which had expanded to include new boy, Al Hersh, who was presently living in a house recently vacated by ex-Byrd Kevin Kelley. Travelling with the Byrds required endurance and stimulation.

"We'd take a lot of uppers," says Carlos Bernal. "We'd take dexedrine and dexamyl, and we took a lot of eskatrol. We'd also take the Biphetamine 30s which is a black upper and has time released downers in it. They call it the California Turnaround because the truck drivers would take a Biphetamine 30 and drive from Los Angeles to New York and then they would take another one on the way back. We used to take those with the coke and whisky to bring you down and mellow you out. When we were on the road, Roger had two briefcases. He had his $3,000 satellite phone in a gold Halliburton and the other Halliburton had three bottles of whisky in it. At all times."

Cocaine abuse was already affecting McGuinn's voice, as he later admitted when discussing his singing on the live portion of *(Untitled)*. Such indulgences were not restricted to pre-show rituals or after hours partying but actually took place while audiences were watching the show. One innocent reviewer complained that the elongated 'Eight Miles High' had now become "somewhat ridiculous, drawn out to nearly a half-hour with Battin soloing on bass for nearly five minutes". What he did not know was that the extended jam had been stretched ever further to accommodate the cocaine hunger of McGuinn and White. "We had lines of coke laid out for them when they came off, leaving Gene and Skip to play on," recalls Al Hersh. "They forgot about everything and were late going back. Sometimes it got ridiculous but that was why. They just completely forgot."

When Terry Melcher joined the tour to play keyboards at a handful of dates, the breaks seemed even longer. The coke made them feel like gods, but also expanded their egos and scrambled their moral antennae. McGuinn suddenly seemed more confident, but increasingly susceptible to rock star affectations. A critic from the *Los Angeles Herald Examiner* sent to review the Byrds' Christmas performance at the Santa Monica Civic Auditorium commented: "Roger McGuinn is stylish, self-impressed, and blissfully arrogant. He's more important than you or I could hope to be. Most of his time was spent making asides to friends in the first row and making withering comments to those in the other hundred rows . . ."

"The road was their vehicle and they played sold out show after sold out show," adds Bernal. "Audiences were tremendous and it was absolutely great for the band. Coke was around. Everybody was doing it, and we didn't want to be left out. It felt good, and it was fun. Everybody was on bad behaviour. The scene was about getting real high, and they were carrying on and being bad boys. We travelled with copious quantities."

Cocaine encouraged selfishness and eventually a disregard for those not caught up in the rock circus. Insidiously, the excesses on the road infiltrated personal relationships, leading to tensions and arguments back home. "With Roger, it was Southern Comfort and cocaine," says his former wife, Dolores. "I feel that's what destroyed it, plus the fact that Skip, Clarence and Gene had never had success like that before. I think it really went to their heads. It was like a second go round for the Byrds with *(Untitled)*. On the road, there were always the providers. They were the guys who woke them up, gave them the Benzedrine and then put them to sleep, and kept them high in between. And then there were all the women . . ."

All the Byrds were married with children at this point, but that would soon change. Gene Parsons was the first of the divorcees, unintentionally setting in motion what seemed like a chain reaction. His wife, Jo Ellen, would shortly be replaced by a new love, Camille. Skip Battin had been a serial seducer and womanizer since first finding fame in the rock 'n' roll era, but had always been discreet enough to maintain a solid marriage. The Byrds' road adventures terminated that happy arrangement. In a surprise turn of events, his wife, Jackie, eventually ended up with Al Hersh, both settling in the former family home in Topanga Canyon. McGuinn, who had been involved with Dolores since the end of 1964, became another marriage casualty. Unlike most of his contemporaries in the rock establishment, he had proven a faithful husband, never straying on the road, despite all the adulation from rapacious groupies since the 'Mr Tambourine Man' days.

"He was absolutely faithful to his wife, Ianthe (Dolores)," says Bernal. "Right up until the end. They were the ideal Hollywood couple . . . But decisions made under the influence of cocaine . . . any kind of sexual or brainstorming job under cocaine, forget about it."

Subud's disapproval of infidelity had not only been accepted by McGuinn, but practiced with true faith. By 1970, he was no longer a believer and temptations were increasingly difficult to resist. Dolores suspected that he was having a fling with one of her friends, and learned the truth while the Byrds were playing a show in the Boston area during November. Phoning the hotel, she asked to speak to 'Mr and Mrs McGuinn' and was promptly directed to their suite where her worst fears were confirmed. To add salt to the wounds, it was her birthday. When confronted, McGuinn was frank about the fling. According to Dolores, he said, "I've been faithful to you all these years and when I was young and had the opportunity, I never took it. So I thought this was my last chance." Their relationship never recovered. Having tasted forbidden fruit, McGuinn – whatever his good intentions – was always likely to be tempted at some future point on the road. When it happened the second time, it had far-reaching consequences.

Linda Gilbert (b. 16 March 1950) was barely out of her teens, when she first met McGuinn, but she was sophisticated beyond her years. Jim Dickson felt she was far more assured than McGuinn and clearly came from a monied background. Her arrival in the midst of his marital discord was dramatic, seemingly prompting a complete reappraisal of his life. "When Linda showed up, it was the timing and everything," says Bernal. "But she was also hot. I remember the night she first showed up at the Whisky A Go-Go. She came in wearing a mink coat, scantily clad underneath, wanting to meet the guitar player. Al and I took her up to meet Roger, and that was it. The lightning bolt. She was a real fox in a mink coat, high heels, abbreviated clothing, giant hooters and, I was told, she was related to J. Paul Getty and all those people. Both her mother and her dad came from money. So Roger rethought – and the next thing you know Ianthe (Dolores) is out of the picture."

It was not an easy separation and the new romance met some challenging obstacles, not least from the abandoned Dolores. On one occasion, she caught them in bed together and almost lost control. "There was a Heineken bottle on the bed's headboard," she recalls. "I held the bottle over her head. I think Linda was pretending to be asleep. Roger was mouthing, 'Don't. Please don't!' I should have just gotten up and walked away, but I was devastated about my family."

After this there was no going back for McGuinn. Dolores claims that his parting words were "You're fired," as if he was dismissing a disgruntled band member. As an example of his black humour, it took some beating. "All I knew was that he didn't like his wife any more," says Al Hersh. "He just wanted it to be over. He just wanted to walk away and have it be done with, which is exactly what he did. That's how he was. He can be a very cold person in a lot of ways."

Like McGuinn, Clarence White once had a seemingly cast iron marriage, but it too was under threat. Adultery on the road and an overfondness for cocaine and partying were again the main symptoms. "Roger got into bug mikes," says Hersh. "So we started bugging each other's rooms. Carlos bugged Clarence's room one night when he had a girl in there." Somehow, White's wife Susie learned of his transgression and further drama followed.

Events reached a head at a party, where the wives literally tracked down their errant husbands. "Ianthe and Susie (White) came in and caught Roger and Clarence," Bernal recalls. "A big horrible scene happened at about two or three in the morning. Linda was there, and another girl with Clarence. They were having a great time but they got into trouble. Susie and Ianthe didn't just come in and go running out. They stuck around for a while and caused a ruckus. They threw some chairs, messed up a pool table and threw bottles. It was a big confrontation."

The fall-out from all of the above was three divorces. White was the only Byrd whose marriage survived, but as long as he remained in the group it was never entirely secure. Later down the line, Susie relocated to Kentucky, along with her two children. It wasn't the end, but she realized that they needed to separate so that Clarence could decide where his life was heading. "I knew they were in trouble," says Dolores. "Their marriage looked like it was breaking up too."

Rock 'n' roll stars are not renowned for seeking marriage guidance, particularly those who were based in Hollywood during the Seventies. The Byrds' Caesarian tendencies were reinforced by their promiscuous, party-loving road crew, who vicariously enjoyed the fantasy high life conjured by their employers. The Byrds no longer needed to hang out in hip places, for they had their very own private members' club, situated on Hesby Street in the Sherman Oaks suburb. It was here that Seiter, Bernal and Hersh created their own saturnalia in a house they dubbed Tweet Manor or the

Byrdhouse. It soon became a haven for recreational drug use, groupie adventures and week-long partying. "The Hesby house was basically a place for the guys to go and get laid," says Hersh. "It was a constant party and all the guys were having affairs there. This went on for a long time. My first function was running that house while Jimmi Seiter was on the road, so I was enjoying the spoils. As you know, Jimmi wanted to be in the band and was playing congas and, little by little, moving in from the side of the stage, trying to be a rock 'n' roll star. Later, he got himself fired and phased himself out, which was when I picked up from him, with Carlos and the sound man, Dinky Dawson."

"Tweet Manor was a clubhouse for the boys," Bernal adds. "The house was pretty big, with three or four bedrooms and big front-room couches to sleep on. That place could accommodate people who wanted to crash. We'd have barbecues and picnics in the swimming pool and stay up for days on pharmaceutical prescriptions. There were large amounts of coke and that was accepted. It was impolite or untoward not to always have a quarter or half an ounce in your possession. For those people I knew or gravitated towards, it was a normal thing. It wasn't a big secret or surprise."

By early 1971, McGuinn was immersed in this hedonistic atmosphere. Rejuvenated and deep in the throes of new love, he was enjoying the fruits of rock stardom, and acting the part. On one occasion, he turned into a demented James Dean, riding his motorcycle directly into the Byrdhouse, then losing control as the vehicle careered through the back door and ended up in the swimming pool. McGuinn himself had to be fished out, but thought little about the incident. It seemed like he was playing the part of a superhero. Before their marriage dissolved, Dolores was always amazed by his love of technology. He liked to play with a laser gun, beaming light through neighbours' windows, then suddenly switching off the gadget to witness the ensuing confusion. Sometimes, he mischievously bugged rooms and listened to people's conversations for his own amusement. "He thought he was 007," she says.

The roadies had similar feelings. "Roger was very impressed with James Bond," Al Hersh notes wryly. "When a James Bond movie came out, he wanted everything Bond had. His bedroom or den was like a James Bond room with the bank of television sets. He had Bond motorcycles and cars and was very enamoured of the whole spy thing. We were bugging each other's rooms. Roger started that with the bug mikes. It was really nuts and out of control with the whole James Bond thing. He really took it on a whole other level and started arming himself with weapons. You're talking about a guy that was capable of doing a couple of quarts of scotch a day and a whole lot of blow. So, yeah, it was like a powder keg there for a while. It could have gone either way."

While these multiple melodramas were unfolding, Terry Melcher agreed to start recording the next Byrds album. The timing was hardly ideal. Whatever emotional turmoil had been visited upon the Byrds was small beer compared to what was going on in Melcher's head. In the aftermath of the Manson murders, he had become increasingly paranoid, albeit not without good reason. Still recoiling from the nightmare of the Tate/Bianca slayings, he had spent many sleepless nights dreading the possibility that extended members of the Family might turn up in the dead of night seeking revenge on behalf of their deranged messiah. Sometimes Melcher felt like a condemned man. He was due to testify against Manson a few months later (23 August) in a trial that already seemed never-ending. Not only was Melcher on medication, but he was self-medicating with coke, pills and an endless supply of vodka. He was constantly shepherded by a burly bodyguard and had armed himself with a shotgun, which he kept close by while parading through his mansion. His long-suffering girlfriend, actress Candice Bergen, offered moral support, while a pet monkey provided light relief and helped take his mind off weightier matters.

Melcher hoped that working on the Byrds' latest project would keep him busy, sane and in control, but others weren't so sure. Jim Seiter had already experienced some of the approaching madness in a bizarre late night interlude that began with a frantic phone call from Candice Bergen. Melcher had washed down some pills with vodka and was liberally discharging his gun, puncturing holes in the ceiling and causing mayhem. The combination of firearms and fire-water meant that he was not only a danger to himself, but anyone else in his vicinity. As an inveterate interventionist during such emergencies, Seiter drove over to Melcher's home, intending to wrest the weapon from his grasp and calm him down. By the time he arrived, the crisis was over and the house preternaturally silent. After a tentative search, he found Melcher in a cage, cradled in the arms of his pet monkey. Rather than waking the pair, he left Melcher to sober up and returned to Hesby to catch up on some much-needed sleep. The next morning, he received a call from the bleary-eyed, befuddled Melcher enquiring, "Hey, what happened last night?" Seiter snapped back: "Go and ask your monkey!", then slammed down the phone in exasperation.

Given the emotional states of everyone involved – musicians and producer – it was remarkable enough that the sessions proceeded in the first place. Even before the players stepped into Columbia's Studio on Sunset and El Centro, McGuinn was promising some radical changes to the musical menu. "I'm fed up to the gills with country music," he said. "I don't care if I never sing another country song in my life. Gene Parsons and Clarence White wouldn't like it, but Skip Battin wouldn't mind. It's not my style, really. I can do a shot but I don't feel at home with it because I'm a city boy from Chicago. I have more of a love for old-time folk and jazz. I was sort of pressurized into country music . . . but it's gotten out of hand."

Curtailing the country influence meant that Clarence White's rendition of 'Home Sweet Home', which had been played at recent concerts, was dropped from the running order during the album rehearsals. Unfortunately, McGuinn had nothing new to contribute. Since his writing spree with Jacques Levy, he had failed to put pen to paper. Constant touring, marital breakdown and non-stop partying had left little time to concentrate on the nuances of songwriting. In different circumstances, this would have been a golden opportunity to transform marital chaos into great art, but McGuinn was in an exuberant rather than introspective mood. Unable to drag a single song from his tired muse, he resurrected the inconsequential 'I Trust', whose forced positivism was a rather evasive reaction to recent tumultuous events.

McGuinn's lackadaisical attitude towards his own writing and disdain for country music unintentionally opened doors for Skip Battin and co-writer Kim Fowley. Ever the opportunist, Fowley seized the moment, safe in the knowledge that he could pen an entire songbook of lyrics, if necessary. Still uncertain about the direction of the new album, McGuinn allowed Battin unprecedented leeway. On 11 January, three Battin/Fowley songs were cut in a single day: 'Citizen Kane', 'Absolute Happiness' and 'Tunnel Of Love'. If nothing else, it confirmed that the new record would be a major departure.

Kim Fowley always thrived when faced with competition or creative indecision. Like a predator scattering weak prey, he was prepared to make the project his own, if allowed. He was full of wild and whirling ideas, some of which were crazy enough to make sense. Sensing songwriting blocks all around him, he came up with a novel idea that would allow McGuinn to retain creative supremacy, without actually having to write anything. This could either be a side project or a follow-up album, depending on how the current sessions progressed. Years before, Jim Dickson and McGuinn had pondered the possibility of the group eventually releasing a 'Byrds Sing Dylan' album, but such a notion would never have been entertained by David Crosby. Graham Nash had left the Hollies after they recorded *Hollies Sing Dylan* which, despite its chart-topping sales, was regarded as a retrograde step. McGuinn probably shared the same ambivalence about being too ingratiated to Dylan and, as if realizing this, Fowley suggested another source. "I was dating Kate Taylor, so I suggested that James Taylor should write for the Byrds. I thought they should do half an album of James Taylor songs and the other half should be by Neil Young: six songs each. Can you imagine the Byrds singing the best of James and Neil, with those two guys guesting? It would have been tremendous."

Fowley's nepotistic ploy was not welcomed by Terry Melcher, who felt his own authority was under challenge. "Terry was threatened by the idea that Peter Asher might show up to co-produce it." This seems unlikely and would never have happened without McGuinn's sanction, but Melcher was quick to curb Fowley's powerplays with some well-chosen words. "Terry told me: 'Remember you're only a lyricist and co-publisher on these Byrds records. I'm still the producer. *Never* forget that.' I said, 'Yes, sir!'"

Although Melcher was ever capable of putting Fowley in his

EXPENSIVE

place and was not unduly concerned about offending either Battin or Parsons, he had only the vaguest idea of how the album might take shape. He looked to McGuinn for guidance and inspiration, employing the same divisive dynamics that had blighted the *Turn! Turn! Turn!* sessions. Having successfully defied David Crosby as a spokesman and songwriter, Melcher had no trouble imposing his viewpoint on the subsidiary members of the latter-day Byrds. What he had not countenanced was the paucity of the material, McGuinn's vacillation, and his own inner demons. "Terry had a thing going on with himself," says Al Hersh. "First of all he was scared for his life during those times and he was totally out of his mind doing the album. Somehow, he thought Manson was going to show up at the studio and kill him. And Chris Hinshaw, his engineer, seemed to be living in fear. They were all completely crazed and those sessions were a joke. Terrible. Terry was in no shape to be doing anything."

It cannot have helped matters when Dolores unexpectedly appeared midway through a session, brandishing a whisky bottle in front of her errant husband. "Everybody was getting divorced, weren't they?" she recalls. "After that recording session, Terry took me to a local bar. Terry was so kind and he was trying to help me out. He said, 'You know, this is happening and you'll have to accept Roger's going . . .'" Having fulfilled this new role as divorce guidance counsellor, Melcher returned to the studio to face more problems with Battin and Parsons, whom he had decided to replace with session musicians on certain tracks. Considering the chaos, Carlos Bernal was impressed that they completed the album on time. "It was only on rare occasions that anybody would be in poor form or really embarrassing. There were a couple of times when Roger was in the recording studio with Terry and you'd see the machine going with the tape flapping and people passed out and asleep in the booth and copious amounts of drugs right out in the open."

Having got this far, Melcher decided to enhance the recordings with a lavish production makeover incorporating additional instrumentation, orchestration and, where necessary, a gospel choir for dramatic effect. His ideas were not merely expansive, but expensive. At a time when McGuinn should have been counting his pennies in preparation for a divorce settlement, he was racking up additional debt to his record company that would probably take years to recoup. When Melcher enquired about a possible album title, McGuinn retorted, with grim irony, "We should call it *Expensive*."

After finishing the album, the Byrds fulfilled some concert bookings in the US before returning to England in May for a series of sell-out shows. On arrival, McGuinn sounded upbeat, even cocky, about the group's current standing. "It would be presumptuous, but I would love the Byrds to be the number 1 group in the world." He was quick to congratulate his old friend George Harrison on the recent international chart-topping single 'My Sweet Lord'. "It's kind of a sneaky prayer, like 'Turn! Turn! Turn!'. And I like that because I'm religious in my own way. I believe everything is alive. I'm the opposite to agnostic."

There was a detectable spikiness when Dylan's name was mentioned. "I wanted to protect him from criticism. But somehow that feeling has gone. I can't protect him any more . . . I don't think we owe [him] anything. He owes me something. Somehow he doesn't appreciate what we did for him. He may appreciate, but he hasn't shown it. 'Mr Tambourine Man' was a big asset to him, and when we continued recording his stuff, it gave him a real boost." Speaking of changes in the Byrds' power structure, he suggested that their new album might come as a surprise. "It's more or less democratic. I allow songs I don't even like very much to go on albums just because someone else wants to do them. It's their expression – each member has his own thing. I think the only consistent factor is my guitar playing and singing . . . I haven't changed tremendously after six years. My voice hasn't changed, it's just got a little deeper, that's all."

The tour opened on 3 May in Bristol, home of the Byrds Appreciation Society, run by 18-year-old Chrissie Brewer. All four members of the group visited Brewer's family home where they entertained themselves poring through scrapbooks of press cuttings going back to 1965. Polaroid pictures capture them looking slightly bemused but smiling as they cramp themselves into the teenager's room to revisit their back pages. Linda is also there, looking resplendent with long hair and a full-length dress, while the bearded

McGuinn sports a dark suit and tie. Before leaving the city, the happy couple were presented with a bottle of Harvey's Bristol Cream as a further testament to British hospitality. It must have provided a welcome break from the rock 'n' roll lifestyle of a touring band to experience such an innocent domestic scene accompanied by some genuine human warmth.

The UK tour culminated in a glorious night at the Royal Albert Hall, on 13 May. Whatever their problems back home or in the studio, there was no sign of any tensions or unprofessional behaviour onstage. Like a well-oiled machine, the Byrds glided effortlessly through an impressively tight set. Their irrepressible road manager Jim Seiter was by now a familiar sight onstage, banging a tambourine alongside Gene Parsons, a surrogate Byrd in all but name. After exhausting their repertoire, the Byrds returned to rapturous encores and finished the evening with a moving, a cappella 'Amazing Grace', a song originally intended for inclusion on *(Untitled)*. The entire performance was recorded that evening, but escaped the rapacious claws of bootleggers. A tape of the show rested in McGuinn's archives for decades, but was unexpectedly unearthed and issued on CD in 2008. As a concert souvenir, it still sounded impressive.

Backstage after the Royal Albert Hall show, the Byrds discussed their latest and as yet unreleased album. From their defensive comments that night, it was clear that they were disappointed about every aspect of the recording. McGuinn revealed that there had been problems with Terry Melcher, adding that he was no longer working for the Byrds as manager or producer. "We got mad," Clarence White explained, "and said, 'We have to get rid of him.' Nobody would say those three words to him: 'You are fired.' So I thought, 'I'll try it', and I fired him. That was good for about three days. I'm not signed with Columbia anyway, so it didn't make any difference. He came back and said, 'I'm ready to work', and finally Roger said those three words, 'You are fired.' That's when he split." Clarence's criticisms were merely a prelude to worse condemnations that would follow later in the year.

A pilot single, 'I Trust'/'Is This My Destiny', was released to coincide with the UK tour, but it was no 'Chestnut Mare'. A personal appearance on *Top Of The Pops* failed to promote sales, radio play was sparse and reviews tepid at best. The group concluded their European jaunt with a series of shows in the Netherlands, then returned home and awaited the critical reaction to their new album.

Byrdmaniax, released on 23 June, received a generally hostile response in America. McGuinn was particularly annoyed by *Rolling Stone*'s review which had described the album's contents as "excrements of pus". The Byrds had hardly helped their promotional cause by damning the record in advance. Given the circumstances, a US chart position of number 46 was pretty good. In subsequent interviews, the group poured scorn on *Byrdmaniax*, while Gene Parsons totally disowned it. As far as the Byrds were concerned, the aesthetic and commercial failure of the album were entirely the responsibility of Terry Melcher. "We were appalled by what we heard," Parsons remembers, "and it was too late. Columbia were saying, 'The budget is *this* and we have to put it out.' They picked the wrong tracks on some of the pieces, and put horns and singers in that had no business being there."

Clarence White, speaking at the time of the release, reiterated Parsons' damning assessment. "Terry Melcher put the strings on while we were on the road. We came back and we didn't even recognize it as our own album. It was like somebody else's work. Our instruments were buried. Melcher had produced some hits on the first two albums, then he almost got us hits with 'Ballad Of Easy Rider' and 'Chestnut Mare', so by the time of *Byrdmaniax*, Roger couldn't believe that Terry could do any wrong."

White and Parsons complained bitterly that Melcher had employed orchestration without their approval and squandered over $100,000 on the project. Even Byron Berline joined the debate over Melcher's extravagances claiming, "On the 'Green Apple Quick Step' session I was there from 9 pm to 5 am. Terry would say, 'We'll do this . . .', and then he'd go off and drink coffee or something. But I didn't care. I got well paid for that."

While the criticisms of Melcher mounted, it was difficult to avoid the feeling that too many people were castigating him solely for his introduction of strings and choruses. Few chose to remember that

EXPENSIVE

he had employed strings effectively on *Ballad Of Easy Rider* and that his track record, up until this point, was impeccable. When I spoke to Melcher, he agreed that the decision to continue recording *Byrdmaniax* was a fatal error, but insisted that the fault was not his alone. "My most vivid recollection of that album was catching McGuinn's wife, Ianthe, in mid-air as she was heading towards McGuinn's neck with a broken whisky bottle. Several members of the group were involved in divorces and they were hiding from their wives. It was complete bedlam in the studio. Everyone had too many problems."

In answering the more controversial questions about the album, Melcher proved remarkably evasive, later admitting that he felt like "a worm squirming on the end of a hook". It seemed only fair, however, to allow him the full opportunity to defend himself against the corrosive comments of the Byrds. The following snatches of interview, then, may serve as Melcher's defence plea.

You claim that you weren't extravagant but how do you explain away the fact that you spent about $100,000 on the album?
"There were wasted weeks. McGuinn rented a Moog which was very expensive. I wasn't getting the guitar parts, so I added other instruments."

Was the orchestration added without their approval?
"I think the orchestration was a big mistake, but the songs were weak."

You're avoiding the question. Was the orchestration added with or without the Byrds' approval?
"I'm not a tyrant or anything. There was a lack of interest on everybody's part. With the divorces, it was a problem. I was trying to save the album, but it was a mistake. I should have called a halt."

You still haven't answered my question. Do you admit that you did add the orchestration without their approval?
"No. Well, I mean I admit that I wasn't in consultation with them a lot and I didn't really deal with Clarence, Battin or Parsons on these matters. But I'm sure it was inconceivable that McGuinn did not know about the orchestration."

Clarence White said, 'Melcher buried our instruments.' Is that true?
"It's possible. If anything got buried it was because it was mediocre."

Parsons described the album as 'Melcher's Folly'. How do you feel about that?
"I didn't get on too well with Gene Parsons. How does he describe *Ballad Of Easy Rider*? I used strings on that album too."

Battin said that you didn't come to too many sessions.
"It's possible. I was having problems too. I should have never let it get past the first session."

Is it true that you wanted to replace Battin and Parsons with session musicians?
"Probably. I thought Gene Parsons was a better guitar player than a drummer."

McGuinn said that the album was taken out of your hands and remixed by an engineer in San Francisco. Were there any substantial differences in the final product?
"I can't remember the differences or even if there were any. All I can say is that my original couldn't have been any worse."

A closer analysis of the album reveals the extent of the supposed damage and the degree to which Melcher's erstwhile good name may be vindicated.

The opening track, 'Glory, Glory', was another song that Gene Parsons borrowed from the Art Reynolds Singers. Melcher obviously felt that a strong vocal backing was required to bring out the gospel flavour and so he introduced a host of backing singers, including Merry Clayton. Unfortunately, the experiment backfired. As Melcher admits: "We were aiming to cut another 'Jesus Is Just Alright', but we didn't make it. Larry Knechtel played piano on this cut but it was too fast. The whole thing was a mess."

By contrast, 'Pale Blue', written by McGuinn, turned out to be one of the stronger songs on the album. An expression of conflicting desire for both freedom and security, its theme is sensitively handled by McGuinn, who provides a touching vocal performance. The use of orchestration seems fully justified here, enhancing the romantic elements in the lyric. But Melcher's true stroke of genius was retaining Parsons' harmonica solos. The juxtaposition of that most simple of instruments, the harmonica, alongside an elaborate string section, instantly transforms the composition. When the Byrds recorded 'Ballad Of Easy Rider' for their CBS album, they wisely dropped the harmonica and allowed Melcher to embellish the song with some free-flowing orchestration. On 'Pale Blue', however, he wanted both light and shade. The harmonica places the song in a folk tradition, making the theme a simple statement of love, unaffected by emotional complexities, while the orchestration provides an underlying pathos. Ultimately, the song succeeds as a result of fusing these disparate elements. The harmonica and strings elucidate the conflicting feelings of domesticity and wanderlust to considerable effect. Here it seems 'Melcher's Folly' actually succeeds. "The idea of orchestration came out of 'Easy Rider'," he confirmed. "I like what you say about the harp and the orchestra working together as I've always liked to use strong contrasts. I thought 'Pale Blue' was pretty close to what we wanted."

It took McGuinn five years to compose a song based on his famous borrowed catchphrase, "I trust it will turn out all right". Alas, it was not worth the long wait. Originally performed as early as March 1970 in concert, this song was not even deemed a serious contender for *(Untitled)*. Melcher tries to add some gravitas to the sentiments with his heavenly host of backing singers, but the effect proves detrimental. White's work appears stifled and McGuinn's Rickenbacker sounds restrained to the point of frustration while the choir scream out the 'I Trust' chorus. All in all, this was an erratic song with some interesting moments that were never developed. In retrospect, Melcher recognized the song's shortcomings. "I think you're right," he concedes. "Now you mention it, there wasn't really any distinctive jingle-jangle Byrds sound."

The derivative Battin/Fowley composition, 'Tunnel Of Love', was memorable only for its lyrics. In the song, the narrator sees a derelict tunnel of love and his mind commutes back into the past to conjure up a ghostly vision of his former self. There is an allusion to the effects of nuclear fallout, water floating with graves and the subject hiding behind a sandbagged door. McGuinn made the composition sound more interesting during a pre-release interview in which he misinterpreted the apocalyptic lyrics as being "about a guy who wakes up to find the world is over and that he is the only person left alive". McGuinn fails to mention the strangely spectral presence of black-robed girls, ushering the troubled narrator to probable doom. Intriguingly, there are strong echoes of William Blake's late eighteenth-century three-stanza poem *The Garden Of Love* from *Songs Of Innocence And Of Experience*. Blake's verse begins with the lines "I went to the Garden of Love . . ." followed by descriptions that appear to be modernized or rephrased by Fowley: "the gates of the Chapel were shut" (cf. "the gates of the tunnel came closed"), "play on the green" (cf. "swim in the stream"), "written over the door" (cf. "standing there by the door"), "and I saw it was filled with graves" (cf. "the water was floating with graves"), "And tomb-stones where flowers should be" (cf. "graves where cotton candy should be"). Even Fowley's distinctive description of "girls in black robes dancing around" seems clearly adapted from Blake's penultimate line in the final verse "'And priests in black gowns, were walking their rounds". Tellingly, the metre and rhythm of both pieces are virtually identical. Amazingly, Fowley, who was solely responsible for the lyrics to Battin's songs, denies that it was inspired by Blake. "It was just based on death," he told me. "I visited Battersea Fun Fair in London, England and I wrote it after I went there." So, how does he explain all of the above lyrical comparisons? "I don't know. Maybe I'm Blake and it came through me while I was sleeping. We get our information from the metaphysical mesh, as Einstein said."

If the lyrics paraphrased a great poet, then the music owed much to early rock 'n' roll. The organ accompaniment, straight out of Fats Domino's 'Blueberry Hill', is complemented by a passable saxophone backing redolent of the Fifties. The other Byrds are virtually nowhere to be heard on the track, which sounds suspiciously like a completely solo outing from Battin. Although the diversity of material makes a pleasant change, McGuinn deserves censure for not taking a firmer stand and insisting that solo efforts be incorporated into a more unified band sound. A classic case of group democracy gone wrong.

Battin's cause was assisted by the implicit support of Parsons and White, who also raised no objections. "I enjoyed the songs," claims Parsons, "but I think they definitely did go off field. They were in their own world in a way and some of them might not have been appropriate for the Byrds but I'm glad we did them anyway. It's a judgement that's really all in the eye of the beholder. I liked the tunes. I realized that they were probably out of whack with what was expected and possibly alienated Roger some, but they were good songs and nobody had any other ones."

Ostensibly, 'Citizen Kane' sounds like another example of McGuinn failing to curb the influence of the notorious Kim Fowley, whose lyrics sometimes stood out like a gross aberration in the Byrds' songbook. Fowley still blames Battin for this, claiming that he was merely writing lyrics under instruction and knew full well that they were inappropriate for the project. "They all yelled about the Fowley/Battin songs, as though I was leading this guy astray but, in reality, Skip didn't want to be a team player. He said, 'After the Byrds I'll want to do this stuff as a solo and introduce it in my spot.'" Melcher's response to Fowley's Tinseltown paean was a cinematic trad jazz overdub that smacked of overkill. Only McGuinn's expressive lead guitar playing identifies the song as 'Byrds' and saves the day. In later years, Battin performed a more sombre version on piano and was quick to stress the composition's autobiographical elements. "Kim wrote that incredibly quickly. It was novelty in one sense, but it was also true. Kim lived that Hollywood life and he saw a lot of that stuff as a kid." Indeed, Fowley had once been removed from his bed as a child so that Errol Flynn, who is namechecked in the song, could service a woman friend.

The *Gene Tryp* composition, 'I Wanna Grow Up To Be A Politician', became another novelty throwaway within the context of *Byrdmaniax*. Musical standards are made when a song transcends its origins and intended context to stand alone magnificently. The great songwriting teams of film and theatre achieved this countless times, but even rock music's most accomplished tunesmiths have struggled when obliged to write to order for a scripted project. With his theatrical background, Jacques Levy was able to provide McGuinn with material that worked in both a dramatic and personal context. The greatest songs composed for *Gene Tryp* – 'Chestnut Mare' and 'Just A Season' – succeeded on both these levels. Alas, 'I Wanna Grow Up To Be A Politician' is too wedded to its narrative theme to break out of a self-imposed theatrical framework. The ham-handed brass band accompaniment merely adds to the artifice, leaving the song locked in theatreland. No doubt, it would have served its purpose quite well as a showtune designed to express the political machinations of the Gene Tryp character who is seen on the campaign trail aboard a wagon painted red, white and blue. Removed from its dramatic format, the song loses both humour and vitality and fails to convince as a stand-alone track on *Byrdmaniax*. McGuinn attempts to get into character with a sprightly vocal, laden with grinning irony, but the sentiments are too stagy and he comes across like a denuded actor, who has no costume or stage design to suspend our disbelief. Whereas we can believe in McGuinn as a lover of the bayou or in pursuit of a chestnut mare, he makes an unconvincing political candidate. Yet, McGuinn's attitude to politics was quite serious at the time. Not long before the album's release, he said, "Politically, I'm becoming much less apathetic. I've always been somewhat left of the centre, but now it's getting so that you have to take a stand. My writing is becoming more political. People have thought of us as representing a political viewpoint since the first album. 'Chimes Of Freedom', even 'The Bells Of Rhymney' were political songs."

Such fleeting expressions of commitment did not alter the fact that during this period of avowed political interest, McGuinn was unwilling, or unable, to express any particular standpoint. Even Battin had indirectly commented upon the Vietnam War in 'Well Come Back Home', but McGuinn remained silent. The only comment we have in song is the unassuming 'I Wanna Grow Up To Be A Politician', a satiric showtune. McGuinn later admitted to me that his inability to express political idealism convincingly during the Seventies was partly a result of his upbringing. "I'm curious about politics, but I'm also very cynical because I came out of Chicago where Richard Daley had been mayor since I was a little kid. I knew the reason he was mayor was not because he was the best person for the job, but because he had the machine."

Following the blandness of McGuinn's political humour, Battin's enticing 'Absolute Happiness' proves a welcome and entirely unexpected highlight. Melcher's use of orchestration is negligible here and has little or no marked effect on the mood of the piece. The song begins with an oddly dramatic narrative before moving into a Buddhist-like speculation on the nature of absolute happiness. Remembering the track, Battin told me: "It was a song about the Buddhist philosophy, as you say. We wrote it after a Buddhist meeting. Kim wasn't involved in Buddhism, but he absorbed the idea."

Strangely enough, Fowley completely contradicts this suggestion, insisting that the words had nothing to do with Buddhism. If Battin had known the true history and intent of the lyric, he might never have provided such a graceful and expressive vocal performance. "It was about this guru who killed somebody in a fight once," Fowley claims. "He had his own religion and a place on Sunset Boulevard, and he had the best girls. They were astounding goddesses and I was trying to fuck one of his blondes. I wrote the song so that I could get laid when she heard it, but she didn't know who the Byrds were. She was such a vegetarian. Then they all went off to Hawaii and he had an untimely death there. He was like a Timothy Leary guru and the song was based on all their religious practices. I went to these ashrams a couple of times and there were all these girls, who looked like *Playboy* models with no underwear on, walking around in white robes. I wanted to join the religion so that I could fuck all of them, but it didn't work out, even for the guy in the song."

The instrumental, 'Green Apple Quick Step', featured Clarence White on mandolin and guitar, his father Eric on harmonica, Parsons on banjo and Byron Berline on fiddle. The playing is so fast that it was difficult to believe that the tape had not been sped up to produce the stunning effects. This was a track for which the Byrds ought to have felt justly satisfied, but this was not the case. Parsons complained bitterly that Melcher had destroyed all the subtleties with Berline's fiddle part. Byron, himself, was equally unimpressed, dismissing the tune as "a spur of the moment thing". Despite the splendid spontaneity, Berline felt alienated during the recording process. "I didn't record live with them," he says. "Terry wanted me to overdub three different fiddle parts. That was impossible! It didn't turn out as well as it should, the mixing was awful. One thing about the song; they put me up in a booth, way upstairs some place. I couldn't see anybody. They had a microphone in the ceiling, about six feet away from my fiddle in order to get that big hollow, echo feel. Terry Melcher is a very strange producer at times."

In spite of Melcher's production tricks, the end project still sounds electrifying, although it clearly offended the traditional tastes of Berline, White and Parsons. When faced with their catalogue of criticisms, Melcher seemed to take the safest way out: "I don't even remember how it goes!"

'(Is This) My Destiny' was another traditional song discovered by White. The whole approach sounds misplaced and out of context, while the steel guitar work and Floyd Cramer keyboards style fails to enliven the mournful tune. White usually had good taste in his choice of song but this nasal dirge was painful to hear on a Byrds album, particularly one urgently in need of stronger original work.

'Kathleen's Song', a track originally cut for *(Untitled)* and printed on early sleeves of that album, was the last *Gene Tryp* composition recorded by the Byrds. Far superior to most of the material on this album, it ranks alongside 'Pale Blue' as one of McGuinn's better songs of the period. Melcher's use of strings, far from proving detrimental, enhances the dramatic elements of the composition, with McGuinn singing the part of the long-suffering heroine whose character closely resembles John Riley's ever patient "fair young maid". McGuinn was initially taken aback when he first heard the orchestration, but voiced no disapproval. "I walked into the studio and discovered a 30-piece orchestra – and walked out again, thinking it was the wrong studio. I asked a guard which studio we were in and got directed right back to the same studio where the orchestra was striking up . . ."

For most commentators, Jackson Browne's 'Jamaica Say You Will' was the strongest cut on the album. Unfortunately, the group were full of complaints about this song too. Parsons claims Melcher substituted a bad take of the song for a version on which White had supposedly given his finest vocal performance. The other Byrds maintain that Melcher unilaterally added strings and horns to the alternate take, without their knowledge or sanction. Clarence White's comments were expressed in a tone of utter disappointment: "On 'Jamaica' I tried to do an excellent recording because I knew Jackson Browne was going to be known as a great singer and incredible songwriter. We did a good track underneath there, but when they added the strings there were almost 40 people in the studio, and they had to listen to the track because we don't always tune on pitch. Instead of tuning to the piano, they had to tune from the earphones. So the whole orchestra is a little sharp and I'm singing flat. I was embarrassed when I heard it."

The disappointment about the mixing seems overstated. Parsons' drumming occasionally lacks prominence while the swirling strings create an unusual, but not unpleasant, effect. The lead guitar sounds impressive, so perhaps the Byrds' criticisms were centred entirely on the weak vocal. Melcher maintains that his actions were positive and beneficial. "Clarence wasn't that great a singer in technical terms. I just chose the version that I thought was the best. Linda Carradine (formerly McGuinn/Gilbert) later told me that there was some friction in the group because Roger didn't like the idea of Clarence singing that song and wanted it for himself."

In conclusion, it seems too sweeping an assertion to dismiss *Byrdmaniax* as a failure on Melcher's part. Some of the material was fairly good and though it lacked the consistent excellence of *(Untitled)*, the album still showed that the Byrds were capable of writing strong songs. Significantly, McGuinn voiced no great dissatisfaction with Melcher's production on 'Pale Blue' or 'Kathleen's Song', and the decision to employ orchestration on those tracks proved an inspired move. Even the severest criticisms of his production techniques on 'Green Apple Quick Step' and 'Jamaica Say You Will' sound unconvincing when we consider the quality of those recordings. Melcher's only real failure was his inability to cope with the Byrds' less impressive material. On 'Glory, Glory', he tries to compensate for the ineffective vocals by introducing backing singers but, rather than succeeding, he merely highlights the group's shortcomings. Instead of attempting to improve their playing, Melcher occasionally buries the instrumentation, but such instances are the exception rather than the rule. His production on *Byrdmaniax* was a spurious controversy to my mind and though the results may have been unusual and disappointing to certain purists, they were not, ultimately, disastrous.

Considering the album's flawed reputation, it is salutary to consider how well it was received in certain critical quarters, mainly in the UK. *Melody Maker* praised almost every track, even while knowing that the Byrds had disowned the work. Reviewer Roy Hollingworth, employing the rock parlance of the day, concluded: "From what I'd already been told, and how I'd regarded the new Byrds album, I was beginning to believe this was going to be a bummer. And – excuse the poetry – nothing would have upset summer more than a Byrds bummer. So I was more than a little worried by the time [the] needle hit the wax. Moral: never take any notice of nasty rumours: they can paint horribly distorted pictures. This is in fact one sweet length of bursting Byrds sunshine so perfect in quality and quantity you'd feel an absolute heel to ask for more."

CHAPTER THIRTY-FIVE

Farther Along

BY mid-1971, the Byrds were trapped at a career crossroads. Many of their old rivals had either broken up or faded into irrelevance at the start of the new decade. It was evident that the Byrds were also under threat, despite the upsurge in interest following *(Untitled)*. Their disappointment with *Byrdmaniax* coincided with a growing realization that they were losing ground to the very artists whom their music had previously inspired. Within a year, the Eagles would emerge to clean-up in the country rock market at precisely the time when McGuinn was abandoning that style. Meanwhile, David Crosby had been let loose like a genie on the West Coast, inspiring and nurturing a new generation of singer-songwriters, including Joni Mitchell and Jackson Browne. Crosby's avuncular affection for fellow writers ensured that he was always in demand as a guest singer and was unstinting in his praise for those who inspired his muse. McGuinn, by contrast, seemed strangely out on a limb. Neither a country rocker nor an introspective singer-songwriter, he was prematurely cast in the role of one of rock's elder statesmen, still carrying the torch for a renowned Sixties' group whose reputation required another strong album to underline their importance and continued relevance. The constant challenge for McGuinn was to discover something new within the Byrds, a task that was becoming increasingly difficult.

In interviews of the period, he betrayed a sense of bemusement at still finding himself searching for meaning in the Byrds. "I don't know what it was in me that made me want to keep the Byrds going," he reflected. "Maybe a sense of security. Maybe the fact that

I thought it was something worthwhile – a reputation, a good brand name. It has quality attached to it."

Once the darlings of Hollywood, the Byrds now found themselves in greater demand on the East Coast and, of course, Europe, where their following had always remained loyal. Touring abroad never made the group much money, but it was good for morale. "It's a swell way to pass the summer and it's a lot of fun," McGuinn noted at the time. Having completed a successful tour of the UK in May 1971, the Byrds returned unexpectedly two months later to play at the Lincoln Folk Festival on 24 July. Although their well-received appearance at the Bath Festival the previous year was a far more prominent event in the rock calendar, Lincoln was arguably of greater historical significance. The festival line-up included a mouthwatering cast of authentic American/Canadian greats (Dion, Sonny Terry & Brownie McGhee, Tom Paxton, Tim Hardin, Buffy Saint-Marie and James Taylor) and representatives of the British folk revival (Pentangle, the Incredible String Band, Steeleye Span, Sandy Denny, Dave Swarbrick and Martin Carthy). As an aficionado of folk, McGuinn must have felt a greater affinity with this event than he had experienced playing at the bigger rock festivals back home. In many ways, Lincoln symbolized a final flowering of rustic solidarity from a subculture unknowingly in retreat. The rock and folk audiences still shared a common cultural heritage, albeit one fractured by commerce and changing trends. The lingering influence of hippie dogma held sway in the more influential pages of the UK music press at a time when no discernible movement could yet be identified to define the amorphous early Seventies. Counterculturalists still paraded the virtues of old heroes, moaned about Dylan's abdication from rock godhead and adjusted with hubristic confidence to a new decade of delightful uncertainty. A reassuring sight at seemingly every rock festival was the mysteriously ubiquitous 'Jesus' – a tall, slim, blond-haired, perpetually white-robed British eccentric whose vitality enlivened every performance. His musical engagement was expressed via a frenzied, palsy-like shaking of head and limbs, a ritual choreography usually accompanied by the inexpert banging of a tambourine. He was there at Lincoln too – the perfect symbol of the age. So were the police who had turned up in search of illicit drugs. They seemed an unnecessary and incongruous presence at such a non-rock gathering. 'Jesus' certainly thought so and berated an inquisitive female officer by rallying the crowd with the words: "How would you like a police dog in your tent?" Onstage, an anonymous announcer retorted: "You're not much of a peacemaker, are you, Jesus?" Apart from a lost dog, that was the only hiccup of the day.

Anticipation was high for the Byrds' showing, and they did not disappoint. Although billed as the 'acoustic Byrds', they opened with an electric 'So You Want To Be A Rock 'n' Roll Star'. The succeeding set was half-electric and half-acoustic and the folk-loving audience reacted equally enthusiastically to the traditional 'Soldier's Joy'/'Black Mountain Rag' and more familiar fare like 'Mr Spaceman' and 'My Back Pages'. Clarence White featured prominently, taking lead vocals on 'Willin'' and introducing a new song: 'Bugler'. Along with the tuneful 'Antique Sandy', 'Bugler' suggested that the next Byrds album might prove something special. Buffy Saint-Marie closed the festival with a startling set and the crowd went away delighted.

Instead of flying back to the States immediately, the Byrds chose to stay in London to complete work on a new album under the supervision of Mike Ross. The entire sessions were completed within the space of a week. It was a decisive move by the Byrds. Their dissatisfaction with *Byrdmaniax* had been voiced publicly, and they were anxious to rectify the damage as soon as possible. The recordings were brought back to the States and mixed by Eric Prestidge at Columbia Studios, Hollywood. Several months would pass, however, before the album was released.

After the beatific vibes of Lincoln, the group faced a raucous homecoming the following week when they appeared at the Lennox Arts Center, Massachusetts, on 31 July. Nearby, a classical concert was underway featuring the Boston Symphony Orchestra performing Prokofiev's *Piano Concerto Number 3*. Aghast at the distant sound of rock music, the classical auditorium complained about the noise and a police delegation was despatched to silence the Byrds. The group were completing the climactic 'Eight Miles High' when Police Chief William Obanhein – familiar to rock audiences as

'Officer Obie' in the film adaptation of Arlo Guthrie's talking blues 'Alice's Restaurant' – strode onstage and threatened to pull the plugs. The evening ended in a brief altercation between Obie and Seiter, accompanied by jeers from the audience.

Despite the democracy displayed by McGuinn in the studio, the Byrds' live act revealed a decline in contributions from the subsidiary members. Having rush recorded their album in London and included fresh fare at Lincoln, the group were not ready to feature too many of the new songs in concert back home. "We're a little bugged with our show because we haven't added enough new material," White admitted at the time. "But the way the schedule has been in the States, we haven't had time at all to rehearse." It was far easier to slot into a familiar live set when playing at colleges and auditoriums whose audiences responded favourably to a well-played, but tight set. "They want to hear certain ones," White said. "'Eight Miles High' we have to do that, and 'Mr Tambourine Man'. But a lot of the new material just doesn't come off onstage – it's just weak . . . Skip [just] did a song called 'Lazy Waters' which is real slow, and in a studio you can really lock it together, but onstage, with all the hassles and everything going on, it just kind of dies. We tried to do it for about three weeks, and the more we did it, the worse it got. And a lot of songs Gene's done are the same type of songs – they just don't cook onstage . . . I'm surprised we're getting away with a song like 'Bugler' because we've had similar songs like 'Truck Stop Girl' that never really did get off the ground onstage. 'Bugler' works enough to get by . . . You have to be very careful on the college circuit, and really do the gig right . . . if they ask for 90 minutes, then you're on for 90 minutes . . . some places have us back every seven months. So it means we're working constantly in colleges, which is good because they're among the better audiences to play to in the States – they sit and they listen real close."

They also watch closely, as McGuinn found out to his cost. In his pre-Byrds days, McGuinn had been nicknamed 'Skinny' McGuinny by his early mentor, Bobby Darin. Over the years, he had retained a conventional slim look, but all that changed in 1971 when he bizarrely metamorphosed into the Michelin Man. During a photo session for Chuck Pulin, there were several unflattering poses, including one in which his stomach was swollen to scary proportions. "I looked pregnant," he admitted. "It didn't scare me [but] it was a shock. Like, 'Jesus, I let it really get out of hand, and I didn't even know it'." The culprit was beer. While touring, he had got into the habit of drinking six packs every day and the new fat tissue told its own story. It took a public humiliation to alert McGuinn to the extent of the problem. At one show, a teenage fan stood up, and shouted, "Hey, Roger!" McGuinn stopped, half-expecting a song request. Instead, the fan patted his stomach, as if he was greeting Santa Claus. "I watched him and I felt, 'Oh, my God, I've been busted in front of a whole audience' – and that's my business, to be slick in front of the audience and not be a fool. That was definitely the best weight-reducing plan, to get in front of an audience." In response, he started doing leg exercises and cut down his beer intake, although he still enjoyed whisky and cocaine. Within a remarkably short time, his girth disappeared as mysteriously as it had arrived, never to reappear, even in middle age.

For the remainder of 1971, the Byrds filled time touring the college circuit, but kept a low profile, with no press, radio or television commitments. In the wake of Melcher's dismissal, McGuinn sought some stability by enlisting a new agent Ron Rainey, of the Agency of Performing Arts (APA). On 8 October, one week after joining the agency, Rainey travelled to Chicago to see the Byrds play a half-full house at the Auditorium Theatre. Despite the low turn out, Rainey thought the show was "fantastic" and established a strong rapport with McGuinn who seemed keen to re-establish the group after what he considered a recent blip. "There was no manager and no one was really driving them," says Rainey. The following week, Rainey received a call from CBS Records, inviting him to attend a meeting with several executives. "They were trying to break two bands, the Blue Oyster Cult and the Mahavishnu Orchestra, who were totally unknown. They wanted the Byrds to headline a college tour, and have these bands underneath them." Rainey was asked how much the Byrds were grossing and came up with a high figure, "probably more than they were making at the time". Unfazed, CBS agreed to bankroll the tour and accepted that, in the event of any shortfall, they would make up the difference.

McGuinn was enthused by this sudden financial injection, which meant the Byrds could continue touring with a guaranteed income, at least for the remainder of the year.

On 23 November 1971, McGuinn married Linda Gilbert, two days before Thanksgiving, but there was no honeymoon. The next evening the group were back at the Hollywood Palladium reliving former glories. During this relatively quiet period, CBS (England) issued *Greatest Hits Volume 2*, a rather presumptuous title considering that, of all the tracks listed, only 'Chestnut Mare' could truly represent the album's title. Meanwhile, the Byrds closed the year with a final flurry of East Coast dates with Blue Oyster Cult and John McLaughlin's Mahavishnu Orchestra. "By the time that was finished the Byrds were the Byrds again," Rainey boasts. "It was an exciting time."

Almost out of the blue, it was announced that the Byrds were to embark on a European tour in January. Although nobody realized it at the time, this was to be the group's last visit to Europe. They played two nights at London's Rainbow Theatre (16–17 January) and were well received, in spite of persistent sound problems during the first performance, made worse by the aching volume previously heaped on sensitive ears by the ironically titled support act, Tranquility. A gig at Midem, in Cannes, followed on 20 January, and the lightning tour ended with a remarkable concert at the Paris Olympia. The Byrds' contract had required that they finish by 8 pm but the show was such a success that the Parisians threatened to break up the theatre unless the group returned for more encores. Fortunately, the venue's management persuaded the Byrds to pacify the crowd by extending their set for an extra quarter of an hour. The quartet flew home from Europe leaving behind them a touch of old-fashioned, mid-Sixties Byrdmania.

To coincide with the European tour, CBS issued the new album, *Farther Along*, two months after its US release. The reviews were again reasonable and some commentators expressed pleasure that the band had reverted to a more austere production. If the album was passable, however, it revealed only fleeting glimpses of the Byrds' excellence. Much of the material sounded rushed and well below their usual standard. In their determination to compensate for *Byrdmaniax*, the group had haphazardly selected material and recorded the new album in unseemly haste. It sounded more an emotive reaction directed against Melcher than an aesthetically pleasing venture. The entire work was structured in an almost identical fashion to *Byrdmaniax*, including the requisite number of Battin/Fowley songs, a new McGuinn composition, the latest Clarence White discovery and even another bluegrass instrumental. Clearly the Byrds were determined to prove that they could produce themselves far more effectively than Melcher, and the choice of material reflected this motive. Unfortunately, the experiment was largely unsuccessful. "We were still pretty upset about *Byrdmaniax*," Parsons admits, "so we decided to record in England where nobody knew what we were doing. We wanted to do it under budget and in our own way. I felt that *Farther Along* was a good album, but it was under produced. It was done really rapidly and it suffered in under production as a reaction to *Byrdmaniax*. I think if we'd been left in the studio twice as long, we'd have come up with some interesting things."

If the Byrds had produced another *(Untitled)* then their point would have been proven, but the erratic *Farther Along*, rather than discrediting Melcher, showed that he was only trying to disguise the group's musical inadequacies. The most perceptive review of the album came from US critic Bud Scoppa, whose diagnosis of the Byrds' current problems was to prove sadly correct: "The Byrds recognized their failure on *Byrdmaniax*, but placed the blame on the lavish production job rather than their own disunity. So what we have on *Farther Along*, evidently rushed out to rectify the problems caused by the last LP, is more disunity, but this time in a basic unadorned state."

Scoppa was right. The responsibility for the shortcomings of *Byrdmaniax* could not be placed solely on the production, and people suddenly began to wonder why Melcher had needed to employ such drastic measures. Was Melcher just an egocentric producer who had overstepped himself, or was he trying to save the Byrds from themselves by attempting to unify the work through orchestration? The question has no easy answer, of course, but a closer look at *Farther Along* underlines the extent of the Byrds' disunity and their unsuccessful attempt to discover a new direction.

The opening 'Tiffany Queen' displays great enthusiasm, with its strident jingle-jangle guitar work and cocksure vocal. McGuinn seems intent on reintroducing the familiar Byrds' sound as an answer to Melcher's strings and girl choruses. Significantly, the arrangement is less cluttered than any track on *Byrdmaniax*. The amusing lyrics and the deliberate imitation Chuck Berry riff firmly grounds the number in Fifties rock 'n' roll. In fact, it is only McGuinn's distinctive Rickenbacker sound that prevents the song from becoming a pure parody rather than an interpretative work. The Byrds' great strength always lay in their ability to convert any musical style to their aesthetic advantage. Here, McGuinn almost succeeds, but the synthesis of Fifties rock 'n' roll and Seventies Byrds was an uneasy coupling. "I dreamt the whole song while we were in London," Roger recalls. "I woke up with the whole thing, the verses and the melody. That was the only time that ever happened to me." The dream was based on a real event involving his new love Linda Gilbert, who playfully planted a Tiffany lamp over her head during a visit to McGuinn's home. "It was at our house," says his former wife, Dolores. "I guess that's when Roger fell in love with her, aided and abetted by Jimmi Seiter, the creep. It's funny because I own that Tiffany lamp. I still have it hanging in my kitchen. Ha!" Considering the short duration between the composing, arranging and recording of the song, it is amazing that it worked at all. As Battin admits: "The whole thing was completed in a 24-hour cycle. It was written during the morning, rehearsed and recorded the same night."

The next track, 'Get Down Your Line' was a passable production, with an impressive echoed vocal from Gene Parsons. Nevertheless, it is far from a classic and pales alongside Parsons' earlier efforts 'Yesterday's Train' and 'Gunga Din'. "It was an experiment," Parsons recalls vaguely. "We thought we had the beginnings of a good record. We were on the verge of a lot of interesting things." Like so many other tracks on the album, 'Get Down Your Line' was pleasant but half-baked, and an age away from the Byrds' greatest moments.

The traditional 'Farther Along' was no doubt the Byrds' answer to 'Glory, Glory' on *Byrdmaniax*. They took care to expand the arrangement but, despite all the work, the song still sounds a little out of place, not least because the Flying Burrito Brothers had already released their own version on 1970's *Burrito Deluxe*. The Byrds' rendition is arguably superior and White's presence and performance are exemplary. That said, this was a song that might have been better appreciated on a solo album. White sought authenticity by modelling his version on that of his great mentor, Rose Maddox. Clarence's phrasing and lyrics echo Maddox's reading and the only major difference is the lack of a dominant fiddle part. McGuinn's involvement and influence are largely undetectable.

'B.B. Class Road', another below average track, was co-written by Byrds sound engineer, Stuart 'Dinky' Dawson. Dawson had the basic idea for the song and Gene Parsons added the melody. Unfortunately, the end result contains no distinguishable Byrds sound whatsoever. Literally, it could be anyone singing and playing. "I was imitating and taking on a different persona," Parsons recalls. "Stuart and I collaborated and it's me growling and howling out the vocal. Dinky may have sung background and was involved in the studio. You can hear broken glass on there, which was his idea." That a mere soundman could be given leave to co-write a song on a Byrds' album was a testament to McGuinn's loss of quality control and general lack of interest in the group throughout this period.

By contrast, 'Bugler', proves a surprise highlight. It stands out magnificently. Probably as a reaction to his disappointment over 'Jamaica Say You Will', White invested all his efforts into this song. The result was nothing less than the best vocal performance of his career. Although Larry Murray (who once played in the Scottsville Squirrel Barkers alongside Chris Hillman) never received the public recognition of either Lowell George or Jackson Browne, there can be little doubt about his excellence as a songwriter. 'Bugler' is so obviously superior to the other tracks on *Farther Along* that it is almost embarrassing. As the last official recording released by White, it remains a tribute to his musicianship and profound influence on the Byrds. We should be thankful that, at a crucial point in the recording, White saved the song from a disastrous end: "It was one of the last songs we did and I could see by the way we were rushing through the album that we weren't getting the mixes right, so I purposely messed up my vocal on 'Bugler' and took it back to Hollywood CBS and dubbed on a bit of mandolin. Then we, just me and the engineer, spent a whole lot of time mixing it."

'America's Great National Pastime' indicates the strong influence that Kim Fowley had over Battin at this point. Although some might insist the lyrics are mildly amusing, the composition is pure novelty. "The idea came from a Coke ad on television that Kim had seen," Battin recalled. "He called me saying he had this great idea for a song and we actually wrote it on the phone in about 15 or 20 minutes." While 'Citizen Kane' retained a vestige of distinctive Rickenbacker work, even that had disappeared on this song. 'America's Great National Pastime' represents the severest loss of musical identity that the Byrds ever suffered, and McGuinn's decision to include it on the album was inexcusable. It was also the final single issued by the Byrds on Columbia (US), but a scheduled UK release was mysteriously cancelled. McGuinn was ambivalent about allowing Battin/Fowley A-side status and, intentionally or otherwise, singlehandedly scuppered its chances prior to release. "What a story," Fowley sighs. "Bill Drake, who programmed the major radio stations in America, called Columbia Records and said, 'If you take out the words "grabbing some ass" on a special edit for our stations, we'll make it a hit. But we can't broadcast that line.' Then Roger stood up and said: 'No! Nobody has ever censored the Byrds before – or now. They didn't censor Dylan, they didn't censor me, and they're not going to censor Skip Battin and Kim Fowley!' I sent a message back: 'It's OK. Take the line out for Bill Drake's stations and we'll have a gold record.' Roger replied: 'No. We're the Byrds. We cannot allow ourselves to be edited. We don't need a hit single.'" Given that both 'My Back Pages' and 'Chestnut Mare' were edited for single release, McGuinn's alleged riposte sounds somewhat disingenuous. Perhaps he realized that securing a novelty hit with 'America's Great National Pastime' might well have damaged rather than enhanced the Byrds' critical reputation.

'Antique Sandy', written by all four Byrds, plus Jim Seiter, has a close thematic link with the *Gene Tryp* number, 'Kathleen's Song'. Whether the Byrds deliberately sought to invite comparison between the folk-flavoured 'Antique Sandy' and the orchestrated 'Kathleen's Song' remains an interesting question. The effects employed, including double-tracked harmonies and electric piano, suggest that the Byrds took some concern over the track, which was surprisingly attractive. "It was an experiment," says Skip Battin. "The four of us had never written a song before. It was about Jimmi Seiter's girlfriend, Sandy. She lived in the woods and had a lot of antiques, but she wasn't particularly afraid of getting eaten by the bear."

"She was a lady I met on the road," adds Seiter. "The guys really liked hanging out with her and they befriended her. Skip actually wanted to write that song and because it was my friend and my experience, I helped. That's the only reason I got credit. I don't recall ever getting a dime from it in publishing though."

Fellow roadie Carlos Bernal was also impressed by the unusual four man composition. "It was a beautiful song. Sandy was a very beautiful hippie, flower child kind of girl. She made friends with Jim Seiter's family and I remember that Jim's dad Joe was a big fan of Sandy too. I didn't know her that well, just peripherally. She was a Woodstocky, pretty, blonde muse that caused these guys to write about her."

'Precious Kate' is also semi-autobiographical, having been inspired by singer Kate Taylor, sister of James and Livingston Taylor. The highly derivative structure and arrangement are painfully ordinary and the composition mediocre at best. "It was an attempt to write a love song based on a true story about Kim and Kate," says Battin. "The 'California Earthquake' line was the only memorable part of the song."

The inclusion of the Fiestas' 'So Fine' was suggested by White, who had long regarded the song as one of his favourites. Unfortunately, it merely underlined how derivative most of the material was on this album. The guitar work sounds so contrived and uninteresting that you wonder why they bothered. If the Byrds were hoping to create a spark of spontaneity by bursting into an old rock number, then the result was a complete failure. The performance lacks any enthusiasm whatsoever, and the arrangement is deathly dull. At best, this sounds like a warm-up number.

While the arrangement of 'Lazy Waters' is better than many of the other tracks, and the harmonies work well, the actual performance seems ultimately unconvincing. In covering the work of fellow Buddhist Bob Rafkin, Battin was seeking a serious song to match the power of 'Absolute Happiness' or 'Well Come Back Home', but this effort fell somewhat short. Battin's vocal is too self-consciously melodramatic to allow the sentiments to come across convincingly, which suggests that he had already become stylized as a purveyor of humorous novelty songs. For Battin, this condemnation was not valid. "'Lazy Waters' *was* a serious song. I was living in the Mendocino woods and working on the road. I'd known the song a long time. It expressed my feelings about life in the country and life on the road."

'Bristol Steam Convention Blues' was inspired by Gene Parsons narrowly missing the Bristol Steam Convention during the last two Byrds' visits to England. The track is obviously meant to stand as the group's reply to Melcher's treatment of their 'Green Apple Quick Step'. Its placing on the album suggests that the Byrds were now replacing their mysterious novelty endings of old with bluegrass instrumentals. Despite the clarity of the production and some fine picking, the number lacked the energy and enthusiasm of 'Green Apple Quick Step' and their attempt to compensate for the loss of Byron Berline's fiddle through the power of their musicianship was ultimately inadequate. If we ignore the comparisons, then the instrumental stands as a reasonable number in its own right, but in deliberately inviting the analogy the Byrds damn their own fine performance.

Farther Along revealed the Byrds in a precarious state, largely of their own making. In attempting to write and record an album within a ludicrous five-day period, they were merely inviting their own doom. The work as a whole seemed almost totally diffused, and although several of the tracks were individually effective, they contributed little to the unity of the piece. Even Skip Battin realized the worst. "When we finished it, I didn't think we had anything. I thought the stuff was rotten – it didn't sound good, it was scattered and there was no unification."

Worse still, each member of the group appeared to be moving

away from the familiar Byrds sound. The prolific Battin/Fowley team had so many new songs that Skip now felt the need to release them in a separate form from the Byrds. Clarence White had strong desires to record a country album and the multi-instrumentalist, Gene Parsons, was negotiating a deal with Warner Brothers. McGuinn was also planning a solo work and seemed far from committed to *Farther Along*. He gave the impression that he had only allowed the sessions to proceed in order to allow the others to show their contempt for Terry Melcher by rushing out an unorchestrated album. White joked that McGuinn seemed more interested in his latest love Linda than in the actual recording, an opinion which Roger later accepted as fact. "Yeah, I was in love, so I didn't care about the music," he told me. "That's probably true. If my emotions were clouded I couldn't possibly function properly. I guess I was in love and just wasn't paying attention to my business. It's a pitfall."

The increasingly fractured state of the group was a lot more serious than a mild case of clouded emotions. There was clearly a gradual polarization between the Byrds as four individuals and the Byrds as a group. While *(Untitled)* had redefined the Byrds' identity, the boundaries were now extending so far that nobody could say what differentiated a Byrds song from a solo work. With *Farther Along*, they betrayed an almost despairing attempt to find some common ground. Like the Beatles during the sessions for *Let It Be*, the Byrds could see no obvious future, so looked to the past for consolation. It seemed that they had to regress in order to maintain their aural unity. The influence of Kim Fowley on Skip Battin meant that a large proportion of their material was uncompromisingly grounded in the Fifties. By now, Battin had been drawn away from his spiritual leanings into the realm of social satire and the glorification of American trivia. Any attempt to create a unified Byrds meant that it was necessary to venture into Battin's territory in order to search for a starting point. McGuinn attempted to bridge that gap by recording the Fifties-flavoured 'Tiffany Queen' and converting rock 'n' roll to Rickenbacker. The experiment was partially successful, but he was unlikely to compose a series of songs in the same vein. White simply presented a bland cover of 'So Fine', as if confirming his inability to compose a nouveau-styled Fifties rocker of his own. Battin and Fowley turned uneasily to satire, drawing amusing parallels between the taste of coke and cocaine and recalling the novelty days of Skip & Flip.

The four Byrds were hopelessly adrift from one another, and the results were painfully apparent on *Farther Along*. Although the album was pleasant enough, it had few saving graces beyond a handful of key cuts. Die-hard followers, myself included, accepted the work unenthusiastically, enjoyed its better moments, and hoped for something more inspired next time around. There was still a lingering belief that the Byrds might climb back to the heights of *(Untitled)* with a stronger set of songs, so the general critical reaction was tolerant rather than condemnatory. Yet, the very idea of an 'ordinary' Byrds album was a sad conceit. The group was still respected as one of the great musical pioneers of the Sixties, but if their exploratory nature was to be replaced by laurel-resting works of questionable significance, then the spirit of the Byrds was already well and truly dead. It was obvious from their live performances that they could produce unspectacular but competent works like *Farther Along* for several years yet before the formula finally exhausted itself. Fortunately, McGuinn was no longer willing to accept such an insidious decline and had already found the perfect antidote to the Byrds' current malaise.

One week after the release of *Farther Along* the front cover of *Disc And Music Echo* presented its readership with an astonishing headline: "Original Byrds To Reform?" Although it seemed totally speculative at the time, McGuinn had already received permission from Columbia to record on David Geffen's Asylum label. The album was to be completed later in the year as a one-off project, and there was no question of the current Byrds disbanding – or so it seemed. Few realized that McGuinn was already reconsidering his future and had been distracted from his commitments to the CBS Byrds for several months. The reunion rumours at least partly explained the aesthetic shortcomings and directionless nature of *Farther Along*. As McGuinn admits: "It was recorded at a time when we were having internal problems and were generally weak. So the attitude of all the songs was weak. Those guys were upset and threatened by the reunion album. Even then, we were talking about the project."

The concern with solo albums, and McGuinn's unrevealed plans about the extent of the Asylum Byrds venture, meant that insecurities were rife. There was no talk of a follow-up album to the disappointing *Farther Along*, but there was much discussion of the prospects of a grand Byrds reunion. The latter-day Byrds felt threatened and uncertain about their future, and McGuinn was unable to alleviate their fears. David Crosby had already voiced his reservations about the group, much to the annoyance of Clarence White, who bit back viciously. "David has some rotten things to say about the new Byrds, and he doesn't know any of us, so he doesn't have the right to say it. Crosby has always been talking about how the original Byrds are much better than the group is now. He has to be some sort of idiot to believe what he's saying."

Increasingly, there was suspicion and dissension in the ranks, with Parsons occasionally flaring up against McGuinn. "He and I had some fairly intense conflicts," Gene remembers. "It did get quite aggressive, actually. He wanted to fire me several times and I quit several times, but Clarence would always get us back together. Clarence was the pacifier, unless he wanted to cause conflict, which he could do. And everyone paid attention then. Clarence was basically the Rock of Gibraltar that held it together."

CHAPTER THIRTY-SIX

Dissolution

BY early 1972, it was difficult to avoid the conclusion that the entire Byrds' organization was winding down. Eddie Tickner, who had been re-enlisted after Larry Spector's departure was let go on the grounds that he was "not progressive enough". Dickson had been brought back for *(Untitled)*, but had now moved on, and Melcher was fired as producer after *Byrdmaniax*. Publicist Billy James and liner note writer Derek Taylor were replaced by an anonymous public relations agency, and long-term road manager and occasional percussionist Jimmi Seiter was dismissed for being, in McGuinn's words, "too outrageous".

Significantly, no Byrds album appeared in America during 1972, and, after *Farther Along*, the only 'new' songs heard in the UK came via their brief contribution to the *Earl Scruggs His Family And Friends* television special, which had been recorded the previous year. The group had been invited to appear by Gary Scruggs, who was a fan of their music. For the souvenir album, the Byrds contributed 'You Ain't Going Nowhere', which was recorded in collaboration with the Earl Scruggs Revue, and 'Nothin' To It', an old bluegrass number made famous by Doc Watson.

This pleasant diversion failed to inspire a fresh burst of creativity. On 12 January, they entered the studio, but only managed to complete a version of David Wiffen's 'Lost My Driving Wheel'. Part of the problem was McGuinn's lack of confidence in his players, a view that had been festering since the recording of *Byrdmaniax* and was made worse by the failure of *Farther Along*. "Melcher was turning everyone's head round on the *Byrdmaniax* album," White remembered. "He was telling Roger, 'You can get a better bass player and drummer for your records.' Terry wanted Roger, Hal Blaine and Joe Osborn 'to cut some good tracks'. He'd go over to Skip and Gene and tell them they should cut their tracks by themselves during the week. And they felt that me and Roger had something going with a middle-man, trying to screw up the whole thing. At that point I started to miss days and not go in, just to avoid any trouble. And I had to tell Roger, 'Terry is taking you some place else. He's taking you away from the group.' Then Terry would say, 'Hey, Roger, – Gene, Clarence and Skip are ganging up on you.' It was impossible. Melcher did what he pleased. Roger let him do everything."

Although McGuinn had agreed to fire Melcher after the album was completed, he never forgot those sarcastic comments on Battin and Parsons. Melcher's respect for session musicians was well known, as was his own musical ability. If there were weaknesses in the Byrds, then Melcher could certainly spot them and he was close enough to McGuinn to voice his opinions without reticence. The doubts lingered and grew with each passing month. "I don't know, maybe Melcher did turn my head," McGuinn later told me. "Terry did hate Skip and Gene. He thought they were terrible musicians. He wanted to get more professional guys."

In April, the Byrds attempted to arrest their decline by recording a single, which was intended for release the following month. Still in their Fifties phase, they cut a new McGuinn composition, 'Born To Rock 'n' Roll', then promptly cancelled its release. "The way we did it was like an old rock 'n' roll song," White recalled. "It was nothing like McGuinn later did it on the reunion album. With us, he just sang it straight." The sad truth was that the song was little better than the stuff on *Farther Along* and provided another unwanted reminder of how far the group had slipped since *(Untitled)*.

The Byrds continued touring the States during the early months of 1972 but all was far from well. They had grown used to glowing live reviews in recent years but suddenly critics were detecting faults in the musical fabric. A weary performance at New York's Academy of Music was described by the trade magazine *Billboard* as "a grim parody". Their reviewer could not help wondering whether the Byrds had simply worn out their repertoire and left themselves with nowhere to go. "Perhaps this act, one of Columbia Records' most venerable bands, was simply tired. Perhaps the chronic PA problems blunted their fire. Or, and this seems to be more likely, the performance's ennui was evidence of creative menopause within one of the most distinctive and certainly influential bands of the last decade."

Occasional negative reviews are to be expected by established stars as well as novices, but this was no cheap put-down. The tone was critical but sympathetic, as if the observer was addressing the decline of a much loved institution. Nor was it a one-off notice. Less than a month later, the Byrds visited Miami, Florida and faced a similarly jaundiced reviewer who felt obliged to comment on their lack of passion and vocal shortcomings. Increasingly, there was a realization that the renaissance promised by *(Untitled)* had not been forthcoming. It was difficult to avoid the conclusion that the group had been reduced to living off former glories. As another reviewer noted: "It can't be pleasant for a group to be greeted by an audience screaming for their oldie-goldies, not knowing or caring about material from their last three album efforts . . . The songs that went over best were the older ones, written by others, witness to the group's creative limbo."

The Byrds could still play a solid, competent show, but the set list lacked adventure or innovation and some of their old bite and passion were missing. McGuinn had promised a new approach, but seemed trapped by the over-familiar. Although he still revered Clarence White as a player, he was tired of the country rock image associated with the group and began to wonder how much further he could take the Byrds' concept. A lack of conviction made him more susceptible to criticisms that he might previously have brushed aside as inconsequential.

John Phillips turned up at one show, took McGuinn aside, and told him bluntly, "Your drummer can't play 4/4 time. He can't play rock 'n' roll, he can only play country." Far from defending Parsons, McGuinn seemed more than willing to accept the views of the former leader of the Mamas & The Papas. "After that I thought

The Byrds with Vito's dancing troupe.

The Jet Set, 1964.

David Crosby, 1964.

The Jet Set (minus Crosby) with model Peggy Moffitt, performing her "off-the-top-of-my-head" action dance.

Byrds' field trip.

Clark, Crosby and McGuinn, early 1965.

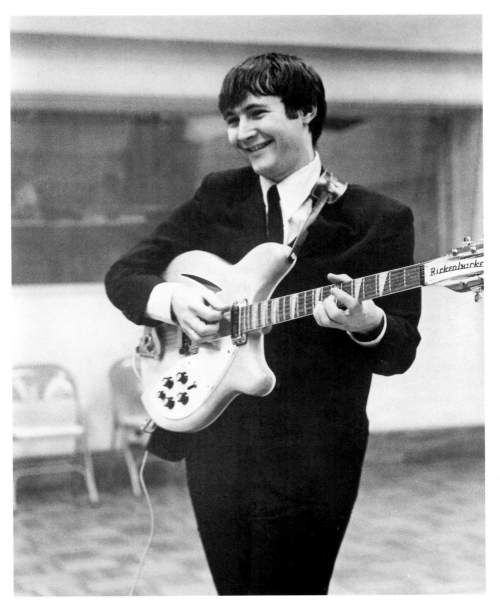

David Crosby, posing with a Rickenbacker guitar, early 1965.

David Crosby, 1965.

The Byrds, early 1965.

Jim Dickson in the studio.

Terry Melcher and McGuinn.

Bob Dylan, flanked by Crosby and McGuinn at Ciro's.

Bob Dylan, onstage with the Byrds at Ciro's, March 1965.

Bob Dylan with the Byrds, March 1965.

Chris Hillman, 1965.

Michael Clarke brushes the hair of Lizzie Donohoe. Looking on are Carl Franzoni, Bryan MacLean and Gene Clark.

Crosby disrupts a photo session, 1965.

Derek Taylor (centre), the Byrds' urbane publicist, with Clark and Hillman.

The Byrds at the Imperial Ballroom, Nelson, Lancashire, 3 August 1965.

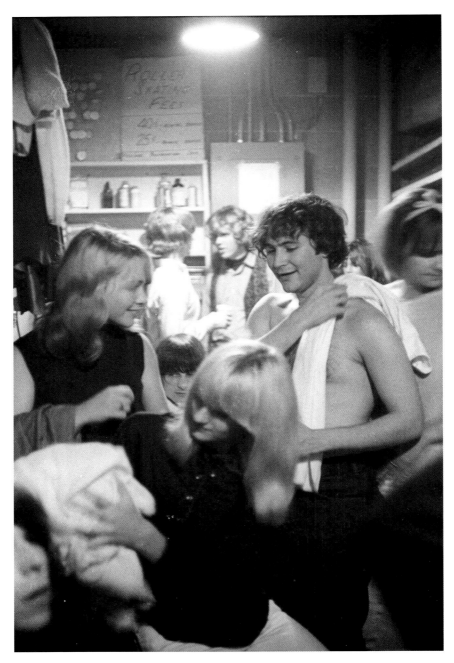
A topless Crosby, backstage at a roller rink, 1965.

Crosby grounded by Gene Clark while the pacific McGuinn brandishes a toy pistol.

The avant-garde look.

Crosby and McGuinn. Fire and Ice.

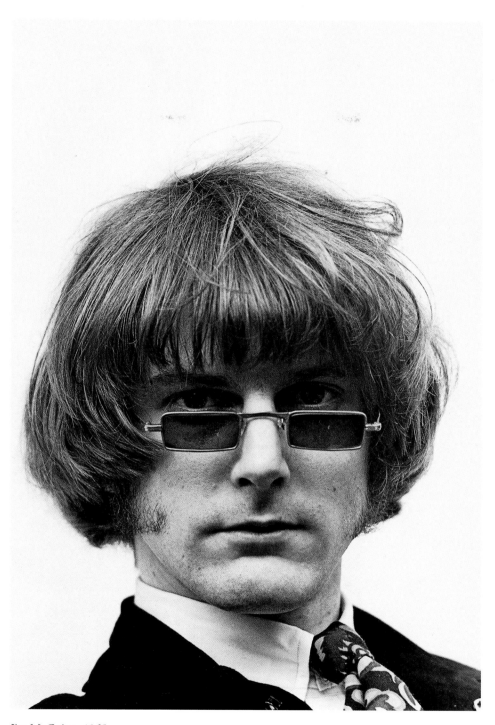
Jim McGuinn, 1965.

1966: The 'raga rock' press conference.

The Byrds live, 1966.

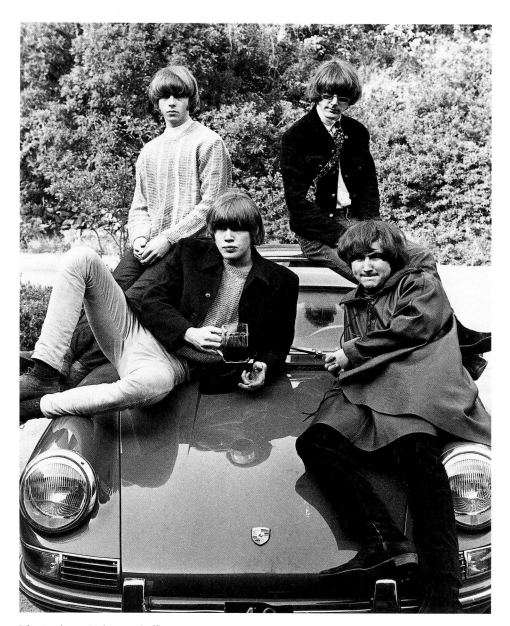
The Byrds, 1966: beer and affluence.

The Byrds up a tree.

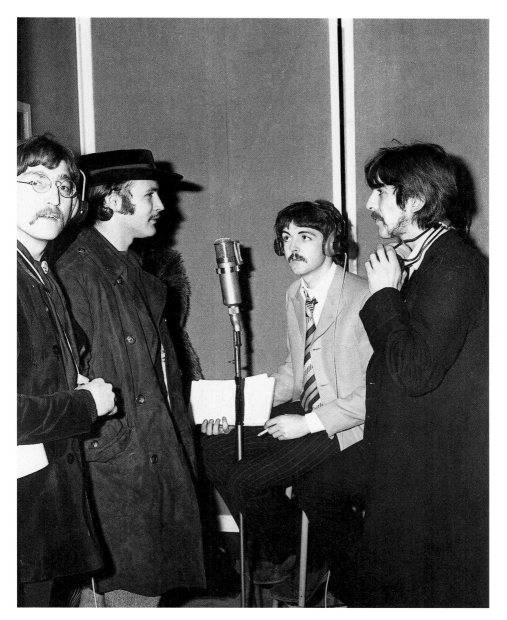

The new Fab Four. Crosby at the *Sgt Pepper's Lonely Hearts Club Band* sessions, 1967.

The Byrds, New York City, July 1967.

The Byrds in the studio.

Crosby (with STP sticker) and McGuinn, 1967.

Exotically garbed in the Summer of Love, 1967.

The Byrds debut as a trio with Kevin Kelley (centre).

Posing for Pan Am. Hillman, Kelley and McGuinn.

Onstage at the Piper Club, Rome, Italy, with Doug Dillard (centre) on 7 May 1968.

The Byrds, 1968: Gram Parsons, Kevin Kelley, Chris Hillman and Roger McGuinn.

The Byrds' long serving road manager, Jim Seiter.

Newport Festival, 4 August 1968. Clarence White joins Hillman, Kelley and McGuinn.

Autumn 1968. White, McGuinn, Hillman and new drummer, Gene Parsons.

Hillman and McGuinn, live 1968.

John York (left) replaces Chris Hillman on bass.

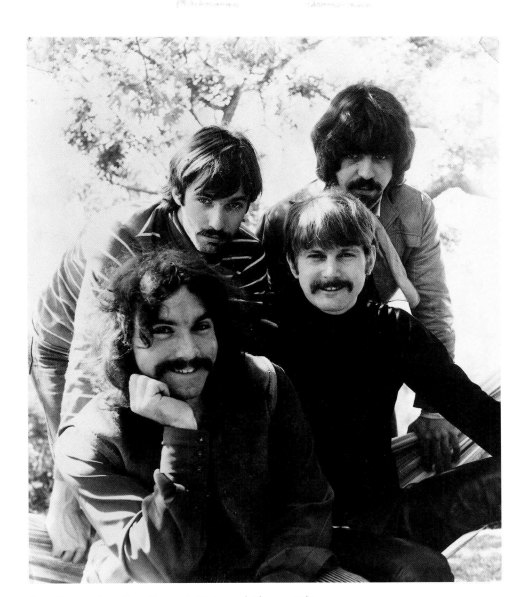
Gene Parsons, John York, Roger McGuinn and Clarence White.

Skip Battin (second from left) replaces John York in the line-up.

McGuinn, White, Battin and Gene Parsons.

John Guerin replaces Gene Parsons. Backstage rehearsal at the County College Of Morris, Dover, New Jersey, 23 September 1972.

The 'Manassas Byrds' at the Capitol Theatre, Passaic, New Jersey, 24 February 1973. Featuring Clarence White, Joe Lala, Chris Hillman and Roger McGuinn, this was the group's final performance as an ongoing entity.

The grand reunion of the original Byrds: McGuinn, Hillman, Crosby, Clarke and Clark.

Crosby joins McGuinn, Clark & Hillman onstage at the Roxy.

The first promotional photograph of McGuinn, Clark & Hillman, standing in reverse order.

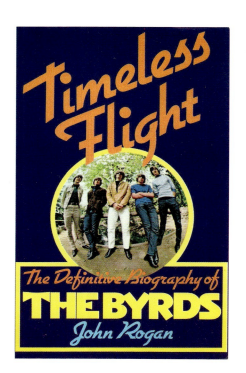
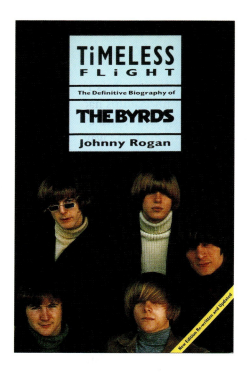
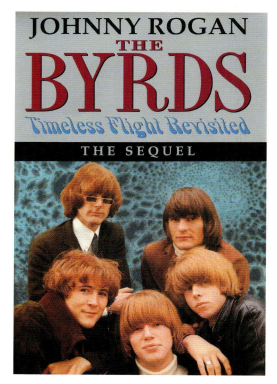

My back pages.

to myself, 'Yes, he's right.' I don't know. I wasn't *that* swayed by what John Phillips had said, it just got things moving." Despite the qualification, it was evident that McGuinn took Phillips' words to heart, in the same way that he had accepted Terry Melcher's earlier criticisms of Parsons and Battin.

Parsons' standing in the group was not helped by his playing on the tour, which sometimes fell below expectations. In a review of their concert at the Symphony Hall in the Atlanta Memorial Arts Center (7 April), he was singled out for some heavy criticism.

"If there was a flaw in last week's performance, it was Gene Parsons' drumming. He seemed to be a bit too loose at times and often his runs and combinations would be too long or overly complicated to allow him to keep a solid rhythm. I had an image once during the show of three well-tuned athletes running effortlessly around a track, being followed by a slightly overweight kid with his shirt hanging out and his shoe untied. See what I mean? It's not always that way. Listen to the Byrds' *(Untitled)* album. There is a live segment on this two-record set that shows what fine drumming Parsons is capable of."

McGuinn didn't need to read this review to realize something was amiss. He knew Parsons was upset about the present apathy enveloping the Byrds, and they had already exchanged harsh words over the distribution of income resulting from a profit-sharing agreement that had been in operation over the past year. McGuinn responded in kind, even allowing his dissatisfaction to slip into the public domain. "His work has been going downhill," he told one reporter. "He had a shot at being very versatile and very adaptable, and I really like the guy, but he didn't grow, he just sort of stagnated. In fact, he dropped a little bit in proficiency. He messes up on songs he doesn't like, which is a symptom of his stubbornness. It's all psychosomatic: he's a good country drummer, but he's fucking up lately, and I think it's because he feels a sense of alienation . . . He's a hell of a good country drummer, but I want to get out of country music." Soon after the Atlanta concert, a whole series of gigs were cancelled, including projected performances in New York, Chicago and England. Retreating temporarily from the backstage tensions, McGuinn spent time formulating new projects, writing songs with Jacques Levy and poring over a rough film script by perennial co-writer, R.J. Hippard.

In July, McGuinn casually made a dramatic announcement to Clarence White: "The time is right, we need another drummer." White was alarmed by the news that his old friend was about to be fired but, considering the recent harsh words over money, he was not entirely surprised. According to Parsons, White told him that he intended to quit the Byrds after their next big pay-day and concentrate on completing the bluegrass solo album he had been planning for many years. In the meantime, Parsons left the Byrds, bitter at the way he had been treated.

"I was fired," he confirms, "but I think Roger used the excuse that I wasn't playing well. He wanted to replace Skip and me with the original Byrds and keep Clarence. I was very vocal about the wages situation. I felt Roger was taking most of the money and we were supposed to have a profit-sharing agreement [exclusively for live work]. We would get statements outlining draws for expenses and when it came time for profit-sharing there wasn't anything left. I felt Roger was more extravagant than the rest of us when you consider his portable telephone and the various gadgetry he would have on the road."

McGuinn, who had already said goodbye to seven former Byrds, was unrepentant about the sacking. "Gene's attitude was wrong and he wasn't trying his best. He was angry with me about the money, although he doesn't feel that any more. We weren't ripping him off. We had a profit-sharing agreement, and there was a bit of misunderstanding about what constituted expense deductions. Gene didn't see the money he was making because he was spending it on the road. I was perfectly honest about the money."

From a more impartial viewpoint, Skip Battin could see both sides of the argument. "McGuinn was definitely in the right on that occasion with Gene. If one person in the band is allowed more on the expense account, then everybody would want a share. But there was also some suspicion in the group that Roger was using the expense account for his own extravagances in a similar way to Gene."

While the group suffered its first membership change in three years, Skip Battin took the opportunity to complete his first solo album, which would be released in Britain early the following year. *Skip* was made up entirely of Fowley/Battin compositions, including a brilliant character sketch of McGuinn entitled 'Captain Video' on which Battin mischievously invited his former colleague to play a Rickenbacker break. Among the other guest credits were Spanky McFarlane, Clarence White and drummers Billy Mundi and John Guerin. Gene Parsons was conspicuous by his absence.

Guerin was also present when the Byrds convened at Wally Heider's Studio in July for a preliminary stab at some tracks which McGuinn had decided to use for their next project. 'Bag Full Of Money', 'Draggin'' and 'I'm So Restless' sounded far superior to most of the material on *Farther Along*, but McGuinn eventually decided to retain these songs, which were subsequently re-recorded for inclusion on his debut solo album.

By September, Guerin was appointed the Byrds' new drummer, although Michael Clarke had previously been tipped for the job. "Roger had a whole lot of ways of getting musicians in the Byrds and sometimes he'd just job it out and say, 'Get me a musician!'" claims Carlos Bernal. "That's how he got John Guerin. He was on *The Tonight Show* and Roger said, 'I want *that* guy! He's the best money can buy.' At that time the hottest drummer in the nation was John Guerin."

Born in Hawaii, on 31 October 1939, Guerin was five years younger than Battin, the second oldest player ever to feature in the group. His background was certainly impressive, including stints and sessions with musicians as diverse as George Shearing, Thelonius Monk, the Monkees, Frank Zappa, Mama Cass, Emitt Rhodes and Helen Reddy. As a studio musician, he had already worked with White and Battin so there were no awkward introductions. "He was pleased to join the Byrds in order to get some gigging experience," Battin confirmed. "I think he wanted a break from session work for a while."

Guerin's arrival coincided with a premature announcement that the group would henceforth be known as Roger McGuinn And The Byrds. This was the strongest indication yet of the internal problems that had been bedevilling the group over the past year. The

McGuinn/White/Parsons/Battin Byrds had always seemed the most easy-going line-up but, in the wake of Gene's departure, Roger had obviously decided to reassert his authority in the strongest possible fashion. Fortunately, the new name was dropped at the last minute, thus saving McGuinn from further accusations of being a hirer/firer. That, in itself, would have been ironic for it was becoming increasingly clear that McGuinn's major mistake had been in allowing the subsidiary members too much say in the choice of songs.

Having digested the criticisms of John Phillips and Terry Melcher, McGuinn was also bamboozled by David Crosby, whose contempt for the new Byrds had already been voiced publicly. With all the talk of the forthcoming Byrds' reunion, McGuinn suddenly woke up to the fact that he had been cruising creatively since the late Sixties. His mind commuted back to the last days of Crosby during *The Notorious Byrd Brothers*, an album that he now rightly saw as a benchmark. "That's what I want to get back into," he told *Crawdaddy*. "I know I'm capable of it, it's just that I've been loaded down by people who weren't sympathetic or tolerant of that in me, who'd veto it, jump on me, gang up on me, make it just really impossible, really a drag. They destroy my creativity, they come around and hassle me. If I pull out the synthesizer at the session, they say, 'Look, this is our session too and we don't want you wasting your time on *that* thing.'"

McGuinn could easily have been talking about the Gram Parsons' era Byrds, but he made it abundantly clear that his barbs were directed against the most recent line-up, whom he promised to keep in order from now on. "It's my band, man," he asserted, "my session, and they're beating me up. I mean bullying me into what they wanted to do, and they did it, and it was a bomb, and I'm glad. Mostly, Skip and Gene. Skip is good, but some of his lyrics are schlock . . . I don't like some of his songs. They're a little cheap, they're a little cheaper than I want to get. So I'm going to make sure they don't get on any of the albums . . . It was an experiment and it failed, back to the drawing board."

The new-look Byrds began performing at the end of September 1972 but failed to undertake a nationwide tour. Guerin wished to remain employed as a session musician, which satisfied McGuinn, who was tired of touring and content to play weekend dates. The sparse itinerary ensured that he was free to prepare himself for the all-important Byrds' reunion album sessions, which took place in October. Prior to the recording, Roger revealed an overwhelming enthusiasm which few had seen in recent years. McGuinn was convinced that the project would be successful, even though he was aware that the expectations of the media and the public might prove too high. Fittingly, the first rehearsal of the reformed Byrds had taken place at his house during the summer and the first song they performed was a new McGuinn composition, 'Sweet Mary'. "It was really quite remarkable," he remembered. "The voices gelled together, and to me, it sounded like we'd never been apart. But then, that can often happen when you get back to a special place that you haven't been to in a very long time. Naturally, everyone was a little nervous. There was a feeling of apprehension among us all . . . some more than others. This was something both David and I were acutely aware of but, underneath the superficial nervousness that we all shared, both Gene and I felt positive that it would really work all over again."

Clark vividly remembered the moment when they cut through the apprehension to discover some common ground. "We all sat down with our guitars and started playing Roger's 'Sweet Mary', then we moved into David's rocker, 'Long Live The King'. We all were silent and we could feel it working. We were singing, but we didn't talk, and then David just stopped and paused, with his hand above the neck of his guitar. He started laughing and said simply, 'Hot nuts!' And the magic started happening."

In spite of the nostalgic reunion, the Byrds played none of their old songs that evening, but concentrated on selecting suitable material for the new work. They had already promised each other that if any member felt uncertain about his commitment to the project, then the planned recording would be shelved. After the euphoric first rehearsal, however, they convinced themselves that the reunion was not only a viable proposition but had the potential to be an aesthetically pleasing venture. By the end of the evening, the original Byrds unanimously agreed to proceed to the historic recording of their first joint album in nearly seven years.

Following the grand reunion festivities, McGuinn returned to White, Battin and Guerin and continued to play at weekends. The extra time allowed him to start work on a dozen tracks for his first solo album, the news of which exacerbated rumours that a Byrds dissolution was at hand. At this point, however, the group was not quite ready for any death notices. Despite pressure from the original Byrds, and the enticement of a potential solo career, McGuinn stubbornly kept the Byrds alive and harboured ambitions of reaching even greater heights. Interviewed by the *NME* backstage at New York's Academy of Music that October, he proclaimed: "We're getting away from country music towards the highest jazz."

This grand statement merely underlined his uncertainty and confusion about which musical direction would prove most beneficial. McGuinn was involved in so many projects that he seemed in danger of falling victim to his own imagination. He wanted to take the Byrds back to *The Notorious Byrd Brothers* period, complete an historic solo album, and allow John Guerin to inspire him to play the highest forms of jazz. In common with his lost plans for a history of twentieth-century music and a Broadway musical, the jazz dream remained unfulfilled. "I just realized how much dedication it would take and I wasn't willing to put enough into it," he later admitted. "I wasn't prepared to practise eight hours a day! I was into jazz when I was with Bobby Darin – from that time until 'Eight Miles High', which was as close to jazz as I ever got. In fact, some people said the 'Eight Miles High' break was good jazz. But I wasn't enough of a jazz singer or player to cut it, so I didn't take the 1972 Byrds into jazz. I think I had delusions of grandeur when I said that."

In spite of McGuinn's confusion, the Byrds soldiered on. Meanwhile, the original line-up converged on Wally Heider's Studios in Hollywood to complete work on the reunion album. There were some fractious moments at the start. "I think some of the guys were a bit edgy," Clark says. "There'd been a lot of hurt in the past and although we brushed it aside there was a sense that it might still be there." One major problem was the continuing commitments of various members, most notably Chris Hillman, who was still touring with Manassas. Crosby was sensitive about Stephen Stills' influence, fearing that he might, intentionally or not, sabotage the project. When Hillman revealed that he had to play a show less than a week after the commencement of the sessions, there was a furious argument with Crosby over the phone. McGuinn also had some weekend dates booked which, although of little consequence, also rankled with Crosby. "Chris was going out with Manassas," McGuinn recalls, "and we'd be in the studio for a couple of days and then all of a sudden he found that he'd have to go out on the road. Then I would have bookings and I'd have to go out too with the so-called Byrds at that time which made Crosby furious because I was using the name Byrds and leaving the real Byrds to go out and do a fake Byrds tour. He was just mad at me for that."

The tensions even spread to the road crew. A photo shoot was arranged at the Troubadour featuring iconic shots of the original group, miming onstage and posing like pussycats on barstools. Outside, Al Hersh and Carlos Bernal were bringing in musical instruments when Crosby stormed over and told them: "Don't touch my guitars." The roadies complied, but were hauled over coals when one of the guitars went missing later that day. It subsequently emerged that the real culprit was Crosby's own road manager, Bruce Berry, who stole the guitar and sold it to fund his heroin habit. A few months later, he would be dead. The tale of the stolen guitar would later become a memorable rap during Neil Young's *Tonight's The Night* tour and Berry would be commemorated by name in the title track of the same album.

Still in McGuinn's employ, Hersh had a greater affinity with the latter-day Byrds than the originals and resented Crosby's domination at the reunion sessions. "David was impossible. I saw them all phone in their parts. We'd come in and David's stuff was already down, and Chris' too. Roger brought in 'Born To Rock 'n' Roll' which was in the same vein as 'Tiffany Queen'. Think about it. It was the same fucking song, except it's jumbled around a bit so that you can't tell it's the same. It was just another dumb ass Chuck Berry rip-off. Roger was just looking for any direction at all, and he couldn't find one. Remarkably, the best stuff was Gene Clark's. For a guy that couldn't string a sentence together, he could write some incredible lyrics. He brought along 'Full Circle', which fitted perfectly."

Five days into the sessions, Clark agreed to partake in an interview, ultimately unpublished, during which he eulogized the reunion. "The original Byrds is now a reality," he proclaimed. "We've expressed the desire to be together for years, but politics kept us apart." Although cagey, he provided a couple of newsworthy revelations that would not become public for some time. Evidently, David Geffen was considering a massive reunion show featuring Buffalo Springfield, the Byrds and Crosby, Stills, Nash & Young. "It's a possibility," Clark said, "whether it's a probability is another thing." Not wishing to be quoted directly, he also confirmed that the CBS Byrds were disbanding and the originals were taking the name back permanently. He was thrilled about the current sessions, noting that four tracks had already been completed, albeit in basic form. "There's a lot of different flavours. There should be after nearly ten years." In words laced with retrospective irony, he added: "We're taking our time, we're not going to rush it. The first Crosby, Stills & Nash album was a product of much thought and much concentration and taking your time without wasting money . . . so was the first Dillard & Clark album and the first Burritos album. Those type of albums are always a product of people not wasting time but actually working and this is the same thing."

Clark was correct in almost every detail except when referring to the reunion album. CS&N's first album had been written well in advance of its recording and played acoustically live in the homes of musician friends months before the participants entered a studio. The debuts of Dillard & Clark and the Flying Burrito Brothers had a similarly long gestation with the players brainstorming ideas and writing together. Unfortunately, the Byrds could not afford the luxury of living, writing or playing together over weeks or months, and they were certainly not "taking their time" as Clark suggested.

After a tentative and troubled beginning, the sessions became less fraught. Partly this was because they were surrendering to the project's self-appointed producer. McGuinn had felt intimidated by Crosby's superstar success, so deferred to his wishes more readily than might otherwise have been the case. Overseeing the production, Crosby placed less emphasis on the signature sound of McGuinn's

DISSOLUTION

Rickenbacker while allowing his colleague fewer lead vocals than on any other record in Byrds' history. McGuinn swallowed these perceived slights without complaint. He was acutely aware that the Byrds was supposed to be a delicate democracy, a point reflected in the distribution of songs. It would have been churlish to complain that Gene Clark had been allowed to sing lead on an additional couple of covers. Everyone knew he needed the reunion kudos the most in order to help relaunch his dwindling solo career. Any other underlying tensions floated away on a cloud of smoke. Crosby's deserved reputation as a connoisseur of pot ensured that the finest marijuana was available throughout the sessions. Other drugs were no doubt available for those inclined. "We had a party while we were in the studio," says McGuinn. "Crosby always had the finest marijuana. It might have distracted us."

Nevertheless, the stoned atmosphere improved group morale and when they listened to the playbacks there was an initial sense of euphoria that they had actually completed the work in such a short spell. The division of material ensured that everybody (bar Clarke, of course) received the same publishing money, but the real benefactor was Neil Young who could hardly have dreamed that he would have the same number of songs on a Byrds album as each of the individual members. During the sessions, an additional song emerged: the traditional 'Fair And Tender Ladies', a tune familiar to Crosby, Clark and McGuinn from their folk days. The first take featured Crosby on lead, but two later attempts were undertaken by Gene Clark, who would return to the song a few years later when working as a duo with McGuinn, and once again on the 1987 album, *So Rebellious A Lover*. Although the song survives among the reunion tapes, it was evidently demoted from contention at the eleventh hour.

Towards the close of the reunion sessions, McGuinn was obliged to fulfil a couple of East Coast dates, including a memorable show in Tampa, Florida on 1 November, supported by folk music legend, Eric Andersen. With Crosby still bristling over the Byrds' shows and work remaining on the Asylum album, McGuinn must have been wondering whether it was worth the effort. He arrived late for the Tampa flight and was marooned at the check-in desk while the other Byrds were already on the plane. John Guerin attempted to delay take off but, in the end, they had to leave without their leader. When the Byrds took the stage at the Curtis Hixon Hall that evening, McGuinn magically appeared. Beaming with enthusiasm, he had a story to tell the audience. "I missed my plane in LA and took a Learjet and it was really fun. Of course, it cost me everything we're going to make tonight, so we're playing for free, but it's really a kick." McGuinn remained chirpy and chatty all evening, offering the spectators belated Halloween greetings, asking them whether they were voting and throwing out smart one-liners such as "apathy is the mother of repression".

Perhaps some of the party atmosphere from the reunion had energized McGuinn that evening, but there was no sign of tension, disillusionment or perfunctory playing. Clarence White appeared eager to take an even more commanding role. His distinctive pull-string pyrotechnic whine on the opening 'Lover Of The Bayou' was a reassuring reminder of the potency of the latter-day Byrds. He was there again on a moving rendition of 'Bugler', re-elevated to the second song in the set. When Battin sang the risible 'America's Great National Pastime', White emerged with an impressive mandolin accompaniment, more prominent than the one heard on the album version. The effect was extraordinary, transforming the novelty song into a country romp. Thereafter, it was pretty much the standard Byrds' set, but Guerin found his niche with a radical reworking of 'Eight Miles High'. It was still an extended jam, over 17 minutes long, but Guerin incorporated some jazzy, percussive flourishes, producing a harder groove than Parsons' more restrained solo. It was now more showy, with less of the intricate interaction between Gene and Skip, but consistent with McGuinn's desire to move in a jazzier direction.

Guerin's arrival tested the sympathy of many long-term fans who had grown used to a stable Byrds line-up since 1969. Gene Parsons was missed, as much for symbolic reasons as musical ones. Those who knew that he had been fired felt sympathy, which was easily, if irrationally, converted into a certain antipathy towards his replacement. Tellingly, such feelings were never entertained by the loyal road crew who were almost in awe of Guerin. "John was hot with the Byrds," says Bernal. "Man, he was sensational. To have the style and technique of a big band drummer like that. Phew! It was really something to see. I was thrilled that I got a chance just to stand right next to the drumkit and watch him play. The celebrity drummer. He was so exciting to listen to. Roger was thrilled too, although they probably had a bit of rivalry. Of course, Roger was the boss and Guerin was working for him. But John let Roger know that he was lucky to have him. He was the nicest guy, a consummate professional and a great guy to work with. Al Hersh and I used to love John Guerin to death. We were always thrilled. We worked closely with John because we knew he was a premium guy and we wanted to make sure we did everything we could to make him feel comfortable and enjoy being on the road with us because he didn't have to do it."

Agent Ron Rainey was also aware of his stature, even then. "He was a great drummer. I don't know if I'd characterize him as a permanent member, but he was there. I remember he was dating Joni Mitchell around that time. But I think when he was in the band it wasn't as 'Byrd-like'. He was a jazz drummer and carried himself a little more importantly than just a member of the band. John had his own roadie to bring his drums in. He was like a hired gun."

The sole problem with Guerin was his limited availability. Working weekend dates was perfect, but everyone knew he was never likely to commit himself further. On a handful of occasions, the Byrds were forced to hire a substitute at short notice, including Jim Moon, the most obscure name ever associated with the group. "Jim Moon was a friend of mine who I used to buy horses from out in Malibu," Bernal recalls. "He later became drummer in Spanky & Our Gang. He lived around Topanga Canyon, near Skip, and was a talented musician who'd played with bands on the Sunset Strip. When Roger was going through drummers because Guerin wasn't there, his name came up. I remember Linda saying, 'You'd like him, Roger. I've met him and he's real nice!' He did one *Midnight Special* television appearance with us with the Wolfman. Roger wore a cowboy shirt with long tassels that were actually ruby red coloured chandelier beads. It was an interesting outfit."

The recording of the reunion album, along with the change of drummer, prompted worried comments from fans about the state of the Byrds in November 1972. Battin was now finding it difficult to fulfil their weekend commitments, as he was busy completing his solo album. Bassist Chris Ethridge was asked to join the Byrds for some shows, fuelling rumours that Battin's days were numbered. "They wanted me to play," Ethridge confirms, "but I'm sure I didn't do it. It wasn't because I didn't want to, but something happened. I might have been already committed to do something else. But I would have been glad to do it because I loved them all." Instead, several dates were postponed and Battin retained his place, at least for the present.

The Byrds ended the year with December dates in Chicago, Philadelphia, Texas and New York. Since the dismissal of Parsons in July, their future had been in the balance but, five months on, they were still alive and gigging. However, most people agreed that their studio work had declined since *(Untitled)* and, although subsequent albums were still selling, there was no sign of the exploratory spirit that had made them pioneers during the 1965–68 period. The Byrds had somehow struggled to the end of 1972, but it was plain that they were on their last legs. Drummer John Guerin was blasé about all the recent changes and spoke as if the Byrds were undergoing an experiment in chaos theory. "At the beginning, anyway, the audience was concerned with the frequent changes in the Byrds. But not any more. It takes them about five minutes to get over it. Anyway, change is healthy. It makes for more innovation and creativity. The Byrds have done more experimenting than any other band. The Byrds have gone into musical areas that no one else has, ever will, or can for that matter." The tone of his words sounded like he was preparing an obituary for some fading institution – which was, of course, largely correct.

By the beginning of 1973, with the release of the reunion album only weeks away, it seemed as though the Byrds were simply winding up their commitments before a final dissolution. When asked whether the group was planning to break up, McGuinn answered teasingly, "Not now, maybe later." It was a comment hardly designed to instil hope and it came as no surprise to learn that the subsidiary members were all covering themselves with various plans for solo careers. Although White had previously told Gene Parsons that he was only staying for the money, he still felt that the group had potential and might continue. "We were hoping for a new light, but things got worse. Roger's head got strange."

The Byrds had a number of shows booked for the first three months of 1973 but ran into trouble within weeks of the New Year when Guerin decided to quit. Although he had enjoyed playing weekend dates with the Byrds, the money was not great and the music, 'Eight Miles High' excepted, did not suit his style of playing. "I liked working with John," says McGuinn, "but he was too jazz-orientated, and perhaps too good a drummer for what I wanted. He wanted more out of the deal. He was just doing it for a gig, he wasn't really part of the group. He had a funny attitude about the whole thing. He kind of looked down on us as something lesser than he was capable of doing. I guess that was true in a way. He's capable of another level of musicianship."

Guerin's sudden departure meant that the Byrds had to find another drummer quickly to honour their commitments. Once again, it was Linda McGuinn who influenced the choice of candidate. Dennis Dragon was the son of the great American composer and conductor Carmen Dragon, who had written scores for many films, from the Forties' Oscar-winning musical *Cover Girl* to the 1956 cold war science fiction classic *Invasion Of The Body Snatchers*, as well as conducting the Hollywood Bowl Symphony Orchestra and the Capitol Symphony. Carmen's sons, Daryl and Dennis, already had some musical experience working with the Beach Boys, and the former would later achieve international success as the male half of the Captain & Tennille.

"Dennis was a close friend of Linda's," Bernal explains. "They were Malibu brats together up the Pacific Coast Highway. Dennis was a very talented kid, but we felt he could never play the same thing twice. That was a bone of contention that came up."

Dragon confirms as much: "As I remember there wasn't much synergy there. I tended to do too many fills and not concentrate on time-keeping. I don't remember much else. My old girlfriend Linda hooked me up with Roger and suggested I drum with them." That said, Al Hersh found the new drummer "fun to tour with – a weird dude, but he cracked me up."

Dragon's services were only required for a few dates at a time when the Byrds were spiralling into the unknown, with confidence at an all-time low. "He was only with us for four weeks, our last drummer," White confirmed. "Jim Moon filled in when John or Dennis couldn't make it. But he didn't have enough experience at the time."

The Byrds still looked as though they might struggle through to their final booking at the Academy of Music on 19 May 1973, but in mid-February McGuinn suddenly lost patience and fired Skip Battin. "A lot of people had told me about Gene and Skip's inadequacies," he reasoned. "I always felt funny about them. I thought Skip was kind of jive." It was most perplexing that after playing with a musician for over three years, in concert halls all over the world, McGuinn could casually conclude that he was below standard. Why had he not spotted Battin's inadequacies years before? All McGuinn could offer me was the flimsy excuse: "I guess I didn't notice. I must have been getting complacent."

By now, Clarence White was growing used to McGuinn's caprice, but still attempted to warn him of the dangers of dismantling the group. Speaking about the last days of the band, he remembered a conversation during which Battin's fate was sealed. McGuinn spoke nonchalantly, as if removing a bass player or a drummer was nothing more than a minor irritant. What seemed a mere whim was probably a little more calculating and had obviously been playing on McGuinn's mind since the recording of *Byrdmaniax* back in 1971.

"Roger said, 'I think we could get a better bass player'," White recalls. "'Well,' I said, 'OK, maybe Joe Osborn is technically a better bass player but even if he wanted to join the Byrds . . . can we relate to each other?' Skip knew our music and could change with us. After something like that has been together for nearly five years, you can't start replacing members. But Roger didn't believe me and had to find out for himself. I think he felt that Terry Melcher was right after all. I said, 'If you feel like getting rid of those guys and don't like their musicianship, don't let me decide, you try it without them. You fire them!' So he did, and ended up with no band!"

Looking back, McGuinn saw his decision to pull the plug on the

DISSOLUTION

Byrds as akin to a mercy killing. "It was a dying spiritual thing there. It wasn't happening. The group was falling apart from within, the same way other groups had before. From ego problems, from old ladies saying, 'I think my old man ought to get more out of this.' Some of those things . . . I hate that, but it happens. It got down to where certain parties in the group thought they were getting cheated on the payroll, which wasn't the truth, and I had to fire them because they were jerks."

Agent Ron Rainey was shocked when McGuinn came in one day and announced, "I'm breaking up the Byrds". "I was representing Roger, not the other Byrds," Rainey points out. "I just said, 'You're *what*? Why?' He had this Mercedes with 'Byrds 1' on the licence plate. He was getting gas in Malibu and the attendant asked him, 'Whatever happened to the Byrds?' He said, 'If the gas attendant where I live doesn't know who the Byrds are, why should I go on?' And that was it. He was the boss and that's what he wanted to do. When Roger makes up his mind about something, that's it. You can't really talk him out of things."

McGuinn's decision was not entirely capricious, although the timing could have been better. Since recording with the original Byrds, he had promised Crosby that he would disband the CBS line-up and the imminent release of the reunion album forced his hand. It made no sense to have two sets of Byrds in existence simultaneously, but McGuinn did not want to leave himself empty-handed. It was obvious that the original Byrds were unlikely to stay together indefinitely and would almost certainly revert to their various solo projects after releasing their album. A worldwide tour remained a tantalizing possibility, but beyond that lay only uncertainty. If McGuinn was to tour, he preferred the security of familiar and respected players like White or Hillman, who could also be used for future reunion ventures. Even Battin understood this brutal logic and was phlegmatic about his dismissal. "McGuinn fired me," he conceded. "At the time I think he wanted to get Hillman and the original Byrds, but he also wanted to keep Clarence. He was probably right. The reunion seemed a good idea. We were falling apart. There was mild resentment and suspicion about the money. I wasn't surprised or annoyed. When Gene got it,

I knew it was just a matter of time. I've had to fire people myself. Sometimes it's necessary."

Kim Fowley was not surprised by McGuinn's decision. He had also been taken to task during the recording of *Byrdmaniax* and was aware that their material was considered inappropriate in many quarters. Although Battin was rightly regarded as easy-going and non-confrontational, Fowley maintains that he always had unrequited ambitions and was carefully considering his future throughout his tenure in the Byrds. "Skip was intelligent, a nice human being and a good guy. The flaw? He wasn't a lead singer. He was a great duet singer and a very good arranger, vocally and musically. I believe he didn't want to always be a part singer or sideman. Remember he had been half of Skip & Flip and had girls screaming for him before he was in the Byrds, so he had that rock star ego trying to be in somebody else's band, which is always a problem emotionally. It clouded his objectivity about where he belonged in the Byrds."

With several dates still to fulfil and no rhythm section, McGuinn phoned Chris Hillman in an attempt to re-enlist him as a Byrd. Hillman was touring with Stephen Stills' Manassas at the time but agreed to help out in return for a fee. What followed was the strange saga of the 'Manassas Byrds'. "Roger had a commitment in New Jersey, just before he ended the band," Hillman remembers. "He had no bass player or drummer, so when he called me I suggested Joe Lala. Actually, Joe is more of a percussionist and, to be truthful, we didn't get a chance to rehearse. Now 50 per cent of the songs he was doing I'd played before but the rest were all new stuff from the *(Untitled)* album onwards. We played bad!"

Their weekend performance at the Capitol Theatre in Passaic, New Jersey, on 24 February, was a desultory affair which only succeeded in convincing Clarence White that they should cancel their farewell show at the Academy of Music in May. Backstage, you could cut the tension with a knife as McGuinn boasted of his plans to tour with the original Byrds in June, including a projected appearance at Madison Square Garden. He did not seem too concerned that neither Hillman nor Lala would be available during April, when the Byrds had further dates to fulfil. "I'm not being the

Byrds," he told a puzzled reporter at the show, "I'm being Jim McGuinn with various other people, including Clarence White at this point. I'll probably have a different bass player and drummer for a time there in the middle and I'll be fluctuating in that area . . . For the time being I've suspended using the name 'Byrds', even though Clarence and myself have been using it with other people for the last few years . . . I feel I've accomplished something by keeping the Byrds alive. In a sense, though, they died five or six years ago and have been resurrected."

The intrepid reporter from *The Free Aquarian* later spoke to Clarence after the gig and found him in a downcast mood. Rather than making excuses for Hillman's playing, he was still lamenting the recent loss of Battin. After speaking to White, the journalist penned a revealing fly-on-the-wall account, documenting the depth of the guitarist's disillusionment.

"Clarence enjoyed playing with Skip Battin because he said Skip was able to drive the band well. He was annoyed and angry when Skip was fired. It made him frustrated because it was clear that he didn't have any control over things that were going down in the group. Clarence said that at one time he felt that playing with the Byrds was consistent with what he wanted to be doing musically but that since Hillman and Lala joined, 'It's become a drag.' He has some hope, certainly a desire, for the Byrds to become a real group again and move forward, but if that doesn't happen then he isn't sure who he will get together with."

The Free Aquarian reviewer left his paper's readership in little doubt who was responsible for the Byrds' substandard performance that weekend: "It was Hillman who messed things up for the band. He is viewing the spring tour as a part-time job or a favour to Roger but he isn't thinking in terms of the music. He even admitted that he doesn't enjoy playing bass any more but that fact didn't stop him from playing so loudly that he drowned out Clarence's guitar through most of the late show. Clarence asked him several times onstage to turn it down, but Chris merely threw his head back, smiled and kept on playing. Hillman had also refused to rehearse with the band and it was evident that he didn't know most of the songs."

Hillman received further censure when it was revealed that he had charged the Byrds $2,000 for his services that weekend. Not surprisingly, Hillman was annoyed at the inaccurate press reports suggesting that he had refused to rehearse and regarded his band fee as a private transaction, which did not warrant petty and exaggerated criticism.

As he countered, with righteous indignation: "Roger asked me, 'How much do you guys want to do this weekend?' We had to cancel everything to do it, so I said, 'How much are you grossing?' and the figure was $25,000 for the weekend. I said, 'Give me and Joe $1,000 a night and we'll do the third night for free.' We were making $500 to $1,000 a night with Stephen Stills, so I don't feel it was unfair. However, I must admit that we didn't play $2,000 worth of music. I wish I could have rehearsed with him but I just didn't know songs like 'Chestnut Mare' and 'Born On The Bayou' ['Lover Of The Bayou'] . . . I flew out there to rehearse, but there was no time to. We only did a weekend. We flew out Friday morning from Colorado. We had a soundcheck for half an hour and that was the time we were supposed to learn those songs. We tried our damnedest. If we'd only had six hours to rehearse, it would have been better."

The real heroes that night at Passaic were the die-hard Byrds followers who, despite being subjected to a poor performance, gave the group a rousing reception and send-off. Even *The Free Aquarian*'s reporter was perplexed by the "surprisingly appreciative audience", who were obviously excited by the return of Hillman and eager to pay tribute to a group whose legend transcended the disappointment of one bad evening.

Following the gig, McGuinn spoke optimistically about the future and seemed hopeful that the present Byrds would complete their commitments. Brushing aside any criticisms, he noted: "It was a spur of the moment proposition that we all got together, and I think that what we can offer now is not technical perfection but spontaneity. Eventually, I hope to get technical perfection with the spontaneity, and get it filled out."

These were brave and diplomatic words from McGuinn in the face of a poor show, but everybody realized that the Byrds had died

DISSOLUTION

a death at Passaic. There was insufficient enthusiasm left in the group to complete their spring schedule and what might have been the start of an exciting new partnership with Hillman failed to take flight. Not long afterwards, McGuinn and White discussed their futures and elected to go their separate ways. After a year of indecision, McGuinn at last dissolved the group that he had led for almost nine years. As McGuinn later noted, with a mixture of humour and arrogance: "Clarence and I fired each other as a joke, but nobody had the right to fire me as I was leader and I'd fired everybody by that time anyway."

CHAPTER THIRTY-SEVEN

Full Circle

THE disbanding of the CBS Byrds in February 1973 coincided with the return of the original set, whose long-awaited Asylum album prompted a barrage of publicity. Headlines proclaimed, 'The Byrds are dead – long live the Byrds', as speculation grew about the permanence of the reunion and possible touring plans for the summer. McGuinn was particularly excited about the venture and spoke with confidence of his desire to reinstate the original Byrds to their rightful position.

"It's a forward step backwards," he said, "and not a hype. Neither is it something that was scraped out of the bottom of a can. It's a brand new product and one which I'm certain will make a lot of people happy. From here on in, the only group of musicians who will be known as the Byrds, and who will record under that name, will be the original five. What I do on my own will be entirely different. You see, the major thing that the original band didn't accomplish was, simply, staying together. Or, at the very least, being open to each other and really attempting to work together. Personally, I always enjoyed the high moments of working with the original Byrds line-up, and this time around it feels like we're most definitely getting back to that."

The strength of the reformed Byrds was seen to lie in the informality of its reunion. While the original members had fallen out partly due to the intensity of their interrelationships, it was hoped that they would avoid those problems by reuniting at regular intervals to undertake tours and record albums. They would not constitute a group in the traditional sense, but rather function as a gathering of individuals under the Byrds' banner. The plan had its prototype in the Crosby, Stills, Nash & Young relationship, whose continued existence as a unit remained one of rock music's great mysteries during the early Seventies.

The consequences of a Byrds' reunion had different implications for the various ex-members. For Michael Clarke, it was a welcome windfall after the financial frustrations of working in the Flying Burrito Brothers. Gene Clark was also in need of attention, having failed to excite commercial interest since leaving the Byrds. His most recent release, the striking *White Light*, was one of the better singer-songwriter albums of the era. Produced by the well-respected guitarist Jesse Ed Davis, it was an evocative but strangely stark recording with echoes of early to mid-period Dylan in its song construction. Its pensive love ballads were loaded with Clark's characteristic and often opaque symbolism, which added intellectual and spiritual depth to the compositions. Unfortunately, the sales were disappointing and Clark's well-cultivated mystique proved no substitute for proper promotion. A proposed follow-up remained uncompleted and the rough tapes of a work in progress later emerged on A&M Holland as *Roadmaster*. Given its fragmented creation, *Roadmaster* was surprisingly good and featured several Clark classics including 'Full Circle Song' and the haunting 'In A Misty Morning'. They even threw in the two Jim Dickson-produced songs recorded with the original Byrds: 'She's The Kind Of Girl' and 'One In A Hundred'. For all that, it was a frustrating release, reserved for Clark aficionados who could afford import copies. Despite the continued patience and support of label president Jerry Moss, Clark's reluctance to tour was a major problem. After a long relationship with the company, his career was in the doldrums.

Chris Hillman was in a more advantageous position. After firing Gram Parsons from the Flying Burrito Brothers, he had recruited Rick Roberts for their third, highly-accomplished album and also appeared on their swansong live LP, *Last Of The Red Hot Burritos*. Hillman co-wrote several songs with Roberts, again displaying his collaborative skills to impressive effect. The Burritos offered aesthetic satisfaction, but failed to perform as well in the marketplace as they deserved. When Stephen Stills offered Hillman the role of his right-hand man in Manassas, Chris eagerly accepted the post. Stills' septet were a revelation and emerged as one of the most accomplished live acts of their era, with a repertoire that effortlessly encompassed rock, bluegrass, blues, country and R&B. Their double album, *Manassas*, was an extraordinarily eclectic collection split into four movements ('The Raven'; 'The Wilderness'; 'Consider' and 'Rock & Roll Is Here To Stay') which crystallized Stills' panoramic musical vision in one neat package. When the group toured the USA in the summer of 1972, they were joined onstage by Graham Nash, Neil Young and McGuinn, the latter featuring on such Byrds' classics as 'The Bells Of Rhymney', 'He Was A Friend Of Mine' and 'So You Want To Be A Rock 'n' Roll Star'.

The sense of reunion and reconciliation fostered during those months was felt most poignantly by David Crosby, whose career had reached startling peaks since founding Crosby, Stills, Nash & Young. In the wake of *Déjà Vu*, he had released his first solo album, *If I Could Only Remember My Name*, a work that transcends its time like few other releases from this era. Rather than producing a plaintive or over-sweetened singer-songwriter album, Crosby poured his soul into a striking experimental mood piece, laced with exquisite harmonies, unusual time signatures and dazzling choral arrangements. With the assistance of various members of the Jefferson Airplane and Grateful Dead, plus other guests including Joni Mitchell and Neil Young, Crosby created his own musical Love-In, cutting through the stoned beatitude with a heightened sense of purpose. The album featured several of his most enduring compositions, the slow-burning 'Music Is Love', the electric CSN&Y allegory 'Cowboy Movie', the sumptuous zither-tinged 'Traction In The Rain' and several wordless meditations, culminating in the classic choral 'Orleans' and the disturbing 'I'd Swear There Was Somebody Here', a Gregorian chant-styled requiem to Crosby's recently deceased girlfriend and former Byrds' fan club president, Christine Hinton. Notwithstanding the achievement of the individual songs, the work needed to be heard in its entirety to appreciate its hidden depths, which were considerable.

Within a month of the release of his solo album, Crosby could be heard again, dominating CSN&Y's live double album, *Four Way Street*. Against all odds, it was he and Nash who performed the previously unissued songs in the set, with Crosby introducing 'The Lee Shore' and reviving 'Triad', the *ménage à trois* ballad that the Jefferson Airplane had recorded after the Byrds coolly rejected the song. Thereafter, Crosby teamed up with Graham Nash for a series of acoustic concerts, whose emotional power and intimacy were probably unrivalled by anything that followed. The duo issued their own album, whose highlights were Crosby's thrilling question and answer songs: 'Where Will I Be' and 'Page 43'. Crosby & Nash's work was released during the same month as Manassas, thereby placing two ex-Byrds back into the US Top 5, and confirming the enormous creative and commercial potential of the CSN&Y/Byrds combination.

With CSN&Y temporarily grounded, entrepreneur David Geffen was even more aware of the importance of an historic Byrds' reunion. Meanwhile, the press paid much attention to the Crosby/McGuinn relationship and spoke in grandiloquent terms about the ending of a feud which had supposedly raged between them for nearly seven years. Now, of course, their futures were inextricably bound together and, as part of the Columbia/Asylum exchange deal, Clive Davis had demanded that Crosby and McGuinn make a joint album for CBS during 1973. Nothing, it seemed, could go wrong. Negotiations were already underway for the original Byrds to tour the USA, and Geffen had just received an offer of $100,000 for one night in London, so a European tour also seemed likely. Many of these ambitious plans might have reached fruition were it not for one fateful twist: the critical reaction to the album.

During and after the recording, Crosby and McGuinn spoke with great enthusiasm about the high quality of the music, and the discovery of a new-found unity which the old Byrds had always lacked. Crosby concluded, "It's a fulfilment of what we could have been; it's what I was hoping for." McGuinn even suggested that the record would take up where *The Notorious Byrd Brothers* had left off, thereby implying that it was an innovative album in the mid-Byrds tradition. Understandably, the critics were waiting for a classic and may even have been expecting the Byrds to surge forward in a new musical direction. In the light of these expectations, it was inevitable that the album would prove anticlimactic. However, the criticism was so widespread that the individual members lost faith in the reunion and this was enough to scupper the extensive touring plans.

In retrospect, the album deserved a fairer hearing than its detractors acknowledge. Admittedly, it was no *Younger Than Yesterday* or *The Notorious Byrd Brothers*, but it was better than anything they had recorded since *(Untitled)*, and that alone made it worthy of a reasonable review. In Britain, both *NME* and *Sounds* applauded the album, but elsewhere the reaction was hostile. The advance publicity ensured that many over-expectant critics were unprepared for anything less than another *The Notorious Byrd Brothers*, and the whole project was dismissed prematurely. McGuinn learned to his cost that reunion recordings were not judged in isolation but set against an artiste's best work. A re-evaluation of the album shows that it had several weaknesses, but there was also evidence of an underlying musical strength which was largely ignored.

'Full Circle' was originally the projected title of the album before it was changed to *Byrds*. No doubt Gene felt critics would mistakenly assume that he had written the song specifically for the reunion venture, which was not the case. "I'd already recorded that song a couple of years earlier and it wasn't really written about anything specific," he told me. "It was just an idea I had." Nevertheless, the wheel of fortune motif was particularly applicable to Clark, who had never really capitalized on his 'original Byrds' status and subsequently fell from grace with the record-buying public. Although undoubtedly one of the strongest cuts on the album, with some striking mandolin work from Chris Hillman where we might have expected to hear McGuinn's 12-string Rickenbacker, the song failed to receive the praise that it so obviously merited.

For his first contribution to the project, McGuinn reverted to the folk style of his pre-Byrds work with 'Sweet Mary', another collaboration with Jacques Levy. The whole approach, complete with nasal vocal and syllable stretching, conjures up visions of the old folk clubs in which McGuinn played while living in Chicago. Hillman's fluttering mandolin set against the 12-string guitar provides a revealing glimpse into what the Byrds might have sounded like if their bassist had not switched instruments in 1964. McGuinn's ex-wife Dolores always assumed the song was written about their broken marriage, citing the key line: "And the last thing I need is a wife". She may well be correct. Lyricist Jacques Levy was well aware of their marital history and as a former clinical psychologist understood the emotional complexities that accompany divorce. The song describes a break-up predicated upon the need for hedonistic pleasures, yet there is also guilt and remorse, along with the knowledge that there is no going back. McGuinn's yearning performance required only a minimum of method acting to sound convincing.

Gene Clark's 'Changing Heart' opens with a Dylanesque harmonica break in true mid-Sixties folk-rock style. The song might have been even stronger if the Rickenbacker had not been mixed into near inaudibility, but the lyrics remain impressive. Whether the song was consciously autobiographical is debatable, but the theme was certainly applicable to Clark's career. He was lavishly praised by fans and media alike when he reached the top with the Byrds but, after reverting to a solo career and attempting to express his soul-searching more effectively, the bright lights deserted him.

David Crosby's decision to cover Joni Mitchell's 'For Free' (from *Ladies Of The Canyon*) came as no great surprise. Their relationship, both personal and professional, was well known and, since producing her first album *Song To A Seagull*, he had frequently named her as his favourite songwriter. His strong vocal performance on 'For Free' compensates for the underdeveloped harmonies. The stark, uncluttered instrumentation draws attention to Crosby's vocal range, while Clarke's impressive drumming is a little reminiscent of the military style playing previously pioneered on *Preflyte*. Coincidentally or not, the theme of 'For Free' fits perfectly with the subject matter of several other tracks on the album. In highlighting the distinction between the famous superstar and the unsuccessful struggling performer, Crosby reiterates the sentiments of both 'Full Circle' and 'Changing Heart'.

McGuinn's 'Born To Rock 'n' Roll' was originally intended as a semi-serious song about how he became a rock musician but, midway through the composition, he suddenly changed his mind and wrote a clichéd tribute to rock 'n' roll. He later admitted that he had a stronger song which he should have included, but selfishly saved for his forthcoming solo album. What remained was a mildly amusing but weak rock 'n' roll number, whose punch was lost amid a completely lacklustre performance. The high energy rock 'n' roll that McGuinn alludes to is conspicuously absent from the recording. Having previously failed to cut a perfect version with the CBS Byrds, and compromised the reunion album with a second unsuccessful attempt, McGuinn inexplicably tried again on his third solo album, with predictably poor results. As he acknowledged: "'Born To Rock 'n' Roll' was a dog. I tried to get it right again on my third solo album, but I've finally given up on it. I realize it's a total disaster. It's stilted and just doesn't work. The reason I tried it again was because it didn't work the first time. But I'll never try it again."

Hillman's co-writing collaboration with Dallas Taylor, 'Things Will Be Better' seems vaguely reminiscent of his contributions to *Younger Than Yesterday*, but clearly lacks the depth or power of songs like 'Time Between', 'The Girl With No Name' or 'Thoughts And Words'. However, in common with several other tracks on the reunion album, Hillman's lyric chronicles the rise and fall of the rock star, concluding that life is a wheel of fortune which can take you to the top just to watch you fall.

The appearance of Neil Young's 'Cowgirl In The Sand', in place of a Dylan cover, prompted many to assume that David Crosby had a strong hand in choosing the material, but this was not the case. Gene Clark had long admired Young as a singer-songwriter and the inclusion of this track from *Everybody Knows This Is Nowhere* was a tribute from one performer to another. "We all discussed doing a Dylan song," says Clark, "but we couldn't find one. It's incredible and a shame that we couldn't find one. Dylan has changed. And we were choosing songs, as we always have done, for their lyrical value; and that to us right away meant Neil Young." Clark's vocal and harmonica playing add a pleasant country flavour to the composition. The harmonies from the other Byrds are impressive and the performance has a unified feel lacking on some of the other tracks.

That in itself was ironic as this may have been one moment when the original Byrds brought in reinforcements.

CSN&Y drummer Johnny Barbata recalls: "David didn't like the track, so he had Wilton Felder – the famous tenor sax player of the Jazz Crusaders – play bass. David had me play drums. The song came out great, and Wilton was a monster on bass; of course he never got credit on the album, until now! I'm sure David wanted to keep the Byrds' mystique intact." Nobody else confirms Barbata's account, so whether Felder's version was merely a guide arrangement that later featured all the Byrds remains uncertain.

'Long Live The King' evolved over several takes from a funky workout featuring some solid R&B drumming from Clarke to this more polished rendition. Thematically, the composition completes the Byrds' examination of the trials and tribulations of superstardom. In Crosby's lyric, the rock business is seen to produce super-heroes only to knock them from their pedestals when the appropriate time arrives. It is interesting that an album so often criticized for its diffusion should provide a thematic link over four separate songs by Crosby, Clark and Hillman. The Byrds were unconsciously predicting the outcome of the reunion venture. They were encouraged to produce a star-studded album, only to see it publicly discredited.

Hillman and Lala's 'Borrowing Time' begs the question whether all four Byrds deserved an equal share in the distribution of songs on the album. Despite an impressive mandolin break and a half-decent melody, this was below average fare which could sensibly have been surrendered in favour of another Clark, McGuinn or Crosby composition. "Gene once again shone the brightest with his songs," Hillman later admitted. "Some of the stuff I put on that album, I have to tell you, were throwaways. I had other songs I was saving . . ."

Crosby's 'Laughing' was already well known to purchasers of his solo album, but he insisted on re-recording the song on the grounds that it had originally been written for the Byrds. Arguably, the arrangement sounds sufficiently different from his solo version to warrant inclusion, with the 12-strings gelling together to form a semblance of the old Byrds sound. Clarke's drumming is the finest on the album and the stop/start technique at the end of each verse provides a suitably dramatic touch. Earlier in the sessions, Crosby had experimented with a radically different version, bathed in vocal echo in an attempt to create the spooky ambience evident on parts of his solo album *If I Could Only Remember My Name*.

The most common criticisms of the reunion record were its disunity and lack of a distinguishable sound. This view might have been justified were it not for '(See The Sky) About To Rain'. Here, Clark's strong lead vocal is backed by sumptuous harmonies and a piercing mandolin break, which adds an extra layer of instrumentation to the enveloping sound. Significantly, Michael Clarke once more reverts to his unusual military-style drumming. In fact, all the components of the original Byrds sound are mixed into this track. The high harmonies increase in prominence as the song progresses, culminating in the percussive stop/start technique at the end of the last verse. For just under one second there is complete silence, followed by a sound which can only be described as pure Byrds. A legion of 12-strings fills the chasm of silence, while the voices soar, after which Clarke, the champion of *4/4*, provides a final blast which is surely the finest drum roll heard on any Byrds track since those magic moments on 'Goin' Back'. The final line of the song is drowned by a stream of reverberating 12-strings which create a stunning wall of sound. At this precise moment, the Byrds find a unique identity and, for this alone, the seven-year vigil for the reformation was worthwhile. Whatever criticism anyone has of the album, there can be no doubt that, within the final minute of this song, five individual musicians combine to produce a distinctive sound that could have been developed on subsequent albums.

The grand reunion was ultimately blighted by the castigating comments of disappointed reviewers and the oversensitive reactions of the Byrds. Probably the most balanced view of the reunion initially came from Gene Clark. "I am disappointed in that album," he said. "Some of the harsh criticism is unjust, because, if you listen to it carefully, the album isn't that bad, but it just hasn't got the punch it could have had if we'd taken the time. Each member of the original Byrds has a lot of credibility and you can't discount them either as live performers or in the studio."

The lymphatic McGuinn was less forgiving, pointing out that

"the album could have been a lot better. At the time we made it I was very excited. But that's how you always are . . . In retrospect, the group should have been more together, rehearsed more." Evidently, his chief colleague felt the same. "Crosby, in retrospect, tells me he didn't [provide] enough slack . . . If I had done one more tune or sung lead on one of the tunes already on there, it would have been better. He also said he shouldn't have done 'Laughing' a second time. When you're involved in the studio, it's really difficult to see the forest from the trees . . . you get wrapped up in it . . . Unfortunately, we forgot that we could never possibly be as good as when we had been together on the road for six months."

Hillman's despondency over the album rapidly festered into disillusionment, reinforced by the realization that they had entered the reunion project more in naïve hope than hard-working commitment. As he explained to me in pained defence: "We only wanted to do it to get back together, to play and see what happened. We weren't really looking at it financially, even though it crossed our minds. We had plans to tour but the album turned out horribly. In all honesty, we didn't have enough time on the album. They gave us one-and-a-half months to do that album, expecting guys to regroup after a five to six year absence. We needed a producer, we needed at least three months to rehearse and we needed material, ours and someone else's. We had none of these, and everybody was so afraid of stepping on the other person's feet because of the tension that had gone down six years prior to that, that it became a bland album. Everybody was being too nice to each other. David re-cut 'Laughing' for some reason, and I didn't put my good songs on the album as I was saving them for my solo album. I felt that everybody was doing the same. I think Gene had the best songs. 'Full Circle' was great. If '(See The Sky) About To Rain' had been edited, it would have made a great single. But they didn't even do that . . . David took the production credit and I'm sure he was sorry he did. I didn't realize he was the producer until the end of the album. I felt we were all the producers, but it came out that he took the credit and he can have it."

It was clear that the reunion album was a rushed venture on which a distinguishable Byrds' sound was unlikely to emerge.

Obviously, the Byrds could not be expected to dissolve their five personalities into a complete whole at the first attempt. The Byrds were aware of this and needed the necessary encouragement to record another. However, they were distracted by the poor reviews, some of which even took umbrage at the lack of a Bob Dylan song, forgetting perhaps that the last Byrds album to contain one of his compositions was *(Untitled)* back in 1970, while earlier works such as *The Notorious Byrd Brothers* and *Fifth Dimension* had intentionally avoided his songwriting talents. The other main criticism centred on the album's lack of unity, but the thematic links discussed earlier suggest that it was somewhat more focused than many detractors realized. With few exceptions, most insights or positive comments on the quality of the musicianship and the compatibility of the membership were sacrificed to preconceived notions about the unsuitability of the product.

After the album's release, the Byrds meekly accepted the worst criticisms as a final judgement. Originally, Crosby and McGuinn had insisted that the album had transcended their wildest expectations, but those effusive comments were soon forgotten once they separated. Before long, they were only too willing to admit that they had overestimated the album's worth. Looking back, Chris Hillman remembers that he was the only person who felt anything less than ecstatic about the album during the period of its recording. "At the time, I went to Elliot Roberts and told him it didn't sound right. I wanted to use Paul Harris on keyboards to fill out the sound but the others felt that we ought to keep it the Byrds. I talked to David three months after that and he said, 'You were right.' I said, 'What the hell does that matter now?'"

Although the album was a relative chart success, reaching the Top 20 and selling in excess of 400,000 copies, the scathing reviews proved more than enough to destroy the enthusiasm and confidence of the thin-skinned Byrds. The plans to tour America and Europe that had seemed so definite weeks before the release of the album were now a bad dream. "It never came about," Hillman casually concludes. "It never even got down to discussing going out on tour after the release of that album."

The Byrds returned to their individual projects and promised to rethink their approach before attempting another get-together. In the meantime, aficionados awaited the Crosby & McGuinn album with anticipation. It was hoped that a joint album might cement relations between the two and encourage them to work together more frequently in the future. Sadly, the much-vaunted collaboration failed to materialize. Although the album was originally a contractual necessity, the exchange deal with Columbia was never completed. "That was a Clive Davis idea," McGuinn explains, "and Clive got fired, so it was no longer valid. Crosby and I never bothered to record together. Nothing was cut."

Instead, fans had to content themselves with McGuinn's first solo album, which was issued at the beginning of July. For the first time in his career, McGuinn produced a record, a decision prompted by David Crosby who encouraged his fellow Byrd to dismiss Terry Melcher who had been working on the project. "Terry was doing a nice job, but David said it was too slick commercially and it needed to be more organic," McGuinn recalls. "I really shouldn't have listened to David." Crosby may have been taking belated revenge on Melcher for disagreements stemming from the Byrds' days, but McGuinn seemed easily swayed. The politics notwithstanding, the finished album was highly impressive, with consistently strong songs performed in a range of musical styles. Many of the critics who slammed the reunion album applauded McGuinn, who suddenly rediscovered the commitment missing from his last couple of albums with the CBS Byrds. "The attitude I had when I was doing it was that I'd hit them with both barrels," he told me. "Kind of show them everything I had." With Melcher's assistance, McGuinn lined up a formidable supporting cast, including session drummers Hal Blaine, John Guerin and Jim Gordon, Beach Boy Bruce Johnston, Spanky McFarlane, Spooner Oldham and the old master Bob Dylan, who provided harmonica on 'I'm So Restless'. "He didn't want to do it," says McGuinn, "but I twisted his arm. I said, '. . . you have so much more experience than I do . . . I don't know how to play harmonica. You do. You're a harmonica player . . .' He said, 'All right, I'll play the middle, but you've got to do the beginning and the end', which is what I did. But I didn't tell anybody so they think it's him all the way. But he played on the middle part and I played on the beginning and end to sound like him . . . He said it was an honour."

Nor was this the best track. Among a strong set, the highlights included a clever surf pastiche 'Draggin'', and the thrilling 'My New Woman', which featured all five original Byrds augmented by saxophonist Charles Lloyd. Everyone agreed that 'My New Woman' would have been perfect for the reunion album. It also showed the power of Crosby and McGuinn when they worked together as a team, something that regrettably happened all too infrequently at this juncture.

McGuinn's album fared less well than expected or deserved, peaking at a disappointing number 137 on *Billboard*. It was the first sign that he might have trouble emulating the commercial appeal or concert receipts of the latter-day Byrds. Agent Ron Rainey recognized his dilemma. "The Byrds were a trademark and McGuinn was arguably the voice of the Byrds and when that disappeared there were still fans of McGuinn but, in reality, breaking out of a big band into a solo career is no mean feat."

Not that McGuinn felt particularly intimidated. He was too busy enjoying himself. Since marrying Linda Gilbert and moving to Malibu, McGuinn had settled into the life of a Seventies rock star. "It was a very tumultuous time," recalls Al Hersh. "They had parties every weekend. Sometimes they'd bleed into the next week. It would be fair to say that they were non-stop. There were people there like Bob Dylan, Brian Wilson, Hal Ashby and a whole hotchpotch of actors and a real interesting mix of people . . . Roger was around guys like Dennis Wilson, who was hanging out at his house. But Dennis was a basket case. He was going through the medicine cabinet and taking dog lining pills. He was out of his mind."

It was a new experience for McGuinn to play the socialite supreme, but with his solo album on release, he felt liberated and full of limitless opportunities. He was particularly proud to have secured that guest appearance from Dylan, who then owned a house in Malibu and seemed happy to visit the McGuinns. "Bob used to come over to my house a lot when we lived in Malibu," Roger reminisces. "We were planning to write songs together. But when we tried we really couldn't come up with anything so we abandoned the idea."

"They had an odd relationship," Hersh adds, "but hung out a lot there." Another visitor at this time was Gene Clark, who stayed at the house for a spell and joined McGuinn onstage during his week-long residency at the Troubadour. Unfortunately, Clark's erratic behaviour put paid to any thoughts of another collaboration. Events reached a dangerous head during a celebrity party when Clark gained access to McGuinn's gun collection. "There were a lot of weapons around," says Hersh, "and Gene got pissed off with Dylan one night and chased him around the backyard with an Uzi. He tripped on something and when he fell his finger hit the trigger and the Uzi was dragging him around the yard. By this time Dylan had cleared out and went somewhere to hide. But Gene was flying around the yard with this Uzi dragging him. McGuinn and Linda had these miniature goats and Gene killed almost all of them. Blew their legs off."

Clark was banished after the incident, but the parties continued. McGuinn was frequently caught up in the madness. "He was getting weird because he was drinking and we were doing a lot of coke," says Hersh. One memorable night, McGuinn found himself locked out of his house and decided to shoot his way in, like a cowboy in a saloon. "Roger was shooting through the wall. He had a bank of television sets and he shot most of those." It was one thing playing the role of James Bond with all his gadgetry, but now McGuinn was turning into Billy The Kid. Thankfully, this phase proved short-lived. "I confiscated all the guns," Hersh concludes. "It was just out of control, really out of control." It took a moment of genuine tragedy to shake everybody out of their rock star complacency.

On 13 July, Roger celebrated his 31st birthday with a house party featuring several old friends, including Clarence White. Although McGuinn had agreed with Crosby that the only Byrds to appear in the future would be the original five, he still missed the contribution of White who had done so much to re-establish the latter-day Byrds as a strong live band. Since leaving the group, he had reformed the Kentucky Colonels, toured Europe and teamed up with David Grisman, Billy Keith and former Seatrain personnel Richard Greene and Peter Rowan in Muleskinner. More importantly, White also commenced work on a solo album, recording a number of songs with Jim Dickson, including 'Waterbed', 'Lucky Me', 'The Last Thing On My Mind', 'Why You Been Gone So Long', 'Never Ending Love' and 'Alabama Jubilee'.

Meanwhile, Dickson's partner Eddie Tickner organized a package tour of East Coast gigs featuring the Kentucky Colonels, Country Gazette and a special bluegrass segment starring White, Gene Parsons, Chris Ethridge and Sneaky Pete Kleinow, plus special guest Gram Parsons. Plans were already underway for this cavalcade of ex-Byrds and ex-Burritos to tour the UK during the autumn, with additional players adding their names to the illustrious list. Sadly, it was not to be. The night after McGuinn's party, on 14 July, White was tragically killed by a drunken driver while loading equipment into a van following a gig. His brother Roland suffered a dislocated arm while attempting to pull him away from the car. White had severe brain damage and passed away several hours later. Gene Parsons' words expressed the feelings of musicians and friends all over the world: "There isn't much to say except that we loved him very much, and we'll miss him for the rest of our lives. For myself, personally, I'll never be able to play music again without thinking of my friend Clarence."

On 19 July, an estimated 100 musicians attended White's funeral at St Mary's Catholic Church in Palmdale. It was a respectful farewell to one of the most talented figures in country and rock music. Although no music was played during the service, Gram Parsons and Bernie Leadon remained at the graveside to sing 'Farther Along'. During the wake that followed, Gram Parsons was noticeably downbeat about the funeral rites. That same evening, he and road manager Philip Kaufman went out to get drunk. According to a number of sources, Parsons and Kaufman made a ritual pact that night, agreeing that when either of them died the other would ensure that the body be taken to the desert and cremated.

Parsons' erratic career had been in steady decline since working with Hillman on *The Gilded Palace Of Sin*. Somewhere along the road to excess, he lost that dream of founding Cosmic American Music. Since *Burrito Deluxe* he had drifted, spending freely without focus. He bought a Harley Davidson, which he promptly crashed while riding with that other excessive Papa John Phillips. While recuperating, Gram moved into Terry Melcher's Benedict Canyon home at precisely the time when the Byrds' producer was attempting to retain his sanity in the wake of the Manson slayings. Alcohol, drugs and women were his familiar means of coping with his worst fears. Melcher fantasized about getting Parsons together with the Byrds at one point, then decided to produce his solo album. In true *Byrdmaniax* fashion, Terry invited singer Merry Clayton along to provide a wailing backing to 'White Line Fever'. Eventually, ten songs were completed, consisting of pop and country standards, plus Parsons' own 'Brass Buttons'. The tapes were safely consigned to a vault, where they remain to this day in pristine condition, having miraculously escaped the scrutiny of previous biographers and archival reissue packagers.

Parsons' excesses were still proving his undoing. After partying with Phillips and Melcher, he reconnected with Keith Richards and became part of the Rolling Stones' touring circus, increasing his heroin habit along the way. At one point, he disappeared to London to work with former Blind Faith bassist Rick (Rik) Grech, whose home recordings with the Georgian were briefly issued in 1995 as *Cosmic American Music*. Parsons still hoped to work with Keith Richards or record for the Rolling Stones' own label. Having inspired their country leanings on songs like 'Country Honk' and 'Wild Horses', he hung out with them in France during the recording of *Exile On Main Street* but was sent home a drugged-up mess.

In a determined effort to salvage his career Parsons turned to the sober-blooded Eddie Tickner who started negotiations with Warner Brothers. Parsons was eager to employ Elvis Presley's band and encouraged Tickner to recruit guitarist James Burton, pianist Glen D. Hardin and drummer Ron Tutt. Tickner also delivered Parsons' fantasy producer – his great idol Merle Haggard. Alas, Haggard pulled out prior to the session, a decision which sent Parsons spiralling downwards into an alcoholic depression.

The disappointment over Haggard was at least partially alleviated by the discovery of a new singing partner. It was Chris Hillman who first brought Emmylou Harris to Parsons' attention.

"I had to damn near break his arm to call her," Hillman remembers, "but he did and, two days later, he went to Washington and met her. It worked, and they went from there." Harris appeared on Parsons' debut solo album, *GP*, his first release after a three-year drought. Gone was the questing spirit of yore, in favour of a pleasant, much-loved country record, overseen by Tickner and co-produced by Parsons and Grech, with assistance from Merle Haggard's engineer, Hugh Davies. Released in January 1973 at a time when the Eagles were taking country rock singles into the charts, Parsons' work seemed to fall between two different audiences. The album failed to reach the *Billboard* Top 200.

Parsons promoted *GP* with a US tour, featuring a back-up band, the Fallen Angels. One of their shows, recorded in front of a radio audience in New York, was released a decade later under the title *Live 1973*. Encouraged by Tickner, Parsons participated in the 'Country Rock Festival' featuring the Kentucky Colonels, Country Gazette and various ex-Burritos. Backstage, Parsons became involved in a fracas with the usually placid Clarence White, who was infuriated by his showboating. Such flare-ups were not uncommon in Parsons' interactions at this point. The previous December, Hillman had bodily thrown him out of his rented house for spoiling the bassist's 28th birthday party with his drunken antics.

Parsons' alcoholism continued to worsen but he rallied sufficiently to record the posthumously released *Grievous Angel*, which contained some striking duets with Emmylou Harris and went some way towards fulfilling his dream of a George Jones/ Tammy Wynette-inspired collaboration. Regrettably, Parsons' self-mythologizing and hedonism overwhelmed both his talent and work rate. The death of Clarence White, whose image, temperament and industry contrasted so markedly with the lifestyle exemplified by Gram, should have had a salutary effect on the singer. Instead, Parsons continued to dice with death, almost killing himself in a fire that razed his home.

Parsons' demise was not far away. On 19 September 1973 he was found dead in a room at the Joshua Tree Inn, the victim of a heart attack brought on by drug toxicity. Lurid and fantasy tales detailing his expiration were soon part of rock folklore. They included the unforgettable image of a woman supposedly masturbating the corpse in a vain attempt to revive the singer while another person inserted ice cubes into his rear. In the end, these outrageously apocryphal accounts were eclipsed by an incident even more unbelievable, yet startlingly true. While plans were underway for Parsons' funeral, the body was stolen from a loading dock at Los Angeles International Airport. Soon after, San Bernardino County sheriff's deputies were alerted to a burned casket containing a corpse. It was situated some 200 miles away in the Mojave Desert area near the Joshua Tree National Monument. The bizarre circumstances surrounding Parsons' death momentarily brought him back into the media spotlight, with press reports reaching as far as the English dailies. At first, the FBI feared that the conflagration might be evidence of some kind of cult, with chilling memories of Manson.

Further investigation revealed that the events were not as sinister as the media had expected. The bodysnatchers were roadies Phil Kaufman and Michael Martin, who had stolen and cremated the body, believing that they had fulfilled the morbid wish that Parsons had expressed following Clarence White's funeral. What remained of Parsons' charred corpse was flown to New Orleans for internment. Back at Kaufman's house, a wake took place at which Bobby 'Boris' Pickett And The Crypt-Kickers sang 'Monster Mash', while friends and associates downed copious amounts of beer. It was a tasteless and irreverent assembly, but the participants felt the rock 'n' roll send-off suited Parsons' lifestyle. Kaufman had even charged a $5 entry fee, primarily to offset legal costs.

The excesses that accompanied his life and followed his death eventually made Parsons a cult figure. Although his record sales remained uneventful, the Gram myth helped keep his music alive for a new generation of fans. His slight catalogue was a lasting reminder of a great, often squandered, talent. Like his contemporary Clarence White, he had a deep and significant influence on the progress of modern country music.

CHAPTER THIRTY-EIGHT

Separation

AFTER experiencing the worst year in the Byrds' history, McGuinn was determined to begin 1974 on a brighter note. He had been touring with a back-up band following the release of his solo album when David Crosby suggested a new challenge: "Why not do a solo tour and get back to your roots?" Crosby was then in the midst of playing college gigs where students and locals paid $5.00 to hear an intimate acoustic set of high quality music and stoned humour. Remembering McGuinn's pre-Byrds days at the Troubadour, Crosby felt that he might also benefit from confronting small audiences after all the ballyhoo of superstar reunions and big money deals.

In January 1974, McGuinn set out on a three-month tour armed only with an acoustic guitar, banjo and Rickenbacker. Despite the technical limitations, he had no trouble reprising the old Byrds hits, including a stunning version of 'Eight Miles High'. "It was difficult, but I used some electronic devices which made it sound like more than one person," he told me. "I used a little pig-nose amplifier, a phase-shifter and a compression amplifier, which made the electric 12-string sound as though a bass were playing. People used to ask me where the bass player was hiding."

Although the solo gigs were challenging, McGuinn felt ambivalent about the tour and sometimes wondered whether it was worth risking his reputation by playing too cheaply. "It was more painful than rewarding," he confided. "People were disappointed that I appeared as a solo act. They thought I'd hit the skids. I wasn't doing it for the money since I could have put another band together and got $3,000 a night. I tried to explain that to people, but they didn't quite understand. The ultimate result of it though was that it gave me a sense of accomplishment and esteem. It was an experiment which I did mainly from David Crosby's request and influence. It took a tremendous amount of courage to do it, and it served as a character-strengthening test."

One of the last dates of the tour was an evening at My Father's Place, a small club in Roslyn, Long Island frequented by journalist Chris Charlesworth, whose appreciation of the set was enhanced by the cheap beer, which retailed at 50 cents a glass. Back at the Holiday Inn, McGuinn was in philosophical mood, acknowledging that his solo album had sold only 47,000 copies but hoping for better next time around. Inevitably, there was discussion of the reunion album, with McGuinn admitting, "It was a bit of an anticlimax, and the last version of the Byrds was the same." Despite the bad reviews, McGuinn was still hopeful that the original five might reconvene, but his tone betrayed a lack of enthusiasm. "Maybe that'll be an anti anticlimax," he warned. "It couldn't be worse than the last one. That one came out on the Asylum label because David was on Asylum and he was calling the shots and had the most power. Asylum were prepared to give us more money than Columbia too, so it didn't make any sense not to go with Asylum. Unfortunately, that was largely a business manoeuvre as opposed to a musical effort. It was very segmented. Each of us had two songs and I know I had another song which was better than some of the stuff that found its way on to the record."

Although the idea of regular musical reunions was an interesting one, McGuinn felt that it was too idealistic to work. He described it as "a big square dance where everybody would play with everybody else over a period of 12 months; David and Graham, me and David, Chris and Stephen," adding laconically, "but it won't work that way." McGuinn was correct. The reformed Byrds may have seemed the perfect vehicle to allow friends to record together and extend their musical ideas without the usual problems of an established group, but such a set-up did not guarantee greatness. With the loss of internal strife, the Byrds also ran the risk of negating the intense enthusiasm that had characterized and defined their best work. It was surely no coincidence that their major achievements, *Younger Than Yesterday* and *The Notorious Byrd Brothers*, had been recorded at a time when either artistic decisions were being challenged, tempers were raging or the group was in the process of self-destruction. It almost seemed that their pleasure in reforming was somehow detrimental to the music. More importantly, the insistence that each member should continue a solo career and remain a Byrd seemed self-contradictory. The group needed more time together as a permanent unit in order to rediscover each other as musicians and personalities. Only when they could communicate, argue and take risks could they hope to record a truly innovative work, and that was an unlikely scenario. The pursuit of individual projects meant that the reformed Byrds would continue to grow away from each other rather than unify.

The lure of reunion money was still in the air in mid-1974 and David Geffen remained determined to transform disappointment into commodity. Lacklustre reviews had not put off promoters, who still saw an onstage reunion of the Byrds as a hot ticket. Characteristically, Geffen and his partner Elliot Roberts hatched even bigger plans, announcing a full-scale mass reunion of Byrds and Buffalo Springfield members to take place on 6 July at the Los Angeles Coliseum. This was the scheme first mentioned, but never published, by Gene Clark at the reunion recording sessions back in October 1972. "It's a business move," McGuinn added. "Elliot Roberts and Bill Graham decided to promote that and get it together. They happened to have all the entertainers necessary to do that except me, and I'm willing to go along with it. If they can get the rest of the group onstage, I'll do it. It sounds like a lot of fun. It will be the Byrds, Buffalo Springfield and Crosby, Stills, Nash & Young in the chronological order they came in. I think it will all be recorded for an album."

The ambitiousness of the project was unprecedented at the time. Three of the most legendary defunct outfits of all time staging a comeback on the same night was a thought that most people could barely conceptualize. On the other hand, having reunited the original Byrds after a near seven-year separation, it seemed that the Geffen/Roberts starmakers were capable of anything. A reunion on this scale, however, was akin to changing the course of rock history. The grand design remained tantalizingly unaccomplished, and all the speculation about a live album and a full-length film of the gig were never realized. Another million-dollar goldmine was passed over. Instead, the original Byrds continued on their parallel courses, burying dreams of Sixties glory and attempting to make sense of a Seventies rock scene in which they were still regarded as important players.

In July 1974, an all-new Roger McGuinn Band was formed. They toured Europe the following month and headlined an open-air concert in London's Hyde Park. The visit coincided with the release of McGuinn's second solo album, *Peace On You* an upbeat but patchy record, which included several strong McGuinn originals ('Gate Of Horn', 'Same Old Sound' and 'The Lady'), a striking Al Kooper arrangement, 'One More Time', and some cover material which largely compromised the package. Overall, it was a pleasant but passionless follow-up to *Roger McGuinn*, with CSN&Y engineer Bill Halverson and his wife Suzanne taking over the production. Even McGuinn felt he had been usurped on his own record. "I wasn't tremendously happy working with Bill. He treated me with disrespect and didn't give me the credit for being able to sing a song from start to finish. He'd record me in segments and Frankenstein it all together. He was, in effect, the artist – and I was the paint. I didn't like that attitude. We wanted a strong professional producer. I didn't realize he was going to turn out to be such an egotistical person."

Any hopes that the Halverson sound might bring a touch of CSN&Y sales to McGuinn's catalogue were blighted when the album peaked at number 92. Still, at least it was a slight improvement in chart statistics from its superior predecessor. For the next year, McGuinn and band continued touring, amid an enveloping mood of complacency. By now, he was starting to use cocaine even more heavily and seemed poorly prepared to meet his record company commitments. With Jacques Levy living in New York and McGuinn still on the West Coast, there was little chance of taking time off to write some new material. "I was having financial difficulties and couldn't afford to get together with him," McGuinn recalls. "It was unpractical. My head was in a weird place – it was just a slump."

Without a writing partner to hand, McGuinn was forced to rely on his own muse, which completely deserted him at this point. In one of the worst decisions of his career, he elected to release an ill-conceived album, several of whose tracks were either written by his backing band or had already appeared on Sneaky Pete's record *Cold Steel*. To compound the problem, McGuinn threw in re-recordings of old material, including 'Lover Of The Bayou' and the Byrds' reunion banality, 'Born To Rock 'n' Roll'. As an exercise in artistic disregard, *Roger McGuinn And Band* took some beating. A chart position of number 165 was probably too generous.

"He owed those albums to CBS," Al Hersh reminds us. "That wasn't so bad. The bad thing was that he wasn't prepared. He had a bunch of crappy songs, some that he'd written years ago. He was starting to rehash them. Look at how many years he was at CBS. He could have done so many great things if he'd had the motivation. But he didn't. Outside of Jacques Levy he didn't really write any more. He needed somebody like that. He wasn't in charge of his destiny or creativity. The next thing should have been a step up but his attitude was like, 'Let's call Dylan and see if he's got any songs that haven't been released yet.' Dylan wasn't going to write with him. It was grasping at straws."

"It was a bad period for me," McGuinn admits. "That band wasn't right and we had an inflated impression of how good we were. I prefer to forget it. If I could erase that album, I would. I'd love to just totally wipe it out. I just couldn't see the wood for the trees at that point. I've had highs and lows in my career and that was just a low point. You *have* to give me some leeway."

His agent Ron Rainey was sympathetic, as ever. "He was going through a lot of changes at the time. Looking back, you can see that McGuinn was at the centre of what was happening from 1965 to the early Seventies. These were very intense periods and there was a lot of pressure. I think McGuinn withstood the pressure for a very long time – the pressure of being in a band, keeping a band together, making records, going on tour, having a wife – and all the things that happen when you grow from your early to late twenties.

SEPARATION

It's a personal observation, but I just think the air went out of him for a while. He was under so much pressure that finally he said, 'I want a break.' So that album manifested itself in him taking a breather. A lot of acts go through down periods. Some come out of them, and some don't."

McGuinn's downward spiral continued when his third marriage ended. He would never again sing his spousal tribute 'M' Linda', although that was no great loss to his set. Linda had met McGuinn during what was arguably the most tempestuous time of his life. But his excesses were infant innocence compared to those of her next husband, actor David Carradine. The good news for McGuinn was that his ex-wife's wealth meant that he was spared the burden of an expensive divorce settlement. This was not the best time for McGuinn. Halfway through the decade, he was spiritually, emotionally and artistically adrift, and sinking fast. As if on cue, his old mentor Bob Dylan arrived with a proposition that was to reignite McGuinn's enthusiasm and kick-start his faltering career. The two bumped into each other one evening when McGuinn was drinking at the Bottom Line in New York. "I hadn't seen him for a while," McGuinn told me. "He was so pleased to see me that he threw a table of drinks over, like in the movies!"

While patrons looked on astonished, Dylan announced with dramatic abandon: "We're going out on the road, why don't you come with us?"

McGuinn considered the suggestion for a second, then sheepishly replied: "I don't think I can because I have these gigs to do", to which Dylan retorted, "You can get rid of those!"

Dylan was correct. McGuinn not only cancelled the gigs but immediately fired his band and joined Dylan's troupe of wandering minstrels for the celebrated Rolling Thunder Revue. One week later, McGuinn was onstage at the Other End with Dylan, Ronee Blakley and David Blue. After some brief rehearsals, the Revue set out on their historic tour on 30 October, with a line-up that included Joan Baez, Joni Mitchell, Allen Ginsberg, Bobby Neuwirth, Ramblin' Jack Elliott, T-Bone Burnett, and a certain 'Kevin Kelley' on piano. McGuinn regularly featured startling versions of 'Eight Miles High' and 'Chestnut Mare', with backing from Guam: Mick

Ronson (guitar/vocals); Rob Stoner (bass/vocals); David Mansfield (steel guitar/dobro); Howie Wyeth (drums/piano) and Luther Rix (percussion). The shows were a revelation to Dylan fans and completely invigorated McGuinn, whose recent lethargy was now a bad memory. Recalling that first tour with the Revue, he says: "It was the most wonderful thing I've done since hanging out with the Beatles in the Sixties."

The Revue embarked on a second tour in the spring of 1976, by which time McGuinn had completed his fourth solo album. This time there were no mistakes. Initially, he had wanted to form a band with Guam, but Mick Ronson's manager Tony DeFries preferred his artiste to stay as a soloist. Fortunately, Ronson was free to offer his services as producer and the results were impressive. *Cardiff Rose*, released in May 1976, was McGuinn's most accomplished solo work and took full advantage of the Rolling Thunder spirit. "It was such a high place that we wanted to take as much of it into the studio as we could," McGuinn enthuses.

It was to McGuinn's lasting benefit that he was able to reconnect with writer friend Jacques Levy, who had recently received the ultimate accolade of collaborating with Bob Dylan for seven songs on *Desire*. McGuinn visited Levy's home and together they thrashed out various song scripts, scouring through books for ideas. Levy had a swing in his flat, which seemed to inspire McGuinn's imagination. "I was swinging on the rope of it like they do on a ship," he recalls, "and I said, 'Hey, Jacques, let's write a pirate song.' So we researched into pirates and got into the jargon and the whole rant and roar of it." After completing 'Jolly Roger' and others, they struck lucky with some class material provided by fellow Revue members. On his last album, McGuinn had been reduced to churning out previously issued material by his backing band. This time around, he had songs in abundance. There was 'Rock 'n' Roll Time', a collaboration with Kris Kristofferson and Bobby Neuwirth written at the time of Clarence White's death. Dylan provided a new song on a sheet of paper titled 'Up To Me'. Finally, McGuinn turned to Joni Mitchell who offered the sumptuous 'Dreamland'. Capturing the humorous esprit of the Rolling Thunder show, McGuinn even mimicked Mitchell's voice on 'Dreamland'. "I was

SEPARATION

just doing that to say, 'Hi Joni,'" he says. "It was the same with 'Up To Me', where I was imitating Dylan's voice. I use the media as a private communications device. I'd been doing that for years and both George Harrison and Dylan have done it to me."

Cardiff Rose deserved to re-establish McGuinn with a hit album, but the lack of a strong promotional single combined with his faltering sales since the Byrds' heyday blighted its progress. Remarkably, the work failed to reach the *Billboard* Top 200, alarming proof of his commercial decline in the wake of that terrible third album. "I was very disappointed," says his agent Ron Rainey. "Guys who do what we do for a living are never satisfied. I moved to California because of Roger McGuinn and I spent a lot of time with him in his house, and we hung out together. I took what I did for Roger very personally. The Rolling Thunder was one of the most exciting things happening at the time. Everybody had worked hard. We put these solo tours together and he'd go out and was a real soldier. At that time executives were moving around at CBS, so maybe some of the consistency wasn't there from days past." Even taking these factors into account, the failure of *Cardiff Rose* was a terrible blow to morale and a major setback for McGuinn, who knew he was unlikely to complete a better album in the near future.

Following the Rolling Thunder outings, McGuinn continued touring with a new group, appropriately named Thunderbyrd. They were reasonably received and worked well as a live act but problems arose towards the end of the year when they entered the studio with producer Don DeVito. "It was painfully obvious that it wasn't going to be a good recording band," McGuinn says. "So I fired them. It sounds very cold, but I fired them and got new guys."

The 'new guys' were a more cohesive bunch, comprising talented guitarist Rick Vito, drummer Greg Thomas and British bassist Charlie Harrison. With DeVito satisfied, they completed what sounded like a rushed album, *Thunderbyrd*, which relied heavily on some cover versions borrowed from artistes as diverse as Peter Frampton, George Jones and Tom Petty. After the non-existent chart performance of *Cardiff Rose*, McGuinn was understandably willing to change tack and seek outside help. "We asked around Hollywood for music publishers to give us commercial material. I had this feeling that it would be nice to have a hit single after all these years. So they submitted 'All Night Long' and 'American Girl'. It was a business thing."

McGuinn's expedient logic made some sense but, the Petty song excepted, he seemed to have little empathy with the remaining material which sounded terribly workmanlike. Apart from another Dylan rarity 'Golden Loom', and the impressively odd 'Russian Hill', the album lacked imagination and failed to improve McGuinn's recent sales record. He could boast a very strong live band with a gutsy feel but in the studio the old magic was only fleetingly observed. With two consecutive records failing to reach the US Top 200, McGuinn's career was coasting towards the rocks.

Psychologically, McGuinn was now in a strange place. The Rolling Thunder interlude had revitalized him momentarily, but he was still in denial and uncertain about the future. Drinking heavily, he resembled the quintessential Seventies rock star, and was also involved in a new relationship with the young actress Season Hubley. In a bizarre coincidence, Hubley had previously been engaged to David Carradine, who was now dating, and would later marry, Roger's ex-wife, Linda. The mid-Seventies was a bewildering and complacent place for McGuinn. There was a directionless quality to his career trajectory and the cross-collateral agreement he had with CBS meant that he was still paying back money for the extravagances of *Byrdmaniax* without the prospect of a major selling solo album to wipe out the historic debt. Bass player Gary Marker, who was dating Walter Cronkite's daughter Kathy at the time, went on a double date with Roger and Season. He had known McGuinn vaguely since recording at CBS Studios with the Rising Sons in 1965 and was bold enough to still call him 'Jim'. That night they went to a club in Studio City to see the jazz fusion guitarist Al Di Meola, who had recently left Chuck Corea's band Return To Forever. Marker was surprised at how insecure the former Byrd had become during this uncertain time. "Jim's sitting there watching Al Di Meola all over the finger-board and he's saying, 'I could do that . . . I could do that.' Finally, I said, 'McGuinn, you're already a legend, you don't have to worry about besting anybody.' He said, 'Oh man, I keep forgetting.'"

SEPARATION

David Crosby's fortunes during these interim years were decidedly healthier, but he too had his darker moments. After the Byrds' reunion, he suffered a similarly depressing year to McGuinn, with death and uncertainty never far away. Still affected by the tragic demise of his partner Christine Gail Hinton, he now watched his mother suffering a slow and painful death from cancer. Other CSN&Y-related deaths later that year included Danny Whitten and Bruce Berry, both victims of heroin abuse. Neil Young's *Time Fades Away* tour proved the first stage of a painful exorcism for Crosby. He and Nash had responded to the Canadian's call when his dispiriting tour of ice hockey and baseball arenas hit problems. "Neil didn't really *need* our help," Crosby stresses, " but he did call us and asked us to come, very specifically. He said it wasn't going well . . . There was another reason why I was out there. My mother was in hospital dying of cancer. I needed the music. It was the only thing to hang on to when Christine died and it was the only thing to hang on to when my mother died. That's why I wanted to be there."

Crosby brought some much-needed human emotion to these shows, never more so than in his rallying cries at the end of the climactic 'Last Dance' which echoed those chilling yowls of pain and exasperation previously heard during the coda of CSN&Y's bitter anthem 'Ohio' back in 1970. He seemed to draw cathartic strength from the audience and learned to forget his pain onstage. In humorous moments, he teased them about their love of old songs and even offered a spontaneous few lines from 'Mr Tambourine Man' for comic effect. Not that it was all good vibes. The acerbic Crosby, so familiar to McGuinn from the final days of the Byrds, rose from the ashes to engage in some psychic combat with Young's prickly mentor, Jack Nitszche. "He's a very bad person," Crosby told me with visible indignation. "When he gets whacko he does bad stuff. Lots of bad stuff. He tries to pick fights with people. He tried to pick one with me. I told him to stay out of my way or I'd take his head off his shoulders, and I meant it."

Crosby and Nash's appearances with Young inevitably prompted rumours of a full-scale CSN&Y reunion. During the summer of 1973, the foursome attempted a new album, tentatively titled

Human Highway. Initially, Young seemed enthused and called in producer/engineer Elliot Mazer, who had previously worked on his biggest-selling album, *Harvest.* "I saw nothing but difficulty," Mazer recalls. After a promising start, the project foundered, a victim of fatal indecision and petty bickering. "It would have been the best CSN&Y album," Crosby told me in a tone of profound regret at all that had been squandered.

Another year passed before the million dollar quartet tried again. This time, they decided to tour rather than record and re-established their standing with a season of outdoor stadium concerts, which were breathtaking in their scope, ambition and sense of event. With sets in excess of three-and-a-half hours, CSN&Y offered some of the greatest live shows of the decade. In different circumstances, the tour might simply have been a gratifying exercise in nostalgia, a chance for audiences to experience their own mini-Woodstocks without the mud. Fortunately, CSN&Y were still extremely productive at this point and the new material they offered sounded impressive. More importantly, history was on their side. During that eventful summer, it seemed as though the ghosts of Sixties' idealism had returned alongside CSN&Y to exact retribution on this new age. When their former nemesis, President Richard Nixon, was forced from office midway through the tour, it must have seemed as if some deific scriptwriter was rewriting their life story. Topical tunes from earlier times like 'Ohio' and 'Chicago' suddenly burned anew while Crosby's politically charged 'Long Time Gone' and 'Almost Cut My Hair' provided fresh passion, devoid of any nostalgic association with past conflicts. There was even a sprinkling of stand-up comedy with Crosby lampooning Nixon's selective memory in a sketch punctuated by the words "I can't recall . . . ". In Boston, Crosby announced, deadpan: "I feel like singing the 'Star Spangled Banner' in honour of how well the Constitution's working." His political sarcasm was eclipsed by the quality of his musicianship and impressive use of harmony. Even Crosby's sometimes adversarial colleague Stephen Stills went out of his way to offer praise. "David is an incredible musician. He's to the point now where he never makes mistakes."

The CSN&Y extravaganza culminated in a remarkable day at

Wembley Stadium on 14 September 1974 which was billed as 'the concert of the century'. Among the support acts were the Band and Joni Mitchell. As Crosby observes with typical frankness: "In 1974, we were probably the biggest group in the world. Stephen liked that. It was enormously satisfying for him to have the Beach Boys, Santana, the Band and Joni Mitchell open for us. That was quite something."

Although cynics could point to the gross receipts as evidence of CSN&Y's moneymaking motivation, the quartet continued to tread an admirably fine line between aestheticism and avarice. They could easily have issued a multimillion selling live album or even a film of the tour, but stubbornly resisted the temptation. Their enduring belief in musical perfection remained a constant. The much anticipated studio album and follow-up to *Déjà Vu* also never happened as they drifted off into various solo and related projects. It was a remarkable decision. Having done all the hard work of touring for months they spurned the chance to transform that live experience into a studio setting. There was one final attempt, but it proved short-lived. "Neil went out of the room and never came back!" Crosby concludes.

At least the exposure lingered long enough to benefit Crosby, whose next record *Wind On The Water*, a second collaboration with Nash, contained some of his best songs, including the autobiographical 'Carry Me' and 'Homeward Through The Haze'. The work culminated in the mini-suite 'To The Last Whale' for which Crosby contributed the choral 'Critical Mass', another monastic mantra which he once described as the 'purest' piece of music he had ever recorded. The US Top 10 album even outsold and outcharted contemporaneous solo efforts by Young and Stills, demonstrating the renewed vitality of Crosby & Nash as a partnership. Crosby continued in exuberant form, providing harmony on albums by various friends, including Joni Mitchell, James Taylor, Dave Mason and Art Garfunkel. There was also *Seastones*, a collaboration with Phil Lesh and Ned Lagin on which he was able to display his more experimental side. "Listen to *Seastones*," he implores. "That's me singing some experimental stuff – very advanced cuckoo music. A lot of what I do is sub-speech, proto-speech, talk that makes you feel as if you're hearing something you understand, but you can't quite catch the words. In the middle is Phil Lesh playing a synthesizer by his bass, and Jerry Garcia playing his guitar through every tone modifier in existence. It made for an astounding thing. The concert we did took you outwards to Mars – edge city."

Like McGuinn with the Byrds, Crosby was frequently measured against his achievements as part of CSN&Y and the media still badgered him about 'reunion' plans. By 1976, the Holy Grail search for the next CSN&Y album had taken another fanciful turn. For several weeks, it seemed that they would complete a record but instead the venture reverted into an anticlimactic Stills/Young collaboration. Bitterness and acrimony followed, with Crosby & Nash accusing their partners of sabotaging the CSN&Y dream for their own selfish ends. Crosby sounded deflated, while the normally diplomatic Nash exploded with anger after reading an interview with Stills in which he joked about not wanting to stick his feet "in the meat grinder again". When another quote appeared suggesting that Crosby & Nash weren't hungry enough, Nash turned on Stills in devastating fashion. "I think it's his cock he keeps putting in the meat grinder. Stephen's fucking with great music, and that's what both of them have been doing for three years. I'm a fool and I'll put my personal things aside . . . But how many times can you keep going up and saying, 'OK, I'll stand here while you hit me again – just don't hit me as hard as you did the last time' . . . How can anybody say we weren't hungry enough? That's crazy, man . . . CSN&Y is, to me, an incredibly special thing that we should not fuck around with. We have no right to as individuals . . . They're panicking, man. I say, if you're scared shitless, and you think your career is going downhill, then to get it back you should make a great CSN&Y album. Right? Then what happened? You tell me, because David and I have no axes to grind. I see Stephen's career going downhill and I see Neil's career going downhill . . . They're desperate and I was saying, 'Don't be desperate. We can have it all. Me and David can have albums, and you and Stephen can have albums and CSN&Y can have albums.'"

Surprisingly, David and Graham again outsold their much-publicized partners with *Whistling Down The Wire*, a pleasant but

SEPARATION

less arresting record with subtler glimpses of Crosby's usual brilliance, most notably on the CSN&Y career commentary 'Taken At All'. Just as it seemed as though further get-togethers were out of the question, Stills swallowed his pride and attempted to make his peace with Crosby & Nash. Abandoned by Young in mid-tour, he was uncertain about his future, vulnerable and keen to reconnect. It cannot have been easy. Crosby was well capable of maintaining a grudge for years, as his interactions with Dickson, Melcher, McGuinn and others ably demonstrated. His sensitivity and susceptibility to profound hurt ran deep, while his defensive self-conviction meant that it was never easy to admit his own shortcomings when cornered. He never found it easy to apologize. But such was his belief in the importance of his music, and in those talented enough to share his vision, that contrition and forgiveness could be employed as painful panaceas. In some ways it was easier to deal with Stills, a passionate man with his heart on his sleeve, than it was to communicate with the more withdrawn figure of McGuinn, who seldom acknowledged feelings of hurt or betrayal. When Stills turned up backstage to confront Crosby & Nash after a show at the Greek Theatre, he was immediately welcomed back into the fold. Crosby's reaction provided a revealing insight into the dynamics of their relationship, which was based on a fiery emotion that McGuinn could never display. Stills was not renowned for his humility, but Crosby understood his pain.

"Well, what would *you* do?" Crosby asks rhetorically. "You want to stand there with a wall in front of you . . . discard all he wrote, be nice and aloof and watch the guy break? The four of us have faced a lot of people, and played an enormous amount of music together, and even times when we're very angry at each other, if somebody went to jump Stephen, I'd take their head off. If he came to me in the middle of the night and said he needed help, 'let me in', my door is always open to him. You don't really love somebody, ever, and then shut if off like a faucet, whether you can stand to be with them for an hour or not. You just don't. When you see them, that's called up in you, and you can't help but want to open to them if there's been that much, and there *has* been that much." By the end of 1976 CS&N, the magic threesome, were working together without Young, and about to take up where their career had first started eight years before.

Chris Hillman also encountered contrasting fortunes between 1973–76. He had joined the Byrds' reunion at the commercial peak of his career with Manassas, whose concerts allowed him to reach back to both the Byrds and the Burritos for favourite material. Inspired by Stills, he had even co-written two of the group's best songs, 'Both Of Us (Bound To Lose)' and 'It Doesn't Matter'. Following up that great double album proved more difficult than anticipated. For *Down The Road*, Hillman contributed 'Lies' and co-wrote the excellent 'So Many Times', but the album proved anticlimactic. Although Manassas undertook another tour, the septet lost its focus during 1973. Stills was increasingly distracted by the prospect of a glorious reunion with his superstar bandmates. As Hillman succinctly noted: "It got to the point where Stephen went with CSN&Y to do a tour and I got an offer for SHF, and that was the end of Manassas."

The Souther, Hillman, Furay Band was one of those projects that looked fascinating on paper, but failed to fulfil its potential. In many respects, it was David Geffen's supergroup by numbers – a boardroom plan to combine the talents of three underachievers and secure the gold albums that had been missing from the careers of the Flying Burrito Brothers and Poco. The trio's eponymous debut album was a slick affair, which featured a couple of decent collaborations between Hillman and drummer Len Fagen ('Heavenly Fire' and 'Rise And Fall'). All too often though, the material was bland, the personalities mismatched, and the group concept virtually non-existent. After a dreadful second album, *Trouble In Paradise*, everyone knew the project was doomed. "I don't know why it didn't work," a puzzled Hillman told me. "It was like three mini solo albums and, of course, we never wrote songs together. There were personality clashes between John David Souther and Richie Furay at times. It had all the ingredients but, once again, like the Byrds' reunion album, we should have taken three months to write and get to know each other. Then we should have put the band together."

After the disbandment of SHF in March 1975, Hillman went on

the road backed by several members of the newly-formed Firefall, playing under the guise of the Chris Hillman Band. For a time, Hillman considered forming a group with Rick Roberts, but instead took advantage of his recent high profile by recording solo. *Slippin' Away* was an album typical of its time – accomplished, uplifting, admirable in parts, but lacking the imagination and bite to achieve classic status. Chris provided some strong self-penned songs, all well played, some commendable, but this was a major label release and the stakes were high. Competing with the leading singer-songwriters of the era, whose ranks included several Byrds' alumni, was never going to be easy. Hillman still looked back enviously at the first Flying Burrito Brothers album when, amid the turmoil of marital discord, he and Gram had both composed their best work.

By 1977, Hillman had hired a touring band and his writing muse was momentarily fired by another divorce. Sessions for his next album *Clear Sailin'* included the startling 'Rollin' And Tumblin'' and Danny O'Keefe's 'Quits', songs which brought a new strength to his repertoire. Though painful, these compositions were sung with true emotion and conveyed Hillman's hurt in a way that he had seldom managed before on vinyl. Despite some highly professional musical backing, Hillman knew that he could not sustain a career as a soloist. As both a vocalist and a composer, he had always been at his most impressive working as the classic right-hand man, bringing out the best in McGuinn, Stills and Parsons. He still dreamed of teaming up again with Doug Dillard, Herb Pedersen, Byron Berline and other country friends for a down-home bluegrass album. In his more morose moments, he even considered winding down his career. "I feel I don't want to go on the road any more," he told me in 1977. "I reckon after a year or two, I'll do something else – probably producing. I've had some offers to produce and I'd prefer to take the last 12–13 years' experience and put it to use by helping new artists or guiding them . . . I've been successful in everything I've done. I'm not the richest guy in the world, but I'm not starving. It's been fun and I've learned a lot – and I'm still learning."

While Hillman was contemplating early retirement, Gene Clark had been left with the disappointment of a career that had left him stranded on the cult fringes. His impressive showing on the Byrds' reunion album had encouraged David Geffen to sign him to Asylum as a solo act. His appointed producer was the effusive Thomas Jefferson Kaye, a free-spirited soul mate whose fearless championing and panoramic vision took Clark to even greater artistic heights. With a budget bursting at the seams, they completed the stupendous *No Other*, one of the most striking and original albums of this or any other era. The album transcended even Clark's most ambitious work, fusing gospel, choral and country in a dazzling array of lyrical images, reinforced by an expansive production that was positively cinematic. *No Other* was Clark's solo *Sgt Pepper's*, a work that should have elevated him to auteur status among the singer-songwriters of his era. Its lyrical landscape was equally extravagant, from the epic 'Chimes Of Freedom'-inspired 'Strength Of Strings' to the abstract narrative mystery of 'From A Silver Phial' and the soaring, spiritually uplifting finale, 'Lady Of The North'. For many, myself included, *No Other* remains one of the most powerfully original albums of all time and a fully realized testament to the immense potential that Clark had shown during his spell in the Byrds. A full and proper analysis of the album is outside the limited scope of this group-related volume, but the full implications of the work, including a track by track breakdown, as well as details about its origins and impact, will be discussed in the lengthy Gene Clark saga included in Volume 2 of this study.

The fate of *No Other* was a sad story and the subject of much frustration at the time. It was largely ignored by record buyers. Despite a decent promotional budget, it failed miserably in the charts, much to Geffen's chagrin and Clark's disappointment. "I thought it was a real achievement," Gene told me in 1977, "and Tommy [Kaye] felt the same. We knew we had done something special but the reaction was very deflating and puzzling. Some critics didn't get it and complained that it was 'over-produced', whatever that means. It didn't sell that well either, and I'm not entirely sure why. I know you thought it was a classic and a great album and more people seem to be appreciating it now than when it was released. Maybe I can build on that for the future."

SEPARATION

As before, Clark had contributed to the record's failure by neglecting to undertake extensive promotion when first asked. Here was an album that needed to be coaxed into the marketplace, but Clark seemed content to allow the disc to succeed on its own merits without a major push. Promotional interviews at the time were conspicuously absent. Subsequently there was a falling out with Geffen which only made matters worse. In desperation rather than hope, Clark undertook a low-key tour appearing at small venues across America with a backing group, the Silverados, but it proved difficult to perform the new record in concert. Ultimately, *No Other* became a word of mouth classic among rock critics, growing in reputation with each passing year, yet still selling extremely poorly.

By 1975, Clark had disappeared to the cult fringes of American rock. He would occasionally pop up playing small gigs across the States, most of which were never reviewed. Ignored by the rock press and without a record contract, his activities were a mystery to those who did not have a frequent and healthy correspondence with fellow aficionados. The extent of his retreat from the rock mainstream was made explicit when reports filtered through that he had formed a new band, Gene Clark And the Mendocino Rhythm Section. Their very name testified to a wilful parochiality. Even the venues at which they appeared, such as 'Joe's Diner', suggested that Clark had temporarily abandoned the Hollywood dream.

In truth, Clark was still confused and deflated after *No Other*. Having produced an album of such scope and ambition, it was difficult to decide which avenue to pursue in the future. Friends told him that he had got "too far out" with that album and needed something more commercial to secure radio play. With producer Thomas Jefferson Kaye again at the helm, Clark completed a more accessible work and took the tapes to Al Coury at RSO Records, who duly offered a deal. *Two Sides To Every Story*, released in 1977, was a more cautious record, lacking the no-holds-barred ambition of *No Other* in favour of a more restrained approach, which leaned more heavily on his country roots. It had some striking songs, notably 'Sister Moon' and 'Past Addresses', but lacked the depth and imagination of either *No Other* or *White Light* and, worst of all, did not sell significantly more copies. Clark spoke of the need to record more commercial material to finance his more abstract work. "I had to find a direction, a form of saying what I had to say in a way that attracted people so that they might notice it, appreciate it, revere it. And *buy* it." Sadly, such compromises proved largely ineffectual. Although he was still a major label artiste, Clark's career was at a crossroads and his future direction seemed beyond prediction.

Surprisingly, the Byrd whose career seemed on the firmest foundations during the mid-to-late Seventies was Michael Clarke. Settled in Hawaii, he had married the wealthy Robin King, who gave birth to their son, Zachary, on 17 July 1973. At the time, there was still desultory talk about another Byrds' reunion, but as the months passed that was soon forgotten. Clarke was unfazed and seemed to be enjoying life. When friends enquired about his plans, he simply said he was now a father in semi-retirement. Amazingly, he had only just celebrated his 27th birthday. As a sideline, he sold exotic plants and at one point performed in an LA based R&B band, the Dependables, an accomplished combination of super session players and touring musicians whose R&B style perfectly suited the drummer's tastes. Always optimistic, Clarke could afford to let fame chase him, rather than vice versa.

Another chance for glory beckoned when fellow ex-Burrito Rick Roberts invited Clarke to relocate to Boulder, Colorado. Rapidly emerging as the new capital of country rock, Boulder was attracting a wealth of Los Angelinos in search of clean mountain air, colourful scenery, empathetic musicians and a homely base in which they could write songs, plot expansive tours and record demos at studios like Mountain Ears or the more celebrated Caribou Ranch. Among the migrants was Stephen Stills, who had recently released a tribute to the state titled 'Colorado'. Roberts had already issued a classic composition of the same title while working with Hillman in the Flying Burrito Brothers. Those songs served as an advertising slogan for Boulder and, hearing of the other players in town, the nomadic Clarke required no persuading to move his family there. Mark Adzick, who co-owned Mountain Ears, was amazed by this sudden influx. "There was a clique of musicians, managers, producers and songwriters who were trying to build Boulder into a

SEPARATION

western Nashville scene. It became a popular place to come. Richie Furay, Chris Hillman, Stephen Stills – I could give you a list – everybody was hanging out there. Some of them were still living in LA but ended up getting houses in the mountains. It was remarkable. If they had contracts which required them to go to Miami, we could still do reference tapes for them."

Rick Roberts carefully handpicked his team who were soon rehearsing. Gigging experience came courtesy of Chris Hillman, who offered the band's nucleus the opportunity to back him on tour. One member who was conspicuously absent from these shows was Hillman's former Byrds' colleague. "I didn't use Mike Clarke in my band because I love him too much," Hillman told me shortly afterwards. "When Michael and I work together, we tend to fight musically. I talked to him and said I'd prefer to keep our friendship intact – it's worth more than our working together and fighting. And this does happen."

With Hillman's help, the new band, including Clarke, recorded some demos and secured a deal with Atlantic Records on 5 August 1975. Roberts named them Firefall, evidently inspired by a fireworks display he had witnessed at Yosemite National Park. The group's eponymous 1976 debut album reached the US Top 30, quickly achieving gold status, while an accompanying single, 'You Are The Woman', climbed into the US Top 10. Soon, they were touring alongside some of the best-selling acts of the era, including the Doobie Brothers and Fleetwood Mac. In effect, the band achieved the kind of mainstream success that David Geffen had envisaged for Souther, Hillman, Furay. Boulder-based producer Jim Mason worked on their second album, *Luna Sea*, another massive seller that spawned a second US Top 10 single, 'Just Remember I Love You'. Further hit singles and albums followed as Clarke unexpectedly found himself earning good money and playing sizeable venues. After the Byrds, Dillard & Clark and the Burritos, he was a chart regular with an impressive CV.

Firefall's David Muse appreciated and understood his importance to the band. "*Rolling Stone* once called him the king of 4/4 and that's exactly what I thought. He *was* the king of 4/4. He was a basic drummer but none of us in Firefall were exactly masters of what we were doing but we all brought something special to it and I felt the same way about Michael and his drumming. A lot of the time he played simple things but that was all that was needed. Many drummers overplay and it just doesn't work . . . I always relate Michael to Ringo Starr. If you look back to the Beatles, he was never considered a great drummer and there was a lot of stuff going down between his bandmates, but I know a lot of drummers consider Ringo their idol. They idolize the guy for what he did. In pop and rock music, it's not exactly about having the best players, it's about having somebody that fits in. And Michael fitted in perfectly for what we were doing."

Even David Crosby was impressed by Clarke's tenacity during this period. "He got better and better after he left the Byrds," he told me. "He's a groove drummer, not a flash drummer. He doesn't play a bunch of hot licks, but he can play a groove quite well. I'm glad he's in Firefall – he deserves it."

CHAPTER THIRTY-NINE

Interlude – Three Byrds Land In London

WITH the Byrds scattered and firmly entrenched in their own individual careers, the possibility of a second reunion seemed out of the question. It was at this point that a happy coincidence brought back faith to many disillusioned hearts. Three original ex-Byrds, McGuinn, Hillman and Clark, were lined up for a tour of Europe in April/May 1977, with each member fronting his own group. It was an ingenious idea on the part of the promoter to present the three ex-Byrds on one show especially at a time when British pop music was entering its most revolutionary period since the early Sixties. Punk was the new rage with the Sex Pistols branded as the scourge of the nation. Since their shocking four-letter word outburst on tea-time television, the media had documented their every outrage, real or imagined, in increasingly garish headlines. With the Queen's Jubilee fast approaching and the single 'God Save The Queen' readied for release on Virgin, having been banned by Gene Clark's former label A&M, punk was at its most potent.

McGuinn, Hillman and Clark were oblivious to such matters as they began their own controversial tour. "I'm not really up to date on the British scene or its politics," Clark told me. "Mendocino, where I live most of the time, is pretty isolated in that sense and even in LA we're caught up in what's happening there now. It was different a few years ago when we were all caught up with the British Invasion. I'm sure it's the same for all of us. It's been so long since I was in England." Warming to the apolitical theme, Clark employed the David Crosby trick of focusing on the music as an end in itself and a force for good. "Music is more important to the world than any form of politics. It's more powerful and international. It transcends language. It can communicate its message emotionally. The language barrier is broken by that emotion contained in music. You can communicate a positive, direct feeling, or offer consolation for a broken heart . . . it breaks all kinds of racial and political barriers. Those distinctions become meaningless. That is why people so revere musical communication. It embraces so much. Its power is immense."

It was soon clear to backstage observers that personal politics would play a more significant part in determining the success or otherwise of the tour. "We had our own people to deal with," says Thunderbyrd's drummer Greg Thomas. "There was Chris Hillman and his ego and Gene Clark and his insanity. It was the clash of the ego tour. They were not speaking to each other. Everybody was putting each other's music down. Roger was the headliner and each one wanted to be the best band."

Despite the competitive spirit, there was some rapport between the musicians in the various camps. Prior to their opening show in Dublin, Clark's drummer Andy Kandanes remembers a lively discussion with Hillman, centring on the pharmaceutical benefits of a certain cough mixture. Hillman was something of an expert on the subject, having witnessed Michael Clarke over-indulge on the magic medicine during the Byrds' 1965 tour, and later in the Burritos. "Oh that stuff's great," someone added, "it's 15 per cent morphine and 10 per cent opium". Kandanes was amazed to discover that it was freely available over the counter in Ireland and was duly despatched to pick up a batch. "I went down to this small pharmacy and there was this little Irish guy who looked about 200 years old. I asked him for some and he came back with a bottle. I said, 'No, I need a case. There are three bands and we all have stomach problems!' He came back and he's blowing dust off this case which must have been sitting there for 50 years." Kandanes returned and distributed the medicine to those in need. Thereafter, the Irish ritual of afternoon tea took on a new mood as Kandanes and his friends added droplets of the mixture to spice up their beverages.

INTERLUDE — THREE BYRDS LAND IN LONDON

The Dublin show was plagued by sound problems but the audience seemed happily distracted by the presence of three Byrds on the bill, an occurrence still seen as a minor miracle. Following the show, a number of the players went back to their hotel, while others found an after hours' club where they drank late into the night. The thrill-seeking Greg Thomas almost sabotaged the schedule when he went missing. Arriving back at their hotel, he had been distracted by the lascivious presence of several sexy strumpets. "There was this well-dressed guy who weighed about 300 lb and he had all these women with him. I thought it would be a good idea to have one. Well, she took me home, and I must have had a blackout. I remember sleeping with her and her girlfriend, then getting up in the morning, not being able to find my shoes and not knowing where I was. I couldn't even remember the directions to find the hotel. I ended up running down the street, just as the bus was leaving. They thought I was lost in action and were going to leave me there. Everyone was saying, 'We thought you were dead.'"

Almost from the outset, it seemed that the visit was cursed with bad luck. The second date, slated for Birmingham on 29 April, was cancelled due to a series of delays caused by zealous customs officials. When McGuinn heard that their instruments had not arrived in time, he was noticeably upset. The troubled tour continued and, despite the dramatic upsurge of punk that summer, media interest remained surprisingly strong. All the music weeklies covered the 'Byrds' event with sizeable spreads. Yet there were also signs of ambivalence, symbolic of a time when many critics felt they should be concentrating on the future, not the past. *Zigzag* magazine, the most Byrds' friendly publication on the planet, had intended to feature the trio on its front cover, complete with in-depth interviews. At the eleventh hour, there was a change of heart and Johnny Rotten was elevated to cover star status at the trio's expense.

In some respects, touring the UK in the summer of 1977 was almost as challenging for the visiting Americans as the infamous 1965 trip had been for the original Byrds. They were interlopers arriving at a time of great change in the music and cultural landscape, seemingly oblivious to the revolution in their midst. In different circumstances, they might have been vilified, but the Sex Pistols were still regarded as a sideshow by the general public and the visiting Americans at least had strength in numbers and a strong curiousity value. In person, the ex-Byrds were a contrasting bunch, far removed from the contemporaneous caricature of laid-back hippies. On the contrary, they were much too spirited and independent of mind for the imagined camaraderie associated with sunny California. McGuinn seemed more aggressive than most imagined and onstage he was belting out a stunning song about a psychopathic killer called 'Shoot 'Em', which would not have sounded out of place in a punk's repertoire. Clark's band were rough and untutored, befitting an outfit seemingly more at home in a Mendocino bar than a concert hall. "I liked that road crazy spirit we had back in those days," says bassist Peter Oliva. "That's what Geno wanted. When you were with us in Europe, we were like the Rolling Stones or something."

Although Hillman's band was the complete opposite – the embodiment of precision and professionalism – he seemed as wired and spiky as McGuinn when roused. Beatific calm was certainly not their style then. Clark, meanwhile, was drinking heavily, egged on by his alcohol-loving partner Thomas Jefferson Kaye. As Hillman later admitted: "It was a very rough period for Roger, Gene and I and a lot of other people in music that came from the Sixties . . . the drug abuse was monumental. There was no crack cocaine or any of that around but there was the regular cocaine and alcohol."

Both substances were in evidence at a huge Mayfair party thrown by RSO, CBS and Warner Brothers to celebrate the tripartite tour. McGuinn, wide-eyed with frizzled hair and dark suit, had that arrogant rock star attitude that only coke can bring to the brain. At least he was generous with his stash – an increasing rarity in the latter part of the Seventies – and the drug clearly released his inhibitions as well as providing a messianic confidence. For the most part he played the role of the cocky visiting American rock god, occasionally veering into surliness.

Clark seemed a more complex creature, nervy, dependent and unpredictable. One reviewer described him as "listless, the epitome of the slightly stumbling overweight bearded hippie who'd drank

INTERLUDE — THREE BYRDS LAND IN LONDON

and smoked too much." It was a painful but acute observation of a man still coming to terms with the tumultuous changes of recent years. Apart from his ever shifting recording status, he had recently been through a painful divorce and surrendered custody of his two children, Kelly and Kai. It was mainly the solicitous presence of his companion, Terri Messina, and the ever watchful Thomas Jefferson Kaye, that kept him grounded. Judging from the amount of coffee he was consuming, the sheer willpower expended in resisting alcohol for elongated periods must have been like slow torture. At the party he let himself go, setting up a table which held something like a dozen bottles of wine and champagne which he sampled in copious quantities. By the end of the evening he was everyone's favourite drunk.

Hillman preferred to maintain an unhealthy distance from his peers. Whatever personal demons he was battling took place in the privacy of his own room. He was brisk, professional and curt with a self-deprecating wit that provided good copy without ever lapsing into sentimentality or overstatement. Like Clark he was recently divorced, but greeted his situation with a caustic humour, cynically observing that such emotional upheavals can always provide a couple of decent songs for a new album. Although outwardly the most together person on the tour, it was difficult to avoid the conclusion that something intense was burning inside his troubled soul. His absences from the central action spoke volumes.

The performances of all three acts were most impressive and extremely good value for money. Clark's KC Southern Band divided critical opinion with their short but provocative set. Many of their songs had a harsh, metallic edge, with a rough R&B groove. Each night, they sounded better and the spontaneity and verve in their performances were unmistakable. "Tommy Kaye was the smart New York guy who knew what was going on and he was a rocker too," recalls Peter Oliva. "He'd crank his guitar right up and that's what gave us that crunchy sound, 'crankah, crankah'." There were a handful of new compositions on display, with the excellent 'Last Of The Blue Diamond Miners' gaining particular attention from the Clark cognoscenti.

By contrast, the Chris Hillman Band sounded perfectly rehearsed, with a solid repertoire mixing Burritos and Manassas songs alongside a strong selection from the new album *Clear Sailin'*. Their set was proof positive of Hillman's continued and much-admired professionalism. McGuinn's Thunderbyrd were also a well-drilled live band, adept at mingling old and new tunes. He sounded at his best on the menacing 'Lover Of The Bayou' and snarling 'Shoot 'Em', which were no doubt given an additional surly bite thanks to his cocaine consumption.

From the start of the tour there was much speculation about a possible reunion onstage. They had resisted such urgings at their first date in Dublin but Hillman hinted that a grand finale might occur later in London. What he failed to reveal, or appeared to have forgotten, was that all three groups were contractually bound to provide a mini-Byrds' reunion at the close of each show. Pressed about the possibility of recording another album as the Byrds, he was surprisingly optimistic. "I'd love to do it," he told me. "I'd like to leave a better taste in everyone's mouth. People were expecting a good album and they didn't get it. People, to this day, will accuse us of doing it for the money, but we didn't make a dime! It was a bad album and it didn't sell. The contractual difficulties involved in getting us together are easy to fix. The problem is to co-ordinate it with each guy, which is something you have to set up six months in advance. The hardest part is getting everyone to agree to it and commit themselves. I've said it before and I'll repeat it now: 'I want to do it again!' I know David and Roger do too."

Gene Clark was equally upbeat that same week and confided, "It could be done, but it has to be handled very gently, very carefully, and in such a way that everyone is still able to carry on their own careers. I know that Chris and Roger and I wouldn't want to split up our current bands and stop our individual careers just because we were doing a Byrds thing, but, if we handled it right, and took the right time, there's no reason why the Byrds shouldn't perform together, and even record something too."

The prospects of such a reunion seemed greatly enhanced on the evening of 30 April at London's Hammersmith Odeon. At the close of Thunderbyrd's set, McGuinn casually announced, "I'd like to ask a couple of buddies of mine to come up here", and out of the

INTERLUDE — THREE BYRDS LAND IN LONDON

wings wandered Chris and Gene, their heads wrapped in tea towels in an hilarious parody of the Rolling Thunder Revue. The trio burst into an impromptu version of 'So You Want To Be A Rock 'n' Roll Star', much to the delight of the previously passive spectators, many of whom rushed to the stage in a desperate attempt to be part of this historic reunion. 'Feel A Whole Lot Better' followed, with Clark beckoning the audience forward and encouraging them to clap and dance. Hillman abandoned his rhythm guitar and switched to his more familiar role as bassist as they moved into 'Mr Tambourine Man'. The evening ended with a spectacular version of 'Eight Miles High', which left the audience gasping. The voices were a little flat, but there was a detectable magic in the strange combination of McGuinn's and Clark's vocals. Twelve years on from their first performance in London, they had turned back the clock and transported many of us into an era that had seemed lost in time.

What began as a mini-Byrds reunion gradually altered into a microcosm of the Byrds' history, complete with personality clashes and a premature dissolution. After that opening gig in London, the trio failed to reunite again, and the following evening I distinctly remember McGuinn beginning 'So You Want To Be A Rock 'n' Roll Star' with the words, "Is Chris there?", only to be greeted by the reply from backstage, "No, he's gone." The following evening, McGuinn gave me his version of events: "It was Gene's paranoia. He left and Chris left too. Gene got a little drunk and I guess he didn't want to stick around and stay sober and wait in the wings and watch Chris' set and my set in frustration."

The three groups performed separately at the next two gigs, Manchester and Leeds, and there was no further talk of surprise guest appearances, despite the small print in their respective contracts. "They didn't take the Byrds segment too seriously," their UK agent told me. "Clark was drunk a lot of the time and McGuinn was high on coke. There was conflict between McGuinn and Hillman. They didn't speak to each other at all. I don't know why. And Hillman's manager Richard Halem resented the fact that we'd paid McGuinn a certain amount of money upfront."

In spite of the underlying tensions, the three ex-Byrds maintained their cool and agreed to undertake a select number of interviews for the original edition of my first book, *Timeless Flight*. Relaxing at a hotel in Leeds, McGuinn ordered some whiskies and agreed to break his silence and talk frankly about his feelings on the Byrds, and particularly David Crosby. As the drinks arrived, the waiter politely asked McGuinn, "Would you like some female company?", a suggestion that appeared to excite Greg Thomas, who urged him to say, 'Yes!' McGuinn brushed aside the offer, and in a world-weary drawl worthy of Dylan, exclaimed: "Man, hookers depress me."

Four years on from the release of the Byrds' reunion album, McGuinn was free from the dictates of diplomacy and ready to tell the real story of the political infighting that compromised the project. Leaning back, he told me: "My real feelings on the matter are that Crosby was trying to get back at me for firing him. Because he had David Geffen, Elliot Roberts and the financial power of Asylum, he had more say in the matter than he ever used to, and that's why Gene did more vocals than he normally would have. Crosby was calling the shots. It was Crosby's *coup d'état*. He was being leader of the group. I think Crosby wanted Gene to do the vocals in place of me. It was one of those things. He wanted to minimize my importance in the group and maximize his, and other people's. In fact, he even stated as a joke, but I believe he meant it, that he wanted to put everyone on the cover except me, and wanted to put a horse in my place."

The very suggestion of a horse infuriated Crosby, who later retorted to me: "I didn't say it. *Never*. That's his style not mine. That particular 'joke' was not funny to me, and I wouldn't have said that to him. I didn't, and I wouldn't have anything to do with it. McGuinn I think was paranoid because he had done it, and I hope he was ashamed of himself."

Although McGuinn's covert suspicions about Crosby's revenge tactics suggested a lingering bitterness, he insisted that there was no acrimony between them. "Let me qualify what I said about Crosby," he added. "I'm still friendly with David. I'm just saying that David was trying to run the show on the Asylum album and it failed. I place the blame on him, though I was at fault too. I'm not saying it was entirely his fault. I was going on the road, Chris was going on the road, and the concentration was diffused. We were having too much of a good time at a party during it and weren't paying attention to our business. But David had a definite ego vendetta going on. I think Crosby was trying to prove that he should have been the leader of the band for the whole time, and with the Byrds reunion album it backfired on him. Especially when it came down to the mixing. That's when he panicked. I saw the beads of sweat on his forehead. That was the bottom line of the entire deal. Crosby is going to hate me for what I've said – but I believe in it."

McGuinn was correct in his view that Crosby would contest his words and deny any serious culpability. "There was no panic," David told me, "and I didn't knife him hardly at all. Maybe I did a couple of times, but compared to what it could have been, it was enormously restrained . . . I got us a bad engineer, who didn't do that badly, but he was the wrong guy. One mistake I think I made was with the Neil Young song '(See The Sky) About To Rain'. It should have been McGuinn lead. That was a definite mistake, not because of any ego trip, but because Roger could have sung it better. That was a mistake."

Summing up the failings of the reunion album and his often competitive relationship with McGuinn, Crosby closed his confessional to me with a scathing reflection: "I think McGuinn's scared of me. I got too big too fast, and that's what he wanted to do. I think McGuinn is jealous and scared of me both . . . Roger's still wishing he were Dylan. I think he's always wished he were Dylan. I think that since CSN&Y, he's resented me, being jealous of me, being afraid of me and not wanted to be put beside me . . . I didn't have a vendetta with him then, and I don't now. It would be foolish to, because I did enormously better than he did, and both he and I know it. And he's got to live with the fact that he said he'd do better without me. That's *his* problem."

From McGuinn's comments that evening in Leeds and Crosby's subsequent rejoinders, it was clear that many of the old wounds had not healed. Any hopes of a reunion were clearly premature, despite what Clark and Hillman may have thought or told the press. The following afternoon, McGuinn's salutary warnings were reinforced by an unexpected and disastrous turn of events. Chris Hillman had quit the tour. A statement was issued alleging breaches of contract by the agency Cream International Artists, which had supposedly failed "to make timely payments to Mr Hillman and to supply the internal transportation between concert cities for him and his band as agreed", thereby making it "impossible for him to continue". The crux of the dispute seemed to be the discovery that McGuinn was paid a large percentage in advance whereas Hillman was receiving monies on a gig-by-gig basis. His manager Richard Halem felt this was unreasonable and demanded that Hillman be paid a week in advance for the remainder of the tour. "I just couldn't meet his demands," claimed Cyriel Van den Hemel of Cream International. "I stuck to the letter of the contract. They've got nothing to complain about. We had no trouble with Clark and McGuinn through the tour, but Hillman was fighting with McGuinn, and Halem was something else."

The news of Hillman's departure came as a great shock. His representatives claimed that he had never cancelled a show in 15 years as a performer, which must have left European concert goers cursing their bad luck for suffering such a rare setback. Although it was not publicized for some reason, Halem did produce a doctor's certificate indicating that Hillman had damaged his hand. As McGuinn says: "He freaked out somehow and he smashed a lamp and I think he cut his hand and flew back to California and that was it." For McGuinn, the affair no doubt provided a chilling reminder of the traumatic days of late 1968 when the volatile Hillman had left the Byrds due to another financial disagreement, slamming his guitar on the floor as a final comment on the situation. Although McGuinn and Clark completed one more date in Glasgow, the remainder of the European tour was cancelled.

The final date at the Apollo Theatre, Glasgow, was a parody of the Byrds' reunion, with a drunken Gene Clark bounding onstage towards the end of the Thunderbyrd set to deliver an horrendous version of 'Mr Tambourine Man', much to McGuinn's annoyance. Clark's bandmates blamed the debacle on a combination of poor communication and Scottish hospitality. Before arriving in Scotland,

INTERLUDE — THREE BYRDS LAND IN LONDON

Clark's pre-gig alcohol intake had been restricted to a few shots of whisky, with Kandanes designated as his chief watcher and moderator. Knowing the tour was over, Clark was in no mood for temperance. "Gene was doing a good job of staying straight, but you knew he was going to fall down somewhere," says Kandanes, "and this was the last night anyway. They left these bottles of malt and cans of beer in the dressing room. Gene drank three quarters of a bottle of Glennfiddich. Then someone came down and said, 'We want Gene to come up and jam.' I said, 'You should have told him that an hour ago before he started drinking.' He was three sheets to the wind and I was afraid he might fall off the stage."

Peter Oliva was amused and amazed to witness Clark acting like a barroom brawler let loose on the big stage. In that strange summer of '77, he had picked up the punk ethic from the bottom of a bottle. "Every brand of Scotch was there on the table," Oliva recalls. "We all had a little nip, but Gene had a little more, I guess. Scotland was the only time he was drunk onstage and that was after we'd stopped playing. When he came out [for the Byrds' segment] he started swinging the mike, like Roger Daltrey. McGuinn and the guys were ducking during 'Mr Tambourine Man' and we were just sitting there laughing. The stage was high and Geno could have broken his neck if he'd fallen into the orchestra pit. But he kept tightrope walking at the edge and swaying with the microphone. I enjoyed the tour. Roger and Gene were into doing it, but it ended too soon. I wish it had gone on to the Continent."

Less than a week before, there had been happy talk of another reunion album from both Clark and Hillman, but such sentiments now sounded hollow and fatuous. Before departing Britain, McGuinn told me his true feelings about such get-togethers in a tone of weary disillusionment. "It's not a great desire on my part at this stage. If the Byrds did reform again it would be so disastrous that I wouldn't want to think about it. I know I said before that I wanted to save the name, but I don't know if it's possible. It might be something that should be left alone. I guess I am putting it away. I feel it's something I don't need and I don't feel that the world needs it really. I think it's something that would gratify the egos of the other Byrds."

CHAPTER FORTY

The Negotiation

THE controversy over the cancelled UK tour followed Hillman across the Atlantic. Cyriel Van den Hemel and his partner Miles Copeland were outraged by the decision and began legal action in an attempt to claw back the losses which had almost forced their company into liquidation. They successfully sued the travel agent, and also went after Hillman and his manager Richard Halem. "We were very angry because we'd taken deposits from people in Europe and could have gone broke over this," says Van den Hemel. "We had bailiffs sitting in the bushes, the way it is in America. We didn't sue McGuinn or Clark. In the end Hillman was the only decent person among them who actually flew over from LA to London and said he was sorry." Eventually the matter was concluded in the High Courts of Justice in the Strand, London, where Hillman took the witness stand and apologized for the unfortunate turn of events. The judge concluded that he was not responsible for reimbursing any monies lost as a result of the cancellation. The elusive Halem failed to appear in Court.

Considering the coldness shown by the ex-Byrds towards each other, and the attendant litigation, few expected to hear of any further get-togethers. However, as if to underline the notorious unpredictability of the group throughout their career, yet another mini-reunion took place during the summer. In July, McGuinn and Clark were approached about the possibility of performing together, informally. The following month, Chris Hillman dropped by Studio Instrument Rentals where McGuinn was rehearsing and they each took a long hard look at their respective careers. A secret

THE NEGOTIATION

pact was made, with Hillman tentatively agreeing to team up with his former colleague later in the year, if all was well. Later that evening, drummer Greg Thomas was dining with McGuinn and guitarist Rick Vito at Dan Tana's, openly boasting: "We just put the Byrds back together. We've been rehearsing all week with Chris Hillman." Such talk was premature, but something was definitely happening. Earlier that month, McGuinn had terminated his contract with Columbia, which was up for renewal after the Thunderbyrd album. "I didn't think they were peddling my product properly," he told me. "Every year they were telling me they were going to do it better next time, and they didn't, so I finally got out of there." In addition to his freedom, McGuinn received a $25,000 pay-off and bided his time while Hillman completed his commitments to Asylum, whose staff were busily promoting the release of his second solo album, *Clear Sailin'*.

Gene Clark was aware of the tentative McGuinn/Hillman summit at SIR and flew down from Northern California to offer his services in the event of any reunion. By mid-September, Clark's manager Ron Eumier had extracted him from his RSO contract, paving the way for a new lucrative record deal with McGuinn, and possibly Hillman. Amid the scheming, the dissolution of Thunderbyrd passed unnoticed, although guitarist Rick Vito and drummer Greg Thomas hoped to retain a place in McGuinn's new project.

In September, the Troubadour celebrated its twentieth anniversary and McGuinn played a short solo set, backed by Rick Vito. Towards the end of the evening, Gene Clark and Greg Thomas joined in on 'Eight Miles High'. That same month, McGuinn and Clark performed a low-key show as an acoustic duo at the Hollywood Canteen on Melrose Avenue. After the gig, Clark's musician friend Tom Slocum suggested they should take the idea further. This reminded them how it had all started 13 years before when Clark had approached McGuinn about forming a duo. Their Peter And Gordon routine had never strayed beyond the Troubadour's Folk Den but now they were ready to experiment with a tour of small colleges and coffee houses.

McGuinn approached his agent Ron Rainey asking for advice.

Rainey was already attempting to negotiate a new solo deal for his client and had recently found an interested party in Rupert Perry, head of A&R at Capitol Records. Rainey was upbeat about booking a small tour for McGuinn/Clark and later used the collaboration as further bait to entice Perry. "Rupert was obviously a fan of the history of the Byrds, so when I said, 'What would you think if I could bring Gene Clark into the fold?', he was all for it." As Rainey well knew, an even greater prize awaited if they could add Hillman to the project. Since connecting with McGuinn in August, Chris had been vacillating about the reunion. He was wary of Clark's involvement, recalling all too clearly how his self-destructive tendencies had blighted two previous residencies as a Byrd. Complicating matters was McGuinn's negativity towards Hillman. There was still some raw tissue that required healing after the recent cold war during the UK tour. Whether they could make a fresh start in such circumstances was a key issue.

Rainey was optimistic. "It was unsaid, but they were ready to move on. We weren't having success with Roger on Columbia, Gene was out in the wilderness and Hillman was coming off Souther, Hillman, Furay and his solo stuff, so he was out there with no band. I thought it was a great idea." One important factor affecting their respective decisions was the women in their lives. In recent times, all three had gone through difficult divorces and found themselves with new partners, all of whom would have a profound effect on their futures for decades to come. Rainey heard that Hillman's new love was Constance Pappas, a former girlfriend of Beach Boy Mike Love, who also worked in an advisory capacity to Seventies superstar, Elton John. "I knew Connie and approached her," says Rainey. "I decided to go after Hillman, who I didn't know, and I got to him. When I met Chris at that time, he was very sceptical of business people. He'd been through his trials and tribulations. So I went back to Rupert and said, 'If I can bring in Hillman, can we do this?' Every time I brought in a Byrd he had to up the ante for each player."

Negotiating with Hillman was not easy. Still smarting from recent events, he was driving a hard bargain. Manager Al Hersh remembers there was initially a stumbling block over the proposed billing of the new project with Chris wanting the provocative 'McGuinn, Hillman & Clark'. Although this may now sound petty and another slap in the face for Clark, who was obviously the superior songwriter, Hillman had good reason for arguing the point. He had just completed a two-record deal with Asylum as a solo, a fitting testament to a beautiful career trajectory which had seen him rise through the ranks in four major bands: the Byrds, the Flying Burrito Brothers, Manassas and SHF. As a matter of professional pride, he felt justified in attempting to achieve second billing. Indeed, this accurately reflected their respective placings on the recent UK tour, where Clark's band were always the bottom of the bill.

Hersh remembers attempting to play the mediator. "When Chris said he wanted McGuinn, Hillman & Clark, I said, 'Well, you got asked last, that's why it should be McGuinn, Clark & Hillman.'" Acknowledging that he was the final player to commit to the project, Hillman relented and said, 'OK'. Rainey drove the deal home with some hard economics. "I told him, 'Look, if you do this, *this* is the amount of money you'll have in your hand when you sign the contract.' It opened his eyes and he said, 'Is this for real?' I said, 'Yes, this is real but, more than that, you guys have to form a band, you'll have to be McGuinn, Clark & Hillman, not the Byrds. This is a new band. So he went for it. They all did. They all saw that it was something that could be worthwhile."

Rumours were rife about a Byrds' reunion during that autumn, but nobody was certain how it might pan out. When pressed about their plans, McGuinn's manager Al Hersh fobbed off enquires with polite denials. For once, it seemed that the former Byrds were conducting their careers with admirable cunning. Their previous full reunion five years ago had been blighted by over-expectation and insufficient rehearsal time. This time around, they intended to build a solid personal and musical relationship before even entering a recording studio.

The McGuinn/Clark tour was a memorable, if short, chapter in their performing histories. Each show would feature solo slots, with an enticing selection of songs, culminating in a joint endeavour during which they would sing 'Knockin' On Heaven's Door', 'Mr

Tambourine Man', 'Chestnut Mare', 'So You Want To Be A Rock 'n' Roll Star' and 'Eight Miles High'. There was enough magic onstage to warrant a duet album, but the participants had clearly set their eyes on a bigger prize. During their closing acoustic gig at Livingstone College on 28 November, McGuinn let slip the news that everybody was hoping to hear. "My future is up in the air. Gene and I are laying the foundations for something, most likely something big. CSN&Y or Eagles, that kind of deal. We're just here laying foundation. The tour's fun and we're making a couple of bucks. It's something to do, keeps us off the streets. There's a story here, or you wouldn't be here."

At this point, the story was still a happy one. McGuinn and Clark were working well together and the modest nature of the enterprise ensured that egos and excesses were kept firmly in check. More importantly, they reconnected as friends and were probably closer than they had been since those innocent days just prior to the formation of the Byrds. "Roger felt that Gene was very talented, especially when they'd started out as folkies," Rainey recalls. "One of the first gigs I booked for them was at the old Aquarius Theatre on Sunset Boulevard, across from the Palladium, a 500 to 600-seater. It went very well and created a buzz. Gene was saying, 'Me and Roger are ready to do this! Let's go!' I remember another night, some time later, at the Roxy. McGuinn started singing and all of a sudden nothing was coming out, just a couple of words. He'd lost his voice. Without missing a beat, Gene walked up to the microphone and sang Roger's parts for the rest of the show, leaving him to play guitar. It was an unbelievable occurrence. Their voices were kind of similar and they had sung the songs so many times that it was as natural as pouring a glass of milk. Gene covered it that night."

By the end of 1977, Hillman was at last ready to join McGuinn and Clark in their grand venture. In the interim, he had been touring as a solo, with harmony backing provided by a friend, Kim O'Kelley. "I was bored," he told me, "so I decided to go out on an acoustic guitar tour with just one guitar, which was something that I'd never done before in my life. It was an interesting experience. It wasn't the most successful thing ever, but I learned a hell of a lot. I played new songs, old songs, everything from the past, and she sang harmony. It was fun."

So far, there was no mention of either Crosby or Clarke in the new set-up, while Hillman's involvement remained a well-kept secret. Clarke was still riding high with Firefall and McGuinn seemed more likely to employ Greg Thomas in his place. David was also enjoying a successful year with the recently reformed Crosby, Stills & Nash, whose summer album *CSN* had climbed to number 2 in the US charts and spawned a Top 10 single, 'Just A Song Before I Go'. Crosby's contributions to the album included the stunning dream sequence 'Shadow Captain', the self-referential 'Anything At All' and the jazzy 'In My Dreams', each song proof enough of his continued power. CS&N's chart triumphs were mirrored in a remarkable series of stadium concerts, their first undertaken as a trio. Despite his busy schedule, Crosby was intrigued to hear of his fellow Byrds' get-togethers and was willing to offer his services, time and other commitments permitting.

News of the ex-Byrds' activities also attracted record company interest. Columbia repented losing McGuinn and started making overtures that were not reciprocated. Asylum were marginal favourites to secure the group, having previously signed the Byrds and provided solo deals for Clark and Hillman. Others insisted that former CBS president Clive Davis would emerge as a front-runner and bag the group for his new label, Arista. Nobody even mentioned Rupert Perry or Capitol Records. Negotiations continued during 1978, with Capitol unexpectedly signing McGuinn, Clark & Hillman later in the year.

Meanwhile, McGuinn had undergone a life transformation. The spiritual search that had taken him from Catholicism through positive thinking, to Subud and LSD, had ended in a hollow agnosticism, characterized by epicurean excess. Burned out from a diet of booze and cocaine, he could only look forward to more short-term ego gratification and drug dependency from his new musical ventures.

The sudden death of Elvis Presley on 16 August 1977 had already affected McGuinn's equilibrium. His adolescent hero had been taking prescription drugs for years and when McGuinn read a newspaper report listing Quaaludes and amphetamines, he was struck by an unerring sense of doom. "I just went, 'Whoa, man!' He was seven years older than I was and I was doing all the drugs he was doing: speed and downers, cocaine and pot. And he died. He was gone." Morbidly calculating their respective ages, McGuinn convinced himself that he would be dead by the mid-Eighties. "I thought, 'Man, I've only got seven years left,' and I panicked. The functioning lobes in my brain began demanding that I investigate what was going on spiritually in the world. Some self-preservation instincts were kicking in." He confided some of his negative feelings to acquaintances like singer Jennifer Warnes, one of several stars with strong Christian beliefs. "I was down at the bottom and the Lord got me," Roger recalls. "He sent Christians around to witness to me, ones that could get through to me – people in the secular end of the business."

McGuinn's epiphany occurred one evening when he suffered what sounded like a panic attack. Pressure seemed to be bearing down on his chest and he felt as though his heart was about to explode. A Christian musician friend advised him to place his faith in the power of prayer. Together they knelt down and offered the plea: "Lord Jesus, we just pray that you come into this man's heart in your own time, slowly but surely, in Jesus' name. Amen." One week later, McGuinn was visiting a house in San Fernando Valley and the stabbing pains in his chest returned. This time, he was convinced that he was being dragged down through the floor to the lower regions of Hell. "I really felt this very strongly," he emphasizes. "I said, 'Oh, God, how can I keep from feeling like this?'" An inner voice replied, "You could accept Jesus", at which point McGuinn submitted. It seemed the final answer to a prayer that had begun 13 years ago at the session for 'Mr Tambourine Man', when he had implored God to take him for a trip. This time, his salvation did not take the form of Eastern meditation, but was firmly grounded in the new wave of Born Again Christianity then sweeping through America.

Changes in McGuinn's life had become increasingly unpredictable as he grappled with the aftermath of addictive behaviour. He cut down his alcohol intake, stopped taking drugs and reassessed his personal relationships. At one point he had become engaged to Season Hubley, but the love affair had evidently run its course. In another strange twist, his first wife Dolores now credits Hubley for suggesting that he should get back together with the family that he had left behind at the start of the Seventies. "When he was dating Susan, he brought her to Tucson and then she sort of convinced him to get back with his family. He said he'd come back at Easter. It was funny but I never told the kids because I had this weird feeling. Easter came and, towards the end of the day, he called my mother's house and said, 'I'm not going to come, I've changed my mind.' My mother grabbed the phone from me and said, 'Roger, don't you ever come to this house again!' It was so upsetting. He said God had told him this . . . But I guess things always work out the way they should . . ."

What had happened to McGuinn over those preceding months was no less extraordinary. With negotiations for the McGuinn, Clark & Hillman project still underway, he undertook some extracurricular activities, enrolling at an acting class. One of the assignments set before the students was an exercise in persuasion, by which they had to convince a fellow member to believe in something to which they were not sympathetic. McGuinn's quarry was Camilla Spaul, a strong-willed 27-year-old budding actress and divorcee, who proved quite a challenge. After setting up two chairs in front of the class, McGuinn produced his guitar and attempted to serenade her with the strains of 'The Christian Life', one of his less convincing performances from *Sweetheart Of The Rodeo*. Back then, McGuinn had attempted to act out Gram Parsons' pleading country vocal with a transparent imitation that sounded more sardonic than convincing. This time he meant it.

Recalling their first eventful evening together, Camilla was less than flattering: "I thought, 'Oh great, a hillbilly musician!' I went, 'Oh no' as it hit me – 'he's going to try and tell me about Jesus onstage in front of all these people.' I was infuriated. I just didn't like him. I didn't like what he had [to say]. I said, 'Look, how long have you been into Jesus?' He said, 'Oh, a couple of months.' I said, 'Wait three more months, you'll get over it.' That's how I felt."

Camilla's cynicism did not last long. His conviction somehow reached her and she too reconverted to Christianity. As McGuinn, laconically noted, "She took a few days, but the Lord got her." Less than two months later, they married on 1 April 1978. It was a rapid chain of events that was to change McGuinn's life irrevocably hereafter. For once, he had even pre-empted his mentor Bob Dylan, whose own conversion to Christianity was still several months away. Before long, they would be studying the Bible together, after which Dylan went on to complete a remarkable series of evangelical albums and concerts, in striking contrast to McGuinn's non-doctrinal music.

Unlike Dylan, McGuinn retained his links with fundamentalist Christianity but interestingly there would be no *Slow Train Coming*, *Saved* or *Shot Of Love* in his canon. Instead, McGuinn restricted himself to broadcasting the same easy-going positivism that he had discovered years earlier when reading Norman Vincent Peale's *The Power Of Positive Thinking*. "As far as songwriting goes, Roger isn't particularly restricted," Camilla McGuinn told me at the time. "We won't write songs which are satanically influenced. We're conscious of the fact that young people will be listening to the albums so subjects such as drugs or sex are avoided. Roger would not want to promote drugs or sexual promiscuity. We're not into religion, we're into Jesus. We might study with other people, but we all study the Bible. We're not averse to using the name Jesus, since He is the main point of our lives. The songs always have Jesus in them simply because Roger loves the Lord, and the Lord is in him. Anything he does reflects his love of Jesus. Roger has written a new song with Chris that uses the name Jesus. The music comes out with the name Jesus because Roger's whole life is surrounded by Jesus. Right now, Roger is an entertainer and not a minister. At the moment his calling is to be as he is. So, as far as a gospel album goes – that's out. But if the Lord wanted us to do something, we'd do it."

Camilla's reservations proved sound. McGuinn never did pursue a gospel album, although a decade on he briefly considered teaming up with fellow Christian and Ciro's habitué Barry McGuire for a work humorously titled *McGuinn & McGuire Just A-Gettin' Higher* in memory of the Mamas & The Papas' sardonic tribute 'Creeque

THE NEGOTIATION

Alley'. Like many other McGuinn projects that too failed to materialize. Although the prospect of McGuinn writing songs denuded of sex and violence sounded less than exciting, it ultimately made little difference to his repertoire. His compositions had always been cerebral and spiritual rather than physical and aggressive, while his only concession to the sinful ways of rock 'n' roll had been in occasional drug songs, and even those were probably misinterpreted. In effect, the new Christian McGuinn, unlike Dylan, was not writing anything radically different from his previous subject matter.

With Hillman now committed to the group, the trio embarked on a short Canadian tour, supporting Eric Clapton. "If we bombed there nobody would know about it," Clark joked. Further small dates followed. Clark was still buzzing from the excitement of the reunion and at times displayed a manic energy which was almost as endearing as it was disconcerting. "I think it was at the Roxy with Roger and Chris, where Gene jumped off the balcony and landed on the stage," Hersh says. "That was unbelievable."

Having agreed to sign with Capitol, McGuinn, Clark & Hillman embarked on an extensive tour of Australia and New Zealand in June 1978. As if already aware of their superstar status, they closed the show with the choral 'Find The Cost Of Freedom', just like Crosby, Stills & Nash. The Antipodean expedition was the longest plane flight Clark had ever taken in his life and although travelling such distances must have been stressful, he was still together at this early stage. "He wasn't drinking very much," his partner Terri Messina recalls. "He'd maybe have a glass of wine at dinner or something . . . he was totally cooled out from all that abusive behaviour." Nevertheless, there remained the unspoken fear that he might yet fall back into his old ways.

Surprisingly, it was not Clark but Hillman who struck the first blow in the battle of the egos. It happened in Australia at a time when they should have been enjoying getting back together on the big stage. Unfortunately, some residual resentments resurfaced unexpectedly. "There was so much animosity," says Al Hersh. "All these old things came out during the McGuinn, Clark & Hillman period. Chris had been kind of a wimp back in the Sixties and he was the guy that always got 'beat up' and vetoed, or never got his way. In the interim he had met Chuck Norris [actor and martial arts specialist] and became a shitkicker. There was this whole thing of 'I'm going to beat the crap out of the guys that beat the crap out of me.' So he was calling in his markers with those that had given him a hard time. It was funny in a way, but it was also sad. There was fisticuffs. We had these dressing rooms and everyone had their own, of course. There was a big gap at the top of the dressing rooms, so you could hear everything the guy next door was saying. Roger was speaking a bunch of crap about Chris, and he flipped out. I was with Chris and he said, 'I'm going to get that motherfucker once and for all.' When he heard Roger bad rapping him, he went into his dressing room and cold cocked him. He knocked him right into the urinal, probably knocked him 30 feet. I was holding on to Chris' pants and he was dragging me. I just wanted to keep the tour going and get it over with."

Quizzed about the episode, Hillman admitted that he'd bodily thrown McGuinn against a wall for the apparently unforgivable crime of referring to him as "Chris, the bass player". It was hardly the worst insult imaginable, but Hillman was no doubt reacting to a perceived attitude rather than the actual words. McGuinn's tone must have been brutally condescending to warrant such an aggressive response. Never a paragon of restraint when riled, Hillman had allowed his emotions to overwhelm him and the consequences could have proven disastrous. McGuinn was known to abhor violence, particularly if it was directed against his own person. In the past, his detachment had saved him from any physical violence in the Byrds, so it must have been shocking to experience such an outburst when the combatants were now in their mid-thirties.

In retrospect, it is amazing that the partnership did not end there and then, but the parties evidently came to an understanding, no doubt part brokered by the ameliorating voice of Al Hersh. Hereafter, McGuinn and Hillman decided to maintain a professional cordiality, while keeping a respectful distance. The tour was completed without any further incident. In concert, they played a selection of songs from their solo years and a sprinkling of Byrds' classics. They were billed at several dates as 'the Founders of the Byrds', which puzzled some onlookers. Many suspected that the group was unable to use the name Byrds because of legal reasons, but McGuinn later told me otherwise. "I made an agreement with David Crosby that I wouldn't use the name without him or Michael in the group. It was a gentlemen's agreement, but I decided to honour it."

David Crosby was happy to learn that they had secured a deal with Capitol and magnanimously offered his services as a backing vocalist, even making a special trip across the country to ensure that he was part of the historic reunion. In December 1977, he had performed alongside McGuinn and Clark at San Francisco's Boarding House. Despite having difficulty remembering some lyrics, he gamely joined in on 'Mr Tambourine Man', 'He Was A Friend Of Mine', 'You Ain't Going Nowhere', 'So You Want To Be A Rock 'n' Roll Star' and 'Eight Miles High'. Although Crosby's cameo appearance seemed a likely one-off between CS&N dates, he later joined his fellow Byrds at the Roxy, this time with Chris Hillman also taking the stage. "They said they needed me at the Roxy because that's where most of the attention would be," he told me. "So I flew down to Los Angeles to do it again. [It was] the best sound that I thought we ever got. It was me and Hillman both singing the same harmony in unison, and Gene and McGuinn singing the same melody in unison. So it was two vocal double lines. We used to do something very like that when Christopher wasn't singing. I would do the harmony, and Gene and Roger would sing the melody. Occasionally, Gene would work out a low harmony, but normally he would sing with Roger."

Crosby's presence would soon become a contentious issue. In addition to his concert guest appearances, he was eager to assist in the studio, but McGuinn played down the offer. "He sat in with us at the Boarding House and the Roxy, and he mentioned he liked what we were doing and would be glad to help us out on records. He was sort of non-committal for a little while, then he came back and said he was committed to Stephen Stills and Graham Nash. When it came to the recording, we didn't get around to calling him. His feelings were a little hurt."

Not for the first or last time, McGuinn had underestimated Crosby's emotional sensitivity. "A little hurt" was a euphemism for something far stronger. Crosby had made a determined effort to build bridges and, filled with positive feelings, he elected to take time off and surprise the trio by offering free vocal accompaniment. Upon arrival at Miami's Criteria Studios, he was crestfallen to discover that they did not require his help and seemed to take perverse satisfaction in cold-shouldering his good intentions. It was enough to bring back those bitter memories of the time they had thrown him out of the group and told him, "We can do better without you."

Crosby expressed his feelings to me, more in sadness than anger. "When they were cutting in Miami as McGuinn, Clark & Hillman, I flew there on purpose to see them, and to go in and ask them if I could sing. And I did. And they didn't want me to. I did it. I came in there real nice and I was humble. I didn't give anyone any shit. I just came in and asked if I could sing. I offered, and I even *asked*. They did a live gig and they didn't even call me. I went there to do it, to sing on the album. Who refused? It was all three of them that refused. They knew why I was there. I flew from Los Angeles to Florida to sing some harmonies to help them. I wasn't trying to shine my own light. The emotion that was foremost in my mind was affection for them and a feeling that I could both focus attention on them and help them to make a better record. It hurt me that they didn't want me to sing because I wanted to do it. I think I could have helped them too."

Crosby's hurt was understandable. What he perceived as a magnanimous act had been cruelly rejected, without good reason. The other Byrds may have misinterpreted his noble intentions as patronizing or simply felt wary of his presence. In the past, McGuinn had been bitterly competitive with Crosby and liked to prove he could survive and thrive without his creative input. The final sessions for *The Notorious Byrd Brothers* had been completed with that attitude uppermost in his mind. Crosby had been an imposing figure during the recording of the reunion album as McGuinn well remembered. Cold-shouldering Crosby smacked of petty vengeance, but it was also a show of independence, even self-preservation. Maintaining the ego balance in McGuinn, Clark & Hillman was a delicate matter and even though Crosby was offering harmony and concord, they already had enough problems dealing with each other.

Al Hersh believes, probably with considerable prejudice, that "David showing up caused a lot of hatred", a perspective that hardly makes sense considering they had specifically invited him to appear at both the Boarding House and the Roxy. That said, there was an element of mischievous cool that Crosby effortlessly exuded.

Andy Kandanes, who was backstage at the Boarding House with Gene Clark, remembers Crosby treating Hersh with open disdain, while teasing McGuinn. "It was funny to see their interaction with David Crosby. I was pretty good friends with David, but he would do stuff. All the press people were there at the Boarding House. He walked in, smoking a joint, and said, 'Hi, Roger.' Then he came over and handed it to me. It was like he used to bust Roger's chops all the time. He was really cool."

Agent Ron Rainey also detected a certain frostiness. "The only time I've ever been in the same room as Crosby was the night at the Roxy when they took a picture. It's still on my wall here. There's McGuinn, Clark, Hillman, Crosby and Stephen Stills. An amazing picture. They showed up and those kinds of things were happening. Crosby was there and he wasn't the most pleasant fellow. I don't know whether he wanted to be involved or not. I just ignored that situation. But, in the business community, who would have said, 'No'? What they did themselves was another thing. If they'd come to me after that show and said, 'Crosby's going to join in', I would have said, 'Wow! I'll get back to Rupert Perry!' But I think McGuinn had taken it as far as he was going to take it. He had Clark and Hillman and I don't think he wanted to press his luck."

CHAPTER FORTY-ONE

The Cocaine Wars

THE recording sessions at Criteria Studios in Miami proceeded reasonably well, but there was a strange atmosphere and emotional distance between McGuinn, Clark and Hillman. Nobody was entirely sure how this had happened, but their original plans to forge a sense of unity and common purpose already looked shaky. They had promised to avoid the problems associated with their previous 'reunion' by taking their time, concentrating on a single project, playing live before recording and getting to know each other. The McGuinn/Clark tour had demonstrated the enormous potential of the enterprise and, at that point, the pair seemed perfectly matched. There was every hope that they might even re-establish their writing partnership, but it was a delicate dynamic. Once Hillman entered the equation things changed. Suddenly, the one-to-one relationship became an uneasy triangle. In theory, Hillman's arrival should have galvanized the trio. He was known as rock's consummate anchor man and the perfect foil for talents as various as McGuinn, Gram Parsons and Stephen Stills. This time around his presence was anything but a unifying force as the recent violent confrontation with McGuinn in Australia demonstrated.

That said, it would be misleading to blame the shift in the group dynamics entirely on Hillman, as he was often a steadying force. Once fame and fortune beckoned, Clark was always likely to be derailed. Indeed, it seems probable that if Hillman had worked with McGuinn as a duo first, then Clark's arrival might have had a similarly disruptive effect. The interaction between the three was built on a complex relationship that began when they were still young men. It embraced friendship, rivalry, cooperation and conflict, depending on the circumstances. They had already elected to snub Crosby partly to avoid trouble, as if his innocent presence might somehow jinx the project. What they had not considered was the distance between themselves, which the new three-way partnership appeared to be exacerbating. Instead of growing closer on the road, they were falling into familiar destructive patterns.

More worryingly, they no longer appeared to have much in common as friends. They kept to themselves and pursued their own interests. The enterprise now more closely resembled a business partnership or a marriage of convenience. At times, they seemed to have become stereotypes of their most prominent traits: McGuinn, the newly abstemious born again Christian; Clark the wild card, getting crazier by the minute; Hillman, still a suitable candidate for anger management classes.

In an attempt at family unity, they agreed to share the same house while recording in Miami, but the arrangement backfired. McGuinn was wary of regressing into the sinful rock 'n' roll intemperance that Clark was now recklessly advocating as the perfect lifestyle choice. Hillman, meanwhile, remained aloof, hiding his feelings behind the comforting mask of 'professional distance'. Technically together, they were in fact leading completely separate existences. Recording the album was their sole common pursuit and, in the circumstances, they did remarkably well to retain their equilibrium in the studio where all differences were seemingly put aside. But the songwriting credits told their own story. There was no sign of any McGuinn/Clark or McGuinn/Hillman collaboration. Creatively, the Byrds were still flying solo.

"We lived in this big mansion all together, but it was very voluble," says Hersh. "It was the same house that Crosby, Stills & Nash lived in when they were there. We also had Joe Lala sleeping on the floor, being into heroin . . ."

The casual reference to Lala's habit was indicative of the prevailing culture. If Hollywood was sin city, then Miami was Babylon incarnate. Recreational drug abuse seemed to be taking place all over town, sometimes on a monumental scale. Cocaine, the favourite drug of rock stars since the dawn of the Seventies, had now seeped into mainstream culture. At that point the so-called 'cocaine economy' in Florida was estimated to be worth $6 billion in cash alone. Banks barely had room to stash the cash and if you analysed a federal bill from Miami in a laboratory, it was almost certain to contain traces of cocaine. The drug seemed to have infiltrated every echelon of society. Audience members and hangers-on were as likely to be found snorting coke as were their idols or employers. Inevitably, there was a response with many rock icons, not to mention their road crews, combining cocaine and heroin. With the spiralling increase in coke consumption, heroin provided the necessary comedown. Not everyone was public about their usage, particularly in later years when they sobered up or had grandchildren, but the long list of names of those indulging during the Seventies included an astonishing number of surprise users. It was at this point that Gene Clark started experimenting with the drug, although there was nothing unusual about that in such circles. The only worry was that, considering his addictive personality, he might develop an overfondness for smack. "Heroin was never his drug of choice, I'll tell you that," says his partner and fellow user Terri Messina. "That was never his big problem like it has been with other people. But he definitely had his ups and downs."

Alcohol remained Clark's main temptation, but once the money came in from Capitol, he was free to indulge more dangerous appetites. So were certain others, including drummer Greg Thomas, who would later become an alcohol and drugs counsellor. Sometimes, the party got out of hand without anybody realizing the consequences. Al Hersh remembers a showcase gig at the Bottom Line which became a pharmaceutical comedy of errors. "Keith Richards had gotten backstage and offered us a giant vial of white powder which I assumed was cocaine. It turned out to be China White. Were you at that show? It was really dramatic. I remember getting dosed thinking we were snorting coke, not China White, and doing heaping beakfuls. We wanted to do a good show, nobody wanted to do heroin, I thought it was coke." Hersh was so concerned that he blacked out the stage, fearful that he, or anyone else in the vicinity who had accidentally indulged, might end up vomiting.

McGuinn remained cautiously remote from any rock 'n' roll excesses. By now married to Camilla and increasingly involved in Christianity, he avoided temptation. Clark, by contrast, was languishing in a palace of indulgence. During the sessions at Criteria, the three ex-Byrds spent their social hours housed in their own quarters, like rival princes at a monarch's court. Sometimes they were reduced to communicating via intermediaries. Gene Clark was using his brother Rick as a personal messenger, delivering despatches back and forth like a war correspondent. Outside the studio a different war was taking place. Colombian and Cuban drug dealers, rivals in the ever expanding narcotics market, were fighting what the press called the 'cocaine wars'. An unprecedented level of violence hit the streets with mass murders reported on news channels with frightening frequency. At its worst, Miami resembled a city on the brink of anarchy.

Back at Criteria, the atmosphere was worsening. Al Hersh, who had been McGuinn's manager since the break-up of the Byrds, knew he was losing the confidence of his employer, who was now a changed man. Although they remained cordial, the old intimacy had been broken and their contrasting lifestyles suggested that it was only a matter of time before the relationship tarnished. Hersh found it difficult to accept the new 'born again' McGuinn, who now represented the antithesis of everything the road manager regarded as the essence of rock 'n' roll rebellion. "He called me one night at four in the morning," says Hersh, "and told me to tune to this channel. I said, 'This can't be right, it's Jerry Falwell.' He said, 'Yeah, watch it, and I'll be over in a minute to talk to you about it.' It was like this big epiphany. Things were never the same after that. Our relationship dwindled."

Although Hersh maintained a positive front at the time, he was bitter about their fractured friendship, as evidenced by a string of acerbic comments. "I didn't respect what Roger was doing," he says, "because I thought, 'Yeah, it saved him from being a hopeless alcoholic, but it also castrated him and made him completely useless.' He went from being my hero, and a lot of other people's hero, into just having nothing to offer." Hersh's harsh assessment and fierce put-down say more about his own antipathy towards

McGuinn than the true problem. McGuinn had certainly not been a hero or anything similar when recording *Roger McGuinn And Band* during the peak of his hedonistic days. Nor had his songwriting been any more prolific during the sessions for *Byrdmaniax* when the cupboard was bare. Creative drought had little or nothing to do with Christianity. It was the absence of a consistent writing partner and the ambivalence of his producers that were clearly the key factors affecting McGuinn's creative output.

Hersh still believed that McGuinn was floundering and subsequently seized upon Camilla's comments about their vetoing songs that glorified the familiar dark litany of sex, drugs and sin. "That's what rock 'n' roll is all about," he maintains. Extraterrestrials were also absent from McGuinn's latest lyrical repertoire but so too were any songs exploring his spiritual enlightenment. Perhaps he was wary of writing anything too serious or radical for fear of misinterpretation. He had four other songs in reserve for the new album, but they were dismissed as "inappropriate".

"Gene's songs were probably the best," Hersh acknowledges. "Roger had nothing. He went from being a rock hero to a total wimp. It was really sad because I'd known him during his hero stage and to see him castrated like that and limited in what he could do creatively . . . Listen to the songs and it shows he had nothing. We were offered these great songs from John Cougar and Tom Petty. McGuinn still thought that Petty was a poseur who was copying his sound and he had only done 'American Girl' reluctantly [with Thunderbyrd]. They should have said, 'Look, we don't have any good songs, we'll take these that are being offered to us.' They did do 'Surrender To Me' which David Soul also recorded. I'd actually picked it and liked it and Chris did a nice job."

Of course, had McGuinn, Clark & Hillman filled the album with cover songs, everybody would have complained about their lack of productivity and bemoaned their artistic decline even more vociferously. In truth, the new songs weren't that bad individually; they just weren't great or worthy enough to stand alongside their best work, either inside or outside the Byrds. This was music not designed to stir the spirit or the mind.

Originally, Hersh had hoped that getting the guys together in a single building might spark some kind of inspired artistic partnership, but it proved impossible to turn back the clock. All that was left was the symbolism, best exemplified onstage where they would sing 'Mr Tambourine Man' with all three members taking a solo verse. Hersh was frustrated. "They were capable of doing it again, if only they had the wherewithal and not the 'distractions'. I hoped that they would all go into a room somewhere in LA and put their heads together, but it never happened . . . The potential was always there. They could have written another 'Eight Miles High' or 'So You Want To Be A Rock 'n' Roll Star'."

The latter view, shared by some long-term fans at the time, including myself, was probably misplaced. We were comparing them to the Byrds and viewing their progress through the cultural prism of the previous decade. The group were now out of time, and even more detached from their older selves than they had been during the late 1972 reunion. As he had proven with *Cardiff Rose*, McGuinn was more likely to come up with something spectacular collaborating exclusively with Jacques Levy than searching for gold with Clark and Hillman. Similarly, Clark could never have conceived anything as magnificent as *No Other* without the empathetic grandiose vision of a Thomas Jefferson Kaye. He would not gain the same support from his current creative competitors, nor his producers, who were unwilling to allow him such freedom. Hillman, at his best when playing right-hand man to McGuinn, Parsons or Stills, no longer felt obliged to subsume his own songwriting ambitions now that he could demand and expect parity. It was difficult to please everybody.

The sessions were overseen by Ron and Howard Albert (the Albert Brothers), who had recently produced Crosby, Stills & Nash's excellent *CSN* and previously worked with Hillman on the great Manassas double album, as well as contributing to its less impressive follow-up, *Down The Road*. McGuinn, Clark & Hillman initially welcomed the hands-on approach of the producers, although there would be belated grumbling from all of the participants. Hersh maintains that he was sceptical from the outset. "Roger always needed something or somebody, and I was always trying to find that person. That's how McGuinn, Clark & Hillman happened because nobody else was going to be that guy, so maybe it'd be them again. We were just treading water . . . The whole record deal at the time was like a time bomb and we never knew when it was going to explode. Everybody was suspicious of me because I was with Roger. I told them, 'Look, I'm going to represent *all* you guys equally.' We made sure they were signed collectively and individually. I wanted to keep it going if one or two of them dropped out, which is what eventually happened. They had no direction or plan and they wouldn't listen to any of us. Then when we got down to Miami to do this thing, John Cougar was there and he offered us a bunch of great songs. We had nothing, man. The songs they had were shit and the Albert Brothers were intent on taking the Byrds out of the skies and making a whole other sound."

Drummer Greg Thomas, who had worked with McGuinn on Thunderbyrd and was a prominent presence during the 1977 UK tour, was taken aback by the scenes in Miami. "If you thought it was bad in London, you should have seen what it was like when I was living with them. We had a big house on the water in Florida and there was me and Gene hanging out together. His brother Rick Clark came out with us, another heavy drinker. Chris and Roger were staying there but it was so bad that I had to leave on the second day when I found out what was going on between everybody. I couldn't take it at the house. It was so tense that I just had to move out and get my own scene. The vibe was so bad that you'd wonder how you could put these people together and make any kind of good music."

Remarkably, these scary portents did not prevent the trio from finding common ground or working professionally during the recording process.

"Somehow everybody pulled it together when we went in the studio with the Albert Brothers," says Thomas. "Occasionally, Gene would get too drunk to be in the studio and you'd have to work with Chris and let Gene sober up. Then he'd come in the next morning at seven o'clock and he'd be loaded again. It was quite insane. Still, it's the last thing they did when they were actually playing together. The music took on this different form. What they were trying to do was make McGuinn, Clark & Hillman sound like a disco band and we had Joe Lala playing percussion with these other players he called the Cuban Army. We had a fabulous time in the studio and they managed to come up with eight or nine songs between them which were pretty good. But they wanted that other feel, which I wasn't much for playing. Being a drummer it's tough to have to play disco music, so instead we made it a cross between the new and the old music. I really liked that album, but I don't know why."

Some of the later negative comments should not distract from the sense of event that accompanied the release of the album at the beginning of 1979. Even the cover artwork caused a stir. The trio looked as though they had been given a makeover by a Hollywood stylist. At the time, manager Al Hersh spoke like a fitness trainer, telling me: "We used that cover to show that the guys are all good looking. They're in really good shape. It wasn't really an image change. They wanted a *Life* magazine kind of cover – sophisticated and classy. Some people were a little shocked by the flashy cover, but these are mature guys and this is a mature album."

Weeks before it was issued, sales representatives were provided with a compilation of the work of the individual Byrds as a taster for this latest reformation. "It was sent out to the entire field staff," Ron Rainey recalls. "There was great feedback. When the Capitol Tower in Hollywood was getting all this feedback from the field, it made the thing grow. There was great anticipation for the album. The buzz was there. I was living in Malibu at the time and all the disc jockeys were talking about the Byrds' 'reunion' and playing their music. Sometimes you can't pay to get that stuff happening."

The trio were also helped by the sterling efforts of Capitol's head of publicity Stephen Peeples, whose press kits were the best in the business. A month before the album's appearance, I was sent a pre-release cassette and offered the chance to interview all three members individually and collectively. Later reports would have you believe that they were at each other's throats, but they seemed harmonious enough at the time. Hillman was bullish about the new album, McGuinn also seemed confident and Clark spoke with reverence, as if he had just undergone a life-altering experience during its recording. Not that he was in any way concerned with artistry.

Chewing an apple and looking a decade younger than he had done on the 1977 UK tour, he spoke like a number crunching market analyst from Capitol's middle management. "So far I've heard this record is a definite hit everywhere. I think this new album is great. I love it and it's a hit already – that's for sure." The promotional patter sounded a little gauche, but was probably accurate. Buoyed by the chart success of the McGuinn composed 'Don't You Write Her Off', the album soon scaled the US Top 100, peaking at number 39. This fell somewhat short of the Byrds' reunion album, but easily eclipsed sales of every solo or offshoot recording by the three individuals, bar Hillman's work in Manassas.

The release of the album under the banner of McGuinn, Clark & Hillman ended months of speculation about the likelihood of the trio using the Byrds name to sell the record. McGuinn had kept his promise to Crosby and maintained the dictum that "there were ever only five Byrds". In contemporary interviews, it was stressed that *McGuinn, Clark & Hillman* was a new project, apparently unconnected with the Byrds. While the sound and production were totally unlike anything previously heard under the Byrds' name, both the press and public felt confused by the distinction. The group that had recorded the albums from *Dr Byrds & Mr Hyde* to *Farther Along* had been accepted as Byrds, yet they featured only one original member. Now there were three originals out there strenuously denying that they were Byrds, yet playing many of that group's songs in concert. So were McGuinn, Clark and Hillman really the Byrds? At the time, Hillman clearly felt that they were not. "We didn't approach this album as the Byrds," he told me. "We didn't have David or Michael. There was more at stake. We didn't have our own personal little things happening at the time, as we did when we were doing the reunion album. I want everybody to realize that we're not the Byrds, and I'm sure they'll know that when they hear the record."

The content of the album went some way towards justifying Hillman's contention. It was clear that the producers, Ron and Howard Albert, had deliberately attempted to avoid simulating the old Byrds sound. They even told McGuinn that the Rickenbacker sounded dated. The problem lay in what they had elected to insert in its place. Much of the album had a slick Seventies' sound in keeping with the high gloss production of the time. The opening 'Long Long Time', written by Hillman and Rick Roberts, would not have sounded out of place on a Firefall album. Like the best of Hillman's solo work, the instrumentation was impressively tight and the harmonies as strong as ever. Much the same could be said of 'Surrender To Me' (written by Rick Vito) which features one of Hillman's finest vocal performances. The producers even borrowed an old Byrds trick from *Younger Than Yesterday* by inserting a backwards tape as a false introduction to the song. While Hillman was in full flight on these tunes, his other contributions were less spectacular. 'Stopping Traffic' and 'Sad Boy' were average rock songs, lacking any real depth or originality. Even the presence of McGuinn and Clark failed to compensate for the weaker material.

McGuinn's contributions were more disappointing. 'Don't You Write Her Off' (co-written with Bob Hippard) was commercial enough to provide a long overdue US Top 40 hit, but even McGuinn agreed that the song was of little consequence. Its calypso beat, complete with references to desert islands and gurus, at least provided some amusing moments. "That was just me joking," McGuinn says. "It's a straight love song. The intent of the first verse is to establish credibility. It's just being silly too." Although the song's chart success allowed McGuinn to claim a pyrrhic victory over his detractors, it did not silence them. "'Don't You Write Her Off' wasn't really a great song," Hersh retorts. "By the time the Albert Brothers had finished butchering it, it was just stupid."

McGuinn's only other contribution to the album, 'Bye Bye Baby', sounded a little more serious. Lyrically, it combined references from 'Chestnut Mare', 'Child Of The Universe' and 'Ballad Of Easy Rider', with its allusions to fillies running wild, a woman with the soul of a child and a flowing river that runs into the sea. It was difficult to escape the uneasy impression that the song was a self-conscious and contrived attempt to recapture lost magic by recycling ideas from earlier classic compositions. Although well recorded, the song's sentiments seemed hollow and unconvincing. At worst, it was a bad acting job from McGuinn.

According to producer Ron Albert, the inclusion of orchestration was entirely due to Mike Lewis, string and horn arranger for Firefall and KC & The Sunshine Band. "Lewis, without any prompting from us, came up with the string part for the track. Chris had his mandolin sitting in the studio all through the sessions, but we just never got round to using it. We thought about trying some mandolin on 'Bye Bye Baby', but after we got the flute part on it, it was so special, so simple, that we just left it alone."

McGuinn looked on dispassionately, accepting the Alberts' overview, probably against his better judgement. "I didn't think it was that big a deal. I went along with it. We were gearing the album to the contemporary market. We may have bent over backwards just a little: we didn't want to be criticized for trying to push the old sound."

With Gene Clark dominating the album on the remaining four tracks, one might have expected some musical adventurousness in the great tradition of *No Other*. Sadly, this was not the case. The lyrically banal 'Little Mama' featured a melody over-reminiscent of Smokey Robinson's 'You Really Got A Hold On Me'. In an attempt to improve the song, Ron Albert borrowed an idea from Paul McCartney. "The first time Gene played this song for me, I heard something more drastic happening in the chorus – the 'everybody's talking about it' part. It seemed a little too melodic, pretty, and I wanted to change the colour a bit. Finally, I figured we should try something really off the wall. I had this idea running around in my head for a while to triple-track snare-drum parts, two cadences built around the straight *2/4* beat. We tried that on 'Little Mama' and it worked great. The idea came from Paul McCartney's 'Let 'Em In', so 'Little Mama' is happening thanks to Paul. That's Blue Weaver on synthesizer. He works with the Bee Gees."

'Backstage Pass', arguably the most serious composition on offer, included some foreboding allusions to being ten feet away from both the Judgement Day and the dreaded airport runway. Hearing Clark acknowledge his fear of flight was intriguing, but the song's emotional power was undermined by a secondary narrative and the insertion of an out of place 'hey ho' chorus, accented by orchestration. Even Ron Albert seemed confused by the conflicting elements in the song. "It's sort of moody in the verses and more upbeat in the choruses and towards the end, maybe reflecting some of Gene's ambiguous feelings about being on the road." Midway through the song Clark included a subtle nod to the Beatles with the phrase "ticket to ride", an allusion previously used on the great 'Artificial Energy'.

'Feeling Higher', co-written by Clark and his girlfriend Terri Messina, was inspired by a UFO sighting following a McGuinn/Clark show. The song begins deceptively as a love song before Clark starts philosophizing about extraterrestrials who come into contact with us, but choose to hide from the "dawning day". During the final verse, the underlying theme becomes more explicit, ending with the hope that mankind will ascend after mastering the secrets of space and time. It was probably the finest song on the album.

Clark's final contribution, 'Release Me Girl', proved the most frustrating moment on offer. During 1977, he had performed a riveting electric version with the KC Southern Band and a fine acoustic adaptation had been previewed during his concerts with McGuinn. Unfortunately, the recorded version was spoiled by insipid orchestration, excessive brass and an incongruous disco beat. As Ron Albert recalls, with severe understatement: "This is the one track that feels the most different from the takes the guys first got. It had a sort of Nashville feel. As it turned out, we really altered it a lot . . . We had Chris and Gene set up a different groove on bass and drums and then asked George Terry to come up with a little guitar line that'd work better. The example I gave George was something sounding a little, but not a lot, like the guitar line in 'Stayin' Alive', so he came up with a variation string part, which ties it all back into the sound we were after. Then we added Lala's percussion and a [Paul] Harris clarinet part with a weird sound and all the pieces just fell together. We did the backing vocals and gave it to Mike [Lewis] and turned him loose. The horn parts he came up with are almost like old-time big band, not slick disco style parts. We weren't too sure about them though, but Gene loved the track when he heard the final mix so we stayed with it."

Indeed, despite some qualifying comments years later, Clark eagerly supported the Alberts at the time and raised no objections either in the studio or in print. He applauded the use of strings and horns, claiming: "Sophistication is the signature of now. But the Byrds' sound is down in there." He did not add that only musical archaeologists schooled in deep excavation could find it.

Although the album crept into the *Billboard* Top 40, the disconcerting production still jarred. Judging from the trio's comments at the time, they seemed determined to avoid 'the Byrds' sound' at all costs. It was only later that McGuinn admitted that he felt compromised by this decision. "Once I went into the studio, the Albert Brothers, who were producing, decided they didn't want the Byrds' sound, which meant they didn't want my sound. I was on the bench for the whole album. The two songs I wrote were the only ones I was involved in. I had no say in the matter at all. I was just an instrument that they decided not to play at all. I was a victim of the whole situation."

In many respects, the desire to avoid the Byrds tag by wilfully introducing a new approach was contradictory. Contrary to popular belief, the most distinguishable feature of the Byrds' work was not some jingle-jangle guitar sound backed by soaring harmonies. What made their work important and adventurous was a constant and insatiable desire to experiment with new ideas. From folk rock to space rock, from ragas to country music, the Byrds had always avoided any pigeonholing classification. Compare 'Mr Tambourine Man' with 'Eight Miles High', or *The Notorious Byrd Brothers* with *Sweetheart Of The Rodeo*, and it becomes clear that the 'Byrds sound' was never stylized in any predictable manner. The aesthetic shortcomings of *McGuinn, Clark & Hillman* had nothing to do with missing Rickenbackers, avoidance of Dylan songs or the fact that McGuinn had only two songs. If the group had attempted to open new, unexplored areas in rock music, as they had done with virtually all of their albums up to, and including, *Sweetheart Of The Rodeo*, then they might have produced a classic. *McGuinn, Clark & Hillman* may have sounded unlike any Byrds album, but that did not mean it was fresh or innovative. On the contrary, it was blatantly reliant upon contemporaneous trends and production tricks, redolent of the Bee Gees, Firefall and other successful acts. Instead of looking forward, in the true Byrds' tradition, McGuinn, Clark & Hillman were imitating their protégés. They wanted to be known as a late Seventies group on record, but in concert they played their elaborately arranged studio cuts with the old, familiar jingle-jangle sound, and also included a large sprinkling of old Byrds' classics. It was an exercise in doublethink; McGuinn, Clark & Hillman were both a new group and they were also the Byrds revisited.

CHAPTER FORTY-TWO

Burn Out

IN February 1979, the group embarked on a European tour, which went smoothly without breaking any box office records. In the post punk climate, the trio were regarded as somewhat passé and their performances seen as nostalgic Byrds outings rather than anything more significant. "Milking it with Roger and his pals," joked *Sounds* in a typically irreverent review. "Accompanied by a drummer and guitarist, Hillman played bass and vocalized unconvincingly, McGuinn acted like a saggy-arsed zomboid puppet, and Clark, while looking cool in tight pants and billowing shirt, gave mumbling, giggling, between-song raps that were like a Cheech & Chong parody of laid-back rockstar jive. It was so weird that at one point Chris Hillman was moved to ask ol' Gene if he was on Mandrax . . . The names were the wrong way round on the marquee outside, but that hardly mattered to the standing room only crowd, who were here to see the Byrds by any other name . . . McGuinn's still great but the other two are duffers."

Iconoclasm was second nature to UK music reviewers in the late Seventies, and McGuinn, Clark & Hillman were easy targets. Funnily enough, although the comments sounded acerbic, the reporters were usually former Byrds fans whose appreciation was hidden beneath acid observations. Still at least there was some temporary harmony in the group. Hillman, a veritable Pyrocles in Australia, suddenly seemed calmer and more reflective. He expressed surprise at how young the audiences were in the UK and quietly wondered how long his latest collaboration might last. "We're giving it a six-month trial," he said. His uncertainty and concern were displayed in more private moments. During a moment of crisis, he accepted some spiritual solace from the born again McGuinn. "I was having trouble in McGuinn, Clark & Hillman and he prayed with me in a taxi cab in London. Isn't that funny? He grabbed my hand and prayed with me. Those are special times. Special things."

Al Hersh, despite his retrospective criticisms, also seemed happy enough at this point, knowing that they had a hit record back home and a busy tour calendar. As a manager, he still fretted about well-meaning 'distractions' that might keep them apart. The 'distractions' Hersh refers to were not drink or drugs but a polite euphemism for the musicians' spouses and loved ones. "With Roger, whoever was his wife took control of his phone book, his social life and, therefore, his entire career. Because of Terri Messina and Roger's wife, Camilla, and even Connie [Hillman's girlfriend, later wife] . . . as savvy as Connie was as a music business person, I felt even she distracted them from being able to put their heads together."

Greg Thomas hinted at the same divisions, which continued when they were on tour. "I was very close to Roger but then he got married and started bringing his wife on the road. That changed everything. He no longer hung out with the band or the players. He stayed with her and made himself unavailable. I was still friends with Chris, but he was very aloof and would always disappear and never hang around with anybody."

The personal dynamics are crucially important when assessing the progress of McGuinn, Clark & Hillman, but they were not simple. One person's 'distraction' was another's salvation. As is often the case in rock 'n' roll reminiscences by road managers or hedonistic musicians, the women in the story are frequently misunderstood or ignored. All too often, they are perceived as temptresses or killjoys intent on breaking up the boys' club. Hersh was already a veteran of the Byrdhouse days when girlfriends and wives came and went but the party always continued.

By the late Seventies, the apparently never ending party was nearing its end. Recreational drug use was rapidly turning ugly and could only last as long as record companies financed pampered stars with large advances and attendant luxuries. Age also played a factor.

By now, the stars of the Sixties were hitting their mid-thirties and many had a history of divorce, and children that they seldom saw, let alone knew. As they headed towards middle age, the more mature or self-aware reassessed their lives and sought relationships designed to last. This was true of several ex-Byrds, even those seemingly dedicated to impossible excesses – notably David Crosby and Gene Clark. It is surely no coincidence that they all found long-term partners during the second half of the Seventies. Jan Dance (Crosby), Terri Messina (Clark), Camilla Spaul (McGuinn) and Connie Pappas (Hillman) forged relationships or marriages spanning decades. They were the new significant others in their musicians' lives and they were not ready to be dismissed as mere 'distractions'. Of course they were always likely to be blamed for breaking up the gang, even when the gang members had long outgrown one another. It was a chauvinistic custom in rock 'n' roll to reproach girlfriends or spouses for fracturing sacred male bonds. A few years earlier Bianca Jagger had been vilified for supposedly creating a rift between Mick and Keith. Similarly, the bitter divisions between Lennon and McCartney were not merely interpreted as business squabbles, but seen as a symptom of the 'distracting' influences of Yoko Ono and Linda Eastman. One of the most insightful satires of the period was the Rutles' 1978 television 'documentary', *All You Need Is Cash*. This hilarious spoof on the Beatles' career was given added authenticity by the inclusion of mock interviews with several of their contemporaries. Playing himself, Mick Jagger suggested that the untimely break-up of the 'Prefab Four' was the result of "women getting in the way". As a sexist summation of the age, those words were remarkably prescient. Looking back at the McGuinn, Clark & Hillman interlude, it is probably accurate to state that Camilla, Terri and Connie were women who were ready to 'get in the way', without apology. They could be forgiven for thinking that it was the roadies, business advisors, fellow musicians and hangers-on who were the true 'distractions' in this saga.

The drug free McGuinn, who chose not to write about sex or violence, may have resembled 'a wimp ' in Hersh's eyes, but at least he was alive and in better control of his future. Hillman may have deferred to his future wife's advice on certain business matters, but that probably made more sense than entrusting everything to another new manager whose interests were more likely to be short-term depending on the artiste's commercial cache and bank balance. Clark had reached the same conclusion and felt a lot more comfortable hanging out with his girlfriend than attempting to parlay with Hollywood moguls or his former Byrds' associates for that matter. More importantly, although they were unaware of what was to come, all three musicians would soon find that they needed their female partners as rocks of support. Bleaker times were on the horizon. Rapid changes in the music industry and public taste meant that even the great Sixties survivors would become commercially vulnerable in succeeding years.

Rock mythology is remarkably resilient, even when faced with irrefutable evidence of changing relationships and impossible situations. The Beatles, long dead in the eyes of their creators, were still the subject of reunion rumours. Lennon's announcement that the dream was over appeared to have fallen on deaf ears. The Byrds suffered similar scrutiny throughout this period. Although McGuinn, Clark & Hillman were wary of being locked in the past, their continued existence ensured that the possibility of a full-scale Byrds' reformation was never far away from anyone's thoughts. "Another reunion of the Byrds remains a very strong possibility," Hillman told me at the time. "I know David and Michael want to do it, and when we have time maybe we'll do it right. And then, we'll just let the Byrds lie."

These vague promises appeared to take on more substance as the decade reached its close. In March 1979, Michael Clarke followed David Crosby's lead by playing onstage with the trio for the first time since the Sixties. Clarke's friend Bob Rassmussen, who worked as a barman in Boulder, was hanging out with the drummer when a call came through from Clark and Hillman, requesting his presence, along with Rick Roberts. "They just thought it would be cool," Rassmussen says. "They were partying, but Roger McGuinn was kind of straight at the time. But they got four fifths of the Byrds onstage." The surprise get-togethers took place at the Paramount, Portland and the Rainbow Music Hall, Denver. Clarke enjoyed the shows, even though he harboured few hopes of a full reunion.

Even while Clarke was re-establishing contact, Crosby was increasingly out on a limb. The highly successful CS&N reunion had run its course and so had his long-standing relationship with Graham Nash. They had recently attempted some recordings as a duo for CBS which ended disastrously when Crosby's drug addiction blighted the sessions. "David was not paying attention and often falling asleep," Nash says. "This led to a monstrous argument between us." A pivotal moment occurred when David's drugs paraphernalia was damaged and he sunk to his knees in despair. "We were in the middle of an incredible jam when his freebase pipe fell and shattered into a thousand pieces," Nash continues, "and that's when I lost it. That's when I realized David needed help." For Nash, this was the final confirmation that cocaine had replaced music as Crosby's primary impulse.

Disillusioned, Nash terminated the sessions and elected to complete the record without Crosby's contributions. "I didn't want to quit working with Graham," Crosby said at the time. "I didn't want to quit working with Crosby, Stills & Nash. That was the best music I made in my whole life. And because it's not happening, it's hurting so bad, man. But I've got to keep going . . . making music, even if it's by myself." Soon after, Capitol Records signed Crosby to a solo deal. With McGuinn, Clark, Hillman and Crosby all on the same record label, somebody in the company was clearly thinking Byrds. Now that Crosby no longer had commitments with CS&N, the odds on some form of Byrds reunion seemed favourable. Alas, any hopes of the original five reconnecting were dashed during the next few months when a strangely familiar history began to repeat itself.

Crosby was not the only ex-Byrd in the grip of cocaine madness. Gene Clark's addictive behaviour was increasing by the month, accompanied by the same fears, neuroses and conflicts that had previously contributed to his twice leaving the Byrds. Hillman first realized how bad it had become during an appearance on *The Dinah Shore Show* to promote the single, 'Don't You Write Her Off'. Clark was fidgety, stressed and in urgent need of a fix. At one point, he threatened to leave the television studio to get his stash and suffered a verbal barracking from Hillman, which caused him to reconsider. "Gene could disappear at the drop of a hat," says Hersh. "You never knew when he was going to take off." That evening, he resembled a rock 'n' roll gypsy in the Keith Richards' mode, complete with neckerchief, Cuban heels and a quirky strumming action on acoustic guitar. On screen he looked cool and dangerous, but his colleagues must have been worried where it might lead.

In May 1979, the group set out on a brief tour of Japan, which included a prestigious show in Osaka. Looking back, it seems incredible that they even persuaded Clark to make the trip, given his aversion to flying. More problems followed. "He missed the plane," Ron Rainey recalls. "I sent somebody from my office to his house to try and find him, but we couldn't raise him. Fortunately, we were leaving a couple of days ahead of the tour, so I left Gene's ticket at the airport and told them, 'Hopefully, he'll be here tomorrow.' And that's what happened, he arrived the next day. But he was unravelling by then."

The culture shock of staying in a foreign land where he did not speak the language or appreciate the customs, tested Clark's nerves to the limit. Soon after, Al Hersh was given a chilling ultimatum. "In Japan, Gene came to me one night and said, 'I'm not going onstage unless you get me some heroin.' I said, 'Gene, that's impossible. We're in Japan!' We knew a promoter who was able to get us a bit of hash, but heroin was out of the question. It was bad that Gene held me up like that – and he was the kind of guy who would not have gone on in those circumstances. We got him something. I don't know what the hell it was, but it placated him until the show was done."

After Japan, relations between Clark and the others hit a new low. McGuinn tried to stay calm, but the fiery Hillman was already spitting lava and close to a full eruption. "Chris was still doing some 'healing' with Roger and he was afraid of being onstage with Gene," says Hersh. "It was like the Clash of the Titans. There were times when they squared off against each other. The Roger thing [in Australia] had been quick. Chris had met the karate guy Chuck Norris and learned how to kick everybody's ass. He got Roger out of the way right away. But when it came to Gene, Chris knew that if it ever happened one, if not both, of them would be dead. Luckily, they somehow avoided it ever happening because if they'd got physical with each other someone would have died. No doubt. I mean, Gene Clark! Look at the build on that guy, man. He was unbelievable, completely blew me away. I would watch them looking at each other and thinking, 'Man, we'd better not mix it!' And thank God they never did. It would have been really really ugly."

The tensions were still evident when McGuinn, Clark & Hillman played for a home crowd at LA's Universal Amphitheatre in July. Arenas and stadiums did not suit the trio, who usually required a smaller venue to connect with the audience, and themselves. If Crosby had been part of the set-up, his passion and sense of event would have cut through the conflicts and created the necessary suspension of disbelief to convince the audience and his fellow players to believe. The others were too cool and rigid to pull off that magic trick in front of an arena crowd. That evening they sounded strangely soulless, even on the classic Byrds songs that everybody loved. Back at the Hammersmith Odeon, their first stage reunion had been thrilling but here they no longer connected. It was an odd homecoming. Capitol's accomplished head of publicity, Stephen Peeples, whose slightly unctuous liner notes had graced the front cover of their album, chose not to attend. He had an alternative engagement watching the Knack, the powerpop quartet whose Beatles pastiches were all the rage in LA that summer. As a barometer of the company's shifting faith in the former Byrds, his absence seemed telling. Sitting next to me at the front of the amphitheatre was Linda Loo Bopp, the young dancer from the Ciro's days, who had accompanied the Byrds on their first American tour in 1965. Her husky voice and model looks meant backstage access was immediate, without any need of passes. But visiting the stars was a strange expedition. Hillman was in a trailer, aloof but seemingly happy to be away from the madding crowd. Suddenly, one of his friends appeared and he became extremely animated, excitedly telling him: "Get into that bathroom!" That phrase was a very familiar one in LA at the time.

McGuinn, meanwhile, could be found in a surrogate tent,

surrounded by a crowd of well-wishers. Sober and friendly, he was barely recognizable when compared to that cocky figure who had swaggered across England like an invading pirate in the summer of 1977. Back then McGuinn was the quintessential stroppy rock star, now he seemed almost preternaturally pleasant. It was rather like experiencing a scene from *Invasion Of The Bodysnatchers*. Cocaine free, he was far less intense or ego driven. All edginess was gone but, like Crosby in later years, he was less fascinating as a result. Something was missing. But at least he was there, unlike Clark who had performed a disappearing act worthy of Houdini. Previously a lover of after hours ligging, he had become a more furtive creature whose habits required a select cognoscenti. Most probably, he had retired to one of his Hollywood haunts or gone back to Terri Messina's place in Laurel Canyon where madness reigned.

The estrangement evident that evening was an accurate reflection of three individuals leading different lives. Drummer Greg Thomas, who had always been McGuinn's right-hand man on tour, switched allegiances and followed the supply line which led inevitably to Clark. "It got worse," he says, referring to the trio's odd interaction. "Roger just did his own thing. Chris was very aloof and would always disappear. So I hung out with Tommy Kaye and Gene at the time. When I became friends with Gene, Roger really despised that. Then I wanted to work with Tommy Kaye. Roger said they were stealing his drummer! McGuinn, Clark & Hillman did a lot of shows in New York, then we'd come back to LA and the only person I could hang out with was Gene. He was always up for hanging out, writing songs and staying up all night doing drugs. Gene's girlfriend Terri lived in Laurel Canyon and we spent a lot of time over there. Things went downhill pretty quickly and everybody was getting very high all the time at that house. We were like the guys that never slept. I thought I was bad, but Gene would definitely overdo it."

In August, events took a darker turn when McGuinn and Hillman started appearing at concerts without Clark. The official line was that he was 'extremely ill'. Students of ancient Byrds history, however, could not help remembering similar explanations prior to Clark's sensational departure in early 1966. In spite of such suspicions, there was some evidence to suggest that his withdrawal might merely be temporary. Hillman confirmed that Gene was receiving treatment in a California hospital for an abscess of the tooth, having poisoned his mouth while performing amateur surgery on a gum with an unsterilized needle. McGuinn later suggested that he was probably strung out.

Clark's colleagues managed to put on a competent show in his absence, although they were occasionally interrupted by shouts of 'Where's Gene?' "We had to get up and say we'd refund money to anybody who wasn't happy," Hersh recalls. "But luckily nobody wanted their money back because nobody missed him." Getting away with a month full of minor dates was one thing, but more urgent bookings lay ahead. Capitol were keen for the group to re-enter the studio and record a second album at the earliest opportunity. Everyone hoped that Clark's convalescence would enable him to write some new material and get healthy for the much anticipated sessions. Such expectations would prove vainer than anyone could possibly have imagined.

In addition to his hedonistic and health issues, Clark was feeling increasingly ostracized by McGuinn and Hillman. Although there was no direct conflict, the atmosphere was decidedly frosty. Their interaction mystified many, including Clark's girlfriend Terri Messina, who never fully understood the group dynamics. "The thing with McGuinn, Clark & Hillman was very personal," she says. "Being close to Gene, I used to ask him, 'Why did you leave the Byrds? They were at the height of their success and you just leave, what's the matter with you?' He would say, 'You'd have to be there. You don't know those other guys.' I told him, 'Well, you're not stupid or that difficult to get along with. Couldn't you have worked it out?' All I got back was 'You'd have to be there.' When I went out on the road with McGuinn and Hillman, I understood what he was talking about and saw the full impact of it. Gene was his own worst enemy. That kind of stuff exists in the business at all levels. I know, I was an actress, I was a film editor and I've been in the entertainment business all my life. There's all kinds of back-stabbing situations you get into. But you've got to get around that stuff. You've got to get over it. All that would really emotionally screw him up . . . He just didn't have the stomach for dealing with a lot of that stuff and dealing with the business . . . But you have to be on top of that and not be flaky. He would like to just be able to do his music and not have to deal with anything else."

Living high on the hog after receiving his record company advance, Clark was distracted by all the rock star trappings and the greater expectations forced upon him. He spent money recklessly, even buying a Porsche, as if reliving his old life as a Hollywood Byrd. His ex-band mate Peter Oliva recalls meeting him at this point and witnessing his largesse. "We went to this disco. I had just gotten married to my second wife. Geno got kind of drunk and took us back to his hotel room and started laying out these $100 bills, maybe a thousand bucks. I guess he was still feeling guilty about what happened to the last band and how it had ended. He said, 'Here, take this! This is for you, man, because you hung in there . . .' So I took it. He was making good money back then."

Clark had assumed that he would be rolling in money after the trio's hit record and world tour but, after all the expenses had been deducted, the profit margins were slighter than he had imagined. As his drug intake increased, he suddenly became paranoid about money, irrationally railing against imagined deceivers. He also resented McGuinn's stronger administrative control, believing that he held the upper hand politically, given his past history with Ron Rainey, Al Hersh and Greg Thomas. His attitude was summed up in the quip: "Give McGuinn an inch and he'll take an army."

The irony was that McGuinn held no such power or influence. His long-standing friendship with Hersh was in terminal decline and all that remained was professional distance. "Roger and I became estranged after years of working together. After he became a born again Christian we just couldn't communicate any more." The nadir occurred prior to a show in Denver when Hersh insulted his employer backstage. McGuinn had stopped taking drugs, but still enjoyed a bottle of wine, an inconsistency that irked Hersh. In a heated moment, he sarcastically taunted: "Roger, you're a hypocritical bastard, you're here drinking a bottle of wine and you're supposed to be this evangelical person." Understandably, McGuinn resented the insult, which he felt was unwarranted. "He said, 'You can't talk to me that way!' I told him, 'I don't understand you.' Then he explained, 'Well, I'm drinking the blood of the Lord.' That's exactly what he said. I had a beer and said, 'Well, I'm drinking piss . . . get onstage.' Our relationship got worse and worse from then on. Everyone was fed up with this pompous bullshit."

Hersh's disdain for McGuinn's religion summed up the chasm between their respective value systems. McGuinn had never been particularly evangelical in his utterances, preferring to keep a respectful distance from his former cronies, whom he knew were still immersed in the drug culture. He had already been advised of the dangers of fraternizing with non-believers and Hersh's attitude vindicated those warnings. Dylan had experienced similar criticisms, but vented his wrath in such songs as 'Slow Train Coming' and 'When You Gonna Wake Up'. Their confrontational scorn brought a new edge to his lyrics, which carried forward into the sarcastic 'Property Of Jesus', a bitter commentary on secular superiority sung in a tone that mixed genuine hurt with sneering derision. Unfortunately, McGuinn had no such outlet, preferring to turn the other cheek rather than playing the avenging angel. His pacific nature probably attracted as much venom from former friends as Dylan's characteristically cutting responses had to his own atheistic critics.

In common with Hersh, Greg Thomas missed the old McGuinn and felt stifled by his unwillingness to engage in any rock 'n' roll hijinks. Witnessing sobriety is anathema to a heavy drinker or drug user because that very state contains an implied judgement against excess, which is intimidating in itself. Thomas' natural reaction was to have fun at McGuinn's expense by playing a practical joke. In other words, ritual humiliation as a defence mechanism. "I got very drunk one night," Thomas recalls. "I think we were in Starkville, Mississippi. We hadn't seen Roger for a couple of weeks, except when he was onstage. He was with his wife and wasn't hanging out with the band. I saw him on roller skates, walking by the pool. That's when it happened. I went up, put my arm around him, grabbed him, then walked him into the deep end of the swimming pool. I was very mischievous then. It's extremely hard to swim with roller skates, so I don't know how he got out. I'd actually told Chris

I was going to do it and he was thrilled because he couldn't stand Roger at the time. But I really loved Roger and can't say a bad thing about him. He's a great person really. I was drunk and I'm really sorry I did that." The indiscretion merely lengthened the division between the various parties, and Thomas left the band soon afterwards. "I was burned out on the music," he concludes, "burned out on the whole scene. McGuinn, Clark & Hillman was like a big accident waiting to happen. I felt I was part of the whole menagerie, but it finally hit the wall."

In November 1979, McGuinn and Hillman entered Criteria Studios to record their second Capitol album, with the assistance of guitarist Johnne 'John' Sambataro and drummer Scott Kirkpatrick. Clark was a ghostly presence, whose appearances at the sessions were limited to a few hours. "Gene started to go nuts again," says Hillman. "We were trying to keep him in line, like 'Come on, Gene, don't do this! You're getting crazy again!' We tried to do this second album and it was really horrible. We couldn't even get him to sing."

Disillusioned, frustrated and suspicious, Clark returned to his old excesses as a means of escape. "He went on a binge because he didn't have the money that he thought he was going to have," his friend Tom Slocum remembers. "Consequently, it screwed up what he had with Terri at the time and also his payments to his ex-wife up in Mendocino."

After the album was completed, McGuinn and Hillman toured without Clark, leaving no doubt in anyone's mind that a split had occurred. Immediately after the sessions I confronted Hersh about Clark's limited involvement and he admitted that Gene had let them down badly while pointing out that his main contribution was a song ironically titled 'Won't Let You Down'. In what now sounds like a fanciful fib, he assured me: "Roger and Chris are like brothers, man." Those words were spoken with such earnestness that it was impossible not to believe he was telling the truth. Perhaps it was a private joke and he meant "brothers in arms". "I was exaggerating," he now admits. "I was saying and doing anything I could because I knew this had a limited shelf life. I didn't see anything beyond what we were doing. I couldn't see Crosby and the other guys getting involved on a major level that would have got the Byrds back together."

Apart from the drugs, the other major reasons behind Clark's third departure from McGuinn and Hillman were all too familiar. Although he had tolerated the extensive touring schedules of the past year, it was evident that he still could not adapt to life on the road. In many respects, this had always been his primary problem as a performer, dating back to the New Christy Minstrels. While Clark had frequently attempted to come to terms with his distaste for touring, his old neuroses always threatened to take him to the brink of a nervous breakdown. "Gene was a handful to travel with," says Hersh, "and we had some weird things happen. We travelled a lot by car and I would be sitting next to him and he'd be sweating all the time, biting his nails, and thinking that around the next curve a truck was going to come and decapitate him. Everybody said he was afraid of flying, but I felt he was afraid of travelling – any kind of travelling. It didn't matter if it was a jet, a boat, a car, a truck or a bus. He just couldn't travel. Period. Maybe he felt out of control of the situation. He would just sit there and I would get these vibes off him. It was just horrible. Indescribable. He wasn't afraid of dying either. It was a strange thing. I don't even know how to explain it."

The downward spiral continued as Clark attempted to find a new path working with some old friends. He invited Andy Kandanes and Peter Oliva to visit Mammoth, where Terri's parents owned a holiday home. During his later days with McGuinn and Hillman, Clark had bought an expensive digital recorder which he was keen to try out. "We were doing some co-writing with Gene," says Kandanes, "mainly for publishing with the possibility of putting another band together and going on tour." It soon became clear that Clark's condition rendered such plans farcical. Frequently strung out, he was also depressed about the likelihood of losing Terri. "That relationship definitely went down in flames because of the drugs," Kandanes adds. "When Peter and I were recording with Gene, they were getting crazy. I ended up grabbing everything and flushing it down the toilet. I told both of them: 'This shit has got to stop right now!' I cared about them and it was horrible for me to see this go on. I just couldn't deal with it any more. Once they got clearer heads they were back to normal, but this stuff was making them crazy. There comes a point when you've got to know when to walk away from all of that."

Not for the last time, Messina parted from Clark shortly afterwards. There was no easy solution to his problems. Tempting fate, he moved from Terri's home into the house of his wild friend and former producer Jesse Ed Davis. Here was a combination made in alcoholic hell. Davis' excesses were legion, including heroin binges with John Lennon and a fondness for liquor which reinforced the stereotypical caricature of the Indian made mad by drink. "Gene loved Jesse, who did *White Light* with him," Slocum says. "But they were a mess. They were lucky to get out of town. They almost got shot one night down in a bar in Hollywood. They were both very drunk and out of control, they were a party on wheels."

Slocum was walking past the restaurant/bar Dan Tana's one evening, when Clark and Davis came spinning through the doors in a brawling fracas that continued on the street. "Gene fell into the arms of this big construction worker, who picked him up," Slocum remembers. "He was about to pummel him. I said, 'Hey, what are you doing? Stop that stuff!' Gene was down on the ground and he wasn't used to looking up at someone who was about to beat the shit out of him. It was crazy alcohol." Clark was still swinging fists wildly and indiscriminately as Slocum bundled him into a taxi which whisked him away.

After his 'lost weekend' with Jesse Ed Davis, Clark finally came to his senses and moved out to Hawaii in an attempt to vanquish his demons. McGuinn and Hillman had already decided to continue without him and although Capitol knew he was needed in the studio, it was clear that the three could no longer work together. Hillman, who had been cynical and wary about Clark's involvement from the outset, was not entirely surprised by the outcome. When the split finally occurred, McGuinn and Hillman initially felt reasonably confident about surviving as a duo. The problem of surmounting Clark's departure had last occurred around the time of the recording of *The Notorious Byrd Brothers*. With the sacking of Crosby, the future of the Byrds had appeared to rest on Clark's contribution to the group. On that occasion, Clark had survived only three weeks and contributed nothing. Without him, the Byrds still managed to create one of their greatest albums. Twelve years later, McGuinn and Hillman found themselves under similar pressure and although they could not produce another *Notorious*, or anything similar, they rallied sufficiently to complete a surprisingly upbeat record.

City was rush released in January 1980 under the banner 'Roger McGuinn and Chris Hillman featuring Gene Clark'. The work had been completed less than two months before, during a 20-day spell in Miami. While the recording had been cut quickly, not everything had run smoothly. Apart from the problems with Clark, McGuinn and Hillman found themselves in conflict with their producers. Since recording their last album, they had come to realize their mistake in allowing the Albert Brothers so much creative control. In spite of the hit single, 'Don't You Write Her Off', and the relative commercial success of *McGuinn, Clark & Hillman*, both performers now felt that the elaborate production was an artistic error. Fresh from the concert platform, they recorded some strong demos, which they presented for immediate recording. The Albert Brothers were unimpressed and argued in favour of a more ornate, professional production. McGuinn and Hillman held their ground, however, and the album was completed in the way that they had originally envisaged.

As Hillman crowed: "We went in with a bunch of new songs to record a rock 'n' roll album using the same kind of fast, basic, hold-the-overdubs, strings and horns approach we used 15 years ago. Add to that the recording technology available today and we cut an album that's really fresh, uptempo and full of energy." Hillman was not far wrong. The back to basics approach resulted in a much more palatable record, which deserved a wider audience. With McGuinn finding fresh inspiration as a songwriter, and Hillman producing some inspired hard-rock items, the album showed considerable promise. Unlike its predecessor, *City* displayed no disdain for the past but embraced the Rickenbacker chime and was a far better representation of the group's live sound.

The title of the album indicated its underlying theme, with four of the ten tracks reflecting the urban motif. "It's time to get back to the city," announced McGuinn, previewing the work. "Chicago is my home town and I almost moved to New York. I need the urban environment, that's why I live in a Century City high-rise. I find that energy really stimulating. Sure, the city can be overwhelming and frightening, but there are ways of dealing with it. It's like the ocean: you can drown or sail across the surface. You can enjoy it as long as you respect its power."

Most of the songs of city life came from Chris Hillman's collaboration with *Crawdaddy* editor Peter Knobler, and were written in a similar vein to 'Stoppin' Traffic' on the previous album. Fortunately, more freedom had gone into the playing on *City* and what might otherwise have sounded fairly average songs were given extra bite. 'Who Taught The Night' had an aggressive feel and funky edge. Much the same could be said of the other Hillman/Knobler collaboration 'Street Talk', with its Shadows' 'Man Of Mystery'-style opening.

The first single from the album, 'One More Chance', cleverly channelled the Sixties Byrds style into an Eighties format. It featured the familiar Rickenbacker sound coupled with a white reggae riff, similar in feel to the Police's 'Walking On The Moon'. In many respects, 'One More Chance' was a celebration of McGuinn's new life as a born-again Christian, but it also worked as an unambiguous love song, without any specific spiritual overtones. McGuinn wisely chose to leave any interpretation open to the listener, merely adding: "It reminds me of the old parable about the knight in armour who thought he was invincible, but he was killed when an arrow found its mark in a crevice between his armour plates. The idea is no matter how hardened you think you are, you're still vulnerable somehow."

Gene Clark's 'Won't Let You Down' emerged as another of the album's highlights, showing the ease with which the trio could imitate the sound of the original Byrds. Although McGuinn had occasionally attempted to achieve similar effects on songs like 'The Lady', this was much more authentic. 'Won't Let You Down' instantly recalled 'Feel A Whole Lot Better', plus subtle snatches of other Byrds' classics. What sounded like a straightforward love song was given added depth by manager Al Hersh's revelation that it was written about the group during their period of crisis. Examined from this perspective, the deceptively ordinary lyrics, optimistic tone and singalong chorus all become charged with irony. The composition opens with Clark offering the group a new, and as yet untitled, song for consideration. What follows is nothing less than an admission of his fall into near alcoholism over the years ("a life of whisky and wine") and how the group "made a new moon" by providing an opportunity to begin a fresh phase in his life. Clark's promise, as stated in the song's title, is severely qualified as early as the second line of the chorus, in which he acknowledges that all he has left to give them is his music, "my world". As Al Hersh caustically remarked, "Gene promised that he would not let them down, but in the end he blew it!"

The highlight of *City* turned out to be the striking title track. With McGuinn's strong Rickenbacker work and a lyric that was a cut above any of his recent compositions, it showed him emerging from a creative slump. According to Camilla McGuinn, the song "came about rapidly" after they sat down to write some suitable lyrics for a tune that Roger wanted to use. The album cover, borrowed from a photo depicting a line of imposing skyscrapers, provided the lyrical inspiration. "The photo was taken at night when light was streaming out of the office windows," Roger recalls. "A Learjet was parked downstairs on ground level. Starting with just the word 'City', Camilla and I started kicking around ideas and came up with someone being lost in the city, something we can all identify with." Although excellent, the song would have been even better if McGuinn had been less sparing with the Rickenbacker break. The snatch of 'Eight Miles High'-style guitar work was arresting but tantalizingly undeveloped, almost as if McGuinn were teasing the listener with tasty morsels from his past.

A less welcome remnant from his past opened side two. The throwaway 'Skate Date' was a lightweight novelty, which sounded like a leftover from the Brill Building era. Amazingly, three writers were credited for this banal composition. "Roger wanted to do a roller-skating song," Camilla told me. "Ever since he was a kid he's always loved roller-skating. He and Chris worked on the song and I completed it. It was written in two separate stages. It's not particularly heavy of course, but I enjoyed it."

McGuinn's recording of Tom Kimmel and Lynn Tobola's 'Givin' Herself Away' proved another welcome high point of *City*. The aggressive vocal style highlighted the irony of the song in which a guy callously sets out in search of a perfectly submissive woman, only to discover a domineering mistress who reduces him to sycophancy. It was the old tale of the hunter becoming the hunted, and the theme allowed McGuinn to spit out the words with venom.

'Deeper In' showed Hillman employing another co-writer, his La Jolla, California, next-door neighbour, Douglas Foxworthy. Alas, the song was little more than average, recalling Hillman's more pedestrian work on the previous album.

Inevitably, it was Gene Clark who provided the strangest and most baffling track, 'Painted Fire'. The rock 'n' roll-style piano and drums gave the song a Fifties feel which sounded totally out of place on the album. Structurally, the track seemed incomplete, as though Clark originally had an interesting idea but lost direction during the writing process. The contrast between the country girl who loves to sit out drinking beer at the weekend and the fashion queen who becomes "everybody's dream" is never fully realized. Having employed the metaphor 'Painted Fire' (referring to an enticingly made-up and dangerously passionate nymphet) Clark failed to create a dramatic vehicle for the theme. As a result, the song seemed strangely fragmentary.

The closing cut on the album, 'Let Me Down Easy', was another reminder of past days, harking back to the style of mid-period Flying Burrito Brothers. A striking steel guitar completed the mixture of musical styles on this album. More importantly, the song demonstrated, both musically and lyrically, that Hillman and Knobler were not restricted to composing thematically repetitive rock songs, as might have been supposed from their other contributions.

Overall, *City* denied the group's public statements prior to the release of the first McGuinn, Clark & Hillman album. At that point, they were anxious to avoid their 'old' sound, but on *City* they were pleased to record a Byrds album Eighties style. Appropriately, they were looking back at their history in order to make sense of the present. Rather than imitating contemporary colleagues and allowing themselves to become a product of late Seventies production, they had decided to use their familiar sound as a springboard to greater achievements. Such a decision should have brought favourable rewards, but it was also a dangerous ploy. The old Byrds Rickenbacker sound had meant ripe pickings for imitators such as Tom Petty, who effortlessly capitalized on McGuinn's pioneering work. Unfortunately, it did not follow that McGuinn, Clark & Hillman would necessarily cut into Petty's market. In the early Seventies, an album such as *City* by three ex-Byrds might have broken through, but by 1980 the market had been milked by a plethora of pretenders, supported by younger audiences who assumed the Byrds were already part of history.

Sadly, *City* did not even receive any compensatory critical commendation. Having produced their finest work in several years, the group lacked one crucial quality: innovation. As a reaction to *McGuinn, Clark & Hillman*, they had made the sensible decision to play to their strengths. McGuinn's typical response was to attempt a sampler of past achievements, a trick he had previously used to good effect on *(Untitled)* and his first solo album. Since then he had occasionally overused old formulas, most noticeably on the ironically titled 'Same Old Sound' and the blatantly self-imitative 'Bye Bye Baby'. For McGuinn, retrospection had become an almost Pavlovian reaction to bad record sales. *City* showed that the familiar jingle-jangle sound could still be put to good use, but it lacked the groundbreaking adventure of their greatest work. McGuinn, Clark & Hillman had answered their critics by attempting the best of the Byrds as the best of McGuinn, Clark and Hillman. Unfortunately, it was neither enough for critical nor commercial success.

Without Gene Clark, McGuinn and Hillman struggled on in the hope of maintaining their partnership. With recording commitments to fulfil, they were placed in the hands of Jerry Wexler and Barry Beckett, whose impressive R&B credentials suggested a completely new direction for the former Byrds. Hillman found himself in the odd position of having an in-law as producer as Wexler had married Rene Pappas, the sister of his wife, Constance.

BURN OUT

By early 1980, the prospect of a Third Coming for the original Byrds was the stuff of dreams. In March of that year, I approached Camilla McGuinn about her husband's possible involvement in such a project but she seemed very dubious. "It's remote," she concluded. "Perhaps it's still possible for a short period. But each of the original Byrds has grown in different ways. Roger and Chris are probably the most stable, so much would depend on them."

With Gene Clark still recovering from the excesses of the previous year, the old dream seemed a long way off. David Crosby, increasingly isolated and already heavily into drugs, seemed a most unlikely candidate for any recordings with the born again McGuinn. But, surprisingly, he was not ready to rule out another reunion. After talking to Camilla, I contacted Crosby the following month to sound out his feelings about his former partner. "I frankly like the guy," he told me. "I feel more distant from him now because of this damn, dumb Jesus thing, but I like him. The Christianity wouldn't necessarily keep us apart. I could still work with him, easily."

CHAPTER FORTY-THREE

The Dark Decade

CROSBY's willingness to work with McGuinn was never likely to be reciprocated during the early Eighties. Even the McGuinn/Hillman partnership no longer looked secure and was virtually blighted with the release of their lacklustre swansong, *McGuinn/Hillman*. At a time when the duo most needed a strong album to convince Capitol of their worth, they produced what sounded like a tired and uninspired contract filler. The hackneyed artwork, complete with the overdone image of a bird spreading its wings, was reflected in the music which largely consisted of mediocre cover versions of songs by Graham Parker, Rodney Crowell, Will MacFarlane and Robbie Steadman. McGuinn and Hillman managed to co-write three numbers, of which only the closing 'Turn Your Radio On' impressed. McGuinn later explained that the duo had a number of suitable compositions ready for inclusion, but these were vetoed by producer Jerry Wexler in favour of extraneous material. This was terribly ironic. It had taken three albums for a writing partnership to emerge and when it did nobody was interested. "We had written 12 songs with a theme," McGuinn elaborates. "They were all related to the idea of entertainment. Jerry Wexler said we had to go for hits and threw out most of the material. He was Chris' brother-in-law, so he was probably trying to help Chris out. He said we had to go for hits but there wasn't anything vaguely like a hit on that album. It was a frustrating project, and a frustrating band tour. The reviews were bad; the audiences didn't like it; there was a lot of anxiety."

Manager Al Hersh had previously expressed his desire for

McGuinn & Hillman to record outside material, but the policy was clearly counter productive. The vain hope that one of the covers might produce a fluke hit was a long shot, which missed by a mile. Instead, the album gave the impression that the duo had run embarrassingly short of ideas and brought the validity of their partnership into question. Hillman complained that Wexler had foolishly attempted to transform them into a white Sam & Dave, thereby sealing their commercial doom. "You couldn't get any whiter guys than McGuinn and I to do this R&B material," he jokes. "So it was a horrible record and even Capitol just hated it." Unsurprisingly, the record failed to register an entry in the *Billboard* Top 200 and its UK release was greeted with universal apathy.

In February 1980, the duo made an ill-advised trip to the UK in a doomed attempt to expand their international appeal. The Byrds had always fared well in Europe, but the times were now against them. Their critical cachet lay in an illustrious past and the rock world was now fixated on youth. Terms like 'new wave' emphasized a disdain for those with nothing fresh to offer. Career patterns of many greats tend to progress in cycles – rise, fall and reconciliation – and the ex-Byrds were firmly placed in the middle category. Capitol brought them over to England with support act Lee Clayton, whose self-titled second album was mightily impressive. Although his live show was compromised by some histrionic guitar work by Philip Donnelly, whose studio contributions had been exemplary, reviewers still showed a preference for the aspirant newcomer. One wrote: "Hampered by a PA that was all shrieking treble, Lee Clayton still stole the show so comprehensively that it was a wonder the police weren't outside his dressing room after the gig with a warrant."

Backstage tensions were hardly helped by the presence of Carlos Bernal, who was then working as Clayton's road manager. "Carlos and Chris never came to terms with the Anya thing," says Al Hersh, referring to Bernal's affair with Hillman's ex-wife back in 1968. "When Clayton was the opening act I thought Chris would kill Carlos because they hadn't really resolved that issue. It came up on that tour and it was really scary too because a lot of weird shit happened." Despite Hersh's fears, there was no reported altercation between the two and Bernal assumed everything had long been forgiven.

Ridicule was now the weapon with which most critics responded to McGuinn & Hillman. They were judged by the quality of their current record which was poor enough to extinguish any vestiges of respect for their previous greatness. Already, it seemed as if they would have to go through a period of purgatory in the critical wilderness before being rediscovered.

Melody Maker caught the mood of the time at its brutal best in a scathing review of their London performance using the sardonic headline: 'Bad Night At The Odeon'. Demonstrating that hell hath no fury like a former fan scorned, critic Allan Jones wrote: "McGuinn and Hillman utterly destroyed any notion of life after death. Dead from the stage up, they were wheeled out of the wings, ludicrously attired in lumberjack shirts and kipper ties. McGuinn still has a voice that can send a shiver through your heart, but I wouldn't throw Hillman a lifebelt if he were drowning. They performed their indifferent new songs with clumsy, misplaced enthusiasm and cannibalized the legend of the Byrds in a disgraceful mercenary manner." Even the encore of Byrds' classics failed to win any redeeming comments, largely due to McGuinn's recent stage gimmick. "He came out on roller skates!" Jones concluded. "Clarence White would've laughed at him. Gram Parsons would've punched the silly bastard out. I would've held his coat."

Although McGuinn/Hillman continued to play low-key gigs together, sometimes backed by drummer Tom Mooney and former Burrito Sneaky Pete Kleinow, there was a jaundiced air about those performances as though they had accepted that this latest collaboration had run its course. At one gig, Hillman was spotted wearing a badge imploring: "How do I get out of this thing?" It was an apposite comment.

What had seemed such a promising reunion back in 1977 was now limping towards an anticlimactic disbandment. Manager Al Hersh, who had worked with McGuinn for more than a decade and experienced the entire MC&H adventure, finally parted company with his employer. On the administrative side, only loyal agent Ron Rainey remained. Even with an act seemingly in terminal decline, he remained optimistic. "We were doing tours for hard tickets, supporting big bands and doing our own shows. It was a money-making operation. Till the end it was making money, otherwise those guys wouldn't have done it."

The senseless murder of John Lennon in December 1980 provided a symbolic reminder of how much had been lost along the way. The liberal dreams and ideals that had characterized the Sixties in the eyes of cultural commentators now seemed like ancient history. Both McGuinn and Hillman would later lament the Seventies as a decade of selfishness and abuse from which they were fortunate to pull through seemingly intact. Now there was a new mood in America of equal or greater symbolism, personified in the inauguration of a former Hollywood idol turned president. One month after Lennon's death, 70-year-old Ronald Reagan began his administration amid a surge of nationalist fervour. By some Almighty providence, the day of his investiture coincided with the long-awaited release of US hostages following 444 days of incarceration in Iran. In the months that followed, it was hard to dispute the theory that Reagan had appointed some deific film-maker to transform his presidential office into a barely credible, partisan B-movie. There was even a villain of the piece in the person of John Warnock Hinckley, a deranged obsessive suffering the pangs of an unrequited passion for actress Jodie Foster. He duly demonstrated the depth of his infatuation by unloading his gun into the lungs of the new president. Remarkably, the ageing Reagan not only survived, but was back at work in the White House within 12 days. This was surely the stuff of a Hollywood movie with a happy ending, in complete contrast to the chilling real life tragedies of John and Robert Kennedy, Martin Luther King or John Lennon. Reagan's survival and indomitable spirit captured the American public's imagination, while simultaneously distracting attention from his various political stratagems.

In spite of their Sixties' liberal credentials, McGuinn and Hillman found themselves unexpectedly caught up in the new conservatism of the Reagan era. Camilla McGuinn had been reading *The Poems Of Henry Van Dyke* and was inspired by the patriotic verse 'America For Me'. Written by the Pennsylvanian poet and Presbyterian minister in June 1909, it combined a love of God and country. Roger added music to Van Dyke's words, producing a beautiful piece, ideally suited for performance and infinitely superior to the questionable cover material on the recent album. They were already playing the song onstage when news came through of Reagan's inauguration address and the simultaneous release of the hostages in Iran. "'America For Me' was causing a huge stir," Rainey recalls, "and television stations in New York wanted to play it when they were showing videos of the hostages being released. I thought we were on the cusp of another hit record. Everybody was getting excited again."

Whatever dwindling prospects McGuinn and Hillman may have had were rendered irrelevant by an event dubbed 'the Bottom Line incident'. It was backstage at the New York club that Hillman's anger again proved his undoing. In a remarkable example of self-sabotage, he assaulted a senior executive from Capitol Records. The repercussions were not long coming. "I was still at home when my phone rang at eight o'clock in the morning," recalls Ron Rainey, who had witnessed the unfortunate happening. "They called me in for a meeting [at Capitol] and they said, 'We're done! They're off the label.' They pulled the moral clause or whatever it was."

It was a sad, if eventful, end to a collaboration that many felt had already run its course. The ever supportive Ron Rainey was disappointed but felt some sympathy towards Hillman, whom he felt had been provoked by his victim. "Chris at that time was a young buck who was full of it, and he had a temper. But his temper was not without reason. That executive wanted Roger to dump Chris and go out as a solo. Chris had been putting up with this for a while. I felt that guy was interfering and driving a wedge between Chris and Roger. We were doing the best we could without Gene, who was now missing in action. It was tough after that to keep the record company's interest. That guy was totally out of line, but Capitol had to protect their person, which I understood. We all understood, but it was patently unfair, in my view."

Roger McGuinn was not so understanding. He had abhorred displays of violence long before his born again conversion and was appalled by this latest outburst. Reacting strongly to excuses made on behalf of his former colleague, he specifically wrote to me

THE DARK DECADE

confirming: "Chris Hillman knew full well he was hitting a Capitol Records man." Not long after, McGuinn decided to terminate their partnership, telling Hillman: "I don't ever want to work with you again."

The decade had barely begun and suddenly the original Byrds were as far away from each other as they had ever been. Talk of further reunions were summarily dismissed as either artistically irrelevant ventures or time-wasting cash-ins. David Crosby, upset by the others' reluctance to allow him to contribute vocals during the first Miami sessions, had evidently hardened in his attitude. "It's history," was his weary riposte to any reunion queries. Chris Hillman seemed equally dismissive and was betraying a discernible antipathy towards big label schemes by uncompromisingly pursuing his interest in bluegrass music. Gene Clark was still willing to tour as the Byrds, but knew that Hillman and McGuinn were none too keen on working with him again. Mike Clarke, for all his recent successes with Firefall, still had problems convincing his fellow Byrds that he was God's gift to the drum kit. Finally, McGuinn was absolutely adamant: the Byrds was dead. He could not envisage a time when the five would reconvene. In the few interviews that he sat through, there seemed a marked reluctance even to talk about the Byrds. It was now the great irrelevance.

The Eighties was to prove the darkest creative period in Byrds history as the individual members either ceased recording or restricted their output to small, independent record labels. The greatest American group of all time were now nothing more than five former legends without a major record contract between them. Godhead had retreated into culthood.

Surprisingly, it was the less prestigious members of the group who fared best during the next few belt-tightening years. The ever-practical Chris Hillman was not content to live on the memories of stardom with the Byrds, Burritos and Manassas, but elected to seek new avenues. Prior to the McGuinn, Clark & Hillman project, he had told me of his desire to forego the rock 'n' roll circus and retire gracefully to become a producer. Confusingly, he also spoke of the possibility of recording a traditional bluegrass album and reinvestigating his pre-Byrds roots. Following the split with McGuinn, he ceased playing altogether for about a year and seriously considered quitting the music business. It was only the intervention of specialist label Sugar Hill that changed his mind. While arranging the re-release of his archive album with the Hillmen, Chris re-established contact with former mentor Jim Dickson and set about recording a new work in a traditional vein. Backed by a trio of country players (Bernie Leadon, Al Perkins and Herb Pedersen) Hillman performed some reasonable but unexciting covers of songs by Bob Dylan, Gram Parsons and others. The predominantly bluegrass *Morning Sky* was obviously a refreshing experience for Hillman who sounded as confident as ever, despite the sparse quality of the material on offer. Without the hype and over-expectation of the Byrds' associated projects, he was rewarded with a clutch of surprisingly positive record reviews. That, at least, compensated for his reduced stature as a 'minor label' recording artiste.

During the same period, he teamed up with former Burrito/Firefall lead singer Rick Roberts for a short tour which ably showed off their talents as acoustic musicians. It was not a happy period for Hillman though, who held few fond memories of the shows. "God those concerts!" he complained. "One of my most embarrassing periods. At the time Rick was having problems. He had lost all his money, couldn't sing, and was totally untogether. Onstage, it was so embarrassing." This was hardly a fair summation of the entire tour, which had many gratifying moments. The set lists were exemplary, incorporating solo work and subtle selections from the repertoires of the Byrds, Burritos, Manassas and Firefall. Their voices gelled too and extant tapes fail to justify Hillman's negative comments about Roberts, who harmonizes well and seems eager to extend their song selection, even including a moving rendition of Stills' tribute to David Crosby's personal grief, 'Do For The Others'. The gigs were pleasantly informal with the duo frequently displaying a humorous rapport in a spontaneous series of one-liners. At one show a cheeky member of the audience shouted "Where's Gram?", only to be told, "How would you like to personally meet him?" Offstage, Hillman repeatedly stressed his pleasure at rediscovering the mandolin after too many years as a rock bassist and guitarist, and seemed determined to continue the retreat into pre-Byrds territory. His turntable choice in 1982 consisted largely of old bluegrass material and songs that he had first learned 20 years before. Although no longer a major label recording star, Hillman was pleased with his music and outwardly seemed reasonably content.

Hillman completed another low-key, traditional country album, *Desert Rose*, which again received fair reviews. He was cleverly using the independent circuit to play his favourite music without having to conform to the dictates of a major label. Although he only recorded a couple of his own compositions during this period, reviewers seemed pleased enough with the covers and few criticized the under-produced recordings or lack of fresh material. Modest ambitions bring their own critical rewards, as Hillman's early Eighties career gratefully reflected.

In common with McGuinn, Hillman began to put aside the excesses of the Seventies and took better care of himself physically. He was now known to rise at 5 am to jog along beaches and also took up cycling, sometimes travelling up to 40 miles across the coast. His personal life was settled once more with a happy marriage to fourth wife Constance Pappas. Hillman's healthiness is next to godliness philosophy was emphasized in his involvement with an evangelical Christian group. In 1984, he collaborated with Bernie Leadon, David Mansfield, Jerry Scheff and Al Perkins on the Christian bluegrass album, *Ever Call Ready*. Hillman was heavily influenced by Perkins at the time and had recently been baptized, but his involvement with the born again movement was relatively brief.

By the mid-Eighties, Hillman was still playing regular concerts and formed a new group, the Desert Rose Band, with a cavalcade of country talent, including Herb Pedersen, Jay Dee Maness, John Jorgenson, Bill Bryson and Steve Duncan. Given Hillman's recent history, it seemed likely that this new group would struggle in the twilight musical arena of small bars and clubs, with only limited distribution of their records. Fortunately, their live performances attracted the interest of the majors and their new label, Curb Records, received the corporate clout of distributors MCA Records. Two albums, *The Desert Rose Band* and *Running*, were surprisingly strong with a freshness and bite reminiscent of the best of the early Flying Burrito Brothers. One of the highlights of the first album was a reworking of 'Time Between', which compared reasonably well with the version on *Younger Than Yesterday*. *Running* was equally accomplished with a sterling selection of songs including the powerful title track, a moving and positive meditation in which Hillman courageously confronts the psychic and emotional upheavals resulting from his father's suicide. It still stands as one of the best compositions of his career.

The revitalization of Hillman as a mature performer was reflected in self-revealing asides during this period. "Songwriting and royalties have kept me real comfortable," he concluded. "I don't have a mansion in Palm Springs and a mansion in Malibu but I'm very comfortable and I'm not excessive in my lifestyle. I'm still here, 25 years later, and I'm still working. There are a lot of people my age who aren't. There were a lot of people that were bigger than me and I never had to fall. I was never a big star. I'm real fortunate . . . we didn't get a great record deal, millions of dollars of advance money or a limousine. We got a chance, and that's all I ever wanted."

Optimistic as he sounded, even Hillman could not have envisaged the commercial success which awaited the Desert Rose Band. As the decade wound to a close, they were being tipped for Grammy awards and zooming to the top of the country charts. From small label obscurity, the irrepressible Hillman had worked his way up the ladder to emerge unexpectedly as a big draw on the ever-profitable country circuit. Chris' true feelings about his success were aptly summed up in a comment to an old friend: "I'm finally getting what I *deserve*."

In common with Hillman, Gene Clark found the Eighties a tough decade, with major labels no longer wishing to take a chance on Seventies singer-songwriters. Clark had been through CBS, A&M, Asylum and RSO as a soloist and produced a formidable body of work, including the awesome *No Other*, yet the sales invariably failed to reflect the artistry. Without the other Byrds, Clark's currency with corporate record companies was weak and so he too was forced to opt for the obscurity of the independent circuit. He briefly teamed up with Hillman, Perkins, Pedersen and Clarke to record some stylish demos with Jim Dickson, including the attractive Rodney Crowell composition 'No Memories Hangin' Round' and a revamped 'Feel A Whole Lot Better'. Dubbing themselves Nyte Flyte, the ensemble played a one-off show at the Palomino in North Hollywood. Unfortunately, the experiment was discontinued. In 1984, Takoma Records released *Firebyrd*, a pleasant, if insubstantial, album, which saw Clark browsing through the Byrds' back pages with reworkings of 'Feel A Whole Lot Better' and 'Mr Tambourine Man'. The latter was particularly interesting for Clark chose to include the verses that the Byrds had omitted from their hit version.

The reliance on Byrds' material, though no reflection on Clark's output, indicated the way he was thinking, and it came as no great surprise when he announced his involvement in a '20th Anniversary' tour. Neither McGuinn, Crosby nor Hillman were remotely interested in resurrecting the Byrds' name so Clark was forced to form his own curiously selected 'supergroup'. The participants were Gene, Michael Clarke, Rick Roberts, Rick Danko and Blondie Chaplin, and the billing carefully announced '20th Anniversary Tribute To The Byrds'. An unintentionally macabre poster amusingly noted: 'Also appearing with their *original* line-up: The Flying Burrito Brothers'. Although the tour was opportunist in intent, few who had witnessed Clark's lack of sales over the years could deny him the chance to make some quick money. Regrettably, the qualifying remarks prior to the Byrds' name were not strictly adhered to by every promoter and news reached England that Clark was intending to tour simply as 'the Byrds'.

Fortunately, this sacrilegious 1985 British Byrds invasion never materialized. Instead, Clark appeared in London on a solo mission and played one of the best sets I saw at that time. A packed audience at Dingwalls was treated to an acoustic 'best of Gene Clark' which included a stunning and remarkable rearrangement of 'Eight Miles High'. Affable, and more communicative than usual, Clark agreed to play a private gig for the author and sample some California wines on his next visit. He promised to return soon with his amorphous band of anniversarians but, ever unpredictable, he changed his plans and remained in the States.

Although generally accepted as the most underrated of the original Byrds, Clark retained a substantial cult following, particularly in Europe. At home, he enjoyed the respect of younger musicians and was pleased to guest on recordings by the Long Ryders and the Three O'Clock. He even gained some retrospective Don Juan notoriety when Michelle Phillips belatedly made public her affair with the tambourine man back in the mid-Sixties. In 1987, Clark recorded the well-received *So Rebellious A Love*r with Carla Olson but, all in all, it was a very quiet decade for the most prolific member of the Byrds.

Michael Clarke had ended the Seventies on an absurdly high note. While the careers of his former colleagues were beginning to founder, Clarke's latest group, Firefall, was enjoying spectacular commercial success. It couldn't last, however, and by the early Eighties Clarke had left the group, which rapidly plunged downhill. For several years, he worked for Jerry Jeff Walker, then joined Clark's 'Byrds' tour and finally set about establishing himself as an 'impressionistic painter'. After years of artistic frustration playing behind America's finest group, Clarke was revealing creativity in an area beyond the scope of his more illustrious former compatriots. Like Hillman, Clarke had come full circle and delved back into his pre-Byrd career for new inspiration. When Crosby had first 'discovered' the fledgling drummer playing congas at Big Sur, Clarke's other main pastime was painting on the beach. Now he was pursuing his second career with vigour. Like everyone else in this story, Clarke was still haunted by the legacy of the Byrds. After being replaced in Gene's anniversarians by former Thunderbyrd drummer Greg Thomas, Michael retired for the best part of three years. Then, in 1988, he unexpectedly decided to revive the Byrds' name. It was a presumptuous move which was to have startling repercussions. Michael Clarke, for perhaps the first time in his life, was about to prove the unlikely catalyst for a serious Byrds reunion.

Roger McGuinn remained something of an enigma during the Eighties when his once prolific recording output evaporated altogether. Like the other Byrds, he avoided the trap of attempting to form another major label superstar aggregation and reverted to his coffee house troubadour persona of the early Sixties. Everyone agreed that McGuinn had changed drastically since his re-conversion to Christianity. Gone was the Dylanesque cynicism, replaced by a beatific impenetrability. Some of the old coolness remained, however, and many felt that behind the man's polite exterior there lurked a sense of wariness and resignation. His Christian ethics did not exclude an interest in money and he was even known to pray for fiscal advantage. Ironically, he had once criticized Skip Battin for doing the same during his Buddhist period. McGuinn was particularly impressed by one prayer session at the time of his conversion when he received a royalty cheque for $30,000. Initially, he had seemed happy to partake in a project with Clark and Hillman, even though they were non-believers, with strong appetites for booze and cocaine, respectively. Gradually, he became extremely wary of aligning himself with agnostics and felt in need of spiritual advice. "I was praying about a financial matter," he remembers. "One of the elders said, 'I sense a need for repentance before we pray about this money.'" The church elders agreed that he was 'unequally yoked' and counselled him against the 'darkness' of agnostic attachments, quoting from Corinthians 6:14: "Be ye not unequally yoked together with unbelievers/For what fellowship had righteousness with unrighteousness?/And what communion hath light with darkness?"

McGuinn had taken some time to act on this advice, but he was now resolute. Hereafter, he studiously avoided reuniting with his former associates and continued as a solo act. "I knew the Lord didn't want me in a situation where I was light with darkness," he says, "and I finally got myself out of that situation. And that's why I'm a solo artiste now. I've been offered a lot of money by agents trying to get the Byrds back together and I can't do it for that reason."

The closest McGuinn came to fraternizing with ex-Byrds during the early Eighties was a tour with the Peace Seekers, whose line-up featured Gene Parsons, Skip Battin, Greg Harris and Jim Goodall. The ensemble undertook a European tour in the summer of 1984 during which they would join McGuinn onstage for sprightly versions of 'Mr Tambourine Man', 'Turn! Turn! Turn!', 'Eight Miles High' and 'So You Want To Be A Rock 'n' Roll Star'. It all went horribly wrong following their shows at London's Dingwalls on 24–25 July. Their tour money was not forthcoming and Parsons was forced to sell his String Bender guitar at the club in order to scrounge enough money for a return flight to America. McGuinn had no such worries having already collected a cheque. When the usually pacific Battin learned that McGuinn had been paid while the group were out of pocket, he exploded in a barely controllable rage. "At Dingwalls, he wanted to kill Roger McGuinn," Gene Parsons recalls. "He broke a bottle in the backroom and I had to subdue him, and then he started coming after me! He said, 'I'm going to kill somebody, I'd rather it be Roger, but I'll kill you if you try and stop me.' Ha! You probably know the story as you were there that night. I thought Roger really took advantage of us. You'd think we'd learn. Skip had had enough. He tipped over." The disillusioned and embittered Peace Seekers left England knowing that their group name had taken on a sadly ironic ring. It was a battle-weary end to another mini-Byrds reunion that would never be repeated.

Such drama aside, McGuinn's life on the road was generally a model of decorum and restraint. Drugs and alcohol were conspicuous by their absence as spirituality reigned. Several of McGuinn's new songs, including 'Light Up The Darkness', testified obliquely to his faith but the evangelical tone seldom permeated his onstage raps or altered a familiar repertoire.

Armed with a Rickenbacker and a smiling, confident stage persona, McGuinn transformed himself into a one-man travelling show. He toured the States and Europe, usually appearing at small clubs and halls, and treating his followers to a formidable selection of past hits, peppered with the occasional new song. At some gigs his wife, Camilla, replaced the standard sound engineer at the mixing desk. Sometimes, the performances seemed clinical and stagy, as though McGuinn were settling into a new role as an anaesthetized, middle-aged trouper on the supper club circuit. However, such reservations would usually be shattered by moments of genius, most notably in the ambitious and dramatic rearrangement of 'Eight Miles High'. Not content to play the easy, singalong tunes, McGuinn would climax his set with a virtuoso performance, complete with the complex interweaving guitar breaks that were always the highlights of this remarkable composition. It says much for McGuinn's faithful and searing solo rendition of 'Eight Miles High' that he could pull off those effects so impressively.

One of the more entertaining and amusing aspects of McGuinn's Eighties performances was the reintroduction of the *Gene Tryp* saga. The play had never been adapted for radio, let alone reached Broadway but, two decades on, the stubborn McGuinn finally incorporated the tale into his stage act. Audiences expecting the usual polite, hackneyed song introductions would smile benignly as McGuinn warmly invited them to imagine a scene set in nineteenth-century America. A wedding is taking place, Gene Tryp appears on the horizon, abruptly whisks away the bride and they live happily together until one day an enormous force field envelops their house, causing Tryp to travel the world. McGuinn would next picture his protagonist on the campaign trail, atop a wagon painted red, white and blue. The catchy 'I Wanna Grow Up To Be A Politician' naturally followed. The scene would then shift to document Tryp's cowboy adventures in which he captures, and finally loses, a beautiful 'Chestnut Mare'. Next, he travels down to New Orleans and confronts a sinister character who calls himself the 'Lover Of The Bayou'. Finally, Tryp grows weary of his travels and muses on his eventful life in the elegiac 'Just A Season'. At this point, McGuinn would take some amusing liberties with the original script in order to throw in a couple of older Byrds hits. Tryp is pictured on a farm and one night a flying saucer lands in his corn field. Several extraterrestrial beings emerge and cordially invite our astonished hero to accompany them on a ride into space. The words of 'Mr Spaceman' provide an apt reply. After whizzing around in a flying saucer, Tryp returns to Earth only to discover that a century has elapsed. It is now July 1965 and Tryp turns on a radio to be greeted by the strains of . . . 'Mr Tambourine Man'. The scene ends.

Audiences responded loudly and appreciatively to McGuinn's witty narrative while he, no doubt, felt relieved to have partly exorcized the troubled ghost of *Gene Tryp* – the most fanciful and frustrating of all his schemes. An exorcism of a different kind was evident in McGuinn's decision to update one of his old Byrds songs as 'Tiffany Queen II'. Sounding better than ever on acoustic, the song boasted some provocative new lyrics. McGuinn remembers a summer back in the early Seventies when he threw parties for "half a million friends", but soon drugs and alcohol took their toll, fistfights ensued, and his mate left to "marry a guy named Carradine". This was a teasing reference to his ex-wife Linda Gilbert, who subsequently wed *Kung Fu* star David Carradine. In the final verse of 'Tiffany Queen II', McGuinn pays tribute to his new bride (Camilla) and presents an idyllic portrayal of life in sun-drenched Florida, swimming daily in the Gulf of Mexico and learning from all his past mistakes. What had seemed a rather ordinary song on *Farther Along* was given a completely new life by the sharp arrangement and explicit autobiographical lyrics.

By the late Eighties McGuinn had amassed a backlog of unreleased titles, stretching back a decade. The quality of the material was decidedly patchy and some compositions, such as 'Woman' and 'The Tears', sounded mawkish. 'Sunshine Love', a poppy cousin to 'Don't You Write Her Off', was catchy but insubstantial, while 'The Price You Pay' resembled a country rock singalong. 'Living Legend', the story of a washed-up rock star reduced to working in a factory, was a return to strength, while the plaintive 'Sweet Memories' recalled the haunting melody of 'Kathleen's Song'. There were also some passable covers, including a reading of the Icicle Works' 'Life In A Northern Town'. Perhaps the most intriguing of the lot was the impressive arrangement of Henry Van Dyke's 1909 poem 'America For Me', first premiered during the McGuinn/Hillman days. Despite fleeting flashes of songwriting flair, there was nothing in his new repertoire to rival songs as startling as 'Chestnut Mare' or 'Just A Season'. With more forethought, he might have reconnected with Jacques Levy, but his old songwriting partner was currently tied up writing lyrics for the stage musical, *Fame*. McGuinn's other accomplished amanuensis, Bob Hippard, was regrettably no longer alive.

"Bob committed suicide," reveals Roger's ex-wife, Dolores. "It was very sad. His wife, Cheryl, had ovarian cancer and she died. She was his life really. She'd worked as a stewardess for Continental Airlines and Bob had been a taxi driver for a while. They lived in this little, modern apartment off Melrose and we used to see them quite often then." Hippard's death escaped the attention of the rock press and McGuinn never mentioned it in print.

Playing the solo troubadour did not prevent McGuinn from making several prestigious guest appearances during the Eighties. On record, he could be heard backing various artistes, including Vern Gosdin, the Beach Boys, Peter Case, Elvis Costello, the Nitty Gritty Dirt Band and Crowded House (on a 3-track CD credited to Byrdhouse). Earlier, in 1984, he had appeared on MTV alongside the highly respected REM, whose work had already been compared to that of the mid-period Byrds. The following year, he joined the Farm Aid benefit concerts and performed at the 25th anniversary of Gerde's Folk City. He toured the world with Bob Dylan and Tom Petty & The Heartbreakers in 1987. McGuinn sang with Dylan on 'Chimes Of Freedom' and even co-wrote a song with Petty, 'King Of The Hill', which they performed on several dates. The cumulative guest appearances ensured that McGuinn's name was not forgotten by music scribes and, as the decade wound to a close, it seemed only a matter of time before a major label signed the Rickenbacker maestro for a well-publicized and long overdue comeback album.

David Crosby's career during the Eighties was less a question of darkness than the prospect of a complete eclipse. The most commercially successful Byrd of the previous decade soon discovered that he was no more capable of securing a major contract than were any of his former partners. Always an excessive, he fell victim to cocaine addiction on a grand scale. I witnessed the extent of his dependency over a couple of days when the freebase pipe was seldom away from his lips. "Please don't mention the drugs", he pleaded, "it's bad enough as it is". Despite this, Crosby remained lucid, sharp and thoroughly in command of proceedings, as though the drug was no more potent than a packet of cigarettes. One of the more remarkable aspects of Crosby's addiction was his ability to carry it off. His colleagues later recalled ghoulish tales of ether-filled rooms and unprecedented degeneracy but, at the beginning of the decade, Crosby still looked in good shape, dressed casually but cleanly, ate well and was conducting his business affairs with assiduous skill and clarity. His acoustic performances were a joy to behold and his articulation onstage and off was undiminished by his habit. He could talk for entire afternoons and evenings, answering often difficult questions with a precision and perspicuity beyond the power of his fellow Byrds. His creativity had not yet been stymied by drugs, despite his later comments to the contrary, and three of his new songs, 'Delta', 'Distances' and 'Drive My Car', all sounded impressive. After the shows, he dug into his bag to produce some new handwritten compositions: 'Melody', 'Paper Glider' and 'Stand And Be Counted'. In reserve, he still had 'King Of The Mountain', 'Samurai' and 'Jigsaw', and Neil Young had recently offered him 'Little Wing' and the old CSN&Y favourite 'Pushed It Over The End'. There were also some wordless melodies and plans for a choral work. Clearly, Crosby's compositional skills remained beautifully intact. Sadly, the creative drought was closer than either of us imagined.

Always a barometer of emotion, Crosby could be arrogant, immodest, humble, aggressive and terribly loving. Temperamentally, he was the perfect foil to McGuinn. It was difficult to imagine two more strikingly different personalities: passionate forcefulness versus cool deliberation. Crosby's passion for the Byrds, as for all his music, was positively tangible. He felt frustrated, held back, at times unforgiving and contemptuous of his fellow Byrds, yet simultaneously affectionate and respectful towards them. Their status was shifting sand, depending on the time period in question; conquering heroes in 1965, brilliant experimentalists during the 'Eight Miles High' period, villains of the piece throughout 1967, and bitter enemies in the wake of *The Notorious Byrd Brothers.*

In spite of his criticisms, Crosby genuinely believed that he could work with the Byrds again and the state of his career in 1980 suggested that this was far from unlikely. Temporarily estranged from Stills and Nash, his only artistic outlet was a long-awaited second solo album. The fact that Capitol Records (McGuinn, Clark & Hillman's label) had signed Crosby indicated that somebody in the company was still hedging their bets on a possible Byrds' reformation. Unfortunately, the flock would soon disperse, in parodic imitation of previous disputes.

THE DARK DECADE

In 1981, Capitol completely humiliated Crosby by rejecting his new album on the grounds that it was musically anachronistic. It was a bitter blow and a sad indication of his declining commercial appeal. He was about to go the way of McGuinn, Clark and Hillman. Starved of a major record label, there was nothing else to do but survive on the revenue offered by small club dates, while patiently awaiting an upswing of fortune.

The vestiges of control that Crosby exercised over his art and life at the dawn of the Eighties were systematically eroded during the succeeding years, as his freebasing intake reached new and dangerously high levels. Professional commitments sapped his energy, while the all-consuming addiction robbed him of vital sleep. During bouts of exhaustion, Crosby would occasionally lose control of his propane torch and accidentally burn holes in his clothing or set alight hotel mattresses. Although his drugs were top quality, increased dependency meant an ever-present danger of scoring impure base. Following one gig, Crosby's body finally cried out for help and he suffered a seizure which might have taken his life. When this horror bulletin reached his remaining friends in California, they decided to act.

One of the more remarkable aspects of Crosby's character is his ability to win the love and loyalty of those who feel they should know better. Jim Dickson described him as "one of the greatest salesmen of the twentieth century". Crosby's personal absorption has an enticing quality which is difficult to fathom. It is easy for people to believe in him, partly because he emanates such a powerful presence and sense of self-worth, curiously aligned to a deep sensitivity and vulnerability.

So it was that a posse of long-suffering friends, including Graham Nash, Jackson Browne, Paul Kantner and Grace Slick, invaded his house in 1981 and attempted to press gang the erring egotist into seeking medical assistance. An emotionally cathartic evening ended with Crosby reluctantly agreeing to enrol in a drug programme at Scripps Hospital in La Jolla, generously financed by Nash. David's commitment is best exemplified by his insistence on freebasing copiously en route. The fiasco was completed 24 hours later when Crosby discharged himself.

When his once loyal friends finally abandoned him as a lost cause, Crosby found a new supporter in the foreboding figure of Jack Casanova. The mysterious Casanova had virtually no experience of the rock world but he convinced David that he could continue to make a living as a 'functioning' base head. To a large extent, Casanova was correct. He kept Crosby on the road, found investors and became the key figure in the singer's drug-centred existence. Crosby paid a high price for his voracious cocaine appetite. As his dependency increased, he found that he could no longer sleep or even eat without an accompanying blast from his ever-present pipe. On commercial air flights he would surreptitiously light up his propane torch and somehow dodge the normally vigilant eyes of suspicious stewards. Even his driving technique was carefully adapted to facilitate his freebase usage; passengers would watch in open-mouthed astonishment as Crosby skilfully steered the car with his knees while gluttonously toking from the pipe that refused to leave his hands. The private doper had now crystallized into a public menace.

Crosby's flagrant self-abuse became national news on 23 March 1982 when he suffered a potentially deadly seizure at the wheel of his car. He was extremely fortunate to escape with his life. Upon regaining consciousness, he discovered to his horror that his car had careered into a freeway divider. A police search of the vehicle unearthed a veritable Pandora's box of narcotics: cocaine, quaaludes and an assortment of drug paraphernalia. To make matters worse, Crosby was carrying a loaded Colt .45. When asked why he carried a gun, the still bemused singer offered the wry reply: "John Lennon". That comment was a revelation in itself. Here was an artiste without a record contract whose self-esteem was still high enough to believe that he might attract a superstar assassin. Hadn't the Byrds once been called 'America's Answer To The Beatles'?

Crosby was immediately released on $2,500 bail but the shock of arrest had no salutary impact on his drug consumption. Fifteen days later, he was appearing at Cardi's nightclub in Dallas, Texas, when police officers arrived supposedly for a routine investigation of liquor violations. Upon entering Crosby's dressing room, they discovered the singer frantically attempting to conceal his freebasing equipment. "Don't do this to me!" Crosby moaned in horror as they searched his bag. Its contents included a gun, a Bunsen burner and a quarter gram of cocaine. He was duly arrested, taken to Dallas City Hall, charged with illegally carrying a loaded firearm and possessing cocaine, then released on bail four hours later. After two arrests within a couple of weeks, Crosby felt like a marked man.

While legal preparations and appeal procedures tortuously dragged on, Crosby continued to feed his ravenous addiction. His self-belief had been reinforced by an unexpected approach from Stills and Nash. Under pressure from Atlantic Records, they'd requested his assistance in converting their joint album into a three-way affair. The volte face made good commercial sense. Remarkably, *Daylight Again* featured Crosby's first released recordings since *CSN* back in 1977. At that time, Crosby had seemed imperious, with an album at number 2 in the charts and stadium tours in abundance. It made his silence over the next five years seem all the more frustrating. *Daylight Again* was a welcome but perplexing package on which Crosby sang the stunning 'Delta', but found there was no room for his other recent gems, 'Distances' and 'Drive My Car'. As a result of this imbalance, Stills ended up with seven songs on the record. The work was still a success and brought Crosby, Stills & Nash chart success, after which they hatched plans for a major tour. For Crosby, this was a financial lifeline and a means for further self-abuse.

Courtrooms, concert tours and continuous cocaine consumption characterized Crosby's chaotic career hereafter. In September 1982, he was arrested once more on an outstanding warrant for an alleged assault and battery suit dating back to 1981. "I'm a gentleman," Crosby pleaded. "I've never hit a girl in my life." The case was quickly dismissed and soon afterwards the driving and drug offence was plea bargained by his formidable attorneys. Crosby was fined $750.00 and placed on three years' probation, a period in which he agreed to enter a drug counselling programme. The Dallas charge, however, would not go away.

The following summer, Crosby found himself back in court in

Texas and newspapers reported that he consistently fell asleep and snored during the proceedings. What seemed a contemptuous gesture was probably nothing more than drug-related exhaustion. Indeed, Crosby was far from nonchalant about his fate and at one point rose to his own defence with an impassioned plea: "Jail is no joke. Handcuffs are no joke. It's real serious. It's been very lonely. Those bars are real. I spent a lot of nights thinking about it. It frightened me. I don't want to do anything ever again that puts me in jeopardy. I want to feel proud of myself and stand for something again."

Judge Patrick McDowell may have been impressed by Crosby's eloquence, but the dispassionate legal arguments of Dallas District Attorney Knox Fitzpatrick proved decisive. While awaiting judgement, Crosby took off on a CS&N tour as speculation mounted that these shows might be the last ever by the trio. The performances were professional enough but void of the passion, power and cultural relevance that CS&N once commanded.

On 5 August 1983, Crosby was sentenced to five years' imprisonment for illegal possession of cocaine and a further three years to run concurrently for firearm offences. An appeal was immediately lodged and the singer was freed on an $8,000 bond. Nash attempted to assist his beleaguered partner by writing a letter to the judge, stating: "I truly believe that what David needs at this juncture of his life is help, guidance and professional supervision. I believe that a confinement in prison would probably kill him."

Outside the courtroom, Crosby told reporters: "I'm being treated like a murderer. They put manacles on my hands and put me in solitary. And I didn't do anything to anybody. I didn't. This is now. This is happening to *me*. They got me for a quarter of a gram pipe residue. For that I'm going to spend five years in a state penitentiary?" Clearly, the case was far from over.

Throughout this nightmarish period, Crosby somehow managed to fulfil his professional obligations. Like the chronic alcoholic who miraculously gets to work every morning, he pulled his weary body through a gruelling series of solo tours arranged by the ever present Jack Casanova. In order to supplement his income, Crosby was reduced to selling drugs as a sideline. His wary backing musicians, ever alert to his smoking mishaps, armed themselves with personal fire extinguishers. Meanwhile, their pyrogenous boss continued to leave a trail of burn stains in his wake, torching hotel suites and damaging furnishings whenever exhaustion loosened the freebase pipe from his hands.

Although Crosby had been ordered to undergo drug counselling, his efforts in this direction were either lacklustre or unsuccessful. For a brief period, he enrolled at Ross General Hospital, Marin County, but the treatment was not to his liking. He was later admitted to Marin General suffering from kidney stones but, midway through treatment, he was caught attempting to smuggle heroin into the hospital and severely reprimanded by his doctor. Incensed, Crosby ripped an intravenous tube from his arm and marched out of the hospital leaving a trail of blood behind him. Thereafter, the news worsened. His girlfriend, Jan Dance, was arrested for attempting to board a plane with a handgun. A subsequent search of her luggage revealed small traces of cocaine, marijuana and heroin residue. Jan was released on probation and reunited with David in Marin County. Now they both lived in fear of imminent incarceration.

While his drug abuse and skirmishes with the law threatened his very existence, Crosby continued to tour, as if giving the lie to suggestions that he was a burned-out coke fiend. His solo shows in the spring of 1984 offered some memorable moments. At the Beacon Theatre, New York, he was in particularly good form. Referring to *Daylight Again*, he complained about Stills' & Nash's reluctance to feature his material: "They only gave me one damn song, it pissed me off, but it was a good one." After playing 'Delta', he invited Roger McGuinn onstage and they played excellent acoustic versions of 'Mr Tambourine Man' and 'Eight Miles High'. "I haven't done that for ten years," Crosby enthused.

During the summer of 1984, CS&N embarked on a summer tour, including an appearance at the fifteenth anniversary of the Woodstock Festival at an open-air concert in New York City. Like a personal trainer, Nash was eagerly informing journalists: "We still have it. We still mean it. It's not for the money. It never was. It's for the music." Although the tour was well-received, it was evident that Crosby was still a serious addict, whose fate had yet to be determined by the courts.

Crosby's carelessness seemed certain to prove his undoing. In October 1984, he was arrested in Ross, California, for reckless driving on a motorcycle. A dip into his bag brought forth a rubber tube, Bunsen burner, pipe, and, inevitably, more cocaine. For good measure there was another offensive weapon, this time a dagger. Attorneys disputed the legality of this latest search and Crosby escaped with a fine for reckless driving. Back in Texas, Knox Fitzpatrick had intensified his attempt to enmesh the beleaguered singer, but Judge McDowell, realizing the extent of Crosby's addiction, took a firm but compassionate stance and ordered the defendant to enter a closed institution to undergo drug rehabilitation.

Faced with a choice between imprisonment or hospitalization, Crosby decided to enrol at the Fair Oaks Hospital in New Jersey. This institution was widely regarded as one of the finest of its kind in America and had achieved considerable prestige among the rock community following the rehabilitation of John Phillips, whose drug problems were arguably even more horrific than those of Crosby.

Hostility and denial characterized Crosby's mood during the early days of treatment at Fair Oaks in January 1985. He was also in considerable physical pain. His ankles resembled balloons, his mouth was full of abscesses and he could not breathe properly while asleep. In spite of these handicaps he made slow but steady progress and might have pulled through but for the psychological dependence on drugs. During the sixth week of his treatment, while walking in the hospital grounds, Crosby abruptly made a break for the outside walls, climbed over and sped off with a friend in an awaiting car, after which he was taken to a hotel in Manhattan for a long overdue freebasing session. Within 48 hours he was arrested in Greenwich Village on another charge of cocaine possession and the usual tired litany of accompanying offences.

Realizing the seriousness of his predicament, Crosby volunteered to return to hospital but his conciliatory gesture had come too late. Unable to pay the $15,000 bond, he was held at the spine-chilling Tombs and Riker's Island before returning to Texas for another trial. His defence attorney made a fresh appeal for hospitalization but Judge McDowell finally lost patience, denied bond and despatched Crosby to Lew Sterrett County prison. For months, the erring singer suffered gruesome withdrawal symptoms, spending most of his time in solitary confinement. "My cell was about six by 13 [feet]. They fed me through a little hole in the door. There were two big fluorescent lights above that never went off. I slept very poorly. I was kicking coke and heroin under the worst possible circumstances. They wouldn't give me an aspirin. I did as cold turkey as you can do it, and it was hell." He also had to suffer the indignity of prison guards playfully teasing him with such quips as "Hey, rock star, come here and mop up this floor." At one point, he was given a job of trust working in the prison cafeteria, but was reprimanded after stealing some bacon and stripped of his privileges. More isolated than ever, he spent most nights crying himself to sleep. Whenever possible, he phoned his business manager, Jack Casanova, and begged him to arrange his release at any cost. Eventually, Graham Nash and CS&N manager Bill Siddons produced the $15,000 to secure his release. David assured them of his intentions to stay straight but, less than two days later, he was freebasing again.

Crosby's inexorable slide back into the narcotic netherworld was tempered by an ever present fear of returning to prison. He became more cautious than before and, for a time, attempted to convince sceptical journalists that he could conquer his addiction. He accompanied Stills and Nash on tour, even appearing at Live Aid alongside the perpetually reluctant Neil Young. The televised performance betrayed how much Crosby had already surrendered to drugs. Visually and vocally, he seemed but a shadow of his once ebullient self. Nevertheless, his celebrity outlaw status continued to attract ghoulish multitudes eager to witness what might prove the *last* performance by Crosby, Stills & Nash. The trio broke the house attendance record at the Concord Pavilion where people waved banners proclaiming, 'David, We Love You'.

By this time, Crosby had constructed his own prison in the form of a backstage van surrounded by his security officers – burly minders whose job was to keep him relatively straight. The freebasing still went on, however. During a gig in Norfolk, Virginia, Crosby was overcome by an attack of nausea and walked offstage midway through the show. While he was recuperating in the restroom, an angry Stills entered and poured a jug of water over his head. As Nash succinctly observed after the show: "It's tough to sing, vomit and shit at the same time." Even his best friends had run short of excuses and explanations for David's behaviour. Graham Nash, once loyal almost to a fault, now seemed convinced that his partner was doomed and informed the press: "David will eventually die, it's only a question of when."

The Grim Reaper showed a strange reluctance to ensnare Crosby but the police authorities had no such reservations. On 23 October 1985, David suffered a flash of *déjà vu* when he drove into a fence on the road to Mount Tamalpais. On this occasion, he remained conscious and unwisely decided to flee from the scene. A car chase ensued and Crosby was arrested for hit-and-run driving. Police again found a gun in his possession, plus the usual assortment of drug paraphernalia. In spite of his countless string of arrests, Crosby again received bail at $5,000, but this latest transgression extinguished any remaining hopes he might have harboured of avoiding a jail sentence.

Judge Patrick McDowell wearily scheduled another hearing in Dallas but this time Crosby failed to appear. Fearing almost certain imprisonment, he decided to become a fugitive. Accompanied by Jan Dance, he fled in search of an impossible redemption. Rather fancifully, he convinced himself that he could escape justice by sailing into the sunset on his boat, the *Mayan*. The plot bore a striking resemblance to his classic fantasy tale 'Wooden Ships'. Now reality was imitating art. The elaborate getaway was ultimately thwarted by the state of the *Mayan*, which had fallen into disrepair following years of neglect and was no longer seaworthy.

The wreck of the *Mayan* appeared to symbolize Crosby's own final defeat. Penniless and barefoot, he pathetically attempted to avoid capture by shaving off his moustache and purchasing cheap wigs to disguise his identity. At this point, he was still consuming a quarter ounce of cocaine and a half gram of heroin per day, but now his supply lines were cut.

THE DARK DECADE

In despair, with nowhere left to go, Crosby abandoned the futile struggle for freedom and turned himself in at the FBI's office at West Palm Beach, Florida. One week later, he was taken to Lew Sterrett Justice Center, then moved to the Government Center and placed in solitary. His parting words to the assembled journalists were a brave "Wish me luck, huh". For the remainder of the year cold turkey, made worse by his poor physical condition, prompted further dark rumours about his longevity. Dallas County's assistant District Attorney was already speaking of him in the past tense: "They say he was a great man with a great deal of talent. I guess the only word I can use to describe him now is 'ruined'. Ruined by drugs."

Crosby had once equated prison with death but now it offered blessed release. Rather than destroying him, his tenure in jail provided salvation. Initially, he suffered severe withdrawal pangs which seemed insurmountable but gradually, almost imperceptibly, his health improved. He was transferred to Huntsville Prison and assigned a job in the prison mattress factory as if to atone for all the beds he had torched during a decade of addiction. As the months passed, Crosby slowly adapted to life behind bars and even began writing new songs, as well as appearing in the prison band. His progress was duly noted and, one year on, his old friends began campaigning for his release. The Texas Board of Parole was similarly impressed and, on 8 August 1986, Crosby was freed. The following year, the Texas Supreme Court concluded that the invasion of his dressing room at Cardi's nightclub in Dallas had been illegal and his conviction was retrospectively overturned.

Crosby emerged from custody overweight, drug free and reformed. One week after his release, he celebrated his 45th birthday by appearing with Nash at Rockefeller's Houston. Short-haired, with stubble replacing his familiar moustache, he took the stage accompanied by wild cheers and treated the audience to several CSN&Y classics, plus the first airing of his song of redemption, 'Compass'. As he noted: "I hadn't written any music for nearly three years. When the words started to come back I knew I was on the way back. I started to be able to think again, to be able not to have dreams about drugs all the time."

Inevitably, Crosby had to face great changes in his life. The recondite Jack Casanova disappeared from his circle without pursuing any claim for a live album and Bill Siddons assumed full managerial responsibilities. He sagaciously encouraged Crosby to sever his old ties in San Francisco and move to Los Angeles. Siddons next tackled his client's tangled business affairs which included a hefty $1 million debt to the IRS. Crosby responded to the crisis by declaring himself bankrupt and seeking a fresh start. The ever loyal Graham Nash purchased his songs, thereby ensuring that his copyrights remained in safe and responsible hands. By now, Crosby was successfully rebuilding his shattered psyche, attending AA meetings and lecturing on the dangers of addiction. Early the following year, the CSN&Y dream team reunited for two acoustic performances at the Arlington Theater, Santa Barbara, in aid of Greenpeace. Crosby arrived at the show on his Harley Davidson, as if reminding the world that he could still live dangerously without drugs. The performances were a revelation and a great shock to those who had assumed the partnership had nothing left to offer. Unlike recent CS&N stadium shows, this was no mere trek through the back catalogue but a chance to demonstrate new material, such as Crosby's still unreleased, 'He's An American'.

One month after the Arlington get-together, an old prophecy was fulfilled when Crosby, Stills, Nash & Young began work on *American Dream*, their first studio album since *Déjà Vu* in 1970. On 16 May 1987, Crosby married Jan Dance at a double wedding ceremony in which Graham and Susan Nash renewed their vows. Among the guests were Stills, McGuinn and Hillman. After the honeymoon, Crosby returned for a new series of CS&N tours, which offered a more vital and varied set than aficionados had heard in many years.

In late 1988, the CSN&Y reunion album *American Dream* was at last released. Despite mixed reviews, the work demonstrated the strength of the quartet, as well as reminding the world of all that had been lost as a result of their failure to record together over the past two decades. The only jarring note was the inappropriate decision to allocate Crosby a mere two songs, the spinetingling 'Compass' and the politically passionate 'Nighttime For The

Generals'. Nevertheless, he seemed resigned to this regrettable imbalance. "It's just how it happened," he told me. "There was some resistance there from somebody, but I don't worry about it. I had two very good songs and was more concerned with the quality rather than the quantity. I'm not worried about the pie-slicing."

The flurry of activity continued with a best-selling autobiography, *Long Time Gone*, and the completion of that seemingly lost second solo album, retitled *Oh Yes I Can*. It was a far less radical record than its great predecessor, *If I Could Only Remember My Name*, but a welcome return nonetheless. During another interview with this author in February 1989, Crosby celebrated his new lease of life. "My health's really excellent. I'm just past three years straight now. I'm a diabetic and I'm dealing with that successfully. I managed to lose 40 lbs since I got out of jail. I figure I've got to lose another 40, so I'm going to the gym, working out and feeling very healthy. I have tremendous energy. There's a kind of slingshot effect that happens when you spent all this time completely drugged out of your mind like a vegetable. Then, when you wake up from it, you go: 'whoosh!' It's like untying weights from the feet of a bird. I feel great. Why wouldn't I? Look at all the stuff that's working out for me."

Crosby went on to provide an inventory of his blessings, detailing his plans at length and letting slip a project that was particularly dear to his heart. After all this activity, there was only one important avenue that still remained unexplored: the Byrds.

CHAPTER FORTY-FOUR

The Third Coming

ALTHOUGH the individual Byrds remained on hold for most of the Eighties, their influence on the music scene was as pervasive as ever. A wealth of fresh, young groups including REM, the Smiths and the Bangles acknowledged the pre-eminence of the Byrds, while Tom Petty, Hüsker Dü and even Roxy Music found themselves borrowing material from the quintet's back catalogue. Music critics accepted that the Byrds were now of classic stature; like the Beatles, early Elvis and mid-period Stones, their best work was deemed above criticism. Pat phrases such as 'Byrds-like Rickenbacker breaks' and 'jingle-jangle guitar work' became familiar journalistic similes that were in danger of becoming clichés. Although never superstars in their time, the Byrds found themselves belatedly eulogized as indisputable greats. Independent record companies recognized their lasting appeal and specialist labels such as Edsel, Rhino, Sierra and Murray Hill kept the group's musical legacy alive by both reopening old catalogues and reissuing the best of their subsequent solo work.

The most ambitious and intriguing archivist adventure was undertaken by Murray Hill, which scoured the tape shelves of Columbia in search of unreleased material from the 1965–67 period. The man behind the project was Bob Hyde, who had the foresight to employ Jim Dickson to remix various cuts, thereby ensuring that the Byrds not only gave their blessing to the project but became actively involved in improving the unearthed material. The most difficult task in the entire archivist expedition was actually finding the tapes and persuading Columbia to sanction their release. Several crucially important unreleased tracks were lost, seemingly forever, while other songs were unavailable in their original multi-track format. Eventually, a large proportion of the unreleased gems were discovered, including the vintage cuts of 'Eight Miles High' and 'Why' on RCA. Meanwhile, back at Columbia, trouble was brewing. The archive album, so near to completion, looked likely to be neutered. The RCA versions were vetoed on the grounds that they weren't recorded at Columbia, while others met corporate resistance because instruments had been added to the original tracks. Eventually, the political obstacles were largely overcome and, in December 1987, Murray Hill released the appropriately titled *Never Before*.

Superbly packaged in a pastiche mid-Sixties sleeve, the contents included a tantalizing sessionography, previously unseen photographs from 1965, a track-by-track breakdown, and some personal reminiscences from Jim Dickson. Fittingly, the vinyl album commences with that most famous of all Byrds songs, 'Mr Tambourine Man', presented in a crisp, previously unreleased, slightly elongated stereo mix. Dickson was always impressed by Terry Melcher's work on the original and felt his decision to create a great mono cut was perfectly sound. It was hoped that the piano work of Leon Russell and the distinctive counter vocal from Gene Clark could be retrieved from the mix but, unfortunately, they had been buried into inaudibility.

According to Dickson, the album's opening track was the least altered. "Outside of 'Mr Tambourine Man' I never put up any of the original mixes. I did with 'Tambourine Man' because it had been sped up and I wanted to get the same pitch. I respected Terry Melcher's mix so much that I didn't want to lose anything he'd gotten in mono. We couldn't really make much of a stereo recording out of it so the only thing we really 'split' were the voices. I took that military drum and put it slightly off-centre to open up the drums a little bit because they were all on one track, except for that overdub of the military drum. I spread it out a little bit so that maybe people might hear it."

The new stereo mix of 'I Knew I'd Want You' was considerably improved, highlighting the excellent musicianship of Hal Blaine,

Larry Knechtel, Jerry Cole and Leon Russell. Another Gene Clark song follows, 'She Has A Way', last heard in more primitive form on *Preflyte*. The Columbia version is far more accomplished with McGuinn's Rickenbacker prominent and Michael Clarke in top form. Like so many Gene Clark songs from the period, 'She Has A Way' had been rejected in favour of extraneous material. Ironically, Bob Dylan, whose work largely replaced that of Clark on the first two albums, had always proved a great admirer of the underrated Kansas songwriter.

The irreverent 'It's All Over Now, Baby Blue' reveals McGuinn at his most acerbic, the exaggerated Dylanesque vocal creating an almost comic effect. As he would later do with 'You Ain't Going Nowhere', McGuinn takes poetic licence with Dylan's lyrics, this time as early as the first line: "You *better go* now, take what you *want* you think will last". The track ultimately emerges as vintage, Byrds folk rock – fast and raucous with some ferocious drumming from Clarke, a distinctive Rickenbacker break that still tingles, and a delightfully offhand arrangement which captures the group at their most playfully arrogant. Dickson believes that the best version was destroyed amid his disagreement with Terry Melcher over the recording. "It was canned. The multi-track is lost. It was probably thrown out. All we had to put on *Never Before* was a quick rough mix. We had a better mix, but it had a flaw in it. McGuinn sounded better on the guitar. Unfortunately, the drums were lost, so we couldn't use it."

The album's title track was a previously unreleased song that Clark had recorded with the Byrds in 1965. He could not remember much about the composition, so tentatively named it 'Never Before' (it was later correctly retitled 'The Day Walk'). Its densely packed verses, full of portentous Dylan-inspired lyrics, are typical of the folk-rock period and indicate the direction Clark would later take during his solo career.

Unfortunately, Clark's involvement in the *Never Before* project was not as extensive as it might have been. "Gene disappeared," Dickson reveals. "He refused to be interested in any way until right at the end when he found that his song was going to be the title track, and it wasn't as bad as he remembered it. He'd more embarrassing cuts to worry about than that, but it was rough on the tape. The ones that got bootlegged would lead you to believe that it was worse than it was. It turned out kind of funky. I liked it because I enjoy hearing Michael play that way. It's the way he likes to play – chunky and hard."

One of the highlights of *Never Before* was the belated unveiling of the RCA version of 'Eight Miles High'. Both Crosby and Hillman had previously acknowledged the superiority of the RCA original, while McGuinn was more cautious, merely conceding that it was probably "more spontaneous". Characteristically, McGuinn's sober analysis seemed closest to the mark. The guitar work did sound more spontaneous on the RCA cut but it was difficult, if not impossible, to dislodge the power of the classic released version from the collective memory. The accompanying 'Why', with its sitar-like guitar breaks, recalls the CBS single track, rather than the less spectacular remake issued on *Younger Than Yesterday*. The song is aptly placed on *Never Before*, prefacing three other David Crosby songs which testify to his creative ascendancy in 1967.

'Triad', the controversial *ménage à trois* ode, emerges with a striking arrangement and a cool yet sexually beguiling vocal. Crosby actually re-recorded a vocal line but, according to Dickson, the substitution is so precise that it is virtually undetectable. Even more impressive is 'It Happens Each Day', one of the first Crosby songs to include his now characteristic use of sea imagery. An irresistible candidate for *Younger Than Yesterday*, it was regrettably incomplete and later abandoned by its writer. In preparing the *Never Before* version, considerable work was done on the old tapes, with Hillman adding some acoustic guitar to flesh out the track. "David was surprised at Chris, who went in and also put some bass on it" Dickson says. "The one that was on there was out of tune. Then David said, 'Who put the guitar on, I don't remember that?' I said: 'Chris did it.' That was when he first realized that Chris had developed as a guitar player."

The revamped track also gave Crosby pause to consider how differently the Byrds might have sounded had he been more active as an acoustic player. "I wish I'd been smarter then and known enough to use acoustic guitar more. I used electric almost exclusively in the

Byrds, and acoustic would have served very well for a lot of the stuff that I was doing on that record." Remarkably, Crosby admitted to me that he had completely forgotten 'It Happens Each Day' ever existed until he heard the unearthed tape. Given the quality of the song and relative scarcity of his compositional output over the years, this blank spot seems all the more extraordinary.

There was no such memory lapse over 'Lady Friend' which Crosby always felt passionately about, deeply resenting its omission from *The Notorious Byrd Brothers*. The long-awaited stereo version features some previously unheard scat singing to accompany the epical brass fade-out. Alas, the original scat vocals in the midsection are no longer audible. Worse still, Clarke's drum work was not deemed strong enough to translate into stereo, so another player was employed by Murray Hill to embellish the sound. This was a ludicrous and unnecessary decision. What should have been a perfect conclusion to a commendable album was drastically compromised by the deletion of Clarke's work. Audiophiles rightly felt that the sound of Eighties' drums was jarring and completely inappropriate.

Such was the impact of *Never Before* that Murray Hill elected to add seven new tracks to the CD version of the work. The luckless Chris Hillman lost some glory, not to mention songwriting royalties, when his compositions were abruptly axed. 'Have You Seen Her Face' was omitted because the new stereo mix added so little to the original track. CBS had already refused to sanction 'Old John Robertson' on the vinyl version because a 'foreign instrument' (a tastefully applied mandolin, which enhanced the track surprisingly well) had been belatedly added. Considering that the 'doctored' Crosby tracks had slipped through the net, this inconsistency was particularly galling.

McGuinn then intervened and took time out to remix the remaining cuts with engineer Ken Robertson. New stereo mixes of the B-sides 'Why' and 'She Don't Care About Time' proved painfully counter-productive, perversely emphasizing weaknesses rather than highlighting strengths. The 45 version of 'Why', for example, loses all of its punch in the crudely diffused stereo mix, exposing Clarke's previously unobtrusive drumming to embarrassing effect and totally burying Hillman's wonderfully subtle gulping bass line. In these instances, the mono mixes were far better left in their original state. 'Don't Make Waves', a suspect choice anyway, was passable, and only vindicated by the cheeky inclusion of Crosby's sarcastic studio comments at the end of the song.

The main attractions of the *Never Before* CD were its long-awaited five unreleased tracks. Chief amongst these was the legendary 'I Know My Rider', a wonderful example of Byrds folk rock with an astonishing Rickenbacker break from McGuinn. Recorded several times during the making of *Fifth Dimension* and *Younger Than Yesterday*, the song was successively rejected by the Byrds, but its charm and vibrancy are undeniable.

The once predominantly instrumental 'Psychodrama City' appears in edited form, but the recording quality is excellent. A revealing example of the jazz-influenced Crosby attempting some talking blues, it was an apt comment on the 'psychodramas' that the Byrds suffered during the 1965–67 period. In the first verse, a blonde fan threatens suicide if she can't have the delectable Crosby, an apparently not uncommon occurrence for the sex-god Byrd. Later in the song, there is an oblique reference to Gene Clark's departure from the Byrds, including the famous incident during which he freaked out on a plane. Crosby casually concludes: "To this day, I don't know why, why he got on at all if he really didn't want to fly." Prior to the release of the CD, while promoting his autobiography *Long Time Gone*, Crosby vehemently denied to me that he had ever written or even sung a composition entitled 'Psychodrama City'. He was adamant. The vocal and the writing credits tell a different story, confirming yet again the amnesiac disregard that the Byrds often betrayed towards their past work. When I subsequently sent a letter to Crosby congratulating him on receiving publishing income for a song he had denied writing, he was, to say the least, unamused.

From Crosby eccentricity to McGuinn whimsy is a clever way of completing a Byrds compilation and the instrumentals 'Flight 713' and 'Moog Raga' both sound intriguing. The former was discovered at the end of the studio tape of 'Get To You' under the rather unimaginative title, 'Song Number 2'. McGuinn belatedly rechristened the composition 'Flight 713', after looking at the studio clock at 13 minutes past seven. An effective instrumental that might have been developed into a strong song, 'Flight 713' allows us a welcome glimpse at McGuinn and Hillman's post-Crosby studio tinkering.

Infinitely more bizarre is the closing 'Moog Raga' which, along with the later 'Fiddler A Dram (Moog Experiment)', displays McGuinn's extravagant essay into electronica. In combining a raga break with an otherworldly synthesizer drone, McGuinn creates a delightful work which simultaneously prompts respect for its innovation, while provoking mild laughter at its obvious novelty. More than anything 'Moog Raga' stands alongside '2-4-2 Fox Trot (The Lear Jet Song)', 'Oh! Susannah' and 'We'll Meet Again' as a wonderfully whimsical way to complete an important work.

Jim Dickson was pleased with *Never Before*, but felt ambivalent about the sensible decision to make it an archival album. "The thing I wanted to do with the album was not the same as Bob Hyde wanted. He wanted a collectors' item and wanted all those things that were unreleased. I said, 'Most of those things were unreleased because they were seriously bad or not completed, and shouldn't be brought out.' I thought we were stretching it to get enough good tracks even to have ten songs. I tried to keep out stuff [on the vinyl album version] that was garbage and ensure that the packaging was good. I wish CBS hadn't lost so many tracks. There were things that I'd loved to have gone in and played with. One of the things I would have been willing to work endlessly on was 'The Bells Of Rhymney'. You have equipment now that can reach into the track . . . Even with the tapes that had been sitting around for 20 years, I could make them sparkle. The engineer sat there astounded how I got the drums out of that 'Eight Miles High' track at all because they were so buried in that quick mix. He was astounded about what we could get out of it."

Dickson was impressed when McGuinn undertook some promotional activity in support of the retrospective and was generally pleased to have worked with some of the Byrds again. "I was happy that Chris and David were supportive enough to come down and work on it. I was unhappy that Chris' song was thrown off and turned him against the project. He was really upset. It was the only song of his that was going to be on the vinyl album and he'd done more work on it all than anybody. He'd helped David's unreleased songs. David did work on his own songs, but Chris did whatever he asked him. He was trying to make up. He's done that many times where he'll come and try and be the good guy and help you out, and make up for what he's done to you the last time. And then he'll do it again! You get tired of being Charlie Brown and watching him being Lucy, and holding that football while you fall on your ass . . . You get tired of that from Chris. You just want to get away. But I'm proud of his growth, I'm happy with his band and I'm glad he's successful."

While Murray Hill were turning back the pages of history, Rhino Records reassembled the *Preflyte* tapes for another intriguing retrospective: *In The Beginning*. Jim Dickson handed over approximately 45 tracks of various cuts recorded in primitive conditions at World-Pacific Studios in 1964. The tapes included many different versions of familiar Byrds songs, including three renditions of 'Boston' and, incredibly, six takes of 'You Movin''. The latter two tracks were the Byrds' early attempts at composing derivative R&B influenced material, exclusively for live performance. Dickson stresses that these were never seriously considered for recording purposes though they were rehearsed ad infinitum so that the Byrds' dancing followers would not be disappointed.

The compilers of *In The Beginning* decided to include as many alternate takes as possible, irrespective of their quality. On 'Mr Tambourine Man' the primitiveness is taken to its retrospective extreme. The sound is so raw and the vocal so wayward that it makes even the previously issued take on *Preflyte* sound sophisticated by comparison. There's also a ramshackle 'You Showed Me', which even the Byrds would be shocked to hear. 'It's No Use', never previously issued in its pre-Columbia state, is another interesting artefact, proving that the group were experimenting with a dense guitar sound even as early as the summer of 1964.

However, the real highlight of the CD was the acoustic and electric treatment of a song never previously released in any form: 'Tomorrow Is A Long Ways Away'. Written by Gene Clark, who rather generously surrenders co-writing royalties to Crosby and

McGuinn on the minimally altered electric version, the song is a revelation. The melody sounds delightful, with a lilt reminiscent of an Elizabethan madrigal. Clark transforms his composition into a folk-rock torch song with a heart-rending solo vocal in the Scott Walker/P.J. Proby school. Unfortunately, it was this aberrant quality which doomed the song to obscurity. Never mind. The song was worth the 25-year wait and, like the rest of *In The Beginning*, allows us a unique opportunity to appreciate the very essence of the Byrds' sound.

The timely retrospectives, *Never Before* and *In The Beginning*, emphasize the point that the magical entity that was the Byrds could never be 'recreated' but only rediscovered in a lost past. No Byrds reunion album could hope to capture the emotional shiver accompanying these demos and rejected outtakes from the Sixties.

Over the years, the Byrds became victims as well as celebrants of their own history. They tried, not without some success, to confine their illustrious name to the past, but the monstrous myth continually returned to haunt and injure their present day projects. Roger McGuinn nobly attempted to close the book on the Byrds in 1973 and, along with Crosby, appeared to concur with the proposition that "there were ever only five Byrds". McGuinn claimed that he owned the Byrds' name and intended to trademark the title to prevent its misuse. Unfortunately, his application expired and although the group name remained unused it was, theoretically at least, up for grabs.

McGuinn's disbanding of the Byrds did not mean that he was disowning or ignoring his past. On the contrary, he continued to play Byrds standards in concert and even named one of his Seventies groups Thunderbyrd. Gene Clark fleetingly betrayed a similar dependence and re-recorded two old Byrds classics, 'Mr Tambourine Man' and 'Feel A Whole Lot Better', for the ominously titled *Firebyrd*. In 1985, Clark became bolder and decided to set out on a '20th Anniversary Byrds Tour'. He received short shrift from the remaining originals, with the exception of drummer Michael Clarke, who was obviously feeling the pinch since the glory days of Firefall. Without McGuinn, Crosby or Hillman, Clark's anniversary tour was decidedly low-key, although mildly interesting for its peculiar tendency to chronologically mismatch latter-day Byrds with two of its original members.

McGuinn was displeased by the tour but charitable enough not to begrudge his ex-partner the chance of picking up some money. In the end, Clark became the victim of wily promoters who felt it made economic sense to jettison the 'Anniversary' mouthful and simply bill the ensemble as 'The Byrds'. When Gene Clark temporarily returned to solo work, Michael Clarke sporadically soldiered on under the banner 'A Tribute To The Byrds'. Again, the inevitable abbreviation followed. At one point, a parodic Byrds line-up briefly turned out comprising Michael Clarke, Skip Battin, John York and Carlos Bernal. Die-hard fans were mortified, Hillman was dismissive, McGuinn seemed indignant. Crosby, incapacitated by cocaine addiction, and later prison, had more important things to worry about.

When David Crosby walked out of Huntsville Prison, Texas, corpulent and clean, he looked like a man ready to reclaim his past. After reforming CSN&Y, he decided that a get-together of the Byrds would be interesting and beneficial to the group's long-term legacy. A passionate, fiercely opinionated man, David Crosby has the unique ability to stir up the emotions of others to such a degree that they become part of his own drama. McGuinn and Hillman listened to his pitch and suddenly decided that the good name of the Byrds should be salvaged for the sake of history – not to mention integrity, reputation and money. At this point, neither Clark nor Clarke were performing under the Byrds' banner but the lingering bad feeling concerning their presumptuous use of the name ensured that they were not invited to participate in the surprise concert that followed.

The new Byrds triumvirate had briefly tested the possibility of a reunion in June 1988 when they appeared as soloists at a celebratory concert for the reopening of the legendary Ash Grove folk club. A wealth of Ash Grove alumni turned up at the Wiltern Theatre and anticipation was high for an onstage Byrds get-together. The audience was not disappointed. As the house lights blinkered, impresario Ed Pearl welcomed "McGuinn, Crosby, Hillman". Backed by John Jorgenson and Steve Duncan of the

Desert Rose Band, the trio provided a greatest hits repertoire consisting of 'Mr Tambourine Man', 'Turn! Turn! Turn!', 'Eight Miles High' and 'So You Want To Be A Rock 'n' Roll Star'. Cheering them on from the audience was Gene Clark, whom Crosby explained was unable to appear due to a recent stomach operation. It was not anticipated that the reunion would be taken any further but, several months later, David Crosby learned about a very different Byrds tour.

Having failed to receive an invitation to join his fellow Byrds, and aware that they might exclude him from future reunions, Michael Clarke became concerned about his future. There were music industry rumours of scarcely believable fortunes to be made if the original Byrds reformed, but McGuinn and the others were dragging their heels on the matter and looked likely to turn down any immediate offers. Roger had already rejected a million dollar deal to play a 45-minute set at the Us Festival in Pasadena, a package intended to include a television special for HBO and a live album for Warner Brothers.

While various Byrds congregated, Clarke was back at his family home in Spokane, occasionally painting and thinking of new employment outside the music business. The extent of his ambition at this point was to complete the high school diploma that he had left unfinished 15 years before. "Michael had not been playing," his mother relates. "At that time someone offered them a lot of money if the Byrds could get back together for one session. It was a big amount of money, but not one of them would get back together for a reunion. Michael was so mad. He was so upset with all of them. I guess his manager Steve Green was the one who said, 'Well, why don't you get a group of your own together?' That's where it all started."

The retaliatory action soon attracted the attention of Crosby who, fomented by Hillman's ire, was concerned about Clarke and Green's intention to resurrect the Byrds, especially when correspondence revealed that a trademark name was being sought. As Crosby told me: "Michael Clarke had fallen on hard times and was in the hands of some unscrupulous people who put him on the road as the Byrds. Then I had this horrible paranoid flash. I called up

McGuinn and Hillman and said: 'What if these guys who have a band on the road copyright the name and then we can't use it?' They said: 'What an awful idea! Do you take special pills to come up with these bad thoughts?' I said: 'I really think they might do that.' And, sure enough, that's what they were up to, so we beat them to it!"

The man behind Michael Clarke was Artists International manager, Steve Green, a specialist in repromoting classic 'oldies' acts. He accepts Crosby's contention that a trademark was sought, but denies that there was anything remotely surreptitious about such a move. "Sure, we tried to trademark the name. If they weren't going to use it, which they hadn't, why shouldn't we? We didn't go about it to hurt them. We were in contact with their attorneys from day one. We didn't try to trademark the name to blow them out of it. We just wanted to get legitimate ownership. We're not trying to steal the name. Even if we'd got the trademark, they'd have had time to oppose it. When you get a trademark, it's not written in concrete. There's a five-year period of opposition. You can oppose it at any time in those five years. We're not trying to pull over anything on anybody. We went about our business to protect our rights."

Green maintains that on the very same day Michael Clarke applied for a federal trademark, a similar application was despatched by Gene Clark. In fact, Clark had begun his application prior to Clarke and was in a stronger position than many assumed. It was an uncanny coincidence and another subplot to a story which was becoming more bizarre by the minute.

One of the more amusing ironies in this whole book is that the undemonstrative Michael Clarke should dramatically emerge as the key figure in effecting another Byrds reunion. For, in order to strengthen their rights to the name, McGuinn, Crosby and Hillman elected to revive the Byrds and play three shows during January 1989 at the Coach House, San Juan Capistrano (4th), the Bacchanal, San Diego (5th), and Ventura Theater (6th). Backed by John Jorgenson and Steve Duncan, the streamlined Byrds performed a plethora of old hits. The Ventura set began with a shaky, but stirring 'Chimes Of Freedom', with Hillman featuring strongly on backing vocals. At the time the song was recorded, Chris was known as the stage-shy Byrd but, 24 years later, he was ready and willing to sing along with the others. A ragged 'It Won't Be Wrong' followed, with Crosby overworking his vocal part to distracting effect. This was probably the one noticeably disappointing rendition. An impressive 'Feel A Whole Lot Better', which McGuinn had played frequently, long after Clark had left the Byrds, restored confidence. The surprise inclusion of Crosby's 'Everybody's Been Burned' was especially moving and probably the highlight of the entire show. Although the under-rehearsed Byrds could not hope to reproduce the superb quality of the recorded version, their late Eighties rendition was still riveting. Another *Younger Than Yesterday* track followed with the evergreen 'My Back Pages'. Even though McGuinn had performed the song for 22 years, he somehow managed to transpose the second verse mistakenly into the final stanza.

A worryingly hoarse Crosby next appeared at the microphone to defend 'Mr Spaceman' from accusations of being a novelty number. "We were serious!" he exclaimed, before the Byrds broke into an excellent version of their 1966 hit. This was succeeded by 'The Bells Of Rhymney', which prompted memories of those wonderfully bell-ringing cymbals of Michael Clarke. The mischievous Hillman then decided to inject some humour into the proceedings by introducing a Byrds song on which Crosby had failed to appear. In a wonderfully sarcastic rewriting of Byrds history, Hillman informed the audience: "About 1968, David left and we begged and begged him not to leave. He went off with Stephen and Graham and he made a million dollars, and Roger and I went to Nashville and we decided we'd crack the country & western market. We missed you on that record!"

With Crosby making shovelling movements in the background, the group launched into the singalong 'You Ain't Going Nowhere'. It proved an interesting version, not only because Crosby was heard prominently, but also due to Hillman being allowed to sing lead vocal on alternate verses. McGuinn completed this new revisionism by altering the lyrics to "pick up your money and pack up your tent" in belated deference to the once aggrieved Bob Dylan.

The most famous Byrds song of all time was saved for late in the set. While introducing 'Mr Tambourine Man', McGuinn wrongly credited Dylan's former road manager Victor Maymudes for introducing the composition to the group, a slip which annoyed Jim Dickson. "The trouble with McGuinn is that he doesn't listen," he sighs. "Like all that history, he doesn't know. He didn't know Miles Davis was involved with CBS. He didn't know where 'Tambourine Man' came from. I had him singing it long before Victor Maymudes came into the studio with Dylan. That's why they came – to hear it. McGuinn was so vague in those days that he didn't pay attention and he doesn't know what went on. I reminded him. I said: 'Jim, every time I tried to explain what was going on to you, you'd say, "I trust everything will work out all right" and you said that over and over and that was the only answer I could ever get.'"

Following the Maymudes' plug, 'Mr Tambourine Man' provided a high moment of nostalgia and was swiftly followed by the Byrds' second US number 1 'Turn! Turn! Turn!', during which Crosby's voice sounded hoarser than ever. The rush of hits continued with 'Eight Miles High'. "They thought it was a drug song, but it isn't", confirmed McGuinn for the umpteenth time. Crosby's chunky upfront rhythm guitar sounded excellent, although the impact of Hillman's bass work was less pronounced and Steve Duncan's professional drumming lacked the aural authenticity of the exiled Michael Clarke. McGuinn, having played 'Eight Miles High' consistently in solo concerts, naturally gave a strong performance which inspired the crowd to cheer loudly. The encore began with McGuinn asking, "Do you all know how to scream?" as the Byrds' greatest hits repertoire ended with a rousing refrain of 'So You Want To Be A Rock 'n' Roll Star'. In striking contrast to 1967, the Byrds came offstage hugging and back-slapping each other and although there were no plans for additional shows, they were clearly pleased by the performances.

Two months later, Crosby was still enthusing about those gigs. "We got up there, man, and tore it up!" he told me. "We hit 'Chimes Of Freedom' and I got chills going up my back. And the audience went: 'Whoop! Up for grabs! Totally nuts!' I'm being very immodest but I'm telling you the truth. We got reviews from people that normally wouldn't give you the sweat off their brow, and they were raves. It was really exciting and, more importantly, it was a hell of a lot of fun."

In spite of his past disagreements with McGuinn and Hillman, Crosby was obviously in magnanimous mood and spoke of his partners with the exuberance of a fan who had just rediscovered old heroes. "When I started playing with Roger and Christopher, I'd forgotten how strong they were. Especially how strong McGuinn is. I confess it. I'm guilty. I didn't remember he was that good. He was fantastic. He's better now than he ever was. We all know that he's got this guitar style which can't be duplicated, but I'd forgotten what a great tale teller he is. Also, the last time I played with Chris Hillman he was just a kid. Now he's Manassas, Burritos and the Desert Rose Band with three number 1 [country] singles in a row. He's a very strong, polished, mature, confident guy."

As the superlatives flowed, Crosby revealed that the new Byrds were intending to record a live album, thereby suggesting that touring plans were afoot. When I pressed him on the non-involvement of Gene Clark, he replied obliquely: "I don't think Gene's ready to do that. Roger and Christopher had an awkward time with Gene when they tried to work with him last. I'm not the one to make a decision about Gene. The other guys made their decision. I'm real happy with it and would like to work with Roger and Christopher."

Contrary to Crosby's suggestion, Gene Clark certainly seemed more than ready to join his colleagues, if the opportunity arose. He had already tried to make his peace by promising that he would not tour under the name Byrds again. In speaking to me of his previously troubled adventures with McGuinn and Hillman, he stressed with pained humility: "I feel a lot of remorse about that."

As paragons of physical health and ageing advocates of non-excessive lifestyles, Crosby, McGuinn and Hillman were obviously choosy about their partners, but it must be stressed that in the wake of this new puritanism, Clark had also reformed his ways. He'd not had a drink in the past year and had even attended the same AA meetings as Crosby. If there was some form of underlying moral criterion to this reunion, then the new Gene Clark could not justifiably be faulted. Although he had also applied to trademark the name, he reassured the others that he would not side with Michael Clarke. While diplomatically sitting on the fence, he clearly felt that a full reunion would be the most sensible solution: "The best thing would be for the five people to sit down and come to some sort of agreement."

After the streamlined reunion concerts, the stakes were upped and as Crosby promised: "We beat them to it." Events reached a head when Clarke's Byrds arrived in Tucson, Arizona, hometown of McGuinn's family. Posters appeared advertising the Byrds "featuring Roger McGuinn". Although the fliers were removed when the mistake was pointed out, the Tucson Garden was flooded with calls and, according to the club owner, many people said they would attend despite McGuinn's absence. When a reporter called the club on the day of the concert enquiring if the billed Byrds were the original group, the wry answer was "as original as we're going to get!" For McGuinn and company, this mix-up was clearly the final straw.

During the spring, a lawsuit was filed in federal court by the three Byrds suing Michael Clarke, Artists International Management, Steve Green and John Does 1-10, for allegedly false advertising, unfair competition and deceptive trade practices. Crosby and manager Bill Siddons seemed confident about the outcome of the legal proceedings but clearly underestimated Green, who had previously fought and won cases involving rival groups of Platters and Drifters. Not surprisingly, Green resisted, employing the argument that McGuinn had abandoned the name Byrds and that the last person to use it for a number of years was his client, Michael Clarke. McGuinn, Crosby and Hillman consistently stressed that Clarke never wrote or sang with the Byrds and therefore his contribution was minimal. Green, rather than making a big deal out of his client's collaborative work on 'Captain Soul' or 'Artificial Energy', bypassed the musical arguments to suggest that Clarke's primary importance to the Byrds was as a sex symbol. Did Michael's good looks ultimately sell as many records as McGuinn's Rickenbacker or Crosby's harmony and green-suede cape? Much appeared to depend on the perspective of a 69-year-old judge.

Green cunningly continued to underplay the entire question of musical authenticity. "We think we're going to win," he argued. "We're not idiots. We don't say that we can recreate what they did in 1965. We're hoping to bring the group into the Nineties and do what Little Feat and others have done by replacing members and going on and having a hit record. We're not sure that we can, but we're getting a tremendous amount of interest."

For Hillman, the above scenario was a nightmare, guaranteed to provoke the same antipathy he had voiced against the various refried Burritos, who had aesthetically cheapened a once great name.

Michael Clarke's reply to the criticisms of his ex-colleagues was the weary: "I won't be denied a living and I don't like to be harassed." Meanwhile, Green claimed that he had attempted to come up with endless permutations of the name that might be acceptable to McGuinn and the others. "We tried 'Michael Clarke salutes the Byrds', 'The Byrds with Michael Clarke', 'An evening with the Byrds featuring Michael Clarke' . . . It sounded all right to us! We tried everything to make them understand that we're not trying to misrepresent them, but their egos are so big that they think we're making money out of them. They don't want parity. I'll go with them being the Byrds if Michael can be the Byrds. I'll go with them 'saluting the Byrds' if Michael can 'salute the Byrds'. Anything they want to do is all right with me."

In defence of McGuinn, Crosby and Hillman, Bill Siddons countered: "We tried to set up meetings with the five musicians and Steve Green refused to let Michael go to the meeting."

Detached observers seemed strongly divided on the issue and, not surprisingly, their opinions were governed by whomever they had spoken to during the dispute. On aesthetic grounds, Michael Clarke was clearly completely out of order and long-term fans were rightly appalled by his use of the name. However, Crosby, McGuinn and Hillman were also censured in some quarters for using the name Byrds and not inviting their former colleagues to participate in the reunion. Crosby brushed aside such criticisms, along with Green's rhetoric, by stating that the one member with an indisputable claim to the name was his former rival, McGuinn. "My contribution aside, if it doesn't have Roger McGuinn in it, it's not the Byrds," he insisted. "I don't care what anybody says. That's the truth. He's the heart and soul of the Byrds. He always has been and he always will be. If he's not there, it isn't the Byrds." Hillman and Siddons concurred with Crosby's viewpoint in separate statements and it seemed likely that this would be the crux of their case.

The most frustrating realization for McGuinn was that he had lost his right to the name Byrds otherwise, as Green admitted, Michael Clarke would have no possible claim. Clarke had signed away his rights to the Byrds name in January 1968, but so too had Crosby and, in any case, all five reconvened officially as 'Byrds' in 1973. Green did not underestimate the strong association in the public's mind between McGuinn and the Byrds, but pinpointed a number of possible flaws in their argument.

"We're not denying that McGuinn was the Byrds or a major force in the group," he told me. "His problem is that he lost his trademark as the Byrds and made so many public statements that he doesn't want to be the Byrds any more. His abandonment seems clear. Roger was only as good as his players. He can't prove that on his own he was successful. They say Michael was marginal, but the Byrds didn't have any real success after he left. Plus, their royalties have actually gone up in the last five years since he went out as the Byrds. They don't seem to want to do anything except stop Michael. That's why their position is weak. Eventually, the courts are going to ask them what they want to do with the name. You can't just take away somebody's living and stop it because you want to bury the group. That will never wash. If McGuinn thought the name was sacrosanct he should have stopped in 1968, but he went on with whomever he could find. That was OK for Roger McGuinn to do, but it's not OK for Michael."

Green had a minor point here, but he ignored the crucial fact that the Byrds were still an 'ongoing' group when McGuinn used the name. With hindsight, Roger concedes that ideally he should have ended the Byrds at a somewhat earlier date, but they were still a lucrative proposition when he diplomatically dissolved the final CBS line-up in 1973. Since then, he had resolutely, many felt nobly, withstood any financial temptations to turn back the clock by trading off the Byrds' name. Even during the Eighties, when he had no record contract, he chose not to use the Byrds as commercial leverage. Clearly, what he now sought was not simply to stop Michael Clarke, but to regulate the use of the name, and decide if, and when, the Byrds should reconvene. It was only the legal battle which persuaded him to modify his previous stance in 1973 when he and Crosby agreed that the only Byrds were the original five.

McGuinn, Crosby and Hillman may have seen themselves as the true guardians of the Byrds but, as the talk of a possible live album and tour continued, where did that leave the presently neutral Gene Clark? Cynics felt that money would eventually topple morality in this scenario, especially as the three Byrds could command a massive advance without Clark and Clarke, thereby splitting the cake three ways rather than five. However, such expediency would not only have been an affront to history but myopic economics. Big-time promoters would always offer far more money for the complete set of original Byrds, rather than a 'best of compilation'. The original quintet had not toured since the end of 1965 and their complete reformation would have been a mouth-watering prospect for any astute impresario. Unlike their great contemporaries, the Beatles, the Beach Boys, the Rolling Stones and the Who, the Byrds had a complete line-up still alive 25 years on. Both Michael Clarke and Gene Clark appreciated the enormous commercial potential of the original Byrds and remained eager to tap that source. While fighting for Michael's rights, Steve Green knew that the real jackpot would be won by masterminding a full-scale reunion.

"There should be five or none, but Michael has to make a living. I'd like to see them all own the trademark: one fifth each. My position has always been consistent. If they want it for five of them, we don't have to go to court. Put it in one name: The Byrds Inc. They tour whenever they want to tour. Nobody's left out. If they trademarked it five ways, we'd drop our application. All we want is a resolution. Even if these guys hate each other, let them do their show, go home, make $10 million for each tour they go on, and split it five ways. It may take only 30 days a year. Michael will then have to find some other way to pay his bills."

Green's fanciful idea about an annual Byrds get-together was obviously out of the question, but even a single live album and a one-off reunion tour would have earned Clarke more than years of playing small-time gigs with his bastardized version of the group. Surely, Clarke and Green would have accepted the Byrds remaining in indefinite suspended animation if McGuinn, Hillman and Crosby agreed to a one-off album/tour and a five-way split under the right conditions. With such an incentive Clarke and Green were determined to fight on. As Green concluded: "If we win the injunction, McGuinn and Hillman are done for."

The injunction hearing, for all its importance, looked like being little more than the first round of an extremely bloody battle ending in a full trial. Such a course of action would have meant a judge ultimately unravelling the complex history of the Byrds in order to reach a solution. Clarke's role in the various comings and goings would no doubt have made particularly interesting reading. We know that Crosby received $15,000 compensation from the Byrds following his dismissal in 1967. A few months later, Clarke was also out but, in signing away his rights, all he received was his drumkit and his royalties. Whether he should have asked for massive compensation for surrendering the value of the name Byrds at that point was a factor that Green's lawyers intended to focus upon in the event of a trial. Within two months of Michael's leaving, McGuinn and Hillman signed a new agreement with CBS Records on 29 February 1968, which offered an advance of $150,000. Clarke thereby missed a welcome windfall by a matter of weeks. How relevant these factors could become was a matter of debate, but with Green collecting affidavits like cigarette cards, and even securing the distant assistance of former Byrds manager Larry Spector, everything seemed set for one of the most exciting, provocative and revealing court cases in rock history.

Days before the injunction hearing, Green ominously warned me: "When everybody's background is brought into this and all the quotes come out, nobody wins. We all lose! Let's figure out what these guys want to do with the Byrds or how Michael can make a living. End of lawsuit."

The injunction hearing finally proved not so much a body blow as a technical knockout awarded to Michael Clarke. The District

Judge William J. Castagna, after hearing both sides of the argument, emerged with an unequivocal judgement.

> The Court has considered the parties' legal memoranda and affidavits, and has heard oral argument. Preliminary injunctive relief is appropriate if the plaintiffs demonstrate: (1) a substantial likelihood of their success on the merits; (2) their own irreparable injury absent injunctive relief; (3) that the plaintiffs' threatened injury outweighs whatever damage the injunction may cause the opposing party; and (4) that the public interest will not be harmed if the injunction issues. Because the plaintiffs have failed to establish their own irreparable injury absent injunctive relief, their motion is declined. Plaintiffs may establish irreparable injury by showing that the defendants' acts will cause a likelihood of public confusion. Here, the plaintiffs' affidavits attempt to demonstrate instances of actual confusion, but these instances are at best minor and inconsequential, and, in addition, are recited by individuals with a bias toward the plaintiffs. The plaintiffs' most significant and unbiased example of actual confusion involves an advertising flyer misidentifying defendant Clarke's band as 'The Byrds featuring Roger McGuinn'. But, rather than suggesting a likelihood of confusion, this isolated incident is the best evidence of a lack of confusion. Since 1984, the defendant Clarke has performed over 300 times throughout the United States using the Byrds' name. And yet the plaintiffs can only credibly identify one incident of confusion. When the sparsity of incidents of confusion is compared to the wide exposure the defendants have received in over 300 concerts over four years, it is apparent that the likelihood of confusion caused by defendant Clarke's actions is indeed remote. But perhaps most important, the plaintiffs have, by their delay, rendered incredible their claim to irreparable injury. As indicated, the plaintiffs have known for at least four years that defendant Clarke has used the name the Byrds in over 300 concert performances. And until now the plaintiffs have taken no meaningful steps to prevent Clarke's continued performances.

> Under these circumstances, where the plaintiffs have delayed applying for injunctive relief for approximately four years, their claim of irreparable injury is simply not credible. For the reasons stated, the plaintiffs have failed to establish their own irreparable injury absent injunctive relief, and it is, therefore ordered that plaintiffs' motion for a preliminary injunction is declined.

Not surprisingly, Michael Clarke's reaction to the news was a combination of excitement and relief: "I've been on pins and needles since the court date but we won a monumental decision. I'm back in business and my life is wonderful."

The news from the other Byrds camp was not so wonderful for they were now facing a possible counter-lawsuit. Within 26 days of Castagna's ruling, McGuinn, Hillman and Crosby voluntarily dismissed their action without prejudice. The great Byrds trial would not now be taking place after all. A stoical Siddons wrote to me: "It just cost too much money to force Michael to stop abusing the Byrds name."

A delighted Steve Green disagreed and felt that his side was magnanimous in victory: "I was confident we'd win but what they did to Michael really damaged us and it's going to take a lot of time to recover. I wanted them to pay my lawyers' fees but I'm going to let it go, and I'll tell you why. We're all talking now and maybe we'll reunite the band for 30 days this year. That might be the best thing. That's all we really wanted anyway. We always wanted that first but, if they didn't want to play, we still wanted to have the ability to go out and play. So if they want to reunite, they'll reunite, and if they don't then Michael will be out there for as long as he wants to be. That's how it finally wound up."

Green's explanation left several important questions unanswered. Although Clarke was in a position to counter-sue and was free to perform as the Byrds, McGuinn, Crosby, Hillman and the neutral Clark retained the talent and drawing power to make the real money. This remained their crucial ace card. Surely, Michael would forgo any rights to the name Byrds in return for a slice of that full-scale reunion cake, which could take the form of large record company advances, plus royalties and substantial concert receipts. Green accepted this logic, but was extremely wary of surrendering his client's hard-fought victory so easily.

"We don't think that will ever happen," he concluded. "It may be their last card but it wouldn't work for Michael because if the album's a bust nothing happens and the tour might not be as big as expected. Michael's still got to work for the rest of his life. It's too much of a gamble. Unless some promoter guarantees them $30 million over the next four to five years for a certain number of dates per year, in which case, of course he'd be fine. But, until that happens, it'd be real touchy whether he would want to be in a situation where it was all or none of them. We're not looking to hurt them. Hopefully, they'll all start talking and get back together and go about their business."

Bill Siddons seemed confident that three or four of the original Byrds (minus Clarke) would possibly get together for a brief reunion and told me: "Our intent all along has only been that if a fan bought a ticket to see the Byrds, at least Roger McGuinn would be in the band."

Siddons' perspective was righteous and fair but underestimated the full implications of Clarke's victory. For now that Clarke had won the injunction proceedings, he was in a strong position to influence the terms of any reunion by bartering the Byrds' name. Without legal redress, the trio's only realistic chance of convincing Clarke to forgo the Byrds name would be to invite him back into their camp, agree to a reunion and hope that he accepted. In spite of Green's reservations about surrendering the name, he must have known that the value of the title Byrds was merely relative. One big reunion killing would be worth years of struggling around the oldies circuit, especially considering that Clarke did not even have a contract with a major record company, and was never likely to secure one.

Despite his earlier comments, Green probably knew that it would be foolhardy to decline a reunion offer on any terms simply to retain a prestigious name that could not automatically guarantee big money. "Michael won't make a fortune unless he can come up with a hit record," Green conceded. "That way he would make more money than any kind of reunion. You just don't know. You've got to weigh it up. We're sitting on it now because the lawsuit has been dismissed. We could file a counter-lawsuit against each and every one of them for what they did. But instead of doing that, in the hope that maybe we can recreate some of that magic, let's try and get back together, play some dates, and if they don't want to, Michael can go out and do it. Now that everybody's under a certain amount of their own control I think you might see more out of it than you ever saw in the past. They're all going in their own directions, and that's good. Maybe now the channels can be opened and we can talk to each other and go out and *make some money*."

CHAPTER FORTY-FIVE

The Hall Of Fame

WITHIN days of the court hearing, McGuinn and Hillman were talking to Clarke in the hope of bartering a deal. Steve Green still spoke wildly of the possibility of reforming the quintet and playing a 30-day tour annually for the next decade. It was all hot air, of course, and by the end of 1989 nothing had come of the reunion rumours. Instead, McGuinn, Crosby and Hillman were reportedly considering touring as the Byrds and defying Clarke to do his worst. Michael responded by taking his changeling Byrds to Europe. While in Spain, Clarke met a young woman, Lee Elliot, whom he would later marry. In the meantime, the group undertook a mini-tour of England, playing predictably small venues, supported by unrecognizable versions of Herman's Hermits and the Merseybeats. With Michael's friend Terry Rogers and occasional sessioner Jerry Sorn, abetted by Skip Battin, the group sounded nothing more than a competent, but eerily soulless, showband running through the Byrds' hit repertoire. Only two new songs were introduced, both written by Rogers: 'Tricou House' and 'Pirates'. The latter provided an unintentionally apposite comment on the entire ersatz venture: "We are a band of pirates, living out this fantasy/We may not be on the ocean, but that's where we ought to be." Byrds' purists probably would have preferred to see them playing beneath the ocean. More than anything, the shows underlined the importance of McGuinn's vocal and Rickenbacker to the true sound of the Byrds.

There was no doubting the antipathy that had occurred as a result of the legal action and disparaging comments were forthcoming from various quarters, although that was nothing new in the Byrds' story. Hillman curtly told me, "I think Michael has been very foolish, and I'll never work with him again. He was never that great a drummer anyway." Clarke responded with irreverent venom: "Screw those guys. They sued me, and I don't like them any more. How's that?" Those last two words sounded very much like a boy showing-off in the firm belief that he had said something very naughty.

Although Hillman confirmed that Gene Clark was no longer in the enemy camp, there was still no sign of the three Byrds inviting him to partake in any reunion. On 24 February 1990, McGuinn, Crosby and Hillman, billed as 'the original Byrds', appeared at a tribute concert for the late Roy Orbison at the Universal Amphitheatre. Turning back the clock, the trio performed alongside their old mentor Bob Dylan for the first time since that wondrous evening at Ciro's back in 1965. Appropriately, they played an elongated version of 'Mr Tambourine Man', with McGuinn and Dylan trading vocals. Dylan stayed onstage for 'He Was A Friend Of Mine', which was dedicated to the memory of Orbison. The Byrds also included familiar versions of 'Turn! Turn! Turn!' and 'Eight Miles High'. Dylan was in a delightfully deadpan mood throughout the proceedings. At one point he turned towards them with a quizzical look and sarcastically whispered, "I thought there were five of you." Afterwards, Dylan was asked if he'd ever played with the Byrds before and, ignoring the passage of 25 years, retorted: "Yeah, I do it all the time."

With the Byrds back in the news, plans were soon afoot for the compilation of a box set, covering the group's illustrious career. One important figure who would not live to see its release was producer Gary Usher, who passed away on 25 May 1990, aged 51, from lung cancer. Usher was highly respected by Byrds' fans for that great trilogy of albums: *Younger Than Yesterday, The Notorious Byrd Brothers* and *Sweetheart Of The Rodeo*. Since those glory days, he had been relatively quiet. In 1969, his part-owned record company Together had been the first to issue *Preflyte*, followed by the archive album, *Early LA*. Unfortunately, the company lost its distributor and any chance of unearthing other archive material or forgotten tapes of the band ended there. During the Seventies,

Usher had produced Canadian power pop hopefuls the Wackers, as well as Bruce Johnston, but his time among the rock elite had now passed. A decade later, there were evidently some recordings attempted with Brian Wilson, but nothing substantial emerged. Increasingly, Usher was remembered for his early work during the surf era, but his contributions to the Byrds were considerable and never fully appreciated, particularly by David Crosby, who remembered that period with an unforgiving air. At the time of his death, Usher was largely uncommemorated in the rock press, but history has been kinder to his recorded legacy.

In August 1990, the Byrds completed several new songs in Nashville for inclusion on their forthcoming box set. Regrettably, Gene Clark was frozen out of the project, leaving McGuinn, Crosby and Hillman to continue their attempt to establish themselves as the 'real' Byrds. "There was no reason for them not to have invited him," Jim Dickson says. "That turned me off worse than anything they had done recently. I know that Chris had always been negative about Gene coming back or Gene being able to do anything. He bad-mouthed Gene to me all along." McGuinn was not exactly supportive either and later conceded that it was unsporting to have treated Clark like a pariah.

With assistance from Heartbreaker Stan Lynch and John Jorgenson of the Desert Rose Band, the streamlined Byrds attempted to stake their claim to the group name with old and new material. 'He Was A Friend Of Mine' was an accomplished and faithful reading of McGuinn's Kennedy tribute, although it seemed strange to hear Hillman's vocal part where Clark would have been featured. The importance of Hillman to the project was underlined by the decision to allow him to sing lead on Julie Gold's much covered 'From A Distance'. His confident performance emphasized how much he had improved as a singer, even since the beginning of the Eighties. In keeping with the Byrds' tradition of covering unreleased Dylan material, McGuinn tackled 'Paths Of Victory'. First recorded by Dylan, as early as 1962, it served as an apposite comment on the group's trials and tribulations over the years. Finally, McGuinn offered his own reflection on the past 25 years with a new composition, 'Love That Never Dies'. The final verse alluded to the group's first hit 'Mr Tambourine Man' and their last 'Chestnut Mare' in the amusing lines, "Throw a dime to the tambourine man and kiss all the horses goodbye". There was even a passing allusion to the title of my first book in the chorus, "Love is a *timeless flight*".

In October 1990, Byrds' aficionados welcomed the release of the eagerly awaited 4-CD box set, which featured 90 tracks from 'Mr Tambourine Man' in 1965 through to the recent recordings of McGuinn, Crosby and Hillman. Boasting over four hours of playing time, with 17 previously unissued recordings, plus the Nashville tracks and a couple of selections from the Orbison tribute, the box set was promoted as the ultimate Byrds' package. In some respects, the track selection picked itself. Being ruthless, but sensible, the compilers omitted the Byrds' novelty songs, space rock excursions and the odder experiments like 'Captain Soul' and 'Mind Gardens', leaving enough room to present a reasonably representative selection from every Byrds album, with additional weight being given to previously unreleased items and the generally superior quality of the earlier recordings. If *Never Before* had not existed, and its contents were revealed here for the first time, then the box would have received universal acclaim, solely on the strength of the new material. As it was, an otherwise strong selection was marred by some strange omissions and quirky anomalies.

The most controversial aspect of the box was the unsubtle politicking that seemed to be present in the track selection and the role of McGuinn as 'musical consultant'. In the booklet, McGuinn praises Crosby, Hillman and White for their contributions to the Byrds but pointedly makes no mention of Gene Clark. The opening disc, featuring highlights from the Byrds' first two albums, reduces Clark's contribution significantly. His superior love ballads, 'I Knew I'd Want You', 'Here Without You' and 'You Won't Have To Cry' are scandalously passed over. Amazingly, the same fate befalls 'Set You Free This Time', one of the greatest Byrds tracks and Clark's finest solo composition as a member of the group. Considering the other omissions, the set needed this former A-side more than ever and its non-appearance, without explanation or apology, was a bitter pill to swallow. The compilers did add an early version of 'She Don't Care About Time', complete with Michael Clarke on harmonica, but this was small consolation.

What no one dared admit was McGuinn's unnecessary and petty avarice in influencing the song selection away from Gene Clark material so that a greater share of the publishing and mechanical royalties from the later Byrds material could be secured. It was all painfully reminiscent of the rivalries over publishing and related income that had first occurred in the group at the end of 1965. "I don't think I really stacked it with a *lot* of my songs," McGuinn counters. "We put Skip Battin songs on there and everybody's songs, so I think Gene got a fair number of songs. He did write an inordinate number of songs for the Byrds. It would have been unbalanced if we'd put all of Gene's songs on there." Even ignoring the fact that, contrary to McGuinn's memory, Battin and York had *no* compositions at all on the box set, he seems to have forgotten his adjustments to the final song listing during which Clark's best work was demoted. At best, McGuinn was blissfully unaware that 'Here Without You' and 'Set You Free This Time' were long regarded as Byrds' standards and a crucial part of the group's history and development. At worst, he deleted them anyway without remorse.

While denying Clark, the track selection shows complete obeisance to the pervasive influence of Bob Dylan. Remarkably, in striking contrast to the distribution of Clark material, the set includes *every* Dylan song recorded by the Byrds, excepting the second version of 'It's All Over Now, Baby Blue'. While much of this material is obligatory, and the role of Dylan in the Byrds' story remains crucial, some of the lesser covers seemed questionable choices. Ironically, the addition of 'Paths Of Victory' and 'Just Like A Woman' meant that more Dylan numbers appeared on the box set than the Byrds actually recorded or released during their years together.

The *Fifth Dimension* selections were less controversial, although Crosby would definitely have included his composition 'What's Happening?!?!' in favour of the lacklustre 'Hey Joe', which suffers from a wide stereo effect that exposes Clarke's embarrassingly wayward drumming. Fortunately, the other tracks from the album sound far better, with '5 D', I See You' and 'John Riley' deserving special mention. 'Eight Miles High', as awesome as ever, is impossible to improve, although I still miss the amusing closing drum roll, which only appeared on the single mono release. The compilers also rectify a couple of unfortunate errors left over from the *Never Before* set. That album's title track had been found at the end of a tape of 'Eight Miles High' and was therefore assumed to be the last song Clark ever recorded with the Byrds. Here, it is revealed as an earlier composition, remarkably from September 1965, and retitled 'The Day Walk'. Crosby's 'Psychodrama City', previously edited on *Never Before*, is finally presented in full, along with the surprise addition of 'Roll Over Beethoven', which the Byrds performed, not especially well, for radio broadcast in Sweden.

The box offers due reverence to *Younger Than Yesterday*, arguably the most important album in the Byrds' canon, with seven impressive selections. 'So You Want To Be A Rock 'n' Roll Star', complete with striking separation, leaps from the speakers, while 'Have You Seen Her Face' is equally pleasing, with some fine drumming from Clarke, whose work throughout this period sounds excellent. Crosby's 'Renaissance Fair' and 'Everybody's Been Burned' are among the highlights, with Hillman's melodic bass particularly notable. Forced to leave out one of Hillman's songs from 1967, the compilers choose 'Thoughts And Words', a difficult and regrettable decision. Thankfully, Crosby's 'It Happens Each Day' is included among the selections from this era and the compilers right the wrongs of recent history by restoring Michael Clarke's drumming to the stereo version of 'Lady Friend'.

It is generally accepted that *The Notorious Byrd Brothers* was among the top two Byrds albums. Alas, it is poorly represented on the box with a paltry four selections (plus the single version of 'Old John Robertson'), the same number allocated to inferior later recordings like *Byrdmaniax* and *Farther Along*. This threatens to make aesthetic nonsense of the entire product. Notable oversights include 'Artificial Energy', 'Natural Harmony', 'Get To You' and 'Change Is Now'. The first of these is particularly puzzling. It may be no coincidence as 'Artificial Energy' was co-written and titled by the exiled Michael Clarke.

After the severely under-represented *Notorious* we receive a delightfully over-represented *Sweetheart Of The Rodeo*. As well as five cuts from the original album, there are a further six previously unissued takes featuring Gram Parsons on lead vocal, including 'The Christian Life', 'You Don't Miss Your Water' and 'One Hundred Years From Now'. These tracks represent the single most important discovery on display, having been the stuff of legend for the best part of 13 years. Three other outtakes are featured: 'Lazy Days', with its strong Chuck Berry influence, seems terribly out of place in the context of *Sweetheart* and would later be re-recorded by the Flying Burrito Brothers; 'Reputation', written by Tim Hardin, is average stuff, despite Parsons' vocal; 'Pretty Polly' works better, with McGuinn providing a reading closer to the Dillards' arrangement than his later psychotic version on *Cardiff Rose*. Overall, the selections from *Sweetheart Of The Rodeo*, almost the length of an entire album, serve as the centrepiece of the box set. They proved a major selling point, even if the ultimate effect, in strictly structural terms, was to create a lopsided view of the Byrds' history.

It is terribly ironic that the Bob Johnston produced *Dr Byrds & Mr Hyde* should receive more generous representation on the box than the superior *The Notorious Byrd Brothers*. The obligatory 'Bad Night At The Whiskey' and 'Drug Store Truck Drivin' Man' are rightly included, but 'King Apathy III' is regrettably chopped in favour of the average 'Nashville West' and a substantially different remix of 'Old Blue'. Faced with the prospect of including the single 'Lay Lady Lay', the compilers denude the track of those wailing backing singers, whose overdubbed presence so offended the Byrds at the time of the record's release. The dreadful 'Stanley's Song', a rare example of a genuinely bad unreleased song from the group, was removed from its place in the chronology and relegated to the final disc of the box so as not to interrupt the flow. It was replaced by Jackson Browne's 'Mae Jean Goes To Hollywood', a lightweight song previously available on Johnny Darrell's *California Stopover*.

The selections from *Ballad Of Easy Rider* sound fresher in the CD age, partly thanks to Terry Melcher's original clarity of production. Clarence White receives a vocal cameo courtesy of an alternate version of 'Oil In My Lamp', while the remaining cuts, especially the title track and 'Jesus Is Just Alright', are splendid. The most shocking omission from the album is Gene Parsons' greatest moment 'Gunga Din', a song that fitted perfectly into the Byrds' canon. John York's pleasant reading of Pentangle's 'Way Behind The Sun' gains admittance to the box as a rarity, providing the Byrds' bassist with his only vocal on the package. Curiously, the track is mistitled 'Way Beyond The Sun' on the record and sleeve, and the members of Pentangle lost their arranging credit and publishing income to McGuinn, presumably as a result of an oversight from the copyright clearance department.

The live tracks from *(Untitled)* are solely represented by 'Positively 4th Street', thereby allowing space to feature a welcome alternate version of 'Lover Of The Bayou', as well as those concert favourites 'Willin'' and 'Soldier's Joy'/'Black Mountain Rag'. The majestic 'Chestnut Mare' and 'Just A Season' are powerful enough to represent the studio segment without need of additional material. An early take of 'Kathleen's Song', once heralded on selected sleeves of *(Untitled)* but later held over for *Byrdmaniax*, appears in less ornate fashion. It would have been a welcome addition to the original double album had McGuinn been more dictatorial about other members' contributions. With Jackson Browne on keyboards, the group also attempt a tentative work-in-progress reading of Dylan's 'Just Like A Woman'.

By the time of *Byrdmaniax*, quality material is thinner on the ground. Battin's notable 'Absolute Happiness' is vetoed as a matter of policy, but the same fate befalls McGuinn's excellent 'Pale Blue', which was probably the album's best original song. A singalong 'I Wanna Grow Up To Be A Politician' pushes its way to the fore as a result of its appearance in McGuinn's solo sets over the years. The instrumental 'Green Apple Quick Step' still sounds resplendent, but 'I Trust' loses what little drama it contained as a result of the decision to diminish the backing singers from a scream to a whisper.

Farther Along fares slightly better with the exuberant 'Tiffany Queen' enlivening proceedings and 'Bugler' providing the other quality track. Battin receives an unexpected lead vocal on 'Lazy Waters', significantly *not* one of his own compositions. Some studio filler from the Byrds' '15 Minute Jam', precised as 'White's Lightning', brings the CBS years to a close. We then leap two decades to hear McGuinn, Crosby and Hillman performing 'Turn! Turn! Turn!' and 'Mr Tambourine Man' at the Roy Orbison tribute and reuniting in Nashville for the four new songs discussed earlier.

After four hours of Byrds' music, the majority of reviewers responded with eulogies, ignoring the aforementioned aesthetic gaffes and questionable decisions. Nor did they concern themselves with criticisms of the packaging, which was transparently shoddy. The box offered a dearth of exciting colour photos, a booklet that leaked ink and CD covers that omitted shots of the various Byrds line-ups in favour of tacky representations of flying birds, a city viewed from the clouds, a red sky at night and a radiating planet. Fortunately, disappointment about the artwork did not detract from the power of the Byrds' music.

Fans were equally excited, but many reiterated the criticisms listed above, coming down particularly hard on the poor artwork, the appalling treatment displayed towards Gene Clark and the structural flaws in the work that had effectively relegated *The Notorious Byrd Brothers* to the level of a minor album. While the box set seemingly stood as the ultimate Byrds' collection, and compared favourably with some of the less thorough sets in the marketplace, its main purpose was to pave the way for a complete remastered series of the individual albums, a task which would commence five years later.

The release of the box set was rapidly followed by the Byrds' induction to the Rock 'n' Roll Hall of Fame at the Waldorf Astoria, New York, on 16 January 1991. It was a strange evening, even by Byrds' standards. With all the recent acrimony over Michael Clarke's ersatz Byrds still fresh, nobody was sure how the participants would react when placed together in the same room. Prior to the ceremony, Gene Clark was characteristically optimistic. "I always hold the hope that we can get rid of all the problems that stand between us, lay down our pride and just play music and enjoy it."

McGuinn shared the same sentiments, adding, "The focus should be on the music not the people now." Borrowing the famous catchphrase that McGuinn always used in the Sixties, Clarke concluded: "I trust that we'll be friends there."

THE HALL OF FAME

On the evening, tensions were present and Clarke found himself sharing a table with Don Henley, safely adrift from his ex-colleagues. He was soon joined by Gene Clark who realized he needed some support. Eventually, the other Byrds invited Michael to their table, agreeing that this was not the time to hold grudges. "We sat down together and enjoyed the evening," says Hillman. "There's not many acts being inducted that can get that far. After all that tumultuous hell of the 20 years that went by – people getting into serious problems emotionally and quitting and getting fired – we sat down and shared in the recognition for the part of our life that we spent together between 1965 and 1968."

Crosby alone felt uncomfortable by Clarke's excessive behaviour. The drummer was soon drunk on wine, which prompted Crosby to suggest some AA counselling. Clarke was clearly in no mood to be patronized by a former addict but, fuelled by alcohol, he promised to stop touring as the Byrds, a declaration that would be forgotten the following morning when he sobered up.

While peace seemed to be descending on the Byrds' camp, the mood of the night changed suddenly when President Bush announced on the giant television screens that Operation Desert Storm had begun. The Byrds had momentarily put aside their differences only to witness the outbreak of the Gulf War. The news dampened any sense of exuberance and it was not until 1.30 am that the group was finally invited onstage to be officially inducted by Don Henley, whose former group the Eagles had benefited so much from the Byrds' heritage.

The strains of 'Mr Tambourine Man' ushered the Byrds on to great applause. McGuinn's acceptance speech was concise and reflective. "Well, I'd just like to thank you very much," he began. "When I was growing up in Chicago, listening to Elvis Presley on my transistor radio, I never dreamed I'd be in the same Hall of Fame that he is, and thank the Lord for it."

David Crosby, still recovering from a serious motorcycle accident a couple of months before, emerged from a wheelchair with the aid of crutches. He stood before the microphone and gave the same Beatle-inspired "Me, I'm just the lucky kind" upbeat message that had once elevated the Byrds to glory at Ciro's. "I'm a very happy guy. I feel a lot of gratitude. I have a lot of gratitude to these men who made it possible for me to make some of the best music of my life. And it occurs to me as I think about it that there are a lot of us, some of the best of us, who are not here and who'll never make it here, and I am incredibly grateful after all the chances I've taken and all the trouble I've been through, to be here tonight to do this, and still be able to play this music. I thank you all."

Chris Hillman, after all his adventures with the Flying Burrito Brothers, Manassas and the Desert Rose Band, recognized that it was the Byrds with whom he would always be associated in the public's mind. "It's taken me so many years to realize how incredibly lucky I was to be part of this group. I was just a kid playing the mandolin in a bluegrass band in 1964 and I got asked to join. I treasure every moment working with these guys, the good and the bad. It was a wonderful time and I love all you guys, I really do. It's such an honour to be in this Hall of Fame with all of the heroes, all the people that influenced me, and I thank you for keeping the Byrds' legacy alive. Thank you."

Gene Clark was the most humble of the five, having just made another attempt to curtail his alcohol abuse with a view to patching things up with his recently estranged partner, Terri Messina. "I think really for myself gratitude is the main thing. I've got to be really thankful for all the people in my life that have supported me through the years, through my good and my bad, and especially my brothers here onstage with me, who I've enjoyed playing with more than anybody else in the whole world. And especially to my beautiful lady, Terri, who has been the most support to me in my whole life. Thank you all very much and I'm proud to be here."

Finally, Michael Clarke displayed modesty and humour, with a characteristic dash of irreverence. "I'd like to say that I appreciate the fact that I'm in here at all! You know, for God's sake, I was just a bongo player on the beach at one point in life, right? So now what am I? I am a Rock 'n' Roll Hall of Famer! Well, thank you all and I appreciate it, and thanks Mom, and hello to all of Gulfport, and 'Hi, baby'."

With the speeches over, McGuinn produced his Rickenbacker, Hillman strapped on a bass and the others, including Michael duetting with Gene, ran through two favourites from 1965: 'Turn! Turn! Turn!' and 'Feel A Whole Lot Better'. This was the first time that the original Byrds had performed on a stage together since the Sixties and, despite all the recent conflict, there was still a lingering hope that they might yet resolve outstanding differences and reunite for a final tour. But it was not to be. The Hall of Fame evening was the last time that the original five Byrds would ever see each other together again.

CHAPTER FORTY-SIX

Fatalities

FOR Gene Clark, the battle was nearly over. While any discussion on the life expectancy of the individual Byrds centred almost exclusively on David Crosby, there were distant warning bells that suggested Gene should take care. It was during the final months of his life that Clark slipped back into the old hedonistic ways. Clark's substance abuse caused concern rather than alarm and it was assumed that once he became involved in a new project all would be well. Following the Hall of Fame induction, his future seemed promising. A long overdue solo album was under consideration, and there was talk of another collaboration with Carla Olson. He was also working on some music for a movie titled *Tainted*, whose opening scene was to feature 'Silver Raven'. Work on the proposed film soundtrack was spread over several months and it was during this period that his co-writer Pat Robinson noticed some worrying changes. "Gene looked OK when he wanted to. He always looked good to me, always in good shape, always well groomed. It was just towards the end there. There was a guy he hung out with that was a little rough and I noticed Gene was looking unshaven . . . Over the period we were working on the *Tainted* movie, all of a sudden he was falling apart. He was coming into the studio looking real funky and his hair was greasy, like he hadn't been taking a shower or something."

While some members of Clark's circle experimented with smack for recreational use, his addictive personality ensured that he was always a dangerous dabbler. "People started taking advantage of Gene because he was falling apart, real quick," Robinson claims.

"Gene was an all-out 'go-all-the-way' kind of guy. And if you were a dabbler, you shouldn't have been dabbling with Gene because he'd hurt himself. Gene was an all-out yahoo with most things. So he was doing himself a lot of harm and people weren't really aware of that."

The renewed drug abuse, combined with Clark's more usual alcoholic excesses, soon took their inevitable toll. "He had 25–30 years of that lifestyle," John York notes. "There was a certain trend that came up in the Sixties, tied to the jazz musician ethic, that if you're not a heroin addict you can't really feel the music, and that kind of nonsense. There's a certain strain of musicians that came up through the Sixties thinking, 'Well, in order for me to even pick up my instrument I have to be totally smashed.' All that drug thing is misplaced devotion . . . The difference between say Roger McGuinn and Gene was that Roger, no matter what he experimented with, was not the kind of person that would ever lose control of the ship, whereas Gene was the kind of guy who would just let it go wherever it's going to go. It was dangerous."

Apart from his other problems, Clark's work in the studio was hampered by gum disease, which had loosened his teeth over the years, forcing him to economize on words in order to prevent sibilance. At times he sounded like a toothless old man and this was particularly noticeable on the session for 'Fallen For You', a song originally intended for inclusion in *Tainted*. In order to rectify the problem, a dental appointment was arranged. "I remember we went out of our way to make sure we got his teeth fixed," Robinson says. "They capped his teeth, but then, just a few days before the session, he knocked them out again. He got in a bit of a wreck in his black Cadillac on Sunset Boulevard. He was pretty wild. He knocked them out on his windshield, broke them off."

Since his tribute to Terri Messina at the Rock 'n' Roll Hall of Fame, Clark had promised to mend his ways and stop the cycle of abuse, but he was forever struggling against the demons within himself. "He did some amazingly scary things," Messina recalls. "He went back into this self-destructive phase . . . he was not only drinking, he was smoking crack. I don't know if anybody told you that, but he was. I had never seen Gene get into crack before. Can you believe that? Even in the years before, when he used to snort coke, which everybody was doing in the late Seventies and early Eighties, some worse than others. But everybody was snorting some coke. He did that and abused it at times, but it was always the alcohol that was his worst problem. Then, he reverted to this state during the last few months of his life. He turned into somebody that was even a stranger to me because I'd never seen him get into crack before. And I hate crack. I had tried it before and I hated it so I couldn't believe he was doing that. I was going, 'What is this?' Then he was getting all these horrible sores on him from doing it. It was weird. You have no idea . . . Thank God you never had to see him like that because it was an absolute nightmare."

Ironically, it was during this darkest period that Clark threatened to complete some of his best work. From his archive, he revived 'Communications', an amazing composition that combined biblical prophecy with extraterrestrial visitations and even speculated on the nature of angels. It was arguably his best song for nearly 20 years, taking up where he had left off with *No Other*. For those who regarded *Firebyrd* and the Carla Olson collaborations as mere pleasant filler, this was the real deal. Like Dylan prior to *Blood On The Tracks*, Clark was also confronting the emotional upheavals in his life and attempting to reconcile his on/off relationship with Terri Messina, which had been strained due to his drink/drug problems and physically violent outbursts. The new songs especially 'Adios Terri', 'Big Bad Mama', 'Pledge To You' and 'If You Knew' were all the more intriguing when viewed in the context of his private life. This was Gene Clark at his most intense, with dashes of wry humour and moments of chilling poignancy.

It was all to end far too soon. During the second week of April 1991, Clark played two sets over five nights at Hollywood's Cinegrill. He was still taking painkillers in the aftermath of the car smash and also drinking heavily, as was his retinue. "He thought he was going to get paid a tremendous amount of money, which was totally wrong," his friend Tom Slocum recalls. "He was getting something like ten grand and he ended up with two grand. I remember having a confrontation there because I didn't even want to go to the gig. It was dark and the hangers-on were so heavy and so numerous. It wasn't a pretty thing. It was several days of weird fucking hell. On one of the shows he walked off in the middle and let the band play and sat down and had a cocktail with some people in the audience and watched the band."

Clad in a tuxedo, Clark looked suddenly old, with the sunken eyes and pallor of a junkie. The performances were erratic and sometimes painful to listen to. He sounded terribly wasted and yet, almost by instinct, he could turn a performance around and transform a set from inertia into one of unbearably raw emotion. His version of 'Here Without You' sounded spinetingling, while two new songs, the startling 'Your Fire Burning' and 'Life And Times', provided further hope of a strong album in the not too distant future.

Those who witnessed Clark's shows at the Cinegrill spoke as though they had seen a ghostly presence. "I felt very sad when I saw him in that state," Carla Olson remembers. "When we left I remember thinking, 'Hold on, Gene! What are you doing to yourself?' We didn't know it was going to be over. He definitely wanted to go out in a storm, that's for sure. I don't think he had any intentions of ending his life or anything like that. I just think he wanted to be Gene Clark 1965 again for one last time. He knew he was riding on a wave and he wanted to ride that wave out."

Although the Cinegrill shows were the last at which Clark would perform, he made one more notable public showing when Roger McGuinn played the Whisky two weeks later. Byrds fan Rick Williams shared a table with Gene that evening and was astonished by the dramatic transformation in the man's appearance: "He looked so good it was as though it was another person – clean-shaven, hair washed, clear-eyed and only drinking 7-Up. He was warm, friendly, articulate and optimistic. Physically, it was an amazing change from the way he looked at the Cinegrill and it made me feel much better for him. He sat across the table from me and said that he hoped Roger would call him up onstage. The show was a nationwide satellite broadcast and I knew in advance that the special guest was Stevie Nicks, and it was her not Gene who was called onstage to share vocals on 'Mr Tambourine Man'. I felt so bad for Gene but he was really gracious to Roger. He just sat there complimenting him."

Clark's capacity to bounce back from the jaws of self-abuse encouraged the belief that he would be around for a long time. David Crosby had already been down a far darker road than Gene and returned alive against ludicrous odds. The words 'detox' and 'rehab' were commonplace among the survivors of the Sixties and Gene Clark seemed together enough to defeat the alcohol and drug dependencies to which he was prone. "Geno was really a nice guy," Pat Robinson stresses. "I was hoping he'd make it through there. It seemed like if you could get through the late forties and into your fifties, then you'd chalk in another 20 years, maybe. If you could only get through that period of adjustment into settling down. I thought Gene had made it, almost. He was dabbling back and forth, and that's when it got dangerous. He would just really go for it too. He was very hard on himself."

Soon after, on the morning of 24 May 1991, Gene Clark was found dead at his home in Sherman Oaks. "One of Gene's musician friends [Jon Faurot] stopped by there," Terri Messina recalls. "They were supposed to get together and do something. He'd talked to Gene and was told to come back later. When he came back, he found him on the floor. He called the paramedics and I guess he called Gene's actor friend Jason Ronard, who called me and I went straight over, but by that time there was nothing that could be done. The paramedics had already been there . . . It was pretty creepy."

Gene Clark's body lay covered up in the living room while a number of friends arrived, including Tom Slocum, Shannon O'Neill and former representative Saul Davis. After saying a final prayer over the corpse, the remaining mourners looked on as ambulance staff removed Clark's body. There was more drama soon after during a bizarre viewing at Van Nuys where an intoxicated David Carradine acted as if he were attending a nineteenth-century Irish wake. He manhandled the cadaver, lifting it from the casket like a ventriloquist eyeing his favourite dummy. Then he screamed at the corpse, "You fucked the girl . . . when she was only . . . Wake up! Wake up!" These were brutal, drunken, unsubstantiated allegations that shocked anyone within earshot, not least because he had identified the girl and mentioned her age. Before he could say any more, he was politely but firmly led away. Clark's body was subsequently flown back to his Missouri birthplace. There, he was laid to rest at St Andrew's Catholic Cemetery on a hill overlooking Tipton. The official cause of death was a heart attack but no one doubted that his history of drug and alcohol abuse had hastened his end.

A number of obituaries were printed, but by far the most moving were the personal reminiscences published in the magazine *Full Circle*. Among these were respectful contributions from former Byrds, including Chris Hillman, Michael Clarke and John York. Clarke prefaced his tribute with a quote from Dylan Thomas' poem *Do Not Go Gentle Into That Good Night*. In a moving valediction, he paid a memorable tribute to the tambourine man:

> Gene was an artist, a true expressionist. Expression is man's most potent instrument of progress. His success is inevitably measured or limited by his ability to communicate his thoughts to others. Gene Clark was one of the most successful and loving people I ever met. A continuous battle raged between Gene and himself, which, in the end, found its way onto paper and into song, where it settled. He was never bothered with the 'trendy' or popular, for the moment type of music. His style was inimical, but limitless and different. In my opinion, Gene Clark has earned, along with all the other folk heroes, a seat in the Folk Heroes' Hall of Fame, and a permanent place in all our hearts.

Michael Clarke's epitaph for his favourite Byrd was all the more poignant considering his own fate. After the Rock 'n' Roll Hall of Fame induction, he continued touring with his own version of the Byrds but, as the months passed, his drinking problems worsened. Not even the sad example of Gene Clark could convince him that he should stop. His stormy third marriage to Lee Elliot already looked on the rocks, and he was increasingly drawn towards a new friend, Susan Paul. Their relationship deepened in the spring of 1992 when she received an unexpected call from the drummer. "I hadn't heard from him for months," she remembers. "He called me and said, 'You once said that if I ever needed a friend . . . Meet me at the airport at 8 o'clock.' I said, 'I don't think so!' but he insisted, 'I've got to see and talk to you.' When I saw him he was about 40 lb thinner. I thought he was sick. He'd chopped his hair off and he looked awful. He told me he and his wife had split. Then he went out of town. He called me and we spoke for hours and hours from New York to Florida. When he came back he called and said he didn't want to be alone. I said, 'Why don't you camp out at my place?' I have a huge house in Tampa with a studio set up in my garage where I work as an interior designer, so he could paint there. He moved in and there was nothing going on between us. It wasn't until several weeks after that we became a couple. I thought he was drinking because he was distraught, but I realized after a few months that it was getting worse and worse and that he had a serious alcohol problem."

Clarke's alcoholism blighted his new relationship and he left Tampa with Susan's salutary parting words, "I'm still going to be here for you, but I can't watch you kill yourself, and I *won't* watch you kill yourself." During the last year of his life, Michael continued his on/off relationship with his third wife, while his physical condition deteriorated. There was still hope that he might turn things around but nobody could convince him to seek help. "I was always talking to him and encouraging him to clean up his act," bandmate Terry Rogers stresses. "But he was like a kid sometimes as far as that stuff was concerned. He didn't want to give it up and he hated doctors. He didn't go to the doctor until the very last minute. He was starting to have some of the effects of liver disease. His legs and his whole middle were swelling, and all that was happening long before he even went to the doctor. I guess the poison had gone through his system."

By late 1993, it was too late. Whereas other musicians were miraculously saved by liver transplants and sudden conversions, Clarke's condition was deemed beyond treatment. The news came as a great shock to many friends who, despite witnessing his decline, still assumed that he would pull through. His physical build and swaggering confidence had given the impression that he could survive anything. During his last days, Clarke seemed almost bemused by the inevitability of his death. With great courage, he still performed, overcoming immense discomfort and a body painfully swollen from the waist down.

FATALITIES

On 19 December 1993, Michael Clarke died from liver failure at his home in Treasure Island, Florida. Despite his estrangement from the Byrds, rumours of Clarke's ill health had obviously caused concern, especially to Chris Hillman, who had spent a long time on the road with the drummer, both as a Byrd and a Burrito. When asked for an obituary, Hillman offered some final thoughts on his former partner:

> Michael was the eternal child, the 'bad boy', the charming, loveable 'man-child'. In another era he would have been cast as one of the Bowery Boys. He was my pal during the glory years of the Byrds 1964/1965. He was the guy who loved collecting and listening to old blues records with me. He was the only other Byrd who truly appreciated the real music, be it Howlin' Wolf or George Jones. I had some fantastic adventures with Mike in the Byrds and later in the Burritos.
>
> He had so much raw talent and so little discipline that it sometimes made me very angry to see him wasting so much of his life. In 1988/89, I tried to encourage and focus him on his art. He had talent and could have become a fine artist. He painted two landscapes for us which we display proudly in our home today.
>
> I was also aware of his ongoing problem. But there was nothing I could do. I'd already been through this movie with Gram. I do remember David Crosby at the Rock 'n' Roll Hall of Fame dinner offering to help Michael as we all struggled to interact around the table that night. I'd heard from someone that Michael was seriously ill. I called his house early that Sunday morning (December 19). His ex-wife Robin answered. I said, "Hello, is Michael home?" "Who's this?" she said. "It's Chris," I replied. "Oh, honey, he just passed away in his mother's arms." I haven't cried like that in a long, long time. I miss him.

Clarke's death emphasized how vulnerable the Byrds were to the lifestyle excesses of the Sixties and Seventies. The shocking demise of the two youngest Byrds prompted pause for reflection on the progress of their most likely casualty. Remarkably, David Crosby had survived both Gene Clark and Michael Clarke, although not before escaping the attention of the Grim Reaper for the umpteenth time. In tandem with the Byrds, Crosby had been attempting to re-establish Crosby, Stills & Nash as a creative force. The collaboration with Young on *American Dream* had not sold as well as expected, but looked likely to kick-start another CS&N record. Unfortunately, the disappointing *Live It Up*, which had not originally been intended as a three-way effort, proved their worst album to date. Nevertheless, the trio continued working together intermittently and became involved in countless causes and fund-raising activities, ranging from high-profile appearances like the Berlin Wall to unpublicized benefit shows for various charities. As Crosby noted: "We really like to make a contribution. It's my feeling that if you don't put some effort into the community and contribute to a community, then you don't have a community. The community is big now. It's worldwide, but it's still the human race. It's still a community and it needs a lot of help."

Like the Byrds, CS&N were forced to look to the past for creative redemption and this was achieved via the highly-praised box set *CSN*, a sterling collection of 77 tracks and a powerful reminder of all that they had achieved during the past two-and-a-half decades. The positive response afforded the set provided a much-needed boost for the trio during the early Nineties. Crosby was acutely aware of the dangers of obscurity and welcomed the renewed focus. "I'll tell you, I care," he said, "at least to the extent that it sells enough, so I can have access to the tools. If it doesn't make me a millionaire, that's OK. But I want to come back in another 18 months and do it again . . . There was a ten-year period when Roger McGuinn couldn't get a record deal, and Roger's a really good musician. I may have my differences with him – but he's a great musician."

Crosby continued to keep himself busy. A new solo album for Atlantic Records, *Thousand Roads*, allowed him to display his talents as an interpretative singer of other people's material, but his decision not to play on the record seemed questionable. Interestingly, it was 'Yvette In English', his songwriting collaboration with Joni Mitchell, that proved the real highlight. A live album, *It's All Coming Back To Me Now . . .* was another welcome testament to his endurance, with the reflective 'Rusty And Blue' dominating the set. Unexpectedly, he even revitalized the acting career that he had scorned prior to joining the Byrds in 1964. Amid a flurry of appearances, he secured cameo roles in the films *Thunderheart* and *Hook*, guested on the television series *Roseanne* and was even immortalized as a cartoon character in *The Simpsons*. He was equally busy in the studio, guesting on albums by artistes including Bob Dylan, Marc Cohn, Willie Nelson, Jimmy Webb, Bonnie Raitt, Stevie Nicks, Jackson Browne and Hootie And The Blowfish.

But nothing was ever straightforward in Crosby's life. Like a character in a morality play or Greek tragedy, he was constantly buffeted by setbacks and sudden changes of fortune. In December 1993, an IRS agent visited his house, seeking to recover a debt approaching $1 million in back taxes. Once again, he was threatened with financial ruin. One month later, an earthquake razed his home. It was enough to make anyone ponder the mysteries of divine intervention.

Crosby found solace in CS&N. During the summer of 1994 they set out on their 25th anniversary tour, playing some of their finest acoustic music and promoting a positive new album *After The Storm*, which included three vital Crosby compositions: a rare songwriting collaboration with Stills ('Camera'), the bluesy 'Till It Shines On You' and, best of all, an impassioned commentary on urban life, street gangs and the homeless ('Street To Lean On'). On the eve of Crosby's 53rd birthday, CS&N turned back the clock by showing up at Woodstock II, re-enacting the scene of their original triumph in 1969. Despite the celebratory nature of the event, it was evident that all was not well with Crosby. He had been experiencing agonizing cramps in his legs, a side-effect of the medication used to ameliorate his still troubled liver. Occasionally, he could be found slumped on the band's bus, almost in tears. After the Woodstock show, the pain became so intense that he was screaming. As the tour progressed, he began to suffer diminished mental capacity when toxic substances in his blood entered his brain. When Stills and Nash queried his unusually 'off' harmonies, he burst into tears and confessed that he was suffering from advanced liver disease. Hepatitis C had gone undetected for over a decade and "it was exacerbated by the years I spent trying to convert myself into a chemical dump site." Could it possibly get any worse?

In September 1994, CS&N curtailed their touring commitments and Crosby was told by specialists at Cedars-Sinai Hospital that he would die unless a liver transplant was completed at the earliest opportunity. He was just recovering from this shock news when his 43-year-old wife Jan announced that she was pregnant. The cosmic irony was not lost on Crosby, who now saw the cycle of life and death approaching his household with a greater immediacy than even he had ever witnessed. "I'd faced death before," he reflects. "God knows, I could and probably should have died at least a dozen times from overdoses and motorcycle wrecks. I never thought I'd live long enough to give a damn. But I'd been clean for nine years, and I only had to look at Jan to know there was every reason to cherish life. After years of seeing specialists and fertility treatments, we'd found out that she was pregnant. Anybody who doesn't think God has a sense of humour isn't watching."

On 5 November, Crosby suffered liver failure and was rushed to the UCLA Medical Center. Fifteen days later, a liver was found but it was discovered to be cancerous. With Crosby's life clock ticking away, it was now uncertain whether another donor might be found in time. Several people visited him in hospital, including Chris Hillman, who was shocked by his condition. "He was dying. At that point, he had about two days to live. A sad, sad sight. He was like a balloon because he couldn't get rid of any liquid from his body. But he never complained . . . he was just sitting there. I told him, 'I really admire how you're dealing with this,' and he said, 'Yeah, but when anybody leaves my room, I just cry.'" Even facing death, Crosby could still provide a caustic career overview for his old friend, telling him bluntly that the age of the singer-songwriter was over for middle-aged white guys like themselves.

Crosby's indomitable spirit helped keep him alive until another liver was prepared, courtesy of a 31-year-old car crash victim. On 28 November, Crosby was wheeled to the operating theatre while singing 'Amazing Grace' at the top of his voice. Some feared this might be his last performance but, after a seven-hour transplant, he was declared "critical but stable". Newspapers were already preparing obituaries, with tabloid column headlines screaming, 'Crosby Critical'. But as his doctor observed: "Who wouldn't be after such an operation?"

Crosby closed 1994 in defiant mood, marvelling once more at his capacity to escape death by a whisker. Temporarily resting from the rock scene, he set about restoring his body to full health. While contemplating the birth of his child, Crosby was shocked when the son that he had abandoned 22 years before dramatically reappeared in his life. The adopted James Raymond had grown up completely unaware of the identity of his biological parents and had only recently sought them out. He was so amazed to discover that David Crosby was his father that he delayed contacting him for two years. When he learned of the liver transplant, he faced a dilemma. "I thought maybe I should meet him," he explained. "But I didn't want to come out of the woodwork. He had just found out he was going to be a father. I didn't want to invade that part of his life."

James Raymond's adoptive father decided to write to Crosby and, after the transplant, an emotional meeting took place at the UCLA Medical Center cafeteria in February 1995. David was amazed to discover that his lost son was a talented musician, who had played in jazz and R&B bands. Music was apparently in his blood. Equally amazing was the fact that James' wife was due to give birth to a son the following day. Having faced near death on an operating table three months before, David Crosby was about to become a grandfather. This miraculous spate of progeny continued when his wife Jan safely gave birth to their son, Django, in May 1995. "All in all, this has been an exalting experience," Crosby concluded. "I've discovered a depth of compassion and feeling I didn't know existed. The mail I get still brings me to tears – strangers offering support, people waiting for transplants asking for advice, people fighting the same fight. Some of us will make it, some won't, but I've been given every reason to believe in starting over."

As if to complete this preposterous fairy tale, Crosby received a $1.2 million settlement resulting from a motorcycle accident back in 1991. This windfall enabled him to pay off the IRS and resume his career. He was feted once again at the Rock 'n' Roll Hall of Fame on 6 May 1997 when Crosby, Stills & Nash were inducted. It was the second time around for Crosby after the Byrds and his speech predictably focused on his miraculous recovery. "I'll be damned . . . I am very honoured to be here. I feel like a very lucky man. For a guy who was supposed to be dead a couple of years ago, I'm doing pretty well."

Crosby's extended lifespan inspired a new musical adventure – CPR – featuring himself, his long lost son, and guitarist Jeff Pevar. Their sound fused the harmonic grace of CS&N with the jazz chops of Steely Dan to create something unexpectedly fresh. CPR toured the club circuit offering Crosby the chance of another artistic renaissance. It seemed to propel him into a sudden songwriting spree. The trio issued a self-titled album on the Samson Music imprint which proved a minor revelation. Among the new songs were 'Morrison', an ambivalent tribute to the doomed Doors' frontman, 'Time Is The Final Currency', a *carpe diem* meditation on mortality and, most startling of all, 'Somehow She Knew', possibly Crosby's most moving and accomplished composition since 'Delta', or even 'Carry Me'. *CPR* was bookended by two live albums, the second of which included a surprise rendition of 'Eight Miles High'. The trio rapidly established a dedicated following among Crosby's fan base and the project was seen as a perfect outlet for his jazzier material.

1997 was not without its darker moments for Crosby. In November, he heard that his only brother, Ethan, was missing, feared dead. Years before, Crosby had told me that his elder sibling was a reclusive character who didn't like to be around people. Given David's gregarious nature, this seemed surprising, particularly as the pair had performed together as kids. Over the years, Ethan's hermit ways had become more pronounced, reinforced by irrational fears of an approaching apocalypse. He lived in complete isolation in Northern California's Trinity National Forest, Mount Shasta, awaiting the aftermath of society's complete breakdown like a character out of Crosby's 'Wooden Ships'. A suicide note was found at his self-built home suggesting he had killed himself in the forest. It was not until the following spring that the body was found in the snow. He had shot himself with his own gun, leaving wild animals to devour part of the corpse.

FATALITIES

Crosby needed some good news as the millennium approached, and history came to his rescue. First there was the release of *Another Stoney Evening*, an archive recording of Crosby & Nash from October 1971 and a treasured companion to their celebrated bootleg, *A Very Stony Evening*. Shortly after, Crosby, Stills & Nash were working on a new album, financing the sessions out of their own pockets. Stills had approached Neil Young to appear on one of the songs and the unpredictable Canadian surprised them all by actually turning up at the studio. Inspired by their evident commitment, he suggested taking the experiment further. "I was just visiting," he recalls, "and the tunes were good. They were making a record. They started it because they wanted to – not because the label told them it was time or anything like that. And that's a great reason to do it. I could hear that from the first note."

Against all expectations, Young committed himself to CSN&Y's first recording since *American Dream* back in 1988. Most fans had despaired of ever hearing another reunion and scepticism was rife about the project, even after it had been scheduled for release. "We didn't let any record company guys in," Young explains. "We didn't tell anybody what we were doing, and we told people to leave if they did show up. It worked well for us because we had no pressure. We never even talked about being CSN&Y or even doing an album. We waited until we were finished and we knew what it was."

During the sessions, the ebullient Crosby was leading the group on 'Turn! Turn! Turn!' and there was even idle speculation that the old Byrds classic might appear on a CSN&Y record. Instead, the foursome pushed ahead, selecting songs, several of which Young had intended for a concomitant solo album. A CSN&Y tour was also promised, but that was generally regarded as the stuff of dreams. The magic foursome had not toured since 1974 and Young's capricious nature could always be relied upon to scupper any such idea at minimal notice. Instead, it was Graham Nash who jeopardized the reunion when he broke both legs in a water-skiing accident in Hanalei Bay, near his Hawaii home. Initial reports warned that he might be crippled for life, but after emergency surgery, in which rods were inserted in his legs, he was assured of a slow recovery.

The projected tour was postponed until the new century but the much touted album, *Looking Forward*, emerged in October 1999. Crosby was thrilled about the record, eagerly insisting that it was a vast improvement on 1988's *American Dream*, although that point was debatable. Once more on a CSN&Y album, Crosby seemed criminally underused with only two songs to his credit – the jazzy 'Dream For Him', a utopian song of hope for his new son was impressive, while 'Stand And Be Counted', a punchy political plea was simpler but effective. Alas, it was difficult to avoid direct comparisons with his last two CSN&Y statements, 'Compass' and 'Nighttime For The Generals', both of which sounded superior to this latest coupling. There was also the lingering suspicion that the participants now had a preconceived notion of what constituted a CSN&Y recording. Neil Young seemed to regard the trio as a vehicle for his lighter, more sentimental work, and even Crosby could be heard arguing that more adventurous compositions such as 'Somehow She Knew' or 'Rusty And Blue' were better suited to CPR due to their melodic complexity. Older fans remembered when CSN&Y was regarded as the natural home for the individual member's most challenging and compelling work. Once there was a time when Young felt that something as ambitious as the triptych suite 'Country Girl' or the lengthy 'Pushed It Over The End' were the stuff of CSN&Y, while Crosby had invested hundreds of hours completing the daredevil 'Déjà Vu' with its strange time signatures and spooky ambience. There was little of this overreaching ambition on the straightforward *Looking Forward*, which was enjoyable, but self-consciously stylized. At least it ended Crosby's century on a satisfactory note.

CHAPTER FORTY-SEVEN

End Of The Century

LIKE Crosby, Chris Hillman had an eventful ten years leading up to the millennium. He had actually begun the decade in the strongest position of any of the Byrds. His Desert Rose Band had already enjoyed a string of country hits and seemed set for continued success with likely crossovers into the rock market. In 1990, their third album, *Pages Of Life*, entered the *Billboard* Top 200 but it proved a false dawn. The following year, long-term steel guitarist Jay Dee Maness announced he was leaving, so Hillman recruited Paul Franklin for *True Love*, which failed to register a place even on the country charts. "I made one of the most monumental blunders anybody can make," Hillman admits. "I stopped listening to my intuitive voice, the voice that says, 'Don't do that, don't write that.' I was seduced by the business side of it . . . I was doing every stupid thing, like a 20-year-old kid thinking, 'Gee, they're going to really get behind it.' I fooled myself."

By mid-1992, the Desert Rose Band were touring with the veteran steel guitarist Tom Brumley, a Buck Owens' alumnus and former member of Rick Nelson's Stone Canyon Band. Already losing heart from recent setbacks, the group suffered a body blow when the talented John Jorgenson also quit and was rapidly replaced by Jeff Ross. Hillman's new line-up returned to Britain almost unnoticed for the ill-fated Witney International Country Music Festival. Backstage, Hillman was in a haughty mood, but managed to summon sufficient ire to brush aside those perennial Byrds' reunion questions. "The Byrds are never going to play again," he emphasized. "Never. It's all over. Seriously. Take my word for it. Crosby and I wanted to do it at the time, but Roger McGuinn decided he wanted to do his solo career. I love Roger dearly, but he distanced himself from David and I right after the Rock 'n' Roll Hall Of Fame award last year. We felt at that time that we could have gone out and done major halls in the States, but Roger didn't want to do that, although about 90 per cent of his show is Byrds' material. And I do love him and respect him, but it's never going to happen again. It never will. Let it go as a memory. It'd never be the same if we brought it back."

The Desert Rose Band's fortunes continued to worsen as news filtered through that they were no longer with MCA and required a new deal. In the interim, Hillman brought in drummer Tim Grogan and another new guitarist Jim Monahan. The line-up changes and record company problems eroded the band's confidence and, by the end of 1993, Hillman seemed ready to throw in the towel. Reflecting on the current country music scene, he spoke with a mixture of bitterness and disillusionment. "It's a volatile business right now. It's becoming so disposable. I think the shelf life of an artiste is cut right in half now. I think record companies might tend to look at an artiste and if he's not going to do big business they let him go a little too quickly rather than developing that artiste, as in the old days. What was once an artistic business has somehow become a commodities business."

Not wishing to become part of a 'commodities business', Hillman disbanded the Desert Rose Band on 1 March 1994, one week after they had played their final gig in Indio, California. "We were very successful," Hillman concluded, by way of epitaph. "We had the longest run of any band that I had ever been in and it was the best band that I've been a part of. The players were top notch. It was a well-oiled machine."

As a salutary reminder of the speed of their commercial decline, a final album, *Life Goes On*, was not even granted a US release and initially could only be bought in Japan and parts of Europe. After the disappointing end to the Desert Rose Band, Hillman took a sabbatical from the music business, filling in time by doing voiceovers for commercials. By 1996, he was ready to record again, teaming up with Herb Pedersen on the traditional but workmanlike

Bakersfield Bound, an album that found a home on Sugar Hill, the specialist label for which he had recorded at the beginning of the Eighties when his career was at a similarly low ebb. It was a chance for Hillman and Pedersen to perform several of their favourite tunes, including some Buck Owens' covers. Stylistically, they modelled themselves on various old-time country/bluegrass brother duos such as the Louvins. On the title track, Hillman and co-writer Steve Hill even attempted to create their own dust bowl ballad, enhanced by some strong playing.

Turning back the clock to 1963, Chris and Herb established a productive collaboration with Tony and Larry Rice for *Out Of The Woodwork*, which completed Hillman's return to his bluegrass roots. He was prominently placed in the credits, singing lead on half of the album's tracks. Although there was an over reliance on familiar songs from his days in the Burritos, Manassas and the Desert Rose Band, the playing and arrangements were often exemplary.

In March 1998, Hillman reunited with McGuinn when both were booked on the same bill at the Florida Folk Festival. Rather than simply playing the expected hits, 'Mr Tambourine Man' and 'Turn! Turn! Turn!', they surprised fans with a well thought out set. After opening with their most successful collaboration, 'So You Want To Be A Rock 'n' Roll Star', McGuinn suggested they perform a couple of songs in tribute to the late Gene Clark: 'Feel A Whole Lot Better' and 'She Don't Care About Time'. The elegiac mood continued with two Gram Parsons-inspired *Sweetheart Of The Rodeo* numbers, 'The Christian Life' and 'Hickory Wind', and ended with an uplifting 'Chimes Of Freedom'.

Three months later, Hillman was back with another record for Sugar Hill, *Like A Hurricane*, his first solo effort since 1984's *Desert Rose*. The Byrds' link was present once more courtesy of 'I'm Still Alive', a composition written about Crosby's dark night of the soul, on which he also sang. Turning back the clock, Hillman revived Jackie De Shannon's 'When You Walk In The Room', the old Searchers' hit that the Byrds had played in 1965 at Ciro's but never recorded. He planned to add McGuinn's Rickenbacker ring to the track, but Roger was unable to make the trip to California. Ten of the songs were co-written with Steve Hill and among the most noteworthy was 'Carry Me Home', which Hillman composed in open tuning. It featured McGuinn's former spiritual mentor Jennifer Warnes on additional vocals. Hillman was engagingly upbeat about the album. "It wasn't intentional but it covers everything from my start in bluegrass through rock 'n' roll, country rock and Desert Rose. I had more fun making this album than any I've done. It was like making records in 1965 with the Byrds, having fun and trying out all kinds of ideas, as opposed to being pressured to conform to what radio wants – which we don't have to do now."

Hillman made a second album with Pedersen and the Rice Brothers before the century closed, but illness prevented him from playing on the tracks or travelling. He had recently been treated for Hepatitis C and there were unsubstantiated rumours that he was at death's door. His friend Joey Stec, who also had the disease, suggests that at one point Hillman was in a coma. "They didn't expect him to live and when he finally came out of the coma his hair turned white."

Hillman dismissed the doom-mongering as exaggeration. "I'm not dying, I'm happy to say. I had Hepatitis and I'm still dealing with it. It's not symptomatic and it's not contagious . . . I was lucky because I caught it early . . . I'm sure people thought, 'Oh, he's got AIDS, he's dying.' No, I'm not dying . . . My doctor said, 'You're as healthy as a horse and for the next five years you could do anything you want, but in the sixth year, we might have a huge problem.'"

Hillman's greatest fear was that he might end up like David Crosby and have to undergo a liver transplant followed by a lifetime's dependence on anti-immune suppressants. As a preventative measure, he undertook treatment involving weekly injections of Interferon. The effects were debilitating and friends reported that he was often so tired that he could barely get out of bed and cross the room. Hillman compared the effects to the aftermath of chemotherapy and it was several months before he was back on his feet. "I don't take it lightly, believe me. I'm dealing with it, and I'm fine." Hillman was happy to publicize his problems, rightly pointing out that Hepatitis C was potentially a silent killer in the rock community with a long list of likely victims, many of whose names we may never know. "I don't have any qualms about telling anyone what I'm going through. In fact, Hepatitis C is a virtual epidemic. You don't have symptoms. It'll sit in your liver for 20 years, and then it'll get you. And everybody my age that had any kind of risky behaviour is subject to having it. For some people it becomes active, and for others it's in their system for the rest of their life, and it never does anything. But it's a killer. There was a gal in the next town over, a beautiful woman, 30 years old with two kids, waiting for a liver transplant. She got it from a blood transfusion. She didn't get the transplant, and she died. So that's why I'll talk to anybody about it. I'm in the process of helping six people who also have it. Thank God the medicine worked on me."

Roger McGuinn also suffered a scare when he was diagnosed with glaucoma at the end of the Nineties. Prior to that he had been in excellent health and enjoyed an eventful decade during which he stayed true to his ideals. In March 1991, two months after the Byrds' induction to the Rock 'n' Roll Hall of Fame, he released his first solo album in over 23 years.

The acclaimed *Back From Rio* displayed all his strengths and sat well alongside the best of his post-Byrds solo work. The crisp production by David Cole was particularly impressive. Here was an album that sounded contemporary and yet harked back to the spirit of the Byrds with the chiming 12-string Rickenbacker prominent on every track. In McGuinn's mind, it was a successful attempt to record a Sixties' inspired album using the technology of the Nineties. With some formidable guest stars, including David Crosby, Chris Hillman, Tom Petty, George Hawkins, Timothy Schmit, Stan Ridgway, John Jorgenson and Stan Lynch, the album became a minor hit, peaking at number 44 in *Billboard*. In promoting the work, the question that McGuinn was most often asked concerned the unusual title, *Back From Rio*. This gave him the chance to recall all the confusion, resulting from his change of Christian name between the releases of *Younger Than Yesterday* and *The Notorious Byrd Brothers*. "The reason I called it *Back From Rio* was because back in the Sixties, when I changed my name from Jim to Roger, a lot of people didn't know that. They thought that Jim was my brother, and that he, for some strange reason, had gone to Rio de Janeiro, maybe to get away from it all. So people would come up to me and say, 'What happened to Jim McGuinn? We heard he went to Rio.' And I'd say, 'Well, no, that's really *me*.' So this is a joke on that, that he's back from Rio, whoever that guy was."

The joke was continued on 'Car Phone', in which a mobile phone user reveals, "He's a guitar player, his name is Jim McGuinn, and he's back from Rio." The song closed with a nod to the Beatles' 'A Day In The Life' in the borrowed line, "He blew his mind out in a car". All this was reminiscent of the musical exchanges between the Fab Four and the Byrds on songs such as 'The Bells Of Rhymney, 'If I Needed Someone' and 'Thoughts And Words'. There was also an allusion to the rise and fall of fellow Sixties' icon John Phillips on 'King Of The Hill', plus an imitation of the studio gimmicks of the period on 'Back From Rio Interlude'. What unified the album though, was the distinctive sound of the Rickenbacker, which was prominently displayed on the cover artwork.

McGuinn promoted the album with a series of personal appearances, including a record company bash at London's Borderline. He also toured briefly with a young Florida group, the Headlights, whose energetic approach added a spark to his concert performances. Arista Records hoped that he might extend his touring schedule, but after the initial promotional spree, McGuinn withdrew. "It was a lot of work – more work than I'd done in a long time. I got used to the casual pace of going out and doing a couple of dates with the acoustic guitar."

By his own admission, McGuinn had never really recovered from the bad experiences that he had suffered on the road during the Seventies, when alcohol and cocaine were in the ascendant and money was squandered recklessly. His solo albums had failed to sell in substantial numbers and road fees with a touring band eroded profits at an alarming rate. It was only during the Eighties that McGuinn realized that he could make as much money playing small gigs on a modest schedule. Moreover, with his wife Camilla joining him, there was never any strain on his marriage resulting from long absences. Rather than sacrificing his quality of life in pursuit of a punishing schedule, McGuinn once again reverted to his folk troubadour role, emulating the example of his early mentors, Bob Gibson and Pete Seeger.

McGuinn's career as a major label artiste had now ceased. Columbia/Legacy issued a rather patchy 20-track compilation from his solo years to take advantage of his higher profile, but it came and went with little fanfare. There was also a guest appearance on Bob Dylan's *The 30th Anniversary Concert Celebration* on which McGuinn performed 'Mr Tambourine Man' and joined Dylan, Neil Young, Tom Petty, Eric Clapton and George Harrison for a desultory superstar version of 'My Back Pages'. "It was great fun," McGuinn remarked of the nostalgic celebration. "It was a whirlwind experience – we flew up there and had rehearsals the day before the show and the next day we did the show . . . It was really great seeing all my old friends, and getting to play with all those guys. I had to show George Harrison how to sing the chorus of 'You Ain't Going Nowhere' because he'd never sung it."

One project that unexpectedly returned to haunt McGuinn was the musical *Gene Tryp*. During the Eighties he had been performing songs from the doomed musical as part of a mini-set within his standard show, but he'd long since abandoned any hope of seeing the work performed onstage. However, thanks to some enterprising drama students in upstate New York, that dream was belatedly realized. The world premiere of *Gene Tryp* finally occurred at Colgate University Theatre in Hamilton between 18–21 November 1992. Retitled *Just A Season: A Romance Of The Old West*, the musical retained most of its original songs, although the lavish sets once promised were obviously not available. McGuinn joined the troupe as an accompanist, playing acoustic 12-string guitar and 5-string banjo and contributing backing vocals. Original director Jacques Levy, who was now head of theatre studies at Colgate, was in attendance and contributed some expansive programme notes.

Levy's account of the musical's tortuous history was revealing. "Roger McGuinn and I met backstage at the famous New York rock palace, the Fillmore East, where Roger's band, the Byrds, was appearing. I talked to him about the notion of our writing a country musical for Broadway and he was intrigued. He agreed to give it a shot, and we started to work together. When the finished draft went to a Broadway producer, his response was so enthusiastic that he immediately announced an upcoming production in *The New York Times*. But it was not to be. Theatre investors in New York were not keen on this 'hick' music, rock-influenced or not. It was an idea whose time had not come. So, instead, we decided to put some of the songs on the next Byrds album. On release, the album quickly hit the charts, and the subsequent single of 'Chestnut Mare' did the same thing. Four songs from the show continue to receive regular airplay here and in Europe, although few listeners realize they were ever part of a play. And though Roger and I went on writing together – for the Byrds and, later, for Roger's solo albums – as far as the show was concerned, we let bygones be bygones. Now, however, with a highly revised book but with many of the original songs retained, after many a year and a long way from the Fillmore East, we are pleased to present the world premiere of *Just A Season*."

The show was divided into two acts, the first featuring 'Chestnut Mare', 'All The Things' and 'Kathleen's Song' (retitled 'Solveig's Song' in deference to Henrik Ibsen), while the second added 'Lover Of The Bayou', 'I Wanna Grow Up To Be A Politician' and 'Just A Season', plus two additional songs, 'The Robbin' Of The Stage' and 'Home On The Hillside'. Although decidedly minor key, it was gratifying to hear that the musical had been staged at last. The small hope remains that some other student drama group might follow suit at a future date.

As the Nineties rolled on, McGuinn gave little indication that he intended to alter his comfortable round of touring small venues. He was enticed abroad in the summer of 1993 to play a couple of gigs in London and Paris specifically for the Hard Rock Café. A press conference was held at the eaterie's French headquarters during which McGuinn made clear that he was neither interested in seeking a major deal for himself nor reforming the Byrds. "David Crosby has been going around trying to get people to convince me to be in the Byrds again," he noted wearily. "But I really don't want to be in the Byrds. I enjoy being a solo artiste for whatever it's worth. I could have a record deal tomorrow if I was looking for one, but I'm not".

In the absence of new songs, McGuinn attempted to refresh his repertoire with such surprises as the Beefeaters' 'Please Let Me Love You', the Beatles' 'I Want To Hold Your Hand', Bob Gibson's 'Springfield Mountain' and the solo oddity, 'Russian Hill'. Over the next couple of years, the set evolved into an autobiographical account of his musical life, embracing Elvis Presley's 'Heartbreak Hotel', the traditional 'Wayfaring Stranger', Bobby Darin's 'Splish Splash', the City Surfers' 'Beach Ball' and the Beatles' 'She Loves You' through to the familiar Byrds' hits. Other surprises included the rarely performed 'Wild Mountain Thyme' and 'You Showed Me'. Lacing the songs with an entertaining narrative revealing his shifts through surf music, traditional folk, Merseybeat and folk-rock, McGuinn added a new dimension to his live shows and impressed many older fans who had never dreamt of hearing such unusual material.

At the end of 1995 McGuinn decided to make some of his music available on the Internet. The Folk Den, then part of the Byrds' Home Page, provided the perfect forum for McGuinn to revisit his old folk roots and preserve the traditions of storytelling in the electronic age. He expressed concern that his favourite music was in danger of being fossilized or forgotten. "I was listening to a Smithsonian Folkways album, and it dawned on me that I wasn't hearing traditional music any more. There was a new trend of folk singers who were singer-songwriters, and they were wonderful. They were writing great songs, but they weren't doing the old standards – the traditional songs that Pete Seeger and all the people I grew up with were doing. I started asking myself, 'What's going to happen in 10 or 20 years when these guys leave the scene and there's nobody doing the traditional songs any more?' They could get lost."

Fulfilling his promise to add a new song to the Folk Den every month, McGuinn produced a veritable mini-album of material, including 'Old Paint' ("a song that tells the story of the special relationship between a cowboy and his horse"), 'Virgin Mary' (a Leadbelly-influenced spiritual often played at the Gate of Horn each Christmas), 'The Argonaut' (the tale of a shipwreck in 1853), 'John Riley' (the classic folk tale that McGuinn first heard played by Joan Baez at Club 47 in Cambridge, Massachusetts), 'To Morrow' (an American folk song about Morrow, Ohio, recorded by McGuinn on reel to reel in 1958 after hearing Bob Gibson's version at the Latin School of Chicago) and 'Easter' (a celebration of the Resurrection, originally performed by Leadbelly on 12-string guitar).

The three surviving original Byrds were still looking towards the future, but it was their golden age past that fascinated the music press. In May 1996, the reissue of the first four Byrds albums on CD brought further critical acclaim and provided another feast for collectors in search of rarities. With six bonus tracks per album, plus extensive liner notes and song annotations, the series proved a logical extension of the work begun on *Never Before* and *The Byrds* box set. As well as boasting a considerable improvement in sound quality, the remastered CDs offered a sterling selection of B-sides, alternate takes and other material, previously unavailable even on bootleg. Although the majority of the session tapes for *Mr Tambourine Man* were stolen from the vaults many years ago, this setback thankfully did not interrupt the flow of new tracks on the remastered first album, which were a delight to hear.

'She Has A Way' was one of numerous Gene Clark tracks that might have appeared on the group's debut album were it not for a push towards a more prominent folk-rock style. The bonus version benefits from access to the multi-tracks, with a different vocal from the take that appears on the box set. There is also an opportunity to hear alternate vocal recordings of 'Feel A Whole Lot Better' and 'You Won't Have To Cry'. By contrast, the Clark/McGuinn collaboration 'It's No Use' offers a strikingly different guitar break. The international hit single 'All I Really Want To Do', with its sprightly vocal and slightly different lyrics, had previously only appeared on the compilation *The Original Singles*. Here, at last, it is rightly added to the Byrds' debut album. Finally, for the first time anywhere, a backing track for the unheard 'You And Me' was discovered in the vaults. With no proof of authorship available, it was belatedly credited to McGuinn/Clark/Crosby. Completists will note that two songs allegedly recorded during the first album sessions ('Words And Pictures' and a cover of Mose Allison's 'I

Love The Life I Live') remain undiscovered, feared forever lost. Sadly, no one connected with the Byrds can confirm whether completed takes of these songs were ever recorded.

The additional tracks on *Turn! Turn! Turn!* are equally intriguing. 'The Day Walk' is familiar from the box set and Murray Hill release. Clark aficionados are also offered the rare B-side 'She Don't Care About Time', an excellent composition previously omitted from the original album in favour of newer material. On the reissue CD it is reinstated alongside a second previously unissued take, which includes a surprise harmonica solo by drummer Michael Clarke. An early version of 'The Times They Are A-Changin'', once considered as a possible follow-up to 'All I Really Want To Do', emerges as an unexpected highlight, arguably outclassing the more familiar released version. "The backing track was taken right from Terry Melcher's mono master," confirms CD producer Bob Irwin. "It has different lyrics, a different outro and the harmonies are more spectacular than on the released version." Another Dylan song follows with 'It's All Over Now, Baby Blue', a different take to that featured on the Murray Hill album. A mix of 'The World Turns All Around Her', featuring bongos, shows the group playfully experimenting in the studio. Finally, there is the mysterious instrumental 'Stranger In A Strange Land' that the compilers actually transferred directly from the bootleg anthology *Journals*. Unfortunately, a vocal version could not be found, but the backing track remains a tantalizing piece. David Crosby admits that the lyrics were a naïve attempt on his part to capture the spirit of the Robert A. Heinlein book of the same title, but that in itself sounds ambitious and commendable. According to Jim Dickson, the song was sold by Tickson Music and tentatively scheduled for a movie soundtrack that never appeared. It was later recorded on a single by the duo Blackburn & Snow and their version, whose backing is faithful to the original, underlines the undoubted quality of the composition.

Three other songs from the *Turn! Turn! Turn!* sessions remain missing. The Dino Valenti composition 'I Don't Ever Want To Spoil Your Party', with a lead vocal from Crosby, was recorded at the same session as 'Stranger In A Strange Land'. Listeners eager to discover what it might have sounded like can stretch their imaginations by consulting the first Quicksilver Messenger Service album where it was re-recorded under the title 'Dino's Song'. The largely unknown and mysteriously titled 'Circle Of Minds' would certainly have been included if available, even in fragmentary form, but no tapes, publishing credits, or even a completed session number could be found. A stolen backing track of the legendary 'Flower Bomb Song' did exist on tape but this was not available to Bob Irwin at Sony and, surprisingly, has yet to feature on a bootleg CD. When I reminded Crosby of the song, he burst into defensive laughter and admitted that it was not only "a very bad song", but probably one of his worst compositions. Written in free verse, it features such memorable asides as "I'm going to make the love gun that will blow your mind". The backing track sounds more impressive than expected and, despite his embarrassment, it would have been intriguing to hear Crosby's hippie philosophizing at such a relatively early period. In many ways, the loss of these Crosby compositions and vocals are the key missing chapter in the early career of the Byrds. Apart from 'The Airport Song' on *Preflyte*, there are no examples of his lead vocal work with the Byrds during 1965–66 nor any indication of the nature of his songwriting.

As the Byrds entered their mid-period, the material available for inclusion as CD bonus tracks was more enthralling. Bob Irwin was justifiably excited about finding the original CBS master of 'Eight Miles High' which, like so many of these tracks, sounds startlingly fresh. The bonus cuts on *Fifth Dimension* bolster the album's reputation considerably. 'Why' (the single version) is presented in true stereo, complete with those wonderful Hillman loping bass runs, regrettably and inexplicably made inaudible on *Never Before*.

" 'Why' was right on the multi-track with the rest of the album," Irwin explains. "So the mix itself was pretty straightforward. Allen Stanton originally recorded most of the songs on one-inch 8-track. Then he did a reduction mix-down to a half-inch 4-track where he printed all his effects. All the echo was printed and the guitars were ganged together. So we created the mixes from the 4-track reduction because that's what gave that album its characteristic sound. 'Why' was printed right on that reel along with everything else. I'd like to take credit for it, but it was a pretty simple task to do it the right way."

'I Know My Rider', another possible single that failed to appear in its time, was taken from the box set, as was its probable B-side, Crosby's satiric 'Psychodrama City'. Fears that contractual problems might prevent Sony from including the original RCA versions of 'Eight Miles High' and 'Why' proved unjustified. At last, listeners could compare these stellar takes with the CBS versions on the same CD and decide for themselves whether Crosby was right in claiming of the RCA 'Eight Miles High': "It was better. It was stronger. It had a lot more flow to it."

Finally, there is a previously unissued instrumental version of 'John Riley', an astonishing example of the Byrds' eclecticism. Working spontaneously in the studio, they casually demonstrate a veritable jazz/folk fusion. Although this has the same chord sequence as the orchestrated 'John Riley', the faster tempo completely transforms the tune. It is a minor revelation. The CD concludes with a hidden bonus track featuring the 'Special Open-End Interview with The Byrds' used as a promotional tool at the time of the album's original US release.

The highlight of the first batch of reissues was undoubtedly the fourth Byrds album, *Younger Than Yesterday*. Listening to the bonus tracks provides a revealing insight into Crosby's developing role as the group's aspiring front man. 'It Happens Each Day', already a favourite since appearing on *Never Before* and the box set, is perfectly placed on the record, fully emphasizing the Byrds' creativity during this fertile period. 'Don't Make Waves', the hastily conceived film theme composed by McGuinn/Hillman, retains its quaint, inconsequential charm. There is another chance to hear the studio talk, missing from the original single, in which Crosby sarcastically exclaims: "Let's double it! Masterpiece!"

'My Back Pages' emerges as the most unusual and distinctive bonus track. McGuinn's guitar solo, played through a Leslie speaker cabinet, alters the entire mood of the song. According to Bob Irwin: "Gary Usher had this marked as being 'the original single version' so, at one time, I think they were going to use that master as the single." It was given a matrix number and everything. It's the same vocal track, I think. It looks like they just bounced it over again and had Roger do a whole new guitar part over the top. It was actually on the master reel. The 'My Back Pages' that was released was on a separate reel all together, for no apparent reason."

The alternate take of Crosby's 'Mind Gardens' is another surprise. Sung at a more relaxed pace, without some of the self-conscious histrionics evident on the original, it proves a more palatable reading. Appropriately, Crosby's 'Lady Friend' follows in stereo, with the original instrumentation intact. There is also a version of the B-side, 'Old John Robertson', minus the phasing which was added to the later album cut.

Despite an extensive search, no tape for the unissued Miles Davis-inspired instrumental 'Milestones' could be found. In all probability, it was removed from the vaults, most likely for inclusion in a television documentary. As a postscript to *Younger Than Yesterday*, astute listeners could hear the original guitar work for 'Mind Gardens'. On the album version, the guitars were 'recorded played backwards' in order to create a sitar-like effect. Separated from the song and 'played forwards', the instrumental segment displays Crosby's delicate finger-picking and McGuinn's tasteful lead work to striking effect.

While old and new fans were assimilating the first batch of Byrds' reissues, McGuinn continued to unveil folk material on the Internet. The latest batch featured 'Springfield Mountain' ("purported to be the first American ballad", documenting the fate of Lieutenant Thomas Merrick, who was mortally wounded by a rattlesnake bite on Springfield Mountain, Massachusetts on 7 August 1761), 'Buffalo Skinners' (a folk tune McGuinn picked up from Herb O'Brien, a bartender at Chicago's Easy Street), 'New York Girls' (the inspiration for 'Jack Tarr The Sailor' on *Ballad Of Easy Rider*), 'Cold Coast Of Greenland' (a whaling song, newly arranged by McGuinn), 'Boatman' (featuring backing vocals from the Ohio River Boys), 'Lost Jimmy Whelan' (a lament for a drowned sailor), 'Golden Vanity' (a sea shanty that McGuinn often performed in Rush Street, Chicago and recorded with the Chad Mitchell Trio), 'What Child Is This' (a hymn to the birth of Christ, set to the melody of Henry VIII's 'Greensleeves'), 'In The Evenin'' (a home recording from 1957 that McGuinn often played at the Café Roué, Chicago), 'Alberta' (a river song chanted by stevedores who worked on the Ohio River), 'Sailor Lad' (a salty sea shanty), 'Brisbane Ladies' (previously played by McGuinn on Hoyt Axton's 1963 album, *Greenback Dollar*, aka *The Balladeer*), 'Wayfaring Stranger' (a reflection on the vanity of human wishes) and 'East Virginia' (an erotic love song recorded on reel to reel at McGuinn's house during the late Fifties).

Although these Folk Den contributions provided fascinating listening for those with access to Internet technology, many fans still hoped that McGuinn might record another album for a major label. When questioned about the prospect of new product, he countered: "I used to put them out every six months with the Byrds, and we did some good ones under those difficult conditions, but I don't really feel like doing that any more." Just as he seemed to be closing the door on the idea of another high profile release, he added, tantalizingly, "Lately, the urge to write has returned."

CHAPTER FORTY-EIGHT

The Absence Of Charity

McGUINN's hint of a possible creative surge was no mere tease. During 1996, he and Camilla completed a series of new songs, including 'Parade Of Lost Dreams', 'Castanet Dance', 'Rebellious Eyes' and 'Made In China', which were distributed to selected record companies as a home-produced CD. Before long, McGuinn was openly discussing the need to complete another album in order to maintain his profile. After five years, even he agreed that it was time to remind audiences that he was no mere artisan on the oldies circuit. Instead of the expected studio album though, McGuinn decided to capture his autobiographical concerts on a live recording. Culled from various shows, *Live From Mars* was released in the US in November 1996 on the Walt Disney label, Hollywood Records. The musical story opened in 1956 with 'Heartbreak Hotel', moving steadily through McGuinn's folk years ('Gate Of Horn'), fascination with Bach ('Chestnut Mare'), studio appearances with Judy Collins ('Turn! Turn! Turn!'), Brill Building hack work ('Beach Ball'), early collaborations with Gene Clark ('You Showed Me'), the discovery of Dylan and folk rock ('Mr Tambourine Man') and fame with the Byrds. In addition to the live extracts, two studio recordings, 'Fireworks' and 'May The Road Rise', were cut with former members of the Jayhawks. Overall, it was a slight but entertaining album, spoiled only by McGuinn's decision to omit one of the most enjoyable segments of his live shows. Regrettably, there was nothing to represent his period as a Beatles imitator, despite the fact that he had regularly included 'She Loves You' and 'I Want To Hold Your Hand' at shows to represent this time. "We had to make some cut-ins and I didn't really have a good version of those on tape," he explained. "I didn't have a definitive version of 'I Want To Hold Your Hand' and the falsetto was a little shaky."

Live From Mars had barely reached UK stores when another McGuinn-related release emerged. *3 Byrds Land In London,* issued on the BBC archive label Strange Fruit, was a welcome reminder of the package tour of 1977 when McGuinn's Thunderbyrd, the Chris Hillman Band and the KC Southern Band all appeared on the same bill. Selections from their first show at the Hammersmith Odeon were broadcast by the BBC at the time, but this was a more complete record. Among the highlights were two previously unreleased Clark songs 'Denver Or Wherever' and 'Hula Bula Man', but alas no 'Last Of The Blue Diamond Miners'. Hillman's segment included eight songs, ranging from the Burritos' 'Hot Burrito # 2' to Manassas' 'It Doesn't Matter', interspersed with selections from his solo albums. McGuinn's Thunderbyrd performed the legendary 'Shoot 'Em', one of his best songs of the era. Unfortunately, its violent content persuaded him to abandon any intention of recording the song following his conversion to born again Christianity. The album concluded with three of the four encores by McGuinn, Hillman and Clark.

The feast of Byrds-related product continued in March 1997 when the second batch of the group's remastered catalogue was issued to critical acclaim. Once again, discerning collectors were offered a mouth-watering collection of bonus tracks, including material only recently discovered in the vaults. For most fans, the jewel in the crown among this quartet of albums was *The Notorious Byrd Brothers*. Its remastered sound quality was exemplary and revealed many of producer Gary Usher's studio tricks to startling effect. The bonus tracks began with 'Moog Raga', previously solely available on the deleted *Never Before*. McGuinn's playful attempt to fuse traditional Indian music with modern synthesizer technology sums up a period when the chief Byrd was at his most ambitious and inventive. This track was originally intended to herald an entire album of synthesizer music, but the experiment was never fully realized.

Probably the biggest surprise among the additional material on *Notorious* was 'Bound To Fall', a backing track conspicuously missing from all previous sessionographies. Written by Mike Brewer, the song was later commandeered by Chris Hillman for inclusion on Manassas' double album in 1972 and was also recorded by Brewer & Shipley. The Byrds' version does not differ markedly from Stephen Stills' reading, but it would have been great to hear McGuinn duetting with Hillman on the vocal track.

David Crosby always bitterly complained that he was written out of the script as a visible contributor to *The Notorious Byrd Brothers*. The controversial 'Triad', previously available on *Never Before* and the box set, was vetoed from the original album on the grounds of 'poor taste' and passed over to the Jefferson Airplane for inclusion on *Crown Of Creation*. Two decades on, it's rewarding to listen to the composition alongside the other songs from the sessions. In the original running order, 'Triad' was in direct competition with 'Goin' Back' for a place on the album, a situation made worse by Crosby's contempt for the Goffin/King composition, which he regarded as lightweight. Although he refused to appear on the released recording of 'Goin' Back', the bonus track herein is an early attempt on which he sings harmony, while McGuinn plays at a slower pace than expected. Crosby returns as an instrumentalist for 'Draft Morning', which includes a 13-second coda previously lost in the segue prior to 'Wasn't Born To Follow'. Finally, 'Universal Mind Decoder' emerges as a prototype of 'Change Is Now', minus the Clarence White touches on the official version, but featuring McGuinn in his more traditional Byrds style.

The remastered *Notorious* also included an extraordinary in-studio argument, captured in all its gruesome glory in the run-off section of the disc. This amazing session reel allows us to eavesdrop on the Byrds at the peak of their petty conflicts. While parts of their conversation recall the uproarious humour of 'The Troggs Tapes', the final mood is probably closer to the Beatles' cold war during *Let It Be*, when Lennon drifted away from the others and a weary Harrison finally despaired of his working relationship with McCartney. As the strains of 'Dolphin's Smile' fade, you realize that this is the last testament of a group about to break up. Within months of this recording, both Crosby and Clarke would be unceremoniously fired in what now seems a final twist of the knife in a long and increasingly bitter family argument.

Amazingly, some of that bitterness still remained in late 1997. Years before, Crosby had railed to me about the internal disputes during this period and famously derided the group's producers, partly to emphasize Dickson's importance and contribution to the Byrds' development. Over the years, he had mellowed somewhat when discussing his last days in the Byrds and his later behaviour during the reunion sessions. He even went out of his way to praise McGuinn's 'genius'. While promoting the reissues, however, the old antagonism returned with a vengeance. When asked about the Byrds' producers, he was scathing in his summation. "The only one who ever did anything was Dickson. The others were all idiots and wouldn't know a song if it bit them on the nose . . . Usher doesn't know his nose from his asshole, OK? And what's his name, the actress' son, Terry Melcher, was even worse – a total idiot. They were all idiots and the Columbia union engineers that used to take breaks in the middle of a song and stuff. They were idiots. All flaming idiots! Dickson wasn't much better because he had a terrible temper and an enormous ego and built up such a core of resentment in us, it made a non-functional situation. You'll notice we did the best work by ourselves . . . *Fifth Dimension* and *Younger Than Yesterday* [were] where we actually started to shine. I don't think they had producers did they?"

McGuinn was appalled when he read Crosby's comments. "I can't believe the nasty things that Crosby said about both Melcher and Gary Usher," he told me soon after. "I thought they did great work. I thought Terry was a great producer, and I still do. I think he had a talent for producing in spite of what Crosby says." Re-reading David's diatribe, what's most notable, besides the absence of charity, is his vagueness about the group's back catalogue. Dickson is praised, then criticized; he can barely remember Terry Melcher's name; Doris Day is simply 'the actress'; and he seems to believe that the Byrds were credited as their own producers, which was *never* the case. Even more oddly, having agreed to promote the remastered albums, Crosby finally admits, after stumbling over song titles and credits, that he has not even listened to any of them. Indeed, it seems likely that he's not heard *The Notorious Byrd Brothers* since he was thrown out of the Byrds and clearly has no intention of revisiting the work. So why did he agree to discuss the remastered albums and their bonus cuts when he was barely aware of their content?

"I'll tell you the truth," he admits. "The only reason I haven't listened is because it's painful to me because of Roger refusing to . . . I really love that music, man. It's not like a lightweight thing with me. He's causing me a lot of pain and I don't think he should. I don't think it's right. I'm trying not to build up a resentment against him because I know it's his right to do it but it really hurts. Imagine the lyric '. . . and each unharmful gentle soul misplaced inside a jail' ['Chimes Of Freedom']. Imagine how that feels to me now as opposed to then . . . the lyrics are now laden with so much more meaning and I want to sing them. I don't care about the money – I have a life. I'm already in a very successful band, to put it mildly, and I don't know . . . I'm glad to fly wingman to the guy. I know he is the central issue there, and I understand that. I just want to do the music."

There is something almost endearing about Crosby's desperate desire to reconnect with the Byrds as a means of confronting and exorcizing the past. It is a passionate need beyond the understanding of McGuinn whose focus was always on sustaining a pleasant present. It seemed the more Crosby railed against the injustice of McGuinn's aloofness, the greater the gap grew between them. It would be easy to interpret an element of psychic vengeance in McGuinn's determined distancing, but it more closely resembles the remote dispassion that a former partner might display towards someone still besotted with a tarnished ideal.

After the internal friction of *The Notorious Byrd Brothers* and Crosby's scorching words, listening to the pastoral *Sweetheart Of The Rodeo* reissue offers sweet relief. It is the best sounding disc among this second batch of reissues, offering instrumentation in stunning clarity. The bonus tracks are a major surprise. Instead of simply lifting all the alternate takes and rehearsal sessions from the box set as expected, series producer Bob Irwin unearths more previously unheard material. The new rehearsal versions of 'The Christian Life', 'Life In Prison' and 'You're Still On My Mind' had never appeared before, even on bootlegs. They offer fresh insights into Parsons' influence over the group's direction during this crucial time. There are also three rare outtakes borrowed from the box set: Tim Hardin's 'Reputation', 'Lazy Days' (later covered more impressively by the Flying Burrito Brothers on their second album) and the traditional 'Pretty Polly', which McGuinn subsequently re-recorded for *Cardiff Rose*. The album ends with a previously undiscovered instrumental which was initially given the grammatically incorrect title: 'All I Have Is Memories'.

The succeeding *Dr Byrds & Mr Hyde* introduces the new set of Byrds – McGuinn, Clarence White, John York and Gene Parsons. Here, McGuinn attempts to impose some aural unity by taking every lead vocal himself. Ironically, in later years, he would do precisely the opposite and allow the quality of the group's work to worsen as a result of misguided democracy.

Despite McGuinn's vocal domination on *Dr Byrds & Mr Hyde*, the country influences imported by White and Parsons are never far away. New bassist John York receives a co-writing credit on 'Candy', which is reconfigured here with an elongated guitar solo in the mid-section. The bonus tracks include the lacklustre 'Stanley's Song', previously unveiled on the box set. This was a rare moment when a McGuinn collaboration with science-fiction writing partner Bob Hippard failed to bear fruit. Also on offer from the box set is the alternate version of 'Lay Lady Lay'. It was initially intended to feature the original single next to this one but, despite entreaties from myself and Irwin, McGuinn could not stomach hearing the female chorus that producer Bob Johnston had overdubbed without the group's permission, so he vetoed this proposal. It is regrettable that the more raucous original single was axed as it would have enabled the public to judge for themselves whether Johnston was correct in adding a gospel choir.

An alternate version of 'This Wheel's On Fire' follows, with Clarence White's country-style picking in evidence, rather than the fuzz guitar trappings heard on the better known rendition. Also on offer is a more spontaneous version of the album's closing medley, during which McGuinn makes a daring and not entirely successful attempt to sing blues. The bonus tracks conclude with a sprightly reading of 'Nashville West', which sounds noticeably looser than the familiar Byrds' version.

The eighth remastered CD in the series highlights the return of Terry Melcher as producer for 1969's *Ballad Of Easy Rider*. The bonus tracks open with 'Way Behind The Sun', featuring John York on lead vocal. "I found the song on a Pentangle album and really liked it," he remembers. "One of the things I was trying to do in the Byrds at that time was bring in other forms of music that they weren't used to, mainly something that was a little blues-oriented." York is also featured as vocalist on an early take of 'Tulsa County Blue' which neatly complements McGuinn's rendition. "I didn't sing it on the album for political reasons," York recalls. "It's funny, you know, I've never heard it. What happened was I did the vocal initially but, at the time, I was really getting fed up with the band and had hinted to Gene and Clarence that I was thinking of leaving if things didn't change. Terry Melcher had tried to get the publishing rights from me for 'Fido' and they were going to release it as a single. But I didn't want to give up the publishing and that ticked him off. Then they came back and told me that they had decided that Roger should sing 'Tulsa County Blue'. At the time, I felt Terry was unhappy that I hadn't given him the rights to 'Fido', but I really don't know if that's true. They told me they felt Roger sounded more like a cowboy than me. It was probably just a matter of a few days later that Roger put his vocal on."

In seeking fresh material, the Byrds also invited Jackson Browne into the studio and received a tape of his songs, from which 'Mae Jean Goes To Hollywood' was recorded. It remained locked in the vaults until the release of the box set. The same fate befell an alternate 'Oil In My Lamp', which has a more punchy arrangement than the released version. Completing the bonus tracks on *Ballad Of Easy Rider* are three tunes never previously available. McGuinn's 'Fiddler A Dram' (mistitled 'Jenny Comes Along' on the tape box/session listing) is an amusing synthesis of folk and electronic rock. The album's title track, available here as an alternate take, displays Clarence White's guitar work more prominently in the mix above the orchestration. Finally, like several others in the reissue series, the album closes with a catchy instrumental, the previously unheard 'Build It Up', composed by White and Gene Parsons.

Overall, the remastering and repackaging of the Byrds' Columbia albums was a conscientious attempt to do justice to one of the most important music catalogues in rock history. Even more than the box set, these recordings confirm the Byrds' standing as one of the most innovative, adventurous and accomplished artistes of their era. Thanks to Nineties' technology, their legacy is now available to a new generation of listeners.

The revitalization of the Byrds' back catalogue did not tempt McGuinn to change his mind about reforming the remnants of the group for another series of concerts. Crosby had been playfully picketing for another get-together but by this point even he realized that McGuinn was adamant about not resurrecting the past. "It's a deep frustration for me," Crosby admitted, "because Roger doesn't want to do it. And I don't know why. He did it with everybody else in the world. But either he or his wife must have some sort of enormous grudge. I'm not sure."

As Crosby's words indicate, reading McGuinn's motives was never easy, as the expulsion of Gene Clark from the previous get-togethers firmly underlined. Although McGuinn had apparently enjoyed the reunion at the Ash Grove and the recordings at Nashville for the box set, his attitude towards Byrds' reunions was always ambivalent. They had only reconvened to try and wrest control of the name from Michael Clarke and that attempt had ended in a well-publicized failure. Midway through 1997, McGuinn stated unequivocally that he would hear no more of reunions. "Frankly, every time I've listened to Crosby it's been a disaster," he told me. "It really has." In many respects. McGuinn was reiterating the words that he had uttered to me exactly 20 years before when he proclaimed: "If the Byrds did reform again it would be so disastrous that I wouldn't want to think about it . . . I feel it's something I don't need and I don't feel that the world really needs it. I think it's something that would gratify the egos of the other Byrds."

One ex-Byrd who no longer needed any ego gratification was Chris Hillman. Like Crosby, he had been politely coaxing a reunion, only to realize that it was a mistake. "At one point, David and I were saying, 'Roger won't go out as the Byrds . . .' And then, I thought, 'Wait a minute, Roger's smarter than all of us. He's right. Why go out as three Byrds? Why put ourselves through that?' Yeah, for the money. Great. But it's not the same. Let the Byrds be a nice memory. Roger's more comfortable playing small venues. I can understand that. He doesn't have to compromise. The Byrds are never going to go out again. Now it's coming from Hillman. It used to be Hillman saying, 'Come on, Roger.' Now I agree with him. Even if we did go out for a six-week tour and made millions of dollars, what does it mean? What am I going to buy? I don't want anything. I just want to pay my bills and have a nice life here . . . I don't have the passion I used to have. I don't think anybody does after 30 years in any job. But I enjoy it more now."

One important feature of the reissue series is that it offers the opportunity to mend those lingering conflicts implicit in the Byrds' story. The passage of time has softened the worst bitterness far more persuasively than any temporary reunion or direct action from aggrieved former members. Perhaps even David Crosby might one day listen to *The Notorious Byrd Brothers*, sample 'Triad' alongside 'Goin' Back' and gain a clearer understanding of the entire picture; Gene Clark, so sorely slighted on the box set, can now rest in peace knowing that his dominance of the group's first two albums has been fully recognized; Gram Parsons went to the grave denouncing *Sweetheart Of The Rodeo* as an unhappy compromise, but now his vocal contributions can be appreciated in all their glory; John York never heard his vocal readings of 'Way Behind The Sun' and 'Tulsa County Blue', now he can; Clarence White's instrumental forays, always an important feature of the latter-day Byrds, can now be appreciated thanks to the inclusion of several additional tunes.

Apart from righting the wrongs of history, the most amazing aspect of the reissue series was that, despite all the additions, McGuinn's importance in the proceedings was in no way diminished. If anything his reputation has been enhanced and the sheer range of his versatility underlined. Indeed, there's a new McGuinn lurking here, a figure we always suspected existed, but perhaps never fully appreciated. Listening to the Byrds' catalogue in its entirety it is hard not to be impressed by McGuinn's determination to survive any change or reversal of fortune, no matter how devastating. Throughout the Byrds' saga, he remained perpetually cool and remarkably unfazed by the apparently never-ending internal strife. Somehow, he developed an indomitable chameleon nature, as if convinced that any musical form could be assimilated and conquered.

Nobody was indispensable in McGuinn's world-view. When he spoke the words "I trust everything will turn out all right" he was not indulging some rhetorical flourish, but positively stating a philosophy which he consistently retained throughout the Byrds' years. Listen to 'Goin' Back' and marvel at the way McGuinn ensures that the Byrds are still the kings of harmony, even as they're effectively reduced to a duo. I've never heard Crosby's solo version of 'Draft Morning' but I doubt that even he sounds as good as McGuinn imitating Crosby. Who else could take over Crosby's vocal role on 'Draft Morning' and sustain the illusion that he's still there? McGuinn attempts to pull off the same trick on *Sweetheart Of The Rodeo* in even more difficult circumstances, convincing himself that he really is country singer Gram Parsons. On *Dr Byrds & Mr Hyde* he handles all the lead singing, even on tracks that would normally be handled by C&W vocalists like Gene Parsons or Clarence White. With 'Tulsa County Blue' on *Ballad Of Easy Rider*, he produces a carbon copy of John York's rendition, and yet makes the song his own. As always, his method is to assimilate, consume and rechannel the work of his collaborators into a sound and vision appropriate to the Byrds.

McGuinn may be a great original but he is also rock's greatest method actor vocalist. Commentaries on his career invariably omit what may well be the most important feature of his early role – his appreciation of the great Stanislavski. Like Marlon Brando and James Dean, McGuinn briefly studied method acting and he never seems to have forgotten that training manual. In some respects, his involvement with the Byrds was a musical and visual representation of that role playing. Even before the Byrds existed, he served his time performing at venues that sought 'Beatles imitators'. The love of change ensured that he would never be a folk purist. His greatest achievement was that leap of imagination by which loving imitation was transformed into genre fusion. He formulated the Byrds' blueprint in his head via a bizarre vocal/instrumental cocktail of Bob Dylan and the Beatles. As he often said, the unique arrangement of 'Mr Tambourine Man' was achieved not so much through spontaneous musical experimentation, but rather via conscious calculation. The Byrds' ability to take disparate musical elements and create something startlingly fresh with ferocious regularity was their ultimate ticket to greatness. You can hear it again on 'Eight Miles High' or 'Why' where John Coltrane and Ravi Shankar combine with Gene Clark folk rock, David Crosby protest and McGuinn's exploratory guitar work to produce music that sounds wonderfully new. Or listen to 'She Don't Care About Time' and 'Chestnut Mare' for folk rock meets Bach. The same process is even parodied with a sardonic wit that has seldom been understood or appreciated on those bizarre closing album tracks like 'We'll Meet Again', 'Oh! Susannah' and '2-4-2 Fox Trot (The Lear Jet Song)'.

Throughout the Byrds, McGuinn never lost faith in his ability to produce the same magic trick performed on 'Mr Tambourine Man': the computer calculation. Such faith ensured that the quality of the group's work was almost always high, even as they were travelling at a remarkable speed through folk, country and space rock. McGuinn loosened his grip towards the end believing, wrongly for once, that even the novelty pop work of Kim Fowley could be consumed and remoulded within the fire of the Byrds. The weaker cuts on the later Byrds albums have unfairly been used to denigrate an often excellent group, but anyone who saw them during this period will testify to their continued reinvention as a powerful live act. Moreover, the best of their studio work after 1969 would still provide a formidable compilation of no small merit.

McGuinn later conceded that he should have ended the Byrds earlier than 1972. A preferred date would have been just after the release of *Sweetheart Of The Rodeo* when Hillman quit. Rock historians and the surviving original Byrds may well agree with this retrospective view, but most of the people who lived through those years are probably thankful that McGuinn chose to soldier on.

THE ABSENCE OF CHARITY

Simultaneously the great original and the great actor, he could sustain a fantasy that never lapsed into mendacity. When Peter Fonda wrote on the back of *Ballad Of Easy Rider*, "Whoever the Byrds are is all right" he was effectively endorsing a statement of faith. What his words really meant were "Whoever McGuinn believes are the Byrds can be the Byrds". Although that philosophy can no longer be applied today, it had some meaning back when the group was still an ongoing venture. It's a message that Michael Clarke knew in his heart to be true and one that David Crosby, the most fervent critic of the post-1967 Byrds, finally acknowledged when he told me: "McGuinn's the heart and soul of the Byrds". Not for the first time, David was overstating a case – Crosby himself was the heart of the Byrds, Clark the soul, Michael Clarke the sinews, Hillman the instinct, and McGuinn the mind – a mind that made him a master of illusion at a time when we all needed to believe.

CHAPTER FORTY-NINE

Survivors

A NEW millennium arrives and, against the odds, three of the original Byrds are still alive and thriving. Both Crosby and Hillman had been touched by intimations of mortality during the past decade and those experiences helped reshape their attitudes towards work and family. Crosby, in particular, resembled a man on a mission, greedy to devour whatever came his way in what everyone assumed were his final years. He once told me that a recovering addict's answer to his inner demons was to keep busy, and he was as good as his word. So was Neil Young, who fulfilled his promise to join CS&N on the road in 2000. The US tour was seen as a triumphant return and its grossing power helped establish the concept of the heritage act, encouraging record companies and promoters to exploit the gods of the past for the benefit of nostalgic baby boomers and younger fans curious to experience genuine giants from rock's golden age. Crosby was now the great survivor and, although this tour was all about CSN&Y, he reminded his audience of earlier times by performing 'Eight Miles High', on which Young played McGuinn's guitar part in his own chaotic style.

Fast approaching his sixties, it might have been expected that Crosby's headline-inspiring exploits were long past, but 2000 had barely begun before he was back on the American news channels. The February edition of *Rolling Stone* featured Crosby on the front page with three women and two children alongside the attention grabbing title: 'The Name Of The Father And The Making Of A New American Family'. It was quite a story. For the previous three years, singer Melissa Etheridge and her lesbian partner, film-maker Julie Cypher, had been questioned in the media about the identity of the biological father of their two children, Bailey and Beckett. Any number of Hollywood hunks and rock stars – from Brad Pitt to Bruce Springsteen – had been suggested as possible celebrity sperm donors, but nobody had worked out it was David Crosby. "They were visiting us in Hawaii," he recalls, "and they saw Django, who is a great kid. There was an obvious longing there, and we said, 'Why don't you have a kid?' Of course it gets extremely difficult when you're a lesbian couple and you can't get legally married and you want to find a sperm donor, so my wife volunteered me." Crosby was happy to oblige and remained discreet about his contribution until the couple broke the story to *Rolling Stone*. "Maybe it's a good thing for a lot of straight families to see that this is not something strange," he said. "I think everyone will understand, except maybe the Christian Coalition and the far right wing. But, I mean, I always wanted to be on Nixon's enemies list and I missed it. So if I piss off these people, it's fine with me."

One person who did react was his former Byrds' partner Chris Hillman, who took the moral highground by informing him that he was committing a mortal sin. Crosby, who seldom aspired to a state of grace, was taken aback, later admitting that he thought Chris' comment was "fascinating, archaic and mildly insane". What it demonstrated was the chasm between their world-views, both theologically and politically. Hillman had morphed into a no-nonsense Republican, reportedly donating $1,000 to George W. Bush's re-election campaign later in the decade and making a number of separate contributions to the Republican Party of California. Crosby was more likely to have called for Bush's head and subsequently wrote a disparaging diatribe about the Christian right. Hillman was not amused. "I still love David. I mean, love the sinner, hate the sin . . . I love David [but] I don't think I could work with him, either. He's got a mouth on him like a Hong Kong sailor, and it's not comfortable. But he respects me. He had written something about Christian fanatics and [George] Bush and all this, and I wrote him back saying 'I'm a Christian fanatic – come on!' And he said 'I'm sorry, I didn't mean you – I respect your beliefs.' And I talk to David, probably more than I talk to Roger."

Crosby's family saga did not end with the Etheridge/Cypher affair. Five years before, a lost son named James Raymond had dramatically appeared in his life and in 2000 it happened again, only this time it was a lost daughter. The Byrds had famously been photographed on the beach with bathing beauty queens in the mid-Sixties and Crosby had impregnated Miss Malibu, otherwise known as Jackie Hyde. She gave birth to a girl, who was placed in adoption and brought up in Mexico under the name Erika Keller. Jackie went on to marry singer Arlo Guthrie and Erika remained unaware of her heritage until she was an adult, bringing up her own children in Florida. After tracking down her biological mother, she learned all about Crosby, who subsequently welcomed her into his life, surprised but unfazed by the knowledge that he had yet more grandchildren.

He continued to perform with his son James in CPR and in 2001 they visited the UK, the highlight of which was a memorable performance at London's Jazz Café. The set kicked off with 'Music Is Love' the mood-setting opener from *If I Could Only Remember My Name* and featured a varied selection of Crosby's best material, including another surprise, the eerie 'Tamalpais High (At About 3)'. Who could have imagined Crosby reviving such adventurous material this late in his career? They even included 'Eight Miles High' in the encore. Before touring economics eventually suspended the CPR experiment, they completed a second album, *Just Like Gravity*. Another solid work, pensive in parts and over an hour in length, it allowed Crosby an important outlet for his songwriting. Most of the compositions were collaborations and, for the eagle-eyed, there was a surprise reworking of a couplet from the Byrds' 'It Happens Each Day' in 'Eyes Too Blue'. Crosby wrote three songs alone and two of these – 'Climber' and 'Just Like Gravity' – had a spooky ambience which underlined what might still be achieved if he could master a complete album in this vein.

Crosby, Stills & Nash were also active during 2001, but their return to the road was dramatically interrupted by 9/11. The events at the World Trade Center soon galvanized them into action, prompting various benefit concerts and personal appearances. America's great personal tragedy seemed to invest them with a new relevance that went beyond the comforting familiarity of the rock nostalgia circuit. Neil Young recognized their symbolic importance as a healing force, which was enough to kickstart another CSN&Y get-together. In January 2002, the foursome toured America again, this time with no album to support, but armed with strong empathetic tunes, including Crosby's evergreen 'Long Time Gone'. Their aim was to offer hope to a grieving nation, and part of the concert receipts were diverted to charitable organizations representing bereaved families.

A small portion of the revenue that Crosby received from the grand reunion was put to surprise use. In March, he succeeded in correcting the wrongs of rock history by preventing further misuse of the Byrds' name on the live circuit. Since Clarke's death, the rights had remained under the part ownership of Florida-based agent Steve Green, who had already proven a tricky adversary in previous negotiations. Crosby was no doubt reluctant to pay him any money for a name which he felt was being misused, but it was still a practical problem that needed to be resolved. Evidently, Crosby did not approach either McGuinn or Hillman for a financial contribution, but elected to sort out the matter using his own money. A payment, reputedly in the region of $20,000, although that figure was never confirmed, transferred the trademark over to Crosby. "I never heard the exact amount of money," says Terry Rogers, who was still touring under the 'Byrds Celebration' name. "But I know David had been in touch with Steve Green at different times and tried to buy the trademark. From what I understood, he finally offered enough money for Steve to do it. It's all about business with Steve, but I'm sure he spent a lot of money over the years in lawyers' fees and things like that. Of course, my lawyers were going back and forth with David Crosby's lawyers to come up with another name that would be acceptable to him." Rogers picketed for the title Younger Than Yesterday, a suitable enough name for a Byrds tribute band. Although it's doubtful Crosby was too happy about that either, he was pleased enough to remove the Byrds' sacred name from misrepresentation by promoters. It was a noble effort which deserved some commendation from McGuinn or Hillman, but they said nothing about the matter to the media.

The cavalcade of concerts and collaborations continued when Crosby & Nash resumed their recording career. Sanctuary Records not only proffered a deal but agreed to release a 2-CD set comprising 20 songs. One of Crosby's best leads was on the James Raymond composition 'Lay Me Down', while David's other material ranged from the anti-corporate rant 'They Want It All' to the long overdue lost classic 'Samurai', and a closing re-run of 'My Country 'Tis Of Thee'. A more cerebral, less immediate work than previous Crosby/Nash offerings from the Seventies, the album was nevertheless a rare and welcome return for the duo, whose subsequent tour emphasized their continuing appeal. In interviews, Crosby sounded as passionate and angry about the Bush administration as he had been when railing against Nixon over 30 years before. "We're about halfway to a police state and in another four years, they'll take it the rest of the way. I have great faith in this country, but there's only so much we can take before the damage gets too much. If we get another four years of Bush, it's going to be very hard for me to live in this country, though I will. But if they reinstate the draft, then I would probably leave, because they're not going to get my young son Django over my dead body."

Crosby's remarkable longevity seemed like a testament to his drug-free life and his story served as a useful parable for counselling agencies in search of a happy ending. Unlike John Phillips – who pre-empted Crosby with a best-selling book, a liver transplant and a series of addresses to former addicts about his phenomenal intake, only to lapse into alcohol abuse and die of heart failure in 2001 – David survived and supposedly stayed straight. The tales of run-ins with the police, search and seizures and possession of weapons were horror stories from his past, or so we thought. In 2004, while on the road with CPR, Crosby left a bag at a hotel in New York. Police were contacted about the exotic contents: a revolver, two knives and a stash of marijuana. Subsequently, Crosby pleaded guilty to possession of a weapon and paid a fine, but it was the chunk of marijuana, not the gun, that proved disconcerting to his friends and fans. It made him a less credible figure in counselling circles, many of which swore by the AA tenets of total abstinence. Crosby argued his case convincingly, allaying fears that he might be falling back into the nefarious drug abuse that had almost destroyed him two decades before. He insisted that the dope was purely for medicinal purposes and helped him sleep better as well as alleviating pain. If he was now tainted as a role model in certain people's eyes, that was their problem. "They should learn that you don't follow people, you follow principles. I don't think pot is a bad thing. Every society in history has had intoxicants, and some are worse than others. Marijuana is certainly not as bad as booze. I haven't done any other kind of alcohol or drug, except for medication, for more than 20 years, and I have no intention of doing so. Pot is the only one that doesn't bite you in the butt."

One year later, Crosby suffered a suspected heart attack, but did not go the way of John Phillips. After an emergency operation at UCLA and a brief convalescence, he was touring again and seemed as indomitable as ever. "He's still abusive," said Hillman, possibly referring to his prickly personality, as much as his smoking. "And he just had a heart attack . . . I mean, this man has nine lives. You'd think, coming out of that situation in prison – and then having a liver transplant – [that] you'd be on your knees thanking God. But that didn't happen, and that's not for me to comment on . . . I still love the guy, you know . . . He's had so many chances . . . There's a part of David that is just a pure, loving, joyful guy, and when I was sick [in 1998] he was there. Crosby was one of those friends. He was there for me . . . He's helped me a few times in my life."

Chris Hillman negotiated the new century in a more understated fashion than his controversial contemporary. After his recent health scare, he seemed determined to continue working on the independent circuit alongside bluegrass pals from his pre-Byrds days. In the summer of 2000, he participated in the one and only 'Byrds' reunion of the decade. Fred Walecki, proprietor of the store Westwood Music, was suffering from cancer and a host of LA's rock fraternity turned out for a benefit concert at the Santa Monica Civic Auditorium. Hillman, McGuinn and Crosby took the stage for a predictable reprise of their two US chart toppers, 'Mr Tambourine

Man' and 'Turn! Turn! Turn!'. The atmosphere was cordial enough but any speculation about further get-togethers was scotched by McGuinn, who claimed Hillman had told him: "You were so right about the Byrds. It would be a big mistake. It would be like the Asylum album – so much anticipation that we could never live up to it. It's better to leave it as a good memory." McGuinn seemed reassured by Hillman's demurral. "So David Crosby is the only one," he added, "and I don't know why he would want to do that. He's been telling everybody, everywhere he goes to ask me to do it. I think it's just a silly idea. We left a really good body of work, and it's out there for people to listen to. I'm proud of it."

Hillman seemed happy enough working with Herb Pedersen and the Rice Brothers and together they issued a third album in 2001. *Running Wild* was another impressive mixture of old and new tunes from the self-styled 'anti-supergroup', including another fond re-working of an unissued song from the Ciro's days, the Beatles' 'Things We Said Today'. Larry Rice, rather than Hillman, sang lead, transforming the song into an old man's lament. Rice also provided the album's finest moment with the closing 'About Love'. Hillman offered a further tip of the hat to Stephen Stills with an unexpected attempt at the great '4+20'. It worked reasonably well, although the song's dark, powerful ending was compromised by Hillman's decision merely to repeat the first verse. With the addition of a rhythm section the material generally sounded punchier without sacrificing the intimacy so evident on their debut four years before.

In 2002, Hillman and Pedersen issued a sequel to *Bakersfield Bound*, titled *Way Out West*. A pot pourri of bluegrass and country songs, this generous 17-song selection neatly mixed new material and old standards such as 'No Longer A Sweetheart Of Mine' and 'Save The Last Dance For Me'. Its striking artwork featured endearing sepia photos of the pair as children, as if they were seeking authenticity in memories of long ago. The songs testified to their appreciation of the music that had moulded them and the album was well received by both old school aficionados and younger listeners. There was also a fleeting opportunity to experience a treasured moment of Hillman's pre-Byrd history when he agreed to partake in a surprise reunion of the Scottsville Squirrel Barkers, who appeared at San Diego's 30th Annual Roots Festival in April 2003.

Hillman's conservatism became more pronounced with each passing year. Increasingly, he spoke of the importance of old-fashioned family values and looked back to his parents' generation for moral guidance. His support for George W. Bush saw him move in a diametrically opposite direction to David Crosby and many other former colleagues from the Sixties who were still pursuing a liberal agenda. Hillman had more in common with McGuinn, although he had long abandoned the born again evangelism evident from his comments in the early Eighties. Since marrying Constance Pappas, Hillman slowly shifted closer to her belief system. "Connie, my wife, was a blessing, an angel sent down to save me, I think. My wife is Greek and grew up in the Orthodox faith. The children were baptized – and I was fine with that. But I was an Evangelical before the children were born, and she was going to church with me. Then I started to question it. It wasn't fulfilling what I was looking for – and I got curious about the Orthodox faith. My wife did nothing. All she did was tell me, 'Oh, I've been praying for you for years.' We venerate the Virgin Mary – the Theotokos, as they say in Greek. Maybe not quite to the extent that the Catholics do, but we do acknowledge her as a very sacred person. As the mother of God, as the woman who was chosen to bear Christ."

Hillman's faith was manifest on 2005's *The Other Side*, a solo album produced by Herb Pedersen that combined bluegrass familiars with gospel-tinged messages. It was an impressively mature album, most notable for telling changes in the singer's delivery. His voice had seasoned into a gruffer instrument, ideally suited to these songs of old wisdom. Hearing his duet with Jennifer Warnes on 'The Water Is Wide' suggested another possible project – a male/female collaboration along the lines of Gram and Emmylou. But it was the album's familiar opening track, 'Eight Miles High', that caused the greatest surprise. On several occasions, Hillman had returned to the Byrds' catalogue for inspiration, but he'd never attempted anything as audacious as this. Transforming the Coltrane-inspired composition into the country idiom and replacing McGuinn's Rickenbacker breaks with fiddle, mandolin and banjo were inspired ideas. Although the song was structurally the same, it sounded completely different and breathtaking in its new, unfamiliar context.

Revisiting old memories, Hillman chose to celebrate some of his favourite times by undertaking a short reunion tour with the Desert Rose Band in 2008. The get-together proved so gratifying that he decided to repeat the experiment two years later. Pre-empting any comments about his motives, he told the press: "This is not – and I emphatically state this – a career move . . . This is not an attempt to reform a band at all. That's the last thing I would want to do. I speak for every member of this band when I say that we're doing this just because we enjoy each other's company. We have a good time together, and we have no pressure. We aren't making a record, we aren't trying to get airplay . . . It may sound corny but this really is a labour of love. I'm 65 years old – what else am I doing this for?" Hillman later boasted that the group was better than ever, while acknowledging that they were probably the most stable band he had encountered in his long career. "The Desert Rose Band was the end of a long journey. The journey isn't over for me, but the Desert Rose Band was almost perfect . . . No baggage, no problems. Nobody getting into goofing around or anything. The consistency level was 95 per cent [for] live performances. And the country community, God bless them, accepted us for who we were."

With a prodigious catalogue behind him, Hillman cut down his recording schedule in the latter part of the decade. In 2009, he played at a fundraising event for the Orthodox Church of the Annunciation in Nipomo, just north of Santa Maria, California. The show was taped by specialist label Rounder Records for a live album, *At Edwards Barn*. A fairly comprehensive review of his career, it included three Byrds songs: 'Turn! Turn! Turn!', 'Eight Miles High' and 'Have You Seen Her Face'. "I think I'm singing better than ever," Hillman now says. "It took me a long time to learn how to sing. In the Byrds and the [Flying] Burrito Brothers, I really wasn't very good. About the time the Desert Rose Band came along, I started getting a grip on it. I sing every Sunday when I'm in town in the tenor section of this choir, and I think it's really enhanced me. It's so different from what I do, which is bluegrass/folk-oriented stuff, and to sing Byzantine liturgical music is really interesting."

SURVIVORS

Understandably, Hillman remains a small label enthusiast. "For someone my age who has come through 47 years in the music business, what are the options? Unless you're Bruce Springsteen or somebody on that level, you make your own album. You pay for it and try to sell it. At a time like this, when there are fewer retail outlets, that usually means at your shows or on your website."

At the end of 2010, Hillman's health again became a matter of concern when he was required to undergo spinal surgery. The operation proved successful, if debilitating, but his body recovered well and he was soon scheduling more concerts for 2011.

Hillman has carved an enviable career without having to exploit the Byrds' name or rely on past glories to bolster his ego. For all that, he realizes that he can never fully escape the group's long shadow. "I will never get out of the nest as far as the Byrds go," he admits. "If I cured cancer tomorrow I would still be an ex-Byrd. That's OK. I can pick and choose when I want to play now. I never thought I would make a living at this. I thought I would end up going back to college. I'm such a lucky guy to be able to do this."

For Roger McGuinn, the new century was all about pursuing his career as an international troubadour. In 1998, he had toured Australia and New Zealand for the first time as a solo artiste, and his calendar was seldom bare over the next few years. He also served as a custodian for the folk heritage, recording a new song every month for his Folk Den website, while also overseeing the wealth of archival Byrds' product that continued to appear in the marketplace. The reissue package of original albums was completed in February 2000 with the arrival of four more remastered CDs.

The biggest surprise was the unveiling of a previously undiscovered concert performance, *Live At The Fillmore – February 1969*. Taken from three nights (6–8 February) at Bill Graham's Fillmore West, the set was never intended for release. Indeed, the taping was almost accidental, as the Byrds were merely the support act on a bill featuring Mike Bloomfield and Pacific Gas & Electric. Those results appeared on a super jam album for CBS in October 1969: *Mike Bloomfield Live At Bill Graham's Fillmore West*. The Byrds' warm-up set was consigned to the vaults and forgotten by everybody. Even a bootleg of the show was never recorded. The performance captures the group during a tricky transitional phase when they were trying to play both country and rock, as if intent on covering all angles. There were the obligatory hits, three in throwaway medley form, five selections from the just released *Dr Byrds & Mr Hyde* and three country covers that had never been released on studio albums: 'Close Up The Honky Tonks', 'Buckaroo' and 'Sing Me Back Home'. An interesting curio from a largely undocumented period in their concert history, its contents have a hit and miss quality, which is hardly surprising in the circumstances.

Hearing the set, decades on, John York felt a strange ambivalence about the recording. "As an historical document, I enjoyed it. It showed that we were really a kick ass rock 'n' roll band. The energy on that, the vitality and the level that we all played on, was amazing. I'd only been in the band a few months and I wasn't doing a lot of vocal work. The mix I think was done from an historical perspective in the sense that a larger voice is up front and Clarence's guitar is really loud. And I think the presence of the other voices is basically bleeding into his mike. I don't think it's an accurate vocal representation of what the band sounded like because we had a more choral blend . . . Mostly, I remember that the level of musicianship was always the highest."

It is regrettable that this line-up was never recorded as headliners when their energy levels and commitment might have been higher. Over the succeeding months, their performances would improve considerably and, following the arrival of Skip Battin, the constant touring would transform the group into one of America's best live acts of the period.

The Byrds were better captured in all their live glory on the sumptuous remastered version of *(Untitled)* which was extended into an epic 2-CD set, *(Untitled)/(Unissued)*. The bonus tracks included six previously unreleased studio takes and eight new live recordings. Arguably, the most remarkable of these was 'All The Things', a rare example of an alternate take that actually eclipses the original version. McGuinn's chiming Rickenbacker is set against an expressive vocal seeped in world-weary regret. It is a powerful acting job from McGuinn with a greater emotional range than expected. White's String Bender fills every sonic space completing the superior effects. The other highlight is a five-minute studio version of 'Lover Of The Bayou' with some powerful harmonica work from Gene Parsons set against a whiny, interweaving guitar attack. In a classic drama school display, the echo-laden McGuinn sounds like he's auditioning for *Gene Tryp* when proclaiming: "I'm the *king* of the bayou". Towards the end he extemporizes wildly, telling us, "Baron Samedi and me are gonna get you and fry you!"

The remaining alternate takes sound more orthodox: 'Yesterday's Train' features a harmonica lead, which was later replaced by a steel guitar; 'Kathleen's Song' is a slighter rendition than the later orchestrated reading on *Byrdmaniax*; 'White's Lightning Pt. 2', despite its flattering title, is not a classic example of Clarence's dazzling playing, but an extended jamming session in which the rhythm section are equally dominant; finally, there's another fine reading of 'Willin'' to complement the version previously premiered on the box set.

The additional live tracks are also revealing. 'You Ain't Going Nowhere' becomes a showcase for White's stringbending, while 'It's Alright Ma (I'm Only Bleeding)' completes the Byrds' exploration of the second side of Bob Dylan's *Bringing It All Back Home*. The latter song is similar to the arrangement used on the *Easy Rider* soundtrack, with Parsons on harmonica and shakers, assisted by an impressive closing flourish from White. It segues into 'Ballad Of Easy Rider', another less ornate performance, with McGuinn providing some movie dialogue: "Hey, hippie, get a haircut or I'm gonna blow your brains out". Familiar versions of 'Old Blue' and 'My Back Pages' are supplemented by two live recordings of 'Take A Whiff (On Me)' and 'Jesus Is Just Alright' borrowed from a performance at the Fillmore East that was actually recorded after the release of *(Untitled)*. Then we're back to the Felt Forum, nearly seven months before, for some fancy jamming on 'This Wheel's On Fire'. The set ends with a 'hidden' track, 'Amazing Grace', the four-part harmony piece that closed their shows like a prayer of celebration.

The remastered *Byrdmaniax* was more sparing in its bonus tracks. A confident 'Just Like A Woman' with Larry Knechtel's organ playing prominent, is followed by a poignant, acoustic version of 'Pale Blue'. But the great surprise is a cover of Gene Clark's 'Think I'm Gonna Feel Better', recorded in October 1970. Clarence White had appeared on the album *Gene Clark With The Gosdin Brothers* so he attempts the lead vocal on this. Alas, the results are so painfully out of tune that it comes as no surprise that the track was buried until this recent excavation. Finally, the hidden track features a rehearsal with Gene Parsons, Clarence White and his father, Eric, on a pleasant romp through 'Green Apple Quick Step'.

At the time of the album's original release, McGuinn had joined in some of the critical drubbing but, possibly influenced by some of the defensive comments printed in my first book *Timeless Flight*, he was now more charitable. "If you listen to the orchestrations, they're not that outrageous. It's just that Gene and Skip didn't like them and were resentful of the fact that Terry did it without consulting them. But I didn't mind them that much." Tellingly, even Gene Parsons admitted that the album wasn't as bad as he remembered all those years ago.

The final Byrds CBS album, *Farther Along*, allows us a glimpse into that perplexing transitional period in early 1972 when the group were still an ongoing venture, but thoughts were firmly on solo recordings. The Melcher-produced 'Lost My Drivin' Wheel' was later revamped by McGuinn for his first solo album, along with 'Bag Full Of Money'. There's also a chance to hear the original and best version of 'Born To Rock 'n' Roll' which has a country lilt here missing from later attempts. In common with *Byrdmaniax*, the bonus cuts are followed by an instrumental in rehearsal, a sprightly 'Bristol Steam Convention Blues'.

The reissue game continued sporadically for the remainder of the decade. There was *The Preflyte Sessions*, which featured their pre-CBS work now extended to a double album; a deluxe version of *Sweetheart Of The Rodeo*, titled the Legacy Edition which, somewhat contentiously, included the International Submarine Band's work on a Byrds release. Along with Sundazed's 180 gram vinyl releases and the inevitable hits compilations, there was no shortage of Byrds' releases for 21st century customers. Improbably, there was even a second box set, *There Is A Season*, issued in

2006. This work seems to have been created in order to rectify the faults of its black predecessor. Almost all the criticisms voiced in the earlier chapter herein are systematically addressed. The song selections, artwork and production are transformed in an attempt to provide the ultimate box set legacy. The first CD carefully reinstates the classic Gene Clark songs that were scandalously omitted from the 1990 version. Indeed CD 1 seems almost flawless, although the decision to include the instrumental 'Stranger In A Strange Land' seems odd given that it no longer had rarity value having already appeared on the reissue of *Turn! Turn! Turn!*. Considering the compilers had been forced to tape their copy from the stolen masters used on the multi-bootleg *Journals*, they might have been better employed utilizing the still unreleased instrumental 'Flower Bomb Song'. Although the latter only appears in inferior quality on tape, it would seem a more likely candidate than a non-vocal outtake that fans already own. Even 'We'll Meet Again' might have been a more appropriate choice. Such minor quibbles aside, there can be no questioning the quality of the first CD, nor the judicious selection.

As before, the premise of the box set seemed to be based on key principles: ignore novelty, arcane or self-consciously experimental tracks (so no 'Oh! Susannah', '2-4-2 Fox Trot', 'CTA 102' or 'Mind Gardens'); banish the subsidiary Byrds, with the exception of the historically important Gram Parsons and Clarence White, and add any remaining significant alternate takes. After the recent reissue programme, of course, there was little to add. The elusive 'Milestones' is still missing in action, and only a brief bootleg tape from an ABC television documentary (not included here due to its poor quality) currently remains. Instead, hard-core collectors had to be content with some unexciting fare: five 'new' live tracks: 'He Was A Friend Of Mine', 'You All Look Alike', 'Nashville West', 'Baby What You Want Me To Do' and 'I Trust'. Rather more interesting was the round-up of previously issued film soundtrack material, notably the once super rare 'Child Of The Universe' from *Candy* in all its bombastic glory, and the two selections from *Banjoman*. It was also pleasing to see Clark's 'Full Circle' and 'Changing Heart' from the Asylum reunion album. Fans of the subsidiary Byrds, whose contributions were deemed expendable, could have few complaints in terms of the historical importance of the missing material, with the glaring exception of 'Gunga Din', an accepted classic among the group's aficionados, even though McGuinn was absent from the recording.

The one negative aspect of the box could be located in its most important section. CD 2 was the jewel in the crown but the compilers clearly faced a structural problem in attempting to do justice to this all-important period. Cramming the best of *Fifth Dimension*, *Younger Than Yesterday* and *The Notorious Byrd Brothers* on to a single CD inevitably meant that several key songs were omitted. Regrettably, these included the great 'Thoughts And Words' and, most problematically, some selections from *The Notorious Byrd Brothers* which, given its flowing nature, arguably deserved a complete re-run. The awesome 'Change Is Now' was deleted in favour of its crude blueprint, 'Universal Mind Decoder', which made little sense considering that the latter had already been released as a bonus track. Equally odd was the absent 'Get To You' which had not even been included on the previous box set despite its strong reputation and regular appearance in McGuinn's repertoire over the years. It was frustrating that CD 2 could not have run to two or three more tracks which could have been achieved technically without any deterioration in sound quality. The absence of several very important songs was made more vexing by the lighter, often inessential offerings given airtime on CDs 3–4. For all that, *There Is A Season* was a fitting tribute to the Byrds and a necessary response to the previous flawed attempt. Probably its biggest treat was the surprise DVD, featuring ten songs, successfully licensed from various television shows.

While the excavation now seems complete, there is always the possibility of more. An extended and remastered version of the Byrds' reunion album would be welcome, and there is always the likelihood of some additional live material. In 2008, a CD of the Byrds' 1971 appearance at the Royal Albert Hall was released, capturing for posterity one of their more memorable shows of the time. Finding earlier material is more difficult. The Byrds were never taped professionally at Ciro's, nor during the 1965 tour, except for a poorly recorded cassette recording by Derek Taylor at Bournemouth. Most assume that nothing else exists up until Monterey, but there is at least one exception. In September 1966, the Byrds played Hollywood's Whisky A Go-Go with Gene Clark in attendance at some shows. The support act was the Daily Flash, managed by Charlie Greene, whose other clients included the Byrds' old rivals Sonny & Cher and the Buffalo Springfield. Greene was keen to record the Daily Flash in concert and hired a mobile unit for the occasion. He also ensured that the entire Byrds' set was recorded and kept the results in his tape archive. In the late Nineties, while I was completing a biography of Neil Young, he offered to unearth the tape and negotiate its release with my assistance. I failed to follow up on this promptly enough and later learned that Greene had died. The whereabouts of his tape archives are presently unknown, but this 1966 show would be a valuable addition to the Byrds' catalogue.

Inevitably, the release of *There Is A Season* resurrected questions about a possible Byrds' reunion, even though McGuinn had long stated that the matter was firmly closed. Crosby was still interested in the idea and with good reason. He had bought back the Byrds trademark in 2002, even though he had no intention of performing in concert under that name without McGuinn. His goodwill gesture deserved some credit, but any lingering hopes of coaxing McGuinn into reconsidering seemed at best forlorn. "All we would need is a drummer," Crosby points out. "It's just not what McGuinn wants to do, and I can't fault him for that. I think he's a genius, and you just can't have everything you want . . . I probably offended him in some way and he's not willing to forgive, but I wish he were. Roger, Chris and I could make some great music. I'm still really good friends with Chris, even though politically we're at opposite ends of the scale, but Roger and I just sure don't agree at all."

When approached for his response, Hillman played the diplomat. "It would be great to play with Roger and David again and grab a drummer and a couple of musicians, but maybe not. Maybe we can't bring that back. Maybe it should remain a good memory as it was in its original form . . . There were wonderful times. There were some pretty funny times. None of them were that heinous to hold through your life as a reason for not communicating. We should be sitting around and enjoying each other's company and friendship."

Privately, McGuinn lambasted the idea. He realized that he could still be cordial with Crosby and Hillman, as long as he kept his distance. Working alongside them brought back memories of previous conflicts and, despite their best endeavours, there was always likely to be some tensions if they ever undertook an extensive tour. It was far easier to resist the temptation. Besides, McGuinn already had enough work assisting with the various Byrds reissues, both as a co-producer and auto-pilot publicist. In concert, he continued to tell the standard Byrds' biography between songs, as if it was now a folk tale. His role as the group's custodian left little time to consider recording new material.

It was not until 2004 that he at last succeeded in completing a follow-up to the acclaimed *Back From Rio*. The new project had been partly inspired by Terry Melcher. While visiting the producer's home in Carmel to contribute to a Beach Boys' revival of 'California Dreamin'', McGuinn was amazed to see that, instead of the expected multi-track studio, Terry had installed a computer in his living room. Working with a mixing board and microphones, Melcher was able to record an entire album on computer at minimal expense. Always a fan of new technology, McGuinn decided to follow suit and complete his own album, overseeing the production, cover design and distribution.

Limited Edition was welcomed by those fans who had almost despaired of ever hearing new work from McGuinn. In interviews, he spoke with conviction of the shortcomings of major labels and extolled the virtues of computer technology. Unfortunately, the album failed to match the rhetoric. Overall, it sounded rather flat and under-produced. There was a fine version of 'If I Needed Someone', the song that George Harrison had once admitted adapting from 'The Bells Of Rhymney' and 'She Don't Care About Time'. The concert favourite 'May The Road Rise To Meet You', already familiar from *Live From Mars*, was still welcome, while 'Echoes Live', the preamble to the acoustic 'Eight Miles High' was breathtaking. Unfortunately, the newer material, co-written with his wife Camilla, lacked bite or inspiration. Part of the problem was that these songs were already stale, dating back to the mid-Nineties. When recording *Back From Rio*, McGuinn had stockpiled a similar selection of old songs, which he and his producer wisely bypassed in favour of freshly recorded compositions, including contributions from songwriters Elvis Costello and Jules Shear. Without a producer or record company to guide or intervene, McGuinn lacked the motivation to write new material and the album failed to match previous heights. It sounded more like a souvenir release than a serious follow-up to *Back From Rio*.

It was difficult to avoid the impression that McGuinn's true heart lay in his Folk Den project rather than any new solo endeavours. This was underlined in 2006 by the release of *The Folk Den Project 1995–2005*, a four disc collection of 100 songs, carefully chosen by McGuinn. Every month for the past decade he had dutifully added a new song to the Folk Den and for this box set he re-recorded the results in 24 bit rr 1 KHz stereo. It was an impressive feat and further confirmation of his determination to reinvent himself as a folk troubadour rather than an ex-rock star.

While McGuinn's profile was relatively low in 2006, Crosby had one of those years where he appeared to be doing everything at once. There was the acclaimed *Voyage*, a CD box set that celebrated his work from the Byrds to the present day. Although he declined to include anything before 1965, it was still a reasonably comprehensive work which ably displayed his talents as a singer-songwriter. Its release was accompanied by the publication of *Since Then*, a sequel of sorts to his outstanding 1989 autobiography, *Long Time Gone*. Alas, the new work lacked the depth and authority of its predecessor. A series of short vignettes in large print, it was punctuated by Crosby's generally familiar views on religion, politics, the decline of the music business, drug abuse, guns, the Christian right and extended families. As before, McGuinn was not interviewed, although Hillman briefly offered some revealing and provocative asides. The same year saw the remastered re-release of Crosby's first solo album, *If I Could Only Remember My Name*, a work that several commentators, myself included, had long promoted as one of the greatest albums of all time. Crosby was no doubt amused when the

Vatican later included the work in its own list of must have albums.

Crosby's vintage year of solo activity was eclipsed by the headline grabbing reunion of CSN&Y. Neil Young had recently recorded a solo album, *Living With War*, an inchoate, corrosive and passionate attack on the Bush administration. When it came time to tour, Young realized that his former comrades could provide the symbolic power that might capture the public's imagination. Back in 1974, President Nixon was impeached during CSN&Y's summer tour, an event that they transformed into a triumph for the old guard of the Sixties counterculture. Thirty two years later, the quartet were back on the road for the Freedom of Speech tour singing 'Let's Impeach The President' and Crosby's finger-pointing 'What Are Their Names' for a new generation, whose political allegiances were far from certain. Crosby's combination of anger and idealism was perfectly suited to this challenge. He had always been at his best when passionately engaged in a project and remained the all-important fuse for CSN&Y's explosive chemistry. Suddenly, CSN&Y were culturally relevant again in a way that few had heard in decades. They were singing about a different president and a different war, but for a handful of months on the road they captured their time once more. For musicians of their age, locked in a past era in most people's consciousness, this was no small feat. Their tour was not some nostalgic re-enactment of the Woodstock era, but a total engagement with the present. Crosby described Young as a force of nature and the Canadian's message hit home. Suddenly, CSN&Y were topical enough to be featured on the news and their shows had an edge and sense of danger, seldom previously revealed.

Crosby sounded like a superannuated super hero who had suddenly regained his lost powers. "Once we learned the new songs and started delivering them and feeling the power of them, we started believing in ourselves again . . . We could do three hours easily and not play anything except hits. But where that road winds up you're essentially dead and have a key in your back, and that's just not good enough. Having a message is part of the job." A DVD documentary, *Déjà Vu,* commemorated the tour which was most notable for the fierce reactions of disgruntled audience members, many of whom felt CSN&Y were betraying America. It was a revealing snapshot of a country divided. Crosby could never be certain whether they would be greeted with cheers or boos at any given concert but, like a good liberal, welcomed both. "If we didn't piss off anybody, we'd be aiming too low. We are causing people to talk and think things they might not have thought and also expressing ourselves, and we think it's an auspicious time to do that."

With three CSN&Y reunions in under a decade, most people assumed that Crosby was now financially set for life. The quartet's grossing power was extraordinary and more than enough to make them all millionaires for the umpteenth time. However, within three years, Crosby claimed he had again run out of money, for reasons unspecified. His medical bills were no doubt hefty, but the money he had made, even in recent times, should have been enough to allow him to live in luxury for the remainder of his days. The most shocking indicator of his fiscal state was laid bare in 2009 when his beloved boat *The Mayan* was put on sale in Santa Barbara for $1 million. An advert was accompanied by a moving quote from Crosby: "After 40 years of sailing my Alden Schooner, and writing many of my best songs aboard her I have reached that point when I must let her go. She has been recently rebuilt by one of the best shipwrights in America and has been professionally maintained. As a real beauty that can be sailed anywhere in the world, she needs someone to love her as I have."

The significance of this decision should not be underestimated. Even at the height of his drug addiction in the Eighties, Crosby had grimly hung on to *The Mayan* as a symbol of all that was good in his life. It was assumed to be his most precious possession, the more so now that he had a young son whom everyone thought would one day inherit the boat. At the time of writing it has yet to be sold. Crosby's perennial good fortune, often at the height of adversity, may yet save the vessel. Health issues have not prevented him from performing and he continues to tour internationally as part of Crosby, Stills & Nash, whose short-term plans include a covers album produced by the redoubtable Rick Rubin, which is now ominously overdue, feared cancelled. Of the three surviving members of the original Byrds, Crosby's longevity is the most extraordinary and unlikely.

CHAPTER FIFTY

The Reaper's Blade

McGUINN, Crosby and Hillman successfully negotiated the first ten years of the 21st century, but there were already a number of casualties among their old circle. On 7 September 1997, their charismatic former publicist Derek Taylor passed away, aged 65. He had already had a serious stomach operation for cancer and lived with the possibility that it might return. It was only a few months before his death that he entertained me at Apple's London headquarters in what was to be his last interview. Echoing the Beatles' inspired title of one of his books, it had been 20 years since we had last met face to face to reflect on his time with the Byrds. In 1997, as in 1977, Taylor was passionate about the subject, feeling, as always, that the Byrds deserved endless re-examination. He still spoke of them with a protective fondness more becoming of a sometimes exasperated father than an ex-public relations representative. Of course, Taylor was always more than a PR man. He lacked the unctuous insincerity so often associated with the job. Instead, he spoke with a realism that was all the more convincing when you realized the extent of his idealism. When Gene Clark left the Byrds in 1966, the familiar record company tactic was to forget he existed. Taylor, by contrast, sent out a press release extolling his virtues, while marvelling at the Byrds' capacity to overcome his loss. That was Taylor at his best – a writer of reasoned epitaphs rather than a re-writer of history. Everyone that met Taylor seems to have fond memories of him. He had a loveable curiosity about all sorts of subjects and could distract you for hours with reflections on everyday life. When I first met him he was a recovering alcoholic with an endearingly childlike wonder at the methodology of abstinence. "Note the way I hold this glass," he observed, midway through our interview. I watched his hands wrapped firmly around a glass of water. "I hold it tight so as not to spill a drop. See, that's typical of an alcoholic." Twenty years later, he had that same analytical approach to his cancer. He noted with grim humour how it made him more effective in talking business at Apple. He could swear at adversaries without apology, if he chose. More than ever, he appreciated the value of the time he had left and seemed stoical about the future. His friends hoped that he might live for many more years. But it was not to be.

Taylor was fondly remembered for his contribution to the Byrds' early career. He was a central character during that stamina-sapping UK tour of 1965, and enjoyed a treasured footnote in rock history by taping the screams of fans at a show in Bournemouth that were later used on 'So You Want To Be A Rock 'n' Roll Star'. His many articles and press releases about the Byrds were always cogent and insightful. "Derek was remarkable," says Jim Dickson. "Not so much as a publicist, but for what he did in emergencies. He would defend whatever misconceptions he could. He'd jump in the breach whenever the Byrds were accused of something. You saw the legal correspondence over 'Eight Miles High'. Derek was in the thick of that fight. When something like that came up, then he'd be good. When nothing was happening he wasn't always a self-starter. We needed a crisis to see Derek at his very best."

Derek Taylor never lost his love for the Byrds. "I loved them as though they were my own children," he once told me. "But, unfortunately, they weren't as well-behaved as my own children." The family allusion was appropriate for a man who always retained a belief in the importance of home life, even amid the excesses of Hollywood. Taylor had six children and spoke of them with a mixture of fondness and wonder. Derek's marriage to Joan remained intact throughout his life – quite an achievement when you consider the staggering number of divorces that he witnessed in the Byrds and among other of his Hollywood associates and clients.

Despite his hard-nosed newspaper upbringing, Taylor became a celebrant of the hippie dream. David Crosby had first turned him on to marijuana on the way back from England and although he still tended to refer to himself as a drinking man, he increasingly veered towards the pleasure principles of the psychedelic chosen. "My life can be divided into two parts," he told me. "Before I took acid and after I took acid." Twenty years later, I reminded him of this comment and, although less willing to divide his life into so sharp a dichotomy, he admitted that the LSD experience was certainly one of several epochs. "Giving up drink, that would be the third stage," he suggested. "The biggest thing of all probably has been giving up drink and becoming reasonably sensible, considerate and a proper husband. Many people who drank like I did lost their wives and marriages. So I really had it all. I had all the fun and wickedness of boozing and all the confidence and liberation I got from these adventures which I wouldn't have undertaken if I was the sober and sensible man I am now."

Even amid the laissez-faire mid-Sixties, Taylor never lost his capacity to work and was a key player in the organization of the Monterey Pop Festival, which featured several of his favourite performers. Originally scheduled to appear, but famously missing from the final cast list, were the Beach Boys. Taylor had taken over as their publicist during that tricky period between their reign as surf kings and reinvention as nouveau hippie aristocrats. He encouraged them to abandon their striped shirts in favour of hipper garb and eulogized Brian Wilson as the group's resident genius. After the Beatles and the Byrds, the Beach Boys were no easy ride. "The Beach Boys were by far the most difficult because they'd already achieved some success and had seen the crown taken away from them. Yet, here was *Pet Sounds* – as good as anything that had ever been done." Taylor faced one of his greatest challenges in dealing with the mercurial Brian Wilson. "Brian was always on about the question 'Who do you love most – me or the Beatles?' That was very painful because it was always the Beatles – and always would be."

In April 1968, Taylor said goodbye to Hollywood. Fittingly, he staged his farewell at Ciro's, inviting the Byrds along to recall old glories. Although Gram Parsons was now in the group, original member Gene Clark rejoined his former colleagues onstage for an appearance that was shambolic but delightfully dangerous. After the Byrds, the Beach Boys, Monterey and a legion of Hollywood clients, Taylor returned to England to rejoin the Beatles. He became press officer (and much else) for Apple, enduring the chaos and creativity that characterized the Beatles' vision of 'Western Communism'. When the Apple dream turned sour and the Beatles split up, Taylor moved on, this time to Warner Brothers, where he was heavily involved in the careers of friends Harry Nilsson and George Melly. Always a maverick, Taylor was treated as such by the corporation he worked for, glorying in such job titles as 'director of special projects' and 'director of creative services'. After a topsy-turvy career in the early Seventies, he led a more settled life at Brundon Mill, Suffolk. Back then, he spoke of his favourite groups – the Beatles, the Byrds and fellow Liverpudlians Deaf School, whom he was eager to promote.

During the latter part of his career, Taylor undertook a number of writing projects while working at a now more sober Apple headquarters. He was involved in various Beatles-related ventures, including the documentary *It Was Twenty Years Ago Today* and the foursome's *Anthology* series. Ever the idealist, he issued his autobiography *Fifty Years Adrift* as an elaborate limited edition hardback, then declined subsequent offers to issue the tome in paperback. During the early Nineties, there were alarming bulletins about his health, peppered by more optimistic prognoses. Up until the end, he remained positive about the future and, a few months before his death, he told me that he was working on another set of memoirs, tentatively titled *In Sunshine Or In Shadow*. The title was a line borrowed from 'Danny Boy' which he felt summed up his final years.

"I think I may be going into shadow now," he reflected. "When you've got cancer you're very much aware of that. It's all uncertain anyway. How long is it? I haven't been told. They can't say. But it's not forever, that's for sure."

Taylor was one of the best conversationalists you could meet, a weaver of myths and dreams blessed with a psychologist's insight. He knew that all gods were tarnished yet somehow never lost faith in the idea of godhead. "I believed that anyone who didn't like the Byrds needed their head examined. I still believe that. How could that be? I have to claim in utter sincerity wishing to make the Byrds famous for its own sake. I knew that they would be good for people. I think now that if I could give one record to a new generation to say, 'Don't worry about this new stuff that's coming out', I would give them all a copy of 'Chimes Of Freedom' with the words and the music. I think that the Byrds is such a treasure trove for a whole new generation that knows nothing about them. There are millions and millions of musically inclined young and middle-aged people who don't know what they're missing."

Taylor's death was a precursor of many fatalities in the new century. The Grim Reaper was like some dormant destroyer suddenly let leash. Clarence White and Gram Parsons had been taken within months of each other back in 1973, while the deaths of Gene Clark and Michael Clarke were separated by just two years at the beginning of the Nineties. In the early 2000s, the roll call of doom continued. On 6 April 2002, the body of 59-year-old Kevin Kelley was discovered at his home in Sherman Oaks. The cause of death was heart failure, brought on by alcohol abuse. Kelley, the first non-original Byrd to die since 1973, was always the most enigmatic figure associated with the group. Few people were even aware of his musical exploits during the Seventies and Eighties when he played with many great musicians in such jazz and country outfits as the unheralded Fever Tree, Jesse, Wolff & Whings, Last Chance, and Gas, Food & Lodging. Nor was he content to be merely a drummer. Switching to guitar, he hoped to establish himself as a singer-songwriter, but the breaks were not forthcoming. Kelley carefully avoided any cash-in or tribute bands and never once attempted to exploit his involvement with the Byrds. While virtually every latter-day Byrd or Burrito hit the revival circuit, Kelley lay low in LA, oblivious to it all. The Byrds was a subject he seldom discussed, although there was clearly some unresolved deep hurt that he anaesthetized with alcohol and dope. When contacted to discuss the liner notes for an archival album featuring tracks from *Sweetheart Of The Rodeo*, he burst into tears on the phone. One of the sadder footnotes of that incident was he never heard his vocal on 'All I Have Are Memories' which was added to the Legacy version of the album after his death. Kelley's final years were unhappy and dogged by conflict with some former members of the Rising Sons concerning the group's publishing over which he had taken unilateral administrative control. With each passing year, Kelley became more insular and in the end retreated to his apartment, lost in a fog of marijuana. "I wouldn't characterize him as being bitter," says his former bandmate and executor Bill Wolff. "But in the last couple of years he kind of gave up – let's put it that way. Up until then he was really still a fighter and the thing that was keeping him down more than anything was his drinking . . . Towards the end he was eating pretty much chicken – and he drank the cheapest Scotch he could find. But he was very much an idealist and he still had a very strong sense of justice and injustice."

Kelley's body was not found until several days after his demise. Jesse Barish, from Jesse, Wolff & Whings had the unenviable task of sorting out his belongings. "I don't think anybody will know what Bill and I knew because we cleaned out his home and we saw the darker side of Kevin's last year. Bill and I looked at each other and said, 'Holy shit, look at how he was living.' Few had seen his physical decline, the weight gain and the drinking and this serious depression that he went into."

Among those attending a special memorial service in his honour was the Rising Sons' Jesse Lee Kincaid. "He had no brothers or sisters, and he was never married. I think that lonely only child [syndrome] dogged him all his life."

"Kevin was a very sensitive person and an Irishman to the core," adds singer Charlie Taylor, another old friend. "He had a melancholy streak eight miles deep and he never could shake it off, but it was what made him who he was. He was a great friend and felt people didn't always shoot straight with him which hurt his soul."

Fifteen months after Kelley's passing, Skip Battin died on 6 July 2003, aged 69. The oldest of the Byrds, he will always be remembered as a multifaceted player and performer, who first found success as a Fifties pop star, then negotiated the Sixties as a rock 'n' roll everyman, working as an arranger, songwriter, custodian of small record labels, and leader of a variety of pseudonymous groups. He collaborated with Van Dyke Parks, covered Dylan songs, acted in films, experimented with youth serums and never gave up. His grandest ambitions with the Evergreen Blueshoes were unrealized but his perseverance paid off when he was asked to join the Byrds in 1969. There, he established himself as a solid bass player and occasional songwriter. His stage presence enlivened their performances in that crucial period from 1969–72. He always hoped to move on to a lucrative solo career, but instead had to play the bread and butter circuit in latter-day versions of the New Riders Of The Purple Sage, the Flying Burrito Brothers and various Byrds tribute outfits. In the Eighties, he toured with Michael Clarke's ersatz 'Byrds' and after the drummer's death continued in the 'Byrds Celebration'. For a brief time they were joined by his former Byrds' pal Gene Parsons but he soon returned to his guitar workshop in Caspar, California. Battin was also ambivalent about touring and dreamt of retiring to his berry farm in Woodburn, Oregon. It was not to be.

"I believe at this time he was suffering the effects of Alzheimer's but we didn't know it," says his third wife, Patricia. "I thought he was smoking too much pot in the evenings in his studio, so I didn't put it together . . . What a terrible thing to happen."

After the dissolution of his third marriage, the farm was sold and he moved into a mobile home in nearby Silverton. There, he became romantically involved with a neighbour, Peggy Taylor. His final years were blighted by the full onset of Alzheimer's disease and he was latterly admitted to the Alterra Clare Bridge care facility in Salem, Oregon. "From what I understand they were very nice to him," says former bandmate Terry Rogers. "They had pictures of him from different eras of his life and I know there was a picture of me with him. They used to play old Byrds records and there was a piano there. So it sounded as good as that kind of deal can be. Peggy thought a whole lot of all of them and appreciated the way they were treating him and everything."

Witnessing his decline was a sad spectacle, particularly for friends and family. On the last occasion I spoke with him, there were obvious lapses in memory and difficulties in concentration, but he could still surprise you when he focused on a particular incident. His most engaging personality trait was an easy-going humility, all the more surprising considering his early pop star success and worldwide fame with the Byrds. The only Byrd to visit Skip at the care home was Gene Parsons. He was moved by their all too brief reunion during which his old friend could barely articulate his feelings into speech. As Gene was leaving, Skip looked forlornly into his eyes and begged him to take him too. It was a sad end for such a vibrant spirit.

Less than six months later, on 5 January 2004, John Guerin expired from a heart attack, aged 64. He had been suffering from complications following influenza and was in hospital in California at the time. Although technically a Byrd (if we accept that he was appointed before their break-up) he never recorded an album with the group and was only a member for a few months, mostly playing weekend dates. Of course, he was far better known as a session musician and, most notably, as a member of the L.A. Express. In later years, he still played with jazz greats such as Oscar Peterson and Sonny Rollins and contributed to Clint Eastwood's acclaimed biopic of Charlie Parker, *Bird*. Guerin's sudden demise was another reminder that the Byrds were now an endangered species.

Besides the three originals, only two other ex-Byrds remain alive at the time of writing. Gene Parsons toured frequently as a duo with Meridian Green, but since the break-up of their marriage, he has effectively retired from the road. Still living in Mendocino, with his current partner Star Decker, he remains busy in his workshop, but shows no great inclination to record or perform. By contrast, the remaining ex-Byrd, John York, performs more frequently than ever. His involvements with Byrds anniversarians and tribute bands during the Eighties were a mere backdrop to a more interesting parallel career as a musical explorer of world music. His interest in Middle Eastern, Native American and Japanese culture have been manifest in a number of small label or privately released experimental works, including *Sacred Path Songs, Claremont Dragon, Koto* and *Arigatou Baby*. He has also collaborated with Chris Darrow and Kim Fowley, and partnered Barry McGuire on world tours.

On 30 September 2004, Jacques Levy died of lung cancer, aged 69. Since working at New York's Colgate University, where he finally premiered *Gene Tryp* in 1992, he had been involved in several off-Broadway shows. His contributions to McGuinn's career, both in the latter-day Byrds and as a soloist, were considerable. Levy's songwriting invigorated albums such as *(Untitled)*, *Roger McGuinn* and *Cardiff Rose* and when he wasn't available as a collaborator, there was a noticeable decline in quality, which was clearly no coincidence. Arguably, he was the best lyric writer McGuinn ever worked with, which is no small compliment. Famously, Levy received the ultimate compliment when he collaborated with Dylan on *Desire*, the best-selling follow-up to *Blood On The Tracks*. As he had done with McGuinn, Levy brought a cinematic touch to Dylan's lyrics and this was reflected in a panoramic musical setting. He also stage-managed Dylan's 1975 Rolling Thunder Revue, again working alongside McGuinn. Jacques stayed friendly with Roger, long after they ceased working together. McGuinn visited him on his deathbed and sang a selection of *Gene Tryp* songs while Levy lay unconscious while breathing on a respirator. In his final hours, he was taken off the respirator and awoken to say farewell to his wife Claudia and two children, Maya and Julien. Although unable to speak due to his cancer, he indicated that he had heard McGuinn who continued to sing and play this final personal tribute. The creative pair shared some private moments together, saying goodbye for the last time.

Less than two months after Levy's passing, Terry Melcher died on 19 November 2004, aged 62. His involvement in the Byrds' saga has been amply documented in earlier chapters and almost every obituary rightly acknowledged his importance in the creation of the group's two biggest US hits: 'Mr Tambourine Man' and 'Turn! Turn! Turn!'. In the early days, some saw Melcher as slightly square in comparison to the hipper elements in the Byrds' circle. Perpetually defined as 'Doris Day's son', it was always difficult for him to find his own identity. Financial privilege often robbed him of motivation, resulting in several unfinished or abandoned projects. Jim Seiter, who remained friendly with Melcher during and after the Byrds, often felt frustrated by his fatal flaw. "Terry's God-given gift, and Lord knows he rarely used it, was to take a song, play it, and show it to you in a way you'd never heard before. He showed me an old R&B song and played it so differently and so funky, it was amazing. A great arrangement. I said, 'Terry, this is so good.' But don't try to get him to do it again, because he wouldn't. Terry was so talented but he didn't have the desire, need or hunger, so why bother?"

After meeting the Byrds, Terry embraced the counterculture more keenly than is often appreciated, involving himself in Monterey and fraternizing with LA's musical elite. The Rising Sons' bassist Gary Marker, who worked with Melcher during 1965–66, felt that he was often misunderstood and underrated. "Terry was a great guy," he eulogizes. "He was strange in that he was raised in that whole Beverly Hills ambience but we got to be friendly because we'd sit around and smoke dope. I remember Billy James being stunned when I told him we were getting loaded together. He said: 'Terry smokes dope?! I can't believe it.' It seemed everybody resented him and thought he was some rich kid who'd been given a free pass at Columbia Records. It really wasn't true. Listen to those old Byrds and Paul Revere & The Raiders records. He was one of the best mixers in the Sixties when it came to stuff like that. He had the Phil Spector approach. He'd say 'I'm mixing this down for that little crappy speaker that's on your dashboard.' Sometimes when he'd mix it down he'd actually run it through a car speaker to see if the mix sounded good. Every [single] was in mono then." McGuinn also remembers Melcher back in 1965 confidently insisting that stereo was a passing fad.

After the death of his much maligned stepfather in 1968, Terry became more involved in his mother's business affairs. He remained friendly with McGuinn, even after being dropped as producer of his first solo album in the early Seventies. Melcher recorded a couple of solo albums, *Terry Melcher* and *Royal Flush*, which were rich in star contributions, but sold poorly. He enjoyed a tempestuous and hedonistic friendship with Gram Parsons, fuelled by alcohol, music and private wealth. He moved to England for a spell and I visited him at a luxury apartment in Mayfair over Christmas 1977. He had aristocratic tastes and was an excellent raconteur with a piercing eye for detail, plus an excellent memory. His musical knowledge was also impressive.

In the mid-Eighties, Melcher invited McGuinn to his home in Carmel, California, to play on the Beach Boys' album *Summer In*

Paradise. Melcher relived some of his earlier chart glories when the group hit number 1 in the US with 'Kokomo', which he co-wrote. For all that, he knew that he would always be remembered in print for his much regretted connection with Charles Manson. The Manson murders inevitably figured in all his obituaries, incongruously placed alongside Doris Day's name.

Melcher drank heavily for much of his life, underwent surgery for prostrate cancer, but it was melanoma that killed him. There were three marriages – Melissa, Jacqueline and Terese – and one son, Ryan.

Articulate and witty, Melcher could still come up with some great lines, even in his twilight years. He liked to refer to Charles Manson as the second most negative influence on his life, knowing that everyone would demand to know the number one candidate. Twinkle-eyed, without missing a beat, he'd say, "David Crosby". It was a brutally funny quip that various people – from Van Dyke Parks to Chris Hillman – have mischievously repeated with relish.

On 2 May 2006, Eddie Tickner died in Phoenix, Arizona, aged 78. He had led an eventful life and, in common with most of the Byrds, had been through three marriages. The first one, back in Philadelphia, had produced two daughters, Marcie and Karen. After settling in Hollywood and forming Tickson Music with Jim Dickson, he experienced all the highs of the Byrds' golden period. It was Tickner who secured them their all-important residency at Ciro's and brought in his second wife, Rita Rendall, as their bookkeeper. While Dickson was the passionate creative force in the group, Tickner was the unflappable one. He always maintained an emotional distance from the madness and reacted with a stoic, often withering humour when faced with their many crises. After the Byrds, he managed Emmylou Harris and the Hot Band for many years and later helped establish Vern Gosdin in Nashville. Among his long list of clients over the decades were Odetta, Etta James, Country Gazette, Carlene Carter, Nicolette Larson and Jonathan Richman & the Modern Lovers. But it was the various ex-Byrds and their associates with whom he always remained most closely connected. Whether it was putting together a deal for the White/Parsons String Bender, negotiating on behalf of Gram Parsons,

Gene Parsons and the various Burrito offshoots, Tickner was always available.

"Eddie was like a second dad," says Gib Guilbeau, whom Tickner persuaded to resurrect the Flying Burrito Brothers, along with Gene Parsons. "He was our manager for a while and it worked out great. We remained close friends forever, until he died. He was a businessman but if he took you under his wing he'd try and get things going for you – and that's what he did with all of us. Whether it was a solo or a group project, he'd say 'Go and cut something, here's some money. Do it!' He paid for studio time for us to cut demos and he'd peddle them for us. If you had a problem or if you needed to know something you'd call Eddie and he'd tell you the straight of it – and most of the time it was real negative. You'd leave there thinking, 'Man I might as well go and blow my brains out!' He'd start off with the negatives – 'Here's what *could* happen, but the good news is if you want to try it, I'll help you.' One thing I found out about Eddie is that you could never impress him. *Ever*."

During the early Eighties, Tickner married McGuinn's former wife, Dolores, and became stepfather to their two sons, Patrick and Henry. Later, he became particularly close to Henry's young children, whom he would regularly baby-sit. "Eddie's a family man at heart," Dickson remarked to me at the time. "It was the same with his own daughters when they had babies. He was very attentive. He likes anybody that innocent. You don't mind if they con you out of a bottle!"

"The children loved Eddie so much," adds Dolores, "it was amazing how close they were." Tickner had a typically lugubrious take on his role as the chosen grandfather. Back in the early days, he and Dickson fed the Byrds on burgers when money was scarce. As a stepfather, he treated Patrick and Henry to similar outings. That ritual continued, as Dolores remembers. "He was taking Henry's children to McDonald's and he said, 'I've bought hamburgers for *three* generations of McGuinn!'"

Tickner was always modest about his successes and never saw himself as a creative manager or svengali figure. "It was funny," says Dolores. "Eddie used to say 'I always choose the song that's *not* a hit.' If there was a song he liked, they'd always choose the opposite one!"

A few months before his death, I visited Tickner in Tucson and told him that I was diving back into the Byrds' story once again. "Don't do it!" he warned. "Let it go. Leave it behind, be like me." His deadpan humour was still in evidence, but he was noticeably thinner and coughing so badly that he was barely able to eat. Later that evening, Dolores took me aside and revealed that he was suffering from a leukaemia related illness. "He tried to overcome it, but he couldn't," she says. "It started with his lungs and then this weight loss. People didn't know how ill he was. He endured all these medical tests. Poor thing . . . With the lung problems he was really short of breath. Then his white blood cell count rocketed . . . He was on medication . . . By the time the white cell count had gone to normal his kidney function had really deteriorated . . . He was in horrible pain and they finally started him on morphine." His condition deteriorated quickly and he died soon after in a hospice.

"It was good you were able to see him," Dolores adds. She had also contacted his two daughters and brother who visited in those final days. "It was shocking," she says. "Eddie and I were together for 22 years, or more." Even as death hovered, Tickner was still doing business deals, negotiating a contract for Tucson's Hacienda Brothers, whom he had put together with a producer. Joey Stec remembers how Eddie helped his girlfriend Takako Kyo (a former member of the all girl group, the Holograms) even after he became sick. "Eddie was wonderful. He was getting Takako a publishing deal and he knew some company in France . . . He was the man. When they were pulling the plug in the hospital, Eddie was still making phone calls trying to get a deal."

The latter may be a slight exaggeration, but was a testament to the care Tickner took with his clients, including those he simply helped as a favour. As a business manager, he was always highly respected in the industry. "At that time in Hollywood, the sun was shining and the deals being made were righteous deals," Carlos Bernal reminisces. "Everybody was getting money and buying new houses, and everybody was happy."

"Eddie was a real good friend, a mentor," says Gene Parsons.

"Eddie was such a nutball, but a fun guy. He was realistic, down to earth, and a very capable manager who knew the business so well. I kept in touch with him right up until the end. I talked to him two weeks before he died. We always enjoyed each other's company. He was one of the most honest guys I ever met."

Emmylou Harris had once provided a memorable one-liner which *Billboard* and other publications quoted as a suitable epitaph: "I always thought Eddie was going to die of terminal integrity."

The succession of Byrds-related deaths in the new century prompted further reflection on the mortality of its surviving members. It is fascinating to see how they have each undergone some form of spiritual odyssey over the decades. McGuinn had always been a searcher, sampling successive salvation through Roman Catholicism, Subud, acid, hedonism and, finally, born again Christianity. Since the end of the Seventies, he has been consistent in his lifestyle and belief system but carefully avoided any overtly evangelistic comments on record or in concert. He rightly points out that many born again performers move into the insular environs of Christian music, often recording for specialist labels. "That's a big business now," he says.

Despite his fundamentalist beliefs, McGuinn rarely mentions religious doctrine, unless specifically asked. Since the late Seventies, when he joined the Church On The Way in Van Nuys, he has followed the teachings of evangelist Jack Hayford. Among the Church's fundamental tenets are belief in the sacred Trinity, the imminence of the Second Coming, the importance of daily Christian living, and the reality of Heaven and Hell, along with acceptance of eternal torment for those who reject Christ the Saviour. Roger and Camilla's religion has obviously permeated every aspect of their lives. As McGuinn explains: "Our daily devotions consist of reading a chapter from the Old Testament, one from the New, a psalm, and a chapter of Proverbs. We always read the chapter that corresponds to the day of the month. Proverbs chapter 1 on the first, and so on. Then we recite some favourite verses from the Bible that we've memorized and pray for family, friends and nations. It takes from 45 minutes to an hour each morning, but it's a wonderful way to start the day."

Interestingly, McGuinn prefers not to dwell on the prospects of Hell for non-believers At the time of Dylan's conversion, albums like *Slow Train Coming* and *Saved* advocated a fierce evangelism, dividing the world between those who had faith and disbelief. In concert, Dylan was informing audiences that they could rock 'n' roll their way right down to the pit. By contrast, McGuinn held back. "When I came to the Lord I prayed about it. I asked the Lord what he wanted me to do with my music and I got to stay where I was when I was called. I got to stick with the secular side of things."

Dylan's religious wrath burned out quickly, but McGuinn retained his faith and despite a certain wariness about working with unbelievers or writing songs promoting promiscuity, violence or immorality, his performing persona has not radically altered. The rock star ego, which was so prominent at the height of his success and through the early Seventies, left him spiritually bereft and he has avoided any temptations which might take him back there. Instead, he has found contentment in a prelapsarian world of folk music, where he can revisit his past in the role of a touring troubadour. "I feel very fulfilled performing in small to medium size theatres in the United States, Europe, Australia and Asia. Fame isn't important to us. We need just enough recognition to get people to come to the venues. It's a simple and very enjoyable life. Travelling around the world with Camilla is like an endless honeymoon."

David Crosby has had enough brushes with death to reflect on the likelihood of modern miracles, but he retains a defiant agnosticism. Back in 1980, he confidently told me: "Nobody can tell you it's slot A or tab B, you have to find it within yourself." Beneath that proclamation of independence lurked a subtle spiritual dimension which manifested itself in his music. Listening to the meditative chanting on *If I Could Only Remember My Name* it is difficult not to detect the presence of a soul in search of psychic salvation. When speaking to Crosby about his harmonic abilities or love of sailing, the conversation invariably takes a transcendent turn. He believes that those gifts were not learned but inherited or passed on by some vaguely described life force. These were feelings that he articulated lyrically and musically, most notably in his reincarnation ode, 'Déjà Vu'. Over the years, he became what might best be described as a reluctant Buddhist. Pushed on his belief system, and the possibility of a spiritual afterlife, he repeats the words uttered to me decades before, but with less stress on "finding it within yourself". Interestingly, he now speaks of 'God', as if the deity was an actual presence, rather than an imaginative abstraction.

"Nobody's got a pipeline to God. Nobody's holding God's hand. Nobody's got the direct word. Nobody can prove shit. So, I can believe anything I want." That last sentence is quintessentially Crosby with all the rebellious spirit of a modern day Tamburlaine defying deific authority and seemingly willing to take on the gods themselves, if necessary. Given all that, what does he believe?

"I believe we go around again. I guess that means I believe in a God. Don't know which one. Don't know what name. I call him a bunch of different names, some of them are pretty funny . . . In terms of my views on the spiritual world . . . I'm pretty happy about all that. My wife is a practising Buddhist. I'm not, I'm kind of a lazy man's Buddhist, which goes like this: 'I think they're *probably* right.' I like having their stuff around. I like having the images. And I love it when Jan prays. I feel comfortable around that one . . . They tried to raise me as a Christian. I'm not real fond of religions that endorse killing. I have a problem with that . . . If I were in a religion I think it would be Buddhism. But even Buddhism gets stuck in dogma. All religions do."

Chris Hillman's spiritual journey was similar to that of McGuinn, but did not end with born again Christianity. At one time, he was heavily influenced by the example of Al Perkins, but soon moved on. "As far as ever going out and actively pushing an agenda through my music, I didn't do that," he says. "I did make some gospel records back in the early Eighties when I was flirting with the born-again movement, and I found it was not comfortable. I found it to be very judgmental." During the Eighties, Hillman investigated his Jewish roots, then committed himself to his wife's faith and became a Greek Orthodox Christian.

Hillman remains an intriguing and complex character, forthright but reflective in his comments. In interviews, he speaks like a pacifist but even friends admit that he is still capable of angry outbursts that are momentarily all-consuming in their intensity.

Nevertheless, he has shown a willingness to change and to learn from his past. During his Byrds' days, he was seen as a counter-cultural icon, but he now inhabits a universe diametrically opposed to many of its open-minded mores. A conservative Republican who speaks of traditional family values as a panacea for many of society's ills, Hillman regularly rails against the empty self-indulgences of the Seventies, a time when he lost many friends and was seduced by the same temptations prevalent among his peer group.

Hillman's past excesses are the least documented of any of the Byrds but the extent of his hedonism should not be under-estimated. He prefers not to reflect too specifically on the baser aspects of those times, and tempers anecdotes with self-reassuring euphemisms which downplay the extent of his own experimenta-tion. "I did things I shouldn't have, and that I would never tell my children about, and I regret that: but I never went to the point of slobbering in the gutter. I think that's because I had a strong upbringing from my parents. What you get from the age of one to 12 will stick with you for life. So, as much as I messed around, I never went over the edge." When the 'edge' means Gram Parsons, David Crosby and Gene Clark, that certainly leaves an awful lot unsaid. Yet Hillman does not seek to justify his mistakes. He was part of a Sixties/Seventies subculture that promoted and celebrated excess until confronted by the new realism of the Eighties when money was scarcer and middle-aged maturity beckoned.

Hillman's memories of the Byrds now sound arguably the most reasonable in terms of retrospective analysis. Like the others he tells a familiar story, almost by rote at times, but with one crucial differ-ence. Both Crosby and McGuinn have admitted their past faults and offered mea culpas at appropriate moments, but Hillman has gone further when displaying his feelings about the group's troubled history. It is as if he has belatedly learnt new perspectives on past events that have called into question his original motivations and feelings. He has displayed a disdain for the cult of celebrity which his critics might say translates rather too easily into bitter criticism of the cult of Gram Parsons. But that is only part of the story.

At other times, Hillman has shown a commendable respect for the dead which is neither glib nor platitudinous. Cynics may question his change of heart but, almost alone among the Byrds, he has gone out of his way to commemorate the lives of Gene Clark and Michael Clarke. Hillman now understands the past conflicts, and his part in them, more fully and objectively. For many years he had a rivalry with Gene Clark which wasn't always pleasant. He also fell out with Michael Clarke over the Byrds' name and some bitter words were exchanged. Yet, unlike his fellows, Hillman has chosen to revisit those times in search of a more charitable perspective on his fallen comrades. Perhaps he could or should have acted differently when they were alive, but he has not forgotten the dead, and in honouring them he also makes peace with himself.

There is an appealing humility in some of his words that can be quite moving. "To this day, and I'll be the first to admit it, I'd never realized how good Gene was until after he'd gone. As much press as Gram Parsons gets, I constantly remind people that Gene wrote some amazing songs, and lots of them. He used these very interesting word-groupings, which were far deeper and heavier than any of the rest of us could come up with."

That same tone of Christian forgiveness and reappraisal is evident in his more positive comments on the surviving Byrds. "I love Roger dearly. I love David. But, my gosh, we have to forgive each other. And we have to remember what a wonderful time we shared together. In our heyday – in the Byrds – it wasn't as bad as it is today. All of the drug use, and babies out of wedlock. It was still pretty innocent. So I look at the Byrds and what a great time I shared with these guys. And we're still alive. And God bless the two that left. I pray for their souls. I pray that God forgives their sins, that they can find eternal rest . . . I think that Roger is absolutely correct in that we should never work together because it can open up old wounds, so to speak. I would love to do something with him musically at some point in time, and that's a possibility, but if it doesn't happen I'll always have great memories . . ."

Hillman may have a long time to consider a get-together with McGuinn, who shows no signs of performance fatigue. Although fast approaching his 70th birthday, he remains in good health and seems blessed with the genes of longevity. His mother celebrated her 100th birthday on 28 July 2010 and McGuinn frequently cites the example of Spanish classical guitarist Andrés Segovia, who was still touring America just before his death in 1987, aged 94. "I'm never going to think of retirement," McGuinn promises. "I think retirement will kill you. It's a form of suicide, it really is. If you don't keep active and keep your self-esteem by doing something you enjoy and that you get some reward for, you're going to die because you're no longer necessary. So I'm going to keep on doing what I'm doing whether anybody likes it or not."

Epilogue

THE Grim Reaper shows no respect for publishing deadlines. While this book was in the final stages of production, I received the shock news that the Byrds' great mentor, Jim Dickson, had died suddenly at his home in Costa Mesa, California, on 19 April 2011. He was 80 years old. He is survived by his brother, Bob, and sister, Martha.

The story of Dickson's life and times are extensively documented in the preceding pages as well as the accompanying endnotes to this volume. He was 33 years old when he put the Byrds together in 1964 but had already enjoyed an eventful life. Always an adventurer, he'd joined the Army at 15 and served in Japan under General Douglas MacArthur. Dickson was too independent of spirit to pursue a military career and returned to LA where he became a hipster, riding with motorcycle gangs, yet still hanging out with the yachting set in Newport. Dickson seemed equally comfortable fraternizing with drop-outs and socialites, as long as they were entertaining and good company. One of his best friends was the Woolworth's heir Lance Reventlow, another adventurer whose love of fast cars and flying would eventually take his life.

Although not conventionally handsome, Dickson was never short of female admirers. During the mid-Fifties, he married 19-year-old actress Diane Varsi, who was later nominated for an Academy Award. "Jim was very successful with women," recalls an old friend from that time, "and he did it purely by charm. There was nothing manipulative about him. It was just that open smile of his and those twinkling blue eyes. Women just loved him. Diane left him *seven* times – and she came back. She was the love of his life, without a doubt, but she was a restless woman, and a gifted one."

Although largely self-educated, Dickson was fairly well-read and always had a keen interest in politics and current affairs. A self-professed radical, he was also one of the few staunch Republicans in the hip musical circles in which he operated. He had an enduring hatred of bureaucracy which coloured many of his political views. One of his keenest passions was researching his family history, a lineage that reached back to far away Scotland and the Buchanan clan. "George Buchanan was my most famous ancestor," he told me "He was a playwright and linguist. He spoke five languages and wrote in Latin. Our family originally came to Baltimore in 1723."

Dickson stumbled into the music business, almost by accident. After an unsatisfactory period working as a salesman, he met jazz hipster Lord Buckley and became his producer. Always innovative, Dickson briefly formed a record label, Vaya, which issued discs by Buckley, the Page Cavanaugh Trio and singer Jimmy Gavin. After working as a distributor, Dickson decided to abandon the music business in favour of film. He found employment as a freelance sound engineer and cameraman, working with Jack Nicholson on Roger Corman's cult comedy *The Little Shop Of Horrors*. For a time, Dickson also considered a career as a photographer, gaining experience in development at the photo lab of his good friend, Barry Feinstein. Soon, he combined his myriad interests by screening avant-garde films at the Renaissance, a Hollywood club that hosted many of the hipper names in jazz, including Miles Davis, Lord Buckley and Lenny Bruce. "There was no sign outside the club, saying it was the Renaissance," one patron recalls. "It was all word of mouth. The only publicity was the local jazz station announcing that Miles Davis or Lenny Bruce would be playing. Everybody knew something was happening at the Renaissance so there were lines on the street. It was amazing. Jim Dickson was always there."

Dickson befriended all the players and began recording many folk, jazz and bluesgrass acts while also working as a freelancer for independent labels such as World-Pacific and Elektra. His production credits included Hamilton Camp, the Dillards, Odetta, Long Gone Miles, Dian & The Greenbriar Boys, Fred Engelberg, the

EPILOGUE

Modern Folk Quartet, and many more. There were also odd experiments involving a long list of musicians from Red Mitchell to Leon Russell. Many archival recordings were consigned to the tape vault and some were later exhumed, notably the early recordings of the Hillmen and David Crosby.

One notable feature of Dickson's pre-Byrds' career was his prescient advocacy of Bob Dylan, whom he saw as the ultimate source of fresh material at a time when something radically different was sorely needed. "We were all making folk records," Dickson told me, "and it seemed there was no material that hadn't been done 20 times by every college folk group. It was ridiculous. There were no new songs. Then Dylan came up with a couple that were outstanding, like 'Blowin' In The Wind' and 'Don't Think Twice'. I knew he had a whole bunch of them and I thought, 'Wow! This is a goldmine.'"

Dickson featured several Dylan songs and adaptations while working with Hamilton Camp ('Paths Of Victory'), the Hillmen ('When The Ship Comes In'), Dian & The Greenbriar Boys ('He Was A Friend Of Mine') and the Dillards ('Walkin' Down The Line'), to name but a few. But the real epiphany came in mid-1964 when he heard a startling series of still unreleased Dylan compositions, spearheaded by 'Mr Tambourine Man' and 'Chimes Of Freedom'. Dickson was awed by their ambition and the sheer force of their poetry. "That was the end all, the be all," he told me.

When Dylan visited Hollywood, Dickson hung out with him and ensured his entourage were allowed free entry to the Ash Grove. Later, he took Dylan sailing on Lance Reventlow's yacht. Despite his reverence for Dylan's writing, Dickson never fawned over the king of folk. The fact that he knew many of Dylan's contemporaries and inner circle – Ramblin' Jack Elliott, Albert Grossman, Victor Maymudes, Barry Feinstein – ensured that he was always treated with respect. Dickson had many fond memories of Dylan encounters and a number of insights into his working methods. Beneath the genius, he detected an astute observer of trends with a business sense that other contemporaries lacked. "Dylan liked covering his bases," he pointed out. "Peter, Paul & Mary made him more money than his own records did. He knew that. He could hustle as much as anybody else, but he was more subtle about it. Dylan had that manner about him. There was a clever humour that he used and not everybody realized it. I went to a concert in Long Beach with Victor one time and I was watching Dylan closely. When he didn't sing, he'd move over to his guitar mike in the little breaks, play a riff, then move back. I'd set up mikes and knew that he could easily have pulled that microphone over and not had to move at all. But he was making that move in a very determined fashion as part of his staging. He paid attention to subtle detail in a lot of the things he did that many people thought were natural. He was much more aware of what he was doing onstage than any of his peers in folk music at that time. He was more studied. Dylan always had a richer background than people gave him credit for. He'd already had a rock 'n' roll band before he started playing folk."

Dickson's fascination with Dylan was at its peak during the period when he first started working with the fledgling Byrds. Having failed to secure David Crosby a recording deal as a solo, he encouraged him to find a group. When Crosby returned with McGuinn and Clark, the Jet Set were born. They had no interest in covering Dylan songs, but Dickson was adamant. He was obsessed with 'Mr Tambourine Man' above all else. He regarded the group was a vehicle for the song, rather than vice versa. As he told me: "'Mr Tambourine Man' was more important to me than the Byrds at that point." Famously, he even invited Dylan to attend a rehearsal session at World-Pacific, thereby sealing the group's commitment to the song. The rest has been documented at length in the early chapters of this book, but one point is crucial. Without Dickson and 'Mr Tambourine Man', there would have been no Byrds.

Having managed the group during their peak period (1965–67), Dickson was fired by letter on the eve of their appearance at the Monterey Pop Festival. They may have hoped to achieve greater autonomy without his overbearing influence. Instead, they were cursed by internal strife, bitterness, uncertainty and fragmentation. Within a few chaotic months, David Crosby and Michael Clarke were ousted from the group and Chris Hillman left the following year. Further line-up changes occurred under McGuinn's sole

EPILOGUE

stewardship and most observers agreed that it was never the same. Dickson was recruited once more for *(Untitled)* and continued to work with various ex-Byrds, including Gene Clark, the Flying Burrito Brothers and Clarence White. He also produced Country Gazette but there was nothing to equal the success of the Byrds.

Still in his mid-forties, Dickson decided to retire from music management. He retained his publishing interests with partner Eddie Tickner, but was uninterested in pursuing new acts. "In 1975, I took the advice of a cartoon in *Esquire* magazine," he once told me. "It said, 'If people don't like the way things are going, why don't they just get on their yachts and sail away?' So I got on my yacht and sailed to Hawaii."

Hawaii had always been a spiritual home for various Byrds when they were in psychic distress. Michael Clarke set up home there for a time and Gene Clark later recuperated on its islands during the worst phase of his drug addiction. Dickson played the father figure to both of them at various points. After a near fistfight with Clark, he realized that the fading star was seriously strung out. In a magnanimous gesture, he invited Gene to stay at his house in the wake of the McGuinn, Clark & Hillman debacle. Michael Clarke, the inveterate rebel, was another lost soul, impossible to tame, but always likeable, in spite of himself. Sometimes, he revealed a child-like deference towards Dickson which even surprised his first wife. "Robin used to say to me, 'Michael always gets the house straight when you come over. You're the only one he ever does that for. It's like you're his daddy!'"

By the end of the Seventies, when I had completed work on *Timeless Flight*, Dickson was back in LA, reportedly in poor health. David Crosby was the one Byrd who prevailed upon me to speak to Dickson at any cost. "Please talk to him, man," he implored. "It'll be the last act of his fucking life, probably." Crosby always insisted that Dickson knew more about the Byrds and had a greater understanding of their purpose than any of the individual members. "He's more articulate than any of us. You have to talk to him. Just think what he has to say . . ." Crosby insisted that no account of the Byrds' career could claim to be valid, let alone definitive, without Dickson's contribution. On reflection, he may well have been right.

It should also be stressed that Crosby showed remarkable courage and disregard for his own reputation in pushing me towards Dickson as the source of higher truth. That was something Dickson consistently failed to acknowledge or appreciate. Crosby's prognosis about Dickson's likely longevity thankfully proved a severe underestimation. In common with Crosby, Dickson emerged as one of the great survivors in this lengthy saga. His indomitable spirit, aligned to what he called "those good Scottish genes", allowed him to escape the Reaper for another three decades. Over the years, Dickson had agonizing back problems and mastered the art of pain management. He had a minor stroke and a list of other medical setbacks, but never complained and retained a remarkable fortitude, even in his darkest moments.

Dickson distanced himself from several of the Byrds at various times, yet he could always be relied upon to bring them back together unexpectedly. Such was the case in the early Seventies when he produced Gene Clark's 'She's The Kind Of Girl' and 'One In A Hundred'. In 1987, while overseeing the archive album *Never Before*, several of the originals agreed to assist with various tracks. Hillman and Crosby provided the greatest input, forging strong links with their former mentor along the way.

Not long after, Dickson disappeared to the unlikely environs of Waldport, Oregon. I visited him there to conduct a week's worth of interviews. He had a limp but was otherwise mobile and the recent excavation of Byrds' material had sharpened his memory of past recordings. He smoked incessantly and the television was a constant backdrop at most times of the day. The sense of a man in weary retirement from the music business was emphasized by the décor which was devoid of memorabilia. Dickson had no gold discs on his wall. Indeed, he had no records in the house at all. Most remarkably, there was no record player or tape recorder on the premises. It was as if he'd had his full quota of music and required no more.

On a nearby table lay David Crosby's recently published autobiography, *Long Time Gone*. Within its pages, Dickson had criticized Crosby for damaging his reputation in the music business, but there were also fond accounts of their seafaring adventures and the moving story of how a shared love of sailing had brought

EPILOGUE

reconciliation. Of course, some of the negative feelings would reassert themselves at different times, but such was the volatile nature of their relationship. We compared 'dedications' in our respective copies of the book. In mine, Crosby had written "Your knowledge is amazing", although more recently we'd had what I considered a playfully heated debate about an unearthed tape titled 'Psychodrama City' which Crosby was in denial about for some strange reason. Dickson's dedication read (from memory): "You have contributed a great deal to my life". It was a heartfelt tribute, but Dickson couldn't help detecting a less empathetic undertone. "Well, I'm glad I did something with my existence on this planet," he joked. "It wasn't all wasted. I contributed to David's life! Hey, I did something."

Even in Waldport, Dickson could not escape the Byrds. He was always preparing royalty statements, which made for interesting reading, and chronicling the progress of various licensing deals for *Preflyte* and other old recordings. Eddie Tickner was a regular caller, as was a newly sober Gene Clark, full of plans to write a book in imitation of David Crosby. Dickson passed him over to me for lengthy conversations, with Clark in uncharacteristically revealing mode. There were amusing tales about Michael Clarke too, who was also likely to call at any time. The relationship with Hillman and Crosby could be hot or cold, depending on the moment, while McGuinn was a distant but respected presence.

Dickson tried to treat them all equally, although that was never an easy task. They rose and fell like shares on the stock market. At this particular moment, he seemed somewhat closer to Clark and Clarke, probably because he felt they needed some support now that McGuinn, Crosby and Hillman were intent on promoting themselves as the original Byrds. Dickson had no strong views either way but usually tended to favour the underdog or the ostracized. Later, he expressed his disappointment that the three had not invited Gene Clark to participate in the 1990 'reunion' recordings in Nashville used on *The Byrds* box set. Earlier, he had told me how he felt McGuinn and Hillman had no right to fire David Crosby, despite his transgressions. His views seemed tempered by a strong sense of justice. Perhaps if Dickson had not been ousted in 1967, he might have prevented Crosby or Clarke from leaving the group. But those are like speculations from an imaginary parallel universe.

The early Nineties ended any dream of the original five reuniting for a concert or recording session. Clark died suddenly at his home and, 19 months later, Clarke succumbed to liver disease. It must have been a strange feeling for Dickson to witness the demise of two of his protégés, the more so considering his own precarious health. "McGuinn seems to survive all right and is healthier than the rest," he told me at the time. "I was shocked and very upset to hear about Michael. He was always the most genial, the easiest to get along with and the least pretentious. He was sort of my favourite."

Dickson could be both tough and sentimental, sometimes in the same paragraph. He was aware of Gene Clark's tragic potential and found it difficult to confront the darker aspects of his life story. "I was back living in North Hollywood when Gene died," he told me, "and I found out the next day. You know all about the subsequent fall-out and the bitterness. I escaped all that. I couldn't bring myself to read the lengthy eulogies you wrote about Gene and Michael. Earlier you'd described Michael dying in his mother's arms and I already had tears in my eyes. I couldn't read on. I thought, 'I can't face this.' I knew it would be too upsetting. Maybe that's a compliment to how coherently you led me through that process. My impulse was to sit down and write you a letter and then I started putting it off."

At various times, Dickson moved to Nashville and Tucson, where Eddie Tickner resided. In 1997, I found him back Hawaii, fishing on the island of Maui. "I'll probably go back to California someday," he said. "I've had a stroke since I last saw you and I don't want any more stress in my life, that's why I came here to fish. I want to survive." As part of his recuperation, Dickson elected to remove two crucial characters from his life whom he now saw as detrimental to his psychic health and blood pressure. "David Crosby knows now that I'm very hostile to him. I don't ever want to see him or Chris Hillman again. I've had enough of them in my life and I just don't need it. No good will come of any of it. I send them cheques but I don't talk to them or do anything. I'm

EPILOGUE

comfortable with that now. It's been a long time." He added that he wished them both well in their careers, but felt relieved to be away from all the old dramas. It was all too stressful.

Dickson's relationships with the surviving Byrds were fascinating to unravel over time. He had known them since they were teenagers or young men and had watched their progress, interaction, triumphs and foibles with a combination of humour, anger and amazement. Although he was no longer in contact with Crosby, he still seemed sensitive to his media outpourings and private observations. "When David was angry with McGuinn for going out as the Byrds without him, he'd say the whole thing was Jim Dickson's idea and McGuinn didn't really have much to do with what the Byrds were about. Well, that's not true, either. In another interview I heard him say, 'Well, the only thing Jim did was tape us and let us listen back to see what we could do.' You get all these different versions and it's whatever suits his purpose at the time he's talking."

The above was terribly unfair to Crosby, who had always been a great supporter of Dickson, even though he had made the mistake of precipitating his departure from the Byrds. Judging Crosby from some edited soundbites heard on a radio or printed in a magazine seemed harsh. I argued that point with Dickson on various occasions, always stressing Crosby's good intentions. Dickson was unsympathetic. His opinions were no doubt coloured by memories of past conflicts, but he took some of my objections on board. He admitted that David was the Byrd he loved *and* hated the most. Theirs was a friendship based on intense emotion, which explained a lot. In more reflective mode, Dickson admitted to me: "I used to think David was devious and Machiavellian when he'd come up with all these stories but now I think he says what he wishes it was in the current time. There is the justification. David Crosby did more damage and injury to me than all the rest of them put together in specific ways. What I've discovered about David is that he'll say whatever he has to say to make his case. In a month from now he might say something completely different if it suits the case that's in his head at the time. He doesn't always try to think back and work out what actually happened because he's seen different versions of everything as his motivations change. I suspect he doesn't quite know what really happened, but he might do if he searched his head."

Crosby's more intemperate comments about Terry Melcher or Gary Usher probably underline Dickson's point about him speaking uncharitably, but he could also be incredibly sympathetic and caring. Passion was always his watchword. "David has all these pieces in his head and he sometimes puts them together in weird ways. You pointed that out on at least one occasion, and you were courageous to do so. I don't think he'll thank you for it. David can be very charming, as you've always claimed. He's the biggest asshole I ever met but he has been remarkably charming. When he wants something, he's just amazing. He can charm the pants off everybody. I've witnessed it, and so have you. He can tell you you're the greatest writer that ever lived and then you can become the worst writer that ever lived. And you know you're not either one!"

Dickson's interaction with McGuinn over the years was mild as milk by comparison. By the end of the millennium he was pleasantly surprised to discover that he felt very comfortable socializing with McGuinn on the rare occasions that they met or corresponded. In many ways, it was the complete antithesis of the intense relationships he had experienced with Crosby and Hillman over the decades. McGuinn was the Byrd that he'd felt least closest to during his tenure as manager, but now this was working to their mutual advantage. Roger's emotional detachment ensured that there was never any danger of conflict or angry misunderstandings. Everything was calm.

Dickson's association with Hillman was the most complex of all his relationships with the original Byrds. It had been characterized by a constant seesawing of emotions over the years. They had worked together on many projects, from the third Flying Burrito Brothers album to Hillman's 1984 solo work, *Desert Rose*. Dickson had also encouraged his charge during the early days of the Desert Rose Band and gained his full support in the initial stages of compiling *Never Before*. But there always seemed a big price to pay, which constantly tested their friendship. Somewhere along the line there would be a massive fall-out, followed by caustic comments, recriminations, periods of exile and then reconciliation. Contrition and forgiveness were also an important part of the dynamic. Sometimes Dickson was mystified by these patterns of behaviour but later came to realize that they had deeper connotations, emanating from Hillman's adolescence. Playing the psychologist, Dickson maintained that he had become a receptacle for the suppressed anger that Hillman felt towards his own father, who had committed suicide during his youth. By adopting the paternal role in the Byrds, Dickson believed that he had triggered something in Hillman's subconscious that ultimately produced anger and conflicting emotions on a strangely cyclical basis. That, at least, was Dickson's theory and the primary reason why he ceased contact with his charge for years and years. He wasn't bitter, simply weary of the emotional rollercoaster.

In May 2006, Dickson's long-term business partner, Eddie Tickner, passed away. Dickson was now back in California, living in an apartment in Costa Mesa and about to have laser surgery to remove cataracts on his eyes. "Somehow, I'm surviving," he told me. "I broke my back twice and they snapped it together pretty good, but I don't walk so well." He took the news of Tickner's death badly. "He was sick for a while, but I didn't realize it was that bad. I miss him. I still talk to Dolores. For a while we were talking on the phone every two days." As well as Dolores, Dickson was also in contact with McGuinn's current wife. "I've had lots of talks and long emails with Camilla," he explained, in almost grateful surprise. "I was rehashing that whole period and she was amazed about what I'd done before the Byrds. Evidently, McGuinn and Camilla met at an acting class and when I said, 'Did you know my first wife was Diane Varsi who had an academy nomination for her first movie?' that opened up a whole other thing. Camilla was intrigued with all that history and how I'd introduced Stanislavski to McGuinn and how I related to other people and their careers. The emails had a lot of questions from Camilla and some from McGuinn, but he didn't have too much to say. He didn't know lots of stuff that went on. I recalled how I went to him for help on the day we were having trouble on the beach filming, and he didn't want to get involved. He'd just say, 'I trust everything will turn out all right'. I told Camilla that and she was astounded! . . . I was never very close to

McGuinn. I don't think anybody ever was though. Camilla called me the 'godfather' of the Byrds and asked if that offended me. I said, 'You can say whatever you want.'"

Camilla was sufficiently intrigued to include a brief but impressive profile of Dickson on her blog at McGuinn's Folk Den website. Dickson seemed secretly pleased that he could implant some new memories into McGuinn's computer brain, correcting Byrds' history in the process.

There was other good news in 2006. After more years than either could remember, Dickson and Hillman were back in contact. Kind words were exchanged and Hillman even visited his former mentor in Costa Mesa. There was a humorous edge to the proceedings as Hillman dealt with his mixed emotions, but the outcome was positive. "Chris talked about the past with remorse," Dickson told me shortly afterwards. "He apologized a lot saying 'we shouldn't have caused you so much trouble' and 'we were kids and we screwed up'. He'd got to thinking about how I'd had to spend so much time trying to keep them together that it was hard to work on various projects." Above all, Hillman seemed to regret that he hadn't had the maturity at the time to "keep the other members in line when it was necessary". It was gratifying to hear that the estranged duo had finally reconnected. But would it last?

Dickson was also a little more positive about Crosby at this point, although there was still no communication between them. David's exploits over recent years were a constant source of discourse among Sixties' survivors. His much publicized sperm donation to lesbian couple Melissa Etheridge and Julie Cypher had been a major news story at the beginning of the new century and now Dickson had a chance to hear Hillman's views on the matter. "Chris surprised me a little bit, but we talked about it. He was a little careful. He didn't say a lot, but he didn't think it was a good thing that David had done. I have no particular judgement about it." Like everyone else, Dickson seemed most amazed by Crosby's capacity for survival. Who would have predicted that David would still be making headlines in the 21st century?

Dickson's energy levels could always be measured by the degree of his indignation with the music industry. When he was involved

EPILOGUE

in a paper trail over licences or suffering problems with record label bureaucracy, his temper was always close to explosion. "I've been trying to call you for months," he told me in early 2006. "I was ready to sink the British Isles over Poptones." Evidently, there was a communication problem with the indie label, which needed resolving and Dickson felt I could help. That was nothing compared to his anger with EMI, who had told him that they would only communicate with Eddie Ticker over statements involving Country Gazette. Dickson explained that Tickner was dead and the contract was with Tickson Music, but it proved to no avail. "I wanted to hang them in the square", he railed. Some of his tribulations were almost comical. Sony were taken to task for producing prolix paper work which was impressively detailed, but unwieldy. "The last statement they sent me it cost them over $100 to mail it. I could hardly carry it to the car with my bad back. Getting it into the house was a problem, it was so heavy. They listed every song by a master number that didn't tell me what the song was. A reconciliation sheet would have been enough."

The frustration with record companies even extended to his own projects, the latest of which was an archival album manufactured by his friend John Delgatto of Sierra Records. Dickson had chosen Delgatto as the custodian of the recordings that remained in his possession, including unreleased Clarence White material, the original 'lost' mix of Gene Clark's *Roadmaster* and various other tapes that have yet to be fully catalogued. One project they completed together was *Sixties Transition*, a compilation of Dickson's work in the years before the Byrds. "It's like a transition from folk to rock, with elements of both," Dickson explained. He hoped to license many rare recordings, including some of the folk/harpsichord experiments undertaken with Leon Russell during the World-Pacific days. "There were also some Hamilton Camp outtakes that were good performances but we were unable to get those. I've never worked on an album that was so frustrating or difficult to put together." Eventually, they decided to release what they could and came up with a compilation featuring material by the Byrds, the Hillmen, David Crosby, Dino Valenti, Dian & The Greenbriar Boys, the Dillards, the Gosdin Brothers, and more.

After numerous delays, it emerged in the autumn of 2007, albeit with limited distribution. One of the surprises was the previously unheard 'Charisma', credited to Bud Shank and David Crosby, and Hamilton Camp's version of 'The Times They Are A-Changin'' which used a rejected backing track originally recorded by the Byrds. "I asked McGuinn's permission," Dickson told me, "and he said, 'Well, if you give me credit you can use it.' Chris was happy too because we were on good terms for the first time in many years. That track brought up memories of Michael. I made a couple of mixes and sent Chris a copy to ask his opinion. He said, 'Is that really Michael? He's playing so good on that.' Chris was upset that he didn't play like that all the time. But I knew Michael had considered that session very seriously. He knew it might be a single and didn't want to make a mistake. It was the same day we did the RCA versions of 'Eight Miles High' and 'Why'."

Dickson was spared the task of asking for Crosby's permission as he had absented himself from the recording. "He'd walked out of that session", Dickson reminded me. On reflection, it was regrettable that Dickson did not contact Crosby as it might have provided the impetus for a long overdue rapprochement. They had shared so much together and survived so many health scares that it would have been fitting to rediscover a new friendship in the autumnal years of their lives. It would have been a great ending to this story. But it was not to be. Crosby already had bigger issues to deal with, and as he had once told me: "Human lives don't go in parallel directions."

In the spring of 2009 I spoke to Dickson once more and learnt of new developments, not all of them positive. "My life's not too bad for somebody who's having a hard time getting around," he said, with stoic assurance. "I can only walk a little bit at a time now and can't stand for very long. I crushed another vertebrae and had to go back for spinal surgery. I'm in worse shape now than when we last spoke. I've got to use a wheelchair for certain things but I can still drive my car and get to the post office. When I go to supermarkets they have an electric wheelchair which I can use if I want, so it's working out."

One confrontation that seriously rattled Dickson came from

EPILOGUE

a familiar quarter. "I had a big row with Chris Hillman," he confided. The complicated circumstances are best saved for another chapter or obituary, but Dickson was shaken by the intensity of it all. Hillman's extended rant was a testament to both his oversensitivity and failure to control his temper. "It was a Chris that I thought was long gone," Dickson recalled with a shudder. He insisted he had no intention of upsetting Hillman and was angry enough about the matter to end their association, but decided to maintain a delicate peace. "I went many years without talking to Chris and it didn't hurt me any," he concluded. "I don't care." Thereafter, they retained a cool but cordial email relationship. As far as I know, they never spoke again or met in person. When Hillman underwent spinal surgery in 2010 Dickson was understandably empathetic and sent fond wishes for a speedy recovery. Hillman was gracious, acknowledging that his own pain was inconsequential in comparison to Dickson's daily grind. The compassionate words were a welcome reminder of better times.

Perhaps it was the contretemps with Hillman or merely passing time, but there seemed a more forlorn aspect to Dickson's personality by early 2009. "I'm 78 now, and I don't really care any more," he told me. "I like to get my royalties that are due. Other than that, I'd rather not think about the Byrds. To me it's all a sleeping dog. When I had my 78th birthday I realized, 'I'm an old man now.' Almost every one I've ever known has already died. There's only two or three of my old friends left." Dickson sounded in need of a friend. As if on cue, an obscure figure from his distant past reappeared to rekindle an old camaraderie.

Singer Jimmy Gavin had been a close friend of Dickson's during the mid-Fifties. Signed to Epic, he had recorded what Dickson considered a groundbreaking experiment in folk rock, 'Johnny Rolling Stone'. An album, teasingly titled *Early Jimmy Gavin*, had also appeared on Dickson's imprint, Vaya Records. Gavin was a familiar face at the Renaissance and enjoyed many adventures with Dickson, including a memorable sailing trip during which they were stranded in Tahiti, only to be rescued by that gallant adventurer Lance Reventlow. Gavin was an early advocate of Subud (later changing his first name to Weston) and a well-travelled individual. He relocated to New York and, by the time the Byrds were breaking big, had moved to London. Over the years, he'd lost contact with Dickson, married, quit the music business and found work as a stone contractor. He thought his singing days were over when he was diagnosed with throat cancer, but pulled through. When his wife was offered a job in Orange County, Gavin decided to track down his old friend.

After attending a Roger McGuinn concert in Virginia, Gavin was introduced to Camilla, who passed on Dickson's number. The retired singer was thrilled to discover that he was living less than 30 minutes away from his former comrade. "That's how we got in touch again. I spent one day every week with Jim for the last two years of his life. I'd stay there all day and I deserve a medal because his house was brown with tobacco. He was a chain smoker and I don't smoke. We got into this routine where I brought my guitar along. I'd had radiation treatment after which I could barely speak for a year, much less sing. When I went to see Jim my voice was just starting to come back. We fell into a lot of reminiscences because we'd had many adventures together. He was still as sharp as a tack."

Gavin confessed that he hadn't performed in public for over 20 years but was ready to return to the concert platform, if the opportunity arose. "I used to have an extremely powerful voice, but it wasn't powerful any more. A classical musician once said, 'Sometimes you have to work with what you have left.' Jim worked with me on repertoire and performance and restored my belief in myself as a performer. We started focusing on songs that you could call 'timeless'. I knew hundreds of songs and, as Jim said, I'd just get up and do a set from what came into my head. Now, every song I do is hand-picked. I've never been surer of myself and it's all Jim's doing. He gave me back my self-confidence and I'm eternally grateful to him."

Dickson mentioned Gavin a lot in conversations during this period and was keen for me to hear his work and learn more about his memories of Hollywood in the Fifties and Sixties. In many ways, he was Dickson's last connection to an era almost lost in time. Memories of old escapades suddenly infiltrated Dickson's dreams. He had vivid reveries of his time sailing his beloved boat, the *Jubilo*,

EPILOGUE

a vessel that symbolized all his youthful dares and dreams. Now he was virtually immobile, a prisoner in his rented apartment beyond whose walls he seldom ventured.

On 17 January 2011, Dickson celebrated, without ceremony, his 80th birthday. It proved a troubled month. He was now permanently locked in his wheelchair and had suffered a serious fall, leading to hospitalization. I spoke to him when he returned home and he was happy to be back to his independent routine. His brother, Bob, visited every week and helped him with groceries and other chores. Gavin had just moved back to London, thereby ending the weekly routine that had revitalized Dickson over the past couple of years.

The last time I spoke to Dickson was less than a month before he died. He asked me to send him a personal report on President Obama's visit to Ireland. He still liked to keep up with all the political news. Even in his final years, he was a fantastic font of untold stories. I'd excavated all his memories of the Byrds during countless conversations and interviews over the past three decades, but he could still surprise you with reflections on some of the subsidiary characters in the story. There were illuminating tales about Dennis Hopper's extraordinary exploits, memories of Bob Dylan that you never found in any of the standard biographies, plus lovely vignettes about the romantic conquests of Gene Clark and Michael Clarke, the history of Hollywood clubland and its unheralded heroes like Benny Shapiro, the strange fate of Vito and the Ciro's dance troupe, memories of aristocratic encounters with the millionaire Lance Reventlow, entertaining interludes about 'Butchie' and her pet Bengal tiger, baby lion, chimpanzee and cheetahs . . . and so much more. Dickson was a wonderful source for such knowledge, which he always imparted with an historian's eye for accuracy. In a world of recycled information it was always exciting to hear a voice that dared challenge conventional opinion with such conviction and authority.

Dickson's death came as a shock, partly because few were aware it had happened. Phone calls were unanswered and his email account was suddenly disconnected. Evidently, he had fallen off his wheelchair and bled to death on the floor of his apartment from an internal injury. John Delgatto broke the news to me in a moving note: "Jim sadly died alone and was discovered days later by his brother. He has been cremated and his ashes will be spread out to sea which I know he wanted. I am so sick, sad and can't stop crying."

Delgatto had only learned of Dickson's demise after reading a short notice in a Los Angeles paper on 1 May. Bob Dickson had been unable to locate any address or phone book in his brother's possession, so many former friends only discovered the news weeks later. Tellingly, the main obituary to appear in London was published more than two months after the event, an absolute age in the world of death notices. There was a lot of pressure to clear Dickson's apartment promptly and a wealth of paperwork, including old contracts, legal documents and other correspondence, was simply thrown away. It was a sad end to a remarkable life.

Back in London, Dickson's friend Jimmy Weston Gavin, recently returned from a visit to Pakistan, was puzzled when his emails to Dickson came back with the words 'failed' followed by the non-explanation, 'technical'. He phoned me for further details and belatedly discovered the bad news. Reflecting on recent events, he wrote a moving eulogy which also serves as a suitable closing paragraph to this first volume:

> Technical? Yes, it was technical. Nothing personal. Another machine shutting down. Pull the plug. Contribute the wheelchair to the charity shop. Pile the rest in the dumpster. The human magpies will sort through it. But mainly it would be black garbage bags tied around a lifetime of photos, pizza delivery menus, bills, bank stubs, a mountain of CDs, undecipherable cardboard boxes of paper, some royalties. A man who had sailed the high seas tied himself to the mast, swallowed uppers, manned the wheel through towering cliffs of wave, sang every country song he'd ever heard, while the doctor and the rest of the crew, convinced that they were doomed, cowered below. The all too usual four days alone in that tobacco stained apartment before anyone knew that he'd caught a good wind out past the harbour lights.

NOTES

Epigraph

page v: "Even such is time . . ." The poem was accompanied by the words: "These verses following were made by Sir Walter Ravleigh the night before he dyed and left att the Gate house". As it turned out, this was not entirely true. The verse was borrowed from an older stanza to which Ralegh had added the final two lines, thereby transforming the meditation into an affirmation of Christian redemption. The epigraph serves several purposes for this book. There are numerous references in the main text to the 'Elizabethan' qualities of the Byrds' early recordings, so it seems appropriate to include a verse from one of the greatest and often unheralded poets of that age. Back in 1989, I was in the middle of an intense interview with the Byrds' former manager Jim Dickson during which we were discussing Gene Clark, Elizabethan madrigals, and the significance of McGuinn's mantra "I trust everything will turn out all right". I recited 'Even Such Is Time' from memory, explaining that it was both Elizabethan and included more than one reference to the word "trust". It also alluded to 'time', which led us back to 'She Don't Care About Time', 'Set You Free This Time', 'a time to be born and a time to die' (from 'Turn! Turn! Turn!'), not to mention the title of my first Byrds' biography, *Timeless Flight*. Dickson nearly fell off his chair. "You have to send that to McGuinn," he told me. "He could turn that into the perfect Byrds song." A few years before, McGuinn had put music to the poem 'America For Me', which proved one of his better songs of the early Eighties. Dickson agreed that 'Even Such Is Time' would be far better. Notice how the poem actually ends with the words "I trust". In line two, it includes the image of time as a kind of unscrupulous banker who places our youth and joys into a trust fund which pays us only with age and dust. The tomb encloses us like the slamming shut of the pages of a biography. In the final couplet, Ralegh transforms what was originally an almost atheistic observation on passing time into devout submission. Scholars have debated the inclusion of the comma in the final line, which may have been a printer's addition. Its presence or otherwise transforms the poem. Minus the comma, it reads as an unambiguous affirmation of resurrection as part of God's grace. But the alternative "The Lord shall raise me up, I trust" suggests hesitation and doubt from the narrator about his worthiness and prospects of eternal life. I prefer the latter which has a darkly humorous undertone, more in keeping with what we know of Ralegh's personality.

Speaking of passing time, I never did send the poem to McGuinn or anyone else connected with the Byrds. Maybe I should do.

Chapter 1: The Secret Origins Of The Byrds

page 23: ". . . Chicago's Old Town School Of Folk Music . . ." The school, located on North Avenue, Chicago, was a non-profit institution founded in November 1957 by Win Stracke and Frank Hamilton. McGuinn enrolled the following October by which time he was playing guitar at one of the coffee houses with a group called the Frets. Frank Hamilton subsequently replaced Erik Darling in the Weavers in September 1962, staying until the following July. During that period, he continued to teach at the Old Town School. There were a number of musicians who achieved success after attending the Old School, including John Prine and Mike Bloomfield. McGuinn remembers teaching Bloomfield how to bend a string for the first time.

page 23: "I was a little shaky . . ." Roger McGuinn, interviewed by the author. London/Florida: 22 May 1997.

page 24: "Fully embracing the West Coast experience, McGuinn relocated to San Francisco . . ." In various interviews, McGuinn has indicated that he auditioned unsuccessfully for the Kingston Trio during this period (summer 1960) as a possible replacement for Dave Guard. However, Guard did not resign from the Kingston Trio until April 1961 and stayed with them until as late as November, when he was replaced by John Stewart.

page 24: "Somebody in John F. Kennedy's . . ." McGuinn, record company biography . . ." *c.* 1976

page 25: "They wouldn't let me sing . . ." ibid.

page 25: "The big band would take a break . . ." Roger McGuinn, interviewed by John Tobler. London: 14 June 1997.

page 25: "He was a great influence on me . . ." McGuinn/Rogan: London/Florida: 22 May 1997.

page 26: "While there, McGuinn and co-writer Frank Gari came up with a Beach Boys pastiche entitled 'Beach Ball' . . ." The City Surfers issued two singles for Capitol: 'Beach Ball' b/w 'Sun Tan Baby' and '50 Miles To Go' b/w 'Powder Puff'. While in New York, McGuinn continued to

NOTES

co-write with Kenny Young and Arty Resnick, but there were no more hits to his name.

page 26: "I wouldn't say that was a responsible part of my life . . ." ibid.

page 26: "I don't even remember writing them . . ." ibid.

page 27: "The way to start off . . ." ibid.

page 27: "I was exempt . . ." ibid.

page 28: "What we need is four of *him* . . ." ibid.

page 28: "I had been mixing the Beatle beat . . ." ibid.

page 28: "I'm just doing the Beatles . . ." ibid.

page 28: "No, what *you're* doing . . ." ibid.

page 30: "Gene and I actually started it . . ." Roger McGuinn interviewed by Pete Johnson. *Hit Parader*: September 1968.

page 30: "I used to make a joke . . ." David Crosby, interviewed by the author. London: 22–23 April 1980.

page 31: "When I started playing music . . ." ibid.

page 32: "Jim Dickson (b. 17 January 1931, Los Angeles, California) . . ." Précising Dickson's pre-Byrds career into a single paragraph leaves out much of the story. As he told me: "I never had any intention of being in the record business. Lord Buckley put me in the record business. Before that I went into the Army at 15. I got out young, got a motorcycle and for the next three to four years, I hung out in motorcycle gangs. We were riding other guys' motorcycles. I finally got tired of having dirty hands and greasy fingernails and got rid of motorcycles forever. I became a salesman and then I met Lord Buckley and wound up making those Lord Buckley records. The next thing I made Page Cavanaugh Trio records, two of them – and some Herb Jeffries (aka Herb Jeffreys) records. I became involved in national distribution for small labels, toured the country and found out about that side of the business. Then I gave up the music business and worked on seven or eight films: on a couple of them I was sound engineer, on one I was assistant camera. I did sound on [Roger Corman's cult comedy thriller] *The Little Shop Of Horrors*. Some of those movies were never finished and some were. When I was contracted to do the sound I had to hire somebody to replace me because I was busy in a cartoon studio doing soundtracks.

"In the two years prior to getting the Byrds going, while I was still doing folk records, I decided to become a photographer and went to work for Barry Feinstein, learning how to print in his lab, and learning about photography. I spent a couple of years at that until he closed the lab. That overlapped with rehearsing with the Byrds. I was taking pictures of the Byrds and later got Barry to do it when he could afford it. I was still interested in photography and making a living. I'd gotten married. I did other odd things. I did some work for Lenny Bruce, some tapes for his court trials. Also albums for Jac Holzman at Elektra. Dian & The Greenbriar Boys, Fred Engelberg (two albums), an album with Marshall Brickman and Eric Weissberg that eventually got used as the *Deliverance* album and I got no credit for it. They put on one new cut and used our album. I had to do that as a house producer, I didn't get a percentage . . . I did the Dillards' albums, Hamilton Camp, a blues singer called Long Gone Miles on World-Pacific, some stuff with the Jazz Crusaders that was never released. Experiments. Hard to think of them all. I did an album with Odetta, Modern Folk Quartet . . . There's somewhere close to 60 albums, and a lot of things that didn't come to fruition.

"I was in films and I was still a semi-stringer for Holzman. Jimmy Gavin was the first folk singer I ever recorded and he knows them all from Wavy Gravy to Pete Seeger. He's worked with every one of those people. He really invented folk rock. He did a song for Epic in the Fifties called 'Johnny Rolling Stone' [b/w 'Rock Island Line'] and it was a single and it didn't go anywhere. I remember hearing it once because the same people that distributed Buckley had it there at that time. Jimmy's worked with virtually everybody I ever knew in folk music at one time or another. It was him, Bob Gibson and Bob Camp at the Troubadour that first made me think that three guys singing together could be magical. They had egos that wouldn't let them go together. It was part of what was in my mind to create something. Gibson and Camp had recorded together at the Gate Of Horn but they couldn't stay together because they both wanted to do it on their own. Jimmy Gavin had more energy but less musicality than either one of them, but together they were just startling. They went onstage at the Club Renaissance one night and blew everything out by singing together. They never did it again. I did an album on a borrowed tape machine with him called *Early Jimmy Gavin* because he was young then too and I figured he could get better, but he went into more of an acting career."

page 33: "I knew Jim Dickson . . ." Eddie Tickner, interviewed by the author. Redondo Beach, California: 20 July 1979.

page 34: "When he wrote songs with verses . . ." Jim Dickson, interviewed by the author. Waldport, Oregon: 26–30 April 1989.

page 34: "I used to have tapes of David . . ." ibid.

page 35: "I could have been a Byrd . . ." Van Dyke Parks, interviewed on Dutch television, Palentino Pictures, in 2002. Parks repeated the story to this author and confirms that it took place well in advance of his forming a group with Skip Battin in 1965, a saga documented at some length in *Volume 2* of this book.

NOTES

page 35: "We started to write a few songs . . ." Gene Clark interviewed by Barry Ballard. *Omaha Rainbow* 15: December 1977. I believe that the hootenanny took place at the Troubadour and the reference is to the lobby of the Folk Den.

page 36: "In folk music . . ." Jim Dickson, interviewed by the author. London/Costa Mesa, California: 24 May 2009.

Chapter 2: The Jet Set

page 37: "It was his idea . . ." Crosby/Rogan. London 22–23 April 1980.

page 38: "I really wasn't suited . . ." *Hit Parader*: July 1966.

page 39: "My childhood was like anyone else's . . ." Michael Clarke, interviewed by the author. London and Manchester: 14–15 October 1989.

page 39: "He could play on anything . . ." Suzy Dick, interviewed by the author. London/Spokane, Washington: 11 May 1997.

page 39: "It didn't have a goddamn bass drum . . ." Clarke/Rogan. London and Manchester: 14–15 October 1989.

page 40: ". . . whose Texas upbringing and Air Force background . . ." According to Suzy Dick: "My husband spent a lot of time in Britain during World War II. He was a gunner and tail gunner on B-17s and helped win the war there. He did the most missions in the Air Force out of England on B-17s."

page 40: "You couldn't punish Michael . . ." Dick/Rogan. London/Spokane, Washington: 11 May 1997.

page 40: "I'd take him to school . . ." ibid. Many years later, Clarke regaled his friend Susan Paul with a high school story which sums up his attitude at the time. "Michael had a habit of indulging stories so there was a lot that I wasn't really sure about his early life," she says. "He told me when he first left home he had nothing but a knapsack on his back. The next day he called his mom from the road to say that he'd taken off with this guy that his parents really disapproved of. He added that a year later he came back [to Spokane] driving a Porsche with a car full of presents for everybody and went to his high school where his music teacher had supposedly told him he wouldn't amount to anything. He walked in and said something off colour to him."

page 40: "My husband wasn't a musician . . ." ibid.

page 40–41: "Michael seemed to be driven . . ." ibid.

page 41: "He had talent, he could paint . . ." ibid. Evidently, all the family either painted or played music. "My husband painted and I have pictures of his," says Suzy Dick. " Jimmy did mountain scenery and pictures. It was a completely different style to Michael's. Michael's sister Judi also paints and it's a different style too: flowers and things like that. So they're all really talented, I tell you. Then I have a younger daughter (Debbie) and she plays the piano. We don't paint; we're the musicians. My husband used to have exhibits of his paintings. He'd take them down to the park here; we have a lot of places where they exhibit paintings. He was just an amateur but he sold quite a few of his paintings. But it was more because he loved to paint. Then he had a stroke in 1984 and couldn't paint with his left hand. He just couldn't make it come out like it should so he had to quit painting. It was really sad, but he got through it."

page 41: "It was his great claim . . ." Dick/Rogan. London/Spokane, Washington: 11 May 1997.

page 41: "I often wondered . . ." ibid.

page 42: "He said he was going down to California . . ." ibid.

page 42: "I remember Michael was walking down . . ." Roger McGuinn, interviewed by the author. Leeds: 4 May 1977.

page 43: "We only used the trio for about a month . . ." Dickson/Rogan. Waldport, Oregon: 26–30 April 1989.

page 44: "Jim and I wrote 'Don't Be Long' . . ." Harvey Gerst, quoted from undated online music discussion.

page 44: "It was my first attempt at recording them . . ." Dickson/Rogan. Waldport, Oregon: 26–30 April 1989.

page 44: "It was a funny thing . . ." Crosby/Rogan. London: 22–23 April 1980.

page 45: "David had got a six-string bass . . ." Dickson/Rogan. Waldport, Oregon: 26–30 April 1989.

page 47: "It was completed in a day . . ." Chris Hillman, interviewed by the author. London: 28 April 1977.

page 47: "It might be one of the best records I ever made . . ." Chris Hillman, speaking at the Library of Congress, Washington D.C.: 16 October 2009.

page 47: "This was my window on authenticity . . ." ibid.

page 48: "We changed their name to the Hillmen . . ." Tickner/Rogan. Redondo Beach, California: 20 July 1979. Hillman was more likely a year older at the time.

page 48: "I'd been taping Chris for over a year . . ." Dickson/Rogan. Waldport, Oregon: 26–30 April 1989.

page 48: "I knew something about Chris Hillman . . ." ibid.

page 49: "He was very flighty . . ." ibid.

page 50: "Michael had enough time . . ." ibid.

NOTES

page 50: "I was a mandolin player . . ." Chris Hillman, interviewed by Pete Frame. *Zigzag* 27: December 1972.

Chapter 3: Preflyte

page 52: "He went out the back door . . ." Dickson/Rogan. Waldport, Oregon: 26–30 April 1989.
page 52: "David without a guitar . . ." ibid.
page 53: "When Gene came in with McGuinn . . ." ibid.
page 53: ". . . there was a hustle . . ." Tickner/Rogan. Redondo Beach, California: 20 July 1979.
page 53: "I don't think I *literally* took . . ." Crosby/Rogan. London: 22–23 April 1980.
page 54: "It was like role playing . . ." David Crosby, interviewed by the author. London: 21 February 1989.
page 54: ". . . a guy named Jimmy . . ." Dickson/Rogan. Waldport, Oregon: 26–30 April 1989. In another quirk of pop history, Jimmy Hannan's backing vocalists on that recording were the Gibb Brothers, later the Bee Gees. By now, of course, McGuinn had long abandoned copying surf hits and was completely caught up in Beatle imitation.
page 54: "Jac wanted to dress them up . . ." ibid.
page 55: "When you'd listen to the playback . . ." ibid.
page 55: ". . . only 15 different actual songs . . ." Although a sixteenth song (an instrumental version of 'The Times They Are A-Changin'') appears on 2001's *The Preflyte Sessions*, this backing track was actually recorded many months later, reputedly for an appearance on the television show *Hullabaloo* in October 1965. The tape was obviously not part of the *Preflyte* group of recordings and the group did not perform the song regularly until their August 1965 tour of England. Also, it should be noted, that there is no reference to the song in the legal documentation (signed by all five Byrds) allowing the World-Pacific material to be licensed to Together Records. That document, incidentally, does include among the list of songs 'Tomorrow Is A Long Ways Away' (which did not appear until 1998's *In The Beginning* on Rhino) and the still unreleased, presumed lost, 'Maybe You Think'.
page 55: "It might have taken us a couple . . ." Crosby/Rogan. London: 22–23 April 1980.
page 56: "It was an exciting process . . ." Dickson/Rogan. Waldport, Oregon: 26–30 April 1989.
page 57: "Gene and McGuinn would both be singing . . ." ibid.

page 57: "I collaborated with Crosby . . ." McGuinn/Rogan. Leeds: 4 May 1977.
page 57: "It got included on *Preflyte* . . ." Dickson/Rogan. Waldport, Oregon: 26–30 April 1989.
page 58: "That was stuff to play at dances . . ." ibid.
page 59: "Looking back . . ." Jim Dickson, interviewed by the author. London/Hawaii: 3 August 1998.
page 59: "Gene's vocal bothered everybody . . ." ibid.
page 60: "It hadn't been released on the previous album . . ." Roger McGuinn interviewed by John Cohen. *Sing Out!* Vol. 18; No. 5: December 1968/January 1969.
page 60: "Dickson had heard Dylan . . ." Tickner/Rogan. Redondo Beach, California: 20 July 1979.
page 60: "Dylan, to me, was a very unassuming guy . . ." Dickson/Rogan. Waldport, Oregon: 26–30 April 1989.
page 61: "They started off hating 'Mr Tambourine Man' . . ." ibid.
page 61: "McGuinn began to like it . . ." ibid.
page 62: "David politicked within the group . . ." ibid.
page 62: "Doing the song at that point . . ." ibid.

Chapter 4: Dylan's Charm Offensive

page 63: "They were doing things nobody else was doing . . ." Anthony Scaduto *Bob Dylan* (London: Helter Skelter/Rogan House, 1996), p. 175.
page 64: "When I told them Dylan was coming . . ." Dickson/Rogan. Waldport, Oregon: 26–30 April 1989.
page 64: "Wow, man! . . ." McGuinn/Rogan. Leeds: 4 May 1977.
page 64: "He didn't have a guitar with him . . ." Jim Dickson, interviewed by the author. London/Costa Mesa, California: 24 May 2009. Whether Chris Hillman had fully committed himself to the group at this stage is uncertain. As Dickson noted earlier, he was still working outside the group and did not agree to throw in his lot with the Jet Set until roughly the late autumn of 1964.
page 65: "Dylan was a very adept song plugger . . ." Dickson/Rogan. Waldport, Oregon: 26–30 April 1989.
page 65: "One of my clients . . ." Tickner/Rogan. Redondo Beach, California: 20 July 1979.
page 65: "She did a lot of other things . . ." Dickson/Rogan. London/Costa Mesa, California: 24 May 2009.
page 66: "I saw one of her musical shows . . ." ibid.
page 66: "She must have made well over $100,000 . . ." ibid.

NOTES

page 66: "At first the songs were dull . . ." McGuinn/Rogan. London/Florida: 22 May 1997.

page 67: "Michael thought he was going to be fired . . ." Dickson/Rogan. Waldport, Oregon: 26–30 April 1989.

page 67: "I just laughed . . ." ibid.

page 67: "When I first started with Eddie . . ." ibid.

page 68: "It was certainly their idea . . ." ibid.

page 69: "CBS' Columbia imprint . . ." In the US and Canada, CBS' recordings were issued under the name Columbia. In other territories, including the UK, they bore the CBS label. This arrangement continued from 1961 to 1990.

page 69: "Rock 'n' roll is musical baby food . . ." Mitch Miller, quoted in *New Musical Express*: January 1958.

page 70: "The musical compositions to be recorded . . ." Contract between CBS Records and the Jet Set: 10 November 1964.

page 70: ". . . each master recording . . ." ibid.

page 70: ". . . by unauthorized dubbing . . ." ibid.

page 70: ". . . a minimum of four 78 rpm sides . . ." ibid.

page 71: "Accordingly, you agree . . ." ibid.

page 71: ". . . 10 per cent of the applicable wholesale price . . ." ibid.

page 72: "I didn't like Jet Set . . ." ibid.

page 72: "McGuinn was enchanted with jets . . ." Dickson/Rogan. London/Costa Mesa, California: 24 May 2009.

page 72: "McGuinn went through the vowels . . ." ibid.

page 72: "We were still trying to think of another name . . ." Gene Clark, interviewed by Barry Ballard. *Omaha Rainbow* 15: December 1977. Clark's account of coming up with the name 'Birdses' is unique to this interview. Nobody else recalls him stating this at the meal, but it is such a peculiar detail that it is more than likely he mentioned it sometime that evening, or earlier.

page 73: "They thought it was a great idea . . ." Tickner/Rogan. Redondo Beach, California: 20 July 1979. McGuinn has caused confusion in the past, notably in a *Rolling Stone* interview with Ed Ward (published 12 October 1970) where he mentioned the dinner conversation but referred to Tickner instead of Dickson. This was probably due to the fact that Tickner was sitting next to him while the tape was rolling. "I remember you saying, 'How about Birds?', he says to Tickner during the interview. "I have a very strong audio-visual memory of that . . . You said 'Birds' and I said, 'No, that's English slang for girls, and we don't want them to think we're a bunch of fags, right?' So you said 'B-u-r-d-s'? And I said, 'Yecchh.' And we got around to Byrds somehow." This appears to be a bowdlerization of comments made to both Tickner and Dickson. Tickner insists that he had nothing to do with the name beyond hosting the Thanksgiving dinner. He credits Dickson and McGuinn for working through the vowels and coming up with the name Byrds. Dickson's own account (see succeeding quote) tallies with Tickner's memory of events.

page 73: "We did go to Thanksgiving . . ." Dickson/Rogan. London/Costa Mesa, California: 24 May 2009.

Chapter 5: Mr Tambourine Man

page 75: "It was only intended . . ." Dickson/Rogan. Waldport, Oregon: 26–30 April 1989.
page 76: ". . . looking as if he was going to come out of his skin . . ." ibid.
page 76: "I went over to Hillman's house . . ." ibid.
page 76: "I went over, kicked down . . ." ibid.
page 77: "Hillman left and ran away . . ." ibid.
page 77: "We actually lived together . . ." Dolores Tickner (formerly McGuinn, née DeLeon), interviewed by the author. London/Tucson, Arizona: 13 January 2007.
page 78: "Later, Chris came in . . ." ibid.
page 78: "He said, 'I hear you're seeing this McGuinn guy . . .'" ibid.
page 78: "I would save my tips . . ." ibid.
page 78: "The four of us . . ." ibid.
page 78: ". . . sexy babes and go-go dancers . . ." ibid.
page 78: ". . . to provide the valium . . ." Dickson/Rogan. Waldport, Oregon: 26–30 April 1989.
page 79: " . . . Its full title Susila Budhi Dharma suggested the 'good character of man' and the force of the inner self with an emphasis on 'patience, submission and sincerity . . .'" Subud literature elaborates on this point, noting "The word Subud is an acronym of *susila*, *budhi* and *dharma*, three words with Sanskrit roots – *susila*, *budhi* and *dharma* – which in Subud are understood to mean: humane behaviour or right living; the inner force or power within all human beings; and surrender to the highest power (great life force, universal life force, the divine, God, Allah, Yahweh, Ishvara, Brahman, Waheguru, the Tao). Combined, these three words represent the aligning of our outer actions (*susila*) with our inner realizations (*budhi*) through surrender to the highest universal power (*dharma*). In addition to the Sanskrit-derived definition, the founder described the word Subud as having its own meaning: originating from the source and returning to the source."

NOTES

page 79: "I'd envisaged something you put in your coffee..." McGuinn/Rogan. London/Florida: 22 May 1997.

page 79: "... to free the individual 'from the influence of the passions'..." In *The Basis And Aim Of Subud*, published by Subud Publications International, there is a translation of the words of Bapak Muhammad Subuh as follows: "As the spiritual training (*latihan kedjiwaan*) of Subud is free from the influence of the passions, desires and thinking, and is truly awakened by the Power of Almighty God, the aim of Subud is naturally toward perfection of character according to the Will of the One who awakens it, namely: Almighty God... It is also necessary to explain that Subud is neither a kind of religion nor a teaching, but is a spiritual experience awakened by the Power of God leading to spiritual reality free from the influence of the passions, desires and thinking."

page 79: "You do what they call an exercise..." Roger McGuinn, interviewed by Pete Frame. *Zigzag* 29: March 1973.

page 80: "I was a staff producer..." Terry Melcher, interviewed by the author. London: 27 December 1977.

page 81: "Do we really need this guy?..." Jim Dickson, interviewed by the author. London/Hawaii: 7 July 1997.

page 81: "That was the most interesting thing for Terry..." Dickson/Rogan. Waldport, Oregon: 26–30 April 1989.

page 82: "When I saw the AFM contract..." Roger McGuinn. Email, dated 6 March 2007.

page 82: "The responsibilities of the leader..." Dickson/Rogan. Waldport, Oregon: 26–30 April 1989.

page 82: "McGuinn playing on that date..." ibid.

page 83: "The bass part was Terry's main contribution..." ibid.

page 84: "Jim, try not to make any string noise..." Terry Melcher, speaking over the intercom at the 'Mr Tambourine Man' session: 20 January 1965.

page 84: "It's a bit draggy..." ibid.

page 84: "Are you in drag?..." ibid.

page 84: "Jim, do some kind of fill..." ibid.

page 84: "Let's take another one..." ibid.

page 84: "Do you want to go on..." ibid.

page 84: "... take me away from the bomb..." Dickson/Rogan. London/Hawaii: 7 July 1997.

page 84: "Underneath the lyrics..." McGuinn/Rogan. London/Florida: 22 May 1997.

page 85: "My problem with all of them..." Dickson/Rogan. London/Hawaii: 7 July 1997.

page 85: "In the spectrum of music . . ." McGuinn/Cohen. *Sing Out!* Vol. 18; No. 5: December 1968/January 1969.
page 85: "Terry mixed out Gene Clark's vocal . . ." Dickson/Rogan. Waldport, Oregon: 26–30 April 1989.
page 86: "Man, you'd be gilding . . ." ibid.
page 86: "Man, we've got the best lead guitar player . . ." ibid.
page 86: "It was a scary business . . ." ibid.

Chapter 6: The New Pop Way Of Living

page 87: "They wanted 'I Knew I'd Want You' . . ." ibid.
page 88: "I was concerned that Grossman would say, 'No' . . ." ibid.
page 88: "She liked to see young people . . ." ibid.
page 89: " . . . nothing more than an extension cord . . ." Dickson/Rogan. Waldport, Oregon: 26–30 April 1989.
page 89: ". . . about three weeks . . ." *ELAC Campus News*: 3 February 1965.
page 89: "I might not have convinced them . . ." Gene Clark, interviewed by the author. London: 2 May 1977.
page 90: "I stayed away . . ." Dickson/Rogan. Waldport, Oregon: 26–30 April 1989.
page 90: "It was awful . . ." Roger McGuinn, interviewed by Penny Valentine. *Sounds*: 14 August 1971.
page 90: "He had this great idea . . ." McGuinn/Rogan. London/Florida: 22 May 1997.
page 91: "I was very angry that Dino . . ." Dickson/Rogan. Waldport, Oregon: 26–30 April 1989.
page 91: "We'd sent Dylan the acetate . . ." ibid.
page 92: "CBS thought I'd pulled some sort of magic trick . . ." Jim Dickson, interviewed by the author. London/Costa Mesa, California: 5 April 2009.
page 92: ". . . off-the-top-of-my-head action dance . . ." *Cosmopolitan*, Volume 158: No. 3: March 1965.
page 92: "It was all very foreign . . ." Dickson/Rogan. London/Costa Mesa, California: 5 April 2009.
page 93: "I can't remember who made the initial contact . . ." Dickson/Rogan. Waldport, Oregon: 26–30 April 1989.
page 93: "Vitautus Alfonso Paulekas . . ." The details of Vito's early life were assembled from the author's interviews with Carl Franzoni and Jim Dickson, assisted by internet postings from J.P. Paulekas, whom I believe is one of his grandchildren.

NOTES

page 94: "The day she was 18 . . ." Carl Franzoni, interviewed by the author. London/Santa Rosa, California: 22 June 2007.

page 94: ". . . on the corner of Laurel Avenue . . ." ibid.

page 94: "His studio was downstairs . . ." ibid.

page 95: "Vito had a studio . . ." Michelle Kerr, interviewed by the author. North Hollywood, California: 29 July 1979.

page 96: "We used to all smoke pot . . ." Chris Hillman, interviewed by Sid Griffin. *Full Circle* 11: January 1992. 'Beatle Bob' may not have been a musician, but he was apparently always ready to try. "He was 'Beatle Bob' until he started to learn how to play saxophone," says Carl Franzoni. "I think he learned to be a saxophonist from Frank Zappa's lead guitarist. Bob then got a new name, a wild name. Then he grew a beard and became the Op Cit. He eventually opened a tattoo parlour in Hollywood." The original Beatle Bob (Bob Roberts) should not be confused with a later 'Beatle Bob' (Robert Matonis) from St Louis, who dances at gigs in the St Louis area. Funnily enough, he first came to prominence when dancing at a venue called Cicero's [cf Ciro's] in the early Eighties.

page 96: "These people were amazing . . ." Roger McGuinn, interviewed by Rob Hughes. *Uncut* 75: August 2003.

page 97: "The Byrds came in off the street . . ." Derek Taylor, interviewed by the author. London: 13 February 1997. Taylor was always passionate about the Byrds. Back in July 1965, he told *Melody Maker* about first hearing 'Mr Tambourine Man' and his initial meeting with Dickson. "He had a kind smile and gentle eyes and looked honest. Which is something in Hollywood. He, too, was broke. But, he said, the Byrds were pretty good and Columbia Records had recorded them . . . He had a copy of it in an envelope and he played it to me. Bob Dylan, he explained, had written the song and had approved the Byrds' version. I said: 'I think it's a hit.' And he said: 'We think so, too.'"

page 97: "It wasn't even on paper . . ." Dickson/Rogan. Waldport, Oregon: 26–30 April 1989.

page 98: "There was some confusion . . ." Franzoni's memory of the Byrds' first involvement with Vito is compressed within an impossibly short period. It is unlikely that they were ever actually 'auditioned' for the Vito concert, having already established themselves as regulars at his studio. The dating of the anti-Vietnam concert is also uncertain. Although Franzoni maintains it was the night before their Ciro's debut, there is no notice in the local press about this gig to confirm an exact date.

page 98: "Franzoni remembers someone sending . . ." In an online interview with John Trubee, Franzoni provided an entertaining account of this episode. "We had a friend who was a very fierce-looking guy. His name was Sam Hanna and he was an actor – he was actually a school teacher. He played in horror movies and scared the shit out of everybody. He had the face of an Arab – big nose, bushy eyebrows, swarthy-looking. He used to come into Vito's apartment, he'd run up the stairs and run through the door and do a tumble and he would say, 'Here I am!' So we talked about the Byrds and what they had done and Sam Hanna took somebody and went over to their apartment. They had a cold water flat on the edge of Beverly Hills and west Hollywood. Sam went up to these guys and said 'Listen, you guys aren't very professional, you don't show up when someone wants to give you a job.'"

page 98: "The group had recently returned . . ." In his first autobiography, Crosby refers to this gig as taking place at the Jack Tar Motel [actually Jack Tar Hotel]. He recalls the Byrds playing three songs and reckons it was the first time they ever "cooked" onstage. He makes no reference to any stolen gear, but Franzoni claims that thieves raided their station wagon, taking everything they could, including the tyres. The Byrds returned to San Francisco during the first week of May for a residency at the Peppermint Tree on Broadway. The venue's large dancehall allowed Vito's crew to show off their weirdness with Franzoni leading the line. Jazz critic and later *Rolling Stone* doyen Ralph J. Gleason offered some amusing thoughts for readers of the *San Francisco Chronicle*, comparing Franzoni's hair to "Medusa's snakes". Gleason recalled attending a Count Basie performance followed by the Byrds at the Peppermint Tree, apparently on the same night. "I went the whole way from Yesterday to Tomorrow. It was fascinating. Nobody dances at a Basie appearance any more and everybody dances to the Byrds. In fact, the dancing is more fun than anything. The Byrds, incidentally, look not like birds, but like the Beatles. The wild and exotic Byrd-watchers on the floor at the Peppermint Tree were a gas. They all seem to be part of the president's physical fitness program doing free-style callisthenics."

page 98: "There were pews there . . ." Franzoni/Rogan. London/Santa Rosa, California: 22 June 2007.

page 98: "We're playing at Ciro's tomorrow night . . ." ibid.

page 98: "When we first turned up . . ." Derek Taylor, interviewed by the author. London: 17 June 1977. One reason for the initially poor turnout was that Ciro's sold alcohol which meant that teenagers were not allowed admission. The more astute solved this problem by obtaining fake IDs.

page 99: "I was never on drugs . . ." Kerr/Rogan. North Hollywood, California: 29 July 1979.

NOTES

page 99: "At last a rock 'n' roll group . . ." *Variety:* 31 March 1965. The previous week, the *Daily Variety* version included a slightly longer review, adding some musical observations: "Guitar breaks are just that: instrumentalizing is kept subordinate to vocal work when the group is singing – as it should be." The paper noted that "opening night audience was small, biz should perk up once word is out that the Byrds, in for a week, are in flight."

page 99: "That anomaly was rectified by a letter dated 12 March . . ." In three prepared letters, McGuinn, Clark and Crosby individually signed a statement addressed to 'T.D. Managers' saying, *inter alia*:

"Gentlemen: This letter is to confirm our prior understanding concerning the change of the name of the musical group of which I am a member from the 'Jet Set' to 'THE BYRDS'. This letter is also to confirm the fact that Michael Clark [sic] and Christopher Hillman have been added as members of 'THE BYRDS' effective as of and from after March 1, 1965."

Chapter 7: Ciro's Magic

page 100: "Coming off the street . . ." Dickson/Rogan. Waldport, Oregon: 26–30 April 1989.

page 100: "On the evocative album sleeve, Dylan had placed . . ." According to Dickson, Dylan's manager Albert Grossman had attempted to buy the Buckley masters during the Fifties and later turned on Dylan to the satirist/comedian.

page 101: "We played some of his other songs . . ." McGuinn/Rogan. London/Florida: 22 May 1997.

page 101: "Dylan was then [the] super-hero . . ." Taylor/Rogan. London: 17 June 1977.

page 101: "I asked Dylan if it was all right . . ." Dickson/Rogan. London/Costa Mesa, California: 24 May 2009.

page 102: "Dylan had finally achieved some credential . . ." Dickson/Rogan. Waldport, Oregon: 26–30 April 1989.

page 102: "In the photo Dylan had his index finger . . ." McGuinn/Rogan. London/Florida: 22 May 1997.

page 102: "Dylan didn't go out of his way . . ." Taylor/Rogan. London: 13 February 1997.

page 102: "They're doing something really new . . ." Bob Dylan, interviewed by Paul Jay Robbins: March 1965. Printed in *Los Angeles Free Press*: September 1965.

page 104: "It was Dylan's relationship with me . . ." Jim Dickson, interviewed by the author. London/Costa Mesa, California: 9 November 2009.

page 104: "It was very funny . . ." Dolores Tickner (formerly McGuinn, née DeLeon)/Rogan. London/Tucson, Arizona: 24–25 February 2007.

page 104: "That wasn't out of her range . . ." Dickson/Rogan. London/Costa Mesa, California: 9 November 2009.

page 104: "He wasn't feeling too well . . ." ibid.

page 104: "Titled *Bash!*, the programme was most notable for the appearance of Jackie De Shannon . . ." Around this time, Jackie De Shannon recorded a dozen demos of folk-rock influenced songs for her publisher Metric Music, including 'Don't Doubt Yourself Babe', 'Splendor In The Grass', 'With You In Mind', 'Too Far Out', 'What's It All About' and 'Girl Of Yesterday'. Although dated May 1965, some of the recordings may have been cut a little earlier and it may be from here that the Byrds borrowed 'Don't Doubt Yourself Babe' which they recorded for their first album on 22 April 1965.

page 104: "The commotion at Ciro's, along with the *Bash!* special . . ." The *Bash!* special included, in addition to Jackie De Shannon and the Byrds, appearances by Eddie Cano, April & Nino (aka Nino Tempo & April Stevens), Brenda Holloway, Cannibal & The Hunters and Frankie Randell. In Christopher Hjort's Byrds' chronology (*So You Want To Be A Rock 'n' Roll Star: The Byrds Day-By-Day 1965–1973*, Jawbone, 2008), he lists the *Lloyd Thaxton Show* (c. late April) as the group's first television appearance, having incorrectly assumed that KCOP's *Bash!* was the same programme, presumably because it was on the same channel. As mentioned in the main text, the *Bash!* special had a different disc jockey, Charlie O'Donnell. In the Byrds' *Lifelines* which were sent out to the music press in the spring/summer of 1965, both David Crosby and Michael Clarke confirm that their television debut was 'KCOP *Bash!*'. The following month's *Lloyd Thaxton Show* was, as far as can be ascertained, the Byrds' second television show.

page 105: ". . . KCOP presenter, Lloyd Thaxton . . ." Quoted in Hjort's book, Thaxton provided an amusing account of the proceedings: ". . . in the middle of our soundcheck, the audio man in the booth told me that the speakers were too loud for the sound control panel to handle. The sound was being naturally distorted. I ran in and told the Byrds they were to turn down the speaker volume controls. I explained that we were not in a stadium, that there were only 15 couples sitting in the small bleachers just five feet away. The group looked at me like I really didn't understand ('the music has to be loud, man!') but, to their credit, they did turn down and made the necessary adjustments. Just in the nick of time: the commercial was over and we were back on air. I picked up my mike and said, 'And here they are, the Byrds!' Then, as if someone gave them a cue from offstage, each member of the group reached down and turned their respective speakers back up to full volume. When the first 'hey' of 'Mr Tambourine Man' hit our mikes, I looked up at the control room window and saw my audio man being literally blown in his seat. The needles on his control board were spinning like a racetrack timing clock . . . It was an exciting performance and the kids loved it."

page 105: "It was picked up by Tom Donahue . . ." Clark/Ballard. *Omaha Rainbow* 15: December 1977. The first pressing was played by Bobby Dale of KEWB – San Francisco.

page 105: "We had the up-and-coming elite . . ." Dickson/Rogan. Waldport, Oregon: 26–30 April 1989.

page 106: "We started the hippie movement . . ." Kerr/Rogan. North Hollywood, California: 29 July 1979.

page 106: "Dickson engineered a lot of that . . ." David Crosby, interviewed by Rob Hughes. *Uncut* 75: August 2003.

page 106: "The dance floor was a madhouse . . ." Derek Taylor, writing in *Melody Maker*: 17 July 1965.

page 107: "It was Sherwood Forest . . ." Kim Fowley, interviewed by the author. London/Redlands, California: 27–28 June 2007.

page 107: ". . . looked at the guitar as if it was a foreign object . . ." Dickson/Rogan. Waldport, Oregon: 26–30 April 1989.

page 107: "What do I do with these drumsticks? . . ." ibid.

page 107: "When David was positive . . ." Dickson/Rogan. London/Hawaii: 7 July 1997.

page 108: "Michael's ability to keep good time . . ." Dickson/Rogan. Waldport, Oregon: 26–30 April 1989.

page 108: "Michael sat in for him . . ." Chris Hillman, interviewed by Rob Hughes. *Uncut* 75: August 2003.

page 109: "Each night was a week . . ." Dickson/Rogan. Waldport, Oregon: 26–30 April 1989.

page 109: "A man whose chin . . ." Art Seidenbaum. *Los Angeles Times*: 28 April 1965.

page 110: "What the Byrds signify . . ." Paul Jay Robbins. *Los Angeles Free Press*: 23 April 1965.

page 110: "We were seen as a symbol . . ." Roger McGuinn, interviewed by Penny Valentine. *Sounds*: 21 August 1971.

page 112: "The Byrds were playing . . ." Lou Adler, quoted in *Melody Maker*: 5 February 1972.

page 112: "When I left the Christy Minstrels . . ." Barry McGuire, interviewed by the author. Rosslare, Co. Wexford, Republic of Ireland: 1–2 August 2008.

Chapter 8: Positive Thinking

page 114: ". . . the recently composed live favourite 'You And Me' . . ." Dickson notes: "They used to play 'You And Me' quite a bit. It was written between the time we had left World-Pacific and started recording at Columbia. That's why it wasn't on *Preflyte*. It probably didn't make the first album because we were doing Dylan songs. The song was probably Gene's, with or without McGuinn."

page 114: "Columbia wanted us to do the first album . . ." Crosby/Rogan. London: 22–23 April 1980.

page 114: "I wanted to use Leon Russell . . ." Dickson/Rogan. Waldport, Oregon: 26–30 April 1989.

page 115: "These people were very hurt . . ." ibid.

page 116: "It was clear that David Crosby . . ." Lizzie Donohue, interviewed by the author. North Hollywood, California: 29 July 1979.

page 116: "Lizzie said I was choking him! . . ." Dickson/Rogan. Waldport, Oregon: 26–30 April 1989.

page 117: "David said, 'No chicks in the limousine' . . ." Dolores Tickner (formerly McGuinn, née DeLeon)/Rogan. London/Tucson, Arizona: 13 January 2007.

page 117: "Long Beach was a disaster . . ." Dickson/Rogan. Waldport, Oregon: 26–30 April 1989.

page 117: "When you open for the Rolling Stones . . ." ibid. Mick Jagger's comments on the Byrds were reported in the UK music paper *Disc* (10 July): "One night, when we were due to be playing at San Diego, the car we were travelling in to the theatre broke down. This made us half an hour late arriving at the theatre, so the Byrds had to stay on stage to keep the audience entertained. By the time we eventually got there they had run out of all their own numbers and were playing ours. What a gas!"

page 118: "We spent seven nights with the Byrds," Brian Jones, unattributed interview, *Disc*: 24 July 1965.

page 118: "We were driving along . . ." Crosby/Rogan. London: 22–23 April 1980.

page 118: "As the momentum gathered, CBS publicist Billy James worked overtime . . ." For further comment on Billy James' contribution see the opening endnote of chapter nine.

NOTES

page 119: "They were very disenchanted . . ." Dickson/Rogan. Waldport, Oregon: 26–30 April 1989.

page 119: "We'd never experienced the pressure . . ." Roger McGuinn, interviewed by the author. Universal City, California: 12 July 1979.

page 119: "Why didn't you tear the coat . . ." Dickson/Rogan. Waldport, Oregon: 26–30 April 1989. *KRLA Beat* (26 May 1965) reported that the Byrds refused to join *Hullabaloo*'s all-star finale to a rendition of Gary Lewis & The Playboys' chart-topping 'This Diamond Ring'. The Byrds' minor act of rebellion was hardly surprising considering the song in question and the showbiz routine. Two years later, the Rolling Stones did something similar by declining to join the revolving roster of artists at the close of UK television's *Sunday Night At The London Palladium*, although it's extremely doubtful that any of the Byrds were ever aware of this coincidence.

page 120: "We didn't look at it that way . . ." Crosby/Rogan. London: 22–23 April 1980.

page 121: "I'd been through Catholicism . . ." McGuinn/Rogan. London/Florida: 22 May 1997.

page 121: "The Byrds' management let them control . . ." Taylor/Rogan. London: 17 June 1977. The references here to Roberts and Azoff are figurative only as they were not in the management business at the same time as Dickson and Tickner. Roberts became Joni Mitchell's and Neil Young's manager later in the Sixties, while Irving Azoff managed the Eagles during the Seventies.

page 121: "Eddie Tickner is more laid-back than me . . ." Dickson/Rogan. Waldport, Oregon: 26–30 April 1989.

page 122: "Rita didn't want any messing . . ." Taylor/Rogan. London: 13 February 1997.

page 123: "What Derek did blew my mind . . ." Dickson/Rogan. Waldport, Oregon: 26–30 April 1989.

page 123: "We'd let them in free . . ." ibid.

page 124: "We had a big hit . . ." Roger McGuinn, interviewed by the author. New York: 26 January 1979.

Chapter 9: The First Album

page 125: "By the time the Byrds reached number 1 on 26 June . . ." It is revealing to consider the impact that the Byrds' success was having on CBS at the time. While researching this period, I unearthed an in-house newsletter from the 'Columbia Records Sales Corp' dated 19 June 1965 and sent by Gene Block to the 'Region Six Sales Personnel' and copied to

Allen Stanton, Terry Melcher and Billy James. A wonderfully strange combination of hip argot and advertising sales talk, it reveals the Byrds as the new saviours of the company and looks forward to the CBS convention in Miami (as discussed in the main text). Titled '*The West Coast Sound* or . . . Catch The Brass Ring', it states . . .

"On February 9, 1965 I sent you a Newsletter titled THE WEST COAST SOUND and next week we have indeed, caught the brass ring. This is in the comparatively short time of four months. NEXT WEEK – THE BYRDS' 'MR TAMBOURINE MAN' GOES TO NUMBER TWO IN *BILLBOARD*. A number 1 before Miami is a shoe in [sic] since it went from six to two in one week. A CONTINENTAL IS ASSURED IN SOMEONE'S GARAGE.

"This record was West Coast all the way. Terry Melcher found the group in Hollywood and produced it. West Coast sound. But the guy who I must give a deep bow to, even more than any sales individual in the region, is Billy James in publicity who really knocked himself out. Then San Francisco who got the first nibble. Then to Los Angeles who made the dam burst. Then the rest of you who believed. To Bob Moering who coordinated . . .

"It caused me to reflect a little. Especially at the *conclusion* of one of the coldest spells Columbia ever had in singles. When we ask you to spend a huge disproportionate amount of time on singles in relation to the dollars received (compared to album), salesmen and promotion men sometimes wonder, 'Why bother? I knock myself out, can't even get a pick – but I write one order on *My Name Is Barbra* or *Dear Heart* and I eat that week.' Nine out of ten (or is it 99 out of 100) times on a single you spend a lot of time (and execs, a lot of profit) and don't even see a plugged nickel back. Well, let's see what has happened so far on one single record called 'MR TAMBOURINE MAN' and an artist known as the BYRDS:

1. The record passed 500,000 nationally already at a time when singles on all labels are slow. (Check out your share of that figure).
2. An album released which in your market has already IN DOLLARS passed what you billed on the single.
3. A new single ships tomorrow by the Byrds and *initial orders alone* in this region exceed 26,000. (Now with drops it just passed 30,000).
4. They'll be the star attraction in this country, passing everything based on all indications. They're being dubbed the newest trend known as 'folk-rock' – meaning taking the place of the folk craze and integrated into rock!

NOTES

5. And last, but not least, as usual when you're hot, other hits come along for the ride. Patti Page is number 10 next week, in case you didn't know. 'Boondocks' coming along nicely. Need I mention Chad & Jeremy? And what about Paul Revere. 'Summer Sounds' is busting nationally and after this region started first – YOU'VE BLOWN IT COMPLETELY.

"On every call remember you are representing the hottest record company in the industry on SINGLES AND DON'T FORGET IT. You are the region that put Columbia back on the map . . . and you did it with WEST COAST SOUND.

"Catch the brass ring? Baby, *you made it gold!* Remember that the next time we ask for your support. LET THERE BE NO ARGUMENT, 'ALL I REALLY WANT TO DO' BY THE BYRDS IS THE SIDE. You have competition, it's good for you. It's a love pat to your tunny [sic]. See ya in Miami."

page 125: "Sonny was a good thief . . ." Charlie Greene, interviewed by the author. London/New York: 20 March 2000. Dickson believes Greene was entirely behind the idea of taping the Byrds.

page 125: "We resented Columbia . . ." Tickner/Rogan. Redondo Beach, California: 20 July 1979.

page 126: "I remember remixing it . . ." Melcher/Rogan. London: 27 December 1977.

page 126: "I was not only disappointed . . ." Taylor/Rogan. London: 17 June 1977.

page 127: "I didn't really mind Sonny & Cher . . ." McGuinn/Rogan. London/Florida: 22 May 1997.

page 127: "I got this overwhelming feeling . . ." ibid.

page 128: "There was always something to unravel . . ." Dickson/Rogan. Waldport, Oregon: 26–30 April 1989.

page 128: "I remember her . . ." ibid.

page 129: "Not a lot of people have found that . . ." ibid.

page 129: "After Jim Dickson picked . . ." McGuinn/Rogan. New York: 26 January 1979.

page 130: "The trouble with a lot of harmony singers . . ." ibid.

page 131: "Although the bells condemn the exploitation . . ." The liner notes on the rear of Pete Seeger's EP *Healing River* state: "In this haunting song, the bells of the churches in Rhymney, Cardiff and Newport intone their discontent; only the prosperous town of Wye finds no reason to complain." Singer Maddy Griffiths, speaking in the BBC Radio 4 documentary *The Bells Of Rhymney*, makes the same point: "The line that always crucifies me, and it still does, is 'Why so worried, sisters why?' That, to me, just encapsulates the whole business of the privileged not understanding the plight of those who have to work with their hands in heavy industries." I would go further in interpreting the Newport bell's suggestion "throw the vandals in court" as another dissenting comment aimed at the miners. While it might be seen to be equally directed at the mine owners, the specific use of the word "vandals", with its connotations of civic disruption, makes the miners the more likely target.

page 131: ". . . wrongly convinced publicist Billy James that the lyric was about a "Welsh mine disaster". That canard . . . carried forward in many later commentaries on the song . . ." Actually, the error was in circulation even before the release of *Mr Tambourine Man*. In the *Los Angeles Times* (7 June) Charles Champlin referred to it as "a Welsh poem about a mining disaster". Evidently, he was primed by Billy James whom he quotes as saying, "When you think about the words in contrast to the dancing, it boggles the mind."

page 132: "I didn't know any better . . ." Pete Seeger, interviewed for the BBC 4 radio documentary, *The Bells Of Rhymney*: broadcast 12 June 2007. In the same programme, McGuinn was asked how the Byrds came to record the song. "We were on a US bus tour and somebody asked me if I knew the song," he said. Here, McGuinn was confusing 'The Bells Of Rhymney' with the other later Seeger adaptation, 'Turn! Turn! Turn!'. The former was performed and recorded months before their bus tour.

page 132: "The only mix of Terry's . . ." Dickson/Rogan. Waldport, Oregon: 26–30 April 1989.

page 133: "Gene did try to emulate the Beatles . . ." Crosby/Rogan. London: 22–23 April 1980.

page 134: "Jackie De Shannon was the first . . ." Dickson/Rogan. Waldport, Oregon: 26–30 April 1989.

page 134: "It was one of those cathartic moments . . ." ibid.

page 135: "When am I going to realize . . ." ibid.

page 135: "I don't know . . ." ibid.

page 135: "I doubted then . . ." Dickson/Rogan. London/Costa Mesa, California: 9 November 2009.

Chapter 10: Hollywood Parties

page 136: "Gene was living with me . . ." Clarke/Rogan. London and Manchester: 14–15 October 1989.

page 137: "At least I'd be in the water . . ." ibid.

page 137: "When I went in, it was major shit . . ." ibid.

NOTES

page 138: "It was a new house . . ." Dickson/Rogan. London/Costa Mesa, California: 9 November 2009.

page 138: "On 4 July, the Byrds appeared at an even more prestigious gathering . . ." Jane Fonda's Independence Day Party in Malibu has often been described incorrectly as her 'birthday party' or '21st birthday party'. Both assertions are incorrect: she was born on 21 December, not 4 July.

page 139: "I was thinking, 'This is really something' . . ." Taylor/Rogan. London: 13 February 1997.

page 139: "Our roadie Bryan McLean . . ." Franzoni/Rogan. London/Santa Rosa, California: 22 June 2007.

page 139: "Jim, this is terrible . . ." Taylor/Rogan. London: 13 February 1997.

page 139: "Well, they always look a mess! . . ." ibid.

page 139: "Socially, it was a very successful evening . . ." ibid.

page 140: "We wanna buy some mod clothes . . ." Jim McGuinn, interviewed by Chris Hutchins. *New Musical Express*: 16 July 1965. In the piece Hutchins confirmed that the interview took place at 3.16 am on the transatlantic phone after "the Byrds had just exhausted themselves playing at Jane Fonda's party".

page 140: "A gruelling tour of the Midwest was organized . . ." The complete itinerary for the Midwest tour booked by the Willard Alexander Agency has never been printed previously. It reads: 5 July: Lakeside Amusement Park, Denver, Colorado (8–12 pm); 6 July: Coliseum Annex, Sioux Falls, South Dakota (8–12 pm); 7 July: Prom Ballroom, St Paul, Minnesota (8–12 pm); 8 July: Inwood Pavilion, Spillville, Iowa (8–12 pm); 9 July: The Cellar, Arlington Heights, Illinois (minimum 9–12 pm); 10 July: Rockford College, Rockford, Illinois (8–12 pm); 11 July: Terp Ballroom, Austin, Minnesota (8–12 pm); 12 July: Curling Club, Duluth, Minnesota (8–12 pm); 13 July: Roof Garden, Arnold Park, Iowa (9 pm–1 am = cancelled?); 14 July: Balmoral Resort, Battle Lake, Minnesota (9 pm–1 am); 15 July: Pia-Mor [Playmor] Ballroom, Rochester, Minnesota (8 pm–12 pm); 16–17 July: Columbia Record Convention, Miami, Florida; 18 July: Idora Park Ballroom, Idora Park, Youngstown, Ohio; 19 July: Stardust Garden Ballroom, Le Sourdesville Lake Amusement Park, Monroe (between Hamilton and Middletown), Ohio (8.30 pm–11 pm); 20 July: Sylvania, Ohio [venue/time unlisted in itinerary]; 21 July: Cedar Point Ballroom, Sandusky, Ohio; 22 July: Auditorium, Bay City, Michigan (8 pm–12 pm); 23 July: Indiana Beach Ballroom, Monticello, Indiana (8.45 pm–12.45 am); 24 July: McCormick Place, Arie Crown Theatre, Chicago, Illinois (show 8 pm); 25 July: Will advise [venue unknown];

26 July: Convention Centre, Gypsy Village, Fontaine Ferry Park, Louisville, Kentucky (8 pm–12 pm); 27 July: Forest Park Shopping Center Arena, Dayton, Ohio (8.30 pm–11.30 pm); 28 July: Grand Haven Roller Rink, 7th Street, Grand Haven, Michigan (8.30 pm–11 pm); 29 July: Starlite Ballroom, St Louis, Missouri; 30 July: Hi Society Youth Center, Peru, Illinois (8 pm–12 pm); 31 July: Westwood Junior School Park Forest, Illinois (8 pm–12 pm).

page 140: "We went out on a dance tour . . ." Tickner/Rogan. Redondo Beach, California: 20 July 1979.

page 141: "I was 17 when we went on tour . . ." Donohue/Rogan. North Hollywood, California: 29 July 1979. Lizzie Donohue's memory of events is supported by Linda Bopp, whom I interviewed in Hollywood on the same night. Years later, Carl Franzoni also confirmed that there were only five female dancers, plus himself and Beatle Bob (who joined the tour at the last minute). The Byrds were reluctant to have another male dancer on the bus, but Franzoni's insistence prevailed. Although Carl could no longer remember a couple of the girls' names, he lit up with recognition when I mentioned Lizzie Donohue. He also recalled one girl who was sent home early from the tour, whom I assume was the 'Jeanine' mentioned in this quote. Of the other Ciro's girls, Michelle Kerr was not on the tour. Nor was the occasionally mentioned Emerald. "Emerald was a black girl, but she didn't go with us either," notes Franzoni. "She just liked to be around the Byrds." Another girl named Sparky, "who worked next door where everybody ate" was not on the tour either and was not mentioned by any of the other Ciro's cast I met. She may have been on the scene a little later than this time period. In some books, various members of the GTOs recall the Vito's crowd but, again, this was considerably later. None of them were on this tour or danced at Ciro's.

page 141: "Somewhere along the trip . . ." Dickson/Rogan. Waldport, Oregon: 26–30 April 1989.

page 142: "The big cheese was Clive Davis . . ." Taylor/Rogan. London: 13 February 1997.

page 143: "I thought Miami . . ." Franzoni/Rogan. London/Santa Rosa, California: 22 June 2007.

page 143: "I always think of dancing . . ." Unedited extract from Efram Turchick's interview with Carl Franzoni featured in the sidebar notes of the double CD, *The Preflyte Sessions*.

page 143: "We would just yell . . ." ibid.

page 143: "The Byrds were the best dance band . . ." Franzoni/Rogan. London/Santa Rosa, California: 22 June 2007.

page 143: "Chris was my favourite Byrd . . ." Frazoni/Turchick, op cit.

NOTES

page 144: "Bryan McLean was like the sixth guy . . ." Franzoni/Rogan. London/Santa Rosa, California: 22 June 2007.
page 144: "McGuinn was the distant guy . . ." ibid.
page 144: "I see what you're saying . . ." ibid.
page 145: "It was amazing . . ." Donohue/Rogan. North Hollywood, California: 29 July 1979.
page 145: "We were all long-haired . . ." Franzoni/Rogan. London/Santa Rosa, California: 22 June 2007.
page 145: "I think I'm on the wrong floor . . . Boy, you're on the wrong world! . . ." David Crosby, interviewed by Chris Dunkley. *Slough Observer*: 2 August 1965.
page 145: "Crosby had got that pound of grass . . ." Franzoni/Rogan. London/Santa Rosa, California: 22 June 2007.
page 146: "He had a sound in his mind . . ." Mike Bloomfield, interviewed on KSAN-FM radio: date unknown, quote unearthed by Christopher Hjort.
page 146: "Lizzie! . . ." Franzoni/Rogan. London/Santa Rosa, California: 22 June 2007.
page 146: "They told me the story . . ." ibid.
page 146: "I had my own . . ." ibid.
page 147: "I didn't do well . . ." Bryan McLean, interviewed by Neil Skok: (online) 22–24 February 1993.

Chapter 11: The British Tour

page 148: "With their Dylan image . . ." Mervyn Conn, quoted in *Melody Maker*: 10 July 1965.
page 148: "What I brought to the Byrds . . ." Taylor/Rogan. London: 13 February 1997.
page 149: "I was much more of a follower. . ." ibid.
page 149: "Eddie believed whatever Derek told him . . ." Dickson/Rogan. Waldport, Oregon: 26–30 April 1989.
page 150: "Unless I am very much mistaken . . ." Chris Hutchins' article, 'Byrds Biggest Craze Since Beatles', *New Musical Express*: 16 July 1965.
page 150: "It was my fault . . ." Franzoni/Rogan. London/Santa Rosa, California: 22 June 2007.
page 151: "Their manager is a very close friend . . ." Mick Jagger, interviewed by Roy Harrod. *Disc*: 10 July 1965.
page 151: "They did it in march time . . ." ibid.
page 151: "I wouldn't want to be drawn . . ." Paul Jones quoted in 'The Byrds by the Jones Boys', interviewer unnamed. *Disc*: 21 July 1965.

page 152: "It seems that the Byrds have brought . . ." Brian Jones, quoted in 'The Byrds by the Jones Boys', interviewer unnamed. *Disc*: 21 July 1965.
page 152: "They didn't go for any showmanship . . ." ibid.
page 152: "You should be very pleased . . ." Taylor/Rogan. London: 13 February 1997.
page 152: "Although the group has had only one hit . . ." Norrie Drummond article, 'Byrds – America's Biggest Ever Group?' *New Musical Express*: 6 August 1965.
page 153: "Where's the hairdryer? . . ." Jimmy Weston Gavin, interviewed by the author. London: 7 January 2011.
page 153: "They had crystals and coloured cubes . . ." Taylor/Rogan. London: 13 February 1997.
page 154: "They floated out of the hotel . . ." Bobby Hamilton, interviewed by the author. London/Worcester: 16 October 1994.
page 154: "The dope smoking was chronic . . ." Taylor/Rogan. London: 13 February 1997.
page 155: "The Byrds walked on to a hearty . . ." Nigel Hunter, reviewing the Fairfield Hall, Croydon show for *Disc*: 14 August 1965.
page 155: "I liked them very much . . ." Paul Jones, also reviewing the Fairfield Hall, Croydon show for *Disc*: 14 August 1965.
page 156: "Blaises was a place . . ." Taylor/Rogan. London: 17 June 1977.
page 157: "The Flamingo Club was awful . . ." Taylor/Rogan. London: 13 February 1997.
page 157: "Enough people packed in for it . . ." Chris Welch, reviewing the Flamingo show for *Melody Maker*: 14 August 1965.
page 158: "The Animals are still the top . . ." Rik Gunnell, quoted in *Melody Maker*: 14 August 1965.
page 158: "I had the five Byrds outside . . ." Taylor/Rogan. London: 13 February 1997.
page 158: "Come back on Monday . . ." ibid.
page 158: "They were always too loud . . ." ibid.
page 160: "'Flopsville' was London's verdict . . ." Chris Welch article, *Melody Maker*: 14 August 1965.
page 160: "I think they are a drag . . ." ibid.
page 160: "It seems a shame . . ." ibid.
page 160: "Another Byrds No. 1?" Singles review by Derek Johnson, *New Musical Express*: 6 August 1965. That same week in *Disc*, Penny Valentine – who would later emerge as a Byrds' supporter – surprisingly noted, "I think this is a marvellous song but Byrds' fan though I have always been, I prefer the Sonny & Cher recording . . ."
page 160: "The Beatles and the Stones . . ." ibid.

NOTES

page 161: "We missed the plane to Manchester . . ." Taylor/Rogan. London: 13 February 1997.

page 162: "I got sick . . ." McGuinn/Johnson. *Hit Parader*: September 1968.

page 162: "That wasn't conducive to working . . ." Clarke/Rogan. London and Manchester: 14–15 October 1989.

page 162: "Mike Clarke was also ill . . ." Taylor/Rogan. London: 17 June 1977.

page 162: "You couldn't make Michael suffer . . ." Dickson/Rogan. Waldport, Oregon: 26–30 April 1989.

page 163: "Their resistance was low . . ." Taylor/Rogan. London: 17 June 1977.

page 163: "The illnesses were wonderful . . ." Clarke/Rogan. London and Manchester: 14–15 October 1989.

page 164: "My prediction that they will knock the Beatles off . . ." Mervyn Conn, quoted in *Melody Maker*: 14 August 1965.

page 165: "If you dig the Byrds' style . . ." *Melody Maker*: 14 August 1965.

page 165: "They look like a rock group . . ." Allen Evans, reviewing the Byrds' debut album. *New Musical Express*: August 1965.

page 165: ". . . with appearances in East Grinstead, Bristol, Hove, Worthing and Ipswich . . ." Even Derek Taylor's legendary diplomatic skills were tested during this phase of the tour. There was criticism in the local press after the Hove date with the *Brighton Evening Argus* complaining about the half-empty town hall. "Only five minutes after they took the stage small groups of people were leaving; the rest looked bored". There was an acerbic rejoinder from local promoter John Smith ("When I say that this group haven't got what it takes I know what I'm talking about"). Faced with this critical fusillade, Taylor defended the Byrds by uncharacteristically turning on the elderly. "I am not disappointed by the small audience. I am never disappointed because I never expect anything. But what can you expect from Hove? Who lives here? Only old people. It is August as well and a great many people are on holiday."

page 165: "Sonny And Cher became a haunting . . ." Taylor/Rogan. London: 13 February 1997.

page 166: "I loved the band . . ." Kenny Lynch, interviewed by the author. Nettlebed, Oxfordshire: 20 March 2011. Plus previous discussions with the author during the mid-to-late Nineties.

page 167: "They thought I was being a good chap . . ." ibid.

page 167: "Whatever mike . . ." ibid.

page 167: "After tuning up for a full five minutes . . ." Keith Altham, commenting on the Byrds' Finsbury Park performance. *New Musical Express*: 20 August 1965.

page 168: "I thought we were good tonight . . ." David Crosby, interviewed by Keith Altham. *New Musical Express*: 20 August 1965.
page 168: "Gene Clark walks around . . ." Gene Clark, interviewed by Keith Altham. *New Musical Express*: 20 August 1965.
page 168: "The Byrds' biggest fault . . ." ibid.
page 168: "We were really studying . . ." Crosby/Hughes. *Uncut* 75: August 2003.
page 169: "The press was, as usual, the press . . ." Taylor/Rogan. London: 17 June 1977.
page 169: "Yes, the press comment has been harsh . . ." Jim McGuinn, interviewed by David Griffiths. *Record Mirror*: 21 August 1965.
page 170: "For an instrumental . . ." Jim McGuinn, quoted in *Blind Date* column. *Melody Maker*: 14 August 1965.
page 170: "It's plain dull . . ." Chris Hillman, quoted in *Blind Date* column. *Melody Maker*: 14 August 1965.
page 170: "Buck Owens did this . . ." ibid.
page 171: "My friend and I went to Slough . . ." *From You To Us* letters column. *New Musical Express*: 20 August 1965.
page 171: "There is absolutely no question . . ." Derek Taylor, addressing the press: 19 August 1965.
page 171: "They did an awful lot of things . . ." Taylor/Rogan. London: 13 February 1997.
page 171: "If we did nothing else . . ." Taylor's recollected quote – Taylor/Rogan. London: 17 June 1977.
page 171: "In Britain . . ." advertisement, *Disc*: 28 August 1965.
page 172: "There was enough good press . . ." ibid.
page 172: "After reading the knocking letters . . ." Letters to *From You To Us*. *New Musical Express*: August 1965.
page 172: "Bravo Byrds . . ." and "How could you . . ." letters to *Melody Maker*: 20 August 1965.
page 173: "The Byrds did try to make friends . . ." Anne Nightingale, newspaper clipping, c. August 1965.
page 174: "We feel there was a slightly negative reaction . . ." Chris Hillman press statement, possibly penned by Derek Taylor. September 1965.

Chapter 12: The Death Of Folk Rock

page 176: "We were sitting around on acid . . ." McGuinn/Rogan. Leeds: 4 May 1977.
page 177: "We don't believe . . ." ibid.
page 177: "We were competitive in the Byrds . . ." ibid.

NOTES

page 177: "The 'right' people were there . . ." Taylor/Rogan. London: 17 June 1977.

page 177: "Reviewers, normally used to the Byrds' legendary coolness . . ." *Rhythm 'n' News* (3 September 1965) reported that the over-18 dance attracted "the hippest of Southern California's 'in crowd'". Evidently, remnants of the Vito's crowd were in attendance. "If conservative adults in the audience thought the performers' outfits were wild, they were equally scandalized by the rest of the crowd. Dressed in everything from jeans to bellbottoms to 'floor-length table cloths', girls clustered in front of the stage, while others stood talking along the sidelines, and the more energetic gyrated – with or without partners – on the massive dance floor."

According to Dyann Starr-King from the *Los Angeles Free Press*: "There was dancing and screaming and a really all-around good time, while the Byrds came on strong with their 'Mr Tambourine Man', 'I'll Feel A Whole Lot Better', 'The Bells Of Rhymney' and many others [including 'Chimes Of Freedom']. Some of the songs were written by Bob Dylan, some by members of the Byrds . . . The dancing was excited and swinging, and the dancers changed between dancing and simply standing happily and watching the group play. Between sets I was surprised and delighted to see several of the Byrds out wandering in the audience, which added even more to the feeling of closeness that the Byrds seem to hold with their audiences. In all, the whole mood of the evening was one of happiness and excitement. From the wild, colourful clothes worn to the dancing and bouncing around – and to the very feeling of the Byrds' music, which can go right through you and leave a warm sensation – it was an evening of fun, of welcome home Byrds, and the magic feeling of everybody having a good time."

page 178: "It was on the same tape . . ." Dickson/Rogan. London/Hawaii: 7 July 1997.

page 178: "Don't they phrase beautifully . . ." George Harrison, in attendance at the Byrds' recording session, documented in *Flip*: Autumn 1965.

page 179: "It was sloppier than anything . . ." Melcher/Rogan. London: 27 December 1977. In the author's first book, *Timeless Flight* (Scorpion/Dark Star, 1981), p. 33, Melcher provided the following comment: "Lennon and McCartney sat in the booth on 'It's All Over Now, Baby Blue', which was really sloppy from start to finish, largely due to the fact that Dylan was there too. It was enough to make anyone nervous." I suspect Melcher actually meant the session for 'The Times They Are A-Changin'' at which George Harrison and Paul McCartney appeared. However, neither Lennon nor Dylan attended that session.

page 179: "It's a pity John's not here . . ." Paul McCartney, in attendance at the Byrds' recording session, documented in *Flip*: Autumn 1965.

page 179: "If I know anything . . ." George Harrison, in attendance at the Byrds' recording session, documented in *Flip*: Autumn 1965.

page 179: "They came down and sealed off CBS . . ." Dickson/Rogan. Waldport, Oregon: 26–30 April 1989.

page 179: "David Crosby had put some drugs." ibid.

page 180: "He'd told the FBI guy . . ." ibid. Dickson adds: "Derek went back through the window, came out into the restroom and said: 'Excuse me for taking so long, I ate something that didn't agree with me.' He came back over and everybody was clean and nothing happened and by that time the cop was talked out of the whole thing and it wasn't going to be a lot of fun anyway. We all walked away and everything was OK – but it was an incredibly uptight moment. A really exciting experience. They were already up from having the Beatles in the studio."

page 180: "I didn't smoke hash . . ." Taylor/Rogan. London: 13 February 1997.

page 180: "George slipped out of a side door . . ." documented in *Flip*: Autumn 1965.

page 181: "When Derek took them to England . . ." Dickson/Rogan. Waldport, Oregon: 26–30 April 1989.

page 181: "I never wanted to be fired . . ." Taylor/Rogan. London: 13 February 1997.

page 181: "The thing about Jim and Eddie . . ." ibid.

page 181: "It took a crisis . . ." Dickson/Rogan. Waldport, Oregon: 26–30 April 1989.

page 182: "What really got to me most was Dylan . . ." McGuinn/Valentine. *Sounds*: 21 August 1971.

page 182: "He had a typewriter . . ." Roger McGuinn, interviewed by David Fricke. *Rolling Stone*: 23 August 1990.

page 182: "There were tons of people . . ." Dolores Tickner (formerly McGuinn, née DeLeon), interviewed by the author. London/Tucson, Arizona: 24–25 February 2007.

page 183: "If that's your partner . . ." ibid.

page 183: "And I was stupid enough . . ." ibid.

page 183: "Crosby was a colourful and unpredictable character . . ." Bob Dylan, *Chronicles Volume One* (Simon & Schuster, 2004) p.132. The odd reference to Crosby "tottering on the brink of death" is probably referring to a later period. While discussing Crosby here, Dylan was simultaneously reminiscing about the time David accompanied him to Princeton to receive an honorary doctorate on 8 June 1970. At that

NOTES

point, Crosby was a major figure in Crosby, Stills, Nash & Young and had just completed a memorable series of gigs at the Fillmore the previous night. Needless to say by that point Crosby was a serious drug user/abuser, which might explain Dylan's comment.

page 183: "Bob wanted a bottle of wine . . ." Clarke/Rogan. London and Manchester: 14–15 October 1989.

page 184: "Everyone was so scared of Dylan . . ." Dolores Tickner (formerly McGuinn, née DeLeon)/Rogan. London/Tucson, Arizona: 24–25 February 2007.

page 184: "They know it all . . ." Bob Dylan, interviewed by Paul Jay Robbins: March 1965. Printed in *Los Angeles Free Press*: September 1965.

page 184: "We were walking down Sunset Boulevard . . ." Dolores Tickner (formerly McGuinn, née DeLeon)/Rogan. London/Tucson, Arizona: 24–25 February 2007.

page 184: "I was thinking . . ." ibid.

page 185: "I'm sure it would have been . . ." ibid.

page 185: "Little Mr Noone . . ." Derek Taylor column. *Disc*: 16 October 1965.

page 185: "I was playing keyboards . . ." Van Dyke Parks, email to the author: 3 July 2007. Parks initially assumed this incident took place onstage at Ciro's "on the Strip". But as Jim Dickson confirmed: "The Byrds didn't have a support act at Ciro's. They played five sets a night." The Trip, of course, was also on the Strip and ads confirm that the Skip Battyn Group were in attendance. Parks is otherwise a reliable witness, although on camera during a filmed interview for the *Under Review* DVD, he assumed his contribution to '5 D' was produced by Terry Melcher, instead of Allen Stanton, and said it was on the *first* Byrds album. These slips of memory were edited during production.

page 186: "He apologized to me . . ." Franzoni/Rogan. London/Santa Rosa, California: 22 June 2007.

page 186: "Gene was like a singing Robert Mitchum . . ." Kim Fowley, interviewed by the author. London/Redlands, California: 27–28 June 2007.

page 187: "You're over-exaggerating . . ." Taylor/Rogan. London: 17 June 1977.

page 188: "David . . . shakes hands with me . . ." P.F. Sloan, quoted in Howard Sounes, *Down The Highway: The Life Of Bob Dylan* (Doubleday, 2001), pp. 229–230

page 189: "It was the first song that Terry tried to push . . ." Dickson/Rogan. Waldport, Oregon: 26–30 April 1989.

page 189: "phoney . . . awful rubbish . . . cashing in on a trend . . ." Mick Jagger and Paul McCartney, quoted in *Melody Maker*: 4 September 1965.
page 189: "I think 'Eve Of Destruction' is a terribly depressing song . . ." Mary Travers, quoted in *Melody Maker*: 25 September 1965.
page 190: "Nothing could be more ridiculous . . ." Tom Paxton, "Folk Rot", published in *Sing Out!*: Autumn 1965.
page 190: "'Eve Of Destruction' protests about nothing . . ." Paul Jones, quoted in *New Musical Express*: September 1965.
page 190: "Hanging desperately to his coat-tails . . ." Tom Paxton, "Folk Rot", published in *Sing Out!*: Autumn 1965.
page 190: "I only read the title 'Folk Rot'," McGuinn/Rogan. London/Florida: 22 May 1997.
page 191: "It was a phenomenon . . ." McGuire/Rogan. Rosslare, Wexford, Republic of Ireland: 1–2 August 2008.
page 193: "We were an easy target . . ." Dickson/Rogan. Waldport, Oregon: 26–30 April 1989.
page 193: "Coming out of folk music . . ." ibid.

Chapter 13: Non-Aristotelian Systems

page 195: "I didn't want to do them . . ." Dickson/Rogan. Waldport, Oregon: 26–30 April 1989.
page 196: "McGuinn came into the booth . . ." ibid.
page 196: "I didn't do it behind his back . . ." ibid.
page 197: "The first time I wanted to get rid of Terry Melcher . . ." ibid.
page 198: "Michael, Chris and David were very short-suited . . ." ibid.
page 198: "When Terry got excited . . ." ibid.
page 198: "Terry brought in a bottle of vodka . . ." ibid.
page 199: "There was resistance to me . . ." Crosby/Rogan. London: 22–23 April 1980.
page 200: "'Stranger In A Strange Land' was a very unsophisticated . . ." David Crosby, interviewed by the author. London: 21 February 1989. Crosby expounded upon the influence of Robert Heinlein's book in a 1967 interview with the *Southern California Oracle, Counter-Culture News*. "I probably gave away five or six hundred copies of that book *Stranger In A Strange Land* in one summer in Sausalito. I gave them away not because they really say this is where it's at, and here's how to live in the world, and you can keep all your money in a bowl, and everything is cool, and you learn how to grok and we'll all learn Martian and all be

telepaths, right? But, there's something about sharing water that's getting high, and there's something about how those people lived that's like what happens every time a bunch of nice people start living in the same place."

page 200: "That was the only Byrds' copyright . . ." Dickson/Rogan. Waldport, Oregon: 26–30 April 1989.

page 200: ". . . the love gun that will blow your mind . . ." Tickner/Rogan. Redondo Beach, California: 20 July 1979. Tickner recited these lyrics from memory, 14 years after the event. He had a grin on his face at the time, as if he thought they were the most amusing and preposterous utterings he had ever heard. They certainly sounded closer to the type of lyrics later witnessed in 1967, but Crosby was always one step ahead of the hippie movement. Still, it was surprising that his lyrics should register so strongly with Tickner, who was not in attendance at the studio. The other Byrds never mentioned the song, let alone the words. As publisher, of course, Tickner may have been attempting to sell this song, in the same fashion as 'Stranger In A Strange Land'. This might also explain why the vocal version is still missing, although that's pure supposition.

page 200: "Everybody, myself included . . ." Dickson/Rogan. Waldport, Oregon: 26–30 April 1989.

page 201: "Suddenly, there were insecurities . . ." Taylor/Rogan. London: 17 June 1977.

page 201: "They could have done it so much better . . ." ibid.

page 201: "The replacement was a song . . ." Coincidentally, McGuinn's former employers the Limeliters were the first to cover the song under the title 'To Everything There Is A Season' on their 1962 album, *Folk Matinee*.

page 202: "It was a standard folk song by that time . . ." McGuinn/Cohen. *Sing Out!* Vol. 18; No. 5: December 1968/January 1969.

page 202: "The fact that he was replaced . . ." Dickson/Rogan. Waldport, Oregon: 26–30 April 1989.

page 203: "McGuinn and I were the only people . . ." Melcher/Rogan. London: 27 December 1977. According to Melcher, Dickson persuaded the Byrds to veto 'Turn! Turn! Turn!' and even officially informed the label that it could not be released. Nobody else recalls this incident and, given McGuinn's continued support for the song, it seems unlikely. Then again, as McGuinn later showed when agreeing to Melcher's dismissal as producer, he was capable of being easily persuaded against his better judgement. Melcher recalls pressing up dozens of acetates of 'Turn! Turn! Turn!' and blitzing radio stations with them in order to push forward its release. This may well be true. Derek Taylor confirms that he offered the disc to KRLA and ran into trouble with the CBS promotions department. Melcher agrees that he suffered the same fate and almost put his job in danger as a result. Of course, any disciplinary action was forgotten once the record was released and rapidly climbed the charts.

page 203: "I thought 'Turn! Turn! Turn!' was an either/or song . . ." Dickson/Rogan. Waldport, Oregon: 26–30 April 1989.

page 204: "That's the essence of the song . . ." Roger McGuinn, interviewed by L.A. Johnson. Paramount Studios, Hollywood, California: 10 July 1995.

page 204: "It's a laundry list . . ." Dickson/Rogan. Waldport, Oregon: 26–30 April 1989.

Chapter 14: Fracas And Fistfights

page 206: "There was friction between McGuinn and Dickson . . ." Melcher/Rogan. London: 27 December 1977.

page 206: "You'll never work in this business again! . . ." Clarke/Rogan. London and Manchester: 14–15 October 1989.

page 207: "I slapped him . . ." ibid.

page 207: "David was punched . . ." reported in *16* (April 1966).

page 207: ". . . the boys shook hands . . ." ibid.

page 207: "They all ganged up on Dickson . . ." Melcher/Rogan. London: 27 December 1977.

page 207: "He was a complete drag about it . . ." Dickson/Rogan. Waldport, Oregon: 26–30 April 1989.

page 208: "David was the one . . ." Clarke/Rogan. London and Manchester: 14–15 October 1989.

page 208: "Someone wasn't looking right . . ." Roger McGuinn, interviewed by Patrick William Salvo. *New Musical Express*: 5 May 1973.

page 208: "I slugged Jim once . . ." Crosby/Rogan. London: 22–23 April 1980.

page 209: "I felt we could make the equivalent . . ." Dickson/Rogan. Waldport, Oregon: 26–30 April 1989.

page 210: "Barry Feinstein arrived . . ." ibid.

page 211: "People have stronger feelings about David Crosby . . ." ibid.

page 211: "McGuinn was horrified . . ." ibid.

page 212: "It was upsetting to me . . ." McGuinn/Rogan. London/Florida: 22 May 1997.

NOTES

page 212: "You're supposed to be the leader . . ." Clarke quote, as remembered by Dolores Tickner (formerly McGuinn, née DeLeon), interviewed by the author. Tucson, Arizona: 28 October 2005. Chris Hillman voiced similar criticisms to Sid Griffin in *Full Circle* 11 (January 1992): "The Byrds never really had a strong leader other than Jim [Dickson] early on. McGuinn is perceived as a leader but he was never a strong leader. He was, in his own right and way, very shy in dealing with other people around him in a close situation. It was never like [him] saying, 'Onward, men! Here we go!' And we needed that. Dickson was our leader, our father, our camp counselor and on the bad side our Svengali, Rasputin."

page 212: "Dickson was becoming too emotional . . ." Melcher/Rogan. London: 27 December 1977.

page 212: "That's pure, unadulterated bullshit . . ." Crosby/Rogan. London: 22–23 April 1980.

page 213: "Melcher's an idiot . . ." ibid.

page 214: "Although Terry liked what he could do . . ." Dickson/Rogan. Waldport, Oregon: 26–30 April 1989.

page 214: "I was hanging out with Terry . . ." McGuinn/Rogan. London/Florida: 22 May 1997.

page 215: "Gene Clark intrigues me . . ." This quote was released by Derek Taylor in promotional asides during late 1965 and 1966. I have no reason to doubt the veracity of the quote, although whether Taylor heard it direct from Dylan or second hand is uncertain. Assuming Dylan's 'intrigue' was based on Clark's development as a songwriter, the quote appears to have been inspired by the recently completed 'Set You Free This Time'. Dylan would probably have been even more intrigued, and possibly flattered, had he ever heard 'The Day Walk', the most Dylanesque of Clark's recent compositions.

page 215: "That's what we all saw . . ." Dickson/Rogan. Waldport, Oregon: 26–30 April 1989.

page 216: "They always encouraged him . . ." ibid.

page 217: "When everyone was contributing equally . . ." Dickson, quoted in liner notes to *Never Before*.

page 217: "The opinion was that Melcher was playing fast favourites . . ." Tickner/Rogan. Redondo Beach, California: 20 July 1979.

page 217: "The restaurant effectively served as a clubhouse for Frank Sinatra . . ." The Villa Capri was also the place where Derek Taylor had first committed himself to the Byrds. As he told me: "The night I decided to leave my Bob Eubank 6290 job and throw in my lot with the Byrds, we decided to go to the Villa Capri, watched over by Frank

Sinatra and friends at the next table. Frank was bored witless with the people he was with, but he was interested in our little group because two of us were English, my wife Joan and me. Eddie and Jim were obviously not English but counterculture-ish. Frank was sitting there and saying 'Who are these guys?' I thought 'This is very bizarre'. I was still quite starstruck. I thought 'Why am I here?' There I was thinking of moving into a skyscraper on Sunset Boulevard and Frank Sinatra's there trying to listen in. Amazing."

page 217: "He liked his music . . ." Dolores Tickner (formerly McGuinn, née DeLeon)/Rogan. London/Tucson, Arizona: 13 January 2007.

page 218: "I think McGuinn and Terry tried to use each other . . ." Dickson/Rogan. Waldport, Oregon: 26–30 April 1989.

page 219: "Terry was trying to bridge the gap . . ." ibid.

page 219: "If I don't have a Bentley . . ." ibid.

page 219: "He's fond of making threats . . ." ibid.

page 220: ". . . unsuitable and appear to be anti-Byrd . . ." letter from CBS Records to Derek Taylor, quoted in *Record Beat*: 15 February 1966.

page 220: "Really, Columbia was quite right . . ." Derek Taylor. *Record Beat*: 15 February 1966.

page 220: "He wears a green and brown suede cloak . . ." Derek Taylor's original uncensored liner notes for *Turn! Turn! Turn!*.

page 220: "Jim McGuinn is the leader . . ." ibid.

page 221: "Hillman is a bluegrass man . . ." ibid.

page 221: ". . . a dozen fistfights . . ." Derek Taylor's 'released' liner notes to *Turn! Turn! Turn!*.

Chapter 15: Turn! Turn! Turn!

page 222: "I had a physical response . . ." Roger McGuinn, interviewed by Harvey Kubernik: 2007. Original interview transcript sent to author.

page 223: "I slipped the single to KRLA . . ." Taylor/Rogan. London: 17 June 1977.

page 223: "Tell Jim [McGuinn] and David . . ." letter from George Harrison to Derek Taylor, quoted in *The Byrds'* box set.

page 224: "Didn't our old grannies . . ." extracted from Derek Taylor's liner notes to *Turn! Turn! Turn!*.

page 224: "We thought that it was better . . ." Crosby/Rogan. London: 22–23 April 1980.

page 224: "It's so unassuming . . ." David Crosby, interviewed by L.A. Johnson. Paramount Studios, Hollywood, California: 15 August 1995.

NOTES

page 224: "I heard that in Catholic schools . . ." McGuinn/Cohen. *Sing Out!* Vol. 18; No. 5: December 1968/January 1969.

page 225: "You take everything on one side . . ." Dickson/Rogan. Waldport, Oregon: 26–30 April 1989.

page 225: "Jac chose and I had my fingers crossed . . ." ibid.

page 225: "We were all satisfied with 'It Won't Be Wrong' . . ." Melcher/Rogan. London: 27 December 1977.

page 226: "When I reached my room . . ." Gene Clark, interviewed in *America Calling* column, *New Musical Express*: 25 February 1966.

page 226: "The Byrds left the studio before Gene . . ." Melcher/Rogan. London: 27 December 1977.

page 226–227: "Never before or since . . ." Michael Gray, *The Bob Dylan Encyclopedia* (Continuum, 2006). In Cameron Crowe's liner notes to the CD anthology *Biograph*, Dylan explained that he wrote the song at Joan Baez's house on the West Coast. "She had a place outside Big Sur. I had heard a Scottish ballad on an old 78 record that I was trying to really capture the feeling of, that was haunting me. I couldn't get it out of my head. There were no lyrics or anything, it was just a melody, had bagpipes and a lot of stuff in it. I wanted lyrics that would feel the same way."

page 227: ". . . the production was lousy . . . sloppy from start to finish . . ." Melcher/Rogan. London: 27 December 1977.

page 227: "They didn't do it as well . . ." Dickson/Rogan. Waldport, Oregon: 26–30 April 1989.

page 227: "It was 'Lay Down Your Weary Tune' . . ." McGuinn/Rogan. Leeds: 4 May 1977. Oddly, McGuinn was not struck by the evident contradiction in Dylan's words. Claiming "that was the first time [Dylan] realized that I could do something different with his material" hardly made sense. Dylan had already complimented the Byrds at World-Pacific, appeared with them onstage at Ciro's, championed them in print, and raved about 'Mr Tambourine Man' to friends and associates. He even wore out a copy of the acetate, such was his enthusiasm.

page 228: "I wrote that song the night John F. Kennedy . . ." ibid. McGuinn remembers composing the lyrics that same evening after visiting Bob Carey from the long established folk group, the Tarriers. McGuinn was feeling down and Carey had good reasons to feel worse. Beset by personal problems, he had been fired from the Tarriers during the late spring due to his unreliability. Like McGuinn he was surviving by working for one of the New York based publishers, the Howie Richmond Organization. Attempts to establish a solo career, plus a brief stint with the Tiffany Singers, were not working out and he would soon hit the bottle. A decade later, he would be found dead on a park bench.

Perhaps some of that darkness could be traced back to that strange evening of 22 November 1963.

While strumming with Carey, McGuinn subconsciously veered into 'He Was A Friend Of Mine', a familiar enough tune in folk circles that had been covered by many, including Bob Dylan. McGuinn modified the melody slightly, then added some poignant words about the assassination. The two-year delay in recording the song largely stemmed from McGuinn's fear that people might think he was somehow cashing in on the president's death. Coincidentally, Jim Dickson also recorded a version of the song on the album he produced for Dian James & The Greenbriar Boys. "Having done it before, I knew it was PD [public domain]," says Dickson, "and McGuinn wrote new lyrics to it. I thought he might do better with it than he did. I wasn't a pro-Kennedy person, but I enjoyed Kennedy. Not for his politics so much, but his image. I liked having a swinging president – that part was fun. A lot of people in McGuinn's generation had put a great deal of hope in Kennedy, and it was not the kind of thing that I'd have wanted to interfere with, even if I'd been able to. The song wasn't something that I thought would be a hit record, but I expected it to appear in documentaries. Other songs about Kennedy show up in all these documentaries they do on television or when they look back at the Kennedy years. It never showed up in those even though it's a perfect song for that."

page 228: "Remember that organ note . . ." Crosby/Rogan. London: 22–23 April 1980.

page 228: "I liked the song very much . . ." Gene Clark, interviewed by the author. New York: 26 January 1979.

page 229: "The song came from my mother . . ." Red Hayes, quoted in *Country Music People*: July 1973.

page 229: "It's a great song, which I've always loved . . ." Dickson/Rogan. Waldport, Oregon: 26–30 April 1989.

page 229: "All he did was grumble . . ." ibid.

page 229: "David Crosby was very aware of that . . ." ibid.

page 229: "He had this good idea . . ." Melcher/Rogan. London: 27 December 1977.

page 230: "We were going to do a great version of that . . ." Dickson/Rogan. Waldport, Oregon: 26–30 April 1989.

page 230: "Crosby and McGuinn wanted to move away . . ." Tickner/Rogan. Redondo Beach, California: 20 July 1979.

page 231: "Terry was too intimidated . . ." Dickson/Rogan. Waldport, Oregon: 26–30 April 1989.

NOTES

page 232: "I'm not too happy . . ." Roger McGuinn, interviewed by Vincent Flanders. Indianapolis Coliseum: 14 February 1970.
page 233: "When the Byrds wrote me a letter . . ." Dickson/Rogan. Waldport, Oregon: 26–30 April 1989.
page 233: "Jim Dickson believed that if he got rid of Melcher . . ." McGuinn/Rogan. Leeds: 4 May 1977.
page 233: "Getting drunk on the set? . . ." Melcher/Rogan. London: 27 December 1977.
page 233: "It wasn't so much that Dickson . . ." Tickner/Rogan. Redondo Beach, California: 20 July 1979.
page 234: "I told him that he'd never have another number 1 . . ." Dickson/Rogan. Waldport, Oregon: 26–30 April 1989.
page 234: "Dickson's vision of the Byrds . . ." Tickner/Rogan. Redondo Beach, California: 20 July 1979.
page 234: "Good or bad I was probably guilty . . ." Dickson/Rogan. Waldport, Oregon: 26–30 April 1989.
page 235: "It must have been the biggest frustration . . ." Crosby/Rogan. London: 22–23 April 1980.
page 235: "I couldn't produce at CBS . . ." Dickson/Rogan. Waldport, Oregon: 26–30 April 1989.
page 235: "McGuinn was a most unlikely case . . ." Taylor/Rogan. London: 13 February 1997.
page 236: "I was being outrageously tactless . . ." ibid.
page 236: "As remarkable as McGuinn would be . . ." Dickson/Rogan. Waldport, Oregon: 26–30 April 1989.
page 237: "Dancers were not rare . . ." Dickson/Rogan. London/Hawaii: 3 August 1998.
page 237: "Jackie showed up in a Thunderbird . . ." ibid.
page 237: "She told me she used to imagine . . ." ibid.
page 237: "She went after David first . . ." ibid.
page 237: "They played at being Sonny & Cher . . ." ibid.
page 239: "The best quality time . . ." McGuire/Rogan. Rosslare, Co. Wexford, Republic of Ireland: 1–2 August 2008.
page 239: "It was the first really good live sound . . ." Dickson/Rogan. Waldport, Oregon: 26–30 April 1989.
page 240: "We'd done the two shows . . ." ibid.
page 240: "Gene picked up a coconut . . ." ibid.
page 240: "We were in this little river . . ." ibid.
page 240: ". . . nervous about Gene's driving . . ." ibid.
page 241: "We lost the car, the $5,000 overrun money . . ." ibid.

Chapter 16: Eight Miles High

page 242: "Columbia wouldn't let us release . . ." Chris Hillman, interviewed by the author. London: 28 April 1977.

page 243: "It was a stunner . . ." Crosby/Rogan. London: 22–23 April 1980.

page 243: "It was just demonstration vocals . . ." Dickson/Rogan. Waldport, Oregon: 26–30 April 1989.

page 243: "David was energetic . . ." ibid.

page 244: "Shankar's sound . . ." David Crosby, quoted in *Melody Maker*: 28 May 1966.

page 244: "I played him Coltrane and Shankar . . ." Crosby/Rogan. London: 22–23 April 1980.

page 244: "David didn't *make* us listen to it . . ." McGuinn/Rogan. London/Florida: 22 May 1997.

page 244: "It was not a sitar on 'Why' . . ." McGuinn/Rogan. Leeds: 4 May 1977.

page 245: "Did I give somebody credit for that? . . ." Crosby/Rogan. London: 22–23 April 1980.

page 245: "When I heard the track 'Why' . . ." Dickson/Rogan. Waldport, Oregon: 26–30 April 1989.

page 246: "Well, I still wanted to get something . . ." ibid. Dickson's championing of 'The Times They Are A-Changin'' indicated his continued love of Dylan. Although he also was thrilled by the Byrds' innovation on 'Eight Miles High', he still believed in recording quality covers. Part of his problem, particularly with David Crosby, was this focus on specific material which fitted his complex vision of the Byrds. It may now sound old-fashioned but Dickson would have persisted with the Dylan covers far into the future. "What I was going to do with the Byrds was record them and have a few Dylan songs all the way along. It was important for McGuinn. To have McGuinn do some Dylan and some Seeger, like he did – 'The Bells Of Rhymney', 'Turn! Turn! Turn!' – but keep it in context so that about three years down the line we'd have enough to put out a double album of Dylan songs with a couple of new ones. Do a couple of Seeger and maybe put out a Seeger album, or put out a best of the Byrds between the third and fourth year and make that the biggest dollar year possible at CBS, so that when it came time at the end of the five-year contract to renegotiate, CBS would come up with a whole lot of money. At that point I intended to release absolute control of it all. Each had different ideas and wanted to go different ways, so let them do it any way they wanted after that. Let's make the good body of work, the win, and if David wants to do his kind of music and they want to play on each other's albums, I won't try to keep it together and make it be the Byrds, or anything. That would complete my goal and I'd have been willing to walk away and say, 'We achieved everything that we hoped to set out for. You guys, with all this under your belt, go and create individually or collectively in any combinations because you'll be secure enough to do it. We'll come away with enough money not to be ever frightened about missing dinner again.'"

Dickson's vision may sound plausible but part of his dream also sounded like a nightmare. It was too reminiscent of the old world of Peter, Paul & Mary covering Dylan. Rather than pushing their own songwriting in the Byrds exclusively, Dickson also wanted them to be seen as Dylan converts. In his concept, they would probably have recorded an album like *Hollies Sing Dylan*, which gave the group a number 1 record in the UK, but also prompted Graham Nash's departure. It is difficult to imagine Crosby sanctioning such a record as late as 1967, and his rebellion over the re-recording of 'The Times They Are A-Changin'' speaks volumes about his attitude towards such an idea.

page 247: "The Trip was good . . ." Linda Loo Bopp, interviewed by the author. North Hollywood, California: 29 July 1979. A strong British contingent was there for the two-week residency at the Trip, including Peter & Gordon, various Yardbirds and pop star pundit, Jonathan King. In a bulletin printed in the UK's *Music Echo*, he wrote: "You might have noticed that my pet hobby-horse recently has been the Byrds. I saw them perform again last week in Los Angeles and they really were unbelievably good. We like to think of ourselves here in England as able to recognize talent when we see it, but somehow they didn't really click on their first visit. The Byrds must come back here very soon, and then, I trust everything will turn out all right. We all know that the voluble and expressive correspondents are the 'anti' brigade. Let's make an exception. Byrd-fans, put pen to paper and bring them over here by popular demand." Surprisingly, the Byrds' Trip residency was well covered in the British music press. I recall that strange combination of curiosity, excitement and slight bafflement after reading Tracy Thomas' transatlantic bulletin in *New Musical Express* (24 February 1966) when she told us: "Currently the Byrds are entertaining SRO-crowds at the Trip, one of the 'in clubs' on the Sunset Strip. Though a few Dylan numbers remain in their customarily reserved set, several hard rock and jazz-rock numbers have crept in from behind the 12-string and tambourine, displaying a versatility and ability in fields other than folk rock that is barely hinted at in their albums."

page 247: "Crosby's cloak . . ." Derek Taylor press release, 1966.

page 247: "It's clear that the Byrds . . ." ibid.

page 249: "I got there late . . ." McGuinn/Johnson. *Hit Parader*: September 1968.

page 249: "Clark's contributions weren't missed . . ." Reviewer: Michael H. Drew. *Milwaukee Journal*: 4 March 1966.

page 250: ". . . nervous condition . . ." ibid.

page 250: " 'Where's Gene?' . . . a Sunday evening show in Chicago . . . a score of screaming fans besieged the stage." *KRLA Beat* (2 April 1966) provided a fascinating report under the headline 'Riot At Byrd's [sic] Concert'. "The Byrds refused to take flight as 300 screaming female fans stormed the stage of the Civic Opera House in one of the wildest rock shows which the city has yet to witness. The Byrds continued performing and absolutely refused to vacate the stage even when House employees rushed from the wings and attempted to unplug the group's electric guitars. In the end it took a total of 30 policemen to quell the screaming audience as the Byrds calmly sang 'Mr Tambourine Man'. Ushers were pushed aside like cardboard boxes as about 20 of the girls managed to make it on stage to their heroes. One girl in the audience received a bruised back and two other members of the Byrds audience were arrested – the first for disorderly conduct and the second for simple assault. The police lieutenant stated that he made the second arrest after being kicked twice in the leg. The audience was primarily female and many wore buttons proclaiming, 'I'm bold', which had to be the understatement of the century! Questioned after the concert, most declared that they had been pleased with the show but apparently the police had other ideas and so stopped it when it was half over."

page 250: "Eddie started working on him . . ." Dickson/Rogan. Waldport, Oregon: 26–30 April 1989.

page 250: ". . . to return to the group . . ." *KRLA Beat*: 12 March 1966.

page 250: ". . . not to undertake any personal appearances . . ." *Record Mirror*: 19 March 1966.

page 250: "I'll be doing more singing now . . ." Chris Hillman, interviewed by Maureen Payne. *Record Mirror*: 19 March 1966.

page 250: "He's clearly not well enough . . ." Eddie Tickner, quoted in *Music Echo*: 12 March 1966.

page 251: "Their first set was disappointing . . ." Reviewer Johnny Mitchell. *Record Beat*: 21 June 1966.

page 251: "I don't think there's a sitar . . ." McGuinn/Rogan. Leeds: 4 May 1977.

NOTES

page 252: "Every kid practically in the United States . . ." *Hit Parader*: July 1966.

page 252: "Most groups accomplish one thing . . ." Further comments from the raga rock press conference, syndicated in various magazines. Unsurprisingly, it was Crosby and McGuinn whose comments dominated the press conference, with Clarke and Hillman reduced to silent acquisition. When one observer questioned their quiet contribution, Derek Taylor snapped back: "They're not dumb. Mike and Chris are just as talkative as Dave and Jim." McGuinn reminded the assembled that Hillman was a fine mandolin player, while Crosby revealed some previously undocumented musical talents that might have surprised Clark and Clarke: "We might play with an electric piano because Mike and Gene both fool with pianos. McGuinn's been fooling with an organ too, and he also plays banjo. We'll play anything that we ourselves can play. If it fits in a piece of music and it swings and we can play it, we use it."

The conference also included a wonderful moment of humility and contrition from Crosby. "I found out that I have an unfortunate habit that's a very stupid one. I used to enjoy putting people down. I'm trying to monitor myself. It's a bad habit. I just shouldn't put people down. It doesn't do you any good or anybody else. There's no constructive purpose to be achieved by it." It would be gratifying to think that Crosby was referring to his treatment of Gene Clark with this unexpected reflection, but he never elaborated on the matter.

page 253: "The Byrds are waiting . . ." Derek Taylor, press release, 1966. His apparent miscalculation regarding the chart performances of 'All I Really Want To Do' (US number 40, not US number 9) and 'It Won't Be Wrong' (US number 63, not US number 39) may have stemmed from using a preferred local LA chart, rather than *Billboard* or *Cash Box*. Or maybe it was simply PR exaggeration.

page 254: "We have dropped 'Rainy Day Women' . . ." *Bill Gavin's Record Report*: 29 April 1966.

page 254: "The irony of it . . ." Derek Taylor, press release: April 1966.

page 254: ". . . with help from fellow Byrds-members . . ." ibid.

page 254: "We could have called the song 'Forty-Two Thousand . . ." McGuinn, quoted in Taylor's press release, April 1966.

page 254–255: "We started it out as six miles high . . ." McGuinn/Frame. *Zigzag* 29: March 1973.

page 255: "You come over here . . ." ibid.

page 255: "I wrote that verse . . ." Crosby/Rogan. London: 22–23 April 1980. Crosby's suggestion about writing "most of the last verse" is contradicted by Clark. McGuinn doesn't remember it either.

915

page 255: "It seems extraordinary . . ." McGuinn, quoted in Derek Taylor's press release: April 1966.

page 256: "Please be advised . . ." Certified letter to Bill Gavin on behalf of the Byrds from Marshall L. McDaniel of McDaniel & McDaniel: 20 May 1966.

page 256: "One week after receiving this demand, Gavin reprinted the relevant portion of the letter . . ." See *Bill Gavin's Record Report,* number 559: 27 May 1966. On 31 May 1966, Edward J. Boessenecker (representing *Bill Gavin's Record Report*) wrote back to Marshall L. McDaniel of McDaniel & McDaniel, explaining: "It was our understanding that the term 'eight miles high' is an expression commonly employed by users of LSD . . . We have given equal publicity to your clients' explanation concerning the origins of these words in the song, and trust that it meets with your approval."

page 257: "Brian never wanted credit . . ." Gene Clark, interviewed by Paul Zollo. *Song Talk*: Spring 1991.

page 257: ". . . after a discussion about William Burroughs . . ." The William Burroughs' reference was mentioned in an interview with Gene Clark by Andy Darlington, first printed in *Rock 'n' Reel* (reprinted *Full Circle* 10: September 1991). Although Clark truncated the timeline and events in his story, there was much here that had a ring of truth. "You know how that song really started?" he said. "It was me and Brian Jones sitting in a hotel room on the road when we were touring with the Stones. We got to be – me, Michael and Brian – [we] all got to be good friends. Brian was a little more social than Mick or Keith, even though I really love Mick, I think he's great. But Brian was always real friendly, so he and I and Michael started hanging out together. I remember we were up eating a couple of steaks, talking and having a couple of Scotches, and we started talking about William Burroughs. And somehow I just got this idea – it came into my mind. I don't know how the conversation led up to it, but I started scribbling down the poetry. And Brian said, 'What are you doing?', and I said, 'This' – showing him. He looked at it, read a little bit of it, and he said, 'That's pretty good, you ought to work on that.' So that's how the song got started. I think I worked on it in private for, gosh, maybe two weeks or something – almost every night in the hotel room. And then we were on the bus – there was all of us in a motor home and we were listening to a lot of John Coltrane and Ravi Shankar because we were programming ourselves . . . We were listening to a lot of Bach too. And I played the song for McGuinn. I remember our road manager turned around and said, 'That's good poetry!' McGuinn goes 'Yeah, I like that too', and then Crosby comes down out of his bunk – he

NOTES

goes 'Yeah, I like that too', and he says, 'I got a line for that one place where the words are shaky.' So he threw in a line. And then McGuinn started working on it. He began to get into the arranging. So that's how it ended up but the original idea came, of course, out of Brian Jones. But he didn't know. At that time he probably didn't halfway remember having the conversation . . ."

page 258: "It was mostly Gene's tune . . ." McGuinn/Rogan. London/Florida: 22 May 1997.

page 258: "I wrote all the words except one line . . ." Gene Clark, interviewed by Paul Zollo. *Jet Lag*: 93 (1991–92).

page 259: "A compulsive fast-moving rhythm . . ." Derek Johnson's review of 'Eight Miles High'. *New Musical Express*: 29 April 1966.

page 259: ". . . a very interesting, appealing record . . .' review in *Melody Maker*: 30 April 1966.

page 259: ". . . odd mixture of musical styles . . . song isn't a knockout . . ." review in *Record Mirror*: 30 April 1966.

page 259: "Before today . . ." review in *Disc*: 30 April 1966.

page 259: ". . . 'Eight Miles High' fared no better than 'Turn! Turn! Turn!' in the UK, charting for one week at number 28 . . ." I am, of course, referring to the all-important *NME* chart. In the less respected *Record Retailer*, 'Eight Miles High' climbed to number 24 while 'Turn! Turn! Turn!' had peaked at number 26.

page 259: "Of course it was a drug song . . ." Crosby/Rogan. London: 22–23 April 1980.

page 260: "Chris always used to wear a straightener . . ." Taylor/Rogan. London: 17 June 1977.

page 260: "McGuinn got smashed with restraint . . ." ibid.

page 261: "It blew us out of the game . . ." ibid. McGuinn's dire conclusion was an understandable but not entirely convincing argument. Over the years, he has exaggerated the impact of the 'banning' even claiming in a 1989 radio interview for the CD formatted *In The Studio* that, "it was really an effective ban back then. It did get us off of, I guess, 90 per cent of the stations". This was far from the truth, for the *Gavin Report* had a relatively minimal effect on the single's overall performance. Research analyst Mark Teehan (writing in *Popular Musicology Online*, 2010) rightly points out that certain journalists and chroniclers have over-emphasized the impact of the *Gavin Report*, no doubt reinforced by the Byrds' critical comments. After analysing "surviving local music surveys", Teehan concludes that the contents of the *Report* were not enough to affect the national performance of 'Eight Miles High'. Although most of his points are objectively sound, his tone occasionally lapses into the same subjectivity with which he associates the proselytizers of the ban. At one point, he rounds up the many commentators on the ban (excluding quotes from this author) with the fiery conclusion: "their claims have been disingenuous and invalid, in effect amounting to an unsubstantiated conspiracy theory."

Unfortunately, in his determination to discredit this canard, he virtually writes off the effects of the *Gavin Report* altogether. The 'ban' may not have had a fatally detrimental effect, but that is very different from suggesting it had no effect at all. Immediately after the *Report* was published the record was removed from playlists at stations in Washington, D.C., Baltimore and Houston, a contention published at the time which Teehan is unable to refute ("Regarding the purported three banned markets . . . it was unfortunate that comprehensive survey data from stations in these three cities has not survived"). That said, a breakdown of the extent of radio play in other areas appears to support his case, and he notes that "only three stations' surveys – ten per cent of the total in our core sample – evinced fallout from the *Gavin Report* [KBOX, Dallas; WHYN, Springfield, Massachusetts and WLOF, Orlando]." Still, one might argue that ten per cent *is* something, however small. Teehan calculates that this "relatively minor damage" would not have affected the chart placing of 'Eight Miles High'. He concludes provocatively: "The Byrds had no possibility of making the national Top 10 – to say nothing of the number 1 position – that was a pipedream." The second part of this comment is sound, but it's doubtful any of the Byrds, or their management, genuinely believed the complex 'Eight Miles High' was commercial enough to reach the top. Derek Taylor had produced an effusive press release, fantasizing about a 'third number 1' but even he suggested this was "blandly optimistic". Given the poor performance of 'It Won't Be Wrong', 'Eight Miles High' actually performed pretty well in the charts, climbing to number 12 in *Cash Box* and number 14 in *Billboard*. The suggestion that it had "no possibility" of reaching the Top 10 is an odd and unconvincing assertion. Without the *Gavin Report* debacle (resulting in a 'ban' in Washington, D.C., Baltimore and Houston and the ten per cent 'fallout' acknowledged by Teehan's own research) who is to say it might not have cost those crucial *two* chart places in *Cash Box* or *four* places in *Billboard* which would otherwise have provided a Top 10 hit? Managers Dickson and Tickner clearly felt damage had been done as evidenced by the previously quoted legal correspondence. This was not done lightly and everyone involved, including publicist Derek Taylor, regarded the potential ban as an impending crisis. After 'Eight Miles High' the Byrds never registered

NOTES

another US Top 20 hit. Probably it's that realization that prompted McGuinn's belief that "it blew us out of the game".

Some consideration should also be given to the views of other managers who encountered similar problems. In late 1966, UK manager/record label mogul Larry Page recalls his consternation upon learning that the Troggs' 'I Can't Control Myself' had fallen foul of the Gavin moral radar. Page flew over from the UK and did everything possible to counter the fallout from a possible 'ban'. "The *Gavin Report* had a lot of power – it could kill you stone dead on radio," he says, with a shudder. These comments underline the crucial point that the *Gavin Report* was taken extremely seriously by everybody at the time. Why else resort to expensive legal intervention as the normally non-litigious Dickson and Tickner felt obliged to do?

Chapter 17: Fear Of Flying

page 262: "He reached the point of crisis . . ." McGuinn/Cohen. *Sing Out!* Vol. 18; No. 5: December 1968/January 1969.

page 263: "Gene didn't like to fly . . ." McGuire/Rogan. Rosslare, Co. Wexford, Republic of Ireland: 1–2 August 2008.

page 263: "Gene was a little squirrelly . . ." Dickson/Rogan. London/Hawaii: 7 July 1997.

page 264: "That was true . . ." Crosby/Rogan. London: 22–23 April 1980.

page 264: "Gene was not Bob Dylan . . ." McGuinn/Rogan. London/Florida: 22 May 1997.

page 264: "Gene could write 15–20 songs a week . . ." Dickson/Rogan. Waldport, Oregon: 26–30 April 1989.

page 265: "I liked the sound and feel of it . . ." ibid.

page 265: "Maybe the guilt factor . . ." *Fusion*: April 1969.

page 265: ". . . had even allowed the B-side 'She Don't Care About Time' to be excluded from *Turn! Turn! Turn!* . . ." One of the detriments of modern criticism in regard to the Byrds' early career is that it often fails to understand the nuances of the era or the audience it is talking about. I have read various reviews and commentaries puzzling over why the group could possibly include 'Oh! Susannah!' at the expense of 'She Don't Care About Time'. Yet, at the time, this was completely logical. The Beatles themselves deliberately excluded singles, both A and B sides, from their albums as a matter of policy. Many of us considered it poor value to feature previously released material, no matter how impressive the particular song. When *Record Mirror* reviewed *Turn! Turn! Turn!* they gave the work a four-star review, with a single caveat: "The worst thing that can be said about this album is that some of the songs have been heard before. Any other comments must be strictly in the raving strata. . . . 'Set You Free This Time' is beautiful and their treatment of 'Oh! Susannah' is a delight." The Byrds would probably have lost a star or two if the B-side 'She Don't Care About Time' had been featured on the album. Record buyers would have complained of a scandalous lack of new songs. It is also salutary to see how well 'Oh! Susannah' was received in its time, a review with which I wholeheartedly concurred back in 1965. 'Oh! Susannah' may not have been a song of distinction, but like 'We'll Meet Again' it was novel, funny and relevant. Later critics may carp, but it must be remembered that the Byrds weren't appealing to that sophisticated an audience in 1965. Their demographic was mainly teenagers, predominantly young ones, and pre-teens too. Songs which may now sound unadventurous or novel were not throwaway items back then. They added variety, and that was extremely important. Between 1965–67 there were still boundaries between different audiences and age groups that needed to be accommodated. The Byrds pushed and knocked down many barriers, but they were not willing to sacrifice everything on the altar of artistry. In 1965, they were still a singles group who made albums in limited time under immense pressure. A secondary argument concerning 'She Don't Care About Time' was that its non-inclusion on the album was a profound slight to the songwriting talents of Gene Clark. Again, this neglects the crucial point that it was heard by over a million more people due to its inclusion on the B-side of 'Turn! Turn! Turn!'. Moreover, its presence there ensured that Clark made more money from the track than he did from probably all his other contributions on *Turn! Turn! Turn!* combined. Securing the B-sides of the first three Byrds' singles, plus the partially written A-side 'Eight Miles High', was what secured Clark his financial fortune. Arguably, it was that collateral that enabled him to leave the Byrds without the fear that he was turning his back on a veritable goldmine.

page 265: "Gene was so prolific . . ." McGuinn/Rogan: Leeds: 4 May 1977.
page 266: "I was making a lot more money . . ." Clark/Zollo. *Song Talk*: Spring 1991.
page 266: "I got the impression . . ." Taylor/Rogan. London: 17 June 1977.
page 266: "The five of us started . . ." *Los Angeles Free Press*: 25 October 1969. Reprinted from *Seattle Helix*. Interview uncredited in either publication, but I believe the journalist was Ed Leimbacher.
page 266: "McGuinn, Christopher . . ." David Crosby, interviewed by Dan Epstein: *Guitar Player*: May 1997.
page 266: ". . . as a singer or performer . . ." ibid.

NOTES

page 266: "Hillman was a good bass player . . ." *Fusion*: April 1969.

page 267: ". . . 'a mediocre bass player' . . . an 'off-the-wall guitarist' . . ." Crosby/Rogan. London: 22–23 April 1980. Needless to say, I could not let these comments pass and mounted a heated and robust defence of Hillman. Crosby did not mind having his perceptions challenged at this point and liked to debate such matters. I reminded him in pretty forceful terms ("Oh, come on, David!") that during his *Rolling Stone* interview he had singled out Hillman for his great bass playing on 'Everybody's Been Burned' and elsewhere. "He wasn't great, man," he retorted. "Christopher did real good job on that and I was real pleased with it, but he wasn't *great*." I didn't even bother to address the gibe against McGuinn as Crosby, in less angry mode, has all too often expressed his appreciation of his playing. Back in the late Sixties, I have little doubt that Crosby regarded Stills as the superior player. Even a decade later, he was telling me that they were jealous of Stills because "they knew he was better than they were" and, of course, we have McGuinn's later comment about Crosby informing him and Hillman that they weren't strong enough musicians to play in his presence (see pp. 351–352). Of course, Crosby is a lot more diplomatic these days and far more generous in his appraisals.

page 267: "I don't believe there was a conspiracy . . ." Tickner/Rogan. Redondo Beach, California: 20 July 1979.

page 267: "I felt an absolute sense of justice . . ." Taylor/Rogan. London: 13 February 1997.

page 267: "I don't think it ever happened . . ." Crosby/Rogan. London: 22–23 April 1980.

page 268: "There was guilt . . ." Dickson/Rogan. Waldport, Oregon: 26–30 April 1989.

page 269: "Although David did tantalize Gene . . ." Tickner/Rogan. Redondo Beach, California: 20 July 1979.

page 269: "I always thought David got smashed with abandon . . ." Taylor/Rogan. London: 17 June 1977.

page 269: "When the Byrds first came together . . ." Dickson/Rogan. Waldport, Oregon: 26–30 April 1989.

page 270: "Gene warned me against taking LSD . . ." Patti McCormick, interviewed by the author. North Hollywood, California: 29 July 1979.

page 270: "I don't know if there was any turmoil . . ." Chris Hillman, unissued video-taped interview by John Tobler. London: June 1990.

page 270: "Gene had the toughest time . . ." Roger McGuinn, interviewed by Tierney Smith. *Goldmine*: 21 July 2006.

page 271: "We'd been together eight months . . ." Gene Clark, interviewed by Frank Beeson. *Bucketful Of Brains*: July 1987.

page 271: "One of the things I noticed..." Dickson/Rogan. London/Costa Mesa, California: 8 November 2009.
page 271: "There's a lot of motion..." David Crosby, interviewed by Kimmi Kobashigawa. *KRLA Beat*: 12 March 1966.
page 272: "We worked a couple of more gigs..." McGuinn/Johnson. *Hit Parader*: September 1968.
page 272: "Several things had happened..." Dickson/Rogan. Waldport, Oregon: 26–30 April 1989.
page 272: "I suspect Crosby probably saw it as an opportunity..." ibid.
page 273: "I guess we were real jealous..." McGuinn/Rogan. London/Florida: 22 May 1997.
page 273: "Well. Whatever, Gene left..." ibid.
page 274: "In a way being four..." McGuinn/Valentine. *Sounds*: 21 August 1971. McGuinn reiterated this point to me, when he spoke about meeting the Beatles some time after Clark's departure. "We'd been in touch with the Beatles and they kind of encouraged us. They said, 'We were better off once we became a foursome'. And we said: 'Yeah, we want to be like the Beatles'. Ha!"
page 274: "It was a meaner, leaner unit..." Taylor/Rogan. London: 13 February 1997.
page 274: "I'd saved the best pictures..." Dickson/Rogan. Waldport, Oregon: 26–30 April 1989.
page 275: "CBS immediately cancelled the whole idea..." ibid.
page 275: "Dickson was in hospital..." McGuinn/Rogan. London/Florida: 22 May 1997.
page 275: "It's not true..." Dickson/Rogan. London/Hawaii: 7 July 1997.
page 277: "After 'Eight Miles High'..." Gene Clark, interviewed by Monty Smith. *Omaha Rainbow* 15: December 1977.
page 277: "It was a fine romance..." Michelle Phillips, *California Dreamin'* (Warner Books, 1986), pp. 84–85.
page 278: "I didn't want to talk to anybody..." Clark/Beeson. *Bucketful Of Brains*: July 1987.
page 278: "It was a new Gene Clark..." Gene Clark, interviewed by Michelle Straubing. *Flip*: May 1966.
page 278: "I had been thinking..." ibid.
page 278: "In order to preserve..." CBS international press memo from Frank Calamita, dated 11 July 1966. It's interesting to observe how late this memo was sent out. Clark had already departed months before but the memo was delayed until new product appeared, specifically the single, '5 D (Fifth Dimension)'. The document also addressed the issue of promo photos, advising: "The Byrds are to be publicized and

NOTES

promoted as a four-man group. The Byrds' contact sheet (number 101) is being revised to include four-man shots. However, in the meantime, anyone ordering photos of the group will automatically receive four-man shots."

page 279: "They have recently survived . . ." Derek Taylor, press release: Spring 1966.

page 280: "To each person . . ." Dickson/Rogan. Waldport, Oregon: 26–30 April 1989.

Chapter 18: Space And Drugs

page 281: "CBS were screaming . . ." Dickson/Rogan. Waldport, Oregon: 26–30 April 1989.

page 282: "There was never any sense of competition . . ." Michelle Phillips, interviewed by the author. Beverly Hills, California: 16 July 1979.

page 283: "It was Chris . . ." Stephen Stills, interviewed by Michael Wale. *Zigzag* 27: December 1972.

page 285: ". . . to make an experimental film . . . but that's my personal project . . ." Jim McGuinn, quoted in *Melody Maker*: 28 May 1966.

page 285: "We're all hoping to act in a picture . . ." ibid.

page 286: "It was almost competitive . . ." Dickson/Rogan. Waldport, Oregon: 26–30 April 1989.

page 286: "Carole was there before Derek Taylor . . ." Dickson/Rogan. London/Costa Mesa, California: 8 November 2009.

page 286: "When I read the first page . . ." ibid.

page 287: "It was funny . . ." Dolores Tickner (formerly McGuinn, née DeLeon)/Rogan. London/Tucson, Arizona: 13 January 2007.

page 287: "He said to me . . ." Roger McGuinn, interviewed by Roy Hollingworth. *Melody Maker*: 8 May 1971.

page 287: "I got the feeling that he was guilty . . ." McGuinn/Cohen. *Sing Out!* Vol. 18; No. 5: December 1968/January 1969.

page 288: "When I wrote '5 D' . . ." A Special Open-End Interview With The Byrds Talking About Their New LP *Fifth Dimension*.

page 288: "'5 D' is a poem . . ." *Hit Parader*: October 1966.

page 288–289: "I was talking about something philosophical . . ." McGuinn/Valentine. *Sounds*: 21 August 1971.

page 289: "It was an ethereal trip into metaphysics . . ." Roger McGuinn, interviewed by Michael Ross, *The Byrds Complete* (Music Sales, 1970).

page 290: "David was just like me . . ." McGuire/Rogan. Rosslare, Co. Wexford, Republic of Ireland: 1–2 August 2008.

page 290: "I got on this spiritual search . . ." ibid.
page 290: "He came to Topanga . . ." ibid.
page 291: "A recent wave of pop songs . . ." *Variety*: Spring 1966. This sudden wave of censorship was greeted with perplexity in parts of the UK music press and, judging from some of the letters printed, there was a general feeling that the US had gone completely overboard in detecting drug connotations where none existed. Not long afterwards, the *NME*'s US correspondent Tracy Thomas was reporting new songs about to be placed in the dock. "The Byrds' 'Eight Miles High' and Dylan's 'Everybody Must Get Stoned' started it all, and now the latest tune to be banned in the search for hidden references to drugs is, of all things, Gary Lewis & The Playboys' 'Green Grass'. The Lovin' Spoonful have been attacked . . . The new Byrds single '5 D' may be taken off radio playlists too. It's about the expansion of awareness, not specifically through drugs; but then, as the critics put it, it doesn't say how to expand."
page 291: "For years, mothers all over the world . . ." Eric Jacobsen, quoted in *Variety*: Spring 1966. The Spoonful's languid 'Daydream' was also considered a possible drug song, although it had more in common with the Kinks' contemporaneous 'Sunny Afternoon' in its theme and execution.
page 292: "Perhaps we were consciously trying . . ." McGuinn/Rogan. Leeds: 4 May 1977.
page 292: "This album, then, cannot be . . ." Album review by Jon Landau. *Crawdaddy*: September 1966. Tellingly, Landau was even unimpressed by the psychedelia styled 'I See You' and 'What's Happening?!?!'. Referring to the "famous Byrds' 'raga rock'", he complained: "I find the intrusion of the Eastern sound into a totally Western melody more an annoyance than anything else, both on this cut ['I See You'] and especially on 'What's Happening?!?!'. The latter is a beautiful song by Dave Crosby but could have been done far more effectively without Indian-sounding instrumental breaks after each verse. The vocal which is either by Crosby or McGuinn, is one of the best on the LP." It is interesting to note that Landau was uncertain about the identity of the lead vocalist, even though it was self-evidently Crosby. Of course, this was the first occasion on which he was heard as a soloist on a Byrds' album. In the *Los Angeles Times*, Pete Johnson, generally a champion of the band, wrote a largely descriptive review of the album and, unlike Landau, chose not to compare the work with its predecessors. Nevertheless, despite his polite tone, he also seemed aware that something was lacking and that the Byrds were in danger of losing ground. "The first wave of folk rock a little more than a year ago swept

the Byrds out of the anonymity of a Sunset Strip house group to a position of leadership in the Colonial rebellion against the dominance of the British sound. Since their emergence they have coasted along on a series of good-sized hit records. They have perhaps slipped a bit in popularity as the folk-rock novelty wore off and as their imitators multiplied, but they remain one of the most tuneful and influential American rock groups."

page 292: "I think it was a disappointment . . ." McGuinn/Valentine. *Sounds*: 21 August 1971.

page 293: "I liked '5 D' . . ." Dickson/Rogan. Waldport, Oregon: 26–30 April 1989.

page 293: "I played it in my folk days . . ." McGuinn/Rogan. London/Florida: 22 May 1997.

page 293: "I went with it . . ." McGuinn/Rogan. Leeds: 4 May 1977.

page 294: "'Mr Spaceman' was too trivial . . ." Dickson/Rogan. Waldport, Oregon: 26–30 April 1989. Dickson would probably have chuckled to himself if he had seen the UK reviews which were full of praise for 'Mr Spaceman' and even singled out the line 'flies in my beard' (albeit misheard) as an example of fine humour. "One of the best performances the American Byrds have beamed to us across the Atlantic so far," effused *Melody Maker*, "with a happy country & western beat and some ear-catching lyrics, including lines like 'I woke up with flies in my beer, and my toothpaste was weird', or something. The Byrds are demanding a trip with a spaceman and promise they won't do anything wrong on the trip. They won't do anything wrong in the chart either." The 'hit' prediction proved false, but only just. 'Mr Spaceman' was played frequently on UK radio (mainly on the popular pirate stations) and very narrowly failed to reach the Top 50. It outsold '5 D' and was in the 'bubbling under' section of the *Record Mirror* chart, which indicated how close it had come to achieving mainstream success. Thematically, rather than musically, it indicated the Byrds' new excursion into 'space rock', while some later critics spotted an underlying country tinge that would emerge more fully on their next album. Interestingly, the venerable Derek Johnson of the *New Musical Express* added another musical generic link that no one else picked up on. "Not exactly what we expect from the Byrds, this is a novelty story-in-song with a topical lyric about visitors from outer space. It's a catchy tune with a contagious bounce – if it wasn't for that rasping strident twang which we associate with this group, I'd say the material was reminiscent of the skiffle days."

page 294: "I'm interested in astronomy . . ." Roger McGuinn, interviewed by Pete Frame. *Zigzag* 30: April 1973.

page 294: "It didn't turn me on . . ." Crosby/Rogan. London: 22–23 April 1980.
page 294: "It's a very strange song . . ." A Special Open-End Interview With The Byrds Talking About Their New LP *Fifth Dimension.*
page 295: "It was one of the very first . . ." Crosby/Rogan. London: 22–23 April 1980.
page 295: " 'I Come And Stand At Every Door' was fine . . ." Dickson/Rogan. Waldport, Oregon: 26–30 April 1989.
page 296: "The reason Crosby did lead on 'Hey Joe' . . ." McGuinn/Rogan. Leeds: 4 May 1977.
page 296: "Some of the songs that David . . ." Dickson/Rogan. Waldport, Oregon: 26–30 April 1989.
page 297: "It was a mistake . . ." Crosby/Rogan. London: 22–23 April 1980.
page 297: "It wasn't really funky . . ." McGuinn/Rogan. Leeds: 4 May 1977.
page 297: ". . . absolute cruel bastards . . ." Clarke/Rogan. London and Manchester: 14–15 October 1989.
page 297: "It was basically my song . . ." ibid.
page 298: "I wasn't trying to perpetuate anything . . ." McGuinn/Rogan. Leeds: 4 May 1977.
page 298: "It was not a vacuum cleaner . . ." ibid.
page 298: "It's another expansion for us . . ." A Special Open-End Interview With The Byrds Talking About Their New LP *Fifth Dimension.*

Chapter 19: Courage

page 299: "They recorded 'I Know My Rider' . . ." Dickson/Rogan. Waldport, Oregon: 26–30 April 1989.
page 299: "The disenchantment with 'I Know My Rider' is difficult to fathom . . ." Perhaps the Byrds felt that the song was too familiar in the folk community. Versions had already appeared by Tossi Aaron, Judy Henske, the Kingston Trio, the Big Three, Alice Stewart, Vince Martin & Fred Neil, Gale Garnett and Judy Roderick. But the Byrds were providing their own distinctive folk-rock version and most of their pop audience would have been unaware of any earlier recordings. The Grateful Dead later covered the song in 1970.
page 299: "Allen Stanton was always difficult . . ." McGuinn/Rogan. Leeds: 4 May 1977.
page 300: "Allen Stanton knew nothing . . ." Crosby/Rogan. London: 22–23 April 1980. It should be remembered, of course, that Stanton

NOTES

whom Crosby felt "knew nothing about music" was responsible for signing the Byrds in the first place.

page 300: "I think he did a reasonable job . . ." Dickson/Rogan. Waldport, Oregon: 26–30 April 1989.

page 301: "The Byrds could play very good . . ." ibid.

page 301: "The first time I worked with them . . ." Jim Seiter, interviewed by the author. London/Los Angeles, California: 18 October 1999.

page 302: "We might as well have sent our four waxwork dummies . . ." John Lennon, interviewed by Ray Coleman. *Disc & Music Echo*: 15 November 1969.

page 304: "Christianity will go . . ." John Lennon, interviewed by Maureen Cleave. *Evening Standard*: 4 March 1966.

page 304: "I'm seriously worried . . ." Derek Taylor, quoted in *West Magazine*: 27 November 1966.

page 304: "It was a big night for me . . ." Barry Tashian, interviewed by the author. London/Nashville, Tennessee: 1 June 2008.

page 305: "David decided that the Byrds . . ." Dickson/Rogan. Waldport, Oregon: 26–30 April 1989.

page 306: "All of a sudden . . ." ibid.

page 306: "extremely sloppy . . . they hit the wrong notes . . ." Reviewer Pete Johnson. *Los Angeles Times*: 3 September 1966. The review continued, "A wall-to-wall deeply piled crowd clapped enthusiastically after a few numbers, but for the most part the applause was spurred more by politeness than appreciation . . . The quartet's second set was improved but still far from the capabilities the Byrds have shown in their records and previous appearances. Despite the lapses in harmony and timing, the Byrds stirred some excitement from the audience with 'Don't Doubt Yourself Babe', 'Hey Joe', 'It Won't Be Wrong', 'Baby, What You Want Me To Do' and 'Chimes Of Freedom'. They botched up 'Mr Tambourine Man', 'I See You', 'Roll Over Beethoven', 'Eight Miles High' and 'All I Really Want To Do'. Since most of these are in their standard repertoire, they have little excuse. The Byrds were once a conscientious, creative group, and it is a shame that they should put such poor effort into a public appearance."

page 306: "Hollywood kids . . ." extract from Tracy Thomas' *America Calling* column, *New Musical Express*: 23 September 1966.

page 307: "At first, they showed me a picture of him . . ." Jim Seiter, interviewed by the author. London/Los Angeles, California: 18 October 1999.

page 307: ". . . a scintillating, polka-dotted . . ." Article: *Byrds Crash The Gate*: late 1966.

page 308: "... loud music dancing ..." from *Hullabaloo*: November 1966.
page 308: "We live in weird times ..." Eddie Tickner, quoted in CBS press release titled 'The Byrd's [*sic*] Million Dollar Insurance Policy': 7 October 1966.
page 308: "Michael went out on the road ..." Tickner/Rogan. Redondo Beach, California: 20 July 1979. Clarke also went out on the road briefly to promote the later 'So You Want To Be A Rock 'n' Roll Star'.
page 308: "There was a separation at the time ..." ibid.
page 309: "moving across the studio floor ..." Derek Taylor, writing in *Disc*: 24 December 1966.
page 309: "I thought it was great ..." Gary Usher, interviewed by Göran Tannfelt. *Full Circle* 7: August 1990. Reprinted from *Surfer's Rule* and *The Cosmic American Music News*. Usher adds: "I guess it was Crosby who shelved it and didn't want to work on it anymore. I could never get them back in the studio to finish it. I always thought it was something that could have been finished up to an excellent record."
page 309: "When I heard they'd done it ..." Dickson/Rogan. Waldport, Oregon: 26–30 April 1989.

Chapter 20: Renaissance

page 310: "... the Sunset Strip continued its metamorphosis into a teenage paradise ..." As early as the summer of 1966, Derek Taylor had commented on this phenomenon in his weekly column in the UK music paper *Disc* (4 June). Observing the scenes on Sunset Boulevard, he wrote: "The girls of Sunset Strip – the little teenagers with bronze skin, long blonde hair, tight bell-bottom jeans, worldly eyes in young faces – these are the hippies who flock into the nightclubs and into the liquor-serving clubs such as the Trip and the Whisky A Go Go ... The 'in' place now is, of course, the Trip, favoured by the Byrds who have their own particular scene. The Byrds and the Lovin' Spoonful are scions of the Strip – lords of all they survey through the afternoon smog of the early twilight when the 15 million lights of Los Angeles flicker into splendid brilliance or crude squalor, depending on your attitude."
page 310: "The LA Sheriff's office enforced draconian laws ..." Evidently, this conflict was a long time coming. In the aforementioned column in *Disc* the previous summer, Derek Taylor had commented on the police presence on the streets and their alleged harassment of the kids. "The Sheriff's Department shows particular interest in these arenas and there

have been complaints – how true they are it's impossible to say – of outrageous 'flashlight treatment'. This is when the Sheriff's men haul their clanking leather-and-steel clad bodies on their motorcycles and march into a coffeehouse brandishing their blazing flashlights in the faces of startled, stone-cold-sober teenagers talking about life, love and music, and liberty to the sound of an acoustic guitar or maybe a mouth-organ. The teenage rebellion is complete on the Strip. Here is a total deadlock between matriarchal, middle-aged American youth and uniformed authority. There is no meeting place between young and old. The young want their folk and rock and freedom; the old want their topless bars."

page 311: "The Byrds, whose politics seldom extended beyond echoing Dylan's decreasingly unfocused protest . . ." My contention that the Byrds were essentially a non-political band refers mainly to this early period. Crosby's role as a political spokesperson for the youth movement, at whatever level, was still over a year away. He wasn't speculating about the Warren Report, Kennedy's assassination or similar matters at this point. Less than a year before at the 'Eight Miles High' press conference, he had publicly distanced himself from political commentary and sounded strangely like McGuinn as he insisted: "We're not a political group. You won't find us on peace marches. Rather than protesting, which is essentially negativity or a reaction, we're more likely to say 'Hey, love somebody'. That's what we are looking for in the way we act, the way we play our music and the way we grow as people. Protest is not a useful tool for us. We prefer the positive, like saying 'UFOs are real'."

page 311: "Baton swinging armed officers . . ." *New York Times* report, reproduced in *CAFF Forum*: c. January 1967.

page 311: ". . . long-haired bellbottomed teenagers . . ." Al Aronowitz, quoted in Derek Taylor, *It Was Twenty Years Ago Today* (New York: Fireside, Simon & Schuster, 1987).

page 311–312: "The Byrds' old friend Peter Fonda and actor pal Brandon deWilde had been handcuffed and arrested . . ." Fonda had ventured onto the streets to photograph the kids, whom he supported. Derek Taylor was shocked after hearing about Fonda's arrest and also joined the protest, accompanied by actor Bob Denver, who was upset when a police officer had spat at his wife, Jeanine (aka Butchie), briefly the former spouse of Chris Hillman.

page 312: "I went in there with my bass . . ." Chris Hillman, speaking at the Library of Congress, Washington D.C.: 16 October 2009.

page 312: "Chris you're cooking . . ." ibid.

page 312: "For the next few days . . ." ibid.

page 313: "Chris had a lot of potential . . ." Usher/Tannfelt. *Full Circle* 7: August 1990. Reprinted from *Surfer's Rule* and *The Cosmic American Music News.*

page 313: "We finished the song . . ." Chris Hillman, speaking at the Library of Congress, Washington D.C.: 16 October 2009.

page 314: "Some people have accused us . . ." McGuinn/Frame. *Zigzag* 30: April 1973. McGuinn elaborated: "We were looking through a teen magazine, maybe *Hullabaloo*. I don't remember who was on the cover. It was more about the turnover: 'Look who's here this week, and who's not.' And there was a sense of our own ability to maintain the level of success that we'd had." The self-referential aspect of the song is crucial to a complete understanding of its satiric importance and underlines that it was never merely some cheap shot directed against a rival group. In recent years, McGuinn has continued to downplay the suggestion that the song was aimed at the Monkees, but their 'manufacture' definitely inspired part of the composition, at least as far as co-writer Hillman was concerned. "Originally, it was tongue in cheek," he says. "It wasn't really a bitter thing as much as just a chuckle at the business. And, really, I still maintain it was against the Monkees. I just thought the Monkees were the epitome of bad, of hideousness. These poor guys . . . they're nice guys but this contrived, horrible ersatz Beatle-type thing. That's what it was." Of course, compared to modern manufactured idols the Monkees were surprisingly innovative. Beneath the hype were many high quality pop singles and several decent albums. As they gained greater control of their career, they took more risks, ultimately committing pop hara-kiri with the surreal anti-war comedy film *Head*, produced by Bob Rafelson and Jack Nicholson. The latter two were part of the extended Byrds' circle and the Monkees' Peter Tork (Thorkelson) was also an old friend of David Crosby. Interestingly, Crosby went out on a limb to praise the group in his interview with the *Southern California Oracle, Counter-Culture News*, published in October 1967. "The cats were dropped into a freak scene and were stunned by it at first, buffeted by it, and attempted to cope with it, and have now outgrown it. They're growing faster than anybody I know, man. And they are going to come out of left field and fuck with the Establishment monstrously, because the Establishment made them huge and they know that they're well aware of what they've got and what they can do with it and they're good cats. They're human beings and they like love and they like nice things." It was gratifying to hear Crosby defying the hip priests of the underground press by praising the Monkees. He was no doubt already aware of the forthcoming film *Head*, whose stoned ambience he would have surely appreciated.

NOTES

page 314–315: "... so it would look good in the papers ..." Referenced in *Fab 208*: March 1966.

page 315: "Here's the twist on it ..." Chris Hillman, interviewed by Michael Walker. *Laurel Canyon: The Inside Story Of Rock-And-Roll's Legendary Neighborhood* (New York: Faber and Faber Inc, 2006), p. 20.

page 316: "They're called 'hippies' or 'happeners' ..." *KRLA Beat*: February 1967. The sense of cultural unrest described in the narrative at this point illustrates a changing of the guard between the Byrds' teenybop and college audiences. However, unlike the San Franciscan hippie bands of the period, the Byrds always retained what might be described as an AM audience. They still had an International Fan Club and the average age of its members was under 16. There were actually two members aged 27 which was regarded as impossibly old at the time. In keeping with tradition, the members' favourite song was 'Mr Tambourine Man'. The results of a club questionnaire, answered by 790 members, was passed over to the teenzine *Flip*, which eagerly focused on the burning question of who was the most popular Byrd. The results read: Jim McGuinn (322 votes), Michael Clarke (251 votes), David Crosby (194 votes) and Chris Hillman (192 votes). It would have been interesting to see how well Gene Clark would have fared if a similar poll had been conducted the previous year.

page 318: "... good British screams ..." Taylor/Rogan: London: 17 June 1977.

page 318: "It all came from that Hugh Masekela session ..." Chris Hillman, unissued video-taped interview by John Tobler. London: June 1990.

page 318: "Chris was a late bloomer ..." Chris Hillman, interviewed by Rich Tupica. *American Songwriter*: 8 October 2010.

page 318: "You better hear ..." ibid.

page 318: "That tells you ..." ibid.

page 319: "We have reason to believe ..." Jim McGuinn, interviewed by Anne Nightingale. *Daily Sketch*: 28 February 1967.

page 319: "We used earphones ..." McGuinn/Frame. *Zigzag* 30: April 1973.

page 319: "At the time we wrote it ..." ibid.

page 320: "... a sly reference to 'CTA 102' in an article printed in *The Astrophysical Journal* ..." Epstein's piece titled 'Quasi-Stellar Radio Sources: 88 GHz Flux Measurements' (*Astrophysical Journal*, Vol. 151: January 1968) noted: "The spectrum of CTA 102 falls off rapidly, giving no indication of an upturn at short wavelengths. As might be expected in this case, we have been unable to detect it; therefore we are unable to comment upon the discussion by McGuinn, Clark, Crosby, Clarke and

Hillman (private communications)." Epstein evidently assumed Gene Clark was still part of the group.

page 320: "I wish that I had been there . . ." Dickson/Rogan. Waldport, Oregon: 26–30 April 1989.

page 320: "He also sang a harmony part . . ." Vern Gosdin, quoted in Alec Palao's liner notes to the Big Beat reissue of the Gosdin Brothers' *Sounds Of Goodbye*.

page 321: "'Time Between' was the first song . . ." Hillman/Rogan. New York: 26 January 1979.

page 321: "Christopher did a real good job on that . . ." Crosby/Rogan. London: 22–23 April 1980.

pages 322: "I would never have done 'Everybody's Been Burned' . . ." Dickson/Rogan. Waldport, Oregon: 26–30 April 1989.

page 323: "The backwards guitar insert . . ." Hillman/Rogan. New York: 26 January 1979.

page 323: "We fought Crosby on that . . ." Chris Hillman, interviewed by Pete Frame. *Zigzag* 30: April 1973.

page 324: "If I had a vote . . ." Dickson/Rogan. Waldport, Oregon: 26–30 April 1989.

page 324: "There was never anything called raga rock . . ." Crosby/Rogan. London: 22–23 April 1980.

page 325: "It was a cop-out . . ." David Crosby, interviewed by Ben Fong-Torres. *Rolling Stone*: 23 July 1970.

page 325: "There wasn't really a dispute . . ." ibid.

page 326: "I thought his stuff . . ." Dickson/Rogan. Waldport, Oregon: 26–30 April 1989.

page 326: "They weren't satisfied with what they had . . ." Jim Seiter, interviewed by the author. Redondo Beach, California: 28 July 1979.

page 326: "When something's on a B-side . . ." Dickson/Rogan. Waldport, Oregon: 26–30 April 1989.

page 327: "The version of 'Why' we did at RCA . . ." Crosby/Rogan. London: 22–23 April 1980.

page 327: "I wouldn't say the solo . . ." Dickson/Rogan. Waldport, Oregon: 26–30 April 1989.

page 327: "The Byrds have real formal constancy . . ." Album review by Sandy Pearlman. *Crawdaddy*: August 1967. Please note that this extract was a necessarily severe précis of the mid-section of Pearlman's piece, teasing out some salient points. Other critics responded cautiously to the work, particularly in America. In *Village Voice* (9 March), Richard Goldstein offered a well-written, analytical appraisal of the work, fearing that the gimmicky 'CTA 102' would become "the most revered cut",

NOTES

complimenting the "more ambitious electronic pieces like 'Thoughts And Words', fretting over 'Mind Gardens' ("a weak and overblown lyric, but a dramatic delivery"), then concluding: "The Byrds are tighter than ever, and the discipline shows in dozens of musical details, each finely polished so you're not distracted from the music. It's difficult to say where the group's evolution will lead and the album offers no clue. But it's a thoughtful work of consolidation and worth buying on that score alone."

Although there was less space in the UK music press, those that did comment were impressed. *Melody Maker* went as far as trumpeting: "If you ignore this album, you are not only foolish – but deaf! Naturally it surpasses all other Byrds works, being rich in sparkling ideas, that most incredible feeling, and what's more – beauty."

page 328: "On the whole . . ." Album review by Tom Phillips. *New York Times*: 6 August 1967.

page 328: "There's also a good deal . . ." ibid.

page 329: "The Byrds first took wing . . ." *Time*: 14 April 1967.

Chapter 21: The Gathering Of The Tribes

page 331: "The Byrds closed the first half . . ." Tracy Thomas, *America Calling* column, *New Musical Express*: March 1967.

page 331: "Since Los Angeles is the first city . . ." Lance Reventlow, *CAFF Forum*: c. January 1967.

page 332: "In the end, the police backed off . . ." Jim Dickson, quoted in Derek Taylor, *It Was Twenty Years Ago Today* (New York: Fireside, Simon & Schuster, 1987), p. 174.

page 332: "Lovely title . . ." Reviewer Penny Valentine. *Disc*: 18 February 1967.

page 332: "No one can deny . . ." Reviewer Derek Johnson. *New Musical Express*: 25 February 1967. Johnson was a little more flippant when confronted with the B-side 'Everybody's Been Burned'. "The era of protest song is not over! Here we have a rippling acoustic guitar backing, folksy quality and a moody depressive feel."

page 333: "I don't know . . ." Reviewer Paul McCartney. *Melody Maker*: 25 February 1967. By the time Crosby visited Abbey Road that week's issue of *Melody Maker* was already on sale and generally available.

page 333: "They pushed two huge coffin-sized speakers . . ." David Crosby, guesting on BBC Radio 2's *Sounds Of The Sixties*: July 1989.

page 334: "Not a chance . . ." There were no eye-witness accounts of the Roundhouse Party published in the music press of the period. I have exchanged stories with several people who attended, including musician

Tony Poole who recalls knocking on the group's hotel room door afterwards and meeting McGuinn and others. A younger female fan wrote to the then Chrissie Brewer (who later ran the Byrds Fan Club from her home in Bristol) shortly after the visit detailing her experiences and those of her teenage friends. The letter captures the innocence of the time, with a keen emphasis on clothes and suppressed adolescent desire.

"Michael was wearing an all fur outfit – jacket, pants, boots, scarf – the lot. He looked big and cuddly and I guess he was making sure he didn't catch cold! He proved himself to be a positive pig by guzzling beer and eating biscuits all the time; in fact the biscuit tin was never out of his hand.

"David was wearing a blue hat made out of a kind of felt material. He also wore a brown suede jacket, black and white pin-stripe pants and brown shoes – not boots. He looked a lot shorter than Chris and the hat concealed where he was thinning at the forehead.

"Chris was enjoying himself by signing his autograph up young ladies' arms and leaning on their backs to sign books, records etc. Jim asked one girl 'Am I hurting you?' when signing her wrist. Jaki (my friend) was busy getting Michael's autograph and whilst signing her membership card he dribbled beer all over it. The smell and stain are still there. Chris was messing around and joking with my friend Anne and in the end he punched her gently in the stomach and called her 'Cheeky' to which Anne nearly collapsed.

"Several of the girls there kissed their favourite Byrds which made me jealous as I hardly had the nerve to even stand near David. They were playing Byrds records over the speakers and I remember whilst 'Hey Joe' was playing I asked David if there was ever a feeling of the group splitting up and he answered 'Not a chance' and repeated it.

"When Jaki asked Jim how Gene was, she said he looked very blank as though he didn't know who she was talking about. Michael was heard to call Jim by the nickname Jimbo on a few occasions and we overheard Michael singing 'Let's Spend The Night Together' in a very deep voice.

"Michael, Chris and Jim were all boozing and Jim spilt some beer. Chris said, 'Don't worry, Jim will lick it up. He's like that.' David was stood at the other end of the room and never had a drink at all – not even good ole British tea! However, when we went upstairs we saw David holding Jim's camera in one hand and a glass of something in the other – and I very much doubt if it was apple juice. He smiled and said they would be leaving soon.

"Michael was the last to leave and Jaki grabbed his hand and went wandering down the stairs with him. Michael came to the party with a girl with long blonde hair but once there he seemed to ditch her. Chris also had a girl and one of the guys there had the cheek to tell Chris he didn't think much of her to look at so Chris informed him that she was a groove in bed! . . .

"It was a horrible day – raining all the time – but walking out from that party you felt like you'd just stepped into Californian sunshine. The Byrds soon flew back to it anyway!"

page 335: "They didn't happen . . ." The Byrds' Speakeasy performance, reviewed by Hugh Nolan. *Disc*: 25 March 1967. Nolan was no enemy of the Byrds and tempered his review with some positive comments about their studio work. He seemed almost mystified by their performance. "The Byrds are an exciting, progressive group whose records get better and better and, on the strength of their new album *Younger Than Yesterday*, can be compared favourably with even the Beatles. But there seems to be some barrier between the group and British audiences. However good their records are they never rise in the Top 50, and their last visit here two years ago remains the glaring example of a well-thought-of group dying the death after being exposed to critical London audiences. Perhaps it was because of their 1965 disaster that this time the Byrds played only one date on their '67 British visit . . . Sad to report maybe they should not even have done that. If there was any justice, they should have got up onstage and knocked everyone out with the beautiful material they are now doing on record. They should have thought, 'Right, you didn't like us last time, so listen to this!' True, they played mostly new material – 'Why', Dylan's 'My Back Pages', Pete Seeger's 'Bells Of Rhymney', and their own 'Renaissance Fair', an LP track they could well release as a single. They did 'Hey Joe' and they did 'So You Want To Be A Rock 'n' Roll Star'. But they did not happen."

If *Disc* was critical, then *Record Mirror* was brutal. Liverpudlian Bill Harry, a Beatles' friend and contemporary, but never a fan of the Byrds, noted: "They appeared at the Speakeasy in London's Margaret Street and chaos reigned. Complete and utter chaos. Capacity crowds of 'faces'; even people like Mick Avory of the Kinks couldn't get in to see them. The Beatles booked a table. The music press turned out in force and, as far as I'm concerned, it was a damp squib. As a group they are fair, probably less talented than half-a-dozen unknown groups in any major city in the British Isles. An enigma? Yes." The tone of Harry's comments resembled nothing less than the bitter partisanship offered by reviewers during the controversial 1965 tour. Interestingly, it was *Melody Maker*, hardly a friend of the Byrds, that offered the most positive response. Their reviewer, Nick Jones, pointed out, apologetically: "Admittedly, the

Byrds didn't present their act but it was an impromptu gig – and, after all, it's the music that's important. And musically the Byrds 1967 are too much. They have a pretty, lyrical freedom of thought and form plus a communicative power irresistible to any receptive listener."

page 335: "We were kind of uptight . . ." Crosby/Fong-Torres, op cit.

page 335: "Listening to the album . . ." letter from CBS Vice President Clive Davis to Eddie Tickner dated 13 March 1967.

page 336: " 'My Back Pages' was my suggestion . . ." Dickson/Rogan. Waldport, Oregon: 26–30 April 1989.

page 338: "Many of the 'tribes' will attend . . ." Radical student and anti-war activist Michael Barnes helped organize the event and recalls a cultural clash with the local press. "I was at UCLA," he told me, "and I knew the folks from the film department. We needed a stage so they brought one out there from UCLA. We started setting up and a bunch of reporters showed up. We didn't think many people would be there. It was a rental park. They said: 'How many people do you expect?' I told them, 'I don't know, maybe 500.' So I got a permit for 500 people and we set the stage up and I had to arrange the bands and all that stuff. These reporters were standing around saying, 'Why are you doing this?' I replied: 'Well because we want to have a little celebration of life.' They said, 'No, what are your political reasons?' And I said, 'Well we don't really have any political reason, apart from sharing and being together' and they just couldn't buy that. It was beyond their comprehension. And man all of a sudden about 5,000 people showed up. It was like 'Oh my God, man, this is amazing. And the day is heaven.' It *was* heaven. The day is etched in my memory forever."

page 339: "The future of the Byrds . . ." Dickson/Rogan. Waldport, Oregon: 26–30 April 1989.

page 340: "It was Crosby versus the rest . . ." Seiter/Rogan. Redondo Beach, California: 28 July 1979.

page 340: "There was a point . . ." Tickner/Rogan. Redondo Beach, California: 20 July 1979.

page 340: "He'd be off, off out of tune . . ." McGuinn/Salvo. *New Musical Express*: 5 May 1973. Crosby was brusquely dismissive of this allegation when I quoted it to him. "First thing, you can't play if it's out of tune . . ."

page 340: "I don't think it's right or fair . . ." Crosby/Rogan. London: 22–23 April 1980.

page 340: "[It was] one of the few times . . ." David Crosby, onstage at the Dorothy Chandler Pavilion, Los Angeles Music Center (10 October 1971), recalling the Byrds' performance at the Fillmore Auditorium, San

NOTES

Francisco, California: 2 April 1967. The Crosby rap is included on the Crosby & Nash bootleg, *A Very Stony Evening*.

page 341: "The electronic complexities . . ." Reviewer Gloria Tully. *San Jose Mercury*: 9 April 1967.

page 342: "David did some of the most unprofessional things . . ." Seiter/Rogan. Redondo Beach, California: 28 July 1979.

page 342: "I remember that, it was at the Whisky . . ." Crosby/Rogan. London: 22–23 April 1980.

page 342: "That was devastating . . ." Seiter/Rogan. London/Los Angeles, California: 18 October 1999.

page 342: "I never went to gigs anymore . . ." Dickson/Rogan. Waldport, Oregon: 26–30 April 1989.

page 342: "The Byrds, one of the best groups in the world . . ." Reviewer Derek Taylor. *Disc*: 3 June 1967.

page 342: "It was their first concert . . ." Suzy Dick/Rogan. London/Spokane, Washington: 11 May 1997.

page 343: "David always underestimated me . . ." Clarke/Rogan. London and Manchester: 14–15 October 1989.

page 344: "We're out to break down those barriers . . ." Jim McGuinn, interviewed on CBS News' *Inside Out: The Rock Revolution*: broadcast, 25 April 1967.

page 344: "Larry Spector was a business manager . . ." Tickner/Rogan. Redondo Beach, California: 20 July 1979.

page 345: "My first meeting with Dennis . . ." Dickson/Rogan. London/Costa Mesa, California: 24 May 2009.

page 345: "It was his hat . . ." ibid.

page 345: "I was puzzled how it happened . . ." Dickson/Rogan. Waldport, Oregon: 26–30 April 1989.

page 345: "Dennis put him in a suit . . ." ibid.

page 346: "It was Larry's mother . . ." ibid.

page 346: "It didn't diminish . . ." ibid.

page 347: "I really liked her a lot . . ." Dolores Tickner (formerly McGuinn, née DeLeon), interviewed by the author. London/Tucson, Arizona: 24–25 February 2007.

page 347: "I heard him railing . . ." Dickson/Rogan. Waldport, Oregon: 26–30 April 1989.

page 347: "Some undercover things . . ." Tickner/Rogan. Redondo Beach, California: 20 July 1979.

page 347: "It was another example of going along with David's bad ideas . . ." McGuinn/Rogan. London/Florida: 22 May 1997.

Chapter 22: Monterey And Mutiny

page 348: "Dickson could be a svengali . . ." Chris Hillman, interviewed by Sid Griffin. *Full Circle* 11: January 1992.

page 348: "The problem is that if you close off . . ." Dickson/Rogan. Waldport, Oregon: 26–30 April 1989.

page 349: "I might have stayed more remote . . ." ibid.

page 350: "I knew Stephen was romancing David away . . ." McGuinn/Rogan. London/Florida: 22 May 1997.

page 351: "You guys aren't good enough . . ." ibid.

page 351: "We went, 'Gee, sorry David!' . . ." ibid.

page 351: "He said, 'Look . . .'" McGuinn/Valentine. *Sounds*: 21 August 1971.

page 351: "We really believed all the peace and love stuff . . ." McGuinn/Kubernik: 2007. Original transcript sent to author.

page 352: "They weren't the complete deal . . ." Bruce Palmer, interviewed by the author. London/Toronto: 24 March 2000.

page 352: "I rehearsed with them . . ." Crosby/Rogan. London: 22–23 April 1980. Crosby's contention that he "had no intention of becoming a member of Buffalo Springfield" was partly qualified 15 years later during an interview with Steve Silberman (*Goldmine* 390: 7 July 1995). Asked: "Did you ever think you might stay in the Buffalo Springfield?", he responded: "If Springfield had held together I would have. I could see that Stephen was a major talent. He might have been a little hard to get along with, but there was no question that there was good energy there. Springfield was a very, very powerful band. They had the essence, the wherewithal, and the jacks-or-better, which is the songs. And they could sing. If they had been able to refine that band and hold it together, there's no telling what they could have accomplished."

page 352: "They were worried about my hanging around with Stills . . ." Crosby/Rogan. London: 22 April 1980.

page 353: "God bless the Beatles! . . ." David Crosby, quoted in *Southern California Oracle, Counter-Culture News*: October 1967. The interviewer was not credited on the page, although I believe it was Stan Russell.

page 354: "Hey, the only answer I can give you . . ." David Crosby, onstage at the International Monterey Pop Festival: 17 June 1967.

page 354: "I was chasing around Monterey . . ." Dickson/Rogan. Waldport, Oregon: 26–30 April 1989.

page 355: "I'd like to tell you all something . . ." Crosby, onstage at Monterey: 17 June 1967.

NOTES

page 355: "You know they're shooting this for television . . ." ibid.
page 355: "I respected Pete Seeger more . . ." McGuinn/Rogan. Leeds: 4 May 1977.
page 356: "I probably did encourage people to drop acid . . ." Crosby/Rogan. London: 22–23 April 1980. Paul McCartney's controversial admission had already appeared in the British glossy magazine *Queen* and was reprinted in *Life* under the subheading 'The New Far-Out Beatles' on 17 June 1967. Speaking of the effects of LSD, McCartney explained: "After I took it, it opened my eyes. We only use one-tenth of our brain. Just think what we could accomplish if we could only tap that hidden part. It would mean a whole new world." No wonder Crosby was impressed. Crosby could also justifiably argue, though he never chose to, that McCartney needed his support. Within two days of Crosby's "I concur", the Beatle was under siege in the pages of the *Daily Mirror*, Britain's then best-selling tabloid newspaper.

In their leader column they wrote: "Beatle Paul McCartney, 25 yesterday, is one of the oldest teenagers on record. At the moment, he is not behaving like a teenager – even an elderly one. He is behaving like an irresponsible idiot. He confesses publicly to have taken the hallucination drug LSD. He says 'maybe' he might take it again. He talks about this dangerous drug in such glowing terms that, despite his statements to the contrary, you might think he was recommending LSD to all his teenage fans – and indeed to the whole world. Perhaps millionaire McCartney ought to see a psychiatrist who will explain just why LSD is regarded as a dangerous drug. Perhaps he ought to see a psychiatrist anyway. Perhaps Mr McCartney ought to consult a lawyer who will tell him that it is an offence to be in unauthorized possession of LSD. This mixed up Beatle may protest that he doesn't advocate LSD for anybody else and that he doesn't want his fans to take it. But he must know his own influence. By talking so enthusiastically about LSD isn't he encouraging his fans to break the law by being in possession of the drug? . . . Most teenagers, fortunately, have more sense than to mess around with dangerous drugs. Most teenagers will continue to regard LSD as a menace."

Later that day, the BBC's rival commercial channel ITV conducted an interview with McCartney at his home in Cavendish Avenue and the results were broadcast that same evening. He admitted having taken LSD "maybe four times". The interviewer even wanted to know where he'd obtained the drug, but, unsurprisingly, McCartney declined to reveal the source. Should McCartney, as a public figure, have kept silent about his drug use? "To say it is only to tell the truth. I'm telling the truth, you know. I don't know what everyone's so angry about."

For the rest, the interviewer quizzed McCartney with the same rhetorical questions that had appeared in the *Daily Mirror*.

Do you think that you have now encouraged your fans to take drugs?
"I don't think it'll make any difference. I don't think my fans are going to take drugs just because I did, you know. But the thing is – that's not the point anyway. I was asked whether I had or not. And from then on, the whole bit about how far it's going to go and how many people it's going to encourage is up to the newspapers, and up to you on television. I mean, you're spreading this now, at this moment. This is going into all the homes in Britain. And I'd rather it didn't. But you're asking me the question. You want me to be honest – I'll be honest."

But as a public figure, surely you've got the responsibility to . . .
"No, it's you who've got the responsibility. You've got the responsibility not to spread this *now*. You know, I'm quite prepared to keep it as a very personal thing if you will too. If you'll shut up about it, I will."

Following Crosby's lead, the other Beatles also came out in support of McCartney, while their normally cautious manager Brian Epstein went on public record admitting that he too had taken LSD (on five occasions) and felt it had made him know himself better.

One month later, on 24 July, a full page advertisement was placed in *The Times*, proclaiming "the law against marijuana is immoral in principle and unworkable in practice". Among the 64 largely distinguished signatories were the four Beatles and their manager. This petition to the Home Secretary advocating a repeal of the law concerning cannabis and its removal from the dangerous drugs list, failed to achieve its primary aim but certainly brought attention to the issue.

The public debate on drug use was part of the alternative zeitgeist and Crosby's political punditry was similar. His casual defence ("it was pretty relevant, I thought") should not be brushed aside as merely glib. Hillman later complained about his sermonizing and McGuinn accused him of simply "trying to be hip", but surely for Crosby it was much more than that. He understood those times and was not afraid to speak out in support of McCartney and LSD. McGuinn effectively put himself in the same position as the *Daily Mirror* and ITV by suggesting that public figures should be discreet on such matters. While some might be tempted to portray McGuinn as the sober voice of reason opposed to Crosby's intemperate lifestyle choices, the issue was never that simple. McGuinn was also a proponent of LSD at the time, but did not discuss such matters onstage or in the pages of the *Oracle*. There is a case for both points of view but, considering Crosby's personality, it was hardly surprising and arguably right and fitting that he should give voice to the LSD debate. Thirteen years later, while in the grip of freebasing addiction, he told me: "I don't know if I'd recommend it now".

page 356: "David's behaviour at Monterey . . ." Taylor/Rogan. London: 13 February 1997.

page 357: "At Monterey, he showed to the world . . ." Seiter/Rogan. Redondo Beach, California: 28 July 1979.

page 357: ". . . pure and unadulterated bullshit . . ." Crosby/Rogan. London: 22–23 April 1980.

page 357: "McGuinn would say things . . ." Dickson/Rogan. Waldport, Oregon: 26–30 April 1989.

page 358: "I remember vividly . . ." Jim Seiter, interviewed by the author. London/Los Angeles, California: 18 October 1999.

page 358: "I don't think playing with them was a big deal . . ." McGuinn/Rogan. London/Florida: 22 May 1997.

page 359: "Early on Monday morning . . ." Ralph Gleason, quoted in Derek Taylor, *It Was Twenty Years Ago Today* (New York: Fireside, Simon & Schuster, 1987), p. 79.

page 360: "Rock 'n' roll groups have to use telepathic messages . . ." Crosby, quoted in *Southern California Oracle, Counter-Culture News*: October 1967.

page 361: "When we had our son . . ." McGuinn/Johnson. *Hit Parader*: September 1968. Evidently, there was no direct contact or discussion about the change of name. As McGuinn explained: "You send to the International Subud secretary in Djakarta, Indonesia, a post office box. You say who you are and you ask what your name should be. Then you get a letter back . . ." It is a little surprising that the name change had not happened even earlier. Already, many of the people associated with Subud that McGuinn had encountered had undergone a name change. For example, Bob (Hamilton) Camp, Jimmy (Weston) Gavin and Lionel (Richmond) Shepard. Patrick McGuinn, incidentally, was born on 19 October 1966.

page 362: "I didn't even know it was happening . . ." McGuire/Rogan. Rosslare, Co. Wexford, Republic of Ireland: 1–2 August 2008.

page 362: "Roger's Cadillac was specially wired . . ." ibid.

page 362: "We were sitting there . . ." ibid.

page 363: "I smoke pot which helps . . ." Crosby, quoted in *Southern California Oracle, Counter-Culture News*: October 1967.

page 363: "Buddha and Christ . . ." ibid.

page 363: "The inside of your head . . ." ibid.

page 364: "I see President Johnson . . ." ibid.
page 364: "That was just an idea of mine . . ." David Crosby, interviewed by Sid Griffin. *Full Circle* 21: April 1996.
page 364: "They went, 'Huh? . . ." ibid.
page 365: "He kicked us out of the studio . . ." Roger McGuinn, interviewed by John Nork. Original transcript submitted to the author. Part published in *Tracking Angle*: February 1997.
page 365: "David went back . . ." Chris Hillman, interviewed by John Nork. Original transcript submitted to the author. Part published in *Tracking Angle*: February 1997.
page 365: "The final mix of 'Lady Friend' . . ." David Crosby, talking on B. Mitchell Reed's radio show on KFWB-AM: 30 August 1967.

Chapter 23: The Great Conflict

page 366: "We were still anxious to do it . . ." Dickson/Rogan. Waldport, Oregon: 26–30 April 1989.
page 367: "The thing that made people underestimate him . . ." Roger McGuinn, interviewed by Cameron Crowe. *Creem*: June 1973.
page 367: "Any greatest hits album is insignificant . . ." Album review by Paul Williams. *Crawdaddy*: September 1967.
page 369: "We first got 'Draft Morning' and 'Dolphin's Smile' together in Hawaii . . ." Hillman/Frame. *Zigzag* 31: issue updated, *c.* May 1973.
page 370: "If you really wanted to . . ." and following exchange from the studio tapes, now included on the CD of *The Notorious Byrd Brothers*.
page 371: "I'm going to buy a boat . . ." Crosby, quoted in *Southern California Oracle, Counter-Culture News*: October 1967. The precise recording date of this uncredited interview is not known. It's possible that the transcript may have evolved from his interview with B. Mitchell Reed which took place on 30 August. If not, it tallies with much of what he said there. The Byrds previously played a benefit for the *Oracle* underground paper on 2 June at the Valley Music Theatre, Woodland Hills, California, so it could also have been completed around that time.
page 372: "I thought up the brass parts . . ." Crosby/Rogan. London: 22–23 April 1980. Crosby's complaint is no doubt valid, but may be overstated. *The Notorious Byrd Brothers* was far from complete at this point and the running order had yet to be established. They may have already told him that they weren't planning to include 'Lady Friend', along with 'Triad', but there is no definitive evidence of this. Crosby

may have been referring to its ultimate omission from the album but, if so, that is a separate issue. After his departure there was no reason to feature the single on *Notorious*, particularly given their disappointment about the song's performance. Since Crosby wasn't too keen about them placing his songs on the album after his departure, he had no reason for retrospective complaint. Whether he could have persuaded them to feature the song on the album had he remained in the group is an interesting question. Given their antipathy towards 'Triad', which he was far more eager to promote, it seems unlikely.

Producer Gary Usher added to this debate, partly justifying the song's omission from the album, although he was evidently unaware or had forgotten about McGuinn and Hillman's lack of enthusiasm for the track. Recalling the selection process, he told Göran Tannfelt: "I think we had probably 12 to 15 things at that time and something had to go. More than likely since Crosby was no longer in the group and 'Lady Friend' being a Crosby song, the song was taken out in favour of a song more in line with where the album was going. Rest assured if David had been in the group at the time of the album's release 'Lady Friend' would have been on the album. I also think the record ['Lady Friend'] should have been recut with a whole different arrangement. It could have been made into a real good Byrds recording. At the time we had the pressure to get the album out and to recut the song and finish it up would have meant getting Crosby back in again. There were a lot of political reasons why it wasn't included on the album." Indeed. Such were the politics that it is conjectural whether Crosby could have overcome the combined wills of McGuinn and Hillman and pushed through 'Lady Friend', let alone 'Triad'.

page 372: "Our latest things are very much in the jazz bag . . ." Roger McGuinn, interviewed by John Bryan. *Open City*: 31 August–7 September 1967.

page 372: ". . . an imitation of some commercial group . . ." ibid.

page 373: "An incredible full sound . . ." Reviewer, Derek Johnson. *New Musical Express*: 2 September 1967. Johnson was unconvinced that it would prove a hit. "It's described as the sound of tomorrow and that may hamper its chances today!"

page 373: "David Crosby is evidently the lead singer . . ." Reviewer, US correspondent, Tracy Thomas. *New Musical Express*: 9 September 1967.

page 373: " 'The Universal Decoder' . . ." Reviewer Pete Johnson. *Los Angeles Times*: 1 September 1967.

page 374: "I see groups that three years ago . . ." David Crosby, talking on B. Mitchell Reed's radio show on KFWB-AM: 30 August 1967.

page 374: "If we get together and help each other . . ." Crosby, interviewed in *Southern California Oracle, Counter-Culture News*: October 1967.

page 375: "We didn't like the song at the time . . ." Chris Hillman, interviewed by Bruce Sylvester. *Goldmine* 436: 11 April 1997.

page 375: "'Triad' wasn't the crux of it . . ." Roger McGuinn, interviewed by Pete Frame. Hollywood, California: 30 October 1973. This interview is exclusive to this book and previous editions.

page 376: "David sat on a couch . . ." Seiter/Rogan. Redondo Beach, California: 28 July 1979.

page 376: "I was driving him home . . ." Seiter/Rogan. London/Los Angeles, California: 18 October 1999.

page 376: "I don't think David thought we would do it . . ." Usher/Tannfelt. *Full Circle* 7: August 1990. Reprinted from *Surfer's Rule* and *The Cosmic American Music News*.

page 377: "They were worried by my hanging out with Stills . . ." Crosby/Rogan. London: 22–23 April 1980.

page 378: "I remember the arguments . . ." Usher/Tannfelt. *Full Circle* 7: August 1990. Reprinted from *Surfer's Rule* and *The Cosmic American Music News*.

page 379: "David was always a very acidic character . . ." Roger McGuinn, interviewed by Pete Johnson. *Los Angeles Times*: April 1968.

page 379: "David got real uptight with me . . ." Seiter/Rogan. Redondo Beach, California: 28 July 1979.

Chapter 24: Crosby Fired! – Clark Hired!

page 380: "People like Clive Davis . . ." Seiter/Rogan. London/Los Angeles, California: 18 October 1999.

page 381: "They came over and said that they wanted to throw me out . . ." Crosby/Rogan. London: 22–23 April 1980.

page 381: "You know we could make great music . . ." Crosby's words, recalled by Roger McGuinn. McGuinn/Rogan. Leeds: 4 May 1977.

page 381: "Yeah, and we could make great music . . ." McGuinn/Rogan. Leeds: 4 May 1977.

page 381: "That's what they said . . ." Crosby/Rogan. London: 22–23 April 1980.

page 381: "I'm a very opinionated person . . ." ibid.

page 382: "Maybe it was a rash decision . . ." McGuinn/Rogan. Leeds: 4 May 1977.

NOTES

page 383: "David Crosby at the time . . ." McGuinn/Frame. Hollywood, California: 30 October 1973. A year before this interview McGuinn was quoted by Michael Watts (*Melody Maker*: 29 January 1972) recalling another of Crosby's supposed faux pas. "Like we were on the *Dick Cavett Show* once and at the end of the programme Cavett said: 'There's a few minutes left, do any of you guys want to say anything?' And he came to Crosby and Crosby said, 'Yeah, I'd like to say I don't like what General Motors are doing polluting the atmosphere.' And Dick said, 'But, David! General Motors are sponsoring the show.' Crosby hasn't got a lot of tact, I guess." This was an amusing tale, but the facts were oddly incorrect. Some years later, I quoted the allegation verbatim to Crosby, who told me: "The Byrds [of his era] never played on *Dick Cavett* . . . Next!" He explained that the only time in the Sixties that he appeared on the show was with Stephen Stills and Joni Mitchell, just after CSN&Y's famous performance at Woodstock. Crosby was correct on both points. His quick riposte momentarily bamboozled me and he rammed the point home by implying that McGuinn's other criticisms should be viewed with similar scepticism.

page 383: "Chris was always the catalyst . . ." McGuinn/Valentine. *Sounds*: 21 August 1971.

page 384: "Chris would call everybody . . ." Seiter/Rogan. London/Los Angeles, California: 18 October 1999.

page 384: "When I heard about it at first . . ." Dickson/Rogan. Waldport, Oregon: 26–30 April 1989.

page 385: "It is 1967 now . . ." Derek Taylor, 'The Byrds In Words But The Real Story Is In Your Own Head'. *Hit Parader*, Vol XXVII, No, 45: March 1968. The most remarkable aspect of this essay is its belated publication date. By the time it reached the newsagents, Michael Clarke had gone and both Kevin Kelley and Gram Parsons had been recruited. In short, the Byrds were barely recognizable from the line-up described by Taylor. The accompanying photos were also old hat, featuring the original five-man group and some shots circa *Younger Than Yesterday*.

page 386: "The Byrds have reached up and down . . ." ibid.

page 387: "Larry was an opportunist . . ." Seiter/Rogan. Redondo Beach, California: 28 July 1979.

page 388: "Jesus, he has a Ferrari . . ." Seiter/Rogan. London/Los Angeles, California: 18 October 1999.

page 388: "He had a chick . . ." ibid.

page 388: "Gene was like some wandering folk troubadour . . ." ibid.

page 388: "Gene would have liked . . ." Dickson/Rogan. Waldport, Oregon: 26–30 April 1989.

page 390: "It was like eggshells . . ." Seiter/Rogan. London/Los Angeles, California: 18 October 1999.
page 390: "Man, that was embarrassing . . ." ibid.
page 390: "Don't worry . . ." ibid.
page 390: "I said, 'Larry, come on . . .'" ibid.
page 390: "Please give me a break! . . ." ibid.
page 391: "We'd only rehearsed once or twice . . ." Seiter/Rogan. Redondo Beach, California: 28 July 1979.
page 391: "The show was a financial success . . ." Review of the Byrds' show at the Marigold Ballroom (10 November). *Connie's Insider: The Upper Midwest's Weekly Trade Music Trade Journal,* Vol 1, no. 15: 18 November 1967.
page 391: "Sadly . . ." Jim Dochniak's recollections on the website Garage Hangover.
page 392: "I swear to God . . ." Seiter/Rogan. London/Los Angeles, California: 18 October 1999.
page 392: "You won't have to worry . . ." ibid.
page 392: "It's mother . . ." Clark/Rogan. London: 2 May 1997.
page 392: "You're damned right . . ." ibid.
page 392: "I don't think they were taunting him . . ." Seiter/Rogan. London/Los Angeles, California: 18 October 1999.
page 393: "We were flying . . ." Clarke/Rogan. London and Manchester: 14–15 October 1989.
page 393: "It's almost like he came in . . ." Chris Hillman, interviewed by John Nork. Original transcript submitted to the author. Part published in *Tracking Angle*: February 1997.
page 393: "None of us were easy to work with . . ." Clarke/Rogan. London and Manchester: 14–15 October 1989.
page 393: "We did a gig as a trio . . ." Seiter/Rogan. Redondo Beach, California: 28 July 1979.
page 394: "The curtains open . . ." Reviewer Jennifer Starkey. *The Happening*: February 1968. The only other contemporary mention of the group's work as a trio that I ever saw occurred in *Teen Set* (March 1968). "Now it's Roger, Chris and Michael," they noted. "A trio of Byrds. Yes, they sound different – heavy blues, lots of bass – but they still do 'Eight Miles High' and make it sound good. And next? Will there be another fourth? Maybe, maybe not. What's really important is that the Byrds still exist, after more than two years of ups and downs, in and outs, in spite of all predictions of extinction. Good luck to them."
page 395: "I remember the performance distinctly . . ." Reviewer Bill Wasserzieher. *Full Circle* 9: April 1991.

NOTES

page 395: "I think he was on the point of quitting . . ." McGuinn/Rogan. Leeds: 4 May 1977. Earlier McGuinn had mentioned another factor in Clarke's leaving. "He just wanted the bread and said he was going to quit after the publishing money came in this time. He just wanted to take his money and split." It is not clear whether Clarke managed to stay around long enough to get his publishing money. All that is certain is that he missed out on the renegotiated CBS contract three months later which would have netted him a substantial sum had he not been fired. Draw your own conclusions.

page 396: "Michael would turn the time round . . ." Crosby/Rogan. London: 22–23 April 1980.

page 396: "Michael and I were really good friends . . ." Seiter/Rogan. London/Los Angeles, California: 18 October 1999.

page 396: "Few knew that the recent line-up changes . . ." 'Byrds Make Trio Debut' trumpeted *New Musical Express* in an impressively benevolent lead review of 'Goin' Back', guaranteed to bring Christmas cheer to bereft fans still reeling from the departures of Crosby and Clark. Nobody knew that Clarke was about to join their ranks, least of all CBS Records. A CBS memorandum dated 7 December 1967 sent to the UK branch of the company suggested that they were still confused and uncertain about the consequences of the recent turbulence. The memo, headed 'The Tearful Parting Of The Ways', advised: "The Byrds. Things are, to say the least, up in the air for the group right now. For your personal enlightenment, David Crosby left to be replaced by Gene Clark. Now, however, Gene has left as well, leaving the Byrds up a tree (excuse bad pun) as a three member group. They haven't decided whether they will add a member or not. As for 'Going [sic] Back', for the press' ears, however, I think the best way to handle the group's present status is to say David Crosby has left the Byrds, period. As for 'Going [sic] Back', Chris Hillman, Roger McGuinn, Mike Clark [sic] get credit for that. David Crosby is going on his own as a solo act. Within the next few days, I'll be sending you new pix and bios of your favourites." At the time of the memo, Clarke was completing work on 'Artificial Energy', the final track to be recorded for *The Notorious Byrd Brothers*. Soon after, he was gone. It should be stressed that news of the comings and goings of various Byrds was frequently late reaching the public during the Sixties. Unlike the weekly UK press, which specialized in news stories, American rock journals were mainly monthly publications with long lead-ins. *Rolling Stone* confidently broke the news of Crosby's departure as happening "last week" in their issue dated 9 November. He had actually left nearly two months before.

Chapter 25: Wanted: The Notorious Byrd Brothers

page 397: "... became interested in Far East religions ..." unearthed from author's archives. Undated CBS/Columbia promotional artiste biography, *circa* May 1968.

page 398: "I suppose McGuinn must have hoped ..." Dickson/Rogan. Waldport, Oregon: 26–30 April 1989.

page 398: "There wasn't a lot of hope ..." McGuinn/Rogan. London/Florida: 22 May 1997.

page 398: "I think the stress ..." McGuinn/Valentine. *Sounds*: 21 August 1971.

page 398: "The album was a critical triumph, greeted with lengthy and effusive reviews in both *Rolling Stone* and *Crawdaddy* ..." The *Rolling Stone* review was penned by Jon Landau, who had previously tackled *Fifth Dimension* for *Crawdaddy*. He lamented the Byrds' live reputation but argued that, like the Beatles, they had now evolved into a studio group. "No one has ever seen the Beatles perform *Sgt Pepper*; but who exactly is complaining?" Complimenting the Byrds on the "never-ending circularity" and "rich, child-like quality" of their music, he attempted to explain the source of its appeal. "It has a timelessness to it, not in the sense that you think their music will always be valid, but in the sense that it is capable of forcing you to suspend consciousness altogether."

'Timeless' was a word that always suited the Byrds and provided a neat summation of their ethereal style. That's probably why it stumbled forth from my own subconscious as a suitable subtitle for this book and its predecessors. It inspired the epigraph too and was, of course, used by McGuinn himself as a chorus to 'Love That Never Dies' when he sang, "love is a timeless flight".

Listening to the Byrds in 1968, Landau clearly felt something similar, acknowledging a sense of familiarity and freshness in identical moments. "*The Notorious Byrd Brothers* is the same old trip but, at the same time, a brand new one. The lyrics have greater force ... and there is a seriousness to even the lighter pieces. Stylistically, the eclecticism is so marked that one suspects McGuinn of having read an article about the Byrds' eclecticism ... C&W, science fiction, light jazz touches, finger-picking rhythms, pop-rock (two fine Goffin–King songs), and touches of strings all play their part on this album. Yet if one doesn't listen closely he may not notice even a fraction of the incongruities which are present. And therein lies a key to the Byrds' ability to assimilate everything they touch."

NOTES

In *Crawdaddy* (May 1968) Sandy Pearlman offered another impressionistic excursion into the Byrds' "sonic preoccupation" and "molecular sound organization" echoing some of the theories advanced in his previous extended essay on *Younger Than Yesterday*. "Trying to tell you how enchantingly beautiful the new Byrds' album is and, right away, we gotta turn to their sonic preoccupation," he began. "Suffice to say, the Byrds have this unique preoccupation with a constant (although simultaneously evolving) primal sound. Certainly this sound has been some kind of major enchantment. It really puts a spell on you: 'cause it really puts a spell on its materials. And that's a function of the Byrds' form. Which form structures the materials into enchantment. So the Byrds' sound is enchanted (and enchanting) in its absolute *otherness* toward rock sound and even the random noise about us. It's peaceful, dependent not upon the ever-implicit (sometimes explicit) internal differential and violence of sound organized as contrast, but rather upon constantly given resolutions. (The Byrds are at some different order of sound, deeply *musical* in the most archaic sense. Think of the music of the spheres. Just think.)."

Pearlman continued in this mode for several pages, coining concepts, extrapolating via constant parenthetic asides and mentioning magic and science in the same breath. After some passing comments on *Fifth Dimension*, he reckoned that with *Younger Than Yesterday* "the Byrds finished all preparations necessary for their impending penetration into the hitherto little known 'molecular sound organization' bag." (Presumably, this was 'little known' for the simple reason that Pearlman had just invented the concept.)

The two 'molecular sound' guys were evidently Phil Spector and Van Dyke Parks whose speciality Pearlman referred to as 'Silent Denial'. As for how the Byrds fitted into all this, he praised "their mastery over all sounds in their repertoire and their perfected form, they can so organize sound molecules as to do away with any 'spaces' between them."

Evidently, the Byrds were also masters of another new concept: 'Absolute Adequacy'. "Absolute adequacy itself describes a band when its sound gets so economical (not merely tight) that excess and inordinancy [sic] just disappear."

Oddly, it was only on his final page that Pearlman directly addressed *The Notorious Byrd Brothers*. Rather eccentrically, he restricted his discussion entirely to the album's first side. "The arrangement which assigns distinct energy roles and levels to the instruments, is so important that it wouldn't at all belittle the Byrds to say that maybe now their greatness lies in arrangement." Back on his 'molecular sound organization' kick, Pearlman marvelled: "they make arrangements filling up the very interstices between sounds. (No holes. No more holes.) In comparison, what we once regarded as the densest sound of all (*Younger Than Yesterday*) now sounds so very, very thin. (Proving only the Byrds can date the Byrds)."

The best of Pearlman's effusion was reserved for 'Artificial Energy'. "On one channel (listen, stereo) drums, brass, bass, traditional Byrds chorale and some electronic noise maker (phase reversal? Moog Synthesizer? Tape loops?). Other channel drums (John Philip Sousa bass drum), brass, Byrds chorale, piano (acoustical), chimes. That's, channel-wise, the catalog of materials. Since sonic density's never mere accumulation, the materials aren't stacked (which would spell weight) atop each other. Rather they're woven, interfering to finally coalesce, not disintegrate." In passing, he claimed that the album's "electronics" made the Rolling Stones' 'She's A Rainbow' and even the Byrds' 'CTA 102' "sound *intentionally* bad".

Fascinated by the album's programming (although strangely he did not mention the Beatles' interwoven *Sgt Pepper's Lonely Hearts Club Band* which was an obvious influence), Pearlman could not resist providing us with yet another new concept: the Turkey Tongue. Rather generously, he credited the Byrds, rather than himself, with its invention. "It was they who invented the Turkey Tongue, a type of Unknown Tongue wherein the *next* cut completes the preceding one. So 'My Back Pages' acted to resolve 'Mind Garden[s]', which was the *turkey* for 'My Back Pages'. Together they constitute the primal Turkey Tongue system." In case we were still in any doubt about what he meant, he provided a series of examples from *The Notorious Byrd Brothers*. "Some of these Turkey Tongues are real spectaculars. 'Artificial Energy' ends with '. . . I'm in jail 'cause I killed a queen', trailed by horns and an electronic noise maker to fadeout, at which point in comes 'Goin' Back', its deliberately paced kineticism slowly wound and all by the traditional Byrds' wind-up intro (think of 'Mr Tambourine Man', think of 'Turn! Turn! Turn!') repeated, quick-cycled, but stately, syncopated patterns. 'Artificial Energy' was as violent as the Byrds ever got (only a multipart chorale preserved an aura of resolution). All aswirl as it was with brass and counter patterns, what not, and then this archaeological find, 'Goin' Back', the self-conscious Byrds' song par excellence (music of the spheres) cuts right across all its implications turning seeming violence to cosmic resolution: that's a Turkey Tongue."

Pearlman's colleague, Paul Williams, saved most of his observations for a rambling appreciation later included in his book *Outlaw Blues*

(E.P. Dutton & Co, 1969). Discursive as ever, Williams meandered indulgently in his conversational way ("The Byrds . . . are about as nice as you could be . . . ") before belatedly hitting home with some insightful observations. "The Byrds more than anybody today have mastered communication. Part of it is that they're not afraid. Not on any of the important levels. They try, but they're not very conscious of what they're 'supposed to be' doing, and this is a saving grace. Such an ominous toy as the Moog becomes in their hands just a thing to make sound with at the beginning of 'Natural Harmony'. They aren't intimidated. They're in control, the music is completely theirs, there is no distance between man and machine because machine is appreciated as simply tool, extension of man, something to do things with. The same is true of the horns, strings, everything on *The Notorious Byrd Brothers*. The listener is absolutely not aware of the strings on 'Goin' Back', not because he can't hear them – they're right there – but because he's hearing the song. In the best art you cannot see the artist's handiwork. You can only feel his presence, in what you're perceiving, you're overwhelmed by that and not concerned with examining it. You relate. Sex can be much closer, more direct, than we think the word 'close' means. So can looking at Picasso. So can listening to the Byrds." Concluding, Williams noted: "The Byrds have abolished time, for themselves, and for all of us if we listen enough." Like Landau and Pearlman, Williams recognized that it was the suspension of time itself that somehow seemed central to the Byrds' music.

In *Jazz & Pop*, Jay Ruby, who would soon conduct an extensive interview with McGuinn, also offered a very personal appreciation of the album in which he applauded the Byrds' world-view as much as their music. "The Byrds have the ability to sound the same and yet subtly introduce new ideas in each of their records. I like the view of the world that they project in their music. It is an innocent place where good people do good things and are saddened, even sometimes outraged by war and other inhuman acts. They are the electronic inheritors of Pete Seeger's world . . . The Byrds have lost their popularity with some people because they appear to be doing the same thing over and over again. This is not true – their changes are just not as dramatic as some others. And even if they were to remain where they are now, the possibilities of their music have not been exhausted. They still move and involve me in the same way they did in 1965."

page 399: "Let's write a song . . ." McGuinn/Rogan. Leeds: 4 May 1977.
page 400: "Rhythms against counter rhythms . . ." Reviewer Sandy Pearlman. *Crawdaddy*: May 1968.
page 400: "It's a good strong track . . ." *Hit Parader*: September 1968.

page 400: "I remember we had a really 'square' . . ." McGuinn/Rogan. Leeds: 4 May 1977.

page 401: "Gary Usher got the tune . . ." McGuinn/Kubernik: 2007. Original interview transcript sent to author.

page 403: "It's not a them-versus-us situation . . ." Crosby, interviewed in *Southern California Oracle, Counter-Culture News*: October 1967.

page 404: "Crosby had written the basic song . . ." Chris Hillman, interviewed by Pete Frame. *Zigzag* 31. The magazine ceased dating issues at this point when Connor McKnight succeeded Pete Frame as editor.

page 404: "It was one of the sleaziest things they ever did . . ." Crosby/Rogan. London: 22–23 April 1980.

page 405: "Man – they used it . . ." ibid.

page 405: "Gary Usher knew Carole King . . ." McGuinn/Rogan. Leeds: 4 May 1977.

page 405: "It was before electronic . . ." Roger McGuinn, interviewed by Dan Epstein. *Guitar Player*: May 1997.

page 405: "King sang, 'And I'll stay awhile . . .' " Not long after, King issued the full original version on the Ode Records album *Now That Everything's Been Said* by the City, whose ranks included her new husband Charles Lackey (bass) and Danny Kortchmar (guitar), who later worked with Crosby & Nash, among others. Interestingly, the drummer was Jim Gordon, who also appeared on *The Notorious Byrd Brothers*.

page 406: "I remember Gene coming to my house . . ." McGuinn/Rogan. London/Florida: 22 May 1997.

page 407: "Actually, it's . . ." McGuinn/Rogan. Leeds: 4 May 1977.

page 407: "I played the bass . . ." Crosby/Rogan. London: 22–23 April 1980.

page 408: ". . . on Hillman's tune . . ." ibid.

page 408: "It's another of those . . ." *Fusion*: April 1969.

page 408: "I grew up in a small town . . ." Hillman/Rogan: 26 January 1979. John Stuart Robertson (born 14 June 1878; died 5 November 1964), originally from Canada, directed 57 films during the early twentieth century, including the famous screen version of *Dr Jekyll And Mr Hyde* in 1929. In the fanzine *Full Circle* (issue 29; April 2001), Don Richmond wrote a brief piece about the director and his wife Josephine. Evidently, Robertson arrived in Rancho Sante Fe in 1928 and built a lavish Spanish colonial abode on a hilltop with spacious grounds, orange trees and riding stables. He established a riding club in the community, which was still there during Hillman's youth. Richmond adds: "Early on, when there was no money in the treasury, John had himself thrown in

NOTES

jail, and paid a fine of $20 to raise money for the club. He spent time at the club daily and often had to reprimand irresponsible young riders (possibly the kind of behaviour that led children to fear him?). Eventually, he had to hire a full-time trainer to watch over things. As time went by, the riding club flourished and grew to between 100 and 200 members, with all the necessary buildings. It's been said that Old John must be cheering from beyond the grave to see the success of his dream."

page 409: "We were just playing . . ." *Fusion*: April 1969.

page 409: " 'Tribal Gathering' was about the feeling . . ." McGuinn/Rogan. Leeds: 4 May 1977.

page 410: "I have found not one absolute . . ." Crosby, interviewed in *Southern California Oracle, Counter-Culture News*: October 1967.

page 410: "It was my idea, my music and my lyrics . . ." Crosby/Rogan. London: 22–23 April 1980.

page 410: "It was my idea to do the 'be-de-lum' introduction . . ." McGuinn/Rogan. Leeds: 4 May 1977.

page 411: "It was purely accidental . . ." Roger McGuinn, interviewed by Pete Johnson. *Hit Parader*: September 1968.

page 411: "It was more a question of how the album would flow . . ." Usher/Tannfelt. *Full Circle* 7: August 1990. Reprinted from *Surfer's Rule* and *The Cosmic American Music News*.

page 411: "If we *had* intended to do that . . ." McGuinn. Radio WHFS Annapolis: 2 March 1989. Recalling the story, McGuinn adds: "We were in Beverly Hills, riding around on horseback and doing some cowboy pictures and different types of poses with horses. We stumbled upon this old abandoned stone house that had four rectangular windows in it. The three of us – David Crosby had just left the group – walked into the old abandoned house and the photographer said, 'That's great!' Michael happened to have his horse with him, so the horse took one of the windows because he didn't want to stand on his own in the dark. The photographer took the picture and a lot of people thought that was the missing man, that the horse represented David Crosby."

page 411: "An accident? . . ." Crosby/Rogan. London: 22–23 April 1980.

page 412: "It came down to McGuinn and me . . ." Chris Hillman, interviewed by Pete Frame. *Zigzag* 31 issue undated, *c.* May 1973.

page 412: "That's dumb . . ." Crosby/Rogan. London: 22–23 April 1980.

page 413: "I feel that was the best stage . . ." McGuinn/Rogan. Leeds: 4 May 1977.

page 413: "I thought *Younger Than Yesterday* . . ." Crosby/Rogan. London: 22–23 April 1980.

Chapter 26: Nashville

page 414: "We were playing these little gigs . . ." McGuinn/Rogan. London/Florida: 22 May 1997.

page 417: "Appropriately enough, it was in a Beverly Hills bank during the Summer of Love . . ." Over recent years, Hillman has sometimes confused the exact time he first met Parsons. But in earlier interviews, he was confident about the dating. "I first met Gram Parsons in a Beverly Hills bank during Summer 1967," he told my colleague Pete Frame decades ago. "He had the same business manager, an awful man called Larry Spector. At the time, Gram was in the International Submarine Band and was making an album with them – even though to all intents and purposes the group had split up. Anyway, a few months later, when we realized we'd have to bring a fourth member into the Byrds again, his name came up."

page 417: "I was with Ian . . ." Gram Parsons, interviewed by Bud Scoppa: 1970. Reprinted in full in Sid Griffin, *Gram Parsons: A Music Biography* (Sierra, 1985). It is worth remembering that this interview took place only a couple of years after the release of *The Notorious Byrd Brothers*, which adds credence to the account. During a promotional interview dated December 1972, Parsons was telling the same story with noteworthy consistency: "I'd met Chris Hillman in a bank. We had on the same kind of jeans and the same looks on our faces. At a session of theirs later on, I mentioned the name 'Flying Burrito Brothers' and they wanted to use it as the title of the album that was eventually called *The Notorious Byrd Brothers*. I wouldn't let them have it. But I joined the group a little after that."

page 417: ". . . moves were afoot earlier . . ." Ian Dunlop, interviewed by the author. London/Cornwall: 12 January 2009.

page 418: "They needed another musician . . ." Gram Parsons, interviewed by Jan Donkers. Radio broadcast. Holland: August 1972.

page 418: "When I hired Gram Parsons . . ." McGuinn/Rogan. Leeds: 4 May 1977.

page 418: "The organ adds needed depth . . ." Review of the Byrds' performance at the University Of Michigan on 23 February 1968, printed in the following day's *Michigan News*.

page 419: "On 29 February 1968 . . ." Details of the terms are taken from three Byrds' CBS contracts, dated 10 November 1964, 10 July 1965 and 29 February 1968, respectively.

page 420: ". . . in order to benefit Michael and Chris . . ." Dickson/Rogan. Waldport, Oregon: 26–30 April 1989.

NOTES

page 421: "I assume Larry Spector's idea . . ." ibid.

page 421: "McGuinn at the time was very aloof . . ." Seiter/Rogan. London/Los Angeles, California: 18 October 1999.

page 421: "He had this black maid . . ." Dolores Tickner (formerly McGuinn, née DeLeon)/Rogan. London/Tucson, Arizona: 13 January 2007.

page 422: "We had given him the opportunity . . ." Chris Hillman, quoted on the internet site, *The Gram Parsons Project*.

page 422: "I knew this music . . ." Chris Hillman, interviewed by David Fricke, quoted in the liner notes to the Legacy edition of *Sweetheart Of The Rodeo*.

page 423: "We thought country was a fun place . . ." Roger McGuinn, interviewed by Thor Christensen. *Dallas Morning Herald*: 3 April 1997.

page 423: ". . . it was like one of the Rolling Stones . . ." McGuinn/Rogan: London/Florida: 22 May 1997.

page 423: "I loved it . . ." Roger McGuinn, interviewed by Sean Egan. *Goldmine*: 28 December 2001.

page 424: "It was going to be a chronological thing . . ." McGuinn/Rogan. Leeds: 4 May 1977.

page 424: "He's sort of up in the air . . ." Roger McGuinn, interviewed by Pete Johnson. *Hit Parader*: September 1968.

page 425: "We were supposed to open for the Turtles . . ." Jon Corneal, interviewed by the author. London/Florida: 24 June 2007.

page 425: "John said it wasn't playing . . ." ibid.

page 426–427: "It was interesting . . ." Roger McGuinn, interviewed by David Fricke, quoted in the liner notes to the Legacy edition of *Sweetheart Of The Rodeo*.

page 427: "I can hear the despair . . ." ibid.

page 427: "I was used to doing . . ." Lloyd Green, interviewed by David Fricke, quoted in the liner notes to the Legacy edition of *Sweetheart Of The Rodeo*.

page 428: "I didn't smoke pot or anything . . ." Lloyd Green, interviewed by Alastair McCay. *Uncut*: March 2008.

page 429: "I'd known the song . . ." McGuinn on his *Folk Den* website.

page 429: "Chris Hillman discouraged me . . ." McGuinn/Rogan. Leeds: 4 May 1977.

page 429: "We had musicians from all over town . . ." Jim Seiter, interviewed by the author. London/Macao, People's Republic Of China: 28 June 2007.

page 429: "Nobody of that calibre . . ." Green/Fricke. Legacy edition of *Sweetheart Of The Rodeo*.

page 429: "I don't think he liked . . ." McGuinn/Rogan. Leeds: 4 May 1977.

page 430: "Ralph was outrageously confrontational . . ." Green/McCay. *Uncut*: March 2008.

page 430: "They dressed casually . . ." In the impressionistic memoir *Grievous Angel,* penned by Jessica Huntley with Polly Parsons, there is a semi-fictionalized account of the group's supposedly 'fashion conscious' *Opry* appearance. "The Byrds had opted for full regalia, Nudie suits, catching the spotlights, colors vibrating, rhinestones glowing . . ." As colour photos from the show confirm, the group were actually underdressed: *nobody* wore a suit; McGuinn and Hillman sported jeans; both Kelley and McGuinn had open-neck shirts; Parsons had a greyish polo neck pullover and brown trousers, rather like those favoured by Rupert The Bear. Needless to say, there wasn't a rhinestone in sight.

page 431: "From my point of view . . ." Chris Hillman, interviewed by Pete Frame for 'The Grievous Angel' family tree, compiled in December 1981, printed in *The Complete Rock Family Trees* (Omnibus Press, 1993).

page 431: "Nobody who was part of that scene . . ." Roger McGuinn, interviewed by Barney Hoskyns. *Mojo* 56: July 1998.

page 431: "I was so embarrassed . . ." Green/Fricke. Legacy edition of *Sweetheart Of The Rodeo.*

page 432: "Initially, they were making fun . . ." Chris Hillman, interviewed by Alastair McCay. *Uncut*: March 2008.

page 432: ". . . suggested that, for the sake of public relations . . ." report by Randy Brooks in *The Vanderbilt Hustler*: 19 March 1968. Remarkably, for such an historically important performance, there has never been a firm consensus on what the Byrds actually played at the Grand Ole Opry. Surprisingly, no broadcast tapes of their appearance could be found in the Opry archives and no bootleg tape has ever surfaced or is known to have been recorded. Over the decades the Opry saga has been repeated many times leading to further confusion. Reconciling the accounts is no easy task. During an interview with Pete Frame, later included within 'The Grievous Angel' in his book, *The Complete Rock Family Trees*, Chris Hillman offered what then seemed a definitive account of the event. "We were the guests on the Tompall and the Glaser Brothers' sections and we went on being introduced as 'The Byrds on Columbia Records'. Just to let you know how hostile the audience felt towards us, they were shouting out stuff like 'tweet tweet' and 'cut your hair' – but we did Merle Haggard's 'Sing Me Back Home' and it changed their minds! They were really appreciative when we finished –

particularly as Lloyd Green was up there playing with us . . . and I've got to hand it to Lloyd Green: it took a lot of balls to get up on stage with a band of long-haired, weirdo, strangers-in-town, knowing that his friends and peers were so antagonistic towards us. We'd told Tompall that we were going to do 'Life In Prison' next, so out he came to make the intro: 'Well, thank you, boys – and now you're going to do another Merle Haggard song aren't you?' But then Gram suddenly got hold of the microphone and said, 'No, I'm going to sing 'Hickory Wind' for my grandmother in Tennessee' . . . and we all had to do 'Hickory Wind'.

Frame's account was evidently repeated more or less verbatim in Ben Fong-Torres' book *Hickory Wind* and carried forward into other studies, including Peter Doggett's *Are You Ready For The Country* and even paraphrased in one of my previous Byrds books. David Meyer's *Twenty Thousand Roads* also uses the Frame quotes but wrongly credits them to Doggett, not realizing that he had borrowed them. However, Meyer then adds a spin of his own: "The band were supposed to do Merle Haggard's 'Sing Me Back Home' and 'Life In Prison'. Glaser announced 'Sing Me Back Home' and the band performed to an unimpressed, blank-faced crowd." So Meyer also believes that the two songs performed were 'Sing Me Back Home' and 'Hickory Wind'. He may well be following, in addition to the aforementioned sources, the liner notes by David Fricke in the Legacy version of *Sweetheart Of The Rodeo*. Therein, it is claimed that 'Sing Me Back Home' *was* performed, adding "Parsons then committed an unpardonable crime: switching songs on air, ditching a *second* Haggard number, 'Life In Prison', for 'Hickory Wind', which he dedicated to his grandmother."

In the absence of any comments on the Opry songs by Gram Parsons or Kevin Kelley, we have road manager Jim Seiter's memories. In Sid Griffin's *Gram Parsons: A Music Biography*, he recalls: "They announced two songs and then Gram says he wants to do two other songs and he wants to dedicate them to his grandmother. They went crazy. I got such a hassle from the Opry officials because we totally broke tradition . . . We did 'Hickory Wind' and I think they sang 'You Ain't Going Nowhere' which came off really well, they got a great response from the people there . . . Hell, *two* songs we're out of there . . ."

All this is complicated by a 1997 interview in *Goldmine* that Hillman conducted with Bruce Sylvester. There, Hillman changes the story, as previously related to Frame, and states that it was 'Sing Me Back Home', not 'Life In Prison' that was the song replaced by 'Hickory Wind'. He has stuck to that version ever since, most recently telling John Einarson in their collaborative book, *Hot Burritos*: "We planned to do 'You Ain't

Going Nowhere' and Merle Haggard's 'Sing Me Back Home' because it had been a recent country hit."

Reconciling these different accounts might seem impossible but, thankfully, at least one newspaper report of the incident, written immediately after the show, throws revealing light on the subject. The report written by Randy Brooks for the university journal, *The Vanderbilt Hustler*, is quoted in full in Christopher Hjort's diary *So You Want To Be A Rock 'n' Roll Star: The Byrds Day-By-Day 1965–1973*. The key parts concerning the Opry appearance are revealing. "The Byrds of 'Mr Tambourine Man', 'Turn! Turn! Turn!' and 'Eight Miles High' fame were in last-minute preparations for their Grand Ole Opry debut Friday night. Their road manager held a cigarette to the lips of Chris Hillman while he stood and played his electric bass. An unidentified man suggested that, for the sake of public relations, they use the current number 1 song, 'Sing Me Back Home', for their encore. The boys had other ideas, and even after the MC introduced that song, guitarist Parsons announced a change of plans and began instead to play 'Hickory Wind', a very pretty and very country tune. . . Both 'Hickory Wind' and 'You Ain't Going Nowhere' drew polite but unenthusiastic response from an audience which only minutes before had cheered heartily for the [Glaser] Brothers and displayed unabashed adoration for Skeeter Davis." Hjort rightly stresses the importance of this source, but it still leaves one problem unresolved. Did the Byrds sing two songs or three? Hjort opts for the latter, writing: "The group has discussed with the MC Tompall Glaser that they will do a pair of Merle Haggard songs, 'Sing Me Back Home' and 'Life In Prison'. After dutifully doing the opening number as agreed, Parsons seizes the moment and tells the crowd and radio audience that he will be singing 'Hickory Wind' instead of the second Haggard song, before rounding off the performance with the new 'You Ain't Going Nowhere'." While plausible, this summation is speculative and veers away from the essential facts contained in the university newspaper report which makes no mention at all of 'Life In Prison' or the existence of any 'third' song. Moreover, everyone else at least seemed to agree that only two songs were performed, not three. My own view, for what it's worth, and taking into account all the above, is that the Byrds performed 'You Ain't Going Nowhere' and 'Hickory Wind', most likely in that order. I think 'Life In Prison' was never in the equation and was probably a mistake – a simple confusion of two different Haggard songs. Hjort now agrees that this is the most probable explanation. Maybe one day, a tape will appear to put the argument completely beyond doubt.

NOTES

page 432: "On the air . . ." Hillman/Sylvester. *Goldmine* 436: 11 April 1997.
page 432: "How dare you . . ." As related by both Parsons and Hillman in numerous interviews.
page 432: "She was always . . ." Hillman/Sylvester. *Goldmine* 436: 11 April 1997.
page 433: "You know what . . ." Hillman/McCay. *Uncut*: March 2008.

Chapter 27: Stonehenge

page 434: "Gene was drunk . . ." Taylor/Rogan. London: 17 June 1977.
page 434: "I couldn't have stopped him . . ." Seiter/Rogan. London/Los Angeles, California: 18 October 1999.
page 435: "He fell flat on his back . . ." Seiter/Rogan. Redondo Beach, California: 28 July 1979.
page 435: "They just kept on playing . . ." Seiter/Rogan. London/Los Angeles, California: 18 October 1999.
page 436: "There are fewer hang-ups . . ." Roger McGuinn, interviewed by Jerry Hopkins. *Rolling Stone*: 11 May 1968.
page 436: "We don't have a title . . ." ibid.
page 437: "We split into two different camps . . ." McGuinn/Rogan. Leeds: 4 May 1977.
page 437: "We hired a piano player . . ." Roger McGuinn. *Fusion*: April 1969.
page 437: "With Buck Owens . . ." Earl Ball, interviewed by David N. Meyer. *Twenty Thousand Roads – The Ballad Of Gram Parsons And His Cosmic American Music* (New York: Villard, 2007), p. 238.
page 438: "I was miserable . . ." Jay Dee Maness, interviewed by David Fricke, quoted in the liner notes to the Legacy edition of *Sweetheart Of The Rodeo*.
page 438: "Gram and Chris took over . . ." McGuinn/Rogan. Leeds: 4 May 1977.
page 439: "Roger, formerly Jim . . ." Reviewer Michael Etchinson. *Los Angeles Herald-Examiner*: 2 May 1968.
page 439: "New singer . . ." ibid.
page 440: "The Byrds basically stayed . . ." Seiter/Rogan. London/Macao, People's Republic Of China: 28 June 2007.
page 440: "In stereo . . ." Album review in *Record Mirror*: 6 April 1968.
page 440: "The other three music weeklies *New Musical Express*, *Melody Maker* and *Disc*, all lavished praise on the album . . ." Remarkably, the UK chart success of *The Notorious Byrd Brothers* brought some unexpected attention from the music press. Letters were printed praising

the Byrds and the end of year readers' poll in the *Melody Maker* saw the album voted the eighth best of the year, while the Byrds also achieved fifth place in the International Group listing. The group was absent from all other UK music press polls, but the endorsement from *Melody Maker* readers was most encouraging.

page 440: "It's true to say . . ." Album review in *Beat Instrumental*: May 1968.

page 440: "We were kind of astonished . . ." Roger McGuinn, interviewed by Tony Wilson and Wina Golden. *Melody Maker*: 20 July 1968.

page 441: "They knew I had a passion for country . . ." Jeff Dexter, interviewed by the author. London: 3 July 2009.

page 441: "Jimmi looked after everything . . ." ibid.

page 442: "Mick Jagger and Marianne Faithfull . . ." Pete Frame, interviewed by Spencer Leigh on BBC, Liverpool, belatedly reproduced in *Country Music People*: September 2006.

page 443: ". . . were called back countless times . . ." Reviewer Norman Jopling. *Record Mirror*: 18 May 1968.

page 443: "It was fantastic . . ." ibid.

page 444: "Seems that everyone . . ." Record review by Derek Johnson. *New Musical Express*: 18 May 1968.

page 444: "This Dylan song . . ." Record review in *Record Mirror*: 11 May 1968.

page 445: "Gram came over . . ." Dexter/Rogan. London: 3 July 2009.

page 445: "Mick and Keith were complete gentlemen . . ." Chris Hillman, quoted on the internet site, *The Gram Parsons Project*.

page 446: "Anya felt Gram was attractive . . ." Dolores Tickner (formerly McGuinn, née DeLeon)/Rogan. London/Tucson, Arizona: 13 January 2007.

page 446: "It was to be an experiment . . ." McGuinn/Rogan. Leeds: 4 May 1977.

page 446: "Gram was a lovely, warm, down-to-earth guy . . ." Keith Richards, quoted in Barney Hoskyns. *Mojo* 56: July 1998.

page 446: "Well, put it this way, *we* wouldn't go . . ." As related to the author by McGuinn and Hillman.

page 448: "Parsons got really mad . . ." Melcher/Rogan. London: 27 December 1977.

page 448: "Things really came out well . . ." Gram Parsons/Donkers. Radio broadcast. Holland: August 1972.

page 449: "It is true that some of Parsons' leads . . ." Gary Usher, interviewed by Göran Tannfelt. *Full Circle* 7: August 1990. Reprinted from *Surfer's Rule* and *The Cosmic American Music News*.

page 449: "There was a genuine concern . . ." ibid.

NOTES

page 450: "... a fortune hunter ..." Christopher Hjort, *So You Want To Be A Rock 'n' Roll Star: The Byrds Day-By-Day 1965–1973* (Jawbone, 2008), p. 200.

page 451: "McGuinn's from Outer Space ..." Tickner/Rogan. Redondo Beach, California: 20 July 1979.

page 451: "He wanted to watch ..." Dolores Tickner (formerly McGuinn, née DeLeon)/Rogan. London/Tucson, Arizona: 13 January 2007.

page 452: "Some people see things ..." Robert F. Kennedy, speaking at the University of Kansas, Missouri: 18 March 1968. The original source of the quotation can be found in George Bernard Shaw's play *Back To Methuselah* : "You see things; and you say, 'Why?' But I dream things that never were; and I say, 'Why not?'"

page 453: "That was the only political benefit ..." Roger McGuinn, quoted in Peter Doggett, *There's A Riot Going On* (Canongate, 2007), p. 158.

page 453: "We were watching the California primary ..." Roger McGuinn, quoted in Bruce Pollock, *When The Music Mattered* (New York, Holt, Rinehart & Winston, 1983), p.90.

page 453: "Then Jacques said ..." ibid.

page 453: "I couldn't sit down ..." ibid.

page 453: "Bobby Kennedy has been shot ..." Dolores Tickner (formerly McGuinn, née DeLeon)/Rogan. London/Tucson, Arizona: 13 January 2007.

page 453: "Roger and Jacques were sitting there ..." ibid.

page 453: "Oh, Roger ..." ibid.

page 453: "Apartheid, the Afrikaans word ..." From 'Suppose God Is Black,' Sen. Robert F. Kennedy. *Look*: 23 August 1966. Kennedy explained in the article that the races of South Africa comprised "three million whites, 12 million blacks, and two million Indian and 'coloured' (mixed blood) people." In one bizarre encounter, he experienced a sliding scale of racial prejudice. "I had asked a group of pro-government editors to define 'coloured'. They considered and said, 'a bastard'. I asked if a child born out of wedlock to a white man and white woman would be coloured. They said the whole area was difficult. Then one of them said it was simply a person who was neither white nor black. A South African, yes; an Indian, yes; A Chinese, yes – but a Japanese, no. Why not a Japanese? Because there were so few, was the answer. It developed, however, that South Africa trades heavily with the Japanese, and perhaps it was more profitable to call them white."

page 454: "I believe in getting through ..." Roger McGuinn, interviewed on the eve of the Byrds' departure to South Africa, 7 July 1968. Printed in *Record Mirror*: 17 August 1968.

page 454: "It was a tremendous gig for Gram . . ." Carlos Bernal, interviewed by the author. London/Los Angeles, California: 10 April 2008.

page 455: "Take your guitar . . ." ibid.

page 455: ". . . there was a tremendous reception . . ." Nick Logan, article/review titled 'Byrds Long-Fly Worth It'. *New Musical Express*: 13 July 1968.

page 455: ". . . a moving rendition of Merle Haggard's 'Sing Me Back Home' which many of us present expected to appear on the next album . . ." After the concert, my notes of the time indicate that they performed an unreleased song which I referred to as 'The Warden'. It did not appear on the subsequent *Sweetheart Of The Rodeo* or any other Byrds' record. Years later, I realized that the song was 'Sing Me Back Home' and have always assumed that I wrote 'The Warden' as those were the opening two words of this then unfamiliar song. However, a review of another show confirms that 'Sing Me Back Home' was actually introduced as 'The Warden', so that may also have happened at the Royal Albert Hall.

page 456: "Someone ordered room service . . ." Dexter/Rogan. London: 3 July 2009.

page 456: "There was a bit of ill feeling . . ." ibid.

page 456: "He picked up the vibe . . ." ibid.

page 456: "We walked around the outside . . ." ibid.

page 457: "That was it . . ." Chris Hillman, interviewed by Pete Frame for 'The Grievous Angel' family tree, compiled in December 1981, printed in *The Complete Rock Family Trees* (Omnibus Press, 1993).

Chapter 28: South Africa

page 458: "He thought he was more important . . ." music press clipping, credited to Michael Thomas.

page 458: "I first heard about the South African tour . . ." Gram Parsons interviewed in *Melody Maker*: 15 July 1968.

page 459: "Something a lot of people don't know . . ." Gram Parsons, *Los Angeles Free Press*: 25 October 1969. Reprinted from *Seattle Helix*. Interview uncredited in either publication, but I believe the journalist was Ed Leimbacher.

page 459: "People to this day . . ." Chris Hillman, unissued video-taped interview by John Tobler. London: June 1990.

page 459: "Gram wasn't going on the tour . . ." Carlos Bernal, interviewed by Pete Frame: 13 May 1971. Published: *Zigzag* 32.

page 459: "I was originally hired . . ." Gram Parsons, interviewed by Jacoba Atlas. *Melody Maker*: 25 July 1970.

NOTES

page 460: "Being with the Byrds . . ." ibid.

page 460: "By refusing to go . . ." Chris Hillman, quoted on the internet site, *The Gram Parsons Project*.

page 460: "The group's already formed . . ." *Melody Maker*: 15 July 1968.

page 460: "He just sort of pocketed it . . ." Gram Parsons, interviewed by Bud Scoppa: 1970. Reproduced in Sid Griffin, *Gram Parsons: A Musical Biography* (Sierra, 1985).

page 461: "It is ironic, putting it mildly, that Jagger and Richards . . ." Robin Denselow, *When The Music's Over: The Story Of Political Pop* (Faber & Faber, 1989), p. 58.

page 461: "Actually, there was no rehearsal . . ." Bernal/Rogan. London/Los Angeles, California: 10 April 2008.

page 461: "It was pretty awkward . . ." ibid.

page 462: "The Byrds were unbelievably bad . . ." *The Sunday Times* (South Africa): 14 July 1968. Months later, McGuinn looked back on this review with a jaundiced eye. Speaking to Jay Ruby in *Jazz & Pop*, he complained that the reviewer was treating them like a traditional showbiz act. "He wanted us to have tuxedos and he said we were wearing scruffy clothes and we looked like gardeners: all these things that we've come to take for granted, like wearing blue jeans and funky shirts, and turning around to get feedback out of your amp, and weird little tricks that we accept here they weren't ready for down there. I'd say they were anywhere from 100 years on some levels to five or ten years behind the scene. And, of course, the segregation thing is terrible and they wouldn't allow any spades in to see us."

page 462: "There were some really nice people there . . ." Bernal/Rogan. London/Los Angeles, California: 10 April 2008.

page 462: "I was walking down the street . . ." Roger McGuinn, interviewed by Chris Salewicz. *New Musical Express*: 7 September 1974.

page 463: "If nothing else . . ." Reviewer Terry Herbst. *The Cape Times*: 16 July 1968.

page 463: "With all the unnerving experiences . . ." Reviewer Garner Thomson. *The Cape Argus*: 16 July 1968.

page 464: "Supporting the Byrds . . ." ibid.

page 464: "The band wasn't really getting along . . ." Bernal/Rogan. London/Los Angeles, California: 10 April 2008.

page 464: "We were roommates . . ." ibid.

page 464: "We hid under a blanket . . ." ibid.

page 465: "It was ridiculous . . ." Reviewer Graeme Pollock. *East Province Herald*: 18 July 1968.

page 465: "People at one of our shows were belching . . ." Roger McGuinn, quoted in *Natal Mercury*: 19 July 1968.

page 466: "Apartheid is all wrong . . ." Chris Hillman, quoted in *Natal Mercury*: 19 July 1968.

page 466: "We got to the third song . . ." Hillman/Rogan. London: 28 April 1977.

page 466: "I did have a nervous reaction . . ." McGuinn/Rogan. Leeds: 4 May 1977.

page 467: "During their second song . . ." Press review of the Byrds' show in Durban.

page 467: "The local press was pretty sympathetic . . ." Dave Gibbon, recalling the Byrds' South African tour in a letter to Pete Frame/*Zigzag*.

page 468: "They were obviously from cranks . . ." Roger McGuinn, quoted in *The Durban Mercury*: 20 July 1968.

page 468: "Rhodesia was a great time . . ." Bernal/Rogan. London/Los Angeles, California: 10 April 2008.

page 468: "The Byrds, still in travel clothes . . ." Reviewer Charles Stoneman. *The Rhodesia Herald*: 26 July 1968.

page 468: "Leaving Rhodesia and going back to South Africa . . ." Bernal/Rogan. London/Los Angeles, California: 10 April 2008.

page 469: "Clarence subsequently moved into session work . . ." Leaving his brothers in the Kentucky Colonels was a big step for Clarence, but nobody tried to hold him back. "He did have a little bit of [a] dilemma there," Gene Parsons told me, "but I don't think he had so much trouble with the Kentucky Colonels. I think they pretty much understood. They had worked and worked and tried to make a living and it was well nigh impossible to make a decent living playing bluegrass in those days. And Clarence had started doing sessions and he was a dyed in the wool musician. His life was playing music and at one point, because he was raising a family, he had to make the decision, 'Am I going to be loyal to this wonderful traditional music that I love and starve to death or am I going to go on and get into a new area?' His family may have dragged their feet for a while but I think they really understood that he was doing what he had to do. And I think they cheered him on."

page 470: ". . . mediocre . . . made little impression on the audience . . ." Reviewer Digby Diehl. *Los Angeles Times*: 6 August 1968. Commenting on their set, Diehl added: "The Byrds, replacing Gram Parsons with Clarence White, sang a series of their hits, such as 'So You Want To Be A Rock 'n' Roll Star' and 'Eight Miles High', interspersed with their new country & western sound on songs such as 'The Warden' ['Sing Me Back Home'], sung by Chris Hillman and Bob Dylan's 'You Ain't Going

NOTES

Nowhere'. Another review mentioned the arrival of the new guitarist in understated fashion. "The Byrds appeared, minus Gram Parsons (who is apparently out for good) and with respected country guitarist Clarence White filling in. They sounded really good, although they still can't sing 'Eight Miles High' without going flat."

Chapter 29: Sweetheart Of The Rodeo

page 471: "At the end of August, *Sweetheart Of The Rodeo* received its American release . . ." One intriguing aspect of the album was its evocative cover. For the one and only time, no photograph of the Byrds appeared on the front or rear sleeve. With Parsons having recently departed, there was evidently not sufficient time to organize a photo session of the recent or new line-up. As a result neither Gram Parsons nor Kevin Kelley ever saw their face on a Byrds' album. The back sleeve favoured a coyote howling at the moon, but it was the front that commanded attention. Usher knew a graphic designer who was consulted about the cover and instructed to send across some archive memorabilia, including Western-inspired postcards and posters. Among the batch was a 1933 postcard of a larger lavish tapestry of rodeo techniques, illustrated by Jo Mora. Usher was thrilled by the concept and sold the idea to McGuinn. It was a radical departure for an album cover, aesthetically impressive and groundbreaking. Whether the absence of McGuinn and company from the sleeve was a factor in the record's poor sales is debatable, but it made no concession to the Byrds' familiar rock audience. This was an entirely new concept. Usher's only regret was that they never had time to compose a song titled 'Sweetheart Of The Rodeo' which might have exploited the cover more successfully.

page 471: "A few songs . . ." Gram Parsons/Donkers. Radio broadcast. Holland: August 1972.

page 472: "It was my idea to do 'I Am A Pilgrim'. . ." Hillman/Rogan. New York: 26 January 1979. Hillman did not comment on the surprise release of the song as a single. It was probably the most uncommercial single they issued in their entire career. With both sides already featured on *Sweetheart Of The Rodeo*, it had little to commend it to hard-core fans and was ignored by disc jockeys. A surprise champion of the song was *NME*'s Derek Johnson, who instinctively knew it would never be a hit, but lavished some praise on the Byrds for trying something different. Under the headline 'Byrds Show Versatility' he wrote: "Rightly or wrongly, I have always regarded the Byrds as a somewhat over-rated group, largely because their early success was dependent almost entirely upon Dylan compositions. But their latest disc marks a complete change of style, and it's refreshing to discover that they do possess a considerable degree of versatility and adaptability. It's an unashamed country number, set to a mid-tempo rhythm, and incorporating lengthy instrumental passages. Mainly soloed to a steel guitar backing, it has an appealingly wistful quality, and a genuine feel for the C&W idiom. The lyric is simple yet expressive, and I found it hard to believe that it was the Byrds performing. I doubt if it will be a hit, but every credit to the group for ringing the changes so effectively."

page 473: "Religion was deeply woven . . ." Barry Tashian, interviewed by the author. London/ Nashville, Tennessee: 1 June 2008.

page 476: "Of all the people . . ." Bob Buchanan, internet interview by David W. Johnson for "Crediting 'Hickory Wind'" on www.folklinks.com.

page 477: "It's his signature song . . ." Chris Hillman, quoted in the liner notes for the Gram Parsons CD *Sacred Hearts & Fallen Angels*.

page 478: "Doing 'Life In Prison' was Gram's idea . . ." Chris Hillman, interviewed by Sean Egan. *Goldmine*: 29 December 2001.

page 479: "Roger and I had access . . ." ibid.

page 482: "Let me tell you a little bit about the place . . ." Roger McGuinn, interviewed by Jay Ruby. *Jazz & Pop*: March 1969. This lengthy interview was the culmination of an editorial debate that had been running in the magazine over the previous months. Columnist Nat Hentoff was scathing about the Byrds' decision to tour South Africa. "To make the South African apartheid scene, as the Byrds did, is to be a traditional careerist. The good soldier. The good professional who does his thing . . . people who create rock music have, like other professionals, a choice to make – between being an active, responsible part of the world or close in on their own tight little island. A choice between old-time showbiz (a gig is there to take) and what a life is all about. It's going to be interesting to see what happens to those rock groups who have been part of the thrust for freedom – freedom of consciousness, freedom of sensuality, freedom to let go and just be. As the bread gets bigger – with all the attendant 'professionalism' required when the material sales are higher and higher – are we going to just go along in the 'professional' manner of the Byrds?"

Hentoff's broadside provoked a spirited response. Canadian R. Woolley wrote to the magazine defending the Byrds, evidently on the basis that art transcends politics. "Let's say the Byrds were all racist supporters of George Wallace. Would this detract from the beauty of 'Goin' Back'? From the precision of 'Eight Miles High'. From the impact

NOTES

of 'He Was A Friend Of Mine' or 'Draft Morning'? A little perhaps, but not sufficiently enough to destroy the worth of the music, at least not to me . . . Do we deny Wagner his greatness because of his nationalistic exaggerations? Or Kipling for his condescending attitudes towards non-whites? Certainly not, however disgusted we may be with these unacceptable beliefs. I congratulate Roger McGuinn and the rest of the Byrds for having the courage to go to South Africa, knowing full well what the reaction would be. It took a strong belief in principle to risk losing the far-too-little stature they have gained."

Inevitably, Hentoff had the last word. Barely able to resist suggesting that Woolley was guilty of woolly thinking, he raised the cultural highground, pointing out: "That Dostoyevsky and Celine were anti-Semitic, that Gieseking played under the Nazis, does not add or cannot detract from the quality of what they produced as art. I would agree with Mr Woolley that if the Byrds were devotees of George Wallace, that fact would not affect – should not affect – one's judgement of the music . . . I do, however, believe in the perfectibility of man, and I would hope that, on reflection, the Byrds and other artists will consider the effect of their acceptance of apartheid. Because that's what it is. If you play before segregated audiences, you accept racism. There's no rationalizing it. If they refuse the next tour of South Africa, they will not be better musicians thereby, but damn it, they'll have shown themselves to be more responsive to the suffering – and the quite literal torture – that is endemic in South Africa today."

Chapter 30: Reconstruction

page 484: "Chris never liked Larry Spector . . ." Bernal/Rogan. London/Los Angeles, California: 10 April 2008.

page 485: "The group was a prototype Burritos . . ." Gene Parsons, interviewed by the author. Caspar, California: 22 July 1979.

page 485: "I'd got Clarence . . ." Chris Hillman, interviewed by Pete Frame. *Zigzag* 32: June 1972.

page 486: "Clarence convinced them . . ." Gene Parsons/Rogan. Caspar, California: 22 July 1979.

page 486: "You make a mistake . . ." Seiter/Rogan. Redondo Beach, California: 28 July 1979.

page 487: "I enjoyed his drumming . . ." Marc McClure, interviewed by the author. London/San Diego, California: 14 April 2007.

page 487: "Kevin was a *great* drummer . . ." Charlie Taylor, interviewed by the author. London/Nashville, Tennessee: 16 September 2007.

page 487: "All of a sudden Kevin was gone . . ." Bernal/Rogan. London/Los Angeles, California: 10 April 2008.

page 488: "We anticipated a negative reaction . . ." Roger McGuinn, interviewed by Judy Sims. *Disc*: 5 October 1968. By the time this interview was printed, much had changed. Hillman was gone and the sales of *Sweetheart Of The Rodeo* indicated that there was a negative commercial reaction to the Byrds' country recordings.

page 489: "It was irresponsible . . ." Roger McGuinn, interviewed by Bud Scoppa. *Crawdaddy*: April 1970.

page 489: "She and I had a torrid affair . . ." Bernal/Rogan. London/Los Angeles, California: 10 April 2008.

page 490: "He was still in the Byrds . . ." ibid.

page 490: "The first time I played . . ." Parsons/Rogan. Caspar, California: 22 July 1979.

page 490: "We ran away to hide . . ." Bernal/Rogan. London/Los Angeles, California: 10 April 2008.

page 491: "At the end of this ruckus . . ." ibid.

page 491: "Gram came to me . . ." Chris Hillman, interviewed for the online website: *The Gram Parsons Project*.

page 492: "McGuinn had to reimburse everybody . . ." Dickson/Rogan. London/Hawaii: 7 July 1997.

page 492: "The game was pretty much over . . ." Tickner/Rogan. Redondo Beach, California: 20 July 1979.

page 493: "At the time, I wasn't interested . . ." John York, interviewed by the author. Hollywood, California: 16 July 1979.

page 493: "I introduced John . . ." Bernal/Rogan. London/Los Angeles, California: 10 April 2008.

page 494: ". . . not very good, vocally or instrumentally . . ." Reviewer Robb Baker: *Chicago Tribune*: 7 January 1969.

page 495: "It was bedlam . . ." McGuinn/Rogan: Leeds: 4 May 1977.

page 495: "It was just a concept of mine . . ." ibid.

Chapter 31: Dr Byrds & Mr Hyde

page 497: "The concept was never realized on the cover . . ." John York, interviewed by the author. London/Rancho Cucamonga, California: 27 October 1996.

page 498: "Initially, McGuinn praised his production on *Dr Byrds & Mr Hyde*, but later reversed that opinion . . ." At the time of the album's release, for example, McGuinn was telling John Carpenter of the *Los*

Angeles Free Press that Johnston "comes into the studio and just vibrates. He's beautiful. Before, about 15 or 20 girls would call or hang out, and behind the glass it was like Disneyland while we were working out there. But Bob is fantastic: comes out there, and you can tell by the feel whether things are coming out all right." Subsequently, Johnston was no longer "fantastic" but something akin to the grand deceiver who had somehow tricked the Byrds. "He cons you into his game," McGuinn observed. Roger may have been reacting to the negative comments of Gene Parsons and Clarence White and was certainly prejudiced against Johnston due to the problems over the later 'Lay Lady Lay', but it was still surprising to read his putdown of the esteemed producer. In *Crawdaddy* (April 1970), he elaborated, "I was disappointed with Bob Johnston. I was disappointed with Bob's mixing, frankly. I didn't know until afterwards that Johnny Cash and Dylan were doing their own mixing. Nobody told me, unfortunately. Bob . . . can keep you occupied for hours with these great stories. He's almost worth it, just for that." These points were reiterated by Gene Parsons in *Zigzag* 41 (March 1974), where he told Pete Frame: "Bob Johnston is a nice enough guy, don't get me wrong, and he's produced plenty of good records – but he wasn't a good producer for us. The album seemed to be the result of poor planning and forethought, really – it was just a bunch of tapes thrown together in one package. The sound was bad, the mixing was bad – we weren't too pleased with what he did, frankly."

page 498: "Bob was a joy to work with . . ." York/Rogan. Hollywood, California: 16 July 1979.

page 499: "I felt I was faking it . . ." Clarence White, interviewed by Pete Frame. London: 22 May 1973. A small part of this interview appeared in *Zigzag*, the rest appeared for the first time in *Timeless Flight: The Definitive Biography Of The Byrds* (Scorpion/Dark Star, 1981), with amendments in this volume. White reiterated some of York's views about the album: "It was Bob Johnston's baby. He'd produced people like Bob Dylan and Johnny Cash, so we naturally thought that he would be great – but then we realized that those people would have their material so well-prepared that all the producer needed to do was come into the studio . . . and just listen. So the producer's role in those sort of cases would be . . . making sure that there was stuff to get, or whatever, making sure the engineer has the sound right, and generally making sure that everything runs smoothly. With a group, especially one that's never recorded before, you need someone to mediate, throw in suggestions and so on."

page 499: "I'd heard it performed . . ." McGuinn, commenting on 'Old Blue' on his *Folk Den* website.

page 499: "I designed the String Bender . . ." Gene Parsons, interviewed by the author. London/Caspar, California: 26 May 1997.

page 500: "It's 'way' . . ." Gib Guilbeau, interviewed by the author. London/Palmdale, California: 18 September 2007.

page 500: "It was just an attempt . . ." McGuinn/Rogan. New York: 26 January 1979.

page 500: "I guess I was imitating Dylan's style . . ." ibid.

page 501: "We'd met the director . . ." York/Rogan. Hollywood, California: 16 July 1979.

page 501: "Roger was willing to . . ." ibid.

page 502: "'Byrds Push Forward Into Country Music' . . ." *New Musical Express*: 3 May 1969. Reviewer Nick Logan wrote: "Just who the Byrds are at any one time is one of the great mysteries of pop. Nevertheless, the release of a new Byrds album ranks among the major events of a pop year and this LP shouldn't be missed." His enthusiasm was mirrored in the rival music weeklies. *Disc* concluded: "The Byrds are ridiculous. They just keep on getting better but remain, always instantly recognizable." They rated the work the Byrds' best since *Younger Than Yesterday*. *Melody Maker* added: "Yes, this is a good one . . . The bassline all the way through is super. It's to the credit of the group that they can switch styles and sound so musical . . ." Not to be outdone in effusion, *Record Mirror*, the most cautious of the bunch, rated the album four stars from five. Overall, it was an impressive sweep and, coupled with a solid chart placing, confirmed that the new version of the Byrds were selling well in Britain and had much to offer.

page 502: "I had the same voice . . ." York/Rogan. Hollywood, California: 16 July 1979.

page 503: "He's always found a way . . ." Gram Parsons, *Los Angeles Free Press*: 25 October 1969. Reprinted from *Seattle Helix*. Interview uncredited in either publication, but I believe the journalist was Ed Leimbacher.

page 504: "He [David] was up till half of the album . . ." Chris Hillman, *Los Angeles Free Press*: 25 October 1969. Reprinted from *Seattle Helix*. Interview uncredited in either publication, but I believe the journalist was Ed Leimbacher.

page 504: "The first of these get-togethers took place at the hip club, the Boston Tea Party . . ." For an extensive report of the show, see *Rolling Stone* (5 April 1969) in which Jon Landau eulogizes the restructured group even claiming, "The Byrds' first set was as perfect as I have ever heard a rock band perform."

page 505: "After the Byrds' . . ." George Guttler, amended version of Flying Burrito Brothers' review. *Full Circle* 22: November 1996.

NOTES

page 506: "Those gigs were really magic . . ." York/Rogan. Hollywood, California: 16 July 1979.

page 506: "We were very different people . . ." Parsons/Rogan. London/Caspar, California: 26 May 1997.

page 506: "I didn't do the research . . ." John York, interviewed by the author. London/Rancho Cucamonga, California: 25 May 1997.

page 507: "Roger's tactic . . ." ibid.

page 507: "God, what is this guy? . . ." ibid.

page 507: "He should wear those . . ." ibid.

page 507: "We loved 'Lay Lady Lay' . . ." York/Rogan. Hollywood, California: 16 July 1979.

page 508: "A great version . . ." Reviewer Derek Johnson, *New Musical Express*: 14 June 1969.

page 508: "Roger and Clarence came down . . ." Melcher/Rogan: 27 December 1977.

page 509: "Graham Nash said . . ." Dickson/Rogan. Waldport, Oregon: 26–30 April 1989. Given its archival content, *Preflyte* performed surprisingly well in the US marketplace, climbing as high as number 84 in *Billboard*, a far better showing than *Dr Byrds & Mr Hyde*.

page 511: "I loved the movie . . ." Outtake liner notes from *Sanctuary III*. Roger McGuinn, interviewed by Jud Cost: Sundazed.com. Back in 1970, McGuinn expressed a similar viewpoint to journalist Penny Valentine in *Disc* (11 July): "I know a lot of people have this idea that the film was about the Byrds. Fonda was a friend of mine and once said that his character was based on me, and Hopper's on Dave Crosby. I don't know – certainly Fonda didn't pump me for the script. That was already written. But I did identify with the film once it was completed. I was shattered at the end."

page 511: "Peter was just Peter . . ." David Crosby, interviewed by Sylvie Simmons. *Mojo*: November 2003.

page 511: "I sabotaged that . . ." Dennis Hopper, interviewed by Peter Biskind: 15 July 1997. Quoted in Peter Biskind, *Easy Riders, Raging Bulls* (New York: Simon & Schuster, 1998), p. 72.

page 512: "We could have done one . . ." Crosby/Simmons. *Mojo*: November 2003.

page 513: "All those people were killed . . ." Crosby/Rogan. London 22–23 April 1980.

page 513: "I was very unhappy . . ." York/Rogan. Hollywood, California: 16 July 1979. York recalls that the fateful gig mentioned here took place in Houston. It was most likely a big show at the city's Sam Houston Coliseum on 5 October. This would suggest that York was replaced by Skip Battin within two weeks of his complaint about the show.

Chapter 32: Uncertain Riders

page 515: "We were flying . . ." John York, interviewed by the author. London/Rancho Cucamonga, California: 25 May 1997. York's account is verified by a contemporaneous interview in *Fusion* 17 (September 1969), in which McGuinn said: "The guy wanted us to do it for free. I said, 'Man, it costs us at least $2,700 to get out and back to California.' He said, 'Well, Dylan's playing for free.' I said, 'Yeah, but he lives just down the road.'" Of course, Dylan famously never played at the festival.

page 517: "I was jealous . . ." McGuinn/Salewicz. *New Musical Express*: 7 September 1974.

page 518: "I was very depressed . . ." York/Rogan. Hollywood, California: 16 July 1979.

page 518: "John, sit down, boy! . . ." York/Rogan. London/Rancho Cucamonga, California: 25 May 1997.

page 518: "Roger never fired me . . ." ibid.

page 518: "There's a rumour going around . . ." Outtake liner notes from *Sanctuary III*. McGuinn/Cost: Sundazed.com

page 518: "I guess he forgot . . ." John York, interviewed by the author. London/Claremont, Los Angeles, California: 11 June 2007.

page 518: "I loved John . . ." Parsons/Rogan. London/Caspar, California: 26 May 1997.

page 519: ". . . it was like being a Beatle . . ." McGuinn/Frame. Hollywood, California: 30 October 1973.

page 519: "I was not a Byrds freak . . ." York/Rogan. Hollywood, California: 16 July 1979.

page 519: "People always say Roger is cold . . ." ibid.

page 521: "I practised and learned every Byrds song . . ." Skip Battin, interviewed by the author. New York: 3 July 1979.

page 521: "There was also talk of Roger playing a junkie . . ." The film, tentatively titled *The Vendors*, never reached the screen. "I agreed to do it but changed my mind." McGuinn explained. "I didn't want to be portrayed as a drug dealer or junkie. Bobby had a camera guy set up and I paid him what it cost to get me out of it. He was pissed; he accepted my resignation but didn't like it because he went out of his way to set it up. I gave him my word and changed my mind. I felt badly about it." (Michael Starr, *Bobby Darin – A Life*, Taylor Trade Publishing, 2004). The aforementioned 'UFO movie' *Ecology 70* was filmed under the name *Saturation 70* by Tony Foutz, but the project was never completed.

NOTES

page 521–522: "... purchasers were confronted with a feeble-looking shot of Gene Parsons' father Lemuel ..." The actual photograph, which I have seen up close, is very evocative and captures its time well. According to Parsons, CBS decided to obscure the shot so that they wouldn't have to pay a fee for using his father's image. This doesn't make much sense as the subject could still be identified and had provided the photograph himself. Presumably he did not push for a fee.

page 522: "It was my idea ..." Melcher/Rogan. London: 27 December 1977.

page 523: "Now she *really* liked ..." McGuinn/Rogan. London/Florida: 22 May 1997.

page 523: "When I wrote that track ..." McGuinn/Valentine. *Sounds*: 21 August 1971.

page 523: "Give that to McGuinn ..." McGuinn/Rogan. London/Florida: 22 May 1997.

page 523: "The screen credit ..." McGuinn/Rogan. Leeds: 4 May 1977.

page 523: "We were in Kansas ..." York/Rogan. London/Rancho Cucamonga, California: 27 October 1996.

page 524: "'Fido' was a problem ..." Melcher/Rogan. London: 27 December 1977.

page 524: "I didn't like Melcher double-tracking ..." York/Rogan. Hollywood, California: 16 July 1979.

page 524: "We used to sing it ..." Gene Parsons, interviewed by Elio Espana, part included in the 2007 DVD, *Under Review*.

page 525: "'Tulsa County Blue' was a copyright ..." Melcher/Rogan. London: 27 December 1977. Melcher also cut the song with the Rising Sons.

page 525: "Gene had this idea ..." York/Rogan. London/Rancho Cucamonga, California: 27 October 1996.

page 526: "I had a whole string section ..." Melcher/Rogan. London: 27 December 1977.

page 526: "Although 'Jesus Is Just Alright' failed to provide the Byrds with a hit single ..." In the UK, the *New Musical Express*' venerable singles reviewer, Derek Johnson was once again taken by surprise. "What's this? The Byrds going gospel? Well, not really! Because although this song is written in the repetitive gospel style, the boys' treatment is more in the country-rock idiom. Highlights are the group's ear-catching vocal harmonies – which at one point give way to jazz-slanted scat – and the fiery percussion which drives the routine along relentlessly."

page 526: "Some of my drumming ..." Parsons/Rogan. London/Caspar, California: 26 May 1997.

page 526: "If you listen to the two records . . ." York/Rogan. London/Rancho Cucamonga, California: 27 October 1996.
page 526: "That was a time of turmoil . . ." York/Rogan. Hollywood, California: 16 July 1979.
page 527: "The story we got . . ." York/Rogan. London/Rancho Cucamonga, California: 27 October 1996.
page 527: "There was some kind of conflict . . ." ibid.
page 527: "I think Roger might have questioned . . ." Parsons/Rogan. Caspar, California: 22 July 1979.
page 527: "The song was based . . ." ibid.
page 528: "It took me a little time . . ." Gene Parsons, interviewed by Bill Buchanan. Public Affairs Radio, Davis, California: 30 March 2009.
page 528–529: "The Zeke Manners song was our joke . . ." Melcher/Rogan. London: 27 December 1977.

Chapter 33: Just A Season

page 533: "Did you see the reaction . . ." Roger McGuinn, interviewed by Pat Long. *The Stag*: 17 December 1969.
page 534: "Dissension had always been . . ." Reviewer Ben Edmonds. *Fusion*: 11 December 1970.
page 535: "We were doing a lot of gigs . . ." McGuinn/Rogan. Leeds: 4 May 1977. McGuinn claimed in print that the Byrds undertook over 200 gigs during 1970, although this may have been a slight exaggeration. Christopher Hjort's heroic attempt to document the Byrds' concert history lists approximately 124 dates for that year.
page 535: "It was my idea to do a double album . . ." Melcher/Rogan. London: 27 December 1977.
page 535: "We may be doing an album with Dylan . . ." *Crawdaddy*: April 1970.
page 536: "It wasn't our fault . . ." McGuinn/Rogan. Leeds: 4 May 1977.
page 536: "Some of the musicians . . ." Roger McGuinn, interviewed by Michael Gray. *Let It Rock* 25: January 1975.
page 536: "What he wanted was us to back him . . ." ibid.
page 537: "When the Airplane . . ." Unpublished letter to *Zigzag*, dated 1973.
page 538: "Getting Dickson was a magnanimous gesture . . ." Melcher/Rogan. London: 27 December 1977. Melcher's comments only tell part of the story. The suggestion that Dickson was solely in charge of editing the live tapes is misleading. He was also present in the studio

NOTES

recording the Byrds. Clarence White's comments on 'Take A Whiff' indicate how Dickson, after listening to the playback, suggested he record the song instead of McGuinn. Critic Bud Scoppa, who attended some of the *(Untitled)* sessions, wrote a fly on the wall account in his 1971 book *The Byrds* detailing an evening on which they completed 'All The Things'. Melcher did not attend the overdub session on which McGuinn worked closely with Dickson throughout.

page 538–539: "Terry got me in for *(Untitled)* . . ." Jim Dickson, interviewed by the author. London/Costa Mesa, California: 10 January 2006.

page 539: "Gene Parsons and Skip Battin were concentrating . . ." ibid.

page 540: "Our son Henry . . ." Dolores Tickner (formerly McGuinn, née DeLeon), interviewed by the author. London/Tucson, Arizona: 24–25 February 2007.

page 540: "Somebody from Columbia . . ." Extracted from a Columbia Records' advertisement for *(Untitled)*.

page 540: "I'll tell you what *really* happened . . ." Melcher/Rogan. London: 27 December 1977.

page 540: "Terry was in total control . . ." Outtake liner notes from *Sanctuary III*. McGuinn/Cost: Sundazed.com

page 541: "The bayou scene was cut . . ." McGuinn/Rogan. Leeds: 4 May 1977.

page 541: "That was a spoof . . ." McGuinn/Cost: Sundazed.com

page 541: "My voice got real hoarse . . ." Roger McGuinn, quoted in Bruce Pollock, *When The Music Mattered* (New York, Holt, Rinehart & Winston, 1983), p.91.

page 542: "There was a time . . ." Parsons/Rogan. London/Caspar, California: 26 May 1997.

page 542: "There was a real charge of energy . . ." Skip Battin, interviewed by the author. London/Oregon: 3 June 1997.

page 543: "I preferred the live segment . . ." McGuinn/Rogan. Leeds: 4 May 1977.

page 543: ". . . proved commercial enough to secure McGuinn his first UK Top 20 hit since . . ." Although the single was an edited version, missing its mid-section, it was played frequently on morning radio in England. The *NME*'s Derek Johnson was still in control of singles reviews, but would soon relinquish his title to younger, less discerning voices. Even at this late stage of his career, he could still spot a hit. "It's been quite a while since we were last treated to a Byrds single, and this is very welcome, even though it's taken from their *(Untitled)* album as, in my estimation, it's one of their best-ever tracks . . . A fast-moving, folk-beaty item, laden with all the familiar Byrds trademarks – with 12-string electric guitar and rattling tambourine dominant. This group's been a bit out of favour lately, but it's in with a chance here."

page 543: "'Chestnut Mare' is the most impressive piece . . ." McGuinn/Ross, *The Byrds Complete* (Music Sales, 1970).

page 544: "We modified the story . . ." Roger McGuinn, interviewed by Pete Frame. London: 13 May 1971.

page 544: "I used to run into Lowell George . . ." White/Frame. London: 22 May 1973.

page 544: "I'd have loved to see Gram back in the Byrds . . ." Melcher/Rogan. London: 27 December 1977.

page 544: "At that time . . ." McGuinn/Rogan. Leeds: 4 May 1977.

page 544: "We wrote it in a hotel . . ." Skip Battin, interviewed by the author. New York: 3 July 1979.

page 545: "The original melody . . ." ibid.

page 545: "Roger said he'd like to do . . ." White/Frame. London: 22 May 1973.

page 545: ". . . too many whiffs . . ." McGuinn/Ross, *The Byrds Complete* (Music Sales, 1970).

page 546: "It was not a true story . . ." Battin/Rogan. New York: 3 July 1979.

page 546: "All white people look the same . . ." Fowley/Rogan. London/Redlands, California: 27–28 June 2007.

page 546: "I was personally touched . . ." Battin/Rogan. New York: 3 July 1979.

page 546: "I'm not a Buddhist . . ." Roger McGuinn, interviewed by Elizabeth Walker. *Rock*: 16 November 1970.

page 547: "The Byrds are alive . . ." Reviewer Ben Edmonds. *Fusion*: 11 December 1970.

page 547: "There are few bands . . ." Reviewer Richard Williams. *Melody Maker*: 7 November 1970. That same day, *Disc* described the work as "probably the most intelligent collection of songs ever assembled on a double LP."

page 547: "radical liberals . . . brainwashed into a drug culture . . ." Vice President Spiro Agnew, speaking at a campaign dinner in Las Vegas, Nevada: 14 September 1970.

page 547–548: ". . . such an attractive light . . ." ibid.

page 548: "A lot of hullabaloo . . ." Eddie Tickner, quoted by Ann Hencken. *The Free-Lance Star*: 16 September 1970.

page 548: "Come on Spiro . . ." This re-run of the 1966 'controversy' at least provided Clarence White with a chance to show his sardonic humour.

NOTES

page 548: "We made a lot of money . . ." McGuinn/Rogan. Leeds: 4 May 1977.

page 550: "I have considered reconstructing . . ." Roger McGuinn, interviewed by Roger and Marco Livingstone. *Sounds*: 4 May 1974.

page 550: "It's *passé* . . ." McGuinn/Rogan. Leeds: 4 May 1977.

Chapter 34: Expensive

page 552: "We'd take a lot of uppers . . ." Bernal/Rogan. London/Los Angeles, California: 10 April 2008.

page 553: ". . . somewhat ridiculous . . ." Reviewer Bobby Nowell, commenting on the Byrds' show at Duke University. *North Carolina Anvil*: 28 November 1970.

page 553: "We had lines of coke laid out . . ." Al Hersh, interviewed by the author. London/Topanga Canyon, California: 12 April 2008.

page 553: "Roger McGuinn is stylish . . ." Reviewer Jerry Dunn Jr. *Los Angeles Herald Examiner*: 29 December 1970.

page 553: "The road was their vehicle . . ." Bernal/Rogan. London/Los Angeles, California: 10 April 2008.

page 554: "With Roger, it was Southern Comfort and cocaine . . ." Dolores Tickner (formerly McGuinn, née DeLeon)/Rogan. London/Tucson, Arizona: 13 January 2007.

page 554: "He was absolutely faithful . . ." Bernal/Rogan. London/Los Angeles, California: 10 April 2008.

page 555: "I've been faithful to you . . ." Dolores Tickner (formerly McGuinn, née DeLeon)/Rogan. London/Tucson, Arizona: 13 January 2007.

page 555: "When Linda showed up . . ." Bernal/Rogan. London/Los Angeles, California: 10 April 2008.

page 555: "There was a Heineken bottle . . ." Dolores Tickner (formerly McGuinn, née DeLeon)/Rogan. London/Tucson, Arizona: 24–25 February 2007.

page 555: "You're fired . . ." Dolores Tickner (formerly McGuinn, née DeLeon)/Rogan. Tucson, Arizona: 28 October 2005.

page 555: "All I knew . . ." Hersh/Rogan. London/Topanga Canyon, California: 12 April 2008.

page 556: "Roger got into bug mikes . . ." ibid.

page 556: "Ianthe and Susie . . ." Bernal/Rogan. London/Los Angeles, California: 10 April 2008.

page 556: "I knew they were in trouble . . ." Dolores Tickner (formerly McGuinn, née DeLeon)/Rogan. London/Tucson, Arizona: 24–25 February 2007.

page 557: "The Hesby house . . ." Hersh/Rogan. London/Topanga Canyon, California: 12 April 2008.
page 557: "Tweet Manor was a clubhouse . . ." Bernal/Rogan. London/Los Angeles, California: 10 April 2008.
page 557: "He thought he was 007 . . ." Dolores Tickner (formerly McGuinn, née DeLeon)/Rogan. Tucson, Arizona: 28 October 2005.
page 557: "Roger was very impressed . . ." Hersh/Rogan. London/Topanga Canyon, California: 12 April 2008.
page 559: "Hey, what happened . . . monkey . . ." Seiter/Rogan. London/Los Angeles, California: 18 October 1999.
page 559: "I'm fed up to the gills . . ." Roger McGuinn, interviewed by Elliot Tiegel. *Record Mirror*: 19 December 1970.
page 559: ". . . Clarence White's rendition of 'Home Sweet Home' . . ." See the 'Unreleased Material' in the Sessionography/Discography session for a fuller discussion of this song and its contemporary lyrics.
page 559: "Since his writing spree with Jacques Levy, he had failed to put pen to paper . . ." When asked if he'd written anything recently by Bud Scoppa in the magazine *Rock*, McGuinn wearily conceded: "Haven't written a single song. I haven't written too much since Jacques Levy and I wrote the songs for *Tryp*. I need somebody to kick me in the ass like Jacques Levy did . . . If I'm sitting around by myself, I'd much rather do something else, like watch television – anything other than sit down and write songs. Really, I don't have the self-discipline."
page 560: "I was dating Kate Taylor . . ." Fowley/Rogan. London/Redlands, California: 27–28 June 2007.
page 560: "Terry was threatened . . ." ibid.
page 560: "Terry told me . . ." ibid.
page 561: "Terry had a thing going on . . ." Hersh/Rogan. London/Topanga Canyon, California: 12 April 2008.
page 561: "Everybody was getting divorced . . ." Dolores Tickner (formerly McGuinn, née DeLeon)/Rogan. London/Tucson, Arizona: 13 January 2007.
page 561: "It was only on rare occasions . . ." Bernal/Rogan. London/Los Angeles, California: 10 April 2008.
page 562: "We should call it *Expensive* . . ." Melcher/Rogan. London: 27 December 1977.
page 562: "It would be presumptuous . . ." Roger McGuinn, interviewed by Caroline Boucher. *Disc & Music Echo*: 15 May 1971.
page 562: "It's kind of a sneaky prayer . . ." ibid.
page 562: "I wanted to protect him . . ." Roger McGuinn, interviewed by Roy Hollingworth. *Melody Maker*: 8 May 1971.

NOTES

page 562: "It's more or less democratic . . ." McGuinn/Boucher. *Disc & Music Echo*: 15 May 1971.

page 563: "We got mad . . ." Clarence White, quoted in *State Beacon*: 26 October 1971. During the May 1971 UK tour, Roger McGuinn also announced, "We fired Terry as manager because he wasn't managing and [he] quit as producer."

page 564: ". . . excrements of pus . . ." Reviewer Richard Meltzer. *Rolling Stone*: 19 August 1971. He called the Byrds "a boring dead group," albeit qualifying his words with a world-weary, "but then again aren't they all?", then adding "Anything unfestering is a bonus."

page 564: "We were appalled . . ." Parsons/Rogan. London/Caspar, California: 26 May 1997.

page 564: "Terry Melcher put the strings on . . ." White/Frame: London: 22 May 1973.

page 564: "On the 'Green Apple Quick Step' session . . ." Byron Berline, interviewed by Pete Frame. London: 14 November 1971.

page 565: "My most vivid recollection . . ." Melcher/Rogan. London: 27 December 1977.

page 565: ". . . a worm squirming . . ." ibid.

pages 565–566: "*You claim that you weren't extravagant . . .*" Interview dialogue between author and Melcher re: *Byrdmaniax*. Melcher/Rogan. London: 27 December 1977.

page 566: "We were aiming . . ." ibid.

page 567: "The idea of orchestration . . ." ibid.

page 567: "I think you're right . . ." ibid.

page 568: ". . . about a guy . . ." Roger McGuinn, interviewed by Steve Peacock. *Sounds*: 6 February 1971.

page 568: ". . . *The Garden Of Love* . . ." Although I have quoted selected lines from *The Garden Of Love* and 'Tunnel Of Love', these were not cherry picked merely to embellish a theory. The reader is advised to consult the poem and song, respectively, and observe the self-evident comparisons, all within three short stanzas.

page 568: "It was just based on death . . ." Fowley/Rogan. London/Redlands, California: 27–28 June 2007.

page 568: "I don't know . . ." ibid.

page 569: "I enjoyed the songs . . ." Parsons/Rogan. London/Mendocino, California: 19 May 2007.

page 569: "They all yelled . . ." Fowley/Rogan. London/Redlands, California: 27–28 June 2007. Continuing his explanation, Fowley recalls: "I said 'You're going to have problems. Why don't we write with Roger or why don't I give you lyrics and you can give them to Roger?'

'No, I want to write with you and I want to be Tom Lehr and Fats Domino, take it or leave it.'"

page 569: "Kim wrote that . . ." Battin/Rogan. New York: 3 July 1979.

page 570: "Politically, I'm becoming much less apathetic . . ." *Crawdaddy*: April 1970.

page 570: "I'm curious about politics . . ." McGuinn/Rogan. Leeds: 4 May 1977.

page 571: "It was a song about the Buddhist philosophy . . ." Battin/Rogan. New York: 3 July 1979.

page 571: "It was about this guru . . ." Fowley/Rogan. London/Redlands, California: 27–28 June 2007.

page 571: ". . . a spur of the moment thing . . ." Berline/Frame. London: 14 November 1971.

page 572: "I didn't record live with them . . ." ibid.

page 572: "I don't even remember . . ." Melcher/Rogan. London: 27 December 1977.

page 572: "I walked into the studio . . ." Roger McGuinn, interviewed by Keith Altham. *Record Mirror*: 19 June 1971.

page 573: "On 'Jamaica' I tried to do an excellent recording . . ." White/Frame: London: 22 May 1973. White's appreciation of Jackson Browne's songwriting was reiterated in a contemporaneous interview with *Melody Maker*'s Richard Williams, where he acknowledged: "I stopped singing after the Kentucky Colonels and I never wanted to do it again until I heard his material. I think that his stuff will influence me into writing – he's so good and he'll be very successful."

page 573: "Clarence wasn't that great a singer . . ." Melcher/Rogan. London: 27 December 1977.

page 574: "From what I'd already been told . . ." Reviewer Roy Hollingworth. *Melody Maker*: 14 August 1971. *Record Mirror* proved equally enthusiastic, describing the work as "more ambitious" than *(Untitled)* and concluding, "it's a near perfect piece of Byrds".

Chapter 35: Farther Along

page 575: "I don't know what it was in me . . ." McGuinn/Valentine. *Sounds*: 14 August 1971.

page 576: "It's a swell way . . ." ibid.

page 577: "How would you like a police dog . . ." As witnessed by the author. Lincoln Folk Festival: 24 July 1971.

page 577: "You're not much of a peacemaker . . ." ibid.

NOTES

page 578: "We're a little bugged . . ." Clarence White, interviewed by Steve Peacock. *Sounds*: 29 January 1972.

page 578: "They want to hear certain ones . . ." Clarence White, interviewed by Michael Benton. *Melody Maker*: 30 May 1973.

page 579: "I looked pregnant . . ." Roger McGuinn, interviewed by Eric Rudolph. *Crawdaddy*: October 1972.

page 579: "Hey, Roger! . . ." ibid.

page 579: "I watched him . . ." ibid.

page 579: "There was no manager . . ." Ron Rainey, interviewed by the author. London/Hollywood, California: 12 January 2007.

page 579: "They were trying to break two bands . . ." ibid.

page 579: ". . . probably more . . ." ibid.

page 580: "By the time that was finished . . ." ibid.

page 581: "We were still pretty upset . . ." Parsons/Rogan. London/Caspar, California: 26 May 1997.

page 581: "The Byrds recognized . . ." Reviewer Bud Scoppa. *Rock*: 13 March 1972.

page 582: "I dreamt the whole song . . ." Roger McGuinn, interviewed by Peter Doggett. *Record Collector* 248: April 2000.

page 582: "It was at our house . . ." Dolores Tickner (formerly McGuinn, née DeLeon)/Rogan. London/Tucson, Arizona: 13 January 2007.

page 582: "The whole thing . . ." Battin/Rogan. New York: 3 July 1979.

page 582: "It was an experiment . . ." Parsons/Rogan. Caspar, California: 22 July 1979.

page 583: "I was imitating . . ." Parsons/Rogan. London/Caspar, California: 26 May 1997.

page 583: "It was one of the last songs . . ." White/Frame. London: 22 May 1973.

page 584: "The idea came from a Coke ad . . ." Skip Battin, interviewed by Barry Ballard. London: 22 September 1976. Part published in *Omaha Rainbow* 11: December 1976.

page 584: "What a story . . ." Fowley/Rogan. London/Redlands, California: 27–28 June 2007. According to Fowley the song ("a combination of social satire and a Coke commercial") was a big hit in Austria. "Somebody covered it with German political lyrics and it did really well."

page 585: "It was an experiment . . ." Battin/Rogan. New York: 3 July 1979.

page 585: "She was a lady . . ." Seiter/Rogan. London/Macao, People's Republic Of China: 28 June 2007.

page 585: "It was a beautiful song . . ." Bernal/Rogan. London/Los Angeles, California: 10 April 2008.

page 585: "It was an attempt to write a love song . . ." ibid. Fowley adds: "I did *all* the lyrics and he did the music. I would come in with lyrics already written and typed and I would sing them to him in Roger McGuinn's voice every time, trying to get him on message. Then he would get mad and rewrite them as Skip Battin. When I did them they were more Roger than Skip ever was. I would sing 'Citizen Kane' like that too but he would say 'No!'. I have demos of me singing 'Citizen Kane' and 'Precious Kate' and at the end of this interview I will mail them to you. You can hear my demos of me imitating Roger singing 'Precious Kate'. Then Skip would get in on it and it never came out like that." Fowley kept his word and sent me the demos. The results show that his argument is only partly convincing, and he evidently forgot that 'Precious Kate' was actually sung by McGuinn on the album, not by Battin.

page 586: "'Lazy Waters' *was* a serious song . . ." ibid.

page 586: "When we finished it . . ." Battin/Rogan. London/Oregon: 3 June 1997.

page 587: "Yeah, I was in love . . ." McGuinn/Rogan. Leeds: 4 May 1977.

page 588: "Original Byrds To Reform?" *Disc & Music Echo*: 29 January 1972. The report added, a touch melodramatically: "This could mark the end of an alleged McGuinn–Crosby dispute which has kept them apart for some years now."

page 588: "It was recorded at a time . . ." McGuinn/Rogan. Leeds: 4 May 1977.

page 589: "David has some rotten things to say . . ." Clarence White, quoted in *State Beacon*: 26 October 1971.

page 589: "He and I had some fairly intense conflicts . . ." Parsons/Rogan. London/Caspar, California: 26 May 1997.

Chapter 36: Dissolution

page 590: "Melcher was turning everyone's head . . ." White/Frame: London: 22 May 1973.

page 591: "I don't know, maybe Melcher . . ." McGuinn/Rogan. Leeds: 4 May 1977.

page 591: "The way we did it . . ." White/Frame: London: 22 May 1973.

page 591–592: ". . . a grim parody . . ." Reviewer Sam Sutherland. *Billboard*: 15 March 1972.

page 592: "Perhaps this act . . ." ibid.

page 592: "It can't be pleasant . . ." Reviewer Jane Ross. *Miami Herald*: 3 April 1972.

NOTES

page 592: "Your drummer can't play 4/4 time . . ." McGuinn/Rogan. Leeds: 4 May 1977.

page 592: "After that I thought . . ." ibid.

page 593: "If there was a flaw . . ." Reviewer Joe Roman. *Great Speckled Bird*: 17 April 1972.

page 593: "His work has been going downhill . . ." Roger McGuinn, interviewed by Eric Rudolph. *Crawdaddy*: October 1972.

page 594: "The time is right . . ." White/Frame. London: 22 May 1972.

page 594: "I was fired . . ." Parsons/Rogan. Caspar, California: 22 July 1979.

page 594: "Gene's attitude was wrong . . ." McGuinn/Frame. Hollywood, California: 30 October 1973.

page 594: "McGuinn was definitely in the right . . ." Battin/Rogan. New York: 3 July 1979.

page 595: "Roger had a whole lot of ways of getting musicians . . ." Bernal/Rogan. London/Los Angeles, California: 10 April 2008.

page 595: "He was pleased to join the Byrds . . ." Battin/Rogan. New York: 3 July 1979.

page 596: "That's what I want to get back into . . ." McGuinn/Rudolph. *Crawdaddy*: October 1972.

page 596: "It's my band . . ." ibid.

page 597: "It was really quite remarkable . . ." Roger McGuinn, interviewed by Roy Carr. *New Musical Express*: 17 March 1973.

page 597: "We all sat down . . ." Gene Clark, interviewed by Chuck Thegze. *Los Angeles Times*: 4 February 1973.

page 598: "We're getting away from country music . . ." Roger McGuinn, interviewed by Julie Webb. *New Musical Express*: 4 November 1972.

page 598: "I just realized how much dedication . . ." McGuinn/Rogan: 4 May 1977.

page 598: "I think some of the guys . . ." Clark/Rogan. London: 2 May 1977.

page 599: "Chris was going out with Manassas . . ." Roger McGuinn, interviewed by Barry Ballard. London: 1 May 1977.

page 599: "Don't touch my guitars . . ." Hersh/Rogan. London/Topanga Canyon, California: 12 April 2008.

page 599: "David was impossible . . ." ibid.

page 600: "The original Byrds is now a reality . . ." Gene Clark, unpublished interview by Jan Donkers. Hollywood, Los Angeles, California: October 1972.

page 600: "It's a possibility . . ." ibid.

page 600: "There's a lot of different flavours . . ." ibid.

page 600: "We're taking our time . . ." ibid.

page 601: "We had a party . . ." McGuinn/Rogan. Leeds: 4 May 1977. McGuinn reiterated these points during an interview with my colleague, Barry Ballard, during the same time period. "Chris was going out with Manassas and would be in the studio for a couple of days and then all of a sudden he found that he would soon have to go out on the road. Then I would have bookings and I'd have to go out too with the so-called Byrds at the time, which made Crosby furious because I was using the name Byrds and leaving the real Byrds to go out and do a fake Byrds tour. He was just mad at me for that. The whole thing was an awful environment too. We had a party environment while we were in the studio and we weren't paying attention to business."

page 602: "I missed my plane in LA . . ." Roger McGuinn, speaking onstage at the Curtis Hixon Hall, Tampa, Florida: 1 November 1972.

page 602–603: "John was hot with the Byrds . . ." Bernal/Rogan. London/Los Angeles, California: 10 April 2008.

page 603: "He was a great drummer . . ." Rainey/Rogan. London/Hollywood, California: 12 January 2007.

page 603: "On a handful of occasions, the Byrds were forced to hire a substitute at short notice . . ." Writer/chronicler Christopher Hjort located a piece in *Variety* which mentioned Jim Moon's real name, Jim Scherz, and confirmed that his first appearance with the Byrds was as early as 6 October 1972 at New York's Academy of Music.

page 603: "Jim Moon was a friend of mine . . ." Bernal/Rogan. London/Los Angeles, California: 10 April 2008.

page 604: "They wanted me to play . . ." Chris Ethridge, interviewed by the author. London/Meridian, Mississippi: 28 March 2009. Interestingly, there was a press report in August 1972 suggesting that Clarence White and Gene Parsons were about to be replaced by Chris Ethridge and former Beach Boy Bruce Johnston "for recording purposes only". Given White's massive studio experience, this did not make much sense even as a rumour. The confusion was probably caused by McGuinn's plans to complete a solo album which would indeed feature both Ethridge and Johnston. There were also rumours that Ethridge did indeed deputize for Battin at some dates, although no concert review has ever confirmed this and Ethridge has no memory of actually playing. Looking back at my own correspondence from the time, I have unearthed a letter to me dated 16 February 1973 concerning Battin's dismissal from the band. It states: "Before Christmas things were at boiling point especially with Skip and Roger. Skip had always been one to stick his neck out and I didn't expect Roger to fire him as much as be crying for his head on a plate. Skip decided he was going to get his solo album out before everybody else and once he did so then he also had the freedom to go it alone if he wanted to. He couldn't be guaranteed to turn up for concerts so they got Chris Ethridge to go along as a stand-by..."

page 604: "At the beginning..." John Guerin, interviewed by Alexander Nesterenko. Undated press cutting, *c.* early 1973.

page 604: "Not now..." McGuinn/Webb. *New Musical Express*: 4 November 1972.

page 605: "We were hoping for a new light..." White/Frame: London: 22 May 1973.

page 605: "I liked working with John..." McGuinn/Rogan. Leeds: 4 May 1977.

page 605: "Dennis was a close friend of Linda's..." Bernal/Rogan. London/Los Angeles, California: 10 April 2008.

page 605: "As I remember there wasn't much synergy..." Dennis Dragon, email message to author: 25 August 2007.

page 606: "... fun to tour with..." Hersh/Rogan. London/Topanga Canyon, California: 12 April 2008.

page 606: "He was only with us for four weeks..." White/Frame: London: 22 May 1973.

page 606: "A lot of people had told me..." McGuinn/Rogan. Leeds: 4 May 1977.

page 606: "I guess I didn't notice..." ibid.

page 606: "Roger said, 'I think we could get a better bass player'..." White/Frame: London: 22 May 1973.

page 607: "It was a dying spiritual thing..." Roger McGuinn, interviewed by Robert Bowman. *Cheap Thrills*: December 1976.

page 607: "I'm breaking up the Byrds..." Rainey/Rogan. London/Hollywood, California: 12 January 2007.

page 607: "I was representing Roger..." ibid.

page 607: "McGuinn fired me..." Battin/Rogan. New York: 3 July 1979.

page 608: "Skip was intelligent..." Fowley/Rogan. London/Redlands, California: 27–28 June 2007.

page 608: "Roger had a commitment..." Hillman/Rogan. London: 28 April 1977.

page 608–609: "I'm not being the Byrds..." Roger McGuinn, interviewed by Joe Edwards and Peter J. Straus. *The Free Aquarian*: March 1973.

page 609: "Clarence enjoyed playing with Skip Battin..." ibid.

page 609: "It was Hillman..." ibid.

page 610: "Roger asked me..." Hillman/Rogan. London: 28 April 1977.

page 610: "It was a spur of the moment proposition..." *The Free Aquarian*: March 1973. The night before the Passaic performance, the 'Manassas

985

Byrds' had commenced their weekend date with an appearance at the Memorial Auditorium, Burlington, Vermont. The critical response pre-empted the negativity shown at Passaic. Reviewer John Hanrahan, writing in the student newspaper *Michaelman*, was also unimpressed by Hillman. "He was not altogether with the group. His bass work was satisfactory, but he was very poor on vocals, forgetting words. Gene Parsons is the drummer for the Byrds and I don't really know if that was him on stage – if it was, he's gotten his hair cut and forgotten how to play the drums. He found himself more than once out of time with the music. The only definite remnants of the Byrds were Roger McGuinn and Clarence White. Roger McGuinn was the only one who tried to make something out of the concert, Clarence White played well, he did not seem to care too much or know too much where he was."

page 611: "Clarence and I fired each other . . ." Roger McGuinn, interviewed by Chris Charlesworth. *Melody Maker*: 4 May 1974.

Chapter 37: Full Circle

page 612: "It's a forward step backwards . . ." McGuinn/Carr. *New Musical Express*: 17 March 1973.

page 615: "It's a fulfilment . . ." David Crosby, interviewed by Judy Sims. *Rolling Stone*: 4 January 1973.

page 616: "In Britain, both *NME* and *Sounds* applauded the album, but elsewhere the reaction was hostile . . ." The reviews could hardly have been more contrasting. *NME*'s Danny Holloway seemed thrilled by almost every aspect of the work. "David Crosby's production was the first thing that really impressed me about the album; the sound is rich and full and the many acoustic instruments are recorded exceptionally well. Crosby has emphasized the Byrds' highs: the cross-picking of guitars and their impressive harmonies . . . What's important is that the Byrds have overcome the novelty of reforming and really do cut it here. The band's direction is no-nonsense, straight-ahead music. There's not any cultural preaching or sloppy outtakes as intros; they've chosen to present their songs as well-played and produced as possible – and without the in-vogue gimmicks, it's difficult for any band to make it. I'm glad to report the Byrds make it on the strength of their music alone . . . After all is said and done, all five of the original Byrds can look back on this one with a lot of pride. And all the old Byrds fans who'll buy it out of duty will be glad to know that they're not being taken for a ride. It's nice to see somebody return with a lot of care. It would've been so easy to have blown it."

NOTES

One week later (7 April), *Melody Maker*'s Mike Oldfield pinpricked the entire enterprise. "It was inevitable, I suppose. After all the ballyhoo surrounding the reformation of the original Byrds the end product was bound to be disappointing. Sadly, though, *Byrds* goes beyond that: it's a dismal and pointless exercise . . . Right up to the reunion, McGuinn has been soldiering on with various personnel, still playing in the Byrds style. All that has been cast aside for the *Byrds*. Not only does it not sound like the Byrds (any version you care to mention) but McGuinn and co don't even sound like a band at all – just a bunch of ego-tripping musicians incapable of writing anything for anyone but themselves. It's this lack of cohesion about the album which must remain its major fault. But if you prefer to look at it as a sampler album for four solo albums with a few fillers thrown in, it doesn't sound too bad . . . You'll have noticed I said four solo albums; in all this self-indulgence Michael Clarke stays quietly in the background, drumming excellently but without spectacular breaks or showing off. His modesty is refreshing. Gene Clark has also tried hard to get into the spirit of the occasion; his 'Full Circle' is the only outstanding cut . . . Unfortunately his singing is poor and overshadowed by some superb background harmonies . . . McGuinn is the big disappointment: why on earth did he let the others do so much singing when he's always been the Byrds' chief vocalist? . . . Hillman's tracks, co-written with members of Steve Stills' Manassas . . . are simple to the point of inane and become tedious with repeated playing. David Crosby's two songs have nothing whatsoever to do with the Byrds; somebody should have woken him up and told him this wasn't a session for CSN&Y or his solo album. 'Long Live The King' and 'Laughing' are both dreary in the extreme and his flat, characterless voice droning on is a pain . . . The remaining three cuts, two by Neil Young, one by Joni Mitchell are dully reproduced. Their inclusion (in preference to, say, any Dylan numbers – long a Byrds speciality – or any group compositions) shows just where the new, reformed Byrds are at. They're just another band from LA." To add salt to the wounds, the review was accompanied by a single photograph of McGuinn, captioned "Byrd McGuinn: the big disappointment", as if he was responsible for its alleged shortcomings.

page 616: "I'd already recorded that song . . ." Clark/Rogan. New York: 26 January 1979.

page 618: "'Born To Rock 'n' Roll' was a dog . . ." McGuinn/Rogan. Leeds: 4 May 1977.

page 618: "We all discussed doing a Dylan song . . ." Gene Clark, interviewed by Chuck Thegze. *Los Angeles Times*: 3 February 1973.

page 619: "David didn't like the track . . ." Johnny Barbata, *The Legendary Life Of A Rock Star Drummer* (self published, no imprint, 1995).

page 619: "Gene once again shone the brightest . . ." Hillman/Egan. *Goldmine*: 28 December 2001.

page 619: "Crosby's 'Laughing' was already well-known to purchasers of his solo album, but he insisted on re-recording the song on the grounds that it had originally been written for the Byrds . . ." It is generally accepted that 'Laughing' was written some time after Crosby was fired from the group. However, the composition's genesis could well have predated that time. The subject of the song's final verse was transcendental meditation guru Maharishi Mahesh Yogi whose beatific aura was punctuated by a girlish giggle. In August 1967, just weeks before Crosby's dismissal, the Maharishi secured massive publicity when the Beatles and their entourage set off to Bangor, Wales, to attend a TM course overseen by the master. Crosby's reaction betrayed the same cynicism with which he had responded to McGuinn's involvement in Subud. 'Laughing' was not issued until as late as 1971, when it appeared on *If I Could Only Remember My Name*, but the inspiration, at least, went back to that time when Crosby was still a Byrd.

page 620: "I am disappointed in that album . . ." Gene Clark, interviewed by Paul Kendall. *Zigzag* 73: June 1977. Plus additional material from the author's interview with Clark in London: 1 May 1977.

page 621: ". . . the album could have been a lot better . . ." Roger McGuinn, interviewed by Barbara Charone. *New Musical Express*: 23 February 1974.

page 621: "Crosby, in retrospect . . ." Roger McGuinn, interviewed by Patrick Snyder-Scumpy. *Crawdaddy*: November 1973.

page 621: "We only wanted to do it . . ." Hillman/Rogan. London: 28 April 1977.

page 622: "At the time, I went to Elliot Roberts . . ." ibid.

page 622: "It never came about . . ." ibid.

page 623: "That was a Clive Davis idea . . ." McGuinn/Rogan. Leeds: 4 May 1977.

page 623: "Terry was doing a nice job . . ." McGuinn/Rogan. London/Florida: 22 May 1997.

page 623: "The attitude I had . . ." Roger McGuinn, interviewed by the author. London: 28 April 1977. Part published *Zigzag* 73: June 1977.

page 623: "He didn't want to do it . . ." Roger McGuinn, interviewed by Robert Bowman and Ralph Alfonso. *Hot Wacks* 14: June/July 1977.

page 624: "The Byrds were a trademark . . ." Rainey/Rogan. London/Hollywood, California: 12 January 2007.

NOTES

page 624: "It was a very tumultuous time . . ." Hersh/Rogan. London/Topanga Canyon, California: 12 April 2008.

page 624: "Bob used to come over . . ." McGuinn/Doggett. *Record Collector* 248: April 2000.

page 625: "They had an odd relationship . . ." Hersh/Rogan. London/Topanga Canyon, California: 12 April 2008.

page 625: "There were a lot of weapons around . . ." ibid.

page 625: "He was getting weird . . ." ibid.

page 625: "Roger was shooting through the wall . . ." ibid.

page 625: "I confiscated all the guns . . ." ibid.

page 626: "There isn't much to say except . . ." Extract from Gene Parsons' letter to Chrissie Oakes (née Brewer) dated 15 July 1973.

page 628: "I had to damn near break his arm . . ." Hillman/Rogan: 28 April 1977. Published in *Dark Star* 10: August 1977.

page 628–629: "They included the unforgettable image . . ." Several sensationalist accounts were provided by interviewees in a profile of Parsons printed in *Crawdaddy*: October 1976. The account of the corpse masturbation has since been dismissed as lurid invention, but the ice cubes story is apparently true.

Chapter 38: Separation

page 630: "Why not do a solo tour? . . ." McGuinn/Rogan. London: 28 April 1977. Published *Zigzag* 73: June 1977.

page 630: "It was difficult, but I used some . . ." ibid.

page 630: "It was more painful . . ." ibid.

page 631: "It was a bit of an anticlimax . . ." McGuinn/Charlesworth. *Melody Maker*: 4 May 1974.

page 631: "A big square dance . . ." Roger McGuinn, interviewed by Barbara Charone. *New Musical Express*: 23 February 1974.

page 632: "It's a business move . . ." *Sounds*: 4 May 1974.

page 633: "In July 1974, an all-new Roger McGuinn Band was formed . . ." The line-up featured Greg Attway, Richard Bowden and David Lovelace from Sneaky Pete Kleinow's Cold Steel and former Stone Canyon Band bassist, Steve Love.

page 633: "I wasn't tremendously happy working with Bill . . ." McGuinn/Rogan. London: 28 April 1977. Part published *Zigzag* 73: June 1977.

page 633: "I was having financial difficulties . . ." ibid.

page 634: "He owed those albums to CBS . . ." Hersh/Rogan. London/Topanga Canyon, California: 12 April 2008.

page 634: "It was a bad period for me . . ." McGuinn/Rogan. London: 28 April 1977. Part published *Zigzag* 73: June 1977.

page 634: "He was going through a lot of changes . . ." Rainey/Rogan. London/Hollywood, California: 12 January 2007.

page 635: "I hadn't seen him for a while . . ." McGuinn/Rogan. London: 28 April 1977. Part published *Zigzag* 73: June 1977.

page 635: "We're going out on the road . . ." ibid.

page 635: "I don't think I can . . ." ibid.

page 635: ". . . a certain 'Kevin Kelley' on piano . . ." Not, of course, the former Byrds' drummer.

page 636: "It was the most wonderful thing . . ." McGuinn/Rogan. London: 28 April 1977. Part published *Zigzag* 73: June 1977.

page 636: "It was such a high place . . ." ibid.

page 636: "I was swinging on the rope . . ." ibid.

page 636: ". . . the sumptuous 'Dreamland' . . ." McGuinn spoke to me at length about the songs on *Cardiff Rose*, but space precludes a lengthy appraisal. He had a funny story about his cover of Joni Mitchell's 'Dreamland'. "She said, 'I have this one song, but you might object to one of the lines in it . . . "I wrapped their flag around me like a Dorothy Moore sarong",' so I said, 'Oh, that's easy, we'll change it to "the Errol Flynn sarong".'"

page 636–637: "I was just doing that to say, 'Hi Joni' . . ." McGuinn/Rogan. London: 28 April 1977. Part published *Zigzag* 73: June 1977. McGuinn adds: "'Partners In Crime' – that was a message to Abbie Hoffman, as Jacques used to be in the Yippie Party."

page 637: "I was very disappointed . . ." Rainey/Rogan. London/Hollywood, California: 12 January 2007.

page 637: ". . . a new group, appropriately named Thunderbyrd . . ." The original Thunderbyrd line-up comprised James Smith (lead guitar) and Commander Cody's old rhythm section, Bruce Barlow (bass) and Lance Dickerson (drums).

page 637: "It was painfully obvious . . ." McGuinn/Rogan. London: 28 April 1977. Part published *Zigzag* 73: June 1977.

page 637: "We asked around . . ." ibid.

page 638: "Jim's sitting there . . ." Gary Marker, interviewed by the author. London/Los Angeles, California: 28 February 2007.

page 639: "Neil didn't really *need* our help," Crosby/Rogan. London: 22–23 April 1980.

page 639: "He's a very bad person . . ." ibid.

page 640: "I saw nothing but difficulty . . ." Elliot Mazer, interviewed by the author. London/New York: 2 January 2000.

NOTES

page 640: "It would have been the best CSN&Y album . . ." Crosby/Rogan. London: 22–23 April 1980.

page 640: "I feel like singing the 'Star Spangled Banner' . . ." David Crosby, onstage at the Boston Garden: 5 August 1974.

page 640: "David is an incredible musician . . ." Stephen Stills, quoted in Johnny Rogan, *Crosby, Stills, Nash & Young: The Visual Documentary* (London: Omnibus Press, 1996), p. 81.

page 641: "In 1974, we were probably the biggest . . ." Crosby/Rogan. London: 22–23 April 1980.

page 641: "Neil went out of the room . . ." ibid.

page 641: "Listen to *Seastones* . . ." Crosby/Rogan. London: 22–23 April 1980.

page 642: "I think it's his cock . . ." Graham Nash, interviewed by Ted Joseph. *Sounds*: 18 September 1976.

page 643: "Well, what would *you* do? . . ." David Crosby, interviewed by Ted Joseph. *Sounds*: 18 September 1976.

page 644: "It got to the point where Stephen . . ." Hillman/Rogan. London: 28 April 1977.

page 644: "I don't know why it didn't work . . ." ibid.

page 645: "I feel I don't want to go on the road anymore . . ." ibid.

page 646: "I thought it was a real achievement . . ." Clark/Rogan. London: 2 May 1977.

page 648: "I had to find a direction . . ." Gene Clark, interviewed by Allan Jones. *Melody Maker*: 14 May 1977.

page 648: "There was a clique of musicians . . ." Mark Adzick, interviewed by the author. London/Minnesota, Minneapolis: 1–2 October 2007.

page 649: "I didn't use Mike Clarke . . ." Hillman/Rogan. London: 28 April 1977.

page 649: "With Hillman's help . . ." The touring Chris Hillman Band included Rick Roberts, Mark Andes and Jock Bartley. When Hillman fell ill, Michael Clarke and Larry Burnett flew to New York to play a showcase gig as Firefall. They were immediately signed to Atlantic, after which Roberts added David Muse to the line-up. As Mark Andes told me: "Rick handpicked them. He was responsible for getting Larry Burnett, whom nobody knew. But Rick was aware of his work as a folk singer in the Washington D.C. area. Rick had already approached Jock Bartley, who agreed to join forces with him. I was the third guy he asked. When I said I would get involved, Larry was brought out and we worked with a couple of drummers before Michael was asked. David Muse was added as a 'textural' guy and stayed with the band."

Recalling his induction, Muse told me: "My friend Rick Roberts invited me out to Boulder. I moved from Atlanta and when I first got there Ricky was out on the road with Stephen Stills. When he got back in town we all did a few gigs with Chris Hillman. But I didn't do that one where they took his place in New York and got the deal for Firefall. They'd already signed the deal with Atlantic when I showed up in Boulder. But it was before they did the first album that I started playing with them and rehearsed with them. That's when I got to meet Michael, at that first rehearsal. Then I went down to Miami and did the first album with them and after that I became a member of the band. Even though I played on the first album I wasn't 'officially' a member at that point."

page 649: "*Rolling Stone* once called him . . ." David Muse, interviewed by the author. London/Tampa, Florida: 12 October 2007.

page 650: "He got better and better after he left the Byrds . . ." Crosby/Rogan. London: 22–23 April 1980.

Chapter 39: Interlude – Three Byrds Land In London

page 651: "I'm not really up to date . . ." Clark/Rogan. London: 2 May 1977.

page 652: "Music is more important to the world . . ." Gene Clark, interviewed by Allan Jones. *Melody Maker*: 14 May 1977.

page 652: "We had our own people to deal with . . ." Greg Thomas, interviewed by the author. London/Los Angeles, California: 3–4 July 2007.

page 652: ". . . 'Oh that stuff's great' . . ." Andy Kandanes, interviewed by the author. London/Cobb, California: 1–2 October 2007.

page 652: "I went down to this small pharmacy . . ." ibid.

page 653: "There was this well-dressed guy . . ." ibid.

page 654: "I liked that road crazy spirit . . ." Peter Oliva, interviewed by the author. London/Vacaville, California: 16 July 2007.

page 654: "It was a very rough period for Roger, Gene and I . . ." Chris Hillman, unissued video-taped interview by John Tobler. London: June 1990.

page 654: ". . . listless, the epitome of the slightly stumbling overweight bearded hippie . . ." Reviewer Steve Clark. *New Musical Express*: 14 May 1977.

page 655: "Tommy Kaye was the smart New York guy . . ." Oliva/Rogan. London/Vacaville, California: 16 July 2007.

page 656: "I'd love to do it . . ." Hillman/Rogan. London: 28 April 1977.

page 656: "It could be done . . ." Clark/Kendall. *Zigzag* 73: June 1977.

page 656: "I'd like to ask . . ." Roger McGuinn onstage at the Hammersmith Odeon. London: 30 April 1977.

NOTES

page 657: "Is Chris there? . . ." Roger McGuinn, onstage at the Hammersmith Odeon: London: 1 May 1977.

page 657: "It was Gene's paranoia . . ." McGuinn/Rogan. Leeds: 4 May 1977.

page 657: "They didn't take the Byrds segment . . ." Cyriel Van den Hemel, interviewed by the author. London: 25 June 1997.

page 658: "Man, hookers depress me . . ." McGuinn aside during our interview. Leeds: 4 May 1977.

page 658: "My real feelings on the matter . . ." McGuinn/Rogan. Leeds: 4 May 1977.

page 658: "I didn't say it . . ." Crosby/Rogan. London: 22–23 April 1980.

page 658: "Let me qualify what I said about Crosby . . ." McGuinn/Rogan. Leeds: 4 May 1977.

page 659: "There was no panic . . ." Crosby/Rogan. London: 22–23 April 1980.

page 659: "I think McGuinn's scared of me . . ." ibid.

page 660: "I just couldn't meet his demands . . ." Cyriel Van den Hemel, quoted in news section. *Sounds*: 14 May 1977.

page 660: "He freaked out somehow and he smashed a lamp . . ." McGuinn/Tobler. London: 14 June 1997.

page 661: "Gene was doing a good job . . ." Kandanes/Rogan. London/Cobb, California: 1–2 October 2007.

page 661: "Every brand of Scotch . . ." Oliva/Rogan. London/Vacaville, California: 16 July 2007.

page 661: "It's not a great desire on my part . . ." McGuinn/Rogan. Leeds: 4 May 1977.

Chapter 40: The Negotiation

page 662: "We were very angry . . ." Van den Hemel/Rogan. London: 25 June 1997.

page 662: ". . . the matter was concluded in the High Courts of Justice . . ." Miles Copeland and Cyriel Van den Hemel were awarded costs, which could not be retrieved. They decided not to pursue the action any further.

page 663: "We just put the Byrds back together . . ." Greg Thomas, quoted by Jim Nash. *BAM*: October 1977.

page 663 : "I didn't think they were peddling . . ." McGuinn/Rogan. New York: 26 January 1979. Part published in *Dark Star* 20: May 1979.

page 664: "Rupert was obviously a fan . . ." Rainey/Rogan. London/Hollywood, California: 12 January 2007.

page 664: "It was unsaid . . ." ibid.
page 664: "I knew Connie . . ." ibid.
page 665: "When Chris said he wanted . . ." Hersh/Rogan. London/Topanga Canyon, California: 12 April 2008.
page 665: "I told him, 'Look, if you do this . . .'" Rainey/Rogan. London/Hollywood, California: 12 January 2007.
page 666: "My future is up in the air . . ." Roger McGuinn, interviewed by Jeff Weinberger. Livingstone College, Salisbury, North Carolina: 28 November 1977.
page 666: "Roger felt that Gene . . ." Rainey/Rogan. London/Hollywood, California: 12 January 2007.
page 666: "I was bored . . ." Hillman/Rogan. New York: 26 January 1979. Part published in *Dark Star* 20: May 1979.
page 668: "I just went, 'Whoa, man!' . . ." Roger McGuinn, interviewed by Jim Carlton. *The Fretboard Journal* no. 8: Winter 2007.
page 668: "I thought, 'Man, I've only got seven years left,' . . ." Promotional interview for *Limited Edition* on McGuinn's website, 2004.
page 668: "I was down at the bottom . . ." Roger McGuinn, interviewed on *The* 700 *Club*.
page 668: "Lord Jesus . . ." ibid.
page 668: "I really felt this very strongly . . ." ibid.
page 669: "When he was dating Susan . . ." Dolores Tickner (formerly McGuinn, née DeLeon)/Rogan. London/Tucson, Arizona: 13 January 2007.
page 669: "I thought, 'Oh great, a hillbilly musician!' . . ." Camilla McGuinn, interviewed on *The* 700 *Club*.
page 670: "She took a few days . . ." McGuinn, interviewed on *The* 700 *Club*.
page 670: "As far as songwriting goes . . ." Camilla McGuinn, interviewed by the author. London/Los Angeles, California: 24 March 1980.
page 671: "If we bombed there . . ." Gene Clark, interviewed by Mary Campbell, Associated Press newsfeature writer. *The Free-Lance Star*: 24 February 1979. Reprinted in *The Rock Hill Herald*: 21 March 1979.
page 671: "I think it was at the Roxy . . ." Hersh/Rogan. London/Topanga Canyon, California: 12 April 2008.
page 671: "He wasn't drinking very much . . ." Terri Messina, interviewed by the author. North Hollywood, California: 1–2 September 1996.
page 671: "There was so much animosity . . ." Hersh/Rogan. London/Topanga Canyon, California: 12 April 2008.
page 673: "I made an agreement . . ." McGuinn/Rogan. New York: 26 January 1979. Part published in *Dark Star* 20: May 1979.

NOTES

page 673: "They said they needed me at the Roxy . . ." Crosby/Rogan. London: 22–23 April 1980.

page 673: "He sat in with us . . ." McGuinn/Campbell. *The Free-Lance Star*: 24 February 1979. Reprinted in *The Rock Hill Herald*: 21 March 1979.

page 674: "We can do better . . ." Crosby/Rogan. London: 22–23 April 1980.

page 674: "When they were cutting in Miami . . ." ibid.

page 675: "David showing up . . ." Hersh/Rogan. London/Topanga Canyon, California: 12 April 2008.

page 675: "It was funny to see their interaction . . ." Kandanes/Rogan. London/Cobb, California: 1–2 October 2007.

page 675: "The only time I've ever been in the same room . . ." Rainey/Rogan. London/Hollywood, California: 12 January 2007.

Chapter 41: The Cocaine Wars

page 677: "We lived in this big mansion . . ." Hersh/Rogan. London/Topanga Canyon, California: 12 April 2008.

page 678: "Heroin was never his drug of choice . . ." Messina/Rogan. North Hollywood, California: 1–2 September 1996.

page 678: "Keith Richards had gotten backstage . . ." Hersh/Rogan. London/Topanga Canyon, California: 12 April 2008. The 'showcase' gig took place at New York's Bottom Line on 23 February 1979 at the time of the album's release.

page 679: "He called me one night . . ." ibid.

page 679: "I didn't respect what Roger was doing . . ." ibid.

page 680: "That's what rock 'n' roll is all about . . ." ibid.

page 680: "Gene's songs were probably the best . . ." ibid.

page 681: "They were capable of doing it again . . ." ibid.

page 681: "The sessions were overseen by Ron and Howard Albert . . ." After completing the album, Ron Albert was called upon by Capitol Records to provide some producer's notes. Evidently, these took the form of an interview, probably conducted by the industrious Stephen Peeples (although no credit was attached). Albert's comments were never included with the album, but they were sent to me at the time. Looking at them today, they provide a revealing glimpse into key areas of the recording process. Having just completed the record, Albert is understandably upbeat and clearly in 'promotional mode'. That said, it's interesting to observe that, as far as he was concerned, the project was problem free and, more importantly, was completed on time. Whatever may have been simmering in the background, McGuinn, Clark &

Hillman were professional enough to put any differences aside and finish the album to their producers' specifications.

Ron Albert: "I can honestly tell you I'm usually a lot more reserved about the projects we do, but this one was special, for all of us. Roger, Gene, Chris and Greg had a good jump on the album already when we started on it because they knew the songs – many of them had been in their live sets over the last several months. The fact that Greg plays drums, Chris plays bass and both Gene and Roger play rhythm meant that the basic tracks were easy to cut. We simply added some great star-talent session guys like George Terry, who hears a song once and has a part worked out by the time the tape rewinds. Same with keyboardist Paul Harris, who was in Manassas with Chris. So it wasn't like we were all hearing and learning the songs for the first time. The guitar and keyboard parts just added another dimension, a spark of freshness to the basics that for the most part were already together within the band.

"It's definitely not a Byrds record – we set out with avoiding that in mind. But because these guys are who they are, enough of the original sound – especially the blend of voices – comes through. Their sound is immediately identifiable, special and like no one else's, one we've heard a lot in the past and grew up with. The unique texture of their voices and harmonies remains intact, and the new album overall has a contemporary sound that makes it like nothing they've ever done before. I don't think there's a cut on the album that sounds dated. It's Fifties–Eighties music that bridges all gaps.

"Another thing I really like about this album is that we finished it way ahead of schedule. The sessions went so smoothly that I always had a feeling that somewhere along the line there would be a serious problem. The ultimate screw-up never happened. There were no problems at all, none of the ego trips that could have led to disaster. Roger, Gene and Chris have evolved way beyond pettiness because they've grown older, they've developed patience and even more respect for each other's ideas. Both Howard and I couldn't be happier with the guys and the album.

"As producers and engineers, Howard and I are very firm believers in what we call the 'Stephen Stills School Of Recording'. As graduates we know that the quicker you can get the basic tracks together with the right kind of feel the better the album will sound. We go for the spontaneity, because even if the basic track has a few clams, they can be repaired. Keeping the basic groove, the sound is almost always much better than it would be if it was done over and over and over again in the quest for the perfect take. The groove must not be sacrificed for technical perfection.

NOTES

Most of this album was cut in this way, with the exception being the first take tunes such as 'Bye Bye Baby' and 'Bad Boy'.

"I think Joe Lala's percussion stuff played a key part in this album. The Latin/Caribbean flavour of his playing is that added ingredient that just helps glue it all together. We've worked with him on so many occasions, he knows what we're after without us hardly saying a word.

"Mike Lewis, the string and horn arranger, has also worked with us on almost everything we've done the last few years, most recently Firefall's *Elan* album. During the early stages of K.C. & The Sunshine Band, his horn charts formed the basis of their sound, which in turn directly influenced the Bee Gees and everything else that's followed. But there aren't really any disco-type horn or string parts on this album.

"Usually when we work with Mike, we play the basic tracks for him, and if we have a concept or idea we'll sing it to him and then leave him alone. From that point, he writes an excessive number of parts, all with different ideas, and then Howard and I will just peel off the stuff that we don't like or don't think will fit. It works extremely well this way because sometimes his ideas are fresher than ours — sometimes we're maybe too close to the track after working it through all the stages. When we're ready to record the parts, he brings in the musicians — they often give him exactly what we want. Howard and I prefer the eight-four-two string section — eight violins, four violas and two cellos."

page 681: "Roger always needed something . . ." Hersh/Rogan. London/Topanga Canyon, California: 12 April 2008.

page 682: "If you thought it was bad in London . . ." Greg Thomas, interviewed by the author. London/Los Angeles, California: 3–4 July 2007.

page 682: "Somehow everybody pulled it together . . ." ibid.

page 683: "We used that cover . . ." Al Hersh, interviewed by the author. New York: 26 January 1979.

page 683: "It was sent out to the entire field . . ." Rainey/Rogan. London/Hollywood, California: 12 January 2007.

page 684: "So far I've heard . . ." Clark/Rogan. New York: 26 January 1979.

page 684: "We didn't approach this album as the Byrds . . ." Hillman/Rogan. New York: 26 January 1979. Part published in *Dark Star* 20: May 1979.

page 685: "That was just me joking . . ." McGuinn/Rogan. New York: 26 January 1979. Published in *Dark Star* 20.

page 685: "'Don't You Write Her Off' wasn't really a great song . . ." Hersh/Rogan. London/Topanga Canyon, California: 12 April 2008.

page 686: "Lewis, without any prompting . . ." Ron Albert's comments on *McGuinn, Clark & Hillman*. Capitol Records press release: February 1979.

page 686: "I didn't think it was that big a deal . . ." McGuinn/Campbell. *The Free-Lance Star*: 24 February 1979. Reprinted in *The Rock Hill Herald*: 21 March 1979.

page 686: "The first time Gene . . ." Ron Albert's comments on *McGuinn, Clark & Hillman*. Capitol Records press release: February 1979.

page 686: "It's sort of moody in the verses . . ." ibid.

page 687: "This is the one track . . ." ibid.

page 688: "Sophistication is the signature . . ." Clark/Campbell. *The Free-Lance Star*: 24 February 1979. Reprinted in *The Rock Hill Herald*: 21 March 1979.

page 688: "Once I went into the studio . . ." Roger McGuinn, interviewed by Brett Milano. *Pulse!*: February 1991.

Chapter 42: Burn Out

page 690: "Milking it with Roger and his pals . . ." Reviewer Sandy Robertson. *Sounds*: 24 February 1979. *New Musical Express'* Max Bell had the same tone, mixing damnation with limited praise, and singling out McGuinn at the expense of the others. "Ah, but you were so much younger then, younger than yesterday . . . and that is the whole truth so help me God. As it is McGuinn, Clark & Hillman (but let's call 'em the Byrds for old times sake) have only themselves to blame for entering into yet another hopeless prima donna reformation with such an evident lack of conviction that I couldn't even make the trouper charge stick. The results were painfully predictable . . . What was this shit? Gene Clark assumed the mantle of stage buffoon, exhorting the audience to clap along . . . The evening started out as a nightmare as they played a selection of the guff from the new Capitol record. Utter bemusement all around, what depths of self-deprivation have they reached? Here's McGuinn looking sullen and bored with his Rickenbacker turned down low, strumming some dumb rhythm chord while someone else [Johnne 'John' Sambataro] gets to play lead guitar. For 50 minutes the spectacle was too depressing with Hillman and the surrogate picker (no Clarence White) getting off on each other . . . McGuinn – who invented one brand of psychedelic pop-rock only to find the Eagles and CS&N make a profit of it – had to stand there justifying his own contributions to popular schlock. What irony. But he *still* had it there to blow you away, which eventually he managed to do for the final 20 minutes. 'So You Want To Be A Rock 'n' Roll Star' and the double piece de resistance 'Eight Miles High' plus 'Feel A Whole Lot Better' showed

NOTES

McGuinn still knows how to reach the ecstatic heights. Nostalgia be damned, the solos and the sound of singing sunshine remained intact."

page 690: "We're giving it a six-month trial . . ." Chris Hillman, interviewed by Danae Brook. *London Evening Standard*: 24 February 1979.

page 691: "I was having trouble . . ." Chris Hillman, interviewed by John Cody. *Canadian Christianity*. com internet site.

page 691: "With Roger . . ." Hersh/Rogan. London/Topanga Canyon, California: 12 April 2008.

page 691: "I was very close to Roger . . ." Greg Thomas/Rogan. London/Los Angeles, California: 3–4 July 2007.

page 693: "Another reunion of the Byrds . . ." Hillman/Rogan. New York: 26 January 1979.

page 693: "They just thought it would be cool . . ." Bob 'Ras' Rassmussen, interviewed by the author. London/Boulder, Colorado: 10 October 2007.

page 694: "David was not paying attention . . ." Graham Nash, interviewed by Dave Zimmer. *Crosby, Stills & Nash: The Authorized Biography* (London: Omnibus Press, 1984), p. 209.

page 694: "We were in the middle of an incredible jam . . ." ibid.

page 694: "I didn't want to quit working with Graham . . ." David Crosby, interviewed by Dave Zimmer. *Crosby, Stills & Nash: The Authorized Biography* (London: Omnibus Press, 1984), p. 214.

page 695: "Gene could disappear . . ." Hersh/Rogan. London/Topanga Canyon, California: 12 April 2008.

page 695: "He missed the plane . . ." Rainey/Rogan. London/Hollywood, California: 12 January 2007.

page 695: "In Japan . . ." Hersh/Rogan. London/Topanga Canyon, California: 12 April 2008.

page 695: "Chris was still doing some 'healing' with Roger . . ." ibid.

page 696: "Get into that bathroom! . . ." Chris Hillman, as witnessed by the author. Universal Amphitheatre, Universal City: 11–12 July 1979. McGuinn, Clark & Hillman's poor showing that evening was made worse by the fact that they were supporting Eddie Money. The billing reflected their non-superstar status.

page 697: "It got worse . . ." Greg Thomas/Rogan. London/Los Angeles, California: 3–4 July 2007.

page 698: "We had to get up . . ." Hersh/Rogan. London/Topanga Canyon, California: 12 April 2008.

page 698: "The thing with McGuinn, Clark & Hillman . . ." Messina/Rogan. North Hollywood, California: 1–2 September 1996.

page 699: "We went to this disco . . ." Oliva/Rogan. London/Vacaville, California: 16 July 2007.

page 699: "Give McGuinn an inch . . ." Tom Slocum, interviewed by the author. Taluca Lake, California: 19–20 November 1996.
page 699: "Roger and I became estranged . . ." Hersh/Rogan. London/Topanga Canyon, California: 12 April 2008.
page 699: "Roger, you're a hypocritical bastard . . ." ibid.
page 699–700: "He said, 'You can't talk to me that way!' . . ." ibid.
page 700: "I got very drunk . . ." Greg Thomas/Rogan. London/Los Angeles, California: 3–4 July 2007.
page 701: "I was burned out . . ." ibid.
page 701: "Gene started to go nuts again . . ." Chris Hillman, interviewed by William Ruhlman. *Goldmine*: 11 January 1991.
page 701: "He went on a binge . . ." Slocum/Rogan. Taluca Lake, California: 19–20 November 1996.
page 701: "Roger and Chris are like brothers . . ." Hersh/Rogan. London/Hollywood, California: 24 March 1980.
page 701: "I was exaggerating . . ." Hersh/Rogan. London/Topanga Canyon, California: 12 April 2008.
page 702: "Gene was a handful . . ." ibid.
page 702: "We were doing some co-writing . . ." Kandanes/Rogan. London/Cobb, California: 1–2 October 2007.
page 702: "That relationship . . ." ibid.
page 703: "Gene loved Jesse . . ." Slocum/Rogan. Taluca Lake, California: 19–20 November 1996.
page 703: "Gene fell into the arms . . ." ibid.
page 704: "We went in with a bunch . . ." Chris Hillman's comments on *City*. Capitol Records press release: January 1980.
page 704–705: "It's time to get back to the city . . ." Roger McGuinn's comments on *City*. Capitol Records press release: January 1980.
page 705: "It reminds me of the old parable . . ." ibid.
page 706: "Gene promised that he would not let them down . . ." Hersh/Rogan. London/Hollywood, California: 24 March 1980.
page 706: ". . . came about rapidly . . ." Camilla McGuinn/Rogan. London/Los Angeles, California: 24 March 1980.
page 706: "The photo was taken at night . . ." Roger McGuinn's comments on *City*, reproduced from a Capitol press release, dated January 1980.
page 706: "Roger wanted to do a roller-skating song . . ." Camilla McGuinn/Rogan. London/Los Angeles, California: 24 March 1980.
page 709: "It's remote . . ." ibid.
page 709: "I frankly like the guy . . ." Crosby/Rogan. London: 22–23 April 1980.

NOTES

Chapter 43: The Dark Decade

page 710: "We had written 12 songs with a theme . . ." Roger McGuinn, interviewed by Brett Milano. *Pulse!*: February 1991.

page 711: "You couldn't get any whiter guys . . ." Chris Hillman, unissued video-taped interview by John Tobler. London: June 1990.

page 711: "Hampered by a PA . . ." Reviewer Allan Jones: *Melody Maker*: 16 February 1980.

page 711: "Carlos and Chris . . ." Hersh/Rogan. London/Topanga Canyon, California: 12 April 2008.

page 712: "McGuinn and Hillman utterly destroyed . . ." Reviewer Allan Jones: *Melody Maker*: 16 February 1980.

page 713: "We were doing tours . . ." Rainey/Rogan. London/Hollywood, California: 12 January 2007.

page 714: "'America For Me' was causing a huge stir . . ." ibid.

page 714: "I was still at home . . ." ibid.

page 714: "They called me in . . ." ibid.

page 714: "Chris at that time . . ." ibid.

page 715: "Chris Hillman knew full well . . ." Roger McGuinn, fax despatched to the author: 1998.

page 715: "I don't ever want to work with you again . . ." Dickson/Rogan. Waldport, Oregon: 26–30 April 1989.

page 716: "God those concerts! . . ." Chris Hillman, interviewed by Jean-Pierre Morisset, May 1985, printed in *Farther Along* 5: Fall/Winter 1986.

page 716: "The set lists were exemplary . . ." For example, during their early show at the Door in Washington D.C. (8 November 1981), they played a varied set featuring 'Step On Out', 'Live And Learn', 'It Doesn't Matter', 'Long Long Time', 'You Are The Woman', 'Bound To Fall', 'Fallen Eagle', 'Sin City', 'Just Remember I Love You', 'Clear Sailin'', 'Wheels', 'Colorado', 'Livin' Ain't Livin''; 'Christine's Tune (Devil In Disguise)' and '(Take Me In Your) Lifeboat'. They then returned for the late show for 'So You Want To Be A Rock 'n' Roll Star', 'Slippin' Away', 'You Are The Woman', 'Bound To Fall', 'Love Is The Sweetest Amnesty', 'My Uncle', 'Do For The Others', 'The Christian Life', 'Dark End Of The Street', 'It Doesn't Matter', 'Hard Times', 'Step On Out', 'Colorado', 'Wake Up Little Susie' and 'Livin' Ain't Livin''. Even within the songs there were several surprises. 'So You Want To Be A Rock 'n' Roll Star' featured Hillman's voice more prominently than on any Byrds' recording; 'Bound To Fall' had fresh exuberance in the duo setting; 'It Doesn't Matter' featured Roberts' original lyrics; 'Colorado' included a mandolin backing, and Hillman's solo songs were performed with conviction. Indeed, it was regrettable that this duo experiment was not revived as it had real potential. Judging from Hillman's disdainful comments, it became unglued towards the end of the tour, but he seems to have forgotten the better moments as evidenced herein.

page 718: "Songwriting and royalties . . ." Chris Hillman, interviewed by Bud Scoppa. *Music Connection*: 15 June–28 June 1987.

page 721: "I was praying about a financial matter . . ." McGuinn, interviewed on *The* 700 *Club*.

page 721: "I knew the Lord . . ." ibid.

page 722: "At Dingwalls, he wanted to kill Roger McGuinn . . ." Gene Parsons/Rogan. London/Mendocino, California: 19 May 2007.

page 724: "Bob committed suicide . . ." Dolores Tickner (formerly McGuinn, née DeLeon)/Rogan. London/Tucson, Arizona: 24–25 February 2007.

page 725: "Please don't mention the drugs . . ." Crosby/Rogan. London: 22–23 April 1980.

page 729: "I'm a gentleman . . ." David Crosby, interviewed by Mark Christensen. *Rolling Stone*: 13 March 1986.

page 730: "Jail is no joke . . ." Crosby, speaking in Dallas before Judge Patrick McDowell: 5 August 1983.

page 730: "I truly believe . . ." Letter from Graham Nash to Judge Patrick McDowell: August 1983.

page 730: "I'm being treated . . ." Crosby, speaking to journalists outside the court in Dallas: 5 August 1983.

page 731: "They only gave me . . ." David Crosby, onstage at the Beacon Theatre, New York: 23 March 1984.

page 731: "I haven't done that . . ." ibid.

page 731: "We still have it . . ." Graham Nash, quoted in Johnny Rogan's *Crosby, Stills, Nash & Young: The Visual Documentary* (London, Omnibus, 1996), p. 135.

page 732: "My cell was about six by 13 . . ." David Crosby, interviewed by Todd Gold. *People*: 27 April 1987.

page 733: "Hey, rock star . . ." David Crosby, interviewed by the author. London: 21 February 1989.

page 734: "It's tough to sing . . ." Graham Nash, quoted in *Rolling Stone*: 13 March 1986.

page 734: "David will eventually die . . ." Graham Nash, interviewed by Edward Kiersh. *Spin*: 1986.

page 735: "They say he was a great man . . ." Statement by Dallas County's assistant District Attorney: 19 December 1985.

NOTES

page 735: "I hadn't written any music . . ." Crosby/Rogan. London: 21 February 1989.
page 736: "It's just how it happened . . ." ibid.
page 737: "My health's really excellent . . ." ibid.

Chapter 44: The Third Coming

page 739: "Outside of 'Mr Tambourine Man' I never put up . . ." Dickson/Rogan. Waldport, Oregon: 26–30 April 1989.
page 740: "It was canned . . ." ibid.
page 740: "Gene disappeared . . ." ibid.
page 741: ". . . more spontaneous . . ." McGuinn/Rogan. Leeds: 4 May 1977.
page 741: "David was surprised at Chris . . ." ibid.
page 741: "I wish I'd been smarter . . ." Crosby/Epstein. *Guitar Player*: May 1997.
page 744: "The thing I wanted to do with the album . . ." Dickson/Rogan. Waldport, Oregon: 26–30 April 1989.
page 744: "I was happy that Chris and David . . ." ibid.
page 748: "Michael had not been playing . . ." Dick/Rogan. London/Spokane, Washington: 11 May 1997.
page 748: "Michael Clarke had fallen on hard times . . ." Crosby/Rogan. London: 21 February 1989.
page 749: "Sure, we tried to trademark the name . . ." Steve Green, interviewed by the author. New York: May 1989.
page 750: "We were serious . . ." David Crosby, onstage at the Ventura Theater, Ventura, California: 6 January 1989.
page 750: "About 1968, David left . . ." Chris Hillman, onstage at the Ventura Theater, Ventura, California: 6 January 1989.
page 751: "The trouble with McGuinn . . ." Dickson/Rogan. London/Hawaii: 7 July 1997.
page 751: "They thought it was a drug song . . ." Roger McGuinn, onstage at the Ventura Theater, Ventura, California: 6 January 1989.
page 751: "We got up there man . . ." Crosby/Rogan. London: 21 February 1989.
page 752: "When I started playing with Roger and Christopher . . ." ibid.
page 752: "I don't think Gene's ready . . ." ibid.
page 752: "I feel a lot of remorse . . ." Gene Clark, interviewed by the author. Waldport, Oregon/Hollywood, California: 28 April 1989.
page 753: "The best thing . . ." Press statement by Gene Clark: early 1989.
page 753: "We beat them to it . . ." Crosby/Rogan. London: 21 February 1989.

page 754: "We think we're going to win . . ." Green/Rogan. New York: May 1989.
page 754: "I won't be denied a living . . ." Press statement by Michael Clarke: Spring 1989.
page 754: "We tried 'Michael Clarke salutes the Byrds' . . ." Green/Rogan. New York: May 1989.
page 754: "We tried to set up meetings . . ." Bill Siddons, letter to the author, dated 29 June 1989.
page 755: "My contribution aside . . ." Crosby/Rogan. London: 21 February 1989.
page 755: "We're not denying that McGuinn was the Byrds . . ." Green/Rogan. New York: May 1989.
page 756: "There should be five or none . . ." ibid.
page 757: "If we win the injunction . . ." ibid.
page 757: "When everybody's background is brought into this . . ." ibid.
page 758: "The Court has considered . . ." United States District Court Middle District of Florida, Tampa Division. Case No. 89–518-CIV-T–15 C. Roger McGuinn, Christopher Hillman and David Crosby aka "The Byrds" v Michael Clarke, Artists International Management Inc, Steve Green and John Does 1–10. Order by District Judge William J. Castagna.
page 759: "I've been on pins and needles . . ." Michael Clarke, interviewed by Bill Orlove. *Boca Raton News*: 23 May 1989.
page 759: "It just cost too much . . ." Bill Siddons, letter to the author, dated 29 June 1989.
page 759: "I was confident we'd win . . ." Green/Rogan. New York: May 1989.
page 760: "We don't think that will ever happen . . ." ibid.
page 760: "Our intent all along . . ." Bill Siddons, letter to the author, dated 29 June 1989.
page 760: "Michael won't make a fortune . . ." Green/Rogan. New York: May 1989.

Chapter 45: The Hall Of Fame

page 763: "I think Michael has been very foolish . . ." Chris Hillman, interviewed by the author. Boston, Massachusetts: 3 May 1989.
page 763: "Screw those guys . . ." Clarke/Rogan. London and Manchester: 14–15 October 1989.
page 763: "I thought there were . . ." Bob Dylan quote, recalled by McGuinn on WXRK-FM. New York: 19 August 1990.

NOTES

page 763: "Yeah, I do it all the time . . ." ibid.
page 764: "There was no reason for them not to have invited him . . ." Dickson/Rogan. London/Hawaii: 7 July 1997.
page 766: "I don't think I really stacked . . ." McGuinn/Tobler. London: 14 June 1997.
page 770: "I always hold the hope . . ." Gene Clark, interviewed by Steve Hochman. *Los Angeles Times*: 4 November 1990.
page 770: "The focus should be on the music . . ." Roger McGuinn, interviewed by Steve Hochman. *Los Angeles Times*: 4 November 1990.
page 770: "I trust that we'll be friends . . ." Michael Clarke, interviewed by Steve Hochman. *Los Angeles Times*: 4 November 1990.
page 771: "We sat down together . . ." Chris Hillman, interviewed by Craig Harris. *Folk Roots*: 1997.
page 771: "Well, I'd just like to thank you . . ." Roger McGuinn's induction speech at the Rock 'n' Roll Hall Of Fame. New York: 16 January 1991.
page 771–772: "I'm a very happy guy . . ." David Crosby's induction speech at the Rock 'n' Roll Hall Of Fame. New York: 16 January 1991.
page 772: "It's taken me so many years . . ." Chris Hillman's induction speech at the Rock 'n' Roll Hall Of Fame. New York: 16 January 1991.
page 772: "I think really for myself . . ." Gene Clark's induction speech at the Rock 'n' Roll Hall Of Fame. New York: 16 January 1991.
page 772: "I'd like to say that I appreciate . . ." Michael Clarke's induction speech at the Rock 'n' Roll Hall Of Fame. New York: 16 January 1991.

Chapter 46: Fatalities

page 774: "Gene looked OK . . ." Pat Robinson, interviewed by the author. London/Agoura, California: 9 November 1996.
page 774: "People started taking advantage . . ." ibid.
page 775: "He had 25–30 years . . ." York/Rogan. London/Rancho Cucamonga, California: 27 October 1996.
page 775: "I remember we went out of our way . . ." Robinson/Rogan. London/Agoura, California: 9 November 1996.
page 775: "He did some amazingly scary things . . ." Messina/Rogan. North Hollywood, California: 1–2 September 1996.
page 776: "He thought he was going to get paid . . ." Slocum/Rogan. Taluca Lake, California: 19–20 November 1996.
page 777: "I felt very sad . . ." Carla Olson, interviewed by the author. London: 24 November 1996.
page 777: "He looked so good . . ." Rick Williams, *Full Circle* 10: September 1991.

page 778: "Geno was really a nice guy . . ." Robinson/Rogan. London/Agoura, California: 9 November 1996.

page 778: "One of Gene's musician friends . . ." Messina/Rogan. North Hollywood, California: 1–2 September 1996.

page 778: "You fucked the girl . . ." As recalled verbatim to the author in separate statements by Tom Slocum and Terri Messina. The name of the girl and her age have been omitted.

page 779: "Gene was an artist . . ." Michael Clarke's tribute to Gene Clark. *Full Circle* 10: September 1991.

page 779: "I hadn't heard from him . . ." Susan Paul, interviewed by the author. London/Tampa, Florida: 13 April 1997.

page 780: "I'm still going to be here for you . . ." ibid.

page 780: "I was always talking to him . . ." Terry Rogers, interviewed by the author. London/Tennessee: 20 January 1997.

page 781: "Michael was the eternal child . . ." Chris Hillman's valedictory tribute to Michael Clarke: *Full Circle* 17: March 1994.

page 782: "We really like to make a contribution . . ." quoted in Johnny Rogan, *Crosby, Stills, Nash & Young: The Visual Documentary* (London, Omnibus, 1996).

page 782: "I'll tell you, I care . . ." David Crosby, interviewed by Peter Doggett. *Record Collector* 160: December 1992.

page 783: ". . . it was exacerbated . . ." David Crosby, interviewed by Todd Gold. *People*: 20 February 1995.

page 784: "I'd faced death before . . ." ibid.

page 784: "He was dying . . ." Chris Hillman, interviewed by Peter Doggett. *Record Collector* 230: October 1998.

page 785: "I thought maybe I should meet him . . ." James Raymond, interviewed by Jason Foster. *San Bernardino Sun*: 1997.

page 785: "All in all . . ." Crosby/Todd. *People*: 20 February 1995.

page 786: "I'll be damned . . ." David Crosby's induction speech at the Rock 'n' Roll Hall Of Fame: 6 May 1997.

page 787: "I was just visiting . . ." Neil Young, interviewed by Joel Selvin. *San Francisco Chronicle*: 9 October 1999.

page 787: "We didn't let any record company guys in . . ." Neil Young, interviewed by Adam Sweeting. *The Guardian*: 29 October 1999.

Chapter 47: End Of The Century

page 789: "I made one of the most monumental blunders . . ." Chris Hillman, interviewed by Richard Cromelin. *Los Angeles Times*: 19 July 1993.

NOTES

page 789: "The Byrds are never going to play again . . ." Chris Hillman, interviewed by Peter Doggett. *Record Collector* 158: June 1992.

page 790: "It's a volatile business . . ." Hillman/Cromelin. *Los Angeles Times*: 19 July 1993.

page 790: "We were very successful . . ." Hillman/Harris. *Folk Roots*: 1997.

page 792: "It wasn't intentional . . ." Chris Hillman, interviewed by Jim Bessman. *Billboard*: 16 May 1998.

page 792: "They didn't expect him to live . . ." Joey Stec, interviewed by the author. London/Los Angeles: 10/12 May 2009.

page 792: "I'm not dying . . ." Hillman/ Doggett. *Record Collector* 230: October 1998.

page 792: "I don't take it lightly . . ." ibid.

page 793: "I don't have any qualms . . ." Chris Hillman, interviewed by Kevin East. 'Carousel Corner', *Sensible Sound*: January 1999.

page 793: "The reason I called it *Back From Rio* . . ." Roger McGuinn, interviewed on Radio Q102, Texas, interspersed with concert live from Electric Ladyland Studios, New York City: March 1991.

page 794: "It was a lot of work . . ." McGuinn; unnamed interview.

page 795: "It was great fun . . ." Roger McGuinn, interviewed by Bill DeYoung. *Goldmine* 426: 22 November 1996.

page 795: "Roger McGuinn and I met backstage . . ." Jacques Levy, programme notes to *Just A Season: A Romance Of The Old West*. World premiere, Colgate University Theatre, Hamilton: 18 November 1992. Directed by Levy, the production included a band comprising Roger McGuinn (guitars), Geoffrey V.S. Ziegler (guitars), Andrew Clark (bass) and Scott Lisson (drums). Act I featured three songs: 'Chestnut Mare' (Peer), 'All The Things' (Peer) and 'Solveig's Song' (Solveig). Act II featured 'Lover Of The Bayou' (Mojo Man, Madame, Hookers), 'I Wanna Grow Up To Be A Politician' (Peer), 'The Robbin' Of The Stage' (the Plummer Gang), 'Just A Season' (Peer) and 'Home On The Hillside' (Peer, Solveig).

page 796: "David Crosby has been going around . . ." Roger McGuinn, press conference, Hard Rock Cafe, Paris: Summer 1993.

page 797: "I was listening to a Smithsonian Folkways album . . ." Roger McGuinn, commenting on his *Folk Den* site.

page 799: "The backing track was taken . . ." Bob Irwin, interviewed by the author. London/New York: November 1995.

page 800: ". . . a very bad song . . ." Crosby/Rogan. London: 21 February 1989.

page 800: "'Why' was right on the multi-track . . ." ibid.

page 801: "It was better . . ." Crosby/Rogan. London: 22–23 April 1980.

page 801: "Gary Usher had this marked . . ." Irwin/Rogan. London/New York: November 1995.
page 803: "I used to put them out . . ." Roger McGuinn, interviewed by the *Columbus Dispatch*: 1995.

Chapter 48: The Absence Of Charity

page 805: "We had to make some cut-ins . . ." McGuinn/Rogan. London/Florida: 22 May 1997.
page 807: "The only one who ever did anything . . ." David Crosby, interviewed by John Nork. *Tracking Angle*: Winter 1997.
page 807: "I can't believe the nasty things . . ." McGuinn/Rogan. London/Florida: 22 May 1997.
page 808: "I'll tell you the truth . . ." Crosby/ Nork. *Tracking Angle*: Winter 1997.
page 810: "I found the song on a Pentangle album . . ." York/Rogan. London/Rancho Cucamonga, California: 27 October 1996.
page 810: "I didn't sing it on the album . . ." ibid.
page 811: "It's a deep frustration for me . . ." Crosby/ Nork. *Tracking Angle*: Winter 1997.
page 811: "Frankly, every time I've listened to Crosby . . ." McGuinn/Rogan. London/Florida: 22 May 1997.
page 811: "If the Byrds . . ." McGuinn/Rogan. Leeds: 4 May 1977.
page 812: "At one point, David and I . . ." Hillman/Sylvester. *Goldmine* 436: 11 April 1997.
page 815: "McGuinn's the heart and soul . . ." Crosby/Rogan. London: 21 February 1989.

Chapter 49: Survivors

page 817: "They were visiting us . . ." 'A Discussion With David Crosby', press release for the book *Since Then*. G.P. Putnam's Sons: 7 November 2006.
page 817: "Maybe it's a good thing . . ." David Crosby, interviewed by Jancee Dunn. *Rolling Stone*: 3 February 2000.
page 817: "I still love David . . ." Chris Hillman, interviewed by John Cody. *Canadian Christianity*: December 2006.
page 819: "I never heard the exact amount . . ." Terry Rogers, interviewed by the author. London/Tennessee: 20 January 1997.
page 819: "But I know David had been in touch . . ." ibid.

NOTES

page 820: "We're about halfway to a police state . . ." David Crosby, interviewed by Peter Doggett. *Record Collector* 303: November 2004.

page 821: "They should learn that you don't follow people . . ." 'A Discussion With David Crosby', press release. G.P. Putnam's Sons: 7 November 2006.

page 821: "He's still abusive . . ." Hillman/Cody. *Canadian Christianity*: December 2006.

page 822: "You were so right about the Byrds . . ." Roger McGuinn, interviewed by Peter Doggett. *Record Collector* 248: April 2000.

page 822: "So David Crosby is the only one . . ." ibid.

page 823: "Connie, my wife . . ." Hillman/Cody. *Canadian Christianity*: December 2006.

page 824: "This is not . . ." Chris Hillman, interviewed by Randy Lewis. *Los Angeles Times*: 28 May 2010.

page 824: "The Desert Rose Band was the end of a long journey . . ." Chris Hillman, speaking at the Library of Congress, Washington D.C.: 16 October 2009.

page 824: "I think I'm singing better . . ." Chris Hillman, interviewed by Dave Irwin. *Tucson Weekly*: 29 April 2010.

page 825: "For someone my age . . ." Hillman/ Lewis. *Los Angeles Times*: 9 November 2009.

page 825: "I will never get out of the nest . . ." Chris Hillman, interviewed by Doug Foley. *Hamilton Spectator*: 2004.

page 825: "Taken from three nights (6–8 February) . . ." Oddly, the album notes and back cover claim it was recorded over two nights, but Bob Irwin confirms it was three. On the first, the Byrds played a full set, a shorter one on the second night and reputedly only five songs on the final night.

page 826: "As an historical document . . ." John York, interviewed by the author. London/Claremont, California: 11 June 2007.

page 828: "If you listen to the orchestrations . . ." McGuinn/Doggett. *Record Collector* 248: April 2000.

page 831: "All we would need is a drummer . . ." David Crosby, interviewed by Tierney Smith. *Goldmine*: 21 July 2006.

page 831: "It would be great . . ." Chris Hillman, interviewed by Tierney Smith. *Goldmine*: 21 July 2006.

page 834: "Once we learned the new songs . . ." 'A Discussion With David Crosby', press release. G.P. Putnam's Sons: 7 November 2006.

page 835: "If we didn't piss off anybody . . ." ibid.

page 835: "After 40 years of sailing . . ." Crosby's comments accompanying an advertisement for the sale of *The Mayan*.

1009

Chapter 50: The Reaper's Blade

page 837: "Note the way I hold this glass . . ." Taylor/Rogan. London: 17 June 1977.

page 837: "I hold it tight . . ." ibid.

page 837: "Derek was remarkable . . ." Dickson/Rogan. Waldport, Oregon: 26–30 April 1989.

page 837: I loved them . . ." Taylor/Rogan. London: 17 June 1977.

page 838: "My life can be divided into two parts . . ." ibid.

page 838: "Giving up drink . . ." Taylor/Rogan. London: 13 February 1997.

page 838: "The Beach Boys were by far the most difficult . . ." ibid.

page 838: "Brian was always on about the question . . ." ibid.

page 839: "I think I may be going into shadow . . ." ibid.

page 839: "I believed that anyone who didn't like the Byrds . . ." ibid. Towards the end, Taylor turned to me pointedly and said, "No matter how indifferent people are and if they say about your writing on the Byrds, 'It's only Johnny Rogan, it's one of his hobby horses.' No! You are *right*. Absolutely. Inside, people hearing that first album, *Mr Tambourine Man,* and *Turn! Turn! Turn!* would hear things that no one else was doing and no one else has bettered. Like the best of the Beatles it survives as fresh as ever. In my opinion, very much better than CSN&Y, and they had much bigger sales in catalogues, and more followers."

page 841: "I wouldn't characterize him as being bitter . . ." William (aka Bill/David) Wolff, interviewed by the author. London/Los Angeles, California: 11 March 2007.

page 841: "I don't think anybody will know . . ." Jesse Barish, interviewed by the author. London/Venice Beach, California: 12–13 April 2007.

page 841: "He had no brothers or sisters . . ." Jesse Lee Kincaid, interviewed by the author. London/Marin County, California: 5 March 2007.

page 841: "Kevin was a very sensitive person . . ." Charlie Taylor/Rogan. London/Nashville, Tennessee: 16 September 2007.

page 842: "I believe at this time . . ." Patricia Battin (née Cartabiano), email interview with the author. Silverton, Oregon: 14 October 2008.

page 842: "From what I understand . . ." Terry Rogers, interviewed by the author. London/East Alton, Illinois: 14–15 July 2007.

page 844: "Terry's God-given gift . . ." Seiter/Rogan. London/Los Angeles, California: 18 October 1999.

page 845: "Terry was a great guy . . ." Marker/Rogan. London/Los Angeles, California: 28 February 2007.

NOTES

page 846: "Twinkle-eyed, without missing a beat . . ." Even after Melcher's death, Crosby was not in forgiving mood. In 2006, he was still insulting the producer's memory. "If there was a record producer who had not the vaguest conception of what he was doing, it would be Terry Melcher," he told *Goldmine* magazine contributor, Tierney Smith. "That was triumph in the face of adversity. He absolutely added nothing and subtracted a great deal. He was an obstacle to be overcome in the production of a great record." McGuinn, Dickson and others have already criticized Crosby's anti-Melcher's comments and Dolores Tickner joined that chorus during an interview with me soon after. "David was always a thorn in everyone's side. Eddie couldn't stand him! I don't know what it was. There was something about David." Quoted by *Vanity Fair* contributor David Kamp, Melcher, speaking about the history of rock in Los Angeles, quipped: "If I had to, I'd blame it all on David Crosby. He broke up the Byrds and joined Buffalo Springfield, and broke them up. And then formed CS&N. I'd have to say that, personally speaking, Crosby was worse for the good feelings of rock 'n' roll than Manson was." Interestingly, this sounds as perverse a reading of Crosby's career as David's own comments on Melcher.

page 847: "Eddie was like a second dad . . ." Gib Guilbeau, interviewed by the author. London/Palmdale, California: 18 September 2007.

page 847: "He was our manager . . ." ibid.

page 847: "Eddie's a family man . . ." Dickson/Rogan. London/Hawaii: 7 July 1997.

page 847: "The children loved Eddie . . ." Dolores Tickner (formerly McGuinn, née DeLeon)/Rogan. London/Tucson, Arizona: 24–25 February 2007.

page 847: "He was taking Henry's children to McDonald's . . ." ibid.

page 847: "It was funny . . ." ibid.

page 848: "Don't do it! . . ." Eddie Tickner, interviewed by the author. Tucson, Arizona: 28 October 2005.

page 848: "He tried to overcome it . . ." Dolores Tickner (formerly McGuinn, née DeLeon)/Rogan. London/Tucson, Arizona: 24–25 February 2007.

page 848: "It was good you were able to see him . . ." ibid.

page 848: "It was shocking . . ." ibid.

page 848: "Eddie was wonderful . . ." Joey Stec, interviewed by the author. London/Los Angeles: 10/12 May 2009.

page 848: "At that time in Hollywood . . ." Bernal/Rogan. London/Los Angeles, California: 10 April 2008.

page 848: "Eddie was a real good friend . . ." Gene Parsons/Rogan.

London/Mendocino, California: 19 May 2007. Another Byrd eager to eulogize Tickner was John York, who told me: "I only knew him during the Byrds. He took us out to Fender one time when Fender wanted to make the String Bender and we all spent the afternoon together. We went to Rickenbacker and Fender. He was a really sweet guy and helped me form a publishing company. When I came back to LA in 1978 he was the first guy I called. I said, 'Eddie I'm back, I want to get involved.' He said, 'John, I'm getting too old. I don't want any more clients. My hands are full with Emmylou, but I wish you luck.' And that was the last time I talked to him."

page 849: "I always thought Eddie was going to die . . ." Emmylou Harris, quoted in Eddie Tickner obituary. *Billboard online*: 3 May 2006.

page 849: "That's a big business now . . ." McGuinn/Cody. *Canadian Christianity*: December 2006.

page 849: "Our daily devotions . . ." McGuinn, *Limited Edition* promotional interview: 2004.

page 850: "When I came to the Lord . . ." McGuinn/Cody. *Canadian Christianity*: December 2006.

page 850: "I feel very fulfilled . . ." McGuinn, *Limited Edition* promotional interview: 2004.

page 850: "Nobody can tell you . . ." Crosby/Rogan. London: 22–23 April 1980.

page 851: "Nobody's got a pipeline to God . . ." David Crosby, interviewed by Dave Zimmer. *Crosby, Stills & Nash: The Biography*. Dave Zimmer & Henry Diltz (New York, Da Capo, 2008), p. 371.

page 851: "I believe we go around again . . ." ibid.

page 851: "As far as ever going out . . ." Hillman/East. 'Carousel Corner', *Sensible Sound*: January 1999.

page 852: "I did things I shouldn't have . . ." Hillman/Doggett. *Record Collector* 230: October 1998.

page 853: "To this day . . ." ibid.

page 853: "I love Roger dearly . . ." Hillman/Cody. *Canadian Christianity*: December 2006.

page 854: "I'm never going to think of retirement . . ." McGuinn/Tobler. London: 14 June 1997.

NOTES

Epilogue

page 855: "Jim was very successful with women . . ." Jimmy Weston Gavin, interviewed by the author. London: 15 June 2011.

page 856: "George Buchanan was my most famous ancestor . . ." Dickson/Rogan. London/Hawaii: 7 July 1997. Dickson spoke a lot about the history of his family and had once visited Scotland to learn more about the Buchanan clan. At one point, I conducted some research on his behalf in return for material on the Byrds. Dickson told me his father was a diesel engineer and an inventor. His mother taught typing and was principal at a night school, among other things. Jim learned printing as a boy and "ended up putting out the school newspaper." Subsequently, he attended trade school, but was always a reluctant pupil. "I wanted to be a beachcomber," he concluded.

page 856: "There was no sign outside the club . . ." Gavin/Rogan. London: 15 June 2011.

page 857: "We were all making folk records . . ." Dickson/Rogan. London/Costa Mesa, California: 24 May 2009.

page 857: "That was the end all . . ." ibid.

page 857: "Dylan liked covering his bases . . ." ibid.

page 858: " 'Mr Tambourine Man' was more important . . ." Dickson/Rogan. Waldport, Oregon: 26–30 April 1989.

page 859: "In 1975 I took the advice . . ." Dickson/Rogan. London/Costa Mesa, California: 9 November 2009.

page 859: "Robin used to say . . ." Dickson/Rogan. London/Costa Mesa, California: 10 January 2006.

page 859: "Please talk to him . . ." Crosby/Rogan. London: 22–23 April 1980.

page 859: "He's more articulate than any of us . . ." ibid.

page 860: ". . . those good Scottish genes . . ." Dickson/Rogan. London/Costa Mesa, California: 10 January 2006.

page 861: "Well, I'm glad I did something . . ." Dickson/Rogan. Waldport, Oregon: 26–30 April 1989.

page 862: "McGuinn seems to survive . . ." Dickson/Rogan. London/Hawaii: 7 July 1997.

page 862: "I was back living in North Hollywood . . ." Dickson/Rogan. London/Hawaii: 3 August 1998.

page 862: "I'll probably go back to California someday . . ." Dickson/Rogan. London/Hawaii: 7 July 1997.

page 862: "David Crosby knows now that I'm very hostile . . ." ibid.

page 863: "When David was angry with McGuinn . . ." ibid.
page 863: "I used to think David was devious . . ." ibid.
page 864: "David has all these pieces in his head . . ." Dickson/Rogan. London/Costa Mesa, California: 24 May 2009. Plus personal correspondence.
page 865: "Somehow, I'm surviving . . ." Dickson/Rogan. London/Costa Mesa, California: 10 July 2006.
page 865: "He was sick for a while . . ." ibid.
page 865: "I've had lots of talks and long emails with Camilla . . ." ibid.
page 866: "Chris talked about the past . . ." ibid.
page 866: ". . . keep the other members in line . . ." ibid.
page 866: "Chris surprised me a little bit . . ." ibid.
page 867: "I've been trying to call you for months . . ." Dickson/Rogan. London/Costa Mesa, California: 10 January 2006.
page 867: "I wanted to hang them in the square . . ." Dickson/Rogan. London/Costa Mesa, California: 8 November 2009.
page 867: "The last statement they sent me . . ." Dickson/Rogan. London/Costa Mesa, California: 24 May 2009.
page 867: "It's like a transition from folk to rock . . ." Dickson/Rogan. London/Costa Mesa, California: 10 January 2006.
page 867: "There were also some Hamilton Camp outtakes . . ." ibid.
page 868: "I asked McGuinn's permission . . ." Dickson/Rogan. London/Costa Mesa, California: 24 May 2009.
page 868: "He'd walked out of that session . . ." ibid. But did Crosby play on the session? "No, he didn't," Dickson confirmed. Later, I unearthed an interview I'd conducted with Dickson a decade earlier (7 July 1997) where he told me: "We went into RCA and cut 'Eight Miles High', 'Why' and 'The Times They Are A-Changin''. I've got the track still. I put Hamilton Camp on it just to see how it would work because we had the track done. When we went into RCA there was a big row with Crosby as soon as it was done because he didn't want me cutting 'The Times They Are A-Changin'' and he walked out without doing the vocal . . . Crosby would sabotage tracks when he didn't like the songs being done." The above seems to imply (although it's by no means entirely clear) that Crosby did play on the backing track, then declined to cut the vocal track. I strongly suspect that Dickson conveniently forgot this and, in order not to have to contact Crosby in 2007, convinced himself that he didn't play on the track either.
page 868: "Human lives . . ." Crosby/Rogan. London: 22–23 April 1980.
page 868: "My life's not too bad . . ." Dickson/Rogan. London/Costa Mesa, California: 5 April 2009.

NOTES

page 869: "I had a big row with Chris Hillman . . ." ibid.

page 869: "It was a Chris . . ." ibid.

page 869: "I went many years without talking to Chris . . ." ibid. Dickson spoke a lot about Hillman and Crosby to me in interviews stretching back to the Eighties. Much of the material was outside the limited scope of this study, but there were a substantial number of revealing anecdotes and insights into their respective personalities. It was all fascinating stuff but way beyond the confines of a group biography like this one. As with Dickson's observations about his time with Gene Clark and Michael Clarke, these extensive accounts have been saved for separate studies of the individuals concerned. This meant further research from me and multi-perspectives from a longer cast of contributors. It's a long and ongoing process. The Clark and Clarke material has already been written and will no doubt follow in *Volume 2*. Much of the Hillman/Crosby research remains locked in my archive and, along with similar material on McGuinn, can only be properly documented in the unlikely event of a third volume in this series. That can only happen after the deaths of the surviving members, as will be evident from the lay-out of material in the next volume. The 'Requiem' theme is all important. Whether I'll still be alive to complete the work is quite another matter, but it is many years away. As ever, it's all about time and death for all of us.

page 869: "I'm 78 now . . ." Dickson/Rogan. London/Costa Mesa, California: 24 May 2009.

page 870: "That's how we got in touch . . ." Gavin/Rogan. London: 15 June 2011.

page 870: "I used to have an extremely powerful voice . . ." ibid.

page 872: "Jim sadly died alone . . ." email from John Delgatto, dated 2 May 2011.

page 872: "Technical . . ." Gavin/Rogan. London: 15 June 2011.

BYRDS SESSIONOGRAPHY

The Columbia/Asylum Recordings, 1965–72, plus the Nashville reunion, 1990.

There are slight variants in precise US release dates of the following albums: *Younger Than Yesterday*, *The Notorious Byrd Brothers*, *Dr Byrds & Mr Hyde*, *Ballad Of Easy Rider* and *(Untitled)*. In this section, I have used most of the dates featured on the notes of Sony CD reissues. See the Albums section for the alternative dates provided by CBS/Columbia at the end of the Sixties which are arguably more accurate.

Usual Personnel: Jim McGuinn (lead 12-string and six-string guitar, vocals); David Crosby (six-string, occasional 12-string guitar, vocals); Gene Clark (vocals, tambourine); Chris Hillman (bass) and Michael Clarke (drums, percussion).

Mr Tambourine Man
Columbia CL 2372 (mono)/CS 9172 (stereo) (US).
CBS BPG 62571 (mono)/SBPG 62571 (stereo) (UK).
Released 21 June 1965 (US).
Released 20 August 1965 (UK).
Recorded at Columbia Studios, Hollywood.
Producer: Terry Melcher.
Engineer: Ray Gerhardt.

Singles from the LP sessions:
'Mr Tambourine Man'/'I Knew I'd Want You'
Columbia 43271 (US)/CBS 201765 (UK).
Released 12 April 1965 (US).
Released 15 May 1965 (UK).

'All I Really Want To Do'/'Feel A Whole Lot Better'
Columbia 43332 (US)/CBS 201796 (UK).
Released 14 June 1965 (US).
Released 6 August 1965 (UK).

BYRDS SESSIONOGRAPHY

Sessions:
20 January 1965. Jim McGuinn (12-string guitar); Jerry Cole (rhythm guitar); Larry Knechtel (bass); Leon Russell (electric piano); Bill Pittman (guitar); Hal Blaine (drums).
72245 'Mr Tambourine Man' single 43271, LP.
72246 'I Knew I'd Want You' single 43271, LP.

8 March 1965. Usual personnel.
72425 'All I Really Want To Do' LP.
72426 'It's No Use' (version I) CD reissue.
72427 'You And Me' unreleased (backing track CD reissue).
72428 'You Won't Have To Cry' (version I) rejected.
72429 'She Has A Way' *Never Before*.
―――― 'She Has A Way' overdub CD reissue.

14 April 1965. Usual personnel.
72493 'It's No Use' (version II) LP.
―――― 'It's No Use' CD reissue.
72494 'The Bells Of Rhymney' LP.
72495 'Feel A Whole Lot Better' single 43332, LP.
72496 'Words And Pictures' unreleased.
72497 'You Won't Have To Cry' (version II) LP.
―――― 'You Won't Have To Cry' CD reissue
72498 'Spanish Harlem Incident' LP.
72499 'I Love The Life I Live' unreleased.
72500 'We'll Meet Again' LP.
―――― 'All I Really Want To Do' alternate take single.
―――― 'Feel A Whole Lot Better' alternate version, CD reissue.

22 April 1965. Usual personnel.
72501 'Chimes Of Freedom' LP.
72502 'Don't Doubt Yourself Babe' LP.
72503 'Here Without You' LP.

Turn! Turn! Turn!
Columbia CL 2454 (mono)/CS 9254 (stereo) (US).
CBS BPG 62652 (mono)/SPBG 62652 (stereo) (UK).
Released 6 December 1965 (US).
Released 22 March 1966 (UK).
Recorded at Columbia Studios, Hollywood.
Producer: Terry Melcher.
Engineer: Ray Gerhardt.

REQUIEM FOR THE TIMELESS — VOLUME 1

Singles from the LP sessions:
'Turn! Turn! Turn!'/'She Don't Care About Time'
Columbia 43424 (US)/CBS 202008 (UK).
Released 1 October 1965 (US).
Released 29 October 1965 (UK).

'It Won't Be Wrong'/'Set You Free This Time'
Columbia 43501 (US)/CBS 202037 (UK).
Released 10 January 1966 (US).
Released 11 February 1966 (UK).

Sessions:
28 June 1965. Usual personnel.
72646 'The Flower Bomb Song' unreleased.
72647 'The Times They Are A-Changin'' (version I) CD reissue.
72648 'She Don't Care About Time' (version I) *The Byrds* box set.
—— 'She Don't Care About Time' (take 1), CD reissue.
72649 'It's All Over Now, Baby Blue' (version I) *Never Before.*
—— 'It's All Over Now, Baby Blue' (take 1), CD reissue.

23 August 1965. Usual personnel.
72728 'The Times They Are A-Changin'' (version II) rejected.
72729 'She Don't Care About Time' (version II) single 43424.
72730 'The World Turns All Around Her' (version I) LP.
—— 'The World Turns All Around Her' (bongo mix), *The Byrds* box set.
—— 'The World Turns All Around Her' (alternate bongo mix), CD reissue.

August 1965. Usual personnel; produced by Jim Dickson and the Byrds; engineered by Tom May.
—— 'It's All Over Now, Baby Blue' (version II) unreleased.

Note: announced on the radio as a new single release but was never scheduled for release. Another candidate for the next Byrds' single was 'The Times They Are A-Changin'' b/w 'She Don't Care About Time'. Columbia Records printed a substantial number of sleeves for the proposed single and it was even given a serial number, Columbia 4-43391, but was subsequently withdrawn.

27 August, 1 September 1965. Usual personnel.
72732   'The Times They Are A-Changin'' (version III) unfinished.
(72734) 'Turn! Turn! Turn!' unfinished.

10 September, 14–16 September 1965. Usual personnel. Add harmonica -1 (Michael Clarke).
72733 'The World Turns All Around Her' (version II) rejected.
72734 'Turn! Turn! Turn!' single 43424, LP.
72736 'It Won't Be Wrong' single 43501, LP.
72737 'Satisfied Mind' unfinished.
72738 'Set You Free This Time' -1, single 43501, LP.
72739 'I Don't Ever Want To Spoil Your Party' unreleased.
72740 'Stranger In A Strange Land' unreleased.
——— 'The Day Walk' ('Never Before') *Never Before*.

18 September. Usual personnel.
——— 'Stranger In A Strange Land' (backing track, take 10), CD reissue.

1 October, 4 October 1965. Usual personnel. Add banjo -1 (McGuinn).
87510 'Wait And See' LP.
87511 'Oh! Susannah' -1, unfinished.

18 October, 20 October, 22 October 1965. Usual personnel.
(87511) 'Oh! Susannah' LP.
87518 'If You're Gone' LP.
87519 'Lay Down Your Weary Tune' LP.

27 October, 28 October 1965. Usual personnel.
——— 'Circle Of Minds' unreleased.
(72732) 'The Times They Are A-Changin'' (version III) LP.
(72737) 'Satisfied Mind' LP.

1 November 1965. Usual personnel.
87528 'He Was A Friend Of Mine' LP.

Fifth Dimension
Columbia CL 2549 (mono)/CS 9349 (stereo) (US).
CBS BPG 62783 (mono)/SPBG 62783 (stereo) (UK).
Released 18 July 1966 (US).
Released 22 September 1966 (UK).
Recorded at Columbia Studios, Hollywood, except where noted.
Producer: Allen Stanton.
Engineer: Ray Gerhardt.

Singles from the LP sessions:
'Eight Miles High'/'Why' (original take)
Columbia 43578 (US)/CBS 202067 (UK).
Released 14 March 1966 (US).
Released 29 April 1966 (UK).

'5 D (Fifth Dimension)'/'Captain Soul'
Columbia 43702 (US)/CBS 202259 (UK).
Released 13 June 1966 (US).
Released 29 July 1966 (UK).

'Mr Spaceman'/'What's Happening?!?!'
Columbia 43766 (US)/CBS 202295 (UK).
Released 6 September 1966 (US).
Released 14 October 1966 (UK).

Sessions:
22 December 1965. Usual personnel. Recorded at RCA Studios, Hollywood. Producer: Jim Dickson. Engineer: Dave Hassinger. Final mix 4 January 1966.
—— 'Eight Miles High' (version I) *Never Before*.
—— 'Why' (version I) *Never Before*.
—— 'The Times They Are A-Changin'' (version IV) unfinished.

24 January, 25 January 1966. Usual personnel.
87687 'Why' (version II) single 43578.
87690 'Eight Miles High' (version II) single 43578, LP.
—— 'Why' (instrumental, take 17) *Another Dimension*.
—— 'Eight Miles High' (instrumental, take 2), *Another Dimension*.

21 February 1966. Usual personnel. Add banjo -1.
87722   'John Riley' (version I) -1, rejected.
——   'John Riley' (instrumental, take 2) *Another Dimension*.
(87796) 'I Know My Rider' (version I) unfinished.

Gene Clark leaves the group at this point.

Personnel: Jim McGuinn (lead 12-string and six-string guitar, vocals); David Crosby (six-string, occasional 12-string guitar, vocals); Chris Hillman (bass) and Michael Clarke (drums, percussion).

28 April, 29 April, 3–6 May 1966. Usual personnel. Add strings -1, clavier -2, harmonica -3 (Michael Clarke), sound effects -4, cowbell -5.
87796 'I Know My Rider' (version I) unfinished.
—— 'I Know My Rider' (instrumental, take 9) *Another Dimension*.
87800 'Mr Spaceman' single 43766, LP.
87801 'What's Happening?!?!' single 43766, LP.
—— 'What's Happening?!?!' *Another Dimension*.
87802 '2-4-2 Fox Trot (The Lear Jet Song)' -4, LP.

―――― '2-4-2 Fox Trot (The Lear Jet Song)' (instrumental, long version). *Another Dimension*.
87803 'John Riley' (version II) -1, CD reissue.
―――― 'John Riley' (instrumental), *Another Dimension*.
87804 'Wild Mountain Thyme' -1, unfinished.
―――― 'Wild Mountain Thyme' (instrumental), *Another Dimension*.
87805 'Hey Joe' -5, unfinished.
87806 'I Come And Stand At Every Door' unfinished.
(87876) 'I See You' unfinished.
―――― 'I See You' (instrumental), *Another Dimension*.
(87877) 'Captain Soul' -3, unfinished.
―――― 'Captain Soul' -3, *Another Dimension*.

12 May, 16–19 May 1966. Usual personnel.
(87796) 'I Know My Rider' (version I) unreleased.
(87804) 'Wild Mountain Thyme' unfinished.
(87805) 'Hey Joe' LP.
(87806) 'I Come And Stand At Every Door' LP.
87876 'I See You' LP.
87877 'Captain Soul' -3, single 43702, LP.

24 May, 25 May 1966. Usual personnel, plus Van Dyke Parks (organ, electric piano -1).
(87803) 'John Riley' (version II) LP.
(87804) 'Wild Mountain Thyme' LP.
87883 '5 D (Fifth Dimension)' -1, single 43702, LP.

Interim Unreleased Single Session:
28 July 1966. Usual personnel. Producer: Allen Stanton. Engineer: Ray Gerhardt.
87993 'I Know My Rider' (version II) *Never Before* CD.
87994 'Psychodrama City' *Never Before* (edited)/*The Byrds* box set (extended)/CD reissue (extended).
―――― 'Psychodrama City' (instrumental, take 1) *Another Dimension*.

Younger Than Yesterday
Columbia CL 2642 (mono)/CS 9442 (stereo) (US).
CBS BPG 62988 (mono)/SPBG 62988 (stereo) (US).
Released 20 February 1967 (US).
Released 7 April 1967 (UK).
Recorded at Columbia Studios, Hollywood.
Producer: Gary Usher.
Engineer: Tom May.

REQUIEM FOR THE TIMELESS — VOLUME 1

Singles from the LP sessions:
'So You Want To Be A Rock 'n' Roll Star'/'Everybody's Been Burned'
Columbia 43987 (US)/CBS 202559 (UK).
Released 9 January 1967 (US).
Released 17 February 1967 (UK).

'My Back Pages'/'Renaissance Fair'
Columbia 44054 (US)/CBS 2468 (UK).
Released 13 March 1967 (US).
Released 12 May 1967 (UK).

'Have You Seen Her Face'/'Don't Make Waves'
Columbia 44157 (US only).
Released 22 May 1967 (US).

28–30 November, 1 December 1966. Usual personnel plus Clarence White (guitar -1), Vern Gosdin (guitar -1), Hugh Masekela (trumpet -2). Add oscillator -3.
88324 'So You Want To Be A Rock 'n' Roll Star' -2, single 43987, LP.
88329 'Have You Seen Her Face' single 44157, LP.
88331 'Milestones' unreleased.
88388 'Time Between' -1, LP.
88389 'Mind Gardens' LP.
—— 'Mind Gardens' alternate version, CD reissue.
88390 'CTA 102' -3, LP.

5–8 December 1966. Usual personnel plus Jay Migliori (sax -1), Clarence White (guitar -2).
88395 'My Back Pages' single 44054, LP.
—— 'My Back Pages' alternate version, CD reissue.
88396 'Thoughts And Words' LP.
88397 'Renaissance Fair' -1, single 44054, LP.
88398 'Everybody's Been Burned' single 43987, LP.
88399 'It Happens Each Day' *Never Before*.
88400 'The Girl With No Name' -2, LP.
—— 'Why' (version III) LP.

3 February 1967. Usual personnel. Add overdubbed organ.
(88395) 'My Back Pages' rejected.

The Notorious Byrd Brothers
Columbia CL 2775 (mono)/CS 9575 (stereo) (US).
CBS 63169 (mono)/S 63169 (stereo) (UK).

Released 3 January 1968 (US).
Released 12 April 1968 (UK).
Recorded at Columbia Studios, Hollywood.
Producer: Gary Usher.
Engineers: Tom May and Don Thompson, except where noted.

Singles from the LP sessions:
'Lady Friend'/'Old John Robertson'
Columbia 44230 (US only).
Released 13 July 1967 (US).

'Lady Friend'/'Don't Make Waves'
CBS 2924 (UK only).
Released 1 September 1967.

'Goin' Back'/'Change Is Now'
Columbia 44362 (US)/CBS 3093 (UK).
Released 20 October 1967 (US).
Released 22 December 1967 (UK).

Sessions:
26 April 1967. Usual personnel.
94793 'Don't Make Waves' single 44157.
—— alternate take MGM LP 4483 (released 5 July 1967).
94794 'Lady Friend' unfinished.

Note: various overdubs were attempted on 'Lady Friend' on 4 May, 10 May, 23 May and 5 June, all incomplete.

14 June, 21 June 1967. Usual personnel. Add string quartet (-1). Add trumpets (-2).
(94794) 'Lady Friend' -2, single 44230.
94897 'Old John Robertson' -1, single 44230.
—— alternate mix with phasing added on LP.

31 July, 1–3 August 1967. Usual personnel, except Crosby plays bass and Hillman six-string guitar (-1), plus Clarence White (guitar -1). Add mandolin, brass (-2). Gunshots (-2) courtesy of Firesign Theatre.
94922 'Change Is Now' ('Universal Mind Decoder'), backing track, -1, CD reissue.
94923 'Draft Morning' -2, backing track/LP. Plus alternate end on CD reissue. Vocals added some time in October.

Note: further work on 'Change Is Now' was done on 14 August 1967.

14–18 August 1967. Usual personnel, except Jim Gordon replaces Michael Clarke (drums). Add piano (-1).
94926 'Dolphin's Smile' LP.
94927 'Tribal Gathering' -1, unfinished.
94928 'Triad' *Never Before*.

Note: further overdubs of 'Tribal Gathering' were attempted on 29–30 August and 29–30 November 1967, all unfinished.

29–30 August 1967. Usual personnel, plus Clarence White (guitar), Red Rhodes (pedal steel guitar), David Crosby (bass).
(94922) 'Change Is Now' single 44362, LP.

5–6 September 1967. Usual personnel, except Jim Gordon replaces Michael Clarke (drums). Add Red Rhodes (pedal steel guitar), Paul Beaver (Moog synthesizer), Dennis McCarthy (celeste), Ann Stockton (harp) and Lester Harris (cello). David Crosby, although present, did not participate.
95118 'Goin' Back' (version I) CD reissue.

David Crosby leaves the group at this point and Gene Clark returns primarily for live performances but leaves again within a few weeks.

9, 11, 16 October 1967. Usual personnel, except Jim Gordon replaces Michael Clarke (drums). Add Red Rhodes (pedal steel guitar), Paul Beaver (Moog synthesizer), Dennis McCarthy (celeste), Ann Stockton (harp), Lester Harris (cello), James Burton (guitar), Terry Trotter (piano), Victor Sazer (violin), Carl West (violin), Dennis Faust (percussion).
95175 'Goin' Back' (version II) single 44362, LP.

23, 30 October, 1 November 1967. Usual personnel. Add Moog synthesizer. Add conga, resonators, electric bongo, electric tabla (-1). Roy Halee, engineer.
95281 'Space Odyssey' LP.
95287 'Moog Raga' -1, *Never Before* (CD).

1 November. Usual personnel.
—— 'Bound To Fall' backing track, CD reissue.

13 November 1967. Usual personnel, except Hal Blaine replaces Michael Clarke (drums). Add Clarence White (guitar -1), Curt Boettcher (backing vocals -1), William Armstrong, Alfred McKibbon, Raymond Kelley, Paul Bergstrom, Jacqueline Lustgarten (strings -1). Vocal processing "through Leslie speakers".
95296 'Get To You' -1 LP.
95297 'Flight 713 (Song No. 2)' *Never Before* CD.

BYRDS SESSIONOGRAPHY

29, 30 November 1967. Usual personnel, except Jim Gordon replaces Michael Clarke (drums). Add Clarence White (guitar -1). Add Moog synthesizer, strings (-2).
93504 'Natural Harmony' -2 LP.
93588 'Wasn't Born To Follow' -1, LP.

5 December, 6 December 1967. Usual personnel. Add Barry Goldberg (piano -1), Gary Weber, Roy Caron, Jay Migliori, Virgil Fums, Richard Hyde (brass -1). Roy Halee, engineer.
(94927) 'Tribal Gathering' LP.
93508 'Artificial Energy' -1, Single 44499, LP.

Michael Clarke leaves the group at this point.

Due to the various comings and goings throughout this turbulent period complete line-ups were not present during the final stages of the recording of *The Notorious Byrd Brothers*. Gene Clark is not registered as appearing on any of the songs recorded, although he was at least present in the studio in October during the final run-through of 'Goin' Back'. Some of Crosby's contributions consisted of a mixture of vocals and backing tracks. As explained in the main text, the Byrds completed 'Draft Morning' with their own lyrics and vocals but Crosby now confirms that he played on the cut, thus verifying the above information: "We cut the track before I left. As I remember we did, then they re-did the vocals. They changed the lyrics, but we cut the instrumental track first. That would explain it. That's what happened." An interview with McGuinn at the time of the album's release (when he could accurately remember the participants' individual contributions) also tallies with the information contained herein: "Crosby's on nothing on the first side of the album. He's on 'Change Is Now' singing harmony, 'Old John Robertson' on high harmony, singing lead with Chris on 'Tribal Gathering' and singing harmony on 'Dolphin's Smile'."

Sweetheart Of The Rodeo
Columbia CL 9670 (mono)/CS 9670 (stereo) (US).
CBS 63353 (mono)/S 63353 (stereo) (UK).
Released 30 August 1968 (US).
Released 27 September 1968 (UK).
Recorded at Columbia Studios, Nashville, Tennessee and Columbia Studios, Hollywood.
Producer: Gary Usher.
Engineers: Roy Halee and Charlie Bragg.

Singles from the LP sessions:
'You Ain't Going Nowhere'/'Artificial Energy'
Columbia 44499 (US)/CBS 3411 (UK).
Released 2 April 1968 (US).
Released 3 May 1968 (UK).

'I Am A Pilgrim'/'Pretty Boy Floyd'
Columbia 44643 (US)/CBS 3752 (UK).
Released 2 September 1968 (US).
Released 18 October 1968 (UK).

New personnel: Roger McGuinn (guitar); Chris Hillman (bass and mandolin); Gram Parsons (guitar); Kevin Kelley (drums). Augmented by Earl P. Ball (piano); Jon Corneal (drums); Lloyd Green (steel guitar); John Hartford (banjo, guitar, fiddle); Roy M. Huskey (bass); Jaydee Maness (steel guitar); Clarence J. White (guitar).

Sessions:
9 March 1968. Usual personnel.
98261 'You Ain't Going Nowhere' single 44499, LP.
98262 'Hickory Wind' LP.
—— 'Hickory Wind' alternate 'Nashville' version (take 8) *Sweetheart Of The Rodeo* Legacy edition.

11 March 1968. Usual personnel.
98263 'Lazy Days' *The Byrds* box set.
—— 'Lazy Days' alternate version *Sweetheart Of The Rodeo* Legacy edition.
—— 'Lazy Days' Sundazed single version.

12 March 1968. Usual personnel.
98264 'Pretty Boy Floyd' single 44643, LP.

13 March 1968. Usual personnel.
98265 'I Am A Pilgrim' single 44643, LP.
98266 'Pretty Polly' *The Byrds* box set.
—— 'Pretty Polly' alternate version *Sweetheart Of The Rodeo* Legacy edition.

14 March 1968. Usual personnel.
98267 'Reputation' *The Byrds* box set.
—— 'Reputation' vocal take, Sundazed single.
98268 'Nothing Was Delivered' LP.

4 April 1968. Usual personnel.
97169 'Life In Prison' LP.
—— rehearsal take included on CD reissue.
—— rehearsal takes 1–4 included on *Sweetheart Of The Rodeo* Legacy edition.

15, 17, 24 April 1968. Usual personnel.
97220 'You Don't Miss Your Water' LP.
97260 'The Christian Life' LP.
—— rehearsal take included on CD reissue.
—— 'The Christian Life' *Sweetheart Of The Rodeo* Legacy edition.
—— rehearsal version, takes 7 and 8.
97319 'You're Still On My Mind' LP.
—— rehearsal take included on CD reissue.
—— rehearsal take 13 and take 48 on *Sweetheart Of The Rodeo* Legacy edition.
97323 'Blue Canadian Rockies' LP.
—— rehearsal version, take 14 on *Sweetheart Of The Rodeo* Legacy edition.

1 May. Usual personnel.
—— 'All I Have Are Memories' instrumental, CD reissue.
—— 'All I Have Are Memories' instrumental, takes 17 and 21 on *Sweetheart Of The Rodeo* Legacy Edition.
—— 'All I Have Are Memories' vocal version master take on *Sweetheart Of The Rodeo* Legacy Edition.

27 May 1968. Usual personnel.
97335 'One Hundred Years From Now' LP.
—— 'One Hundred Years From Now' *The Byrds* box set.
—— plus overdubbing on 97220.
—— rehearsal take included on CD reissue.
—— rehearsal takes 12–15 included on *Sweetheart Of The Rodeo* Legacy edition.

Gram Parsons, Kevin Kelley and Chris Hillman leave during the time between this and the next recording.

Dr Byrds & Mr Hyde
Columbia CL 9755 (mono)/CS 9755 (stereo) (US).
CBS 63545 (mono)/S 63545 (stereo) (UK).
Released 3 February 1969 (US).
Released 25 April 1969 (UK).
Recorded Columbia Studios, Hollywood.
Producer: Bob Johnston.
Engineers: David Diller, Tom May and Neil Wilburn.

Single from the LP sessions:
'Bad Night At The Whiskey'/'Drug Store Truck Drivin' Man'
Columbia 44746 (US)/CBS 4055 (UK).

Released 7 January 1969 (US).
Released 7 March 1969 (UK).

New personnel: Roger McGuinn (guitar, vocals); Clarence White (lead guitar); Gene Parsons (drums, guitar, five-string banjo); John York (vocals, bass).

Sessions:
7 October 1968. Usual personnel.
97734 'Old Blue' single 44868, LP.
97735 'King Apathy III' LP.

8 October 1968. Usual personnel.
97736 'Drug Store Truck Drivin' Man' single 44746, LP.
97737 'This Wheel's On Fire' unfinished.

14 October 1968. Usual personnel.
97749 'Your Gentle Way Of Loving Me' LP.

15 October 1968. Usual personnel.
97750 'Nashville West' LP.
97751 'Bad Night At The Whiskey' single 44746, LP.

16 October 1968. Usual personnel.
97752 'Stanley's Song' *The Byrds* box set.

21 October 1968. Usual personnel. Add Jacques Levy (screams -1). Recorded Music Row, Nashville, Tennessee.
——— 'Nashville West' -1, alternate version, Nashville recording, CD reissue.

4 December 1968. Usual personnel. Add brass and orchestration (-1)
97857   'This Wheel's On Fire' LP.
——— 'This Wheel's On Fire' alternate version, CD reissue.
97858   'Medley: 'My Back Pages'/'B.J. Blues'/'Baby, What Do You Want Me To Do' LP.
——— 'Medley: 'My Back Pages'/'B.J. Blues'/'Baby, What Do You Want Me To Do', alternate version, CD reissue.
97951   'Child Of The Universe' LP.
——— 'Child Of The Universe' -1, *Candy* soundtrack.
100506 'Candy' LP (edited), CD reissue (extended version).

Ballad Of Easy Rider
Columbia 9942 (stereo) (US).
CBS S 63795 (stereo) (UK).
Released 27 October 1969 (US).

Released 16 January 1970 (UK).
Recorded Columbia Studios, Hollywood.
Producer: Terry Melcher.
Engineer: Jerry Hochman.

Singles from the LP sessions:
'Lay Lady Lay'/'Old Blue'
Columbia 44868 (US)/CBS 4284 (UK).
Released 2 May 1969 (US).
Released 6 June 1969 (UK).

'Wasn't Born To Follow'/'Child Of The Universe'
CBS 4572 (UK only).
Released 26 September 1969 (UK).

'Ballad Of Easy Rider'/'Oil In My Lamp'*
Columbia 44990 (US only).
Released 1 October 1969 (US).
*Note: some copies of Columbia 44990 were released with 'Wasn't Born To Follow' in place of 'Oil In My Lamp'.

'Jesus Is Just Alright'/'It's All Over Now, Baby Blue'
Columbia 45071 (US)/CBS 4753 (UK).
Released 15 December 1969 (US).
Released 20 February 1970 (UK).

Usual personnel: Roger McGuinn (vocals, guitar, synthesizer); Clarence White (lead guitar, vocals); Gene Parsons (drums, guitar, vocals, five-string banjo); John York (vocals, bass). Parsons claims McGuinn did not participate on 'There Must Be Someone' and 'Gunge Din'.

Sessions:
27 March 1969. Usual personnel.
———— 'Lay Lady Lay' *The Byrds* box set.

18 April 1969. Usual personnel. Add female chorus.
105809 'Lay Lady Lay' single 44868.

17 June 1969. Usual personnel.
106034 'Jesus Is Just Alright' single 45071, LP.

18 June 1969. Usual personnel. Add strings.
106035 'Ballad Of Easy Rider' single 44990, LP.
———— 'Ballad Of Easy Rider' long version, CD reissue.
106036 'Jack Tarr The Sailor' unfinished.

19 June 1969. Usual personnel.
106039 'Oil In My Lamp' *The Byrds* box set.
106040 'Deportee (Plane Wreck At Los Gatos)' unfinished.

23 June 1969. Usual personnel.
(106040) 'Deportee (Plane Wreck At Los Gatos)' LP.
106041 'Build It Up' CD reissue.
106042 'Way Behind The Sun' *The Byrds* box set.

24 June 1969. Usual personnel.
106043 'Fiddler A Dram (Moog Experiment)' CD reissue.
106044 'There Must Be Someone' unfinished.

1 July 1969. Usual personnel.
(106036) 'Jack Tarr The Sailor' LP.
(106039) 'Oil In My Lamp' single 44990, LP.

2 July 1969. Usual personnel.
(106044) 'There Must Be Someone' LP.

22 July 1969. Usual personnel.
106139 'It's All Over Now, Baby Blue' single 45071, LP.

23 July 1969. Usual personnel. Add Byron Berline fiddle.
104002 'Tulsa County Blue' LP.
——— 'Tulsa County (Blue)' alternate version, CD reissue.

24 July 1969. Usual personnel. Add Glen Hardin (Hammond organ, -1).
104003 'Gunga Din' -1, LP.

28 July 1969. Usual personnel.
104027 'Mae Jean Goes To Hollywood' *The Byrds* box set.

15 August 1969. Usual personnel.
104030 'Fido' LP.

26 August 1969. Usual personnel.
104040 'Armstrong, Aldrin And Collins' LP.

John York leaves at this point.

(Untitled)
Columbia G 30127 (stereo) (US).
CBS S 64095 (stereo) (UK).
Released 16 September 1970 (US).
Released 13 November 1970 (UK).
Recorded Columbia Studios, Hollywood.

Producers: Terry Melcher and Jim Dickson.
Engineer: Chris Hinshaw.

Single from the LP sessions:
'Chestnut Mare'/'Just A Season'
Columbia 45259 (US)/CBS 5322 (UK).
Released 23 October 1970 (US).
Released 1 January 1971 (UK).

New personnel: Roger McGuinn (vocals, guitar, synthesizer); Clarence White (vocals, guitar); Gene Parsons (drums, guitar, vocals, five-string banjo); Skip Battin (bass, vocals).

1 March 1970. Live material recorded at Felt Forum, Madison Square Garden Center, New York.
——— 'You Ain't Going Nowhere' CD *(Untitled)/(Unissued)*.
——— 'Old Blue' CD *(Untitled)/(Unissued)*.
——— 'It's All Right Ma (I'm Only Bleeding)' CD *(Untitled)/(Unissued)*.
——— 'Ballad Of Easy Rider' CD *(Untitled)/(Unissued)*.
——— 'My Back Pages' CD *(Untitled)/(Unissued)*.
——— 'This Wheel's On Fire' CD *(Untitled)/(Unissued)*.

Sessions:
26–28 May, 31 May 1970. Add Gram Parsons, backing vocals (-1); Byron Berline, fiddle (-2), Sneaky Pete Kleinow, steel guitar (-3). Parsons claims McGuinn did not appear on 'Yesterday's Train'.
106946 'All The Things' -1, CD *(Untitled)/(Unissued)*.
107027 'Lover Of The Bayou', CD *(Untitled)/(Unissued)*.
107030 'Yesterday's Train', CD *(Untitled)/(Unissued)*.
107032 'You All Look Alike' -2, unfinished.
107036 'Yesterday's Train' -3, LP.
107037 'Hungry Planet' LP.
107038 'Willin'' CD *(Untitled)/(Unissued)*.
107039 'Well Come Back Home' LP.

1–5 June, 9 June, 11 June 1970. Usual personnel. Add Gram Parsons, backing vocals (-1), Byron Berline, fiddle (-2). Includes live material recorded in concert at Queen's College, New York, 28 February 1970.
106946 'All The Things' -1, LP.
106996 '15 Minute Jam' *The Byrds* box set (extracted as 'White's Lightning').
106996 'White's Lightning Part 2' CD *(Untitled)/(Unissued)*.
107011 'Willin'' *The Byrds* box set.
107012 'Take A Whiff (On Me)' LP.

107027 'Lover Of The Bayou' LP.
107032 'You All Look Alike' -2, LP.
107630 'Just A Season' single 45259, LP.
107631 'Chestnut Mare' LP.
——— 'Chestnut Mare' edited single 45259.
107633 'Kathleen's Song' *The Byrds* box set.
107633 'Kathleen's Song' CD *(Untitled)/(Unissued)*.
107642 'Truck Stop Girl' LP.
107645 'Amazing Grace' bonus track *(Untitled)/(Unissued)*.
107646 'Eight Miles High' rejected.
107667 'Eight Miles High' LP.
107668 'Mr Tambourine Man' LP.
107669 'Mr Spaceman' LP.
107670 'It's Alright Ma (I'm Only Bleeding)' *(Untitled)/(Unissued)*.
107671 'Nashville West' LP.
107672 'So You Want To Be A Rock 'n' Roll Star' LP.
107673 'Positively 4th Street' LP.
107674 'Lover Of The Bayou' rejected.
——— 'Soldier's Joy'/'Black Mountain Rag' *The Byrds* box set.
——— 'Just Like A Woman' *The Byrds* box set.
——— 'You All Look Alike' *There Is A Season* box set.
——— 'Nashville West' *There Is A Season* box set.

23 September 1970. Live material recorded at Fillmore East, Manhattan, New York.
——— 'Take A Whiff (On Me)' CD remastered.
——— 'Jesus Is Just Alright' CD remastered.
——— 'Baby, What You Want Me To Do' *There Is A Season* box set.
——— 'I Trust' *There Is A Season* box set.

Byrdmaniax
Columbia KC 30640 (stereo) (US).
CBS S 64389 (stereo) (UK).
Released 23 June 1971 (US).
Released 6 August 1971 (UK).
Recorded Columbia Studios, Hollywood.
Producer: Terry Melcher.
Engineer: Chris Hinshaw.

Singles from the LP sessions:
'I Trust (Everything Is Gonna Work Out Alright)'/'(Is This) My Destiny'

BYRDS SESSIONOGRAPHY

CBS 7253 (UK only).
Released 7 May 1971 (UK).

'Glory, Glory'/'Citizen Kane'
Columbia 45440 (US)/CBS 7501 (UK).
Released 20 August 1971 (US).
Released 1 October 1971 (UK).

Sessions:
6 October 1970. Usual personnel. Add Terry Melcher (piano) and female chorus (-1)
107894 'I Trust (Everything's Gonna Work Out Alright)' -1, LP.
107895 'Think I'm Gonna Feel Better' CD remastered.

9 January 1971. Usual personnel.
110643 '(Is This) My Destiny' single 7501, LP.

11 January 1971. Usual personnel. Add Paul Polena, horns (-1); Paul Polena, string arrangement (-2), Larry Knechtel, organ (-3).
110650 'Citizen Kane' -1, single 45440, LP.
110652 'Absolute Happiness' -2, LP.
110655 'Tunnel Of Love' -3, LP.

17 January 1971. Usual personnel. Add Paul Polena, string arrangement (-1), female chorus (-2).
110639 'Just Like A Woman' CD, remastered
110640 'Jamaica Say You Will' -1, LP.
110641 'Glory, Glory' -2, single 45440, LP.

19 January 1971. Usual personnel.
110638 'I Wanna Grow Up To Be A Politician' LP.

24 January 1971. Usual personnel. Add Byron Berline, fiddle and Eric White, harmonica.
110649 'Green Apple Quick Step' LP.
——— 'Green Apple Quick Step' rehearsal, CD reissue.

26 January 1971. Usual personnel. Add Paul Polena, string arrangement (-1).
110658   'Pale Blue' -1, LP.
110658   'Pale Blue' CD remastered
(107633) 'Kathleen's Song' -1, LP.

Farther Along
Columbia KC 31050 (stereo) (US).
CBS S 64676 (UK).

REQUIEM FOR THE TIMELESS — VOLUME 1

Released 17 November 1971 (US).
Released 21 January 1972 (UK).
Recorded: CBS Studios, London.
Producer: The Byrds.
Engineer: Mike Ross.

Single from the LP sessions:
'America's Great National Pastime'/'Farther Along'
Columbia 45514 (US only; UK release cancelled).
Released 29 November 1971 (US).

Sessions:
22 July. Usual personnel.
115588 'Lazy Waters' LP.
115589 'Bugler' LP. Remixed in Hollywood, August 1971.
115590 'Antique Sandy' LP.

25 July. Usual personnel. Parsons claims McGuinn did not participate on 'B.B. Class Road'.
115543 'Farther Along' single 45514, LP.
115594 'Tiffany Queen' LP.
115595 'B.B. Class Road' LP.

27 July. Usual personnel. Except McGuinn was not featured on 'Bristol Steam Convention Blues'.
115591 'America's Great National Pastime' single 45514, LP. Remixed in Hollywood, August 1971.
115592 'Bristol Steam Convention Blues' LP.

28 July. Usual personnel.
115585 'So Fine' LP.
115586 'Get Down Your Line' LP.
115587 'Precious Kate' LP.

Earl Scruggs, His Family And Friends
Columbia 30584 (US).
CBS S 64777 (UK).
Released 20 October 1971 (US).
Released March 1972 (UK).
Recorded: Doug Underwood Ranch, Nashville.
Producer: Neil Wilburn.
Engineers: Ed Hudson and Freeman Ramsey.

BYRDS SESSIONOGRAPHY

Sessions:
26 April 1971. Usual personnel, augmented by Earl and Randy Scruggs and the Earl Scruggs Revue.
108783 'You Ain't Going Nowhere' LP.

28 April 1971. Usual personnel, augmented by Randy Scruggs.
108784 'Nothin' To It' LP.

The Final Columbia Sessions.

12 January 1972. Usual personnel, plus unknown session musicians.
115709 'Lost My Drivin' Wheel' *Farther Along* CD reissue.

18 April 1972. Usual personnel.
115930 'Born To Rock 'n' Roll' *Farther Along* CD reissue.

Gene Parsons leaves the group at this point.

July/August 1972. Recorded at Wally Heider's Studio. Usual personnel, except that John Guerin replaces Gene Parsons on drums.
———— 'Bag Full Of Money' *Farther Along* CD reissue.
———— 'Draggin'' unreleased.
———— 'I'm So Restless' unreleased.

Note: 'Born To Rock 'n' Roll' was intended as a single and would probably have been backed by 'Lost My Drivin' Wheel'. The tracks recorded during July/August 1972 were later salvaged and re-recorded for McGuinn's first solo album.

Byrds
Asylum SD 5058 (stereo) (US).
Asylum SYLA 8754 (stereo) (UK).
Released 7 March 1973 (US).
Released 24 March 1973 (UK).
Recorded Wally Heider's Recording Studio # 4, Hollywood.
Producer David Crosby.
Engineer Doc Storch (Sandy Fisher).
Second Engineer Raghu Markus.

Singles from the LP sessions:
'Full Circle'/'Long Live The King'
Asylum 11016 (US)/Asylum AYM 517 (UK).
Released 11 April 1973 (US).
Released 22 June 1973 (UK).

'Things Will Be Better'/'For Free'
Asylum AYM 516 (UK only).
Released 24 April 1973 (UK).

'Cowgirl In The Sand'/'Long Live The King'
Asylum 11019 (US only).
Released June 1973 (US).

'Full Circle'/'Things Will Be Better'
Asylum AYM 545 (UK only).
Released 6 July 1973 (UK). Reissued 8 August 1975 (UK).

Personnel: Roger McGuinn (six and 12-string electric/acoustic guitar, Moog, banjo, vocals); Gene Clark (six-string acoustic guitar, harmonica, tambourine, vocals); David Crosby (six and 12-string electric/acoustic guitar, vocals); Michael Clarke (drums, congas, percussion); Chris Hillman (six and 12-string electric/acoustic guitar, mandolin, bass, vocals).

Sessions:
October–November 1972. Personnel as above.
——— 'Full Circle' LP.
——— 'Sweet Mary' LP.
——— 'Changing Heart' LP.
——— 'For Free' LP.
——— 'Born To Rock 'n' Roll' LP.
——— 'Things Will Be Better' LP.
——— 'Cowgirl In The Sand' LP.
——— 'Long Live The King' LP.
——— 'Borrowing Time' LP.
——— 'Laughing' LP.
——— '(See The Sky) About To Rain' LP.
——— 'Fair And Tender Ladies' unreleased.

Tape reels indicate further work, possibly overdubbing, was done as follows:

2 November: 'Fair And Tender Ladies' (later version); 'Long Live The King' (early version); 'Fair And Tender Ladies' (early version); '(See The Sky) About To Rain'; 'Laughing' (later version); 'Long Live The King' (third version); 'Fair And Tender Ladies' (new version); 'Long Live The King' (with new acoustic guitar from Gene Clark).

3 November: 'Fair And Tender Ladies' (early version).

9 November: '(See The Sky) About To Rain' (Clark, McGuinn, Crosby, guitars).

13 November: 'Laughing' (Crosby and McGuinn, 12-string guitars).

15 November: 'Long Live The King' (third version: new 12-string guitar, Crosby).

On at least one of the takes of 'Cowgirl In The Sand', Johnny Barbata (drums) and Wilton Felder (bass) were featured, and Dallas Taylor supposedly added congas and possibly tambourine to 'Things Will Be Better'.

The Nashville Sessions.
McGuinn, Crosby and Hillman reunited under the Byrds' banner to record four songs for inclusion on:
The Byrds Box Set (Columbia/Legacy 46773) (US)/Columbia Legacy 4676112 (UK).
Released 19 October 1990 (US).
Released 7 December 1990 (UK).
Recorded: Treasure Isle Recorders, Nashville, Tennessee.
Producer: Don DeVito and "the Byrds": Roger McGuinn, David Crosby and Chris Hillman. Recorded by Ed Seay, assisted by Mike Poole, mixed by Tim Geelan.

Sessions:
6–8 August "Usual" personnel. Add John Jorgenson, mandolin, Stan Lynch, drums (-1), John Jorgenson, bass/lead guitar, Stan Lynch, drums and Al Kooper, keyboards, (-2).
——— 'He Was A Friend Of Mine' *The Byrds* box set.
——— 'Paths Of Victory' -1, *The Byrds* box set.
——— 'From A Distance' -1, *The Byrds* box set.
——— 'Love That Never Dies' -2, *The Byrds* box set.

In addition to all of the above, the Byrds also recorded countless undated tapes in their pre-Byrds days at World-Pacific, selections of which can be heard on *Preflyte*, *In The Beginning* and *The Preflyte Sessions*. Several live recordings have also been retrospectively unearthed and released under the Byrds' banner. These include some contributions from their radio appearance in Stockholm, Sweden on 28 February 1967 (broadcast 29 March) including 'Roll Over Beethoven' (*The Byrds* box set), 'He Was A Friend Of Mine' (*There Is A Season* box set) and 'Hey Joe' (*Another Dimension*). The appearances with *Earl Scruggs, His Family And Friends* and contributions to *Banjoman* are detailed in the 'Byrds Guest Slots/Rarities (Vinyl)' section. There are also two memorable live recordings *Live At The Fillmore – February 1969* (issued in 2000) and *Live At The Royal Albert Hall 1971* (issued 2008), plus the single 'Lover Of The Bayou' b/w 'You Ain't Going Nowhere' (titled *Live In Holland 1971*) also issued in 2008.

BYRDS UNRELEASED MATERIAL

Following the CD remastered series of the original Byrds' albums, with extensive bonus tracks and the two box sets, most of the known material by the Byrds has finally reached the marketplace. Only a small number of songs remain unissued. The list below is a breakdown of the still unreleased tracks that the Byrds completed in the studio between 1964–72. Although many of the tapes of the early songs appear to have been lost or destroyed, slim hopes remain that some of this material might yet surface somewhere.

'Maybe You Think'. Listed in documentation pertaining to the World-Pacific recordings in 1964, this track survived the period and was evidently a contender for *Preflyte* along with 'Tomorrow Is A Long Ways Away'. Since then it appears to have been mislaid and was not on the tapes presented to Rhino for *In The Beginning*. Nor does it appear on the authoritative *The Preflyte Sessions*. The song was not registered for copyright purposes until as late as 31 October 1966. Apart from this track, no other previously unreleased songs are known to be still in existence from the pre-Columbia days even though the group cut numbers by Chuck Berry, the Beatles and the Searchers, amongst others, during rehearsals at World-Pacific.

'You And Me'. The Byrds performed this song on stage frequently during early 1965 and it was recorded for their debut album on 8 March 1965. It was later deleted in favour of newer material. Only a backing track of the song could be found in the CBS archives.

'Words And Pictures'. Recorded on 14 April 1965 for *Mr Tambourine Man*, this was also missing from the tape shelves at CBS and is unlikely ever to be found.

'I Love The Life I Live'. Recorded the same day as 'Words And Pictures', this Crosby favourite was allegedly written by Mose Allison and appeared on a Georgie Fame EP during the same period. Once again, the original tape could not be found.

'Turn! Turn! Turn!' (stereo mix). The stereo mix did not appear on the Sony CD remastered series and was also not included on the later 180 gram vinyl releases. However, it has not been lost and, just before the release of the *Turn! Turn! Turn!* remastered CD, I discovered it existed in Dickson's archives. Possibly Sundazed were unaware of this while working on the 180 gram vinyl series, which is regrettable.

'Flower Bomb Song'. One of the earlier examples of Crosby's songwriting, this was regarded as totally inappropriate by both Dickson and the group, yet it was recorded for *Turn! Turn! Turn!*. When I reminded Crosby of the song he burst into defensive laughter and admitted that it was not only "very bad" but one of his worst compositions. Originally written in free verse, Eddie Tickner claims that it contained such memorable lines as "I'm going to make the love gun that will blow your mind." It would certainly have been intriguing to hear Crosby's hippie philosophizing at such an early period, but the tape has been lost, feared destroyed. Several fascinating takes of the backing track were subsequently found in the tape vaults. The loss of the vocal is all the more tantalizing after hearing the instrumental arrangement.

'Stranger In A Strange Land'. Another Crosby song, this time scheduled for a movie that never appeared. The song was inspired by the Robert Heinlein book of the same title. Crosby admitted that it was a fairly naïve piece of work, although he may merely have been aping Jim Dickson's long-standing criticisms. Tickson Music sold the copyright of the song, such was their lack of confidence in the piece. A cover version was subsequently issued as a single on Verve Records by Blackburn & Snow, with Crosby's pseudonymous writing credit 'Samuel F. Omar' (an acronym of SFO Music). Despite the criticisms of Dickson and Crosby, the composition and performance are both strong and, judging from Blackburn & Snow's version, this would have been an excellent addition to *Turn! Turn! Turn!*. In many ways, these unreleased Crosby songs are a key missing chapter in the early history of the Byrds. Apart from 'The Airport Song' on *Preflyte* there are no examples of his lead vocal work with the Byrds during 1964–65 nor any indication of his songwriting, good or otherwise. Even Crosby at his most excessive was never less than interesting and the loss of these tracks is therefore all the more regrettable. Since this song was ultimately intended for release on a soundtrack album it is possible that copies were taken from the master tape and sent to the proposed film makers. We can only hope. An impressive backing track was belatedly discovered in CBS's tape vault, bootlegged and subsequently included on the *Turn! Turn! Turn!* reissue.

'I Don't Ever Want To Spoil Your Party'. Yet another Crosby favourite which bore the kiss of death. This was written by his good friend Dino Valenti and recorded at the same session as 'Stranger In A Strange Land'. Gene Clark may also have attempted a lead vocal on the song. The tape was lost, but listeners anxious to hear what the original might have sounded like should check out the first Quicksilver Messenger Service album where it was re-recorded under the title, 'Dino's Song'.

'Circle Of Minds'. Although listed in the CBS files as having been recorded by the Byrds, no session number was assigned to this track. If the song was anywhere near as interesting as its title, then it was another serious loss to the Byrds' canon.

'Milestones'. Recorded for *Younger Than Yesterday* at a time when Hillman was hitting form having just returned from a Hugh Masekela session, this was a tantalizing example of the Byrds' determined excursion into jazz territories. According to Hillman and his colleagues, this instrumental was taken from the 1958 album of the same name by Miles Davis. However, nobody has previously pointed out that 'Milestones' was only listed as an album title on copies of that record at the time, not a track. It is rather like a new group announcing that they had recorded a Byrds' song called 'Younger Than Yesterday'. The instrumental that Chris is referring to was 'Miles', which was retitled 'Milestones' on later issues of the album. The title 'Miles' was probably used to distinguish the composition from an earlier bebop melody also titled 'Milestones', which Davis recorded in 1947. Certainly, 'Miles' could have been adapted by the Byrds very effectively. Sadly, this tape was also missing from the CBS archives. All that survives is a rough instrumental extract recorded for an ABC Television broadcast on 3 December 1966.

'15 Minute Jam'. Listed as a track from the *(Untitled)* sessions, this was a studio jam, a small section of which was issued on *The Byrds* box set under the title 'White's Lightning'. The remainder, or most of it, can be heard under the title 'White's Lightning Part 2' on the second box set, *There Is A Season*. During the final stages of selecting tracks for their double album, the Byrds were evidently unsure about the final running order. As well as album sleeves listing 'Mae Jean', there were others printed which referred to 'Kathleen' and 'Tag'. 'Kathleen' emerged on the next album, *Byrdmaniax*, as 'Kathleen's Song', while 'Tag', which directly followed the live 'Eight Miles High' on the sleeve, was obviously 'Hold It!', the familiar signature tune that the group tagged on to the end of their live performances.

'Home Sweet Home'. While promoting *Byrdmaniax*, McGuinn told Steve Peacock (*Sounds*: 6 February 1971) that among the songs to be included was ". . . one called 'Home Sweet Home' which is about going home and realizing how things have changed and how you have changed also, a boy remembering how his mother sang him a lullaby . . ." Sung by Clarence White, this was played live at several shows of the period. Its first known appearance in the set occurred at Bloomfield College, New Jersey on 24 October 1970. Although there is no reference in the official session listing, it was played during rehearsals for the *Byrdmaniax* sessions, but a tape has yet to be found. The composer of the title is not known by this author. Several citations on the internet claim that the Byrds' 'Home Sweet Home' is the traditional song originally written by John Howard Payne with music by Henry Rowley Bishop in 1823, but this is a different composition. The traditional song begins: "Mid Pleasures and palaces though I may roam/Be it ever so humble, there's no place like home/A charm from the sky seems to hallow us there/Which, seek through the world, is ne'er met with elsewhere." Clarence White's rendition of 'Home Sweet Home' is a contemporary composition, beginning "But it only made me worry to go round and round so slowly, the questions and the answers still the same. Last time I was home it was all so strange to see the home had grown so small . . ." The song closes with a reference to a truck, again confirming that this is a contemporary, rather than traditional, composition: "The morning sunlight struck and we got up and fixed the truck, and the old man drove me back out to the road." Clarence White may be using a bluegrass melody based on the traditional song in Byrds-style, but who wrote the lyrics?

'Draggin''. For many years, there was speculation about songs recorded during early 1972 for inclusion on what might have been the follow-up to *Farther Along*. On the remastered CD of *Farther Along*, the bonus tracks included the long missing 'Lost My Drivin' Wheel', 'Born To Rock 'n' Roll' and 'Bag Full Of Money' all from this period. In addition, there was 'Draggin'' recorded at Wally Heider's in July/August 1972 and credited to 'the Byrds'. It is probable that McGuinn was already intending to save this cut for his first album, where it subsequently appeared.

'I'm So Restless'. The final track listed at the Heider sessions in July/August, this was another essentially solo item by McGuinn which also appeared on his eponymous first album. Although the Byrds were still functioning as a group at this stage, it is debatable whether McGuinn ever intended these last couple of cuts to appear under their aegis.

Inevitably, there are some songs assumed to have been recorded by the Byrds that do not appear in CBS files. Of the latter tracks the most surprising omission is 'Sing Me Back Home' which was strongly rumoured as a recorded song prior to *Sweetheart Of The Rodeo*. Although it featured heavily in the Byrds' sets of the period, it may not, in retrospect, have been attempted in the studio. The session listing also fails to elucidate the complete story of the recording of *Sweetheart Of The Rodeo*, although much can be gleaned from the Legacy version of *Sweetheart Of The Rodeo*. Finally, it is interesting to note that several of the songs that the Byrds performed live or on radio/television were not apparently attempted in the studio. These predominantly cover songs include 'Things We Said Today', 'When You Walk In The Room', 'Maggie's Farm', 'Not Fade Away', 'I'm A Loser', 'Do You Believe In Magic?', 'Roll Over Beethoven', 'Get Out Of My Life Woman', '(Excuse Me) I Think I've Got A Heartache', 'Foggy Mountain Breakdown', 'Sing Me Back Home', 'Under Your Spell Again', 'Long Black Veil', 'Take A City Bride', 'I Shall Be Released', 'Six Days On The Road', 'Close Up The Honky Tonks', 'California Blues', 'Roll In My Sweet Baby's Arms', 'Blue Suede Shoes', 'Buckaroo', 'Home Sweet Home', 'The Water Is Wide' and 'Salt River'.

BYRDS DISCOGRAPHY
(Volume 1)

This discography, in keeping with the scope of Volume 1, concentrates entirely on *Byrds* releases, including singles, albums, bootlegs, plus a listing of television appearances.

In Volume 2, I will be including a complete breakdown of the releases and guest appearances of each individual Byrd, including all their various offshoot adventures as soloists and band performers both before and after the Byrds. This is an extensive undertaking of similar or greater length to the discography herein, but obviously steps outside work recorded during the timeframe of the Byrds. The next volume will also feature complete copyright listings detailing the song registrations of Roger McGuinn, Gene Clark, David Crosby, Michael Clarke, Chris Hillman, Kevin Kelley, Gram Parsons, Clarence White, Gene Parsons, John York and Skip Battin. A further section will feature unreleased compositions from all of the above.

SINGLES (US/UK)

1964/65 (as the Beefeaters)
'Please Let Me Love You'/'Don't Be Long'
Elektra 45013 (US)/Pye International 7N-25277 (UK).
Released 7 October 1964 (US).
Released 8 January 1965 (UK).
Reissued Bounty B 45102, 1965 (US).
Reissued Elektra 2101 007, 1970 (UK).

1965
'Mr Tambourine Man'/'I Knew I'd Want You'
Columbia 4-43271 (US)/CBS 201765 (UK).
Released 12 April 1965 (US).
Released 15 May 1965 (UK).

'All I Really Want To Do'/'Feel A Whole Lot Better'*
Columbia 4-43332 (US)/CBS 201796 (UK).
Released 14 June 1965 (US).
Released 6 August 1965 (UK).

* In the (US) only the B-side was repromoted as an A-side after release. The single take of 'All I Really Want To Do' in both territories is different from that used on the first album.

'Turn! Turn! Turn!'/'She Don't Care About Time'
Columbia 4-43424 (US)/ CBS 202008 (UK).
Released 1 October 1965 (US).
Released 29 October 1965 (UK).

1966
'Set You Free This Time'/'It Won't Be Wrong'
Columbia 4-43501 (US)/CBS 202037 (UK).
Released 10 January 1966 (US).
Released 11 February 1966 (UK).

'It Won't Be Wrong'/'Set You Free This Time'*
Columbia 4-43501 (US)/CBS 202037 (UK).
Released 24 January 1966 (US).
Released 18 February 1966 (UK).

* CBS switched sides after the first week of release in the UK and after the second week of release in the US.

'Eight Miles High'/'Why'
Columbia 4-43578 (US)/CBS 202067 (UK).
Released 14 March 1966 (US).
Released 29 April 1966 (UK).

'5 D (Fifth Dimension)'/'Captain Soul'
Columbia 4-43702 (US)/CBS 202259 (UK).
Released 13 June 1966 (US).
Released 29 July 1966 (UK).

'Mr Spaceman'/'What's Happening?!?!'
Columbia 4-43766 (US)/CBS 202295 (UK).
Released 6 September 1966 (US).
Released 14 October 1966 (UK).

BYRDS DISCOGRAPHY

1967
'So You Want To Be A Rock 'n' Roll Star'/'Everybody's Been Burned'
Columbia 4-43987 (US)/CBS 202559 (UK).
Released 9 January 1967 (US).
Released 17 February 1967 (UK).

'My Back Pages'/'Renaissance Fair'
Columbia 4-44054 (US)/CBS 2468 (UK).
Released 13 March 1967 (US).
Released 12 May 1967 (UK).

'Have You Seen Her Face'/'Don't Make Waves'
Columbia 4-44157 (US only).
Released 22 May 1967 (US only).

'Lady Friend'/'Old John Robertson'
Columbia 4-44230 (US only).
Released 13 July 1967 (US only).

'Lady Friend'/'Don't Make Waves'
CBS 2924 (UK only).
Released 1 September 1967 (UK only).

'Goin' Back'/'Change Is Now'
Columbia 4-44362 (US)/CBS 3093 (UK).
Released 20 October 1967 (US).
Released 22 December 1967 (UK).

1968
'You Ain't Going Nowhere'/'Artificial Energy'
Columbia 4-44499 (US)/ CBS 3411(UK).
Released 2 April 1968 (US).
Released 3 May 1968 (UK).

'I Am A Pilgrim'/'Pretty Boy Floyd'
Columbia 4-44643 (US)/CBS 3752 (UK).
Released 2 September 1968 (US).
Released 18 October 1968 (UK).

1969/70
'Bad Night At The Whiskey'/'Drug Store Truck Drivin' Man'
Columbia 4-44746 (US)/CBS 4055 (UK).
Released 7 January 1969 (US).
Released 7 March 1969 (UK).

'Lay Lady Lay'/'Old Blue'
Columbia 4-44868 (US)/CBS 4284 (US).
Released 2 May 1969 (US).
Released 6 June 1969 (UK).

'(I) Wasn't Born To Follow'/'Child Of The Universe'
CBS 4572 (UK).
Released 26 September 1969 (UK only).

'Ballad Of Easy Rider'/'Oil In My Lamp'.*
Columbia 4-44990 (US).
Released 1 October 1969 (US only).

* Some copies were released with '(I) Wasn't Born To Follow' in place of 'Oil In My Lamp'.

'Jesus Is Just Alright'/'It's All Over Now, Baby Blue'
Columbia 4-45071 (US)/CBS 4753 (UK).
Released 15 December 1969 (US).
Released 20 February 1970 (UK).

1970/71
'Chestnut Mare'/'Just A Season'
Columbia 4-45259 (US)/CBS 5322 (UK).
Released 23 October 1970 (US).
Released 1 January 1971 (UK).

'I Trust (Everything Is Gonna Work Out Alright)'/'(Is This) My Destiny'
CBS 7253 (UK only).
Released 7 May 1971 (UK only).

'Glory, Glory'/'Citizen Kane'
Columbia 4-45440 (US)/CBS 7501 (UK).
Released 20 August 1971 (US).
Released 1 October 1971 (UK).

1971/72
'America's Great National Pastime'/'Farther Along'
Columbia 4-45514 (US)/CBS 7712 (UK).
Released 29 November 1971 (US).
Released 7 January 1972 (UK scheduled only).
In the UK the single appears to have been withdrawn prior to release, although it was available through most of Europe.

BYRDS DISCOGRAPHY

1973
'Full Circle'/'Long Live The King'
Asylum 11016 (US)/Asylum AYM 517 (UK).
Released 11 April 1973 (US).
Released 22 June 1973 (UK).

'Things Will Be Better'/'For Free'
Asylum AYM 516 (UK only).
Released 24 April 1973 (UK only).

'Cowgirl In The Sand'/'Long Live The King'
Asylum 11019 (US only).
Released June 1973 (US only).

'Full Circle'/'Things Will Be Better'
Asylum AYM 545 (UK only).
Released 6 July 1973 (UK only).
Reissued 8 August 1975 (UK only).

2002
'You Movin''/'Boston'
Sundazed KS7 01 (US only).
Released May 2002 (US).
Original demos from the 1964 World-Pacific rehearsals. Alternate versions to those appearing on *The Preflyte Sessions*.

2004
Cancelled Flytes
Sundazed PVS 72860/S 7001 (US only).
This special edition box set included five picture sleeve 7-inch vinyl singles, none of which had previously been coupled.
'Chimes Of Freedom'/'The Bells Of Rhymney'
S 160/PV 72861.
'It's All Over Now, Baby Blue'/'She Don't Care About Time'
S161/PV 72862.
'The Times They Are A-Changin''/'She Has A Way'
S 162/PV 72863.
'I Know You Rider' (mono mix)/'Psychodrama City' (mono mix)
S163/PV 72864.
'My Back Pages'/'It Happens Each Day'
S164/PV 72865.
Released September 2004 (US only).

2007
'Lazy Days'/'Reputation'
Sundazed S 189/PV 704201 (US only).
Released 27 March 2007 (US only).

2008
Live In Holland 1971
Sundazed S 196 (US only).
'Lover Of The Bayou'/'You Ain't Going Nowhere'.
Released May 2008 (US only).

Please note that re-issued singles and back-to-back hits after the group's break-up have not been included. The single version of 'All I Really Want To Do' is an alternate take and both 'My Back Pages' and 'Chestnut Mare' are edited.

EPs (UK)

1966
The Times They Are A-Changin'
CBS EP 6069 (UK).
'The Times They Are A-Changin''; 'The Bells Of Rhymney'; 'It's No Use'; 'We'll Meet Again'.
Released February 1966 (UK).

Eight Miles High
CBS EP 6077 (UK).
'Mr Tambourine Man'; 'All I Really Want To Do'; 'Turn! Turn! Turn!'; 'Eight Miles High'.
Released October 1966 (UK).
This EP features the single version of 'All I Really Want To Do'.

1983
The Byrds
Pickwick SCOOP 33 7SR 5016 (UK).
'Lay Lady Lay'; 'Turn! Turn! Turn!'; 'So You Want To Be A Rock 'n' Roll Star'; 'Chestnut Mare'; 'All I Really Want To Do'; 'Goin' Back'.
Released September 1983 (UK).

BYRDS DISCOGRAPHY

1989
Solid Gold
CBS 654571 (UK).
'Mr Tambourine Man'; 'Turn! Turn! Turn!'; 'All I Really Want To Do';
'Lay Lady Lay'.
Released May 1989 (UK).

1990
Four Dimensions
CBS 656544 (UK).
'Mr Tambourine Man'; 'Turn! Turn! Turn!'; 'Eight Miles High'; 'Feel A Whole Lot Better'.
Released December 1990 (UK).

BYRDS ORIGINAL VINYL ALBUMS (US & UK)

The following is a list of the Byrds' original official LPs, excluding greatest hits compilations which can be found under 'Byrds Compilations (US & UK)' and the entries for individual artistes. Please note that reissues and various artiste sampler albums, greatest hits compilations, commemoration sets, promotional records, reissued and renumbered releases and two-for-one packages are not included here. In the UK all the Byrds' albums from *Mr Tambourine Man* to *Dr Byrds & Mr Hyde* were issued in both mono and stereo. In America, mono pressings also ended with *Dr Byrds & Mr Hyde*, having already become rarer since *The Notorious Byrd Brothers*. There are slight variants in precise US release dates of the following albums: *Younger Than Yesterday*, *The Notorious Byrd Brothers*, *Dr Byrds & Mr Hyde*, *Ballad Of Easy Rider* and *(Untitled)*. In this section, I have used the original dates offered by CBS/Columbia back at the end of the Sixties, which I believe are correct. The Byrds' sessionography includes unexplained variants, which have since been employed in the notes of Sony reissues.

For details of Sony's remastered CDs with bonus tracks consult the Byrds CD Remastered Original Albums later in this discography.

1965
Mr Tambourine Man
Columbia CL 2372 (mono); Columbia CS 9172 (stereo) (US).
CBS BPG 62571 (mono); CBS SBPG 62571 (stereo) (UK).
'Mr Tambourine Man'; 'Feel A Whole Lot Better'; 'Spanish Harlem

Incident'; 'You Won't Have To Cry'; 'Here Without You'; 'The Bells Of Rhymney'; 'All I Really Want To Do'; 'I Knew I'd Want You'; 'It's No Use'; 'Don't Doubt Yourself Babe'; 'Chimes Of Freedom'; 'We'll Meet Again'.
Released 21 June 1965 (US).
Released 20 August 1965 (UK).

1965/66
Turn! Turn! Turn!
Columbia CL 2454 (mono); Columbia CS 9254 (stereo) (US).
CBS BPG 62652 (mono); CBS SBPG 62652 (stereo) (UK).
'Turn! Turn! Turn!'; 'It Won't Be Wrong'; 'Set You Free This Time'; 'Lay Down Your Weary Tune'; 'He Was A Friend Of Mine'; 'The World Turns All Around Her'; 'Satisfied Mind'; 'If You're Gone'; 'The Times They Are A-Changin''; 'Wait And See'; 'Oh! Susannah'.
Released 6 December 1965 (US).
Released 22 March 1966 (UK).

1966
Fifth Dimension
Columbia CL 2549 (mono); Columbia CS 9349 (stereo) (US).
CBS BPG 62783 (mono); CBS SBPG 62783 (stereo) (UK).
'5 D (Fifth Dimension)'; 'Wild Mountain Thyme'; 'Mr Spaceman'; 'I See You'; 'What's Happening?!?!'; 'I Come And Stand At Every Door'; 'Eight Miles High'; 'Hey Joe (Where You Gonna Go)'; 'Captain Soul'; 'John Riley'; '2-4-2 Fox Trot (The Lear Jet Song)'.
Released 18 July 1966 (US).
Released 22 September 1966 (UK).

1967
Younger Than Yesterday
Columbia CL 2642 (mono); Columbia CS 9442 (stereo) (US).
CBS BPG 62988 (mono); CBS SBPG 62988 (stereo) (UK).
'So You Want To Be A Rock 'n' Roll Star'; 'Have You Seen Her Face'; 'CTA 102'; 'Renaissance Fair'; 'Time Between'; 'Everybody's Been Burned'; 'Thoughts And Words'; 'Mind Gardens'; 'My Back Pages'; 'The Girl With No Name'; 'Why'.
Released 6 February 1967 (US).
Released 7 April 1967 (UK).

BYRDS DISCOGRAPHY

1968

The Notorious Byrd Brothers
Columbia CL 2775 (mono); Columbia CS 9575 (stereo) (US).
CBS 63169 (mono); CBS S 63169 (stereo) (UK).
'Artificial Energy'; 'Goin' Back'; 'Natural Harmony'; 'Draft Morning'; 'Wasn't Born To Follow'; 'Get To You'; 'Change Is Now'; 'Old John Robertson'; 'Tribal Gathering'; 'Dolphin's Smile'; 'Space Odyssey'.
Released 15 January 1968 (US).
Released 12 April 1968 (UK).

Sweetheart Of The Rodeo
Columbia CL 9670 (mono); CS 9670 (stereo) (US).
CBS 63353 (mono); CBS S 63353 (stereo) (UK).
'You Ain't Going Nowhere'; 'I Am A Pilgrim'; 'The Christian Life'; 'You Don't Miss Your Water'; 'You're Still On My Mind'; 'Pretty Boy Floyd'; 'Hickory Wind'; 'One Hundred Years From Now'; 'Blue Canadian Rockies'; 'Life In Prison'; 'Nothing Was Delivered'.
Released 30 August 1968 (US).
Released 27 September 1968 (UK).

1969

Dr Byrds & Mr Hyde
Columbia CL 9755 (mono); CS 9755 (stereo) (US).
CBS 63545 (mono); CBS S 63545 (stereo) (UK).
'This Wheel's On Fire'; 'Old Blue'; 'Your Gentle Way Of Loving Me'; 'Child Of The Universe'; 'Nashville West'; 'Drug Store Truck Drivin' Man'; 'King Apathy III'; 'Candy'; 'Bad Night At The Whiskey'; 'Medley: 'My Back Pages'/'B.J. Blues'/'Baby, What Do You Want Me To Do'.
Released 5 March 1969 (US).
Released 25 April 1969 (UK).

1969/70

Ballad Of Easy Rider
Columbia CS 9942 (stereo) (US).
CBS S 63795 (stereo) (UK).
'Ballad Of Easy Rider'; 'Fido'; 'Oil In My Lamp'; 'Tulsa County Blue'; 'Jack Tarr The Sailor'; 'Jesus Is Just Alright'; 'It's All Over Now, Baby Blue'; 'There Must Be Someone'; 'Gunga Din'; 'Deportee (Plane Wreck At Los Gatos)'; 'Armstrong, Aldrin And Collins'.
Released 10 November 1969 (US).
Released 16 January 1970 (UK).

1970
(Untitled)
Columbia G 30127 (stereo) (US).
CBS S 64095 (stereo) (UK).
'Lover Of The Bayou'; 'Positively 4th Street'; 'Nashville West';
'So You Want To Be A Rock 'n' Roll Star'; 'Mr Tambourine Man';
'Mr Spaceman'; 'Eight Miles High'; 'Chestnut Mare'; 'Truck Stop Girl';
'All The Things'; 'Yesterday's Train'; 'Hungry Planet'; 'Just A Season';
'Take A Whiff'; 'You All Look Alike'; 'Well Come Back Home'.
Released 14 September 1970 (US).
Released 13 November 1970 (UK).

1971
Byrdmaniax
Columbia KC 30640 (stereo) (US).
CBS S 64389 (stereo) (UK).
'Glory, Glory'; 'Pale Blue'; 'I Trust'; 'Tunnel Of Love'; 'Citizen Kane'; 'I Wanna Grow Up To Be A Politician'; 'Absolute Happiness'; 'Green Apple Quick Step'; '(Is This) My Destiny'; 'Kathleen's Song'; 'Jamaica Say You Will'.
Released 23 June 1971 (US).
Released 6 August 1971 (UK).

1971/72
Farther Along
Columbia KC 31050 (stereo) (US).
CBS S 64676 (stereo) (UK).
'Tiffany Queen'; 'Get Down Your Line'; 'Farther Along'; 'B.B. Class Road'; 'Bugler'; 'America's Great National Pastime'; 'Antique Sandy'; 'So Fine'; 'Lazy Waters'; 'Bristol Steam Convention Blues'.
Released 17 November 1971 (US).
Released 21 January 1972 (UK).

1973
Byrds
Asylum SD 5058 (US).
Asylum SYLA 8754 (UK).
'Full Circle'; 'Sweet Mary'; 'Changing Heart'; 'For Free'; 'Born To Rock 'n' Roll'; 'Things Will Be Better'; 'Cowgirl In The Sand'; 'Long Live The King'; 'Borrowing Time'; 'Laughing'; '(See The Sky) About To Rain'.
Released 7 March 1973 (US).
Released 24 March 1973 (UK).

BYRDS DISCOGRAPHY

ARCHIVAL ALBUMS (Vinyl)

Preflyte
Together ST-T-1001 (US).
'You Showed Me'; 'Here Without You'; 'She Has A Way'; 'The Reason Why'; 'For Me Again'; 'Boston'; 'You Movin''; 'The Airport Song'; 'You Won't Have To Cry'; 'I Knew I'd Want You'; 'Mr Tambourine Man'.
Released 29 July 1969 (US).

Originally issued in the US only on Gary Usher's label Together. The album was later issued in the UK (January 1973) on Kim Fowley's short-lived label, Bumble (GEXP 8001) and reissued in the US (April 1973) by Columbia (C 32183). It was later issued on CD in the UK (July 2001) by Poptones (MC 5044 CD) and by the same label (December 2001) on vinyl (MC33150441LP). A further straight reissue appeared on CD in the US in February 2006 by Sundazed (SC 6234). See also 'Archival CDs' and '180 Gram Vinyl' sections for the extended *The Preflyte Sessions* released in November 2001 on Sundazed (SC11116).

The Original Singles Volume I
CBS 31851 (UK)/Columbia FC 37335 (US).
'Mr Tambourine Man'; 'I Knew I'd Want You'; 'All I Really Want To Do'; 'Feel A Whole Lot Better'; 'Turn! Turn! Turn!'; 'She Don't Care About Time'; 'Set You Free This Time'; 'It Won't Be Wrong'; 'Eight Miles High'; 'Why'; '5 D (Fifth Dimension)'; 'Captain Soul'; 'Mr Spaceman'; 'What's Happening?!?!'; 'So You Want To Be A Rock 'n' Roll Star'; 'Everybody's Been Burned'.
Released 8 August 1980 (UK).
Released February 1981 (US).

This was the only compilation to include the original singles masters in mono. Originally conceived in the UK, it was subsequently issued in the US Columbia (FC 37335). Beware the later US CD reissue, in which I was not involved, as they have not used the original singles masters in every case. Indeed, they even use 'Why' from *Younger Than Yesterday* and do not appear to have had access to the original singles mixes as CBS UK did when putting together the vinyl version.

The Original Singles Volume II
CBS 32103 (UK).
'My Back Pages'; 'Renaissance Fair'; 'Have You Seen Her Face'; 'Don't Make Waves'; 'Lady Friend'; 'Old John Robertson'; 'Goin' Back'; 'Change Is

Now'; 'You Ain't Going Nowhere'; 'Artificial Energy'; 'I Am A Pilgrim'; 'Pretty Boy Floyd'; 'Bad Night At The Whiskey'; 'Drug Store Truck Drivin' Man'; 'Lay Lady Lay'; 'Old Blue'.
Released February 1982 (UK).

The second volume was not issued in the US. CBS approached me to compile a third volume but I told them they were scraping the barrel, not least because there were not enough singles to make up a full 16-track compilation.

Never Before
Re-Flyte MH 70318 (US).
'Mr Tambourine Man' (previously unreleased stereo mix); 'I Knew I'd Want You' (new stereo mix); 'She Has A Way' (previously unreleased); 'It's All Over Now, Baby Blue' (previously unreleased); 'Never Before' (previously unreleased – later correctly retitled 'The Day Walk'); 'Eight Miles High' (previously unreleased alternate RCA version); 'Why' (previously unreleased alternate RCA version); 'Triad' (previously unreleased); 'It Happens Each Day' (previously unreleased); 'Lady Friend' (previously unreleased stereo mix, with re-recorded drums).
See Archival CDs for extended version.
Released 1 December 1987 (US).

In The Beginning
Rhino R1 70244 (US).
'Tomorrow Is A Long Ways Away'; 'Boston'; The Only Girl I Adore'; 'You Won't Have To Cry'; 'I Knew I'd Want You'; 'The Airport Song'; 'Please Let Me Love You'; 'You Movin''; 'It Won't Be Wrong'; 'It's No Use'; 'You Showed Me'; 'She Has A Way'; 'For Me Again'; 'Here Without You'.
See Archival CDs for extended version.
Released August 1988 (US).

Another Dimension
Sundazed SEP 2 10-168 (US).
10-inch double album vinyl release. 'Eight Miles High' (instrumental take 2); 'Why' (instrumental take 17); 'Ryder (I Know My Rider)' (instrumental take 9); 'John Riley I' (instrumental take 2); '2-4-2 Fox Trot (The Lear Jet Song)' (long version instrumental, minus sound effects); 'Psychodrama City' (instrumental take 1); 'John Riley II' (completed early master, no string overdubs); 'Wild Mountain Thyme' (completed early master, no string overdubs); 'Hey Joe (Where You Gonna Go)' (*Radiohuset*, Stockholm, Sweden); 'I See You' (completed master, longer version, without

overdubs); 'What's Happening?!?!' (completed master, long version, partial alternate vocal); 'Captain Soul (30 Minute Break)' (completed early master, longer version, without overdubs).
Released 26 April 2005 (US).

In addition to the above, several vinyl archive albums were released retrospectively between the Sixties and the Eighties. See later section for the modern releases on 180 gram vinyl.

BYRDS GUEST SLOTS/RARITIES (Vinyl)

The albums below feature appearances by the Byrds, including rare versions of songs generally not available elsewhere. Sole US or UK releases are indicated in parentheses.

Early LA
Together ST-T-1014 (US).
This album featured two tracks by the Jet Set, 'The Only Girl' and 'You Movin'', plus two sumptuous solo recordings from Crosby – 'Willie Jean' and 'Come Back Baby'.
Released 1969 (US).

Don't Make Waves
MGM 4483 ST (US).
An alternate take of the title track is available on this soundtrack.
Released 5 July 1967 (US).

Candy
ABC ABCS OC-9 (US).
Stateside SSL 10276 (UK).
The soundtrack contains an alternate mix of 'Child Of The Universe', including full orchestration and brass, radically different from the version on *Dr Byrds & Mr Hyde*.
Released January 1969 (US).
Released April 1969 (UK).

Easy Rider
Dunhill DSX-5006 (US).
Stateside SSL 5018 (UK).
Although the version of 'Wasn't Born To Follow' is the same as that on *The Notorious Byrd Brothers*, McGuinn (backed by Gene Parsons) appears on two

rare solo outings: 'Ballad Of Easy Rider' and 'It's Alright Ma (I'm Only Bleeding)'.
Released October 1969 (US).
Released January 1970 (UK).

Earl Scruggs, His Family And Friends
Columbia 30584 (US).
CBS 64777 (UK).
This features the McGuinn/White/Parsons/Battin line-up of the Byrds, augmented by the Earl Scruggs Revue on 'You Ain't Going Nowhere' and 'Nothin' To It'.
Released October 1971 (US).
Released March 1972 (UK).

Banjoman
Sire SA 7527(US).
Sire SRK 6026 (UK).
With Guerin replacing Parsons, this film soundtrack included the Byrds performing 'Mr Tambourine Man' and 'Roll Over Beethoven'.
Released January 1977 (US).
Released February 1979 (UK).

The soundtrack album *Homer* (Atlantic 2400 137) includes the previously issued 'Turn! Turn! Turn!'. The US-only Various Artistes compilations *Garden Of Delights* (Elektra S-3-10) and *Elektrock* (Elektra 60403) feature the Beefeaters' 'Please Let Me Love You', and 'Please Let Me Love You'/ 'Don't Be Long', respectively.

BYRDS VINYL COMPILATIONS (US & UK)

The following list of compilations excludes special samplers, two-for-one packages, promotional items for radio play and releases outside the US or UK, unless specified.

The Byrds' Greatest Hits
Columbia CL 2716 (US).
CBS SBPG 63107 (UK).
'Mr Tambourine Man'; '(I'll) Feel A Whole Lot Better'; 'The Bells Of Rhymney'; 'Turn! Turn! Turn!'; 'All I Really Want To Do'; 'Chimes Of Freedom'; 'Eight Miles High'; 'Mr Spaceman'; '5 D (Fifth Dimension)'; 'So You Want To Be A Rock 'n' Roll Star'; 'My Back Pages'.
Released 7 August 1967 (US).
Released 20 October 1967 (UK).

BYRDS DISCOGRAPHY

Preflyte
Together ST-T-1001 (US).
Bumble GEXP 8001 (UK).
See Archival Albums (Vinyl) for track listing.
Originally issued in the US only on Gary Usher's label Together. The album was later issued in the UK (January 1973) on Kim Fowley's short-lived label Bumble (GEXP 8001) and reissued in the US by Columbia (C 32183) the same year.
Released 29 July 1969 (US).
Released January 1973 (UK).

The Byrds' Greatest Hits Vol. 2
CBS S 64650 (UK).
'Ballad Of Easy Rider'; 'Jesus Is Just Alright'; 'Chestnut Mare'; 'You Ain't Going Nowhere'; 'I Am A Pilgrim'; 'Goin' Back'; 'I Trust (Everything Is Gonna Work Out Alright)'; 'Lay Lady Lay'; 'Drug Store Truck Drivin' Man'; '(I) Wasn't Born To Follow'; 'The Times They Are A-Changin''; 'Get To You'.
Released October 1971 (UK).

Best Of Volume 2
Columbia KC 31795 (US).
'Ballad Of Easy Rider'; 'Wasn't Born To Follow'; 'Jesus Is Just Alright'; 'He Was A Friend Of Mine'; 'Chestnut Mare'; 'Tiffany Queen'; 'Drug Store Truck Drivin' Man'; 'You Ain't Going Nowhere'; 'Citizen Kane'; 'I Wanna Grow Up To Be A Politician'; 'America's Great National Pastime'.
Released 10 November 1972 (US).

History Of The Byrds
CBS 68242 (UK).
'Mr Tambourine Man'; 'Turn! Turn! Turn!'; 'She Don't Care About Time'; 'Wild Mountain Thyme'; 'Eight Miles High'; 'Mr Spaceman'; '5 D (Fifth Dimension)'; 'So You Want To Be A Rock 'n' Roll Star'; 'Time Between'; 'My Back Pages'; 'Lady Friend'; 'Goin' Back'; 'Old John Robertson'; 'Wasn't Born To Follow'; 'You Ain't Going Nowhere'; 'Hickory Wind'; 'Nashville West'; 'Drug Store Truck Drivin' Man'; 'Gunga Din'; 'Jesus Is Just Alright'; 'Ballad Of Easy Rider'; 'Chestnut Mare'; 'Yesterday's Train'; 'Just A Season'; 'Citizen Kane'; 'Jamaica Say You Will'; 'Tiffany Queen'; 'America's Great National Pastime'.
Released April 1973 (UK).

Return Of The Byrds
Columbia Realm 2V 8006-7 (US).

REQUIEM FOR THE TIMELESS — VOLUME 1

'Mr Tambourine Man'; 'Lay Down Your Weary Tune'; 'You Ain't Going Nowhere'; 'Spanish Harlem Incident'; '5 D (Fifth Dimension)'; 'The Bells Of Rhymney'; 'I Knew I'd Want You'; 'So You Want To Be A Rock 'n' Roll Star'; 'Tiffany Queen'; 'Goin' Back'; 'It's No Use'; 'Jesus Is Just Alright'; 'Mr Spaceman'; 'All I Really Want To Do'; 'He Was A Friend Of Mine'; 'Drug Store Truck Drivin' Man'; 'The Times They Are A-Changin''; 'Have You Seen Her Face'; 'My Back Pages'; 'Lady Friend'.
Released 7 May 1976 (US).

Greatest Hits
CBS Embassy EMB 31381 (UK).
'Mr Tambourine Man'; 'Turn! Turn! Turn! (To Everything There Is A Season)' '5 D (Fifth Dimension)'; 'So You Want To Be A Rock 'n' Roll Star'; 'Eight Miles High'; 'Wasn't Born To Follow'; 'I Am A Pilgrim'; 'This Wheel's On Fire'; 'Jesus Is Just Alright'; 'Chestnut Mare'; 'Glory, Glory'; 'America's Great National Pastime'.
Released July 1976 (UK).

The Byrds
CBS 88320 (UK).
'Mr Tambourine Man'; 'The Bells Of Rhymney'; 'Feel A Whole Lot Better'; 'All I Really Want To Do'; 'The Times They Are A-Changin''; 'Turn! Turn! Turn!'; 'Lady Friend'; 'Mr Spaceman'; '5 D (Fifth Dimension)'; 'Eight Miles High'; 'So You Want To Be A Rock 'n' Roll Star'; 'My Back Pages'; 'Dolphin's Smile'; '(I) Wasn't Born To Follow'; 'Goin' Back'; 'Hickory Wind'; 'I Am A Pilgrim'; 'You Ain't Going Nowhere'; 'This Wheel's On Fire'; 'Drug Store Truck Drivin' Man'; 'Nashville West'; 'Gunga Din'; 'It's All Over Now, Baby Blue'; 'Ballad Of Easy Rider'; 'Jesus Is Just Alright'; 'Chestnut Mare'; 'Jamaica Say You Will'; 'I Trust (Everything Is Gonna Work Out Alright)'; 'Lay Lady Lay'; 'Farther Along'.
Released December 1978 (UK). Mail order only.

The Byrds Play Dylan
Columbia PC 36293 (US)/CBS 31795 (UK).
'The Times They Are A-Changin''; 'Mr Tambourine Man'; 'All I Really Want To Do'; 'Chimes Of Freedom'; 'Spanish Harlem Incident'; 'My Back Pages'; 'Lay Down Your Weary Tune'; 'It's All Over Now, Baby Blue'; 'You Ain't Going Nowhere'; 'This Wheel's On Fire'; 'Nothing Was Delivered'; 'Lay Lady Lay'; 'Positively 4th Street'.
For the UK release of this record, I resequenced the tracks, placing them in chronological order, as follows: 'Mr Tambourine Man'; 'All I Really Want To Do'; 'Chimes Of Freedom'; 'Spanish Harlem Incident'; 'The Times

BYRDS DISCOGRAPHY

They Are A-Changin''; 'Lay Down Your Weary Tune'; 'My Back Pages'; 'You Ain't Going Nowhere'; 'Nothing Was Delivered'; 'This Wheel's On Fire'; 'It's All Over Now, Baby Blue'; 'Lay Lady Lay'; 'Positively 4th Street'.
Released November 1979 (US).
Released February 1980 (UK).

The Original Singles Volume I
CBS 31851 (UK).
Columbia FC 37335 (US).
See Archival Albums (Vinyl) for track listing.
This was the only compilation to include the original singles masters in glorious mono. Originally conceived in the UK, it was subsequently issued in the US Columbia (FC 37335). Beware the CD reissue, in which I was not involved, as they have not used the original singles masters.
Released August 1980 (UK).
Released February 1981 (US).

The Original Singles Volume II
CBS 32103 (UK).
See Archival Albums (Vinyl) for track listing.
The second volume was not issued in the US. CBS approached me to compile a third volume but I told them they were scraping the barrel, not least because there were not enough singles to make up a full 16-track compilation.
Released February 1982 (UK).

The Very Best Of The Byrds
Columbia CS P-P2 17596 (US).
'Mr Tambourine Man'; 'America's Great National Pastime'; 'Lay Lady Lay'; 'Farther Along'; 'Turn! Turn! Turn!'; 'Oh! Susannah'; 'It's All Over Now, Baby Blue'; 'So You Want To Be A Rock 'n' Roll Star'; 'Eight Miles High'; 'Chimes Of Freedom'; 'Bugler'; 'Spanish Harlem Incident'.
Released November 1983 (US).

The Byrds Collection
Castle Communications CCSLP 151 (UK).
'Lady Friend'; 'Chestnut Mare'; 'The Bells Of Rhymney'; 'He Was A Friend Of Mine'; 'Why'; 'Everybody's Been Burned'; 'Eight Miles High'; 'The Girl With No Name'; 'Goin' Back'; 'So You Want To Be A Rock 'n' Roll Star'; '5 D (Fifth Dimension)'; 'Old John Robertson'; 'Here Without You'; 'Wasn't Born To Follow'; 'Draft Morning'; 'It Won't Be Wrong'; 'John Riley'; 'My Back Pages'; 'Mr Tambourine Man'; 'Turn! Turn! Turn!'; 'Have You Seen Her Face'; 'Feel A Whole Lot Better'; 'All I Really Want To Do'; 'You Ain't Going Nowhere'.

REQUIEM FOR THE TIMELESS — VOLUME 1

The CD version (CCSCD 151) of this double album excluded the following tracks: 'He Was A Friend Of Mine'; 'Why'; 'Here Without You'; 'John Riley'; 'Feel A Whole Lot Better'.
Released September 1986 (UK).

Never Before
Re-Flyte MH 70318 (US).
'Mr Tambourine Man'; 'I Knew I'd Want You'; 'She Has A Way'; 'It's All Over Now, Baby Blue'; 'Never Before'; 'Eight Miles High'; 'Why'; 'Triad'; 'It Happens Each Day'; 'Lady Friend'.
Released 1 December 1987 (US).

In The Beginning
Rhino R1 70244 (US).
'Tomorrow Is A Long Ways Away'; 'Boston'; 'The Only Girl I Adore'; 'You Won't Have To Cry'; 'I Knew I'd Want You'; 'The Airport Song'; 'Please Let Me Love You'; 'You Movin''; 'It Won't Be Wrong'; 'It's No Use'; 'You Showed Me'; 'She Has A Way'; 'For Me Again'; 'Here Without You'.
Released August 1988 (US).

Please note, some further compilations can be found in the Byrds Vinyl Albums 180 gram section later in the discography.

BOX SETS (CDs)

The Byrds
Columbia Legacy 46773 (US).
Columbia Legacy 4676112 (UK).
Disc 1: 'Mr Tambourine Man'; 'Feel A Whole Lot Better'; 'Chimes Of Freedom'; 'She Has A Way'; 'All I Really Want To Do'; 'Spanish Harlem Incident'; 'The Bells Of Rhymney'; 'It's All Over Now, Baby Blue'; 'She Don't Care About Time'; 'Turn! Turn! Turn!'; 'It Won't Be Wrong'; 'Lay Down Your Weary Tune'; 'He Was A Friend Of Mine'; 'The World Turns All Around Her'; 'The Day Walk (Never Before)'; 'The Times They Are A-Changin''; '5 D (Fifth Dimension)'; 'I Know My Rider'; 'Eight Miles High'; 'Why'; 'Psychodrama City'; 'I See You'; 'Hey Joe'.
Disc 2: 'Mr Spaceman'; 'John Riley'; 'Roll Over Beethoven'; 'So You Want To Be A Rock 'n' Roll Star'; 'Have You Seen Her Face'; 'My Back Pages'; 'Time Between'; 'It Happens Each Day'; 'Renaissance Fair'; 'Everybody's Been Burned'; 'The Girl With No Name'; 'Triad'; 'Lady Friend'; 'Old John

BYRDS DISCOGRAPHY

Robertson'; 'Goin' Back'; 'Draft Morning'; 'Wasn't Born To Follow'; 'Dolphin's Smile'; 'Reputation'; 'You Ain't Going Nowhere'; 'The Christian Life'; 'I Am A Pilgrim'; 'Pretty Boy Floyd'; 'You Don't Miss Your Water'.
Disc 3: 'Hickory Wind'; 'Nothing Was Delivered'; 'One Hundred Years From Now'; 'Pretty Polly'; 'Lazy Days'; 'This Wheel's On Fire'; 'Nashville West'; 'Old Blue'; 'Drug Store Truck Drivin' Man'; 'Bad Night At The Whiskey'; 'Lay Lady Lay'; 'Mae Jean Goes To Hollywood'; 'Ballad Of Easy Rider'; 'Oil In My Lamp'; 'Jesus Is Just Alright'; 'Way Behind The Sun'; 'Tulsa County (Blue)'; 'Deportee (Plane Wreck At Los Gatos)'; 'Lover Of The Bayou'; 'Willin''; 'Soldier's Joy'/'Black Mountain Rag'; 'Positively 4th Street'.
Disc 4: 'Chestnut Mare'; 'Just A Season'; 'Kathleen's Song'; 'Truck Stop Girl'; 'Just Like A Woman'; 'Stanley's Song'; 'Glory, Glory'; 'I Trust'; 'I Wanna Grow Up To Be A Politician'; 'Green Apple Quick Step'; 'Tiffany Queen'; 'Bugler'; 'Lazy Waters'; 'Farther Along'; 'White's Lightning'; 'Turn! Turn! Turn!'; 'Mr Tambourine Man'; 'He Was A Friend Of Mine'; 'Paths Of Victory'; 'From A Distance'; 'Love That Never Dies'.
Released October 1990 (US).
Released December 1990 (UK).

12 Dimensions – The Columbia Recordings 1965–1972
Columbia 497610 2/4976102000 (UK).
To coincide with the final batch of CD remastered reissues, the UK branch of Sony issued this commemorative cube-sized box set, which featured the dozen reissues plus four cardboard photos and a Pete Frame family tree.
Released February 2000 (UK).

There Is A Season 4 CD box set
Columbia Legacy 82876773882 (US).
Columbia Legacy 82876877002 (UK).
Disc 1: 'The Only Girl I Adore'; 'Please Let Me Love You'; 'Don't Be Long'; 'The Airport Song'; 'You Movin''; 'You Showed Me'; 'Mr Tambourine Man'; '(I'll) Feel A Whole Lot Better'; 'You Won't Have To Cry'; 'Here Without You'; 'The Bells Of Rhymney'; 'All I Really Want To Do' (single version); 'I Knew I'd Want You'; 'Chimes Of Freedom'; 'She Has A Way'; 'It's All Over Now, Baby Blue'; 'Turn! Turn! Turn!'; 'It Won't Be Wrong'; 'Set You Free This Time'; 'The World Turns All Around Her'; 'The Day Walk'; 'If You're Gone'; 'The Times They Are A-Changin'' (withdrawn version); 'She Don't Care About Time' (single version); 'Stranger In A Strange Land'.
Disc 2: 'Eight Miles High'; 'Why' (single version); '5 D (Fifth Dimension)'; 'Wild Mountain Thyme'; 'Mr Spaceman'; 'I See You'; 'What's Happening?!?!';

REQUIEM FOR THE TIMELESS — VOLUME 1

'I Know My Rider'; 'So You Want To Be A Rock 'n' Roll Star'; 'Have You Seen Her Face'; 'Renaissance Fair'; 'Time Between'; 'Everybody's Been Burned'; 'My Back Pages'; 'It Happens Each Day'; 'He Was A Friend Of Mine' (live); 'Lady Friend'; 'Old John Robertson' (single version); 'Goin' Back'; 'Draft Morning'; 'Wasn't Born To Follow'; 'Tribal Gathering'; 'Dolphin's Smile'; 'Triad'; 'Universal Mind Decoder'.

Disc 3: 'You Ain't Going Nowhere'; 'I Am A Pilgrim'; 'The Christian Life' (Gram Parsons vocal); 'You Don't Miss Your Water' (Gram Parsons vocal); 'Hickory Wind'; 'One Hundred Years From Now' (Gram Parsons vocal); 'Lazy Days' (alternate version); 'Pretty Polly' (alternate version); 'This Wheel's On Fire' (alternate version); 'Drug Store Truck Drivin' Man'; 'Candy' (elongated version); 'Child Of The Universe' (soundtrack version); 'Pretty Boy Floyd' (live); 'Buckaroo' (live); 'King Apathy III' (live); 'Sing Me Back Home' (live); 'Lay Lady Lay' (alternate version); 'Oil In My Lamp' (alternate version); 'Tulsa County (Blue)'; 'Jesus Is Just Alright'; 'Chestnut Mare'; 'Just A Season'; 'Kathleen's Song' (alternate version); 'All The Things' (alternate version).

Disc 4: 'Lover Of The Bayou' (live); 'Positively 4th Street' (live); 'Old Blue' (live); 'It's Alright Ma (I'm Only Bleeding)' (live); 'Ballad Of Easy Rider' (live); 'You All Look Alike' (live); 'Black Mountain Rag' (live); 'Baby What You Want Me To Do' (live); 'I Trust' (live); 'Take A Whiff (On Me)' (live); 'Glory, Glory'; 'Byrdgrass'; 'Pale Blue'; 'I Wanna Grow Up To Be A Politician'; 'Nothin' To It'; 'Tiffany Queen'; 'Farther Along'; 'Bugler'; 'Mr Tambourine Man' (*Banjoman* soundtrack version); 'Roll Over Beethoven' (*Banjoman* soundtrack version); 'Full Circle'; 'Changing Heart'; 'Paths Of Victory'.

DVD: 'Mr Tambourine Man'; '(I'll) Feel A Whole Lot Better'; 'All I Really Want To Do'; 'Turn! Turn! Turn!'; 'It Won't Be Wrong'; 'Set You Free This Time'; 'So You Want To Be A Rock 'n' Roll Star'; 'Mr Tambourine Man'; 'Eight Miles High'; 'Mr Spaceman'.

Released September 2006 (US).
Released October 2006 (UK).

The Complete Columbia Albums Collection
Columbia Legacy 886978738028 (US).
Available exclusively through Pop Markets.com, this box was not dissimilar to the aforementioned UK release, *12 Dimensions*. It includes the 11 remastered/reissued Byrds CDs but, unlike its UK predecessor, does not feature *Live At The Fillmore – February 1969*. However, it does offer the 2-CD Legacy Edition of *Sweetheart Of The Rodeo*. A booklet was also included in the package.
Released May 2011 (US).

BYRDS DISCOGRAPHY

BYRDS CD REMASTERED ORIGINAL ALBUMS

The history of the Byrds' releases on CD has been, to say the least, chaotic. This was particularly true in the early days of the format when the group were poorly represented in the burgeoning CD market. Various reissue labels picked up releases in random fashion. Initially the UK market only offered *The Byrds' Greatest Hits* (CBS 63107/32068). Edsel Records successfully licensed *Younger Than Yesterday* (Edsel ED 227), *The Notorious Byrd Brothers* (Edsel ED 262) and *Sweetheart Of The Rodeo* (Edsel ED 234), while Castle Communications offered *The Byrds Collection* (CCS CD 151). The Beat Goes On label briefly licensed *Fifth Dimension* (CD 106) and *Dr Byrds & Mr Hyde* (CD 107). Finally, UK's Sony/Columbia reissued unremastered versions of the catalogue from *Mr Tambourine Man* through to *Farther Along*. The release schedule was haphazard, and the serial numbers inconsistent, with different digits on the sleeves and discs. None of these releases had extra tracks or other distinguishing features.

American CD releases were also slight at first, with Columbia slowly issuing: *Mr Tambourine Man* (CK 9172), *Turn! Turn! Turn!* (CK 9254), *Fifth Dimension* (CK 9349), *Younger Than Yesterday* (CK 9442), *The Byrds' Greatest Hits* (CK 9516), *The Notorious Byrd Brothers* (CK 9575), *Sweetheart Of The Rodeo* (CK 9670), *Ballad Of Easy Rider* (CK 9942), *(Untitled)* (CGK 30127), *Best Of The Byrds* (CK 31795) and *The Original Singles, Volume I* (CK 37335). The quality of the recordings left much to be desired and, once more, there were no extras. Previously unissued CD Byrds' material was made available in the late Eighties on *Never Before* (Re-Flyte D 22808) and *In The Beginning* (Rhino R2 70244), as fully documented in the 'Archival Albums (CDs)' section below.

Following the release of the box set, *The Byrds* (see Box Set section), Sony/Legacy set about rehabilitating the group's back catalogue by re-releasing the original albums in remastered form, complete with original artwork, plus some fascinating bonus tracks.

Mr Tambourine Man
Columbia Legacy CK 64845 (US).
Columbia Legacy 483705 2 (UK).
Original album plus bonus tracks: 'She Has A Way' (previously unissued version); '(I'll) Feel A Whole Lot Better' (previously unissued alternate take); 'It's No Use' (previously unissued alternate take); 'You Won't Have To Cry' (previously unissued alternate take); 'All I Really Want To Do' (single

version); 'You And Me' (previously unissued instrumental backing track).
Released 20 April 1996 (US).
Released 7 May 1996 (UK).

Turn! Turn! Turn!
Columbia Legacy CK 64846 (US).
Columbia Legacy 483706 2 (UK).
Original album plus bonus tracks: 'The Day Walk' (Never Before)' (box set version); 'She Don't Care About Time' (single version); 'The Times They Are A-Changin'' (previously unissued alternate take); 'It's All Over Now, Baby Blue' (previously unissued alternate take); 'She Don't Care About Time' (previously unissued alternate take); 'The World Turns All Around Her' (previously unissued alternate mix); 'Stranger In A Strange Land' (previously unissued instrumental backing track).
Released 20 April 1996 (US).
Released 7 May 1996 (UK).

Fifth Dimension
Columbia Legacy CK 64847(US).
Columbia Legacy 483707 2 (UK).
Original album plus bonus tracks: 'Why' (single version); 'I Know My Rider (I Know You Rider)' (box set version); 'Psychodrama City' (box set version); 'Eight Miles High' (RCA version from *Never Before*); 'Why' (RCA version from *Never Before*); 'John Riley' (previously unissued alternate take, instrumental backing track). Plus extra hidden bonus track featuring "A Special Open-End Interview With The Byrds Talking About Their New LP *Fifth Dimension*."
Released 20 April 1996 (US).
Released 7 May 1996 (UK).

Younger Than Yesterday
Columbia Legacy CK 64848 (US).
Columbia Legacy 483708 2 (UK).
Original album plus bonus tracks: 'It Happens Each Day' (box set version); 'Don't Make Waves' (single version); 'My Back Pages' (previously unissued alternate take); 'Mind Gardens' (previously unissued alternate take); 'Lady Friend' (single version); 'Old John Robertson' (single version). Plus extra hidden bonus track featuring the original backing track for 'Mind Gardens' before it was "recorded played backwards".
Released 20 April 1996 (US).
Released 7 May 1996 (UK).

BYRDS DISCOGRAPHY

The Notorious Byrd Brothers
Columbia Legacy CK 65151 (US).
Columbia Legacy 486751 2 (UK).
Original album plus bonus tracks: 'Moog Raga' (*Never Before* version); 'Bound To Fall' (previously unissued instrumental backing track); 'Triad' (box set version); 'Goin' Back' (previously unissued alternate version); 'Draft Morning' (elongated version); 'Universal Mind Decoder' (previously unissued demo instrumental backing track for 'Change Is Now'). Plus extra hidden bonus tracks featuring the radio advertisement for the album with Gary Usher, plus the rehearsal for 'Dolphin's Smile', including the infamous studio argument.
Released February 1997 (US)/(UK).

Sweetheart Of The Rodeo
Columbia Legacy CK 65150 (US).
Columbia Legacy 486752 2 (UK).
Original album plus bonus tracks: 'You Got A Reputation' (box set version); 'Lazy Days' (box set version); 'Pretty Polly' (box set version); 'The Christian Life' (previously unissued rehearsal take); 'Life In Prison' (previously unissued rehearsal take); 'You're Still On My Mind' (previously unissued rehearsal take); 'One Hundred Years From Now' (previously unissued rehearsal take); 'All I Have Is Memories' (previously unissued instrumental). Plus extra hidden bonus track featuring the radio advertisement for the album.
Released February 1997 (US)/(UK).

Dr Byrds & Mr Hyde
Columbia Legacy CK 65113 (US).
Columbia Legacy 486753 2 (UK).
Original album plus bonus tracks: 'Stanley's Song' (box set version); 'Lay Lady Lay' (box set version); 'This Wheel's On Fire' (previously unissued alternate take); 'Medley: 'My Back Pages'/'B.J. Blues'/'Baby, What You Want Me To Do' (previously unissued alternate take); 'Nashville West' (previously unissued alternate take).
   In deference to Jimmy Reed's original, the Byrds' grammatically correct 'Baby, What *Do* You Want Me To Do' has been retitled 'Baby, What You Want Me To Do'.
Released February 1997 (US)/(UK).

Ballad Of Easy Rider
Columbia Legacy CK 65114 (US).
Columbia Legacy 486754 2 (UK).
Original album plus bonus tracks: 'Way Behind The Sun' (box set version);

'Mae Jean Goes To Hollywood' (box set version); 'Oil In My Lamp' (box set version); 'Tulsa County' (previously unissued alternate take); 'Fiddler A Dram (Moog Experiment)' (previously unissued instrumental); 'Ballad Of Easy Rider' (previously unissued alternate take); 'Build It Up' (previously unissued instrumental). Plus extra hidden bonus tracks featuring two radio advertisements for the album. The previously titled 'Tulsa County Blue' loses the 'Blue' here.

First pressings of the album mistakenly label 'Way Behind The Sun' as 'Way Beyond The Sun', with McGuinn erroneously receiving a writing credit. Released February 1997 (US)/(UK).

(Untitled)/(Unissued)
Columbia Legacy C2K 65847 (US).
Columbia Legacy 495077 2 (UK).
Original album plus bonus tracks: 'All The Things' (previously unissued alternate take); 'Yesterday's Train' (previously unissued alternate take); 'Lover Of The Bayou' (previously unissued studio version); 'Kathleen's Song' (previously unissued alternate take); 'White's Lightning Part 2' (previously unissued studio recording); 'Willin'' (previously unissued); 'You Ain't Going Nowhere' (previously unissued live recording); 'Old Blue' (previously unissued live recording); 'It's Alright Ma (I'm Only Bleeding)' (previously unissued live recording); 'Ballad Of Easy Rider' (previously unissued live recording); 'My Back Pages' (previously unissued live recording); 'Take A Whiff (On Me)' (previously unissued live recording); 'Jesus Is Just Alright' (previously unissued live recording); 'This Wheel's On Fire' (previously unissued live recording). Plus hidden bonus track featuring 'Amazing Grace', the song which usually ended Byrds' sets of the period.

The White/McGuinn arranging credit on 'Take A Whiff (On Me)' has been partly reassigned to Leadbelly (Huddie Ledbetter), plus John and Alex Lomax. Incorrectly, in my view, 'Well Come Back Home' has been retitled 'Welcome Back Home'.
Released February 2000 (US)/(UK).

Byrdmaniax
Columbia Legacy CK 65848 (US).
Columbia Legacy 495079 2 (UK).
Original album plus bonus tracks: 'Just Like A Woman' (previously unissued take); 'Pale Blue' (previously unissued take); 'Think I'm Gonna Feel Better' (previously unissued). The newly discovered 'Think I'm Gonna Feel Better' sung by Clarence White was a surprise attempt at a Gene Clark recording first issued in 1967. Plus hidden bonus track 'Green Apple Quick Step' featuring Clarence White's father on harmonica.

Gene Parsons has been erroneously added to the composing credits on 'Pale Blue', which previously featured McGuinn's name only. This appears to be an administrative error as he was not featured on the original album. Parsons confirmed to me that he did not co-write the track, nor is it registered in his publishing copyrights.
Released February 2000 (US)/(UK).

Farther Along
Columbia Legacy CK 65849 (US).
Columbia Legacy 495078 2 (UK).
Original album plus bonus tracks: 'Lost My Drivin' Wheel' (previously unissued take); 'Born To Rock 'n' Roll' (previously unissued take); 'Bag Full Of Money' (previously unissued take). These final songs were recorded for possible inclusion on another Byrds' album but instead were carried forward and re-cut by Roger McGuinn, although a new version of 'Born To Rock 'n' Roll' also appeared on the Byrds' 1973 reunion album. Plus hidden bonus track, 'Bristol Steam Convention Blues' (rehearsal take).
Released February 2000 (US)/(UK).

In addition to the Sony/Columbia reissue series, the specialist label Mobile Fidelity Sound Lab released gold-plated CDs taken from the original first generation master tapes, using half-speed mastering for superior audio quality. The CDs were licensed as limited editions in SACD (Super Audio Compact Disc) as follows:

(Untitled)
Mobile Fidelity Sound Lab UDCD 22 (US).
The original album with no bonus tracks, issued before Sony's remastered version.
Released 21 April 1998 (US).

Mr Tambourine Man
Mobile Fidelity Sound Lab UD SACD 2014 (US).
This is the mono mixed version of the original album, accompanied by the six stereo bonus tracks included on the Sony remastered reissue.
Released September 2005 (US).

The Notorious Byrd Brothers
Mobile Fidelity Sound Lab UD SACD 2015 (US).
This is the mono mixed version of the original album, accompanied by the six stereo bonus tracks included on the Sony remastered reissue.
Released May 2006 (US).

ARCHIVAL ALBUMS (CDs)

Never Before
Re-Flyte D 22808 (US).
'Mr Tambourine Man' (previously unreleased stereo mix); 'I Knew I'd Want You' (new stereo mix); 'She Has A Way' (previously unreleased); 'It's All Over Now, Baby Blue' (previously unreleased); 'Never Before' (previously unreleased – later correctly retitled 'The Day Walk'); 'Eight Miles High' (previously unreleased alternate RCA version); 'Why' (previously unreleased alternate RCA version); 'Triad' (previously unreleased); 'It Happens Each Day' (previously unreleased); 'Lady Friend' (previously unreleased stereo mix, with re-recorded drums).
Bonus tracks: 'I Know My Rider (I Know You Rider)' (previously unreleased); 'Why' (single version, previously unreleased stereo mix); 'She Don't Care About Time' (previously unreleased stereo mix); 'Flight 713 (Song Number 2)' (previously unreleased instrumental); 'Psychodrama City' (previously unreleased); 'Don't Make Waves' (single version, previously unreleased stereo mix); 'Moog Raga' (previously unreleased instrumental).
Released 1 May 1989 (US).

In The Beginning
Rhino R2 70244 (US).
'Tomorrow Is A Long Ways Away'; 'Boston'; 'The Only Girl I Adore'; 'You Won't Have To Cry'; 'I Knew I'd Want You'; 'The Airport Song'; 'The Reason Why'; 'Mr Tambourine Man'; 'Please Let Me Love You'; 'You Movin''; 'It Won't Be Wrong'; 'You Showed Me'; 'She Has A Way'; 'For Me Again'; 'It's No Use'; 'Here Without You'; 'Tomorrow Is A Long Ways Away' (acoustic version).
Released August 1988 (US).

Monterey International Pop Festival
Rhino R2 70506 (US)/Castle Communications ROK CD 102 (UK).
Includes the following tracks by the Byrds:
'Renaissance Fair'; 'Have You Seen Her Face'; 'Hey Joe'; 'He Was A Friend Of Mine'; 'Lady Friend'; 'Chimes Of Freedom'; 'So You Want To Be A Rock 'n' Roll Star'.
Released November 1992 (US).
Released February 1994 (UK).

BYRDS DISCOGRAPHY

3 Byrds Land In London 1977
Strange Fruit SFRSCD 001 (UK).
Gene Clark: 'Kansas City Southern'; 'Denver Or Wherever'; 'Release Me Girl'; 'Hula Bula Man'.
The Chris Hillman Band: 'Hot Burrito # 2'; 'Rise And Fall'; 'Nothing Gets Through To You'; 'Rollin' And Tumblin''; 'Playing The Fool'; 'Quits'; 'The Witching Hour'; 'It Doesn't Matter'.
Roger McGuinn's Thunderbyrd: 'Lover Of The Bayou'; 'American Girl'; 'Mr Spaceman'; 'Why Baby Why'/'Tiffany Queen'; 'Golden Loom'; 'It's Gone'; 'Chestnut Mare'; Dixie Highway'; 'Shoot 'Em'.
McGuinn, Hillman, Clark [Roger McGuinn's Thunderbyrd, with Chris Hillman and Gene Clark]: 'So You Want To Be A Rock 'n' Roll Star'; 'Mr Tambourine Man'; 'Eight Miles High'.
Released 3 February 1997 (UK).

3 Byrds In London 1977 – Live At The BBC
Mastertone 8228 (US).
Gene Clark: 'Kansas City Southern'.
The Chris Hillman Band: 'Hot Burrito # 2'; 'It Doesn't Matter'.
Roger McGuinn's Thunderbyrd: 'Lover Of The Bayou'; 'American Girl'; 'Mr Spaceman'; 'Why Baby Why'/'Tiffany Queen'; 'Golden Loom'; 'Chestnut Mare'.
McGuinn, Hillman, Clark [Roger McGuinn's Thunderbyrd, with Chris Hillman and Gene Clark]: 'So You Want To Be A Rock 'n' Roll Star'; 'Mr Tambourine Man.'
The US version was a retitled and resequenced single CD, minus several tracks from the UK release.
Released June 1998 (US).

Live At The Fillmore – February 1969
Columbia Legacy CK 65910 (US).
Columbia Legacy 495080 2 (UK).
'Nashville West'; 'You're Still On My Mind'; 'Pretty Boy Floyd'; 'Drug Store Truck Drivin' Man'; 'Medley: 'Turn! Turn! Turn!'/'Mr Tambourine Man'/'Eight Miles High'; 'Close Up The Honky Tonks'; 'Buckaroo'; 'The Christian Life'; 'Time Between'; 'King Apathy III'; 'Bad Night At The Whiskey'; 'This Wheel's On Fire'; 'Sing Me Back Home'; 'So You Want To Be A Rock 'n' Roll Star'; 'He Was A Friend Of Mine'; 'Chimes Of Freedom'. This newly unearthed live album was released along with the final three CDs in the reissue series.
Released February 2000 (US)/(UK).

REQUIEM FOR THE TIMELESS — VOLUME 1

12 Dimensions – The Columbia Recordings 1965–1972
Columbia 497610 2/4976102000 (UK).
See Box Sets section.

The Preflyte Sessions
Sundazed SC 11116 (US).
Disc 1: 'The Reason Why' (version 2, *Preflyte*); 'You Won't Have To Cry' (electric version, *Preflyte*); 'She Has A Way' (previously unissued version 4); 'You Showed Me' (electric version, *In The Beginning*); 'Here Without You' (version 2, *In The Beginning*); 'Don't Be Long' (single); 'I Knew I'd Want You' (electric version 2, *In The Beginning*); 'Boston' (previously unissued version 2); 'Tomorrow Is A Long Ways Away' (electric version, *In The Beginning*); 'For Me Again' (previously unissued version 2 electric); 'It's No Use' (previously unissued version 2); 'You Movin'' (previously unissued version 3); 'Please Let Me Love You' (single); 'The Airport Song' (*Preflyte*); 'Mr Tambourine Man' (electric version, *Preflyte*); 'She Has A Way' (previously unissued version 3); 'I Knew I'd Want You' (electric version 1, previously unissued); 'Boston' (previously unissued instrumental version); 'You Showed Me' (previously unissued instrumental version); 'The Times They Are A-Changin'' (previously unissued instrumental version).
Disc 2: 'The Only Girl I Adore' (*Early LA*); 'Tomorrow Is A Long Ways Away' (acoustic version, *In The Beginning*); 'You Showed Me' (acoustic version, *Preflyte*); 'I Knew I'd Want You' (acoustic version, *Preflyte*); 'You Won't Have To Cry' (acoustic version, *In The Beginning*); 'Mr Tambourine Man' (acoustic version, *In The Beginning*); 'Willie Jean' (David Crosby, *Early LA*); 'Come Back Baby' (David Crosby, *Early LA*); 'Jack Of Diamonds' (David Crosby, previously unissued); 'Get Together' (David Crosby, previously unissued); 'She Has A Way' (previously unissued, version 1); 'Here Without You' (version 1, *Preflyte*); 'For Me Again' (version 1, *Preflyte*); 'It's No Use' (version 1, *In The Beginning*); 'You Movin'' (version 1, *Preflyte*); 'Boston' (version 1, *Preflyte*); 'She Has A Way' (version 2, *Preflyte*); 'You Movin'' (previously unissued, version 2); 'The Reason Why' (previously unissued, version 1); 'It's No Use' (previously unissued, version 3).

All these tracks, bar one, were recorded in 1964, prior to the group's signing to CBS. However, the inclusion of 'The Times They Are A-Changin'' is misleading, as it was recorded (probably not even at World-Pacific) as a backing track in late 1965 and is not part of the 'Preflyte' sessions.
Released November 2001 (US).

BYRDS DISCOGRAPHY

Sweetheart Of The Rodeo
Columbia Legacy COL 510921 2 (US).
Disc 1: Original LP: 'You Ain't Going Nowhere'; 'I Am A Pilgrim'; 'The Christian Life'; 'You Don't Miss Your Water'; 'You're Still On My Mind'; 'Pretty Boy Floyd'; 'Hickory Wind'; 'One Hundred Years From Now'; 'Blue Canadian Rockies'; 'Life In Prison'; 'Nothing Was Delivered'.
Disc 1: Additional Master Takes: 'All I Have Are Memories' (Kevin Kelley vocal, previously unissued); 'Reputation' (First Box Set version); 'Pretty Polly' (First Box Set version); 'Lazy Days' (First Box Set version); 'The Christian Life' (master take, Gram Parsons vocal; First Box Set version); 'You Don't Miss Your Water' (master take, Gram Parsons vocal; First Box Set version); 'One Hundred Years From Now' (master take, Gram Parsons vocal; First Box Set version); radio spot for *Sweetheart Of The Rodeo*.
Disc 2: The International Submarine Band: 'Sum Up Broke' (mono Columbia single); 'One Day Week' (mono Columbia single); 'Truck Drivin' Man' (mono Ascot single); 'Blue Eyes' (*Safe At Home* version); 'Luxury Liner' (*Safe At Home* version); 'Strong Boy' (*Safe At Home* version).
Disc 2 Working Demos, Outtakes and Rehearsal Versions: 'Lazy Days' (alternate version, previously unreleased); 'Pretty Polly' (alternate version, previously unreleased); 'Hickory Wind' (alternate 'Nashville' version, take 8, previously unreleased); 'The Christian Life' (rehearsal version, take 5, Gram Parsons vocal, previously unreleased); 'The Christian Life' (rehearsal version, take 8, Gram Parsons vocal, previously unreleased); 'Life In Prison (rehearsal version, takes 1 and 2, Gram Parsons vocal, previously unreleased); 'One Hundred Years From Now' (rehearsal version, takes 12 and 13, Gram Parsons vocal, previously unreleased); 'One Hundred Years From Now' (rehearsal version, takes 14 and 15, Gram Parsons vocal, previously unreleased); 'You're Still On My Mind' (rehearsal version, take 13, Gram Parsons vocal, previously unreleased); 'You're Still On My Mind' (rehearsal version, take 48, Gram Parsons vocal, previously unreleased); 'All I Have Are Memories' (alternate instrumental, take 21, previously unreleased); 'Blue Canadian Rockies' (rehearsal version, take 14).
Released September 2003 (US).

Cancelled Flytes
Sundazed PVS 72860/S 7001 (US).
(Unissued on CD). See Singles section.
Released September 2004 (US).

Another Dimension
Sundazed SEP 2 10-168 (US).
(Unissued on CD). See Archival Albums (Vinyl).
Released 26 April 2005 (US).

REQUIEM FOR THE TIMELESS — VOLUME 1

Sixties Transition
Sierra SXCD 6027 (US).
Compilation of Jim Dickson productions, including work with Dino Valenti, David Crosby, Bud Shank/David Crosby, Dian & The Greenbriar Boys, the Hillmen, the Byrds, the Dillards, the Gosdin Brothers and Hamilton Camp. Includes four selections from *Preflyte* – 'You Showed Me', 'The Airport Song', 'I Knew I'd Want You' and 'Mr Tambourine Man', the *Early LA* versions of Crosby's 'Willie Gene' and 'Come Back Baby', the previously unreleased 'Charisma (featuring Crosby on rhythm guitar), plus Hamilton Camp's version of 'The Times They Are A-Changin'' featuring a backing track from the Byrds (minus Crosby, who reputedly declined to contribute).
Released September 2007 (US).

Live At The Royal Albert Hall 1971
Sundazed SC 11177(US)/SC 11177 (UK).
'Lover Of The Bayou'; 'You Ain't Going Nowhere'; 'Truck Stop Girl'; 'My Back Pages'; 'Baby, What You Want Me To Do'; 'Jamaica Say You Will'; 'Black Mountain Rag'/'Soldier's Joy'; 'Mr Tambourine Man'; 'Pretty Boy Floyd'; 'Take A Whiff (On Me)'; 'Chestnut Mare'; 'Jesus Is Just Alright'; 'Eight Miles High'; 'So You Want To Be A Rock 'n' Roll Star'; 'Mr Spaceman'; 'I Trust (Everything's Gonna Work Out Alright)'; 'Nashville West'; 'Roll Over Beethoven'; 'Amazing Grace'.
Released May 2008 (US).
Released June 2008 (UK).

The Byrds have also appeared on several soundtrack albums (see under Archival Albums). More recent releases include 1995's *Forrest Gump* (Epic 476941-2) which features the previously issued 'Turn! Turn! Turn!' and 1999's *The Limey* (Flash Cut Records 54352-2) which includes 'It Happens Each Day'. Although outside the scope of this discography, I should briefly mention the two Australian releases *Byrd Parts* Raven RVCD 77 (released 1998) and *Byrd Parts 2* Raven RVCD 165 (released 2003). The first features mainly Byrds' family tracks, including rare but previously released songs from David Crosby, the Jet Set, the Hillmen, the Beefeaters, Jackie De Shannon (supposedly with the Byrds backing her on 'Splendor In The Grass'), David Hemmings (including Clark's rare composition 'Back Street Mirror'), Fred Neil & Gram Parsons, the International Submarine Band, Dillard & Clark, Terry Melcher, Clarence White & Ry Cooder, Nashville West, Gene Parsons and McGuinn, Clark & Hillman. The second collection focuses on 'Byrds-related' tracks (including guest appearances by ex-Byrds) on predominantly previously released recordings by Hoyt Axton, the Les Baxter Balladeers, David Crosby, the City Surfers, Judy Collins, Gene Clark (including the otherwise unavailable 'Why Can't I Have Her Back Again' and 'If I Hang Around'), Rose Garden, Peter Fonda, Johnny Rivers, Clarence White, the Everly Brothers, Johnny Darrell, Earl Scruggs with the Byrds, Delaney & Bonnie, the Flying Burrito Brothers, McGuinn & Hillman, the Textones and Gene Clark & Carla Olson.

VINYL ALBUMS 180 gram

The UK label Simply Vinyl was the first to licence Byrds' material for release on 180 gram vinyl. Below are the albums they issued. Note that the release campaign was not in strict chronological order. Soon after, the US label Sundazed issued a far more extensive reissue campaign with complete access to the Sony archives. For greater clarity, each label's catalogue is listed separately here. As this discography is US/UK based I have not included similar releases in other territories, but the Netherlands-based Music On Vinyl have so far released 180 gram versions of *Sweetheart Of The Rodeo* (MOV 064) and the 3-LP edition *(Untitled)/(Unissued)* (MOVLP 381).

Simply Vinyl 180 gram releases:

Mr Tambourine Man
Simply Vinyl 62571/SVLP 0032 (UK).
As per original vinyl album.
Released July 1998 (UK).

Turn! Turn! Turn!
Simply Vinyl 49219/SVLP 0037 (UK).
As per original vinyl album.
Released November 1998 (UK).

Fifth Dimension
Simply Vinyl 62783/SVLP 0047 (UK).
As per original vinyl album.
Released November 1998 (UK).

Younger Than Yesterday
Simply Vinyl 62988/SVLP 00007 (UK).
As per original vinyl album.
Released October 1997 (UK).

REQUIEM FOR THE TIMELESS — VOLUME 1

The Notorious Byrd Brothers
Simply Vinyl 63169/SVLP 00006 (UK).
As per original vinyl album.
Released October 1997 (UK).

Sweetheart Of The Rodeo
Simply Vinyl 63353/SVLP 0057 (UK).
As per original vinyl album.
Released November 1998 (UK).

Dr Byrds & Mr Hyde
Simply Vinyl 486753/SVLP 0070.
As per original vinyl album.
Released February 1999 (UK).

The Very Best Of The Byrds
Simply Vinyl 487995/SVLP 375 (UK).
'Mr Tambourine Man'; 'All I Really Want To Do'; 'Chimes Of Freedom'; 'Feel A Whole Lot Better'; 'Turn! Turn! Turn!'; 'The Times They Are A-Changin''; 'The World Turns All Around Her'; 'It Won't Be Wrong'; 'He Was A Friend Of Mine'; 'Eight Miles High'; '5 D (Fifth Dimension)'; 'Mr Spaceman'; 'So You Want To Be A Rock 'n' Roll Star'; 'My Back Pages'; 'Renaissance Fair'; 'Goin' Back'; 'Wasn't Born To Follow'; 'Dolphin's Smile'; 'You Ain't Going Nowhere'; 'One Hundred Years From Now'; 'You're Still On My Mind'; 'Hickory Wind'; 'Ballad Of Easy Rider'; 'Jesus Is Just Alright'; 'It's All Over Now, Baby Blue'; 'Lay Lady Lay'; 'Chestnut Mare'.
Released April 2002 (UK).

(Untitled)/(Unissued)
Simply Vinyl 495077/SVLP 381 (UK).
3-LP set. Original album plus bonus tracks: 'All The Things' (previously unissued on vinyl, alternate take); 'Yesterday's Train' (previously unissued on vinyl, alternate take); 'Lover Of The Bayou' (previously unissued on vinyl, studio version); 'Kathleen's Song' (previously unissued on vinyl, alternate take); 'White's Lightning Part 2' (previously unissued on vinyl, studio recording); 'Willin'' (previously unissued on vinyl); 'You Ain't Going Nowhere' (previously unissued on vinyl, live recording); 'Old Blue' (previously unissued on vinyl, live recording); 'It's Alright Ma (I'm Only Bleeding)' (previously unissued on vinyl, live recording); 'Ballad Of Easy Rider' (previously unissued on vinyl, live recording); 'My Back Pages' (previously unissued on vinyl, live recording); 'Take A Whiff (On Me)' (previously unissued on vinyl, live recording); 'Jesus Is Just

Alright' (previously unissued on vinyl, live recording); 'This Wheel's On Fire' (previously unissued on vinyl, live recording); 'Amazing Grace' (previously unissued on vinyl, live recording).
Released June 2002 (UK).

Sundazed 180 gram vinyl releases

Mr Tambourine Man
Sundazed LP 5057 (US).
Original stereo album, plus bonus tracks: 'She Has A Way'; 'You And Me' (instrumental).
Released July 1999 (US).

Turn! Turn! Turn!
Sundazed LP 5058 (US).
Original stereo album, plus bonus tracks: 'She Don't Care About Time' (single version); 'Stranger In A Strange Land' (instrumental); 'The Times They Are A-Changin'' (first version).
Three of the songs herein – 'Turn! Turn! Turn!', 'He Was A Friend Of Mine' and 'The Times They Are A-Changin'' are in mono only.
Released July 1999 (US).

Fifth Dimension
Sundazed LP 5059 (US).
Original stereo album, plus bonus tracks: 'I Know My Rider (I Know You Rider)'; 'Why' (single version); 'Eight Miles High' (RCA version).
Released July 1999 (US).

Younger Than Yesterday
Sundazed LP 5060 (US).
Original stereo album, plus bonus tracks: 'It Happens Each Day'; 'Don't Make Waves'; 'My Back Pages' (alternate version).
Released July 1999 (US).

Sanctuary
Sundazed LP 5061 (US).
'All I Really Want To Do' (single version); 'I'll Feel A Whole Lot Better' (alternate version, previously on CD); 'You Won't Have To Cry' (alternate version, previously on CD); 'It's No Use' (alternate version, previously on CD); 'She Don't Care About Time' (version 1, previously on CD); 'It's All Over Now, Baby Blue' (version 1, previously on CD); 'The World Turns All Around Her' (alternate mix, previously on CD); 'The Day Walk'; 'Why' (RCA version); 'John Riley' (instrumental, previously on CD); 'Psychodrama

City'; 'Mind Gardens' (alternate version, previously on CD); 'Lady Friend' (stereo mix, previously on CD); 'Old John Robertson' (single version).
Released July 2000 (US).

Sanctuary II
Sundazed LP 5065 (US).
'Universal Mind Decoder' (instrumental); 'Draft Morning' (alternate ending, previously on CD); 'Bound To Fall' (instrumental); 'Goin' Back' (alternate take, previously on CD); 'Triad'; 'Moog Raga'; 'This Wheel's On Fire' (version 1, previously on CD); 'Nashville West' (alternate version, previously on CD); 'Stanley's Song'; 'Time Between' (previously unissued alternate backing track – take 3); 'Have You Seen Her Face' (previously unissued acoustic/vocal reference mix); 'Mind Gardens' (instrumental, alternate take, previously issued on CD).
Released December 2000 (US).

The Preflyte Sessions
Sundazed LP 5114 (USA).
2-LP 180 gram vinyl set.
Disc 1: 'The Reason Why' (version 2); 'You Won't Have To Cry' (electric version); 'She Has A Way' (version 4, previously unreleased); 'You Showed Me' (electric version); 'Here Without You' (version 2); 'Don't Be Long' (single); 'Boston (version 2, previously unreleased); 'Tomorrow Is A Long Ways Away' (electric version); 'It's No Use' (version 2, previously unreleased); 'You Movin'' (version 3, previously unreleased); 'Please Let Me Love You' (single); 'The Airport Song'; 'Mr. Tambourine Man' (electric version); 'I Knew I'd Want You' (electric version, previously unreleased).
Disc 2: 'The Only Girl I Adore'; 'Tomorrow Is A Long Ways Away' (acoustic version); 'You Showed Me' (acoustic version); 'I Knew I'd Want You' (acoustic version); 'Willie Jean' (David Crosby); 'Come Back Baby' (David Crosby); 'Jack Of Diamonds' (David Crosby, previously unreleased); 'Get Together' (David Crosby, previously unreleased); 'She Has A Way' (version 1, previously unreleased); 'Here Without You' (version 1); 'For Me Again' (version 1); 'It's No Use' (version 1); 'Boston' (version 1); 'The Reason Why' (version 1, previously unreleased).
Released November 2001 (US).

Sanctuary III
Sundazed LP 5066 (US).
'Ballad Of Easy Rider' (alternate mix); 'Oil In My Lamp' (alternate version); 'Mae Jean Goes To Hollywood'; 'Fido' (previously unreleased alternate mix); 'Lover Of The Bayou' (studio version); 'White's Lightning, Part 1'; 'All The

Things' (alternate version); 'Kathleen's Song' (alternate version, take 3); 'Way Behind The Sun'; 'Build It Up' (instrumental); 'It's All Over Now, Baby Blue' (alternate mix); 'White's Lightning, Part 2'.
Released December 2001 (US).

Sanctuary IV
Sundazed LP 5090 (US).
'The Christian Life' (Gram Parsons vocal version); 'Pretty Polly'; 'One Hundred Years From Now' (Gram Parsons vocal version); 'You're Still On My Mind' (rehearsal version, take 43); 'You Don't Miss Your Water' (Gram Parsons vocal version); 'All I Have Is Memories' (instrumental); 'Life In Prison' (rehearsal version, take 11); 'You Got A Reputation'; 'One Hundred Years From Now' (rehearsal version, take 2); 'The Christian Life' (rehearsal version, take 11); 'Lazy Days'.
Released May 2002 (US).

The Columbia Singles '65–'67
Sundazed LP 5130/P2 55624 (US).
'Mr Tambourine Man'; 'I Knew I'd Want You'; 'All I Really Want To Do'; 'Feel A Whole Lot Better'; 'The Bells Of Rhymney' (alternate version); 'Chimes Of Freedom' (alternate version); 'She Don't Care About Time' (alternate version); 'It's All Over Now, Baby Blue' (alternate version); 'The Times They Are A-Changin'' (alternate version); 'Turn! Turn! Turn!'; 'She Don't Care About Time'; 'Set You Free This Time'; 'It Won't Be Wrong'; 'He Was A Friend Of Mine'; 'Eight Miles High'; 'Why'; '5 D (Fifth Dimension)'; 'Captain Soul'; 'Mr Spaceman'; 'What's Happening?!?!'; 'So You Want To Be A Rock 'n' Roll Star'; 'Everybody's Been Burned'; 'My Back Pages'; 'Renaissance Fair'; 'Have You Seen Her Face'; 'Don't Make Waves'; 'Lady Friend'; 'Old John Robertson'; 'Goin' Back'; 'Change Is Now'. This 2-LP vinyl set features material taken from the Sony reissued, remastered albums.
Released September 2002 (US).

Mr Tambourine Man
Sundazed LP 5197 (US).
Original mono album. No bonus tracks.
Released January 2006 (US).

Turn! Turn! Turn!
Sundazed LP 5198 (US).
Original mono album. No bonus tracks.
Released January 2006 (US).

REQUIEM FOR THE TIMELESS — VOLUME 1

Fifth Dimension
Sundazed LP 5199 (US).
Original mono album. No bonus tracks.
Released January 2006 (US).

Younger Than Yesterday
Sundazed LP 5200 (US).
Original mono album. No bonus tracks.
Released January 2006 (US).

The Notorious Byrd Brothers
Sundazed LP 5201 (US).
Original mono album. No bonus tracks.
Released February 2006 (US).

Sweetheart Of The Rodeo
Sundazed LP 5215 (US).
Original stereo album.
Released July 2007 (US).

Another Dimension
Sundazed SEP 2 10-168 (US).
10-inch double album vinyl release. 'Eight Miles High' (instrumental, take 2); 'Why' (instrumental, take 17); 'Ryder (I Know My Rider)' (instrumental, take 9); 'John Riley I' (instrumental, take 2); '2-4-2 Fox Trot (The Lear Jet Song)' (long version instrumental, minus sound effects); 'Psychodrama City' (instrumental, take 1); 'John Riley II' (completed early master, no string overdubs); 'Wild Mountain Thyme' (completed early master, no string overdubs); 'Hey Joe (Where You Gonna Go)' (*Radiohuset*, Stockholm, Sweden); 'I See You' (completed master, longer version, without overdubs); 'What's Happening?!?!' (completed master, long version, partial alternate vocal); 'Captain Soul (30 Minute Break)' (completed early master, longer version, without overdubs).
Released 26 April 2005 (US).

Live At The Royal Albert Hall 1971
Sundazed LP 5189 (US).
2-LP Vinyl set. 'Lover Of The Bayou'; 'You Ain't Going Nowhere'; 'Truck Stop Girl'; 'My Back Pages'; 'Baby, What You Want Me To Do'; 'Jamaica Say You Will'; 'Black Mountain Rag'/'Soldier's Joy'; 'Mr Tambourine Man'; 'Pretty Boy Floyd'; 'Take A Whiff (On Me)'; 'Chestnut Mare'; 'Jesus Is Just Alright'; 'Eight Miles High'; 'So You Want To Be A Rock 'n' Roll Star'; 'Mr Spaceman'; 'I Trust (Everything's Gonna Work Out Alright)'; 'Nashville

West'; 'Roll Over Beethoven'; 'Amazing Grace'.
Released May 2008 (US).

In August 2008, Sundazed also released *Dr Byrds & Mr Hyde* (Sundazed LP 5072) in the US, but this did not appear on 180 gram vinyl.

BYRDS CD COMPILATIONS

This section features US/UK compilations only (excepting the interesting Australian release *Full Flyte*). It does not feature straight reissues of original albums, multi-disc repackaged original albums, duplicated issues of certain compilations, radio only promotions, or specific limited edition releases. Please note that certain Continental releases have infiltrated the UK market, some legally, some not. In this sense, any compilations discography is ultimately selective.

The Byrds Play Dylan
CBS 466307 2 (UK).
'Mr Tambourine Man'; 'All I Really Want To Do'; 'Chimes Of Freedom'; 'Spanish Harlem Incident'; 'The Times They Are A-Changin''; 'Lay Down Your Weary Tune'; 'My Back Pages'; 'You Ain't Going Nowhere'; 'Nothing Was Delivered'; 'This Wheel's On Fire'; 'It's All Over Now, Baby Blue'; 'Lay Lady Lay'; 'Positively 4th Street'.
CD release of vinyl issue CBS 31795 (February 1980). Reissued 1990, and on numerous occasions thereafter.

The Byrds Collection
Castle CCSLP 151/CCSCD 151 (UK).
'Lady Friend'; 'Chestnut Mare'; 'The Bells Of Rhymney'; 'Everybody's Been Burned'; 'Eight Miles High'; 'The Girl With No Name'; 'Goin' Back'; 'So You Want To Be A Rock 'n' Roll Star'; '5 D (Fifth Dimension)'; 'Old John Robertson'; 'Wasn't Born To Follow'; 'Draft Morning'; 'It Won't Be Wrong'; 'John Riley'; 'My Back Pages'; 'Mr Tambourine Man'; 'Turn! Turn! Turn!'; 'Have You Seen Her Face'; 'All I Really Want To Do'; 'You Ain't Going Nowhere'.
Appeared as both 120 gram vinyl release and on CD.
Released September 1986 (UK).

The Very Best Of The Byrds
CBS 4634189 2 (Holland/UK).
'So You Want To Be A Rock 'n' Roll Star'; 'Goin' Back'; 'Wild Mountain Thyme'; 'Nothing Was Delivered'; 'Chimes Of Freedom'; 'Draft Morning';

'I Come And Stand At Every Door'; 'Artificial Energy'; '5 D (Fifth Dimension)'; 'You Ain't Going Nowhere'; 'Renaissance Fair'; 'Change Is Now'; 'What's Happening?!?!?'; 'Have You Seen Her Face'; 'My Back Pages'; 'Get To You'; 'The Bells Of Rhymney'; 'Eight Miles High'; 'I See You'; 'Natural Harmony'.
Released 1988 (Holland/UK). Issued by license via Holland.

The Byrds Box Set
Columbia Legacy 46773/4676112 (US)/(UK).
See 'Box Sets' section.
Released October 1990 (US)/December 1990 (UK).

Full Flyte
Raven RVCD 10 (Australia).
'Mr Tambourine Man'; 'Feel A Whole Lot Better'; 'All I Really Want To Do'; 'Turn! Turn! Turn!'; 'Chimes Of Freedom'; 'She Don't Care About Time'; 'Eight Miles High'; '5 D (Fifth Dimension)'; 'Mr Spaceman'; 'So You Want To Be A Rock 'n' Roll Star'; 'Have You Seen Her Face'; 'Renaissance Fair'; 'My Back Pages'; 'Everybody's Been Burned'; 'Why'; 'Lady Friend'; 'Goin' Back'; 'Wasn't Born To Follow'; 'Old John Robertson'; 'Artificial Energy'; 'You Ain't Going Nowhere'; 'Hickory Wind'; 'You're Still On My Mind'; 'Drug Store Truck Drivin' Man'; 'Gunga Din'; 'Ballad Of Easy Rider'; 'Chestnut Mare'.
Released February 1991 (Australia).

Free Flyte
Sony Music Special Products A 17733 (US).
'Mr Tambourine Man'; 'Turn! Turn! Turn!'; 'Eight Miles High'; 'All I Really Want To Do'; 'Feel A Whole Lot Better'; 'You Won't Have To Cry'; 'You Ain't Going Nowhere'; 'She Has A Way'; 'So You Want To Be A Rock 'n' Roll Star'; 'Mr Spaceman'.
Released 1991 (US).

Greatest Hits Re-mastered
Columbia 467843 2 (UK).
A 1994 straight reissue of *The Byrds Greatest Hits*, but included here because of the 'Remastered' claim. It was later superseded by the 1999 reissue on Columbia Legacy (see below).

20 Essential Tracks From The Boxed Set: 1965–1970
Columbia Legacy CK 47884/471665-2 (US)/(UK).
'Mr Tambourine Man'; 'Feel A Whole Lot Better'; 'All I Really Want To Do'; 'Turn! Turn! Turn!'; '5 D (Fifth Dimension)'; 'Eight Miles High'; 'Mr

Spaceman'; 'So You Want To Be A Rock 'n' Roll Star'; 'Have You Seen Her Face'; 'Lady Friend'; 'My Back Pages'; 'Goin' Back'; 'Ballad Of Easy Rider'; 'Jesus Is Just Alright'; 'Chestnut Mare'; 'I Wanna Grow Up To Be A Politician'; 'He Was A Friend Of Mine'; 'Paths Of Victory'; 'From A Distance'; 'Love That Never Dies'.
Released January 1992 (US)/March 1993 (UK).

The Byrds Play Dylan
Columbia 983399 2 (UK).
'Mr Tambourine Man'; 'All I Really Want To Do'; 'Chimes Of Freedom'; 'Spanish Harlem Incident'; 'The Times They Are A-Changin''; 'Lay Down Your Weary Tune'; 'My Back Pages'; 'You Ain't Going Nowhere'; 'Nothing Was Delivered'; 'This Wheel's On Fire'; 'It's All Over Now, Baby Blue'; 'Lay Lady Lay'; 'Positively 4th Street'.
Released 1994 (UK). Another reissue.

Definitive Collection
Columbia 480548 9 (UK).
Disc 1: 'Mr Tambourine Man'; 'Chimes Of Freedom'; 'The Bells Of Rhymney'; 'Feel A Whole Lot Better'; 'All I Really Want To Do'; 'Turn! Turn! Turn!'; 'Set You Free This Time'; 'Eight Miles High'; '5 D (Fifth Dimension)'; 'Mr. Spaceman'; 'So You Want To Be A Rock 'n' Roll Star'; 'My Back Pages'; 'Have You Seen Her Face'; 'Goin' Back'; 'Wasn't Born To Follow'; 'Lady Friend'; 'You Ain't Going Nowhere'; 'Lay Lady Lay'; 'Ballad Of Easy Rider'; 'Jesus Is Just Alright'; 'Chestnut Mare'; 'I Trust (Everything's Gonna Work Out Alright)'; 'I Wanna Grow Up To Be A Politician'; 'Glory, Glory'; 'America's Great National Pastime'.
Disc 2 (Live recordings): 'Lover Of The Bayou'; 'Mr Tambourine Man'; 'Eight Miles High'; 'Mr Spaceman'.
Released December 1995 (UK). Issued by licence via Holland.

The Byrds Play Dylan
Columbia 467757/466307 (UK).
The disc was re-released again in 1996 (see 1994 for same track listing). There are two different serial numbers, one on the actual record (466307) and another on the cover and artwork (467757). The earlier serial number is from the 1990 issue, which suggests they were putting old CDs in new covers.

Nashville West
Sony Music Special Products A 28123 (US).
'Hickory Wind'; 'Old Blue'; 'Nashville West'; 'Old John Robertson'; 'Drug Store Truck Drivin' Man'; 'Satisfied Mind'; 'Life In Prison'; 'America's

Great National Pastime'; 'Yesterday's Train'; 'Truck Stop Girl'.
Released January 1996 (US).

The Very Best Of The Byrds
Columbia 487995 2 (UK).
'Mr Tambourine Man'; 'All I Really Want To Do'; 'Chimes Of Freedom'; 'Feel A Whole Lot Better'; 'Turn! Turn! Turn!'; 'The Times They Are A-Changin''; 'The World Turns All Around Her'; 'It Won't Be Wrong'; 'He Was A Friend Of Mine'; 'Eight Miles High'; '5 D (Fifth Dimension)'; 'Mr Spaceman'; 'So You Want To Be A Rock 'n' Roll Star'; 'My Back Pages'; 'Renaissance Fair'; 'Goin' Back'; 'Wasn't Born To Follow'; 'Dolphin's Smile'; 'You Ain't Going Nowhere'; 'One Hundred Years From Now'; 'You're Still On My Mind'; 'Hickory Wind'; 'Ballad Of Easy Rider'; 'Jesus Is Just Alright'; 'It's All Over Now, Baby Blue'; 'Lay Lady Lay'; 'Chestnut Mare'.
Released June 1997 (UK).

The Best Of The Byrds
Columbia 488146 2 (UK).
'Mr Tambourine Man'; '5 D (Fifth Dimension)'; 'Feel A Whole Lot Better'; 'We'll Meet Again'; 'All I Really Want To Do'; 'I Am A Pilgrim'; 'Eight Miles High'; 'My Back Pages'; 'Turn! Turn! Turn!'; 'Wait And See'; 'The Times They Are A-Changin''; 'Lay Lady Lay'; 'Ballad Of Easy Rider'; 'Spanish Harlem Incident'; 'Mr Spaceman'; 'Chimes Of Freedom'.
Released July 1997 (UK).

Super Hits
Columbia Legacy 504725 2 (UK).
Columbia Legacy CK 65637 (US).
'Mr Tambourine Man'; 'Turn! Turn! Turn! (To Everything There Is A Season)'; 'Eight Miles High'; 'So You Want To Be A Rock 'n' Roll Star'; 'Renaissance Fair'; 'Artificial Energy'; 'Chestnut Mare'; 'He Was A Friend Of Mine'; 'I Wanna Grow Up To Be A Politician'; 'America's Great National Pastime'.
Released July 1998 (US).
Released December 2000 (UK).
Reissued with new cover June 2005 (UK).

The Byrds Greatest Hits
Columbia/Legacy CK 66230 (US).
'Mr Tambourine Man'; 'Feel A Whole Lot Better'; 'The Bells Of Rhymney'; 'Turn! Turn! Turn!'; 'All I Really Want To Do'; 'Chimes Of Freedom'; 'Eight Miles High'; 'Mr Spaceman'; '5 D (Fifth Dimension)'; 'So You Want To Be A Rock 'n' Roll Star'; 'My Back Pages'.

BYRDS DISCOGRAPHY

Bonus tracks: 'It Won't Be Wrong'; 'Set You Free This Time'; 'Have You Seen Her Face'.
Released April 1999. Sony later issued a SACD version.

The Byrds
Sony Music Special Products A 30827 (US).
'Feel A Whole Lot Better'; 'All I Really Want To Do'; 'Here Without You'; 'The World Turns All Around Her'; 'It Won't Be Wrong'; 'CTA 102'; 'Renaissance Fair'; 'The Girl With No Name'; 'Wasn't Born To Follow'; 'This Wheel's On Fire'.
Released January 2000 (US).

The Byrds Play The Songs Of Bob Dylan
Columbia 501946 2 (UK).
'Mr Tambourine Man'; 'It's All Over Now, Baby Blue'; 'The Times They Are A-Changin''; 'You Ain't Going Nowhere'; 'Lay Lady Lay'; 'All I Really Want To Do'; 'Chimes Of Freedom'; 'My Back Pages'; 'Just Like A Woman'; 'This Wheel's On Fire'; 'Nothing Was Delivered'; 'Positively 4th Street'; 'Spanish Harlem Incident'; 'Lay Down Your Weary Tune'; 'It's Alright Ma (I'm Only Bleeding)' (live); 'Lay Lady Lay' (alternate version); 'The Times They Are A-Changin'' (alternate version); 'Mr Tambourine Man' (live version); 'Chimes Of Freedom' (live version); 'Paths Of Victory'.
Released May 2001 (UK).

The Byrds Play Dylan
Columbia/Legacy CK 85430 (US).
'All I Really Want To Do'; 'Chimes Of Freedom'; 'It's All Over Now, Baby Blue'; 'Lay Down Your Weary Tune'; 'Lay Lady Lay'; 'Mr Tambourine Man'; 'My Back Pages'; 'Nothing Was Delivered'; 'Positively 4th Street'; 'Spanish Harlem Incident'; 'The Times They Are A-Changin''; 'This Wheel's On Fire'; 'You Ain't Going Nowhere'; 'It's Alright Ma (I'm Only Bleeding)'; 'Just Like A Woman'; 'Lay Lady Lay'; 'The Times They Are A-Changin''; 'Mr Tambourine Man'; 'Chimes Of Freedom'; 'Paths Of Victory'.
Released June 2002 (US).

The Essential Byrds
Columbia Legacy 504725 2 (UK).
Columbia Legacy C2K 89110 (US).
Disc 1: 'Mr Tambourine Man'; 'Feel A Whole Lot Better'; 'All I Really Want To Do'; 'The Bells Of Rhymney'; 'Chimes Of Freedom'; 'Turn! Turn! Turn!'; 'She Don't Care About Time'; 'It Won't Be Wrong'; 'Lay Down Your Weary Tune'; 'Set You Free This Time'; 'He Was A Friend Of Mine'; 'The Times They Are A-Changin''; 'Eight Miles High'; '5 D (Fifth

Dimension)'; 'Wild Mountain Thyme'; 'Mr Spaceman'; 'So You Want To Be A Rock 'n' Roll Star'; 'Have You Seen Her Face'; 'Time Between'; 'Renaissance Fair'; 'My Back Pages'; 'Dolphin's Smile'.
Disc 2: 'Artificial Energy'; 'Old John Robertson'; 'Goin' Back'; 'Natural Harmony'; 'Wasn't Born To Follow'; 'You Ain't Going Nowhere'; 'Hickory Wind'; 'Nothing Was Delivered'; 'This Wheel's On Fire'; 'Drug Store Truck Drivin' Man'; 'Your Gentle Way Of Loving Me'; 'Ballad Of Easy Rider'; 'Jesus Is Just Alright'; 'It's All Over Now, Baby Blue'; 'Lover Of The Bayou'; 'Chestnut Mare'; 'Glory, Glory'; 'Jamaica Say You Will'; 'I Wanna Grow Up To Be A Politician'; 'Tiffany Queen'; 'Antique Sandy'; 'Farther Along'.
Released April 2003 (US).
Released May 2004 (UK).
Reissued: 10 January 2011 (US/UK).

Mojo Presents . . . An Introduction To The Byrds – 24 Classic Songs
Columbia 512778 2 (UK).
'Feel A Whole Lot Better'; 'The Bells Of Rhymney'; 'Mr Tambourine Man'; 'She Don't Care About Time'; 'The World Turns All Around Her'; 'I See You'; 'I Know My Rider (I Know You Rider)'; '5 D (Fifth Dimension)'; 'Eight Miles High'; 'Everybody's Been Burned'; 'Have You Seen Her Face'; 'Lady Friend'; 'So You Want To Be A Rock 'n' Roll Star'; 'Change Is Now'; 'Draft Morning'; 'Goin' Back'; 'Hickory Wind'; 'One Hundred Years From Now'; 'You Ain't Going Nowhere'; 'Drug Store Truck Drivin' Man'; 'Gunga Din'; 'Chestnut Mare'; 'Bugler'.
Released September 2003 (UK).

Mr Tambourine Man – The Best Of The Byrds
Sony Music Media SMM 516489-2 (Germany/UK).
2-CD set. Disc 1: 'Mr. Tambourine Man'; 'All I Really Want To Do'; 'Eight Miles High'; 'Feel A Whole Lot Better'; 'Just A Season'; 'You Ain't Going Nowhere'; 'Jamaica Say You Will'; 'This Wheel's On Fire'; 'Everybody's Been Burned'; 'Why'; 'Goin' Back'; 'Don't Make Waves'.
Disc 2: 'Turn! Turn! Turn!'; 'Ballad Of Easy Rider'; 'Jesus Is Just Alright'; 'Chestnut Mare'; 'Nashville West'; 'Tribal Gathering'; 'Lay Lady Lay'; 'I See You'; 'What's Happening?!?!'; 'Thoughts And Words'; 'Bugler'; 'From A Distance'.
Released April 2004 (Germany/UK). Available in UK as a European import, presumably licensed, which is the only reason why it is included here.

America's Great National Treasure
Sony/BMG A 96086 (US).
'Mr Tambourine Man'; 'Eight Miles High'; 'Hey Joe'; 'Goin' Back';

'Hickory Wind'; 'Jamaica Say You Will'; 'Have You Seen Her Face'; 'America's Great National Pastime'; 'Triad'; 'Ballad Of Easy Rider'.
Released January 2006 (US).

The Very Best Of The Byrds
Sony/BMG 82876 855142 (UK).
'Mr Tambourine Man'; 'Feel A Whole Lot Better'; 'All I Really Want To Do' (album version); 'Turn! Turn! Turn!'; 'The World Turns All Around Her'; 'It's All Over Now, Baby Blue' (*Ballad Of Easy Rider* version); '5 D (Fifth Dimension)'; 'Eight Miles High'; 'I See You'; 'So You Want To Be A Rock 'n' Roll Star'; 'Have You Seen Her Face'; 'You Ain't Going Nowhere'; 'Hickory Wind'; 'Goin' Back' (alternate version); 'Change Is Now'; 'Chestnut Mare' (unedited version); 'Chimes Of Freedom'; 'The Times They Are A-Changin''; 'Dolphin's Smile'; 'My Back Pages'; 'Mr Spaceman'; 'Jesus Is Just Alright'; 'This Wheel's On Fire'; 'Ballad Of Easy Rider'. Although I provided the liner notes, I was not consulted over the 'Very Best Of' content which was compiled and sequenced by Sony's Tim Fraser-Harding.
Released May 2006 (UK).

Byrds: A Collection
Sony BMG 88697 12448 2 (UK).
'Turn! Turn! Turn!'; 'Mr Tambourine Man'; 'Have You Seen Her Face'; 'Chestnut Mare'; 'Eight Miles High'; 'All I Really Want To Do'; 'It Won't Be Wrong'; 'Feel A Whole Lot Better'; 'Wasn't Born To Follow'; 'My Back Pages'; 'He Was A Friend Of Mine'; 'Draft Morning'; 'Goin' Back'; 'You Ain't Going Nowhere'; 'It's All Over Now, Baby Blue'.
Released July 2007 (UK).

The Byrds Play Dylan
Sony BMG 8869 725267 2 (UK).
'Mr Tambourine Man'; 'All I Really Want To Do'; 'Chimes Of Freedom'; 'Spanish Harlem Incident'; 'The Times They Are A-Changin''; 'Lay Down Your Weary Tune'; 'My Back Pages'; 'You Ain't Going Nowhere'; 'Nothing Was Delivered'; 'This Wheel's On Fire'; 'It's All Over Now, Baby Blue'; 'Lay Lady Lay'; 'Positively 4th Street'.
Released February 2008 (UK).

Playlist: The Very Best Of The Byrds
Columbia Legacy 88697 39219 2 (US).
'Mr Tambourine Man'; 'Spanish Harlem Incident'; 'Feel A Whole Lot Better'; 'Turn! Turn! Turn!'; 'He Was A Friend Of Mine'; 'Eight Miles High'; 'Mr Spaceman'; 'So You Want To Be A Rock 'n' Roll Star'; 'My Back Pages'; 'Change Is Now'; 'One Hundred Years From Now'; 'Ballad Of Easy

Rider'; 'Chestnut Mare'; 'I Wanna Grow Up To Be A Politician'. Plus CD ROM track featuring digital liner notes booklet, photos and discography.
Released October 2008 (US).

Steel Box
Sony BMG 88697 459812 (UK).
This is exactly the same running order as *The Byrds Play Dylan* Sony BMG 8869 725267 2 (UK). Even the serial numbers are almost the same. Only the cover is different.
Released March 2009 (UK).

Eight Miles High – The Best Of The Byrds
Sony/Camden 8869 763627 2 (UK).
'Mr Tambourine Man'; 'Turn! Turn! Turn!'; 'Eight Miles High'; 'Feel A Whole Lot Better'; 'Wasn't Born To Follow'; 'Spanish Harlem Incident'; 'So You Want To Be A Rock 'n' Roll Star'; 'All I Really Want To Do'; 'Ballad Of Easy Rider'; 'Mr Spaceman'; 'One Hundred Years From Now'; 'He Was A Friend Of Mine'; 'Wild Mountain Thyme'; 'Hickory Wind'; 'Goin' Back'; 'Chestnut Mare'.
Released December 2009 (UK).

There have also been a series of albums issued, mainly on the Continent, under the name 'Byrds' which do not feature the group, despite including their photograph on the CD artwork. Some of these misleading items also include tracks featuring Pat Robinson and Gene Clark from the Eighties. A discussion of these songs will be featured in full in the discography of Volume 2 under 'Gene Clark'.

BYRDS BOOTLEGS

BOOTLEG ALBUMS

Byrds Live At Buddy's In England Fly Records 502.
'You Ain't Going Nowhere'; 'Lover Of The Bayou'; 'Old Blue'; 'Well Come Back Home'; 'Medley: 'My Back Pages'/'B.J. Blues'/'Baby, What Do You Want Me To Do'; 'He Was A Friend Of Mine'; 'Willin''; 'Soldier's Joy'/ 'Black Mountain Rag'; 'Take A Whiff'.
Originally released in the UK in 1971, this was the first known Byrds bootleg. The extract is taken from a show at Het Concertgebouw on 7 July 1970 and broadcast by VPRO. The quality is reasonable/good and would probably receive a grade 7 on the old 'Trademark of Quality' scale. A more complete recording is available on the bootleg CD *Live In Amsterdam*.

Hey, Mr Tambourine Man [no label details].
'Old Blue'; 'Soldier's Joy'/'Black Mountain Rag'; 'Mr Tambourine Man'; 'Pretty Boy Floyd'; 'Take A Whiff'; 'Chestnut Mare'; 'You Ain't Going Nowhere'; 'Truck Stop Girl'; 'Medley: 'My Back Pages'/'B.J. Blues'/'Baby, What Do You Want Me To Do'; 'Jamaica Say You Will'; 'So You Want To Be A Rock 'n' Roll Star'; 'Roll Over Beethoven'.
Released in Holland in 1971. The compilers have erroneously credited John York as bassist instead of Skip Battin. In terms of quality, this album is equal to the more famous *Buddy's*. The recording date is again uncertain but, judging from the material, I would suspect that it was taped during the group's May 1971 tour.

Byrds Live At Lincoln Straight Records [no serial number on disc].
'Willin''; 'Antique Sandy'; 'Soldier's Joy'/'Black Mountain Rag'; 'I Wanna Grow Up To Be A Politician'; 'Mr Spaceman'; 'Bugler'; 'You Ain't Going Nowhere'; 'Medley: 'My Back Pages'/'B.J. Blues'/'Baby, What Do You Want Me To Do'; 'Jesus Is Just Alright'; 'Glory, Glory'.
Recorded live at the Lincoln Folk Festival on 24 July 1971. The quality varies from barely acceptable to absolutely atrocious. This is partly explained by the fact that the best portion of the album was not recorded at Lincoln at all but pirated from *Live At Buddy's*. This easily ranks as the worst ever Byrds bootleg album in terms of quality. It is a shame that such a memorable concert was not captured in all its vitality.

REQUIEM FOR THE TIMELESS — VOLUME 1

Kralingen Triple album set.
'You Ain't Going Nowhere'; 'Medley: 'My Back Pages'/'B.J. Blues'/'Baby, What Do You Want Me To Do'; 'Jesus Is Just Alright'; 'All The Things'; 'So You Want To Be A Rock 'n' Roll Star'.
Recorded at the Netherlands open-air festival on 27 June 1970, this bootleg was released during 1971. The triple album set also included material by the Jefferson Airplane and It's A Beautiful Day. In terms of quality, the album was below the standard of *Live At Buddy's* but infinitely superior to *Live At Lincoln*. The festival was later transformed into a movie *Stamping Ground* (also known as *Love And Music*) which included the Byrds' performance of 'Old Blue'. Additional footage from the movie features the group playing 'Soldier's Joy'/'Black Mountain Rag'; 'All The Things'; 'Nashville West'; 'Turn! Turn! Turn!'; 'Mr Tambourine Man'; 'Buckaroo'; 'Eight Miles High'; 'So You Want To Be A Rock 'n' Roll Star'; 'Mr Spaceman' and 'Amazing Grace'.

Byrds: Older Than Yesterday Cocaine Records.
Side A: Gene Clark Band [KC Southern Band]: 'Release Me Girl'; 'Hula Bula Man'. Chris Hillman Band: 'Quits'; 'The Witching Hour'; 'It Doesn't Matter'.
Side B. Roger McGuinn Band [Thunderbyrd]: 'Lover Of The Bayou'; 'American Girl'; 'Mr Spaceman'; 'Golden Loom'; 'It's Gone'.
Side C. Roger McGuinn Band [Thunderbyrd]: 'Dixie Highway'; 'Shoot 'Em'. McGuinn, Hillman & Clark: 'So You Want To Be A Rock 'n' Roll Star'; 'Mr Tambourine Man'; 'Eight Miles High'.
Side D. Studio (1964–70). 'Willin'' (from an English concert 1970); Beefeaters: 'Please Let Me Love You'; 'Don't Be Long'. Byrds: 'Don't Make Waves'; 'Don't Make Waves' (alternate take); 'She Don't Care About Time'; 'Lady Friend'; 'Lay Lady Lay'; 'Willin''.
This was released in Holland in 1979 in order to celebrate the Byrds' 15th anniversary. The first three sides feature material taken primarily from the 1977 Hammersmith Odeon concert (30 April 1977), erroneously dated September 1977 by the compilers. The final side features further rarities. Although useful in its time, the record was subsequently made redundant by the release of *3 Byrds Land In London*.

Doin' Alright For Old People Excitable Recordworks 4506-1.
'Jolly Roger'; 'Chestnut Mare'; 'Mr Tambourine Man'; 'You Ain't Going Nowhere'; 'Turn! Turn! Turn!'; 'Knockin' On Heaven's Door'; 'Bye Bye Baby'; 'So You Want To Be A Rock 'n' Roll Star'; 'Eight Miles High'; 'Feel A Whole Lot Better'.
The sleeve notes claim that this was recorded at the Boarding House, San

Francisco on 10 February 1978. This was an important album as it contained the work of four Byrds (McGuinn, Clark, Hillman and Crosby). Crosby appears on 'Mr Tambourine Man', 'You Ain't Going Nowhere', 'Eight Miles High' and 'Feel A Whole Lot Better'. The excellent quality is again explained by the fact that the show was taped from a KSAN radio broadcast. The group played two separate dates at the Boarding House in December and February. See the CD Bootlegs and Bootleg Tapes sections for a longer version of the concert.

Easy Riders Penguin EGG 5.
'He Was A Friend Of Mine'; 'Willin''; 'It's Alright Ma (I'm Only Bleeding)'; 'Ballad Of Easy Rider'; 'Chestnut Mare'; 'Chimes Of Freedom'; 'Get Out Of My Life Woman'; 'Mexico' [*sic*]; 'Come Back Baby (From Way Behind The Sun)'[*sic*]; 'Drug Store Truck Drivin' Man'.
Released in 1981, this reasonable quality recording was particularly interesting for its second side, which was taken from the Boston Tea Party concert at Massachusetts in February 1969. John York takes lead vocal on 'Tulsa County Blue' (mistitled as 'Mexico' on the album) and 'Way Behind The Sun'.

Live In Washington 9/12/71 Black Cat Records.
'Lover Of The Bayou'; 'So You Want To Be A Rock 'n' Roll Star'; 'Mr Spaceman'; 'I Wanna Grow Up To Be A Politician'; 'Soldier's Joy'/ 'Black Mountain Rag'; 'Mr Tambourine Man'; 'Pretty Boy Floyd'; 'Nashville West'; 'Tiffany Queen'; 'Chestnut Mare'; 'Jesus Is Just Alright'; 'Eight Miles High'; 'B.J. Blues'; 'Roll Over Beethoven'; 'Citizen Kane'.
Not released until the Eighties, this bootleg was taken from a live broadcast on Radio WANU. The quality is at best mediocre and the material, with the exception of 'Citizen Kane', is over-familiar and duplicated on many other bootlegs and tapes.

Mr Tambourine Man.
'Jamaica Say You Will'; 'Old Blue'; 'Soldier's Joy'/'Black Mountain Rag'; 'Mr Tambourine Man'; 'Pretty Boy Floyd'; 'Take A Whiff'; 'Chestnut Mare'; 'Jesus Is Just Alright'; 'You Ain't Going Nowhere'; 'Truck Stop Girl'; 'Medley: 'My Back Pages'/'B.J. Blues'/'Baby, What Do You Want Me To Do'; 'Jamaica Say You Will'; 'So You Want To Be A Rock 'n' Roll Star'; 'Roll Over Beethoven'.
An average and unspectacular collection featuring the McGuinn, White, Parsons, Battin Byrds. The inclusion of a second live 'Jamaica Say You Will' is an interesting anomaly, although on certain pressings neither actually appears on the record, despite being featured on the sleeve.

Boston Tea Party Handmade Records FC 002.
'You Ain't Going Nowhere'; 'Old Blue'; 'Long Black Veil'; 'Goin' Back'; 'Get Out Of My Life Woman'; 'Ballad Of Easy Rider'; 'Jesus Is Just Alright'; 'Tulsa County Blue'; 'Sing Me Back Home'; 'Lay Lady Lay'; 'Time Between'; 'Medley: 'My Back Pages'/'B.J. Blues'/'Baby, What Do You Want Me To Do'; 'Take A City Bride'; 'It's All Over Now, Baby Blue'; 'Turn! Turn! Turn!'; 'Mr Tambourine Man'; 'Eight Miles High'; 'I Shall Be Released'; 'Drug Store Truck Drivin' Man'.
An excellent quality double album taken from the belatedly available 1969 Boston Tea Party tape. This collection omits the following tracks: 'He Was A Friend Of Mine', 'Mr Spaceman', 'This Wheel's On Fire', 'Jesus Is Just Alright', 'Nashville West', 'Fido' and, most strangely in view of its rarity at the time, John York's reading of 'Way Behind The Sun'.

Goin' Back D541.
'You Don't Miss Your Water'; 'Hickory Wind'; 'Feel A Whole Lot Better'; 'Chimes Of Freedom'; 'The Christian Life'; 'Turn! Turn! Turn!'; 'Medley: 'My Back Pages'/'B.J. Blues'/'Baby, What Do You Want Me To Do'; 'Mr Spaceman'; 'Lay Lady Lay'; 'Medley: 'My Back Pages'/'B.J. Blues'/'Baby, What Do You Want Me To Do'; 'Goin' Back'; 'Way Behind The Sun'; 'Jesus Is Just Alright'; 'Turn! Turn! Turn!'; 'Mr Tambourine Man'; 'Eight Miles High'; 'Goin' Back'.
Another good quality, albeit unoriginal, bootleg combining the Piper Club concert and the Boston Tea Party. The first two tracks from the Piper Club gig, 'You Ain't Going Nowhere' and 'Old John Robertson', are omitted and in selecting the tracks from the Boston Tea Party the compilers fall into the trap of repetition by electing to use the 'Medley' twice in the space of a single album.

The Byrds Back Pages Colombia Guinn 202.
'She Has A Way'; 'It's All Over Now, Baby Blue'; 'Tabernacle Hillside' [sic]; 'It Happens Each Day'; 'John Riley'; 'I Know You Rider'; 'Psychodrama City'; 'Triad'; 'Hey Joe'; 'My Back Pages'; 'Mr Tambourine Man'; 'He Was A Friend Of Mine'; 'So You Want To Be A Rock 'n' Roll Star'; 'Roll Over Beethoven'; 'The Bells Of Rhymney'.
A bootleg of British origin released in 1987, this was compiled from the rough tapes of *Never Before* which had been circulating among collectors prior to the album's release. Thus, the vocals on a couple of the cuts are barely audible and 'Triad' is an instrumental backing track only. Not knowing the actual title of Gene Clark's 'Never Before' ('The Day Walk') at the time of the bootleg's release, the compilers jokingly called it 'Tabernacle Hillside' (borrowed from the lyrics of 'So You Say You Lost Your Baby' on

Clark's first solo album). 'Psychodrama City' includes the lengthy instrumental introduction deleted from *Never Before*. Side two consists of the 1967 Stockholm radio performance, now available on CD, and the final track, 'The Bells Of Rhymney', is taken from an unidentified US television show circa early 1966. Finally, the cover artwork boasts some bogus liner notes from Derek Taylor, cleverly designed in the style of the rear cover of *Turn! Turn! Turn!*.

The Byrds Back Pages: A Collector's Guide B 6470.
'Please Let Me Love You'; 'Don't Be Long'; 'Hey Joe'; 'My Back Pages'; 'Mr Tambourine Man'; 'He Was A Friend Of Mine'; 'So You Want To Be A Rock 'n' Roll Star'; 'Roll Over Beethoven'; 'Don't Make Waves'; 'Child Of The Universe'; 'You Ain't Going Nowhere'; 'Turn! Turn! Turn!'; 'Ballad Of Easy Rider'; 'It Won't Be Wrong'; 'The Water Is Wide'; 'Mr Tambourine Man'; 'Nashville West'; 'Lover Of The Bayou'; 'Jesus Is Just Alright'; 'Old John Robertson'; 'So You Want To Be A Rock 'n' Roll Star'; 'He Was A Friend Of Mine'.
A mishmash of an album containing the Beefeaters single, the Swedish radio tracks, and a couple of cuts from the Piper Club. Haphazardly put together, 'Jesus Is Just Alright' is not actually listed on the sleeve whereas 'So You Want To Be A Rock 'n' Roll Star' and 'He Was A Friend Of Mine' are, but do not appear on the album. The inclusion of 'The Water Is Wide' is of potential interest but sadly the track has been taken from a slow-running tape and is no doubt chronologically misplaced, along with 'It Won't Be Wrong'. Finally, the title and liner notes are pirated from my own work, with a cursory thanks to John R. Cheers! The source of the article was a piece I wrote in issue 13 of *Dark Star* titled "The Byrds Back Pages: A Collector's Guide To The Byrds". Needless to say, I had no involvement in the bootleg and was not aware of its existence until it was pointed out to me by the ever vigilant and indefatigable collector Barry Ballard.

Byrds On The Wyng Wally Jig 001.
'You Won't Have To Cry'; 'She Has A Way'; 'Turn! Turn! Turn!'; 'I Don't Believe Me' [*sic*]; 'Eight Miles High'; 'Why'; 'Ways To Show It' [*sic*] ; 'Triad' (instrumental)'; 'I Knew I'd Want You' [*sic*]; 'Eight Miles High'; 'Hey Joe'; 'I Know You Rider'; 'Disembodied Spirit' [*sic*]; 'Scrambled Egg Jam' [*sic*]; 'Mr Tambourine Man'; 'Thoughts And Words'; 'It's All Over Now, Baby Blue'.
Undoubtedly the most interesting vinyl Byrds bootleg to date, this included material from the CBS archives not generally available elsewhere. Only the sound quality disappoints. 'You Won't Have To Cry' and 'She Has A Way' were taken from the first CBS album sessions and featured a brief snatch of

Terry Melcher on instruction vocals. 'Turn! Turn! Turn!' and 'Triad' are instrumental backing tracks. The RCA versions of 'Eight Miles High' and 'Why' are the same as those on *Never Before* and there are some brief segments from the *Younger Than Yesterday* sessions. 'I Knew I'd Want You', although listed on the sleeve, does not appear on the album. 'It Happens Each Day' (mistakenly titled 'Disembodied Spirit') is the original version, unimproved by Crosby and Hillman, while 'Scrambled Egg Jam' is a fictitious coinage for the instrumental version of 'John Riley', which appeared on one of the CBS tapes. 'I Know My Rider (I Know You Rider)' is a rougher take than the one included on *Never Before* but McGuinn's lead guitar breaks still sound effective and there is the delightful bonus of some scat singing from Crosby. An alternate take of 'Eight Miles High' from the Columbia sessions is a minor revelation, mainly because it sounds so rough, spontaneous and unfocused. Michael Clarke's drumming is extremely heavy-handed and very different from his work on the completed single version. Most chaotic of all, however, is a truly shambolic rendition of 'Hey Joe' with Crosby all over the place and Clarke sounding as though he is banging a dustbin lid. Unbelievable. The album also contains a real mystery. A girl singer complete with a Byrds-sounding backup group provides a couple of Dylan covers: 'I Don't Believe You' (which the producer insists on calling 'I Don't Believe Me') and 'It's All Over Now, Baby Blue'. It turns out that these were guide vocals and demos specifically imported by Terry Melcher to encourage the group to increase its Dylan repertoire. The group was an unknown local combo and the producer Jack Nitzsche. Overall, the result is a fascinating insight into what was happening to the Byrds in the studio during one of the most fascinating phases of their career.

Eight Miles High Live In Nurnberg Do It Do It 005.
This is a release by Michael Clarke's 'Byrds', appropriately enough on a bootleg. I mention it reluctantly in passing for completists only.

BOOTLEG CD RELEASES

The Monterey Pop Festival 1967 Volume I Living Legend LLR CD 017/018.
Released by Living Legend Records, this 17-track excellent quality CD features three tracks by the Byrds taken from their appearance at the Monterey Pop Festival: 'He Was A Friend Of Mine', 'Hey Joe' and 'So You Want To Be A Rock 'n' Roll Star'. The same selections can be heard on Monterey Pop releases on Black Panther, Document and Evil Records.

Crosby provides his own inimitable introductions to the songs, including the famous reference to the Kennedy assassination. The compilers have erroneously credited Bob Dylan with the authorship of 'He Was A Friend Of Mine'. Although Dylan did record a song of that name as a demo for Leeds Music in early 1962, the lyrics to the Byrds' version were written by McGuinn. This set was made largely redundant by the official release of the Monterey box set on Rhino.
Released 1988.

The Live Byrds Bulldog BGCD 022.
'You Ain't Going Nowhere'; 'Old John Robertson'; 'You Don't Miss Your Water'; 'Hickory Wind'; 'Feel A Whole Lot Better'; 'Chimes Of Freedom'; 'The Christian Life'; 'Turn! Turn! Turn!'; 'Medley: 'My Back Pages'/ 'B.J. Blues'/'Baby, What Do You Want Me To Do'; 'Mr Spaceman'.
Subtitled "It was more than 20 Years Ago . . . recorded live at Piper Club, Roma May 2, 1968" this CD is a fairly average quality reproduction of the famous Piper Club tape which has been in circulation on the bootleg tape market for years.
Released 1988.

Live In Stockholm 1967 Swinging Pig TSP CD 006.
Introduction; 'Hey Joe'; Introduction; 'My Back Pages'; Introduction; 'Mr Tambourine Man'; Introduction; 'He Was A Friend Of Mine'; Introduction; 'So You Want To Be A Rock 'n' Roll Star'; Introduction; 'Roll Over Beethoven'.
This excellent quality recording was taken from a live broadcast on Radiohuset (Studio 4), Stockholm. A brief note mentions that the recording took place in April 1967, though I suspect it may have been between 28 February and 3 March when the group visited Stockholm on a promotional tour. Christopher Hjort, my younger colleague in such chronicles, writes that it indeed took place on 28 February and was titled *Tonarskvall: The Byrds I Sverige* [The Byrds In Sweden]. On the CD listing McGuinn once again loses the writing credit of 'He Was A Friend Of Mine' to Bob Dylan.
Released 1988.

Stockholm 1967/Boston Tea Party Koine K 890102.
'Hey Joe'; 'My Back Pages'; 'Mr Tambourine Man'; 'He Was A Friend Of Mine'; 'So You Want To Be A Rock 'n' Roll Star'; 'Roll Over Beethoven'; 'You Ain't Going Nowhere'; 'Old Blue'; 'Goin' Back'; 'Get Out Of My Life Woman'; 'Ballad Of Easy Rider'; 'Jesus Is Just Alright'; 'Tulsa County Blue'; 'Mr Spaceman'; 'Lay Lady Lay'; 'My Back Pages'; 'It's All Over Now, Baby

Blue'; 'Turn! Turn! Turn!'; 'Mr Tambourine Man'; 'Eight Miles High'.
A predictable mixture of the Stockholm broadcast and the over-familiar Boston Tea Party.
Released 1989.

Dream Rock Black Panther BPCD 019.
'Hey Joe'; 'My Back Pages'; 'Mr Tambourine Man'; 'He Was A Friend Of Mine'; 'So You Want To Be A Rock 'n' Roll Star'; 'Roll Over Beethoven'; 'You Ain't Going Nowhere'; 'Old Blue'; 'Goin' Back'; 'Get Out Of My Life Woman'; 'Ballad Of Easy Rider'; 'Jesus Is Just Alright'; 'Tulsa County Blue'; 'Mr Spaceman'; 'Lay Lady Lay'; 'My Back Pages'; 'It's All Over Now, Baby Blue'; 'Turn! Turn! Turn!'; 'Mr Tambourine Man'; 'Eight Miles High'.
The first six tracks are from the Stockholm radio broadcast February 1967, and the remainder from the Boston Tea Party, February 1969.
Released 1989.

Never Again SPA 02-CD-3315.
'Hey Joe'; 'My Back Pages'; 'Mr Tambourine Man'; 'He Was A Friend Of Mine'; 'So You Want To Be A Rock 'n' Roll Star'; 'The Bells Of Rhymney'; 'Roll Over Beethoven'; 'He Was A Friend Of Mine'; 'Hey Joe'; 'So You Want To Be A Rock 'n' Roll Star'; 'Turn! Turn! Turn!'; 'I Don't Believe You'; 'Eight Miles High'; 'I Know My Rider'; 'Scrambled Egg Jam' [John Riley]; 'It's All Over Now, Baby Blue'.
The first seven tracks are from the Stockholm radio broadcast, followed by three selections from Monterey and studio demos taken from the bootleg LP *Byrds On The Wyng*.
Released 1989.

Tambourines & 12-Strings – The Best Of Live In Concert Living Legend LLR CD 067.
'Jesus Is Just Alright'; 'Tulsa County Blue'; 'He Was A Friend Of Mine'; 'Mr Spaceman'; 'Lay Lady Lay'; 'Ballad Of Easy Rider'; 'It's All Over Now, Baby Blue'; 'Way Behind The Sun'; 'Mr Tambourine Man'; 'Hey Joe'; 'So You Want To Be A Rock 'n' Roll Star'; 'I Shall Be Released'; 'My Back Pages'; 'Lover Of The Bayou'; 'This Wheel's On Fire'; 'Eight Miles High'; 'Chestnut Mare'; 'Amazing Grace'.
Another uneasy combination of tracks from the Boston Tea Party, the Stockholm radio broadcast, rounded off with five songs from Amsterdam, July 1970.
Released 1990.

Live In Amsterdam Swinging Pig TSP-CD-046-1/2.
Introduction; 'You Ain't Going Nowhere'; 'Lover Of The Bayou; 'Old

Blue'; 'Well Come Back Home'; 'Medley: 'My Back Pages'/'B.J. Blues'/'Baby, What Do You Want Me To Do'; 'He Was A Friend Of Mine'; 'Willin''; 'Fiddle Tune' ['Soldier's Joy'/'Black Mountain Rag']; 'Take A Whiff'; 'This Wheel's On Fire'; 'It's Alright Ma (I'm Only Bleeding)'; 'Ballad Of Easy Rider'; 'Jesus Is Just Alright'; 'All The Things'; 'Country Jig' ['Buckaroo'/'Nashville West']; 'Medley: 'Turn! Turn! Turn!'/'Mr Tambourine Man'/'Eight Miles High'; 'So You Want To Be A Rock 'n' Roll Star'; 'Positively 4th Street'; 'Mr Spaceman'; 'You Don't Miss Your Water'; 'Chestnut Mare'; 'Chimes Of Freedom'; 'Amazing Grace'.
A strong selection taken from the Het Concertgebouw, Amsterdam, 7 July 1970, broadcast by VPRO.
Released 1990.

Live In Boston 1970 The Early Years 02-CD-3326.
'You Ain't Going Nowhere'; 'He Was A Friend Of Mine'; 'Old Blue'; 'Long Black Veil'; 'Goin' Back'; 'Get Out Of My Life Woman'; 'Ballad Of Easy Rider'; 'Jesus Is Just Alright'; 'Tulsa County Blue'; 'Mr Spaceman'; 'Sing Me Back Home'; 'This Wheel's On Fire'; 'Lay Lady Lay'; 'Medley: 'My Back Pages'/'B.J. Blues'/'Baby, What Do You Want Me To Do'; 'Take A City Bride'; 'It's All Over Now, Baby Blue'; 'Way Behind The Sun'; 'Medley: 'Turn! Turn! Turn!'/'Mr Tambourine Man'/'Eight Miles High'; 'I Shall Be Released'.
Although titled 'Live In Boston 1970', this was, of course, the Boston Tea Party show of a year later. The sleeve also wrongly credits some of the above songs under such crazy titles as 'You Ain't Goin' Home', 'Bye Bye Blues', 'Nobody Knows But Me', 'Get Off My Life Woman', 'Ridin' Down To Mexico' and 'Angeline'. To top it all, two tracks listed at the end, 'Drug Store Drivin' Man' and 'Nashville West' are not even on the disc. A truncated version of this CD was reissued in 1991 titled *Live USA,* with the above errors intact. It was reissued again in 1994 in better quality as *Boston Tea Party* on Yellow Dog.
Released 1990.

Fly Into A Passion Genuine Pig TGP-CD-123.
'Lover Of The Bayou'; 'You Ain't Going Nowhere'; 'Jesus Is Just Alright'; 'It's Alright Ma (I'm Only Bleeding)'; 'This Wheel's On Fire'; 'Medley: 'My Back Pages'/'B.J. Blues'/'Baby, What Do You Want Me To Do'; 'Willin''; 'Medley: 'Turn! Turn! Turn!'/'Mr Tambourine Man'/'Eight Miles High'; 'So You Want To Be A Rock 'n' Roll Star'; 'Mr Spaceman'.
Recorded at New York State University, October 1970, although it's billed as September 1970. Probable source is a US Retrorock radio show from 1981.
Released 1990.

Eight Miles High Triangle PYCD 034.
'Lover Of The Bayou'; 'This Wheel's On Fire'; 'Old Blue'; 'Well Come Back Home'; 'It's Alright Ma (I'm Only Bleeding)'; 'Ballad Of Easy Rider'; 'Jesus Is Just Alright'; 'All The Things'; 'Buckaroo'/'Nashville West'; 'Medley: My Back Pages'/'B.J. Blues'/'Baby, What Do You Want Me To Do'; 'He Was A Friend Of Mine'; 'Willin''; 'Turn! Turn! Turn!'; 'Mr Tambourine Man'; 'Eight Miles High'; 'Hold It!'.
Another chance to hear the Het Concertgebouw, Amsterdam, 7 July 1970, broadcast by VPRO.
Released 1990.

Electric Carnival Diamonds In Your Ear CD 23.
'You Ain't Going Nowhere'; 'He Was A Friend Of Mine'; 'Old Blue'; 'Long Black Veil'; 'Goin' Back'; 'Get Out Of My Life Woman'; 'Ballad Of Easy Rider'; 'Jesus Is Just Alright'; 'Tulsa County Blue'; 'Mr Spaceman'; 'Sing Me Back Home'; 'This Wheel's On Fire'; 'Lay Lady Lay'; 'Time Between'; 'Take A City Bride'; 'It's All Over Now, Baby Blue'; 'Way Behind The Sun'.
Alas, the Boston Tea Party show yet again, this time available as a limited edition (500) picture CD with a McGuinn/Hillman/Clarke poster.

Journals Cedrem CD 81–89.
'Mr Tambourine Man' (backing tracks, takes 1–22); 'I Knew I'd Want You' (backing track, unspecified take); 'It's No Use' (overdubbed vocals, with instruments, takes 1–7); 'The Bells Of Rhymney' (overdubbed vocals, with instruments, takes 1–5); 'The Bells Of Rhymney' (overdubbed vocals, with instruments, take 12); 'The Bells Of Rhymney' (overdubbed vocals, with instruments, take 17); 'Feel A Whole Lot Better' (overdubbed vocals, with instruments, takes 1–3); 'It's All Over Now, Baby Blue' (backing tracks, takes 1–6); 'The World Turns All Around Her' (backing tracks, takes 1–20); 'It's All Over Now, Baby Blue' (alternate session, backing tracks, takes 1–14); 'It Won't Be Wrong' (backing tracks, takes 1–20); 'Satisfied Mind' (backing tracks, takes 1–18); 'Set You Free This Time' (backing tracks, takes 1–12); 'Set You Free This Time' (alternate session, backing tracks, takes 1–26); 'Set You Free This Time' (second session, overdub 1, take 1); 'Set You Free This Time' (second session, backing tracks, take 29); 'Stranger In A Strange Land' (backing tracks, takes 1–12); 'Stranger In A Strange Land' (backing tracks, takes 14–17); 'Wait And See' (backing tracks, takes 1–26); 'Oh! Susannah' (backing tracks, takes 1–7); '5 D (Fifth Dimension)' (backing tracks, takes 1–26); The 5D Interview. Bonus CD: including a selection of the above takes of 'Mr Tambourine Man' (takes 1–2, 19–20); 'I Knew I'd Want You'; 'It's No Use' (takes 5–6); 'The Bells Of Rhymney' (takes 1–2); 'Feel A Whole Lot Better' (takes 1–2); 'It's All Over Now, Baby

Blue' (takes 2–4); 'The World Turns All Around Her' (takes 14–15); 'It's All Over Now, Baby Blue' (alternate session, take 7); 'It Won't Be Wrong' (takes 5–8); 'Satisfied Mind' (takes 17–18); 'Set You Free This Time'(takes 1–4, 18); 'Stranger In A Strange Land' (takes 1–2, 9–10); 'Wait And See' (takes 23–26); '5 D (Fifth Dimension)' (takes 18–26).

News that master tapes of the Byrds' first two albums were stolen from CBS studios inevitably resulted in a series of bootlegs, but few would have foreseen something quite as elaborate as this extravaganza. Nine CDs, consisting mainly of instrumental backing tracks from 1965, comprise this pricey package which, according to the insert, was manufactured in 1994 and issued as a limited edition of 1,000 copies. The discs appear in a gold-painted box which resembles a thin biscuit tin. Although the packaging is initially impressive, with a booklet featuring various bootlegged articles, it is immediately noticeable that the tin is actually too small to accommodate its contents. Such considerations will not unduly bother hard-core collectors, who will be more interested in the tracks on display. The bad news is that there are no new songs here at all, and the chance of including 'Flower Bomb Song' as a unique extra on CD is squandered. At least we do get various takes of 'Stranger In A Strange Land', one of which was actually borrowed for use as a bonus cut on the remastered reissue of *Turn! Turn! Turn!*.

The above reservations aside, *Journals* provides an opportunity to hear countless takes of 14 songs spread across many hours of tape. The compilers have elected to feature backing tracks, although judging from other bootleg CDs and tapes, there were a number of vocal versions of various songs that might have been added to break the monotony. The absence of so many vocal tracks robs the collection of authoritative status. More worryingly, the whole is extremely hard listening. Indeed, part of the challenge lies in changing the way in which you normally listen to recordings. Hearing take after take does not provide easy entertainment, but it is nevertheless revelatory. The listener is forced to maintain a suspension of disbelief as each track melts into the next, repeating introductions endlessly and never allowing the comfort of a vocal to transform an evolving idea into a fully fledged song. The effect is rather like listening to avant-garde recordings in which patience and concentration are required in order to appreciate the subtleties of the art form. Here, too, the mind has to adjust to repetition and focus on the value of each individual track. Like Melcher, you have to listen to the songs with the ear of a producer, sorting out the valuable from the debris.

Between songs, there is plenty of interaction between musicians and producer, but careful attention is required. Originally, I played the CDs through expensive speakers but still found that important dialogue was not audible. It is only through the headphones that the full drama emerges, with angry, bored or humorous comments enlightening the music en route. There is also a wonderful unpredictability about the backing tracks as you're never sure if a take is going to last three seconds or three minutes. Any lapse in concentration means that you're likely to miss an entire take and, once the mind wanders, the listening experience is cheapened, resulting in boredom or frustration. This is like a class in aural dissection, fascinating for the student, but hard-going for the non-committed. Approached the right way, however, these discs are a revelation, showing in often painful progression, the Byrds' growth as recording artistes. The recordings are also a tribute to the influence of producer Terry Melcher, whose suggestions and appraisals show an astute understanding of the Byrds during this crucial time. No doubt the compilers did not consider *Journals* as a conceptual work in avant-garde terms but, accidentally or otherwise, that's what it is. If you get through this with enjoyment, then it's likely your whole approach to music listening may be altered.

Appropriately, the package commences with the Byrds' first recording and chart topper. As they prepare for the first take of 'Mr Tambourine Man', Hal Blaine asks, "Do you want Leon in or out on the fade?" Considering the fate of Leon Russell, Melcher concludes, "He's out! He's out for the first four bars and the last four, which are repeats. He knows."

Issuing instructions, Melcher asks bassist Larry Knechtel to "do the '*A*'s a little off-tempo." A slow, tentative backing track follows, confirmed by Melcher's: "It feels a little bit slow!"

Blaine clicks his drumsticks, performs a military flourish and counts in take 2 of 'Mr Tambourine Man'. A strong version follows and it's clear that the musicians are on the mark. Melcher is sufficiently enthused to suggest, "We'll play that back." Then, as if realizing that they couldn't possibly get such a great take that quickly, he prevaricates. "Wait a minute," he warns. "Hal, let me hear the bass drum a little bit."

'Mr Tambourine Man' (take 3) features a more prominent, albeit fuzzy, bass and Blaine hits a cymbal hard causing reverberation midway through the take.

For the fourth take, Melcher shows concern about the tempo, advising Jim McGuinn to "start it off a hair slow." McGuinn's opening solo sounds much improved here.

Hal Blaine counts to six, as the group move into take 5. "Hal, do that pick-up on the snare and do it heavy," Melcher interrupts. A sixth take follows, which the group concludes without further interruption. It's reasonable, but perhaps not quite what they want.

The seventh take collapses midway through the song. "Did someone fuck up?" Melcher enquires.

"Yeah, I did, sorry, man," says a contrite McGuinn.

In an attempt to lighten the mood, Blaine jokes, "Cool it, there's a fag in the booth for Christ's sake."

Take 8 barely gets beyond an opening guitar strum before Melcher insists, "We'll take that again." Focusing on McGuinn, he advises, "Jim, try not to make any string noise when you come in there because when I review it . . . you'll say I'm sloppy, or something like that."

The opening of take 9 definitely sounds slow, a view with which Melcher soon concurs. Thirty-four seconds in, he calls a halt. "It felt a hair too slow," he points out. "Just a hair."

"What kind?" demands Hal Blaine. "Are you talking pubic again?"

"Pubic. Yes. Genital type," Melcher responds, going along with the schoolboy humour.

Melcher is so caught up in the banter that he momentarily loses track of the takes, calling take 9 for a second time. This one doesn't last long. "It's a bit draggy," Melcher notes, adding, "Are you in drag, Bill?"

By contrast, the tenth take of 'Mr Tambourine Man' shows the group speeding up. "That was a little bit too fast," Melcher warns. "There won't be anywhere left to go . . . we would have had a double time by bar 62 or bar 61."

The eleventh take of 'Mr Tambourine Man' is halted within a minute. "Hold it a sec," Melcher urges. "Jim, do some kind of fill in 21, like bar 21 and 22 go into 'Take me for a trip . . .' "

This is attempted on take 12, but it is not to Melcher's satisfaction. "20 or 21 don't feel right," he tells them. "There should be a lot of feel there. Everyone play like they were leader."

The thirteenth take of 'Mr Tambourine Man' lasts a mere 17 seconds. "Hold it!" Melcher says. "Hey, Jim, can you do that fill . . . do a little slide into it."

Another bad intro on the fourteenth take causes Melcher to push the button after 24 seconds. "I'll tell you what," he says, evidently with a new idea. "Bill and Larry, when you come into the *D*, slide up from the *A*."

On the fifteenth and sixteenth takes, they mess up the opening and the seventeenth is also unsatisfactory. "Now, it's too slow," Melcher complains. "Bill and Larry forget the *A-D* slide there – it's not even enough."

Take 18 is also halted. "Hold it a second," Melcher interrupts. "Everybody really attack bar 5. Jerry and Bill and Leon – everybody. When everybody comes in, there just isn't enough there. And a little more attack on the first note too, Jim."

Take 19 is stopped after a minute due to the drumming. "Let's take another one," says Melcher. "That just didn't feel right."

"Take 79," they joke, as the twentieth take begins. This time it sounds much tighter. "That was real good," enthuses Melcher. "Up until the half..."

Take 21 is the most impressive yet. Two minutes in, Melcher regrettably halts proceedings. 'Hold it!,' he implores. "There was a little trouble right there. The feel was perfect until right there."

"Is this 22?" Melcher asks as they prepare to perform the umpteenth backing track of 'Mr Tambourine Man'. Unsure if they are tiring or not, Melcher gives them the option to stop. "Do you want to go on or do you want to rest for a minute?" he enquires. "You want to rest! Well, let's try one more while it feels good. One more while you're resting!" He then adds, jokingly: "You've been resting through the whole thing anyway, for Christ's sake."

A very impressive take follows, with some solid and emphatic drumming from Blaine. This is almost certainly the backing track that they used on the single. "OK, let's play that back," Melcher announces triumphantly.

After the 22 takes of 'Mr Tambourine Man', there is only one take of 'I Knew I'd Want You' featured on *Journals*. It's so impressive that you suspect it must have been attempted very late in the sessions.

On seven versions of 'It's No Use', we get to hear the vocals as well as the instruments. The first take is incredibly solid and appears to need little adjustment. "Let's take one more," Melcher suggests.

The second take is arguably even better, with the vocals sounding perfectly on key. Alas, take 3 is interrupted after 30 seconds presumably due to technical problems. Its successor shows a decline in the quality of the vocal harmonies, which are more ragged than before. "I'm sure we'll get it this time," Melcher promises.

Take 5 of 'It's No Use' is pulled less than a minute in. "OK," Melcher says hopefully, skipping a take in his computation: "Lucky seven!" This final version is indeed impressive, with Crosby's voice more prominent than before. It proves enough.

The seven takes of vocal overdubs on the backing track of 'The Bells Of Rhymney' provide a further endearing insight into the group's harmonic blend. "Merthyr's spelt 'M-U-R-T-H-U-R'," announces Crosby, presumably ironically. "Oh, and it's 'miners' and 'mine owner'," he adds, as if addressing himself. One minute in, Melcher calls a halt.

With Michael Clarke's drumming sounding as powerful as needed, McGuinn and Clark's vocals are closely intertwined on take 2, as they sing double lead. They still sound a little uncertain in places and have enormous problems harmonizing on the final "aahhs" towards the conclusion of the song. At the end, McGuinn says, "I have a couple of corrections to make. Contrary to your suggestion, it's not . . ." – at which point, the tape cuts out so that we never discover what McGuinn was referring to.

On take 3 of 'The Bells Of Rhymney', McGuinn's vocal lead is dominant, with Clark's thrust into the background. The timing sounds a little awry and Jim's voice is severely strained, cracking up badly at the end.

McGuinn's voice is still strained on take 4, especially when he tries to sing the words "silver bells". Towards the end, he once again finds it impossible to reach the high notes.

Throughout take 5, the harmonies are much improved but, at the end, McGuinn is so off-key that he sounds as though he is being strangled.

There is a break in the tape at this point and we move on to take 12. Generally, it sounds much better, although perhaps not quite in sync vocally. At least the previously appalling closing vocals are at last working out.

Another jump in the tape takes us to take 17. This is the perfect version on which everything comes together, including that wonderful final harmony on which they had clearly worked so hard.

'Feel A Whole Lot Better' overdub 1, take 1, is quite a spirited version, with Gene Clark's enunciation prominent and his vocal surprisingly spontaneous. After one minute and 34 seconds, Melcher stops the track, demanding, "Who sings the high part?" He then instructs engineer Ray Gerhardt to "put up the voices considerably".

The second vocal overdub on 'Feel A Whole Lot Better' is wonderful, with a truly expressive lead vocal from Gene Clark. He also changes the lyrics slightly, singing, "Now I have to say" instead of "Now, I've got to say".

The third take sounds faultless, a classic example of the Byrds singing and playing at their best.

The ultimately abandoned 'It's All Over Now, Baby Blue' is available on *Journals* courtesy of various backing tracks, the best of which are probably better than the complete vocal/instrumental take featured on *Never Before*. The opening take features some extremely hard drumming from Clarke. At one minute 12 seconds, Melcher asks quizzically: "How come everyone's not playing?"

Instead of take 2, Melcher announces take 1 again. An adequate backing track follows. "Let's play that back," Melcher suggests, presumably attempting to discover how close he is to a finished version. They then play take 2, which lasts a mere 30 seconds before Melcher interrupts, "Jim, you and Chris aren't in tune yet."

Take 3 is interesting, but Melcher is not convinced. "It really doesn't . . ."

he adds, but is cut off before making his point. The succeeding take 4 is again reasonable, but Clarke's drums switch from the right to the left channel towards the end.

Take 5 of 'It's All Over Now, Baby Blue' finishes prematurely. Melcher offers encouraging words. "It's making it," he enthuses, "except that you're still out of tune with Chris. When it comes together on a mono that's when it gets noticeable."

The final take 6 on *Journals* is the best yet, with a chiming jingle-jangle Rickenbacker break from McGuinn. "That sounded pretty good," Melcher concedes.

A surprisingly long time is spent completing the backing track of 'The World Turns All Around Her' which is given a degree of attention more usually lavished upon a potential single. The first take lasts a mere handful of seconds before Melcher announces, "David, you were either out of tune or you hit a wrong note." Melcher's assistant feels the blame lies elsewhere: "Somebody's out of tune. Jim, I think."

Take 2 is quite percussive and chugs along reasonably well. Melcher makes no comment at all as they move into the third take. "'My World Turns All Around Her'," the producer announces, before correcting himself. A few seconds in, he calls another halt. "Let's start again," he suggests. "The last chord before it goes into rhythm sounded a little strange." After this, the group tunes up for a while in preparation for a new assault.

"'My World Turns All Around Her' take 4," Melcher announces, having still not learned the correct title of the song. Unfortunately, both this and take 5 founder on the opening chords.

Take 6 also sounds slightly off, causing Melcher to focus on Clarke's heavy-handed drumming. "Hey, we can get a better cymbal sound by putting it out with mallets," Melcher jokes. "Like, when you try hitting it that hard, it just starts running into itself." Fearing an impasse, Jim Dickson intervenes from the booth with the suggestion: "Do another one, right away!"

Melcher adds: "Yeah, Mike, don't worry about those big cymbal crashes. It'll sound better with mallets. We'll put them on later."

As we enter what seems to be the seventh take of 'The World Turns All Around Her', Melcher again loses count and announces, "six". Throughout, they continue to complain about Clarke's over-use of cymbals. Take 7 sounds a little distorted, but otherwise reasonable. "The intro was especially strong," Melcher comments encouragingly.

Take 8 is pretty good, but not quite as magical as the final version. While waiting, the Byrds play a country lick in bluegrass vein until Melcher insists, "Let's get on with the business in hand".

Clarke seems more interested in the country excursion than 'The World Turns All Around Her' and exclaims: "We gotta do a country song like that."

Take 9 does not get beyond the introduction, while on take 10 they play for only three seconds before messing up. "That was good till there," Melcher says, damning them with faint praise and prompting uproarious laughter.

Takes 11, 12 and 13 are all plagued by false starts but Melcher allows the latter take to proceed. A very good take follows. This time, it is Michael Clarke who suggests the inevitable, "Let's do it again," adding, "I screwed up."

"Watch those fills there, Mike," Melcher warns. "It's the first backbeat – it's a little late."

Take 14 does not get past the introduction, but take 15 is a very sprightly version.

"One more time," says Mike.

"OK – that was a good one," Melcher suggests, for once not pressing for another take.

"No, man, I've got a better one," Clarke insists, clearly getting into the song.

"You missed a cymbal crash, I think, once," Melcher notes, as if trying to find something wrong in order to justify Clarke's comments.

"I missed a whole lot of shit," Michael adds, with unnecessary humility.

Despite the talk, take 16 fumbles after the intro and there is little comment on take 17, which is nevertheless impressive. Feeling their way into the song, the Byrds play a great introduction to take 18 and then stop. "That was good," Melcher encourages.

Take 19 is another non-starter and take 20 goes a little awry two thirds of the way through, but otherwise sounds fine. With enough takes to choose from for 'The World Turns All Around Her', we move on.

The opening chords of 'It's All Over Now, Baby Blue' are preceded by the words, "Friday version, take 1' which suggests that this may not be the version listed in the sessionography on 28 June, which was a Monday. The group sound like they are still warming up on take 2, which is far too slow. The Byrds barely hit a chord on take 3, before the take is cut. The next take features Michael playing very loudly and heavy as the group attempts to find a groove.

"... 'Baby Blue', take 2, er 3. . . . 5!" announces Melcher, who seems to have lost his bearings. This take doesn't even start and in the background you can just hear Crosby lecturing Clarke about his playing.

Clarke plays some brusque fills on take six, but at times sounds like he is battering his drums into submission. Towards the end, they move into a jam, which sounds both intriguing and amusing.

The aggressive playing of Clarke is also the keynote of take 7, as he leads the others into the chorus. After 48 seconds, Melcher halts proceedings. "Right there, you speed up," Crosby points out, his comments presumably directed at Clarke.

Take 9 is another heavy percussive effort, with Clarke seemingly determined to play the hell out of the song. At least they are allowed to perform the entire backing track on this occasion.

The engineer gets involved in the action on take 10, demanding:

"Where the hell are you going with the microphone, Michael?"

"I'm lowering it a little bit," the drummer replies.

"What good is it doing down there?" asks the engineer

"I don't want so much cymbal in it," Michael responds, with proud logic.

"I'll drop it a little bit in here, you know," the engineer points out. "Just tell me if you've got too much."

With the technical problem solved, take 10 proceeds with a false intro. The succeeding take is also unsatisfactory and take 12 sounds too restrained. Take 13 is clearly going nowhere, but there is a breakthrough on the final take 14, which seems closer to the sound they are searching for, with Clarke's drumming very upfront, but not overwhelming.

Melcher's tendency to labour over potential singles is evident from the time spent on 'It Won't Be Wrong'. After two false starts, the producer discusses the original version of the song, when it was issued as the Elektra B-side, 'Don't Be Long'.

"I heard the intro on the other record," he says. "It was a good thing. Is that what you're playing now?"

They then discuss who will play on the record and settle down for an impressively tight take 3, which has a firm groove. Listening to McGuinn's Rickenbacker in isolation from the vocals allows you to appreciate his playing even more. After a mistake midway through the song, Melcher points out, "The spot that seems to be funny is the intro and the breaks. Nobody seems to be exactly sure but . . . let's take another one."

Takes 4–6 are stopped within seconds, with Melcher explaining: "Since everything else is right, let me just keep stopping until we get the intro right."

During take 7, Melcher is still dissatisfied and asks, "Hey, Michael, why don't you lay out of the intro and do that part the second time the intro comes up. You know, like halfway through." The continuing take 7 is slightly slower and less forceful, but they at least get through the entire song without further comment. "Do you want to hear that?" Melcher asks, before adding the pun, "'Don't Be Long', Jim, because we're on take 8."

Take 8 lasts barely a few seconds, and take 9 has a dreadful opening, prompting Melcher's exclamation, "No! I guess some people have to look at their chords."

The tenth take causes Melcher to complain about some noise. "Somebody's dropped a drumstick or something," he points out. In an attempt to add some atmosphere to the track, Michael suggests that they should "turn off the lights again."

Crosby agrees, insisting: "Turn off the lights. Shut them off!"

Melcher is a little perplexed and wonders whether they can play properly without the lights. "Does everyone know how to finger without looking?" he asks. "I'm sure Michael needs to see his drums."

Exasperated by such reasoning, the drummer cheekily retorts, "Fuck off. Just do it. Shut them off! Leave them on or shut them off!"

"That makes sense," Melcher chirps back with inescapable logic.

After all the backchat, take 11 merely lasts a few seconds. Take 12 is much better, but still a little tentative in parts. "It was good except for one or two . . ." Melcher concludes, not even bothering to finish his sentence.

Take 13 is another false start, which causes Melcher to admonish, "That was a little loose."

By take 14, McGuinn adds a semi-drone effect which sounds most impressive. Terry is still seeking a better take though and tells them, "There have been a couple of bad chords and things. Do you want to check . . . the tuning or something? It's either you or Gene, Jim." The reference to Gene in relation to tuning suggests that he was playing guitar on the track, which is something of a rarity at these sessions.

Take 15 breaks down halfway through the song. Explaining their error, Melcher points out: "What went wrong was that the break wasn't tight and didn't sound right . . . the rest of it was good."

Take 16 of 'It Won't Be Wrong' is the best yet, although McGuinn's solo during the break could be improved.

After a failed take 17, they push through a formidable take 18, after which Clarke throws in a celebratory drum roll. The session ends with two more takes, both of which are very solid and eminently suitable for release.

The session for 'Satisfied Mind' is one of the most laborious to listen to on *Journals*, although it does show the Byrds slowly clawing their way towards a complete version of the song. Takes 1–2 are false starts, with Melcher telling McGuinn: "Jim, your footwork's coming through a little bit."

After fumbling the openings of takes 3–4, they manage to get through the song, but Clarke's drumsticks sound like knitting needles. The usually shy Chris Hillman makes a rare essay into speech asking, "Gene, there's a harmonic break before the second chorus, isn't there? In the second verse?"

Turning to Clarke, Melcher announces, "As soon as you're ready. Really hit that bass drum, man."

Take 6 stumbles before it has begun. Melcher, realizing something is very wrong, tells McGuinn, "Jim, the sound isn't right yet on that guitar. Can you try taking off a little more tremolo?"

The seventh take is faded after a few seconds and this time Clarke is blamed. Melcher asks, "Are you coming in after that first beat, Michael?"

Clarke, increasingly frustrated by the song, replies, "What? I don't know what beat I'm coming in on, man. I don't even know this fucking song."

"You should come in on the bass drum where Chris comes in," Melcher points out helpfully.

"Why don't you get Hal Blaine?" Clarke retorts sarcastically, clearly wishing he was somewhere else.

On take 8, Clarke thuds through the song with noticeable weariness. Admittedly, it's a pretty dull arrangement to have to work on for any length of time. "Let me make a suggestion here," says Melcher, before being cut off.

Take 9 barely begins and by take 10 a tambourine has been added to the equation in place of Clarke's thudding drums.

Perseverance brings some rewards on take 11, but take 12 sounds wayward once more. "I think we'll need one more," Melcher announces, optimistically.

Alas, take 13 lasts only a few seconds. "A little less tremolo, Jim," Melcher asks, repeating his request on take 6.

By take 14, Melcher feels that the intros are too far apart from each other. "Can everyone start from the top . . . come in together or something?" he asks hopefully.

Take 14 is short and sweet, take 16 adequate until the end when they fumble badly. "What take is this?" Melcher demands, clearly lost amid the sheer number of re-runs.

They slog through take 17 but, as Melcher tells them, "The intro didn't make it."

The final take sees the introduction of an acoustic guitar, which sounds good. With the tambourine prominent, it betrays a Salvation Army feel. By the end of the take, it is clear that the song is at last fully formed. Who would have imagined that this apparently simple arrangement would have caused them so much trouble?

The largest number of takes on *Journals*, covering almost one-and-a-half CDs details the lengthy backing track history of 'Set You Free This Time'. Take 1 barely begins before Melcher suggests, "Jim, take it again. I think I have a problem getting the echo right." It's not righted on takes 2 or 3 either, prompting further comments from Melcher. "Jim can you turn your amplifier down a little bit." McGuinn then carefully counts in take 4 and we're off, with Gene accompanying them on acoustic guitar. A sedate but accomplished version follows, with a slightly different ending to the released version.

Take 5 of 'Set You Free This Time' lasts less than a minute. Melcher stops proceedings, saying: "Wait a second! That was the right sound, Jim. How clean do you want that intro?"

Clarke's drums are more prominent on take 6, a complete version of which sounds impressive. "Do you want to hear it?" Melcher asks, hinting that we may be near a finished take, although that will prove over-optimistic.

Take 7 only lasts a few seconds before Melcher insists: "Do it again, the intro was one tempo."

Gene, meanwhile, asks the other Byrds, "Can we speed it up a little bit?"

Take 8 begins at a painfully slow tempo. "It's become a funeral dirge," Melcher complains.

Crosby concurs: "Yeah, it's too slow."

The group speeds up on take 9, which is pretty accomplished. It's difficult to imagine them getting much better than this, and Melcher instinctively feels that they should not spend too much longer on the track. "Let's give this track like to three," he suggests. "Let's not go on and on."

Gene partly agrees, "Because we've got a good enough take already."

"There's several," Melcher notes encouragingly.

"Well, that one we just did," Clark points out, eager for Melcher to use the ninth take.

Take 10 is interrupted during the intro. "Take it again," Melcher announces. "I'm sorry, Jim, we had too much of you."

There's a faulty intro on take 11, but they rally for take 12, which is very good. Melcher makes it clear that the only reason to carry on is to master the introduction. "Well, that intro was a little loose," he insists.

We then switch to a completely different session for 'Set You Free This Time' and, judging from the opening takes, it was probably recorded earlier than the one we have just heard.

The first two takes last a few seconds only and, after take 3, Melcher wonders, "Is that what you meant to play there?"

"That's what he wants," Crosby says, presumably referring to Clark.

"It sounds like a dischord thing there," Melcher suggests.

"Why don't you let us take one and quit stopping," an impatient Clarke retorts, clearly put out by Melcher's fussiness at this point.

"Why don't you fuck yourself," Melcher replies punkishly.

The following take goes nowhere and ends quickly. At this point, Clark practises his vocal line. Melcher, meanwhile, considers his recent harsh comment to Mike Clarke, which he only meant in jest. "I was only kidding, Mike," he assures the drummer, who has suddenly gone rather quiet.

"Do you want to hear one of the intros back?" Melcher adds.

"No," screams Michael, seemingly backed by everybody else.

Even Gene shows uncharacteristic annoyance at Melcher's frequent intrusions at this point. "Hey Terry," he says, "hold on a minute, will you please?" Turning to McGuinn, Clark asks that he stay in "*D*".

With the Byrds deep in concentration, Melcher seems almost sheepish about announcing take 6. It stumbles along to completion, but isn't the best take by a long way. At the end, Clark explains what he wants during the different verses.

Take 7 begins noticeably out of tune. "Let's do a tuning session," Gene insists.

Having tuned their instruments, the group move into take 8, with Gene telling them, "Remember the ending, OK? Hey, if it's done right it would blag right into the lyrics of the song, man." Alas, the take barely begins before a fault is found.

There's another false start on take 9, with Melcher apologizing and playing the diplomat. "Sorry, take it again," he says. "Michael's . . . cymbals are blocking him up." They all laugh at this.

Clarke enjoys messing around on the tenth take, playing those familiar military beats that he has been using since the World-Pacific versions of 'Mr Tambourine Man'. He is clearly getting into the song at this point and this take is treated like a rehearsal. During the latter part of the song, Clarke discovers a groove and gets audibly enthused.

Takes 11–12 both have faulty intros, prompting Melcher to announce: "Let's take it again. Nobody was together."

Commenting on the track, Clark points out, "We don't have to do that. It's just that it sounds so groovy with the vocal."

Eager and enthusiastic to play on, Clarke retorts: "Come on, let's just do it!"

They then urge Michael to play a drum roll to inspire them and he is pleased to oblige.

Gene hesitates, adding, "I hate to be out of tune, man". He then retunes his guitar in preparation for take 13, but they falter again during the introduction.

"Start again!" Melcher insists. "The feel there was perfect. Settle into the groove like after 8 bars."

"How can you be out of tune when you just tuned?" Mike asks.

"It's the fog today," Gene jokes in response.

"Whenever you're ready, 14" Melcher announces.

"They're arguing over who's flat now," Gene tells him. "You'll have to wait till that's finished!"

A strong take follows, with Clarke's drumming very upfront. Melcher, still unsure about the conclusion asks, "Was that an ending, or is there a fade on it, Gene?"

Take 15 lasts for only a few chords and take 16 proves unsatisfactory. "Do it again," Melcher implores. "That wasn't a good one."

As they prepare for take 17, Crosby is unsure about his contribution.

Clark, responding with maximum encouragement, informs his partner, "Oh wait a minute. You have a groovy thing there that you're doing . . . Dig that swing! It's a swing, man."

Melcher is also more upbeat. "That was a good intro like that," he enthuses.

Michael Clarke disagrees. "I didn't like that," he insists.

Melcher next turns to McGuinn telling him, "Jim, coming in alone was a good thing."

"Yeah, I like it a lot," Crosby agrees.

"How many beats do you want before we start the song?" Clark asks.

"Can you go to 'D'?" Crosby replies. "That's where we start the song."

"OK, all right, fine," Gene agrees.

A fairly good version follows all this conversation.

Take 19 of 'Set You Free This Time' sounds adequate, but the feel isn't quite right. "That wasn't as good as 14," Melcher rightly notes.

After take 20 founders, Melcher suggests, "It sounded better with McGuinn coming in the first lick alone."

Take 22 isn't what Melcher requires. "No," he says. "It sounds like someone should hit a chord there."

We move on to the next CD for take 23, which again features Clarke's familiar military beat. Overall, this one sounds the most sprightly take for some time.

Take 24 barely begins, but Gene does manage to instruct the others more clearly about what he wants and an adequate performance follows.

Clark is still encouraging his fellow players at the start of take 26, which turns out well. "Do you want to hear that one?" Melcher asks, sensing a winner.

An overdub follows, before Michael Clarke demands, "Still, one more time." After expending so much effort on the song, his insistence on continuing is commendable.

Melcher agrees, but warns, "This has to be the last one – 29."

Thankfully, they close with an impressive take, vindicating the work already done.

Arguably the highlight of *Journals* emerges next with the 17 takes of 'Stranger In A Strange Land', the Crosby composition that failed to appear on their second album. Take 1 begins with a tambourine and that distinctive riff. It's unbearably tantalizing to hear the backing track without the vocals, all the more so when you recall how few vocals of Crosby's there are with the Byrds. This take ends after a minute, but Michael Clarke carries on, discovering a groove of his own. "Hey, slower," he concludes, authoritatively.

Melcher, meanwhile, has some wise words for McGuinn: "The idea, Jim, about fading a track in, the track should have everything going when we fade it in. It should sound like the fade, you know. It should be the whole track coming in."

An excellent riffing session follows with the Byrds obviously getting into the track. Take 2 chugs along briefly, after which a discussion follows about the track but, unfortunately, the microphone fails to pick up the conversation.

"Stranger Than Fiction!" Melcher portentously announces as we move into take 3. This is the best yet — a great garage-style riff slightly reminiscent of Them's 'Gloria'. It makes you feel desperate to hear the vocal. Crosby once told me that he wasn't impressed by this song, especially its lyrics, but he also felt *Preflyte* was appalling and should never have been released, so you can't always rely on his opinions of old material. Listening to the backing track of the song, it sounds so distinctive that you can almost picture the composition on the finished album. Imagine *Turn! Turn! Turn!* with a Crosby composition and lead vocal and consider the implications. The very sound texture of the Byrds would have been subtly altered, as it was so dramatically on 'The Airport Song', the only Crosby lead extant from the Byrds' World-Pacific sessions.

McGuinn adds some little flourishes to take 3, but it's Michael Clarke who is really pushing the song. At the end, he again demands a change in the tempo with the words, "slower".

The fourth take of 'Stranger In A Strange Land' is stopped in its prime. Melcher chides, "It was perfect until right there, until that change, which wasn't smooth at all."

Take 5 is also cut after about a minute. "There was a mistake there," Melcher points out, "and one a couple of bars back . . . it's a good feel."

Determined to do his best, Clarke asks, "I'd like to know when that change comes in."

Crosby agrees to assist, replying, "OK, I'll go through it."

Melcher is still not impressed by the opening of take 6 and they swiftly move on to the next take, which sounds a lot slicker, if slightly less spontaneous than its predecessors.

Take 8 is a false start. "Hold it!" Melcher tells them. "You made some noise."

Take 9 is also broken up. "Let's do it again," Melcher suggests. "It was better when you were doing the breaks coming in, Michael."

Take 10 of 'Stranger In A Strange Land' is more aggressive and although the tambourine is still in the mix, it is now less noticeable. Chris appears to be enjoying playing the bass line and working well with Michael, who sounds determined to play in his favourite R&B style.

Clarke is really up for take 11 and wants the others to help him maintain the right groove throughout. "Hey, man," he asks, "just like look at me when those breaks come in!"

A good, extremely solid version follows, with Mike drumming hard and getting better all the time.

Melcher is also enthusiastic: "That's one of the best intros on it. It's good Mike laying back until after Jim comes in. That was good."

Take 12, is a false start, as Melcher exclaims, "Do that again . . . the intro just didn't flow."

Melcher then jumps to take 14, which is adequate, although the ending doesn't sound quite right.

Takes 15–16 are both false starts, but they pull it together on take 17 in which Crosby plays a neat, shuffling rhythm and Hillman adds some arresting bass work. Everything coalesces for a grand finale, but it does not prove enough to win the track a place on the album.

One of the surprises of *Journals* is the amount of time they spend on a seemingly straightforward song like 'Wait And See' which, again, is treated with the kind of attention normally allocated to a potential single. The backing track throughout is amazingly refreshing and much better than expected. From take 1 onwards they sound extremely well rehearsed. Indeed, this could have been a one take song. Maybe Melcher agrees as he asks, "You want to hear it?"

Take 2 only features the opening chords. Melcher tells McGuinn: "Jim, don't play the opening that hard because it's distorting. It's not picking up."

Take 3 is fairly good, but there's a false start on its successor. They seem to find form on take 5 which rocks forcibly, if a little rickety, with Chris' bass prominent. Hillman appears to fluff a note, but it's not that noticeable. Despite its spontaneity and power, Melcher sees a number of errors. "That wasn't too good," he concludes.

The tambourine is upfront on take 6, but Hillman's bass cuts in and out of the speakers. "Sorry," Melcher apologizes, "something happened and the bass didn't get on the track. Something went dead – one of the plugs."

Take 7 merely consists of them slowly tuning up, and there's a false start on take 8, with the group suddenly sounding cold. Melcher resumes take 8, which features some excellent, solid drumming from Clarke. Again, the bass is prominent, which enables us to focus on every note. Michael offers some exuberant moments but, overall, Melcher is disappointed. "That was a little sloppy," he concludes "Do you want to hear it?"

The timing is suspect on take 9. Melcher explains his reservations to McGuinn: "Jim, the intro's got one tempo going and the song starts and it's like twice as fast. Is that intended?"

"No!" Crosby interrupts, not alone.

"I didn't think so," Melcher retorts.

"Slow it down," Crosby tells the others.

A promising take follows, but goes a little awry towards the end.

Take 11 is a false start, but Melcher is encouraged by the opening. "That was good with the bass in there like that," he enthuses. "Keep it like that. It makes it."

As take 12 begins, Gene is asked, "Are you putting in the tambourine before anybody comes in?"

The group lose their way midway through the song, and the whole thing disintegrates. Melcher reveals: "Somebody missed a guitar note in the place where the drum drops out, so we'll take it again."

After a false start on take 13, they run through an adequate attempt on take 14, although it is far from perfect.

A tuning intermission follows before take 15, which breaks down halfway through. The succeeding take has another of those false starts, prompting Melcher to suggest, "It would be better if there was a drum pick-up or something because no one comes in together." They re-run take 16 and it sounds much tighter.

By take 17, there's confirmation of a change of plan regarding the inclusion of Gene Clark's tambourine. Melcher tells them, "Well, since we aren't taking a tambourine on this, it doesn't make that much difference. He and Michael aren't really together anyway. I've turned the tambourine mike off."

After all that, there's another false start and the take concludes within a few seconds. The same thing happens on take 18. "That wasn't together, either," Melcher complains.

Take 19 is pretty good, spoiled only by a few mistakes towards the end. Melcher also notes that there is some feedback.

By take 20, Melcher is still concerned about the introduction. He points out: "It really feels bad when the intro has one tempo going and then it starts up faster . . . It should be a constant feeling."

Clarke also has some advice. "You guys are speeding up!" he tells the other Byrds.

Melcher's involvement in every aspect of the recording is underlined 20 seconds into the revised take, when he offers some sound advice. "Hold it!" he announces. "When you leave that spot open . . . when the spot's left open in between the intro and when the rhythm starts without the drum thing, you can hear different people's guitars chording at different times and things – it's pretty sloppy. If you just put one drumbeat before it, it will just pull it together, OK?"

Having been told what to do, the group fumble through two false starts, and it is not until take 23 of 'Wait And See' that they are back on track with a complete take. It's reasonable enough, but could be much better. "Get on the road with the show!" Melcher admonishes them.

Take 24 only lasts a few seconds. "Jim, tune with Chris will you?" Melcher asks.

Take 25 opens dramatically only to be interrupted by a screaming Michael Clarke who exclaims, "Hey! My drum wasn't on."

Although it's still not perfect, take 26 sounds good enough and, with all the other tracks they've completed, surely there is enough to piece a decent song together. Fortunately, Melcher is at last satisfied. "That was good," he enthuses, no doubt relieved to have completed 'Wait And See'.

'Oh! Susannah' opens with McGuinn playing a rather slow introduction. Clarke's drums come bursting through and he just lets rip. Towards the end, Melcher points out, "That note right there, Jim, it's not quite in tune. It stuck out every time. I think it's a little flat with that string there."

Deciding on a course of action, Melcher asks, "Do you want me to stop every time the breaks are not together? Otherwise, do you want to play it through a couple of times?"

Although the tape reveals no answer to Melcher's question, the group evidently decide to play the song all the way through each time.

Take 2 features a superior intro from McGuinn, although it is still marginally slow. Clarke then leaps forth like a greyhound from a trap, tearing away on the drums. He seems to enjoy thrashing away on this track although, according to Jim Dickson, he was very sceptical about its inclusion. Towards the end of the song, Clarke begins to play around with the military beat which will be a feature of the completed recording.

The third take of 'Oh! Susannah' is the most sprightly yet. Clarke's playing levels out, sounding less manic and more focused. McGuinn's solos are also better but he misses a note around the two-minute mark. Thereafter, the take collapses into cacophony, causing ripples of laughter from the group.

Take 4 prompts Michael to instruct McGuinn: "Hey, Jimmy, play it slower!"

On take 5, McGuinn takes Clarke's advice too literally and opens with an agonizingly slow solo. Melcher interrupts to tell the guitarist, "Jim, start again because there was talking."

Although take 6 also sounds a little slow during the intro, you can hear the contrast that Clarke is seeking. His drumming is intense, solid and impressive in places, while Hillman's bass also shows improvement. This would have been a rival to the finished version, except that they mess up the intro during the concluding verse.

The final take 7 of 'Oh! Susannah' features Clarke playing at his hardest, while McGuinn picks out the notes with careful precision. Towards the end, Clarke begins to add the military drumbeat that will be completed for the released version.

The 26 takes of '5 D (Fifth Dimension)' feature Allen Stanton in charge and his approach is far more reserved than that of the exuberant Melcher. Admittedly, the Byrds were far more experienced in the studio by this time but, even so, you suspect that Melcher would have had much to say about the development of these takes, most of which are stopped without explanation. After three false starts, the Byrds manage to complete a take, and Stanton offers a playback. Further problems blight the next two takes, but they find a solid beat on take 7 and the results are fairly good.

Takes 8–11 are fumbling efforts and there are discussions about the song, but unfortunately they are conducted away from the mike. After an adequate take 12, they suffer more false starts on takes 13–15. They get through take 16 without a problem, which at this point is a welcome development.

Take 17 fades after 50 seconds and take 18 barely lasts a minute. Two further false starts occur on takes 19–20, but they pass the minute mark on take 21. After a short-lived take 22, Clarke hits his drums in frustration. There's a breakthrough of sorts on take 23 with one of the best takes of the evening. It is followed by another, which reveals Hillman's improving bass playing. Unfortunately, they can't seem to sustain the momentum and take 25 lasts a mere 30 seconds, resulting in more discussions.

Take 26 is definitely one of the best and sounds as close as they are likely to get to a satisfactory version. Although they lose it at the 2 minute 41 second mark, they're virtually there. Perhaps realizing this, Clarke expresses his disappointment with the exclamation, "It was shitty . . . bullshit."

The CD ends with the famous *Fifth Dimension* interview, taken from a vinyl record, rather than the master tape. Its inclusion is now redundant as a result of its official release on the *Fifth Dimension* CD.

A final bonus disc is merely a sampler of what we've already heard, clearly directed at those who can't stomach listening to the entire package. The compilers feature various takes from every song attempted except 'Oh! Susannah', which is omitted despite the fact that it was one of the few numbers where Melcher allowed them to play without interruption. So ends the longest, most exhausting and expensive Byrds' bootleg package ever conceived.
Released 1994.

Lyve Twytter Discurios DIS 114CD.
'Lover Of The Bayou'; 'You Ain't Going Nowhere'; 'Jesus Is Just Alright'; 'It's Alright Ma (I'm Only Bleeding)'; 'Ballad Of Easy Rider'; 'This Wheel's On Fire'; 'Medley: 'My Back Pages'/'B.J. Blues'/'Baby, What Do You Want Me To Do'; 'Willin''; 'Medley: 'Turn! Turn! Turn!'/'Mr Tambourine Man'/'Eight Miles High'; 'So You Want To Be A Rock 'n' Roll Star'; 'Mr Spaceman'; 'All The Things'; 'Country Jig' ['Buckaroo'/'Nashville West']; 'You Don't Miss Your Water'; 'Chestnut Mare'; 'Chimes Of Freedom'; 'Amazing Grace'.
An adequate if unoriginal bootleg with more selections from Amsterdam 1970.
Released 1990.

Two Tea For Two Great Dane GDR CD 9112.
'You Ain't Going Nowhere'; 'He Was A Friend Of Mine'; 'Old Blue'; 'Long Black Veil'; 'Goin' Back'; 'Get Out Of My Life Woman'; 'Ballad Of Easy Rider'; 'Jesus Is Just Alright'; 'Tulsa County Blue'; 'Mr Spaceman'; 'Sing Me Back Home'; 'This Wheel's On Fire'; 'Lay Lady Lay'; 'Time Between'; 'Take A City Bride'; 'It's All Over Now, Baby Blue'; 'Way Behind The Sun'.
Another unnecessary rehash of the Boston Tea Party.
Released 1990.

The Byrds Live DV More Record CDDV 5503.
'Mr Spaceman'; 'Chestnut Mare'; 'Chimes Of Freedom'; 'Lover Of The Bayou'; 'Old Blue'; 'My Back Pages'; 'It's Alright Ma (I'm Only Bleeding)'; 'Ballad Of Easy Rider'; 'So You Want To Be A Rock 'n' Roll Star'; 'Medley: 'Turn! Turn! Turn!'/'Mr Tambourine Man'/'Eight Miles High'.
Unfortunately, the over-familiar Amsterdam show again.
Released 1990.

Turn! Turn! Turn! The Easy Rider Years Live 930160.
'Hey Joe'; 'So You Want To Be A Rock 'n' Roll Star'; 'Old Blue'; 'My Back

Pages'; 'Chestnut Mare'; 'Chimes Of Freedom'; 'Take A Whiff'; 'Positively 4th Street'; 'Lay Lady Lay'; 'All The Things'; 'Get Out Of My Life Woman'; 'Jesus Is Just Alright'; 'He Was A Friend Of Mine'; 'It's Alright Ma (I'm Only Bleeding)'; 'Ballad Of Easy Rider'; 'This Wheel's On Fire'; 'Well Come Back Home'; 'Lover Of The Bayou'; 'Medley: 'Turn! Turn! Turn!'/ 'Mr Tambourine Man'/'Eight Miles High'.
This double CD combines three of the most familiar bootlegged items in the Byrds' canon: Monterey, Amsterdam 1970 and the Boston Tea Party 1971. Released 1993.

Doin' Alright For Old People Aulica A148.
'Jolly Roger'; 'Chestnut Mare'; 'Mr Tambourine Man'; 'You Ain't Going Nowhere'; 'Turn! Turn! Turn!'; 'Knockin' On Heaven's Door'; 'Bye Bye Baby'; 'So You Want To Be A Rock 'n' Roll Star'; 'Eight Miles High'; 'Feel A Whole Lot Better'.
This was the almost complete Byrds' reunion featuring McGuinn, Clark, Hillman & Crosby at San Francisco's Boarding House on 6 December 1977. Released 1993.

Willin' Oil Well RSC CD 046.
'Hey Joe'; 'My Back Pages'; 'Mr Tambourine Man'; 'He Was A Friend Of Mine'; 'So You Want To Be A Rock 'n' Roll Star'; 'Roll Over Beethoven'; 'Lover Of The Bayou'; 'Willin''; 'Soldier's Joy'/'Black Mountain Rag'; 'Positively 4th Street'.
A potpourri featuring six tracks from the Stockholm radio broadcast, three selections from Queen's College, New York, 28 February 1970, one from the Felt Forum, New York, January 1970, and finally four tracks taken from the Full Throttle CD in the box set.

Never Ever Before Whoopy Cat Records WKP 0018.
'Mr Tambourine Man' (backing tracks, takes 1–2, takes 5–9; takes 13–14); 'Mr Tambourine Man' (vocal overdub, take 15), 'Mr Tambourine Man' (complete version, wide stereo); 'I Knew I'd Want You' (backing track, take 1); 'It's No Use' (vocal overdubs, with instruments, takes 5–6); 'The Bells Of Rhymney' (vocal overdubs, with instruments, takes 1–2, take 5); 'Feel A Whole Lot Better' (vocal overdubs, with instruments, takes 1–2); 'You Won't Have To Cry' (vocal overdubs, with instruments, takes 1–2); 'We'll Meet Again' (vocal overdub 2, with instruments, take 1); 'She Don't Care About Time'; 'Set You Free This Time' (backing tracks, takes 15–17); 'It's All Over Now, Baby Blue' (backing track, take 1); 'It's All Over Now, Baby Blue' (alternate session, backing tracks, takes 1–2); 'The World Turns All Around Her' (backing tracks, takes 14–15); 'She Has A Way' (vocal

overdub, with instruments, take 1); 'Turn! Turn! Turn!' (backing track); 'Eight Miles High' (vocal overdub and alternate backing track, take 9); 'Why' (vocal overdub and alternate backing track, take 8).

Released in 1994, this CD bootleg was one of the most enjoyable to emerge, mixing rare backing tracks and vocal overdubs from the Byrds' first three albums. Although a number of the takes also appear on *Journals*, this CD is a much more palatable offering, carefully selecting material and including some impressive vocal tracks, noticeably absent from the bootleg boxed set. One of the highlights is a vocal overdub of 'Mr Tambourine Man', with the instruments muted. Hearing the Byrds singing angelic three-part harmony on this most famous of songs is nothing short of astonishing and creates a ghostly ambience that lingers long after the track has finished. 'The Bells Of Rhymney' features Crosby's amusing preamble in which he misspells Merthyr as Murther. The takes of 'Feel A Whole Lot Better' are interesting, with some additional conversation between Melcher and Dickson. There's a moving, alternate vocal overdub of 'You Won't Have To Cry' that sounds impressive. The same applies to 'We'll Meet Again', in which McGuinn offers a more emotive vocal reading than on the more accomplished released version. The track ends with some parachronistic instructions from Melcher ("Hal, a lot more cymbal, OK"), which actually precede the recording of 'I Knew I'd Want You', which is curtailed here after a single note.

The compilers suggest that the version of 'She Don't Care About Time' included on the disc comes from the Columbia session of 28 June 1965. However, it seems oddly like a live performance, with the drums sounding as if they were recorded in a different room. It surely isn't the Byrds, but almost certainly a Flamin' Groovies cover.

After backing tracks of 'Set You Free This Time', 'It's All Over Now, Baby Blue' and 'The World Turns All Around Her', there's a rare chance to hear the earliest version of 'Turn! Turn! Turn!', allegedly recorded on 1 September 1965, soon after the Beatles visited the studio. Finally, and best of all, there are two fascinating, alternate versions of 'Eight Miles High' and 'Why' recorded at Columbia following the RCA attempts. It would be fascinating to hear all the takes from these sessions as these are worthy of high praise, even though they are still rough. 'Eight Miles High' sounds substantially different in places, with the Coltrane riff more noticeable. Finally, 'Why' is a spontaneous rush of inventive raga rock, with McGuinn's alluring Indian drone even more pronounced, albeit less disciplined, than on the released version. Rock has seldom been more inventive than this.
Released 1994.

REQUIEM FOR THE TIMELESS — VOLUME 1

Tambourines & 12-Strings Gold Standard B-26-94-10.
'I Knew I'd Want You' (take 1); 'It's No Use' (take 6); 'The Bells Of Rhymney' (take 2); '(I'll) Feel A Whole Lot Better' (take 2); 'It Won't Be Wrong' (take 8); 'The World Turns All Around Her' (take 15); 'Satisfied Mind'; 'Set You Free This Time' (takes 1–4, 8); 'Stranger In A Strange Land' (takes 1–2); 'Wait And See' (take 24); 'Wait And See (takes 25–26); 'Oh! Susannah' (take 1); '5 D (Fifth Dimension)' (takes 1–7); '5 D (Fifth Dimension)' (take 12); 'It's All Over Now, Baby Blue' (takes 4–5); 'Mr Tambourine Man' (takes 4–6); 'Goin' Back'; 'Don't Make Waves'; 'He Was A Friend Of Mine'; 'Medley: 'My Back Pages'/'B.J. Blues'/'Baby, What Do You Want Me To Do'; 'Byrds Churp'.
Not to be confused with the aforementioned *Tambourines & 12-Strings*, this is a far more interesting CD featuring studio material from 1965–1966. Filling out the CD are the soundtrack version of 'Don't Make Waves', two tracks from a show at San Francisco's Avalon Ballroom and a joke ending – an interview from 1965.
Released 1994.

In The Studio Capricorn CR-2006.
'Mr Tambourine Man'; 'I Knew I'd Want You'; 'It's No Use'; 'The Bells Of Rhymney'; '(I'll) Feel A Whole Lot Better'; 'It's All Over Now, Baby Blue'; 'The World Turns All Around Her'; 'It's All Over Now, Baby Blue'; 'It Won't Be Wrong'; 'Satisfied Mind'; 'Set You Free This Time'; 'Stranger In A Strange Land'; 'Wait And See'; '5 D (Fifth Dimension)'.
This reprises the ninth CD on the 9-CD bootleg box set, *Journals*.
Released 1994.

All American Trichant Records CD DE 1007.
'You Ain't Going Nowhere'; 'Old Blue'; 'Well Come Back Home'; 'Medley: 'My Back Pages'/'B.J. Blues'/'Baby, What Do You Want Me To Do'; 'He Was A Friend Of Mine'; 'Willin''; 'Soldier's Joy'/'Black Mountain Rag'; 'This Wheel's On Fire'; 'It's Alright Ma (I'm Only Bleeding)'; 'Ballad Of Easy Rider'; 'Jesus Is Just Alright'; 'Nashville West'; 'Mr Tambourine Man'; 'Eight Miles High'; 'So You Want To Be A Rock 'n' Roll Star'; 'Mr Spaceman'.
Reputedly recorded at the American University, Washington, April 1970.
Released 1995.

Live At The Boarding House Frontline FLCD 18.
'Release Me Girl'; 'Silver Raven'; 'Bound To Fall'; 'It Doesn't Matter'; 'Ballad Of Easy Rider'; 'Jolly Roger'; 'Chestnut Mare'; 'Crazy Ladies'; 'Train Leaves Here This Morning'; 'Mr Tambourine Man'; 'You Ain't Going Nowhere'; 'Turn! Turn! Turn!'; 'Knockin' On Heaven's Door'; 'Bye Bye

Baby'; 'So You Want To Be A Rock 'n' Roll Star'; 'Eight Miles High'.
A more complete recording of the McGuinn, Clark, Hillman & Crosby get-together at San Francisco's Boarding House on 6 December 1977. Released 1995.

Unsurpassed Masters – 1965 On The Air OTA-008.
'Mr Tambourine Man'; 'You Won't Have To Cry'; 'We'll Meet Again'; 'Mr Tambourine Man' (takes 1–2); 'Mr Tambourine Man' (takes 19–20); 'I Knew I'd Want You'; 'It's No Use'; 'The Bells Of Rhymney' (takes 1–2); '(I'll) Feel A Whole Lot Better' (takes 1–2); 'It's All Over Now, Baby Blue' (takes 2–4); 'The World Turns All Around Her' (takes 14–15); 'It's All Over Now, Baby Blue' (take 7); 'It Won't Be Wrong' (takes 5–7, 18); 'Satisfied Mind' (takes 17–18); 'Set You Free This Time' (takes 1–4, 18); 'Stranger In A Strange Land' (takes 1–2, 9–10); 'Wait And See' (takes 23–26); '5 D (Fifth Dimension)' (takes 23–26); 'I Knew I'd Want You'.
Another glimpse into the Columbia recording sessions already catalogued on earlier releases. The first three tracks on this CD are borrowed from *Never Ever Before*, while the final 'I Knew I'd Want You' is from *Preflyte*.

Ash Grove Deep Six-37.
'Lover Of The Bayou'; 'You Ain't Going Nowhere'; 'Well Come Back Home'; 'Old Blue'; 'Medley: 'My Back Pages'/'B.J. Blues'/'Baby What You Want Me To Do'; 'He Was A Friend Of Mine'; 'Truck Stop Girl'; 'Break My Mind' (with Gram Parsons & Linda Ronstadt); 'I'm Movin' On' (John Hammond Jr, lead vocal); 'Take A City Bride' (Gib Guilbeau, lead vocal); 'Chestnut Mare'; 'This Wheel's On Fire'; 'It's All Right Ma (I'm Only Bleeding)'; 'Ballad Of Easy Rider'; 'Jesus Is Just Alright'; 'Turn! Turn! Turn!'; 'Mr Tambourine Man'; 'Eight Miles High'.
Originally, this was available on CDR with the erroneous date of 1 January 1970. The show actually took place on 23 August 1970. See Bootleg Tapes (Studio and Concert) for additional information.

By the mid to late Nineties, the bootleg industry was saturated with CDRs, often made by fans and enthusiasts. These instant creations meant that any concert, studio recording or compilation hybrid could be mocked up with a title and cover. This liberation from professional bootleggers was in many ways a welcome development, although it now challenges the very notion of what constitutes a bootleg. Many such releases may only be a handful in number (or even a single copy) and few were aimed at the marketplace with a view to making a profit.

REQUIEM FOR THE TIMELESS — VOLUME 1

BOOTLEG TAPES (Studio and Concert)

The continued interest in the Byrds will probably ensure that more obscure bootlegged taped material will continue to be released in the future. The following is a list of extant live/studio tapes.

1964 The World-Pacific Recordings.
'Tomorrow Is A Long Ways Away' (acoustic) (I); 'Tomorrow Is A Long Ways Away' (I); 'I Knew I'd Want You' (I); 'I Knew I'd Want You' (U); 'I Knew I'd Want You' (P); 'I Knew I'd Want You' (U); 'Boston' (U); 'Boston' (U); 'Boston' (P/I); 'The Airport Song' (P/I); 'It Won't Be Wrong' (B); 'It Won't Be Wrong' (I); 'Please Let Me Love You' (B); 'Please Let Me Love You' (I); 'The Only Girl' (E); 'Mr Tambourine Man' (I); 'Mr Tambourine Man' (P); 'The Reason Why' (U); 'The Reason Why' (P/I); 'You Won't Have To Cry' (P); 'You Won't Have To Cry' (I); 'She Has A Way' (U); 'She Has A Way' (U); 'She Has A Way' (U); 'You Movin'' (E); 'You Movin'' (U); 'You Movin'' (U); 'You Movin'' (U); 'You Movin'' (P/I); 'You Movin'' (U); 'For Me Again' (U); 'For Me Again' (P/I); 'For Me Again' (U); 'You Showed Me' (I); 'You Showed Me' (P); 'You Showed Me' (U); 'It's No Use' (U); 'It's No Use' (I); 'It's No Use' (U); 'It's No Use' (U); 'It's No Use' (U); 'Here Without You' (U); 'Here Without You' (P); 'Here Without You' (I). This extraordinary tape represents what was left from the World-Pacific recordings. For the sake of convenience, I have provided a key to the tracks as follows: (I)= tracks released on *In The Beginning*; (P)= *Preflyte*; (B)= Beefeaters; (E)= *Early LA* and (U)= previously unreleased. The only problem that the tape presented to me was the identification of the *Preflyte* and *In The Beginning* version of 'She Has A Way'. The ending of version two of the song on the tape sounds the same as the cuts on *Preflyte* and *In The Beginning* but the opening appears noticeably different. It may be that there was a fourth version which has not been included here. Also missing is 'Maybe You Think', which appeared on the documentation relating to the original tapes that were licensed in 1969, but has since disappeared. For anyone intrigued by the Byrds' early experiments at World-Pacific these recordings are mandatory listening.

1964 The Brown Tapes.
'You Won't Have To Cry'; 'You Showed Me'; ' I Knew I'd Want You'; 'Mr Tambourine Man'; 'You Won't Have To Cry'; 'You Showed Me'; 'I Knew I'd Want You'; 'Mr Tambourine Man'; 'The Airport Song'; 'The Reason Why'; 'The Reason Why'; 'Tomorrow Is A Long Ways Away'; 'The Only Girl'.

BYRDS BOOTLEGS

This is a copy of the original reel to reel containing brown coloured tape from which *Preflyte* and much of *In The Beginning* were taken. Different mixes are no doubt evident.

1964 *The Dickson Masters.*
'Tomorrow Is A Long Ways Away' (version 2); 'I Knew I'd Want You' (version 4); 'Boston' (version 3); 'The Airport Song' (version 1); 'It Won't Be Wrong' (version 2); 'Please Let Me Love You' (version 2); 'The Only Girl' (version 1); 'Mr Tambourine Man' (version 2); 'The Reason Why' (version 2); 'You Won't Have To Cry' (version 2); 'She Has A Way' (version 8); 'You Movin'' (version 6); 'For Me Again' (version 3); 'It's No Use' (version 4); 'It's No Use' (version 1); 'Here Without You' (version 4); 'Tomorrow Is A Long Ways Away' (version 1); 'You Won't Have To Cry' (version 1); 'You Showed Me' (version 1); 'I Knew I'd Want You' (version 1); 'Mr Tambourine Man' (version 1); 'The Airport Song' (version 1); 'She Has A Way' (version 1); 'You Movin'' (version 1); 'The Reason Why' (version 1); 'You Won't Have To Cry' (version 1); 'Here Without You' (version 1); 'She Has A Way' (version 1); 'You Movin'' (version 1); 'Mr Tambourine Man' (version 1); 'Tomorrow Is A Long Ways Away' (version 1); 'The Reason Why' (version 1); 'It's No Use' (version 1); 'I Knew I'd Want You' (version 1); 'Boston' (version 1); 'For Me Again' (version 1); 'You Showed Me' (version 1); 'Boston' (version 1); 'You Movin'' (version 1); 'It's No Use' (version 1); 'She Has A Way' (version 1); 'For Me Again' (version 1); 'Here Without You' (version 1); 'You Movin'' (version 2); 'It's No Use' (version 1).
Taken from an additional six reels of tape (some copies), these provide a further insight into the Byrds' World-Pacific recordings, though virtually all of this is available elsewhere on tape.

1965–67 *The Columbia Recording Sessions.*
'You Won't Have To Cry'; 'She Has A Way'; 'Turn! Turn! Turn!' (instrumental backing track); 'It's All Over Now, Baby Blue'; 'Never Before'; 'Eight Miles High'; 'Why'; 'It Happens Each Day'; 'John Riley' (instrumental); 'Mr Tambourine Man'; 'I Knew I'd Want You'; 'I Know My Rider'; 'Psychodrama City'; 'Triad' (instrumental backing track); 'Moog Raga'; 'Everybody's Been Burned' (version 1); 'Everybody's Been Burned' (version 2); 'Everybody's Been Burned' (version 3); 'Everybody's Been Burned' (version 4); 'Everybody's Been Burned' (version 5); 'Everybody's Been Burned' (version 6); 'Everybody's Been Burned' (version 7); 'Thoughts And Words' (version 1); 'Thoughts And Words' (version 2); 'Thoughts And Words' (version 3); 'Thoughts And Words' (version 4); 'Thoughts And

Words' (version 5); 'Thoughts And Words' (version 6); 'Thoughts And Words' (version 7); 'Thoughts And Words' (version 8); 'Thoughts And Words' (version 9); 'Thoughts And Words' (version 10); 'Thoughts And Words' (version 11); 'Thoughts And Words' (version 12); 'Thoughts And Words' (version 13); 'Renaissance Fair' (version 1); 'Renaissance Fair' (version 2); 'Renaissance Fair' (version 3).

The most complete of the bootlegged rough tapes from which the majority of *Never Before* was compiled, this is a treasure trove of Byrds ephemera. The tracks are roughly in chronological order and the recording dates span early 1965 to early 1967. The familiar voice of Terry Melcher introduces the first take of 'You Won't Have To Cry' from the *Mr Tambourine Man* album sessions. This version is a little more restrained than the final LP cut, but immediately reveals how far the group have progressed since those tentative World-Pacific demos only months before. The musicianship is noticeably tighter and the vocal harmonies far more effective as a result of endless hours of rehearsal. But the recording is far from perfect or complete. The pounding tambourine featured on the album is conspicuous by its absence here, and was probably overdubbed separately by Melcher after the session had finished. As the track fades, the still dissatisfied producer suggests: "Let's take one more."

The tape next cuts to a Columbia take of Gene Clark's 'She Has A Way', one of several World-Pacific songs that failed to win a place on their first album. The listener is allowed to eavesdrop on a fascinating studio conversation in which the participants attempt to pull the song into shape. Melcher seems unsure how many parts there are in the harmony, while Crosby disputes the merits of an earlier take.

Crosby: "They put a fade-out on the ending!"

Melcher: "Hold it! You don't have to keep singing over the fade. Right. You just stop somewhere."

Melcher then proceeds to sing several lines of the song himself, and his rendition is pretty good. Thumping his hands on the studio mixing desk to provide a percussive accompaniment, he instructs Crosby to "just let go after 'wanna settle down, whoa, whoa'." A much improved version of the song follows, with McGuinn's guitar particularly evident. The drumming is even more astonishing. Months before, Michael Clarke had played the number like a schoolboy in a military cadet band. Suddenly, he has transformed into a competent studio musician. Clarke's rapid improvement and unquestionable involvement in all these songs is one of the many surprises on the tape, especially to those cynics who had suspected that session drummers were recruited at crucial moments.

The instrumental 'Turn! Turn! Turn!' follows and although it sounds strange without McGuinn's distinctive vocal, it is nonetheless pleasant and instructive. 'It's All Over Now, Baby Blue' is the same take used for *Never Before* as is the succeeding 'Never Before' ('The Day Walk'). Here, however, the vocal is buried so low in the mix that it is barely audible. Thankfully, it was later rescued and tidied up for inclusion on *Never Before*. The RCA versions of 'Eight Miles High' and 'Why' are good quality recordings and I can still recall the shock of pleasure upon hearing them for the first time over two decades on. 'It Happens Each Day' underwent significant alteration before being included on *Never Before*. Both Hillman and Crosby worked on the track adding guitar and bass. The drumming also sounds different on the *Never Before* version.

Arguably the only carping omission from the *Never Before* CD round-up of unreleased tracks was the amazing instrumental of 'John Riley', which did not emerge until the CD remastered release of *Fifth Dimension*. There is some strong banjo work on the track, possibly the work of Doug Dillard, although it could equally, or more likely, be McGuinn. The instrumental steams along at a tremendous pace before falling apart after several minutes. A splendid tour de force.

The version of 'Mr Tambourine Man' on this tape is the same as the number 1 single apart from an elongated fade-out and the sound of Hal Blaine clicking his drumsticks and counting to six in the lead-in to the song. 'I Knew I'd Want You' offers no such extras and sounds the same as the original flip-side. 'I Know My Rider' is the version chosen for the *Never Before* CD rather than the other outtake on *Byrds On The Wyng*. Even this rough version is nothing less than astonishing. Crosby's vocal is prominent, the harmonies are well-executed and McGuinn lets rip with two Rickenbacker solos which combine judicious economy with maximum power. At the end of the take, an evidently excited Crosby enthuses: "Let's do it again!" Suddenly, you find yourself wishing they had done just that on the tape.

'Psychodrama City' suffers from a barely audible vocal which was vastly amplified on the *Never Before* CD. The redeeming feature of this rough version is that we get to hear the lengthy introduction, which was later edited out of the recorded track, only to be reinstated on the box set.

Following 'Psychodrama City' we get to hear an amusing interlude during which Michael Clarke treats us to a drum solo, just to prove that he can play with the best of them. An impatient Gary Usher interrupts: "Hold it! Hold it, Mike!", and the tape cuts to the next recording. The instrumental backing track for 'Triad' demonstrates the quality of the Byrds' playing to moving effect. Towards the end of the track, Usher reveals that they are about to move into ninth take. Unfortunately, we do not get to hear the vocal part which was slightly amended on *Never Before*. The eerie 'Moog Raga', with its ethereal drone is a slightly longer version of the track that McGuinn remixed for the *Never Before* CD. It brings the first side of this lengthy tape to an appropriate close.

The remainder of the tape consists of approximately 40 minutes of studio backing tracks from the sessions for *Younger Than Yesterday*. Although tedious listening at times, these tortuous retakes provide an interesting insight into the way in which the Byrds fashioned and improved their albums. 'Everybody's Been Burned', one of the greatest Byrds songs, requires several attempts before McGuinn masters the tricky arrangement.

Clarke, meanwhile, is having great problems keeping time, and Usher is finally moved to complain: "Michael, it's falling down before you even get started." After restarting for the umpteenth time, they finally produce a much improved backing track with Hillman's solid bass lines high in the mix.

Unfortunately, Gary Usher is still not satisfied with the results and turns his polite wrath on the tousled-haired bassist: "Chris, would you turn your volume down a little please! Not on your guitar, but on your amplifier!" Ten minutes into the tape we leave the Byrds still struggling with the intricacies of 'Everybody's Been Burned' and move to another song.

"The mike sounds good," chirps Hillman, as the Byrds launch into the instrumental backing track of 'Thoughts And Words'. The first take sounds good, but there is some hesitation about halfway through. Two more completed takes follow, but Usher is still not entirely satisfied. "Keep this sound, it sounds good that way," he advises Crosby, before spurring on the flagging Hillman.

Usher continually frames his questions and criticisms in disarmingly polite rhetorical asides: "Chris, are you driving as hard as you can, please?" The fourth take begins spectacularly enough with the cleanest sound yet, but unfortunately it breaks down. Two more takes follow in quick succession until a frustrated Mike Clarke terminates the proceedings with a heavy-handed drum roll. The ferociously polite Usher responds with a schoolmasterly enquiry: "Michael, may I hear for a minute what you're going to play?" The errant drummer obliges and a seventh take ensues. This too ends in an explosion of drums, and Clarke receives further advice from his producer.

Take eight features some great bass playing by Hillman, while Clarke also suddenly hits form. But it is still not quite right.

Take nine is perfunctory, take ten reveals Hillman experimenting with the bass line. Take 11 falls apart before it has even begun. Take 12 sounds like the big breakthrough. Usher goes for the killer take, but cannot resist ticking off Clarke one last time: "Mike, make sure you hit the very last note with the band. Can you hear me? You didn't do it this time."

"I don't want to do it", retorts the exasperated drummer, who clearly has his own ideas about how he should sound.

"Oh, you don't want to do it! All right. Thirteen!" Usher sounds surprised but content. The thirteenth take includes vocals, and it is a stunner. Although identical to the version on *Younger Than Yesterday*, its appearance after a dozen frustrating and tortuous takes allows us to appreciate the song in an entirely new way. Although the familiar backwards guitar break is incorporated into the track, it no longer sounds a studio trick, but appears to be happening live, and Crosby's interweaving harmony with Hillman is wondrous to behold. Even Usher is sufficiently moved to offer a congratulatory understatement: "It's not bad."

The final few minutes of the tape present 'Renaissance Fair', complete with delicately precise guitar work and a surprisingly driving rhythm from Hillman and Clarke. Three fragmented takes follow before the tape abruptly ends.

1965–66 *The Byrds' Session Tapes, Vol I.*
'The Times They Are A-Changin'' (first version, vocal, with instruments); 'The Times They Are A-Changin'' (instrumental backing track, insert 1, take 1); 'The Times They Are A-Changin'' (instrumental backing tracks, inserts takes 2–3,); 'It's All Over Now, Baby Blue' (instrumental backing track, take 1); 'The World Turns All Around Her' (instrumental backing tracks, takes 1–3); 'It Won't Be Wrong' (instrumental backing tracks, takes 1–3, 9–12); 'Satisfied Mind' (instrumental backing tracks, takes 1–5); 'Set You Free This Time' (instrumental backing tracks, takes 2–6); '5 D (Fifth Dimension)' (instrumental backing track); 'Flower Bomb Song' (instrumental backing tracks, takes 2–6); 'Stranger In A Strange Land' (instrumental backing tracks, takes 15–17); 'Wait And See' (instrumental backing tracks, take 1, take 10); 'Oh! Susannah' (instrumental backing track, take 1).
In addition to the bootleg CD issues of Byrds' material from the early Columbia days, extracts from the sessions also appeared on tape. Many of these were subsequently included on *Journals*, but there are some excellent moments here, including the attempts at 'The Times They Are A-Changin'' and, most importantly, that beautiful lilt 'Flower Bomb Song', which sounds great in instrumental form, despite the fact that its lyrics were derided by Dickson, Tickner and Crosby. The sequencing, by which 'Flower Bomb Song' and 'Stranger In A Strange Land' follow one another, adds to the overwhelming sense of frustration that we will probably never be able to hear the Crosby vocals to these intriguing backing tracks.

1965–66 *The Byrds Session Tapes, Vol. II.*
'Wait And See' (instrumental backing tracks, take 1, take 10); 'Satisfied Mind' (instrumental backing tracks, takes 1–5); 'The World Turns All Around Her' (instrumental backing tracks, takes 1–3, take 9); 'It Won't Be Wrong' (instrumental backing tracks, takes 1–3, 9–10, 11–12); 'Mr Tambourine Man' (complete stereo track); 'Feel A Whole Lot Better' (overdub 2, take 1); 'The Times They Are A-Changin'' (version 1, vocals, with instruments); 'We'll Meet Again' (vocals, with instruments); 'Mr Tambourine Man' (vocal version, with instruments); 'The Times They Are A-Changin'' (alternate vocal version, with instruments); 'She Don't Care About Time' (alternate vocal version, with instruments); 'Don't Doubt Yourself Babe' (instrumental backing tracks, takes 5–8); 'You Won't Have To Cry' (vocal overdub, with instruments, take 1); 'Mr Tambourine Man' (instrumental backing tracks, takes 3–6, 15–20); 'I Knew I'd Want You' (instrumental backing track); 'Set You Free This Time' (instrumental backing tracks, takes 2–6); '5 D (Fifth Dimension)' (instrumental backing track); 'Oh! Susannah' (instrumental backing track, take 1); 'Flower Bomb Song' (instrumental backing tracks, takes 2–6); 'It's No Use' (vocal overdub 1, take 1, with instruments); 'The Bells Of Rhymney' (take 2, vocals and instruments); 'Feel A Whole Lot Better' (vocal overdub, with instruments, takes 1–2); 'Stranger In A Strange Land' (instrumental backing tracks, takes 15–17); 'The Times They Are A-Changin'' (insert 1, take 1, instrumental backing track).

   Although much of this material appears on the previous tape, the quality is marginally superior, depending on your source. There are a number of highlights, including 'The Bells Of Rhymney' with Clark's voice placed much higher in the mix than McGuinn's. It provides an intriguing glimpse into how the folk-rock Byrds songs might have sounded if Gene had been retained as lead vocalist. The quirky 'We'll Meet Again', a live favourite in mid-1965, is enchanting, with McGuinn sounding a little more expressive, especially when singing, "Some sunny day-yea". Finally, check out 'Don't Doubt Yourself Babe' for some more in-studio chat and listen as Michael Clarke delights in banging away on the drums.

1965 *Bournemouth Gaumont, 15 August 1965.*
'The Times They Are A-Changin''; 'Don't Doubt Yourself Babe'; 'All I Really Want To Do'; 'Chimes Of Freedom'; 'The Bells Of Rhymney'; 'We'll Meet Again'; 'Mr Tambourine Man'.
The screams for 'So You Want To Be A Rock 'n' Roll Star' were taken from this show and when Jim Dickson heard the live version of 'The Times They Are A-Changin'' on this tape, he insisted that the Byrds record the song as a

single. They never did. Despite several attempts the only completed studio take was the casual version on *Turn! Turn! Turn!*.

1967 *Everybody's Been Burned.*
This acoustic demo of 'Everybody's Been Burned' is spinetingling stuff. It would be even more interesting to hear how Crosby tackled the song back in 1964. Although earlier tapes of Crosby are available, including 'Jack Of Diamonds' and 'Get Together' from 1964, the earliest attempts at 'Everybody's Been Burned' from that period have yet to surface.

1967 *Radio Hus, Stockholm, 28 February 1967.*
As documented in the CD section, this tape contains six tracks recorded for radio in 1967. Some tapes include an additional cut, 'The Bells Of Rhymney' but this was taken from a US television show in early 1966.

1967 *Monterey Extract, 17 June 1967.*
Now superseded by the official release of the Byrds' set at Monterey, this short tape consisted of a radio broadcast from KMET (1973) which included a brief segment of 'So You Want To Be A Rock 'n' Roll Star' and 'He Was A Friend Of Mine'.

1967 *Monterey: The Audience Tape, 17 June 1967.*
'Hey Joe'; 'He Was A Friend Of Mine'; 'Lady Friend'; 'Chimes Of Freedom'; 'I Know My Rider'; 'So You Want To Be A Rock 'n' Roll Star'. The quality of the tape is surprisingly good given the time of its recording. There is a rough, almost aggressive quality about the Byrds' performance which reflects the tensions in the group at the time. Highlights of the tape are the rarely heard live versions of 'Lady Friend' and 'I Know My Rider' which betray a hard metallic edge. McGuinn's sitar-like guitar break still entrances, almost creating a wall of sound effect. The startling addition of live brass on 'So You Want To Be A Rock 'n' Roll Star' ends the performance on a high note. This audience tape does not include 'Renaissance Fair' and 'Have You Seen Her Face' which were also played that evening.

1965–67 *The Never Before Outtakes.*
'Old John Robertson'; 'Lady Friend' (take 4); 'Psychodrama City'; 'Turn! Turn! Turn!'; 'John Riley' (instrumental); 'Mr Tambourine Man'; 'The Times They Are A-Changin''; 'I Know My Rider' ; 'I Know My Rider'. An intriguing selection featuring several rare versions of familiar songs. 'Old John Robertson' is Hillman's revamped mix, complete with the attractive mandolin overdub vetoed by CBS. 'Lady Friend' is a take, minus drums. 'Psychodrama City' is the uncut, original tape, recorded as a rough, two-track mix. The 'Turn! Turn! Turn!' stereo backing track was

mysteriously lost (since rediscovered) some time between the release of *Never Before* and the CD version of *Turn! Turn! Turn!*. The fascinating instrumental version of 'John Riley' sounds like a different mix from the one that belatedly appeared as a bonus track on the *Fifth Dimension* CD. The rough two-track stereo mix of 'Mr Tambourine Man' underlines the limitations that faced the compilers in completing the disc. 'The Times They Are A-Changin'' clearly emanates from the sessions for the second album, complete with studio talk. The first version of 'I Know My Rider' is an early attempt from the sessions for *Fifth Dimension*, while the second track is the first Murray Hill version, mixed by Ken Robertson and Bob Hyde, which was later amended by McGuinn.

1965–68 *Rhythm Track Mixes.*
'So You Want To Be A Rock 'n' Roll Star'; 'Have You Seen Her Face'; 'CTA 102'; 'Renaissance Fair'; 'Time Between'; 'Everybody's Been Burned'; 'Thoughts And Words'; 'Mind Gardens'; 'My Back Pages'; 'The Girl With No Name'; 'Why'; 'Eight Miles High'; 'Wasn't Born To Follow'; 'All I Really Want To Do'; 'You Ain't Going Nowhere'; 'Draft Morning'.
These recordings are rough studio mixes with the vocals turned down to the level of barely audible. As a result, the Byrds' rhythm work is highlighted to remarkable effect. There are some real revelations on this tape. Crosby's chunky rhythm guitar on 'Eight Miles High', herein transformed into a lead instrument, is nothing less than astonishing. 'Time Between' features Crosby's harmony vocal in the chorus separated and presented in an entirely new way. 'Draft Morning' is another surprise. Buried underneath the sound of gunfire is an impressive Hillman mandolin break that you can now hear independently for the first time. Even 'Mind Gardens' has a few surprises, the raga-like guitars creating a swirling ethereal feel which is emphasized by the absence of Crosby's vocal. It would be fascinating to hear the remainder of the Byrds' canon in this format.

1968 *The Piper Club, Rome, 7 May 1968.*
'You Ain't Going Nowhere'; 'Old John Robertson'; 'You Don't Miss Your Water'; 'Hickory Wind'; 'Feel A Whole Lot Better'; 'Chimes Of Freedom'; 'The Christian Life'; 'Turn! Turn! Turn!'; 'Medley: 'My Back Pages'/'B.J. Blues'/'Baby, What Do You Want Me To Do'; 'Mr Spaceman'.
Now also available on CD on Bulldog Records, the original rough-taped version offers a better quality reproduction.

1968 *Middle Earth, 11 May 1968.*
'Tribal Gathering'; 'Eight Miles High'; 'You Don't Miss Your Water'; 'The Christian Life'; '5 D (Fifth Dimension)'; 'Turn! Turn! Turn!'; 'Medley: 'My

Back Pages'/'B.J. Blues'/'Baby, What Do You Want Me To Do'; 'Foggy Mountain Breakdown'; 'Pretty Boy Floyd'; 'Hickory Wind'; 'Under Your Spell Again'; '(Excuse Me) I Think I've Got A Heartache'; 'So You Want To Be A Rock 'n' Roll Star'; 'Mr Tambourine Man'; 'Chimes Of Freedom'; 'Goin' Back'; 'Feel A Whole Lot Better'; 'The Bells Of Rhymney'; 'We'll Meet Again'; 'Sing Me Back Home'.

A below average quality recording, although it does contain four unreleased songs. Gram Parsons plays electric piano on some cuts, which helps to improve the quality of the rock songs.

1968 *Middle Earth, Roundhouse, London, 6 July 1968.*
'So You Want To Be A Rock 'n' Roll Star'; 'Chimes Of Freedom'; 'You Ain't Going Nowhere'; 'Medley: 'My Back Pages'/'B.J. Blues'/'Baby, What Do You Want Me To Do'; 'Hickory Wind'; 'Sing Me Back Home'; 'The Christian Life'; 'You've Got Me Under Your Spell Again'; 'You Don't Miss Your Water'; 'Eight Miles High'; 'The Bells Of Rhymney'; 'Space Odyssey'; 'Tribal Gathering'.

There has often been confusion between the two Middle Earth tapes, (including the dating) as a result of the switch of venue to the Roundhouse. The set lists above are based on correspondence from the time. The tapes that survive have evidently been misdated. Some sources believe this tape was the 11 May set list.

1968 *Venue unknown.*
'So You Want To Be A Rock 'n' Roll Star'; 'Chimes Of Freedom'; 'You Ain't Going Nowhere'; 'Medley: 'My Back Pages'/'B.J. Blues'/'Baby, What Do You Want Me To Do'; 'Hickory Wind'; 'Sing Me Back Home'; 'The Christian Life'; 'You've Got Me Under Your Spell Again'.

A fair quality recording with some hard drumming from the little heard Kevin Kelley. The set is similar to that performed at the Middle Earth gig in 1968 although this appears to have been recorded at a small club. They did play Blaises on 12 May, but I cannot confirm that this was taped there.

1968 *Newport Pop Festival, Costa Mesa, California, 4 August 1968.*
'So You Want To Be A Rock 'n' Roll Star'; 'You Ain't Going Nowhere'; 'Sing Me Back Home'; 'Eight Miles High'; 'Medley: 'My Back Pages'/'B.J. Blues'/'Baby, What Do You Want Me To Do'; 'You Don't Miss Your Water'; 'Chimes Of Freedom'; 'Turn! Turn! Turn!'.

A poor quality tape of historical importance as the first taped recording of Clarence White in the group, playing his second gig with the Byrds.

1968 *Avalon Ballroom, San Francisco, California, 2 November 1968.*
'Old Blue'; 'Medley: 'My Back Pages'/'B.J. Blues'/'Baby, What Do You

Want Me To Do'; 'Mr Spaceman'; 'Time Between'; 'Goin' Back'; 'Blue Suede Shoes'; 'He Was A Friend Of Mine'; 'So You Want To Be A Rock 'n' Roll Star'; 'Drug Store Truck Drivin' Man'; 'This Wheel's On Fire'; 'Stanley's Song'; 'Pretty Boy Floyd'; 'Eight Miles High'; 'One Hundred Years From Now'; 'You Don't Miss Your Water'; 'Hickory Wind'; 'King Apathy III'; 'Bad Night At The Whiskey'; 'Nashville West'.
The Byrds played at the Avalon on 1–3 November. This tape is an excellent quality recording. Note the inclusion of the cover of 'Blue Suede Shoes' and the outtake 'Stanley's Song'.

1968/69 *Avalon Ballroom, San Francisco, California, 2 November 1968/ Fillmore West, San Francisco, California, 15 June 1969.*
'So You Want To Be A Rock 'n' Roll Star'; 'Goin' Back'; 'This Wheel's On Fire'; 'Jesus Is Just Alright'.
An excellent quality stereo recording from a radio broadcast of the Byrds' performance at the Avalon Ballroom (2 November 1968). Bob Cohen, owner of the Avalon, allowed KSAN to broadcast three of the songs in their *What Was That – Suddenly Lost Summer* documentary. 'Jesus Is Just Alright', taken from a Fillmore West gig (15 June 1969), was donated by Bill Graham. The Byrds line-up at both concerts was McGuinn, White, Parsons and York.

1969 *Boston Tea Party, Boston, Massachusetts, 22 February 1969.*
'You Ain't Going Nowhere'; 'He Was A Friend Of Mine'; 'Old Blue'; 'Long Black Veil'; 'Goin' Back'; 'Get Out Of My Life Woman'; 'Ballad Of Easy Rider'; 'Jesus Is Just Alright'; 'Tulsa County Blue'; 'Mr Spaceman'; 'Sing Me Back Home'; 'This Wheel's On Fire'; 'Lay Lady Lay'; 'Time Between'; 'Medley: 'My Back Pages'/'B.J. Blues'/'Baby, What Do You Want Me To Do'; 'Take A City Bride'; 'It's All Over Now, Baby Blue'; 'Way Behind The Sun'; 'Jesus Is Just Alright'; 'Turn! Turn! Turn!'; 'Mr Tambourine Man'; 'Eight Miles High'; 'I Shall Be Released'; 'Drug Store Truck Drivin' Man'; 'Nashville West'; 'Fido'.
The Byrds appeared for three nights, 20–23 February, and this tape is dated 22 February. John York takes lead vocal on 'Long Black Veil', 'Tulsa County Blue' and 'Way Behind The Sun'. The recording quality is excellent and the material is of particular interest as it includes non-recorded items such as Bob Dylan's 'I Shall Be Released' and Lee Dorsey's 'Get Out Of My Life Woman'. The tape has since been widely bootlegged on CD. The Flying Burrito Brothers were the support act and joined the Byrds on stage over the weekend.

1969 *Rhode Island University, North Kingston, Rhode Island, 9 May 1969.*
'You Ain't Going Nowhere'; 'Turn! Turn! Turn!'; 'Mr Tambourine Man';

'Eight Miles High'; 'Old Blue'; 'Long Black Veil'; 'Jesus Is Just Alright'; 'Take A City Bride'; 'Goin' Back'; 'This Wheel's On Fire'; 'Medley: 'My Back Pages'/'B.J. Blues'/'Baby, What Do You Want Me To Do'; 'I Shall Be Released'; 'Oil In My Lamp'; 'Bad Night At The Whiskey'; 'He Was A Friend Of Mine'; 'So You Want To Be A Rock 'n' Roll Star'; 'Sing Me Back Home'; 'Lay Lady Lay'.
The recording quality is impressive.

1969 *Fillmore West, San Francisco, California, 14 June 1969.*
'This Wheel's On Fire'; 'Nashville West'; 'So You Want To Be A Rock 'n' Roll Star'; 'Goin' Back'; 'Wasn't Born To Follow'; 'Ballad Of Easy Rider'; 'Jesus Is Just Alright'; 'Get Out Of My Life Woman'; 'Eight Miles High'; 'He Was A Friend Of Mine'; 'Hold It!'.

1969 *'Newport 69', Devonshire Downs, Northridge, California, 22 June 1969.*
'Sing Me Back Home'; 'You Ain't Going Nowhere'; 'Old Blue'.
A poor quality handful of songs from an important date. Hopefully, a more complete and better recording will emerge at some future date.

1969 *Palm Beach International Raceway, West Palm Beach, Florida, 29 November 1969.*
'You Ain't Going Nowhere'; 'Old Blue'; 'It's All Over Now, Baby Blue'; 'Jesus Is Just Alright'; 'Positively 4th Street'; 'Mr Spaceman'; 'Ballad Of Easy Rider'; 'Wasn't Born To Follow'; 'My Back Pages'; 'Take A City Bride'; 'Close Up The Honky Tonks'/'You're Still On My Mind'; 'Drug Store Truck Drivin' Man'; 'So You Want To Be A Rock 'n' Roll Star'; 'Nashville West'; 'Turn! Turn! Turn!'; 'Mr Tambourine Man'; 'Eight Miles High'; 'Hold It!'.
This below par quality tape is listed as 30 November, although the Byrds were scheduled to play on 29 November.

1970 *Fillmore West, San Francisco, California, 2–4 January 1970.*
First set: 'You Ain't Going Nowhere'; 'Feel A Whole Lot Better'; 'Old Blue'; 'You All Look Alike'; 'Positively 4th Street'; 'Jesus Is Just Alright'; 'Mr Spaceman'; 'It's All Over Now, Baby Blue'; 'Take A City Bride'; 'Turn! Turn! Turn!'; 'Mr Tambourine Man'; 'Eight Miles High'; 'Baby, What You Want Me To Do'; 'Hold It!'.
Second set: 'Feel A Whole Lot Better'; 'This Wheel's On Fire'; 'Positively 4th Street'; 'Roll Over Beethoven'; 'Medley: 'Close Up The Honky Tonks'/'You're Still On My Mind'/'Sing Me Back Home'; 'So You Want To Be A Rock 'n' Roll Star'; 'You Don't Miss Your Water'; 'Jesus Is Just Alright'; 'Nashville West'; 'Turn! Turn! Turn!'; 'Mr Tambourine Man'; 'Eight Miles High'.

REQUIEM FOR THE TIMELESS — VOLUME 1

At the dawn of the Seventies, the Byrds' set still included a large sprinkling of country songs, reminiscent of their collaborations with the Flying Burrito Brothers. This tape is available in both average and soundboard quality.

1970 *Ash Grove, Hollywood, California, 6–8 February 1970.*
'Lover Of The Bayou'; 'You Ain't Going Nowhere'; 'Well Come Back Home'; 'Old Blue'; 'Medley: 'My Back Pages'/'B.J. Blues'/'Baby, What Do You Want Me To Do'; 'Willin''; 'Take A Whiff'; 'Soldier's Joy'/'Black Mountain Rag'; 'Truck Stop Girl'; 'This Wheel's On Fire'; 'Ballad Of Easy Rider'; 'Jesus Is Just Alright'; 'Nashville West'; 'Chestnut Mare'; 'Eight Miles High'; 'Hold It!'.
This excellent quality tape was recorded on one of the three nights at the Ash Grove. Reviews mention that the Byrds also performed 'You All Look Alike' and 'Amazing Grace'. It is noticeable that they have already prepared the bulk of the material for *(Untitled)*, recording sessions for which would not begin until the end of May. The album would not be released until as late as September.

1970 *Felt Forum, Madison Square Garden Center, New York, 1 March 1970.*
'Lover Of The Bayou'; 'You Ain't Going Nowhere'; 'Old Blue'; 'You All Look Alike'; 'My Back Pages'; 'Positively 4th Street'; 'He Was A Friend Of Mine'; 'Willin''; 'Soldier's Joy'/'Black Mountain Rag'; 'Eight Miles High'; 'Jesus Is Just Alright'; 'Ballad Of Easy Rider'; 'So You Want To Be A Rock 'n' Roll Star'; 'Hold It!'.
An excellent, if incomplete, tape of one of the shows used for the live section of *(Untitled)*.

1970 *T.C Williams High School, Alexandria, Virginia, 7 March 1970.*
'Lover Of The Bayou'; 'You Ain't Going Nowhere'; 'I Trust (Everything Is Gonna Work Out Alright)'; 'Medley: 'My Back Pages'/'B.J. Blues'/'Baby, What Do You Want Me To Do'; 'Truck Stop Girl'; 'Soldier's Joy'/'Black Mountain Rag'; 'Mr Tambourine Man'; 'Take A Whiff'; 'This Wheel's On Fire'; 'It's Alright Ma (I'm Only Bleeding)'; 'Jesus Is Just Alright'; 'Eight Miles High'; 'Positively 4th Street'; 'So You Want To Be A Rock 'n' Roll Star'; 'Mr Spaceman'.
Most remarkable for the early appearance of 'I Trust (Everything Is Gonna Work Out Alright)', a song that was not even attempted for *(Untitled)* and did not emerge until 1971 on *Byrdmaniax* and as a UK single.

1970 *Loyola College, Baltimore, Maryland, 15 April 1970.*
'Lover Of The Bayou'; 'You Ain't Going Nowhere'; 'Well Come Back Home'; 'Medley: 'My Back Pages'/'B.J. Blues'/'Baby, What Do You Want Me To Do'; 'Truck Stop Girl'; 'Soldier's Joy'/'Black Mountain Rag'; 'Mr

Tambourine Man'; 'Take A Whiff'; 'This Wheel's On Fire'; 'It's Alright Ma (I'm Only Bleeding)'; 'Ballad Of Easy Rider'; 'Jesus Is Just Alright'; 'Eight Miles High'; 'So You Want To Be A Rock 'n' Roll Star'; 'Mr Spaceman'; 'Hold It!'.
Another excellent quality recording.

1970 *American University, Washington DC, 18 April 1970.*
'You Ain't Going Nowhere'; 'Old Blue'; 'You All Look Alike'; 'Medley: 'My Back Pages'/'B.J. Blues'/'Baby, What Do You Want Me To Do'; 'He Was A Friend Of Mine'; 'Willin''; 'Soldier's Joy'/'Black Mountain Rag'; 'This Wheel's On Fire'; 'It's Alright Ma (I'm Only Bleeding)'; 'Ballad Of Easy Rider'; 'Jesus Is Just Alright'; 'Nashville West'; 'Turn! Turn! Turn!'; 'Mr Tambourine Man'; 'Eight Miles High'; 'Hold It!'; 'So You Want To Be A Rock 'n' Roll Star'; 'Mr Spaceman'; 'Hold It!' (reprise); 'Amazing Grace'.
On some tapes this is listed as 'Georgetown University'.

1970 *Freedom Hall, Louisville, Kentucky, 12 June 1970.*
'Lover Of The Bayou'; 'You Ain't Going Nowhere'; 'Old Blue'; 'You All Look Alike'; 'Medley: 'My Back Pages'/'B.J. Blues'/'Baby, What Do You Want Me To Do'; 'He Was A Friend Of Mine'; 'Willin''; 'Soldier's Joy'/ 'Black Mountain Rag'; 'This Wheel's On Fire'; 'Jesus Is Just Alright'; 'Chimes Of Freedom'; 'Nashville West'; 'Turn! Turn! Turn!'; 'Mr Tambourine Man'; 'Eight Miles High'; 'Hold It!'; 'So You Want To Be A Rock 'n' Roll Star'; 'Mr Spaceman'.
This excellent quality soundboard recording was also issued on the bootleg CD *Rollin' Down The Road* (Rattlesnake RS 126).

1970 *Kralingen Festival, Rotterdam, Netherlands, 27 June 1970.*
'You Ain't Going Nowhere'; 'Old Blue'; 'Medley: 'My Back Pages'/'B.J. Blues'/'Baby, What Do You Want Me To Do'; 'Soldier's Joy'/'Black Mountain Rag'; 'It's Alright Ma (I'm Only Bleeding)'; 'He Was A Friend Of Mine'; 'Chimes Of Freedom'; 'You All Look Alike'; 'Jesus Is Just Alright'; 'All The Things'; 'Buckaroo'; 'Nashville West'; 'Just A Season'; 'Turn! Turn! Turn!'; 'Mr Tambourine Man'; 'Eight Miles High'; 'So You Want To Be A Rock 'n' Roll Star'; 'Mr Spaceman'; 'Ballad Of Easy Rider'; 'Amazing Grace'.
This much bootlegged set has appeared in various permutations, the above is the complete set, as far as I know.

1970 *Bath Festival, 29 June 1970.*
'It's Alright Ma (I'm Only Bleeding)'; 'Ballad Of Easy Rider'; 'Willin''; 'Soldier's Joy'; 'Baby, What You Want Me To Do'; 'Drug Store Truck Drivin' Man'; 'You Don't Miss Your Water'; 'Jesus Is Just Alright'; 'Turn!

Turn! Turn!'; 'Mr Tambourine Man'; 'Eight Miles High'; 'Mary Don't You Weep'; 'Black Mountain Rag'; 'Just A Season'; 'Amazing Grace'; 'So You Want To Be A Rock 'n' Roll Star'; 'You Ain't Going Nowhere'; 'Old Blue'; 'Wasn't Born To Follow'; 'Glory, Glory'; 'Take A Whiff'.

Although listed as 28 June, the Byrds did not appear until the early hours of Monday 29 June. This recording has been cut up and issued in various permutations. As with Kralingen, this appears to be the complete set list. Recording quality varies, depending on source, but this one is probably the best.

1970 *De Doelen, Rotterdam, Netherlands, 5 July 1970.*
'Lover Of The Bayou'; 'You Ain't Going Nowhere'; 'Old Blue'; 'Well Come Back Home'; 'Medley: 'My Back Pages'/'B.J. Blues'/'Baby, What Do You Want Me To Do'; 'He Was A Friend Of Mine'; 'Willin''; 'Soldier's Joy'/'Black Mountain Rag'; 'This Wheel's On Fire'; 'Hold It!'; 'It's Alright Ma (I'm Only Bleeding)'; 'Ballad Of Easy Rider'; 'Jesus Is Just Alright'; 'All The Things'; 'Buckaroo'/'Nashville West'; 'Turn! Turn! Turn!'; 'Mr Tambourine Man'; 'Eight Miles High'; 'Hold It!' (reprise); 'So You Want To Be A Rock 'n' Roll Star'; 'Drug Store Truck Drivin' Man'; 'Mr Spaceman'; 'Wasn't Born To Follow'; 'Mary Don't You Weep'; 'Amazing Grace'; 'Chimes Of Freedom'; 'Just A Season'; 'Chestnut Mare'; 'Glory, Glory'; 'Amazing Grace'.

A poor quality tape of a formidable set, which includes the rare traditional 'Mary Don't You Weep' recently introduced at the Bath Festival.

1970 *Het Concertgebouw, Amsterdam, Netherlands, 7 July 1970.*
'You Ain't Going Nowhere'; 'Lover Of The Bayou'; 'Old Blue'; 'Well Come Back Home'; 'Medley: 'My Back Pages'/'B.J. Blues'/'Baby, What Do You Want Me To Do'; 'He Was A Friend Of Mine'; 'Willin''; 'Soldier's Joy'/'Black Mountain Rag'; 'Take A Whiff'; 'This Wheel's On Fire'; 'It's Alright Ma (I'm Only Bleeding)'; 'Ballad Of Easy Rider'; 'Jesus Is Just Alright'; 'All The Things'; 'Buckaroo'/'Nashville West'; 'Turn! Turn! Turn!'; 'Mr Tambourine Man'; 'Eight Miles High'; 'Positively 4th Street'; 'Mr Spaceman'; 'You Don't Miss Your Water'; 'Chestnut Mare'; 'Chimes Of Freedom'; 'Amazing Grace'.

This was the full tape from which *Live At Buddy's* was taken, recorded at the Het Concertgebouw, Amsterdam. The quality is excellent and far superior to the vinyl bootleg album it spawned.

1970 *Central Park, New York, 20 July 1970.*
'Lover Of The Bayou'; 'Old Blue'; 'Well Come Back Home'; 'Medley: 'My Back Pages'/'B.J. Blues'/'Baby, What Do You Want Me To Do'; 'He Was A

Friend Of Mine'; 'Willin''; 'Soldier's Joy'/'Black Mountain Rag'; 'Take A Whiff'; 'This Wheel's On Fire'; 'It's Alright Ma (I'm Only Bleeding)'; 'Ballad Of Easy Rider'; 'Jesus Is Just Alright'; 'Turn! Turn! Turn!'; 'Mr Tambourine Man'; 'Eight Miles High'; 'Hold It!'.
The recording quality is fairly impressive.

1970 *Meadowlands, East Rutherford, New Jersey, 25 July 1970.*
'Lover Of The Bayou'; 'Jesus Is Just Alright'; 'Ballad Of Easy Rider'; 'This Wheel's On Fire'; 'Willin''; 'Turn! Turn! Turn!'; 'Mr Tambourine Man'; 'Eight Miles High'; 'So You Want To Be A Rock 'n' Roll Star'.
The date may be incorrect as the Byrds were booked to play at the Playhouse In The Park, Philadelphia, Pennsylvania, on this evening.

1970 *Fillmore West, San Francisco, California, 13 August 1970.*
'Lover Of The Bayou'; 'You Ain't Going Nowhere'; 'Well Come Back Home'; 'Old Blue'; 'Medley: 'My Back Pages'/'B.J. Blues'/'Baby, What Do You Want Me To Do'; 'This Wheel's On Fire'; 'It's Alright Ma (I'm Only Bleeding)'; 'Ballad Of Easy Rider'; 'Jesus Is Just Alright'; 'All The Things'; 'Nashville West'; 'Turn! Turn! Turn!'; 'Mr Tambourine Man'; 'Eight Miles High'; 'Hold It!'.
This strong quality tape was the first night of the Byrds' appearance at the Fillmore West, which covered 13–16 August.

1970 *Ash Grove, Hollywood, California, 23 August 1970.*
'Lover Of The Bayou'; 'You Ain't Going Nowhere'; 'Well Come Back Home'; 'Old Blue'; 'Medley: 'My Back Pages'/'B.J. Blues'/'Baby, What Do You Want Me To Do'; 'He Was A Friend Of Mine'; 'Truck Stop Girl'; 'Break My Mind' (featuring Gram Parsons, Linda Ronstadt); 'I'm Moving On' (featuring John Hammond Jr); 'Take A City Bride' (featuring Gib Guilbeau); 'Chestnut Mare'; 'This Wheel's On Fire'; 'It's Alright Ma (I'm Only Bleeding)'; 'Ballad Of Easy Rider'; 'Jesus Is Just Alright'; 'Turn! Turn! Turn!'; 'Mr Tambourine Man'; 'Eight Miles High'.
The Byrds were joined on stage by Gram Parsons, Linda Ronstadt, John Hammond Jr and Gib Guilbeau on the Sunday of a weekend appearance at the Ash Grove.

1970 *University Of The Pacific, Stockton, California, 20 September 1970.*
'I Trust (Everything Is Gonna Work Out Alright)'; 'Well Come Back Home'; 'Medley: 'My Back Pages'/'B.J. Blues'/'Baby, What Do You Want Me To Do'; 'Truck Stop Girl'; 'Soldier's Joy'/'Black Mountain Rag'; 'Take A Whiff'; 'This Wheel's On Fire'; 'It's Alright Ma (I'm Only Bleeding)'; 'Ballad Of Easy Rider'; 'Jesus Is Just Alright'; 'Turn! Turn! Turn!'; 'Mr Tambourine Man'; 'Eight Miles High'; 'Hold It!'; 'So You Want To Be A

Rock 'n' Roll Star'; 'Mr Spaceman'; 'The Christian Life'; 'Lover Of The Bayou'; 'Hold It!'.
Interesting to witness the familiar opener 'Lover Of The Bayou' shifted to the end of the set, plus a surprise return for 'The Christian Life'. Evidently, the latter was done by spontaneous request. As McGuinn says: "I'd like to do one little thing. This cat right here in a blue shirt who asked me backstage if I'd sing 'Christian Life'. Do you remember it, Clarence? What key is it in? D? OK – kick it off!" McGuinn sings it far more sincerely than he did on *Sweetheart Of The Rodeo* and White provides some strikingly intricate flourishes. 'I Trust' has already started when the tape begins and is performed in gospel call-and-response style with lots of exclamations from McGuinn.

1970 *State University, Plattsburgh, New York, 11 October 1970.*
'Lover Of The Bayou'; 'You Ain't Going Nowhere'; 'Jesus Is Just Alright'; 'It's Alright Ma (I'm Only Bleeding)'; 'This Wheel's On Fire'; 'Medley: 'My Back Pages'/'B.J. Blues'/'Baby, What Do You Want Me To Do'; 'Willin''; 'Medley: 'Turn! Turn! Turn!'/'Mr Tambourine Man'/'Eight Miles High'; 'So You Want To Be A Rock 'n' Roll Star'; 'Mr Spaceman'.
Some tapes incorrectly list this as September 1970.

1970 *Bloomfield College, New Jersey, 24 October 1970.*
'Lover Of The Bayou'; 'You Ain't Going Nowhere'; 'Old Blue'; 'Positively 4th Street'; 'Medley: 'My Back Pages'/'B.J. Blues'/'Baby, What Do You Want Me To Do'; 'Home Sweet Home'; 'Truck Stop Girl'; 'Soldier's Joy'/'Black Mountain Rag'; 'Mr Tambourine Man'; 'Take A Whiff'; 'Chestnut Mare'; 'It's Alright Ma (I'm Only Bleeding)'; 'Ballad Of Easy Rider'; 'Jesus Is Just Alright'; 'Eight Miles High'.
The first known live performance of Clarence White's rendition of 'Home Sweet Home'. Just after 'Lover Of The Bayou', McGuinn plays a few bars from Chuck Berry's 'Johnny B. Goode' and sings part of the chorus.

1970 *Rochester Institute Of Technology, Rochester, New York, 7 November 1970.*
'I Trust (Everything Is Gonna Work Out Alright)'; 'You Ain't Going Nowhere'; 'Lover Of The Bayou'; 'Well Come Back Home'; 'Medley: 'My Back Pages'/'B.J. Blues'/'Baby, What Do You Want Me To Do'; 'Truck Stop Girl'; 'Soldier's Joy'/'Black Mountain Rag'; 'Mr Tambourine Man'; 'Take A Whiff'; 'This Wheel's On Fire'; 'It's Alright Ma (I'm Only Bleeding)'; 'Ballad Of Easy Rider'; 'Jesus Is Just Alright'; 'Eight Miles High'; 'Hold It!'; 'Chestnut Mare'.
One of several shows during this period featuring Terry Melcher guesting on keyboards.

BYRDS BOOTLEGS

1970 *Drew University, Madison, New Jersey, 14 November 1970.*
'You Ain't Going Nowhere'; 'Lover Of The Bayou'; 'Well Come Back Home'; 'Truck Stop Girl'; 'Soldier's Joy'/'Black Mountain Rag'; 'Mr Tambourine Man'; 'Take A Whiff'; 'Jesus Is Just Alright'.
Tape recording incomplete. The Byrds were supported by the Flying Burrito Brothers at this show.

1970 *Old Dominion University, Norfolk, Virginia, 22 November 1970.*
'Lover Of The Bayou'; 'You Ain't Going Nowhere'; 'I Trust (Everything Is Gonna Work Out Alright)'; 'Medley: 'My Back Pages'/'B.J. Blues'/'Baby, What Do You Want Me To Do'; 'Truck Stop Girl'; 'Soldier's Joy'/'Black Mountain Rag'; 'Mr Tambourine Man'; 'Take A Whiff'; 'This Wheel's On Fire'; 'It's Alright Ma (I'm Only Bleeding)'; 'Jesus Is Just Alright'; 'Eight Miles High'; 'Hold It!'; 'Positively 4th Street'; 'So You Want To Be A Rock 'n' Roll Star'; 'Mr Spaceman'.
The seventh anniversary of President John F. Kennedy's assassination does not inspire McGuinn to add 'He Was A Friend Of Mine' to the set.

1970 *Music Hall, Cleveland, Ohio, 26 November 1970.*
'Medley: 'My Back Pages'/'B.J. Blues'/'Baby, What Do You Want Me To Do'; 'Home Sweet Home'; 'Soldier's Joy'/'Black Mountain Rag'; 'Mr Tambourine Man'; 'Take A Whiff'; 'You Ain't Going Nowhere'; 'Jesus Is Just Alright'; 'So You Want To Be A Rock 'n' Roll Star'; 'Mr Spaceman'; 'Chestnut Mare'; 'I Trust (Everything Is Gonna Work Out Alright)'.
An incomplete tape of a memorable evening when they were supported by the still struggling Elton John.

1970 *State University, New York, 6 December 1970.*
'Lover Of The Bayou'; 'You Ain't Going Nowhere'; 'Positively 4th Street'; 'Old Blue'; 'Medley: 'My Back Pages'/'B.J. Blues'/'Baby, What Do You Want Me To Do'; 'Home Sweet Home'; 'Soldier's Joy'/'Black Mountain Rag'; 'Mr Tambourine Man'; 'Take A Whiff'; 'Jesus Is Just Alright'; 'Eight Miles High'.
Another excellent soundboard recording.

1970 *Oberlin College, Oberlin, Ohio, 18 December 1970.*
'Lover Of The Bayou'; 'You Ain't Going Nowhere'; 'Medley: 'My Back Pages'/'B.J. Blues'/'Baby, What Do You Want Me To Do'; 'Home Sweet Home'; 'Soldier's Joy'/'Black Mountain Rag'; 'Mr Tambourine Man'; 'Take A Whiff'; 'Jesus Is Just Alright'; 'Eight Miles High'; 'Hold It!'.
A short set, possibly with some missing songs, but including Clarence White's rendition of 'Home Sweet Home'.

1971 *Carnegie Hall, New York, 17 February 1971.*
'Lover Of The Bayou'; 'You Ain't Going Nowhere'; 'Medley: 'My Back Pages'/'B.J. Blues'/'Baby, What Do You Want Me To Do'; 'Jamaica Say You Will'; 'Soldier's Joy'/'Black Mountain Rag'; 'Pretty Boy Floyd'; 'Mr Tambourine Man'; 'Chestnut Mare'; 'Jesus Is Just Alright'; 'Eight Miles High'; 'Hold It!'; 'I Wanna Grow Up To Be A Politician'; 'So You Want To Be A Rock 'n' Roll Star'; 'Mr Spaceman'.
A pretty good audience recording.

1971 *Viking Hall, Upsala College, East Orange, New Jersey, 26 February 1971.*
'Lover Of The Bayou'; 'You Ain't Going Nowhere'; 'Truck Stop Girl'; 'Medley: 'My Back Pages'/'B.J. Blues'/'Baby, What Do You Want Me To Do'; 'Jamaica Say You Will'; 'Soldier's Joy'/'Black Mountain Rag'; 'Mr Tambourine Man'; 'Take A Whiff'; 'Chestnut Mare'; 'Jesus Is Just Alright'; 'Eight Miles High'; 'Hold It!'; 'So You Want To Be A Rock 'n' Roll Star'.

1971 *Trenton State College, Trenton, New Jersey, 19 March 1971.*
'Lover Of The Bayou'; 'You Ain't Going Nowhere'; 'Truck Stop Girl'; 'Medley: 'My Back Pages'/'B.J. Blues'/'Baby, What Do You Want Me To Do'; 'Jamaica Say You Will'; 'Soldier's Joy'/'Black Mountain Rag'; 'Mr Tambourine Man'; 'Pretty Boy Floyd'; 'Take A Whiff'.
An incomplete set from the period.

1971 *Fairfield Halls, Croydon, 6 May 1971.*
'Lover Of The Bayou'; 'You Ain't Going Nowhere'; 'Truck Stop Girl'; 'Medley: 'My Back Pages'/'B.J. Blues'/'Baby, What Do You Want Me To Do'; 'Jamaica Say You Will'; 'Soldier's Joy'/'Black Mountain Rag'; 'Mr Tambourine Man'; 'Pretty Boy Floyd'; 'Take A Whiff'; 'Chestnut Mare'; 'Jesus Is Just Alright'; 'Eight Miles High'; 'Hold It!'; 'So You Want To Be A Rock 'n' Roll Star'; 'Mr Spaceman'; 'Roll Over Beethoven'; 'Hold It!' (reprise); 'Goin' Back'; 'This Wheel's On Fire'.
Recording quality is impressive.

1971 *University Of Liverpool, Liverpool, 8 May 1971.*
'Lover Of The Bayou'; 'You Ain't Going Nowhere'; 'Truck Stop Girl'; 'Medley: 'My Back Pages'/'B.J. Blues'/'Baby, What Do You Want Me To Do'; 'Jamaica Say You Will'; 'Soldier's Joy'/'Black Mountain Rag'; 'Mr Tambourine Man'; 'Pretty Boy Floyd'; 'Take A Whiff'; 'Chestnut Mare'; 'Jesus Is Just Alright'; 'So You Want To Be A Rock 'n' Roll Star'; 'Mr Spaceman'; 'Hold It!' (reprise); 'Old Blue'; 'Mary Don't You Weep'; 'Roll Over Beethoven'; 'Amazing Grace'.
Oddly, some tapes claiming to be from this show, have a slightly different track listing.

1971 *City Hall, Sheffield, 9 May 1971.*
'Lover Of The Bayou'; 'You Ain't Going Nowhere'; 'Truck Stop Girl'; 'Medley: 'My Back Pages'/'B.J. Blues'/'Baby, What Do You Want Me To Do'; 'Jamaica Say You Will'; 'Soldier's Joy'/'Black Mountain Rag'; 'Mr Tambourine Man'; 'Pretty Boy Floyd'; 'Take A Whiff'; 'Chestnut Mare'; 'Jesus Is Just Alright'; 'Eight Miles High'; 'Hold It!'; 'So You Want To Be A Rock 'n' Roll Star'; 'Mr Spaceman'; 'Hold It!' (reprise); 'Old Blue'; 'Mary Don't You Weep'.
A rare chance to hear 'Mary Don't You Weep' played in the UK.

1971 *Free Trade Hall, Manchester, 11 May 1971.*
'Lover Of The Bayou'; 'You Ain't Going Nowhere'; 'Truck Stop Girl'; 'Medley: 'My Back Pages'/'B.J. Blues'/'Baby, What Do You Want Me To Do'; 'Jamaica Say You Will'; 'Mr Tambourine Man'; 'Pretty Boy Floyd'; 'Take A Whiff'; 'Chestnut Mare'; 'Jesus Is Just Alright'; 'Hold It!'; 'So You Want To Be A Rock 'n' Roll Star'; 'Mr Spaceman'; 'It's Alright Ma (I'm Only Bleeding)'; 'Ballad Of Easy Rider'; 'Wasn't Born To Follow'; 'Hold It!' (reprise).
This is a rather poor recording but others on the UK tour at Liverpool, Sheffield, Croydon were slightly better. A truncated version of this concert is available of soundboard quality.

1971 *Vorst Nationaal, Brussels, Belgium, 18 May 1971.*
'Lover Of The Bayou'; 'You Ain't Going Nowhere'; 'Truck Stop Girl'; 'Medley: 'My Back Pages'/'B.J. Blues'/'Baby, What Do You Want Me To Do'; 'Soldier's Joy'/'Black Mountain Rag'; 'Pretty Boy Floyd'; 'Take A Whiff'; 'Jesus Is Just Alright'; 'Mr Spaceman'; 'Hold It!'.
This was a show recorded by Belgium television and the quality is excellent.

1971 *Tupholme Manor Park, Bardney, Nr. Lincoln, Lincolnshire, 24 July 1971.*
'So You Want To Be A Rock 'n' Roll Star'; 'Mr Spaceman'; 'I Wanna Grow Up To Be A Politician'; 'Bugler'; 'Soldier's Joy'/'Black Mountain Rag'; 'Mr Tambourine Man'; 'Antique Sandy'; 'Pretty Boy Floyd'; 'Willin''; 'You Ain't Going Nowhere'; 'Medley: 'My Back Pages'/'B.J. Blues'/'Baby, What Do You Want Me To Do'; 'Jesus Is Just Alright'; 'Hold It!'; 'Chestnut Mare'; 'Glory, Glory'.
Unlike the poor quality bootleg album, *Live At Lincoln*, part of which did not even include material recorded that day, this tape is a thorough representation of one of the Byrds' most memorable appearances of the period.

1971 *Fairleigh Dickinson Hall, New Jersey, 11 September 1971.*
'Lover Of The Bayou'; 'So You Want To Be A Rock 'n' Roll Star'; 'Mr

Spaceman'; 'Bugler'; 'I Wanna Grow Up To Be A Politician'; 'Medley: 'My Back Pages'/'B.J. Blues'/'Baby, What Do You Want Me To Do'; 'Soldier's Joy'/'Black Mountain Rag'; 'Mr Tambourine Man'; 'Pretty Boy Floyd'; 'Roll In My Sweet Baby's Arms'; 'Tiffany Queen'; 'Chestnut Mare'.
Notable for the first appearance on bootleg tape of 'Roll In My Sweet Baby's Arms', with Battin singing lead.

1971 *Woods Brown Amphitheatre, American University, Washington, DC, 12 September 1971.*
'Lover Of The Bayou'; 'So You Want To Be A Rock 'n' Roll Star'; 'Mr Spaceman'; 'I Wanna Grow Up To Be A Politician'; 'Soldier's Joy'/'Black Mountain Rag'; 'Mr Tambourine Man'; 'Pretty Boy Floyd'; 'Nashville West'; 'Citizen Kane'; 'Tiffany Queen'; 'Chestnut Mare'; 'Jesus Is Just Alright'; 'Eight Miles High'; 'Hold It!'; 'Roll Over Beethoven'.
The American University broadcasted this concert on radio, thus the excellent quality.

1971 *Palladium, Hollywood, California, 24 November 1971.*
'Lover Of The Bayou'; 'So You Want To Be A Rock 'n' Roll Star'; 'Mr Spaceman'; 'Bugler'; 'I Wanna Grow Up To Be A Politician'; 'Medley: 'My Back Pages'/'B.J. Blues'/'Baby, What Do You Want Me To Do'; 'Truck Stop Girl'; 'Chestnut Mare'; 'Jesus Is Just Alright'; 'Eight Miles High'; 'Feel A Whole Lot Better'; 'Roll Over Beethoven'.
An excellent quality recording.

1972 *Rainbow Theatre, London, England, 17 January 1972.*
'Lover Of The Bayou'; 'So You Want To Be A Rock 'n' Roll Star'; 'Mr Spaceman'; 'Bugler'; 'I Wanna Grow Up To Be A Politician'; 'Medley: 'My Back Pages'/'B.J. Blues'/'Baby, What Do You Want Me To Do'; 'Soldier's Joy'/'Black Mountain Rag'; 'Mr Tambourine Man'; 'Pretty Boy Floyd'; 'Roll In My Sweet Baby's Arms'; 'Tiffany Queen'; 'Chestnut Mare'; 'Jesus Is Just Alright'; 'Chimes Of Freedom'; 'Eight Miles High'; 'Nashville West'; 'Feel A Whole Lot Better'; 'Roll Over Beethoven'.
This was the second night at the Rainbow. The previous night's performance, although memorable, was blighted by sound problems. Tape quality is merely average.

1972 *MIDEM Conference, Cannes, France, 20 January 1972.*
'Lover Of The Bayou'; 'So You Want To Be A Rock 'n' Roll Star'; 'Mr Spaceman'; 'Roll In My Sweet Baby's Arms'; 'Medley: 'My Back Pages'/'B.J. Blues'/'Baby, What Do You Want Me To Do'; 'Eight Miles High'; 'Amazing Grace'; 'Roll Over Beethoven'.

BYRDS BOOTLEGS

1972 *Live At The Olympia, Paris, France, 22 January 1972.*
'Lover Of The Bayou'; 'So You Want To Be A Rock 'n' Roll Star'; 'Mr Spaceman'; 'Roll In My Sweet Baby's Arms'; 'Medley: 'My Back Pages'/'B.J. Blues'/ 'Baby, What Do You Want Me To Do'; 'Eight Miles High'; 'Amazing Grace'; 'Roll Over Beethoven'.
This performance was filmed and broadcast in France, thus the excellent quality.

1972 *Kenyon College, Gambier, Ohio, 11 February 1972.*
'Lover Of The Bayou'; 'Bugler'; 'America's Great National Pastime'; 'Chimes Of Freedom'; 'Lost My Drivin' Wheel'; 'I Wanna Grow Up To Be A Politician'; 'Medley: 'My Back Pages'/'B.J. Blues'/'Baby, What Do You Want Me To Do'; 'Soldier's Joy'/'Black Mountain Rag'; 'Mr Tambourine Man'; 'Farther Along'; 'Roll In My Sweet Baby's Arms'; 'B.B. Class Road'; 'Mr Spaceman'; 'Tiffany Queen'; 'Chestnut Mare'.
This set is noticeable for the inclusion of five songs from *Farther Along*, plus 'Lost My Drivin' Wheel'.

1972 *Blackham Coliseum, University Of Southwest Louisiana, Lafayette, Louisiana, 5 April 1972.*
'Lover Of The Bayou'; 'Bugler'; 'America's Great National Pastime'; 'Chimes Of Freedom'; 'I Wanna Grow Up To Be A Politician'; 'Medley: 'My Back Pages'/'B.J. Blues'/'Baby, What Do You Want Me To Do'; 'Soldier's Joy'/ 'Black Mountain Rag'; 'Mr Tambourine Man'; 'Roll In My Sweet Baby's Arms'; 'B.B. Class Road'; 'So You Want To Be A Rock 'n' Roll Star'; 'Mr Spaceman'; 'Tiffany Queen'; 'Chestnut Mare'; 'Nashville West'; 'Eight Miles High'; 'Turn! Turn! Turn!'; 'Feel A Whole Lot Better'.
A rare chance to hear 'B.B. Class Road' in concert. Tape quality is only average though.

1972 *Dean Junior College, Franklin, Massachusetts, 29 October 1972.*
'Lover Of The Bayou'; 'Bugler'; 'America's Great National Pastime'; 'Chimes Of Freedom'; 'I Wanna Grow Up To Be A Politician', 'Medley: 'My Back Pages'/'B.J. Blues'/'Baby, What Do You Want Me To Do'; 'Soldier's Joy'/ 'Black Mountain Rag'; 'Mr Tambourine Man'; 'Take A Whiff'; 'So You Want To Be A Rock 'n' Roll Star'; 'Mr Spaceman'; 'Chestnut Mare'; 'Jesus Is Just Alright'; 'Eight Miles High'; 'Hold It!'; 'Roll Over Beethoven'.
This tape is wrongly labelled 12 September 1972 on some tapes.

1972 *Curtis Hixon Hall, Tampa, Florida, 1 November 1972.*
'Lover Of The Bayou'; 'Bugler'; 'America's Great National Pastime'; 'Chimes Of Freedom'; 'I Wanna Grow Up To Be A Politician'; 'Medley:

'My Back Pages'/'B.J. Blues'/'Baby, What Do You Want Me To Do';
'Soldier's Joy'/'Black Mountain Rag'; 'Mr Tambourine Man'; 'Take A
Whiff'; 'So You Want To Be A Rock 'n' Roll Star'; 'Mr Spaceman';
'Chestnut Mare'; 'Eight Miles High'; 'Nashville West'; 'Feel A Whole Lot
Better'; 'Roll Over Beethoven'.
This concert is of particular interest as it was the first bootleg tape to feature
drummer John Guerin, who had recently been recruited to the group
following the dismissal of Gene Parsons. The quality is very good and the
jazzier version of 'Eight Miles High', featuring Guerin's drumming, is
particularly interesting.

1972 *Tower Theatre, Philadelphia, Pennsylvania, 15 December 1972.*
'Lover Of The Bayou'; 'Bugler'; 'America's Great National Pastime';
'Chimes Of Freedom'; 'I Wanna Grow Up To Be A Politician'; 'Medley:
'My Back Pages'/'B.J. Blues'/'Baby, What Do You Want Me To Do';
'Soldier's Joy'/'Black Mountain Rag'; 'Mr Tambourine Man'; 'So You Want
To Be A Rock 'n' Roll Star'; 'Mr Spaceman'; 'Chestnut Mare'.
Excellent quality, but seemingly incomplete.

1973 *Kansas State University, Manhattan, Kansas, Missouri, 20 January 1973.*
'America's Great National Pastime'; 'Chimes Of Freedom'; 'I Wanna Grow
Up To Be A Politician'; 'Medley: 'My Back Pages'/'B.J. Blues'/'Baby, What
Do You Want Me To Do'; 'Soldier's Joy'/'Black Mountain Rag'; 'Mr
Tambourine Man'; 'So You Want To Be A Rock 'n' Roll Star'; 'Mr
Spaceman'; 'Chestnut Mare'; 'Roll Over Beethoven'; 'Hold It!'; 'Eight Miles
High'.
This show, part of a tribute to Earl Scruggs, was filmed and two songs, 'Mr
Tambourine Man' and 'Roll Over Beethoven', later appeared on the
soundtrack album, *Banjoman*, and were also included on the second Byrds'
box set, *There Is A Season*.

1973 *Cowtown Palace, Kansas City, Missouri, 21 January 1973.*
'Lover Of The Bayou'; 'Jesus Is Just Alright'; 'Wasn't Born To Follow';
'The Bells Of Rhymney'; 'Take A Whiff'; 'Old Blue'; 'Ballad Of Easy Rider';
'It Won't Be Wrong'; 'The Water Is Wide'; 'Mr Tambourine Man'; 'Turn!
Turn! Turn!'; 'Nashville West'; 'Eight Miles High'; 'Hold It!'.
This is something of an oddity for various reasons. Firstly, the set list is
almost completely different from the previous night's show (see above).
Equally strangely, a contemporaneous review of the show claims they played
"three or four" songs from *Farther Along* (*none* are listed here!), plus 'Feel A
Whole Lot Better', 'So You Want To Be A Rock 'n' Roll Star' and 'Chestnut
Mare' (which are also missing). Although it's possible the tape is simply

incomplete, the inclusion of oddities such as 'It Won't Be Wrong' and 'The Water Is Wide' ring alarm bells. While it would be pleasing to report that the Byrds were changing their set with gay abandon, this was not the case. Either the date is incorrect or part of the concert was recorded at a later show during McGuinn's solo adventures. Most likely, the tape includes a 'drop in' segment from the later 'Lee Jeans Living Rock Concert' which featured 'Turn! Turn! Turn', 'Ballad Of Easy Rider', 'It Won't Be Wrong', 'The Water Is Wide', 'Mr Tambourine Man', 'Nashville West', 'Lover Of The Bayou' and 'Jesus Is Just Alright', part or all of which I suspect was broadcast at the start of McGuinn's solo career.

1973 *Cornell University, Ithaca, New York, 10 February 1973.*
'Lover Of The Bayou'; 'Take A Whiff'; 'America's Great National Pastime'; 'Chimes Of Freedom'; 'I Wanna Grow Up To Be A Politician'; 'Medley: 'My Back Pages'/'B.J. Blues'/'Baby, What Do You Want Me To Do'; 'Soldier's Joy'/'Black Mountain Rag'; 'Mr Tambourine Man' (acoustic); 'Mr Tambourine Man' (electric); 'So You Want To Be A Rock 'n' Roll Star'; 'Old Blue'; 'Mr Spaceman'; 'Chestnut Mare'; 'Eight Miles High'; 'Hold It!'; 'Turn! Turn! Turn!'; 'Feel A Whole Lot Better'; 'Roll Over Beethoven'.
This is the last known bootleg tape of the CBS-era Byrds, recorded two weeks before their break-up. Oddly, although I have photos and contemporaneous correspondence of the 'Manassas Byrds' (Hillman and Lala) at the final performance at Capitol Theatre, Passaic, New Jersey (24 February), those in attendance evidently neglected to tape the show, unaware that it was the end of an era.

1977 *Boarding House, San Francisco, California, 6 December 1977.*
'Release Me Girl'; 'Silver Raven'; 'Bound To Fall'; 'It Doesn't Matter'; 'Ballad Of Easy Rider'; 'Jolly Roger'; 'Chestnut Mare'; 'Crazy Ladies'; 'Train Leaves Here This Morning'; 'Mr Tambourine Man'; 'You Ain't Going Nowhere'; 'Turn! Turn! Turn!'; 'Knockin' On Heaven's Door'; 'Bye Bye Baby'; 'So You Want To Be A Rock 'n' Roll Star'; 'Eight Miles High'; 'Feel A Whole Lot Better'.
Of the many concerts by McGuinn and Clark during this period, this recording is of importance because it features both Hillman and Crosby, and was the nearest thing from the period to a full Byrds reunion. It was broadcast in February 1978. Crosby wanders on and off the stage but can be heard clearly on 'Mr Tambourine Man' and 'Eight Miles High'.

1977 *Boarding House, San Francisco, California, 8 December 1977.*
'Release Me Girl'; 'Silver Raven'; 'Train Leaves Here This Morning'; 'Ballad

Of Easy Rider'; 'Wasn't Born To Follow';' 'Jolly Roger'; 'Chestnut Mare'; 'Crazy Ladies'; 'Mr Tambourine Man'; 'He Was A Friend Of Mine'; 'She Don't Care About Time'; 'You Ain't Going Nowhere'; 'Wild Mountain Thyme'; 'Chimes Of Freedom'; 'Knockin' On Heaven's Door'; 'Feel A Whole Lot Better'; 'So You Want To Be A Rock 'n' Roll Star'; 'Eight Miles High'. This is listed as 8 December, and does not appear to feature Hillman. Not to be confused with the above.

1977 *Boarding House, San Francisco, California, 8 December 1977.*
'Mr Tambourine Man'; 'Chestnut Mare'; 'Crazy Ladies'; 'Turn! Turn! Turn!'; 'Feel A Whole Lot Better'; 'She Don't Care About Time'; 'You Ain't Going Nowhere'; 'Chimes Of Freedom'; 'He Was A Friend Of Mine'; 'My Back Pages'; 'Little Mama'; 'Knockin' On Heaven's Door'; 'So You Want To Be A Rock 'n' Roll Star'; 'Eight Miles High'.
Listed as 'late show' 8 December, this features McGuinn, Clark & Crosby. It was preceded by three solo slots from Clark ('Denver Or Wherever', 'Silver Raven'), Crosby ('The Lee Shore', 'Drive My Car') and McGuinn ('Dreamland', 'Jolly Roger').

1989 *Coach House, San Juan, Capistrano, California, 4 January 1989.*
'I Am A Pilgrim'; 'Desert Rose'; 'Darkness On The Playground'; 'Ballad Of Easy Rider'; 'Wasn't Born To Follow'; 'It's Alright Ma (I'm Only Bleeding)'; 'Chestnut Mare'; 'Tracks In The Dust'; 'Compass'; 'Guinnevere'; 'Almost Cut My Hair'; 'Chimes Of Freedom'; 'It Won't Be Wrong'; 'Feel A Whole Lot Better'; 'Everybody's Been Burned'; 'My Back Pages'; 'Mr Spaceman'; 'The Bells Of Rhymney'; 'You Ain't Going Nowhere'; 'Mr Tambourine Man'; 'Turn! Turn! Turn!'; 'Eight Miles High'.
The first night of McGuinn, Crosby and Hillman's Byrds' reunion, including solo sets. This excellent quality recording was broadcast on FM.

1989 *Bacchanal, San Diego, California, 5 January 1989.*
'I Am A Pilgrim'; 'Desert Rose'; 'Darkness On The Playground'; 'Tiffany Queen'; 'Ballad Of Easy Rider'; 'Wasn't Born To Follow'; 'It's Alright Ma (I'm Only Bleeding)'; 'Chestnut Mare'; 'Tracks In The Dust'; 'Compass'; 'Guinnevere'; 'Almost Cut My Hair'; 'Chimes Of Freedom'; 'It Won't Be Wrong'; 'Feel A Whole Lot Better'; 'Everybody's Been Burned'; 'My Back Pages'; 'The Bells Of Rhymney'; 'You Ain't Going Nowhere'; 'Mr Tambourine Man'; 'Turn! Turn! Turn!'; 'Eight Miles High'; 'So You Want To Be A Rock 'n' Roll Star'; 'He Was A Friend Of Mine'.

1989 *Ventura Theater, Ventura, California, 6 January 1989.*
'Chimes Of Freedom'; 'It Won't Be Wrong'; 'Feel A Whole Lot Better'; 'Everybody's Been Burned'; 'My Back Pages'; 'Mr Spaceman'; 'The Bells Of

Rhymney'; 'You Ain't Going Nowhere'; 'Mr Tambourine Man'; 'Turn! Turn! Turn!'; 'Eight Miles High'; 'So You Want To Be A Rock 'n' Roll Star'.

As documented in the main text, this concert in Ventura was the final part of a brief series of Byrds reunion gigs, featuring three-fifths of the original group: McGuinn, Hillman and Crosby. The quality of the tape is excellent but it was not transformed into a vinyl bootleg.

1991 *Rock 'n' Roll Hall Of Fame Induction, Waldorf Astoria, New York, 16 January 1991.*
'Mr Tambourine Man' (house band only); 'Turn! Turn! Turn!'.
The five Byrds, including Michael Clarke on vocals, appeared together on stage for the first time since 1966, along with guitarist John Jorgenson and drummer Steve Duncan from the Desert Road Band. This tape includes their historic, slightly ragged rendition of 'Turn! Turn! Turn!'.

2000 *Fred Walecki Tribute, Santa Monica, California, 8 August 2000.*
'Mr Tambourine Man'; 'Turn! Turn! Turn!'.
McGuinn, Crosby and Hillman were billed as the Byrds for this benefit concert.

Since the availability of cheap CDRs, it is possible for anyone to create their own CD of a concert, complete with a catchy title and artwork. Countless new titles will continue to appear, but are no longer likely to be manufactured by professional bootleggers in large quantities. This probably signals the death knell for the traditional bootleg, with fans taking over the means of production. It also makes further listing largely superfluous as many new titles are regurgitated favourites possibly representing merely a handful of copies which can be instantly duplicated. The popular use of MP3 means that a single copy of a CDR can be posted on the Internet for download purposes on a constant basis.

TELEVISION APPEARANCES/ VIDEOS/DVDS

The Byrds have yet to appear on any legal video compilation of their television appearances, excepting the DVD collection included with the box set, *There Is A Season*. The following is a selective listing of the Byrds' television appearances. Precise dating is often complicated as a result of confusion in listings between recording and first broadcast. Additionally, broadcast dates vary in different regions and many shows were repeated. Here, I have attempted to use the first actual broadcast date, where known. Alas, many of the shows listed below were wiped and remain only in memory. Bootleg tapes are available where indicated, but the chances of further material appearing diminish with each passing year, although forgotten videos and old reels are no doubt still out there somewhere. I am particularly indebted to Ray Frieders who, in the aftermath of the extensive listing in *Timeless Flight Revisited*, provided additional information, including details of specific US television stations and programmes, as well as identifying other artistes featured on key shows. Finally, it should be noted that unreleased footage of the Byrds from 1965–66 exists in private collections. Black and white filmed footage of the Byrds backstage, regrettably without sound, was recently unearthed; the opening sequence of the unreleased promotional film for 'Set You Free This Time', which ended with the infamous fracas on the beach, was also taped; finally, McGuinn has some film (without sound) of the Byrds arriving in London in February 1967 and travelling across the city by taxi which he subsequently premiered on YouTube. During the same period, he also filmed the group sightseeing in London and attending the fan club convention at the Roundhouse on 25 February 1967. Obviously, there is extensive footage of post-Byrds solo and offshoot group activities not featured here.

1965

26 March 1965 *Bash!:* song details not known, possibly 'Mr Tambourine Man'. KCOP–TV13, Los Angeles, California. This was the Byrds' television debut. The show was hosted by KRLA disc jockey Charlie O'Donnell and served as a talent showcase. In addition to the Byrds, other guests that evening included Eddie Cano, April & Nino (April Stevens & Nino Tempo), Freddy

TELEVISION APPEARANCES/VIDEOS/DVDS

Cannon, Brenda Holloway, Cannibal & The Headhunters, Jackie De Shannon and Frankie Randell. The presence of De Shannon on the same show at this stage is noteworthy, as she was an early champion of the group.

26 April 1965 *Lloyd Thaxton Show*: 'Mr Tambourine Man'. For their second appearance on KCOP, the Byrds performed on this syndicated show. They played their first single live, but the footage has not survived.

8 May 1965 *Shivaree*: 'Mr Tambourine Man'; 'I Knew I'd Want You'. First shown on Los Angeles' KABC–TV, this was later repeated in different regions. Hosted by Gene Weed, Glen Campbell was among the other guests.

11 May 1965 *Hullabaloo*: 'Mr Tambourine Man'; 'Feel A Whole Lot Better'. Recorded in colour at NBC's studios in Burbank, California, this survives in black and white and can be found on *Hullabaloo Volume 9* (MPR Home Video). 'Feel A Whole Lot Better' was also featured on the DVD included with the 2006 box set, *There Is A Season*. Hosted by Frankie Avalon, the other guests on the show included Sam The Sham & The Pharaohs, Barbara McNair, Peter And Gordon, the Supremes, Joanie Summers and the Hullabaloo Dancers.

22 May 1965 *Flip Them In Fresno*. Filmed at the Radcliffe Convention Centre in Fresno, California, this featured the Byrds on their short tour with the Rolling Stones. The footage, without sound, was available on mail order on 8 mm film through the magazine *Teen Screen*.

27 May 1965 *Lloyd Thaxton Show*: 'Feel A Whole Lot Better'. The Byrds also recorded 'Mr Tambourine Man' (see 8 June) and 'Chimes Of Freedom' (see 6 August) on this syndicated show. Only 30 of the Thaxton shows were archived, alas none with the Byrds.

8 June 1965 *Lloyd Thaxton Show*: 'Mr Tambourine Man'.

12 June 1965 *Shivaree*: 'Mr Tambourine Man'; 'I Knew I'd Want You'. A repeat of the show from 8 May for East Coast viewers.

23 June 1965 *Shindig!*: 'Mr Tambourine Man'; 'Not Fade Away'; 'Long Tall Sally'. McGuinn and Crosby are featured on the medley of 'Long Tall Sally'. On the cover of the Rolling Stones' 'Not Fade Away', McGuinn growls in imitation of Mick Jagger while Hillman mimics the style of Bill Wyman with his bass in a rigid upright position. Other guests featured on this edition, hosted by Jimmy O'Neill, include the Everly Brothers, Melinda Marx, Jody Miller, the Kingsmen, the Righteous Brothers, the Stoneman Family, Billy Preston, Nicki Lynn, Dave Berry and Will Nelson. The show survives on film.

Summer 1965: *Shebang*: probably 'Mr Tambourine Man'. Recorded in colour at Los Angeles' KTLA–TV 5, this appearance, hosted by Casey Kasem, no longer survives in the archives of Dick Clark Productions. A more precise date was not available.

1 July 1965 *Top Of The Pops*: 'Mr Tambourine Man'. This was the Byrds' first appearance on UK television, either via a taped performance sent over from America or simply a record plug with visual accompaniment. This edition of the programme on BBC 1 has not survived.

7 July 1965 *Where The Action Is*: 'Mr Tambourine Man'; 'Feel A Whole Lot Better'. Syndicated by ABC–TV in California, this Dick Clark-hosted show also included Jackie De Shannon, Paul Revere & The Raiders and Steve Alaimo. The Byrds were filmed at a swimming pool. A section of 'Mr Tambourine Man' was broadcast decades later on *Entertainment Tonight* [see 25 June 1988]. Perhaps it was this show that Dickson recalled while I was discussing the Byrds' television appearances with him. "There was one video that I've never seen again that was done at that time," he recalls. "It was 'Mr Tambourine Man'. They had a kaleidoscopic camera effect that they did on it. It was done at a local Hollywood studio. I sent them this special soundtrack with all this new equipment and it was beautiful. I've never been able to get my hands on that to see it again. I think it was ABC, but I'm not sure. Of all the ones we did, that was the one that wasn't embarrassing. It was actually very artful. I was surprised that it didn't surface more. Most of them were in black and white but this was in colour and it was gorgeous – and I never saw it again. It was probably lip-synced but beautifully done, because of the camera work. They were getting several angles and doing some effects that they were experimenting with that day and it was great. I don't know where it went."

15 July 1965 *Top Of The Pops*: 'Mr Tambourine Man'. A repeat showing of the Byrds' footage from the show on 1 July as the record was climbing the charts.

17 July 1965 *Shivaree*: 'All I Really Want To Do'; 'Feel A Whole Lot Better'. The Byrds' second appearance on *Shivaree* also survives on film. Other artistes appearing on the Gene Weed-hosted show were Chris Crosby, Mel Carter, Brady & Grady and Melinda Marx.

17 July 1965 *Hollywood A Go Go*: 'Mr Tambourine Man'; 'Feel A Whole Lot Better'; 'All I Really Want To Do'. Recorded on 23 June at Los Angeles' KHJ–TV, this syndicated show survives in the archives of David Eagle Productions. Hosted by Sam Riddle, the black and white show also featured Jackie Wilson, Ian Whitcomb, the Challengers and Lenny Welch.

TELEVISION APPEARANCES/VIDEOS/DVDS

22 July 1965 *Top Of The Pops*: 'Mr Tambourine Man'. With their single hitting number 1 this week, the Byrds were featured again at the end of the show.

— July 1965 *Teen Town*: unknown. Researcher Christopher Hjort mentions this show, but there are no further details of where or when it was broadcast.

4 August 1965 *Scene At 6:30*: 'Mr Tambourine Man'; 'All I Really Want To Do'. Filmed for Manchester, England's Granada TV, footage of this broadcast has evidently been lost.

5 August 1965 *Where The Action Is*: 'All I Really Want To Do'; 'The Bells Of Rhymney'. Mimed performance filmed on location with swimmers (no doubt emanating from the same source as their previous appearance on 5 July). The show also featured Jewel Akens and Steve Alaimo.

6 August 1965 *Ready, Steady, Go!*: 'Mr Tambourine Man', 'All I Really Want To Do'. Special edition heavily focused to the Byrds during their summer tour of Britain and filmed live. Other guests on this edition included Sonny & Cher, the Who (minus Roger Daltrey), the Walker Brothers, Brian Poole & The Tremeloes, the Rockin' Berries, Tom Jones and the Artwoods.

6 August 1965 *Lloyd Thaxton Show:* 'Chimes Of Freedom'. Back in the States, there was another appearance on the syndicated Thaxton Show.

9 August 1965 *Gadzooks*: 'All I Really Want To Do'. Recorded at London's Television Theatre, this BBC 2 show has not survived. Also appearing were Sonny & Cher (a haunting for the Byrds), Roger Whittaker and Friday Brown. See the main text for the story of how Michael Clarke almost missed the show.

11 August 1965 *Discs A Go-Go:* 'All I Really Want To Do'. Recorded at Television Centre, Bristol, this is another lost appearance. For the third consecutive time, Sonny & Cher share the same programme with the group.

12 August 1965 *Top Of The Pops*: 'All I Really Want To Do'. Sonny & Cher were again on the same programme, promoting 'I Got You Babe', along with a cavalcade of current chart acts, including the Walker Brothers, the Dave Clark Five, the Kinks, the Fourmost, Marianne Faithfull, Jonathan King, the Shadows and Horst Jankowski.

19 August 1965 *Top Of The Pops*: 'All I Really Want To Do'. The Byrds' celebrated performance survives and is now available on the DVD portion of

the box set, *There Is A Season*. The Byrds perform their second single, which had just climbed to number 4 in the UK. Almost inevitably, Sonny & Cher were once again featured.

21 August 1965 *Thank Your Lucky Stars*: 'All I Really Want To Do'. Hosted by Jim Dale, this was the third leading UK pop show of the era. It was broadcast by ABC-TV on ITV. Other guests included the Walker Brothers, the Rockin' Berries, Frank Ifield, Alma Cogan, Barbara Kay and the Transatlantics.

26 August 1965 *Top Of The Pops*: 'All I Really Want To Do'. The Byrds were already back in the States when their single made its third appearance on *Top Of The Pops*. For the umpteenth time, Sonny & Cher are also included on the same programme, this time at their zenith as 'I Got You Babe' has hit the number 1 spot.

— August 1965 French television: 'Mr Tambourine Man'; 'Chimes Of Freedom'; 'Feel A Whole Lot Better'. No further details.

— September 1965 *Ninth Street West*: unknown. Hosted by Sam Riddle, the Byrds' fan club newsletter mentions that the Byrds appeared on the show which was broadcast by KHJ-TV, Los Angeles, CA.

8 September 1965 *Mike Douglas Show*: 'Feel A Whole Lot Better'. This syndicated talk show from Philadelphia may survive in the archives of Eyemark Entertainment. Most memorable for the unique sight of Carl Franzoni dancing to the Byrds, along with the host, Mike Douglas.

16 September 1965 *Shindig!*: 'California Sun'; 'Feel A Whole Lot Better'; 'The Bells Of Rhymney'. Recorded at Los Angeles' ABC studios, this tape has survived. The opening 'California Sun' by the McCoys includes McGuinn singing a few words.

1 October 1965 *Hollywood A-Go-Go*: 'Mr Tambourine Man'; 'Feel A Whole Lot Better'; 'Turn! Turn! Turn!'.

16 October 1965 *Shivaree*: 'Turn! Turn! Turn!'; 'Feel A Whole Lot Better'. Another syndicated show that survives, this was recorded at ABC Television's Los Angeles studio and originally broadcast on KABC Channel 7. The group are also featured backing Dobie Gray on 'My Baby'. On 'Feel A Whole Lot Better' McGuinn wears a folk singer's hat. Also featured on the show were Dobie Gray, Suzy Clark, the Toys and Donovan (who possibly provided the hat).

TELEVISION APPEARANCES/VIDEOS/DVDS

22 October 1965 *Lloyd Thaxton Show*: 'Turn! Turn! Turn!' [assumed]. *The Washington Post* indicates an appearance on this date. Barry McGuire's 'Eve Of Destruction' was also featured.

23 October 1965 *Shindig!*: 'Turn! Turn! Turn!'; 'Chimes Of Freedom'; 'I'm A Loser'. This was the Byrds' third and final appearance on the show. The version of 'I'm A Loser' is a mimed medley featuring the other stars on this edition – Bobby Sherman, Dobie Gray, the Blossoms, the Shangri-Las, Glen Campbell and the Eligibles.

3 November 1965 *Lloyd Thaxton Show*: 'Turn! Turn! Turn!'. With guests the Spokesmen.

6 November 1965 *Hollywood A Go Go*: 'Turn! Turn! Turn!'. Another tape that survives in the archives, this included guest appearances from Ian Whitcomb, Bobby Vee, Len Barry, Duane Eddy, Jeannie Smith and the Bobby Fuller Four. [See also 27 November].

24 November 1965 *Lloyd Thaxton Show*: 'Turn! Turn! Turn!'. A repeat of the syndicated show from 3 November.

27 November 1965 *Hollywood A Go Go*: 'Turn! Turn! Turn!'; 'It Won't Be Wrong'. This black and white tape also survives in the archives. The dating may be suspect as it features the same guest appearances mentioned on 6 November. Perhaps this was a syndicated repeat. 'It Won't Be Wrong' is also listed, seemingly prematurely [see 5 February 1966 entry].

29 November 1965 *Hullabaloo*: 'The Times They Are A-Changin''; 'Do You Believe In Magic?'. This NBC show, in colour, was originally scheduled for 4 October 1965, but was evidently postponed for eight weeks. The version of 'Do You Believe In Magic?' is part of the show's medley. Other acts featured included Michael Landon, Jackie De Shannon, Chad & Jill and Paul Revere & The Raiders.

29 November 1965 *The Big TNT Show*: 'Mr Tambourine Man'; 'The Bells Of Rhymney'; 'Turn! Turn! Turn!'. Recording date: film released in LA on 19 January 1966. This movie, hosted by David McCallum, also features Joan Baez, Ray Charles, Petula Clark, Donovan, Bo Diddley, the Lovin' Spoonful, Roger Miller, the Modern Folk Quartet, the Ronettes and Ike & Tina Turner.

12 December 1965 *Ed Sullivan Show*: 'Turn! Turn! Turn!'; 'Mr Tambourine Man'. Recorded at CBS Studios, New York, this was the Byrds' sole appearance on the Sullivan Show. The performance, in colour, survives, while the programme lists guest appearances from Al Hirt, Alan King, the

Swingle Singers, Barbara McNair, Wayne Newton and the Bratislava Slovakian Folkloric Company.

25 December 1965 *Top Of The Pops*: 'Mr Tambourine Man'. BBC 1's round-up of the year featured the hits that reached number 1 on their chart in 1965, including the Byrds. One of the most memorable shows of the era, hosted by Jimmy Savile, Alan Freeman, Pete Murray and David Jacobs, the songs featured were courtesy of the Beatles ('I Feel Fine'; 'Help!'; 'We Can Work It Out'/'Day Tripper'), Georgie Fame & The Blue Fames ('Yeh, Yeh'), the Moody Blues ('Go Now'), the Righteous Brothers ('You've Lost That Lovin' Feelin''), the Kinks ('Tired Of Waiting For You'), the Seekers ('I'll Never Find Another You'; 'The Carnival Is Over'), Tom Jones ('It's Not Unusual'), the Rolling Stones ('The Last Time'; 'Satisfaction'; 'Get Off Of My Cloud'), Unit 4+2 ('Concrete And Clay'), Sandie Shaw ('Long Live Love'), Elvis Presley ('Crying In The Chapel'), the Hollies ('I'm Alive'), Sonny & Cher ('I Got You Babe'), the Walker Brothers ('Make It Easy On Yourself') and Ken Dodd ('Tears').

26 December 1965 *Top Of The Pops*: 'Mr Tambourine Man'. A repeat of the previous afternoon's show.

1966
19 January 1966 *The Big TNT Show* [see entry for 29 November 1965].

5 February 1966 *Hollywood A Go Go*: 'Mr Tambourine Man'; 'It Won't Be Wrong'; 'Set You Free This Time'; 'Turn! Turn! Turn!'. This was the final episode of the show. On 'Set You Free This Time', McGuinn and Crosby switch their trademark images, with Jim wearing his partner's green suede cape and David sporting granny glasses. The show, hosted by Sam Riddle, also featured James Darren, Freddy Cannon, David Watson, the Everly Brothers, Brenda Bantam & the Bantams, Karen Verros and Bob Lind. The show was supposedly repeated in syndication on 19 February. Footage still exists.

13 February 1966 *Dave Hull's Hullabaloo*. Performance footage of the Byrds onstage, unfortunately without sound, was filmed on this date. Approximately 18 minutes' long, the film also shows the group backstage and in rehearsal. The footage was acquired from the estate of the late fine art photographer John Dietrich (the son of Howard Hughes' Chief Executive Officer, Noah Dietrich) by Byrds' collector Whin Oppice in 2007.

15 February 1966 *Lloyd Thaxton Show:* 'Mr Tambourine Man'; 'Set You Free This Time'. Broadcast in colour, but does not survive.

TELEVISION APPEARANCES/VIDEOS/DVDS

21 February 1966 *Where The Action Is*: 'Set You Free This Time'; 'Turn! Turn! Turn!'. Filmed in black and white on location in the Santa Inez Mountains. The show also features Freddy Cannon and Steve Alaimo. This edition was repeated on 27 February. Footage survives.

22 February 1966 *Murray The K's All-Star Special*: 'Turn! Turn! Turn!'. Famously featuring only four Byrds as Gene Clark had fled the plane to New York before take-off in Chicago. Also featured on the show were the Ramsey Lewis Trio, Jay & The Americans, the Four Tops, Little Anthony & The Imperials, the Four Seasons, Joe Tex and the Shangri-Las. Apparently, no tape survives.

24 March 1966 *Where The Action Is*: 'Set You Free This Time'; 'It Won't Be Wrong'. Evidently filmed at the same time as the 21 February broadcast. McGuinn and Clark sing 'Set You Free This Time' atop a tree. Footage survives in Dick Clark Media Archives of all four Byrds' performances on *Where The Action Is*.

19 June 1966 *Murray The K Special:* unknown, monthly syndicated special. Also featuring Allen & Rossi, Little Anthony & The Imperials, Patty Michaels, Shades Of Blue, the Vibrations, Mitch Ryder and Jackie Wilson. No surviving footage.

16 July 1966 *Summertime On The Pier*: unknown, featured on KYBC-TV, New Jersey [sourced by Christopher Hjort: no further details, no tape exists].

17 September 1966 *Boss City*: unknown. Also featuring the Monkees, the Four Tops, Lee Dorsey, the Sandpipers, Count Five and the Daily Flash. [sourced by C. Hjort: no further details].

15 October 1966 *Clay Cole's Diskotek*: unknown. Also featuring Maxine Brown, the Blues Project, the Zephyrs and Meadowlark Lemon of the Harlem Globetrotters. Recorded at New York's WPIX–TV 11. No known footage survives.

3 December 1966 [recording date]: *The Songmakers*: 'Turn! Turn! Turn!'; 'Milestones'. This US ABC-TV documentary includes a rare excerpt of 'Milestones' filmed during a studio rehearsal. On 'Turn! Turn! Turn!', the Byrds perform with Judy Collins. The show also featured the Mamas & The Papas, Simon & Garfunkel, Dionne Warwick, Smokey Robinson & The Miracles, Judy Collins, Burt Bacharach, Hal David, Johnny Mercer, the Paul Butterfield Blues Band, the Blues Project, Tom Paxton, Henry Mancini and Sammy Fair. The show was broadcast on 24 February 1967. No known complete tape is available.

REQUIEM FOR THE TIMELESS — VOLUME 1

1967

24 February 1967: *The Songmakers* [see entry for 3 December 1966].

5 March 1967 *Drop In*: 'So You Want To Be A Rock 'n' Roll Star'; 'Mr Tambourine Man'; 'Eight Miles High'. Filmed in Stockholm, Sweden, these performances appeared on various videos before being released officially as part of the DVD with the 2006 Byrds box set, *There Is A Season*.

19 March 1967 *Eamonn Andrews Show*: cancelled. Sometimes listed erroneously. Although the Byrds were scheduled to appear on this high-rating UK ITV show in a pre-published itinerary, they failed to secure a booking.

30 March 1967 *Top Of The Pops*: 'So You Want To Be A Rock 'n' Roll Star'. Recorded during their UK trip, several weeks before, this was their *sole* performance of 'So You Want To Be A Rock 'n' Roll Star' on the show. Despite reports elsewhere, there was no repeat. Other guests featured were Cat Stevens, Cliff Richard, Dave Dee, Dozy, Beaky, Mick & Tich, Dusty Springfield, Engelbert Humperdinck, Sandie Shaw, the Alan Price Set, Frank & Nancy Sinatra (on film) and the Jimi Hendrix Experience. Sadly, the performance was evidently wiped and no copy of the tape has since surfaced.

3 April 1967 *Diamoci Del Tu*: 'Mr Spaceman'. Filmed in Milan, Italy, for Radiotelevisione Italiana (RAI), this was recorded during the Byrds' brief visit to the country at the beginning of March, following their sojourn in Sweden. Hillman appears to be playing a Hofner-style bass.

15 April 1967 *Boss City*: unknown. Sourced by C. Hjort, no further details, except that Jefferson Airplane were also on the programme.

25 April 1967 *Inside Pop: The Rock Revolution*: 'Captain Soul'. Broadcast by CBS Network News Special, this one-hour documentary was an ambitious undertaking, partly narrated by conductor Leonard Bernstein. It was most memorable for Brian Wilson performing 'Surf's Up' on piano, a seemingly lost classic that would not be revived until years later as the title track of the Beach Boys' 1971 album. Other artistes included on the show were the Beatles, the Hollies, Herman's Hermits, Frank Zappa, Janis Ian and Tim Buckley. McGuinn was also interviewed and provided some political opinions, which came as a surprise. 'Captain Soul' is featured on the soundtrack.

17 June 1967 *Monterey Pop Festival*: 'Hey Joe'; 'Chimes Of Freedom'; 'He Was A Friend Of Mine'. These selections from the Byrds' appearance at

TELEVISION APPEARANCES/VIDEOS/DVDS

Monterey were belatedly broadcast in 1997 on the VH1 Special, *Monterey Pop: The Lost Performances*.

25 July 1967 *The Tonight Show*: 'Renaissance Fair'; 'Lady Friend'; 'Have You Seen Her Face'. Sadly, Johnny Carson's shows from the Sixties were not archived.

29 July 1967 *American Bandstand*: 'Eight Miles High'; 'Lady Friend'. This tape still exists in the Dick Clark Media Archives.

22 October 1967 *Smothers Brothers Comedy Hour*: 'Mr Spaceman'; 'Goin' Back'.

— October 1967 *Where The Girls Are* [see 23 April 1968 entry].

2 November 1967 *Joey Bishop Show*: unknown. Live performance, presumably including Gene Clark. No tape survives.

4 November 1967 *Boss City*: unknown. Sourced by C. Hjort, who suggests that they were probably promoting 'Goin' Back'. No tape exists, however.

14 November 1967 *Groovy*: 'Goin' Back'. Footage lost, presumed wiped.

1968
23 April 1968 *Where The Girls Are*: 'Mr Spaceman'; 'Good Day Sunshine'. Probably the strangest video of the Byrds – for any number of reasons. Despite the broadcast date, this NBC recording hails back to October 1967 during Gene Clark's short but troubled comeback in the group. It must have puzzled viewers familiar with the Byrds' tortuous history, as by now we were well into the Gram Parsons' era. Even more confusingly, here were the Byrds miming 'Mr Spaceman', a single released in 1966, thereby taking us even further back. One of the segments for the song featured Jimmi Seiter on bass and the Association's Ted Bluechel on drums, performing alongside McGuinn and Clark. Oddly, another part of the song is filmed outdoors, this time with McGuinn, Gene Clark and Michael Clarke. The complete absence of Hillman, and Michael Clarke's missing appearance in the studio, remain unexplained. The rendition of the Beatles' 'Good Day Sunshine' features the show's host, actor/singer Noel Harrison and vocalist Barbara McNair performing with McGuinn, Gene Clark, Jimmi Seiter and Ted Bluechel.

28 April 1968 *Boss City*: 'Eight Miles High'; 'So You Want To Be A Rock 'n' Roll Star'. Previously, this has been wrongly credited as *Sam Riddle's Ninth Street West Show* which had ceased production by this time. *Boss City* was also hosted by Sam Riddle, which explains the confusion. Tape wiped.

11 May 1968 *American Bandstand*: 'Eight Miles High'; 'You Ain't Going Nowhere'. Evidently, this was recorded the same day as the preceding *Boss City*. Regrettably, this performance was not included in the Dick Clark Media Archives.

— May 1968 *Where The Girls Are*: 'Renaissance Fair'; 'Lady Friend'; 'Have You Seen Her Face'. Although I have seen this in tentative television listings, it is a chronologically incorrect reference to the 25 July 1967 edition of *The Tonight Show*. No tape now exists.

28 September 1968 *Playboy After Dark*: [see 28 February 1969]. 'You Ain't Going Nowhere'; 'This Wheel's On Fire'.

1969

28 February 1969 *Playboy After Dark*: 'You Ain't Going Nowhere'; 'This Wheel's On Fire'; 'Mary Had A Little Lamb'. Taped exactly five months before, this colour syndicated show, recorded at CBS' Los Angeles studios, was first seen in Chicago and later reached the West Coast as late as 30 May and 5 July. Hosted by *Playboy* founder Hugh Hefner, who exchanges pleasantries with McGuinn on the show, it also includes the Byrds singing 'Mary Had A Little Lamb' with the entire cast, conducted by Pete Barbutti. Those in attendance include Marvin Gaye, Sally Marr (mother of Lenny Bruce, who provided the Byrds with their first 'paid' gig in 1965), Pat Henry and Marvin Worth. Footage still exists via *The Playboy Channel*.

— March 1969 *La Carabina de Ambrosio*: 'You Ain't Going Nowhere'. During their visit to Mexico, the Byrds evidently appeared on this show, if John York's memory is to be believed. No other details are available.

22 June 1969 *Newport '69*: 'You Ain't Going Nowhere'; 'Sing Me Back Home'; 'Old Blue'. Bootleg video. Evidently, the whole set was not filmed, but these three songs appear on various tapes.

30 June 1969 *Dick Cavett Show*: 'Jesus Is Just Alright'. Recorded live at ABC Television Studios, New York. No known footage has survived.

1970

17 January 1970 *Memphis Talent Party*: 'Jesus Is Just Alright'; 'Mr Tambourine Man'. Mimed versions, including the original Byrds' 1965 recording of 'Mr Tambourine Man', which the Skip Battin era line-up lip-synch with little conviction. Bootleg copies are in regular circulation.

8 February 1970 *Groovy Show*: unknown. A successor to the television show *Groovy*, now hosted by disc jockey Robert W. Morgan, this featured the

Byrds, plus other guests Little Richard, and the Dells. No tape survives to confirm what they played.

24 June 1970 *Journaal*: footage from Dutch television of the Byrds arriving at Amsterdam's Schiphol Airport. No songs though.

27 June 1970 *Stamping Ground*: 'Old Blue'. Available on the video collection *California Screamin' Volume Four* (Castle Hendring/CCTV, 1989).

11 October 1970 *Fanfare: Welcome To Fillmore East:* 'Eight Miles High'; 'Jesus Is Just Alright'; 'Take A Whiff (On Me)'. Recorded by New York's National Educational Television (NET) on the preceding 23 September, this hour-long promotion for Bill Graham's venue also featured Van Morrison, the Allman Brothers, Albert King, Elvin Bishop, the Flock and Sha Na Na. Audio selections of the Byrds performing 'Take A Whiff (On Me)' and 'Jesus Is Just Alright' were later added to the CD *(Untitled)/(Unissued)*, while 'Baby, What You Want Me To Do' and 'I Trust' can be found on the 2006 box set, *There Is A Season*.

1971
10 January 1971 *Fanfare: Flatt And Scruggs Show*: 'You Ain't Going Nowhere'; 'Nothin' To It'. This tribute to Earl Scruggs, recorded the previous year, featured the Byrds fraternizing and playing with the Scruggs family. Hosted by Joan Baez, the show also featured Bob Dylan, Doc Watson, Bill Monroe and the Morris Brothers. CBS released an album version in November 1971, and CBS/Fox later issued a home video of the event titled *Scruggs*. The Public Broadcasting System donated the footage to the Library of Congress Preservation Collection.

18 February 1971 *Top Of The Pops*: 'Chestnut Mare'. This edition has apparently not survived.

6 May 1971 *Top Of The Pops*: 'I Trust (Everything Is Gonna Work Out Alright)'. Also missing, presumed lost.

22 May 1971 *Beat Club*: 'Soldier's Joy'/'Black Mountain Rag'; 'Chestnut Mare'; 'Mr Tambourine Man'; 'So You Want To Be A Rock 'n' Roll Star'; 'Eight Miles High'. Recorded a few days earlier at Bremen Television Studios. Evidently, the acoustic 'Mr Tambourine Man' was omitted from the broadcast, but still exists on tape. 'So You Want To Be A Rock 'n' Roll Star' was not actually broadcast on this date but held over for a subsequent showing as late as 28 October 1972.

27 May 1971 *Disco 2*: 'Jesus Is Just Alright'; 'Take A Whiff (On Me)'; 'Truck Stop Girl'. Recorded on 17 May, this BBC 2 music programme was hosted by Richard Williams. In colour, but presumed wiped.

23 June 1971 *Midweek*: 'Jesus Is Just Alright' (rehearsal); 'You Ain't Going Nowhere'; 'Truck Stop Girl'; 'Medley: 'My Back Pages'/'B.J. Blues'/'Baby, What Do You Want Me To Do'; 'Jamaica Say You Will'; 'Jesus Is Just Alright'; 'Eight Miles High'; 'Mr Tambourine Man'; 'Pretty Boy Floyd'; 'Take A Whiff (On Me)'; 'So You Want To Be A Rock 'n' Roll Star'; 'Mr Spaceman'; 'Roll Over Beethoven'. Recorded on 31 May in the Netherlands, including interviews with McGuinn and Gene Parsons.

22 July 1971 *David Frost Show*: 'So You Want To Be A Rock 'n' Roll Star'; 'Mr Spaceman'; 'Soldier's Joy'/'Black Mountain Rag'; 'Mr Tambourine Man'; 'I Wanna Grow Up To Be A Politician'; 'Citizen Kane'. Available in audio, but film presumed lost.

28 October 1971 *Pop Shop: That's For The Byrds*: 'Lover Of The Bayou'; 'You Ain't Going Nowhere'; 'Truck Stop Girl'; 'Medley: 'My Back Pages'/'B.J. Blues'/'Baby, What Do You Want Me To Do'; 'Soldier's Joy'/'Black Mountain Rag'; 'Pretty Boy Floyd'; 'Take A Whiff (On Me)'; 'Jesus Is Just Alright'; 'Mr Spaceman'. Filmed by Belgium's RTBF TV at the Vorst Nationaal, Brussels, Belgium on 18 May 1971.

1972
18 January 1972 *ITV Today*: 'Roll In My Sweet Baby's Arms'; plus Roger McGuinn interview.

5 February 1972 *Les Byrds A L'Olympia*: 'Lover Of The Bayou'; 'So You Want To Be A Rock 'n' Roll Star'; 'Mr Spaceman'; 'Roll In My Sweet Baby's Arms'; 'Medley: 'My Back Pages'/'B.J. Blues'/'Baby, What Do You Want Me To Do'; 'Eight Miles High'; 'Amazing Grace'; 'Roll Over Beethoven'. Broadcast on France's Channel 2, this featured selections from the Byrds' memorable show at the Paris Olympia on the preceding 22 January. Available in audio, but no known film footage available.

9 March 1972 *Country Suite*: 'Roll In My Sweet Baby's Arms'; 'Soldier's Joy'/'Black Mountain Rag'; 'Mr Tambourine Man'; 'Farther Along'. Broadcast in Nashville and hosted by Billy Ed Wheeler, this was a rare opportunity to see 'Roll In My Sweet Baby's Arms', a song never recorded in the studio by the Byrds. The date of this performance in Nashville evidently took place two months earlier, possibly on 1 January. The tape regularly appears on the bootleg market.

TELEVISION APPEARANCES/VIDEOS/DVDS

28 October 1972 *Beat Club*: 'So You Want To Be A Rock 'n' Roll Star'. Originally recorded back in May 1971 [see broadcast details for 22 May 1971], this belated showing meant that only 'Mr Tambourine Man' remained unseen.

1973
2 February 1973 *Midnight Special*: 'Mr Tambourine Man', 'So You Want To Be A Rock 'n' Roll Star'. A unique opportunity to see the latter-day Byrds (McGuinn, Battin and White) performing with drummer Jim Moon. The show, hosted by Helen Reddy, included guest appearances from Ike & Tina Turner, Curtis Mayfield, Don McLean, Rare Earth, Kenny Rankin, the Impressions and George Carlin. Complete footage exists.

1975
1 November *Banjoman* (film): 'Roll Over Beethoven'; 'Mr Tambourine Man'. Recorded back on 20 January 1973 with Earl Scruggs, His Family & Friends at Kansas State University, Manhattan, Kansas, this film was finally issued in November 1975. In addition to the concert, the film features early footage of Earl Scruggs and among the guests are Joan Baez, Ramblin' Jack Elliott, Tracy Nelson, Mother Earth, David Bromberg, the Nitty Gritty Dirt Band, Doc Watson and Merle Watson. The Byrds line-up, featuring John Guerin on drums, were featured on the soundtrack album, which was not issued in the US until as late as January 1977. They could be seen performing 'Mr Tambourine Man' and 'Roll Over Beethoven'. The latter track also made a belated reappearance on the 2006 box set, *There Is A Season*.

1988
25 June 1988 *Entertainment This Week*: 'Mr Tambourine Man'. Recorded eight days before broadcast, this US programme featured news of the Byrds trio (McGuinn, Crosby and Hillman) performing under that name for a show at the Ash Grove. Included in the programme was a version of 'Mr Tambourine Man' recorded by the original five in July 1965 from *Where The Action Is*.

1990
18 April 1990 *After Hours*: 'Eight Miles High'. Recorded at the Roy Orbison Tribute on 24 February 1990, this featured the 'Byrds' trio (McGuinn, Crosby & Hillman) talking about their career and reunion.

6 May 1990 *Roy Orbison Concert Tribute*: 'Turn! Turn! Turn!'; 'Mr Tambourine Man'; 'Eight Miles High'. Recorded on 24 February at the

Universal Amphitheatre, Los Angeles, this belated showing of the *Roy Orbison Concert Tribute* on CNN regrettably omitted 'Eight Miles High' from the broadcast. The star-studded evening included guest appearances from John Fogerty, Emmylou Harris, Larry Gatlin, Levon Helm, John Hiatt, John Lee Hooker, Chris Isaak, Booker T. Jones, B.B. King, k.d. lang, Benny Mardones, Mike McDonald, Iggy Pop, Bonnie Raitt, the Stray Cats, Was (Not Was), Dwight Yoakam, the Shrunkenheads, Dean Stockwell and Patrick Swayze. The Byrds line-up was augmented by guitarist/vocalist John Jorgenson and drummer Steve Duncan. Audio versions of 'Turn! Turn! Turn!' and 'Mr Tambourine Man' (on which Bob Dylan joined them) were later featured on the first Byrds box set in 1990.

8 August 1990 *Showbiz Today*: 'Mr Tambourine Man'; 'Eight Miles High'; 'So You Want To Be A Rock 'n' Roll Star'. Another appearance from the three Byrds (McGuinn, Crosby & Hillman) promoting the 1990 box set on which they included four newly recorded songs in Nashville. On the show, they discuss their past career, interspersed with 'Mr Tambourine Man' (from *Hollywood A Go Go*), 'Eight Miles High' (from the Roy Orbison Tribute) and 'So You Want To Be A Rock 'n' Roll Star' (from their 'reunion' show at the Ventura Theater on 6 January 1989).

Some unofficial DVDs featuring selections of some television appearances in questionable quality are around, plus the double DVD documentary film, *The Byrds: Under Review*.

Index

Singles releases are in roman type and albums are in *italics*. Persons listed in parentheses refer to the name of the recording or performing artists of the particular song. Composers, where cited, are listed separately under their own names.

'About Love' (Rice, Rice, Hillman & Pedersen), 822
'Absolute Happiness' (Byrds), 560, 571, 586, 769
Acuff, Roy, 432
'Adios Terri' (Gene Clark), 776
Adler, Lou, 111–113, 188–189, 191, 350, 362
Adzick, Mark, 648–649
Africa/Brass (John Coltrane), 222
After The Storm (Crosby, Stills & Nash), 783
Aftermath (Rolling Stones), 293
Agnew, Spiro, Vice President, 547–548
'Airport Song, The' (Byrds), 57–58, 230, 271, 800
'Alabama Jubilee' (Clarence White), 626
Albert, Howard, 681–682, 684–688, 704
Albert, Ron, 681–682, 684–688, 704
'Alberta' (Roger McGuinn), 803
Ali, Muhammad, 95, 403
'Alice's Restaurant' (Arlo Guthrie), 578
'All I Have Are Memories' (Byrds), 437, 479, 809, 840
'All I Really Want To Do' (Bob Dylan), 101, 204, 281
'All I Really Want To Do' (Byrds), 8, 14, 101, 115, 125–127, 132–133, 140, 155, 160–161, 164–165, 170, 182, 189, 195, 253, 263, 281, 543, 798–799
'All I Really Want To Do' (Cher), 125–127, 164–165, 182, 187
'All Night Long' (Roger McGuinn), 638
'All The Things' (Byrds), 544, 550, 826
'All The Things' (1992 'musical' version), 796
All You Need Is Cash (television 'documentary'), 692
'All You Need Is Love' (Beatles), 353, 361
Allison, Mose, 798
'Almost Cut My Hair' (Crosby, Stills, Nash & Young), 538, 640
Alpert, Herb, & The Tijuana Brass, 316
Altham, Keith, 166–168, 173

'Amazing Grace' (Byrds), 563, 827
'Amazing Grace' (David Crosby), 784
America For Me (poem) (Henry Van Dyke), 713–714, 724
'America For Me' (Roger McGuinn), 713–714, 724
'America's Great National Pastime' (Byrds), 584, 602
American Dream (Crosby, Stills, Nash & Young), 736–737, 782, 787–788
'American Girl' (Roger McGuinn), 638, 680
'American Girl' (Tom Petty & The Heartbreakers), 638, 680
'Anathea' (David Crosby), 31
Anderson, Lynn, 427
Animals, The, 2, 64, 146, 153, 158, 192, 226
Another Side Of Bob Dylan (Bob Dylan), 129, 246
Another Stoney Evening (Crosby & Nash), 787
'Antique Sandy' (Byrds), 577, 584–585
'Anything At All' (Crosby, Stills & Nash), 667
Appalachian Swing (Kentucky Colonels), 505
Archainbound, George, 477
'Are You Afraid To Die' (Louvin Brothers), 473
'Argonaut, The' (Roger McGuinn), 797
Arigatou Baby (John York), 843
Ark, The (Chad & Jeremy), 498
'Armstrong, Aldrin And Collins' (Byrds), 512, 528–529
Aronowitz, Al, 311
Art And Paul, 24
'Artificial Energy' (Byrds), 395, 399–400, 411, 687, 753, 767
Ashby, Hal, 624
Asher, Jane, 153
Asher, Peter, 153, 560
Aspinall, Neil, 161
Association, The, 350, 436
At Edwards Barn (Chris Hillman & Herb Pedersen), 824
Atkins, Susan, 531

Autry, Gene, & The Cass County Boys, 477–478
Avedon & Penn, 275
Axton, Hoyt, 24, 27–28, 34, 803
Azoff, Irving, 121

'B.B. Class Road' (Byrds), 583
Babitz, Eve, 540
'Baby Don't Go' (Sonny & Cher), 187–188
'Baby What Do You Want Me To Do' (Byrds), 101, 443, 501–502, 829
'Baby What You Want Me To Do' (Jimmy Reed), 101, 501
Bacall, Lauren, 139
Bach, J.S., 102, 110, 205, 288, 543, 804, 814
Back From Rio (Roger McGuinn), 793–794, 832–833
'Back From Rio Interlude' (Roger McGuinn), 794
Back Porch Majority, The, 29
'Back Street Mirror' (David Hemmings), 366
'Back Street Mirror' (Gene Clark), 366
'Backstage Pass' (McGuinn, Clark & Hillman), 686–687
'Bad Night At The Whiskey' (Byrds), 495–497, 501, 768
Baez, Joan, 85, 164, 192, 236, 297, 499, 516, 635, 798
'Bag Full Of Money' (Byrds), 595, 828
'Bag Full Of Money' (Roger McGuinn), 595, 828
Bakersfield Bound (Chris Hillman & Herb Pedersen), 791
Baldry, Long John, 334
Ball, Earl, 437–438, 474
'Ballad Of Easy Rider' (Byrds), 523, 536, 564, 567, 685, 810–811, 827
Ballad Of Easy Rider (Byrds), 521–531, 533–534, 545, 547, 565–566, 768, 802, 810, 813, 815
Ballad Of Evergreen Blueshoes, The (Evergreen Blueshoes), 520
Balladeer, The (Hoyt Axton), 803
Band, The, 426, 481, 498, 516, 535–536, 560, 562, 641
'Bang Bang' (Cher), 259
Bangles, The, 738
Banjoman (soundtrack), 829
Barbata, Johnny, 619
Barish, Jesse, 841
Barrick, John, 141, 177, 240
Barrymore, John, 386
Barrymore, John, Jr, 182
Basement Tapes, The (Bob Dylan), 426–427, 493, 498
Basie, Count, 45, 140, 231

Bath Festival, 536–537
Battin, Jackie, 554
Battin, Patricia, 842
Battin, Skip, 15, 185, 520–521, 536, 539–540, 542, 544–547, 553–554, 559–561, 565–569, 571, 578, 582, 584–589, 591, 593–596, 598, 602–604, 606–609, 721–722, 747, 762, 766, 769, 826, 828, 841–843
Baxter, Les, 6, 32
'Be A Soldier' (Terry Day), 80
'Beach Ball' (City Surfers), 26, 54, 80, 365, 797
'Beach Ball' (Roger McGuinn), 797, 804
Beach Boys, The, 26, 73, 80–81, 83, 178, 241, 253, 293, 300–301, 305, 338, 530–531, 623, 641, 664, 725, 756, 832, 838–839, 845–846
Beatle Bob (see Bob Roberts)
Beatles For Sale (Beatles), 97
Beatles, The, 1–4, 6–8, 13–15, 19, 21, 27–29, 38–39, 54–56, 59, 63–64, 66, 68–71, 73, 75–76, 87, 89, 97, 107, 110, 126–127, 133, 139, 148–150, 156, 158–160, 163–164, 167–168, 170–174, 176–182, 184, 187, 191, 194, 201, 212, 219–220, 223, 238, 242, 244, 247, 251, 255, 260–261, 264, 271, 274–275, 292–293, 298–299, 301–306, 313, 315, 317, 322–323, 330, 332–333, 335, 337–338, 348–349, 353, 356, 361, 378, 399, 438, 440–441, 455, 481, 483, 497, 510, 519, 548, 587, 636, 650, 687, 692–693, 728, 738, 756, 794, 797, 804, 806, 813–814, 822, 838–839, 845
Beatty, Warren, 138
Beau Brummels, The, 87
Beaver, Paul, 403, 414, 495
Beckett, Barry, 708
Bee Gees, The, 686–688
Beefeaters, The, 44, 54–55, 73, 225, 275, 797
Bees, The, 492
'Before The Beginning' (Peter Jay & The Jaywalkers), 170
Beggar's Opera, The (play) (John Gay), 285
Bell, Alexander Graham, 429
Bell, William, 474
'Bells Of Rhymney, The' (Byrds), 67, 96, 102, 108, 112, 130–132, 140, 143, 155, 160, 203, 223, 334, 373, 415, 439, 442, 570, 744, 750, 794, 832
'Bells Of Rhymney, The' (Cher), 125
'Bells Of Rhymney, The' (Gram Parsons/Shilos), 415
'Bells Of Rhymney, The' (Judy Collins), 202

INDEX

'Bells Of Rhymney, The' (Manassas, with Roger McGuinn), 614
'Bells Of Rhymney, The' (Pete Seeger), 131–132, 203
Bennett, Tony, 69
Bergen, Candice, 523, 558
Bergman, Peter, 337
Berline, Byron, 525, 546, 564, 571–572, 586, 645
Bernal, Carlos, 454–455, 459, 461–465, 467–468, 484, 487, 489–491, 493, 552–557, 561, 585, 595, 599, 603, 605, 711–712, 747, 848
Berry, Bruce, 599, 639
Berry, Chuck, 42, 58, 89, 428, 515, 527, 599, 768
Best Of Lord Buckley, The (Lord Buckley), 100
'Big Bad Mama' (Gene Clark), 776
Big Brother & The Holding Company, 350
Big Three, The, 282
Big TNT Show, The (film), 235
Bird (film), 843
Birds, The, 72–73, 152, 255
Birds, The (film), 150
'Birdses' (Dino Valenti), 72–73
Black, Big, 354
Black, Cilla, 2
Blackburn & Snow, 200, 351, 799
Blaine, Hal, 81, 83–84, 115, 119, 188, 371, 591, 623, 739
Blake, William, 568
Blakley, Ronee, 635
Blind Faith, 516, 627
Blonde On Blonde (Bob Dylan), 293, 426
Blood On The Tracks (Bob Dylan), 776, 844
Blood, Sweat & Tears, 516
Bloomfield, Mike, 146, 355, 825
'Blowin' In The Wind' (Bob Dylan), 857
'Blue Canadian Rockies' (Byrds), 437, 444, 477–478
Blue Canadian Rockies (film), 477
'Blue Canadian Rockies' (Gene Autry & The Cass County Boys), 477–478
Blue Diamond Boys, The, 47–48
'Blue Grass Chopper' (Hillmen), 48
Blue Grass Favorites (Scottsville Squirrel Barkers), 47
Blue Oyster Cult, 579–580
'Blue Ribbons' (Joe Meyers & The Sharks), 29
'Blue Suede Shoes' (Byrds), 493
'Blue Suede Shoes' (Carl Perkins), 493
'Blue Suede Shoes' (Elvis Presley), 493
'Blueberry Hill' (Fats Domino), 568
'Bluebirds Over The Mountain' (Beach Boys), 531
Bluechel, Ted, 436

Blues Magoos, The, 351
'Boatman' (Roger McGuinn), 802
Bob Dylan Greatest Hits (Bob Dylan), 367
Bock, Dick, 33, 92
Bogart, Humphrey, 96, 386
Bonney, William ('Billy The Kid'), 476, 625
Bono, Sonny, 111, 125–127, 166, 195–196
Bonzo Dog Doo-Dah Band, 14
Booker T & The MGs, 350
Bopp, Linda, 99, 141, 146, 247, 696
'Born To Be Wild' (Steppenwolf), 522
'Born To Rock 'n' Roll' (Byrds), 591, 599, 617–618, 828
'Born To Rock 'n' Roll' (Roger McGuinn), 618, 634
'Borrowing Time' (Byrds), 619
'Boston' (Byrds), 58, 87, 108, 745
Boston Symphony Orchestra, 577
'Both Of Us (Bound To Lose)' (Manassas), 644
'Bound To Fall' (Brewer & Shipley), 806
'Bound To Fall' (Byrds), 806
Bowie, David, 451
Bown, Alan, 14
Boyle, Katie, 4
Boz, 166
Brando, Marlon, 182–183, 813
'Brass Buttons' (Gram Parsons), 627
'Breezes Of Patchouli' (Donovan), 159
Brewer & Shipley, 806
Brewer, Chrissie (see Chrissie Oakes)
Brewer, Mike, 806
Brickman, Marshall, 32
Briggs, Billy, 416
Bringing It All Back Home (Bob Dylan), 7, 100, 112, 195, 827
'Brisbane Ladies' (Hoyt Axton), 803
'Brisbane Ladies' (Roger McGuinn), 803
'Bristol Steam Convention Blues' (Byrds), 586, 828
Brooks, Elkie, 166
Broonzy, Big Bill, 23
'Brotherhood Of The Blues' (David Crosby), 34
Brown, James, 95
Brown, Michael, 24
Browne, Jackson, 529, 572–573, 575, 583, 727, 768–769, 783, 810
Brubeck, Dave, 40
Bruce & Terry, 80, 198
Bruce, Lenny, 25, 88–89, 231, 856
Brumley, Tom, 789
Bryson, Bill, 717
Buchanan, Bob, 476
Buchanan, George, 856
'Buckaroo' (Byrds), 494, 826
Buckley, Lord, 32, 89, 93, 100, 856
Buckley, Tim, 351, 447, 549

'Buffalo Skinners' (Roger McGuinn), 802
Buffalo Springfield, The, 282–283, 312, 331, 350, 352, 357–359, 377, 379, 383, 517, 540, 600, 632, 831
Buffalo Springfield Again (Buffalo Springfield), 540
'Bugler' (Byrds), 46, 577–578, 583–584, 602, 769
'Build It Up' (Byrds), 811
Burdon, Eric, & The Animals, 350
Burnett, T-Bone, 635
Burrito Deluxe (Flying Burrito Brothers), 428, 537, 583, 626
Burroughs, William, 257
Burton, James, 469, 627
Bush, George, President, 771
Bush, George W., President, 817, 820, 823
'But You're Mine' (Sonny & Cher), 188
Butchie (see 'Butchie' Cho)
Butler, Anya, 136, 321, 421, 445–446, 489–491, 711
Butler, Michael, 549
Butler, Richard Cadbury, 136
Butterfield Blues Band, The, 516
Butterfield, Paul, 145, 246, 516
'Bye Bye Baby' (McGuinn, Clark & Hillman), 685–686, 708
Byrd, Admiral, 73
Byrdhouse, 725
Byrdmaniax (Byrds), 15, 558–575, 577, 581–583, 590, 606, 608, 627, 638, 680, 767, 769, 827–828
Byrds, The,
  American Bandstand appearance, 436
  Ballad Of Easy Rider, recording/appraisal of, 512, 521–530, 534
  Bath Festival (1970) appearance, 536–537
  Battin, Skip, appointment, 520–521
  Battin, Skip, death, 841–843
  Battin, Skip, firing, 606
  beach incident/fracas, 207–211
  Beatles, meetings/relationship with, 156–157, 173, 176–180, 223, 302–305, 333
  Big TNT Show, appearance in , 235
  British tour (1965), 8–9, 148–175
  British tour (1971), 562–563
  Byrdmaniax, recording/appraisal of, 559–560, 564–574
  Byrds, recording/appraisal of, 597–601, 612–613, 615–622, 658–659
  CAFF, involvement in, 310–312, 331–332
  Capitol Theatre, Passaic, N.J. (1973) final appearance, 608–611
  Caravan Of Stars tour (1965), 222, 236–237
  CBS Byrds, break-up of, 606–608

CBS Records, first signing, 70–72
CBS Records, modification/renewal of contract, 99, 419–420
Ciro's residency, 78, 99–103, 105–113, 123
Clark, Gene, death, 778, 862
Clark, Gene, leaving group, 10, 13, 249–251, 262–280, 390–394
Clarke, Michael, appointment, 39, 42–43
Clarke, Michael, death, 780–781, 862
Clarke, Michael, leaving group, 395–396
Cosmopolitan spread, 92–93
country music, shift towards, 422–433, 436
court case/conflict over Byrds name, 749, 753–761
Crosby, David, firing of, 13, 51–52, 376, 380–385, 861
Dickson, Jim, death, 855–872
Dickson, Jim, firing as manager, 347–349
Dr Byrds & Mr Hyde, recording/appraisal of, 497–502
draft problems, 136–138
drug use during Byrds' period, 96, 141, 153–154, 171, 177, 179–180, 240–241, 259–261, 290–291, 340–341, 363, 391, 552–554, 557
Dylan, Bob, connection with, 7, 63–66, 100–104, 182–184, 227, 287–288, 472, 518, 535–536, 562, 624–625, 857
early recordings of, 44, 54–60, 508, 738–741, 745–746
ersatz Byrds/'tribute' bands/partial 'Byrds', 746–748, 762–764
Farther Along, recording/appraisal of, 577, 580–586
Fifth Dimension, recording/appraisal of, 291–298
film, thwarted ambitions to complete, 285–287, 366
first number 1 single, reaction to, 118
first paid gig, 88–89
first television appearance, 104–105
Flying Burritos Brothers, concert collaborations, 504–506
Fonda, Jane, Independence Day Party appearance, 138–140
formation of group, 21, 36, 42–43, 50
Grand Ole Opry appearance, 430–433
Hall of Fame induction, 770–773
Hillman, Chris, appointment, 45, 49–50
Hillman, Chris, departure from group, 489–490
Hullabaloo appearance, 119, 282
image, 81, 119–121, 123–124, 161, 166–168, 170, 247, 260–261
influence of group, 19, 281–282, 338–339, 738

INDEX

Byrds, The (*contd*)
  instruments, purchase of, 66–67
  Kelley, Kevin, death, 840–841
  Kelley, Kevin, dismissal, 485–487
  Kennedy, Robert F. ('SRO for RFK' show), 452–453
  Lincoln Folk Festival (1971) appearance, 576–577
  Manassas Byrds, 608–611
  Melcher, Terry, appointment as producer, 80–81, 508
  Melcher, Terry, death, 844–846
  Melcher, Terry, firing of, 232–235, 563–566, 590
  Middle Earth, London (1968) appearance, 441–444
  Midwest/coast to coast tour (1965), 140–147
  Monterey Pop Festival (1967) appearance, 349–350, 353–359, 858
  'Mr Tambourine Man', rehearsal/recording of, 60–62, 81–86
  Mr Tambourine Man, first album, recording/appraisal of, 114, 116, 127–135
  naming of group, 71–74
  Nashville visit, 423, 425, 427–433
  Newport Pop Festival (1968) appearance, 470
  Notorious Byrd Brothers, The, recording/appraisal of, 370–371, 376–377, 398–413, 440
  original Byrds reunions, 588–589, 597–601, 612–613, 615–622, 770–773
  Parsons, Gene, appointment as drummer, 485–486
  Parsons, Gene, firing, 594
  Parsons, Gram, arrival, 13, 415, 417–418
  Parsons, Gram, death, 16, 628–629
  Parsons, Gram, leaving, 456–461
  Piper Club, Rome (1968) appearance, 439–440
  Playboy After Dark (1968) appearance, 493
  radio ban threatened, 11, 253–257, 290–291
  raga rock/Eastern music exponents, 176–177, 222, 242–245, 251–253
  Rainbow London (1972) appearance, 580
  Ready, Steady, Go! appearance, 8, 157, 165
  Rolling Stones' tour, 116–118
  Royal Albert Hall (1968) appearance, 455
  Royal Albert Hall (1971) appearance, 563
  Seiter, Jim 'Jimmi', appointment as road manager, 301
  Shindig! appearance, 118, 124
  Sonny & Cher, rivalry, 125–127, 165–166, 181–182, 187–188, 195
  South African tour, 446, 461–468, 482–483
  Spector, Larry, appointment as manager, 344–347
  stage act, criticisms of, 13–14, 158–160, 164–175, 301, 305–306, 339–343, 380, 391–395
  Stanton, Allen, relationship with, leaving of, 299–300
  Stonehenge visit, 441, 445–446
  Sweetheart Of The Rodeo, recording/appraisal of, 427–430, 437–438, 449, 471–482
  Taylor, Derek, appointment of, 96–98
  Taylor, Derek, death, 836–840
  Taylor, Derek, Farewell Party, 434–435
  Tickner, Eddie, death, 846–849, 865
  Tonight Show appearance, 366, 380
  Top Of The Pops appearances, 2, 8, 15, 161, 334, 564
  trio, brief period working as, 397–398, 414
  Trip residency, 184–186, 247
  Turn! Turn! Turn!, recording/appraisal of, 201, 206, 223–234
  (Untitled), recording/appraisal of, 535, 538–539
  Usher, Gary, appointment as producer, 300
  Usher, Gary, death, 763–764
  Usher, Gary, leaves as producer, 497–498
  Village Gate appearance, 307–308
  volatility/fighting/conflict within, 51–52, 75–77, 91, 116, 206–221, 228, 267–268, 339–343, 350–353, 355–360, 365, 369–372, 374–385, 387, 390–396, 404–405, 410–412, 438, 458–460, 466, 489, 503–504, 507, 590–593, 596, 606, 658–660, 722, 858
  Where The Action Is appearance, 140
  Where The Boys Are appearance, 436
  Whisky A Go-Go appearances, 13, 306, 341–342, 373–374, 388, 493, 496, 555, 831
  White, Clarence, appointment of, 469
  White, Clarence, death, 15, 626
  York, John, appointment of, 492
  York, John, firing, 518–520
  Younger Than Yesterday, recording/appraisal of, 309, 317–329, 335–336
Byrds (Byrds), 15, 48, 591, 597–601, 604, 607, 612, 615–624, 631, 644, 658–659, 829–830
Byrds Celebration, 819, 842
Byrds' Greatest Hits, The (Byrds), 367–368
Byrds, The (box set) (Byrds), 763–770, 798, 808–811, 827, 861

Caesar & Cleo, 111
CAFF (Community Action For Facts And Freedom), 311–312, 331–332, 337, 345, 349
Cajun Gib & Gene, 486, 499–500
'California Dreamin'' (Beach Boys), 832
'California Dreamin'' (Mamas & The Papas), 281
California Stopover (Johnny Darrell), 768
'Camera' (Crosby, Stills & Nash), 783
Camp, Hamilton (aka Bob Camp), 32, 36, 228–229, 856–857, 867–868
Campbell, Glen, 82–83
'Campdown Race' (Stephen Foster), 232
'Can't Buy Me Love' (Beatles), 38
'Candy' (Byrds), 501, 809, 829
Candy (film), 500–501, 510, 829
Candy (film soundtrack), 500, 510, 829
Candy (novel) (Terry Southern), 93, 510
Canned Heat, 516
Captain & Tennille, The, 605
'Captain Soul' (Byrds), 297, 505, 753, 765
'Captain Video' (Skip Battin), 595
'Car Phone' (Roger McGuinn), 794
Cardenas, Rene, 33
Cardiff Rose (Roger McGuinn), 636–638, 681, 768, 809, 844
Carlos, Walter, 495
Caron, Leslie, 139
Carpenter, John, 337
Carr, Gary, 46
Carradine, David, 638, 724, 778
Carradine, Linda, 555–556, 562–563, 573, 580, 582, 587, 605, 624–625, 635, 638, 724
Carroll, Diahann, 138
'Carry Me' (Crosby & Nash), 641, 786
'Carry Me Home' (Chris Hillman), 792
Carson, Johnny, 352, 366
Carter, Carlene, 846
Carter, June, 525
Carter-Fea, Jim, 156
Carthy, Martin, 576
Casanova, Jack, 728, 730, 733, 736
Case, Peter, 725
Cash, Johnny, 192, 498
Cassidy, Ed, 398
Castagna, William J., Judge, 753, 757–759
'Castanet Dance' (Roger McGuinn), 804
Castaways, The, 486
'Catch The Wind' (Donovan), 159
Cates, Joseph, 65
'Cathy's Clown' (Everly Brothers), 5
Cavanaugh, Page, 32, 856
'Cease To Exist' (Charles Manson), 531
Cellar Full Of Noise, A (autobiography) (Brian Epstein), 97

Chad & Jeremy, 142, 497–498
Champion The Wonder Horse, 477
Chandler, Gene, 6
'Change Is Now' (Byrds), 373, 407–408, 422, 440, 481, 501, 767, 806, 830
'Changing Heart' (Byrds), 617, 829
Chaplin, Blondie, 719
Chaplin, Charlie, 315
'Charisma' (Bud Shank/David Crosby), 868
Charles, Ray, 34, 170, 231, 477
Charlesworth, Chris, 631
Cheech & Chong, 690
Cher, 111, 125–127, 146, 164, 166–167, 259
'Cherry Pie' (Skip & Flip), 520
'Chestnut Mare' (Byrds), 15, 24, 543–544, 547, 550, 563–564, 570, 580, 584, 610, 635, 685, 724, 765, 796, 814
'Chestnut Mare' (McGuinn & Clark), 666
'Chestnut Mare' (1992 'musical' version), 796
'Chestnut Mare' (Roger McGuinn), 723, 769, 804
Chicago, 515
'Chicago' (Crosby, Stills, Nash & Young), 640
'Child Of Our Times' (Barry McGuire), 113
'Child Of The Universe' (Byrds), 500, 685
'Chimes Of Freedom' (Bob Dylan), 60, 205, 646, 725, 808, 857
'Chimes Of Freedom' (Byrds), 60, 116, 132, 134–135, 155, 159–160, 165, 204, 354, 373, 434, 439, 442, 455, 570, 646, 749–751, 808, 840
'Chimes Of Freedom' (Roger McGuinn & Chris Hillman), 791
Cho, 'Butchie', 99, 103–104, 136, 141, 146, 249, 346, 871
'Christian Life, The' (Byrds), 203, 437, 443, 473–474, 505, 669, 768, 809
'Christian Life, The' (Louvin Brothers), 473–474
'Christian Life, The' (Roger McGuinn), 669
'Christian Life, The' (Roger McGuinn & Chris Hillman), 791
'Christine's Tune' (Flying Burrito Brothers), 503
Churchill, Winston, 5
'Circle Of Minds' (Byrds), 800
Ciro's (nightclub), 96, 98–112, 114, 123, 125, 127–129, 131–133, 135, 158, 166, 184, 188, 215, 247, 268, 270, 274, 283, 286, 297, 300, 307, 311, 339, 345–346, 385–386, 415, 434, 436, 438, 470, 510, 520, 670, 763, 771, 791, 822, 830, 838
'Citizen Kane' (Byrds), 560, 569, 584
'Citizen Kane' (Skip Battin), 569

INDEX

'City' (Roger McGuinn & Chris Hillman, Featuring Gene Clark), 706
City (Roger McGuinn & Chris Hillman, Featuring Gene Clark), 701, 704–708
City Surfers, The, 26, 797
Clancy Brothers, The, With Tommy Makem, 293
Clapton, Eric, 671, 795
Claremont Dragon (John York), 843
Clark, Carlie (Gene's former wife), 701
Clark, Dave, 151, 153
Clark, Dick, 42, 222, 257, 294
Clark, Gene, 8, 10–11, 13, 17–19, 21, 28–30, 35–38, 42–43, 48–49, 51–53, 55–59, 61–62, 64, 66, 68, 70, 72–75, 81–82, 85–87, 89–90, 92–93, 99, 105, 107, 112, 114–119, 128–130, 133, 136–137, 143, 146, 153, 161, 168, 178–179, 186–187, 196–197, 199–200, 202, 205–212, 215, 217–221, 225–231, 236–241, 247–251, 254–255, 257–258, 260–282, 286–288, 291–292, 299–300, 303–304, 306–308, 320, 330, 338, 343, 366, 368–369, 385, 387–394, 403, 406, 413, 418, 420–421, 434–436, 438, 492–494, 537–539, 597–601, 613, 616–620, 625, 632, 645–649, 651–652, 654–667, 669, 671, 673–699, 701–709, 715, 718–721, 726–727, 739–741, 743, 745–750, 752–753, 756, 759, 763–767, 770–779, 782, 798–799, 804–805, 811–812, 814–815, 828–829, 831, 836, 838, 840, 852–853, 858–862, 867, 871
  absences/leaving of McGuinn, Clark & Hillman, 697–698, 701–704, 708
  alcohol abuse/drinking, 17, 153, 199, 269–270, 391, 434–435, 625, 654–655, 660–661, 682, 703, 709, 775–778
  autobiography ambition, 861
  birth, 28
  Byrds' CBS contract, 70, 99
  'Byrds' '20th Anniversary Tour' involvement, 719, 746–747
  childhood, 29
  Cinegrill gig, final performance, 776–777
  Clarke, Michael, relationship with, 42, 136–137, 237, 272–273, 393, 779
  communication skills, lack of, 18, 187, 599
  Crosby, David, relationship/conflict with, 36, 53, 75, 89, 92, 206, 229, 236, 267–269, 272
  custody loss of children, 655
  dangerous driving, 240, 775–776
  Davis, Jesse Ed, friendship with, 613, 703
  death, 19, 778, 840, 862
  demotion on *Byrds* box set, 765–766, 829
  Dickson, Jim, relationship with, 199, 209–210, 263, 269, 538, 719, 859–862, 871
  Dillard & Clark work, 494, 537, 600
  divorce, 655
  dominance at start of Byrds' career, 51, 89, 107
  draft evasion, 136–137, 403
  drug use/abuse, 153, 239–240, 248–249, 269–270, 601, 677–679, 690, 694–695, 697–698, 702–703, 709, 774–777, 859
  Dylan, Bob, relationship with, 64, 215, 225, 248, 265, 388, 618
  early groups, 29–30
  'Eight Miles High', composing of, 254–255, 257–258, 266, 280
  exile from 'Byrds' reunion, 752–753, 756, 763–765, 811, 861
  extraterrestrial interests, 687, 776
  fall into cult fringes, 647–648, 718–720
  fear of flying/reluctance to tour, 236, 249–250, 262–263, 269–272, 275–277, 299, 390–393, 613, 695, 702
  financial extravagances, 143, 388, 699
  Firebyrd recording, 718–719
  first recording ['Blue Ribbons'], 29
  funeral, 779
  Gene Clark With The Gosdin Brothers, recording of/reaction to, 300, 304, 385
  guitar work/usurpation as guitarist, 43, 66, 75, 89, 92, 206, 221, 267–268, 368–369
  gum disease, 128, 775
  gun use/accidentally shooting goats, 625
  Hall of Fame induction, 770–774
  Hillman, Chris, relationship with, 266, 392, 435, 664, 675–676, 694–696, 698–699, 718–719, 764, 853
  image, 8, 93, 119, 161, 168, 186, 208, 238–239, 260, 262, 279, 389–390
  Japan tour (1979), 695
  Jet Set formation, 21, 30, 35–38
  Kaye, Thomas Jefferson, relationship with, 17, 646–647, 654–655, 681, 697
  leaving Byrds, 10, 13, 249–251, 262–280, 390–394, 261–280, 286, 299
  Levy, Jackie, relationship with, 237–238, 248, 273
  McGuinn, Clark & Hillman, formation of, 662–666, 669
  McGuinn, Clark & Hillman saga, 666–709
  McGuinn, Jim/Roger, relationship with, 30, 35–36, 249–250, 255, 265–266, 270, 272–273, 389, 392, 403, 406, 421, 597, 625, 661–666, 698–699, 777
  Messina, Terri, relationship with, 655, 687, 690, 692–693, 697–698, 702–703, 772, 775–776

Clark, Gene (*contd.*)
  muscle strength, 8, 119, 208–209, 240, 269, 279, 696
  naming of Byrds, alleged involvement in, 72–74
  nervous breakdown, 249–250, 269–273, 277–278, 390–394, 702
  neurotic/self-destructive tendencies, 276–277, 390–394, 434–435, 625, 652, 677, 695, 774–778
  New Christy Minstrels induction, 29–30
  No Other achievement/appraisal, 19, 646–647, 681, 686, 718, 776
  onstage friction with Byrds/guest appearances, 250–251, 268, 306–307, 390–391, 434–435, 438, 657, 660–661
  passivity, 43, 82, 202, 206, 211, 218, 263, 267
  Phillips, Michelle, affair with, 277–278, 282, 720
  publishing income, resentment/envy from other Byrds, 197–198, 200, 206–207, 218, 220–221, 226, 230, 236, 263, 265–266, 273
  returns to Byrds, 13, 385, 387–394, 418, 597–598, 600–601
  Roadmaster recording, 613
  romantic entanglements, 128–129, 146, 229, 237–238, 248, 264–265, 273, 277–278, 388–389
  'Set You Free This Time'/promotional film/beach fracas, 207–211, 265
  singing style/lead vocal showcases, 55–59, 61, 68, 81–82, 85–86, 92, 117, 128, 130, 133, 186, 239, 263, 273, 279, 435, 618, 620, 666, 687, 746, 775, 777, 798
  Slocum, Tom, friendship with, 703, 776–777
  songwriting, 10, 19, 29, 55–59, 62, 81, 87, 114, 116, 128–130, 133, 178, 199–200, 205–207, 215, 221, 225–231, 236–238, 247–248, 254–255, 257–258, 263–268, 273, 279, 366, 388–389, 403, 599, 601, 616–617, 619, 621, 655, 680, 686–687, 701, 705–707, 740–741, 745–746, 766–767, 775, 777, 799, 804–805, 829, 853
  spirituality/psychic interests/abilities, 89–90, 186–187, 276–277
  stomach operation, 748
  Taylor, Derek, Farewell Party guest appearance, 434–435, 438, 838
  touring as duo with McGuinn, 662–666, 676
  Two Sides To Every Story, last major label recording, 647–648
  UK tour (1977), 651–661
  UK tour (1979), 690
  UK tour (1985), 719
  violence, 703, 775–776
  White Light recording, 613, 703
  world tour (1978), 671–672
  York, John, connection with, 492–493, 775
Clark, Kai (Gene's second son), 655
Clark, Kelly (Gene's first son), 655
Clark, Petula, 2, 315
Clark, Rick, 679, 682
Clarke, Arthur C., 410
Clarke, Michael, 8, 13, 19, 21, 39–44, 47, 49–50, 53, 56, 60, 64–67, 70, 81, 83, 92, 99, 107–108, 117–119, 122, 132, 134, 136–138, 143, 146, 154, 161–163, 168, 170, 179, 183, 198–199, 202, 206–209, 211–212, 215, 217–218, 220–221, 230–232, 237–238, 260, 266–267, 272, 276, 280, 286, 293, 295, 297, 308, 342–343, 358–359, 368–371, 374, 378, 384, 387–388, 393–396, 398–399, 402–403, 407, 411, 420, 436, 439, 494, 505, 510, 595, 598, 601, 613, 617, 619–620, 648–650, 652, 667, 673, 684, 693–694, 715, 718–720, 740–742, 746–751, 753–763, 766–767, 770–773, 779–782, 799, 807, 811, 815, 819, 840, 842, 853, 858–859, 861–862, 868, 871
  alcohol use/abuse, 358, 771, 779–780
  birth, 39
  Boulder, Colorado, move to, 648
  cardboard boxes, playing on, 43, 50, 56, 65, 108, 266
  CBS contract, appended to, 70, 81, 99
  childhood/adolescence, 39–41
  Clark, Gene, relationship with, 42, 136–137, 237, 272–273, 393, 779
  cough mixture ingestion, 154, 162–163, 652
  Crosby, David, relationship/conflict with, 42–43, 206–209, 212, 220, 343, 370–371, 396, 650, 748–749, 754, 760, 771, 781, 806
  death, 19, 780–781, 819, 840, 862
  Dependables, working with, 648
  Dickson, Jim, relationship with, 43, 50, 67, 108, 132, 162–163, 208–209, 218, 232, 859, 861–862
  Dillard & Clark, touring with, 494
  draft evasion, 136–138, 403
  drug use/abuse, 154
  drumming ability/style of playing, 39–41, 43, 50, 53, 60, 64–67, 83, 107–108, 117–119, 132, 134, 143, 202, 230–232, 266, 295, 359, 368, 394, 396, 399, 407, 617, 619–620, 649–650, 715, 740–742, 750–751, 763, 766–767, 781, 868
  Dylan, Bob, friendship with, 64–65, 183

INDEX

Clarke, Michael (*contd.*)
  education, 39–41, 748
  Elliot, Lee, marriage to, 762, 779
  ersatz Byrds, working with, 719–720, 746–749, 753–763, 770, 779, 842
  eulogy to Gene Clark, 779
  father, relationship with, 39–40, 342–343
  Firefall, joining of, success with, 649–650, 667, 715, 720, 746
  Flying Burrito Brothers, recruitment to, 494
  Green, Steve, connection with, 748–749, 753–757, 759–762
  Hall of Fame induction, 770–773, 779
  harmonica playing, 179, 297, 799
  Hawaii 'fever', love of, 369, 371, 395, 439, 648, 859
  hedonistic behaviour, 41
  Hillman, Chris, relationship with, 371, 494, 649, 753–755, 759, 763, 771–773, 781, 868
  horse featured on *Notorious Byrd Brothers* sleeve, 411
  image, 8, 42–43, 118–119, 161, 168, 238, 260, 753
  Jones, Brian, connection/look, 8, 42–43, 118
  King, Robin, relationship with/marriage to, 648, 781, 859
  'Lady Friend' reissue, controversy over removal of drums, 742
  lawsuit/conflict over Byrds name, 396, 748, 753–761, 811
  leaving/fired from Byrds, 13, 374, 395–396, 807, 858
  liver disease, 780, 862
  marriages, 648, 762, 779
  McGuinn, Clark & Hillman, appearances with, 693–694
  McGuinn, Jim/Roger, relationship with, 42–43, 162, 212, 297, 370–371, 395, 595, 673, 748–749, 754–755, 757, 759–760, 770–773
  Melcher, Terry, connection/friendship with, 132, 199, 206
  Morello, Joe, influence of, 40–41
  mother, relationship with, 39–41, 342–343, 748, 781, 862
  name change to Clarke, 41–42
  Nyte Flyte sessions, 718–719
  painting/artwork, 42, 720, 748, 780–781
  Paul, Susan, relationship with, 779–780
  personable nature/boyish charm, 64–65, 162–163, 206–207, 221, 267, 384, 387, 396, 781, 862
  personal appearances for promotion, 308
  photogenic looks, 286
  punishment, imperviousness to, 40, 370
  rebelliousness, 39–40, 369–371, 374
  restive spirit, 40–42, 374, 395
  sex appeal/multiple girlfriends, 40–41, 118, 146, 217, 237, 260, 395, 510, 871
  son, birth of, 648
  songwriting/compositions, 297, 395, 399, 753
  tambourine playing, 280, 293
  teasing of, 208–209, 370–371
  Troubadour (1968) guest appearance with Byrds, 439
  20th Anniversary Byrds Tribute, 719, 746
  UK tour (1989), 762–763
  violence/conflicts, 206–209, 211–212, 215, 220, 369–371, 374, 763
  Walker, Jerry Jeff, recording/touring with, 720
  working in Byrds as trio, 394–395
Clarke, Robin (see Robin King)
Clarke, Zachary (Michael's son), 648
Claxton, William, 92
Clayton, Lee, 711
Clayton, Merry, 566, 627
Clear Light, 343
Clear Sailin' (Chris Hillman), 645, 656, 663
'Climber' (CPR), 818
Clooney, Rosemary, 69
'Close Up The Honky Tonks' (Byrds), 494, 826
Clough, Michael, 32
Clyde & Gary, 520
Coburn, James, 182
Cocker, Joe, 14, 515–516
'Coffee Blues' (Mississippi John Hurt), 291
Cohn, Marc, 783
'Cold Coast Of Greenland' (Roger McGuinn), 802
Cold Steel (Sneaky Pete Kleinow), 634
Cole, David, 793
Cole, Jerry, 81, 83–84, 740
Collins, Jackie, 148
Collins, Joan, 148
Collins, Joe, 148
Collins, Judy, 27, 131, 201, 295, 528, 804
'Colorado' (Flying Burrito Brothers), 648
'Colorado' (Manassas), 648
'Colours' (Donovan), 159
Coltrane, John, 222, 242, 244, 251–253, 258, 294, 337, 360, 418, 814, 823
'Come Back Baby' (David Crosby), 34
'Communications' (Gene Clark), 776
'Compass' (Crosby, Stills, Nash & Young), 735–736, 788
'Compass' (David Crosby), 735
Conn, Mervyn, 148, 150, 152, 163–164, 171
Connor, 'Coon Dog', 415
Connor, Chris, 35

1169

Cooder, Ry, 77, 397, 525
Cooke, Sam, 111
Cooper, Michael, 445
Copeland, Miles, 662
Corea, Chuck, 638
Corman, Roger, 30, 32, 428, 509, 856
Corneal, Jon, 424–425, 428
Cosmic American Music (Gram Parsons/Rick Grech), 627
Costello, Elvis, 725, 833
Cougar, John, 680, 682
Country Boys, The, 469
Country Gazette, 626, 628, 846, 859, 867
'Country Girl' (Crosby, Stills, Nash & Young), 788
'Country Honk' (Rolling Stones), 627
Country Joe & The Fish, 350, 355, 516
Coury, Al, 647
Cover Girl (musical), 605
'Cowboy Movie' (David Crosby), 614
Cowboy Songs And Other Frontier Ballads (John Lomax), 423
'Cowgirl In The Sand' (Byrds), 618
'Cowgirl In The Sand' (Neil Young), 618
CPR, 786, 788, 818, 820
CPR (CPR), 786
Cramer, Floyd, 572
Crawford, Celia (Cindy), 31
Cream, 315
Creedence Clearwater Revival, 515–516
'Creeque Alley' (Mamas & The Papas), 362, 670–671
Crewe, Bob, 316
'Critical Mass' (Crosby & Nash), 641
Cronkite, Kathy, 638
Cronkite, Walter, 638
Crosby & Nash, 615, 631, 641–643, 787, 820
Crosby Nash (Crosby & Nash), 820
Crosby, Aliph (David's mother), 30–31, 36, 214, 245, 639
Crosby, Chip (Ethan) (David's brother), 30–32, 786
Crosby, David, 6, 8, 13, 17–19, 21, 30–38, 42–45, 48–49, 51–60, 62, 64–66, 68, 70, 73, 75, 78, 81–82, 85–86, 89–92, 99–101, 105–107, 112, 114–121, 123, 130, 132–136, 140–145, 153, 156, 159, 161–162, 166, 168, 171, 176–180, 183–185, 187–188, 193, 196, 198–202, 206–224, 228–231, 233–241, 243–248, 251–252, 254–255, 257–260, 263–269, 271–273, 279–280, 282–285, 288, 290, 293–300, 303–306, 309, 311–312, 314–315, 318–330, 333–344, 346–347, 350–361, 363–385, 387, 389, 394, 396, 398, 400, 402–405, 408–414, 417–418, 420–422, 433, 438, 452, 460, 470, 481, 484, 492–494, 502, 504, 506–513, 516–518, 532, 537–539, 541, 543, 552, 560–561, 575, 589, 596–601, 607, 613–615, 617–625, 630–632, 639–643, 650, 652, 658–659, 667, 673–675, 677, 684, 692–694, 696–697, 701, 703, 709–710, 715–716, 719–720, 725–737, 741–757, 759, 762–772, 774, 778, 781–793, 796, 798–802, 806–808, 811–823, 831–838, 846, 850–853, 857–864, 866–868
   acquisition of 'Byrds' title, 819–820, 831
   acting aspirations, 31, 783
   Altamont appearance, 532
   arrests, 728–729, 732, 734
   articulacy/persuasive personality, 51, 114, 141, 183–187, 207–208, 252, 268–269, 282, 298, 341, 374, 376, 380–382, 404–405, 411–412, 658–659, 726
   autobiographies, 737, 833
   bass playing, 44–45, 49, 368–369, 373, 407–408, 412
   Baxter, Les, work as 'Balladeer', 6, 32
   Beefeaters' record, reaction towards, 44
   birth, 30
   brother, Ethan/Chip, death of, 786
   burglary activity, 30–31
   Capitol Records' rejected by, 727
   CBS, signing to, 70
   childhood/adolescence, 30
   children/offspring, 31, 785, 817–818
   Clark, Gene, relationship/conflict with, 36, 53, 75, 89, 92, 206, 229, 236, 267–269, 272
   Clarke, Michael, relationship/conflict with, 42–43, 206–209, 212, 220, 343, 370–371, 396, 650, 748–749, 754, 760, 771, 781, 806
   confidence/self-belief/arrogance, 86, 115, 117, 121, 134–135, 141, 145, 183, 185–186, 207–208, 268, 309, 329, 341–343, 351, 357–358, 360, 365, 372, 374, 376, 380–382, 411–412, 599, 658–659, 726–727, 851
   conflict/violence in Byrds, 51–53, 116, 133–134, 162–163, 201, 206–215, 245, 265, 268, 296, 323, 339–340, 342–343, 350–352, 355–361, 365, 367, 369–383, 404–405, 411–412, 631, 658–659, 726, 806–808
   contradictions, 18, 86, 99, 135, 184–185, 210, 269, 344–345, 365, 367, 380, 517, 726, 807–808
   countercultural interests, 200, 284–285, 311–312, 320, 337–339, 341, 359–360, 363–364, 371–372, 374, 409

INDEX

Crosby, David (*contd.*)
  court appearances, 729–730, 732
  CPR, formation of/recordings, 786, 818, 820
  Crosby, Stills & Nash, first album, recording of, 494, 600
  Crosby, Stills & Nash 1977 stadium tour, 667
  Crosby, Stills & Nash recordings, 517, 600, 729, 782–783, 787
  Crosby, Stills, Nash & Young, formation/early success, 516–517, 537–538
  Crosby, Stills, Nash & Young 1974 Tour, 640–641, 787
  Crosby, Stills, Nash & Young, recordings, 537–538, 614–615, 640–642
  Crosby, Stills, Nash & Young reunion (1987/88), 736–737, 782, 787–788
  Crosby, Stills, Nash & Young reunion (1997/99), 787–788
  Crosby, Stills, Nash & Young reunion (2000), 816
  Crosby, Stills, Nash & Young reunion (2002), 819
  Crosby, Stills, Nash & Young reunion (2006), 834–835
  Dance, Jan, relationship with/marriage to, 692, 731, 734, 736, 784–785, 851
  diabetes, 737
  Dickson, Jim, friendship/conflict with, 32, 36–37, 116, 119, 121, 133–135, 199, 201, 206–215, 218–220, 234–236, 243–244, 246, 296, 321–324, 358, 384–385, 421, 508–509, 538, 641, 744–745, 807, 859–864, 866, 868
  disillusionment with Byrds, 51, 335, 339–343, 350–352, 355–361, 365, 367–368, 370–372, 374–383
  draft exemption, 136, 403
  drug use/abuse, 17–18, 31, 42, 86, 141, 145, 171, 176, 179–180, 200, 211, 219, 259–260, 269, 290, 340–341, 355–357, 363–364, 374, 601, 694, 709, 725–735, 737, 820–821, 838
  Dylan, Bob, charm offensive on/friendship with, 183, 188, 246
  Eastern music, interest in/incorporation of, 176–177, 222–223, 243–245, 251–252, 303, 324–325
  Easy Rider, alleged depiction in movie, 511
  education, 30–31
  firing from Byrds, 13, 51–52, 376, 380–385, 460, 703, 757, 858, 861
  folk singer ambitions, pre-Byrds, 31–33, 35, 38, 100

  freebasing, 17–18, 694, 725–735
  gun possession, 513, 728–730, 734
  Hall of Fame induction: Byrds, 771–773, 786
  Hall of Fame induction: Crosby, Stills & Nash, 785–786
  heart attack (suspected), 821
  Hillman, Chris, relationship with, 49, 312, 315, 321, 342, 355–356, 358–359, 365, 367, 372, 374–381, 383–385, 398, 404–405, 407, 412, 599, 674, 693, 741, 747, 749, 752, 784, 790–792, 812, 817–818, 821–822, 831–832, 853, 866
  Hinton, Christine Gail, relationship with, 639
  honesty/magnanimity/sensitivity, 18, 193, 282–283, 297, 341, 344–345, 352–353, 360, 363, 372, 374–375, 381–382, 404–405, 411–412, 658–659, 673–675, 726–727, 752, 782, 784, 807–808
  horse depiction on *Notorious Byrd Brothers* sleeve, 411–412, 658
  If I Could Only Remember My Name, appraisal, 19, 614, 619–620, 737, 833, 850
  image, 8, 51, 119–120, 145, 161, 166, 218, 220, 247, 335, 337, 366, 417, 753
  imprisonment, 730, 732–733, 735
  intervention by long-suffering friends, 727
  Jet Set formation, 21, 30, 35–38
  Live Aid appearance, 733
  liver disease/transplant, 783–785, 792, 821
  material concerns, 218–219, 782
  McGuinn, Clark & Hillman, guest appearances with, 673, 675, 693
  McGuinn, Clark & Hillman, rejected by, 673–675, 677, 715
  McGuinn, Jim/Roger, relationship with, 36, 120, 199, 206, 212, 214, 216–218, 233–236, 288, 347, 350–351, 353, 355–359, 361, 365, 367, 370–372, 375–385, 398, 404–405, 410–412, 504, 508, 517–518, 597, 599–601, 607, 615, 621, 623–624, 630–631, 641, 658–659, 673–675, 709–710, 726, 747, 749, 752, 754–755, 765, 793, 796, 807–808, 811–812, 815, 822, 831–832, 863
  Melcher, Terry, aversion towards, 81, 198–199, 206, 212–214, 217–218, 228, 233–236, 561, 623, 641, 807, 846, 864
  Mitchell, Joni, relationship with, 383, 575, 617, 641
  Morrison, Jim, disdain for, 341, 357, 786
  mother, relationship with, 30, 36, 214, 245, 639
  'Mr Tambourine Man', objections to recording song, 62, 64–65

1171

Crosby, David (contd.)
  Nash, Graham, relationship with, 334, 373, 508–509, 615, 642–643, 673, 694, 726–727, 731, 733–734, 736, 783, 787
  negative view of post-*Notorious* Byrds, 413, 589, 596
  Nitzsche, Jack, conflict with, 639
  onstage charisma/charm/sarcasm/set brevity/controversy, 82, 100, 107, 143, 159, 168, 305–306, 335, 339–340, 342–343, 354–358, 373, 377, 379–380, 640
  passionate personality/enthusiasm, 18, 51–52, 118, 206–215, 243–244, 339–341, 351, 363–364, 366, 368, 374–375, 381–382, 411–412, 575, 640, 658–659, 673–675, 726, 752, 808, 851
  political views/pronouncements, 344, 355–357, 359, 364, 403–404, 452, 481, 517, 640, 736, 782, 820, 831, 833–835
  producer of *Byrds*, 600–601
  production work, 600–601, 617, 621
  Raymond, James, relationship with, 785–786, 818
  rebelliousness attitude, 121, 123, 134–135, 141–142, 145, 183, 193, 201, 207–210, 217, 220, 238–239, 245–246, 268, 296, 299, 339–340, 342–343, 350–351, 355–357, 363–367, 369–372, 374, 376–380, 382–383, 411–412, 433, 599, 816–817
  Recordsville, reluctance to visit, 18
  release from prison, 735, 747, 821
  religion, speculation about, 850–851
  Renaissance Faire visit, 284–285
  reunions with Byrds/offshoots, 597–601, 747–752, 762–763, 811–812, 821–822
  rhythm guitar playing, 53–54, 89, 266, 268, 342, 751, 802
  sailing, 218, 363, 371–372, 383–384, 409–410, 734, 835
  science fiction interest, 200, 375
  sexual interests, 30–31, 290, 363, 375
  Sgt Pepper's sessions, attendance, 333
  singing/harmonic skills, 31, 34–35, 38, 43, 57–58, 60, 68, 81, 130, 201, 293–296, 321, 336, 364–365, 409, 517, 601
  sociability/generosity, 118, 183, 218, 240, 244, 269, 304–305, 333–334, 337–338, 352–353, 360, 374–376, 470, 575, 614–615, 673–675, 726–727, 782–783
  solo recordings, pre-Byrds, 31, 34–35
  son, Django, birth of/upbringing, 785, 820
  songwriting/compositions, 31, 34, 57–58, 199–200, 230–231, 239, 245, 254–255, 257–260, 294–295, 298–299, 318,
320–330, 333, 336, 364–365, 367, 369, 372, 374–376, 382, 403–404, 409–410, 481, 494, 517, 537–538, 597, 614–615, 617–619, 621, 667, 726, 735–737, 741–743, 745–746, 767, 782–783, 786, 788, 798–802, 806, 818, 820, 834
  sperm donator, 816–817, 866
  Stills, Stephen, relationship with, 350–352, 357–360, 377, 598–599, 640, 642–643, 667, 673, 694, 716, 726, 729, 731, 734, 783
  survival, 17, 725–735, 774, 778, 781–782, 816, 820–821, 835–836, 850, 860, 866
  tax problems, 736, 783
  Time Fades Away tour, 639
  Troubadour humiliation, 52–53, 100
  Usher, Gary, disdain towards, 375–376, 378, 402, 764, 807, 864
  usurpation of Gene Clark as guitarist, 43, 66, 75, 89, 92, 206, 221, 267–268, 368–369
  Voyage (box set) career overview, 833
  Woodstock, association with, 516–518, 731, 783
Crosby, Django (David's son), 785, 817, 820
Crosby, Floyd (David's father), 30, 32
Crosby, Jan (David's wife), 692, 731, 734, 736, 784–785, 851
Crosby, Stills & Nash, 494, 512, 517, 600, 643, 667, 671, 677, 681, 694, 729–731, 733–734, 736, 750, 782–787, 816, 818–819, 835
Crosby, Stills & Nash (Crosby, Stills & Nash), 494, 512, 517, 600
Crosby, Stills, Nash & Young, 16, 381, 511, 516–517, 532, 538, 552, 600, 613–615, 619, 632–633, 639–644, 659, 666, 726, 735–737, 787–788, 816, 819, 834–835
'Cross The Plains' (David Crosby), 31
Crowded House, 725
Crowell, Rodney, 710, 719
Crowley Michael (see Michael Crumm)
Crown Of Creation (Jefferson Airplane), 375, 806
'Cruising 600' (Jet Set), 71
Crumm, Michael (aka Michael Crowley), 29
'Crying In The Chapel' (Elvis Presley), 5
CSN (box set) (Crosby, Stills & Nash), 782
CSN (Crosby, Stills & Nash), 667, 681, 729
'CTA 102' (Byrds), 319–320, 528, 829
Curry, Donna, 285
Cypher, Julie, 817–818, 866

D'Lugoff, Art, 307
Daily Flash, The, 337, 352, 831
Daley, Richard, Mayor, 570

INDEX

Daltrey, Roger, 661
Dance, Jan (see Jan Crosby)
Daniel, Luke, 475
Daniels, Jeff, 475
Danko, Rick, 719
Darin, Bobby, 25–28, 80, 191–193, 452, 521, 578, 598, 797
Darrell, Johnny, 768
Darrow, Chris, 843
Dating Game, The (television programme), 97
David Copperfield (novel) (Charles Dickens), 13
David, Hal, 130
Davies, Dave, 153
Davies, Hugh, 628
Davies, Idris, 130
Davis, Clive, 142, 335–336, 367, 380, 535–536, 615, 623, 667
Davis, Jesse Ed, 613, 703
Davis, Miles, 68–69, 88, 231, 309, 751, 802, 856
Davis, Saul, 778
Davis, Skeeter, 432
Dawn, The, 337
Dawson, Stuart 'Dinky', 557, 583
'Day In The Life, A' (Beatles), 333, 548, 794
'Day Tripper' (Beatles), 2, 242
'Day Walk, The' (Byrds), 214, 231, 264, 740–741, 767, 799
Day, Doris, 69, 80, 88, 198, 214, 217, 807, 844, 846
'Daydream' (Lovin' Spoonful), 281
Daylight Again (Crosby, Stills & Nash), 729, 731
De Shannon, Jackie, 104, 111, 133–134, 245, 791
Deaf School, 839
Dean, James, 103–104, 173, 509, 540, 557, 813
Decker, Star, 843
'Dedicated To The One I Love' (Mamas & The Papas), 338
'Dedicated To The One I Love' (Shirelles), 338
'Deeper In' (Roger McGuinn & Chris Hillman, Featuring Gene Clark), 707
DeFries, Tony, 636
'Déjà Vu' (Crosby, Stills, Nash & Young), 538, 788, 850
Déjà Vu (Crosby, Stills, Nash & Young), 517, 537–538, 614, 641, 736
Déjà Vu (DVD documentary) (Crosby, Stills, Nash & Young), 834–835
DeLeon, Dolores (see Dolores Tickner)
Delgatto, John, 867, 872
Deliver (Mamas & The Papas), 338, 406
'Delta' (Crosby, Stills & Nash), 726, 729, 786

'Delta' (David Crosby), 726, 731
Denny, Sandy, 576
Denselow, Robin, 461
'Denver Or Wherever' (Gene Clark), 805
Denver, Bob, 346
Dependables, The, 648
'Deportee (Plane Wreck At Los Gatos)' (Byrds), 528
'Deportee (Plane Wreck At Los Gatos)' (Judy Collins), 528
Desert Rose Band, The, 46, 321, 717–718, 748, 752, 764, 772, 789–792, 824, 864
Desert Rose (Chris Hillman), 717, 791, 864
Desert Rose Band, The (Desert Rose Band), 717–718
Desire (Bob Dylan), 844
DeVito, Don, 637
deWilde, Brandon, 312, 346, 416
Dexter, Jeff, 441, 443, 445, 456–457
Di Fiore, Roger, 240
Di Meola, Al, 638
Diamond, Neil, 91
Dian & The Greenbriar Boys, 32, 856–857, 867
Dick, Debbie (Michael Clarke's sister), 39
Dick, James (Michael Clarke's father), 39–40, 137
Dick, Judi (Michael Clarke's sister), 39
Dick, Suzy (Michael Clarke's mother), 39–42, 342–343, 748, 772, 781, 862
Dickens, Charles (singer), 166
Dickson, Bob, 855, 871–872
Dickson, Harley, 76–76, 79, 286
Dickson, Jim, 32–37, 39, 43–46, 48–62, 75–78, 81–93, 96–97, 99–109, 111, 114–119, 121–123, 125–126, 128–130, 132–136, 138–142, 149, 151, 160, 176–181, 187, 193, 195–220, 224–225, 227–246, 250, 256, 260, 263–265, 268–276, 280–283, 286, 293–296, 299–302, 305–306, 308–309, 311–312, 320–324, 326–328, 332, 336–337, 339, 342, 344–350, 354, 357–358, 366, 378, 383–385, 388–389, 393, 398, 420–421, 426, 429, 469, 492, 499, 508–510, 537–539, 541, 545, 555, 560, 590, 613, 626, 643, 716, 719, 727, 738–741, 744–745, 751, 764, 799, 807, 837, 846–847, 855–872
Dickson, Martha, 855
Diddley, Bo, 117, 134, 222, 238, 515
Dill, Danny, 505
Dillard & Clark, 16, 494, 537, 600, 649
Dillard, Doug, 86, 439–443, 447, 645
Dillards, The, 32, 283, 429, 441, 499, 768, 856–857, 867

1173

'Dino's Song' (Quicksilver Messenger Service), 800
Dion, 28, 576
Disney, Walt, 804
'Distances' (David Crosby), 726, 729
'Distant Drums' (Jim Reeves), 478
Dixon, Sammy, 459
'Do For The Others' (Chris Hillman & Rick Roberts), 716
'Do For The Others' (Stephen Stills), 716
Do Not Go Gentle Into That Good Night (poem) (Dylan Thomas), 779
'Do The Freddie' (Freddie And The Dreamers), 7
'Do You Believe In Magic?' (Lovin' Spoonful), 282
Dobbs, Fred C., 183
Dochniak, Jim, 391
Doherty, Denny, 305
'Dolphin's Smile' (Byrds), 369–370, 374, 376, 409–410, 806–807
Domino, Fats, 568
'Don't Be Long' (Beefeaters), 44, 225
'Don't Doubt Yourself Babe' (Byrds), 117, 133–134, 155, 245, 306
'Don't Doubt Yourself Babe' (Jackie De Shannon), 245
'Don't Let It Down' (Dino Valenti), 73
'Don't Make Waves' (Byrds), 365, 513, 743, 801
Don't Make Waves (film), 365, 513
'Don't Think Twice' (Bob Dylan), 857
'Don't Worry Baby' (Beach Boys), 83
'Don't You Write Her Off' (McGuinn, Clark & Hillman), 684–685, 704, 724
Donahue, Tom, 105
Donnelly, Philip, 711
Donohue, Lizzie, 116, 141, 145–146
Donovan, 151, 159, 166, 168, 191
Doobie Brothers, The, 526, 649
Doonican, Val, 315
Doors, The, 327, 331, 338, 341, 351, 357, 440, 515, 786
Dorsey, Lee, 297, 505
Douglas, Craig, 4
Douglas, Ed, 46–47
Down The Road (Manassas), 644, 681
Dr Byrds & Mr Hyde (Byrds), 497–504, 507, 533, 541, 543, 684, 768, 809, 813, 826
Dr Faustus (play) (Christopher Marlowe), 285
Dr John, 541
Dr Strangelove (film), 135, 510
'Draft Morning' (Byrds), 369, 403–405, 410, 511, 806, 813
'Draft Morning' (David Crosby), 813
'Draggin'' (Byrds), 595

'Draggin'' (Roger McGuinn), 595, 624
Dragon, Carmen, 605
Dragon, Daryl, 605
Dragon, Dennis, 605–606
Drake, Bill, 584
'Dream Baby' (Roy Orbison), 477
'Dream For Him' (Crosby, Stills, Nash & Young), 788
'Dreamland' (Joni Mitchell), 636–637
'Dreamland' (Roger McGuinn), 636–637
Dreyer, Julia, 326
Drifters, The, 753
Driscoll, Julie, & The Brian Auger Trinity, 427, 498
'Drive My Car' (David Crosby) 726, 729
'Drug Store Truck Drivin'' Man (Byrds), 430, 496–497, 768
Drummond, Norrie, 152–153
Duchess, The, 222
Duncan, Steve, 717, 747, 749, 751
Dunlop, Ian, 416–417
Dylan, Bob, 3–4, 6–10, 24, 27, 31, 41, 48, 59–65, 69, 82, 84–85, 87–88, 91–92, 100–105, 108, 110–112, 115, 117–118, 121, 125–129, 131–132, 134, 142–143, 145–146, 148, 151, 155, 157, 159–160, 164–165, 168, 170–171, 173, 178–179, 182–184, 187–188, 190–196, 199, 201–204, 215, 225–227, 230–233, 239, 242, 246, 248, 254, 258, 264–265, 271, 274, 281, 287, 290, 292–293, 311, 320, 325–326, 328–329, 335–336, 347, 349, 354, 388, 405, 416, 426–427, 429–430, 435–436, 444, 471–472, 479–482, 490, 496, 498, 500–501, 503–504, 507–508, 510–511, 518, 523, 526, 529, 549, 576, 584, 613, 617–618, 622–625, 634–638, 658–659, 670–671, 700, 716, 721, 725, 740, 750–751, 763–764, 766, 769, 776, 783, 795, 799, 804, 814, 827, 841, 844, 850, 857–858, 871

Eagles, The, 575, 628, 666, 771
Earl Scruggs His Family And Friends (Earl Scruggs His Family And Friends), 590
Early Jimmy Gavin (Jimmy Gavin), 869
Early LA (Various Artistes), 34, 38, 763
Early Years, The (Gram Parsons/Shilos), 415
Earth Island, 545
'East Virginia' (Roger McGuinn), 803
'Easter' (Leadbelly), 798
'Easter' (Roger McGuinn), 798
Eastman, Carole, 286–287, 366
Eastwood, Clint, 843
Easy Rider (film), 93, 406, 509–512, 521–523, 529, 533, 827

INDEX

Easy Rider (soundtrack album), 406, 509, 511, 513, 521–522, 530
Easybeats, The, 14
'Echoes' (Gene Clark), 385
'Echoes Live' (Roger McGuinn), 832
Eddy, Duane, 526
Edmonson, Travis, 31
'Eight Days A Week' (Beatles), 255
'Eight Miles High' (Byrds), 10, 19, 242–243, 246–248, 251–261, 266, 277, 280, 287–288, 291, 294, 296, 302, 307, 326, 329, 354, 356, 389, 391, 399, 402, 407, 414, 418, 434, 442, 444, 455, 522, 536, 542–543, 548, 553, 577–578, 598, 602, 605, 630, 635, 657, 681, 688, 706, 726, 739, 741, 744, 751, 767, 800–801, 814, 837, 868
'Eight Miles High' (Chris Hillman), 823
'Eight Miles High' (Chris Hillman & Herb Pedersen), 824
'Eight Miles High' (CPR), 786, 818
'Eight Miles High' (Crosby, Stills, Nash & Young), 816
'Eight Miles High' (David Crosby with Roger McGuinn), 731
'Eight Miles High' (Gene Clark), 719
'Eight Miles High' (introduced as 'McGuinn, Crosby, Hillman'), 748
'Eight Miles High' (McGuinn & Clark), 666
'Eight Miles High' (McGuinn & Clark, with David Crosby), 673
'Eight Miles High' (McGuinn, Crosby & Hillman, billed as 'the original Byrds'), 763
'Eight Miles High' (Roger McGuinn), 663, 722–723, 832
'Eight Miles High' (Roger McGuinn, with the Peace Seekers), 721
Einstein, Albert, 289, 540, 568
Electric Flag, The, 355, 359, 416
Eliot, T.S., 130
Ellington, Duke, 45
Elliot, Cass, 282, 305, 595
Elliot, Lee, 762, 779–780
Elliott, Ramblin' Jack, 60–61, 635, 857
'Elusive Butterfly' (Bob Lind), 283
Emerald, 99
Emery, Ralph, 429–430, 432, 496
'Emptiness, The' (Gene Clark), 214
Engelberg, Fred, 32, 856
Epstein, Brian, 97, 139, 148, 161, 212, 303, 348–349
Epstein, Eugene, Dr, 319–320
Etheridge, Melissa, 817–818, 866
Ethridge, Chris, 416, 604, 626
Eubanks, Bob, 97

Eumier, Ron, 663
Evans, Allen, 165
'Eve Of Destruction' (Barry McGuire), 113, 188–191, 204, 290
Ever Call Ready (Ever Call Ready), 717
Evergreen Blueshoes, The, 520, 842
Everly Brothers, The, 5, 22, 38, 59, 473
Everybody Knows This Is Nowhere (Neil Young), 618
'Everybody's Been Burned' (Byrds), 34–35, 321–322, 328, 373, 750, 767
'Everybody's Been Burned' (David Crosby), 34–35, 321–322
'Everybody's Talkin'' (Nilsson), 523
'Everyone's Gone To The Moon' (Jonathan King), 192
'Excuse Me, I Think I've Got A Heartache' (Byrds), 443
Exile On Main Street (Rolling Stones), 627
'Eyes Too Blue' (CPR), 818

Fagen, Len, 644
'Fair And Tender Ladies' (Byrds), 601
'Fair And Tender Ladies' (Gene Clark & Carla Olson), 601
'Fair And Tender Ladies' (Hillmen), 48
'Fair And Tender Ladies' (Roger McGuinn/Gene Clark), 601
Faith, Percy, 69–70
Faithfull, Marianne, 2, 334, 442, 445
Fall Of The House Of Usher, The (film), 30
Fallen Angels, The, 628
'Fallen For You' (Gene Clark), 775
Falwell, Jerry, 679
Fame, Georgie, & The Blue Flames, 153, 157–158
Fame (musical), 724
Fantastic Expedition Of Dillard & Clark (Dillard & Clark), 494, 600
Farlowe, Chris, 157
Farrow, Mia, 138
'Farther Along' (Byrds), 582–583
Farther Along (Byrds), 15, 577, 580–589, 590–591, 595, 684, 724, 767, 769, 828
'Farther Along' (Flying Burrito Brothers), 583
'Farther Along' (Gram Parsons & Bernie Leadon), 626
'Farther Along' (Rose Maddox), 583
Faurot, Jon, 778
'Feel A Whole Lot Better' (Byrds), 9, 116, 119, 126–129, 133, 161, 167, 239, 439, 442, 467, 705, 750, 773, 798
'Feel A Whole Lot Better' (Gene Clark), 719, 746
'Feel A Whole Lot Better' (Roger McGuinn & Chris Hillman), 791

1175

'Feel A Whole Lot Better' (Roger McGuinn/ Thunderbyrd, with Gene Clark & Chris Hillman), 657
'Feeling Higher' (McGuinn, Clark & Hillman), 687
Feinstein, Barry, 32–33, 89, 101, 141, 208–210, 274, 305, 510, 856–857
Felder, Wilton, 619
Fever Tree, 840
'Fiddler A Dram (Moog Experiment)' (aka 'Jenny Comes Along') (Byrds), 529, 744, 810
'Fido' (Byrds), 512, 523–524, 529, 810
Fiestas, The, 585
'15 Minute Jam' (Byrds), 769
Fifth Dimension (Byrds), 11, 291–299, 305, 325, 402, 412, 502, 743, 766, 800, 807, 830
Fifty Years Adrift (autobiography) (Derek Taylor), 839
Finch, Peter, 138
'Find The Cost Of Freedom' (Crosby, Stills, Nash & Young), 511
'Find The Cost Of Freedom' (McGuinn, Clark & Hillman), 671
Firebyrd (Gene Clark), 719, 746, 776
Firefall, 645, 649–650, 685–686, 688, 715–716, 720
Firefall (Firefall), 649
Firesign Theatre, The, 404
'Fireworks' (Roger McGuinn), 804
Fitzgerald, Ella, 35
Fitzpatrick, Knox, 730, 732
'5 D (Fifth Dimension)' (Byrds), 79, 288–290, 293, 297, 302, 399, 402, 408, 443, 522, 766
Five Easy Pieces (film), 286
Flatt & Scruggs, 443
Fleetwood Mac, 649
'Flight 713 (Song Number 2)' (Byrds), 743–744
'Flower Bomb Song' (Byrds), 199–200, 264, 323, 800, 829
Floyd, Charles Arthur ('Pretty Boy'), 475
Flying Burrito Brothers, The, 16, 416, 428, 438, 460, 477, 485, 491, 494, 501, 503–504, 532, 537, 583, 600, 613, 626, 628, 644–645, 648–649, 665, 707, 712, 715–716, 752, 754, 768, 772, 781, 791, 809, 824, 840, 842, 847, 859, 864
Flying Burrito Brothers, The (Flying Burrito Brothers), 613
Flynn, Errol, 96, 569
'Foggy Mountain Breakdown' (Byrds), 443
'Foggy Mountain Breakdown' (Flatt & Scruggs), 443
Folger, Abigail, 512

Folk Den Project 1995–2005, The (box set) (Roger McGuinn), 833
Folk Songs From The Southern Appalachians (Cecil Sharp), 423
Fonda, Henry, 139, 509
Fonda, Jane, 138–140, 509–510
Fonda, Peter, 103, 139, 176–177, 214, 218, 311–312, 344, 346–347, 416, 509–511, 523, 815
Fontana, Wayne, 4
'For Free' (Byrds), 617
'For Free' (Joni Mitchell), 617
'For Me Again' (Byrds), 59
'For What It's Worth' (Buffalo Springfield), 331
Ford, Perry, 156
Ford, Tennessee Ernie, 6
Foster, Jodie, 713
Foster, Stephen, 231–232
Foundations, The, 447
Four Freshmen, The, 409
'409' (Beach Boys), 300
'4+20' (Rice, Rice, Hillman & Pedersen), 822
Four Seasons, The, 372
Four Way Street (Crosby, Stills, Nash & Young), 615
Fowley, Kim, 95, 106–107, 186–187, 520, 545–546, 559–561, 567–569, 571, 581, 584–585, 587–588, 595, 608, 814, 843
Fox, James, 138–139
Foxworthy, Douglas, 707
Frame, Pete, 442
Frampton, Peter, 637
Frankenstein (book) (Mary Shelley), 79
Franklin, Paul, 789
Franzoni, Carl, 93–95, 98, 109–110, 112, 136, 138–139, 141–147, 150, 186, 282
Fraser, Robert, 315, 446
Fraser, Ronald, 139
Fraternity Of Man, The, 343
Freddie And The Dreamers, 7, 159
Freiberg, David, 3, 326
'From A Distance' (Byrds), 764
'From A Distance' (Julie Gold), 764
'From A Silver Phial' (Gene Clark), 646
Frykowsky, Voytek, 512
Fugs, The, 307
'Full Circle' (Byrds), 599, 616–617, 621, 829
'Full Circle Song' (Gene Clark), 613
Furay, Richie, 359, 644, 649
Fury, Billy, 124
Fusion, 398

Gable, Clark, 386
'Games' (Crosby & Nash), 517
Ganton, Louise, 22–23
Garcia, Jerry, 642

INDEX

Garfunkel, Art, 641
Gari, Frank, 26
Garland, Judy, 96
Gas Company, The, 520
Gas, Food & Lodging, 488, 840
'Gate Of Horn' (Roger McGuinn), 23, 633, 804
Gateway Singers, The, 24
Gauchos, The, 95
Gavin, Bill, 253–254, 256
Gavin, Jimmy [aka Weston Gavin], 32, 36, 153, 856, 869–872
Gay, John, 285
Gaye, Marvin, 493
Geffen, David, 588, 600, 615, 632, 644, 646–647, 649, 658
Gene Clark With The Gosdin Brothers (Gene Clark), 300, 307, 385, 828
Gene Tryp (musical), 450–451, 453, 521, 530, 539, 541, 544–545, 549–550, 569–570, 572, 584, 598, 723, 795–796, 827, 843–844
'Gentle On My Mind' (Dean Martin), 499, 523
Gentle Soul, The, 525
George, Lowell, 544, 583
Gerhardt, Ray, 197
Gerlach, Fred, 77
Gerlach, Nick, 77–78, 841
Gernreich, Rudy, 92
Gerry & The Pacemakers, 159
Gershwin, George, 31
Gerst, Harvey, 44, 248
'Get Down Your Line' (Byrds), 582
'Get Off Of My Cloud' (Rolling Stones), 2, 192
'Get Out Of My Life Woman' (Byrds), 505
'Get Out Of My Life Woman' (Lee Dorsey), 297, 505
'Get To You' (Byrds), 389, 406–407, 411, 743, 767, 830
'Get Together' (David Crosby), 33–35, 200
'Get Together' (Dino Valenti), 200
Getty, J. Paul, 555
Giant (film), 509
Gibson & Camp, 499
Gibson, Bob, 22, 36, 91, 795, 797–798
Gilbert, Linda (see Linda Carradine)
Gilded Palace Of Sin, The (Flying Burrito Brothers), 494, 503, 537, 600, 626
Gillespie, Dizzy, 487
Gilligan's Island (television programme), 346
Ginsberg, Allen, 287, 635
'Girl With No Name, The' (Byrds), 326, 443, 618
'Give Me Your Word' (Tennessee Ernie Ford), 6
'Givin' Herself Away' (Roger McGuinn & Chris Hillman, Featuring Gene Clark), 707

Glaser, Tompall, 432–433
Glaser, Tompall, & The Glaser Brothers, 432
Gleason, Ralph, 359
'Glory, Glory' (Byrds), 566, 573, 583
Glover, Jimmy, 29
'God Bless The Child' (David Crosby), 31
'God Save The Queen' (Sex Pistols), 651
Goffin, Gerry, 26, 375, 401, 405–406, 511, 806
'Goin' Back' (Byrds), 13, 375–378, 383, 390, 396, 401–402, 411, 443, 620, 806, 812–813
'Goin' Back' (Dusty Springfield), 401
Gold, Julie, 764
Golden Apples Of The Sun, The (Judy Collins), 295
'Golden Loom' (Bob Dylan), 638
'Golden Loom' (Roger McGuinn), 638
Golden State Boys, The, 47
'Golden Vanity' (Chad Mitchell Trio), 802
'Golden Vanity' (Roger McGuinn), 802
Good, Jack, 124
Goodall, Jim, 722
Goodman, Benny, 45
Gordon, Jim, 374, 376, 396, 402, 623
Gosdin Brothers, The, 47–48, 300, 307, 385, 477, 527, 529, 867
Gosdin, Rex, 47, 300, 307, 385
Gosdin, Vern, 47, 300, 307, 320, 385, 527, 529, 846
GP (Gram Parsons), 628
Graduate, The (film), 451
Graham, Bill, 379, 825
Grand Ole Opry (radio show), 430–433, 439, 505
Grant, Cary, 96, 103
Grapefruit, 14
Grateful Dead, The, 337, 350, 440, 470, 516, 614
Gray, Michael, 226–227
'Great Selchie Of Shule Skerry' (Judy Collins), 295
Great White Wonder, The (bootleg) (Bob Dylan), 426
Great, Johnnie B., 166
Greatest Hits Volume 2 (Byrds), 580
Grech, Rick (Rik), 627–628
'Green Apple Quick Step' (Byrds), 564, 571, 573, 586, 769
Green Grass Group, The, 49
'Green Green' (New Christy Minstrels), 29, 112
Green, Lloyd, 427–432, 435, 437–438, 472, 496
Green, Meridian, 843
Green, Steve, 748–749, 753–757, 759–762, 819

Greenback Dollar (see *The Balladeer*)
Greene, Charlie, 111, 125, 283, 312, 831
Greene, Richard, 625
'Greensleeves' (Henry VIII), 802
Grievous Angel (Gram Parsons & The Fallen Angels), 628
Grisman, David, 625
Grogan, Tim, 790
Grossman, Albert, 23, 88, 91–92, 122, 347, 349, 426, 857
Grusin, Dave, 500–501
Guam, 635–636
Guerin, John, 595–596, 598, 602–606, 623, 843
Guilbeau, Gib, 485–486, 499–500, 525, 847
'Guinnevere' (Crosby, Stills & Nash), 382, 517
'Gunga Din' (Byrds), 527–529, 582, 769, 830
Gunnell, Rik, 157–158
Gunther, Carl, 97, 178, 274
Guthrie, Arlo, 516, 578, 818
Guthrie, Woody, 31, 45, 475–476, 522, 528
Guttler, George, 505
Gwalia Deserta (poetry anthology) (Idris Davies), 130

Hacienda Brothers, The, 848
Haggard, Merle, 416, 432, 443, 455, 478–479, 505, 627–628
Hair (musical), 549
Halee, Roy, 377
Halem, Richard, 657, 660, 662
Hall, Denise, 160
Hall, Francis C., 66
Halverson, Bill, 633
Halverson, Suzanne, 633
Hambley, Scott, 46
Hamilton, Bobby, 154
Hamilton, Frank, 23
Hamlet (play) (William Shakespeare), 323
Hammond, John, 69, 87
Hammond, Ollie, 184
'Hanging On' (Gosdin Brothers), 527
Hannan, Jimmy, 26, 54
Happens (David Hemmings), 366
Hard Day's Night, A (film), 38, 54, 66, 162, 168
Hardin, Glen D., 627
Hardin, Tim, 351, 428, 516, 576, 768, 809
Hardy, Francoise, 2
Harris, Emmylou, 627–628, 823, 846, 849
Harris, Greg, 722
Harris, Paul, 622, 687
Harrison, Charlie, 637
Harrison, George, 66, 97, 156, 176–180, 205, 220, 223, 244, 252, 274, 303–305, 377, 562, 637, 795, 806, 832
Hartford, John, 431, 472

Hartley, Keef, 516
Harvest (Neil Young), 640, 817
Hassilev, Alex, 23
Hassinger, Dave, 242, 245
Hastings, Doug, 352
'Have You Seen Her Face' (Byrds), 313, 318–319, 321, 354, 366, 443, 742, 767
'Have You Seen Her Face' (Chris Hillman & Herb Pedersen), 824
'Have You Seen Your Mother, Baby, Standing In The Shadow?' (Rolling Stones), 302
Havens, Richie, 516
Hawkins, George, 793
Hayes, Red, 228–229
Hayford, Jack, 849
Hazlewood, Lee, 416, 448
'He Was A Friend Of Mine' (Byrds), 9, 227–228, 355–356, 373, 434, 481, 764, 829
'He Was A Friend Of Mine' (Dian & The Greenbriar Boys), 857
'He Was A Friend Of Mine' (Manassas, with Roger McGuinn), 614
'He Was A Friend Of Mine' (McGuinn & Clark, with David Crosby), 673
'He Was A Friend Of Mine' (McGuinn, Crosby & Hillman, billed as 'the original Byrds'), 763
Headlights, The, 794
'Heartbreak Hotel' (Elvis Presley), 8, 22, 797
'Heartbreak Hotel' (Roger McGuinn), 797, 804
'Heave Away' (Roger McGuinn), 525
'Heavenly Fire' (Souther, Hillman, Furay Band), 644
Hedgehopper's Anonymous, 192
Hefner, Hugh, 493
Heider, Wally, 595, 598
Heinlein, Robert A., 200, 375
'Help!' (Beatles), 2, 8, 164, 170
Help! (film), 220, 286
Hemmings, David, 366
Hendrix, Jimi, 315, 350, 360, 515–516
Henley, Don, 771
Henry VIII, King, 802
Henske, Judy, 105
'Here Without You' (Byrds), 58, 129–130, 765–766
'Here Without You' (Gene Clark), 777
Herman's Hermits, 7, 185, 316, 762
Hersh, Al, 552–558, 561, 599, 603, 606, 624–625, 634, 664–665, 671–672, 675, 677–683, 685, 691–692, 695–696, 698–702, 706, 710–712
'Hey Joe' (Byrds), 134–135, 143, 177, 273, 296–297, 322, 334, 354, 373, 766
'Hey Joe' (Leaves), 177, 296

INDEX

'Hey Joe' (Love), 296
'Hey Little Cobra' (Rip Chords), 80
'Hey Nelly Nelly' (Judy Collins), 202
'Hickory Wind' (Byrds), 419, 427–428, 432, 448, 455, 476–478, 482, 493, 543
'Hickory Wind' (Gram Parsons/Flying Burrito Brothers), 505
'Hickory Wind' (Roger McGuinn & Chris Hillman), 791
High Noon (film), 30
Highway 61 Revisited (Bob Dylan), 7, 188
Hill, Steve, 791–792
Hill, Vince, 315
Hillman, Chris, 8, 17–18, 21, 45–50, 64, 66, 70, 75–78, 81, 92, 96, 99, 108, 112, 119, 129, 136, 143–144, 154, 156, 159, 161–163, 168, 170, 173–175, 198, 202, 206, 209, 211–212, 215–216, 218, 221, 228–229, 238, 240, 242, 244, 248, 250, 260, 266–267, 270, 276, 279–280, 283, 288, 293, 297, 312–315, 318–323, 325–326, 330, 334, 339–344, 348–349, 351–352, 354–359, 365–369, 371–375, 377–384, 387–390, 392–400, 402–409, 412, 414, 417–423, 425–426, 429, 431–433, 435–438, 440, 442–446, 448–450, 457–461, 464–466, 468–469, 472, 477–479, 484–495, 503–505, 519, 537–539, 583, 597–599, 601, 607–611, 613–616, 618–619, 621–622, 626–628, 631, 644–645, 648–649, 651–652, 654–657, 659–667, 669, 671–677, 680–698, 700–721, 724, 726–727, 736, 741–742, 744–757, 759, 762–765, 767, 770–772, 779, 781, 784, 789–793, 798–799, 801, 805–806, 811–812, 814–825, 831–832, 836, 846, 851–853, 858–866, 868–869
   acerbity, 170, 344, 383, 457–458, 484, 504, 655, 695–696, 711, 748, 851, 869
   African music, interest in, 312–313
   Apartheid, views on, 465–466
   apologia to UK, 173–175
   assassination threat, 467–468
   bass playing, 49–50, 66, 129, 156, 216, 221, 312, 320–321, 330, 404, 609, 657, 672, 741, 743, 751, 767
   Bernal, Carlos, feud with, 489–491, 711–712
   birth, 45
   Buffalo Springfield, championing of, 283
   Burrito Deluxe recording, 537
   Byrds, disenchantment with recording, 621–622, 656
   Capitol Records' signing, 667, 671
   CBS contract 1968, 419–420
   CBS, name added to 'Byrds' contract, 70, 81, 99, 297, 488
   childhood, 45
   Clark, Gene, relationship with, 266, 392, 435, 664, 675–676, 694–696, 698–699, 718–719, 764, 853
   Clarke, Michael, relationship with, 371, 494, 649, 753–755, 759, 763, 771–773, 781, 868
   coldness, 355–356, 359, 392, 458, 464, 484, 677
   Crosby, David, relationship with, 49, 312, 315, 321, 342, 355–356, 358–359, 365, 367, 372, 374–381, 383–385, 398, 404–405, 407, 412, 599, 674, 693, 741, 747, 749, 752, 784, 790–792, 812, 817–818, 821–822, 831–832, 853, 866
   Desert Rose Band disbandment, 790
   Desert Rose Band recordings, 717–718, 789–790
   Desert Rose Band 'reunion', 824
   destruction of home, 314–315
   Dickson, Jim, relationship with, 46–48, 50, 75–77, 215–216, 348, 537, 716, 719, 744–745, 859, 861–866, 868–869
   divorces/break-ups, 489–491, 655
   draft evasion, 136
   drug use/abuse, 96, 240, 654, 721, 852
   early musical career, 45–47
   eulogy to Michael Clarke, 781, 853
   father's suicide, reaction to, 46, 215, 718, 865
   favoured by Carl Franzoni, 143–144
   final gigs with Byrds (1973), 608–611
   Flying Burrito Brothers, establishing of, 438, 485, 491
   Flying Burrito Brothers, The, recording, 613
   Gilded Palace Of Sin, The, recording, 494, 503, 537
   girlfriends, 75, 78, 664, 691
   Hall of Fame induction, 771–772
   health kick, 717–718, 752
   Hemmings, David, guest collaboration, 366
   Hepatitis C treatment, 792–793, 821
   High Court appearance, 662
   Hillmen, The, 48–49
   humour, 17, 371, 655, 657, 701, 750, 846
   image, 8, 161, 238, 260, 423, 503, 683
   James, Catherine, incident, 75–77, 215
   Jet Set, joining of, 49–50
   Kelley, Kevin, relationship with, 397–398, 485–487
   Knobler, Peter, collaboration with, 705, 707
   Last Of The Red Hot Burritos, recording, 613
   leaving Byrds, 77, 489–490

Hillman, Chris (contd.)
   Manassas, involvement with, 598–599, 608, 614, 644, 665, 681, 715, 752, 772, 791, 805–806
   mandolin playing, 46–48, 50, 221, 616, 716, 742, 772, 823
   marriages, 136, 321, 445–446, 664, 691–692, 717, 823
   McGuinn, Clark & Hillman recordings, 676, 680–682, 684–688, 701, 704–708
   McGuinn, Clark & Hillman tours, 671–676, 690, 695–696, 698
   McGuinn, Jim/Roger, relationship with, 78, 313–314, 318, 374, 398, 406, 412, 421–422, 429, 432, 438, 446, 449, 464, 466–467, 479, 484, 489, 503–505, 608–610, 656–657, 660–664, 671–672, 675–676, 682, 691, 695, 700–701, 710–715, 721, 747, 752, 765, 790–791, 812, 822, 832, 853
   McGuinn/Hillman duo, 710–715
   Norris, Chuck, involvement with, 672, 695
   O'Kelley, Kim, tour, 666–667
   Parsons, Gram, relationship with, 417–418, 422–424, 433, 438, 445–446, 450, 458, 460, 477–478, 485, 491, 494, 503, 626–628
   Pedersen, Herb, collaboration with, 790–792, 822
   professionalism, 17, 654–655, 677
   religion/spirituality, 691, 717, 817, 823, 851
   remorse/maturity/forgiveness, 851–853, 864–866
   Republican sympathies, 817, 823, 852
   retirement threat, 715
   reunions with 'Byrds', 747–753, 763, 821–822
   Rice Brothers, collaboration with, 791–792, 822
   Roberts, Rick, relationship/collaboration with, 613, 648–649, 685, 716
   Scottsville Squirrel Barkers, working with, 46–47, 822–823
   shyness, 48, 64, 168, 173, 340, 342, 344, 750
   singing, 48, 279, 319, 354, 443–444, 477–478, 505, 673, 680, 750, 764, 806, 822–825
   solo albums, 645, 655–656, 664–665, 716–717, 791–792, 823, 864
   songwriting/compositions, 313, 318–323, 326, 365, 368, 374, 399, 402, 406–409, 425, 491, 503, 618–619, 621, 644–645, 685, 705–707, 718, 767, 791–792, 798, 801

Souther, Hillman, Furay Band interlude, 644–645, 664–665
Spector, Larry, ambivalent relationship with, 420–421, 484–485, 489, 491, 503
spinal surgery, 825, 869
surliness/sarcasm/ego, 215–216, 229, 340, 342, 344, 383, 392, 457–458, 464, 504, 652, 672
suspicious nature, 18, 664
UK tour (1977), 651–661
violence/temper tantrums in Byrds and beyond, 75–77, 211–212, 457, 484, 489–491, 671–672, 676–677, 695–696, 714–715
White, Clarence, championing of, 469–470, 472, 485
Hillman, Constance ('Connie'), 664, 691–692, 708, 717, 823, 851
Hillmen, The, 48–49, 60, 76, 716, 857, 867
Hillmen, The (Hillmen), 48, 716
Hinckley, John Warnock, 713
Hinshaw, Chris, 561
Hinton, Christine, 247, 614, 639
Hippard, Cheryl, 724–725
Hippard, R.J. [Bob], 24, 28, 319, 493, 528, 594, 685, 724–725, 809
Hirshhorn, Caryl, 65–66
Hirshhorn, Naomi, 65–68, 90, 97, 492
Hitchcock, Alfred, 150
Hodges, Eddie, 80
Hoffman, Dustin, 451
Hoh, Eddie, 493
'Hold It!' (Byrds), 501–502, 543
Holdridge, Cheryl, 103–104
Hollies Sing Dylan (Hollies), 560
Hollies, The, 148, 153, 307, 334, 373, 382, 517, 560
Hollingworth, Roy, 574
Holly, Buddy, 69, 238
Hollywood Bowl Symphony Orchestra, 605
Holograms, The, 848
Holzman, Jack, 32, 44, 54, 65, 202, 225, 275
'Home On The Hillside' (1992 'musical' version), 796
'Home Sweet Home' (Byrds), 559
Homer, 297, 407
'Homeward Through The Haze' (Crosby & Nash), 641
Hook (film), 783
Hootie And The Blowfish, 783
Hopkins, Jerry, 436
Hopper, Dennis, 93, 103, 139, 182, 311, 344–346, 509–512, 871
Hord, Eric, 243
Hot Band, The, 846
'Hot Burrito # 2' (Chris Hillman Band), 805

INDEX

'Hot Burrito # 2' (Flying Burrito Brothers), 805
Houdini, Henry, 697
'House Of The Rising Sun' (Animals), 64
Houston, Cisco, 45
Howard, Harlan, 443
Hubley, Season, 638, 669
'Hula Bula Man' (Gene Clark), 805
Human Highway (unreleased album) (Crosby, Stills, Nash & Young), 640
Humble Pie, 516
Humperdinck, Engelbert, 315
Humphrey, Hubert, Vice President, 452
'Hungry Planet' (Byrds), 544–545
'Hungry Planet, The' (Earth Island), 545
Hunter, Meredith, 532
Hunter, Nigel, 155
Hurt, Mississippi John, 291
Husker Du, 738
Huskey, Roy, 431, 472
Hussein, King, 415
Hutchins, Chris, 150
Hutton, Barbara, 103
Hyde, Bob, 738, 744
Hyde, Jackie, 818

'I Am A Pilgrim' (Byrds), 428, 444, 472–473, 505
'I Am A Pilgrim' (Kentucky Colonels), 505
'I Belong' (Kathy Kirby), 6
'(I Can't Get No) Satisfaction' (Rolling Stones), 2, 8, 117, 164, 170, 192
'I Come And Stand At Every Door' (Byrds), 295–296, 525
'I Don't Believe You' (Bob Dylan), 195
'I Don't Ever Want To Spoil Your Party' (Byrds), 201, 799
'I Don't Ever Want To Spoil Your Party' (Dino Valenti), 201, 799
'I Feel Fine' (Beatles), 2
'I Got You Babe' (Sonny & Cher), 126, 165–166, 170, 187
'I Hear A Symphony' (Supremes), 223
'I Hear Singing' (Chris Hillman), 313
'I Knew I'd Want You' (Byrds), 9, 58, 81, 86–87, 133, 204, 739–740, 765
'I Know My Rider' (David Crosby), 34
'I Know My Rider' (I Know You Rider) (Byrds), 291, 299, 354, 373, 743, 801
'I Love The Life I Live' (Byrds), 799
'I See You' (Byrds), 294, 306, 766
'I Trust' (Byrds), 15, 559, 563–564, 567, 769, 829
'I Wanna Be Your Man' (Rolling Stones), 302
'I Wanna Grow Up To Be A Politician' (Byrds), 569–570, 769

'I Wanna Grow Up To Be A Politician' (1992 'musical' version), 796
'I Wanna Grow Up To Be A Politician' (Roger McGuinn), 723
'I Want To Hold Your Hand' (Beatles), 38, 63, 797
'I Want To Hold Your Hand' (Roger McGuinn), 797, 804–805
'I'd Swear There Was Somebody Here' (David Crosby), 614
'I'm Alive' (Hollies), 148
'I'm Henry VIII, I Am' (Herman's Hermits), 185
'I'm So Restless' (Byrds), 595, 623–624
'I'm So Restless' (Roger McGuinn), 595
'I'm Still Alive' (Chris Hillman), 791
Ibsen, Henrik, 450, 796
Icicle Works, 724
If I Could Only Remember My Name (David Crosby), 19, 614, 620, 737, 818, 833, 850
'If I Needed Someone' (Beatles), 223, 322, 794
'If I Needed Someone' (Roger McGuinn), 832
'If You Gotta Go, Go Now' (Manfred Mann), 192, 427
'If You Knew' (Gene Clark), 776
'If You're Gone' (Byrds), 229–230, 526
Impressions (John Coltrane), 294
'In A Misty Morning' (Gene Clark), 613
'In My Dreams' (Crosby, Stills & Nash), 667
'In My Room' (Beach Boys), 300
In The Beginning (Byrds), 56, 59, 745–746
'In The Evenin'' (Roger McGuinn), 23, 802–803
Incredible String Band, The, 516, 576
Ingles, Jackie, 253
Ingram, Bobby, 32
Inside Pop: The Rock Revolution (television documentary), 344
International Submarine Band, The, 416–419, 424–425, 428, 434, 437, 448, 476, 828
Invasion Of The Bodysnatchers (film), 605, 697
Ireland, Jill, 139
Irish Ramblers, The, 27
Iron Butterfly, 515
Irwin, Bob, 799–801, 808–809
'Is It Really Monday?' (David Crosby), 517
'Is This My Destiny' (Byrds), 563, 572
'It Ain't Me Babe' (Johnny Cash), 192
'It Ain't Me Babe' (Turtles), 188
'It Doesn't Matter' (Chris Hillman Band), 805
'It Doesn't Matter' (Manassas), 644, 805
'It Happens Each Day' (Byrds), 409, 741–742, 767, 801, 818
'It Was I' (Skip & Flip), 520

It Was Twenty Years Ago Today (television documentary), 839
'It Won't Be Wrong' (Byrds), 44, 225, 248, 253, 750
It's All Coming Back To Me Now . . . (David Crosby), 782–783
'It's All Over Now, Baby Blue' (Bob Dylan), 146, 195, 799
'It's All Over Now, Baby Blue' (Byrds), 142, 195–197, 201–202, 217–218, 505, 526–527, 529, 740, 766, 799
'It's All Over Now, Baby Blue' (Joan Baez), 192
'It's All Right Ma (I'm Only Bleeding)' (Bob Dylan), 510
'It's All Right Ma (I'm Only Bleeding)' (Byrds), 827
'It's All Right Ma (I'm Only Bleeding)' (Roger McGuinn), 511
'It's Been Raining' (David Crosby), 31
'It's Good News Week' (Hedgehopper's Anonymous), 192
'It's My Life' (Animals), 192
'It's No Use' (Byrds), 57, 133, 745, 798
Ivy League, The, 151

'Jack O' Diamonds' (David Crosby), 34
'Jack Tarr The Sailor' (Byrds), 525, 802
Jackson, Mahalia, 453
Jacobsen, Eric, 291
Jagger, Bianca, 692
Jagger, Mick, 42, 117–118, 151, 153, 189, 217, 315–316, 353, 439, 442, 445–447, 456, 459–461, 692
'Jamaica Say You Will' (Byrds), 572–573, 583
'Jamaica Say You Will' (Jackson Browne), 572
James, Billy, 105, 118, 131, 142, 590, 845
James, Catherine, 75–77, 215
James, Dian, 76
James, Etta, 846
James, Harry, 400
James, Jesse, 476
Jan & Dean, 80
Jay, Peter, & The Jaywalkers, 170
Jayhawks, The, 804
Jazz Crusaders, The, 619
Jefferson Airplane, 282, 293, 327, 337–338, 342–343, 350–351, 357, 375–377, 379, 440, 470, 515–516, 537, 548, 614–615, 806
Jefferson Airplane Takes Off (Jefferson Airplane), 282, 293
Jeffries, Herb, 32
Jenkins, Roy, 258
Jesse, Wolff & Whings, 840–841
Jesu Joy Of Man's Desiring (Bach), 205
Jesus (festival attendee), 576–577

'Jesus Is Just Alright' (Art Reynolds Singers), 525
'Jesus Is Just Alright' (Byrds), 525–526, 566, 768, 827
'Jesus Is Just Alright' (Doobie Brothers), 526
Jet Set, The, 21, 37–39, 42–44, 49–66, 68–72, 74, 88, 92, 271, 394, 858
Jet Set, The (identically named US group), 394
Jet Set, The (UK Decca label act), 71
Jet Set, The (UK Delta label act), 71
Jethro Tull, 515
'Jigsaw' (David Crosby), 726
'John Birch Society, The' (Chad Mitchell Trio), 24
'John Riley' (Byrds), 297–298, 407, 572, 766, 801
'John Riley' (Joan Baez), 798
'John Riley' (Roger McGuinn), 797–798
John Wesley Harding (Bob Dylan), 426, 481
John, Elton, 664
'Johnny Rolling Stone' (Jimmy Gavin), 869
'John's Music Box' (Mamas & The Papas), 406
Johnson, Art, 521
Johnson, Derek, 160–161, 164, 259, 332, 373, 444, 508
Johnson, Lou, 6
Johnson, Lyndon Baines, President, 29, 364, 403, 452
Johnston, Bob, 498, 502, 507–508, 536, 768, 809
Johnston, Bruce, 80, 623, 764
'Jolly Roger' (Roger McGuinn), 525, 638
Jones, Allan, 712
Jones, Brian, 8, 42–43, 118, 152, 156–157, 257, 274, 353, 442, 446
Jones, George, 429, 437, 475, 628, 637, 781
Jones, Paul, 151, 155–156, 190
Jones, Tom, 316
Joplin, Janis, 516
Jordan, Louis, 139
Jorgerison, John, 717, 747, 749, 764, 789, 793
Journals (bootleg set) (Byrds), 799, 829
Journeymen, The, 415
Joyce, Ana, 172
'Juanita' (Flying Burrito Brothers), 503
Judy Collins 3 (Judy Collins), 131, 201–202
'Jumpin' Jack Flash' (Rolling Stones), 446
'Just A Season' (Byrds), 545, 550, 570, 724, 769
'Just A Season' (1992 'musical' version), 796
'Just A Season' (Roger McGuinn), 723
Just A Season: A Romance Of The Old West (musical), 795–796
'Just A Song Before I Go' (Crosby, Stills & Nash), 667

INDEX

'Just Like A Woman' (Byrds), 766, 769, 827
'Just Like A Woman' (Manfred Mann), 427
'Just Like Gravity' (CPR), 818
Just Like Gravity (CPR), 818
'Just Remember I Love You' (Firefall), 649
'Just You' (Sonny & Cher), 188

Kaleidoscope, 343
Kandanes, Andy, 652, 661, 675, 702
Kantner, Paul, 31, 282, 377, 727
'Kathleen's Song' (Byrds), 572–573, 584–585, 724, 769, 827
Kaufman, Philip, 626, 629
Kaye, Thomas Jefferson, 17, 646–647, 654–655, 681, 697
KC & The Sunshine Band, 686–687
KC Southern Band, 655, 805
Keith, Billy, 625
Keller, Erika, 818
Kelley, Kevin, 16, 77, 397–398, 414, 422–423, 431, 437, 440, 444, 464–465, 468, 472, 474, 479, 485–488, 534, 552, 645, 840–841
Kelley, Kevin [Rolling Thunder Revue musician], 635
Kelly, Gene, 139
Kelly, Ned, 476
Kennedy, Jackie, 10
Kennedy, John Fitzgerald, President, 9–10, 24, 227–228, 274, 304, 355–356, 452, 481, 713, 764
Kennedy, Robert F., Senator, 452–454, 481, 713
Kentucky Colonels, The, 469, 505, 524, 625–626, 628
Kerouac, Jack, 41
Kerr, Michelle, 95, 98–99, 106, 123
Kerry, Bob, 79
'Kicks' (Paul Revere & The Raiders), 283
Kimmel, Tom, 707
Kincaid, Jesse Lee (see Nick Gerlach)
Kindling (Gene Parsons), 505
'King Apathy III' (Byrds), 500–501, 768
'King Midas In Reverse' (Hollies), 373
'King Of The Hill' (Roger McGuinn), 725, 794
'King Of The Mountain' (David Crosby), 726
King, B.B., 146, 515
King, Carole, 26, 375, 401, 405–406, 511, 806
King, Jonathan, 192
King, Martin Luther, Dr, 452, 481, 713
King, Robin, 648, 781, 859
Kingston Trio, The, 24, 29, 33, 45, 415, 452
Kinks, The, 2, 8, 153, 251
Kipling, Rudyard, 229
Kirby, Kathy, 6
Kirkpatrick, Scott, 701

Kirshner, Don, 549
Kitt, Eartha, 23
Kız Çocuğu (aka 'The Little Girl') (poem) (Nâzim Hikmet Ran), 295
Kleinow, Sneaky Pete, 438, 450, 505, 544, 626, 634, 712
Knack, The, 696
Knechtel, Larry, 81, 133, 188, 525, 566, 740, 827
Knobler, Peter, 705, 707
'Knockin' On Heaven's Door' (McGuinn & Clark), 665
'Kokomo' (Beach Boys), 846
Kooper, Al, 633
Korzybski, Alfred, 204
Koto (John York), 843
Kristofferson, Kris, 636
Kubrick, Stanley, 135, 410
Kyo, Takako, 848

'La Bamba' (Gauchos), 95
L.A. Express, 843
LaBianca, Leno, 512, 516, 530, 558
LaBianca, Rosemary, 512, 516, 530, 558
Ladies Of The Canyon (Joni Mitchell), 617
'Lady Friend' (Byrds), 354, 364–368, 372–373, 377, 396, 400, 742, 767, 802
'Lady Of The North' (Gene Clark), 646
'Lady, The' (Roger McGuinn), 633, 705
Lagin, Ned, 641
Laine, Denny, 156
Laine, Frankie, 69, 80
Lala, Joe, 608–610, 619, 677, 683, 687
Lambert, Kit, 136, 321, 491
Lance, Major, 105, 108
Land Of Giants (New Christy Minstrels), 29
Landau, Jon, 292
Landis, Don, 288
Larson, Nicolette, 846
Last Chance, 840
'Last Dance' (Neil Young), 639
'Last Of The Blue Diamond Miners' (Gene Clark), 655, 805
Last Of The Red Hot Burritos (Flying Burrito Brothers), 613
'Last Thing On My Mind, The' (Clarence White), 617
'Last Time, The' (Rolling Stones), 2
'Laugh At Me' (Sonny), 187
'Laughing' (Byrds), 382, 619–621
'Laughing' (David Crosby), 382, 517, 620
Lawford, Peter, 72
'Lay Down Your Weary Tune' (Bob Dylan), 184, 226–227
'Lay Down Your Weary Tune' (Byrds), 184, 226–227

'Lay Lady Lay' (Bob Dylan), 507–508
'Lay Lady Lay' (Byrds), 507–508, 768, 809
'Lay Me Down' (Crosby & Nash), 820
'Lazy Days' (Byrds), 428, 479, 768, 809
'Lazy Days' (Flying Burrito Brothers), 428, 768, 809
'Lazy Days' (International Submarine Band), 428
'Lazy Waters' (Byrds), 578, 586, 769
Leadbelly [Huddie Ledbetter], 23, 545, 548, 797–798
Leadon, Bernie, 505, 626, 716–717
Lear, John, 272, 298
Lear, William P., 272
Leary, Timothy, 307, 571
Leaves, The, 177, 296
Led Zeppelin, 515, 536
'Lee Shore, The' (Crosby, Stills, Nash & Young), 615
Lee, Brenda, 6
Lee, Peggy, 35
Legends, The, 415
Lennon, John, 19, 85, 140, 156, 168, 176–177, 179, 216, 242, 302–305, 510, 692–693, 703, 713, 728, 806
Lesh, Phil, 641–642
'Let 'Em In' (Paul McCartney/Wings), 686
Let It Be (Beatles), 587, 806
'Let Me Down Easy' (Roger McGuinn & Chris Hillman, Featuring Gene Clark), 707
'Let's Impeach The President' (Crosby, Stills, Nash & Young), 834
'Let's Spend The Night Together' (Rolling Stones), 315–316
Levy, Claudia, 844
Levy, Jackie, 237–238, 248
Levy, Jacques, 447, 450–453, 500, 521, 540–541, 544, 549–551, 559, 569–570, 594, 616–617, 633–634, 636, 681, 724, 795–796, 843–844
Levy, Julien, 844
Levy, Maya, 844
Lewis, Gary, & The Playboys, 7
Lewis, Jerry, 96
Lewis, Ken, 151
Lewis, Mike, 686–687
Leyton, John, 139
Lieberson, Goddard, 142
'Lies' (Manassas), 644
'Life And Times' (Gene Clark), 777
Life Goes On (Desert Rose Band), 790
'Life In A Northern Town' (Icicle Works), 724
'Life In A Northern Town' (Roger McGuinn), 724
'Life In Prison' (Byrds), 437, 448, 478–479, 809

'Life In Prison' (Merle Haggard), 478–479
'Light My Fire' (Doors), 338
'Light Up The Darkness' (Roger McGuinn), 722
Lightning Seeds, The, 57
Like A Hurricane (Chris Hillman), 791
'Like A Rolling Stone' (Bob Dylan), 8, 145, 164
Limeliters, The, 23–24, 36
Limited Edition (Roger McGuinn), 832–833
Lincoln Festival, 576–578
Lind, Bob, 283
Liston, Sonny, 95
Little Feat, 544, 754
'Little Jimmy Whelan' (Roger McGuinn), 802
'Little Mama' (McGuinn, Clark & Hillman), 686
'Little Ole Wine Drinker Me' (Dean Martin), 258
Little Richard, 105, 111
Little Shop Of Horrors, The (film), 32, 510, 856
'Little Wing' (David Crosby), 726
'Little Wing' (Neil Young), 726
Live Aid, 733
Live!!! Almost!!! (Dillards), 429
Live At The Bitter End (Chad Mitchell Trio), 24
Live At The Fillmore – February 1969 (Byrds), 494, 825–826
Live At The Royal Albert Hall 1971 (Byrds), 563, 830
Live From Mars (Roger McGuinn), 550, 804–805
Live It Up (Crosby, Stills & Nash), 782
Live 1973 (Gram Parsons & The Fallen Angels), 628
'Living Legend' (Roger McGuinn), 724
Living With War (Crosby, Stills, Nash & Young), 834
Lloyd, Charles, 624
Lomax, John, 423
Lombard, Carole, 386
'Lonely Sea' (Beach Boys), 300
'Long Black Veil' (Byrds), 505
Long Gone Miles, 856
'Long Live Love' (Sandie Shaw), 5
'Long Live The King' (Byrds), 597, 619
'Long Long Time' (McGuinn, Clark & Hillman), 685
Long Ryders, The, 720
Long Time Gone (autobiography) (David Crosby & Carl Gottlieb), 737, 743, 833, 860–861
'Long Time Gone' (Crosby, Stills & Nash), 481, 517
'Long Time Gone' (Crosby, Stills, Nash & Young), 640, 819
Looking Forward (Crosby, Stills, Nash & Young), 788
'Lost My Driving Wheel' (Byrds), 590, 828

INDEX

'Lost My Driving Wheel' (Roger McGuinn), 828
Louvin Brothers, The, 47, 473–474, 791
Love, 282, 296
Love & Theft (Bob Dylan), 232
Love, Mike, 664
'Love That Never Dies' (Byrds), 764–765
'Love's Gonna Live Here' (Buck Owens), 170
'Love's Gonna Live Here' (Ray Charles), 170
'Lover Of The Bayou' (Byrds), 541, 550, 602, 610, 769, 827
'Lover Of The Bayou' (1992 'musical' version), 796
'Lover Of The Bayou' (Roger McGuinn), 634, 656, 723
Lovin' Spoonful, The, 123, 253, 281–282, 291, 307
'Lucky Me' (Clarence White), 626
Lulu, 2
Lynch, Kenny, 166–167
Lynch, Stan, 764, 793
Lynn, Vera, 135, 159

'M'Linda' (Roger McGuinn), 635
MacArthur, Douglas, General, 855
MacFarlane, Will, 710
'Mack The Knife' (Bobby Darin), 25
MacLean, Bryan, 139, 141, 144, 147, 282
Maddox, Rose, 583
'Made In China' (Roger McGuinn), 804
'Mae Jean Goes To Hollywood' (Byrds), 529, 768, 810
'Mae Jean Goes To Hollywood' (Johnny Darrell), 768
'Maggie's Farm' (Bob Dylan), 215, 491
'Maggie's Farm' (Byrds), 215
Mahal, Taj, 77, 397, 474
Mahavishnu Orchestra, 579–580
Makeba, Miriam, 312–313, 446, 461, 483
Mamas & The Papas, The, 253, 277–278, 281–282, 338, 350, 361–362, 406, 492, 592, 670
'Man Of Mystery' (Shadows), 705
Man Who Fell To Earth, The (film), 451
Manassas, 598–599, 608, 614–615, 644, 665, 681, 684, 715–716, 752, 772, 791, 806
Manassas (Manassas), 614–615, 644, 681, 806
Mancini, Henry, 453
Mancini, Mary, 94
Mandela, Nelson, 465
Maness, Jay Dee, 434, 437–438, 474, 717, 789
Manfred Mann, 155, 190, 192, 427
Mann, Barry, 80
Manners, Zeke, 528–529

Mansfield, David, 636, 717
Manson, Charles, 530–532, 558, 561, 627, 629, 846
Mantovani, 316
Mao, Chairman, 481
Marcos, Ferdinand, President, 303
Marcos, Imelda, 303
Marker, Gary, 398, 638, 845
Marlowe, Christopher, 285
Marr, Sally, 88–89
Martin, Dean, 96, 258
Martin, Michael, 629
Mary Poppins (soundtrack), 71
Masekela, Hugh, 312, 314, 318, 328, 331, 346–347, 350, 354, 360, 400
Mason, Bonnie Jo, 111
Mason, Dave, 641
Mason, Jim, 649
Mathis, Johnny, 69
'May The Road Rise (To Meet You)' (Roger McGuinn), 804, 832
May, Tom, 196–197
Mayall, John, 157
'Maybe You Think' (Byrds), 55
Maymudes, Victor, 60, 64, 103, 490–491, 751, 857–858
Mazer, Elliot, 640
Mbulu, Letta, 312–313
McCallum, David, 139
McCarthy, Eugene, Senator, 452
McCartney, Linda (née Eastman), 307, 692
McCartney, Paul, 66, 153, 157–158, 178–180, 217, 226, 303, 305, 318, 330, 332–333, 353, 355–356, 686, 692, 806
McClure, Marc, 487
McCormick, Patti, 270
McDaniel, Marshall, 256
McDowell, Patrick, Judge, 730, 732–734
McDowell, Roddy, 138
McFarlane, Spanky, 595, 623
McGhee, Brownie, 576
McGuinn, Camilla, 275, 669–670, 679–680, 691–692, 706–707, 709, 713, 722, 724, 794, 804, 833, 849–850, 865–866, 870
McGuinn, Clark & Hillman, 17, 664–667, 669, 671–709, 726, 859
McGuinn, Clark & Hillman (McGuinn, Clark & Hillman), 681–688, 704, 708
McGuinn, Dolores aka Ianthe (see Dolores Tickner)
McGuinn, Dorothy (Jim/Roger McGuinn's mother), 21, 120, 169, 217, 853
McGuinn, Henry (Jim/Roger McGuinn's second son), 540, 669, 847
McGuinn/Hillman (McGuinn/Hillman), 710–711

McGuinn, James (Jim/Roger McGuinn's father), 21, 169, 217
McGuinn, Jim (Roger), 3, 8, 13, 15, 17–19, 21–30, 35–38, 42, 44–45, 49, 51–57, 59–62, 64, 66–68, 70–74, 76–85, 89–93, 96, 98–99, 101, 103–104, 107, 110–112, 116–117, 119–124, 127–129, 131–134, 136, 140–141, 143–144, 146, 153–154, 156, 161–163, 165–170, 176–179, 182–187, 190–191, 193, 195–196, 198–225, 227–236, 238–241, 243–245, 247–255, 257–258, 260–267, 269–275, 279–280, 282–290, 292–300, 303–304, 309, 313–315, 318–321, 323, 325–327, 329–330, 333–334, 336–337, 339–341, 343–344, 347, 350–359, 361–384, 387–401, 404–415, 418–432, 435–468, 470, 472, 474–477, 479–485, 488–530, 532–551, 553–573, 575–576, 578–585, 587–612, 614–625, 630–639, 642, 645, 651–654, 656–677, 679–715, 717, 719–727, 731, 736, 740, 743–760, 762–766, 768–772, 775, 777, 782, 790–798, 801–816, 818–823, 825–828, 830–833, 836, 843–845, 849–854, 858–859, 861–866, 868, 870
- alcohol use/abuse, 428, 553–554, 558, 579, 625, 635, 638, 658, 667–668, 679–680, 794
- aloofness/coolness/distancing/lack of emotion/suppression of feelings, 67, 119, 144, 167, 185, 211–212, 236, 244, 340, 344, 353, 355, 359, 361, 460, 484, 490, 503–504, 506–507, 519–520, 643, 691, 764, 808, 813, 832, 864
- anxiety attacks, 270, 466–467
- apathy, 482, 500, 504, 507, 529, 568, 583–584, 589, 604
- aversion to Byrds' reunions, 661, 715, 719, 746–748, 753–756, 760, 762, 796, 808, 811–812, 831–832, 853
- Battin, Skip, relationship/interaction with/firing of, 539, 545–547, 559–560, 591, 593–594, 596, 606–608, 722, 766, 828
- Beatles' influence, 27–29, 38–39, 55, 66, 68, 89, 131, 140, 156–157, 176–181, 191, 223, 242, 244, 271, 274, 303, 333, 335, 441–442, 510, 794
- birth, 21
- box set politicking, 765–766
- Byrds reunions, 588–589, 596–601, 607, 612–613, 615–622, 631–633, 747–752, 763–765, 772–773
- CBS contract termination, 663
- CBS signing, 70
- children, 361, 387, 540, 847

chronology of twentieth-century music concept, 424, 436–437, 442, 481, 495, 598
- Clark, Gene, relationship with, 30, 35–36, 249–250, 255, 265–266, 270, 272–273, 389, 392, 403, 406, 421, 597, 625, 661–666, 698–699, 777
- Clarke, Michael, relationship with, 42–43, 162, 212, 297, 370–371, 395, 595, 673, 748–749, 754–755, 757, 759–760, 770–773
- Coltrane, John, interest in/reaction to music of, 222, 251–253, 294
- considers leaving Byrds, 90–91
- conversion, 668, 721
- country, musicologist interest in, 423
- Crosby, David, relationship with, 36, 120, 199, 206, 212, 214, 216–218, 233–236, 288, 347, 350–351, 353, 355–359, 361, 365, 367, 370–372, 375–385, 398, 404–405, 410–412, 504, 508, 517–518, 597, 599–601, 607, 615, 621, 623–624, 630–631, 641, 658–659, 673–675, 709–710, 726, 747, 749, 752, 754–755, 765, 793, 796, 807–808, 811–812, 815, 822, 831–832, 863
- cynicism, 266, 273, 314, 340, 356, 372, 503–504, 721, 764–766
- Darin, Bobby, work with/influence of, 25–28, 191–193, 578
- DeLeon, Dolores, relationship with/marriage to, 77–78, 103–104, 117, 183–185, 201, 217, 260, 287, 361, 387, 445, 540, 554–557, 561, 565, 582, 617, 669
- Dickson, Jim, relationship with, 36, 43, 61, 67, 72–74, 82–83, 91, 122, 129, 197–198, 202–207, 210–215, 218–219, 231–236, 245, 275–276, 300, 327, 336–337, 347, 354, 538–539, 545, 590, 744, 751, 764, 864–866, 868
- diplomacy/apology for poor performances, 169
- disbanding of CBS Byrds, 604, 606–611
- draft exemption, 27, 136
- drug use, 17, 79, 96, 123, 153–154, 176–177, 179–180, 260, 291, 352, 391, 541, 548, 552–554, 558, 625, 654, 656, 667–668, 794, 849
- Dylan, Bob, interaction with/influence of, 60–62, 64–65, 101–102, 104, 111–112, 127, 146, 182–184, 227, 232, 287–288, 292, 325–326, 329, 336, 354, 426–427, 429–430, 444, 472, 479–480, 496, 498–500, 523–524, 526, 535–536, 541, 562, 623–624, 634–638, 659, 670–671, 725, 740, 750–751, 763, 766, 795

INDEX

McGuinn, Jim (Roger) (contd.)
  Easy Rider, involvement in/contribution to, 509–512, 533
  education, 21–22
  filming experiments/notions, 285–286, 314–315, 334, 366
  firing of Crosby, 13, 51–52, 376, 380–385, 460, 703, 757, 858, 861
  Folk Den recordings, 797–798, 802–803, 833
  folk music, introduction to, 22–23
  Gene Tryp musical/Jacques Levy collaboration, 450–451, 453, 521, 530, 539, 541, 544–545, 549–550, 569–570, 572, 584, 598, 723, 795–796, 827, 843–844
  Gilbert, Linda, relationship with/marriage to/divorce from, 555–557, 562, 573, 580, 582, 587, 624–625, 635, 638, 724
  glaucoma, 793
  Grand Ole Opry appearance, 430–432
  guitar playing, 8, 22, 39, 43, 59–60, 66–67, 82–85, 91, 116, 127–129, 131, 133–134, 143, 146, 156, 196, 201, 203, 205, 223–225, 227–228, 231, 236, 243–245, 248, 251, 253, 259, 288, 295, 299, 318, 321, 327, 333, 341, 354, 407, 429, 439–440, 501, 505, 526, 539, 542–543, 567, 569, 582, 595, 601, 616–617, 619–620, 684–685, 688–689, 705–706, 708, 722–724, 740–741, 743, 751–752, 793, 801–802, 826
  guns, fascination with, 557–558, 625
  Hall of Fame induction, 770–773
  Hillman, Chris, relationship with, 78, 313–314, 318, 374, 398, 406, 412, 421–422, 429, 432, 438, 446, 449, 464, 466–467, 479, 484, 489, 503–505, 608–610, 656–657, 660–664, 671–672, 675–676, 682, 691, 695, 700–701, 710–715, 721, 747, 752, 765, 790–791, 812, 822, 832, 853
  Hippard, R.J. (Bob), suicide, 724–725
  horse depiction of Crosby on Notorious Byrd Brothers sleeve, 411–412, 658
  Hubley, Susan, relationship with, 638, 669
  illness on tour, 162–163, 463, 465–467
  image, 8, 13, 68, 90, 92, 110–111, 120–121, 123–124, 140, 153, 156, 161, 166–168, 170, 173, 185, 235, 238, 247, 260, 366, 394, 423–424, 431, 462, 506–507, 683
  impressionable ways, 591–593, 596, 606
  infidelities, 554–556, 561
  intellectual persona, 187, 288–290, 336
  languid wit, 187, 280, 294, 371, 392–393, 462–463, 465, 533, 555–556
  Lennon, John, connection/interaction with, 140, 156–157, 176, 242
  Levy, Jacques, death, 843–844
  longevity, 853–854, 862
  marriages, 26, 387, 580, 670
  material concerns/financial discussions/problems, 218–219, 287–288, 290, 492, 494–495, 504, 533, 535, 547–548, 561–562, 564–565, 579, 593–594, 607, 610, 713, 721–722, 755–757, 760–762, 765–766, 794
  McGuinn, Clark & Hillman recordings, 676, 680–682, 684–688, 701, 704–708
  McGuinn, Clark & Hillman tours, 671–676, 690, 695–696, 698
  McGuinn/Hillman duo, 710–715
  McGuire, Barry, friendship with, 112, 290, 362, 670
  Melcher, Terry, involvement with, 80, 195–196, 199, 203, 206–207, 212–214, 217–219, 231–233, 235, 508, 512, 522–524, 526, 535, 538, 540, 553, 560–567, 569–574, 579, 581–582, 590–591, 593, 623, 807, 828, 832, 845–846
  method acting, 85, 161, 196, 449, 474, 570, 669, 768, 813–815
  'Mr Tambourine Man', playing on, 81–86, 127, 444
  name change to Roger, 361, 793–794
  naming of Byrds, involvement in, 72–74
  pacific nature/aversion to violence, 67, 119, 208–209, 211–212, 489, 495, 672, 695, 700, 714–715, 722
  Parsons, Gene, relationship/interaction with/firing of, 506, 527, 539, 542, 559, 589, 591–594, 596, 606–607, 722, 828
  Parsons, Gram, interaction with/rivalry, 422–424, 431–433, 436–450, 454–460, 496, 503, 507, 544
  political/apolitical stance, 344, 355, 364, 452–454, 466, 481, 548, 570–571, 713–714, 823, 832
  positive philosophy, 120–121, 190–191, 204, 280, 289–290, 329, 351–353, 361–362, 390, 398, 436, 454, 484, 488, 567, 751
  pre-Byrds' groups/collaborations, 23–26
  role as 'leader' of Byrds, 82, 212, 262, 351, 412, 436–438, 442–445, 498–499, 519, 534, 560, 568, 583–584, 593–596, 606, 611
  Rolling Thunder Revue, involvement in, 635–637
  science fiction, interest in, 289, 293–294, 319–320, 363–364, 410, 441, 497

McGuinn, Jim (Roger) (contd.)
    session work, 27, 201–202, 366, 528, 725
    singing/vocal style, 8, 57, 61, 68, 85, 129, 131–132, 134, 178, 196, 227–231, 235–236, 243, 273, 295, 297, 299, 400, 404, 410, 435–436, 449, 467, 474–477, 479, 498–499, 501–502, 505, 525, 528, 541, 543–545, 570, 572, 587, 591, 673, 707, 813
    solo albums, 623–624, 630, 633–638, 681, 793–794, 804–806, 832–833
    songwriting drought, 425–426, 529–530, 559–560
    songwriting/compositions, 24, 26–27, 44, 54, 56–57, 79, 129, 133, 200, 225, 227–228, 239, 245, 248, 254–255, 257–258, 264, 288–289, 293–294, 298, 313–314, 318–320, 330, 365, 368, 374, 389, 399–400, 404–408, 410, 511, 522–523, 541, 543–545, 550–551, 563, 566–567, 569–570, 572, 582, 584, 587, 591, 595, 597, 599, 616–618, 623–624, 633–634, 636–638, 670–671, 680, 684–686, 688, 705–707, 722, 724–725, 743–744, 746, 764–765, 798, 804, 832–833
    Sonny & Cher, attitude towards, 127, 165–168, 181–182, 187
    South Africa visit/controversy, 446, 454, 456–470, 482–483
    Spaul, Camilla, relationship with/marriage to, 669–670, 691, 693, 706–707, 709, 713–714, 722, 724, 794, 811, 832–833, 849–850, 865–866
    spirituality/Christianity, 79–80, 84–85, 121, 127, 177, 287–290, 363, 546–547, 562, 667–668, 677, 679–680, 691, 700, 705, 709, 714, 721, 805, 823, 849–850
    spying/James Bond fascination, 557–558, 625
    Stanton, Allen, uneasy relationship with, 299–300
    Subud, involvement in, 78–80, 84, 121, 177, 361, 363, 495–496, 546, 554, 667, 849
    synthesizer/electronica experimentation, 388, 414, 436–437, 481, 495, 498, 529, 545, 565, 596, 743–744, 805, 424
    'Turn! Turn! Turn!', discovery of, 201–203
    UK 1977 tour with Clark & Hillman, 653–661
    Usher, Gary, death/reaction to, 763–764, 807
    weight gain, 578–579
    White, Clarence, appointment/relationship with, 469–470, 527, 543, 545, 553, 556, 559, 573, 589, 591–592, 594, 608–611, 625–626
    York, John, relationship/interaction with/firing of, 506–507, 513–514, 518–520, 524, 527, 810
McGuinn, Linda (see Linda Carradine)
McGuinn, Patrick (Jim/Roger McGuinn's first son), 361, 669, 847
McGuinn, Roger (see Jim McGuinn)
McGuire, Barry, 29, 105, 112–113, 188–191, 194, 204, 239, 263, 269, 290, 362, 670, 843
McKenzie, Scott, 350, 353, 361
McLaughlin, John, 580
McPeake Family, 293
McQueen, Steve, 93, 138
'Medley: 'My Back Pages'/'B.J. Blues'/'Baby What Do You Want Me To Do'' (Byrds), 501–502, 809–810
Melanie, 516
Melcher, Jacqueline, 846
Melcher, Marty, 197
Melcher, Melissa, 846
Melcher, Ryan, 846
Melcher, Terese, 846
Melcher, Terry, 26, 80–88, 111, 114–116, 126, 128–129, 132, 134, 142, 178–179, 189, 195–199, 201, 203, 205–207, 212–214, 217–220, 225–227, 229, 231–236, 242, 283, 299, 332, 348, 398, 448, 508, 512–513, 522–526, 529–532, 535, 538–540, 544, 553, 558–567, 569, 571–574, 579, 581–582, 586–587, 590–591, 593, 596, 606, 623, 739–740, 768, 799, 807, 810, 828, 832, 844–846, 864
Melly, George, 839
'Melody' (David Crosby), 726
'Memphis' (Johnny Rivers), 58
'Memphis Tennessee' (Chuck Berry), 58
Men, The, 44
Meredith, Burgess, 182
Merrick, David, 549
Merrick, Thomas, Lieutenant, 802
Merry Christmas (New Christy Minstrels), 29
Merry-Go-Round, The, 351
Merseybeats, The, 762
Messina, Terri, 655, 671, 678, 687, 691–693, 697–699, 701–703, 772, 775–776, 778
Meyers, Joe, & The Sharks, 29
Michell, John, 441
Mighty Day On Campus (Chad Mitchell Trio), 24
'Mighty Quinn' (Manfred Mann), 427
Migliori, Jay, 320
Mike Bloomfield Live At Bill Graham's Fillmore West (Mike Bloomfield), 825
Miles, Buddy, 359–360

INDEX

'Milestones' (Byrds), 309, 802, 829
'Milestones' (Miles Davis), 309, 802
Miller, Beverly, 285
Miller, Mitch, 69–70
Miller, Roger, 28
Miller, Steve, 350–351
'Mind Gardens' (Byrds), 323–325, 328–329, 765, 802, 829
Mineo, Sal, 105–106, 311
Mingus, Charles, 487
Mitchell, Chad, 24–25, 42, 165, 461, 802
Mitchell, Guy, 69
Mitchell, Joni, 383, 575, 603, 614, 617, 635–637, 641, 782
Mitchell, Red, 857
Mitchum, Robert, 186
Mock, Earl, & The Mockingbirds, 520
Modern Folk Quartet, 32, 857
Moffitt, Peggy, 92–93
Mojo Men, The, 351
Monahan, Jim, 790
Monck, Chip, 358
Money, Zoot, 157
Monk, Thelonious, 595
Monkees, The, 313, 315, 470, 595, 657
Monroe, Marilyn, 96
'Monster Mash' (Bobby 'Boris' Pickett And The Crypt-Kickers), 629
Monterey (International Monterey Pop Festival), 281, 349–359, 361–362, 374, 377, 380, 409, 417, 439, 447, 838–839, 845, 858
Monterey Pop (film), 357
Moody Blues, The, 334
'Moog Raga' (Byrds), 414, 743–744, 805
Moon, Jim, 603, 606
Mooney, Tom, 712
More Bob Dylan Greatest Hits (Bob Dylan), 472
Morello, Joe, 40–41
Morning Sky (Chris Hillman), 716
'Morrison' (CPR), 786
Morrison, Jim, 341, 357, 786
Moss, Jerry, 615
'Motherless Children' (David Crosby), 31, 34–35
Mothers Of Invention, The, 282, 293
'Move Over Darling' (Doris Day), 80
Move, The, 14, 455
'Mr Soul' (Buffalo Springfield), 359
'Mr Spaceman' (Byrds), 293–294, 308, 319, 390, 436, 528, 542, 577, 750
'Mr Spaceman' (Roger McGuinn), 723
'Mr Tambourine Man' (Bob Dylan), 60–61, 63–64, 82, 100, 127, 146, 151, 205, 469, 857

'Mr Tambourine Man' (Byrds), 7–8, 14, 19, 59–62, 64–65, 81–87, 89–91, 97, 99–100, 105, 112, 114, 118–119, 123, 125, 129, 140, 146, 148–152, 155, 157, 160–161, 164, 167, 171, 186, 188, 190, 198, 204, 213, 216, 223–224, 227, 230, 232, 235–236, 238, 246, 252–254, 263, 280, 307, 325, 334, 354, 368, 434–435, 441–442, 444, 472, 519, 537, 542, 554, 562, 578, 639, 668, 688, 739, 745, 751, 765, 770–771, 791, 814, 821, 844, 858
Mr Tambourine Man (Byrds), 9, 101, 116, 125–135, 164–165, 207, 236, 349, 368, 410, 510, 564, 798
'Mr Tambourine Man' (David Crosby with Roger McGuinn), 731
'Mr Tambourine Man' (introduced as 'McGuinn, Crosby, Hillman'), 748
'Mr Tambourine Man' (McGuinn & Clark), 665–666
'Mr Tambourine Man' (McGuinn & Clark, with David Crosby), 673
'Mr Tambourine Man' (McGuinn, Clark & Hillman), 681
'Mr Tambourine Man' (McGuinn, Crosby & Hillman, billed as 'the original Byrds'), 763
'Mr Tambourine Man' (mistitled 'Tambourine Man') (Gene Clark), 719, 746
'Mr Tambourine Man' (Roger McGuinn), 723, 777, 795, 804
'Mr Tambourine Man' (Roger McGuinn, with the Peace Seekers), 721
'Mr Tambourine Man' (Roger McGuinn/Thunderbyrd, with Gene Clark), 660–661
'Mr Tambourine Man' (Roger McGuinn/Thunderbyrd, with Gene Clark & Chris Hillman), 657
'Mrs Brown You've Got A Lovely Daughter' (Herman's Hermits), 185
Muleskinner, 625
Mundi, Billy, 595
Murray The K, 249
Murray, Larry, 46, 583
Muse, David, 649–650
Music From Big Pink (Band), 481
'Music Is Love' (CPR), 818
'Music Is Love' (David Crosby), 614, 818
'My Back Pages' (Bob Dylan), 193, 325, 329, 795
'My Back Pages' (Byrds), 325–326, 329, 334–335, 354, 367, 372, 426, 443, 501, 505, 577, 584, 750, 801–802, 827
'My Country 'Tis Of Thee' (Crosby & Nash), 820

My Fair Lady (soundtrack), 70–71
'My Generation' (Who), 192
'My New Woman' (Roger McGuinn), 624
'My Old Kentucky Home' (Stephen Foster), 232
'My Sweet Lord' (George Harrison), 562
'My Uncle' (Flying Burrito Brothers), 503

Nash, Graham, 334, 373, 382, 508–509, 560, 614–615, 631, 639, 642, 673, 694, 726–727, 729–731, 733–736, 750, 787
Nash, Rose, 334
Nash, Susan, 736
Nashville Skyline (Bob Dylan), 482, 507–508
Nashville West, 469, 485–486, 500, 810
'Nashville West' (Byrds), 500, 541, 768, 829
'Nashville West' (Nashville West), 500
Natch'l Blues, The (Taj Mahal), 474
'Natural Harmony' (Byrds), 402, 408, 767
'Needles And Pins' (Searchers), 111, 116
Neil, Fred, 31
Nelson, Rick, 789
Nelson, Willie, 783
Nesmith, Mike, 470
Neuwirth, Bobby, 64, 91, 635–636
Never Before (see 'The Day Walk')
Never Before (Byrds), 243, 327, 738–744, 746, 765, 767, 798, 800–801, 805–806, 860, 864
'Never Ending Love' (Clarence White), 626
'Never Learn Not To Love' (Beach Boys), 531
New Christy Minstrels, The, 25, 29, 49, 69, 112, 165, 186, 188, 236, 263, 269, 271–272, 389, 702
New Generation, The, 337
New Kentucky Colonels, The, 16
New Lost City Ramblers, The, 46
New Riders Of The Purple Sage, 842
'New York Girls' (Roger McGuinn), 525, 802
Newhart, Bob, 366
Newman, Randy, 80
New-Romanesque Ensemble, The, 285
Nicholson, Jack, 103, 105–106, 286, 510, 856
Nicks, Stevie, 777, 783
Nightingale, Anne, 172–173
'Nighttime For The Generals' (Crosby, Stills, Nash & Young), 736–737, 788
Nilsson, Harry, 839
Nitzsche, Jack, 111, 195, 639
Nitty Gritty Dirt Band, The, 725
Nixon, Richard, President, 640, 820, 834
'No Longer A Sweetheart Of Mine' (Chris Hillman & Herb Pedersen), 822
'No Memories Hangin' Round' (Gene Clark), 719
No Other (Gene Clark), 19, 646–647, 681, 686, 718, 776

Nolan, Hugh, 335
Noone, Peter, 185
Norris, Chuck, 672, 695
'Norwegian Wood' (Beatles), 223, 244, 251
'Not Fade Away' (Rolling Stones), 117–118, 133–134
'Nothin' To It' (Byrds), 590
'Nothing Was Delivered' (Byrds), 428, 479–480
Notorious Byrd Brothers, The (Byrds), 13, 15, 19, 338, 395, 398–415, 417–419, 425, 436, 440, 442, 469, 481, 504, 511, 539, 596, 598, 615–616, 622, 632, 674, 688, 703–704, 726, 742, 763, 767–768, 770, 793, 805–806, 808, 812, 830
'November Nights' (Peter Fonda), 416
Nuese, John, 416, 425
Nyro, Laura, 350
Nyte Flyte, 719

O'Brien, Herb, 802
O'Connor, Emil, 80
O'Donnell, Charlie, 104
O'Keefe, Danny, 645
O'Kelley, Kim, 666–667
O'Neill, Shannon, 778
Oakes, Chrissie, 562
Oates, Warren, 286
Obama, Barack, President, 871
Obanhein, William, 577–578
Odetta, 23, 32–33, 109, 118, 846, 856
Odyssey, The (Homer), 297
Of Cabbages And Kings (Chad & Jeremy), 497–498
'Oh Pretty Woman' (Roy Orbison), 50
'Oh! Susannah' (Byrds), 9, 231–232, 298, 501, 744, 814, 829
'Oh! Susannah' (Stephen Foster), 231–232
Oh Yes I Can (David Crosby), 737
'Ohio' (Crosby, Stills, Nash & Young), 639
Ohio River Boys, The, 802
'Oil In My Lamp' (Byrds), 524, 768, 810
'Old Blue' (Byrds), 499, 523, 768, 827
'Old Blue' (Dillards), 499
'Old Blue' (Gibson & Camp), 499
'Old Blue' (Joan Baez), 499
'Old Blue' (Pete Seeger), 499
'Old John Robertson' (Byrds), 408–409, 422, 443, 742, 767, 802
'Old Paint' (Roger McGuinn), 797
Oldham, Andrew Loog, 152, 349
Oldham, Spooner, 623
Oliva, Peter, 654–655, 661, 699, 702
Olson, Carla, 720, 774, 776–777
'Omaha Rainbow' (John Stewart), 452
'One Hundred Years From Now' (Byrds), 437, 477, 768

INDEX

'One Hundred Years From Now' (Gosdin Brothers), 477
'One In A Hundred' (Gene Clark), 537, 613, 860
'One More Chance' (Roger McGuinn & Chris Hillman, Featuring Gene Clark), 705
'One More Time' (Roger McGuinn), 633
1–2–3–4, More, More, More, More (book) (Don Landis), 288–289
'Only Girl, The' (Jet Set), 38
Ono, Yoko, 692
Orbison, Roy, 50, 477, 763, 765, 770
Original Singles, The (Byrds), 798
'Orleans' (David Crosby), 614
Osborn, Joe, 591, 606
Osborne Brothers, The, 473
Other Side, The (Chris Hillman), 823
Otis Blue (Otis Redding), 474
Out Of The Woodwork (Rice, Rice, Hillman & Pedersen), 791
Owens, Buck, 45, 170, 416, 418, 437–438, 443, 789, 791

Pacers, The, 415
Pacific Gas & Electric, 825
'Page 43' (Crosby & Nash), 615
Page, Larry, 165, 167
Page, Patti, 69
Pages Of Life (Desert Rose Band), 789
'Paint It, Black' (Rolling Stones), 251
'Painted Fire' (Roger McGuinn & Chris Hillman, Featuring Gene Clark), 707
Paisley, Ian, Reverend, 415
'Pale Blue' (Byrds), 566–567, 572–573, 769, 828
Pallenberg, Anita, 445–446
Palmer, Bruce, 352
Palmer, Earl, 43
'Paper Glider' (David Crosby), 726
'Paperback Writer' (Beatles), 299, 302
Pappas, Constance (see Constance Hillman)
Pappas, Rene, 708
'Parade Of Lost Dreams' (Roger McGuinn), 804
Parents Can't Win (book) (James & Dorothy McGuinn), 21–22
Pariser, Alan, 349
Parker, Charlie, 843
Parker, Colonel Tom, 69
Parker, Graham, 710
Parks, Van Dyke, 35, 185–186, 288, 293, 520, 525, 841, 846
Parmley, Don, 47
Parsons, Avis, 415
Parsons, Camille, 554
Parsons, Gene, 15, 485–486, 490, 498–500, 502, 505–506, 511, 518–519, 521–529, 539–544, 553–554, 559, 561, 563–567, 569, 572–573, 578, 581–587, 589, 591–596, 602, 604–607, 626, 721–722, 769, 809–811, 813, 827–828, 840, 842–843, 846–849
Parsons, Gram, 13, 16, 415–418, 421–425, 427–433, 435–450, 454–464, 469–479, 484–485, 488, 491, 493–494, 496, 503–507, 513, 521, 537, 543–544, 596, 626–629, 669, 676, 681, 712, 716, 768, 781, 809, 812–813, 823, 829, 838, 845–846, 852–853
Parsons, Jo Ellen, 554
Parsons, Lemuel, 522
Parsons, Robert ('Bob'), 415
'Past Addresses' (Gene Clark), 647
'Paths Of Victory' (Byrds), 541, 764, 766
'Paths Of Victory' (Hamilton Camp), 857
Paths Of Victory (Hamilton Camp), 228
Patterson, Phyliss, 284
Paul, Susan, 779–780
Paulekas, Szou, 94, 105, 139
Paulekas, Vitautus Alfonso (Vito), 93–95, 98–99, 105, 112, 116, 123, 139–141, 143, 150, 186, 247, 282, 871
Paxton, Gary, 499, 510, 526
Paxton, Tom, 189–193, 576
Peace On You (Roger McGuinn), 23, 633
Peace Seekers, The, 721–722
Peale, Norman Vincent, 120–121, 290, 670
Peanut Butter Conspiracy, The, 337
Pearl, Ed, 46, 78, 184, 747
Pearlman, Sandy, 327, 400
Pedersen, Herb, 645, 716–718, 790–792, 822–823
Peeples, Stephen, 683, 696
Peer Gynt (verse play) (Henrik Ibsen), 450, 544
'Penny Lane' (Beatles), 315–317, 332
Pentangle, 576, 769, 810
Perkins, Al, 716–718, 851
Perkins, Carl, 22, 493
Perry, Rupert, 664, 667, 675
Pet Sounds (Beach Boys), 293, 305, 838
Peter And Gordon, 30, 56, 153, 663
Peter, Paul & Mary, 31, 37, 42, 65, 189, 307, 331, 857
Peterson, Oscar, 843
Petty, Tom, 637, 680, 707, 725, 738, 793, 795
Pevar, Jeff, 786
Phillips, John, 349–350, 353, 513, 592–593, 596, 627, 732, 794, 820–821
Phillips, Michelle, 277–278, 282, 521, 720
Pickens, Slim, 135

Pickett, Bobby 'Boris', And The Crypt-Kickers, 629
Pinza, Ezio, 544
'Pirates' ('Byrds', Michael Clarke version), 762
Pit And The Pendulum, The (film), 30
Pitt, Brad, 817
Pittman, Bill, 82, 84
Platters, The, 753
'Please Let Me Love You' (Beefeaters), 44, 54–55, 797
'Please Let Me Love You' (Roger McGuinn), 797
'Please Please Me' (Beatles), 38
'Pledge To You' (Gene Clark), 776
Pledges, The, 520
Poco, 501, 644
Poems Of Henry Van Dyke, The (poetry collection) (Henry Van Dyke), 71
Pohlman, Ray, 43
Poindexter, Hal, 47
Poitier, Sidney, 139
Polanski, Roman, 512–513
Police, The, 705
Polland, Pam, 525
Pollock, Graeme, 465
Porgy & Bess (soundtrack), 71
Porter, Cole, 322
'Positively 4th Street' (Bob Dylan), 314, 496, 541
'Positively 4th Street' (Byrds), 541, 769
Posta, Adrienne, 156
Power Of Positive Thinking, The (book) (Norman Vincent Peale), 120–121, 670
Precht, Bob, 238
'Precious Kate' (Byrds), 585
Preflyte (Byrds), 56–60, 83, 119, 508–509, 513, 617, 740, 745, 763, 800, 861
Preflyte Sessions, The (Byrds), 35, 56, 828
Presley, Elvis, 5, 8, 22, 69, 238, 275–276, 291, 430, 493, 667–668, 738, 771, 797
Prestidge, Eric, 577
'Pretty Boy Floyd' (Byrds), 428, 443, 475–476, 482, 505, 528
'Pretty Boy Floyd' (Woody Guthrie), 475–476, 528
'Pretty Polly' (Byrds), 428–429, 479, 768, 809
'Pretty Polly' (Dillards), 429, 768
'Pretty Polly' (Roger McGuinn), 768, 809
Pretty Things, The, 156, 334
'Price Of Love, The' (Everly Brothers), 5
'Price You Pay, The' (Roger McGuinn), 724
Price, Ruth, 35
Proby, P.J., 746
'Property Of Jesus' (Bob Dylan), 700
'Psychodrama City' (Byrds), 299, 743, 767, 801, 861

Pulin, Chuck, 578
'Pushed It Over The End' (Crosby, Stills, Nash & Young), 727, 788
'Pushed It Over The End' (David Crosby), 727
'Pusher, The' (Steppenwolf), 522

'Queen Of The Hop' (Bobby Darin), 25
Quicksilver Messenger Service, 326, 337, 350, 470, 800
Quill, 516
'Quits' (Chris Hillman), 645

Rafkin, Bob, 586
Raim, Walter, 202
Rainey, Ron, 579–580, 603, 607, 624, 634–635, 637, 663–666, 675, 695, 699, 712–715
'Rainy Day Women # 12 & 35' (Bob Dylan), 254, 258, 287, 496
Raitt, Bonnie, 783
Ramblin' (New Christy Minstrels), 29
Ran, Nâzim Hikmet, 295
Rassmussen, Bob, 693
Raven, The (film), 30
Rawls, Lou, 350
Raymond, James, 31, 785–786, 818, 820
Reagan, Ronald, President, 713–714
'Reason Why, The' (Byrds), 59
Reasons, The, 469, 485–486
Rebel Rousers, The, 526
Rebel Without A Cause (film), 509, 540
'Rebellious Eyes' (Roger McGuinn), 804
Redding, Otis, 350, 474
Reddy, Helen, 595
Reed, B. Mitchell, 374
Reed, Jimmy, 101, 501
Reeves, Jim, 316, 477–478
'Relax Your Mind' (Chris Hillman), 313, 425
'Release Me' (Engelbert Humperdinck), 315
'Release Me Girl' (McGuinn, Clark & Hillman), 687–688
REM, 725, 738
Remains, The, 304, 416
'Remember Love' (Chris Hillman), 313, 425
'Renaissance Fair' (Byrds), 16, 285, 320–321, 328–329, 334, 354, 366, 373, 402, 409, 767
Rendall, Rita, 73, 122, 346–347, 846
'Reputation' (Byrds), 428, 479, 768, 809
'Reputation' (Tim Hardin), 428, 809
Return To Forever, 638
'Reuben's Train' (Scottsville Squirrel Barkers), 47
Reventlow, Count, 103
Reventlow, Lance, 103–104, 122, 138, 312, 331, 855, 857, 869, 871

INDEX

Revere, Paul, & The Raiders, 142, 199, 222, 253, 283, 845
'Revolution' (Beatles), 481
Revolver (Beatles), 293, 304–305
Reynolds, Art, 525–526, 529, 566
Rhodes, Emitt, 595
Rhodes, Jack, 228
Rhodes, Red, 396
Rice, Larry, 791–792, 822
Rice, Rice, Hillman & Pedersen (Rice, Rice, Hillman & Pedersen), 792
Rice, Tony, 791–792, 822
Richard, Cliff, 124
Richards, Joey, 495–496
Richards, Keith, 217, 315, 353, 442, 445–447, 456, 459–461, 627, 678, 692, 695
Richman, Jonathan, & The Modern Lovers, 846
Ridgway, Stan, 793
Riot On Sunset Strip (film), 311
Rip Chords, The, 80
'Rise And Fall' (Souther, Hillman, Furay Band), 644
Rising Sons, The, 77, 397–398, 474, 638, 841, 845
Rivers, Johnny, 58, 316, 350, 492
Rix, Luther, 636
Roach, Max, 487
Roadmaster (Gene Clark), 613, 867
'Robbin' Of The Stage, The' (1992 'musical' version), 796
Robbins, Paul Jay, 102, 110, 184, 339
Roberts, Billy, 296
Roberts, Bob, 95–96, 99
Roberts, Elliot, 121, 622, 632, 658
Roberts, Rick, 613, 645, 648–649, 685, 693, 716, 719
Robertson, John, 408–409
Robertson, Ken, 742
Robinson, Pat, 774–775, 778
Robinson, Smokey, & The Miracles, 351, 686
'Rock & Roll Woman' (Buffalo Springfield), 352, 357
'Rock 'n' Roll Time' (Roger McGuinn), 638
'Rock And Roll Music' (Beatles), 6
Rock Family Trees (book) (Pete Frame), 442
Roger McGuinn (Roger McGuinn), 595, 623–624, 633, 844
Roger McGuinn And Band (Roger McGuinn), 618, 634, 680
Rogers, Terry, 762, 780, 819, 842
'Roll Over Beethoven' (Beatles), 89
'Roll Over Beethoven' (Byrds), 89, 505, 767
'Roll Over Beethoven' (Chuck Berry), 89
'Rollin' And Tumblin'' (Chris Hillman), 645

Rolling Stones, The, 2, 8, 14, 116–118, 133–134, 152–153, 160, 163–164, 170–171, 192, 247, 251, 257, 261, 271, 274, 293, 302, 315–317, 349, 353, 423, 441–442, 445–446, 455, 460, 481, 532, 627, 654, 738, 756
Rolling Thunder Revue, 635–637, 657, 844
Rollins, Sonny, 843
Ronard, Jason, 778
Ronson, Mick, 635–636
'Rose Marie' (Slim Whitman), 6
Roseanne (television series), 783
Rosemary's Baby (film), 513
Rosenberg, Fred, 310
Ross, Jeff, 789
Ross, Mike, 577
Rothchild, Paul, 43
Rotten, Johnny, 653
Roustabouts, The, 469
Rowan, Peter, 625
Roxy Music, 738
Royal Flush (Terry Melcher), 845
Rubber Soul (Beatles), 223, 252
Rubin, Rick, 835
'Ruby Tuesday' (Rolling Stones), 315–316
Rum Runners, The, 29
Rumors, The, 415
'Runaround Sue' (Dion), 28
'Running' (Desert Rose Band), 46, 717–718
Running (Desert Rose Band), 717–718
Running Wild (Rice, Rice, Hillman & Pedersen), 822
Rupe, Art, 111
Russell, Leon, 81, 84–85, 114–115, 385, 739–740, 857, 867
'Russian Hill' (Roger McGuinn), 638, 797
'Rusty And Blue' (CPR), 788
'Rusty And Blue' (David Crosby), 783, 788
Rutles, The, 692

Sacred Path Songs (John York), 843
'Sad Boy' (McGuinn, Clark & Hillman), 685
Safe At Home (International Submarine Band), 424, 434, 448
'Sailor Lad' (Roger McGuinn), 803
Saint-Marie, Buffy, 105, 191, 576–577
Salt 'n' Pepa, 57
Sam & Dave, 711
Sambataro, Johnne 'John', 701
'Same Old Sound' (Roger McGuinn), 633, 708
'Samurai' (Crosby & Nash), 820
'Samurai' (David Crosby), 726
'San Francisco' (Scott McKenzie), 353
Sandburg, Carl, 234
Santana, 515, 641
Satan Is Real (Louvin Brothers), 473

'Satisfied Mind' (Byrds), 228–229, 418
'Satisfied Mind' (Hamilton Camp), 228–229
'Satisfied Mind' (International Submarine Band), 418–419
'Satisfied Mind' (Porter Wagoner), 228
'Saturday Night' (New Christy Minstrels), 29
'Save The Last Dance For Me' (Chris Hillman & Herb Pedersen), 822
Saved (Bob Dylan), 670, 850
Scheff, Jerry, 717
Schmit, Timothy, 793
Schorr, Jane, 26
Schorr, Walter, 26
Science And Sanity: An Introduction To Non-Aristotelian Systems And General Semantics (book) (Alfred Korzybski), 204
'(See The Sky) About To Rain' (Byrds), 620–621, 659
Scoppa, Bud, 581
Scottsville Squirrel Barkers, The, 46–48, 583, 823
Scruggs, Earl, 433, 590
Scruggs, Gary, 433, 590
Searchers, The, 105, 111, 116, 157, 791
Seastones (Phil Lesh & Ned Lagin), 641–642
Seatrain, 625
Sebastian, John, 123, 282, 362, 516
Sebring, Jay, 512
Secombe, Harry, 315
Sedaka, Neil, 26
'See My Friend' (Kinks), 251
Seeds, The, 351
Seeger, Mike, 46
Seeger, Pete, 23, 46, 69, 131–132, 159, 201–204, 293, 295–296, 355, 499, 795, 797
Seekers, The, 316
Segovia, Andrés, 854
Seiter, Jim ('Jimmi'), 301, 306–307, 326, 340, 342, 357–358, 376, 379–380, 384, 387–388, 390–396, 421, 429, 434–436, 439–441, 447, 454–455, 486–487, 490, 556–559, 563, 578, 582, 584–585, 590, 844–845
Seiter, Joe, 585
Sellers, Peter, 135
Sennes, Frank, 96
Sennes, Jr, Frank, 123
Sentinel, The (short story) (Arthur C. Clarke), 410
'Set You Free This Time' (Byrds), 10, 207–208, 225–226, 228, 247–248, 257, 265, 510, 765–766
Sex Pistols, The, 651, 654
Sgt Pepper's Lonely Hearts Club Band (Beatles), 317, 333, 353, 378, 646

Sha Na Na, 516
'Shadow Captain' (Crosby, Stills & Nash), 667
Shadows, The, 71, 705
Shaffer, Sue Anne (see Szou Paulekas)
Shakespeare, William, 20, 317, 323, 480
Shank, Bud, 868
Shankar, Ravi, 176–177, 222–223, 243–244, 252, 303, 350, 360, 377, 516, 814
Shapiro, Benny, 68, 182, 349, 871
Shapiro, Michelle, 68
Sharp, Cecil, 423
Shaw, George Bernard, 452
Shaw, Sandie, 2, 5
'She Don't Care About Time' (Byrds), 178, 205, 223, 265, 742, 766, 799, 814, 832
'She Don't Care About Time' (Roger McGuinn & Chris Hillman), 791
'She Has A Way' (Byrds), 58–59, 114, 129, 740, 798
'She Loves You' (Beatles), 38, 797
'She Loves You' (Roger McGuinn), 797, 804
'She Said She Said' (Beatles), 176, 510
'She's The Kind Of Girl' (Gene Clark), 537, 613, 860
Shear, Jules, 833
Shearing, George, 40, 595
Shelley, Mary, 79
Shepard, Lionel (see Richmond Shepard)
Shepard, Richmond, 79
Shepard, Sam, 450
Shilos, The, 415–416
Shirelles, The, 338
'Shoot 'Em' (Roger McGuinn), 654, 656, 805
Shooting, The (film), 286
Shore, Dinah, 694
Shot Of Love (Bob Dylan), 670
Shrimpton, Chrissie, 153
Siddons, Bill, 733, 736, 753–755, 759–760
'Silhouettes' (Herman's Hermits), 7
'Silver Raven' (Gene Clark), 774
Simon & Garfunkel, 27, 281–282, 350, 397
Simon, Paul, 281–282
Simpsons, The (television animated cartoon series), 783
Sims, Judy, 488
'Sin City' (Flying Burrito Brothers), 421, 491, 503
Sinatra, Frank, 25, 35, 96, 140, 217, 271, 315
Sinatra, Nancy, 315
Since Then (book) (David Crosby & Carl Gottlieb), 833
'Sing Me Back Home' (Byrds), 432, 443, 455, 494, 505, 826
'Sing Me Back Home' (Merle Haggard), 432, 443, 478
Sir Douglas Quintet, 492

INDEX

'Sister Moon' (Gene Clark), 646
Sixties Transition (Various Artistes), 867–868
'Skate Date' (Roger McGuinn & Chris Hillman, Featuring Gene Clark), 706–707
Skip & Flip, 520–521, 588, 608
Skip (Skip Battyn), 595
Slick, Grace, 352, 727
Slippin' Away (Chris Hillman), 645
Sloan, P.F. (Phil), 112–113, 188–189, 351
Slocum, Tom, 663, 701, 703, 776–778
Slow Train Coming (Bob Dylan), 700
Slow Train Coming (Bob Dylan), 670, 850
Sly & The Family Stone, 516
Small Faces, The, 11
Smile (Beach Boys), 338
Smith, Joe, 34
Smith, Keely, 2
Smiths, The, 738
Smothers Brothers, The, 390
Snively, John, 415
'So Fine' (Byrds), 585, 587–588
'So Fine' (Fiestas), 585
'So Many Times' (Manassas), 644
So Rebellious A Lover (Gene Clark & Carla Olson), 601, 720, 776
'So You Want To Be A Rock 'n' Roll Star' (Byrds), 11, 14, 16, 170, 178, 313–315, 317–318, 332, 334, 346, 354–355, 367, 373, 400, 443, 455, 487, 522, 537, 542, 577, 681, 751, 767, 837
'So You Want To Be A Rock 'n' Roll Star' (Manassas with Roger McGuinn), 614
'So You Want To Be A Rock 'n' Roll Star' (McGuinn & Clark), 666
'So You Want To Be A Rock 'n' Roll Star' (McGuinn & Clark, with David Crosby), 673
'So You Want To Be A Rock 'n' Roll Star' (performance introduced as 'McGuinn, Crosby, Hillman'), 748
'So You Want To Be A Rock 'n' Roll Star' (Roger McGuinn & Chris Hillman), 791
'So You Want To Be A Rock 'n' Roll Star' (Roger McGuinn, with the Peace Seekers), 721
'So You Want To Be A Rock 'n' Roll Star' (Roger McGuinn/Thunderbyrd, with Gene Clark & Chris Hillman), 657
'Soldier's Joy'/'Black Mountain Rag' (Byrds), 577, 769
'Solveig's Song' (1992 'musical' version), 796
'Somebody To Love' (Jefferson Airplane), 338
'Somehow She Knew' (CPR), 786, 788
Sommer, Bert, 516
Somohadiwidjojo, Bapak Muhammad Subuh, 78–79

Song To A Seagull (Joni Mitchell), 617
'Song With No Words (Tree With No Leaves)' (David Crosby), 517
Songs Of Innocence And Of Experience (poetry volume) (William Blake), 568
Sonny & Cher, 9, 105, 111, 125–127, 165–167, 170, 181–182, 187–188, 194, 223, 237, 283, 316, 453, 470, 831
Sorn, Jerry, 762
Soul, David, 680
Sound Of Music, The (soundtrack), 7, 315–316
'Sounds Of Silence, The' (Simon & Garfunkel), 281
Sousa, John Philip, 108, 400
South Pacific (soundtrack), 70
Souther, Hillman, Furay Band, The, 644, 649, 664–665
Souther, Hillman, Furay (Souther, Hillman, Furay Band), 644
Souther, John David, 644
Southern, Terry, 93, 510
'Space Odyssey' (Byrds), 410–411, 443, 525, 528
'Spanish Harlem Incident' (Bob Dylan), 129
'Spanish Harlem Incident' (Byrds), 129
Spanky & Our Gang, 603
Sparks, Randy, 29, 49, 90
Spaul, Camilla (see Camilla McGuinn)
Spector, Larry, 312, 344–347, 366, 378–379, 381, 383, 385, 387–390, 393, 396, 415–421, 425, 455, 484, 488–493, 503–504, 507, 510, 512, 590, 757
Spector, Phil, 4, 111, 165, 235–236
'Splendor In The Grass' (Jackie De Shannon), 133
'Splish Splash' (Bobby Darin), 25, 797
'Splish Splash' (Roger McGuinn), 797
Spoon River (musical), 65
Springfield, Dusty, 2, 401
'Springfield Mountain' (Roger McGuinn), 797, 802
Springsteen, Bruce, 817, 825
St John, Jill, 72, 103, 311
'Stand And Be Counted' (Crosby, Stills, Nash & Young), 788
'Stand And Be Counted' (David Crosby), 726
Stanislavski, Konstantin, 85, 813, 865
'Stanley's Song' (Byrds), 493, 768, 809
Stanton, Allen, 69–70, 72–74, 199, 220, 235, 246, 248, 288–289, 293, 299–300, 398, 800
Staplehurst, Sid, 10–11
Starr, Ringo, 650
'Stayin' Alive' (Bee Gees), 687
Steadman, Robbie, 710

1195

Stec, Joey, 792, 848
Steele, Alison, 252, 259
Steeleye Span, 576
Steely Dan, 786
Steppenwolf, 515
Stewart, Billy, 6
Stewart, John, 452
'Still I'm Sad' (Yardbirds), 251
Stills, Stephen, 283, 331, 350–352, 357–360, 377, 511, 520, 598–599, 610, 613–614, 631, 640–645, 648–649, 673, 675–676, 681, 716, 726, 729, 731, 733–734, 736, 750, 783, 787, 806, 822
Stills/Young Band, 642–643
Stockhausen, Karlheinz, 319
Stone Canyon Band, 789
Stone, Brian, 111, 125, 283, 312
Stoner, Rob, 636
'Stopping Traffic' (McGuinn, Clark & Hillman), 685, 705
'Stranger In A Strange Land' (Blackburn & Snow), 200, 799
'Stranger In A Strange Land' (Byrds), 199–200, 231, 264, 323, 375, 799
Stranger In A Strange Land (novel) (Robert A. Heinlein), 200, 375
Straubing, Michelle, 278
'Strawberry Fields Forever' (Beatles), 315–317, 332, 378
'Street Fighting Man' (Rolling Stones), 481
'Street Talk' (Roger McGuinn & Chris Hillman, Featuring Gene Clark), 705
'Street To Lean On' (Crosby, Stills & Nash), 783
Streisand, Barbra, 69
'Strength Of Strings' (Gene Clark), 227, 646
Strike, Lisa, 71
'Subterranean Homesick Blues' (Bob Dylan), 3, 100–101
Sullivan, Ed, 38, 238–239, 316, 366
'Sum Up Broke' (International Submarine Band), 416
Summer In Paradise (Beach Boys), 845–846
'Summertime' (David Crosby), 31
'Sunshine Love' (Roger McGuinn), 724
Supremes, The, 223
Surf Riders, The, 29
Surfin' Safari (Beach Boys), 300
Surratt, Paul, 416
Surrealistic Pillow (Jefferson Airplane), 338
'Surrender To Me' (David Soul), 680
'Surrender To Me' (McGuinn, Clark & Hillman), 680, 685
Swarbrick, Dave, 576
'Sweet Mary' (Byrds), 597, 616
'Sweet Memories' (Roger McGuinn), 724

Sweetheart Of The Rodeo (Byrds), 14, 326, 444, 447, 471–482, 486–488, 492, 495–496, 501–502, 505, 522, 528, 669, 688, 750, 763, 768, 791, 808, 812–814, 840
Sweetheart Of The Rodeo (The Legacy Edition) (Byrds), 828, 840
Sweetwater, 516
'Switch Blade Sam' (Jeff Daniels), 475

Tabu (film), 30
Tainted (film), 774–775
'Take A City Bride' (Byrds), 505
'Take A City Bride' (Gene Parsons), 505
'Take A Whiff (On Me)' (Byrds), 538, 545, 548, 827
'Take A Whiff (On Me)' (Leadbelly), 545, 548
'Taken At All' (Crosby & Nash), 643
'Talkin' John Birch Paranoid Blues' (Bob Dylan), 24, 239
'Talkin' L.A.' (David Hemmings), 366
'Tamalpais High (At About 3)' (CPR), 818
Tammy And The Doctor (film), 509
Tashian, Barry, 304–305, 416, 473
Tate, Sharon, 512–513, 516, 530–531, 558
Tatum, Art, 487
Taylor, Charlie, 487, 841
Taylor, Dallas, 618
Taylor, Derek, 13, 96–99, 101–102, 106, 121–123, 126–127, 139–140, 142, 147–150, 152–154, 156–159, 161–163, 165, 169–174, 177–181, 185, 187, 201, 219–221, 223–224, 235–236, 247, 251, 253–256, 260–261, 265–270, 272, 274, 279–280, 285–286, 303–305, 309, 312, 314, 318, 331, 342, 344, 356–357, 385–387, 434, 531, 538, 544, 590, 831, 836–840
Taylor, James, 560, 576, 585, 641
Taylor, Joan, 179, 837
Taylor, Kate, 560, 585
Taylor, Livingston, 585
Taylor, Peggy, 842
'Tears, The' (Roger McGuinn), 724
Temple, Shirley, 463
Ten Years After, 516
Terry, George, 687
Terry Melcher (Terry Melcher), 845
Terry, Sonny, 576
'That's All I Want' (Terry Day), 80
'That's What You Want' (Gene Clark), 214
Thaxton, Lloyd, 105
The Flying Saucer Vision: The Holy Grail Restored (book) (John Michell), 441
'The Russians Are Coming! The Russians Are Coming!' (International Submarine Band), 416

INDEX

Them, 166
There Is A Season (box set) (Byrds), 828–829, 831
'There Must Be Someone' (Byrds), 527, 529
'There Must Be Someone' (Gosdin Brothers), 527
'There's A Higher Power' (Louvin Brothers), 473
'There's Always Something There To Remind Me' (Sandie Shaw), 130
They Shoot Horses Don't They (film), 93
'They Want It All' (Crosby & Nash), 820
'Things We Said Today' (Beatles), 89, 107, 822
'Things We Said Today' (Byrds), 89, 107
'Things We Said Today' (Rice, Rice, Hillman & Pedersen), 822
'Things Will Be Better' (Byrds), 618
'Think I'm Gonna Feel Better' (Byrds), 828
'Think I'm Gonna Feel Better' (Gene Clark), 828
'This Is My Song' (Petula Clark), 315
'This Wheel's On Fire' (Band), 498
'This Wheel's On Fire' (Byrds), 493, 498–499, 809, 827
'This Wheel's On Fire' (Julie Driscoll & The Brian Auger Trinity), 427, 498
Thomas, Dylan, 131, 779
Thomas, Greg, 637, 652–653, 658, 663, 667, 678, 682–683, 691, 697, 699–701, 720
Thomas, Tracy, 331
Thomson, Garner, 464
'Thoughts And Words' (Byrds), 322–323, 443, 618, 767, 794, 830
Thousand Roads (David Crosby), 782
3 Byrds Land In London 1977 (Roger McGuinn/Thunderbyrd, The Chris Hillman Band, Gene Clark, KC Southern Band), 805
'Three Finger Breakdown' (Scottsville Squirrel Barkers), 47
Three O'Clock, The, 720
Through The Morning, Through The Night (Dillard & Clark), 537
Thunderbyrd, 637–638, 652, 656, 680, 682, 720, 805
Thunderbyrd (Roger McGuinn), 637–638
Thunderheart (film), 783
'Ticket To Ride' (Beatles), 2, 399
Tickner, Dolores, 77–78, 103–104, 117, 182–185, 201, 217, 260, 287, 347, 361, 421, 435, 445–446, 451–453, 540, 554–557, 561, 565, 582, 617, 669, 724, 847–848, 865
Tickner, Eddie, 33, 48, 53, 60, 65–68, 72–74, 78, 90, 96–97, 106, 111, 121–123, 125–126, 140, 148–149, 181, 211–212, 217, 230, 233–234, 250, 256, 267–269, 275–276, 283, 286, 301–302, 308–309, 340, 344, 346–347, 378, 385, 420, 451, 485, 492, 510, 538, 548, 590, 626–628, 846–849, 859, 861–862, 865, 867
Tickner, Karen, 846
Tickner, Marcie, 846
'Tiffany Queen' (Byrds), 582, 587, 599, 723, 769
'Tiffany Queen II' (Roger McGuinn), 724
'Till It Shines On You' (Crosby, Stills & Nash), 783
'Time Between' (Byrds), 313, 319–321, 422, 443, 493, 618, 718
'Time Between' (Desert Rose Band), 718
'Time Between' (Flying Burrito Brothers), 505
'Time Cube' (Roger McGuinn), 529
Time Fades Away (Neil Young), 639
'Time For Love' (Chris Hillman), 313, 425
'Time Is The Final Currency' (CPR), 786
Timeless Flight: The Definitive Biography Of The Byrds (book) (John Rogan), 658, 765, 828, 859
'Times They Are A-Changin', The' (Bob Dylan), 3, 113, 230
Times They Are A-Changin', The (Bob Dylan), 226
'Times They Are A-Changin', The' (Byrds), 142, 155, 178–179, 187, 195–196, 201–202, 230, 245–246, 799
Times They Are A-Changin', The (EP) (Byrds), 230, 247
'Times They Are A-Changin', The' (Hamilton Camp), 868
'To Morrow' (Bob Gibson), 798
'To Morrow' (Roger McGuinn), 23, 798
'To The Last Whale' (Crosby & Nash), 641
Tobola, Lynn, 707
Tom & Jerry, 27
'Tomorrow Is A Long Ways Away' (Byrds), 59, 284, 745–746
'Tomorrow Never Knows' (Beatles), 242, 305
Tonight In Person (Limeliters), 23–24
Tonight's The Night (Neil Young), 599
Tork, Peter, 305
Townsend, Irving, 68
Townshend, Pete, 156
'Traction In The Rain' (David Crosby), 614
Travers, Mary, 101, 105, 109, 189, 305
Tree, Christopher, 337
Trent, Jackie, 2
'Triad' (Byrds), 200, 373–377, 615, 741, 806, 812
'Triad' (Crosby, Stills, Nash & Young), 615
'Triad' (Jefferson Airplane), 375–376, 470, 615, 806

'Tribal Gathering' (Byrds), 338, 374, 409, 443
'Tricou House' ('Byrds', Michael Clarke version), 762
Trip, The (club), 184–186, 246–247, 250–251, 301–302, 312
Trip, The (film), 416, 428, 509–510
Troggs, The, 806
Trouble In Paradise (Souther, Hillman, Furay Band), 644
Troxel, Jim, 526
'Truck Stop Girl' (Byrds), 544, 578
'Truck Stop Girl' (Little Feat), 544
True Love (Desert Rose Band), 789
'Tulsa County' (Gentle Soul), 524
'Tulsa County' (June Carter), 524
'Tulsa County Blue' (Byrds), 523–524, 810, 812–813
'Tunnel Of Love' (Byrds), 560, 567–568
'Turn Your Radio On' (McGuinn/Hillman), 710
'Turn! Turn! Turn!' (Byrds), 9, 201–207, 222–225, 229, 233–234, 236, 238, 242, 253, 259, 263, 296, 354, 373, 440, 442, 454, 465–466, 472, 542, 545, 562, 751, 770, 773, 791, 822, 844
Turn! Turn! Turn! (Byrds), 9, 207, 211, 223–232, 257, 265, 281, 291, 329, 343, 369, 399, 508, 526, 547, 561, 564, 799, 829
'Turn! Turn! Turn!' (Chris Hillman & Herb Pedersen), 824
'Turn! Turn! Turn!' (Crosby, Stills, Nash & Young), 787
'Turn! Turn! Turn!' (Judy Collins), 201–202
'Turn! Turn! Turn!' (McGuinn, Crosby & Hillman, billed as 'the original Byrds'), 763
'Turn! Turn! Turn!' (performance introduced as 'McGuinn, Crosby, Hillman'), 748
'Turn! Turn! Turn!' (Roger McGuinn), 804
'Turn! Turn! Turn!' (Roger McGuinn, with the Peace Seekers), 721
Turner, Lana, 96
Turtles, The, 56, 188, 253, 337, 425, 545
Tutt, Ron, 627
20/20 (Beach Boys), 531
Twinkle, 2
'Twist And Shout' (Beatles), 38
'2–4–2 Fox Trot (The Lear Jet Song)' (Byrds), 298, 744, 814, 829
Two Sides To Every Story (Gene Clark), 647
2001: A Space Odyssey (film), 410
Tyner, McCoy, 418

U2, 57
'Unchained Melody' (Les Baxter), 6
'Under My Thumb' (Rolling Stones), 117

'Under Your Spell Again' (Buck Owens), 418, 443
'Under Your Spell Again' (Byrds), 418, 443
'Universal Mind Decoder' (Byrds), 368, 373, 407, 806, 830
'Universal Soldier' (Buffy Saint-Marie), 191
'Universal Soldier' (Donovan), 191
(Untitled) (Byrds), 15, 535, 538–548, 550, 553–554, 563, 567, 572–573, 575, 581, 587–588, 590–593, 604, 608, 616, 622, 708, 769, 826–827, 844, 859
(Untitled)/(Unissued) (Byrds), 826–827
'Up To Me' (Roger McGuinn), 636–637
'Upon A Painted Ocean' (Barry McGuire), 113
Usher, Gary, 300, 309, 313, 323, 326, 365, 375–378, 399–402, 404–405, 411–412, 437, 449, 478–479, 497, 627, 643, 763–764, 801, 805, 807, 864

Vadim, Roger, 139–140
Valenti, Dino, 31, 33, 42–43, 72–73, 75, 90–91, 200–201, 296, 799, 867
Valentine, Elmer, 184, 283, 312
Valentine, Penny, 332
Van den Hemel, Cyriel, 660, 662
Van Dyke, Henry, 713–714, 724
Vanilla Fudge, 515
Varsi, Diane, 32, 286, 345, 510, 855, 865
'VC 10' (Jet Set), 71
Velvet Underground, The, 307
Ventures, The, 6
Very Stony Evening, A (bootleg) (Crosby & Nash), 787
Village Vanguards, The, 415
Vincent, Gene, 22, 124
'Virgin Mary' (Roger McGuinn), 797
Vito (see Vitautus Alfonso Paulekas)
Vito, Rick, 637, 663, 685
Voight, Jon, 549
Voyage (box set) (David Crosby), 833

W.C. Fields Electric String Band, 492
Wackers, The, 764
Wagoner, Porter, 228, 427
'Wait And See' (Byrds), 230–231, 264
Walecki, Fred, 821
Walker, Cindy, 477–478
Walker, Jerry Jeff, 720
Walker, Scott, 334, 746
'Walkin' Down The Line' (Dillards), 857
'Walking On The Moon' (Police), 705
'Wall Song, The' (Crosby & Nash), 517
'Wanderer, The' (Dion), 28
'War's Mystery' (David Hemmings), 366
Warnes, Jennifer, 668, 792, 823
Warwick, Dionne, 351

INDEX

Washington, Geno, & The Ram Jam Band, 157
Washington, George, President, 331
'Wasn't Born To Follow' (Byrds), 405–406, 409, 511, 806
'Wasn't Born To Follow' (Carole King), 405–406
Wasserzieher, Bill, 395
'Water Is Wide, The' (Chris Hillman), 823
'Waterbed' (Clarence White), 626
Watson, Doc, 590
Watts, Charlie, 153
Watts, Shirley, 153
'Way Behind The Sun' (Byrds), 523, 769, 810, 812
'Way Behind The Sun' (Pentangle), 769, 810
Way Out West (Chris Hillman & Herb Pedersen), 822
'Wayfaring Stranger' (Roger McGuinn), 797, 803
Wayne, John, 263
'We Can Work It Out' (Beatles), 2, 242
'We Didn't Ask To Be Brought Here' (Bobby Darin), 192
We Five, 188, 222
'We Gotta Get Out Of This Place' (Animals), 192
We Must Survive (Earth Island), 545
'We'll Meet Again' (Byrds), 9, 135–136, 155–156, 298, 410, 442, 501, 510, 529, 744, 814, 829
Weaver, Blue, 686
Weavers, The, 23, 45
Webb, Jimmy, 783
Webber, Jean Carole (see 'Butchie' Cho)
Webster, Guy, 82, 219–220, 411
Webster, Paul Francis, 82
Webster, Roger, 82
Wednesday Morning 3AM (Simon & Garfunkel), 281
Weil, Cynthia, 80
Weissberg, Eric, 32
Welch, Chris, 157, 160, 172–173
'Well Come Back Home' (Byrds), 546–547, 570, 586
Werber, Frank, 33, 200
Wertz, Kenny, 46
Weston, Doug, 28, 337
Wexler, Jerry, 708, 710–711
'What Are Their Names' (Crosby, Stills, Nash & Young), 834
'What Child Is This' (Roger McGuinn), 802
'What's Happening?!?!' (Byrds), 294–295, 320–321, 334, 766
'When Love Goes Bad' (Chris Hillman), 313, 425

'When The Ship Comes In' (Hillmen), 48, 857
'When You Gonna Wake Up' (Bob Dylan), 700
'When You Walk In The Room' (Byrds), 104, 791
'When You Walk In The Room' (Chris Hillman), 791
'When You Walk In The Room' (Searchers), 104, 791
Where Have All The Flowers Gone (Pete Seeger Tribute Album) (Various Artistes), 132
'Where Will I Be' (Crosby & Nash), 615
Whisky A Go-Go (venue), 283, 306, 312, 341–342, 373–374, 388, 493, 496, 555, 831
Whistling Down The Wire (Crosby & Nash), 642–643
White Light (Gene Clark), 613, 647, 703, 719
'White Line Fever' (Gram Parsons), 627
'White Rabbit' (Jefferson Airplane), 338, 548
White, Clarence, 15–16, 320, 326, 328, 396, 403, 405, 407, 422, 437, 461, 469–470, 472, 484–486, 488, 493, 498–503, 505, 508, 518, 521, 524–528, 538–541, 543–545, 553–554, 556, 559, 563–567, 569, 571–573, 577–578, 581, 583–585, 587, 589–592, 594–596, 598, 602–603, 605–609, 611, 625–626, 628–629, 636, 712, 765, 768, 806, 809–813, 826–829, 840, 846, 859, 867
White, Eric, 469
White, Eric, Snr, 571, 828
White, Joanne, 469
White, Josh, 23, 45
White, Roland, 46, 469, 626
White, Susie, 556
'White's Lightning' (Byrds), 769
'White's Lightning Pt 2' (Byrds), 827
Whitman, Slim, 6
Whitten, Danny, 639
'Who Taught The Night' (Roger McGuinn & Chris Hillman, Featuring Gene Clark), 705
Who, The, 2, 8, 136, 192, 321, 334, 350, 491, 516, 756
'Why' (Byrds), 243–246, 248, 251–252, 295, 326–327, 334, 739, 741–743, 800–801, 814, 868
'Why You Been Gone So Long' (Clarence White), 626
Wiffen, David, 590
Wild Angels, The (film), 509–510
'Wild Horses' (Flying Burrito Brothers), 537
'Wild Horses' (Rolling Stones), 627
'Wild Mountain Thyme' (Byrds), 27, 293, 298, 797

'Wild Mountain Thyme' (Roger McGuinn), 797
Wilkins, Marijohn, 505
Williams, Andy, 69–70, 112, 452–453
Williams, Hank, 45, 416, 430, 503
Williams, Larry, 111
Williams, Paul, 367
Williams, Richard, 547
Williams, Rick, 777
Williams, Tennessee, 415
'Willie Gene' (aka 'Willie Jean') (David Crosby), 34
'Willin'' (Byrds), 577, 769, 827
Wills, Bob, 430, 477
Wills, Bob, & The Texas Playboys, 477
Wilson, Brian, 273, 300, 305, 338, 624, 764, 838
Wilson, Carl, 305
Wilson, Dennis, 81, 530–531, 624
Wilson, Tom, 281
Wind On The Water (Crosby & Nash), 641
Winters, Kinky, 35
'With A Little Help From My Friends' (Beatles), 548
Wolf, Howlin', 781
Wolff, Bill, 841
'Won't Let You Down' (Roger McGuinn & Chris Hillman, Featuring Gene Clark), 701, 705–706
'Wooden Ships' (Crosby, Stills & Nash), 371, 382, 517, 734, 786
Woodstock Festival, 515–516, 538, 585, 640, 731, 783, 834
'Words And Pictures' (Byrds), 798
'World Turns All Around Her, The' (Byrds), 228, 799
Worthington, Cal, 47
Wyeth, Howie, 636
Wyman, Bill, 156
Wynette, Tammy, 628

Yanovsky, Zal, 292, 362
Yardbirds, The, 2, 8, 251, 327
Yarrow, Peter, 42
'Yellow Rose Of Texas, The' (Mitch Miller), 69
'Yellow Submarine' (Beatles), 298
'Yesterday's Train' (Byrds), 544, 582, 827
York, John, 492–493, 497–498, 501–502, 505–507, 513–516, 518–521, 523–527, 529, 534, 536, 747, 766, 769, 775, 779, 809–810, 812–813, 826, 843
'You Ain't Going Nowhere' (Byrds), 14, 427, 429–430, 432, 435–436, 440, 444, 462, 471–472, 479, 482, 493, 496, 505, 740, 750, 827
'You Ain't Going Nowhere' (Byrds & Earl Scruggs Revue), 590
'You Ain't Going Nowhere' (Roger McGuinn), 795
'You Ain't Going Nowhere' (Roger McGuinn & Gene Clark, with David Crosby), 673
'You All Look Alike' (Byrds), 546, 829
'You And Me' (Byrds), 114, 798
'You Are The Woman' (Firefall), 649
'You Don't Know Me' (Ray Charles), 477
'You Don't Miss Your Water' (Byrds), 443, 474–475, 505, 768
'You Don't Miss Your Water' (Otis Redding), 474
'You Don't Miss Your Water' (Taj Mahal), 474
'You Don't Miss Your Water' (William Bell), 474
'You Got Me Hooked' (Jet Set), 71–72
'You Movin'' (Byrds), 58, 108, 745
'You Really Got A Hold On Me' (Smokey Robinson), 686
'You Showed Me' (Byrds), 56–57, 745
'You Showed Me' (Lightning Seeds), 57
'You Showed Me' (Roger McGuinn), 797, 804
'You Showed Me' (Salt 'n' Pepa), 57
'You Showed Me' (Turtles), 56–57
'You Sit There' (David Crosby), 517
'You Were On My Mind' (We Five), 188
'You Won't Have To Cry' (Byrds), 58, 129, 765, 798
'You're Still On My Mind' (Byrds), 437, 448, 475, 809
'You're Still On My Mind' (George Jones), 475
'You're Still On My Mind' (Jeff Daniels), 475
Young Rascals, The, 369
Young, Neil, 283, 352, 359, 530, 560, 599, 601, 614, 618, 639–644, 659, 726, 733, 782, 787–788, 795, 816, 819, 831, 834
Young, Steve, 520
Younger Than Yesterday (Byrds), 12, 15, 285, 309, 317–329, 331, 333–335, 338, 354, 385, 402, 409, 412–413, 420, 443, 469, 481, 502, 616, 618, 622, 632, 685, 718, 741, 743, 750, 763, 767, 793, 801–802, 807, 830
Younger Than Yesterday (tribute band), 819
'Your Fire Burning' (Gene Clark), 777
'Your Gentle Way Of Loving Me' (Byrds), 499–500
'Your Gentle Ways Of Lovin' Me' (Cajun Gib & Gene), 499–500
Yum Yum, Karen, 95, 99, 141
'Yvette In English' (David Crosby), 782

Zappa, Frank, 282, 595
Zebra In The Kitchen (film), 463
Zorba The Greek (film), 6